BIBLIOGRAPHY OF
BRITISH HISTORY

1789–1851

BIBLIOGRAPHY OF
BRITISH HISTORY

1789–1851

ISSUED UNDER THE DIRECTION OF
THE AMERICAN HISTORICAL ASSOCIATION
AND THE ROYAL HISTORICAL SOCIETY
OF GREAT BRITAIN

EDITED BY

LUCY M. BROWN

AND

IAN R. CHRISTIE

OXFORD
AT THE CLARENDON PRESS
1977

Oxford University Press, Walton Street, Oxford OX2 6DP

OXFORD LONDON GLASGOW NEW YORK
TORONTO MELBOURNE WELLINGTON CAPE TOWN
IBADAN NAIROBI DAR ES SALAAM LUSAKA ADDIS ABABA
KUALA LUMPUR SINGAPORE JAKARTA HONG KONG TOKYO
DELHI BOMBAY CALCUTTA MADRAS KARACHI

ISBN 0 19 822390 0

© *Oxford University Press 1977*

*Printed in Great Britain
at the University Press, Oxford
by Vivian Ridler
Printer to the University*

PREFACE

TWENTY-FIVE years have elapsed since the publication of Pargellis and Medley's volume in this series. During that time the conditions in which historical studies are pursued have greatly changed. The research worker of today has the benefit of a great many more bibliographical aids than he had twenty-five years ago; to take a few examples there are the British National Bibliography, the publications of the British Library's catalogue and its five-year cumulations, and the many guides and catalogues of local record offices and record societies. All these make it possible for the historian of the early nineteenth century to enter into the welter of his source material with greater confidence and less bewilderment than would have been possible a generation ago. On the other hand, historians are tending to divide into self-sustaining groups: for example, labour history, urban history, and the history of ideas now have separate identities as subjects, and the risk of one party not knowing what the other is thinking is proportionately greater.

The present work has been compiled with these circumstances in mind. We have tried to keep it more or less to the length of the previous volume in the series, and this has meant that we have had to be ruthlessly selective. The vast flood of imprints between 1789 and 1851, let alone what followed afterwards, clearly made any attempt at a comprehensive listing impossible. At the same time we have attempted to extend our guidance over as full a range of topics as did our predecessors in the series. We hope that by so doing we shall do something to counteract the centrifugal forces at work in our subject.

This limitation has led us to shape the assistance we offer to users of this bibliography in certain particular ways. The various sections and subsections have been prepared with the object of providing, first, a representative sample of the more prolific forms of contemporary imprints, such as pamphlets and essays; secondly, an outline of each field as treated in the literature concerned with it, drawing attention to leading features and/or personalities; thirdly, reference, where this is possible, to up-to-date authoritative treatment; and fourthly, an indication of further immediate guidance to be found, for instance, in specialist bibliographies, in reading lists in books, or by reference to specialist journals or series. We have not followed a uniform pattern from section to section, and roughly speaking the amount of detail given varies inversely with the quality of specialist bibliography otherwise available, to which the user can turn. Thus, for example, no attempt has been made to list the vast contemporary literature in the form of travel journals, contemporary memoirs, and missionary accounts, which describes the various countries then being developed as parts of the second British Empire. The user is referred for guidance to this to such specialist compilations as Tremaine and Staton on Canada (4328), E. C. Baker on the Windward and Leeward Isles (4484, 4487), Schmidt on South Africa (4520), Ferguson on Australia (4686) and Hocken on New Zealand (4749). Attention is drawn to such specialist series as the Van Riebeeck Society publications (4518) and the Archives Year Book for South African history (4524), and to specialist journals such as the Journal of Indian History (4573), but no attempt has been made to list in detail all the relevant individual volumes of such series or the relevant articles in such periodicals.

Economy of space has taken a different form in the section on English Literature in the chapter on Cultural History, by the omission of details of editions of writers' works, for which reference can be made to the British Library catalogue and the New Cambridge Bibliography of English Literature. We have been concerned to list editions of their correspondence, key biographies, and studies relating to their work and their contemporary influence.

The use of this bibliography is therefore often rather as a guide to where information may be found than to the information itself. With this view, we have included a number of guides of a fairly general nature in the opening sections of chapter 1, 'General Reference Works'.

Most of the books listed in this bibliography are to be found in the British Library (formerly British Museum Library). Others can be located for the most part in one or other of the specialist libraries and society libraries in London (see pp. 3, and 9–10 below). Unless otherwise stated the place of publication is London. No systematic attempt has been made to give the American place of publication for the many modern works published simultaneously both in Britain and in the United States and normally only the British edition is given. Titles are usually arranged chronologically, so that the most recent books on a subject come last, but in some cases arrangement is roughly in chronological order of content or in order of importance. First editions are normally listed, but not always if superseded by a later. In the case of some contemporary works of reference, such as legal handbooks, which were regularly revised over a period of many years, the earliest and latest editions within the period

1789 to 1851 have been indicated. Later editions are also noted to indicate revisions, enlargements, or popularity. Cross references are not exhaustive and in respect of some subjects and persons are supplemented by the entries in the index. Geographical sections in the later chapters do not contain all titles dealing with those areas, and other sections should be consulted: for instance, general monographs on economic history often contain much material on particular localities.

ACKNOWLEDGEMENTS

Our first and fullest thanks are due to our two principal assistants, Mrs. Miriam Alman and Mrs. Catherine Dowden. In turn they each served the project for a number of years, and their special expertise as librarians was indispensable. Mrs. Dowden gave additional help with the shaping of the General Reference section. We are also grateful to Mrs. J. Penney and Miss Elaine South, who helped with the collection and checking of material, to Mrs. Jane Rowland, who checked the index, and to Mrs. Audrey Munro, who put much of the draft material into fair typed form.

We also wish to thank the many people who kindly gave of their time and energy in response to our importunate requests for advice. We profited greatly from their help, and we take upon ourselves full responsibility for any errors of omission or commission in relation to material at which they looked.

Mr. T. D. O'Rourke and Mr. W. Kellaway made suggestions concerning the General Reference section, and Mr. John Brooke vetted the account there given of the Historical MSS. Commission and National Register of Archives. The section on British diplomatic history benefited from advice and suggestions offered by Professor H. C. Allen, Professor M. S. Anderson, Professor C. R. Boxer, Dr. Isabel de Madariaga, Professor Ragnhild Hatton, and Professor R. A. Humphreys. Professor C. W. Dugmore looked through our initial collection on Religious History, and Professor W. R. Ward gave further guidance after this section had taken shape; while Mr. E. G. W. Bill went over our description of the MSS. collections in Lambeth Palace Library. The Office of the Church Commissioners kindly made available information about the nature of their records.

The section on naval history was much improved by advice from Mr. John Munday and Mrs. D. Rowland, and the late Professor M. A. Lewis went through the material at an early stage and made many helpful suggestions. Professor A. H. John allowed us to call on his wide knowledge of the economic and social history of the period and also of the history of

Wales. Professor R. R. Davies helped to correct the initial vagaries of our spelling of Welsh titles. Dr. L. O. J. Boynton made us free of his expertise on furniture, glassware, and architecture, Dr. Audrey Lambert gave help with our material on maps, and Mrs. K. D. Wilson gave advice with the section on English literature. We are indebted for advice on the History of Science to the late Dr. A. Armitage, to Professor D. McKie, Professor C. A. Rogers, Dr. W. A. Smeaton, and Professor J. S. Wilkie. Dr. Ethel Drus, Professor J. D. Fage, Professor G. S. Graham, Professor W. L. Morton, and Professor George Shepperson gave advice on various aspects of British colonial history, and we are also grateful to the West India Committee for permission to examine pamphlets only available in London in the Committee's library.

We are also grateful to the librarians and staffs in many libraries, both in Great Britain and in the United States, who helped with our queries about pamphlet collections and about rare copies of privately printed books, and who gave us valuable advice on the sources for local history. Over the years we have made heavy drafts on the services of staff in the British Museum Library, and wish to record our particular thanks for their help. Two major private libraries in London—the London Library and the Library of the Royal Commonwealth Society—deserve special mention as providing indispensable facilities for the preparation of this bibliography.

Our thanks go finally to Mr. E. A. Smith, who read the final draft, and to Mr. J. M. Collinge, who scrutinized the galley proofs; we received from both of them valuable last-minute additions.

Our last acknowledgement is of a different kind, and in one view the most important of all. An enormous debt of gratitude is owed to the Ford Foundation for its very generous grant to the Joint Committee of the American Historical Association and the Royal Historical Society, without which this bibliography could not have been undertaken.

L.M.B.

I.R.C.

NOTE

On a few pages in the first half of this volume the large-print and the small-print portions of an entry have been split on either side of a leaf. Users finding an entry in large print apparently complete at the foot of a right-hand page are advised to make sure that no further information follows immediately overleaf.

CONTENTS

Contents

LIST OF ABBREVIATIONS

acad.	academy
add.	Additions, additional
Add. MSS.	Additional Manuscripts, British Library (formerly British Museum)
agric.	agriculture, agricultural
A.H.A.	American Historical Association
A.H.R.	*American Historical Review*
anon.	anonymous
antiq.	antiquarian, antiquities
app.	appendix
arch.	architecture
archaeol.	archaeological
ASLIB	Association of Librarians
assoc.	association
Balt.	Baltimore
B.B.C.S.	*Bulletin of the Board of Celtic Studies*
bibliog.	bibliography, bibliographical
biog.	biography, biographical
Birm.	Birmingham
B.M. or B.L.	British Museum, otherwise British Library*
Bull.	bulletin
c.	*circa*
Cal., Calif.	California
Camb.	Cambridge
Camb. Hist. J.	*Cambridge Historical Journal*
Can. Hist. R.	*Canadian Historical Review*
chap.	chapter
C.H.B.E.	*Cambridge History of the British Empire*
chem.	chemical
chron.	chronological
C.M.S.	Church Missionary Society
coll.	collection
Colo.	Colorado
comm.	commission
comp.	compiler, compiled
Conn.	Connecticut
cons.	constitutional
D.N.B.	*Dictionary of National Biography*
doc.	document
eccles.	ecclesiastical
econ.	economic
Econ. H.R.	*Economic History Review*

* In 1973 the British Museum Library and the Manuscript Department became parts of the British Library.

ed.	editor, edited
Edin.	Edinburgh
edn.	edition
E.H.R.	*English Historical Review*
Eng.	English, England
enl.	enlarged
Fla.	Florida
gaz.	gazette
geol.	geological
H.A.H.R.	*Hispanic American Historical Review*
H.C.	House of Commons
hist.	history, historical, historisch
H.L.	House of Lords
H.M.C.	Historical Manuscripts Commission
I.H.R.	Institute of Historical Research, University of London
illus.	illustration, illustrated
impr.	impression
inst.	institute
instn.	institution
intro., introd.	introduction
irreg.	irregularly
j., jour.	journal
J.H.S.E.	Jewish Historical Society of England
l., lib.	library
Law Quart. Rev.	*Law Quarterly Review*
Linn. Soc.	Linnean Society
lit.	literature, literary
L.M.S.	London Missionary Society
mag.	magazine
Manch.	Manchester
Mass.	Massachusetts
med.	medieval, medical
mem.	memorials, memoirs
misc.	miscellany, miscellaneous
mod.	modern
MS., MSS.	manuscript, manuscripts
N.C., N. Car.	North Carolina
N.C.B.E.L.	*New Cambridge Bibliography of English Literature*
n.d.	no date
no.	number
n.p.	no place
NRS	Navy Records Society
n.s.	new series
N.Y.	New York
N.Y.P.L.	New York Public Library
Oxf.	Oxford
p., pp.	page(s)
P & M	Pargellis and Medley

Parl. papers	Parliamentary papers
Penn.	Pennsylvania
Phil.	Philadelphia
phil.	philosophy, philosophical
Phil. Trans.	*Philosophical Transactions of the Royal Society*
Pol. Sci. Q.	*Political Science Quarterly*
P.R.O.	Public Record Office
proc.	proceedings
pseud.	pseudonym
pt.	part
pub., publ.	published
pub(n).	publication
q., quart.	quarterly
q.v.	*quod vide*
R., Rev.	Review
rec.	record
rep.	report
repr.	reprint, reprinted
rev.	review, revised
R.O.	Record Office
roy.	royal
s., ser.	series
S.A.A.R.	South African Archival Records
Scot.	Scottish
sess.	session
S.H.R.	*Scottish Historical Review*
S.O.A.S.	School of Oriental and African Studies, University of London
soc.	society
S.P.C.K.	Society for Promoting Christian Knowledge, London
S.P.G.	Society for the Propagation of the Gospel
stats.	statistical
suppl.	supplement
trans.	transactions, translated
univ.	university
v., vol.	volume
Va.	Virginia
V.C.H.	*Victoria County History*
Wash.	Washington
+	continuing

I

GENERAL REFERENCE WORKS

A. BIBLIOGRAPHIES AND CATALOGUES

1. BIBLIOGRAPHY OF BIBLIOGRAPHY

1 BESTERMAN (THEODORE). A world bibliography of bibliographies. 4th edn. 5 v. Lausanne. 1965–6.

A most thorough and comprehensive guide to literature of all countries on all subjects. Louise-Noelle Malclès, *Les sources du travail bibliographique*, 3 v. in 4, Paris, 1950–8, is excellent, though more selective and weighted towards France. R. L. W. Collison, *Bibliographies, subject and national; a guide to their contents, arrangement and use*, 3rd edn., rev. and enlarged, 1968, gives a selective listing of major bibliographies, with particular attention to special library catalogues. A. J. Walford, *Guide to reference material*, 2nd edn., 3 v., 1966, lays stress on recent reference books and bibliographies relating to Great Britain; v. 2, most relevant for historians, includes *c.* 5,000 items. Constance M. Winchell, *Guide to reference books*, 8th edn., Chicago, 1967, with suppls., is also most valuable. *The American Historical Association's guide to historical literature*, ed. by G. F. Howe, new edn., N.Y., 1961, is highly selective and somewhat limited on British nineteenth-century history. For current lists of books and articles containing bibliographies see *The bibliographic index: a cumulative bibliography of bibliographies*, 1937, in progress, now biennial with periodical cumulations; similar but weighted on German material is *Bibliographische Berichte. . . . Im Auftrage des deutschen Bibliographischen Kuratoriums*, Frankfurt-a-Main, 1959, in progress.

2. BIBLIOGRAPHIES AND CATALOGUES RELATING TO BRITISH HISTORY

See Graham Pollard, 'General lists of books printed in England', *I.H.R. Bulletin*, 12 (1935), 164–74. The principal trade list is *The English catalogue of books . . .* 1835+, 1864+, with authors and subjects in one alphabet: *Index to the English catalogue of books, 1837–1889*, 4 v., 1858–93, is a guide to subjects. *Whitaker's cumulative book list* provides a useful supplement from 1924. From 1950 British books are listed under an extremely detailed subject arrangement in the *British National Bibliography*, 1951+, published weekly, with cumulations every three, six, nine, and twelve months, and periodic cumulated subject and author catalogues. For books on the United States market see the *United States catalog; books in print, 1899*, Minneapolis, 1900, 4th edn., N.Y., 1928, supplemented by the *Cumulative book index: a world list of books in the English language*, N.Y., 1933+; full for U.S., British and Canadian imprints but selective for other English-speaking countries. A wide range of material is listed under various subject groupings in the *New Cambridge bibliography of English literature* (2650).

2 ALTHOLZ (JOSEF LEWIS). Victorian England, 1837–1901. (Conference on British Studies, bibliographical handbooks.) Camb. 1970.

A selective guide; 2,500 entries. Ian R. Christie, *British History since 1760: a select bibliography* (Historical Assoc., Helps for students of history, 81), 1970, is a brief listing mainly of recent monographs. For literature on the period immediately preceding 1789 see S. Pargellis and D. J. Medley, *Bibliography of British History: the eighteenth century, 1714–1789*, Oxf., 1951.

3 FREWER (LOUIS B.) *ed.* Bibliography of historical writings published in Great Britain and the empire, 1940–1945. Oxf. 1947.

Publication in the United Kingdom only is covered in the series *Bibliography of historical works issued in the United Kingdom:* (1) *1946–56*, comp. by Joan C. Lancaster, 1957, (2) *1957–60*, (3) *1961–65*, (4) *1966–70*, comp. by W. Kellaway, 1962, 1967, 1972.

4 HALKETT (SAMUEL) *and* LAING (JOHN). Dictionary of anonymous and pseudonymous English literature. New and enl. edn. by James Kennedy, William Allan Smith, and Alfred Forbes Johnson. 7 v. 1926–34.

Of the two additional vols. ed. by D. E. Rhodes and A. E. C. Simon, 1956, 1962, v. 9 includes further nineteenth-century material. See too William Cushing, *Initials and pseudonyms; a dictionary of literary disguises*, N.Y., 1885–8, London, 1886, and *Anonyms; a dictionary of revealed authorship*, Camb., Mass., 1889, London, 1890; A. Taylor and F. J. Mosher, *The bibliographical history of anonyma and pseudonyma*, Chicago, 1951.

5 HISTORICAL ASSOCIATION, LONDON. Annual bulletin of historical literature, 1911+. 1912+.

Surveys in the form of critical essays of leading books and articles appearing each year on history in all fields; rather restricted selection. Much fuller is the *International bibliography of historical sciences*, 1926+, Paris, 1930+.

6 INSTITUTE OF HISTORICAL RESEARCH (London University). [Annual list of] Historical research for university degrees in the United Kingdom. I.H.R. Bulletin. Theses supplement 1+. 1933+.

Superseded in 1954 by annual lists of 'theses completed' and 'theses in progress'. See too *Doctoral dissertations accepted by American universities*, ed. by D. B. Gilchrist and E. A. Henry, 22 v., N.Y., 1934–1954/5, continued as *Index to American doctoral dissertations*, 1957+; *Current research in British Studies by American and Canadian scholars*, Marquett, Mich., 1953+ (quadrennial). W. F. Kuehl, *Dissertations in history; an index to dissertations compiled in history departments of United States and Canadian universities, 1873–1970*, Kentucky, 2 v., 1965–72, is a useful cumulated list. The ASLIB *Index to theses accepted for higher degrees in the universities of Great Britain and Ireland*, ed. by P. D. Record, M. Whitrow, G. M. Paterson, and J. E. Hardy, 1950/1, in progress, gives guidance to work in adjacent disciplines. For theses available on film see *Microfilm abstracts*, Ann Arbor, 1935+, continued as *Dissertation abstracts*, 1952+.

7 A LONDON BIBLIOGRAPHY of the social sciences, being the subject catalogue of the British library of political and economic science at the London School of Economics, the Goldsmiths' library of economic literature at the University of London, the libraries of the Royal Statistical Society and the Royal Anthropological Institute. Comp. under the direction of Bertie Mason Headicar and Clifford Fuller. 4 v. 1931–2. Numerous supplements, 1934+.

The largest subject bibliography of its kind, touching many aspects of nineteenth-century British history. Supplements list only accessions to the library at LSE and appear with exceptional promptness. Particularly valuable for government publications, which are listed separately at the end of each subject entry.

8 PEDDIE (ROBERT ALEXANDER). Subject index of books published
   before 1880. 4 v. 1933–48.

> Earlier compilations worth consultation are Robert Watt, *Bibliotheca britannica*, 4 v.,
> Edin., 1824, and S. A. Allibone, *Critical dictionary of English literature and British and
> American authors . . .*, 3 v., Philadelphia, 1859–71, suppl. by J. F. Kirk, 2 v., Phil., 1891.
> For books published after 1880 see B.M. Subject Index (10).

9 ROYAL HISTORICAL SOCIETY. Writings on British history, 1901–33;
   a bibliography of books and articles on the history of Great Britain from about
   A.D. 400 to 1914, published during the years 1901–33 inclusive. Comp. by
   Hugh Hale Bellot. 5 v. in 7. 1968–70.

> V. 1: auxiliary sciences and general works; v. 4: the eighteenth century, 1714–1815;
> v. 5: 1815–1914. Subject arrangement and full index. Similar guidance through the
> literature from 1934 is provided in *Writings on British history*, ed. by A. T. Milne,
> D. J. Munro and J. M. Sims, 1937, in progress. For publications of learned societies
> as contributions to their periodicals or as separates see E. L. C. Mullins (21), and Terry
> and Matheson (3871).

B. LIBRARY RESOURCES. GUIDES AND CATALOGUES

For general guidance to libraries and institutions holding printed information,
see the *ASLIB directory*, ed. by Brian J. Wilson, 2 v., 1968–70, v. 1: *information
sources in science, technology and commerce*; v. 2: *information sources in medicine,
the social sciences and the humanities*. A. J. Philip, *An index to the special collections
in libraries, museums and art galleries, public, private and official, in Great Britain
and Ireland*, 1950, provides information on special collections in small libraries;
see also *The libraries, museums and art galleries year book*, ed. by E. V. Corbett,
1971, revised irregularly. *Government information and the research worker*, ed.
by R. Staveley and Mary Piggott, 2nd edn., 1965, covers resources and publications of government libraries and information centres. On libraries in London,
R. A. Rye, *The students' guide to the libraries of London*, 3rd edn., 1927; L. M.
Harrod, *The libraries of greater London; a guide*, 1951; R. Irwin and R. Staveley,
eds., *The libraries of London*, 2nd rev. edn., 1961, give guidance which is to some
extent out of date owing to reorganization and redeployment of book collections.
R. B. Downs, *American library resources, a bibliographical guide*, Chicago, 1951,
is a bibliography of bibliographies rather than a description of resources. Lee Ash
and D. Lorenz, eds., *Subject collections*, 3rd edn., 1967, is a guide to special
collections in libraries in the United States and Canada. K. F. Brown, *A guide
to the reference collections of the New York public library*, N.Y., 1941, is descriptive.

10 BRITISH MUSEUM. DEPARTMENT OF PRINTED BOOKS.
    General catalogue of printed books. Photolithographic edition to 1955. 263 v.
    1959–66. Suppl. for 1956–1965. 50 v. 1968. Suppl. for 1966–70. 26 v. 1971–2.

> *Subject index of the modern works added to the British Museum . . . 1881–1900*, ed. by
> G. K. Fortescue, 3 v., 1902–3, follows on from Peddie (8) and is continued by further
> subject indexes published at five-yearly intervals.

11 LIBRARY OF CONGRESS. The national union catalog: pre-1956
    imprints. Chicago. 1968+.

> In course of completion in about 610 vols.; continued in *The national union catalog;*

a cumulative author list, 1956+, 1958+; will supersede *A catalog of books represented by Library of Congress printed cards issued [1898] to July 31, 1942*, 167 v., Ann Arbor, 1958–60, and supplements 1942–1947, 42 v., Ann Arbor, 1948, *1948–1952*, 24 v., A.A., 1953, continued by *The national union catalog . . . 1953–57*, 28 v., A.A., 1958. *The Library of Congress catalog. Books: subjects, 1950–54*, Ann Arbor, 1955, followed by cumulations in various series provides the fullest and most up-to-date subject catalog of its kind.

12   HALE (RICHARD WALDEN) Jr., *ed.*, Guide to photocopied historical materials in the United States and Canada. Ithaca. 1961.

See *Union list of microfilms; rev., enl. and cumulated edition* (Philadelphia bibliographical center and union library catalog committee on microphotography), Ann Arbor, 1951, *supplement, 1949–59*, Ann Arbor, 1961. Eva M. Tilton, *A union list of publications in opaque microforms*, 2nd edn., 1964, covers 26 U.S. and European publishers. Library of Congress, *National register of microfilm masters*, 1965+, Washington, 1965+, pub. irregularly. See too LC, union catalog division, *Newspapers on microfilm*, 6th edn., 1967, which includes some British material.

C. PERIODICALS AND SOCIETY PUBLICATIONS

1. BIBLIOGRAPHY

13   GRAHAM (WALTER JAMES). English literary periodicals. N.Y. 1930.

A basic narrative introduction. See Felix Speer, *The periodical press of London, theatrical and literary, excluding the daily newspaper, 1800–1830*, Boston, 1937; W. S. Ward, *Index and finding list of serials published in the British Isles, 1789–1832*, Lexington, K., 1953; J. H. Wiener, *A descriptive finding list of unstamped British periodicals, 1830–1836*, 1970.

14   FREITAG (RUTH S.), *comp.* Union lists of serials; a bibliography. Washington. 1964.

15   BRITISH UNION-CATALOGUE OF PERIODICALS. A record of the periodicals of the world, from the seventeenth century to the present day, in British libraries. Ed. by J. D. Stewart, Muriel E. Hammond, and E. Saenger. 4 v. 1955–8.

Supplement to 1960, 1962; continued in *British union-catalogue of periodicals incorporating world list of scientific periodicals: new periodical titles*, ed. by K. I. Porter, 1964, quarterly, first cumulation covering 1960–68, 1970. For American resources see *Union list of serials in libraries of the United States and Canada*, 3rd edn., covering pubns. to Dec. 1949, ed. by Edna B. Titus, 5 v., N.Y., 1965; continued for periodicals begun after 1950 by *New serial titles*, 1953+, with periodic cumulations. See too *Ulrich's international periodicals directory. A classified guide to current periodicals, foreign and domestic*, 3rd edn., 2 v., 1969–70. Mary Toase ed., *Guide to current British periodicals*, 1962.

16   BOEHM (ERIC H.) *and* ADOLPHUS (LALIT) *eds.* Historical periodicals; an annotated world list of historical and related serial publications. Santa Barbara, Cal., Munich, 1961.

Lists some 4,500 periodicals. P. Caron and M. Jaryc, *World list of historical periodicals and bibliographies*. Oxf., N.Y., 1940, is still useful as a guide to discontinued periodicals. For the English language periodicals of main interest to the student of British history see J. L. Kirby, *A guide to historical publications in the English language* (Hist. Assoc., Helps for students of history, 80), 1970.

2. Guides to Contents

See Daniel Carl Haskell, *A check list of cumulative indexes to individual periodicals in the New York public library*. N.Y., 1942, repr. Detroit, 1969.

17 POOLE'S INDEX TO PERIODICAL LITERATURE. N.Y. 1882.

Index mainly to American but also to a few British periodicals, 1802–81. Five quinquennial supplements, 1888–1908, continue it to 1906. See Marion V. Bell and Jean C. Bacon, *Poole's index; date and volume key*, Chicago, 1957. *Index to the periodicals of [1890–1902]*, 1–13, 1891–1903, is useful for titles not in Poole. Poole's *Index* was continued in *International Index to Periodicals . . . 1907–15+*, N.Y., 1916+, continued from 1958 as *International index; a guide to periodical literature in the social sciences and humanities*, and from 1965 as the *Social sciences and humanities index*. See too the *Canadian index; a guide to Canadian periodicals and films* (Canadian Library Assoc.), Ottawa, 1947+; author and subject index, 1948–59, Ottawa, 1962.

18 THE WELLESLEY INDEX to Victorian periodicals, 1824–1900: tables of contents and identification of contributors with bibliographies of their articles and stories. Ed. by Walter E. Houghton. 1966, in progress.

A comprehensive guide to articles and reviews; in time will largely supersede the *Nineteenth century readers' guide to periodical literature, 1890–1899, with supplementary indexing, 1900–1922*, 2 v., N.Y., 1944.

19 THE SUBJECT INDEX TO PERIODICALS [1915–16]+. Library Assoc. 1919+.

Annual to 1961, thereafter continued in three series: *British Education Index*; *British Humanities Index*; *British Technology Index*; all 1962+. The fullest guide to British magazine articles published after 1915.

20 HISTORICAL ABSTRACTS, 1775–1945. A quarterly of abstracts of historical articles on the period 1775–1945, appearing currently in periodicals the world over. Ed. by E. H. Boehm. Santa Barbara, Cal., and Vienna. 1955+.

Class arrangement with subject index; index to periodicals in March issue; subject index, v. 1–5, 1963.

21 MULLINS (EDWARD LINDSAY CARSON). Texts and calendars: an analytical guide to serial publications. 1958.

See also E. L. C. Mullins, *A guide to the historical and archaeological publications of societies in England and Wales, 1901–1933*, 1968, and A. T. Milne, *A centenary guide to the publications of the Royal Historical Society, 1868–1968; and of the former Camden Society, 1838–1897*, 1968.

3. Periodicals and Society Publications

(a) *Contemporary Magazines and Reviews*

22 The annual register. 1758+.

An increasingly valuable chronological record over the years after 1789; general index 1758–1819, 1826.

23 Athenaeum; a journal of literature, science, the fine arts, music and the drama. 153 v. 1828–1921. Weekly.

In 1828, absorbed the *Literary chronicle and weekly review* (1819–28). See L. A. Marchand, *The Athenaeum; a mirror of Victorian culture*, Chapel Hill, 1941.

24   Blackwood's Edinburgh Magazine. Edinburgh. 1817+. Monthly.

General Index to . . . vols. 1–50, 1855. A. L. Strout, comp., *A bibliography of articles in Blackwood's magazine, 1817–1825*, Lubbock, 1959, with an appendix showing authorship of articles in Blackwood's contributors' book, 1825–70. On economic articles see F. W. Fetter (1753). See also (18).

25   Critical review; or, Annals of literature. By a society of gentlemen. 144 v. 1756–1817. Monthly.

A major rival of the *Monthly review*.

26   Dublin review. Lond. and Dublin. 1836+. Quarterly.

List of contents by vols. in *The Dublin review, 1836–1936*, [1936]. Index by subject, *Index . . . from vol. 1, May 1836 to vol. 52, 1863*, 1864. Also, 'General list of articles, vols. 1–118 (1836–1896)', 118 (1896). See (18).

27   Edinburgh review, or, Critical journal . . . 1802–1929. 250 v. Edin., Lond., N.Y. 1803–1929. Quarterly.

General index . . . 1802[–89], v. 1. [–170], 6 v., Edin., Lond. 1813–91. E. Schneider, I. Griggs, and J. D. Kern, 'Early Edinburgh reviewers; a new list', *Modern philology*, 43 (1946), 192–210, covers vols. 1–19 (1802–12). S. Halpern, 'Sydney Smith in the *Edinburgh Review*; a new list', *Bulletin of the New York Public Library*, 66 (1962), 589–602; see Brougham (207); Clive (3955). On economic articles see F. W. Fetter (1753). See also (18); the *Wellesley Index* gives full analysis from 1802.

28   European magazine, and London review. 89 v. 1782–1826. Monthly.

Then merged in the *Monthly magazine and British register*, appearing under various titles, 1796–1843, the organ of the unitarian radicals; see G. Carnall, 'The *Monthly Magazine*', *Review of English Studies*, n.s. 5 (1954), 158–64.

29   Examiner. A Sunday paper, on politics, domestic economy, and theatricals. 1808–81. Weekly.

The pace-setter and most outstanding of the weeklies. See E. C. Blunden, *Leigh Hunt's 'Examiner' examined . . . 1808–1825*, 1928.

30   Fraser's magazine for town and country. 80 v. [1830–69]. New series, 26 v., 1870–1882.

31   Gentleman's magazine. 302 v. 1731–1907. Monthly.

General index . . . 1731[–1818], 4 v., 1780–1821; *A complete list of the plates and woodcuts . . . to 1818*, 1821.

32   Monthly review. 247 v. 1749–1845.

A general index, 5 v. 1786–1818. B. C. Nangle, *The Monthly review, second series, 1790–1815; indexes of contributors and articles*, Oxford, 1955.

33   New monthly magazine [and literary journal]. 149 v. 1814–71.

A leading anti-radical monthly.

34   Quarterly review. 1809+.

General indexes, v. 20, 40, 60, 80, 100, 121, 140, 160, 181, 201, 222, 243. On contributors
see H. Shine and Helen Chadwick, *The Quarterly Review under Gifford; identification
of contributors, 1809–1824*, Chapel Hill, 1949. See Croker (194). On economic articles
see F. W. Fetter (1753). See also (18).

35   Scots magazine. 79 v. Edin. 1739–1817. Monthly.

Absorbed in the *Edinburgh magazine, or, Literary miscellany* in 1804. Succeeded by the
Edinburgh magazine and literary miscellany, 18 v., Edin., 1817–26. Styled after the
Gentleman's magazine.

36   Statistical Society of London journal. 1838+.

Miscellaneous information on social and economic questions.

37   Westminster review. 181 v. 1824–1914. Quarterly.

Some variations of title; absorbed the *Foreign quarterly review* (1827–46). See Nesbitt
(523), Bowring (2293). On economic articles see F. W. Fetter (1753).

(b) *Modern Scholarly Journals*

Other, more specialized publications will be found in the appropriate sections.
See Kirby (16).

38   American historical review. American Historical Assoc. N.Y. 1896+.
     Quarterly.

General index to vol. I[–70], 1895[–1965], 6 v., N.Y., 1906–68. For issues to 1945 see
F. D. Scott and Elaine Teigler, eds., *Guide to the American historical review, 1895–1945;
a subject-classified explanatory bibliography* . . ., Annual report of A.H.A., 1944, Wash.
1945, vol. I, pt. 2, 65–292.

39   American political science review. Baltimore, 1906+. 1907+. Quarterly.

Index . . . v. 1–57 [1906–63], 1964.

40   University of Birmingham historical journal. Birmingham. 12 v. 1947–70.

Continued as *Midland history*, 1971+; two issues a year.

41   Cambridge historical journal . . . 13 v. 1923–57.

Continued as the *Historical journal*, 1958+; quarterly.

42   English historical review. London, N.Y. 1886+. Quarterly.

*General index of articles, notes, documents, and selected reviews of books . . . vols. I[–70],
1886[–1955]*, 5 v., Lond., N.Y., 1906–63.

43   Historische Zeitschrift. Munich. 1859+. Quarterly 1859–76; bi-monthly
     1877+.

Register zu Bd. I[–130], 1859[–1906], 3 v., 1888–1925.

44   History; the journal of the Historical association. [n.s.] 1916+.

Three issues a year. Index to v. 1–50 (1916–65), comp. by Olwen Hufton, 1970.

45 History today. Monthly. 1951+.

Mainly for non-professional readers, but includes occasional research papers.

46 Institute of historical research (London university). Bulletin. 1923+. Lond., N.Y. 1925+.

Three times a year till v. 21 (1946–8), then two nos. to annual vol. Table of contents, v. 1–25 (1923–52), 1952.

47 International review of social history. Assen, Netherlands. 1956+. Three times a year.

Articles in English, French, and German; annotated bibliographies.

48 Journal of British studies. American Historical Assoc. Conference on British studies. Hartford, Conn. 1962+.

Two nos. to annual vol.

49 Journal of ecclesiastical history. 1950+.

Two nos. to annual vol.; quarterly from 1970.

50 Journal of modern history. Chicago. 1929+. Quarterly.

51 Journal of the history of ideas: a quarterly devoted to cultural and intellectual history. Lancaster, Pa., and N.Y. 1940+.

Index v. 1–25, 1966.

52 Northern history: a review of the history of the north of England. Leeds. 1966+. Annual.

53 Notes and queries . . . 1849+. Lond., High Wycombe. 1850+. Weekly. Monthly from 1953.

General index . . . series the 1st[–15th], 1849[–1955], 15 v., Lond., High Wycombe, 1856–1955.

54 Past and present: A journal of historical studies. Past and present society, Oxford. 1951+.

Begun in 1951 with sub-title, 'A journal of scientific history'; originally 2, later 3, and from 1969 4 nos. a year.

55 Political science quarterly. Boston. 1886+.

Index . . . v. I[–45], 1886[–1930], Boston, 1931; *Index . . . v. 46–65, [1931–50],* 1951.

56 Political studies. Political studies assoc. of the U.K. Oxford. 1953+. Quarterly.

Index to v. 1–10, 1963.

57 Renaissance and modern studies. Nottingham 1957+. Annual.

58 Royal historical society, London. Transactions . . . 1869+. 1872+. Annual.

For guide to contents, see Milne (21).

59   Victorian studies. Bloomington, Ind. 1957+. Quarterly.

Contains annual Victorian bibliography, formerly included (1933–57) in *Modern Philology.*

D. HANDBOOKS

60   HELPS FOR STUDENTS OF HISTORY. Ed. by Charles Johnson and James P. Whitney. 51 v. S.P.C.K. Lond., N.Y. 1918–24.

Reprinted in 11 v. grouped by subject, 1969; continued by the Historical association, no. 52+, 1950+; outline guides, bibliographies, and explanations of groups of source material.

61   HANDBOOK OF DATES for students of English history. Ed. by C. R. Cheney. Rev. edn. 1970.

62   CHUBB (THOMAS). The printed maps in the atlases of Great Britain and Ireland. A bibliography, 1579–1870. 1927.

63   HANDBOOK OF BRITISH CHRONOLOGY. Ed. by Sir F. M. Powicke and E. B. Fryde. 2nd edn. 1961.

Dates of tenure of major officers of state, archbishops, and bishops, chronological list of parliaments and related assemblies up to 1832.

E. PAMPHLET COLLECTIONS

For this period, as for the eighteenth century, libraries holding pamphlet literature may conveniently be placed in the three classes defined in S. Pargellis and D. J. Medley, *Bibliography of British History. The eighteenth century, 1714–1789,* 1951, pp. 11–12, (*q.v.*) viz: 1. Those libraries which contain pamphlets dealing with special subjects; 2. Those libraries which contain special collections or collections made by particular individuals; 3. Those libraries which contain large numbers of pamphlets forming part of no special collection. For general guidance the researcher can turn to works listed in the introductory note to Section B above. The following observations supplement the information in Pargellis and Medley, *loc. cit.*

Among libraries in London in class 1, not specifically noticed by Pargellis and Medley, are the Admiralty library, now the Naval library, Ministry of Defence (naval literature), the British library of political and economic science located at the London School of Economics and Political Science—see (7), the Bank of England library, the Institute of Bankers library, the Institution of Civil Engineers, and the Institution of Electrical Engineers (economic and technological literature), the library of Jews' College, especially its Green Memorial library (Anglo-Jewish history), Liberal Club (political), and the library of the Royal Commonwealth Society (colonial). A number of the Greater London public libraries include in their holdings pamphlets relating to the history of their districts (so do many provincial libraries—some of these are mentioned in G. Kitson Clark and G. R. Elton, *Guide to research facilities in history in the universities of Great Britain and Ireland,* 2nd edn. 1965). Lambeth Palace Library and the library of the Church Commissioners hold collections on ecclesiastical matters.

Among libraries in London holding special collections or collections made by individuals referring to the period 1789–1851 are: The University of London (the Goldsmiths' library of economic literature, including Richard Oastler's collection of tracts on factories and the J. U. Raistrick collection on early railway history); University College London library (the Joseph Hume collection on political affairs and a small Chadwick collection on social questions); the Guild-hall library (the J. R. D. Tyssen collection of the writings of Hackney noncon-formist ministers, including the works of Belsham, Burder, Lindsay, Price, Priestley, Wakefield, and others); the English Church Union theological library and reading room (the Archdeacon G. A. Denison collection).

Provincial holdings include the pamphlet accumulations of two great political families. A large collection of pamphlets of the period *c.* 1790–1850 made by the Earls Grey of Howick is housed in the library of the University of Newcastle upon Tyne. Another substantial part of this collection is located together with the Grey MSS. in the department of palaeography, the University of Durham. The University of Liverpool library holds the Knowsley collection acquired from the Earl of Derby, including some 1,500 pamphlets of the years 1830–65. These groups contain material on all matters of public interest. Collections mainly on economic and social affairs include the Joseph Cowen tracts (of socialist interest) in the University of Newcastle library and a group on anti-slavery in the John Rylands library, Manchester. The Overstone collection at Reading University library contains a comprehensive holding of early nine-teenth-century works on political economy.

For Scottish history the general collection in the National Library of Scotland, Edinburgh, is in part supported by the University of St. Andrews library, which was a copyright library until 1836. Aberdeen University library holds three special collections, the King, Thomson, and Herald collections, the first with a predominantly theological emphasis. In the University of Glasgow library the David Murray and John Smith collections contain material on all aspects of Scottish life. The Mitchell library, Glasgow, holds (i) the Stirling's Library Pamphlets, covering a wide range of subjects; (ii) the Whitefoord–Mackenzie collection, also wide-ranging and strong on the religious controversy of the Disruption; (iii) a group of 27 volumes relating to the history of the Church of Scotland; (iv) a small group of political tracts published *c.* 1830–50.

The Foster collection in the library of the Queen's University of Belfast includes nearly 300 bound volumes of pamphlets published mostly between 1750 and 1814, more than half of them on Irish affairs, a collection formed by the last Speaker of the Irish House of Commons. There is also Irish material in the Bradshaw collection, Cambridge University library, earlier acquisitions being listed in *A catalogue of the Bradshaw collection of Irish books in the University Library*, Cambridge, 3 v., 1916.

Apart from general pamphlet holdings in the great libraries in the United States, special reference may be made to the following: at Harvard University library, pamphlets on British political affairs, *c.* 1760–1825, in collections origin-ally formed by George Pitt, Lord Rivers, and by Augustus Frederick, Duke of

Sussex (see A. C. Potter, *The Library of Harvard University*, Camb., Mass., 1915); at Columbia University, N.Y., the Edwin R. A. Seligman collection on economic history, and in the Sterling Library, Yale University libraries, the collection 'Economic Tracts', both including material on Great Britain. In Canada McGill University library holds a substantial number of pamphlets relating to British affairs in its Redpath collection, and also a separate collection of Canadian pamphlets.

F. MANUSCRIPTS

The National Register of Archives maintained by the Royal Commission on Historical Manuscripts is the central clearing-house for information about the large numbers of archives still in private hands in the United Kingdom or which have been deposited in repositories since 1945. The Register comprises over 18,000 lists, varying from brief reports to detailed catalogues, on which are based detailed personal, subject, and topographical indexes, the first of these being printed out by computer. Brief summaries of lists added to the Register appear in the 22nd and subsequent *Report(s) of the Royal Commission on Historical Manuscripts*, publ. irregularly. The Commission also issues typescript source lists for business history and the history of architecture and the fine and applied arts, based on information held in the National Register of Archives. John Brooke, *The Prime Ministers' Papers, 1801–1902*, 1968, constitutes a valuable guide to archives of major significance for the student of nineteenth-century politics, other than sources for extreme radicalism. From 1923 to 1975 the *Bulletin* of the Institute of Historical Research (46) listed migrations of MSS., including those reported in dealers' catalogues. The recording of deposits of MSS. was taken over by the *Bulletin* of the National Register of Archives in 1955 and has continued as an annual publication since that date, under the title, *List of Accessions to Repositories*, since 1957 published by the Stationery Office for the Royal Commission on Historical Manuscripts. *Archives*, 1949+, the journal of the British Records Association, includes informative articles on holdings of manuscripts in a variety of repositories; *Business Archives*, new series, 1969+, the journal of the Business Archives Council, includes articles and notes on business records.

The archives of government departments in the Public Record Office, London, form by far the most extensive and important collection of manuscript source material for British history in the early nineteenth century. Among its other deposits are the papers of the prime ministers, William Pitt and Lord John Russell. The British Museum has substantial relevant holdings, including the papers of the prime ministers, Lord Grenville, Perceval, Liverpool, Goderich, and Peel, the letter-books of Palmerston as foreign secretary, and the papers of many lesser political figures. In aggregate a very great mass of manuscript material is also now held in provincial repositories—county record offices, major public libraries, and university libraries; such holdings include the papers of Canning in Leeds Central Library and of Earl Grey at the University of Durham. For a list of principal repositories see *Record Repositories in Great Britain*, 5th edition, 1973, HMSO for the Royal Commission on Historical Manuscripts.

Philip Hepworth, *Archives and manuscripts in libraries*, 2nd edn., 1964, includes a list of published guides and catalogues to collections in British libraries. F. G. Emmison, *Introduction to archives*, 1964, rev. edn., 1972, is a good brief introduction, mainly on local records; see too the 'Short guides to records' under the general editorship of L. M. Munby, published in *History*, vols. 47–56 (1962–71), issued in book form, 1972.

1. GUIDES AND CATALOGUES

For guides to collections of general national interest in the National Libraries of Wales and Scotland, see (3798) and (3872). For London see P. E. Jones and R. Smith (3751).

64   GUIDE to the contents of the Public Record Office. 3 v. 1963–8.

V. 1, Legal records; v. 2, State papers and departmental records; v. 3, documents transferred to the P.R.O., 1960–66, plus considerable additions and corrections to vols. 1–2. Sir Hilary Jenkinson, *Guide to the public records*, pt. 1: *Introductory*, 1949, repr. 1950, is a valuable general account of the way in which the collections have been amassed and maintained. Handbooks to particular sections of the records include: no. 3, *The records of the colonial and dominions office*, 1964, and no. 13, *The records of the foreign office, 1782–1939*, 1969. There is detail on some runs in the P.R.O. *Lists and indexes*, 55 v., 1892–1936, supplementary series, 1961+. The List and Index Society, *Select catalogue of unpublished search room lists in the Public Record Office*, 1965, lists guides and indexes which the society has since been publishing by subscription in photographic copy. P.R.O., *Catalogue of microfilm*, 1967, lists material for which master film had already been made to that date. The annual *Report of the keeper of public records and . . . report of the Advisory Council on public records, 1959+*, 1960+, includes yearly listings of accessions, mainly subsumed up to 1966 in the *Guide*.

65   PARLIAMENT. Guide to the records of parliament. By Maurice F. Bond. 1971.

Describes 'the complete range of records preserved within the Palace of Westminster: the records of both Houses of Parliament; all documents which have been presented to the two Houses or purchased by them; and the papers which have accumulated in the various parliamentary and non-parliamentary offices of the Palace'.

66   BRITISH MUSEUM. List [Catalogue] of additions to the manuscripts in the British Museum . . . 1836+. 1843+.

The guide to the main collections (Additional MSS. and Egerton MSS.) of concern for British history after 1789, with incomplete indexes of correspondents. See too *Index to the Additional MSS., with those of the Egerton collection . . . acquired . . . 1783–1839*, 1949. For recent accessions unindexed draft catalogues can be consulted in the Museum's manuscript room. So far there is one separate index for a major nineteenth-century collection: *Catalogue of additions to the manuscripts. . . . The Gladstone papers*, 1953. The *British Museum quarterly*, 1926+, includes notes on accessions. For other collections see *The catalogues of the manuscript collections in the British Museum*, rev. edn., 1962.

67   LONDON UNIVERSITY. Catalogue of the manuscripts and autograph letters in the University library. Comp. by R. A. Rye. 1921.

Includes some correspondence of Richard Cobden; now out of date, and for additional accessions consultation of the library's working catalogue is essential. A new up-to-date catalogue is in preparation. For an interim report see Joan Gibbs and Paul Kelly,

'Manuscripts and archives in the University of London library', *Archives* xi (1973–4), 161–71.

68	BODLEIAN LIBRARY. A summary catalogue of western manuscripts in the Bodleian library. Ed. by F. Madan and H. H. E. Craster. 7 v. in 8. Oxf. 1895–1953.

Deals with accessions up to 1915 only. For information on more recent accessions see the annual *Report of the curators*, and the *Bodleian quarterly record*, 1–8 (1917–38), continued as the *Bodleian Library record*, 1+, 1938+.

69	CAMBRIDGE UNIVERSITY LIBRARY. Summary guide to accessions of western manuscripts (other than medieval) since 1867. Comp. by A. E. B. Owen. Camb. 1966.

Holdings include letters of William Pitt, David Ricardo, Sir James Stephen, William Smith, M.P.

70	DURHAM UNIVERSITY LIBRARY. Summary list of the additional manuscripts accessioned and listed between September 1945 and September 1961. By David Ramage. Durham. 1963.

Grey of Howick MSS. and other collections. For greater detail see the following typed duplicated lists: 'List of political and public correspondence of the second Earl Grey . . . 1787–1843', and 'List of personal and family correspondence of the second Earl Grey . . . 1762–1875', 2 v., 1956–7, comp. by M. Jack; and 'A list of the correspondence of the third Earl Grey, 1818–1894', comp. by J. E. Fagg, 1960, for the University of Durham department of palaeography and diplomatic.

71	JOHN RYLANDS LIBRARY, MANCHESTER. 'Hand-list of the collection of English manuscripts in the . . . library, 1928'. By Moses Tyson. *John Rylands Lib. Bull.* 13 (1929), 152–219.

Tyson also comp. 'Hand-list of additions . . . 1928–35', *ibid.* 19 (1935), 230–54, 458–85. F. Taylor comp., *Supplementary hand-list of western manuscripts in the . . . library*, 1937, Manchester, 1937, and *Handlist of additions . . . 1937–1951*, Manchester, 1951. Holdings include Wedgwood papers, Thrale-Piozzi papers, Melville papers relating to East Indian affairs, Hibbert-Ware papers, Oldknow papers, records of the Moravian church.

72	SHEFFIELD CITY LIBRARIES. Guide to the manuscript collections. [Prepared by R. Meredith]. Sheffield, 1956.

Supplement 1+, *1956–1962+*, Sheffield, 1962+.

73	HAMER (PHILIP MAY) *ed.* A guide to archives and manuscripts in the United States. National Historical Publications Commission. New Haven. 1961.

Comprehensive, and giving reference to printed guides for particular repositories. See too the *National union catalog of manuscript collections*, Ann Arbor, Mich., 1962, Hamden, Conn., 1964, Washington, D.C., 1965+. The William L. Clements library, Ann Arbor, Michigan, has substantial holdings relating to later Georgian British history; see the *Guide to the manuscript collections . . .*, ed. by H. H. Peckham, 1942. Jean Preston, 'Collections of English historical manuscripts in the Huntington library [San Marino, Calif.]', *Archives*, 6 (1963–4), 95–107, notes papers of Richard Carlile, Thomas Clarkson, Zachary Macaulay, Richard, Earl Howe, the Hastings family, and the Grenvilles of Stowe. Other information occasionally appears in the *Huntington Library quarterly*, 1931+.

74 CRICK (BERNARD ROWLAND) *and* ALMAN (MIRIAM) *eds.* A guide to manuscripts relating to America in Great Britain and Ireland. 1961.

Covers much material relating as much to British as to American history. See too L. K. Born, *British manuscripts projects; a checklist of the microfilms prepared in England and Wales for the American Council of Learned Societies, 1941–5*, Washington, 1955.

2. HISTORICAL MANUSCRIPTS COMMISSION REPORTS

The early reports compiled for the Royal Commission on historical manuscripts tended to be brief general descriptions of material in private hands and in borough, cathedral, and other corporate archives. Practice changed fairly rapidly towards production of partial and then of reasonably full calendars of collections of interest for general political history. The early reports can still be of some help in establishing the existence of collections, though in many instances these have now changed hands or passed into a repository, and often more up-to-date information is obtainable through the National Register of Archives (p. 11).

There is no complete guide to the series. For a list, see the most recent updated issue of United Kingdom Government Publications, *Publications of the Royal Commission on Historical Manuscripts, sectional list no. 17*, pub. irregularly. For reports issued up to 1911 see the index, pt. 1, *Topographical*, ed. by R. A. Roberts, 1914, pt. 2, *Persons*, ed. by Francis Bickley, 2 v., 1935–8. For the later reports see the index of persons, *Guide to the reports of the Historical Manuscripts Commission, 1911–1957*, ed. by A. C. S. Hall, 3 v., 1966; a topographical index for this period is in preparation. The Commission's early surveys of cathedral muniments, besides being summary, were incomplete, and Dorothy M. Owen (p. 101) is more helpful. Similarly local records can now better be approached in other ways—see Tate (508) and pp. 73–4, 428.

Till very recently the Commission paid little attention to records for nineteenth-century history, and only a few of its publications have much material for the period 1789–1851. Those of principal interest are:

75 BATHURST. Series 76. Manuscripts of Earl Bathurst preserved at Cirencester Park, 1665–1834. 1923.

Chiefly the political corresp. of Henry, 3rd Earl Bathurst, secretary of state for war and colonies, 1812–27.

76 CARLISLE. Series 42. Manuscripts of the earl of Carlisle at Castle Howard. Fifteenth report, appendix 6. 1897.

Includes a few important letters on Irish affairs and some items of royal corresp.

77 CHARLEMONT. Series 28. Manuscripts of the earl of Charlemont, part 2. 1894.

Corresp. of James, 1st earl of Charlemont, on Irish and general politics, 1784–1799.

78 GRENVILLE. Series 30. The manuscripts of J. B. Fortescue, formerly preserved at Dropmore. Thirteenth report, appendix 3, Fourteenth report, appendix 5, and Fortescue MSS., vs. 3–10. 10 v. 1892–1927.

The political corresp. of William, Lord Grenville, 1789–1820. A very full calendar, though not complete; the collection is now British Museum Additional MSS. 58855–59494.

79 LONSDALE. Series 33. The manuscripts of the earl of Lonsdale. Thirteenth report, appendix 7. 1893.

Includes political and family corr. of James and William, earls of Lonsdale, 1789–1815, substantial on 1806–7, from the papers now in the Cumberland and Westmorland R.O.

80 RAWDON HASTINGS. Series 78. The manuscripts of Mr. R. Rawdon Hastings, formerly at Ashby de la Zouch. V. 3. 1934.

Political and miscell. corr. of Francis, 2nd earl of Moira, 1790–1815, including letters of the Prince of Wales and other members of the royal family.

81 GLADSTONE. The autobiographica of W. E. Gladstone. Ed. by John Brooke and Mary O. Sorensen. 1971.

Also *Autobiographical memoranda of W. E. Gladstone*, ed. by John Brooke and Mary O. Sorensen, 1972, in progress, v. 1: *1832–1845*, 1972; the first publications in the Commission's new series on Prime Ministers' papers, 1801–1902 (see Brooke, p. 11).

The following calendars are of less interest but contain some material for the period 1789–1830: Series 8: Ninth report, appendix 2, Elphinstone MSS. (history of India); Alfred Morrison MSS. (miscell.; see also Nelson (1248), Hamilton (2070), Blessington (2717)); Series 15: Tenth report, appendix 6, Abergavenny MSS. (general politics), Braye MSS. (letters of the Cardinal Duke of York); Series 35: Fourteenth report, appendix 4, Kenyon MSS. (general and legal); Series 55: Various collections, v. 6, Cornwallis Wykeham-Martin MSS. (naval); Series 64: MSS. of the earl of Verulam (personal and political); Series 72: Laing MSS. in the University of Edinburgh library, v. 2 (miscell. and Scottish politics); Series 81: Graham of Fintry MSS., supplementary report (family and military affairs).

II

POLITICAL HISTORY

A. HISTORIES

1. 1789–1851 (general)

For political caricature see George (2914).

82 HUGHES (THOMAS SMART). The history of England by Hume and Smollett continued from the death of George II to the present time. 6 v. 1835–6.

Carried to the accession of Queen Victoria and largely rewritten, 7 v., 1855. Full narrative from contemporary printed material.

83 A HISTORY OF ENGLAND. Ed. by Sir Charles Oman. Vol. 6: England under the Hanoverians, by Sir Charles Grant Robertson, 15th edn. 1948. Vol. 7: England since Waterloo, by Sir John Arthur Ransome Marriott, 15th edn. with a new select bibliog. by M. R. D. Foot, 1954.

More up to date in treatment than *The Political History of England*, ed. by William Hunt and Reginald L. Poole, v. 10: *1760–1801*, by W. Hunt, 1905; v. 11: *1801–1837*, by George C. Brodrick and J. K. Fotheringham, 1906; v. 12: *1837–1901*, by Sidney J. Low and Lloyd C. Sanders, 1907. Sir Herbert Eustace Maxwell, *A century of empire, 1801–1901*, 3 v., 1909, is still worth consulting. See too William Law Mathieson, *England in transition, 1789–1832: a study of movements*, 1920.

84 TREVELYAN (GEORGE MACAULAY). British history in the nineteenth century and after, 1782–1919. 1922. New edn. 1937.

With Briggs (88) the best one-volume history of the period. Esmé Cecil Wingfield-Stratford, *The history of British civilization*, 2nd rev. edn., 1945, has brief but suggestive chapters on the period.

85 FEILING (*Sir* KEITH GRAHAME). The second Tory party, 1714–1832. 1938. Rep. 1951.

A more general analysis of politics than its title suggests. See also the penetrating analysis in Archibald S. Foord, *His Majesty's Opposition, 1714–1830*, Oxf., 1964. Some technical points are discussed in Arthur Aspinall, 'English party organization in the early nineteenth century', *E.H.R.* 41 (1926), 389–411. On party ideas see Reginald James White, ed., *The conservative tradition*, 1950; Alan Bullock and Maurice Shock, eds., *The liberal tradition from Fox to Keynes*, 1956; Simon Maccoby, *The English radical tradition, 1763–1914*, 1952, and *English Radicalism, 1786–1832: From Paine to Cobbett*, 1955, and *English Radicalism, 1832–1852*, 1935. Simple outlines are provided by William Harris, *The history of the radical party in parliament*, 1885, and Clement Boulton Roylance Kent, *The English radicals: an historical sketch*, 1899. J. W. Derry, *The radical tradition: Tom Paine to Lloyd George*, 1967, discusses Paine, Cobbett, Bentham, Owen, the Chartists, Cobden, Bright, and J. S. Mill. H. W. C. Davis, *The age of Grey and Peel*, Oxf., 1929, is a suggestive survey.

86 COLE (GEORGE DOUGLAS HOWARD) *and* POSTGATE (RAY-MOND WILLIAM). The common people, 1746–1946. 2nd edn. rep. 1956.

Bibliog. 689–708. Complementary to this work are G. D. H. Cole, *A short history of the British working class movement, 1789–1947*, new edn., 1948, and G. D. H. Cole and Alexander W. Filson, *British working class movements: select documents, 1789–1875*, 1951. A limited selection of extracts is in *The challenge of socialism*, ed. by Henry M. Pelling, 1954.

87 ENGLISH HISTORICAL DOCUMENTS. General ed. David Charles Douglas. Vol. 11: 1783–1832, ed. by Arthur Aspinall and E. Anthony Smith, 1959. Vol. 12. I: 1833–1874, ed. by George Malcolm Young and William Day Handcock, 1956.

Rich representative collections, with valuable introductions and bibliogs.

88 BRIGGS (ASA). The age of improvement. 1959.

An excellent survey of 1783–1867 incorporating the results of recent scholarship.

89 OXFORD HISTORY OF ENGLAND. Ed. by Sir George Clark. [Vol. 12]: The reign of George III, 1760–1815, by John Steven Watson, Oxf., 1960. [Vol. 13]: The Age of Reform 1815–1870, by Sir Ernest Llewellyn Woodward, Oxf., 1938, 2nd edn., 1962.

Standard, with select bibliogs.

90 WEBB (ROBERT KIEFER). Modern England; from the eighteenth century to the present. N.Y., 1968. London, 1969.

Standard. See too J. W. Derry, *Reaction and reform, 1793–1868; England in the early nineteenth century*, 1963; W. B. Willcox, *The age of aristocracy, 1688–1830*, Boston, 1966.

91 CANNON (JOHN). Parliamentary reform, 1640–1832. Camb. 1973.

Standard, with valuable reappraisals. See also E. Royle, *Radical politics, 1790–1900; religion and unbelief*, Harlow, 1971.

2. 1789–1815

92 BELSHAM (WILLIAM). History of Great Britain from the revolution, 1688, to the conclusion of the treaty of Amiens. 12 v. 1805.

In part a reissue of his *Memoirs of the reign of George III*, which ended at 1783; continued in *Memoirs of George III from the treaty of Amiens . . . to the termination of the regency*, 2 v., 1824; Foxite in tone, provoking an answering work by Robert Bisset, *The history of the reign of George III, to [1802]*, 6 v., 1803, 2nd edn. with adds. to 1820, 6 v., 1820. More detached are Charles Coote, *History of England*, vol. 10 [1783–1802], 1803, John Aikin, *Annals of the reign of George III*, 2 v., 1816, 2nd edn. 2 v., 1820, and authors who 'continued' Smollett's *History of England*: James Robins (Robert Scott, *pseud.*), 4 v., 1824; William Jones, 3 v., 1825; J. R. Miller, 1825, 2nd edn., 1828. Jean Edmond Tournachon de Montvéran, *Histoire critique et raisonnée de la situation de l'Angleterre au 1er Janvier 1816*, 8 v., Paris, 1819–22, is a survey of British development over the previous thirty years.

93 ADOLPHUS (JOHN). History of England from the accession to the decease of George III. 7 v. 1840–5.

Written from a conservative viewpoint. Thomas S. Hughes, *The history of England* ...
[*1760–1837*], 5 v., 1834–6, reflects a similar view. Liberal in tone is W. N. Massey,
A history of England during the reign of George III, 4 v., 1855–63, 2nd edn. 4 v., 1865.

94　O'GORMAN (FRANCIS). The whig party and the French Revolution. 1967.

Principally on the years 1789–94. Some aspects of the party's situation are set forth in
Whig organization in the general election of 1790; selections from the Blair Adam papers,
ed. by D. E. Ginter, Berkeley and London, 1967; for others see J. W. Derry, *The regency
crisis and the whigs, 1788–9*, Camb., 1963. More centred on the role of Fox is L. G.
Mitchell, *Charles James Fox and the disintegration of the whig party, 1782–1794*, 1971.
See too Herbert Butterfield, 'Charles James Fox and the Whig opposition in 1792',
Camb. Hist. J. 9 (1949), 293–330.

95　VEITCH (GEORGE STEAD). The genesis of parliamentary reform. 1913. Repr. 1964.

Standard; bibliog. 366–8. Philip A. Brown, *The French Revolution in English History*,
1918, gives a rather different emphasis. Eugene Charlton Black, *The Association*, Camb.,
Mass., 1963, gives a concise account of pro- and anti-reform organizations in the
'nineties. Brief but suggestive is Robert Birley, *The English Jacobins from 1789 to 1802*,
Oxf., 1924; and for examples of radical thought see *The debate on the French Revolution,
1789–1800*, ed. by Alfred Cobban, 2nd edn., 1960. W. A. L. Seaman, 'Reform politics
at Sheffield, 1791–1797', *Trans. Hunter Arch. Soc.*, 7 (1957), 215–28, and Freda Knight,
The strange case of Thomas Walker: ten years in the life of a Manchester radical, 1957,
are recent studies of local radicalism. Some contrasts with France in the 'nineties are
drawn in G. A. Williams, *Artisans and sans-culottes*, 1968. See too Carl B. Cone, *The
English Jacobins*, N.Y., 1968; J. Wardroper, *Kings, lords and wicked libellers*, 1973;
Thompson (1810).

96　BARNES (DONALD GROVE). George III and William Pitt, 1783–1806: a new interpretation based upon a study of their unpublished correspondence. Stanford Univ. [Cal.] 1939.

An examination of Pitt's and the king's attitudes to various problems of policy based,
apart from the king's papers, on printed material. The assessment of Pitt's politics in
William Thomas Laprade, *England and the French Revolution, 1789–1797*, Baltimore,
1909, has not won general acceptance.

97　ROBERTS (MICHAEL). The Whig Party, 1807–1812. 1939.

Very full examination of political structure and manœuvres. See too his papers, 'The fall
of the Talents, March 1807', 'The leadership of the Whig party in the House of Commons, 1807–1815', 'The ministerial crisis of May–June 1812', *E.H.R.* 50 (1935), 61–77,
620–38, 51 (1936), 466–87.

98　BRYANT (*Sir* ARTHUR WYNNE MORGAN). The years of endurance: 1793–1802. 1942.

With his *Years of victory, 1802–1812*, 1944, and *The age of elegance, 1812–1822*, 1950,
a well-written narrative of the years of war with France and of return to peace. Francis
John MacCunn, *The contemporary English view of Napoleon*, 1914, examines the attitudes
of the politicians and of leading writers.

99　DARVALL (FRANK ONGLEY). Popular disturbances and public order in Regency England; being an account of the Luddite and other disorders in

England during ... 1811–1817, and of the attitude and activity of the authorities. 1934. Repr. 1969.

Frank Peel, *The risings of the Luddites, Chartists, and Plugdrawers*, Heckmondwike, 1888, drew on oral tradition about the Luddites. See M. I. Thomis, *The Luddites; machine-breaking in Regency England*, Newton Abbot, 1970; and Henson (1547), E. P. Thompson (1810), Blackner and Thomis (3664).

3. 1815–1851

100 WALPOLE (*Sir* SPENCER). A history of England from the conclusion of the great war in 1815. Rev. edn. 6 v. 1890.

Old fashioned and out of date but still of use for the narrower field of political narrative. Harriet Martineau, *History of England during the thirty years' peace, 1816–1846*, 2 v., 1845–50, has the merits and defects of a work from a contemporary radical viewpoint. More strictly descriptive is William Johnston, *England as it is . . . in the middle of the nineteenth century*, 2 v., 1851. Reinhold Pauli, *Geschichte Englands seit den Friedenschlüssen von 1814 und 1815*, 3 v., Leipzig, 1864–75, is discriminating. W. N. Molesworth, *History of England from . . . 1830*, 3 v., 1871–3, is useful but overlooked salient sources.

101 HALÉVY (ELIE). History of the English people in the nineteenth century. Trans. by E. I. Watkin. 2nd rev. edn. 6 v. 1949–52.

V. 1: *England in 1815*; v. 2: *The liberal awakening, 1815–1830*; v. 3: *The triumph of reform, 1830–1841*; v. 4: *Victorian years, 1841–1895*; valuable especially for its concern with social and religious forces, and indispensable. Recent surveys and discussions include G. S. R. Kitson Clark, *An expanding society: Britain, 1830–1900*, Camb., 1967; N. H. Brasher, *Arguments in history: Britain in the nineteenth century*, 1968; C. J. Bartlett, *Britain pre-eminent; studies of British world influence in the nineteenth century*, 1969; D. E. D. Beales, *A history of England*, v. 7: *From Castlereagh to Gladstone, 1815–1885*, 1969.

102 CROOK (DAVID PAUL). American democracy in English politics, 1815–1850. Oxf. 1965.

Examines the uses to which ideas about the U.S.A. were put by British politicians. G. D. Lillibridge, *Beacon of freedom: the impact of American democracy upon Great Britain, 1830–1870*, Phil., London, 1955, examines American influence on British radical reformers. See too Patricia Hollis, *The pauper press* (3500).

103 MITCHELL (AUSTIN VERNON). The Whigs in opposition, 1815–1830. Oxf. 1967.

A valuable study covering both political structure and party politics. See too A. V. Mitchell, 'The Whigs and parliamentary reform before 1830', *Historical Studies, Australia and New Zealand*, 12 (1965–67), 22–42.

104 MACHIN (GEORGE IAN THOM). The Catholic question in English politics, 1820–1830. Oxf. 1964.

105 WHITE (REGINALD JAMES). Waterloo to Peterloo. 1957.

Primarily concerned with social unrest and agitation for reform. Donald Read, *Peterloo: the 'massacre' and its background*, Manchester, 1958, is a thorough study of this subject in the Manchester area. For other interpretations see R. Walmsley, *Peterloo: the case re-opened*, Manchester, 1969, and Joyce Marlow (*pseud.* for Joyce M. Connor), *The*

Peterloo massacre, 1969. Manchester Public Libraries pub. *Peterloo . . . a bibliography*, comp. by M. E. Leighton, 1969, and *Peterloo, 1819: a portfolio of contemporary documents*, ed. by H. Horton, 1969. See also Bamford (2205), Cobbett (188), Hunt (2255); Thompson (1810).

106 ASPINALL (ARTHUR). 'The Canning ministry'. *E.H.R.* 42 (1927), 201–26.

See too his 'The Goderich ministry', *ibid.*, 533–59; 'The last of the Canningites', *ibid.*, 50 (1935), 639–69; 'The Canningite party', *Trans. Roy. Hist. Soc.*, 4th ser., 17 (1934), 177–226. Herbert Randolph ed. *Canning's administration: narrative of formation, with correspondence*, from the papers of Sir Robert Wilson, 1872; see also (179).

107 BUTLER (JAMES RAMSAY MONTAGU). The passing of the great reform bill. 1914. New impr. 1964.

Standard. Among writings by contemporaries are John A. Roebuck, *History of the Whig ministry of 1830 to the passing of the reform bill*, 2 v., 1852; A. J. Maley, *Historical recollections of the reign of William IV*, 1860; W. N. Molesworth, *The history of the reform bill of 1832*, 1865. M. G. Brock, *The great reform act*, 1973, is an indispensable reassessment. Various aspects are discussed in: A. S. Turberville and F. Beckwith, 'Leeds and parliamentary reform, 1820–1832', *Thoresby Misc.* 12 (1943), 1–89; A. Briggs, 'The background of the parliamentary reform movement in three English cities (1830–2)', *Camb. Hist. J.* 10 (1950–2), 293–317; E. Hughes, 'The bishops and reform, 1831–1833: some fresh correspondence', *E.H.R.* 56 (1941), 459–90; N. Gash, 'English reform and French revolution in the general election of 1830', in *Essays presented to Sir Lewis Namier*, ed. by Richard Pares and A. J. P. Taylor, 1956, 257–88; D. C. Moore, 'The other face of reform', *Victorian Studies* 5 (1961–2), 7–34, and 'Concession or cure: the sociological premises of the first reform act', *Hist. J.* 9 (1966), 39–59; N. McCord, 'Some difficulties of parliamentary reform', *ibid.* 10 (1967), 376–90; J. Milton Smith, 'Earl Grey's cabinet and the objects of parliamentary reform', *ibid.* 15 (1972), 55–74. See also William IV (216), Attwood (1434), Grey (176), Russell (205), Durham (206), Graham (220).

108 McDOWELL (ROBERT BRENDAN). British Conservatism, 1832–1914. 1959.

See Peel (199–200). N. Gash discusses Peel and conservative politics in 'Peel and the party system, 1830–1850', *Trans. Roy. Hist. Soc.*, 5th ser. 1 (1951), 47–69. Conservative attitudes to social questions are considered in Richard L. Hill, *Toryism and the people, 1832–1846*, 1929; and see Oastler (1725), Shaftesbury (2518).

109 SOUTHGATE (DONALD GEORGE). The passing of the whigs, 1832–1886. 1962.

110 LITTLETON (EDWARD JOHN, *1st baron Hatherton*). Memoir and correspondence relating to political occurrences in June and July 1834. Ed. by Henry Reeve. 1872.

111 McCORD (NORMAN). The anti-corn-law league, 1838–1846. 1958.

Indispensable. The standard contemporary history is Archibald Prentice, *History of the anti-corn-law league*, 2 v., 1853, new edn. with introd. by W. H. Chaloner, 2 v., 1968. Economic motives of M.P.s are discussed in John Alun Thomas, 'The repeal of the corn laws, 1846', *Economica*, 9 (1929), 53–60. A. A. W. Ramsay, 'The crisis in the cabinet, 1845', *Cornhill mag.*, 160 (1939), 188–201, examines a little-known intrigue relating to repeal. Important aspects are treated in G. S. R. Kitson Clark, 'The electorate and the repeal of the corn laws', *Trans. Roy. Hist. Soc.*, 5th ser., 1 (1951), 109–26; 'The repeal of the corn laws and the politics of the 'forties', *Econ. H.R.*, 2nd ser., 4 (1951–2), 1–13; and 'Hunger and politics in 1842', *J. of Mod. Hist.* 25 (1953), 355–74. See too G. L. Mosse, 'The anti-league, 1844–1846', *Econ. H.R.* 17 (1947), 134–42; D. Spring, 'Earl Fitzwilliam and the corn laws', *A.H.R.* 59 (1953–4), 287–304, Mary Lawson-Tancred (1661). On the corn laws see (1509) and (1659–1663).

112 HOVELL (MARK). The Chartist movement. Ed. and completed with a memoir by T. F. Tout. Manchester. 1918. 2nd imp. 1950.

A classic, and the best general narrative. R. G. Gammage, *History of the Chartist movement, 1837–1854*, new edn., Newcastle on Tyne, 1894, includes much first-hand material. Edouard Dolléans, *Le chartisme, 1830–1848*, 2 v., Paris, 1912–13, is excellent. More summary general surveys are Neil Stewart, *The fight for the charter*, 1937, and Reginald Groves, *But we shall rise again: a narrative history of Chartism*, 1938. Theodore Rothstein [Fedor A. Rotshtein], *From Chartism to labourism*, 1929, by a Russian communist, presents some interesting material. *From Cobbett to the Chartists*, ed. by Max Morris, 2nd edn., 1951, is a collection of extracts from contemporary sources. See also Dorothy Thompson, *The early Chartists*, 1971; J. T. Ward, *Chartism*, 1973; David Jones, *Chartism*, 1975.

113 BRIGGS (ASA) *ed.* Chartist studies. 1959.

Valuable examinations of regional variations in Chartism. For particular areas see David Williams, *John Frost: a study in Chartism*, Cardiff, 1939; L. C. Wright, *Scottish Chartism*, 1953; A. Wilson, *The Chartist movement in Scotland*, Manchester, 1970. On various aspects see H. U. Faulkner, *Chartism and the churches: a study in democracy*, N.Y., 1916; F. F. Rosenblatt, *The Chartist movement in its social and economic aspects*, N.Y., 1916; P. W. Slosson, *The decline of the Chartist movement*, N.Y., 1916; Alice M. Hadfield, *The Chartist land company*, Newton Abbot, 1970. John Warner and W. A. Gunn, *John Frost and the Chartist movement in Monmouthshire*, 1939, is a valuable bibliography. For social background to Chartism see Hammond (1807), and on the problem of public order Mather (2627).

114 COLE (GEORGE DOUGLAS HOWARD). Chartist portraits. 1941.

Indispensable. See also John Saville, ed., *Ernest Jones: Chartist*, 1952; A. R. Schoyen, *The Chartist challenge: a portrait of George Julian Harney*, 1958; Donald Read and Eric Glasgow, *Feargus O'Connor, Irishman and Chartist*, 1961; A. Plummer, *Bronterre. A political biography of Bronterre O'Brien, 1804–1864*, 1971. See too Frost, J. (113), Frost, T. (2350), Holyoake (2354), Linton (2326), Lovett (2322), Stephens (1725), Cooper (2329).

115 STEWART (ROBERT). The politics of Protection: Lord Derby and the Protectionist party, 1841–52. Camb. 1971.

116 CONACHER (JAMES B.). The Peelites and the party system, 1846–52. Newton Abbot. 1972.

W. D. Jones and A. B. Erickson, *The Peelites, 1846–1857*, Columbus, Ohio, 1972.

B. POLITICAL PAMPHLETS AND POLITICAL ESSAY JOURNALS

Works with bibliographical lists of pamphlets relating to particular subjects are Veitch and Black (95), Maccoby (85), Cobban (95), Roberts (97), Gray (182), Pearl (188), Driver (1725), Hill (108), Warner and Gunn (113). For the period

1813–1828, *The Pamphleteer*, 29 v., 1813–28, general index v. 29, reproduced over 500 pamphlets: well over the 150 actually classed as 'political' are of political interest. See also *Edinburgh Review, Examiner, Quarterly Review, Westminster Review*. Brougham's contributions to the *Edinburgh* are identified in New (207). Albany Fonblanque reprinted his contributions to the *Examiner* in *England under seven administrations*, 3 v., 1837. The following small list out of a vast field has been selected to be representative of writers and opinions.

117 HEYWOOD (SAMUEL). The right of Protestant Dissenters to a compleat toleration asserted; containing an historical account of the Test Laws. 2nd edn. 1789.

Other contributions to this campaign were Capel Lofft, *An history of the corporation and test acts*, Bury, 1790, and *A vindication of the . . . history*, 1790; Anna Letitia Aikin (afterwards Barbauld), *An address to the opposers of the repeal of the Corporation and Test Acts*, 1790; Christopher Wyvill, *A defence of Dr. Price and the reformers of England*, 1792.

118 WOLLSTONECRAFT (MARY). A vindication of the rights of men. 1790.

One of the best replies to Burke's *Reflections* (518); followed by her *A vindication of the rights of women*, 1792. Burke was also attacked in William Belsham, *Examination of an appeal from the New to the Old Whigs*, 1792.

119 BOWLES (JOHN). The retrospect; or, a collection of tracts published at various periods of the war. 1798.

Six essays, 1793–6, justifying the war with France. Burke's attacks on peace feelers provoked Samuel Ferrand Waddington, *A review of Mr. Burke's three letters on a regicide peace*, 1796; see too Edmund Burke, *A letter . . . to . . . the Duke of Portland, on the conduct of the minority in parliament. Containing fifty-four articles of impeachment against . . . C. J. Fox*, 1797. Thomas Erskine, *A view of the causes and consequences of the present war with France*, 35 edns. in 1797, was answered by John Gifford, *pseud.* of John Richards Green, *A letter to . . . Thomas Erskine*, 1797, and *A second letter . . .* 1797, and by John Bowles, *French aggression proved*, 1797. Herbert Marsh, *The history of the politics of Great Britain and France*, 2 v. 1800, a detailed defence of the ministry, was attacked in William Belsham, *Remarks on a late publication styled, The history* (etc.), 1800: both wrote rejoinders.

120 DYER (GEORGE). The complaints of the poor people of England. 2nd edn. corr. and enl. 1793.

A comprehensive statement of the demand for constitutional reform in the interests of the underprivileged lower orders of society.

121 STUART (DANIEL). Peace and reform against war and corruption, in answer to a pamphlet written by Arthur Young, entitled, The example of France a warning to Great Britain. 1794.

Representative of the views of the aristocratic Society of the Friends of the People. For more radical opinions see Joseph Gerrald, *A convention the only means of saving us from ruin*, 1793; John Thelwall, *The natural and constitutional right of Britons to annual parliaments, universal suffrage, and freedom of popular association*, 1795, and *The rights of nature against the usurpations of establishments*, 1796. [Vicesimus Knox], *The spirit of despotism*, ed. by W. Hone, 1821, was circulated secretly in 1795.

122 ASSOCIATION FOR PRESERVING LIBERTY AND PROPERTY against republicans and levellers. Association Papers. Pt. I: Publications printed by special order of the society. Pt. II: Liberty and property preserved. 1793.

Its conservative and loyalist ideas were also voiced by Robert Nares, *Principles of government deduced from reason*, 1792; Thomas Somerville, *Observations on the constitution and present state of Great Britain*, 1793; Arthur Young, *The constitution safe without reform*, Bury, 1795; John Reeves, *Thoughts on English government* [three letters], 1795–99. Anti-revolution propaganda was continued in the *Anti Jacobin*, 1797–8, and the *Anti-Jacobin Review and Magazine*, ed. by John Gifford, *pseud.* of John Richards Green, v. 1–61, 1798–1821.

123 MACKENNA (THEOBALD). Constitutional objections to the government of Ireland by a separate legislature, in a letter to John Hamilton esq., occasioned by his remarks on a Memoire on the projected union. 3 edns. Dublin. 1799.

The connected question of Catholic emancipation was argued in John Reeves, *Considerations on the coronation oath*, 1801, and Sir John Joseph Dillon, *The question as to the admission of Catholics to Parliament*, 1801.

124 BELSHAM (WILLIAM). Remarks on the late definitive treaty of peace, signed at Amiens, March 25, 1802. 1802.

Defended the treaty, which was attacked virulently in William Cobbett, *Letters to Lord Hawkesbury and Henry Addington on the peace with Bonaparte*, 1802. British renewal of the war was defended in William Hunter, *A vindication of the cause of Great Britain*, 1803.

125 [BENTLEY (THOMAS RICHARD)]. A few cursory remarks upon the state of parties during the administration of . . . Henry Addington. By a near observer. 9 edns. 1803.

This defence of Addington was attacked in *A plain answer to . . . The cursory remarks*, 1803; *Observations on a ministerial pamphlet entitled, Cursory remarks*, 1803; *General review of men and measures, occasioned by Remarks of Near and Accurate Observers*, 1804. Lord Archibald Hamilton, *Thoughts on the formation of the late and present administrations*, 1804, was a Foxite attack on both Addington and Pitt.

126 BROUGHAM (HENRY PETER). An inquiry into the state of the nation. 6 edns. 1806.

A Foxite discussion of the war situation, which evoked *An answer to the Inquiry . . . with strictures on the . . . present ministry*, 1806. [Charles James Fox], *The state of the negotiation . . . with details of its progress*, 4 edns., 1806, exhibits Fox's war aims.

127 [HORNER (F.) *and* BENNET (H. G.)]. A short account of a late short administration. 1807.

Rare: reprinted in (192). Lord Grenville's resignation on the Catholic question was discussed in [John Allen], *Letters of Scaevola on the dismissal of his Majesty's late ministers*, 2 pt., 1807; and *The state of the case. Addressed to Lord Grenville and Lord Howick*, 1807.

128 [COBBETT'S] [WEEKLY] POLITICAL REGISTER. 89 v. 1802–35.

Became the major popular radical journal of its time. On the radical revival from 1807 see *An exposition of the circumstances which gave rise to the election of Sir Francis Burdett*

... *for* ... *Westminster, and of the principles which governed the committee who conducted that election*, 1807; Capel Lofft, *On the revival of the cause of reform*, 1810; Walter Honywood Yate, *Political and historical argument proving the necessity of a parliamentary reform*, 2 v., 1812; William Roscoe, *A review of the speeches of* ... *G. Canning on the late election for Liverpool*, 1812. John Ranby, *An inquiry into the supposed increase of the influence of the crown*, 1811, assailed the reformers' views.

129 McCALLUM (PIERRE FRANC). Le Livre rouge; or, a new and extraordinary Red-Book; containing a list of the pensions ... together with a view of the receipts and expenditure of the public money. Designed as a companion to the Court Calendar. 1810.

One of a series of 'exposures' of the Establishment, followed by *The Black Book; or, Corruption unmasked*, 1819, republ. as *The Extraordinary Black Book*, 1831, *The Black Book, an exposition of abuses in church and state*, ed. by John Wade, 1835. See also William Benbow, *The crimes of the clergy*, 1823; William Carpenter, *The people's book*, 1831, and *A peerage for the people*, 1837.

130 CLARKE (WILLIAM). The authentic and impartial life of Mrs. .... Clarke ... with a compendious view of the ... investigation of the conduct of ... the Duke of York, 1809.

Extra fuel to this *cause célèbre* was provided by Mary Anne Clarke, *The rival princes, or a faithful narrative of facts*, 2 v., 1810.

131 ROSCOE (WILLIAM). Occasional tracts relative to the war between Great Britain and France. 1810.

Includes three attacks on war policy, 1808–10, the first of which provoked *Letter to William Roscoe esq., containing strictures on his late publication, Considerations on ... the present war*, Liverpool, 1808. Samuel Whitbread, *A letter from Mr. Whitbread to Lord Holland on the present situation in Spain*, 1808, signified a rift in the Opposition. Thomas Chalmers, *An inquiry into the extent and stability of national resources*, Edinburgh, 1808, rebutted arguments for peace on grounds of economic exhaustion.

132 [STERLING (E.)]. The letters of Vetus. 2 pt. 1812.

Supported the pretensions of Wellesley to be Minister. See *Authentic correspondence and documents explaining the proceedings of* ... *Wellesley, and* ... *Moira*, 5th edn., 1812. *Letter to the Lords Grey and Grenville on their late conduct, by a plain Englishman*, 1812, attacked the Opposition.

133 HAMPDEN CLUB. A collection of reports of the proceedings. 2 v. [1814–22].

A made-up set in the British Library, London. T. J. Wooler, ed., *The Black Dwarf*, 12 v., 1817–24, a weekly devoted to radical reform. See too George Ensor, *Radical reform, restoration of usurped rights*, 1819; and for conservative views, John Somers Cocks, Lord Somers, *A defence of the constitution* ... *against the innovating and levelling attempts of the friends to annual parliaments and universal suffrage*, 1817. Francis Philips, *An exposure of the calumnies circulated* ... *against the magistrates and the yeomen cavalry of Manchester and Salford*, 1819, was answered by *Notes and observations* ... *on the papers relative to the internal order of the country* ... *By a member of the Manchester committee*, 1820.

134 RUSSELL (*Lord* JOHN). A letter to ... Lord Holland on foreign politics. 1819.

Attacked Castlereagh and stated Whig policy. On Whig sympathy for the Greeks see

Thomas Erskine, Lord Erskine, *A letter to the Earl of Liverpool on the subject of the Greeks*, 2nd edn., 1822, 4th edn., 1823.

135   [CREEVEY (THOMAS)]. A guide to the electors of Great Britain upon the accession of a new king, and the immediate prospect of a new parliament. 1820.

States a Whig election programme.

136   ENSOR (GEORGE). Addresses to the people of Ireland, on the degradation and misery of their country. Dublin. 1823.

For Ensor's vigorous assertion of Irish and Catholic claims, see also his *Irish affairs at the close of 1825*, 1826. Those of British Catholics were asserted in Henry Howard, *Historical references in support of the remarks on the erroneous opinions entertained respecting the Catholic religion*, Carlisle, 1827. Anti-Catholic was John Freeman Mitford, Lord Redesdale, *A political view of the Roman Catholic question, especially regarding the supremacy usurped by the Church of Rome*, 1829.

137   [BROUGHAM (HENRY PETER)]. The country without a government; or, plain questions upon the unhappy state of the present administration. 1830.

Brougham followed with *The result of the general election; or, what has the Duke of Wellington gained by the dissolution?* 4 edns., 1830, provoking a well-written answer, *Observations on two pamphlets . . . attributed to Mr. Brougham*, 1830. See too *A brief exposition of the foreign policy of Mr. Canning, as contrasted with that of the existing administration*, 1830.

138   GROTE (GEORGE). Essentials of parliamentary reform. 1831.

Reflecting the views of the philosophical radicals, as does Charles Buller, *On the necessity of a radical reform*, 1831, and Henry William Tancred, *A legal review of the origin of the system of representation . . . with observations on the reform necessary*, 1831. Popular radical attitudes are presented in William Carpenter, *An address to the working classes on the reform bill*, 1831. Sir Francis Palgrave, *Conciliatory reform*, [1831], suggested representation of classes. Opposition to the Reform Bill was voiced in Sir John Walsh, *Observations on the ministerial plan of reform*, 1831, and *Popular opinions on parliamentary reform considered*, 1831; and in *Sixty-eight reasons for opposing the reform bill now pending in parliament*, 1832. Henry Peter Brougham, Lord Brougham and Vaux, *Friendly advice, most respectfully submitted to the Lords on the reform bill*, 1831, was one of many appeals from both sides to the upper House.

139   WALSH (*Sir* JOHN). On the present balance of parties in the state. 1832.

An able analysis. *The reform ministry and the reform parliament* [ed. by Denis Le Marchant], 7 edns., 1833, praises the Whigs, who were attacked in Benjamin Disraeli, *What is he? By the author of Vivian Grey*, 1833; *Vindication of the English constitution*, 1835; *Letters of Runnymede*, 1836. James Bernard Bernard, *Appeal to the conservatives*, 1835, called for an alliance with the working classes against Whigs and Radicals. A good analysis of soaring conservative fortunes is given in P. J. Budworth, *The prospects and policy of a Tory administration*, 1838.

140   RUSSELL (*Lord* JOHN). Letter to the electors of Stroud, on the principles of the reform act. 7 edns. 1839.

An attempt to check further agitation for reform, answered in *Lord Brougham's reply to Lord John Russell's letter*, 4 edns., 1839.

141 [DISRAELI (BENJAMIN)]. England and France; or, a cure for the ministerial Gallomania. 1832.

Later attacks on Palmerston's foreign policy included [Richard Cobden], *England, Ireland and America*, 1835, and *Russia*, 1836; [William Gargill], *Mehemet Ali, Lord Palmerston, Russia, and France*, 1840, and *The foreign affairs of England administered by . . . Viscount Palmerston*, 1841.

142 LOVETT (WILLIAM) *and* COLLINS (JOHN). Chartism: a new organization of the people. 1840. New edn. with introd. by Asa Briggs, 1969.

A general explanation of organization and purpose of Chartism. See too *The people's charter*, 1836; *The rotten House of Commons* [1837].

143 ANTI-CORN LAW CIRCULAR. nos. 1–57. Manchester 1839–41.

The organ of the Anti-Corn Law League. Continued as the *Anti-Bread Tax Circular*, 1841–3, and then *The League*, 1843–6. For repeal were Thomas Perronet Thompson, *Corn-law fallacies, with the answers*, 3rd edn., 1839, and William Wolryche Whitmore, *A letter on the corn laws to the Manchester Chamber of Commerce*, 1839, and *A second letter*, 1839; against: John Broadhurst, *Reasons for not repealing the corn laws*, 1839; George Calvert Holland, *The millocrat*, 1841; John Almack, jun., *Character, motives and proceedings of the Anti-Corn-Law leaguers, with a few general remarks on the consequences that would result from a free trade in corn*, 1843; George Game Day, *Defeat of the Anti-Corn Law League in Huntingdonshire*, 1844. See also Thomas Perronet Thompson, *Catechism on the Corn Laws*, 1827; Ebenezer Elliott, *Corn Law Rhymes*, 3rd edn., 1831.

144 VYVYAN (*Sir* RICHARD). A letter . . . to his constituents upon the commercial and financial policy of Sir Robert Peel's administration. 1842.

A trenchant expression of back-bench discontent.

145 URQUHART (DAVID). The statesmen of France and the English alliance. 1847.

An attack on Palmerston's handling of the Spanish marriages question. Urquhart also ed. the anti-Russian periodicals, *The Portfolio*, 6 v., 1836–7, and *The New Portfolio*, 4 v., 1842–3.

C. CORRESPONDENCE, JOURNALS, MEMOIRS, AND BIOGRAPHIES

(Arranged roughly in chronological order of content.) In *H.M.C.* see especially Bathurst (75), Grenville (78), Gladstone (81). Some of the more important and accessible MSS. collections are noted, but the user should consult pp. 11–15.

146 GEORGE III. The later correspondence of George III. Ed. by Arthur Aspinall. 5 v. Camb. 1962–70.

A very full selection of corr. from the royal archives and many other collections; with few exceptions does not reproduce letters in print, of which there are many in Stanhope and Rose, *Pitt and Napoleon* (147), *Dropmore* (78), and a few in Pellew (180), Twiss (173), and in Bonamy Dobrée, ed. *The letters of King George III*, 1935. Edward Holt, *The public and domestic life of . . . George the third*, 2 v., 1820, is a eulogistic account, as is Robert Huish, *The public and private life of . . . George the third*, 1821. John Heneage Jesse, *Memoirs of the life and reign of King George III*, 2nd edn., 3 v., 1867, cites widely but is untrustworthy. Two excellent modern studies are S. Ayling, *George the third*,

1972, and John Brooke, *King George III*, 1972. The king's medical history is ably explored in Ida Macalpine and R. Hunter, *George III and the mad business*, 1969. For interpretations of the king's political role see also Barnes (96) and Pares (442). For his family see *Social Hist.* (1976–2001).

147   PITT. Life of the right honourable William Pitt. By Philip Henry, 5th Earl Stanhope. 4 v. 1861–2. 2nd edn. 4 v. 1862–3. New edn. 3 v. 1879.

Indispensable, printing much correspondence from Pitt's papers in the P.R.O. and other collections. Other letters are in *Secret correspondence connected with Mr Pitt's return to office in 1804* [ed. by Stanhope, priv. printed], 1852; Stanhope, *Miscellanies*, 1st ser., 2nd edn., with some supplementary letters, 1863; Rosebery, *Pitt and Wilberforce*, 1897, including Wilberforce's memoir of Pitt; Edward Gibson, Lord Ashbourne, *Pitt: some chapters of his life and times*, 1898; and John Holland Rose, *Pitt and Napoleon: essays and letters*, 1912. John Gifford, *pseud.* of John Richards Green, *A history of the political life of W. Pitt*, 3 v., 1809, has useful appendices; see too *The speeches of . . . William Pitt*, 4 v., 1806. R. Coupland, ed., *The war speeches of William Pitt the younger*, Oxf., 1915, 3rd edn., 1940. Sir George Pretyman Tomline, *Memoirs of . . . Pitt*, 2 v., 1821, extending only to 1793, was written with informed personal knowledge; see also Lord Rosebery, *Bishop Tomline's estimate of William Pitt*, (repr. from the *Monthly Rev.*), 1903. John Holland Rose, *William Pitt and the national revival* [to 1791], 1911, and *William Pitt and the great war*, 1911, both pub. in one vol., 1923, is a comprehensive study; see too his *A short life of . . . Pitt*, 1925. Other lives are by Lord Rosebery, 1891; Charles Whibley, 1906; Felix Salomon, *William Pitt der jüngere*, Leipsic, 1906; Philip Whitwell Wilson, 1930; Edward Keble Chatterton, *England's greatest statesman*, Indianapolis, 1930; Hermann Proebst, *William Pitt, Begründer der britischen Macht*, Berlin [1938]; Jacques Chastenet de Castaing, Paris, 1941; J. W. Derry, 1962. See too Barnes (96) and the assessment in Goldwin Smith, *Three English Statesmen*, 1867. John Ehrman, *The younger Pitt*, 1969, in progress, is exhaustive.

148   DUNDAS. The life of Henry Dundas, first Viscount Melville. By Cyril Matheson. 1933.

An able study of one of Pitt's closest collaborators. Holden Furber, *Henry Dundas, first viscount Melville, 1742–1811*, Oxf., 1931, treats especially of his Scottish and Indian politics. There is also a brief life by James Alex. Lovat-Fraser, Camb., 1916. Many of his surviving papers are in Register House, Edinburgh, and in the National Library of Scotland.

149   LEEDS. The political memoranda of Francis fifth duke of Leeds, now first printed from the originals in the British Museum. Ed. by Oscar Browning. Camden Soc. n.s. 35. 1884.

Cabinet memoranda and political notes. Leeds was For. Sec. till 1791.

150   RICHMOND. The radical duke: the career and correspondence of Charles Lennox, third duke of Richmond. By Alison Gilbert Olson. 1961.

Richmond was a minor member of Pitt's cabinet till the end of 1794.

151   WILBERFORCE. The life of William Wilberforce. By his sons Robert Isaac Wilberforce and Samuel Wilberforce. 5 v. 1838.

Uses Wilberforce's diaries. His sons also ed. *The correspondence of . . . Wilberforce*. 2 v. 1840. Pitt's letters and other docs. are in *Private papers of William Wilberforce*, ed. by Anna Maria Wilberforce, 1897, repr. N.Y., 1968. See also (658), and lives by R. Coupland, 1923, R. Furneaux, 1974.

152 ROSE. The diaries and correspondence of the Right Hon. George Rose: containing original letters of the most distinguished statesmen of his day. Ed. by Rev. Leveson Vernon Harcourt. 2 v. 1860.

Rose was Pitt's subordinate at the Treasury and a fervent 'Pittite'. See B.L. Add. MSS. 42772–95.

153 STANHOPE. The life of Charles, third Earl Stanhope. By Ghita Stanhope and G. P. Gooch. 1914.

Letters 1780–1815. For a briefer recent assessment see A. Newman, *The Stanhopes of Chevening*, 1969. Stanhope's papers are in Kent R.O.

154 BUCKINGHAM AND CHANDOS. Memoirs of the court and cabinets of George the third, from original family documents. By Richard Plantagenet T. N. B. C. Grenville, 2nd duke of Buckingham and Chandos. 4 v. 1853–5.

Correspondence 1782–1810 of Lord Temple, later first marquess of Buckingham, his brother William Wyndham Grenville, Lord Grenville, and their family and political connections. Valuable but the editing poor. Further selections of the correspondence up to 1840 by the same editor are, *Memoirs of the court of England during the Regency, 1811–1820*, 2 v., 1856; *Memoirs of the court of George IV*, 2 v., 1859; *Memoirs of the courts and cabinets of William IV and Victoria*, 2 v., 1861. From the Stowe MSS. now in the Huntington Library, Cal.

155 FOX. Memorials and correspondence of Charles James Fox. Ed. by Lord John Russell. 4 v. 1853–7.

A selection from the 'made-up' collection of Fox's letters now British Library Add. MSS. 47559–601, 51457–51519. [J. Wright], *The speeches of . . . Fox*, 6 v., 1815. Early accounts are B. C. Walpole, *Recollections of the life of C. J. Fox*, 1806; Ralph Fell, *Memoirs of the public life of . . . Fox*, 2 v., 1808; Philopatris Varvicensis, *pseud.* of Samuel Parr, *Characters of . . . C. J. Fox*, 2 v., 1809, which was severely criticized in *Some particulars in the character of . . . C. J. Fox . . . in a letter from Philotheus Antoniensis*, 1809; and John Bernard Trotter (Fox's secretary), *Memoirs of the latter years of . . . Charles James Fox*, 1811. Lord John Russell, *The life and times of . . . Fox*, 3 v., 1859–66, examines Fox's career from the viewpoint of early Victorian Whiggism, and J. L. Le Breton Hammond, *Charles James Fox: a political study*, 1903, from that of a late Victorian liberal. J. W. Derry, *Charles James Fox*, 1972, is the best scholarly biography, showing full understanding of the context of Fox's career. L. D. Reid, *Charles James Fox*, 1969, makes a thorough study of Fox as an orator and debater.

156 COURTENAY (JOHN). Incidental anecdotes and a biographical sketch. 1809.

Slight but frank autobiographical recollections of political life by one of Fox's parliamentary followers.

157 NICHOLLS (JOHN). Recollections and reflections personal and political as connected with public affairs during the reign of George III. 2 v. 1820–2.

Some sidelights on Fox's role in politics, by another of his parliamentary followers.

158 CAMDEN. Lord Chancellor Camden and his family. By Henry S. Eeles. 1934.

Pp. 190–266 is a sketch of the career of William Pitt's friend, John Jeffreys Pratt, later 2nd Earl Camden, sometime lord lieutenant of Ireland; there is no good biog. Camden's papers are in Kent R.O.

159 SMITH. Dissent in politics, 1780–1830. By Richard W. Davis. 1971.

Largely a study of the career of William Smith, M.P. (1756–1835), based upon his surviving papers.

160 BURKE. A checklist of the correspondence of Edmund Burke; arranged in chronological order and indexed under the names of 1200 correspondents. By Thomas W. Copeland and Milton Shumway Smith. Camb. 1955.

A preparation for the splendidly produced *Correspondence of Edmund Burke*, ed. by T. W. Copeland and others, 9 v., Camb., 1958–70. A few letters to Burke not included in this edition are to be found in *Correspondence of . . . Edmund Burke*, ed. by Charles William, Earl Fitzwilliam, and Sir Richard Bourke, 4 v., 1844. See too *The epistolatory correspondence of . . . Edmund Burke and Dr French Laurence*, 1827; J. P. Gilson, ed., *Correspondence of Edmund Burke and William Windham*, Roxburghe Club, 1910. For Burke's collected speeches see *The speeches of Edmund Burke*, 4 v., 1816. For Burke's works see *Pol. theory* (518).

161 BURKE. Burke and the nature of politics. By Carl B. Cone. 2 v. Lexington, Kentucky. 1957–64.

The fullest study, though not always clearly defining the context of Burke's activities. Francesco Cordasco comp., *Edmund Burke: a handlist of critical notices and studies*, N.Y., 1950. Early surveys were Charles McCormick, *Memoirs of . . . Burke*, 1797, a party attack, and Robert Bisset, *The life of Edmund Burke*, 1798, 2nd edn., 2 v., 1800, an eulogistic reply. Sir James Prior, *Memoir of the life and character of . . . Edmund Burke*, 1824, 2nd edn., 2 v., 1826 (fuller than the 5th edn. rev. 1854), and Thomas MacKnight, *History of the life and times of . . . Burke*, 3 v., 1858–60, are uncritical but use original material and are still of value. Some anecdotes are preserved in 'Extracts from Mr. Burke's table talk at Crewe Hall. Written down by Mrs. Crewe', in *Miscellanies of the Philobiblon Soc.* 7 (1862–3). T. W. Copeland, *Edmund Burke. Six essays*, 1950, provides valuable analyses of certain biographical problems. Dixon Wecter, *Edmund Burke and his kinsmen, a study of the statesman's financial integrity and private relationships*, Boulder [Colo.], 1939, has little on the period. There are older lives by John Morley, 1867, Bertram Newman, 1927, R. H. Murray, 1931, and Sir Philip Magnus, 1939. On Burke and Ireland, see Mahoney (4085).

162 SHERIDAN. Speeches of the late right honourable Richard Brinsley Sheridan (several corrected by himself). Ed. by a constitutional friend. 5 v. 1816. 3 v. 1842.

Of the early memoirs, that by John Watkins, 1817, is uninformed, and partly corrected in Alicia Lefanu, *Memoirs of . . . Mrs Frances Sheridan*, 1824. Thomas Moore, *Memoirs of . . . Sheridan*, 1825, 2nd edn., 2 v., 1825, 5th edn., with cor., 2 v., 1827, includes letters and was written with personal knowledge, as was also [William Earle], *Sheridan and his times*, 2 v., 1859. William Smyth, *Memoir of Mr Sheridan*, Leeds, 1840, is prejudiced. Among later writers William Fraser Rae, *Sheridan: a biography*, 2 v., 1896, and Walter Sydney Sichel, *Sheridan: from new and original material; including a manuscript diary by Georgiana, duchess of Devonshire*, 2 v., 1909, made able use of the Sheridan MSS. Percy Fitzgerald, *Lives of the Sheridans*, 2 v., 1886, uses the Garrick correspondence. Michael T. H. Sadler, *The political career of . . . Sheridan*, 1912, prints some letters of Mrs. Sheridan. Some new materials were used in Raymond Crompton Rhodes, *Harlequin Sheridan: the man and the legends. With a bibliography and appendices*, Oxf., 1933. Other lives are by Mrs. Margaret Oliphant, 1883; Lloyd Charles Sanders, 1890; Eliza Marian Butler, 1931; Kenelm Foss, 1939. Cecil Price, ed., *The letters of . . . Sheridan*, 3 v., Oxf., 1966.

163 WINDHAM. The Windham papers: the life and correspondence of the Right Hon. William Windham, 1750–1810. [Edited by Lewis Melville.] Intro. by the earl of Rosebery. 2 v. 1913.

A selection from the papers now British Library Add. MSS. 37842–935. Mrs. Henry Baring, ed., *The Diary of the Rt. Hon. William Windham*, 1866. Thomas Amyot ed. his *Speeches*, 3 v., 1812.

164 FRANCIS. Memoirs of Sir Philip Francis, K.C.B., with correspondence and journals. Commenced by the late Joseph Parkes and completed by Herman Merivale. 2 v. 1867.

Letters, 1758–1813, of an associate of Fox and dabbler in radical politics. See B.L. Add. MSS. 34287, 40756–65, 47781–3.

165 WYVILL (CHRISTOPHER). Political papers, chiefly respecting the attempt of the county of York and other considerable districts . . . to effect a reformation of the Parliament of Great Britain. 6 v. [1794–1808].

V. 4–6 Letters 1789–1807 including corr. with C. J. Fox. On Wyvill's later career see J. R. Dinwiddy, *Christopher Wyvill and reform* (Borthwick papers no. 39), York, 1971.

166 MINTO. Life and letters of Sir Gilbert Elliot, first earl of Minto, from 1751 to 1806. Ed. by the Countess of Minto. 3 v. 1874.

Politics and diplomacy; a Foxite who joined Pitt after the French Revolution. Minto's papers are in the National Library of Scotland.

167 AUCKLAND. The journal and correspondence of William, Lord Auckland. With a preface and introduction by . . . the bishop of Bath and Wells. 4 v. 1861–2.

From the papers, now British Library Add. MSS. 34412–71.

168 LANSDOWNE. Life of William, earl of Shelburne, afterwards first Marquess of Lansdowne. By Lord Edmond Fitzmaurice. 2nd rev. edn. 2 v. 1912.

About the last sixty pages touch on his politics after 1789, with material from his papers.

169 TOOKE. Memoirs of John Horne Tooke. By Alexander Stephens. 2 v. 1813.

Letters, 1766–1812. W. Hamilton Reid, *Memoirs of the public life of . . . Tooke*, 1812, adds very little; Minnie Clare Yarborough, *John Horne Tooke*, N.Y., 1926, is a sound scholarly study, bibliog. 243–7.

170 WHITBREAD. Samuel Whitbread, 1764–1815; a study in opposition. By Roger Thomas Baldwin Fulford. 1967.

With full use of family papers, but concentrating on the personal rather than on the general issues which these illuminate. Whitbread's papers are now in Bedfordshire R.O.

171 GOWER. Lord Granville Leveson Gower (first Earl Granville): private correspondence, 1781 to 1821. Ed. by Castalia, Countess Granville. 2 v. 1916.

Letters of a minor politician and diplomat.

172   CORNWALLIS. Correspondence of Charles, first Marquis Cornwallis. Ed. by Charles Ross. 3 v. 1859.

Letters, India, Ireland, and domestic politics, to 1805; some of the papers are now in the P.R.O.

173   ELDON. The public and private life of Lord Chancellor Eldon, with selections from his correspondence. By Horace Twiss. 3 v. 1844.

Political corr. 1783–1835. See too William E. Surtees, *A sketch of the lives of Lords Stowell and Eldon, comprising with additional matter, some corrections of Mr Twiss's book on the Chancellor*, 1846; *Lord Eldon's anecdote book*, ed. by Anthony L. J. Lincoln and Robert L. McEwen, 1960; and Albert Farnsworth, 'Lord Chancellor Eldon', *Law Quart. Rev.* 72 (1956), 178–81.

174   BENTINCK. Lord William Bentinck. The making of a liberal imperialist, 1774–1839. By John Rosselli. 1974.

175   TIERNEY. George Tierney. By Herbert Keen Olphin. 1934.

Letters from Tierney's papers, now in Hampshire R.O.

176   GREY. Lord Grey of the Reform Bill; being the life of Charles, second Earl Grey. By George Macaulay Trevelyan. 1920.

A fully documented study of Grey, whose career of reform extended from the 'Friends of the People' to the Reform Act. *Some account of the life and opinions of . . . Grey*, by his son Charles Grey, 1861, ends at 1817. Guy de Strange, ed., *The correspondence of Princess Lieven and Earl Grey, 1824–1834*, 2 v., 1890; Grey's papers are now at the Department of Palaeography and Diplomatic, University of Durham.

177   CASTLEREAGH. The rise of Castlereagh. By H. Montgomery Hyde. 1933.

An excellent, fully documented study, ends at 1801. *Memoirs and correspondence of Viscount Castlereagh, second Marquess of Londonderry, edited by his brother*, Charles W. Vane, third Marquess of Londonderry, 12 v., 1848–53, is a good collection, but not complete, and omits much family correspondence. Sir Arthur Alison, *Lives of Lord Castlereagh and Sir Charles Stewart*, 3 v., 1861, prints other documents. A. Hassall, *Viscount Castlereagh*, 1908, makes no use of new archival material, and Sir J. A. R. Marriott, *Castlereagh*, 1936, very little. Rather better is Ione Leigh, *Castlereagh*, 1951. See also *For. rel.* (301), (309). C. J. Bartlett, *Castlereagh*, 1966, is a sound survey.

178   CANNING. Some official correspondence of George Canning. Ed. with notes by Edward J. Stapleton. 2 v. 1887.

Letters, 1821–27. Roger Therry, comp., *The speeches of . . . George Canning. With a memoir of his life*, 3rd edn., 6 v., 1836. Other collections include, *The speeches and public addresses of . . . George Canning during the late election in Liverpool, and on a public occasion in Manchester*, 1812, and *Speeches . . . delivered on public occasions in Liverpool*, 1825. [Thomas Forster, comp.,] *A biographical memoir of . . . Canning. To which is added the whole of his satires, odes, songs, and other poems*, Brussels, 1827. Robert Walsh, ed., *Select speeches of . . . Canning*, Phil., 1835. Canning's papers are now in Leeds Public Library.

179   CANNING. The rise of George Canning. By Dorothy Marshall. 1938.

Excellent biographical study fully documented from the Canning papers, covers Canning's early career up to 1806. The best general biography is Harold W. V. Temperley

Life of Canning, 1905, more full and up to date than Frank Harrison Hill, *George Canning*, 1887, Walter Alison Phillips, *George Canning*, 1903, or Sir John A. R. Marriott, *George Canning and his times*, 1903. Josceline Bagot, *George Canning and his friends*, 2 v., 1909, is anecdotal but prints many letters, mainly from the Bagot papers. John F. Newton, *Early days of . . . Canning*, 1828, has info. about him as an undergraduate. Augustus G. Stapleton, *The political life of . . . Canning, from . . . September 1822 to . . . August 1827*, 3 v., 1831, and *George Canning and his times*, 1859, written with personal knowledge by his confidential secretary, reproduce some papers, but are uncritical, as is also Robert Bell, *The life of . . . Canning*, 1846. Arthur Aspinall, *The formation of Canning's ministry*, Camden Soc., 3 s., 59 (1937), provides full documentation from a wide range of sources. See also *For. rel.* (310). Valuable recent studies are P. J. V. Rolo, *George Canning*, 1965, and Wendy Hinde, *George Canning*, 1973.

180   SIDMOUTH. The life and correspondence of . . . Henry Addington, first Viscount Sidmouth. By George Pellew. 3 v. 1847.

Letters from Addington's papers, now in the Devon Record Office. On Addington and the income tax see Farnsworth (1424). P. Ziegler, *Addington*, 1965, bibliog. 457–62, is excellent.

181   COLCHESTER. The diary and correspondence of Charles Abbot, Lord Colchester. Ed. by his son, Charles, Lord Colchester. 3 v. 1861.

Colchester was Speaker, 1802–17. Many of the family papers are now in the P.R.O.

182   PERCEVAL. The life of the Right Hon. Spencer Perceval, including his correspondence with numerous distinguished persons. By Spencer Walpole. 2 v. 1876.

Prints a selection of letters, 1795–1812. Charles V. Williams, *The life and administration of . . . Perceval*, 1812, brings together a number of his speeches. Philip Treherne, *The Right Hon. Spencer Perceval*, 1909, is slight. Denis Gray, *Spencer Perceval, 1762–1812, the evangelical prime minister*, Manch., 1963, is a scholarly work. See B.L. Add. MSS. 49173–95.

183   LIVERPOOL. The life and administration of Robert Banks, second earl of Liverpool . . . compiled from original documents. By Charles Duke Yonge. 3 v. 1868.

Prints a limited selection of letters from the Liverpool papers, now British Library Add. MSS. 38237–38415. There is no good biography. *Memoirs of the public life and administration of the Earl of Liverpool*, 1827, is little more than a chronicle based on published parliamentary debates. Sir Charles A. Petrie, *Lord Liverpool and his times*, 1954, makes little use of the copious manuscript material. William Ranulf Brock, *Lord Liverpool and Liberal Toryism, 1820–1827*, 1941, 2nd edn., 1967, is a good rather brief study. J. E. Cookson, *Lord Liverpool's administration, 1815–1822*, 1975, is detailed and scholarly.

184   TAYLOR. The Taylor Papers. Ed. by Ernest Taylor. 1913.

A selection from surviving political papers of Sir Herbert Taylor, secretary successively to the Duke of York, George III (from 1805), Queen Charlotte, and William IV: much was destroyed at his death.

185   BURDETT. Sir Francis Burdett and his times (1770–1844). By Melville Watson Patterson. 2 v. 1931.

A sketch of a Westminster radical and social reformer, based on material in several private collections. Burdett's papers are in the Bodleian Library, Oxford.

186   BARING. Journals and correspondence of Francis Thornhill Baring, 1st Baron Northbrook, from 1808 to 1852. Ed. by the Earl of Northbrook and F. H. Baring. Winchester. 1905.

Baring was chancellor of the exchequer under Melbourne, 1839–41.

187   PLACE. The life of Francis Place, 1771–1854. By Graham Wallas. 4th edn. 1925.

Excellent on early 19th cent. radical politics. Place's papers are British Library Add. MSS. 27789–859, 28869, 35142–54, 36623–8. See Mary Thale, ed., *The autobiography of Francis Place*, Camb., 1972, and D. J. Rowe, ed., *London radicalism, 1830–1843*, 1970.

188   COBBETT. The progress of a ploughboy to a seat in parliament; as exemplified in the history of the life of William Cobbett, member for Oldham. Ed. by William Reitzel. 1933.

A compilation from autobiographical passages in Cobbett's writings, illustrating the career of this stalwart critic of the early nineteenth-century 'establishment'; in particular from Cobbett's own *Life and adventures of Peter Porcupine*, Phil., 1796. Morris L. Pearl, *William Cobbett: a bibliographical account of his life and times*, 1953, based upon the Cole collection of MSS. and pubns. at Nuffield Coll., Oxf., has detailed notices of nearly 200 works by Cobbett and many others relating to him. The best life is by George Douglas Howard Cole, 3rd edn., 1947. G. D. H. Cole and Margaret Cole, eds., Cobbett's *Rural Rides*, 3 v., 1930, and a selection, *The opinions of William Cobbett*, 1944; G. D. H. Cole also ed., *Letters from William Cobbett to Edward Thornton written in the years 1797–1800*, 1937. Lewis Melville drew on unpublished material for *The life and letters of William Cobbett in England and America*, 2 v., 1913; other lives by Edward Smith, 2 v., 1878; Edward Irving Carlyle, 1904; Gilbert Keith Chesterton, 1925; Marjorie Bowen, *Peter Porcupine*, 1953. See also J. W. Osborne, *William Cobbett: his thought and his times*, New Brunswick, N.J., [1966]; James Sambrook, *William Cobbett*, 1973; Pierce W. Gaines, *William Cobbett and the United States, 1792–1835*, 1973.

189   HOLLAND. Memoirs of the Whig Party during my time. By Henry Richard Vassall, Lord Holland. Ed. by his son, Henry Edward, Lord Holland. 2 v. 1852–4.

Holland's *Further Memoirs of the Whig Party* (1807–1821) were ed. by Lord Stavordale, 1905; together a leading source for Whig politics c. 1790–c. 1820. See also (2133). Holland's papers are B.L. Add. MSS. 51520–957.

190   CREEVEY. The Creevey papers: a selection from the correspondence and diaries of . . . Thomas Creevey, M.P. Ed. by Sir Herbert Maxwell. 2 v. 1903. 3rd edn. 1905.

Witty and informative political gossip, c. 1802–38. *Creevey's life and times: a further selection from the correspondence* . . ., ed. by John Gore, 1934, was compiled to illustrate the social history of the time.

191   WARD. Memoirs of the political and literary life of Robert Plumer Ward. By Edmund Phipps. 2 v. 1850.

Diaries and correspondence 1795–1846, including many letters from the Mulgrave papers.

192   HORNER. Memoirs and correspondence of Francis Horner. By Leonard Horner. 2 v. 1843. 2nd edn. with addns. 2 v. 1853.

From papers now in the British Library of Political and Economic Science, London.

193 GODERICH. 'Prosperity' Robinson. The life of Viscount Goderich, 1782–1859. By Wilbur Devereux Jones. 1967.

Well-researched; sometimes uncritical of its subject.

194 CROKER. The Croker Papers. The correspondence and diaries of John Wilson Croker . . . secretary to the admiralty from 1809 to 1830. Ed. by Louis J. Jennings. 3 v. 1884.

Correspondence, 1809–1857, of a government servant, M.P., and writer. Myron F. Brightfield, *John Wilson Croker*, Berkeley, Cal., 1940, uses unprinted material from Croker's papers now in the William L. Clements library.

195 LIEVEN. The letters of Dorothea, Princess Lieven, during her residence in London, 1812–1834. Ed. by Lionel G. Robinson. 1902.

Correspondence of a well-informed diplomat's wife, from the papers now British Library Add. MSS. 47236–47435. Other documents are printed in *The unpublished diary of Princess Lieven*, ed. H. W. V. Temperley, 1925; *The private letters of Princess Lieven to Prince Metternich, 1820–1826*, ed. by P. Quennell, 1937; *Letters of Princess Lieven to Lady Holland, 1847–57*, ed. by E. A. Smith, Roxburghe Club, 1956. H. M. Hyde, *Princess Lieven*, 1938, has bibliographical information but is mainly about her private life; see too Priscilla, countess Zamoyska, *Arch intriguer: biography of Dorothea de Lieven*, 1957. See also Grey (176), Aberdeen (215), Wellington (201), Palmerston (217).

196 WELLESLEY. Memoirs and correspondence of . . . Richard, Marquess Wellesley. Ed. by Robert Rouière Pearce. 3 v. 1846.

After returning from India in 1805, W. became a considerable figure in British politics. Lewis Melville, ed., *The Wellesley Papers. The life and correspondence of . . . Wellesley, 1760–1842 . . . including hitherto unpublished correspondence*, 2 v., 1914. See too *Authentic correspondence and documents explaining the negotiations for the formation of an administration*, 5th edn., 1812; *The despatches and correspondence of . . . Wellesley during his Lordship's mission to Spain . . . in 1809*, ed. by R. M. Martin, 1838. There are other lives by W. T. McC. Torrens, 1880; G. B. Malleson, 1888, W. H. Hutton, 1893, but no adequate modern biography. See also under *India* (4577). See also Iris Butler, *The eldest brother*, 1974. Wellesley's papers are B.L. Add. MSS. 12564–13915, 37274–37318, 37414–16.

197 GEORGE IV. The correspondence of George, Prince of Wales, 1770–1812. Ed. by Arthur Aspinall. 8 v. 1963–71. The letters of King George IV, 1812–1830. Ed. by Arthur Aspinall. 3 v. Camb. 1938.

Early lives by Robert Huish, 1830, and George Croly, 1841, are anecdotal. Those by Percy H. Fitzgerald, 1881, and Shane Leslie, 1926, exploited previously unused material. R. T. B. Fulford, *George the fourth*, rev. enl. edn., 1949, used material in the royal archives. Doris Leslie, *The Great Corinthian*, repr. 1967, and Dorothy M. Stuart, *Portrait of the Prince Regent*, 1953, add little. See too Joanna Richardson, *George IV, a portrait*, 1966. There is interesting detail in A. Aspinall, 'George IV and Sir William Knighton', *E.H.R.* 55 (1940), 57–82. See also *Social Hist.* (1980, 1983, 1994–6).

198 GREVILLE. The Greville Memoirs, 1814–1860. Ed. by Lytton Strachey and Roger Fulford. 8 v. 1938.

The only complete edn., superseding that by Henry Reeve and the selections by P. W. Wilson and P. Morrell; memoirs of an extremely knowledgeable minor placeman. See also A. H. Johnson, ed., *Letters of Charles Greville and Henry Reeve, 1836–65*, 1924. In lighter vein is the diary of his brother Henry, 1832–52, see *Leaves from the diary of Henry Greville*, ed. by Viscountess Enfield, 1883.

199   PEEL. Sir Robert Peel from his private papers. By Charles Stuart Parker.
3 v. 1891–99.

Selected letters from Peel's papers, now British Library Add. MSS. 40181–40617. Other
letters are printed in George Peel, *The private letters of . . . Peel*, 1920, and in *Memoirs
by the Right Hon. Sir Robert Peel*, ed. by Lord Stanhope and E. Cardwell, 2 v., 1856–7.
Peel's collected *Speeches* are in 4 v., 1853.

200   PEEL. Mr. Secretary Peel: the life of Robert Peel to 1830. Sir Robert
Peel: the life of Sir Robert Peel after 1830. By Norman Gash. 2 v. 1961–72.

An exhaustive and authoritative, fully documented biography. George Kitson Clark,
Peel and the Conservative Party, 1832–1841, 1929, is excellent; his *Peel*, 1936, is a brief
sketch. Lives by W. Cooke Taylor, 1846, J. C. Symons, 1856, Lord Dalling, 1874,
G. Barnett Smith, 1881, Justin McCarthy, 1891, are out of date or of little value.
Rosebery, *Sir Robert Peel*, 1899, is a brief but suggestive essay. Anna A. W. Ramsay,
Sir Robert Peel, 1928, is of value, though with some lacunae; see too Sir Tresham Lever,
The life and times of Sir Robert Peel, 1942. Sir Lawrence Peel, *A sketch of the life and
character of Sir Robert Peel*, 1860, provides data on family history and domestic back-
ground; see also Jonathan Peel, *The Peels: a family sketch*, 1877. For foreign views of
Peel in his own time see H. Künzel, *Leben und Reden Sir Robert Peels*, 2 v., Brunswick,
1851, and François Pierre Guillaume Guizot, *Sir Robert Peel*, Paris, 1856, Eng. edn.,
1857.

201   WELLINGTON. The dispatches and general orders of . . . the Duke of
Wellington . . . from 1799 to 1815. Compiled by Lieut. Col. [John] Gurwood.
13 v. 1834–9.

Contains the cream of Wellington's military correspondence, but marred by excisions
and poor indexing. *Supplementary despatches, correspondence, and memoranda . . .* edited
by the second Duke, 14 v., 1858–72, prints material omitted by Gurwood. The second
duke also carried the edited correspondence on to 1832 in *Despatches, correspondence,
and memoranda . . . from 1818 to 1832*, 8 v., 1867–80. *Wellington at war, 1794–1815*,
ed. by Antony Brett-James, 1961, is a selection of the wartime letters. The seventh Duke,
ed., *A selection from the private correspondence of the first Duke of Wellington*, Roxburghe
Club [Camb.], 1952. Sir Charles Webster, ed., 'Some letters of the Duke of Wellington
to his brother William Wellesley-Pole', *Camden miscellany*, 18 (1948). Minor collections
relating to the Duke's later years are: *Correspondence of Lady Burghersh with . . . Wellington*, ed. by Rose Weigall, 1903; *My dear Mrs Jones: the letters of . . . Wellington to
Mrs Jones of Pantglas*, 1954; *Letters of . . . Wellington to Miss J.*, ed. by Christine T.
Herrick, 1924; *A great man's friendship. Letters of . . . Wellington to Mary, marchioness
of Salisbury*, ed. by Lady Burghclere, 1927. The *Speeches of . . . Wellington in Parliament*
were arranged by Gurwood and ed. by William Hazlitt, 2 v., 1854. The seventh Duke
ed., *Wellington and his friends*, 1965, a selection of Wellington's letters to Mr. and Mrs.
Arbuthnot, the Earl and Countess of Wilton, Princess Lieven, and Miss Burdett-Coutts.
Victor de Pange, ed., *The unpublished correspondence of Madame de Staël and the Duke
of Wellington*, translated by Harold Kurtz, 1965.

202   WELLINGTON. History of the life of Arthur, Duke of Wellington.
From the French of M. Brialmont . . . with emendations and additions by the
Revd. George Robert Gleig. 4 v. 1858–60.

Gleig had personal knowledge of the Duke and was given access to unpublished corr.
Maxwell Hamilton Maxwell, *Life of . . . Wellington*, 3 v., 1838–41, ends with Waterloo;
Joachim Haywood Stocqueler, *The life of . . . Wellington*, 2 v., 1852–3, drew copiously
on contemporary printed material, particularly for the Duke's later career. For reminiscences of contemporaries see: *Three years with the Duke; or, Wellington in private life,
by an ex aide-de-camp* [Lord W. Lennox], 1953; Philip Henry, fifth Earl Stanhope, *Notes*

of conversations with . . . Wellington, 1831–51, 1888; *The conversations of . . . Wellington with George William Chad*, ed. by the seventh Duke, Camb., 1956; *Personal reminiscences of. . . Wellington*, by the first Earl of Ellesmere, ed. by his daughter Alice, Countess of Strafford, 1903; *Personal reminiscences of . . . Wellington*, by G. R. Gleig, ed. by Mary E. Gleig, 1904. See also Arbuthnot (203). *Wellington; . . . the public and private life . . . as told by himself, his comrades and his intimate friends*, by George Lathom Browne, 1888, is a collection of extracts from periodicals, memoirs, and the dispatches; as is also Sir William Fraser, *Words on Wellington*, 1889. Philip Guedalla, *The Duke*, 1931, is a good modern biography; see too Richard Aldington, *Wellington*, 1946, and Sir Charles Petrie, *Wellington: a reassessment*, 1956. The older *Life* by Sir Herbert Eustace Maxwell, 2 v., 1899, is still of value. Jacques Chastenet de Castaing, *Wellington, 1769–1852*, Paris, 1945, draws on French sources not used by Guedalla. Appraisals by military historians are in Frederick Sleigh, Earl Roberts, *The rise of Wellington*, 1895; Edmond Bonnal, *Wellington, général en chef, 1808–1814*, Paris, 1912, 1 v. only pub.; Sir John William Fortescue, *Wellington*, 1925; Charles R. M. F. Cruttwell, *Wellington*, 1936; and *Wellingtonian studies*, ed. by Michael Howard [Aldershot, 1959]. Charles Harvard Gibbs-Smith and Harold Victor T. Percival comp., *The Wellington Museum—Apsley House*, 2nd edn. rev. 1952. Elizabeth Longford, *Wellington*, 2 v., 1969–72, is excellent.

203 ARBUTHNOT. The correspondence of Charles Arbuthnot. Ed. by Arthur Aspinall. Camden Soc. 3rd s. 65. 1941.

Arbuthnot was closely associated with Wellington. See too *The journal of Mrs Arbuthnot, 1820–1832*, ed. by Francis Bamford and the Duke of Wellington, 2 v., 1950.

204 RAIKES. Private correspondence of Thomas Raikes with . . . Wellington and other distinguished contemporaries. Ed. by Harriet Raikes. 1861.

Letters 1812–1847. *A portion of the journal kept by Thomas Raikes . . . from 1831 to 1847*, 4 v., 1856–7, contains reminiscences of social and political life in London and Paris.

205 RUSSELL. The life of Lord John Russell. By Spencer Walpole. 2 v. 1889.

Prints a selection of memoranda and corr. 1803–75, from the papers now in the P.R.O. For other letters see *The early correspondence of . . . Russell* [to 1840], ed. by Rollo Russell, 2 v., 1913, and *The later correspondence of . . . Russell*, ed. by George P. Gooch, 2 v., 1930. *Selections from speeches of Earl Russell, 1817 to 1848, and from despatches, 1859 to 1865*, 2 v., 1870, has an autobiographical introduction; see too Russell, *Recollections and suggestions, 1813–1873*, 1875. *Lady John Russell. A memoir* (2321) includes incidental political info. See too Alexander Wyatt Tilby, *Lord John Russell. A study in civil and religious liberty*, 1930. J. Prest, *Lord John Russell*, 1972, is valuable but partisan.

206 DURHAM. The life and letters of the first Earl of Durham. By Stuart Johnson Reid. 2 v. 1906.

Corr. 1809–40. Other accounts are Chester William New, *Lord Durham. A biography*, 1929; Leonard Cooper, *Radical Jack*, 1959.

207 BROUGHAM. The life of Henry Brougham to 1830. By Chester William New. Oxf. 1961.

Fully documented. Indispensable despite inaccuracies is *The life and times of Henry, Lord Brougham, written by himself*, ed. by his son, 3 v., 1871, with letters and extracts from his diaries: Brougham's papers are now at University College London. Letters from Brougham form about half the collection printed in *Brougham and his early friends: letters to James Loch, 1798–1809*, arr. by R. H. M. Buddle Atkinson and G. A. Jackson, 3 v., 1908, priv. printed. See too Brougham's *Works*, 11 v., 1855–61, 2nd edn., 11 v.,

1872; *Lord Brougham's opinions . . . on politics, theology, law, science, education, literature . . .* (from his speeches and writings), 1837; and his *Speeches . . . upon questions relating to public rights, duties, and interests,* 4 v., Edinburgh, 1838. Ralph Thomas, comp., *A bibliographical list of Lord Brougham's publications . . . by the author of 'The handbook of fictitious names',* 1873. Arthur Aspinall, *Lord Brougham and the Whig Party,* Manch., 1927, rep. 1939, is thorough and masterly in treatment, from printed sources, and see his paper, 'Lord Brougham's "Life and Times"', *E.H.R.* 59 (1944), 87–112. A good short biog. is Frances Hawes, *Henry Brougham,* 1957. See also (528).

208   LYNDHURST. A life of Lord Lyndhurst; from letters and papers in possession of his family. By Sir Theodore Martin. 1883.

Letters and speeches relating to conservative party politics, 1828–60; also much on legal matters. See also Campbell (567).

209   HUSKISSON. The Huskisson papers, 1797–1830. Ed. by Lewis Melville. 2 vol. 1931.

Huskisson's papers are now British Library Add. MSS. 38734–70. His *Speeches* were coll., 3 v., 1831. There is no full biog. Alexander Brady, *William Huskisson and liberal reform,* 1928, is a study of changes in economic policy with which H. was concerned; see also Schuyler (4300). Charles Ryle Fay, *Huskisson and his age,* 1951, is an impressionist survey. See also George Stead Veitch, 'Huskisson and Liverpool', *Trans. Hist. Soc. of Lancs. & Chesh.* 80 (1929), 1–50, also pr. separately; and Anna L. Lingelbach, 'William Huskisson as president of the board of trade', *A.H.R.* 43 (1937–8), 759–74.

210   HERRIES. Memoir of the public life of J. C. Herries. Ed. by Edward Herries. 2 v. 1880.

A pious family defence, provoked by Spencer Walpole's *History*; cites some political correspondence and memoranda.

211   HOBHOUSE. The diary of Henry Hobhouse, 1820–1827. Ed. by Arthur Aspinall. 1947.

Hobhouse was under-secretary at the Home Office, 1817–1827.

212   MELBOURNE. Lord Melbourne's papers. Ed. by Lloyd Charles Sanders. 1889.

A selection of corr. 1800–1846. The best biography is by Lord David Cecil: *The Young Melbourne,* 1939, and *Lord M.,* 1954. Less penetrating is Bertram Newman, *Lord Melbourne,* 1930. William T. McC. Torrens, *Memoir of . . . Melbourne,* 2 v., 1878, drew upon letters in various private collections but is out of date, as is Henry Dunckley, *Lord Melbourne,* 1890. William Henry L. E. Bulwer [Lord Dalling], *Private memoir of the late Lord Melbourne* [1848], is a brief but suggestive contemporary assessment.

213   STANLEY. The Earl of Derby. By George Saintsbury. 1892.

A short essay. See too Thomas Edward Kebbel, *Life of . . . Derby,* 1893. There is no full study of his earlier career: Wilbur Devereux Jones, *Lord Derby and Victorian Conservatism,* Oxf., 1956, deals mainly with his career after 1851. See also Stewart (115).

214   ELLENBOROUGH. A political diary 1828–30, by Edward Law, Lord Ellenborough. Ed. by Lord Colchester. 2 v. 1881.

A valuable record, further portions of which for 1830–3 are printed in *Three early nineteenth century diaries,* ed. by Arthur Aspinall, 1952. Some of Ellenborough's papers concerning his later career have been donated to the P.R.O.

215 ABERDEEN. The life of George, fourth Earl of Aberdeen. By Frances Balfour. 2 v. 1923.

Makes use of the Aberdeen papers, now British Library Add. MSS. 43039–358, as does also the more limited study, Sir Arthur Gordon, *The Earl of Aberdeen*, 1893. For other letters see *The correspondence of Lord Aberdeen and Princess Lieven*, ed. by Ernest Jones Parry, Camden Soc., 3rd s., 60, 62, 2 v., 1938.

216 WILLIAM IV. The correspondence of . . . Earl Grey and . . . William IV . . . Nov. 1830 to June 1832. Ed. by Henry George, third Earl Grey. 2 v. 1867.

Percy H. Fitzgerald, *The life and times of William IV*, 2 v., 1884, is full and informative. Based on contemporary printed material and gossip was Robert Huish, *The history of the life and reign of William the fourth, the Reform Monarch of England*, 1837. Joseph Fitzgerald Molloy, *The Sailor King*, 2 v., 1903, and Grace E. Thompson, *The Patriot King*, 1932, are anecdotal. Better balanced, but without references, is Walter Gore Allen, *King William IV*, 1960. P. Ziegler, *King William IV*, 1971, is excellent.

217 PALMERSTON. The life of Henry John Temple, Viscount Palmerston. With selections from his diary and correspondence. By William Henry L. E. Bulwer [Lord Dalling]. 3 v. 1870–4.

This work was completed after Dalling's death by Evelyn Ashley, *The life of Viscount Palmerston, 1846–65. With selections from his speeches and correspondence*, 2 v., 1876. Ashley also wrote a revised version of the joint work incorporating some fresh documents, *The life and correspondence of . . . Palmerston*, 2 v., 1879. John Campbell, Marquis of Lorne, *Viscount Palmerston*, 1892, prints a few more family letters, but is otherwise of little value. The best older general study is Herbert C. F. Bell, *Lord Palmerston*, 1936, with wide use of documents including the royal archives. Noel W. B. Pemberton, *Lord Palmerston*, 1954, competently summarizes recent scholarship. Philip Guedalla, *Palmerston*, 1926, is a brilliant impressionist portrait. Lord Sudley, ed., *The Lieven–Palmerston correspondence, 1828–1856*, 1943. See also Connell (236) and *For. rel.* (311–325). Recent biographies by D. G. Southgate, *The most English minister*, 1966, and J. Ridley, 1970, are of value.

218 ALTHORP. Memoir of John Charles, Viscount Althorp, third Earl Spencer. By Denis Le Marchant. 1876.

Includes some letters; the author was a close friend and private secretary to Althorp. Ernest Myers, *Lord Althorp*, 1890, includes material from several private archives. See Earl Spencer, 'John Charles, Viscount Althorp, third Earl Spencer', *Quarterly Rev.* 283 (1945), 468–80.

219 POULETT THOMSON. Memoir of the life of . . . Charles Lord Sydenham. By George Poulett Scrope. 1843.

Undue editorial reticence renders inadequate this sketch of Sydenham's career in domestic politics; the work is fuller on his Canadian administration.

220 GRAHAM. The life and letters of Sir James Graham . . . 1792–1861. Ed. by Charles Stuart Parker. 2 v. 1907.

Arvel B. Erickson, *The public career of Sir James Graham*, 1952, is valuable and cites new material. William T. McC. Torrens, *The life of . . . Graham*, 2 v., 1863, is erratic and limited. See also J. T. Ward, *Sir James Graham*, 1967.

221 PRAED. A poet in Parliament: the life of Winthrop Mackworth Praed, 1802–1839. By Derek Hudson. 1939.

222   EWART. William Ewart, M.P., 1798–1869: portrait of a radical. By William Arthur Munford. 1960.

Includes material from family papers; Ewart had interests in education, criminal law reform, army discipline.

223   PARKES. Joseph Parkes of Birmingham. By Jessie Kathleen Buckley. 1926.

A radical, and political agent, an adviser on the Reform Act of 1832. See also G.B.A.M. Finlayson, 'Joseph Parkes of Birmingham', *I.H.R. Bull.* 46 (1973), 186–201.

224   ROEBUCK. Life and letters of John Arthur Roebuck ... with chapters of autobiography. Ed. by Robert Eadon Leader. 1897.

Utilitarian, author of the critical essays, *Pamphlets for the people*, 2 v., 1835.

225   DUNCOMBE. The life and correspondence of Thomas Slingsby Duncombe. Ed. by his son, Thomas H. Duncombe. 2 v. 1868.

Letters and diaries of a radical politician, 1813–61.

226   MOLESWORTH. Life of the Right Hon. Sir William Molesworth. By Millicent Garrett Fawcett. 1901.

Letters 1828–55, of a radical with strong interests in colonial affairs.

227   THOMPSON. General T[homas] Perronet Thompson, 1783–1869: his military, literary and political campaigns. By Leonard George Johnson. 1957.

Letters 1803–66. Thompson was proprietor of the *Westminster Review*, 1829–35.

228   MACAULAY. The life and letters of Lord Macaulay. By George Otto Trevelyan. 2 v. 1876.

Slight additions were made to the 2nd edn., 2 v., 1877. A modern study is Richmond Croom Beatty, *Lord Macaulay: Victorian liberal*, Norman, Oklahoma, 1938. Older lives by Henry H. Milman, 1862, and Frederick Arnold, 1862, are of value. His sister, Lady Trevelyan, ed., *The Works of Lord Macaulay*, 8 v., 1866. See also A. N. L. Munby, *Macaulay's library*, Glasgow, 1966; J. R. Griffin, *The intellectual milieu of Lord Macaulay*, Ottawa, 1965. Thomas Pinney, ed., *The Letters of . . . Macaulay*, Camb., 1974, in progress. J. L. Clive, *Thomas Babington Macaulay*, 1973, in progress.

229   GREY. Memoir of Sir George Grey. By Mandell Creighton. Priv. pr. Newcastle-upon-Tyne 1884.

Grey was under-secretary for colonies, 1834, 1835–9, and Home Secretary, 1846–52.

230   GLADSTONE. The life of William Ewart Gladstone. By John Morley. 3 v. 1903. 2 v. 1905–6.

V. 1 deals with the period, includes extracts from diaries and some correspondence. Gladstone's public papers are now British Library Add. MSS. 44086–835. Arthur Tilney Bassett comp., *Gladstone's speeches. Descriptive index and bibliography*, 1916, lists a number of the early speeches but prints only one before 1851. *Correspondence on church and religion of W. E. Gladstone*, selected . . . by Daniel C. Lathbury, 2 v., 1910, has material on the period. Among Gladstone's own early publications were: *The course of commercial policy at home and abroad*, 1843; *Remarks upon recent commercial legislation*, 1845; *The state in its relations with the Church*, 1838; *Church principles considered in their results*, 1840; *Two letters to the Earl of Aberdeen on the state prosecutions of the Neapolitan government*, 1851. See too his *A chapter of autobiography*, 1868; *Gleanings of past years*, 7 v., 1879; *Later gleanings . . . theological and ecclesiastical*, 1897. The best single-volume lives are Sir Philip Magnus, *Gladstone. A biography*, 1954, and Erich Eyck, *Gladstone*, 1938. Studies dealing with Gladstone's career in this period are: Francis E. Hyde, *Mr Gladstone at the Board of Trade*, 1934; Francis W. Hirst, *Gladstone as a financier and economist*, 1931, and *Gladstonian finance and economy*, 1938. A good life of Gladstone's wife is Georgina Battiscombe, *Mrs Gladstone*, 1956. More limited in range is their daughter's account: Mary Drew, *Catherine Gladstone*, 1919. A Tilney Bassett, ed., *Gladstone to his wife*, 1936. M. R. D. Foot, ed., *The Gladstone diaries*, v. 1 +, Oxf. 1968 +. See also (81), and for family background (2240).

231 HERBERT. Sidney Herbert, Lord Herbert of Lea. By Lord Stanmore. 2 v. 1906.

V. 1, pp. 1–169, family and political correspondence 1832–52 of one of the leading Peelites.

232 CLARENDON. The life and letters of George William Frederick, fourth Earl of Clarendon. By Sir Herbert Maxwell. 2 v. 1913.

Family and political corr. from *c.* 1800. George [J. T. H.] Villiers, *A vanished Victorian*, 1938, has letters from the Palmerston papers and other private collections. Clarendon's papers are in the Bodleian Library, Oxf.

233 GRANVILLE. The life of Granville George Leveson-Gower, second Earl Granville. By Lord Edmond Fitzmaurice. 2 v. 1905.

234 DISRAELI. The life of Benjamin Disraeli, earl of Beaconsfield. By William Flavelle Monypenny and George Earle Buckle. 6 v. 1910–20. Rev. edn. 2 v. 1929.

A spacious survey on the grand scale, with very full citations from Disraeli's papers. B. R. Jerman, *The Young Disraeli*, Princeton, N.J., 1960, with much new material, is excellent. Small collections of letters are printed in *Lord Beaconsfield's letters, 1830–52* [ed. by Ralph Disraeli], 1882, and *Letters from . . . Disraeli to Frances Anne, marchioness of Londonderry*, 1837–61, ed. by the marchioness of Londonderry, 1938. Valuable for Disraeli's political ideas are his novels, Bradenham edn., 12 v., 1926–7; see too Walter S. Sichel, *Disraeli. A study in personality and ideas*, 1904; *Whigs and Whiggism: political writings by Benjamin Disraeli*, ed. by William Hutcheon, 1913; *The radical Tory: Disraeli's political development illustrated from his original writings and speeches*, ed. by H. W. J. Edwards, 1937; Richard Faber, *Beaconsfield and Bolingbroke*, 1961; and Graubard (518). Sir Edward Clarke, *Benjamin Disraeli: the romance of a great career*, 1926, is a well-balanced, judicious short survey based on Monypenny and Buckle; more popular are David Churchill Somervell, *Disraeli and Gladstone; a duo-biographical sketch*, 1926, and Hesketh Pearson, *Dizzy: the life and nature of Benjamin Disraeli, earl of Beaconsfield*, 1951. R. N. W. Blake, *Disraeli*, 1966, is standard. R. W. Stewart, *Benjamin Disraeli: a list of writings by him, and writings about him, with notes* (The Scarecrow Author Bibliographies, no. 7), Metuchen, N.J., 1972.

235 MANNERS. Life of Lord John Manners and his friends. By Charles Whibley. 2 v. 1925.

Based on the Rutland papers; an analysis of the 'Young England' group in politics in the 'forties.

236 VICTORIA. The letters of Queen Victoria. First series. Ed. by Arthur Christopher Benson and the first Viscount Esher. 3 v. 1907.

A limited selection of the letters in the royal archives, 1837–61. There are more letters in *Regina v. Palmerston: the correspondence between Queen Victoria and her Foreign and Prime Minister, 1837–1865*, [ed. by] Brian Connell, 1962, and (a very few before 1851) in *The Queen and Mr Gladstone*, ed. by Philip Guedalla, 2 v., 1933, and *Further Letters of . . . Victoria*, ed. by Henry Hector Bolitho, 1938. In *The girlhood of . . . Victoria*, 2 v., 1912, Viscount Esher edited a selection from her diaries between 1832 and 1840. Sidney Lee, *Victoria: a biography*, 1902, with bibliog., is standard; Giles Lytton Strachey, *Queen Victoria*, 1921, is a brilliant interpretation of personality; Edward Frederick Benson, *Queen Victoria*, 1935, is conventional; H. H. Bolitho, *The reign of . . . Victoria*, 1949, is popular, but includes some unpublished material and records a number of court traditions and oral reminiscences. Kurt Jagow, *Königin Victorias Mädchenjahre*, Berlin, 1938, uses material from German archives. Dormer Creston, *pseud.* of Dorothy Julia Baynes, *The youthful Queen Victoria: a discursive narrative*, 1952, is a good personal portrait based on secondary material. See also Mackintosh (444). See too Elizabeth Longford, *Victoria, R.I.*, 1964.

237 ALBERT, PRINCE CONSORT. The life of . . . the Prince Consort. By Sir Theodore Martin. 5 v. 1876–80.

Includes some letters, but indiscriminate, written almost entirely as a panegyric. Other corr. is in *The Prince Consort and his brother: two hundred new letters*, ed. by Henry Hector Bolitho, 1933, and *Prinzgemahl Albert, ein Leben am Throne: eigenhändige Briefe und Augzeichnungen*, ed. by Kurt Jagow, Berlin, 1937—slight changes were made in the English version, *Letters of the Prince Consort, 1831–1861*, sel. and ed. by K. Jagow and trans. by Edgar T. S. Dugdale, 1938. Sir Arthur Helps, ed., *Principal speeches and addresses of . . . the Prince Consort*, 1862. Charles Grey, *The early years of . . . the Prince Consort*, 1867, was by the Queen's secretary, with her authority and guidance. Popular sketches are Francis B. Chancellor, *The Prince Consort*, 1931; Henry Hector Bolitho, *Albert the Good*, 1932, and *Albert and Victoria*, 1938. More critical in treatment are Roger Fulford, *The Prince Consort*, 1949; and Frank Eyck, *The Prince Consort: a political biography*, 1959, bibliog. 259–64, a valuable attempt at a conspectus rising above either a purely British or purely German viewpoint; both overestimate his political influence: see Mackintosh (444).

238 STOCKMAR. Memoirs of Baron Stockmar, by his son Baron E. von Stockmar. Eng. trans. ed. by Friedrich Max Müller. 2 v. Brunswick. 1872.

A personality behind the scenes at Victoria's court, whose influence is sometimes exaggerated, as by Pierre Crabitès, *Victoria's guardian angel: a study of Baron Stockmar*, 1937.

239 COBDEN. The life of Richard Cobden. By John Morley. 1881. Rev. edn. 1903.

Many letters, 1826–65, and bibliog. Cobden's *American diaries* were ed. by Elizabeth Hoon Cawley, Princeton, 1952. Primary for his political views are *The political writings of Richard Cobden*, 2 v., 1867; and *Speeches on questions of public policy, by Richard Cobden, M.P.*, ed. by John Bright and James Edwin Thorold Rogers, 2 v., 1870. A few documents are printed in Edward Hughes, 'The development of Cobden's economic doctrines and his methods of propaganda: some unpublished correspondence', and Fritz Trautz, 'Richard Cobden's associations with Germany', *Bull. J. Rylands L.* 22 (1938), 1–14, and 34 (1952), 459–68. Personal information was used in John McGilchrist, *Richard Cobden, the apostle of free trade*, 1865; Henry Ashworth, *Recollections of Richard Cobden, M.P. and the anti-corn law league*, 1877; J. E. Thorold Rogers, *Cobden and modern political opinion*, 1873. Sir Edward W. Watkin, *Alderman Cobden of Manchester: letters and reminiscences*, 1891, prints many letters not seen by Morley, and is of value for Cobden's local background, as is also William E. A. Axon, *Cobden as a citizen: a chapter in Manchester history*, 1907. Ian Bowen, *Cobden*, 1935, a brief, competent sketch, makes use of unpublished letters; Charles Taquey, *Richard Cobden: un révolutionnaire pacifique*,

Paris, 1939, bibliog. 236–9, examines Cobden as an agitator and propagandist. Francis W. Hirst, *Richard Cobden and John Morley*, Swindon, 1941, is a thoughtful lecture. See also Read (240). F. W. Steer, ed., *The Cobden papers; a catalogue*, Chichester, 1964, and Patricia Gill, ed., *The Cobden and Unwin papers; a catalogue*, Chichester, 1967. For other papers see (67) and British Library Add. MSS. 43647–78. See also (141).

240 BRIGHT. The life of John Bright. By George Macaulay Trevelyan. 1913. 2nd edn. 1925.

Standard, letters 1835–87, and citing material later pub. in *The Diaries of John Bright*, ed. Robert A. J. Walling, 1930. Bright's *Speeches* were ed. by James Edwin Thorold Rogers, 2 v., 1868; George Barnett Smith, *The life and speeches of John Bright*, 2 v., 1881, is also worth consulting. William Robertson, *Life and times of John Bright*, 1877, included info. given by friends. Joseph Travis Mills, *John Bright and the Quakers*, 2 v., 1935 has much info. Brief, but a useful summary, is Margaret E. Hirst, *John Bright*, 1945. See too J. Ausubel, *John Bright: Victorian reformer*, 1966; D. Read, *Cobden and Bright: a Victorian political partnership*, 1967; J. L. Sturgis, *John Bright and the empire*, 1969. Some of Bright's papers are now British Library Add. MSS. 43383–92.

241 BENTINCK. Lord George Bentinck: a political biography. By Benjamin Disraeli. 1852.

Concerned mainly with Bentinck as leader of the protectionists, 1845–8.

242 TANCRED. A Victorian M.P. and his constituents; the correspondence of H. W. Tancred, 1841–1859. Ed. by B. S. Trinder. (Banbury Hist. Soc. Pubs. 8). Banbury. 1969.

D. FOREIGN AFFAIRS

1. Sources

(a) *Manuscript*

243 LIST OF FOREIGN OFFICE RECORDS TO 1878, preserved in the Public Record Office. P.R.O. Lists and Indexes. No. 52. 1929.

The classes of documents are: general correspondence, mainly arranged by states; treaties, embassy and consular archives; archives of commissions, including slave trade papers; confidential prints, being duplicate sets of important political papers specially printed for distribution within the Foreign Office and missions abroad (of limited extent for the period 1789–1851); chief clerk's department—accounts, correspondence, papers, and ledgers; passport office; and private papers, including those of Sir Arthur Aston, Lord Cowley, James Henderson, Lewis Hertslet, John Augustus, Lord Hervey, Lord Howard de Walden, Francis James Jackson and Sir George Jackson, Henry Manvers Pierrepont, Lord Stratford de Redcliffe, Lord Stuart de Rothesay (Sir Charles Stuart), and Sir Woodbine Parish. Collections donated or deposited in the Public Record Office apart from the Foreign Office papers which contain diplomatic material include the Cave, Chatham, Cornwallis, and Granville papers.

244 BRITISH LIBRARY. Chief diplomatic collections.

Add. MSS. 29714–18, 28060–8, Egerton MSS. 3498–3505. Marquis of Carmarthen (Duke of Leeds), to 1791.
Add. MSS. 34428–71. William Eden, 1st Lord Auckland, to 1793.
Add. MSS. 37080–85. 4th Earl of Bute, to 1796.

Egerton MSS. 2634–41, Add. MSS. 34048, 37077, 39793, 40714–6, 41197–200, 42069–
82. Sir William Hamilton, to 1800.
Add. MSS. 46822–38. Francis Drake, *c.* 1790–1813.
Add. MSS. 39841–2. William Wyndham Grenville, Lord Grenville, to the Austrian
Ambassador, 1793–1801.
Add. MSS. 48383–416. Sir Arthur Paget, 1791–1809.
Add. MSS. 37286–94. Marquis Wellesley, 1809–12.
Add. MSS. 41511–66. W. A'Court, 1st Lord Heytesbury, 1812–32.
Add. MSS. 32603–9. Sir Woodbine Parish, the 1820s.
Add. MSS. 36299–300. Lord Strangford, 1821–5.
Add. MSS. 47236–435. The Lieven Papers. Plus new accession, 1973.
Add. MSS. 42781–95. Sir George Henry Rose, 1814–23.
Add. MSS. 42791–809. Hugh Henry Rose, Lord Strathnairn, 1836–56.
Add. MSS. 48417–509, 49963–9. The Palmerston letter books, from 1830.
Add. MSS. 43039–358. Lord Aberdeen, 1813–55.
Add. MSS. 58855–59494. William W. Grenville, Lord Grenville. See (78).

245 THOMAS (DANIEL H.) *and* CASE (LYNN M.). Guide to the diplomatic archives of Western Europe. Phil. London. 1959.

Indispensable, covering fourteen countries; essays on the nature of the archive collections of each followed by lists of guide and reference works and of printed collections
of documents. More limited information on archives of East European countries (includ-
ing Russia), and of Turkey, is given in Société des Nations, Institut International de
Coopération Intellectuelle, *Guide International des Archives: Europe*, Paris, Rome, 1934.
Exceptional in its specialized guidance is *Catálogo XVII* of the Archivo General de
Simancas: *Secretaría de Estado. Documentes relativo a Inglaterra (1254–1834)*, ed. by
Julián Paz and Ricardo Magdaleno, Madrid, 1947.

(b) *Printed*

(i) *Collections of letters, papers, and instructions*

See also under prime ministers and foreign secretaries in *Political Biography*
(pp. 26–42).

246 FOREIGN OFFICE. British and foreign state papers. 1829+.

Treaties and other documents, all but a few introductory items being for the period
from 1812 onwards. The contents of the volumes are roughly in chronological order,
though publication was at first irregular, beginning with v. 15. V. 64 is a general index,
chronological and alphabetical, to vs. 1–63, covering 1373–1873. There was no regular
publication of papers before 1812, but many which were printed are conveniently located
in the section, 'Chronicle: State Papers', in the *Annual Register*. Parliamentary sessional
papers (see 387) include accounts of diplomatic correspondence laid before parliament.
H. W. V. Temperley and Lillian Penson, *A century of diplomatic blue books, 1814–1914*,
Camb., 1938, lists the blue books and discusses ministerial policy on the release of
diplomatic news. See also by the same compilers, *Foundations of British foreign policy
from Pitt to Salisbury, or documents old and new, selected and edited with historical introductions* [1792–1902], Camb., 1938. For printed correspondence of prime ministers and
foreign secretaries see in *Political Biography*. Clive Parry, ed., *Law officers' opinions to
the foreign office, 1793–1860 . . .*, v. 1+, Farnborough, 1970+.

247 COLENBRANDER (HERMAN THEODOOR). Gedenkstukken der
algemeene geschiedenis van Nederland, 1795–1840. 10 pts. in 22 v. The
Hague. 1905–22.

248 BIANCHI (NICOMEDE). Storia documentata delle diplomazia europea in Italia [1814–61]. 8 v. Turin. 1865–72.

Includes references to British diplomatic activities from the Sardinian and other archives.

249 MEMOIRES DU PRINCE DE TALLEYRAND. Ed. with a preface by the Duc de Broglie. 5 v. Paris. 1891–2.

See also Pallain (274), (282), (305).

250 METTERNICH. Mémoires, documents et écrits divers laissés par le prince de Metternich. Publiés par son fils le prince Richard de Metternich, classés et réunis par M. A. de Klinkowstroem. 8 v. Paris. 1880–4.

The English edition only reached the fifth vol. (to 1835).

251 COWLEY. Diary and correspondence of Henry Wellesley, first Lord Cowley, 1790–1846. Ed. by his grandson, Col. F. A. Wellesley. [1930].

Letters and memoranda of the British ambassador to Spain, 1809–22, Vienna, 1823–31, Paris, 1841–6.

252 VNESHNAYA POLITIKA ROSSII XIX I NACHALA XX VEKA. Moscow. 1960+.

First series: v. I (1801–4); II (1804–6) . . . Much material from Russian archives dealing with British policy.

(ii) *Treaties*

253 TÉTOT (—). Répertoire des traités de paix, de commerce, d'alliance . . . depuis la paix de Westphalie jusqu'à nos jours. Table générale des recueils de Dumont, Wenck, Martens, Murhard, Samwer, de Clercq, Léonard, Angeberg, Lesur, Hertslet, Neumann, Testa, Calvo, Elliot, Cantillo, Castro, Soutzo, State Papers . . . donnant l'indication du volume et de la page du recueil où se trouve le texte de chaque traité. 2 v. Paris. 1866–73.

Some collections of later date than 1873 are listed in Denys Peter Myers, *Manual of collections of treaties and of collections relating to treaties*, Camb., Mass., 1922, which covers a wider variety of materials than Tétot.

2. GENERAL

254 RAGATZ (LOWELL JOSEPH). A bibliography for the study of European history, 1815 to 1939. Ann Arbor. 1942.

About 15,000 titles; three supplements, 1943, 1945, 1956. J. S. Bromley and A. Goodwin, *A select list of works on Europe and Europe overseas, 1715–1815*, Oxf., 1956, gives about 2,500 titles, and Alan L. C. Bullock and Alan J. P. Taylor, *A select list of books on European history, 1815–1914*, Oxf., 1957, about 1,500. Charles Morley, *Guide to research in Russian history*, Syracuse, N.Y., 1951, includes printed sources. On the Napoleonic period see also Friedrich Max Kircheisen (940).

255 MARTENS (KARL, *Freiherr von*). Manuel diplomatique ou précis des droits et des fonctions des agens diplomatiques; suivi d'un recueil d'actes et d'offices pour servir de guide aux personnes qui se destinent à la carrière politique. 1822. 5th edn. rev. and ed. by F. H. Geffken, Leipzig, 2 v. 1866.

See also Ernest Lehr, *Manuel theorique et pratique des agents diplomatiques et consulaires français et étrangers*, Paris, 1888, rev. edn. by H. Richter, 1932. The classic modern exposition is Sir Ernest Mason Satow, *A guide to diplomatic practice*, 2 v., 1917, 4th edn., ed. by Sir Nevile Bland, 2 v., 1957.

256 CHARMATZ (RICHARD). Geschichte der auswärtigen Politik Österreichs im xix^{ten} Jahrhundert. 2 v. Leipzig. 1912–14. 2nd corrected edn. 2 v. Leipzig and Berlin. 1918.

257 WARD (*Sir* ADOLPHUS WILLIAM) *and* GOOCH (GEORGE PEABODY) *eds*. The Cambridge history of British foreign policy, 1783–1919, 3 v. 1922–3.

V. 1, 1783–1815, v. 2, 1815–1866. The 2nd vol. is less solidly based on the documents of the FO archives. Among single-volume surveys Heinrich David, *Englands Europäische Politik im xix Jahrhundert von den französichen Revolutionskriegen bis zum Tode Palmerstons*, Bern, 1924, is valuable, and Robert William Seton-Watson, *Britain in Europe, 1789–1914*, Camb., 1937, bibliog. 677–88, is excellent. Opposition criticism of government policy is discussed in Alan J. P. Taylor, *The trouble makers: dissent over foreign policy, 1792–1939*, 1957. Kenneth Bourne, *The foreign policy of Victorian England, 1830–1902*, 1970, presents selected documents, with a substantial introd.

258 BECKER Y GONZALES (JERÓNIMO). Historia de las relaciones exteriores de España durante el siglo xix. 3 v. Madrid. 1924–6.

V. 1, 1800–40, v. 2, 1840–68. Much detail and full citations of diplomatic correspondence.

259 LACOUR-GAYET (GEORGES). Talleyrand, 1754–1838. 4 v. Paris. 1928–34.

Enlightening on a number of episodes of British diplomacy.

260 SRBIK (HEINRICH, *Ritter von*). Metternich: der Staatsmann und der Mensch. 2 v. Munich. 1925–6.

Standard. Srbik followed this with a third volume: *Quellenöffentlichungen und Literatur: eine Auswahlübersicht von 1925–1952*. Munich, 1954, a source for bibliography of Metternich up to 1952.

261 GOEBEL (JULIUS LUDWIG). The struggle for the Falkland islands; a study in legal and diplomatic history. New Haven. 1927.

Examines British, Spanish, and Argentine claims to sovereignty in the islands.

262 HEADLAM-MORLEY (*Sir* JAMES WYCLIFFE). Studies in diplomatic history. Ed. Kenneth and Agnes Headlam-Morley. 1930.

Suggestive discussions of various diplomatic themes, in papers written by an adviser to the Foreign Office, 1920–8.

263 SWAIN (JAMES EDGAR). The struggle for the control of the Mediterranean prior to 1848; a study of Anglo-French relations. Boston, Mass. 1933.

Concise, well-documented; bibliog. 139–45.

264 ABBOTT (WILBUR CORTEZ). An introduction to the documents relating to the international status of Gibraltar, 1704–1934. N.Y. 1934.

Brief intro. and bibliog. of printed and MS. sources.

265 BINDOFF (STANLEY THOMAS) *and others*. British diplomatic representatives, 1789–1852. (Camden Soc., 3rd s. v. 50). 1934.

Includes refs. to issue of credentials and instructions, but omits biographical details. Edmund B. D'Auvergne, *Envoys extraordinary*, 1937, includes sketches of some notable diplomats. See too Ernest Jones Parry, 'Under-secretaries of state for foreign affairs, 1782–1855', *E.H.R.* 49 (1934), 308–20 and Bindoff, 'Unreformed diplomatic service' (457).

266 PHILLIPS (WALTER ALISON) *and* REEDE (ARTHUR H.). Neutrality: its history, economics and law. V. 2: The Napoleonic period. N.Y. 1936.

267 ALMADA (JOSÉ DE). A aliança inglêsa. Subsídios para o seu estudo. 2 v. Lisbon. 1946–7.

A general survey from 1373 to 1904. See also his *Para a história da aliança Luso-Britanica*, Lisbon, 1955, and Leitão (308).

268 LUCA (STEFAN-PASCAL). Les rivalités franco-anglaises et l'élaboration de l'unité italienne, 1789–1849. Geneva. 1941.

A critical essay, based on printed material; bibliog. 163–71.

269 BINDOFF (STANLEY THOMAS). The Scheldt question to 1839. 1945.

270 HATZE (MARGRIT). Die diplomatisch-politischen Beziehungen zwischen England und der Schweiz im Zeitalter der Restauration. Basle. 1949.

271 RENOUVIN (PIERRE) *ed.* Histoire des relations internationales. 12 v. Paris. 1953–8.

V. 4: *La Révolution française et l'Empire Napoléonien*, by André Fugier, 1954; v. 5: *Le XIXe siècle. 1. De 1815 à 1871: l'Europe des nationalités et l'éveil de nouveaux mondes*, by Pierre Renouvin, 1954. Emile Bourgeois, *Manuel historique de politique étrangère*, 4 v., Paris, 1892–1926, v. 2: *Les révolutions, 1789–1830*; v. 3: *Le temps présent, 1830–1877*, is brilliant but prejudiced.

272 KUKIEL (MARIAN). Czartoryski and European unity, 1770–1861. Princeton, N.J., London. 1955.

Bibliog. 323–34; some material on Britain's attitude at various times to the Polish question.

273 WIENER (JOEL HOWARD). Great Britain: foreign policy and the span of empire, 1689–1971. A documentary history. 4 v. 1972.

3. BRITAIN AND EUROPE

(Arranged according to chronological order of content)

(a) 1789–1815

(i) *Sources*

274 BROWNING (OSCAR). The despatches of Earl Gower, English ambassador at Paris, from June 1790 to August 1792. Camb. 1885.

Also includes material from the diary kept by the 2nd Visc. Palmerston at Paris in 1791. Anglo-French diplomacy is also illustrated in *La mission de Talleyrand à Londres en 1792*, ed. by Georges Pallain, Paris, 1889.

275 DIARIES AND CORRESPONDENCE OF JAMES HARRIS, first earl of Malmesbury. Ed. by his grandson, the third earl. 4 v. 1844.

V. 3 includes his journal and correspondence relating to his missions, 1793–7.

276 THE PAGET PAPERS: diplomatic and other correspondence of . . . Sir Arthur Paget, 1794–1807. Ed. by Sir Augustus B. Paget. 2v. 1896.

277 SCOTT (JAMES BROWN) *ed*. The armed neutralities of 1780 and 1800: a collection of official documents preceded by the views of representative publicists. N.Y. 1918.

See too Sir Francis Taylor Piggott and George William Thomson Omond, *Documentary history of the armed neutralities, 1780 and 1800*, 1919.

278 THE DIARIES AND LETTERS OF SIR GEORGE JACKSON, K.C.H., from the peace of Amiens to the battle of Talavera. Ed. by Lady Jackson. 2 v. 1872.

She also ed. *The Bath archives. A further selection from the diaries and letters of Sir George Jackson . . . from 1809–1816*, 2 v., 1873. Jackson, a junior diplomat, served in Germany and, in 1808–9, in Spain.

279 BROWNING (OSCAR) *ed*. England and Napoleon in 1803: being the despatches of Lord Whitworth and others. 1887.

280 AURIOL (CHARLES). La France, l'Angleterre, et Naples, 1803–6. 2 v. Paris. 1904.

Very full; dispatches from British and French archives and some private collections. Some material on Hugh Elliot's mission to Naples, 1803–6, is in Emma E. E. Elliot-Murray Kynynmound (countess of Minto), *A memoir of the right honourable Hugh Elliot*, Edin., 1868.

281 ROSE (JOHN HOLLAND) *ed*. Select dispatches from the British foreign office archives, relating to the formation of the Third Coalition against France, 1804–5. (Camden Soc. 3rd s., v. 7). 1904.

Dispatches from the ambassadors at St. Petersburg; and Lord Harrowby's mission to Berlin. See too C. S. B. Buckland, ed., 'Letters from Genz and others in Vienna to the Hon. H. M. Pierrepont, 1803–1806', *E.H.R.* 53 (1938), 98–113, and Sir Robert Adair, *Historical memoir of a mission to the court of Vienna in 1806. With a selection from his dispatches*, 1844.

282 WEBSTER (*Sir* CHARLES KINGSLEY) *ed*. British diplomacy, 1813–15; select documents dealing with the reconstruction of Europe. 1921.

Georges Pallain, ed., *Correspondence of Prince Talleyrand and King Louis XVIII during the congress of Vienna*, Engl. edn., 2 v., 1881.

283 BURGHERSH. Correspondence of Lord Burghersh . . . 1808–1840. Ed. by Rachel Weigall. 1912.

Mainly concerned with Italian affairs, 1814–15.

284 KLÜBER (JOHANN LUDWIG). Akten des Wiener Congresses in den Jahren 1814 und 1815. 9 v. Erlangen. 1815–35.

Comte d'Angeberg (*pseud.* of Leonard Boryko Chodzko), ed., *Le Congrès de Vienne et les traités de 1815; précédé et suivi des actes diplomatiques qui s'y rattachent; avec une introduction historique par J. B. Capefigue*, 2 v., Paris, 1863, including memoranda and diplomatic notes and with references to documents printed in other collections.

(ii) *Later Works*

285 ANDERSON (MATTHEW SMITH). Britain's discovery of Russia, 1553–1815. 1958.

Half the work is on the years 1791–1815. Also excellent on this period is Dietrich Gerhard, *England und der Aufstieg Russlands: zur Frage des Zusammenhanges des europäischen Staaten und ihres Ausgreifens in die aussereuropäische Welt in Politik und Wirtschaft des 18 Jahrhunderts*, Munich and Berlin, 1933. Andrei A. Lobanov-Rostovsky, *Russia and Europe, 1789–1825*, Durham, N. Car., 1947, is a scholarly survey based on printed material only. Robert Howard Lord, *The second partition of Poland; a study in diplomatic history*, 1916, has little on British diplomacy. See also Salomon's *Pitt* (147), of value for his use of the Prussian archives.

286 CARLSSON (SIGNE). Sverige och Storbritannien, 1787–1790; studier i den Gustavianska tidens diplomatiska historia. Lund. 1944.

Bibliog. 318–23; based on a wide range of MSS. sources, including Russian archives. Lydia Wahlström, *Sverige och England under revolutionskrigens början*, Stockholm, 1917, deals with Anglo-Swedish relations in the early years of the revolutionary wars. Also valuable is *Den Svenska utrikespolitikens historia*, Del III, *1792–1810*, by S. C. O. Carlsson, Del IV, *1810–1814*, by Torvald Höjer, two parts in one vol., Stockholm, 1954.

287 NORRIS (JOHN MACKENZIE). 'The policy of the British cabinet in the Nootka crisis.' *E.H.R.* 70 (1955), 562–80.

288 VREEDE (GEORG WILLEM). Inleiding tot eene geschiedenis der nederlandsche diplomatie. 6 v. Utrecht. 1856–65.

Vs. 4–6 deal with the diplomacy of the Batavian republic and the reign of Louis Bonaparte (1795–1810).

289 FORTESCUE ([*Sir*] JOHN WILLIAM). British statesmen of the great war, 1793–1814. Oxf. 1911.

Rather superficial but stimulating. Ephraim Douglas Adams, *The influence of Grenville on Pitt's foreign policy, 1787–1798*, Wash., 1904, is brief and limited. J. M. Sherwig, 'Lord Grenville's plan for a concert of Europe, 1797–99', *J. of Mod. Hist.* 34 (1962), 284–93.

290 STOKER (JOHN TEASDALE). William Pitt et la révolution française (1789–1793). Paris. 1935.

Based on British and French diplomatic archives. More general is Jules Dechamps, *Les îles britanniques et la révolution française*, Paris, 1949. David Williams, 'The missions of David Williams and James Tilly Matthews to England, 1793', *E.H.R.* 53 (1938), 651–68, deals with attempts to preserve or restore peace through unofficial channels in the spring of 1793.

291 SHERWIG (JOHN MARTIN). Guineas and gunpowder. British foreign aid in the wars with France, 1793–1812. Camb., Mass. [1969].

292 SALEMI (LEONARDO). I trattati antinapoleonici dell'Inghilterra con le
Due Sicilie, 1793–1812. Palermo. 1937.

See too Mario Pastore, ed., *La legazione sarda in Londra* (1730–1860) (Indici dell'
archivio storico, v. 4), Rome, 1952.

293 GUYOT (RAYMOND). Le directoire et la paix de l'Europe des traités de
Bâle à la deuxième coalition (1795–1799). Paris. 1911.

Good use of British archives; bibliog. 4–36. Aspects of British war diplomacy and
intrigue are treated in H. Mitchell, *The Underground War against Revolutionary France.
The Missions of William Wickham, 1794–1800,* Oxf., 1965.

294 DRIAULT (J. EDOUARD). Napoléon et l'Europe. 5 v. Paris. 1910–27.

V. 1: *La politique extérieure du Premier Consul (1800–1803)*; v. 2: *Austerlitz. La fin du
Saint-Empire (1804–1806)*; v. 3: *Tilsit. France et Russie sous le premier empire. La
question de Pologne (1806–1809)*; v. 4: *Le grand empire (1809–1812)*; v. 5: *La chute de
l'empire: la légende de Napoléon (1812–1815)*. A good brief survey is Robert Balmain
Mowat, *The diplomacy of Napoleon,* 1924. Otto Brandt, *England und die Napoleonische
Weltpolitik, 1800–1803,* Heidelberg, 1916, and P. Coquelle, *Napoleon and England,
1803–1813,* Engl. edn. by Gordon D. Knox, 1904, are scholarly studies. On the
resumption of war against Napoleon, see C. Gill, 'The relations between England and
France in 1802', *E.H.R.* 24 (1907), 61–78; J. Deschamps, 'La rupture de la paix
d'Amiens', *Révue des études Napoléoniennes,* 44 (1939), 172–207; H. Butterfield, *Charles
James Fox and Napoleon; the peace negotiations of 1806,* 1962.

295 CARR (RAYMOND). 'Gustavus IV and the British government, 1804–9'.
E.H.R. 60 (1945), 36–66.

See also S. Clason, 'Gustav IV Adolf och General Moore', *Historisk Tidskrift,* 32
(Stockholm, 1912), 1–52, 233–95. Carl V. V. Key Åberg, *De diplomatiska förbindelserna
mellan Sverige och Storbritannien under Gustav IV Adolfs Krig emot Napoleon intill
konventionen i Stralsund,* Uppsala, 1890, and *De diplomatiska förbindelserna mellan
Sverige och Storbritannien under Gustav IV Adolfs senaste regeringsar* [1807–9], Uppsala,
1891, drew only on the Swedish archives. S. C. O. Carlsson, *Gustav IV Adolf,* Stockholm, 1946, and S. Johnson, 'Legend ock verklighet kring Gustav Adolfs brytning med
Napoleon', *Svensk Tidskrift,* 1950, 462 ff., use English documents and illustrate English
policy.

296 MØLLER (E.). 'England og Danmark-Norge i 1807'. *Historisk Tidskrift,* 8 (Copenhagen, 1912), iii, 311–422.

297 RAMÍREZ DE VILLA-URRUTIA (WENCESLAO, *Marquis de Villa-
Urrutia*). Relaciones entre España e Inglaterra durante la guerra de la independencia; apuntes par la historia diplomática de España de 1808 a 1814.
3 v. Madrid. 1911–14.

See also Jeronimo Becker y Gonzales, *Acción de la diplomacia española durante la guerra
de la independencia,* in *Publicaciones del congreso historico internacional de la independencia
y su epoca (1807–1815),* t. 1, Zaragoza, 1909.

298 ROSSELLI (JOHN). Lord William Bentinck and the British occupation
of Sicily, 1811–14. Camb. 1956.

See too Charles William Crawley, 'England and the Sicilian constitution of 1812', *E.H.R.*
55 (1940), 251–74.

299 BUCKLAND (CHARLES STEPHEN BUCKLAND). Metternich and the British government from 1809 to 1813. 1932.

Bibliog. vii–xxiii. See also his *F. von Gentz's relations with the British government, 1809–12*, 1933. Fedor von Demelitsch, *Metternich und seine auswartige Politik*, Stuttgart, 1898, is an excellent study from the Vienna archives on the years 1809–12, though uncritical of Metternich's premises.

300 RENIER (GUSTAV JOHANN). Great Britain and the establishment of the kingdom of the Netherlands, 1813–1815; a study in British foreign policy. 1930.

Bibliog. 346–50. Heinz Fischer, *Die oranischen Erblande und die Vergrösserung der Niederlande, 1813–15*, Frankfort, 1936; Ernst Moritz Klingenburg, *Die Entstehung der deutsch-niederländischen Grenze im Zusammenhang mit der Neuordnung des niederländisch-niederrheinischen Raumes, 1813–15*, Leipzig, 1940.

301 WEBSTER (*Sir* CHARLES KINGSLEY). The foreign policy of Castlereagh, 1812–1815. Britain and the reconstruction of Europe. 1931. Repr. 1950.

See too his *The congress of Vienna, 1814–15*, new edn., 1934. Other studies of the years of peace-making include Karl Goldmann, *Die preussisch-britischen Beziehungen . . . 1812–1815*, Wurzburg, 1934; Edward Vose Gulick, *Europe's classical balance of power: a case history of the theory and practice of one of the great concepts of European statecraft*, Ithaca, N.Y., and London, 1955. See also (177).

(b) 1815–1851

(i) *Sources*

302 HYDE (HARFORD MONTGOMERY). 'The Lieven archives'. *Bull. I.H.R.* 12 (1934–35), 152–63.

See also Lieven (176), (195), (201), (215), (244).

303 DAUDET (ERNEST) *ed.* L'ambassade du Duc Decazes en Angleterre (1820–1821). Paris. 1910.

Anti-British bias, but well documented.

304 CHATEAUBRIAND (FRANÇOIS RENÉ DE, *Visc.*) Correspondance générale . . . Ed. by Louis Thomas. 5 v. Paris. 1912–14.

Includes diplomatic corr. during his embassy in London and his attendance at the Congress of Verona. For other material see: Chateaubriand, *Congrès de Verone. Guerre d'Espagne. Negotiations: colonies espagnoles*, 2 v., Paris, 1838. Richard Bentley pub. an English version under title, *The congress of Verona: comprising a portion of Memoirs of his own times. By M. de Chateaubriand*, 2 v., 1838; François Marie Adhémar, Comte D'Antioche, *Chateaubriand, ambassadeur à Londres, 1822, d'après ses dépêches inédites*, Paris, 1912; and Comte Marcellus, *Correspondance entre . . . Chateaubriand et . . . Marcellus, chargé d'affaires . . . à Londres*, 2 v., Paris, 1858.

305 PALLAIN (GEORGES) *ed.* Correspondance diplomatique de Talleyrand. Ambassade de Talleyrand à Londres, 1830–1834. Paris. 1891.

306 DEMOULIN (ROBERT). 'La correspondance des consuls anglais en Belgique pendant la révolution de 1830'. *Acad. Roy. de Belgique Comm. Roy. Hist. Bull.* 98 (1934), 417–535.

Text, notes, and index of names.

307 GUIZOT (FRANÇOIS PIERRE GUILLAUME). Mémoires pour servir a l'histoire de mon temps. 8 v. Paris. 1858–67.

Includes his memoirs of his embassy in England and his later connections with Anglo-French diplomatic relations.

308 LEITÃO (RUBEN ANDRESEN). Documentos dos arquivos de Windsor. Coimbra. 1955. Novos Documentos dos arquivos de Windsor. Coimbra. 1958.

Documents, 1846–7 and 1847–53, in English and French, with introduction, notes, and bibliography.

(ii) *Later Works*

309 WEBSTER (*Sir* CHARLES KINGSLEY). The foreign policy of Castlereagh, 1815–1822. Britain and the European alliance. 1925. 2nd edn. rep. 1947.

Old-fashioned but still of value is Walter Alison Phillips, *The confederation of Europe; a study of the European alliance, 1813–1823, as an experiment in the international organization of peace,* 1914, 2nd edn., 1920. Other studies are: Sir Harold Nicolson, *The congress of Vienna: a study in allied unity, 1815–1818,* 1945, N.Y., 1946, reflective; Jacques-Henri Pirenne, *La Sainte Alliance (1815–18),* 2 v., Neuchatel, 1946–9, emphasizing Anglo-Russian rivalry; H. G. Schenk, *The aftermath of the Napoleonic wars: the concert of Europe, an experiment,* 1947, provocative, but neglectful of conventional diplomatic material; Maurice Bourquin, *Histoire de la Sainte Alliance,* Geneva, 1954; Henry Alfred Kissinger, *A world restored: Metternich, Castlereagh, and the problems of peace, 1812–1822,* 1957, uncritical of Metternich's premises. There are a few side-lights on Anglo-French relations in Jules Dechamps, *Chateaubriand en Angleterre,* Paris, 1934. See also (177).

310 TEMPERLEY (HAROLD WILLIAM VAZEILLE). The foreign policy of Canning, 1822–27. 1925.

Standard. See also (178), (179).

311 WEBSTER (*Sir* CHARLES KINGSLEY). The foreign policy of Palmerston, 1830–1841: Britain, the liberal movement, and the Eastern question. 2 v. 1951.

A scholarly definitive study. See also his papers: 'Lord Palmerston at work, 1830–1841', *Politica,* 1 (1934), 129–44; 'Palmerston and the liberal movement, 1830–41', *ibid.* 3 (1938), 299–323; 'Palmerston, Metternich, and the European system, 1830–41', *British Academy proc. for 1934,* xx (1936), 125–58; 'Urquhart, Ponsonby and Palmerston', *E.H.R.* 62 (1947), 327–51. Gavin B. Henderson, 'The foreign policy of Lord Palmerston', *History,* 22 (1937–8), 335–44, is critical. A contemporary's attack on Palmerston's handling of policy after 1830 is A. G. Stapleton, *Intervention and non-intervention in the foreign policy of Great Britain, 1790–1865,* 1866. See also (217).

312 BOOGMAN (JOHAN CHRISTIAAN). Nederland en de Duitse bond, 1815–51. 2 v. Groningen. 1955.

Limited reference to British diplomacy.

313 GLEASON (JOHN HOWES). The genesis of Russophobia in Great Britain. A study of the interaction of policy and opinion. Camb. Mass. and London. 1950.

On the years 1815–1841; well documented from British archives. A valuable brief review is Charles William Crawley, 'Anglo-Russian relations, 1815–1840', *Camb. Hist. J.* 3

(1929), 47–73. Theodor Schiemann, *Geschichte Russlands unter Kaiser Nikolaus I*, 4 v., Berlin, 1904–19, a classic, covers also the reign of Alexander I. See too Frederick Stanley Rodkey, 'Anglo-Russian negotiations about a "permanent quadruple alliance", 1840–1841', *A.H.R.* 36 (1930–31), 343–9; William Habberton, *Anglo-Russian relations concerning Afghanistan, 1837–1907*, Urbana, Ill., 1937. On Baltic aspects see C. F. Palmstierna, *Sverige, Ryssland och England, 1833–1855*, Stockholm, 1932.

314 ROSSELLI (NELLO). Inghilterra e regno di Sardegna dal 1815 al 1847. Turin. 1954.

Bibliog. 911–28. See too Margaret C. W. Wicks, *The Italian exiles in London, 1816–1848*, Manch., 1937, and Emilia Morelli, *Mazzini in Inghilterra*, Florence, 1938.

315 GUICHEN (EUGÈNE DE). La révolution de 1830 et l'Europe. Paris. 1916.

Incorporates material from an exceptional range of European archives.

316 SMIT (CORNELIS). De conferentie van Londen. Het vredesverdrag tussen Nederland en Belgie van 19 April 1839. Leiden. 1949.

Little use of archives. See too Rudolf Steinmetz, *Englands Anteil an der Trennung der Niederlande, 1830*, The Hague, 1930, and for background, René Dollot, *Les origines de la neutralité de la Belgique et le système de la barrière* (1609–1830), Paris, 1902.

317 GUYOT (RAYMOND). La première entente cordiale [1830–1846]. Paris. 1926.

From British and French archives, with attention to the commercial and financial aspects of Anglo-French relations. Older but worth consulting is John [Richard] Hall, *England and the Orleans monarchy*, 1912.

318 PARRY (ERNEST JONES). The Spanish marriages, 1841–1846; a study of the influence of dynastic ambition upon foreign policy. 1936.

Excellent. See too his 'A review of the relations between Guizot and Lord Aberdeen, 1840–52', *History* 23 (1938), 25–36, and A. B. Cunningham, 'Peel, Aberdeen and the Entente cordiale', *Bull. I.H.R.* 30 (1957), 189–206.

319 FLOURNOY (FRANCIS ROSEBRO). British policy towards Morocco in the age of Palmerston (1830–1865). Baltimore and London. 1935.

A study well documented from British, French, and U.S. archives.

320 GREER (DONALD MALCOLM). L'Angleterre, la France et la révolution de 1848: le troisième ministère de Lord Palmerston au foreign office, 1848–1851. Paris. 1925.

321 SPROXTON (CHARLES). Palmerston and the Hungarian revolution. Camb. 1919.

322 TAYLOR (ALAN JOHN PERCIVALE). The Italian problem in European diplomacy, 1847–9. Manch. 1934.

323 ECKINGER (KARL). Lord Palmerston und der Schweitzer Sonderbundskrieg. Berlin. 1938.

324 HJELHOLT (HOLGER). British mediation in the Danish–German conflict, 1848–1850. 2 vs. Copenhagen. 1965, 1966.

With full use of British public and private archives.

325 BULLEN (ROGER). Palmerston, Guizot, and the collapse of the entente cordiale. 1974.

4. BRITAIN AND THE NEAR AND MIDDLE EAST

326 I. HAKKI UZUNÇARŞILI. On Dokuzuncu Asir Başlarina Kadar Türk-Ingiliz Münasebâtina Dair Vesikalar (*French title*: Documents concernant les relations Turco-Anglaises jusqu'au début du XIXe siècle). *Belleten*, XIII/51 (1949), 573–650.

Relates mainly to the period from 1793; in Turkish, with French summary. A guide to Turkish historical literature is Enver Koray, *Türkiye Tarih Yayinlari Bibiyografyasi 1721–1955*, 2nd edn., Istanbul, 1959.

327 ANDERSON (MATTHEW SMITH). The Eastern Question. 1966.

Standard. Sir John Arthur Ransome Marriott, *The Eastern Question*, 4th edn., Oxf., 1940, is an older brief survey from the commencement of the nineteenth century. The standard expositions from the French side are Edouard Driault, *La question d'Orient depuis ses origines jusqu'à la paix de Sèvres*, Paris, 1921, dealing lightly with the period up to 1851, and J. Ancel, *Manuel historique de la question d'Orient, 1792–1925*, Paris, 1926. See too A. Adu Boahen, *Britain, the Sahara, and the Western Sudan, 1788–1861*, Oxf., 1964.

328 CHARLES-ROUX (FRANÇOIS). L'Angleterre et l'expédition française en Égypte. Paris. 1925.

Valuable detailed examination of the way in which British policy was shaped by French initiative. For background see the same author's *Autour d'une route. L'Angleterre, l'Isthme de Suez, et l'Egypte au xviiie siècle*, Paris, 1922. Georges Douin and E. C. F. Jones, *L'Angleterre et l'Egypte: la politique mameluke, 1801–7*, 2 v., Cairo, 1929–30, is primarily a collection of documents from the British Foreign Office and War Office archives.

329 PURYEAR (VERNON JOHN). Napoleon and the Dardanelles. 1951.

A scholarly survey covering 1802–15. Sir Robert Adair, *The negotiations for the peace of the Dardanelles in 1808–9*, 2 v., 1845, is an account by the British negotiator. See too Paul Frederick Shupp, *The European powers and the Near Eastern question, 1806–7*, N.Y., 1931, Paul Rüter, *Die Turkei, England und das russisch-französische Bundnis, 1807–1812*, Emsdetten, 1935, and A. M. Stanislavskaya, *Russko-Angliyskie otnosheniya i problemy sredizemnomor'ya (1798–1807 gg.)*, Moscow, 1962.

330 YAKSCHITCH (GRÉGOIRE). L'Europe et la résurrection de la Serbie, 1804–34. 2nd edn. Paris. 1917.

331 BAGGALLY (JOHN WORTLEY). Ali Pasha and Great Britain. Oxf. 1938.

Deals with Albanian affairs during and just after the Napoleonic period.

332 CRAWLEY (CHARLES WILLIAM). The question of Greek independence: a study of British policy in the Near East, 1821–1833. Camb. 1930.

Standard; bibliog. 251–9. The view from the French archives is Gaston Isambert, *L'Indépendance grèque et l'Europe*, Paris, 1900; also valuable is the early part of Edouard Driault and Michel L'Héritier, *Histoire diplomatique de la Grèce de 1821 à nos jours*, 5 v., Paris, 1925–6, based on the Austrian, British, and French archives. Important are Douglas Dakin, *British and American philhellenes during the war of Greek independence, 1821–1833*, Thessalonika, 1955, and *British intelligence of events in Greece, 1824–1827: a documentary collection*, Athens, 1959. Also of relevance for British policy is A. V. Fadeev, *Rossiya i vostochny krisis 20-kh godov xix veka*, Moscow, 1958.

333 DODWELL (HENRY HERBERT). The founder of modern Egypt. A study of Muhammad 'Ali. Camb. 1931.

Examines the British concern with Egypt under Muhammad 'Ali from the archives of the Foreign Office and the India Office. See too Pierre Crabitès, *Ibraham of Egypt*, 1935; Shafik Ghorbal, *The beginnings of the Egyptian Question and the rise of Mehemet Ali*, 1928.

334 BAILEY (FRANK EDGAR). British policy and the Turkish reform movement: a study in Anglo-Turkish relations, 1826–1853. Camb., Mass., London. 1942.

See also Frederick S. Rodkey, 'Lord Palmerston and the rejuvenation of Turkey, 1830–41', *J. of Mod. Hist.* 1 (1929), 570–93, 2 (1930), 193–225; H. Temperley, 'British policy towards parliamentary rule in Turkey, 1830–41', *Camb. Hist. J.* 4 (1933), 156 seq.

335 RODKEY (FREDERICK STANLEY). The Turko-Egyptian question in the relations of England, France, and Russia, 1832–1841. Urbana [Ill.]. 1924.

Adolf Hasenclever, *Die Orientalische Frage in den Jahren 1838–41*, Leipzig, 1914, is a detailed and critical study based on Austrian and Prussian archives. See also G. H. Bolsover, 'Lord Ponsonby and the Eastern question (1833–39)', *Slavonic and East Eur. Rev.* 13 (1934), 98–118; 'Palmerston and Metternich on the Eastern question in 1834', *E.H.R.* 51 (1936), 237–56; and 'David Urquhart and the Eastern question, 1833–7: a study in publicity and diplomacy', *J. Mod. Hist.* 8 (1936), 444–67. There is a life of Urquhart by Gertrude Robinson, Oxf., 1920. See also (145).

336 PURYEAR (VERNON JOHN). International economics and diplomacy in the Near East: a study of British commercial policy in the Levant, 1834–1853. Stanford, [Cal.], London. 1935.

Presents some controversial conclusions. Britain's economic interests in the Ottoman empire in relation to diplomacy are also discussed in Frank Edgar Bailey, 'The economics of British foreign policy, 1825–50', *J. Mod. Hist.* 12 (1940), 449–84. See also Philip E. Mosely, *Russian diplomacy and the opening of the Eastern Question in 1838 and 1839*, Camb. [Mass.], 1934; and F. Waddington, 'La politique de Lord Palmerston et le traité de 15 Juillet 1840', *Rev. Hist. Diplomatique*, 49 (1935), 1–27, 174–201.

337 TEMPERLEY (HAROLD WILLIAM VAZEILLE). England and the Near East. V. 1: The Crimea. 1936.

Standard; outlines the 'Eastern question' from the beginning of the century but is more full on the years after 1840. Vernon John Puryear, *England, Russia and the Straits question, 1844–56*, Berkeley [Cal.], London, 1931, is controversial. A. B. Cunningham, ed., *The early correspondence of Richard Wood, 1831–1841* (Roy. Hist. Soc., Camden 4th ser. 3), 1966; valuable for British interest in Syria.

338 KELLY (JOHN BARRETT). Britain and the Persian Gulf, 1795–1880. 1968.

L. S. Semenov, *Rossiya i mezhdunarodnye otnosheniya na Srednem Vostoke v 20-kh godakh XIX v.*, Leningrad, 1963, is largely concerned with Anglo-Russian relations in Persia in the 1820s. See also M. E. Yapp, 'The control of the Persian mission, 1822–1836', *Univ. of Birmingham Hist. J.* 5 (1960), 162–79.

5. ANGLO-AMERICAN RELATIONS

(a) *General*

339 BEMIS (SAMUEL FLAGG) *and* GRIFFIN (GRACE GARDNER). Guide to the diplomatic history of the United States, 1775–1921. Wash. 1935.

Bibliog. and guide to archives. Some more recent MSS. accessions are listed in Crick and Alman (74).

340 BEMIS (SAMUEL FLAGG). The American secretaries of state and their diplomacy. 10 v. N.Y. 1927–9.

Standard. See too his *A diplomatic history of the United States*, 4th rev. edn., 1950; Thomas Andrew Bailey, *A diplomatic history of the American people*, 4th edn., N.Y., 1950; Julius W. Pratt, *A History of United States foreign policy*, N.Y., 1955; Richard William Van Alstyne, *The rising American empire*, 1960.

341 ALLEN (HARRY CRANBROOK). Great Britain and the United States: a history of Anglo-American relations, 1783–1952. 1954.

Standard. An enlarged version of pt. 1 has been pub. under the title *The Anglo-American relationship since 1783*, 1960. Other excellent surveys are William Archibald Dunning, *The British Empire and the United States: a review of their relations during the century of peace following the Treaty of Ghent*, 1914; and John Bartlet Brebner, *North Atlantic triangle: the interplay of Canada, the United States, and Great Britain*, Toronto, London, 1945. On the diplomats, see Beckles Willson, *America's ambassadors to England, 1785–1928: a narrative of Anglo-American diplomatic relations*, 1928, and *Friendly relations: a narrative of Britain's ministers and ambassadors to America (1791–1930)*, 1934.

(b) *Detailed Studies (in chronological order of subject)*

342 BURT (ALFRED LEROY). The United States, Great Britain, and British North America, from the revolution to the establishment of peace after the war of 1812. New Haven, [Conn.], London. 1940.

Centred on Canadian issues. Samuel Flagg Bemis, *Jay's Treaty: A study in commerce and diplomacy*, N.Y., 1923, is exhaustive, but weighted on the American side, and its emphasis is corrected in C. R. Ritcheson, *Aftermath of Revolution. British policy towards the United States, 1783–1795*, Dallas, 1969. Bradford Perkins, *The first rapprochement: England and the United States, 1795–1805*, Phil., London, 1955, *Prologue to war: England and the United States, 1805–1812*, Berkeley, London, 1961, and *Castlereagh and Adams: England and the United States, 1812–1823*, Berkeley, 1964, are excellent, as also is Reginald Horsman, *The causes of the war of 1812*, 1962, with full bibliog. 269–92. An older book worth consulting is Frank Arthur Updyke, *The diplomacy of the war of 1812*, Baltimore, 1915. Bernard Mayo, ed., *Instructions to the British ministers to the United States, 1791–1812*, Wash., 1941. See too Jerald A. Coombs, *The Jay Treaty*, Berkeley, London, 1970.

343 SOULSBY (HUGH GRAHAM). The right of search and the slave trade in Anglo-American relations, 1814–62. Baltimore. 1933.

344 WILLIAMS (MARY WILHELMINA). Anglo-American isthmian diplomacy, 1815–1915. Wash. 1916.

Standard, but in need of revision.

345 BOURNE (KENNETH). Britain and the balance of power in North America, 1815–1908. 1967.

Discusses interactions of defence policy and diplomacy.

346 PERKINS (DEXTER). The Monroe doctrine, 1823–1826. Camb., Mass. London. 1927.

Perkins also wrote more general surveys, *The Monroe doctrine, 1826–1867*, Baltimore, 1933, and *Hands off: a history of the Monroe doctrine*, Boston, 1941. See also Leonard Axel Lawson, *The relation of British policy to the declaration of the Monroe doctrine*, N.Y., 1922; and Edward H. Tatum, *The United States and Europe, 1815–23: a study in the background of the Monroe doctrine*, Berkeley, 1936.

347 MERK (FREDERICK). Albert Gallatin and the Oregon problem: a study in Anglo-American diplomacy. Camb., Mass. London. 1950.

See also his *The Oregon Question: Essays in Anglo-American diplomacy and politics*, Camb., Mass. 1967.

348 ADAMS (EPHRAIM DOUGLASS). British interests and activities in Texas, 1838–46. Baltimore. 1910.

349 JONES (WILBUR DEVEREUX). The American problem in British diplomacy, 1841–1861. 1974.

6. BRITAIN AND LATIN AMERICA

(a) *General*

350 HUMPHREYS (ROBERT ARTHUR). Latin American history: a guide to the literature in English. N.Y., London. 1958.

See also his paper, 'The historiography of the Spanish American revolutions', *H.A.H.R.* 36 (1956), 81–93.

351 MULHALL (MICHAEL GEORGE). The English in South America. Buenos Aires. 1878.

Old-fashioned but wide ranging, as is also W. H. Koebel, *British exploits in South America*, N.Y., 1917.

352 HISPANIC AMERICAN HISTORICAL REVIEW. Baltimore; afterwards Durham, N.C. V. 1+. 1918+.

Guide . . . 1918–1945, ed. Ruth Lapham Butler, Durham, N.C., 1950; *Guide . . . 1946–1955*, ed. Charles Gibson and E. V. Niemeyer, Durham, N.C., 1958.

353 MANNING (WILLIAM RAY). Diplomatic correspondence of the
United States concerning the independence of the Latin-American nations.
3 v. N.Y. 1925.

See too J. F. Rippy, *Rivalry of the United States and Great Britain over Latin America,
1808–30*, Baltimore, 1929; Luis Cuervo Marquez, *Independencia de las colonias hispano-
americanos; participación de la Gran Bretaña y de los Estados Unidos, Legion Britanica,*
2 v., Bogotá, 1938; Williams (344).

354 IRELAND (GORDON). Boundaries, possessions and conflicts in South
America. Camb., Mass. 1938.

Also *Boundaries, possessions and conflicts in Central and North America and the Caribbean,*
Camb., Mass., 1941. Indispensable works of reference.

355 WEBSTER (*Sir* CHARLES KINGSLEY) *ed.* Britain and the independence of Latin America, 1812–30: select documents from the Foreign Office
archives. 2 v. 1938.

Indispensable. V. 1: Introduction; correspondence with Latin America; v. 2: Communications with European states and the United States. William W. Kaufmann, *British
policy and the independence of Latin America, 1804–28*, New Haven, London, 1951, is
standard; and see R. A. Humphreys, *Liberation in South America, 1806–1827: the
career of James Paroissien*, 1952. Some details of British policy are discussed in J. T.
Lanning, 'Great Britain and Spanish recognition of the Hispanic American states',
H.A.H.R. 10 (1930), 429–56; John Rydjord, 'British mediation between Spain and her
colonies, 1811–1813', *ibid.* 21 (1941), 29–50. See also R. A. Humphreys and G. S.
Graham (1130).

(b) *Regions*

(i) *Río de la Plata (Argentina, Uruguay, Paraguay)*

356 BEVERINA (JUAN). Las invasiones inglesas al Río de la Plata, 1806–7.
2 v. Buenos Aires. 1939.

Most detailed. See too Carlos Roberts, *Las invasiones inglesas del Río de la Plata*, Buenos
Aires, 1938; John Street, 'La influencia Británica en la independencia de las provincias
del Río de la Plata, con especial referencia al periodo comprendido entre 1806 y 1816',
Revista Hist. 19 (1953), 181–257, 329–91, 21 (1954), 1–83, 224–317, full bibliog. 303–17;
and 'Lord Strangford and Río de la Plata, 1808–15', *H.A.H.R.* 33 (1953), 477–510;
*Misiones diplomáticas; Misiones de Matías Irigoyen, José Agustin de Aguirre, Tomás
Crompton, y Mariano Moreno*, v. 1, Buenos Aires, 1937; Enrique Ruíz Guinazu, *Lord
Strangford y la revolucion de mayo*, Buenos Aires, 1937; *Correspondencia de Lord Strang-
ford y de la estación naval británica en el Río de la Plata con el gobierno de Buenos Aires,
1810–22*, Buenos Aires, 1941.

357 FERNS (HENRY STANLEY). Britain and Argentina in the nineteenth
century. Oxf. 1960.

Luis Alberto de Herrera, *La misión Ponsonby*, 1930 [no place of pub.], is a full study,
with docs. from the British archives, 1824–9. See too his 'La Paz de 1828', *Rev. Inst.
Hist. y Geog. Uruguay*, año *1937*, 13 (1938), 1–106, año *1938*, 14 (1939), 1–76, año *1939*,
15 (1940), 55–98; E. J. Pratt, 'Anglo-American commercial and political rivalry on the
Plata, 1820–30', *H.A.H.R.* 11 (1931), 302–35; John Frank Cady, *Foreign intervention in
the Rio de la Plata, 1838–50*, Phil., London, 1929, Spanish edn., Buenos Aires, 1943.
For some aspects of British immigration see James Dodds, *Records of the Scottish settlers
in the River Plate and their churches*, Buenos Aires, 1897. On the Falklands question see
Goebel (261).

358 KIERNAN (VICTOR GORDON). 'Britain's first contacts with Paraguay', *Atlante*, 3 (1955), 171–91.

An excellent account covering 1823–53.

(ii) *Brazil*

359 MANCHESTER (ALAN KRIBBS). British pre-eminence in Brazil; its rise and decline. Chapel Hill, N. Car. 1933.

Surveys both the diplomatic and economic fields. See too his paper, 'The recognition of Brazilian independence', *H.A.H.R.* 31 (1951), 80–96. Caio de Freitas, *George Canning e o Brasil*, 2 v., Sao Paulo, 1958, is a thorough, scholarly study. See also Cochrane (360).

(iii) *Chile and Peru*

360 MONTANER BELLO (RICARDO). Historia diplomática de la independencia de Chile. Santiago. 1941.

For British participation, see Thomas Cochrane, 10th earl of Dundonald, *Narrative of services in . . . Chile, Peru and Brazil*, 2 v., 1859, and J. Miller, *Memoirs of General [W.] Miller in the service of the republic of Peru*, 2 v., 1828. C. W. Centner has discussed 'The Chilean failure to obtain British recognition, 1823–1828', in *Revista de Hist. de América*, 15 (1942), 285–97.

(iv) *Venezuela and Colombia*

361 'LA MISIÓN DE BOLIVAR Y LÓPEZ MÉNDEZ A LONDRES'. *Acad. Nac. Hist. Venezuela Bol.* 18 (1935), 643–710.

On the mission of 1810; includes documents. See too Luis Correa, ed., 'La misión a Londres de Bolivar y López Méndez; documentos adquiridos por el Dr. Carlos Urdaneta Carrillo', *ibid.* 21 (1938), 47–66; Vicente Lecuna, ed., 'Documentos referentes a misiones enviadas por el Liberador a Londres y Barbadoes en 1814', *ibid.* 297–312; William Spence Robertson, 'The beginnings of Spanish American diplomacy', in *Essays in American History dedicated to Frederick Jackson Turner*, N.Y., 1910, repr. 1951; Alfred Hasbrouck, *Foreign legionaries in the liberation of Spanish South America*, N.Y., 1928.

(v) *Central America*

362 HUMPHREYS (ROBERT ARTHUR). The diplomatic history of British Honduras, 1638–1901. 1961.

For the Guatemalan view see José Luis Mendoza, *Inglaterra y sus pactos sobre Belice*, Guatemala, 1942: there is an Eng. trans. by Lilly de Jongh Osborne, 1947. See too R. W. Van Alstyne, 'The Central American policy of Lord Palmerston, 1846–8' *H.A.H.R.* 16 (1936), 339–59.

(vi) *Mexico*

363 RYDJORD (JOHN). Foreign interest in the independence of New Spain. Durham, N. Car. 1935.

A useful survey up to 1815; bibliog. 309–22. See too C. R. Salit, 'Anglo-American rivalry in Mexico, 1823–1830', *Revista de Hist. de América*, 16 (1942), 65–84.

(vii) *Caribbean*

364 CALLAHAN (JAMES MORTON). Cuba and international relations: a historical study in American diplomacy. Baltimore. 1899.

Limited reference to Gt. Britain. See too H. L. Hughes, 'British policy towards Haiti, 1801–5', *Can. Hist. R.* 25 (1944), 397–408.

7. BRITAIN AND THE FAR EAST AND PACIFIC

365 PRITCHARD (EARL HAMILTON). The crucial years of early Anglo-Chinese relations, 1750–1800. Pullman, Wash. 1936.

Excellent, with full bibliog. 403–30.

366 MORSE (HOSEA BALLOU). The international relations of the Chinese empire. 3 v. 1910–18.

V. 1: *The period of conflict, 1834–60.* The best general authority. See too William Conrad Costin, *Great Britain and China, 1833–1860*, Oxf., 1937. Arthur John Sargent, *Anglo-Chinese commerce and diplomacy*, Oxf., 1907, emphasizes commercial aspects of Anglo-Chinese relations. Pin-Chia Kuo, *A critical study of the first Anglo-Chinese war, with documents*, Shanghai, 1935, with critical bibliog. 200–8, can be supplemented by Arthur Waley, *The Opium War through Chinese eyes*, 1958, and J. K. Fairbank, 'Chinese diplomacy and the Treaty of Nanking, 1842', *J. of Mod. Hist.* 12 (1940), 1–30. Hsin-Pao Chang, *Commissioner Lin and the Opium War*, Camb., Mass., 1964, makes extensive use of Chinese materials. Alastair Lamb, *Britain and Chinese Central Asia*, 1960, deals with the question of Tibet. On the treaty ports see Fairbank (1496).

367 BEASLEY (WILLIAM GERALD). Great Britain and the opening of Japan, 1834–58. 1951.

A scholarly study; bibliog. 210–22.

368 TARLING (NICHOLAS). Anglo-Dutch rivalry in the Malay World, 1780–1824. 1962.

369 BROOKES (JEAN INGRAM). International rivalry in the Pacific islands, 1800–75. Berkeley and Los Angeles. London. 1941.

Also valuable is John M. Ward, *British policy in the South Pacific, 1796–1893*, Sydney, 1948. See also Koskinen (4782).

III

CONSTITUTIONAL HISTORY

A. GENERAL WORKS

1. CONTEMPORARY TREATISES

For treatises and pamphlets on constitutional theory, see *Political theory* (517–30).

370 BLACKSTONE (*Sir* WILLIAM). Commentaries on the laws of England. 11th edn. cont. to the present time by John Williams. 4 v. 1791. 21st edn. with . . . notes by J. F. Hargrave (and others). 4 v. 1844.

Important despite Blackstone's and his successors' neglect of constitutional conventions. Similar in approach is Henry John Stephen, *New commentaries on the laws of England, partly founded on Blackstone*, 4 v., 1841–5.

371 PLOWDEN (FRANCIS [PETER]). The constitution of the United Kingdom of Great Britain and Ireland, civil and ecclesiastical. 1802.

Much legal antiquarianism, but thoughtful and intelligent.

372 RUSSELL (*Lord* JOHN). An essay on the history of the English government and constitution from the reign of Henry VII to the present time. 1821. 2nd edn. greatly enl. 1823. Other edns. 1865, 1873.

Half on post-1760; valuable as giving the political practitioner's views.

373 BOWYER (*Sir* GEORGE). The English constitution; a popular commentary on the constitutional law of England. 1841.

Legalistic, but with important variations of treatment from that of Blackstone.

374 SMITH (JOSHUA TOULMIN). Local self-government and centralization: the characteristics of each, and its practical tendencies as affecting social, moral, and political welfare and progress, including comprehensive outlines of the English constitution. 1851.

By a bitter opponent of current tendencies to centralization. Similar in approach was his *Government by commissions illegal and pernicious*, 1849.

375 BAGEHOT (WALTER). The English constitution. 1867. Rev. edn. 1872.

Most valuable for its insight into the growth of conventions after 1832. See too his *Essays on parliamentary reform*, 1883 [written 1859–72], and Henry George, 3rd Earl Grey, *Parliamentary government*, 1858, rev. edn., 1864.

2. SOURCE BOOKS

376 COSTIN (WILLIAM CONRAD) *and* WATSON (JOHN STEVEN), *comps.* The law and working of the constitution: documents, 1660–1914. 2 v. 1952.

V. 2: 1784–1914; in fullness supersedes all other specialist collections, but gives no commentaries. David Lindsay Keir and Frederick Henry Lawson, *Cases in constitutional law*, 1928, 3rd edn. rev. 1948, has few cases for the period but useful introductory surveys. See also Douglas (87). H. J. Hanham, *The nineteenth century constitution. Documents and commentary*, Camb., 1969, is excellent.

3. LATER WORKS

377 MAY (*Sir* THOMAS ERSKINE), *Baron Farnborough*. The constitutional history of England since the accession of George the third, 1760–1860. 2 v. 1861–3. 2nd edn. 1863–5. 3rd edn. in 3 v. 1871. New edn. ed. and cont. to 1911 by Francis Holland. 1912.

Much valuable information, but lacking in historical insight. Less weighty but an interesting contrast in approach is Charles Duke Yonge, *The constitutional history of England from 1760 to 1860*, 1882.

378 AMOS (SHELDON). Fifty years of the English constitution, 1830–1880. 1880.

A perceptive study in the Bagehot tradition.

379 ANSON (*Sir* WILLIAM REYNELL). The law and custom of the constitution. V. 1, Parliament. V. 2, The Crown. 2 v. 1886–92. 2nd edn. 1892–6. 3rd edn. (v. 2 in 2 pts.) 1897–1908. V. 1, 4th edn. 1909. 5th edn. ed. by Maurice L. Gwyer. 1922. V. 2, 4th edn. ed. by Arthur Berriedale Keith. 1935.

An able analysis of the contemporary constitution from a lawyer's point of view, with much historical matter pertinent to the first half of the 19th century. Alpheus Todd, *On parliamentary government in England. Its origin, development and practical operation*, 2 v., 1867–9, 2nd edn., 2 v., 1887–9, new edn. by Spencer Walpole, 2 v., 1892, was a less successful attempt on the same lines, badly arranged but a mine of information.

380 HOLDSWORTH (*Sir* WILLIAM SEARLE). A history of English law. v. 13. Ed. by A. L. Goodhart and H. G. Hanbury. 1952.

Includes a valuable survey of 'constitutional background', 1793–1832.

381 EMDEN (CECIL STUART). The people and the constitution; being a history of the development of the people's influence in British government. Oxf. 1933. 2nd edn. 1956.

Henry Jephson, *The platform: its rise and progress*, 2 v., 1892, analyses various political campaigns.

382 KEIR (*Sir* DAVID LINDSAY). The constitutional history of modern Britain [from 1485]. 1938. 6th edn. 1960.

A brilliant general survey. Briefer, on similar lines, is Frederick George Marcham, *A constitutional history of modern England, 1485 to the present*, N.Y., 1960. The last part of Frederic William Maitland, *The constitutional history of England*, Camb., 1906, is a luminous survey of developments, 1702–1888. Kingsley B. S. Smellie, *A hundred years of English government*, 1937, 2nd edn. rev., 1950, gives perceptive treatment to the early Victorian period.

B. PARLIAMENT

See House of Lords Record Office supplementary memorandum, *A handlist of articles in periodicals and other serial publications relating to the history of Parliament*, comp. by H. S. Cobb, duplicated, 1973; see also Bond (65).

1. BOTH HOUSES

(a) *Statutes*

383 PICKERING (DANBY) *ed*. The statutes at large from Magna Charta to . . . 1761. 24 v. Continued to 1806. Vs. 25–46. Camb. 1762–1807.

With indexes. Other edns. covering the late 18th century are *The statutes at large . . . to [1800]*, by Owen Ruffhead, 18 v., 1763–1800, also edn. of 1769–1800, and new edn. by Charles Runnington, 14 v., 1786–1800. For the 19th century see *The statutes of the United Kingdom, with notes, references and an index*, by T. E. Tomlins and others, 29 v., 1804–1869. The British Library has various made-up sets of Public and Private Acts. Joseph Chitty, *A collection of statutes of practical utility with notes thereon; intended as a circuit and court companion*, 2 v., 1829–37, 2nd edn. by W. N. Welsby and E. Beavan, 4 v., 1851–4, is useful. See also *An index to the statutes public and private passed [1801] to . . . [1865]*, 2 v., 1867. Other chronological indexes were comp. by Richard Lowndes, 1831, and George Crabb, 3 v., 1841–4. Indexes to private and local Acts are George Bramwell, *Analytical table of the private statutes [1727–1812]*, 1813; Thomas Vardon, *Index to the local and personal and private acts: 1798–1837*, 1840; Statute Law Committee, *Index to local acts . . . [1801–1899]*, 1900. See Sheila Lambert, *Bills and acts: legislative procedure in eighteenth-century England*, Camb., 1971, ch. 9, 'Promulgation of the statutes'.

(b) *Debates*

384 GREAT BRITAIN, Parliament. A bibliography of parliamentary debates of Great Britain. [Comp. by John A. Woods and others]. 1956.

385 COBBETT (WILLIAM) *and* HANSARD (THOMAS CURSON) *eds*. [Cobbett's] Parliamentary History of England . . . to 1803. 36 v. 1806–20.

Taken over by Hansard in 1812, when the title was changed. Continued by the same editors in *[Cobbett's] Parliamentary Debates, 1803–20*, 41 v., 1803–20, and then by Hansard in *Parliamentary Debates*, new ser., 25 v., 1820–30, and Hansard's *Parliamentary Debates*, 3rd ser., 350 v., 1830–91. *General index to the first and second series . . . [1803–30]*, ed. by Sir John Philippart, 2 v., 1832–3. Other reports sometimes including matter omitted in this series are: John Almon and John Debrett, *The Parliamentary Register*, 83 v., 1775–1804; William Woodfall, and others, *An impartial report of the debates*, 33 v., 1794–1803; John Stockdale, *The Parliamentary Register; or, An impartial report of the debates*, 29 v., 1804–13, continuing both Debrett and Woodfall; *The Senator*, 28 v., 1790–1801; *The Mirror of Parliament*, ed. John Henry Barrow, 1st ser., 37 v., 1828–37, 2nd ser., 24 v., 1838–41.

386 ASPINALL (ARTHUR). 'Le Marchant's reports of debates in the House of Commons, 1833.' *E.H.R.* 58 (1943), 78–105.

(c) *Parliamentary Papers*

Before 1801 papers may be found as (1) separates, (2) in the journals and their appendices, (3) in the reprinted collection of reports not inserted in the journals

cited as 'First Series' (388), and (4) in the surviving artificially 'bound sets' in
110 v. put together by Charles Abbot, speaker of the Commons (389). In 1801
for the Commons and in 1804 for the Lords, the printing of the papers was
reorganized, papers being numbered consecutively for each session. For a list
of catalogues and indexes see Percy and Grace Ford, *A guide to parliamentary
papers. What they are: How to find them: How to use them*, Oxf., 1955; and 'Bibliographical aids to research. II. British Parliamentary Papers: Catalogues and
indexes', *Bull. I.H.R.* 11 (1933–4), 24–30.

(i) *House of Lords*

387   A GENERAL INDEX TO THE SESSIONAL PAPERS printed by
order of the House of Lords or presented by special command [1801–59].
1860. Repr. 1938.

See *A guide to House of Lords papers and petitions* (H.L. R.O. memorandum 20), 1959.

(ii) *House of Commons*

388   REPORTS FROM COMMITTEES OF THE HOUSE OF COMMONS
. . . not inserted in the journals. 1715–1801. 16 v. 1803–6.

V. 16 is a detailed general index, which includes a list of the reports appearing in the
journals and not reprinted in this series.

389   CATALOGUE OF PAPERS PRINTED BY ORDER OF THE HOUSE
OF COMMONS, 1731–1800. 1807. Facs. repr. 1954.

This is a catalogue of the Abbot collection in 110 v., one set of which exists in the
British Library. There is an almost complete set in the library of University College
London.

390   CATALOGUE OF PARLIAMENTARY REPORTS, and a breviate of
their contents, arranged . . . according to the subjects, 1696–1834. Parl. Papers
1834 [626] L.I.

The facsimile reprint with an introd. by Percy and Grace Ford, Oxf., 1953, includes a
select list of House of Lords papers not given in the original.

391   PARSONS (KENNETH A. C.), *comp.* A checklist of the British parliamentary papers (bound set), 1801–1950. Camb. priv. pr. 1958.

For the period 1801 to 1851, a *General Index to the Bills, Reports, accounts, and other
papers printed by order . . . 1801–1832,* 1833, was followed by further general indexes
for 1832–44, 1845, and for 1845–50, 1850. There are also indexes for different classes:
General index to the Bills printed by order . . . 1801–1852, 1854 [O.8], LXX. 1; *General
index to the reports of Select Committees, 1801–1852,* 1854 [O.9], LXX. 569; *General
index to the accounts and papers, reports of commissioners, estimates . . . 1801–1852,* 1854,
facsimile repr., 1938. Hilda Vernon Jones, comp., *Catalogue of parliamentary papers,
1800–1900, with a few of earlier date,* 1901, gives summaries but is incomplete and
omits sessional numbers. Selective and without summaries is Percy and Grace Ford,
comps., *A select list of British Parliamentary Papers, 1833–1899,* Oxf., 1953.

(d) *Procedure*

392   MAY (*Sir* THOMAS ERSKINE), *Baron Farnborough.* A treatise upon

the law, privileges, proceedings, and usage of parliament. 1844. 10th edn. much
enl. 1893. 16th edn. 1957.

See also under Lords, and Commons.

393 CLIFFORD (FREDERICK). A history of private-bill legislation. 2 v.
1885–7.

See also Williams (435) and Spencer (498).

394 WITTKE (CARL FREDERICK). The history of English parliamentary
privilege. [Columbus, Ohio]. 1921.

Informative but not always reliable.

2. House of Lords

(a) *Journals and Procedure*

For judicial proceedings see *Legal History*

395 JOURNALS OF THE HOUSE OF LORDS.

Vs. 38–83 cover the period 1789–1851. *General index to the journals . . . 1780–1819*,
vs. 36–52, 1832; *General index . . . 1820–1833*, v. 53–64, 1855; *General index . . . 1833–
1852/3*, vs. 65–85, 1891. The House of Lords record office has a typescript report (memo
no. 13) 'The journals, minutes and committee books of the House', 1956.

396 REMEMBRANCES: or a complete collection of the standing orders of
the House of Lords . . . compared with the Journals. John Debrett, *Parliamentary Papers*, 3 v. (1797), v. II, 527–76.

*Standing orders of the House of Lords [1698–1831] relative to the bringing in and pro-
ceeding on private bills*, 1834. The first complete collection made by the House itself
appeared in 1844. A second complete text was printed in 1849 and was also included
in Sessional Papers H.L. 1849 (47, p. 1).

397 ROGERS (JAMES EDWIN THOROLD) *ed.* A complete collection of
the protests of the Lords with historical introductions. Edited from the
Journals of the Lords. 3 v. Oxf. 1875.

V. 2, 1741–1825; v. 3, 1826–74. There are occasional omissions.

(b) *Later Works*

398 PIKE (LUKE OWEN). A constitutional history of the House of Lords.
1894.

Standard. See also Weston (540).

399 TURBERVILLE (ARTHUR STANLEY). The House of Lords in the
age of reform, 1784–1837. 1958.

Bibliog. 429–38. See too his papers, 'The House of Lords and the advent of democracy,
1837–1867', *History*, 29 (1944), 152–83, and 'The House of Lords and the Reform Act
of 1832', *Proc. Leeds Phil. & Lit. Soc., Lit. and Hist. section*, 6 (1945), 61–92. D. Large,
'The decline of "the party of the crown" and the rise of parties in the House of Lords,
1783–1837', *E.H.R.* 78 (1963), 669–95.

400 FERGUSSON (*Sir* JAMES). The sixteen peers of Scotland: an account of the elections of the representative peers of Scotland, 1707–1959. Oxf. 1960.

401 HOUSE OF LORDS RECORD OFFICE. Leaders and whips in the House of Lords, 1783–1964 (H.L. R.O. memorandum 31). 1964.

See also *The financial administration and records of the Parliament office, 1824–1868; A list of representative peers for Scotland, 1707–1963, and for Ireland, 1800–1961;* and *Officers of the House of Lords, 1485–1971* (H.L. R.O. memoranda 37 (1967), 39 (1968), and 45 (1971); *The origin of the office of chairman of committees in the House of Lords* (H.L.R.O. memorandum 52 (1974)); J. C. Sainty, 'The origin of the leadership of the House of Lords', *Bull. I.H.R.* 47 (1974), 53–73.

(c) *The Peerage*

For lists of peers and peerages see *Social Biography* (2037–40); for Scottish peers see (3949).

402 CRUISE (WILLIAM). A treatise on the origin and nature of dignities, or titles of honour. 1810. 2nd edn. 1823.

The first systematic study of peerage law.

403 REPORTS FROM THE LORDS COMMITTEES touching the dignity of a peer of the realm. 5 v. H.L. 1820 (117–20), 1829 (222).

Subject-matter index to 1829 edn., 1837.

404 PALMER (*Sir* FRANCIS BEAUFORT). Peerage law in England. 1907.

405 RICHARDS (GERDA CROSBY). 'The creations of peers recommended by the younger Pitt.' *A.H.R.* 34 (1928), 47–54.

The enlargement of the peerage was criticized by [Sir Samuel Egerton Brydges], *Reflections on the late augmentation of the English peerage,* 1798, and [Sir Nicholas Harris Nicolas], *A letter to the Duke of Wellington on the propriety and legality of creating peers for life,* 1830, 3rd edn., 1834. Joshua Wilson, *A biographical index to the present House of Lords,* 1808, gives details of political conduct.

3. HOUSE OF COMMONS

(a) *Journals, Debates, and Procedure*

406 JOURNALS OF THE HOUSE OF COMMONS.

V. 44–106, 1789–1851. General index vols. were pub. for v. 35–55 (1774–1800), 1827, for v. 56–75 (1801–20), 1825, for v. 75–92 (1820–37), 1839, and for v. 93–107 (1837–52), 1857. See D. Menhennet, *The journal of the House of Commons; a bibliographical and historical guide* (H.C. library documents 7), 1971.

407 HATSELL (JOHN). Precedents of proceedings in the House of Commons. New edn. 4 v. 1818.

V. 1: Privileges of parliament; v. 2: Members, speakers, etc.; v. 3: Lords and supply; v. 4: Conferences and impeachments. See also: *Règlemens observés dans la Chambre des*

Communes pour débattre les matières et pour voter. Traduit [*by* P. E. L. *Dumont*] *de l'Anglois* [*of Sir Samuel Romilly*]. *Mis au jour par le Comte de Mirabeau*, Paris, 1789; *A collection of rules and standing orders of the House of Commons . . . A new edition*, 1799; *Standing orders of the House . . . relating to private bills and other matters, 1685–1830. With tables of fees*, 1830—another issue rev. to date, 1846.

408 HOUSE OF COMMONS. Divisions, 1836–1894. 62 v. 1836–94. *General index.* v. 1: *1836–52*, 1855.

409 REDLICH (JOSEF). The procedure of the House of Commons; a study of its history and present form . . . translated from the German by A. Ernest Steinthal. With an introduction and supplementary chapter by Sir Courtenay Ilbert. 3 v. 1908.

Standard. Gilbert Francis Montriou Campion, *An introduction to the procedure of the House of Commons* [1929], 3rd edn., 1958, includes a historical survey.

410 DASENT (ARTHUR IRWIN). The speakers of the House of Commons from the earliest times to the present day. 1911.

Still of value is Alexander Manning, *The lives of the speakers of the . . . Commons*, 1850. Michael MacDonagh, *The speaker of the House* [1914], is anecdotal. See too P. A. C. Laundy, *The office of Speaker*, 1964. On other officials see P. K. Marsden, *The officers of the Commons, 1363–1965*, 1966.

411 TREWIN (JOHN COURTENAY) *and* KING (EVELYN MANS-FIELD). Printer to the House: the story of *Hansard*. 1952.

Used the diary edited by Percy and Grace Ford in *Luke Graves Hansard; his diary, 1814–1841: a case study in the reform of patronage*, Oxf., 1962. See also Arthur Aspinall, 'The reporting and publishing of the House of Commons' debates, 1771–1834', in *Essays presented to Sir Lewis Namier*, ed. Richard Pares and A. J. P. Taylor, 1956, 227–57. Michael MacDonagh, *The reporters' gallery*, 1913, is anecdotal.

(b) *Personnel, Elections, and Structure of the House*

(i) *Parliamentary Lists*

412 WILSON (JOSHUA). A biographical index to the present House of Commons. Corrected to March 1806. [1806].

Another edn. corr. to Feb. 1808 [1808]. Best of the lists produced by publishers from time to time, till a more regular handbook was provided by Dod (413).

413 DOD (CHARLES ROGER PHIPPS). The Parliamentary [Pocket] Companion. 1833+.

Annual; biogs. of M.P.s and notes of elections.

414 SMITH (HENRY STOOKS). The parliaments of England from 1st George I, to the present time. 3 v. 1844–50.

Gives representation by constituencies, with polling figures; not always accurate.

415 MEMBERS OF PARLIAMENT . . . [Return of the names of every member of the lower house of parliaments of England, Scotland, Ireland, 1213–1874]. H.C. 1878 (69, 69–I, 69–II), LXII; 1890–1 (169) LXII. 281.

Known as *The official return of members of parliament*. See also Judd (438).

(ii) *Elections (general)*

416   SIMEON (JOHN). A treatise on the law of elections in all its branches. 1789. 2nd edn. enl. 1795.

Other similar guides are: Richard Troward, *A collection of the statutes now in force relative to elections*, 1790, 2nd edn., 1796; Samuel Heywood, *A digest of the law respecting county elections*, 1790, and *A digest of so much of the law respecting borough elections, as concerns cities and boroughs in general*, 1797; Francis Newman Rogers, *The law and practice of elections*, 1820, 7th edn., 1847; Charles Favell Forth Wordsworth, *The law and practice of elections (for England and Wales) as altered by the Reform Act, including the practice on election petitions*, 1832, 3rd edn., 1847, and *The law . . . (for Scotland) as altered . . .*, 1832. See too *Report from the select committee on county election polls*, H.C. 1826–7 (349), IV, 1105, and *Report on election polls of cities and boroughs, ibid.* (394) 1111.

417   SMITH (E. ANTHONY). 'The election agent in eighteenth century politics.' *E.H.R.* 84 (1969), 12–35.

418   FRASER (SIMON). Reports of the proceedings before select committees of the House of Commons in . . . cases of controverted elections . . . determined during the first session of the seventeenth parliament of Great Britain. 1791. Reports . . . during the second session. 1793.

Other similar compilations are: Robert Henry Peckwell, *Cases of controverted elections, 1802–1806*, 2 v., 1805–6; Uvedale Corbett and Edmund Robert Daniell, *Reports of cases of controverted elections in the sixth parliament of the United Kingdom*, 1821. For further such reports for the years after 1832, see Sweet and Maxwell (547), v. 2, under 'elections', and Parl. Papers (391), and Hanham (421). See also (419) and (421).

419   OLDFIELD (THOMAS HINTON BURLEY). The representative history of Great Britain and Ireland; being a history of the House of Commons, and of the counties, cities, and boroughs of the United Kingdom. 6 v. 1816.

Details the electoral state of each constituency; his *A key to the House of Commons*, 1820, adds little. See also Adam (Pargellis and Medley, 3338).

420   RANKIN (MICHAEL HENRY). Present state of representation in England and Wales . . . with an appendix containing a summary . . . the Reform and Boundary Acts, and a copious index. 1832.

The Maxima Charta of 1832, 1832, gives a fairly full precis of the Acts in non-technical language. Samuel Lewis, *Parliamentary history* (v. 5 of his *A topographical dictionary of England*), 1835, has maps showing boundary changes of the constituencies in 1832. See too the boundary commission reports, parl. papers 1831–2, H.C. 141. xxxviii–xli, H.C. 408. xlii, H.C. 519. xliii.

421   SMITH (HENRY STOOKS). The register of parliamentary contested elections. 1841.

Similar is George Crosby, *Crosby's general political reference book*, Leeds, 1838, reissued as v. 1 of his *Crosby's parliament record*, 2 v., Leeds, 1849. More detailed on its period is Charles R. P. Dod, *Electoral facts from 1832 to 1852 impartially stated*, 1852, 2nd edn., 1853, new edn. by H. J. Hanham, Brighton, 1972. See too J. R. Vincent and M. Stenton, eds., *McCalmont's parliamentary poll book, 1832–1918*, Brighton, 1971.

(iii) *Particular Elections*

422 KLIENEBERGER (HANS RUDOLF). Durham elections: a list of material relating to parliamentary elections in Durham, 1675–1874. Durham. 1956.

423 CLIFFORD (HENRY). A report of the two cases of controverted elections of . . . Southwark [in 1796] . . . with . . . an account of the two subsequent cases of the city of Canterbury. 1797. Repr. 1802.

424 HISTORY OF THE WESTMINSTER and Middlesex elections in the month of November 1806. 1807.

425 SMITH (E. ANTHONY). 'The Yorkshire elections of 1806 and 1807'. *Northern History*, 2 (1967), 62–90.

426 CARPENTER (SAMUEL). A statement of the evidence . . . upon the controverted election for Saltash. 1808.

427 ASPINALL (ARTHUR). 'The Westminster election of 1814.' *E.H.R.* 40 (1925), 562–9.

William Thomas, 'Whigs and Radicals in Westminster. The election of 1819', *Guildhall Miscellany* 3 (1969–71), 174–217.

427A AN IMPARTIAL STATEMENT of all the proceedings, connected with the progress and result of the late elections. 1818.

A valuable compilation based on newspaper reports, etc.

428 MARKHAM (JOHN). The 1820 parliamentary election at Hedon; a study of electioneering in a Yorkshire borough before the passing of the Reform Act. Beverley. [1971].

429 GREAVES (ROBERT WILLIAM). 'Roman Catholic relief and the Leicester election of 1826.' *Trans. Roy. Hist. Soc.*, 4th ser. 22 (1940), 199–223.

430 [A COLLECTION of election addresses, handbills, songs, squibs, etc., issued Feb.–July 1826, during the contests for the representation of the county of Northumberland in parliament]. 3 v. Newcastle. 1826.

The Poll Book of the contested election for the northern division of . . . Northumberland . . . July 1841, including the addresses and authentic papers issued by the various candidates, Newcastle, 1841. Typical of similar productions concerning many large constituencies.

431 MARSHALL (LEON S.). 'The first parliamentary election in Manchester.' *A.H.R.* 47 (1941–2), 518–38.

432 KEMP (BETTY). 'The general election of 1841.' *History*, n.s. 37 (1952), 146–57.

(iv) *Later Works*

433 GREGO (JOSEPH). A history of parliamentary elections and electioneering in the old days . . . from the Stuarts to Queen Victoria. 1886.

An entertaining digest of election material, newspaper reports, with contemporary illustrations.

434 BEAN (WILLIAM WARDELL). The parliamentary representation of the six northern counties of England . . . and their cities and boroughs. From 1603 to the general election of 1886. With lists of members and biographical notices. Hull. 1890.

In addition to the lists and parliamentary histories for various constituencies listed under *Bean* at Pargellis and Medley, 434, see:

Cornwall H. Spencer Toy, *The Cornish pocket borough*, Penzance, 1968.

Devon J. J. Alexander, 'Devon county members of parliament. Pt. VII: The later oligarchical period (1760–1832)', *Trans. Devonshire Assoc.*, n.s. 50 (1918), 589–601, and pt. VIII Supplement, *ibid.* 57 (1925), 311–20. See too other papers by him on Bere Alston, *ibid.* 41 (1909), 152–78, Dartmouth and Tavistock, *ibid.* 43 (1911), 350–402; on Exeter, *ibid.* 62 (1930), 195–223; also by W. H. Wilkin on Honiton, *ibid.* 66 (1934), 253–78, and by Daphne Drake on Barnstaple, *ibid.* 72 (1940), 251–64. H. J. Hanham, 'Ashburton as a parliamentary borough, 1640–1888', *Trans. Devonshire Assoc.*, n.s. 98 (1966), 206–56.

Durham Sir Cuthbert Sharp, *A list of the knights and burgesses who have represented the county and city of Durham*, Durham, 1826, 2nd edn., Sunderland, 1831.

Hampshire Sir Frederick Black, *An outline sketch of the parliamentary history of the Isle of Wight*, Newport, 1929.

Lewes Wallace H. Hills, *The parliamentary history of . . . Lewes, 1295–1885*, Lewes, 1908.

Malton E. A. Smith, 'Earl Fitzwilliam and Malton. A proprietary borough in the early nineteenth century', *E.H.R.* 80 (1965), 51–69.

Shrewsbury Edward Edwards, *Parliamentary elections of the borough of Shrewsbury, from 1283 to 1859*, Shrewsbury, 1859.

435 PORRITT (EDWARD and ANNIE GERTRUDE). The unreformed House of Commons; parliamentary representation before 1832. 2 v. Camb. 1903. 1909.

Standard on the system of representation and the organization of business in the House before the Reform Act. Orlo Cyprian Williams, *The historical development of private bill procedure and standing orders in the . . . Commons*, 2 v., 1948–9 and *The clerical organization of the . . . Commons, 1661–1850*, Oxf., 1954, are definitive. Helen Elizabeth Witmer, *The property qualification of members of parliament*, N.Y., 1943, is a valuable digest of much scattered material. See too Betty Kemp, 'The stewardship of the Chiltern Hundreds', in *Essays presented to Sir Lewis Namier*, ed. by R. Pares and A. J. P. Taylor, 1956, 204–26; Patrick Howarth, *Questions in the House: the history of an unique British institution*, 1956; Peter Fraser, 'Public petitioning and parliament before 1832', *History*, n.s. 46 (1961), 195–211 and 'The growth of ministerial control in the nineteenth-century House of Commons', *E.H.R.* 75 (1960), 444–63; Valerie Cromwell, 'The losing of the initiative by the House of Commons, 1780–1914', *Trans. Roy. Hist. Soc.*, 5th s. 18 (1968), 1–23.

436 THOMAS (JOHN ALUN). The House of Commons, 1832–1901; a study of its economic and functional character. 1939.

More limited detailed surveys are S. F. Woolley, 'The personnel of the parliament of 1833', *E.H.R.* 53 (1938), 240–62; W. O. Aydelotte, 'A statistical analysis of the parliament of 1841: some problems of method', *Bull. I.H.R.* 27 (1954) 141–55, and 'The House of Commons in the 1840s', *History*, n.s. 39 (1954), 249–62, and 'Parties and issues in early Victorian England', *J. of British Studies*, 5 no. 2 (Mar. 1966), 95–114.

437 GASH (NORMAN). Politics in the age of Peel: a study in the technique of parliamentary representation, 1830–1850. 1953.

A valuable detailed study; some of its judgements are slightly revised in the same author's *Reaction and reconstruction in English politics, 1832–1852*, Oxf., 1965. Charles Seymour,

Electoral reform in England and Wales: the development and operation of the parliamentary franchise, 1832–1885, New Haven, 1915, is still of value. See too N. Gash, 'The influence of the crown at Windsor and Brighton in the elections of 1832, 1835, and 1837', *E.H.R.* 54 (1939), 653–63, and 'F. R. Bonham, Conservative "political secretary", 1832–47', *ibid.* 63 (1948), 502–22; D. E. D. Beales, 'Parliamentary parties and the independent member, 1810–1860', in R. Robson, ed., *Ideas and Institutions of Victorian Britain*, 1967; D. Close, 'The formation of a two-party alignment in the House of Commons between 1832 and 1841', *E.H.R.* 84 (1969), 257–77.

438 JUDD (GERRIT PARMELE) *IV*. Members of parliament, 1734–1832. 1955.

Valuable for reference.

439 VINCENT (JOHN RUSSELL). Pollbooks; how Victorians voted. 1967.

The largest British collection is at I.H.R. See Hanham (421) for pollbooks published after 1832.

440 GWYN (WILLIAM BRENT). Democracy and the cost of politics in Britain. 1962.

440A. NOSSITER (T. J.). Influence, opinion and political idiom in Re-formed England. Case studies from the the North-east, 1832–74. Brighton. 1975.

C. THE CENTRAL GOVERNMENT

1. THE CROWN

441 GRETTON (RICHARD HENRY). The king's majesty: a study in the historical philosophy of modern kingship. 1930.

A perceptive essay.

442 PARES (RICHARD). King George III and the politicians. Oxf. 1953.

A study of the role of the king in politics based on thorough examination of printed material, carrying discussion through to 1830. See also B. W. Hill, 'Executive monarchy and the challenge of parties, 1689–1832', *Hist. J* 13 (1970), 379–401. For a discussion of royal influence in the early Victorian period see Mackintosh (444), pp. 111–28.

443 KEMP (BETTY). King and Commons, 1660–1832. 1957.

See also A. S. Foord, 'The waning of "the influence of the crown"', *E.H.R.* 62 (1947), 484–507. See Rose (446).

2. THE CABINET

444 ASPINALL (ARTHUR). 'The cabinet council, 1783–1835.' *Proceedings of the British Academy*, v. 38 (1952), 145–252.

See too his paper, 'The grand cabinet, 1800–1837', *Politica*, 3 (1938), 324–44, and W. I. Jennings, 'Cabinet government at the accession of Queen Victoria', *Economica*, 11 (1931), 404–25, and 12 (1932), 63–78. John Pitcairn Mackintosh, *The British cabinet*, 1962, has valuable historical chapters on the period 1789–1851. See also Pares (442).

3. CENTRAL ADMINISTRATION

(a) *General*

445 THE ROYAL KALENDAR; or, complete and annual register.

Annual list of holders of political, public, and court offices; in 1814 amalgamated with its rival, *The court and city register*, becoming *The royal kalendar or court and city register*. Another similar guide was the *British imperial calendar . . . or general register*, 1809+, pub. irreg. See also (454).

446 ROSE (GEORGE). Observations respecting the public expenditure and the influence of the crown. 1810.

A valuable discussion of the then government establishments, though the figures of office-holders are not exhaustive.

447 CHITTY (JOSEPH) *jun*. A treatise on the law of the prerogatives of the crown and the relative rights and duties of the subject. 1820.

A mine of information on the legal position, but no awareness of the incipient growth of ministerial responsibility. Some material on the extension of the powers of officials is included in the *Committee on ministers' powers report*, H.C. 1931–32 (Cmd. 4060), xii. 341.

448 TAYLOR (*Sir* HENRY). The statesman. 1836. Repr. with an introd. essay by Leo Silberman. Camb. 1957.

Enlightening on the position of senior civil servants. See too (461), (2211).

449 [THOMAS (FRANCIS SHEPPARD)]. Notes of materials for the history of public departments. 1846.

An early guide to public offices, which gives basic information about staffs, establishments, reorganization of departments.

450 PUBLIC INCOME AND EXPENDITURE . . . 1688–[1869]. H.C. 1868–9 (366, 366–I), XXXV.

Tables of figures and explanatory memoranda.

451 COHEN (EMMELINE WALEY). The growth of the British civil service, 1780–1939. 1941.

A careful connected account based mainly on official papers. See too Sir John Craig, *A history of red tape: an account of the origin and development of the civil service*, 1955.

452 PARRIS (HENRY). Constitutional bureaucracy. The development of British central administration since the eighteenth century. 1969.

For the debate on the rationale of this development see: O. MacDonagh, 'Emigration and the state, 1833–55', *Trans. Roy. Hist. Soc.*, 5th ser. 5 (1955), 133–59; 'The nineteenth-century revolution in government: a reappraisal', *Hist. J.* 1 (1958), 52–67; and *A pattern of government growth* (1750); H. Parris, 'The nineteenth-century revolution in government: a reappraisal reappraised', *Hist. J.* 3 (1960), 17–37; Jenifer Hart, 'Nineteenth-century social reform: a Tory interpretation of history', *Past and Present*, 31 (1965), 39–61; Valerie Cromwell, 'Interpretations of nineteenth-century administration', *Victorian Studies*, 9 (1965–6), 245–55. There is a well-balanced summary in chapter 5 of Fraser (2502). See also Roberts (2502) and recent monographs under *Social Policy, passim*.

453 LUBENOW (WILLIAM CORNELIUS). The politics of government growth; early Victorian attitudes towards state intervention, 1833–1848. Newton Abbot. 1971.

Bibliog. 220–31. See also J. B. Brebner, '*Laissez-faire* and state intervention in nineteenth-century Britain', *J. of Econ. Hist.* 8 *Supplement* (1948), 59–73; Arthur J. Taylor, *Laissez-faire and state intervention in nineteenth-century Britain*, 1972. Tory-radical attitudes are discussed in Hill (108); see also Oastler (1725). Gillian R. Sutherland, ed., *Studies in the growth of nineteenth-century government*, 1972.

454 SAINTY (JOHN CHRISTOPHER), *comp.* Office-holders in Modern Britain. V. 1: Treasury officials, 1660–1870. 1972. V. 3: Officials of the Boards of Trade, 1660–1870. 1974. V. 4: Admiralty officials, 1660–1870. 1975. V. 5: Home Office, officials, 1782–1870, 1975.

(b) *Treasury and Revenue Services*

455 ROSEVEARE (HENRY). The treasury. The evolution of a British institution. 1969.

An excellent detailed account. See also his study with documents, *The treasury, 1660–1870. The foundations of control*, 1973. For a contemporary account see Francis Sheppard Thomas, *The ancient exchequer of England; the treasury; and origin of the present management of the exchequer and treasury of Ireland*, 1848. See too Sir George Albert Bonner, *The office of the king's remembrancer in England*, 1930. There is some information for the years just after 1789 in John E. D. Binney, *British public finance and administration, 1774–1792*, Oxf., 1958; William R. Ward, *The English land tax in the eighteenth century*, 1953; and Edward Hughes, *Studies in administration and finance, 1558–1825*, Manch., 1934.

456 ATTON (HENRY) *and* HOLLAND (HENRY HURST). The King's customs. 2 v. 1908–10.

Contemporary works on law and practice include James Smyth, *The practice of the customs*, 1812, 2nd edn., 1821; Nicholas Jickling, *A digest of the laws of the customs*, 2 v., 1815; James Deacon Hume, *The laws of the customs*, 1826, suppls. 1827–9, 1832, 2nd edn., 1833, suppls. 1834, 1835–6; Joseph Green Walford, *The laws of the customs*, 1846.

(c) *Foreign Office*

457 JONES (RAY). The nineteenth-century foreign office; an administrative history. 1971.

Stanley Thomas Bindoff, 'The unreformed diplomatic service (1812–1860)', *Trans. Roy. Hist' Soc.*, 4th ser. 18 (1935), 143–72. See also Hutton, *Burges* (2096) and Parry (265).

(d) *Home Office*

458 NELSON (RONALD ROY). The home office, 1782–1801. Durham, N. Car. 1969.

A thorough examination of the office during its first twenty years. Sir Frank Newsam, *The home office*, 1954, includes a brief sketch of nineteenth-century developments. See also Peel (199, 200), Melville Lee (2620).

(e) *War Office*

459 GORDON (HAMPDEN). The war office. 1935.

Very brief outline to 1854. See also Clode (1063).

(f) *Board of Trade*

460 SMITH (*Sir* HUBERT LLEWELLYN). The board of trade. 1928.

Includes brief historical outline. For detail see Roger Prouty, *The transformation of the board of trade, 1830–1855*, 1957; and Lucy Brown, *The board of trade and the free-trade movement*, Oxf., 1958, and 'The board of trade and tariff problems, 1840–42', *E.H.R.* 68 (1953), 394–421. See also Hyde, *Gladstone* (230), Badham, *Hume* (2310), Cockcroft, *Chalmers* (2142).

(g) *Colonial Office*

461 YOUNG (DOUGLAS MACMURRAY). The colonial office in the early nineteenth century. 1961.

Bibliog. 288–304; a scholarly study of administrative development, *c.* 1794–1830. See too Manning (4200). Henry L. Hall, *The colonial office: a history*, 1937, covers 1835–85. See also Stephen (2246), Taylor (448), Knaplund (4305).

(h) *Post Office*

462 ROBINSON (HOWARD). The British post office. A history. Princeton, N.J. 1948.

Bibliog. 447–58. Standard. Of older histories, Herbert Joyce, *The history of the post office . . . to 1836*, 1893, is still of value. Joseph Clarence Hemmeon, *The history of the British post office*, Camb., Mass., 1912, is concerned mainly with economic aspects; for the philatelic see Chapman F. D. Marshall, *The British post office*, 1926, with excellent critical bibliog. On the mail-coach men see Vale (1961), and on the penny post Sir Rowland Hill (2265).

(i) *Miscellaneous*

463 HOLOHAN (VINCENT WHEELER). The history of the King's Messengers. 1935.

464 MITCHISON (ROSALIND). 'The old board of agriculture (1793–1822)'. *E.H.R.* 74 (1959), 41–69.

See also (2140).

465 CLOKIE (HUGH MACDOWALL) *and* ROBINSON (JOSEPH WILLIAM). Royal commissions of inquiry; the significance of investigations in British politics. 1937.

See also Smith (374).

D. LOCAL GOVERNMENT

County and borough record offices contain an enormous amount of MS. material, very little of which has been printed. Hubert Hall, *A repertory of British archives*

(Roy. Hist. Soc. 1920), pt. 2 and 3, 93–254, gives a list of sources, which is being increasingly supplemented by guides put out by the local repositories (see under *Local History*). There is valuable bibliographical information in Webb (466) and more limited guidance in George Laurence Gomme, *The literature of local institutions*, 1886.

1. GENERAL

466 WEBB (SIDNEY *and* BEATRICE). English local government from the revolution to the municipal corporations act. 9 v. 1906–29.

An exhaustive, scholarly survey, indispensable for the period up to 1835; v. 1: *The parish and the county*; v. 2 and 3: *The manor and the borough*; v. 4: *Statutory authorities for special purposes*; v. 5: *The story of the king's highway*; v. 6: *English prisons under local government*; v. 7–9: *English poor law history*.

467 REDLICH (JOSEF) *and* HIRST (FRANCIS W.). Local government in England. 2 v. 1903.

A study of the contemporary situation but with a valuable historical survey on the early Victorian period. Rudolf Gneist, *Self-government; Communal-Verfassung und Verwaltungsgerichte in England*, Berlin, 1871, is learned but less sound in interpretation.

468 KEITH-LUCAS (BRYAN). The English local government franchise: a short history. Oxf. 1952.

An excellent survey, mainly 18th and 19th centuries. More general in period is Edwin Cannan, *The history of local rates in England*, 1896, 2nd edn., 1912.

2. COUNTY GOVERNMENT

(a) *Local Records*

469 BOSWELL (EDWARD). The civil division of the county of Dorset. 2nd edn. Dorchester. 1833.

Lists of officers and a general guide to local administration.

470 DAVENPORT (JOHN MARRIOTT). Lords lieutenant and high sheriffs of Oxfordshire, 1086–1868. Oxf. [1868].

471 STRANGE (HAMON LE). Norfolk official lists, from the earliest period to the present day. Norwich. 1890.

472 COX (JOHN CHARLES). Three centuries of Derbyshire annals, as illustrated by the records of the quarter sessions of the county of Derby, from Queen Elizabeth to Queen Victoria. 2 v. 1890.

473 KENYON (ROBERT LLOYD) *and* WAKEMAN (*Sir* OFFLEY) *eds.* Shropshire county records. Orders of the Shropshire quarter sessions. 4 v. in 2. [Shrewsbury. 1902–11].

V. 3–4: 1783–1889; documents include inclosure awards and plans relating to roads, bridges, and railways.

474 HERTFORD COUNTY RECORDS. Ed. by William John Hardy and William Le Hardy. 10 v. 1905–57.

Sessions of the county and of the Liberty of St. Alban.

475 POWELL (DOROTHY L.). Guide to archives and other collections of
documents relating to Surrey. Quarter sessions records with other records of
the justices of the peace for the county of Surrey. Surrey Record Soc. no. 32.
1931.

476 STEPHENS (*Sir* LEON EDGAR). The clerks of the counties, 1360–
1960. 1961.

Nominal rolls for clerks for each county, with brief biog. notes.

(b) *General Treatises*

477 BURN (RICHARD). The justice of the peace and parish officer. 17th edn.
continued to the present time by John Burn. 4 v. 1793. 29th edn. corr. and
greatly enl. 6 v. 1845.

An alphabetical digest covering every branch of civil, criminal, and public law with
which the J.P. might be concerned. See too Henry James Pye, *Summary of the duties
of the justice of the peace out of sessions*, 1808, 4th edn., 1827.

478 DOGHERTY (THOMAS). The crown circuit companion; containing
the practice at the assizes on the crown side, and of the courts of general and
general quarter sessions of the peace . . . to which are added, the clerk of
assize's circuit companion . . . and also the duty of the sheriffs. 7th edn. enl.
and improved. 1799.

479 RASTALL *afterwards* DICKINSON (WILLIAM). A practical guide to
the quarter sessions and other sessions of the peace. 1815. 6th edn. rev. 1845.

480 IMPEY (JOHN). The practice of the office of sheriff and under sheriff . . .
also the practice of office of coroner. 1786. rev. edn. 1817. 6th edn. 1831.

Sir William Henry Watson, *A practical treatise on the law relating to the office and duty
of sheriff*, 1827, 2nd edn., 1848; Sir John Jervis, *A practical treatise on the office and
duties of coroners*, 1829, 2nd edn. by W. N. Welsby, 1854.

481 MULLINS (EDWARD). A treatise on the magistracy of England and
the origin and expenditure of county rates. 1836.

Critical, with reference to Hume's plan for elected county councils.

(c) *Special Studies*

482 STYLES (PHILIP). The development of county administration in the
late XVIIIth and early XIXth centuries. (Dugdale Society Occasional Papers,
no. 4.) Oxf. 1934.

An admirable brief survey, based on Warwickshire quarter session records, 1773–1837.

483 FRANCE (REGINALD SHARPE). The Lancashire sessions act, 1798.
Preston. 1945.

A detailed study of district rivalries in local administration.

484 OSBORNE (BERTRAM). Justices of the peace, 1361–1848: a history of the justices of the peace for the counties of England. Shaftesbury. 1960.

See also Esther A. L. Moir, *The justice of the peace*, Harmondsworth, 1969, and *Local government in Gloucestershire, 1775–1800; a study of the justices of the peace*, Bristol, 1969.

3. Boroughs and Municipalities

See also *Local History*.

(a) *Local Records*

485 [STEVENSON (WILLIAM HENRY)] *ed*. Records of the borough of Nottingham: being a series of extracts from the archives of the corporation of Nottingham. 9 v. Nottingham and London. 1882–1956.

V. 7–9, 1760–1900.

486 PICTON (*Sir* JAMES ALLANSON). City of Liverpool. Municipal archives and records. 2 v. Liverpool. 1883–6.

V. 2, 1700–1835. See also (504).

487 EARWAKER (JOHN PARSONS). The court leet records of the manor of Manchester . . . 1552 . . . 1686, and . . . 1731 to . . . 1846. 12 v. Manchester. 1884–90.

V. 9–12, an excellent set of town records for the years 1787–1846. See also (503).

488 HEWITSON (ANTHONY) *ed*. Preston court leet records: extracts and notes. Preston. 1905.

489 MAYO (CHARLES HERBERT) *ed*. The municipal records of the borough of Dorchester, Dorset. Exeter. 1908.

490 POWELL (DOROTHY L.). Guide to archives and other collections of documents relating to Surrey. Borough records. Surrey Record Soc. no. 29. 1929.

491 BUTCHER (EMILY ELIZABETH) *ed*. Bristol corporation of the poor: selected records, 1696–1834. Bristol Record Soc. Pub. V. 3. Bristol. 1932.

A. B. Beaven, ed., *Bristol lists, municipal and miscellaneous*, Bristol, 1899.

492 HARTOPP (HENRY). Roll of the mayors of the borough and lord mayors of the city of Leicester, 1209 to 1935. With biographical, genealogical, heraldic and historical data. Leicester. [1936.]

Hartopp also comp. *Register of the freemen of Leicester, 1770–1930, including the apprentices sworn before successive mayors*, Leicester, 1933. See *Records of the borough of Leicester*, v. 5: *Hall books and papers, 1689–1835*, and v. 6: *The chamberlain's accounts, 1688–1835*, both ed. by G. A. Chinnery, Leicester, 1965–7.

493 BLAIR (CHARLES HENRY HUNTER). The mayors and lord mayors of Newcastle upon Tyne, 1216–1940, and the sheriffs of the county of Newcastle upon Tyne, 1399–1940. Gateshead on Tyne. 1940.

494 MACMAHON (KENNETH AUSTIN) *ed.* Beverley corporation minute books (1707–1835). Yorkshire Arch. Soc. Record Series 122. [Leeds.] 1958.

495 STEER (FRANCIS WILLIAM), *ed.* Minute book of the common council of the city of Chichester, 1783–1826. Lewes. 1963.

(b) *General Treatises*

496 WILLCOCK (JOHN WILLIAM). The law of municipal corporations, together with a brief sketch of their history, and a treatise on mandamus and quo warranto. 1827.

Other similar guides were William Glover, *A practical treatise on the law of municipal corporations*, 1836; Thomas James Arnold, *A treatise on the law relating to municipal corporations*, 1851.

497 FIRST REPORT OF THE COMMISSIONERS appointed to inquire into the municipal corporations in England and Wales. Parl. papers, 1835 (116), XXIII–XXVI.

A mine of information; index, 1839 (402), XVIII. See too the *Second Report* (on London and Southwark), 1837 (239), XXV. Of value for background is Henry Alworth Merewether and Archibald J. Stephens, *The history of the boroughs and municipal corporations of the United Kingdom, from the earliest to the present time*, 3 v., 1835, new edn. ed. by G. H. Martin, Brighton, 1973. See G. B. A. M. Finlayson, 'The municipal corporation commission and report, 1833–5', *Bull. I.H.R.* 36 (1963), 36–52, and 'The politics of municipal reform, 1835', *E.H.R.* 81 (1966), 673–92.

498 SPENCER (FREDERICK HERBERT). Municipal origins: an account of English private bill legislation relating to local government, 1740–1835; with a chapter on private bill procedure. 1911.

See also (393).

(c) *Special Studies*

499 BUNCE (JOHN THACKRAY). History of the corporation of Birmingham; with a sketch of earlier government of the town. 3 v. Birmingham. 1878–1902.

V. 1 traces the development of borough government up to and past the grant of the charter of 1838. See also (504A).

500 BEAVEN (ALFRED BEAVEN). The aldermen of the city of London, *temp.* Henry III–1908. 2 v. 1908–13.

Biographical and other notes on the aldermen, livery companies, parliamentary representation. Thomas Emerson, *A concise treatise on the courts of law of the city of London*, 1794.

501 MANCHEE (WILLIAM HENRY). The Westminster city fathers (the burgess court of Westminster) 1585–1901. Being some account of their powers and domestic rule of the city prior to its incorporation in 1901. 1924.

502 COZENS-HARDY (BASIL) *and* KENT (ERNEST A.). The mayors of Norwich 1403 to 1835; being biographical notes on the mayors of the old corporation. Norwich. 1938.

503 REDFORD (ARTHUR) *and* RUSSELL (INA STAFFORD). The history of local government in Manchester. 3 v. 1939–40.

See too Shena Dorothy Simon, *A century of city government: Manchester, 1838–1938,* 1938, and Earwaker (487).

504 WHITE (BRIAN DAVID). A history of the corporation of Liverpool, 1835–1914. 1951.

Ramsay Muir and Edith May Platt, *A history of municipal government in Liverpool from the earliest times to the municipal reform act of 1835,* 1906, includes a few documents of the period 1789–1835. See also Peet (510).

504A HENNOCK (E. P.) Fit and proper persons. Ideal and reality in nineteenth-century urban government. 1973.

A study with particular reference to Birmingham and Leeds.

4. PARISH

(a) *General Treatises*

505 PAUL (JOHN). The parish officer's complete guide; or, The laws relating to the respective duties of churchwarden, overseer . . . constable, and surveyor of the highways. 6th edn. 1793.

506 REPORT FROM THE SELECT COMMITTEE appointed to inquire into the general operation and effect of the laws and usages under which select and other vestries are constituted in England and Wales. H.C. 1830 (25, 215) IV, 425, 569.

507 SMITH (JOSHUA TOULMIN). The parish. Its powers and obligations at law . . . its officers and committees. 1854. 2nd edn. 1857.

508 TATE (WILLIAM EDWARD). The parish chest: a study of the records of parochial administration in England. 3rd. edn. rev. Camb. 1969.

An essential introd. to the study of parish history.

(b) *Records and Special Studies*

509 BATTYE (THOMAS). A disclosure of parochial abuse, artifice and peculation in the town of Manchester. 2nd edn. Manchester. 1796.

An account of the author's own investigations; on his writings, see Webb, *The parish and the county* (466), 70, note.

510 PEET (HENRY) *ed.* Liverpool vestry books, 1681–1834. 2 v. Liverpool. 1912–15.

511 PEYTON (SIDNEY AUGUSTUS) *ed.* Kettering vestry minutes. Kettering. 1933.

512 CUTLACK (S. A.). The Gnossal records, 1679 to 1837. Poor law administration. Staffs. Record Soc. Coll. 1936.

513 OXLEY (JAMES EDWIN) *ed*. Barking vestry minutes and other parish documents. Colchester. 1955.

514 SHEPPARD (FRANCIS HENRY WOLLASTON). Local government in St. Marylebone, 1688–1835: a study of the vestry and turnpike trust. 1958.

5. MISCELLANEOUS

515 KYD (STEWART). A treatise on the law of corporations. 2 v. 1793–4.

Deals with all classes of corporate body, as does James Grant, *A practical treatise on the law of corporations in general,* 1850.

516 SHERWOOD (RICHARD) *ed*. The constitution of the Isle of Man, consisting of part the third of the commissioners of inquiry for the Isle of Man made in the year 1792. Douglas. 1882.

See too *The lex scripta of the Isle of Man,* 1819; William Mackenzie, *Index to all the statute of Tynwald laws of the Isle of Man,* 1861; Spencer Walpole, *The land of home rule. An essay on the history and constitution of the Isle of Man,* 1893.

E. POLITICAL THEORY

For connected material see also under *Philosophy* (2793–2822).

1. SOURCES

517 PALEY (WILLIAM). The principles of moral and political philosophy. 5th edn. 1788. With final corrections. 2 v. 1790.

Regarded for many years as a standard work.

518 BURKE (EDMUND). The works of . . . Burke. 12 v. 1808–13. 8 v. (Bohn edn.). 1894–1900.

See especially:

a. Reflections on the revolution in France, and on the proceedings in certain societies in London relative to that event. 1790.

b. Appeal from the new to the old whigs. 1791.

c. Two letters . . . on the proposals for peace with the regicide directory of France. 1796–7. A third letter . . . 1797.

See Sir James Mackintosh, *Vindiciae Gallicae: a defence of the French revolution and its English admirers,* 1791, apart from the American Tom Paine's *Rights of Man* the most serious of the replies provoked by the *Reflections;* also Wollstonecraft and Belsham (118).

W. B. Todd, *A bibliography of Edmund Burke,* 1964. The literature of comment is copious: John MacCunn, *The political philosophy of Burke,* 1913; Alfred Cobban, *Edmund Burke and the revolt against the eighteenth century; a study of the political and social thinking of Burke, Wordsworth, Coleridge, and Southey,* 1929, 2nd edn., 1960; Mario Einaudi, *Edmondo Burke e l'indirizzo storico nelle scienze politiche,* Turin, 1930; Annie M. Osborn, *Rousseau and Burke,* 1940; Charles Parkin, *The moral basis of Burke's political thought,* Camb., 1956; P. J. Stanlis, *Edmund Burke and the natural law,* Ann Arbor, Mich., 1958; F. P. Canavan, *The political reason of Edmund Burke,* 1960; S. R. Graubard, *Burke, Disraeli and Churchill: the politics of perseverance,* 1961; J. T. Boulton, *The language of politics in the age of Wilkes and Burke,* 1963; R. R. Fennessy, *Burke, Paine and the Rights of Man; a difference of political opinion,* The Hague, 1963; C. P.

Courtney, *Montesquieu and Burke*, Oxf., 1963; H. U. Willi, *Die Staatsauffassung Edmund Burkes, 1729–1797*, Winterthur, 1964; H. G. Schumann, *Edmund Burkes Anschauungen vom Gleichgewicht in Staat und Staatensystem*, Meisenheim am Glan, 1964; H. C. Mansfield, *Statesmanship and party government; a study of Burke and Bolingbroke*, 1965; G. W. Chapman, *Edmund Burke, the practical imagination*, Camb., Mass., 1967; R. A. Kirk, *Edmund Burke; a genius reconsidered*, New York, 1967; B. T. Wilkins, *The problem of Burke's political philosophy*, Oxf., 1967; F. O'Gorman, *Edmund Burke; his political philosophy*, 1973. R. J. S. Hoffman and P. Levack, *Burke's politics*, N.Y., 1949, is a well-chosen selection from the writings. See also Mario Einaudi, 'The British background of Burke's political philosophy', *Pol. Sci. Q.* 49 (1934), 576–98; J. G. A. Pocock, 'Burke and the ancient constitution: a problem in the history of ideas', *Hist. J.* 3 (1960), 125–43; Paul Lucas, 'On Edmund Burke's doctrine of prescription', *ibid.* 11 (1968), 35–63; D. Cameron, *The social thought of Rousseau and Burke*, 1973. For biography see (160, 161).

519 HALL (ROBERT). Apology for the freedom of the press and for general liberty. 1793. 7th edn. 1822.

520 SPENCE (THOMAS). The restorer of society to its natural state. 1801.

The fullest expression of his socialist views, but see also especially his *The constitution of a perfect commonwealth*, 2nd edn., 1798. Many of his pamphlets are collected in *Spence and his political works*, ed. by Arthur W. Waters, Leamington Spa, 1917. See too Olive D. Rudkin, *Thomas Spence and his connections*, 1927; Allen Davenport, *Life, writings and principles of Thomas Spence*, [1936]; P. M. Kemp-Ashraf, Introduction to Supplement, 'Selected writings of Thomas Spence, 1770–1814', *Essays in honour of William Gallacher*, Berlin, 1966.

521 GODWIN (WILLIAM). An inquiry concerning political justice and its influence on general virtue and happiness. 2 v. 1793. Ed. with a critical intro. and notes by F. E. L. Priestley, 3 v. Toronto. 1946.

Other leading statements of his ideas are *The inquirer; reflections on education, manners, and literature*, 1797, and *Thoughts on man, his nature, productions, and discoveries*, 1831. C. K. Paul, *William Godwin: his friends and contemporaries*, 2 v., 1876, is standard; other lives by H. Roussin, Paris, 1913; Ford K. Brown, 1926; George Woodcock, 1946. H. N. Brailsford, *Shelley, Godwin and their circle*, [1913], is excellent. See too D. Fleischer, *William Godwin: a study in liberalism*, 1951; B. R. Pollin, *Education and enlightenment in the works of William Godwin*, N.Y., 1963, and ed., with J. W. Marken, *Uncollected writings of William Godwin, 1785–1822*, Gainsville, Fla., 1968, and *Godwin criticism; a synoptic bibliography*, Toronto, [1967]; E. E. Smith and Esther Greenwell, *William Godwin*, N.Y., 1965.

522 CARTWRIGHT (JOHN). The constitutional defence of England. 1796.

Cartwright pursued his demands for constitutional reform further in *The state of the nation, in a series of letters to the Duke of Bedford*, 1805; *England's Aegis*, 2 v., 1806; *The comparison: in which mock reform, half reform, and constitutional reform are considered*, 1810; and *The English constitution produced and illustrated*, 1823, perhaps the most strictly theoretical of his works. Frances D. Cartwright, ed., *Life and correspondence of Major Cartwright*, 2 v., 1826, prints some surviving letters. See also J. W. Osborne, *John Cartwright*, Camb., 1972; Naomi C. Miller, 'John Cartwright and radical parliamentary reform', *E.H.R.* 83 (1968), 705–28.

523 BENTHAM (JEREMY). The collected works of Jeremy Bentham. General ed. J. H. Burns. 1968, in progress.

In two series, works and correspondence; until completion the main collection remains

Sir John Bowring, ed., *The works of Jeremy Bentham*, 11 v., Edin., 1838–43. See especially:

a. Introduction to the principles of morals and legislation, Bowring, v. 1, 1–154, sep. imps. 1789, 1823, and ed. by J. H. Burns and H. L. A. Hart, 1970.

b. A fragment on government, Bowring, v. 1, 221–95; sep. imps. 1776, 1823, and ed. by E. C. Montague, Oxf., 1891.

c. An essay on political tactics, Bowring, v. 2, 299–373.

d. The book of fallacies, Bowring, v. 2, 375–487; sep. imp. 1824, and rev. edn. with a preface by Harold A. Larrabee, 1952.

e. Anarchic fallacies, Bowring, v. 2, 489–534.

f. A plan of parliamentary reform in the form of a catechism, Bowring, v. 5, 433–557; sep. imps. 1817, 1818.

g. Constitutional code, Bowring, v. 9, 1–662.

h. Bowring omitted *A comment on the Commentaries, being a critical examination of the introduction to Sir William Blackstone's Commentaries on the laws of England*, ed. by C. W. Everett, Oxf., 1928. Hilda G. Lundin, *The influence of Jeremy Bentham on English democratic development*, 1920, is brief; see too MacCunn (534). G. L. Nesbitt, *Benthamite reviewing. The first twelve years of the Westminster Review, 1824–36*, N.Y., 1934, examines the propaganda of Bentham's circle. James Mill (525), provides a succinct summary of the utilitarians' views on representation and reform. For Bentham's life see (2113) and for his writings on jurisprudence (652) and philosophy (2805). Mary Mack, *Jeremy Bentham: an odyssey of ideas, 1748–92*, 1962, is controversial; see too D. J. Manning, *The mind of Jeremy Bentham*, 1968; B. Parekh, ed., *Bentham's political thought*, 1973.

524   OWEN (ROBERT). A new view of society; or, Essays on the principle of the formation of the human character. 3 pt. 1813–14.

Other important sources for his ideas are *The book of the new moral world*, 7 pt., 1836–44, and *The life of Robert Owen written by himself*, with an appendix, 2 pt., 1857–8. The fullest biog. is by Frank Podmore, 2 v., 1906. G. D. H. Cole, *The life of Robert Owen*, 1925, rev. edn., 1930, is excellent. Other lives by Margaret Cole, 1953, A. L. Morton, 1962. See also J. F. C. Harrison, *Robert Owen and the Owenites in Britain and America; The quest for the new moral world*, 1969.

525   MILL (JAMES). An essay on government. Ed. by Ernest Barker. Camb. 1937.

A classic, originally printed in the fifth edn. of the *Encyclopaedia Britannica*.

526   COLERIDGE (SAMUEL TAYLOR). The statesman's manual; or, The bible the best guide to political skill and foresight. 1816.

For Coleridge's more mature political thought see *On the constitution of the church and state, according to the idea of each*, 1830. His daughter, Sarah Coleridge, ed., *Essays on his own times: forming a second series of The Friend*, 3 v., 1850. There is a good selection in R. J. White, *The political thought of . . . Coleridge*, 1938, and a good account of his political works in J. A. Colmer, *Coleridge: critic of society*, Oxf., 1959. See too D. P. Calleo, *Coleridge and the idea of the modern state*, 1966; and (2725). R. J. White, ed., *Political tracts of Wordsworth, Coleridge and Shelley*, Camb., 1953.

527   BERNARD (JAMES BERNARD). Theory of the constitution, compared with its practice in ancient and modern times. 1834.

A conservative polemic.

528   BROUGHAM (HENRY PETER, 1st Baron Brougham and Vaux). Political philosophy. 3 pt. in 2 v. 1842–3.

529 CARLYLE (THOMAS). The works of . . . Carlyle. 30 v. 1896–9.

See especially *Sartor Resartus*, 1834; *Chartism*, 1839; *On heroes, hero-worship, and the heroic in history*, 1842; *Past and present*, 1843; *Latter-day pamphlets*, 1850. See F. W. Roe, *The social philosophy of Carlyle and Ruskin*, 1921; Julian Symons, *Thomas Carlyle, the life and ideas of a prophet*, 1952; A. J. La Valley, *Carlyle and the idea of the modern*, 1968. For his life and correspondence see also (2300).

530 KINGSLEY (CHARLES). Alton Locke. 1850.

This novel, and *Yeast*, 1848, state Kingsley's Christian socialist view of social problems. The biog. by his wife, Frances E. Kingsley (2327), is indispensable. Other studies are Charles W. Stubbs, *Charles Kingsley and the Christian social movement*, 1899; Margaret F. Thorp, *Charles Kingsley, 1819–1875*, Princeton, 1937; Guy Kendall, *Charles Kingsley and his ideas*, 1947; Robert B. Martin, *The dust of combat: A life of Charles Kingsley*, 1959, bibliog. 294–9. See also Maurice (707), Binyon (535), Christensen (722).

2. Later Works

531 HALL (WALTER PHELPS). British radicalism, 1791–1797. N.Y. 1912.

A detailed study of pamphlet literature. See also Maccoby (85).

532 MAITLAND (FREDERIC WILLIAM). 'A historical sketch of liberty and equality as ideals of English political philosophy from the time of Hobbes to the time of Coleridge.' In *Collected papers . . .*, ed. by H. A. L. Fisher, i (1911), 1–161.

533 McNIECE (GERALD). Shelley and the revolutionary idea. 1969.

534 STEPHEN (LESLIE). The English utilitarians. 3 v. 1900. Repr. 3 v. 1950.

Standard. See Elie Halévy, *La formation du radicalisme philosophique*, 3 v., Paris, 1901; trans. by Mary Morris, 1928; new edn. with bibliog. by C. W. Everett, 1952; Ernest Albee, *A history of English utilitarianism*, 1902; John Plamenatz, *The English utilitarians*, 2nd edn., Oxf., 1958. Briefer is William L. Davidson, *Political thought in England: the utilitarians from Bentham to J. S. Mill*, 1915. John MacCunn, *Six radical thinkers*, 1910, has a short penetrating appreciation of Bentham. See too Joseph Hamburger, *James Mill and the art of revolution*, New Haven, 1964, *Intellectuals in politics; John Stuart Mill and the philosophic radicals*, New Haven, 1965, and 'James Mill on universal suffrage and the middle class', *J. of Politics*, 24 (1962), 167–90; W. Thomas, 'James Mill's politics: the "Essay on Government" and the movement for reform', *Hist. J.* 12 (1969), 249–84, W. R. Carr, 'James Mill's politics reconsidered', *ibid.* 14 (1971), 553–80, and W. Thomas, 'James Mill's politics: a rejoinder', *ibid.* 735–50.

535 BINYON (GILBERT CLIVE). The Christian Socialist movement in England. 1931.

A general account. See also (722).

536 HEARNSHAW (FOSSEY JOHN COBB). The social and political ideas of some representative thinkers of the age of reaction and reconstruction, 1815–1865. 1932.

Robert Henry Murray, *Studies in the English social and political thinkers of the nineteenth century*, 2 v., Camb., 1929, v. 1: *From Malthus to Kingsley*, ranges more widely. Also excellent are Clarence Crane Brinton, *The political ideas of the English romanticists*, 1926, and *English political thought in the nineteenth century*, 1933, 2nd edn., Camb. Mass., 1949; John Bowle, *Politics and opinion in the nineteenth century*, 1954; W. A. Dunning, *History of political theories from Rousseau to Spencer*, 1922.

537   BEER (MAX). A history of British socialism. New edn. 2 v. 1929.

Standard. G. D. H. Cole, *A history of socialist thought*, v. 1: *The forerunners, 1789–1850*, 1953, provides excellent treatment in a more general setting. See too Esther Lowenthal, *The Ricardian socialists*, 1911.

538   PANKHURST (RICHARD KEIR PETHICK). The Saint Simonians, Mill and Carlyle: a preface to modern thought. 1957.

539   HIMMELFARB (GERTRUDE). Victorian minds. 1968.

Discusses Burke, Bentham, Malthus, J. S. Mill. See also Letwin (2800).

540   WESTON (CORINNE COMSTOCK). English constitutional theory and the House of Lords, 1556–1832. 1965.

541   HARRISON (WILFRID). Conflict and compromise; history of British political thought, 1593–1900. 1965.

542   PALLISTER (ANNE). Magna Carta: the heritage of liberty. Oxf. 1971.

IV

LEGAL HISTORY

A. REFERENCE AND SOURCES

1. MANUSCRIPTS

For fuller guidance, see (64).

(a) *Equity*

Reports in equity cases are found principally in the records of the Court of
Chancery and to a less extent, up till 1841, in those of the Court of Exchequer.
The main classes to be searched are:

CHANCERY
Chancery Proceedings; Entry Books of Decrees and Orders; Decree Rolls.
EXCHEQUER
Bills and Answers; Decrees, Original and Entry Books; Orders, Original
and Entry Books; Depositions taken by Commission, and Baron's Deposi-
tions; Reports and Certificates.

(b) *Common Law*

The main classes to be searched are:

(1) Crown Cases
COURT OF KING'S BENCH
Crown Rolls; Controlment Rolls (till 1834); Indictments.
CLERKS OF ASSIZE
Minute Books, Crown Books, Indictments, and other records arranged by
circuits: Oxford Circuit; Midland Circuit (no records before 1818);
Western Circuit; South Eastern Circuit; North Eastern Circuit; Chester
and North Wales Circuit (few records before 1831); South Wales Circuit
(formed 1876; records from 1834).

(2) Civil Cases
COURT OF KING'S BENCH
Plea or Judgment Rolls.
COURT OF COMMON PLEAS
Plea Rolls; Recovery Rolls (to 1837); Feet of Fines (to 1838); Register of
Judgments (from 1838).
COURT OF THE EXCHEQUER OF PLEAS
Plea Rolls; Order Books; Rule Books.
CLERKS OF ASSIZE
Minute Books and other records, as above.

HIGH COURT OF ADMIRALTY

Instance Court

Oyer and Terminer Records; Libels; Acts; Assignation Books; Instance Papers; Letters of Marque, Bonds, and Declarations.

Prize Court

Assignation Books; Prize Papers.

Prize Appeals Court

Appeals Papers; Assignation Books; Case Books.

2. REPORTS OF COMMISSIONS

543 PARLIAMENT. INDEX TO REPORTS of commissioners on law and courts of justice, 1810–1845. 1846 (673–I), (673–II), pt. 1 and 2, xli. i.

Indexes and brief abstracts of the following: *Report of commissioners on saleable offices in courts of law*, 1810 (358) ix. 125; [*First*] *report of commissioners* [*on*] *duties, salaries, and emoluments of the officers of the courts*, 1816 (428) viii. 91; [*Second*] do. 1818 (156) vii. 225; [*Third*] 1818 (292) vii. 243; [*Fourth*] 1819–20 (3) ii. 175; [*Fifth*] 1822 (125) xi. 99; [*Sixth*] 1823 (462) vii. 27; [*Seventh*] 1823 (43) ix. 25; [*Eighth*] 1824 (240) ix. 75; *First report . . . by the commissioners appointed to inquire into the practice and proceedings of the superior courts of common law*, 1829 (46) ix. 1; *Second* do. 1830 (123) xi. 547; *Third* 1831 (92) x. 375; *Fourth* 1831–2 (239) xxv pt. 1 and 2. 1; *Fifth* 1833 (247) xxii. 195; *Sixth* 1834 (263) xxvii. 449; *Report of the commissioners* [*on*] *the practice of the court of Chancery*, 1826 (143) xv. 1; *Report of the commissioners appointed to inquire into the practice and jurisdiction of the ecclesiastical courts*, 1832 (199) xxiv. 1; *Report* [*of*] *the commissioners appointed to inquire into the law of England respecting real property*, 1829 (263) x. 1; *Second* do. 1830 (575) xi. 1; *Third* 1832 (484) xxiii. 321; *Fourth* 1833 (226) xxii. 1; *Report of the commissioners for inquiring into bankruptcy and insolvency*, 1840 (274) xvi. 1, and supplement 1841 (289) xii. 1.

3. BIBLIOGRAPHY

544 MARVIN (JOHN GALE). Legal bibliography; or, A thesaurus of American, English, Irish and Scotch law books; together with some continental treatises. Phil. 1847.

Comprehensive, with useful annotations. See also Richard Whalley Bridgman, *A short view of legal bibliography*, 1807, selective; John Clarke, *Clarke's Bibliotheca legum; or, Complete catalogue of the Common and Statute law-books of the United Kingdom . . . originally comp. by J. Worrall*, 1810, 5th edn., 1824; William Reed, *Bibliotheca nova legum Angliae*, 1809, and suppl., 1812.

545 MIDDLE TEMPLE LIBRARY. A catalogue of the printed books in the library. By Cyril Edward Alfred Bedwell. 3 v. Glasgow. 1914.

Supplement, 1914–24, by Herbert A. C. Sturgess, Glasgow, 1925. The most up to date and comprehensive of the catalogues of the Inns and other societies. Much material on English law is listed in *Harvard University Law School Library Catalogue* 2 v., Camb., [Mass.], 1909, and the *Catalogue of the New York University Law Center law collection*, comp. and ed. by Julius J. Marke, N.Y., 1953.

546 HOLDSWORTH (*Sir* WILLIAM SEARLE). A history of English law. V. 13. Ed. by A. L. Goodhart and H. G. Hanbury. 1952.

Includes valuable comprehensive critical analyses of legal treatises of the period. See also Sir Percy H. Winfield, *The chief sources of English legal history*, Camb., [Mass.], 1925, a collection of lectures with select bibliogs.

547 SWEET AND MAXWELL LTD. A legal bibliography of the British commonwealth of nations. Comp. by William Harold Maxwell and others. 2nd edn. 7 v. 1955–64.

V. 1: *English law to 1800,* classified by subject with author index; v. 2: *English law, 1801–1954,* alphabetical with subject index; v. 3: *Canadian and British-American colonial law from the earliest times to* ... *1956;* v. 4: *Irish law to 1956;* v. 5: *Scottish law to 1956, together with a list of Roman law books;* v. 6: *Australia, New Zealand, and their dependencies;* v. 7: *The British Commonwealth excluding the United Kingdom, Australia, New Zealand, Canada, India and Pakistan.* Comprehensive, but omitting some works listed in Clarke and Reed (544), and without critical annotation. See too R. P. Brittain, *Bibliography of medico-legal works in English,* South Hackensack N.J., and London, 1962, and Cumming (2581).

548 LONDON UNIVERSITY. INSTITUTE OF ADVANCED LEGAL STUDIES. A survey of legal periodicals: union catalogue of holdings in British libraries. 2nd edn. 1957.

549 INDEX OF LEGAL PERIODICAL LITERATURE. Boston [Mass.].

Publ. annually, 1887–1937.

550 SWEET AND MAXWELL LTD. Guide to law reports and statutes. 4th edn. 1962.

Comprehensive, but does not reproduce all the information given in William Harold Maxwell and Charles R. Brown, *A complete list of British and colonial law reports and legal periodicals,* 3rd edn., 1937, suppl., 1946, or in Charles C. Soule, *The lawyer's reference manual of law books and citations,* 1882, which gives information about American reprints. See also Sir John Charles Fox, *A handbook of English law reports; from the last quarter of the eighteenth century to* ... *1865.* Pt. 1: *House of Lords, Privy Council, and Chancery reports,* 1913.

4. DICTIONARIES

551 TOMLINS (Sir THOMAS EDLYNE). The law dictionary ... originally compiled by Giles Jacob ... now greatly enlarged and improved. 2 v. 1797; 4th edn. by Thomas Colpitts Granger. 2 v. 1835; suppl. by D. Williams. 1838.

Less ambitious were other law dictionaries by Thomas Walter Williams, 1816; James Whishaw, 1829; Henry James Holthouse, 1839, 2nd edn. 1846; John Jane Smith Wharton, 1848.

5. ABRIDGEMENTS

552 [BACON (MATTHEW).] A new abridgment of the law. By a gentleman of the Middle Temple. 5th edn. by Sir Henry Gwillim. 7 v. 1798. 7th edn. 8 v. 1832.

Well arranged and so more popular than Charles Viner, *A general abridgment of law and equity,* 2nd edn., 24 v., 1791–4; suppl., 6 v., 1799–1806. Also in high repute was Sir John Comyns, *A digest of the laws of England,* 3rd edn., enl. and cont. by Stewart Kyd, 6 v., 1792, 5th edn., cor. and continued by A. Hammond, 8 v., 1822.

553 BLAXLAND (GEORGE). Codex legum Anglicanarum; or, A digest of principles of English law, arranged in the order of the Code Napoleon. 1839.

Deals with civil rights, personality, property rights, and contracts.

554 PETERSDORFF (CHARLES). A practical and elementary abridgment of the cases argued and determined in the courts of King's Bench, Common Pleas, Exchequer . . . 1660, to 4 Geo. IV. 15 v. 1825–30.

This was supplemented by *A practical and elementary abridgment of the Common law . . . 1824 to . . . 1840*, 5 v., 1841–4. John Frederick Archbold, *Summaries of the laws of England*, 2 v., 1848–9, deals in v. 1 with pleadings, evidence, practice and proceedings of courts; in v. 2 with hereditaments and tenures; no more publ.

6. Law Reports

555 THE ENGLISH REPORTS. Full reprint, 1220–1865. 178 v. 1900–32.

Brings together the compilations of the numerous contemporary reporters. More than half the contents relate to the century ending 1865; for guidance see W. H. Maxwell and C. R. Brown (550).

556 HOWELL (THOMAS BAYLY). A complete collection of state trials and proceedings for high treason and other crimes and misdemeanors from the earliest period to . . . 1783 . . . and continued from . . . 1783 to [1820] by Thomas Jones Howell. 33 v. 1816–26.

General index by David Jardine, 1828. Sir John MacDonell and John E. P. Wallis ed., *Reports of state trials, new series, 1820-58*, 8 v., 1888–98.

7. Periodicals

See also (548), (549).

557 LAW JOURNAL. 12 v. 1823–34.

Continued as the *Law Journal Reports*, v. 13+, 1835+.

558 LAW MAGAZINE; or, Quarterly Review of Jurisprudence. 55 v. 1828–56.

Indexes to v. 1–12, 13–31, 32–43. Combined in 1856 with *The Law Review*, 23 v., 1844–56, and became the *Law Magazine and Law Review*. The contents include some biographical matter as well as articles on points of law. See also *The Legal Observer*, 52 v., 1831–56, the *Law Times*, v. 1+, 1843+.

559 LAW QUARTERLY REVIEW. v 1+. 1885+.

Index to v. 1–72 by Peter Allsop, 1957. Includes historical articles, as does also the *Cambridge Law Journal*, v. 1+. 1921+.

B. HISTORY AND BIOGRAPHY

1. History of the Law

560 HOLDSWORTH (*Sir* WILLIAM SEARLE). A history of English law. 17 v. 1903–72. 6th rev. edn. 1938–72.

A splendidly comprehensive survey. Material on the late eighteenth century and early nineteenth century occurs in v. 1 (on the organization and reform of the courts) and in nearly all vols. from v. 7 onwards, in which sections of the subject are traced through, sometimes well into the nineteenth century. V. 13 deals with the development of public and criminal law, 1793–1832; see also Radzinowicz (2581). V. 14–16, extensive treatment of the period 1832–75. V. 17, general index.

561 ASSOCIATION OF AMERICAN LAW SCHOOLS. Select essays in
Anglo-American legal history. Edited by a committee of the Association. 3 v.
Bost. 1907–9.

562 JENKS (EDWARD). A short history of English law. 1912. 6th edn. 1949.

A good brief outline. Geoffrey R. Y. Radcliffe and Geoffrey Cross, *The English legal
system*, 1937, 3rd edn., 1954, also short, is more up-to-date. Harold Potter, *Historical
introduction to English law and its institutions*, 1932, 4th edn. by A. K. R. Kiralfy, 1958,
is more technical in approach.

563 DICEY (ALBERT VENN). Lectures on the relation between law and
public opinion in England during the nineteenth century. 2nd edn. rep. w.
introd. by E. C. S. Wade. 1962.

A classic, and indispensable. For recent critical discussion of its themes see all entries
under Parris (452).

564 ABEL-SMITH (BRIAN) *and* STEVENS (ROBERT BOCKING).
Lawyers and the courts; a sociological study of the English legal system, 1750–
1965. 1967.

2. BIOGRAPHY

See also Eldon (173), Brougham (207), Lyndhurst (208).

565 TOWNSEND (WILLIAM CHARLES). The lives of twelve eminent
judges of the last and of the present century. 2 v. 1846.

[James Grant], *The bench and the bar*, 2 v., 1837, John Payne Collier, *Criticisms on the
bar*, 1819, Archer Polson, *Law and lawyers*, 1858, record the authors' personal knowledge and impressions.

566 WOOLRYCH (HUMPHRY WILLIAM). Lives of eminent serjeants-
at-law of the English bar. 2 v. 1869.

Brief biogs.

567 FOSS (EDWARD). Biographia juridica. A biographical dictionary of the
judges of England . . . 1066–1870. 1870.

Puts in alphabetical form and abridges the contents of his *The judges of England, with
sketches of their lives and . . . notices connected with the courts at Westminster . . . 1066–
1864*, 9 v., 1848–64. Also valuable is his *Tabulae curiales: or, Tables of the superior
courts of Westminster hall, showing the judges who sat in them from 1066 to 1864; with the
attorney- and solicitor-generals of each reign*, 1865. The works of John, 1st baron Campbell, *The lives of the lord chancellors and keepers of the great seal of England*, 5th edn., 10
v., 1868, and *The lives of the chief justices of England . . . till the death of Lord Tenterden*,
3rd edn., 4 v., 1874, though full of plagiarisms and misrepresentation, contain material
not to be found elsewhere: see Sir Edward Burtenshaw Sugden, 1st baron St. Leonards,
Misrepresentations in Campbell's lives of Lyndhurst and Brougham, 1869. James Beresford Atlay, *The Victorian chancellors*, 2 v., 1906–8, though unoriginal, is worth consulting.

568 ABINGER. A memoir of . . . James [Scarlett], first Lord Abinger . . .
including a fragment of his autobiography and selections from his correspondence and speeches. By Peter Campbell Scarlett. 1877.

569 CAMPBELL. Life of John, Lord Campbell, Lord High Chancellor of Great Britain; consisting of a selection from his autobiography, diary and letters; by his daughter . . . Mrs. Hardcastle. 2 v. 1881.

Campbell pub. a collection of his *Speeches*, Edin., 1842.

570 DENMAN. Memoir of Thomas, first Lord Denman. By Sir Joseph Arnould. 2 v. 1873.

571 ERSKINE. Erskine. By James Alexander Lovat-Fraser. Camb. 1932.

Of interest is H. Duméril, *Lord Erskine: étude sur le barreau anglais à la fin du xviiie siècle*, Paris, 1883. Lloyd Paul Stryker, *For the defense: Thomas Erskine, the most enlightened liberal of his times, 1750–1823*, N.Y., 1949, draws on a wide range of printed material. James Ridgway ed. his *Speeches . . . on subjects connected with the liberty of the press*, 2nd edn., 4 v., 1813–16, and *Speeches . . . on miscellaneous subjects*, 1827.

572 HILL. The recorder of Birmingham: a memoir of Matthew Davenport Hill, with selections from his correspondence. By his daughters Rosamund and Florence Davenport Hill. 1878.

573 KENYON. The life of Lloyd, first Lord Kenyon. By George Thomas Kenyon. 1873.

574 LANGDALE. Memoirs of Henry [Bickersteth], Lord Langdale. By Sir Thomas Duffus Hardy. 2 v. 1852.

Includes letters 1797–1851.

575 MACKINTOSH. Memoirs of the life of . . . Sir James Mackintosh; ed. [from his letters and his journal] by his son Robert James Mackintosh. 2nd edn. 2 v. 1836.

His son also ed. his *Miscellaneous works*, 3 v., 1846.

576 ROMILLY. Memoirs of the life of Sir S. Romilly, written by himself; with a selection from his correspondence; ed. by his sons. 3 v. 1840.

Romilly's *Speeches* were pub., 2 v., 1820. Cecil George Oakes, *Sir Samuel Romilly, 1757–1818*, 1935, is a well-balanced study, with full bibliog. 393–423. See too P. Medd, *Romilly*, 1968.

577 STOWELL. Lord Stowell; his life and the development of English prize law. By Edward Stanley Roscoe. 1916.

See too Surtees (173).

3. INNS OF COURT: TRAINING

578 GOLDSMITH (GEORGE). The English bar; or, Guide to the Inns of Court. 1843. 3rd edn. 1849.

Informative on the regulations of the various inns. See too Thomas Lane, *The student's guide; being a concise account of the . . . Society of Lincoln's Inn*, 1803, 4th edn., 1823.

579 LINCOLN'S INN. The Records of the . . . Society . . . Admissions. Ed. by William Paley Baildon. 2 v. 1896.

V. 1: 1420–1799; v 2: 1800–1893. Baildon also ed., *The records of the Society . . . The black books*, 4 v., 1897–1902; v. 4: 1776–1845.

580　INNER TEMPLE. A calendar of the Inner Temple records. Ed. by Reginald Arthur Roberts. 5 v. 1896–1936.

> V. 5: 1751–1800. See also *Masters of the bench . . . 1450–1883, and Masters of the Temple, 1540–1883,* 1883, and *Supplement . . . 1883–1901; to which is appended a list of the Treasurers, 1505–1901,* 1901.

581　MIDDLE TEMPLE. The Middle Temple bench book: being a register of benchers . . . from the earliest records to the present time. 2nd edn. By J. Bruce Williamson. 1937.

> *Register of admissions to the . . . Society . . . from the fifteenth century to . . . 1944,* comp, by Herbert A. C. Sturgess, 3 v., 1949; v. 2: 1782–1909.

582　GRAY'S INN. The register of admissions to Gray's Inn, 1521–1889. Comp. by Joseph Foster. Priv. pr. 1889.

> Reginald James Fletcher ed. *The pension book of Gray's Inn . . . 1569–[1800],* 2 v., 1901–10; v. 2: 1669–1800.

583　SMITH (PHILIP ANSTIE). A history of education for the English bar, with suggestions as to subjects and methods of study. 1860.

> Thomas Ruggles, *The barrister: or, Strictures on the education proper for the bar,* 2 v., 1792, 2nd edn., 1818, suggests contemporary shortcomings. Samuel Warren, *A popular and practical introduction to law studies,* 1835, 2nd edn., 1845, is a guide to what was then regarded as the leading standard literature of the profession. See also Harold Greville Hanbury, *The Vinerian Chair and legal education,* Oxf., 1958.

4. The Legal Profession

584　THE LAW LIST. Annual from 1841.

> This was preceded by *Browne's general law list,* nos. 1–16, 1775–97, followed by the *New law list,* by J. Hughes, 1798–1802, and then *Clarke's new law list,* 1803–40.

585　KELLY (BERNARD WILLIAM). Short history of the English bar. 1908.

> A too brief outline of a neglected subject.

586　NORTON-KYSHE (JAMES WILLIAM). The law and privileges relating to the Attorney-General and Solicitor-General of England, with a history from the earliest periods. 1897.

587　CHRISTIAN (EDMUND BROWN VINEY). A short history of solicitors. 1896.

> Robert Robson, *The attorney in eighteenth century England,* Camb., 1959, bibliog. 172–7, has a good deal pertaining to the years after 1800. *The records of the Society of Gentlemen Practisers in the courts of law and equity called the Law Society; comp. from MSS. in the possession of the Incorporated Law Society of the United Kingdom* [ed. by Edwin Freshfield], 1897, prints records for 1739–1810. Robert Maugham, *A treatise on the law of attornies, solicitors, and agents,* 1825, was a well-executed pioneer work, soon followed by the more comprehensive book by John Merrifield, *The law of attornies . . . also on the law of costs,* 1830.

C. COURTS AND PROCEDURE

1. GENERAL

588 CARTER (ALBERT THOMAS). A history of the English courts; being a 7th edn. of A history of English legal institutions. 1944.

A brief outline. Henry Aldridge, *History and antiquities and jurisdiction of all the courts of law*, 1835, gives a clear simple account of the working of the courts. A full and learned account, for civil law practice, is Joseph Chitty, Snr. *The practice of the law in all its departments; with a view of rights, injuries and remedies*, 4 v. in 1, 1833–8, 3rd edn., 3 v., 1837–42. See too William Bagley, *The new practice of the courts of law at Westminster*, 1840.

589 CHITTY (JOSEPH) *Snr.* A practical treatise on pleading; and on the parties to actions, and the forms of actions with . . . precedents of pleadings. 2 v. 1809. 7th edn. corr. and enl. by Henry Greening. 3 v. 1844.

A book of high repute, as was also Henry John Stephen, *A treatise on the principles of pleading in civil actions*, 1824, 5th edn., 1843.

590 BULLER (*Sir* FRANCIS). An introduction to the law relative to trials at *nisi prius*. 5th edn. corr. with add. 1790. 7th edn. 1817.

For long standard, not fully replaced by Isaac Espinasse, *A digest of the law of actions at* nisi prius, 2 v., 1789, 4th edn. 1812; but largely superseded by William Selwyn, *Abridgment of the law of* nisi prius, 2 v., 1808, 11th edn., 1845.

591 TIDD (WILLIAM). The practice of the Court of King's Bench in personal actions. 2 v. 1790–4. 9th edn. 2 v. 1828, and 3 suppls. 1830–3.

An authoritative statement of the law of procedure. To the 3rd edn., 1803, were added references to cases of practice in the Court of Common Pleas; in the 7th edn., 1821, law and practice of extents, rules of court, and decisions in the Exchequer of Pleas. John Frederick Archbold, *The practice of the Court of King's Bench in personal actions and ejectment*, 2 v., 1819, went to eight edns. by 1845; the 4th edn., 2 v., 1835, included also the practice of the Courts of Common Pleas and Exchequer. See too Thomas Lee, *Dictionary of the practice in civil actions in the courts of King's Bench and Common Pleas*, 2 v., 1811–12, 2nd edn., 1825.

592 BOLTON (GEORGE). The practice of the criminal courts, including the proceedings before the magistrates in petty and quarter sessions, and at the assizes. 1835.

A selective treatise, dealing with the more common offences.

593 MARRIOTT (*Sir* JAMES). Formulare instrumentorum: or, A formulary of authentic instruments, writs, and standing orders, used in the High Courts of Admiralty of Great Britain. 1802.

Arthur Browne, *A compendious view of the civil law and the law of the Admiralty*, 2 v., 1798–9, 2nd edn., 1802; Edwin Edwards, *A treatise on the jurisdiction of the High Court of Admiralty of England*, 1847.

594 SPENCE (GEORGE). The equitable jurisdiction of the Court of Chancery . . . comprising its rise, progress and final establishment. 2 v. 1846–9.

A standard learned history with much information on the contemporary state of chancery jurisdiction. John Mitford, 1st baron Redesdale, *A treatise on the pleadings in suits in the Court of Chancery*, 2nd edn., 1787, reached 5th edn., 1847; see too George Cooper, *A treatise of pleading on the equity side of the High Court of Chancery*, 1809, and John Newland, *The practice of the High Court of Chancery, with forms of pleadings and procedure*, 1813, 3rd edn., 1830. Henry Maddock, *A treatise on the principles and practice of the High Court of Chancery*, 2 v., 1815, 3rd edn., 1837, valuable, was the first general work on the subject; surpassed in some respects by George Jeremy, *A treatise on the equity jurisdiction of . . . Chancery*, 1828. The work of Chancery after 1830 was dealt with in further treatises and guides by William Thomas Jemmett, 1830, Joseph Story, 1836, 1838; John Sidney Smith, 2 v., 1834–5, Edmund Robert Daniell, 3 v. 1837–41, Thomas Kennedy, 2 v., 1843–52; Josiah William Smith, 1845, John Adams, 1850.

595 FOWLER (DAVID BURTON). The practice of the Court of Exchequer upon proceedings in equity. 2 v. 1795. 2nd edn. 2 v. 1817.

On the common law side of the Exchequer, James Manning, *The practice of the office of pleas, and the Court of Exchequer at Westminster, with a summary of the law of extents*, 3 v., 1819.

596 HANDS (WILLIAM). A practical treatise on fines and recoveries in the Court of Common Pleas. 1800. 4th edn. 1825.

597 SWEET (JOSEPH). The practice of the county courts by writs of justicies: with forms, declarations, costs, etc. 1828. 2nd edn. 1835.

A guide for the public, whereas George Barclay Mansell, *The practice by justicies and plaint in the county court: with practical forms*, 1834, was intended also for practitioners. See too James Edward Davis, *A manual of the law of evidence in the trial of actions and other proceedings in the new county courts*, 1848.

598 SWAN (ROBERT). A practical treatise on the jurisdiction of the ecclesiastical courts relating to probates and administration. 1830.

599 BUCKLEY (WILLIAM). The jurisdiction and practice of the Marshalsea and Palace courts, with tables of costs and charges. 1825. 2nd edn. 1827.

Samuel Abrahams, *The Palace court in constitution and practice, with reasons for its immediate abolition*, 1848.

600 LEWIS (THOMAS). On the constitution, jurisdiction, and practice of the sheriffs' courts of London. 1833.

601 WINDER (W. H. D.). 'The courts of requests'. *Law Quart. Rev.* 52 (1936), 369–94.

An authoritative survey.

602 TANCRED (HENRY WILLIAM). A treatise on informations in the nature of a *quo warranto*; with . . . some account of the proceedings in the Court of the Eyre. 1830.

603 IMPEY (WALTER J.). A treatise on the law and practice of the writ of *mandamus*. 1826.

604 GUDE (RICHARD). The practice of the Crown side of the Court of King's Bench, and the practice of the Sessions. 2 v. 1828.

605 MACQUEEN (JOHN FRASER). A practical treatise on the appellate jurisdiction of the House of Lords and Privy Council, together with the practice on parliamentary divorce. 1842.

An accurate and authoritative account. See also William Robert Sydney, *A treatise on the jurisdiction and modern practice in appeals to the House of Lords, and in proceedings on claims to dormant peerages*, 1824; John Palmer, *The practice in the . . . Lords, on appeals, writs of error, and claims of peerage*, 1830, and *The practice on appeals from the colonies to the Privy Council*, 1831, suppl., 1834; Arthur Stanley Turberville, 'The House of Lords as a court of law, 1784–1837', *Law Quart. Rev.* 52 (1936), 189–219; William F. Finlason, *The judicial committee of the Privy Council . . . especially in ecclesiastical cases*, [1878].

2. EVIDENCE

606 PEAKE (THOMAS). A compendium of the law of evidence. 1801. 2nd edn. with add. 2 pts. 1804–6. 5th edn. 1822.

Later authoritative guides were Samuel March Phillipps, *A treatise on the law of evidence,* 1814, 10th edn., 1852, and Thomas Starkie, *A practical treatise of the law of evidence and digest of proofs, in civil and criminal proceedings*, 3 v., 1824, 4th edn., 1853. John Pitt Taylor, *A treatise on the law of evidence as administered in England and Ireland*, 2 v., 1848, makes comparisons with foreign practice. More specialized are Richard Newcombe Gresley, *A treatise on the law of evidence in the Courts of Equity*, 1836, 2nd edn., 1847, and John Tamlyn, *Treatise on the law of evidence, principally with reference to the practice of the Court of Chancery and in the Masters' offices*, 1845.

607 BEST (WILLIAM MAWDESLEY). A treatise on the principles of evidence and practice as to proofs in courts of common law; with elementary rules for conducting the examination and cross-examination of witnesses. 1849.

More emphasis on principles than in other contemporary treatises.

3. JURIES

608 BENTHAM (JEREMY). The elements of the art of packing, as applied to special juries, particularly in the cases of libel law. 1821.

A critical survey of practice, particularly that of the years 1800–10.

609 UNIACKE (CROFTON). The new jury law; forming a title of the code of legal proceedings according to the plan proposed for the statute law of the realm. 1825.

See too James Kennedy, *A treatise on the law and practice of juries as amended by the Statute 6 George IV, c. 50, including the coroner's inquest*, 1826.

4. CONTEMPORARY CRITICISM

See also Brougham (207).

610 MILLER (JOHN). An inquiry into the present state of the civil law of England. 1825.

Deals mainly with reform of court procedure and of the law of real property. Miller returned to the charge with *On the present unsettled condition of the law and its administration*, 1839.

611 MAYHEW (THOMAS). A complete history of an action at law . . . together with observations proving the present practice to be extravagant and unjust. 1828.

A critical analysis of an action for debt through its various stages.

612 PARKES (JOSEPH). A history of the Court of Chancery, with practical remarks on the recent commission, report, and evidence, and on the means of improving the administration of justice in the English courts of equity. 1828.

Learned and thorough. See too Sir James Bland Burges (afterwards Lamb), *An enquiry into . . . delay attributed to the judicial proceedings of the House of Lords and the Court of Chancery*, 1824; William Long Wellesley, *View of the Court of Chancery*, 1830; Arthur James Johnes, *Suggestions for the reform of the Court of Chancery by a union of the jurisdictions of equity and law: with a plan for a new tribunal for cases of lunacy*, 1834.

613 COOPER (CHARLES PURTON). A brief account of some of the most important proceedings in Parliament, relative to the defects in the administration of justice in the Court of Chancery, the House of Lords, and the Court of Commissioners of Bankrupts. 1828.

D. THE LAW

1. COMMON LAW

(a) *Bailments*

614 JONES (*Sir* WILLIAM). An essay on the law of bailments. 2nd edn. with notes by John Balmanno, 1798. 4th edn. 1833.

An extremely able exposition.

(b) *Commercial Law*

615 CHITTY (JOSEPH) *Snr*. A treatise on the laws of commerce and manufactures and the contracts relating thereto. With an appendix of treaties, statutes and precedents. 4 v. 1820–4.

A sound guide. John William Smith, *A compendium of mercantile law*, 1834, 3rd edn., 1843, was the first study of a more modern type. See too George Ross, *A treatise on the law of vendors and purchasers of personal property*, 1811, 2nd edn., 1821; Colin, Baron Blackburn, *Treatise on the effect of the contract of sale*, 1845.

616 COOKE (WILLIAM). Compendious system of bankrupt laws. 2 v. 3rd edn. 1793.

The most complete of the earlier works, reached the 8th edn., 1823. Also standard was John Frederick Archbold, *The law and practice in bankruptcy*, 1825, 10th edn., 1844. See too Edward Erastus Deacon, *The law and practice of bankruptcy*, 2 v., 1827, 2nd rev. edn., 1848; and on actions over debts due to the Crown, Sir Edward West, *A treatise of the law and practice of extents*, 1817.

617 BAYLEY (*Sir* JOHN). A short treatise on the law of bills of exchange, cash bills, and promissory notes. 1789. 4th edn. with add. 1822. 6th edn. by G. M. Dowdeswell. 1849.

A standard work with similar title by Joseph Chitty, *Snr.*, was publ. 1799, 9th edn., 1840. Both were superseded by Sir John Barnard Byles, *A practical treatise of law of bills of exchange*, 1829, 6th edn., 1851. A useful modern outline treatment is James Milnes Holden, *The history of negotiable instruments in English law*, 1955.

618   WATSON (WILLIAM). A treatise on the law of partnership. 1794. 2nd edn. 1807.

A rapidly developing subject, later dealt with in books with similar title by Niel Gow 1823, 4th edn., 1840, and John Collyer, 1832, 2nd edn., 1840; and in Charles F. F. Wordsworth, *The law of railway, banking, mining, canal, and other joint stock companies*, 1836, 5th edn., 1851.

619   PALEY (WILLIAM). A treatise on the law of principal and agent; chiefly with reference to mercantile transactions. 1812. 3rd edn. 1833.

620   KYD (STEWART). A treatise on the law of awards. 1791. 2nd edn. 1799.

For the later development of law on this subject see James Stamford Caldwell, *A treatise on the law of arbitration*, 1817, 2nd edn., 1825; Sir William Henry Watson, *A treatise on the law of arbitration and awards*, 1825, 3rd edn., 1846; Francis Russell, *Treatise on the power and duty of an arbitrator, and the law of submissions and awards*, 1849.

621   COLLIER (JOHN DYER). An essay on the law of patents for new inventions. 1803.

Richard Godson, *A practical treatise on the law of patents for inventions and of copyright, with two supplements*, 1823–35, 2nd edn. with suppls., 1844, 1851; William M. Hindmarch, *A treatise on the law relating to patent privileges*, 1846.

622   MAUGHAM (ROBERT). A treatise on the laws of literary property. 1828.

George Ticknor Curtis, *A treatise on the law of copyright . . . in England and America*, Boston, London, 1847. See also John James Lowndes, *An historical sketch of the law of copyright*, 1840.

(c) *Contract*

623   POTHIER (ROBERT JOSEPH). A treatise on the law of obligations or contracts . . . Trans. from the French, with an introduction, appendix and notes, illustrative of the English laws on the subject, by William David Evans. 2 v. 1806. 3rd edn. 1853.

Samuel Comyn, *Treatise on the law of contracts*, 2 v., 1807, 2nd edn., 1824, was regarded as the best guide for many years, until superseded by standard works with similar titles by Joseph Chitty, *Jnr.*, 1826, 4th edn., 1850, and Charles Greenstreet Addison, 1845–7, 2nd ed., 1849. See also Richard Meredith Jackson, *The history of quasi-contract in English law*, Camb., 1936.

(d) *Criminal Law*

624   RUSSELL (*Sir* WILLIAM OLDNALL). A treatise on crimes and misdemeanours. 2 v. 1819. 3rd edn. 1843.

A classic, dealing with the whole of English criminal law except treason. Guides on the effects of law reforms are John Frederick Archbold, *Peel's Acts*, 2 v., 1827, 3rd edn., 1835; Charles Sprengel Greaves, *Lord Campbell's Act for further improving the administration of criminal justice*, 1851.

625 EAST (*Sir* EDWARD HYDE). A treatise of the pleas of the Crown. 2 v. 1803.

Standard, till superseded by John Frederick Archbold, *The law and practice relating to pleading and evidence in criminal cases*, 1822, 11th edn., 1849. Also useful is Thomas Starkie, *A treatise on criminal pleading*, 2 v., 1814, 3rd edn., 1828.

626 STARKIE (THOMAS). A treatise on the law of slander and libel. 1813. 2nd edn. 1830.

Francis Ludlow Holt, *History and digest of the law of libel*, 1812, 2nd edn., 1816, expressed a high Tory view, which was attacked in Richard Mence, *The law of libel*, 1824.

627 PALEY (WILLIAM). The law and practice of summary convictions on penal statutes by justices of the peace. 1814. 3rd edn. 1838.

A complete and clear summary.

628 COTTU (CHARLES). On the administration of criminal justice in England; and the spirit of the English government; tr. from the French. 1822.

A remarkable account by a visiting French lawyer.

629 STEPHEN (*Sir* JAMES FITZJAMES). A history of the criminal law of England. 3 v. 1883.

Standard. See also Radzinowicz (2581).

630 NOKES (GERALD DACRE). A history of the crime of blasphemy. 1928.

Learned and readable.

(e) *Land Law*

631 CRUISE (WILLIAM). A digest of the laws of England respecting real property. 6 v. 1804–6. 4th edn. rev. and enl. by H. H. White. 7 v. 1835.

Later more concise guides are Walter Henry Burton, *An elementary compendium of the law of real property*, 1828, 7th edn., 1850; Joshua Williams, *Principles of the law of real property*, 1845; George Crabb, *The law of real property in its present state*, 2 v., 1846. Admirable treatises on different aspects include Charles Fearne, *An essay on the learning of contingent remainders and executory devises*, 4th edn. enl., 2 v., 1791–5, 10th edn., 1844; John Joseph Powell, *A treatise upon the law of mortgages*, 3rd edn., 2 v., 1791, 6th edn. enl., by T. Coventry, 2 v., 1826; Charles Watkins, *A treatise on copyholds*, 2 v., 1797–9; 3rd edn. rev., 2 v. 1821, and John Scriven, *A practical treatise on copyhold tenure and court keeping*, 1816, 4th edn., 1846; William Woodfall, *The law of landlord and tenant*, 1802, 7th edn., 1829, remodelled and enl. by S. B. Harrison, 1st edn., 1831, 6th edn., 1849; Sir Edward Burtenshaw Sugden, 1st baron St. Leonards, *A practical treatise of the law of vendors and purchasers of estates*, 1805, 12th edn., 1851; and *A practical treatise of powers*, 1808, 7th edn., 1845; Andrew Amos and J. Ferrand, *A treatise on the law of fixtures*, 1827, 2nd edn., 1847; Thomas Platt, *A practical treatise on the law of covenants*, 1829.

632 HUMPHREYS (JAMES). Observations on the actual state of the English laws of real property, with the outlines of a code. 1826.

An outline for systematic reform; criticized by John James Park in *A contre-projet to the Humphreysian code; and to the projects of redaction of Messrs Hammond, Uniacke and Twiss*, 1828.

633 WATKINS (CHARLES). Principles of conveyancing . . . with an introduction on the study of that branch of law. 1800; 8th edn. pt. 1, 1838; 9th edn.
pt. 2, 1845, both by H. H. White.

An introductory work, on a subject which attracted other very competent writers:
Charles Barton, *Elements of conveyancing*, 6 v., 1802–5, 3rd edn., 3 v., 1826; Richard
Preston, *A treatise on conveyancing*, 3 v., 1806, 5th edn., 1819–29; William M. Bythe-
wood and Thomas Jarman, *A selection of precedents . . . forming a system of conveyancing*,
10 v., 1821–34; 2nd edn., 10 v., 1829–35, index vol. by G. Sweet, 1836; James Stewart
The practice of conveyancing, 3 v., 1827–34, 2nd edn., 1832–40; Solomon Atkinson, *The
theory and practice of conveyancing*, 2 v., 1829, 2nd edn., 1829–41; John James Park,
*A treatise on the law of dower; particularly with a view to the modern practice of con-
veyancing*, 1819.

634 CHITTY (JOSEPH) *Snr*. A treatise on the game laws and on fisheries.
2 v. 1812. 2nd edn. 1826.

Comprehensive. See also Patrick Brady Leigh, *The game laws*, 1831, 2nd edn., 1838;
John Locke, *The game laws*, 1836, 3rd edn., 1849.

635 SIMPSON (ALFRED WILLIAM BRIAN). An introduction to the
history of the land law. 1961.

Bibliog. 262–5. Older works worth consulting are Sir Kenelm Edward Digby, *An introduction to the history of the law of real property*, Oxf., 1875, 5th edn., 1897; Jean E. R.
De Villiers, *The history of legislation concerning real and personal property in England
during the reign of Queen Victoria*, 1901; Sir William Searle Holdsworth, *An historical
introduction to the land law*, Oxf., 1927.

(f) *Tort*

636 WINFIELD (*Sir* PERCY HENRY). The province of the law of tort.
Camb. 1931.

Has some historical matter. Charles Greenstreet Addison, *Wrongs and their remedies;
being a treatise on the law of torts*, 1860, though primarily a statement of the law in about
1860, has many references to early nineteenth-century developments.

(g) *The Family*

637 CLANCY (JAMES). Rights, duties and liabilities of husband and wife,
at law and in equity. 1814. 3rd edn. 1827.

John Fraser MacQueen, *The rights and liabilities of husband and wife*, 1849.

638 MORGAN (HECTOR DAVIES). The doctrine and law of marriage,
adultery and divorce. Oxf. 1826.

Contains much legal information as well as theology.

(h) *Inheritance*

639 MITFORD (EARDLEY). The law of wills, codicils and revocations.
2nd edn. 1801. 6th edn. 1817.

A guide for the public as well as for practitioners. See also Roper Stote D. Roper,
A treatise upon the law of legacies, 1799, 4th edn. with addns. by H. H. White, 2 v.,
1847; William Roberts, *A treatise upon wills and codicils*, 1809, 3rd edn., 2 v., 1826,
suppl., 1837; Henry Sugden, *An essay on the law of wills as altered by the 1 Victoria, c. 26*,
1837; Thomas Jarman, *A treatise on wills*, 2 v., 1844.

640 TOLLER (*Sir* Samuel). The law of executors and administrators. 1800. 7th edn. 1838.

Sir Edward Vaughan Williams, *The law of executors and administrators*, 2 v., 1832, 4th edn., 1849.

641 SANDERS (FRANCIS WILLIAMS). An essay on the nature and laws of uses and trusts, including a treatise on conveyances at common law. 1791. 5th edn. 1844.

Thomas Lewin, *A practical treatise on the law of trusts and trustees*, 1837, 2nd edn., 1842.

(i) *Reform*

On the reform of the criminal law see (2581–2619). See also biographies of Bentham (2113), Brougham (207), Mackintosh (575), Romilly (576).

642 SOCIETY FOR PROMOTING the amendment of the law. Annual reports of the council. 1844–56.

See also the *Law Review* (558).

643 [ODGERS (WILLIAM BLAKE) *and others*]. A century of law reform: twelve lectures on the changes in the law of England during the nineteenth century. 1901.

See too Sir William Searle Holdsworth, 'The movement for reforms in the law, 1793–1832', *Law Quart. Rev.* 56 (1940), 33–48, 208–28, 340–53.

2. Ecclesiastical Law

644 BURN (RICHARD). The ecclesiastical law. 5th edn. 4 v. 1788. 9th edn. by Sir Robert J. Phillimore, 4 v. 1842.

645 PHILLIMORE (*Sir* ROBERT JOSEPH). The ecclesiastical law of the Church of England. 2 v. 1873, suppl. 1876; 2nd edn. 2 v. 1895.

A thorough, systematic survey, with a fair amount of historical material.

3. Equity

646 BALLOW (HENRY). A treatise of equity. Rev. and brought up to date by John Fonblanque. 2 v. 1793–4. 5th edn. 2 v. 1820.

The only textbook at the turn of the century. Charles Barton, *An historical treatise of a suit in equity*, 1796, was a guide for students, as was later George Goldsmith, *The doctrine and practice of equity*, 1838, 4th edn., 1849. Henry [Wilmot] Seton, *Forms of decrees in equity and orders connected therewith*, 1830, was standard. Critical was Ralph Barnes, *An inquiry into equity practice, and the law of real property, with a view to legislative revision*, 1827.

647 KERLY (*Sir* DUNCAN MACKENZIE). An historical sketch of the equitable jurisdiction of the Court of Chancery. Camb. 1890.

4. Maritime Law and Marine Insurance

See also Stowell (577).

648 [PLUMER] WARD (ROBERT). A treatise of the relative rights and duties of belligerent and neutral powers in maritime affairs. 1801.

A *pièce d'occasion* discussing the problems raised by the Armed Neutrality, as was also Sir Christopher Robinson, *Collectanea maritima: being a collection of public instruments . . . tending to illustrate the history and practice of prize law*, 1801. See too Domenico Alberto Azuni, *The maritime law of Europe*, tr. from the French [by William Johnson], 2 v., N.Y., 1806.

649 ABBOTT (CHARLES), 1st baron Tenterden. A treatise of the law relative to merchant ships and seamen. 1802. 8th edn. by William Shee. 1847.

The authoritative work, throughout this period.

650 MOORE (STUART ARCHIBALD). A history of the foreshore and the law relating thereto. 3rd edn. 1888.

651 PARK (*Sir* JAMES ALLAN). A system of the law of marine insurance, with three chapters on bottomry; on insurance on lives; and on insurance against fire. 1787, 8th edn. 1842.

A highly successful work, which systematized the decisions of Lord Mansfield. Also in good repute was Samuel Marshall, *A treatise on the law of insurance*, 2 v., 1802, 3rd edn., 1823. Later standard works were James Lees, *The laws of shipping and insurance*, 2nd edn., 1845, and Sir Joseph Arnould, *A treatise on the law of marine insurance and average*, 2 v., 1848.

5. Jurisprudence

652 BENTHAM. The works of Jeremy Bentham. Ed. by John Bowring. 11 v. 1838–43.

Especially: (a) *An introduction to the principles of morals and legislation* (v. 1, 1–154; also sep. imps., see (523); (b) *General view of a complete code of laws* (v. 3, 157–210); (c) *Principles of the civil code* (v. 1, 299–364); (d) *Principles of penal law* (v. 1, 365–580); (e) *The rationale of reward* (v. 2, 189–266); (f) *Introductory view of the rationale of evidence* (v. 6, 1–187); (g) *The rationale of judicial evidence* (v. 6, 189–585; v. 7, 1–644; also sep. imp. ed. by John Stuart Mill, 5 v., 1827). Other important legal writings published later from Bentham's MSS. are *The theory of legislation*, (trans. from the French of Etienne Dumont by Richard Hildreth) ed. with an introd. by Charles Kay Ogden, 1931, 1950; and *The limits of jurisprudence defined*, ed. Charles Warren Everett, N.Y., 1945, re-ed. in *Collected Works* under the title, *Of laws in general*, by H. L. A. Hart, 1970. See also George Williams Keeton and Georg Schwarzenberger, eds., *Jeremy Bentham and the law: a symposium*, 1948; and Sir William Holdsworth, 'Bentham's place in English legal history', *California Law Rev.* 28 (1940), 568–86. For Bentham's life see (2113) and for his political thought (523).

653 MACKINTOSH (*Sir* JAMES). A discourse on the study of the law of nature and nations. 1799. 5th edn. 1835.

654 BICHENO (JAMES EBENEZER). Observations on the philosophy of criminal jurisprudence; being an investigation of the principles necessary to be kept in view during the revision of the criminal code. 1819.

Other writers on this theme included John Thomas Barber Beaumont, *An essay on criminal jurisprudence, with the draft of a new penal code*, 1821; Anthony Hammond,

Sketch of a digest of the laws of England, with introductory essays on the science of natural jurisprudence, 1820, and *On the reduction to writing of the criminal law of England*, 1829. See also *Social history* (pp. 322–7).

655 AUSTIN (JOHN). The province of jurisprudence determined, *and* The use of the study of jurisprudence; with an introd. by Herbert Lionel Adolphus Hart. 1954.

Bibliog. note xix–xxi.

656 REDDIE (JAMES). Inquiries, elementary and historical, in the science of law. 1840. 2nd edn. 1847.

V

ECCLESIASTICAL HISTORY

A. CHURCH OF ENGLAND

1. SOURCES

(a) *Manuscripts*

Public Record Office: References to material will be found in the indexes to the following classes—Chancery; Home Office; Treasury.

Office of the Church Commissioners: Minute books, correspondence, and deeds of the Church Building Commissioners from 1818; the minute book of the Commissioners of Enquiry into the working of the ecclesiastical courts, 1830; minute books of the Commissioners of Enquiry into the ecclesiastical revenues of England and Wales, 1832; minute books, correspondence, and other papers of the Ecclesiastical Commission from 1836, including miscellaneous reports from parishes and pre-1836 estate records of the former ecclesiastical corporations (some of which have been dispersed to county record offices); minute books of Queen Anne's Bounty, with correspondence, deeds, and returns of 'poor' livings.

Diocesan Records. For a brief guide see Dorothy M. Owen, *The records of the established church, excluding parochial records*, British Records Assoc., Archives and the user, no. 1, 1970.

Lambeth Palace Library: (1) *archives*—records of the Archbishop of Canterbury and the Vicar General; Faculty Office; Court of Arches; Temporalities; Fulham Papers, being diocesan papers of the Bishop of London (but not including registers, which are at the Guildhall). See *Index to the Act Books of the archbishops of Canterbury, 1663–1859*, comp. by E. H. W. Dunkin, extended and ed. by Claude Jenkins and E. A. Fry (British Record Soc., Index Library, v. 55, 63), 2 v., 1929–38; Jane Houston, ed., *Index of cases in the records of the court of arches . . .*, 1972. (2) *manuscripts*—see E. G. W. Bill, comp., *Catalogue of manuscripts in Lambeth Palace Library. Manuscripts 1222–1860*, Oxf., 1972, and typescript catalogue at the Library for more recent accessions. (3) *deposits*—papers of John Keble, Isaac Williams, the Cambridge Camden Society's reports, and papers of the Incorporated Church Building Society, 1800–40 (not yet catalogued).

Some diocesan and archdiaconal records are now being more fully listed: see, F. W. Steer and Isabel M. Kirby, comps., *Diocese of Chichester. A catalogue of the records*, 2 v., Chichester, 1966–7, v. 1: *Bishop and archdeacons*; v. 2: *Dean and chapter*; Isabel M. Kirby, comp., *Diocese of Gloucester. A catalogue of the records*, 2 v., Gloucester, 1968, v. 1: *Bishop and archdeacons*; v. 2: *Dean and chapter*; and *Diocese of Bristol. A catalogue of the records of the bishop and archdeacons and of the dean and chapter*, Bristol, 1970; Buckinghamshire R.O.,

Records of the archdeaconry of Buckingham, Bucks. R.O., occasional publns. 2, Aylesbury, 1961.

(b) *Devotional and Critical Works*

See also under 5 (i) Evangelical Party, and 5 (iv) Tractarians.

657 MICHAELIS (JOHANN DAVID). Introduction to the New Testament. Trans. from the German by Herbert Marsh. 4 v. 1793–1801.

Its appearance provoked considerable controversy. Later works on biblical criticism include William Van Mildert, *An inquiry into the general principles of scripture-interpretation*, 1815; and Thomas Hartwell Horne, *Introduction to the critical study and knowledge of the holy scriptures*, 3 v., 1818–21.

658 WILBERFORCE (WILLIAM). A practical view of the prevailing religious system of professed Christians in the higher and middle classes, in this country, contrasted with real Christianity. 1797. 15th edn. 1824.

This may be regarded as the Evangelical party's manifesto in the Calvinistic controversy which convulsed the church at the turn of the century. See too John Overton, *The true churchman ascertained*, 1802. Charles Daubeny attacked Wilberforce in *A guide to the church*, 1798, and Overton in *Vindiciae Ecclesiae Anglicanae*, 1803. For other views see Sir Richard Hill, *An apology for brotherly love*, 1798, and James Bean, *Zeal without innovation*, 1808. George Pretyman Tomline, *A refutation of Calvinism*, 1811, 8th edn., 1823, was one of the most popular attacks on Calvinism within the church: it was answered in Thomas Scott, *Remarks on the refutation of Calvinism*, 2 v., 1811. See also Richard Mant, *Two tracts intended to convey correct notions of regeneration and conversion*, 1817, and Alexander Knox, *The doctrine respecting baptism held by the Church of England*, 1820.

659 VAN MILDERT (WILLIAM). An historical view of the rise and progress of infidelity, with a refutation of its principles and reasonings. 2 v. 1806.

An attack on scepticism, later taken up in Richard Whately, *Historic doubts relative to Napoleon Buonaparte*, 1819, Thomas Rennell, *Remarks on scepticism*, 1819, and Thomas Hartwell Horne, *Deism refuted; or, Plain reasons for being a Christian*, 1819.

660 MARSH (HERBERT). An inquiry into the consequences of neglecting to give the Prayer Book with the Bible. Camb. 1812.

This blow in the Calvinistic controversy in special reference to the British and Foreign Bible Society was answered in William Otter, *A vindication of churchmen who become members of the . . . Society*, Camb., 1812, and Isaac Milner, *Strictures on some of the publications of the Rev. Herbert Marsh*, 1813.

661 MILLER (JOHN). The divine authority of holy scripture asserted. Oxf. 1817.

662 BROWNE (ISAAC HAWKINS). Essays, religious and moral, 1815.

He also wrote *Essays on subjects of important enquiry in metaphysics, morals, and religion*, 1822.

663 RENNELL (THOMAS). Proofs of inspiration: or, The grounds of distinction between the New Testament and the apocryphal volume. 1822.

Other works on the theme of the inspired authority of scripture include John Davison, *Discourses on prophecy*, 1824; John Bird Sumner, *The evidence of Christianity derived*

from its nature and reception, 1824; Daniel Wilson, *The evidence of Christianity stated* ...
in a popular and practical manner, 2 v., 1828–30; Samuel Hinds, *An enquiry into the
proofs, nature, and extent of inspiration and into the authority of scripture*, Oxf., 1831.

664   ARNOLD (THOMAS). Sermons. 3 v. 1829–34.

665   JEBB (JOHN). Piety without asceticism; or, The Protestant Kempis. 1831.

An anthology for the guidance of churchmen. Jebb was in some respects a forerunner
of the Tractarians (section 5 (iv) below).

666   BURTON (EDWARD). Lectures upon the ecclesiastical history of the
first three centuries. Oxf. 2 v. 1831–3.

667   PALMER ([*Sir*] WILLIAM). Origines Liturgicae. Oxf. 1832.

A scholarly examination of a hitherto neglected subject. See also John Jebb, *The choral
service of the United Church of England and Ireland*, 1843; Benjamin Harrison, *Historical
enquiry into the true interpretation of the rubrics* ... *respecting the sermon and communion
service*, 1845.

668   SMITH (JOHN PYE). On the relation between the Holy Scriptures and
some parts of geological science. 1839.

An Independent who defended the discoveries of science against those who rejected
them on the ground of conflict with scripture.

669   JELF (RICHARD WILLIAM). An inquiry into the means of grace.
Oxf. 1844.

A definition of beliefs of the Church of England as contrasted with the beliefs of Protestant and Catholic dissent. Jelf was Principal of King's College London, 1844–68.

2. CONTEMPORARY REFERENCE WORKS

670   CLEAVER (WILLIAM). A list of books intended for the use of the
younger clergy and other students of divinity within the diocese of Chester.
Oxf. 1791. 2nd edn. 1792.

The duties of the clerical profession, Romsey, 1810, is a contemporary treatise on pastoral
theology. George Pretyman Tomline, *Elements of Christian theology*, 2 v., 1799, 12th
edn., 1818, was prepared especially for ordination candidates. For criticism of training
see Sir William Cockburn, *Strictures on clerical education in the university of Cambridge*,
1809. A later view of clerical duties is in William Hale Hale, *Duties of deacons and priests
compared*, 1850. Charles Lloyd's list of books in divinity recommended in 1828 to his
pupils, in J. Parker, *Biblioteca Parva Theologica*, 2 pt., 1851, provoked controversy.

671   THE CLERGYMAN'S ASSISTANT, or A collection of acts of parliament, forms and ordinances, relative to certain duties and rights of the parochial clergy. [Comp. by John Robinson]. 1806. 1822. 1828.

672   VALOR ECCLESIASTICUS temp. Hen. VIII auctoritate regia insti-
tutus. Ed. by J. Caley, with intro. and indexes by J. Hunter, 6 v. 1810–1834.

Still of service in the nineteenth century in establishing the claims to revenues of the
trustees of Queen Anne's bounty.

673 THE CLERICAL GUIDE, or ecclesiastical directory: containing a complete register of the prelates and other dignitaries of the church, a list of all the benefices . . . 1817. 1822. 1829. New edn. 1836.

The Clergy List, published annually from 1841, includes assistant clergy.

674 HODGSON (CHRISTOPHER). An account of the augmentation of small livings, by 'The governors of the Bounty of Queen Anne . . .' and of benefactions by corporate bodies and individuals, to the end of . . . 1825. 2 pts. 1826–35.

Contains lists of benefactors and of augmented livings.

675 MEMORIALS AND COMMUNICATIONS addressed to his late Majesty's commissioners of enquiry into the state of the established church . . . in 1836 and 1837. 1838.

676 TIMPSON (THOMAS). British ecclesiastical history. 1838.

A textbook, but, on late eighteenth and early nineteenth century topics, based on a rich collection of material. Edward Mahon Roose, *Ecclesiastica; or, the church, her schools, and her clergy*, 1842, includes short sketches of several divines of the early nineteenth century.

677 TAYLOR (WILLIAM COOKE). The bishop. A series of letters to a newly-created prelate. 1841.

An outline of a bishop's duties.

678 A COLLECTION OF THE LAWS AND CANONS of the church of England . . . Translated . . . with explanatory notes . . . by John Johnson . . . A new edn. with notes and a preface by John Baron. 2 v. Oxf. 1850–51.

679 CENSUS OF GREAT BRITAIN. 1851. Religious worship in England and Wales, abridged from the official report made by H. Mann. 1854.

See *Report on the 1851 census of religious worship*, P.P. (1852–3), LXXXIX; K. S. Inglis, 'Patterns of religious worship in 1851,' *J. of Eccles. Hist.* 11 (1960), 74–86. For other reports to parliament see the general indexes listed at (391).

680 LE NEVE (JOHN) *and* HARDY (THOMAS DUFFUS). Fasti ecclesiae anglicanae, or, A calendar of the principal ecclesiastical dignitaries in England and Wales, and of the chief officers in the universities of Oxford and Cambridge. 3 v. Oxf. 1854.

New edn. by Joyce M. Horn, 1969, in progress, v. 1: St. Paul's London; v. 2: Chichester diocese, covers 1541–1857.

3. JOURNALS, BIOGRAPHIES, AND COLLECTED WORKS

(Arranged roughly in chronological order of content)

681 HURD. The works of Richard Hurd. 8 v. 1811.

Francis Kilvert ed. *Memoirs of the life and writings of . . . Richard Hurd*. 1860.

682   HORSLEY. The charges of Samuel Horsley. Dundee. 1813.

H. Horsley edited *Sermons*, 2 v., Dundee, 1810, and *Speeches in parliament*, 2 v., Dundee, 1813. There is a life by Heneage H. Jebb, 1909.

683   BARRINGTON. Sermons, charges and tracts [of Shute Barrington]. 1811.

684   PORTEUS. The works of . . . Beilby Porteus, with his life by the Rev. Robert Hodgson. 6 v. 1811.

685   WATSON. Anecdotes of the life of Richard Watson, bishop of Llandaff; written by himself at different intervals, and revised in 1814. 1817. 2nd edn. 2 v. 1818.

He also wrote *Miscellaneous tracts on religious, political and agricultural subjects*, 2 v., 1815.

686   PALEY. The works of William Paley . . . with a life by Alexander Chalmers. 5 v. 1819. New edn. by Edmund Paley. 6 v. 1830.

G. W. Meadley ed. *Memoirs of William Paley*, 1809, 2nd edn., 1810.

687   BATHURST. Memoirs of the late Dr. Henry Bathurst, lord bishop of Norwich. 2 v. 1837.

Mrs. Tryphena Thistlethwayte, *Memoirs and correspondence of Dr. H. Bathurst, bishop of Norwich*, 1853.

688   PARR. Works of Samuel Parr, with memoirs of his life and writings. By John Johnstone. 8 v. 1828.

William Field, *Memoirs . . . of Samuel Parr*, 2 v., 1888.

689   KNOX. Remains of Alexander Knox. [Ed. by J. J. Hornby]. 4 v. 1834-7.

Charles Forster ed. *Thirty years correspondence between John Jebb and Alexander Knox*, 2 v., 1834.

690   VAN MILDERT. Sermons . . . and charges of William Van Mildert . . . to which is prefixed a memoir of the author. By Cornelius Ives. 1838.

691   WATSON. Memoir of Joshua Watson. By Edward Churton. 2 v. 1861.

Alan Brunskill Webster, *Joshua Watson: the story of a layman, 1771-1855*, 1954.

692   SMITH. The letters of Sydney Smith. Ed. by Nowell C. Smith. 2 v. Oxf. 1953.

Smith's *Works*, were pub., 4 v., 1839-40. The letters of *Peter Plymley*, ed. by George C. Heseltine, 1929, were originally written by him in support of Catholic emancipation. Stuart J. Reid, *A sketch of the life and times of the Rev. Sydney Smith*, 2 v., 1884, was based on family documents and the recollections of personal friends. Other lives are by George W. E. Russell, 1905, Osbert Burdett, 1934, Hesketh Pearson, 1934.

693   CAREY. The diocese of Exeter in 1821: Bishop Carey's replies to queries before visitation. Ed. by Michael Cook. (Devon and Cornwall Record Society, n.s. 3, 4.) 2 v. Exeter. 1958-60.

V. 1: Cornwall; v. 2: Devon.

694 RICHMOND. A memoir of . . . Legh Richmond. By Thomas Shuttleworth Grimshaw. 1828.

The author of *Annals of the poor*, 1826. For other illustrations of clerical life, see *Memoir of the Rev. John George Breay . . . prebendary of Lichfield*, by a member of his congregation, 2nd edn., 1841; John Freeman, *Life of the Rev. William Kirby*, 1852; *The diary of the Rev. William Jones* (2077); *The journal of . . . John Skinner* (2291).

695 KAYE. The works of John Kaye, bishop of Lincoln. 8 v. 1888.

Includes a memoir by W. F. J. Kaye.

696 COPLESTON. Memoir of Edward Copleston, bishop of Llandaff, with selections from his diary and correspondence. By Will. James Copleston. 1851.

Copleston was a champion of church restoration. Richard Whately, ed., *Remains of the late Edward Copleston*, 1854.

697 PHILLPOTTS. The life, times, and writings of Dr. H. Phillpotts, lord bishop of Exeter. By Reginald Neale Shutte. 1863.

Unfinished, ending at 1832; see George C. B. Davies, *Henry Phillpotts, bishop of Exeter, 1778–1869*, 1954. Important aspects of Phillpotts's career are discussed in Richard Stanton Lambert, *The Cobbett of the West. A study of Thomas Latimer and the struggle between press and pulpit at Exeter*, 1939, and John C. S. Nias, *Gorham and the bishop of Exeter*, 1951. See Boggis (3563).

698 STANLEY. Addresses and charges of Edward Stanley . . . bishop of Norwich, with a memoir by his son, Arthur Penrhyn Stanley, 1851.

As bishop Stanley was a vigorous reformer. His son also ed. *Memoirs of Edward and Catherine Stanley*, 1879.

699 HORNE. Reminiscences personal and bibliographical of Thomas Hartwell Horne. With notes by his daughter, Sarah A. Cheyne, and a short introduction by J. B. M'Caul. 1862.

700 BLOMFIELD. Bishop Blomfield and his times. An historical sketch. By George Edward Biber. 1857.

Church building in greater London owed much to his drive. See too *Memoir of Charles James Blomfield, bishop of London, with selections from his correspondence*, ed. by his son, Alfred Blomfield, 2 v., 1863.

701 WHATELY. The life and correspondence of Richard Whately, D.D., late Archbishop of Dublin. By Elizabeth Jane Whately. 2 v. 1866.

On Whately's career at Dublin see also Fitzpatrick (4255).

702 BULL. Parson Bull of Byerley. By John Clifford Gill. 1963.

Excellent on the parish career of the Rev. George Stringer Bull; for his association with the Ten Hours movement see (1725).

703 LONSDALE. The life of John Lonsdale, bishop of Lichfield; with some of his writings. By Edmund Beckett Denison. 1868.

703A SUMNER. Life of Charles Richard Sumner, D.D., bishop of Winchester during a forty years episcopate. By George Henry Sumner. 1876.

704 THIRLWALL. Letters literary and theological of Connop Thirlwall. Ed. by John J. S. Perowne and Louis Stokes. 1881.

Perowne also ed. *Remains literary and theological of Connop Thirlwall*, 3 v., 1877–8. See too *Letters to a friend . . .*, ed. by A. P. Stanley, dean of Westminster, 1881, and J. C. Thirlwall (3864).

705 STOWELL. Memoirs of the life and labours of the Rev. Hugh Stowell. By John Buxton Marsden. 1868.

706 HOOK. The life and letters of Walter Farquhar Hook. By William R. W. Stephens. 2 v. 1878.

707 MAURICE. The life of Frederick Denison Maurice, chiefly told in his own letters. Ed. by [John] Frederick Maurice. 2 v. 1884. Repr. 1972.

Gives a full list of his works. Other lives by C. F. G. Masterman, 1907, Olive J. Brose, 1972. Augustus J. C. Hare, *Memorials of a quiet life*, 3 v., 18th edn., 1884, and *Story of my life*, 6 v., 1896–1900, include material about the Maurice circle. Maurice's influence is discussed in J. S. Lidgett, *The Victorian transformation of theology*, 1934. See also Walter M. Davies, *An introduction to F. D. Maurice's theology*, 1964. F. M. McClain, *Maurice: man and moralist*, 1972. See also Gloyn (718), Christensen (722).

708 WILBERFORCE. The letter-books of Samuel Wilberforce, 1843–68. Transcribed and ed. by R. K. Pugh, with the assistance of J. F. A. Mason. (Oxford Record Soc. Publns. 47.) Oxf. 1970.

Mainly about his Oxford episcopate. A. R. Ashwell and R. G. Wilberforce, *Life of . . . Samuel Wilberforce . . . with selections from his diary and correspondence*, 3 v., 1880–2, is indispensable; see also S. Meacham, *Lord Bishop; the life of Samuel Wilberforce, 1805–1873*, 1970; D. Newsome, *The parting of friends; A study of the Wilberforces and Henry Manning*, 1966.

709 NEALE. The influence of John Mason Neale. By Arthur Geoffrey Lough. 1962.

Lists Neale's published works; he was a founder of the Cambridge Camden Soc.—see (729).

710 HAMPDEN. Some memorials of Renn Dickson Hampden. Ed. by Henrietta Hampden. 1871.

711 WORDSWORTH (CHARLES). Annals of my early life, 1806–1846. 1891.

W. E. Hodgson, ed., Wordsworth's *Annals of my life, 1847–1856*, 1893.

4. LATER WORKS

712 STOUGHTON (JOHN). Religion in England from 1800 to 1850: a history, with a postscript on subsequent events. 2 v. 1884.

A valuable continuation of his *Religion in England under Queen Anne and the Georges, 1702–1800*, 2 v., 1878. These works also appeared as part of a general series, 8 v., 1901.

713 PROBY (WILLIAM HENRY BAPTIST). Annals of the 'Low-Church' Party in England down to the death of Archbishop Tait. 2 v. 1888.

Critical and unsympathetic but informative.

714 OVERTON (JOHN HENRY). The English church in the nineteenth century, 1800–33. 1894.

High-Church bias, but excellent. For the years just before 1800 see J. H. Overton and F. Relton, *The English church . . . (1714–1800)*, 1906; C. J. Abbey and J. H. Overton, *The English church in the eighteenth century*, 2 v., 1878; C. J. Abbey, *The English church and its bishops, 1700–1800*, 2 v., 1887. A. W. Rowden, *The primates of the four Georges*, 1916, is useful but has inaccuracies. R. B. McDowell discusses 'The Anglican episcopate, 1780–1945', in *Theology*, 50 (1947), 202–9.

715 CORNISH (FRANCIS WARRE). History of the English church in the nineteenth century. 2 v. 1910.

The old standard work. See too L. Elliott-Binns, *Religion in the Victorian era*, 2nd edn., 1964.

716 HUNT (JOHN). Religious thought in England in the nineteenth century. 1896.

A valuable outline. See too V. F. Storr, *The development of English theology in the nineteenth century, 1800–1860*, 1913. Daniel H. M. Davies, *Worship and theology in England*, v. 3: *From Watts and Wesley to Maurice*, Princeton, 1961, is excellent. See also B. M. G. Reardon, *From Coleridge to Gore; a century of religious thought in Britain*, 1971. On Coleridge see J. D. Boulger, *Coleridge as a religious thinker*, New Haven, 1961, and J. R. Barth, *Coleridge and Christian doctrine*, Camb., Mass., 1969. On British reactions to the religious ideas of Lamennais, see William G. Roe, *Lamennais and England*, 1966.

717 ALLEN (WILLIAM OSBORN BIRD) and McCLURE (EDMUND). Two hundred years: the history of the Society for Promoting Christian Knowledge, 1698–1898. 1898.

W. K. L. Clarke, *A history of the SPCK*, 1959. His *Eighteenth century piety*, [1944], includes essays relating to the later years of George III's reign.

718 CARPENTER (SPENCER CECIL). Church and people, 1789–1889. A history of the Church of England from William Wilberforce to 'Lux Mundi'. 1933.

For other treatment see Cyril E. Hudson and M. B. Reckitt, *The church and the world: v. 3: church and society in England from 1800*, 1940; C. K. Gloyn, *The church in the social order. A study of Anglican social theory from Coleridge to Maurice*, Forest Grove, Oregon, 1942; C. R. Sanders, *Coleridge and the Broad Church Movement*, Durham, N.C., 1942; R. A. Soloway, *Prelates and people; ecclesiastical social thought in England, 1783–1852*, 1969; G. Kitson Clark, *Churchmen and the condition of England, 1832–1885*, 1973.

719 FLOYER (JOHN KESTELL). Studies in the history of English church endowments. 1917.

W. R. Le Fanu, *Queen Anne's Bounty. A short account of its history and work*, 2nd edn. rev. by Fred. G. Hughes, 1933, is a useful outline. G. F. A. Best, *Temporal pillars; Queen Anne's Bounty, the Ecclesiastical Commissioners, and the Church of England*, Camb., 1964, is excellent.

720 CAMERON (ALLAN THOMAS). The religious communities of the church of England. 1918.

See also Thomas J. Williams, *Priscilla Lydia Sellon; The restorer after three centuries of the religious life in the English church*, 1965, and T. J. Williams and A. W. Campbell, *The Park Village sisterhood*, 1965.

721 PROCTOR (FRANCIS). A new history of the Book of Common Prayer. Rev. by Walter Howard Frere. 3rd impr. corr. 1925.

R. C. D. Jasper, *Prayer Book revision in England, 1800–1900,* 1954.

722 CHRISTENSEN (TORBEN). The origin and history of Christian socialism, 1848–54. Aarhus. 1962.

C. E. Raven, *Christian socialism, 1848–1854,* 1920; N. C. Masterman, *John Malcolm Ludlow: the builder of Christian socialism,* 1963. See also (535).

723 LONGDEN (HENRY ISHAM). Northamptonshire and Rutland clergy from 1500. 16 v. Northampton. 1938–52.

A monumental biographical dictionary, of far more than merely local interest.

724 CROSS (FRANK LESLIE). The Oxford dictionary of the Christian church. Rev. rep. 1958.

Also valuable for reference is Sidney L. Ollard and Gordon Crosse, *A dictionary of English church history,* 1912, 3rd rev. edn. 1948.

725 BROWN (CHARLES KENNETH FRANCIS). History of the English clergy, 1800–1900. 1953.

Standard; good bibliog. On particular aspects see Fred. W. B. Bullock, *A history of training for the ministry of the church of England in England and Wales from 1800–1874,* St. Leonards, 1955; Diana McClatchey, *Oxfordshire clergy, 1777–1869. A study of the established church, and of the role of its clergy in local society,* Oxf. 1960.

726 MATTHEWS (WALTER ROBERT) *and* ATKINS (WILLIAM MAYNARD) *eds.* A history of St. Paul's cathedral and the men associated with it. 1957.

George L. Prestige, *St. Paul's in its glory . . . 1831–1911,* 1955.

727 PORT (MICHAEL HARRY). Six hundred new churches. A study of the church building commission, 1818–1856, and its church building activities. 1961.

728 ARNOLD (RALPH). The Whiston matter. The Reverend Robert Whiston versus the Dean and Chapter of Rochester. 1961.

An account of a dispute about administration of chapter funds.

729 WHITE (JAMES FLOYD). The Cambridge movement; the ecclesiologists and the Gothic revival. Camb. 1962.

Bibliog. 237–53. Discusses the influence of the Cambridge Camden Society, formed 1839. See also Neale (709). For a more general look at the role of the universities see V. H. H. Green, *Religion at Oxford and Cambridge,* 1964.

730 CHADWICK (WILLIAM OWEN). The Victorian Church. 2 v. 1966–70.

V. 1: 1829–59, bibliog. 575–83. The best up-to-date survey. A. R. Vidler, *The church in an age of revolution; 1789 to the present day,* 1962, is more general in treatment.

731 RANSOME (MARY) *ed.* The state of the bishopric of Worcester, 1782–1808. (Worcestershire Hist. Soc., n.s., v. 6). Birmingham. 1968.

732 EDWARDS (DAVID LAWRENCE). Leaders of the Church of England, 1828–1944. 1971.

On the Arnolds, Newman, Keble, Wilberforce, Shaftesbury, and Maurice. A. R. Vidler, *F. D. Maurice and company; nineteenth century studies*, 1966, discusses Coleridge, Hare, and others.

5. Special Subjects

(a) *The Evangelical Party and its Critics*

See Wilberforce (151), Buxton (2601).

For the beginnings of the Evangelical movement, see Pargellis and Medley (2), p. 101.

(i) *Contemporary Works, Memoirs, Correspondence*

733 HILL. The life of . . . Rowland Hill. Ed. by Edwin Sidney. 1834. 5th edn. 1861.

Vernon J. Charlesworth, *Rowland Hill, his life, anecdotes, and pulpit-sayings*, 1876.

734 CECIL. The works of . . . Richard Cecil, with a memoir of his life. By Josiah Pratt. 4 v. 1811. Another edn. 1854.

735 MORE. Works of . . . Hannah More. 8 v. 1801. Other edns. 19 v. 1818. 11 v. 1830. 6 v. 1834.

See (2122).

736 MILNER. The life of Isaac Milner, dean of Carlisle . . . comprising a portion of his correspondence and other writings hitherto unpublished. Ed. by Mary Milner. 1842.

737 RAIKES. Robert Raikes: the man and his work. Biographical notes collected by Josiah Harris. Unpublished letters by Robert Raikes. Letters from the Raikes family. Ed. by J. Henry Harris. 1899.

Alfred Gregory, *Robert Raikes, journalist and philanthropist*, 1877, is perhaps the best biog. There is Raikes corr. in Joseph Ivimey, *Memoir of W. Fox . . . founder of the Sunday-school society*, 1831.

738 SCOTT. The works of . . . Thomas Scott. Edited by John Scott. 10 v. 1823–25.

739 BURGESS. The life of Thomas Burgess . . . bishop of Salisbury. By John Scandrett Harford. 1840.

740 SIMEON. Memoirs of the life of . . . Charles Simeon . . . with a selection from his writings and correspondence. Ed. by William Carus. Camb. and London, 1847.

Abner W. Brown, *Recollections of the conversation parties of the Rev. C. Simeon*, 1863. There is a life by Handley Carr Glynn Moule, 1892. See too Harriet Scolefield, *Memoir of . . . James Scolefield . . . Regius Professor of Greek*, 1855; Scolefield was a contemporary of Simeon at Cambridge.

741 PHILPOT. The seceders, 1829–1869: the story of a spiritual awakening as told in the letters of J. C. Philpot and W. Tiptaft. Ed. by J. H. Philpot. 2 v. 1930.

742 PRATT. Memoir of the Rev. Josiah Pratt. By Josiah and John Henry Pratt. 1849.

He was secretary to the C.M.S. 1802–24. For another leading figure in the society see Thomas Rawson Birks, *Memoir of the Rev. E. Bickersteth*, 2 v., 1852.

743 COX (ROBERT). Liturgy revised. 1830.

An expression of evangelical desire for alterations, including the exclusion of the Athanasian creed; see too Charles Nourse Wodehouse, *Petition to the House of Lords for Ecclesiastical Improvements*, 1832.

744 STEPHEN (JAMES). Essays in ecclesiastical biography and other subjects. 2 v. 1849. 4th edn. 1860.

Authoritative on the evangelical party in the early years of the century. For some later figures see Mary Seeley, *The later evangelical fathers*, 1879. John Campbell Colquhoun, *William Wilberforce: his friends and his times*, 1866, is a valuable supplement to Stephen; see too (151) and John Scandrett Harford, *Recollections of William Wilberforce*, 1864. John King, *Memoir of the Rev. T. Dykes*, 1849, deals with evangelicalism in Hull and district. James Jerram, *The Memoirs and a selection from the letters of the . . . Rev. C. Jerram*, 1855, is among the best accounts of the evangelicals of the second generation.

(ii) *Later Works*

745 OVERTON (JOHN HENRY). The evangelical revival in the eighteenth century. 1886.

A standard account which includes much material for the period after 1800. Other treatments are George Reginald Balleine, *A history of the evangelical party in the church of England*, 1908, and Leonard Elliott-Binns, *The evangelical movement in the English church*, 1928. Charles Hugh Egerton Smyth, *Simeon and church order*, Camb., 1940, surveys the movement in Cambridge. Stanley Brown-Serman, 'The evangelicals and the Bible', *Hist. Mag. Protestant Episcopal Church*, 12 (1943), 157–79, deals with the teaching of Scott and Simeon. Ernest Marshall Howse, *Saints in politics*, 1952, discusses the 'Clapham sect'. John Stewart Reynolds, *The Evangelicals at Oxford, 1735–1871: a record of an unchronicled movement*, Oxf., 1953, is destructive of ill-based generalizations by earlier scholars. See Brown (2506), Heasman (2507).

746 VENN (JOHN). Annals of a clerical family. 1904.

A valuable biographical approach to the story of the movement. Marcus Lawrence Loane, *Oxford and the evangelical succession*, 1950, and *Cambridge and the evangelical succession*, 1952, are studies of religious leaders in the universities. Arthur Skevington Wood, *Thomas Haweis, 1734–1820*, 1957, is a valuable work of reference but uninteresting as biography. See also S. Meacham, *Henry Thornton of Clapham, 1760–1815*, Camb., Mass., 1964; David Spring, 'The Clapham Sect: some social and political aspects', *Victorian Studies* 5 (1961–2), 35–48.

(b) *Church, State, and Reform*

(i) *Sources*

747 A REPORT from the clergy of a district in the diocese of Lincoln, convened for the purpose of considering the state of religion in the several parishes of the said district. 1800.

A reactionary early move for 'reconstruction'; followed later by *The state of the established church; in a series of letters to . . . Spencer Perceval*, 2nd edn. 1810; and Richard Yates, *The church in danger*, 1815.

748 [BERENS (EDWARD)]. Church reform. By a churchman. 1828.

Further pamphlet discussion followed: John Acaster, *The church in danger from herself*, 1829, and *Remedies for the church in danger*, 1830; Edward Burton, *Thoughts upon the demand for church reform*, Oxf., 1831, and *Sequel to remarks upon church reform*, 1832; Lord Robert Henley, *A plan of church reform*, 1832; Thomas Arnold, *Principles of church reform*, 1833; Uvedale Price, *Reform without reconstruction . . . without legislative interference*, 1833. Whig policy provoked argument on a number of topics: Samuel Roffey Maitland, *The Translation of bishops*, 1834; William Lisle Bowles, *The patronage of the English bishops*, 1836, and *A final defence of the rights of patronage in deans and chapters*, 1838; Charles H. Elsley, *Church leases considered*, 1837; William Selwyn, *The substance of an argument . . . against those clauses of the benefices pluralities bill, which confer additional powers on the ecclesiastical commissioners*, 1838; Sydney Smith, *A letter to Lord John Russell . . . on the church bills*, 1838; Newton Smart, *The ecclesiastical commission considered*, 1839; Robert Isaac Wilberforce, *Church courts and discipline*, 1843; William Wellwood Stoddart, *The royal supremacy in the church with reference to the appellate jurisdiction*, 1851.

749 HOUSE OF COMMONS. Reports of commissioners on the state of the Established Church, with reference to duties and revenues. First R., 1835 (54) XXII. 1; second R., 1836 (86) XXXVI. 1; third R., 1836 (280) XXXVI. 47; fourth R. 1836 (387) XXXVI. 67.

750 PALMER (WILLIAM). A treatise on the Church of Christ. 1838.

This work was regarded by contemporaries as an outstanding statement of the claims of the church to support from the state. Palmer also wrote, *An enquiry into the possibility of obtaining means for church extension without parliamentary grant*, 1841, and *A renewed enquiry . . .*, 1848, on the same subject.

751 ACTS RELATING TO THE ECCLESIASTICAL COMMISSIONERS FOR ENGLAND. 1846.

Orders in council ratifying schemes of the ecclasiastical commissioners for England [and Wales], 15 v., 1836–62; a general index up to 1854 was pub. in 1855.

752 FINAL REPORT of the Metropolis Churches' Fund from July 1836 to May 1854. 1854.

(ii) *Later Works*

753 SCULLY (FRANCIS MICHAEL). L'évolution de l'opinion anglaise sur les rapports entre l'église établie d'Angleterre et l'état à l'époque des réformes 1829–1839. Paris. 1938.

See too Alex. R. Vidler, *The orb and the cross. A normative study in the relations of church and state with reference to Gladstone's early writings*, 1945.

754 BROSE (OLIVE JOHNSON). Church and parliament. The reshaping of the church of England, 1828–1860. 1959.

William Law Mathieson, *English church reform, 1815–40*, 1923, discusses the earlier years but is less thorough. For particular aspects see A. C. Wood, ed., 'Clerical non-residence in Nottinghamshire, 1803–1838', *Thoroton Soc. Rec. ser.* 11, pt. 1 (Nottingham, 1943), 43–67; P. J. Welch, 'Bishop Blomfield and church extension in London' and 'Contemporary views on the proposals for the alienation of capitular property in England (1832–1840)', *J. Eccles. Hist.* 4 (1953), 203–15, 5 (1954), 184–95; O. J. Brose, 'The Irish precedent for English church reform: the church temporalities Act of 1833', *ibid.* 7 (1956), 204–25; P. J. Welch, 'Blomfield and Peel: a study in cooperation between church and state, 1841–1846', *ibid.* 12 (1961), 71–84.

755 THOMPSON (KENNETH ALFRED). Bureaucracy and church reform; the organizational response of the Church of England to social change, 1800– 1965. 1970.

Bibliog. 422–53; useful though some failures of insight on the early nineteenth century.

(c) *Tithes*

(i) *Sources*

756 COVE (MORGAN). An essay on the revenues of the church of England; with an enquiry into the necessity, justice, and policy of an abolition or com- mutation of tithes. 1795. 3rd edn. greatly enl. 1816.

See too James Miller, *A letter to . . . Earl Grey . . . on the origin and nature of church property and the connexion of tithes with . . . agricultural distress,* 1831, one of many pamphlets provoked by the Whig tithe bill.

(ii) *Later Works*

757 EASTERBY (WILLIAM). The history of the law of tithes in England. Camb. 1888.

An able exposition of the legal intricacies of the subject. Henry William Clark, *A history of tithes,* 1891, 2nd edn., 1894, includes information on ecclesiastical finance. Henry Lansdell, *The sacred tenth; or, Studies in tithe-giving ancient and modern,* 2 v., Brighton and N.Y., 1906, is biased but has a useful bibliog. A few other bibliog. notes will be found in W. Harold Maxwell, *Catalogue of modern law books,* 1895. W. R. Ward, 'The tithe question in England in the early nineteenth century', *J. Eccles. Hist.* 16 (1965), 67–81. See also (1673).

758 CORMACK (ALEXANDER ALLAN). Teinds and agriculture, an historical survey. Oxf. 1930.

On tithe in Scotland; extensive bibliog.

(d) *The Tractarians and their Opponents*

(i) *Sources*

759 HUGH. Nineteenth century pamphlets at Pusey House; an introduction for the prospective user. By Father Hugh. 1961.

E. R. Fairweather, ed., *The Oxford Movement,* N.Y., 1964, is a good collection of the main sources.

760 TRACTS FOR THE TIMES. 6 v. 1838–41.

761 NEWMAN (JOHN HENRY). The prophetical office of the church viewed relatively to Romanism and popular Protestantism. 1837.

The classical defence of the church of England as the 'via media'. His *Essay on the development of doctrine*, 1845, marked the transfer of his loyalty to Rome. His *Apologia pro vita sua*, 1864 (also ed. with an intro. by Wilfrid Ward, 1913, and by Martin J. Svaglic, Oxf. 1967) is a deeply revealing account.

762 PALMER (WILLIAM). A narrative of events connected with the publication of Tracts for the Times, with reflections on existing tendencies to Romanism. 1843. Rev. enl. edn. 1883.

763 WARD (WILLIAM GEORGE). The ideal of a Christian church considered in comparison with existing practice. 1844.

In part a rejoinder to William Palmer's *Narrative*.

764 MOLESWORTH (JOHN EDWARD NASSAU). Remarks upon the cases of Dr. Hampden and the Revd. J. P. Lee, in reference to a proposed modification of the law of electing bishops . . . 1848.

765 CHURCH (RICHARD WILLIAM). On the relations between church and state. Rep. 1881.

(ii) *Correspondence, Memoirs, Biography*

766 FROUDE. Remains of the late reverend R[ichard] H[urrell] F[roude], M.A. Ed. by J. H. Newman and J. Keble. 2 v. 1838.

Louise Imogen Guiney, *Hurrell Froude*, 1904.

767 FABER. The life and letters of Frederick William Faber. By John Edward Bowden. 1869.

A recent reassessment based on Faber's papers in the London Oratory is Ronald Chapman, *Father Faber*, 1961.

768 KEBLE. A memoir of John Keble. By Sir John Taylor Coleridge. 1869.

There are lives by Walter Lock, 1893, Lord Irwin, 1932, and Kenneth Ingram, 1933. See too [E.] Georgina Battiscombe, *John Keble, a study in limitations*, 1963.

769 DENISON (GEORGE ANTHONY). Notes of my life, 1805–1878. 1878.

Denison was at Oriel Coll. at the beginning of the movement.

770 MOZLEY (THOMAS). Reminiscences chiefly of Oriel College and the Oxford Movement. 2 v. 1882.

By Newman's brother-in-law. See too Anne Mozley, ed. *Letters of the Rev. J. B. Mozley, D.D.*, 1885.

771 PATTISON (MARK). Memoirs. 1885.

F. C. Montague, 'Some early letters of Mark Pattison', *Bull. John Rylands L.* 18 (1934), 156–76.

772 TAIT. The life of Archibald Campbell Tait, Archbishop of Canterbury. By Randall Thomas Davidson and William Benham. 2 v. 1891.

Tait, while at Oxford, was a broad-minded observer of the movement but condemned Tract 90.

773   STANLEY. The life and correspondence of Arthur Penrhyn Stanley, D.D. by Rowland E. Prothero. 2 v. 1893.

See also George Granville Bradley, *Recollections of Arthur Penrhyn Stanley*, 1883.

774   WILLIAMS. The autobiography of Isaac Williams, B.D. Ed. by Sir George Prevost. 1892.

Owain W. Jones, *Isaac Williams and his circle*, 1971.

775   PUSEY. The life of Edward Bouverie Pusey. By Henry Parry Liddon. 4 v. 1893–7.

There are also lives by G. W. E. Russell, 1907, and Leonard Prestige, 1933.

776   CHURCH. The life and letters of Dean Church. By Mary C. Church. 1894.

Basil Alec Smith, *Dean Church. The Anglican response to Newman*, 1958, is a scholarly survey.

777   BLACHFORD. The letters of Frederick [Rogers] Lord Blachford. Ed. by G. E. Marindin. 1896.

778   TUCKWELL (W.). Reminiscences of Oxford. 1901.

779   NEWMAN. The letters and correspondence of John Henry Newman during his life in the English Church. Edited by Anne Mozley. 2 v. 1891.

Still the standard printed source for the Anglican period. See too *Correspondence of John Henry Newman with John Keble and others, 1839–1845*, ed. by Fathers of the Birmingham Oratory, 1917. *The letters and diaries of John Henry Newman*, XI: *Littlemore to Rome, October 1845 to December 1846*, ed. by Charles Stephen Dessain, 1961, is the first vol. of a projected series providing a full edition in 20 v. for the Catholic period, to be followed by 10 for the Anglican period; the editing is of the highest standard. See also (2289).

780   NEWMAN. Young Mr. Newman. By Maisie Ward. 1948.

A full survey of Newman's career up to 1845, based on his papers at the Birmingham Oratory. Sean O'Faolain, *Newman's Way*, 1952, adds fresh material about Newman's family background. See too Meriol Trevor, *Newman. The pillar of the cloud*, 1962, v. 1 of a 2-v. biography, which takes his career up to 1853. Wilfrid Ward, *The life of John Henry Cardinal Newman*, 2 v., 1912, is cursory on the Anglican period. Various aspects are discussed in C. F. Harrold, *John Henry Newman. An expository and critical study of his mind, thought, and art*, 1945; R. D. Middleton, *Newman at Oxford: his religious development*, 1950; Terence Kenny, *The political thought of John Henry Newman*, 1957; S. J. Coulson, A. M. Allchin, and Meriol Trevor, *Newman; a portrait restored*, 1965; S. J. Coulson and A. M. Allchin, eds., *The rediscovery of Newman; an Oxford symposium*, 1967; S. J. Coulson, *Newman and the common tradition*, Oxf., 1970. S. C. Dessain, *John Henry Newman*, 1966, is excellent. See also R. W. Greaves, 'Golightly and Newman, 1824–1845', *J. Eccles. Hist.* 9 (1958), 209–28; William Robbins, *The Newman Brothers*, 1966.

(iii) *Later Works*

781   BROWNE (EDWARD GEORGE KIRWAN). History of the Tractarian movement. Dublin. 1856.

He also pub. a rev. form, *Annals of the Tractarian movement from 1842 to 1860*, 1861.

782 CHURCH (RICHARD WILLIAM). The Oxford Movement: twelve years, 1833–1845. 1891.

Excellent, combining scholarship and personal recollection. See too James Anthony Froude, 'The Oxford counter-reformation', in *Short studies on great subjects*, v. 4, 1885.

783 FABER (GEOFFREY). Oxford Apostles. 1933.

An able analysis from a secular point of view, which was challenged in Christopher Dawson, *The spirit of the Oxford Movement*, 1933. Also excellent is Yngve Brilioth, *The Anglican revival*, 1925. See too S. L. Ollard, *A short history of the Oxford movement*, 1915; Charles P. S. Clarke, *The Oxford movement and after*, 1932. Robert Dudley Middleton, *Magdalen Studies*, 1936, is a study of the leaders of the movement.

784 PECK (WILLIAM GEORGE). The social implications of the Oxford movement. N.Y. 1933.

Edmund Arbuthnott Knox, *The Tractarian movement, 1833–1845*, 1933, examines the movement in a European setting. See too Henry R. T. Brandreth, *Œcumenical ideals of the Oxford movement*, 1947, and *Dr. Lee of Lambeth: a chapter in parenthesis in the history of the Oxford movement*, 1951. Owen Chadwick, ed., *The mind of the Oxford Movement*, 1960, a valuable anthology.

785 HÄRDELIN (ALF). The tractarian understanding of the eucharist. Stockholm. 1965.

Bibliog. 345–61; a careful and detailed study. See also T. Dearing, *Wesleyan and Tractarian worship; an ecumenical study*, 1966.

B. NONCONFORMITY

1. General

(a) *Sources*

786 EVANS (JOHN). A sketch of the denominations into which the Christian world is divided; accompanied with a persuasive to religious moderation. 1795. 9th edn. 1807.

787 KINGSBURY (WILLIAM). An apology for village preachers; or an account of the proceedings and motives of protestant dissenters and serious Christians of other denominations, in their attempts to suppress infidelity and vice, and to spread vital religion in country places . . . with . . . replies to objections. 1798.

Job Orton, *Letters to dissenting ministers*, 2 v., 1806, was concerned with failure to maintain influence among the congregations.

788 THE EVANGELICAL MAGAZINE. V. 1+. 1793+.

The organ of the new evangelical nonconformity. Cont. after 1812 as *The Evangelical Magazine and Missionary Chronicle*, index to first 24 v., 1817. Periodical sources become abundant in this period: see *The Protestant Dissenter's Magazine*, 6 v., 1794–9; *The Eclectic Review*, 1805+; and *The British Review and London Critical Journal*, 23 v., 1811–25; also under different denominations.

789 BOGUE (DAVID) *and* BENNETT (JAMES). A history of the dissenters from the revolution in 1688 to the year 1808. 4 v. 1808-12. 2nd edn. by J. Bennett. 2 v. 1833.

Bennett continued the work with a vol. on the period 1808-38, 1839.

790 WILSON (WALTER). The history and antiquities of dissenting churches and meeting houses in London, Westminster, and Southwark; including the lives of their ministers, from the rise of nonconformity to the present time. 4 v. 1808-14.

791 A SKETCH of the history and proceedings of the deputies appointed to protect the civil rights of the Protestant dissenters. To which is annexed a summary of the laws affecting Protestant dissenters. With an appendix of statutes and precedents and legal instruments. 1814.

792 DR. WILLIAMS'S LIBRARY, LONDON. Catalogue of the Library . . . founded pursuant to the will of . . . Daniel Williams . . . who died in the year 1716. 2 v. 1841.

V. 1, author cat. of books, v. 2, author cat. of tracts, pamphlets, sermons, etc. A third vol. with two supplements 1870-85 lists accessions to 1885, including material printed before 1841. Doris M. Johnson, ed., *Catalogue of accessions . . . 1900-1950* (1955) and Inez Elliott, *Catalogue of accessions . . . 1951-1960* (1961). The Library (now in Gordon Square, London, W.C.1) holds considerable MSS. collections.

793 RAWSTON (GEORGE). My life, by an ex-dissenter. 1841.

A personal criticism of contemporary nonconformity. For another personal view, see (2303).

(b) *Later Works*

794 SKEATS (HERBERT S.). A history of the free churches of England, from . . . 1688 to . . . 1851. 1868. 2nd edn. 1869.

795 NIGHTINGALE (BENJAMIN). Lancashire nonconformity, or, Sketches historical and descriptive of the Congregational and old Presbyterian churches in the county. 6 v. Manchester, 1890-3.

The best of the local histories. For others see Godfrey Davies, *Bibliography of British history: Stuart period, 1603-1714*, 2nd edn. ed. by Mary F. Keeler, Oxf., 1970, nos. 1324, 1393. Anne Durning Holt, *Walking together*, 1938, contains interesting sketches of dissent in Liverpool.

796 McLACHLAN (HERBERT). English education under the test acts. Being the history of the nonconformist academies, 1662-1820. Manchester. 1931.

Other works by this leading modern historian of Unitarianism are *Warrington academy* [Manchester], 1943, Chetham Soc. v. 107, n.s.; and *The story of a nonconformist library*, Manchester, 1923. Also of value are Irene Parker, *Dissenting academies in England; their rise and progress and their place among the education systems of the country*, Camb., 1914, and Valentine David Davis, *A history of Manchester college. From its foundation in Manchester to its establishment in Oxford*, 1932.

797 MINEKA (FRANCIS EDWARD). The dissidence of dissent. The *Monthly Repository*, 1806–1838, under the editorship of Robert Aspland, W. J. Fox, R. H. Horne, and Leigh Hunt. With a chapter on religious periodicals, 1700–1825. Chapel Hill. 1944.

Bibliog. 429–38. A scholarly study of a periodical of major importance for the study of nonconformist religious thought.

798 MANNING (BERNARD LORD). The protestant dissenting deputies. Ed. by Ormerod Greenwood. Camb. 1952.

A definitive study based on the minute books of the deputies, tracing their campaigns to protect and extend Dissenters' legal rights.

799 COWHERD (RAYMOND GIBSON). The politics of English dissent: the religious aspects of liberal and humanitarian reform movements from 1815 to 1848. N.Y. 1956.

A rather undiscriminating survey. For the opening years of the period see Evelyn D. Bebb, *Nonconformity and social and economic life, 1660–1800*, 1935, and A. H. Lincoln, *Some political and social ideas of English dissent, 1763–1800*, Camb., 1938. See also F. R. Salter, 'Political nonconformity in the 1830s', *Trans. Roy. Hist. Soc.* 5th s. 3 (1953), 125–43.

800 DONALDSON (BARBARA). The registrations of dissenting chapels and meeting houses in Staffordshire, 1689–1852; extracted from the return in the General Register Office made under the Protestant Dissenters Act of 1852 (15 and 16 Vic. c. 36). (Staffordshire Record Soc. Collections, 4th s., v. 3.) Kendal. 1960.

801 HENRIQUES (URSULA RUTH QUIXANO). Religious toleration in England, 1787–1833. 1961.

802 WARD (WILLIAM REGINALD). Religion and society in England, 1790–1850. 1972.

Deals extensively, *inter alia*, with attitudes towards 'establishment'.

2. BAPTISTS

For archival material see the holdings of the Baptist Missionary Society.

803 THE BAPTIST ANNUAL REGISTER. Ed. by John Rippon. 4 v. 1793–1802.

The Baptist Magazine, v. 1+, 1809+.

804 FULLER (ANDREW). The works of . . . 8 v. 1824.

Other editions, 1838, 1840, 1845, 1852. A. G. Fuller, ed., *The principal works and remains of the Rev. Andrew Fuller, with a new memoir of his life* (Bohn Standard Library), 1846.

805 CAPPE (NEWCOME). Critical remarks on many important passages of scripture; together with dissertations upon several subjects . . . to which are prefixed memoirs of his life, by the editor, Catharine Cappe. 2 v. York. 1802.

See too John Sheppard, *An inquiry on the duty of Christians with respect to war; including an examination of the principles of the London and American peace societies*, 1820.

806   GADSBY (JOHN) *ed.* The works of the late William Gadsby. 1851.

Also, *A memoir of ... William Gadsby ... compiled from authentic sources,* 2nd edn., 1847.

807   HALL (ROBERT). The works of Robert Hall ... Published under the superintendence of Olinthus Gregory. 6 v. 1831–2.

808   IVIMEY (JOSEPH). A history of the English Baptists, including an investigation of the history of baptism in England. 4 v. 1811–30.

V. 4 deals with the reign of George III.

809   WHITLEY (WILLIAM THOMAS). A Baptist bibliography; being a register of the chief materials for Baptist history, whether in manuscript or print, preserved in Great Britain, Ireland and the colonies. 2 v. 1916–22.

A comprehensive bibliog. which includes some material relating to nonconformity in general. See too Edward Caryl Starr, *A Baptist bibliography,* v. 1 +, Phil., and Rochester, N.Y., 1947 +, in progress.

810   WHITLEY (WILLIAM THOMAS) *ed.* Minutes of the general assembly of the general Baptist churches in England, with kindred records, 1654–1728, 1731–1811. 2 v. 1909–10.

811   BAPTIST HISTORICAL SOCIETY. Trans. 7 v. 1908–20.

Cumulative index, comp. by Douglas C. Sparkes, 1966. Continued in *The Baptist Quarterly, incorporating the Transactions of the Baptist Historical Society,* 1922 +, which prints source material.

812   UNDERWOOD (ALFRED CLAIR). A history of the English Baptists. 1947.

Also valuable are W. T. Whitley, *A history of British Baptists,* 1923, 2nd edn., 1932, and *The Baptists of London, 1612–1928,* 1928. Biographical sketches of interest include, Edwin Paxton Hood, *Robert Hall,* 1881, and [Sir William H. Winterbotham], *The Rev. William Winterbotham: A Sketch,* 1893. For wider surveys see Robert George Torbet, *A history of the Baptists,* Phil., 1950, rev. edn., 1952, and Ernest A. Payne, *The Baptist Union: a short History,* 1959.

3. Congregationalists

For archival material see the holdings of the Congregational Union, at Congregational Memorial Hall.

813   SURMAN (CHARLES EDWARD). A bibliography of Congregational church history, including numerous cognate Presbyterian/Unitarian records and a few Baptist. Erdington, 1947.

Typescript 17 ff., copy in B.L. Other guides are Henry Martyn Dexter, *The Congregationalism of the last three hundred years, as seen in its literature,* N.Y. 1880; and the *Transactions of the Congregational Historical Society,* 1901 +, which prints records and bibliogs.

814   HINTON (JOHN HOWARD). A review of the Congregational system, in connection with a department of its local history, being the first circular letter of the Berks and West London Association. Oxf. 1926[?]

Other contemporary materials are in John Shenton Bright, *Apostolic Independency; exemplified in the history, doctrines, discipline, and ordinances, of the congregational*

churches, commonly called independent, 1842; *The works of William Jay, collected and
revised by himself*, 12 v. Bath, 1842–8; *The autobiography of* . . . *W. Jay*, ed. George
Redford and J. A. James, 1854; Cyrus Jay, *Recollections of William Jay*, 1859; William
Hendry Stowell, *Memoir of the life of R. W. Hamilton, D.D.*, 1850; Seymour Teulon
Porter, *Lectures on the ecclesiastical system of the Independents*, Glasgow, 1856; William
Stowell, ed., *A memoir of the life and labours of the Rev. W. H. S[towell]*, 1859; Thulia
S. Henderson, *Memoir of the Rev. E[benezer] Henderson* [1859]; John R. Leifchild,
*John Leifchild, his public ministry, private usefulness, and personal characteristics. Founded
upon an autobiography*, 1863; and (2252).

815 DALE (ROBERT WILLIAM). History of English Congregationalism.
Completed and ed. by Alfred William Winterslow Dale. 2nd edn. 1907.

Still of value are John Waddington, *Congregational history 1700–1800*, 1876, and *Congregational history, continuation to 1850*, 1878. Albert Peel, *History of the Congregational
Union of England and Wales, 1831–1931*, 1931, is excellent. Peel ed. *The life of Alexander
Stewart, prisoner of Napoleon and preacher of the gospel; written by himself to 1815*, 1948;
see too his *The noble army of congregational martyrs*, 1948. William Gordon Robinson,
William Roby, 1766–1830, and the revival of Independency in the north, 1954, and *History
of the Lancashire Congregational Union, 1806–1951*, 1955, are useful regional studies.
Robert Tudur Jones, *Congregationalism in England, 1662–1962*, 1962, is standard.
W. T. Owen, *Edward Williams, D.D., 1750–1813*, Cardiff, 1963, is well documented.
See too J. G. Miall, *Congregationalism in Yorkshire*, 1868.

4. PRESBYTERIANS AND UNITARIANS

816 THE MONTHLY REPOSITORY of theological and general literature.
36 v. 1806–37.

Includes valuable biog. notices of leading dissenting ministers.

817 MURCH (JEROM). A history of the Presbyterian and General Baptist
churches in the west of England; with memoirs of some of their pastors. 1835.

818 CHANNING. The works of William E. Channing. 6 v. 1840–44.

A more full *Complete Works*, was pub. in 1884. See too Russell Lant Carpenter, ed.,
Memoirs of the life of the Rev. Lant Carpenter, 1842; Robert Brook Aspland, *Memoir of
the life, works, and correspondence of the Rev. Robert Aspland*, 1850; *Memorial edition of
the collected works of W[illiam] J[ohnson] F[ox]*, 12 v. 1865–8; William James, *Memoir
of the Rev. T. Madge, late minister of Essex Street Chapel, London*, Bristol, 1871.

819 JAMES (THOMAS SMITH). The history of the litigation and legislation
respecting Presbyterian chapels and charities in England and Ireland between
1816 and 1849. 1867.

820 DRYSDALE (ALEXANDER HUTTON). History of the Presbyterians
in England, their rise, decline, and revival. 1889.

Thomas McCrie, jr., *Annals of English presbytery. From the earliest period to the present
time*, 1872.

821 COLLIGAN (JAMES HAY). The Arian movement in England. Manchester. 1913.

Alexander Gordon, *Heads of English Unitarian history*, 1895.

822 PRESBYTERIAN HISTORICAL SOCIETY of England. Journal.
1914+.

823 UNITARIAN HISTORICAL SOCIETY. Trans. 1916–18+.

See Walter H. Burgess, 'Work in the field of Unitarian history', I (1916–18), 1–9.
An American society, with the same name, publishes *Proceedings*, 1925+.

824 McLACHLAN (HERBERT). The Unitarian movement in the religious
life of England. V. 1: Its contribution to thought and learning, 1700–1900.
1934.

Raymond Vincent Holt, *The Unitarian contribution to social progress in England*, 1938;
Earl Morse Wilbur, *A history of Unitarianism in Transylvania, England, and America*,
Camb., Mass., 1952.

5. Methods

For archival material see the holdings of the Methodist Missionary Society, and
the Methodist Church Archives.

(a) *Bibliography*

825 OSBORN (GEORGE). Outlines of Wesleyan bibliography; or, A record
of Methodist literature from the beginning. In two parts: the first containing
the publications of John and Charles Wesley . . . the second those of Methodist
preachers. 1869.

Richard Green, comp. *The Works of John and Charles Wesley . . . an exact account of all
the publications . . . with . . . descriptive and illustrated notes, 1896*, 2nd edn. 1906; and
*Anti-Methodist publications issued during the eighteenth century. A chronologically arranged
and annotated bibliography*, 1902, which includes material up to 1810. See too H. C.
Decanver, *pseud.* of Curtis H. Cavender, *Catalogue of works in refutation of Methodism,
from its origin in 1729, to the present time*, Phil., 1846, N.Y., 1868.

826 SHARP (JOHN ALFRED). A catalogue of manuscripts and relics . . .
books and pamphlets, etc., belonging to the Wesleyan Methodist conference,
and preserved at the office of the conference. 1921.

(b) *Sources*

827 MINUTES of the Methodist conferences. 12 v. 1812–55.

Minutes from 1744 to 1854.

828 THE ARMINIAN MAGAZINE. 20 v. 1778–97.

Continued as *The Methodist Magazine*, 1798–1821, and as the *Wesleyan Methodist
Magazine* (3rd s.), 1822–44 (4th s.), 1845–54.

829 GENERAL RULES of the Methodists of the New Connection; revised
and approved at their twenty-seventh annual conference. Hanley, 1823.

John Blackwell, *Life of the Rev. Alexander Kilham . . . one of the founders of the Methodist
New Connection in the year 1797, including a full account of the dispute which occasioned
the separation*, 1838.

830 INGRAM (ROBERT ACKLOM). The cause of the increase of Methodism and Dissension, and of the popularity of what is called Evangelical preaching, and the means of obviating them, considered in a sermon. 1807.

[James Henry Leigh Hunt], *An attempt to show the folly and danger of Methodism . . . By the editor of the Examiner*, 1809; *Methodism displayed and Christianism detected . . . By a member of the church of England*, 1813, are representative examples of the attack upon Methodism.

831 CROWTHER (JONATHAN). A . . . portraiture of Methodism; or, The history of the Wesleyan Methodists; including their rise, progress, and present state. 1811.

Crowther was widely travelled in the British Isles, and became president of conference in 1819.

832 JACKSON (THOMAS). The centenary of Wesleyan Methodism: a brief sketch of the rise, progress, and present state of the Wesleyan Methodist societies throughout the world. 1839.

Jabez Bunting comp., *Memorials of the late rev. Richard Watson*, 1833. Watson was one of the early preachers in the New Connection; see also Watson's *Works*, 12 v., 1834–7; *The miscellaneous works of Adam Clarke* [ed. by J. Everett], 13 v., 1836–7; J. B. B. Clarke, *An account of the infancy, religious and literary life of Adam Clarke*, 3 v., 1833.

833 TURNER (GEORGE). The constitution and discipline of Wesleyan Methodism: an essay. 1841.

An expanded version, exposing 'misrepresentations', was pub. in 1850.

834 WARD (WILLIAM REGINALD). The early correspondence of Jabez Bunting. (Roy. Hist. Soc., Camden, 4th s., 11.) 1972.

On Bunting see also (836).

(c) *Later Works*

835 SMITH (GEORGE). History of Wesleyan Methodism. 3 v. 1857–61.

Abel Stevens, *The history of the religious movement of the eighteenth century, called Methodism*, 3 v., N.Y., 1858–61, amplifies and corrects Smith's account, the two together forming an excellent record.

836 BUNTING. The life of Jabez Bunting, D.D. By Thomas Percival Bunting, completed by G. Stringer Rowe. 2 v. 1859–1887.

On the leader of the final separation from the church of England. On other leading personalities see: W. Entwisle, *Memoir of Joseph Entwisle*, 1848; Adeline Waddy, *The life of . . . Samuel Waddy*, 1878; Richard Chew, *James Everett: a biography*, 1875.

837 PETTY (JOHN). The history of the Primitive Methodist Connection, from its origin to the conference of 1860. New edn. 1864.

H. B. Kendall, *The origin and history of the Primitive Methodist Church*, 2 v., 1906, rev. edn., 1919. On the founders see J. T. Wilkinson, *William Clowes, 1780–1851*, 1951, and *Hugh Bourne, 1772–1852*, 1952.

838 CROTHERS (THOMAS DICKSON) *and others*. The centenary of the Methodist New Connection. 1897.

839 WESLEY HISTORICAL SOCIETY. Proceedings. [Burnley] 1896–7+.

840 TOWNSEND (WILLIAM JOHN), WORKMAN (HERBERT BROOK) and EAYRS (GEORGE) eds. A new history of Methodism. 2 v. 1909.

Select bibliog., v. 2, 535–50. J. F. Hurst, *History of Methodism*, 3 v., 1901, is a good general survey; v. 1, in three parts, deals with England. See too S. G. Dimond, *The psychology of the Methodist revival, an empirical and descriptive study*, 1926, and G. C. Cell, *The rediscovery of John Wesley*, N.Y., 1935, a study of Wesley's theology. Rupert E. Davies and E. G. Rupp, eds., *A history of the Methodist church in Great Britain*, v. 1, 1965, in progress, includes a valuable conspectus by John Walsh of Methodism at the end of the eighteenth century.

841 EDWARDS (MALDWYN LLOYD). After Wesley: A study of the social and political influence of Methodism in the middle period (1791–1849). 1935.

An informative survey. W. J. Warner, *The Wesleyan movement in the industrial revolution*, 1930, discusses the influence of Wesley's economic ethics. See also Ernest R. Taylor, *Methodism and politics, 1791–1851*, Camb., 1935; R. F. Wearmouth, *Methodism and the working class movements of England, 1800–1850*, 1937.

842 NORWOOD (FREDERICK A.). 'Methodist historical studies, 1930–1959'. *Church History* 28 (1959), 391–417.

See also F. A. Norwood, 'Wesleyan and Methodist historical studies, 1960–70; a bibliographical article', *ibid.* 40 (1971), 182–99.

843 ROSE (EDWARD ALAN) comp. A register of Methodist circuit plans, 1777–1860. Manchester. 1961–5.

Supplements, 1965, 1970.

844 SHAW (THOMAS). The Bible Christians, 1815–1907. 1965.

845 KENT (JOHN HENRY SOMERSET). The age of disunity. 1966.

See also Robert Currie, *Methodism divided*, 1968.

846 ARMSTRONG (ANTHONY). The church of England, the Methodists, and society, 1700–1850. 1973.

847 SEMMEL (BERNARD). The Methodist revolution. 1974.

6. QUAKERS

(a) *Bibliography*

848 SMITH (JOSEPH). A descriptive catalogue of Friends' books, or, Books written by members of the Society of Friends . . . from their first rise to the present time. 2 v. 1867.

This work, with Smith's *Supplement to a descriptive catalogue*, 1893, and his *Bibliotheca anti-Quakeriana*, 1873, provides an almost complete guide.

(b) *Sources*

(i) *Manuscripts*

The library of the Society of Friends, Friends House, Euston Road, London, N.W.1, has an extensive collection, and there are other important holdings at the Friends Meeting Houses at Birmingham, Bristol, Colchester, Kendal, Leeds, Manchester, Norwich, York, and Dublin.

(ii) *Writings, Journals, and Letters*

849 THE FRIENDS' LIBRARY comprising journals, doctrinal treatises, and other writings of members of the religious society of Friends. Ed. by William Evans and Thomas Evans. 14 v. Phil. 1837–50.

Piety promoted, 11 v., 1701–1829, repr. by William and Thomas Evans, eds., 4 v., Phil., 1854, includes many short biog. notices.

850 EPISTLES from the yearly meeting of Friends, held in London, to the quarterly and monthly meetings in Great Britain, Ireland, and elsewhere; from 1681 to 1857. 2 v. 1858.

851 SCOTT. A journal of the life, travels, and gospel labours, of that faithful servant, and minister of Christ, Job Scott. N.Y. 1797. Repr. Warrington. 1798.

Scott came to England from Rhode Island in 1792, and spent much of the remaining years of his life in Ireland.

852 CLARKSON (THOMAS). A portraiture of Quakerism, as taken from a view of the moral education, discipline, peculiar customs, religious principles, political and civil economy, and character of the Society of Friends. 3 v. 1806.

A detached but sympathetic survey.

853 CREWDSON (ISAAC). A beacon to the Society of Friends. 1835.

For the ensuing argument see, *The beacon controversy between the Society of Friends and I. Crewdson*, 1836.

854 HOPPER. Isaac T. Hopper: a true life. By Lydia Maria Francis (*afterwards* Child). 1853.

855 GURNEY. Memoirs of Joseph John Gurney: with selections from his journal and correspondence. By Joseph Bevan Braithwaite. Norwich. 2 v. 1854.

On his banking activities see Swift (1448), and for his family (2104).

856 GRELLET. Memoirs of the life and gospel labours of Stephen Grellet. Ed. by Benjamin Seebohm. 2 v. 1860.

William Guest, *Stephen Grellet*, 1880. In the years after 1815 Grellet travelled widely in England and on the Continent.

857 FRIENDS' HISTORICAL SOCIETY. Journal. 1903–4+.

Includes original documents and articles, and publishes monographs as supplements.

858 FRIENDS' HISTORICAL SOCIETY of Philadelphia. Bulletin. Phil. 1906+.

V. 27 (1938), 37–43, gives a list of research projects on Quakerism.

(c) *Later Works*

**859 JONES (RUFUS MATTHEW). The later periods of Quakerism. 2 v.
1921.**

The standard account, from 1725 to the 20th century. There are briefer surveys in
Alfred Neave Brayshawe, *The Quakers; their story and message*, 1921, 2nd edn. partly
rewritten, 1927; Elizabeth Braithwaite Emmott, *The story of Quakerism*, 1929.

**860 HIRST (MARGARET E.). The Quakers in peace and war; an account of
their peace principles and practice. 1923.**

Chaps. 8–10 on the later eighteenth and the nineteenth centuries.

861 RUSSELL (ELBERT). The history of Quakerism. N.Y. 1942.

862 GRUBB (ISABEL). Quakerism and industry before 1800. 1930.

Arthur Raistrick, *Two centuries of industrial welfare; the London (Quaker) Lead company, 1692–1905*, 1938, pub. as a suppl. to the *Journal of the Friends' Hist. Soc.*, examines
the application of Quaker ethics in business.

**863 PENNEY (NORMAN) *ed.* Pen pictures of London yearly meeting, 1789–
1833: being extracts from the notes of R. Cockin and others. 1930.**

**864 McKENZIE (ISABEL). Social activities of the English Friends in the
first half of the nineteenth century. N.Y. 1935. (Privately printed.)**

See Allen (2510) and Sturge (2259).

**865 LIDBETTER (HUBERT). The Friends meeting house; an historical
survey of the places of worship of the Society of Friends. . . . York. 1961.**

866 ISICHEI (ELIZABETH ALLO). Victorian Quakers. 1970.

7. OTHER SECTS

Bereans

**867 [THOMSON (JAMES) *and* McMILLAN (DAVID)] *eds.* The works of
John Barclay. With a memoir of the author. Glasgow. 1852.**

Barclay, the founder of the Bereans, d. 1798.

Free Church of England

**868 VAUGHAN (FRANK). A history of the Free Church of England,
otherwise called the reformed episcopal church. Bath. [1936].**

Irvingites

**869 SHAW (PLATO ERNEST). The Catholic Apostolic Church, sometimes
called Irvingite. A historical study. N.Y. 1946.**

Brief bibliog. Gavin Carlyle, ed., *The collected writings of Edward Irving*, 5 v., 1864–5,
and *The Prophetical works of Edward Irving*, 2 v., 1867–70. There are lives of Irving by
Washington Wilks, 1854, and Margaret O. Oliphant, 2 v., 1862; see also A. L. Drummond, *Edward Irving and his circle*, 1937.

Moravians

870 HUTTON (JOSEPH EDMUND). A history of the Moravian Church. 2nd edn. rev. and enl. 1909.

John Holmes, *History of the Protestant Church of the United Brethren*, 2 v., 1825–30, is still useful.

Plymouth Brethren

871 NEATBY (WILLIAM BLAIR). A history of the Plymouth Brethren. 1901.

See also F. R. Coad, *A history of the Brethren movement*, Exeter, 1968; H. H. Rowdon, *The origins of the Brethren, 1825–50*, 1967.

Southcottians

872 ROBERTS (DANIEL). Observations relative to the divine mission of Joanna Southcott. 1807.

Swedenborgians

873 HINDMARSH (ROBERT). Rise and progress of the New Jerusalem church in England, America, and other parts. Ed. by E. Madely. 1861.

Universalists

874 ROWELL (GEOFFREY). 'The origins and history of Universalist Societies in Britain, 1750–1850.' *J. Eccles. Hist.* 22 (1971), 35–56.

W. A. Smith, *Shepherd Smith the Universalist: the story of a mind*, 1892.

C. ROMAN CATHOLICISM

1. REGISTERS AND SOURCE DOCUMENTS

875 CATHOLIC RECORD SOCIETY. Publications. V. 1+. 1905+.

Chiefly lists of Catholic missions in England, of English Catholic institutions abroad, of English members of religious orders. The registers of missions are under town or family and consist of names of those baptized, confirmed, and buried.

876 DUBLIN REVIEW. 1836+.

Founded by Wiseman, an intellectual focus for Catholicism. Other influential periodicals were *The Tablet*, 1840+, and *The Rambler*, 1848+ (the organ of the Liberal Catholics).

877 ANSTEY (THOMAS CHISHOLM). A guide to the laws of England affecting Roman Catholics. 1842.

See too James Paton, *British history and papal claims, from the Norman conquest to the present day*, 2 v., 1893.

878 OLIVER (GEORGE). Collections illustrating the history of the Catholic religion in the counties of Cornwall, Devon, Dorset, Somerset, Wilts, and

Gloucester. In two parts, historical and biographical, with notices of the Dominican, Benedictine, and Franciscan orders in England. 1857.

Oliver also comp. *Collections towards illustrating the biography of the Scotch, English, and Irish members of the Society of Jesus,* 1845.

879 BRADY (WILLIAM MAZIERE). Annals of the Catholic hierarchy in England and Scotland . . . 1585–1876. Rome. 1877.

The 3rd vol. reprinted of *The Episcopal succession in England, Scotland and Ireland,* 3 v., Rome, 1876–7, containing accounts taken from the archives in Rome of vicars apostolic and bishops who governed the Catholic church in England.

880 FOLEY (HENRY). Records of the English province of the Society of Jesus. Historic facts illustrative of the labours and sufferings of its members in the sixteenth and seventeenth centuries. 7 v. in 8. 1877–83.

V. 5, 6, and 7 include some 19th-century material.

881 GILLOW (JOSEPH). A literary and biographical history, or bibliographical dictionary, of English Catholics, from the breach with Rome, in 1534, to the present time. 5 v. 1885–1902.

882 BUTLER (CHARLES). Historical memoirs of the English, Irish, and Scottish Catholics since the reformation. 3rd edn. cor. and rev. 4 v. 1822.

Includes some contemporary material, as does John Milner, *Supplementary memoirs of English Catholics,* 1820. John Kirk, *Biographies of English Catholics in the eighteenth century,* edited by John Hungerford Pollen and Edwin Burton, 1909, includes men still active in the early 19th century.

2. DEVOTIONAL AND CRITICAL WORKS

883 BERINGTON (JOSEPH). The faith of Catholics, confirmed by Scripture, and attested by the Fathers of the first five centuries of the Church. 1813.

884 MILNER (JOHN). The End of Religious Controversy, in a friendly correspondence between a religious society of Protestants and a Roman Catholic Divine. 3 v. 1818. 5th edn. rev. 1824.

Milner's chief theological publication. He also published a *Vindication* of it, 1822. See too his *The Divine Right of Episcopacy,* 1791 and *Ecclesiastical Democracy detected,* 1822; *A serious expostulation with the Rev. Joseph Berington, upon his theological errors concerning miracles and other subjects,* 1797; *The Catholic Scriptural Catechism,* 1820; *On devotion to the Sacred Heart of Jesus,* 1821.

885 BUTLER (CHARLES). The Book of the Roman Catholic Church. 1825.

A work of controversy addressed to Southey, which drew many replies, to which Butler made rejoinder in *A Letter to the Right Rev. C. J. Blomfield,* 1825; and *Vindication of the Book of the Roman Catholic Church,* 1826.

886 ROCK (DANIEL). The Liturgy of the Mass, and Common Vespers for Sundays, with annotations and illustrative plates. 2 pt. 1832.

This exposition was followed by *Hierurgia; or, The Holy Sacrifice of the Mass, with notes and dissertations elucidating its doctrines and ceremonies, and numerous illustrative plates.* 2 v., 1833. A controversial work is his *Transubstantiation vindicated from the strictures of the Rev. Maurice Jones,* 1830.

887 WISEMAN (NICHOLAS PATRICK STEPHEN). Lectures on the principal doctrines and practices of the Catholic Church. 1836.

His works include *The Real Presence . . . proved*, 1836; *High Church Claims*, 1841, a comment on some of the views of the Tractarians; *Three lectures on the Catholic hierarchy*, 1850.

3. LATER WORKS

888 AMHERST (WILLIAM JOSEPH). The history of Catholic emancipation and the progress of the Catholic church in the British Isles . . . from 1771 to 1820. 2 v. 1886.

Frederick Charles Husenbeth, *The life of the Right Rev. John Milner, D.D.*, Dublin, 1862, sketches the career of the vicar-apostolic for the western and midland districts of England in the early 19th century. See too Bernard Ward, *Catholic London a century ago*, 1905.

889 GERARD (JOHN). Centenary record: Stonyhurst college, its life beyond the seas, 1592–1794, and on English soil, 1794–1894. Belfast. 1894.

Peter Keenan Guilday, *The English Catholic refugees on the continent, 1558–1795*. Vol. I. *The English colleges and convents in the Catholic Low Countries, 1558–1795*, 1914, gives the broader background of Catholic education at the beginning of the period. For its development, see Arthur Stapylton Barnes, *The Catholic schools of England*, 1926.

890 ZIMMERMAN (BENEDICT). Carmel in England: A history of the English mission of the discalced Carmelites, 1615 to 1849, drawn from documents preserved in the archives of the order. 1899.

891 WARD (BERNARD NICHOLAS). The dawn of the Catholic revival in England, 1781–1803. 2 v. 1909.

The best history of the subject, ably continued in his work, *The eve of Catholic emancipation; being the history of the English Catholics during the first thirty years of the nineteenth century*, 3 v., 1911–12. Philip Hughes, *The Catholic question, 1688–1829: a study in political history*, 1929, is a careful study; see also Machin (104). See too Maude D. M. Petre, *The ninth Lord Petre: or, Pioneers of Roman Catholic emancipation*, 1928.

892 WARD (BERNARD NICOLAS). The sequel to Catholic emancipation [1830–50]. 2 v. 1915.

Standard. For another treatment see Denis R. Gwynn, *The second spring, 1818–1852. A study of the Catholic revival in England*, 1942. W. B. Ullathorne, *History of the restoration of the Catholic hierarchy*, 1871, is an account at first hand. On proselytizing see Conrad Charles, 'The origins of the Parish Mission in England and the early Passionist apostolate, 1840–1850', *J. Eccles. Hist.* 15 (1964), 60–75, and Leetham (893). From a foreign viewpoint is Paul M. P. Thureau-Dangin, *La renaissance catholique en Angleterre*, 3 v., 1906–9, Eng. edn., 2 v., 1914.

893 WARD (WILFRED PHILIP). W. G. Ward and the Catholic revival. Rev. edn. 1912.

Other leading biographies are: W. P. Ward, *The life and times of Cardinal Wiseman*, 2 v., 1897; other lives by Denis R. Gwynn, rev. edn. 1950, and Brian Fothergill, 1963; E. de Lisle, *Life and letters of Ambrose Phillips de Lisle*, 2 v., 1900; C. R. H. Leetham, *Luigi Gentili, a sower for the second spring*, 1965.

894 ELLIS (JOHN TRACY). Cardinal Consalvi and Anglo-Papal relations, 1814–1824. Washington. 1942.

An able survey, based only on printed material.

895 WATKIN (EDWARD INGRAM). Roman Catholicism in England from the Reformation to 1950. 1957.

A useful introductory outline. David Mathew, *Catholicism in England, 1535–1935. Portrait of a minority: its culture and tradition*, 1936, is an urbane survey. Mary D. R. Leys, *Catholics in England, 1559–1829; a social history*, 1961. See also Henriques (801).

896 MILBURN (DAVID). A history of Ushaw College; a study of the origin, foundation and development of an English Catholic seminary, with an epilogue, 1908–1962. Durham. 1964.

897 NORMAN (EDWARD ROBERT). Anti-Catholicism in Victorian England. 1968.

G. F. A. Best, 'The Protestant constitution and its supporters, 1800–1829', *Trans. Roy. Hist. Soc.*, 5th s., 8 (1958), 105–27, and 'Popular Protestantism in Victorian England', in *Ideas and institutions of Victorian Britain*, ed. R. Robson, 1967, 115–42.

D. CHRISTIAN MISSIONS

Archival material in addition to that already mentioned above is held by the S.P.G., the S.P.C.K., the C.M.S., and the L.M.S. For missionaries' diaries and autobiographies see Matthews (2006).

898 SMITH (THOMAS). The history and origin of the missionary societies. 2 v. 1824–39.

899 COX (FRANCIS AUGUSTUS). History of the Baptist Missionary Society from 1792 to 1842. 1842.

See: James Hoby, *Memoir of William Yates, D.D., of Calcutta*, 1847; [John Taylor], *Biographical and literary notices of William Carey*, Northampton, 1886; Frank D. Walker, *William Carey, missionary, pioneer, and statesman*, 1926; B. R. Pearn, 'F. Carey and the English Baptist mission in Burma (1807–22)', *J. Burma Research Soc.* 28 (1938), 1–91; Eli D. Potts, *British Baptist missionaries in India, 1793–1837; the history of Serampore and its missions*, Camb., 1967.

900 SHERRING (MATTHEW ATMORE). The history of Protestant missions to India . . . 1706 to 1882. 1884.

901 LOVETT (RICHARD). The history of the London Missionary Society, 1795–1895. 2 v. 1899.

John Morison, *The fathers and founders of the London Missionary Society*, 2 v., [1840]. Margaret J. Cowie, comp., *The London Missionary Society in South Africa; a bibliography*, Cape Town, 1969; see too W. C. Northcott, *Robert Moffat; pioneer in Africa, 1817–1870*, 1961; I. Schapera, *Missionary correspondence, 1841–1856, of David Livingstone*, 1961.

902 STOCK (EUGENE). History of the Church Missionary Society. 4 v. 1899–1916.

Standard on the missionary work of the evangelicals. See Charles Hole, *The early history of the Church Missionary Society for Africa and the East to the end of A.D. 1814*, 1896. William Goode, *A memoir of the late Rev. William Goode*, 1828, gives letters of a leading member of the society.

903 WESLEYAN METHODIST Missionary Society. Reports. 1812–1900.

William Moister, *A history of Wesleyan missions*, 1871.

904 PASCOE (CHARLES FREDERICK). Two hundred years of the S.P.G. ... 1701–1900. 1901.

Henry Paget Thompson, *Into all lands: the history of the Society for the Propagation of the Gospel in foreign parts, 1701–1950*, 1951.

905 CANTON (WILLIAM). A history of the British and Foreign Bible Society. 5 v. 1904–10.

On its beginnings see John Owen, *The history of the origin and first ten years of the British and Foreign Bible Society*, 2 v., 1816, and *Extract of letters on the object and connexions of the British and Foreign Bible Society*, 1819. George Browne, author of *The history of the ... Society ... to ... its jubilee in 1854*, 2 v., 1859, was a former secretary. On the first president see *Memoirs of ... Lord Teignmouth* (4576).

906 HODGKIN (HENRY THEODORE). Friends beyond seas. 1916.

An account of the foreign missions of the Society of Friends.

907 HUTTON (JOSEPH EDMUND). History of Moravian Missions. 1923.

John Taylor Hamilton, *A history of the missions of the Moravian church in the eighteenth and nineteenth centuries*, 1901.

908 LATOURETTE (KENNETH SCOTT). A history of the expansion of Christianity. 7 v. 1937–45. Repr. 1947.

V. 4: The great century in Europe and the United States of America, 1800–1914.
V. 5: The great century in the Americas, Australasia, and Africa, 1800–1914.
V. 6: The great century in northern Africa and Asia, 1800–1914.
A valuable general survey. See too Ernest Alexander Payne, *The church awakes: the story of the modern missionary movement*, 1942.

909 GROVES (CHARLES PELHAM). The planting of Christianity in Africa. 4 v. 1948–58.

The standard work. V. 1 and 2 cover the late 18th and the early 19th centuries. See also Johannes Du Plessis, *A history of Christian missions in South Africa*, 1911; Horton Davies and Robert H. W. Shepherd, comps., *South African missions, 1800–1950*, Edinburgh, 1954.

910 TIBAWI (ABDUL LATIF). British interests in Palestine, 1800–1901; a study of religious and educational enterprise. 1961.

E. JUDAISM

I. BIBLIOGRAPHY AND SOCIETIES

911 ROTH (CECIL). Magna bibliotheca Anglo-Judaica; a bibliographical guide to Anglo-Jewish history. New edn. rev. and enl. 5698–1937.

A rev. edn. of Joseph Jacobs and Lucien Wolf, *Bibliotheca Anglo-Judaica*, 1888, Roth's more than 2,000 entries are selective, uncritical, and arranged by subject. Abraham S. Wolf Rosenbach, *An American Jewish bibliography, being a list of books and pamphlets by Jews or relating to them printed in the United States from the establishment of the press in the colonies until 1850*, [Baltimore], 1926, is arranged chronologically. Ruth P. Lehmann, *Nova bibliotheca Anglo-Judaica, 1937–60*, 1961, new edn., 1973, under title, *Anglo-Jewish bibliography, 1937–70*, up-dates Roth.

912 BLOCH (JOSHUA) *ed.* Journal of Jewish bibliography; a quarterly edited in collaboration with eminent scholars. N.Y. 1938.

913 JEWISH QUARTERLY REVIEW. 20 v. 1888–1908. n.s. Phil. 1910+.

There is a *Classified index to volumes i–xx*, 1909–30, Phil., 1932. A critical and scholarly journal dealing with Jewish literature, theology, history, and religion.

914 AMERICAN JEWISH HISTORICAL SOCIETY. Publications. Balt. N.Y. 1893+.

Index, v. 1–20, 1914.

915 JEWISH HISTORICAL SOCIETY OF ENGLAND. Transactions. 1895+.

This society also issues, irregularly, a *Miscellanies* series, 1925+. Index to *Transactions*, v. 1–12, and to *Miscellanies*, pt. 1, in J.H.S.E. *Miscellanies*, pt. 2 (1935), 107–12.

2. CONTEMPORARY ACCOUNTS

916 BLUNT (JOHN ELIJAH). A history of the establishment and residence of the Jews in England, with an enquiry into their civil disabilities. 1830.

See too Francis Henry Goldsmid, *Remarks on the civil disabilities of British Jews*, 1830.

917 MARGOLIOUTH (MOSES). The history of the Jews in Great Britain. 3 v. 1851.

3. LATER WORKS

918 PICCIOTTO (JAMES). Sketches of Anglo-Jewish history. 1875.

Reprints from the Jewish Chronicle. New edn. with prologue, notes, and an epilogue, by Israel Finestein, 1956.

919 HENRIQUES (HENRY STRAUS QUIXANO). The Jews and the English law. Oxf. 1908.

920 BARON (SALO WITTMAYER). A social and religious history of the Jews. 3 v. N.Y. 1937.

Comprehensive, with full bibliog. A greatly enlarged edn. is in progress, N.Y., 1952+.

921 ROTH (CECIL). A history of the Jews in England. Oxf. 1941. 3rd rev. edn. Oxf. 1964.

Does not entirely supersede Albert M. Hyamson, *A history of the Jews in England*, 1908, 2nd edn. rev., 1928. For public opinion about Jews, see Montagu Frank Modder, *The Jew in the literature of England to the end of the nineteenth century*, Phil., 1939. C. Roth, *Essays and portraits in Anglo-Jewish history*, Phil., 1962.

F. HYMNOLOGY

922 JULIAN (JOHN) *ed.* A dictionary of hymnology, setting forth the origin and history of Christian hymns of all ages and nations. 1892. Rev. edn. 1925.

923 HYMNS ANCIENT AND MODERN for use in the services of the church with accompanying tunes. Historical edition, with notes on the origin of both hymns and tunes and a general historical introduction. Illustrated by facsimiles and portraits. 1909.

924 BENSON (LOUIS FITZGERALD). The English hymn, its development and use in worship. 1915.

An excellent guide, with footnotes, but no bibliog.

925 RAINBOW (BERNARR J. G.). Choral revival in the Anglican church, 1839–1872. 1970.

See also White (729).

VI

MILITARY HISTORY

A. GENERAL

1. MANUSCRIPTS

The War Office papers in the Public Record Office provide the main body of material, but there is additional matter in the records of the Home Office, the Colonial Office, the Audit Office, and the Paymaster General's Office. See (64). British Library, Department of Manuscripts, class catalogue no. 50 (Military), provides an incomplete but useful guide to the military material in the Library's collections. On the holdings of the Royal United Service Institution, see the *Calendar of military manuscripts . . .*, comp. by Sir Lonsdale Hale, 1914. Marryat R. Dobie, comp., 'Military manuscripts in the National Library of Scotland', *J. of the Soc. for Army Hist. Res.* 27 (1949), 118–20. For other collections, see C. T. Atkinson, 'Material for military history in the reports of the Historical Manuscripts Commission', *ibid.* 21 (1942), 17–34. Wellington's papers remain at the time of writing in the possession of the family.

2. BIBLIOGRAPHIES AND CATALOGUES

926 HIGHAM (ROBIN) *ed.* A guide to the sources of British military history. 1972.

Deals with naval as well as military warfare, and also the economic and technological background; arrangement alphabetical order of authors within century-long periods, without much detailed breakdown by subject; indispensable.

927 POHLER (JOHANN). Bibliotheca historico-militaris. Systematische Uebersicht der Erscheinungen aller Sprachen auf dem Gebiete der Geschichte der Kriege und Kriegswissenschaft. 4 v. Cassel. 1887–99. Repr. 4 v. N.Y. 1961.

928 WAR OFFICE LIBRARY. Catalogue. By Francis J. Hudleston. 3 pts. 1906–12.

Pt. 3: subject index. Suppls. to pt. 1–2 [accessions to 1915], 1916; annual suppls., to pt. 3, 1–29, *1912–40*, 1913–41. *The catalogue of the library of the Royal United Service Institution*, 3rd edn., 1908, and *The subject list of works on military and naval arts, in the library of the Patent Office*, 1907, contain some works not in the War Office Library.

929 CRAIG (HARDIN), *comp.* A bibliography of encyclopaedias and dictionaries dealing with military, naval and maritime affairs, 1577–1971. 4th edn. Houston, Texas. 1971.

Duplicated typescript; international in scope; publications listed in chronological order of appearance.

3. General Works

930 FORTESCUE (*Sir* JOHN WILLIAM). A history of the British army. 13 v. and 6 atlases. 1899–1930.

> V. 4–12 deal with the period 1789–1851. A standard work, but in some respects unsatisfactory. Campaigns are dealt with at length, but the detail is not always trustworthy; army administration is treated superficially, and the author's judgements on policy are sometimes extremely biased.

931 LLOYD (ERNEST MARSH). A review of the history of infantry. 1908.
> Bibliog. 291–6.

932 SEBAG-MONTEFIORE (CECIL). A history of the volunteer forces from the earliest times to . . . 1860; being a recital of the citizen's duty. 1908.

> Sir George Jackson Hay, *An epitomized history of the militia* [cover-title, *The constitutional force*], [1906?], gives attention to the origins and special services of militia units existing in 1905. J. R. Western, *The English militia in the eighteenth century; the story of a political issue, 1660–1802,* 1965, gives much information for the years just after 1789. See also Sir Henry W. W. McAnally, *The Irish militia, 1793–1816: a social and military study,* 1949. A. S. White and E. J. Martin, comp., 'A bibliography of volunteering', *J. of the Soc. for Army Hist. Res.* 23 (1945), 2–29, 24 (1946), 88–91.

933 JOURNAL of the Society of [for, after Jan. 1929] Army Historical Research. 1921+.

> Articles, notes, source materials, plates, and maps. General indexes to v. 1–12 (1921–33) and 13–28 (1934–50). Also of value are the *Journal of the Royal United Service Institution,* 1857+; *Military affairs: journal of the American Military Institute,* Wash., 1937+; *The Irish Sword: the journal of the Military History Society of Ireland,* Dublin, 1949+.

934 BARNETT (CORRELLI DOUGLAS). Britain and her army, 1509–1970; a military, political and social survey. 1970.

> Bibliog. 501–5. Also useful is E. W. Sheppard, *A short history of the British army,* 4th edn., 1950. J. F. C. Fuller, *The conduct of war, 1789–1961; a study of the impact of the French, Industrial and Russian revolutions on war and its conduct,* 1961, is opinionated but stimulating.

935 LESLIE (N. B.). Battle honours of the British and Indian armies, 1695–1914. 1970.
> A valuable work of reference.

B. MILITARY OPERATIONS

1. The French Wars, 1789–1815

For campaigns in India and the colonies, see the appropriate regional section. For prisoners of war see (1267).

(a) *General*

For Wellington see also (201), (202).

936 DUMAS (MATHIEU), *Count*. Précis des événemens militaires; ou, Essais historiques sur les campagnes de 1799–1814. 19 v. Paris. 1817–26.

> Charles Théodore Beauvais, ed., *Victoires, conquêtes, désastres, revers et guerres civiles des Français, 1791–1815,* 28 v., Paris, 1818–25.

937 JOMINI (ANTOINE HENRI DE), *baron.* Histoire critique et militaire des guerres de la Révolution. New edn. 15 v. Paris. 1820–4.

938 CLAUSEWITZ (KARL VON). Hinterlassene Werke . . . über Krieg und Kriegführung. 10 v. Berlin. 1832–7.

V. 4–8 deal with campaigns in the period.

939 CAMON (HUBERT). La guerre napoléonienne. 5 v. Paris. 1903–10.

940 KIRCHEISEN (FRIEDRICH MAX). Bibliography of Napoleon; a systematic collection critically selected. 1902.

Supplements are printed in the *Revue des études napoléoniennes,* Paris, 1912+. Pieter Geyl, *Napoleon: for and against,* trans. from the Dutch, 1949, takes in the work of more recent French historians. Leading biographical works include those of Jomini (4 v., Paris, 1827; Eng. tr., N.Y., 1864), Pierre Lanfrey (5 v., Paris, 1867–75, and later edns. in English), J. H. Rose (2 v., 11th edn., 1934), Theodore A. Dodge (4 v., Boston, 1904–7), Jacques Bainville (1932). See also Maximilien Yorck von Wartenburg, *Napoleon as a general,* trans. from the German, 2 v., 1902. John Eldred Howard, ed., *Letters and documents of Napoleon,* v. 1: *The rise to power* [*1784–1802*], 1961.

941 SCHWERTFEGER (BERNHARD HEINRICH). Geschichte der königlich deutschen Legion, 1803–16. 2 v. Hanover and Leipzig. 1907.

See also N. L. Beamish, *History of the King's German Legion,* 2 v., 1832–7. L. F. C. C. von Ompteda, *A Hanoverian-English officer a hundred years ago. Memoirs of Baron Ompteda,* comp., baron L. von Ompteda, trans. by John Hill, 1892, tells of the baron's service in the Legion in England, Ireland, Gibraltar, and Denmark.

942 BOURDEAU (ÉMILE HIPPOLYTE). Campagnes modernes. 4 pts. Paris. 1912–21.

A detailed account of French military activities, 1792–1815; pt. 4 includes over a hundred maps and diagrams.

943 OMAN (*Sir* CHARLES WILLIAM CHADWICK). Studies in the Napoleonic wars. 1929.

943A GLOVER (RICHARD). Britain at bay. Defence against Napoleon, 1803–14. 1973.

(b) *The Low Countries, 1793–5*

See also Abercromby (954).

944 BROWN (ROBERT). An impartial journal of a detachment from the brigade of foot guards . . . 25 Feb. 1793 . . . [to] 9 May 1795. 1795.

945 HASTINGS (FRANCIS RAWDON-HASTINGS) *1st Marquis of.* A journal kept in the British army, from the landing of the troops under the command of Earl Moira at Ostend in June 1794 to their return to England in the following year. Liverpool. 1796.

See too *An historical journal of the British campaign on the Continent in . . . 1794 with the retreat through Holland in 1795,* Birmingham, 1797, from the military diary of Captain L. T. Jones.

946 CALVERT. The journals and correspondence of General Sir Harry Calvert . . . comprising the campaigns in Flanders and Holland in 1793–4 . . . ed. by his son, Sir Harry Verney. 1853.

947 GRAHAM. Memoirs of General [Samuel] Graham. Ed. by his son, James J. Graham. Priv. pr. Edin. 1862.

948 CHUQUET (ARTHUR). Les guerres de la Révolution. 11 v. Paris. 1886–96.

V. C. E. Dupuis, *La campagne de 1793 à l'armée du nord et des Ardennes*, 2 v., Paris, 1906–9, and M. H. M. Coutanceau, *La campagne de 1794 à l'armée du nord*, 5 v., Paris, 1903–8, were pub. under the direction of the French military staff.

949 BURNE (ALFRED HIGGINS). The noble duke of York: the military life of Frederick, Duke of York and Albany. 1949.

See also Taylor, Sir Herbert (184).

950 HARNESS. Trusty and well beloved: the letters home of William Harness, an officer of George III. Ed. by Caroline M. Duncan-Jones. 1957.

(c) *Miscellaneous, 1793–1802*

951 WAR OFFICE. Intelligence division. British minor expeditions, 1746–1814; comp. in the Intelligence branch of the Quartermaster General's department. 1884.

(d) *Holland, 1799*

952 WALSH (EDWARD). A narrative of the expedition to Holland, in the autumn of . . . 1799. 1800.

953 BUNBURY (*Sir* HENRY EDWARD). Narratives of some passages in the great war with France, 1799–1810. 1810. New edn. with an introd. by Sir J. W. Fortescue. 1927.

Bunbury was one of the best contemporary military writers. This work is also valuable for other campaigns. See also the memoir of him by his son, Sir Charles J. F. Bunbury, priv. pr., 1868.

954 ABERCROMBY. Lieutenant-General Sir Ralph Abercromby, 1793–1801; a memoir by his son, James, Lord Dunfermline. Edin. 1861.

955 GACHOT (J. EDOUARD). Les campagnes de 1799: Jourdan en Allemagne et Brune en Holland. Paris. 1906.

956 MACKESY (PIERS). Statesmen at war. The strategy of overthrow, 1798–99. 1974.

(e) *Egypt, 1799–1801*

957 WILSON (*Sir* ROBERT THOMAS). History of the British expedition to Egypt. 1802.

See Giovanni Costigan, *Sir Robert Wilson, a soldier of fortune in the Napoleonic wars*, Madison, Wisc., 1932.

958 TAFFANEL DE LA JONQUIÈRE (CLÉMENT ÉTIENNE LUCIEN MARIE DE). L'expédition d'Egypte, 1798–1801. 5 v. Paris. 1899–1907.

959 BURGOYNE (*Sir* JOHN MONTAGU). A short history of the naval and military operations in Egypt, 1798–1802. 1885.

See too *Dyott's diary, 1781–1845*, ed. Reginald W. Jeffery, 2 v., 1907, and J. F. Miot, *Mémoires pour servir à l'histoire des expéditions en Egypte et en Syrie*, 2nd edn., 1814.

(f) *Peninsular War, 1808–1814*

(i) *Bibliography*

960 AYRES DE MAGALHÃES SEPULVEDA (CHRISTOVAM). Dicionário bibliográfico da guerra peninsular. 4 v. Coimbra. 1924–30.

C. 15,000 titles; compendious but uncritical.

(ii) *Letters, Journals, Memoirs, and Biographies*

In alphabetical order of individuals. About 100 are listed in Oman, *Wellington's army* (1010). For others see Ayres (960), Bryant (98), Ward (1010).

961 COLE (JOHN WILLIAM). Memoirs of British generals distinguished during the Peninsular war. 2 v. 1856.

A. I. Shand, *Wellington's lieutenants*, 1902, includes sketches of one or two men not in Cole. Near-contemporary biographies include H. B. Robinson, *Memoirs of . . . Sir Thomas Picton*, 2nd edn., 2 v., 1836; Sir Denis Le Marchant, *Memoirs of the late Maj. Gen. Le Marchant*, priv. pr., 1841; Edwin Sidney, *Life of Lord Hill*, 1845. See also Sir Lowry Cole (4319).

962 ANGLESEY. One-leg: the life and letters of Henry William Paget, 1st Marquess of Anglesey, 1763–1854. By the [7th] Marquess of Anglesey. 1961.

963 BLAKENEY (ROBERT). A boy in the Peninsular war . . . an autobiography. Ed. by Julian Sturgis. 1899.

Blakeney was a subaltern in the 28th foot.

964 BRAGGE. Peninsular portrait, 1811–14: the letters of Captain William Bragge, 3rd (King's Own) Dragoons. Ed. by S. A. C. Cassels. 1963.

965 BUNBURY (THOMAS). Reminiscences of a veteran. . . . 3 v. 1861.

966 BURGOYNE. Life and correspondence of Field Marshall Sir John [Fox] Burgoyne. By George Wrottesley. 2 v. 1873.

967 CAMPBELL. The life of Colin Campbell, Lord Clyde. By Laurence Shadwell. 2 v. 1881.

968 COMBERMERE. Memoirs and correspondence of Field Marshal Viscount Combermere . . . from his family papers. By Mary, Viscountess Combermere and W. W. Knollys. 2 v. 1866.

969 COSTELLO. The adventures of a soldier; or, Memoirs of Edward Costello. 1841. 2nd edn. 1852. New edn. by Antony Brett-James. 1967.

970 CRAUFURD. General [Robert] Craufurd and his Light Division. By Alexander Henry Gregan Craufurd. 1891.

971 [DANIEL (JOHN EDGECOMBE)]. Journal of an officer in the commissariat department . . . 1811–15. 1820.

972 DICKSON. The Dickson manuscripts; being diaries, letters . . . [and] other papers of . . . Major-General Sir Alexander Dickson . . . Series 'C': 1809–18. Ed. by John H. Leslie. 2 v. 1908–12.

973 DOUGLAS. The life of General Sir Howard Douglas, from his notes, conversations and correspondence. By Stephen Watson Fullom. 1863.

974 D'URBAN. The Peninsular journal of Major-General Sir Benjamin D'Urban . . . 1808–17. Ed. by I. J. Rousseau. 1930.

975 FRAZER. Letters of Col. Sir Augustus Simon Frazer . . . written during the Peninsular and Waterloo campaigns. Ed. by Edward Sabine. 1859.

976 GLEIG (GEORGE ROBERT). The subaltern. 1825. Repr. 1915.

977 GOMM. Letters and journals of Field-Marshal Sir William Maynard Gomm . . . from 1779 to Waterloo, 1815. Ed. by Francis C. Carr-Gomm. 1881.

978 GORDON (ALEXANDER). A cavalry officer in the Corunna campaign, 1808–9: the journal of Captain Gordon of the 15th Hussars. Ed. by H. C. Wylly. 1913.

979 GRAHAM. Freshly remembered: the story of Thomas Graham, Lord Lynedoch. By Cecil Aspinall-Oglander. 1956.
See also Antony Brett-James, *General Graham, Lord Lynedoch*, 1959.

980 GRATTAN (WILLIAM). Adventures of the Connaught Rangers, 1808–14. 2 v. 1847. Abridged by Charles Oman. 1902.

981 GRONOW (REES HOWELL). The reminiscences and recollections of Captain Gronow . . . 1810–60. 2 v. 1889.

982 HARRIS (JOHN). Recollections of Rifleman Harris (old 95th). Ed. by Henry Curling. 1848. Repr. with introd. by Sir John Fortescue. 1928.

983 HAY (*Sir* ANDREW LEITH). A narrative of the Peninsular war. 2 v. Edin. 1831.

984 KINCAID (*Sir* JOHN). Adventures in the Rifle Brigade in the Peninsula, France, and the Netherlands, 1809–15. 1830. Repr. with introd. by Sir John Fortescue. 1929.
Kincaid also wrote, *Random shots from a rifleman*, 1835.

985 LARPENT. The private journal of F. S. Larpent, Judge-Advocate General. Ed. by Sir G. Larpent. 3 v. 1853.

986 LAWRENCE. The autobiography of Serjeant William Lawrence, a hero of the Peninsular and Waterloo campaigns. Ed. by G. N. Bankes. 1886.

987 LESLIE. The military journal of Colonel Charles Leslie, 28th Regiment, 1807–32. Aberdeen. 1837.

988 LONG. Peninsular cavalry general (1811–13): the correspondence of Lieutenant-General Robert Ballard Long. Ed. by T. H. McGuffie. 1951.

989 LUARD. Scarlet Lancer. By James Lunt. 1964.

The adventures of John Luard, 1805–42, including service in the Peninsular war and at Waterloo.

990 MOORE. Sir John Moore. By Carola Mary Anima Oman. 1953.

Sir John F. Maurice ed., *The diary of Sir John Moore*, 2 v., 1904, a valuable source for all campaigns and activities in which Moore was engaged.

991 NAPIER. Passages in the early military life of General Sir George Thomas Napier. Ed. by William Craig E. Napier. 1884.

992 PAGET. Letters and memorials of General Sir Edward Paget. Collected and arranged by his daughter, Harriet Mary Paget. Ed. by Eden Paget. Priv. pr. 1898.

993 PAKENHAM. Pakenham letters, 1800–1815. Ed. by Thomas Pakenham, Lord Longford. Priv. pr. 1914.

Mainly letters written by Sir Edward Michael Pakenham, and also exclusively concerned with the Peninsular war.

994 ROBERTSON (*Sergeant* D.). The journal of Sergeant D. Robertson. Perth. 1842.

His military diaries, 1797–1818.

995 SCHAUMANN (AUGUST LUDOLF FRIEDRICH). On the road with Wellington; the diary of a war commissary in the Peninsular campaigns. Trans. and ed. by Anthony M. Ludovici. 1924.

996 [SHERER (MOYLE)]. Recollections of the Peninsula. 1823.

997 SIMMONS. A British rifleman: the journals and correspondence of Major George Simmons, Rifle Brigade, during the Peninsular war and the campaign of Waterloo. Ed. by Willoughby Verner. 1899.

998 SMITH. The autobiography of Lieutenant-General Sir Harry Smith. Ed. by G. C. Moore Smith. 2 v. 1902.

His army career, 1787–1846; valuable for military, public, and private life.

999 TOMKINSON (WILLIAM). The diary of a cavalry officer in the Peninsular and Waterloo campaigns, 1809–15. Ed. by James Tomkinson. 1894.

Very full accounts of experiences, by the lieutenant-colonel, 16th light dragoons.

1000 WARRE (*Sir* WILLIAM). Letters from the Peninsula, 1808–12. Ed. by Edmond Warre. 1909.

1001 WHEATLEY (EDMUND). The Wheatley diary; a journal and sketch book kept during the Peninsular war and the Waterloo campaign. Ed. with an introd. and notes by Christopher Hibbert. 1964.

1002 WHEELER (WILLIAM). The letters of Private Wheeler, 1809–28. Ed. by B. H. Liddell Hart. 1951.

1003 WHITTINGHAM. A memoir of the services of Lieutenant-General Sir Samuel Ford Whittingham. Ed. by Major-General Ferdinand Whittingham. 1868.

Much material on the Peninsular war, and on later service in India.

1004 WOODBERRY (GEORGE). Journal du Lieutenant Woodberry: campagnes de Portugal et d'Espagne, de France, de Belgique et de France, 1813–5. Trans. and ed. from the English MS. by Georges Hélie. Paris. 1896.

(iii) *General Histories*

1005 FOY (MAXIMILIEN SEBASTIEN), *count*. History of the war in the Peninsula under Napoleon . . . published by the Countess Foy; trans. from the French. 2 v. 1827.

Contains much valuable information from the French side. See also Nicolas Jean-de-Dieu Soult, Duke of Dalmatia, *Mémoires sur les opérations . . . en 1809*, Paris, 1821; *Mémoires de Masséna*, ed. by Jean Baptiste Frederic Koch, 7 v., Paris, 1848–50; Louis Gabriel Suchet, Duke of Albuféra, *Memoirs of the war in Spain, 1808–14*, 1829.

1006 NAPIER (*Sir* WILLIAM FRANCIS PATRICK). History of the war in the Peninsula and in the south of France, 1807–14. 6 v. 1828–40.

An excellent first-hand account on some points, but often marred by prejudice. Vividly written, it 'killed' Robert Southey's *History of the Peninsular war*, 3 v., 1823–32. Lord Londonderry, *Narrative of the Peninsular war . . . 1808–13*, 2 v., 1828, provides valuable information from his own letters to his brother, Castlereagh. The Londonderry MSS. are now in Durham C.R.O.; see S. C. Newton, ed., *The Londonderry Papers, Durham*, 1969.

1007 GÓMEZ DE ARTECHE Y MORO (JOSÉ). Guerra de la independencia: historia militar de España de 1808 á 1814. 14 v. Madrid. 1868–1903.

1008 OMAN (*Sir* CHARLES WILLIAM CHADWICK). A history of the Peninsular war. 7 v. Oxf. 1902–30.

A full definitive narrative. Other discussions of the military events are: L. W. G. Butler, *Wellington's operations in the Peninsula, 1808–14*, 2 v., 1904; Sir Charles W. Robinson, *Wellington's campaigns, Peninsula–Waterloo, 1808–15: also Moore's campaign of Corunna*, 3 pts., 1905–6; Christopher Hibbert, *Corunna*, 1961.

1009 GRASSET (ALPHONSE LOUIS). La guerre d'Espagne, 1807–13.
3 v. Paris. 1914–32.

Officially sponsored, as were D. E. P. Balagny, *Campagne de l'empereur Napoléon en
Espagne, 1808–9*, 5 v., Paris, 1902–7; Finlay C. Beatson, *With Wellington in the Pyrenees
. . . July 25 to Aug. 2, 1813* [1914]; H. J. M. C. Vidal de la Blache, *L'Evacuation de
l'Espagne et l'invasion dans le Midi, juin 1813–avril 1814*, 2 v., Paris, 1914.

1010 WARD (STEPHEN GEORGE PEREGRINE). Wellington's head-
quarters; a study of the administrative problems of the Peninsula, 1809–14.
1957.

Sir Charles W. C. Oman, *Wellington's army, 1809–14*, 1912, is authoritative for the
organization of the army, its day-to-day life, and its psychology; appendix by C. T.
Atkinson, 'Divisional and brigade organization and changes, 1809–14', pp. 343–73.
Godfrey Davies, *Wellington and his army*, Oxf., 1954, is mainly concerned with the
internal economy of the army and not with military operations.

1011 GLOVER (MICHAEL). Wellington as military commander. 1968.

An authoritative assessment. See also: M. Glover, *Wellington's Peninsular victories;
Bussaco, Salamanca, Vitoria, Nivelle*, 1963; D. D. Horward, *The battle of Bussaco:
Massena v. Wellington*, Tallahassu, Fla, 1965, well documented from French as well as
English sources; P. Young and J. P. Lawford, *Wellington's masterpiece: the battle and
campaign of Salamanca*, 1973; Jac Weller, *Wellington in the Peninsula, 1808–14*, 1962,
with special attention to tactics and terrain.

1012 GLOVER (MICHAEL). Britannia sickens; Sir Arthur Wellesley and
the Convention of Cintra. 1970.

(g) *Waterloo*

1013 JAMES. Surgeon James's journal, 1815. Ed. by Jane Vansittart. 1964.

1014 VERNER. Reminiscences of William Verner (1782–1871), 7th Hussars;
an account of service . . . including the battle of Waterloo. Ed. by Ruth W.
Verner (Society for Army Historical Research, special publns. 8). 1965.

1015 SIBORNE (WILLIAM). History of the war in France and Belgium in
1815; containing minute details of the battles of Quatre Bras, Ligny, Wavre
and Waterloo. 2 v. 1844. 4th edn. under title, The Waterloo campaign, 1815.
Birmingham. 1894.

Comprehensive. See also Cavalié Mercer, *Journal of the Waterloo campaign kept throughout the campaign of 1815*, 2 v., 1870. Repr. with introd. by Sir John Fortescue, 1927.

1016 GLEIG (GEORGE ROBERT). Story of the battle of Waterloo. 1847.

By Wellington's later biographer.

1017 CHESNEY (CHARLES CORNWALLIS). Waterloo lectures: a study
of the campaign of 1815. 1868. 4th edn. 1907.

See too Sir James S. Kennedy, *Notes on the battle of Waterloo*, 1865; William Leeke,
The history of Lord Seaton's regiment . . . at the battle of Waterloo, 2 v., 1866–71.

1018 SIBORNE (HERBERT TAYLOR). Waterloo letters. 1891.

A selection from a collection of letters now in the B.L.

1019 ROPES (JOHN GODMAN). The campaign of Waterloo; a military history. 1893.

An impartial discussion of various disputed points.

1020 WOOD (*Sir* HENRY EVELYN). Cavalry in the Waterloo campaign. 1895.

1021 DALTON (CHARLES). The Waterloo roll call; with biographical notes and anecdotes. 2nd edn. 1904.

1022 BAS (FRANÇOIS DE) *and* T'SERCLAES DE WOMMERSON (JACQUES AUGUSTIN J. A. F. L. G. DE) *count*. La campagne de 1815 aux Bays-Bas d'après les rapports officiels néerlandais. 3 v. and suppl. Brussels. 1908–9.

1023 BECKE (ARCHIBALD FRANK). Napoleon and Waterloo; the emperor's campaign with the Armée du Nord, 1815. 2 v. 1914. Rev. edn. 1936.

Henry Houssaye, *1815, Waterloo*, trans. from the 31st French edn. by A. E. Mann and ed. by A. Euan Smith, 1900, is a full, vivid, and accurate narrative from the French viewpoint. Among other discussions by French authors are Auguste Antoine Grouard, *Stratégie Napoléonienne—la critique de la campagne de 1815*, Paris, 1904; E. Lenient, *La solution des énigmes de Waterloo*, Paris, 1915; Henri Lachouque, *Le secret de Waterloo*, Paris, 1952.

1024 WELLER (JAC). Wellington at Waterloo. 1967.

Good battlefield illustrations, but weak on French battle dispositions.

(h) *Miscellaneous, 1802–15*

1025 STEWART. Cumloden papers. Priv. pr. Edin. 1871.

From the military journals of Sir William Stewart, 1794–1809, concerning service in various theatres of war.

1026 WILSON (*Sir* ROBERT THOMAS). Private diary of travels, personal services, and public events, during mission and employment with the European armies in the campaigns of 1812, 1813, 1814. From the invasion of Russia to the capture of Paris. Ed. by Herbert Randolph. 2 v. 1861. New edn. by A. Brett-James. 1964.

Includes letters. H. Randolph also ed., *Life of General Sir Robert Wilson*, 1862, dealing with his adventures up to 1807.

1027 BAIRD. The life of Sir David Baird. By Walter Harold Wilkin. 1912.

Baird served at the Cape of Good Hope, in Denmark, and at Corunna, and also in India.

2. THE WAR OF 1812

1028 JAMES (WILLIAM). A full and correct account of the military occurrences of the late war between Great Britain and the United States. 2 v. 1818.

See also H. M. Brackenridge, *History of the late war between the United States and Great Britain*, Baltimore, 1816, 6th edn., Phil., 1836.

1029   FAY (HEMAN ALLEN) *ed.* Collection of the official accounts, in detail, of all the battles fought by sea and land between the navy and army of the United States and the navy and army of Great Britain during 1812–15. N.Y. 1817.

See also John Brannan, ed., *Official letters of the military and naval officers of the United States during the war with Great Britain in 1812–15*, Wash., 1823.

1030   BEIRNE (FRANCIS FOULKE). The War of 1812. N.Y. 1949.

See also Herbert W. Wilson, 'The war of 1812–15', in *C.M.H.*, v. 7, 335–48, bibliog., 797–9; A. R. Gilpin, *The war of 1812 in the old northwest*, East Lansing, Mich., 1958; Reginald Horsman, *The war of 1812*, 1969.

3. 1815–51

1031   GIBSON (TOM). The Maori wars. The British army in New Zealand, 1840–1872. 1974.

C. THE ART OF WAR

1. TACTICS

1032   DUNDAS (*Sir* DAVID). Principles of military movements, chiefly applied to infantry; illustrated by manœuvres of the Prussian troops, and by an outline of the British campaigns in Germany during the war of 1757. 1788. 2nd edn. 1795.

Dundas also pub., *Rules and regulations for the formations, field-exercises, and movements of H.M. forces*, [1792], new edns., 1794, 1798, 1801; *Instructions and regulations for the formations and movements of the cavalry*, 1799, and several later edns. See too J. G. Le Marchant, *Elucidation of certain points in H.M. regulations for cavalry*, 1797–8; Robert Smirke, *Review of a battalion of infantry, including the eighteen manœuvres*, 1799.

1033   JAMES (CHARLES). The regimental companion; containing the relative duties of every officer in the British Army. 1799. 7th edn. 4 v. 1811–13.

See T. H. McGuffie, 'The significance of military rank in the British army between 1790 and 1820', *Bull. I.H.R.* 30 (1957), 207–24.

1034   JAMES (CHARLES). A new and enlarged military dictionary. 1802. 4th edn. 1816.

035   JACKSON (ROBERT). A systematic view of the formation, discipline and economy of armies. 1804. 3rd edn. 1845.

1036   LOPEZ SUASSO DIAZ DE FONSECA (ANTONIO), *baron.* A treatise on the British drill and exercise of the company. 2nd edn. 1816.

See also his work, *The theory of the infantry movements*, 3 v., 1825, new edn., 1846.

1037   BECKE (ARCHIBALD FRANK). An introduction to the history of tactics, 1740–1905. 1909.

1038 FULLER (JOHN FREDERIC CHARLES). Sir John Moore's system of training. 1925.

1039 TURNER (ERNEST SACKVILLE). Gallant gentlemen: a portrait of the British officer, 1600–1956. 1956.

1040 SMYTH (*Sir* JOHN GEORGE). Sandhurst: the history of the Royal Military Academy, Woolwich, the Royal Military College, Sandhurst, and the Royal Military Academy, Sandhurst, 1741–1961. 1961.

See too Hugh S. Thomas, *The story of Sandhurst*, 1961. R. H. Thoumine, *Scientific soldier*, 1968, is an excellent study of General Le Marchant as a military educationist.

1041 GLOVER (RICHARD). Peninsular preparation; the reform of the British army, 1795–1809. Camb. 1963.

An excellent survey, and indispensable.

1042 LUVAAS (JAY). The education of an army; British military thought, 1815–1940. 1965.

Includes a substantial chapter on the period 1815–54. See also R. L. Blanco, 'Reform and Wellington's post-Waterloo army, 1815–1854', *Military Affairs*, 29 (1965), 123–31.

2. ARTILLERY, FORTIFICATIONS, AND SMALL-ARMS

1043 ADYE (RALPH WILLETT). The little bombardier, and pocket gunner. 1801. 8th edn. rev. by William G. Eliot. 1827.

See also J. M. Spearman, *The British gunner*, 1828, 4th edn., 1850.

1044 GORDON (ANTHONY). A treatise on the science of defence for the sword, bayonet, and pike in close action. 1805.

1045 BRADDOCK (JOHN). A memoir on gun-powder, in which are discussed the principles both of its manufacture and proof. 1832.

1046 PASLEY (*Sir* CHARLES WILLIAM). Rules, chiefly deduced from experiment, for conducting the practical operations of a siege. Chatham. 1829.

1047 STRAITH (HECTOR). A treatise on fortification . . . with observations on the increased effects of artillery. Croydon. 1833. 6th edn. 2 v. 1852.

See also Sir Henry Yule, *Fortification for officers of the army and students of military history, with notes*, 1851.

1048 GREENER (WILLIAM). The gun; or, A treatise on the various descriptions of small fire-arms. 1835. 3rd edn. 1885.

1049 HIME (HENRY WILLIAM LOVETT). Gunpowder and ammunition, their origin and progress. 1904.

1050 CHARBONNIER (PROSPER JULES). Essais sur l'histoire de la balistique. Paris. 1928.

1051 PETERSON (HAROLD LESLIE) *ed.* Encyclopaedia of firearms. 1964.

Gives historical data on nineteenth-century firearms. Hugh B. C. Pollard, *A history of firearms*, 1926, is a manual and history for aid in identification. See too: W. Y. Carman, *A history of firearms from earliest times to 1914*, 1955; John N. George, *English guns and rifles*, Plantersville, S. Car., 1947; H. L. Blackmore, *British military firearms, 1650–1850*, 1961; Ian Glendenning, *British pistols and guns, 1640–1840*, 1951, consisting mainly of plates; A. W. F. Taylerson and others, *The revolver, 1818–1865*, 1968; De Witt Bailey, *British military longarms, 1715–1815*, 1971, and *British military longarms, 1815–1865*, 1972.

1052 HOGG (OLIVER FREDERICK GILLILAN). Artillery; its origin, heyday and decline, 1970.

An excellent survey. See also O. F. G. Hogg, *Royal Arsenal* (1572), and Basil P. Hughes, *British smooth-bore artillery; the muzzle loading artillery of the eighteenth and nineteenth centuries*, 1969.

1053 HAYWARD (JOHN FORREST). The art of the gunmaker. v. 2: Europe and America, 1660–1830. 1963.

See also W. K. Neal and D. H. L. Back, *The Mantons: gunmakers*, 1967, and *Forsyth and co., patent gunmakers* [1969].

1054 WILKINSON-LATHAM (JOHN). British cut and thrust weapons. Newton Abbot. 1971.

See also the same author's *British military swords from 1800*, 1966, and *British military bayonets*, 1967. Older surveys are Alfred Hutton, *Fixed bayonets*, 1890; C. J. Ffoulkes and E. C. Hopkinson, *Sword, lance, and bayonet; a record of the arms of the British army and navy*, Camb., 1938.

D. LISTS AND REGISTERS

1055 ARMY. A list of the general and field officers as they rank in the army. [pub. by authority]. [1754–1868].

The *Army List*, afterwards *The Monthly Army List*, 1814+.

1056 ARMY. List of officers of the royal regiment of artillery from . . . 1716 to the present date. 1869.

A rev. edn. of John Kane, *List of officers of the royal regiment of artillery, as they stood in 1763, with a continuation to the present time*, 1815.

1057 PHILIPPART (JOHN). The royal military calendar, containing the services of every general officer in the British army, from the date of their first commission. 3 v. 1815. 3rd edn. 5 v. 1820.

1058 JOHNSTON (WILLIAM). Roll of commissioned officers in the medical service of the British army, who served on full pay . . . 20 June 1727 to 23 June 1898. Ed. by Harry A. L. Howell. Aberdeen. 1917.

E. ARMY ADMINISTRATION

1059 REIDE (THOMAS). Treatise on military finance. 1795. 9th edn. 1805.

1060 WILSON (*Sir* ROBERT THOMAS). An enquiry into the present state of the military force of the British empire, with a view to its re-organization, addressed to the Rt. Hon. William Pitt. Priv. pr. 1804.

1061 PASLEY (*Sir* CHARLES WILLIAM). Essay on the military policy and institutions of the British empire. Pt. 1. 1810.

See also Edward Sterling, *Views of military reform*, 2nd edn., 1811.

1062 [SCOTT (ROBERT BISSET)]. The military law of England . . . and the practice of courts martial. 1810.

With an app. of precedents. See also: S. P. Adye, *A treatise on courts martial*, 3rd edn., 1786, 8th edn., 1810; William Hough, *The practice of courts-martial*, 1825, 3rd edn., 1835, and *Military law authorities: chronological exposition* . . . [*1781–1836*], 1839; Sir C. J. Napier, *Remarks on military law and the punishment of flogging*, 1837; Thomas F. Simmons, *The constitution and practice of courts martial*, 1830, 3rd edn., 1843, R. M. Hughes, *The duties of judge advocates*, 1845. For a later survey see C. M. Clode, *The administration of justice under military and martial law*, 1872.

1063 CLODE (CHARLES MATHEW). The military forces of the crown; their administration and government. 2 v. 1869.

Invaluable, if now outdated. For various aspects see also: E. B. de Fonblanque, *Treatise on the administration and organization of the British army, with especial reference to finance and supply*, 1858; Sir John W. Fortescue, *The British army, 1783–1802*, 1905, and *The county lieutenancies and the army, 1803–14*, 1909; J. S. Omond, *Parliament and the army, 1642–1904*, Camb., 1933.

1064 FORBES (ARTHUR). A history of the army ordnance services. 3 v. 1929.

1065 MASSÉ (CHARLES HENRI). The predecessors of the Royal Army Service Corps, 1757–1888. Aldershot. 1948.

1066 CLAVER (SCOTT). Under the lash: a history of corporal punishment in the British armed forces, including a digest of the report of the Royal Commission, 1835. 1954.

F. HISTORY OF SPECIAL BRANCHES

1. ARTILLERY, ENGINEERS, CAVALRY

1067 CONNOLLY (THOMAS WILLIAM JOHN). History of the Royal sappers and miners, from the formation of the corps in March 1772. 2nd edn. 2 v. 1857.

1068 DUNCAN (FRANCIS). History of the Royal regiment of artillery, compiled from the original records. 3rd edn. 2 v. 1879.

George G. Walker, *The Honourable Artillery Company, 1537–1947*, 2nd edn., Aldershot, 1954, includes a wealth of quotation from the Company's archives. See also John H. Leslie, *The services of the Royal regiment of artillery, in the Peninsular war, 1808–14*, 1912; and H. W. L. Hime, *History of the Royal regiment of artillery, 1815–53*, 1908. *The journal of the Royal Artillery*, 1905 +, was preceded by *Minutes of Proceedings of the Royal Artillery Institution* from 1858.

1069 PORTER (WHITWORTH) *and* WATSON (CHARLES MOORE). History of the corps of Royal engineers. 3 v. 1889–1915.

1070 ROGERS (HUGH CUTHBERT BASSET). The mounted troops of the British army, 1066–1945. 1959.

> Much misc. information, and illustrations of uniforms and equipment. Leonard Cooper, *British regular cavalry, 1644–1914*, 1966, includes brief surveys of engagements. And see Geoffrey Tylden, *Horses and saddlery*, 1965.

1071 PAGET (GEORGE C. H. V.), *7th Marquess of Anglesey*. A history of the British cavalry, 1816–1919. V. 1: 1816–50. 1973.

2. Medical

1072 JACKSON (ROBERT). A system of arrangement and discipline for the medical department of armies. 1805.

1073 HUNTER (JOHN). A treatise on the blood, inflammation, and gun-shot wounds. 1794. New edn. 1828.

1074 GUTHRIE (GEORGE JAMES). On gun-shot wounds of the extremities. 1815. 2nd edn. 1820.

> By the leading British military surgeon of the time. See too John Hennen, *Observations on some important points in the practice of military surgery*, Edin., 1818, 3rd edn., 1829; Sir George Ballingall, *Outlines of . . . military surgery*, 1833, 3rd edn., 1844.

1075 GARRISON (FIELDING HUDSON). Notes on the history of military medicine. Wash. 1922.

> Originally printed in *The Military Surgeon*, Nov. 1921–Aug. 1922. See too, *The autobiography and services of Sir James McGrigor, late director general of the army medical department*, 1861; A. A. Gore, *The story of our services under the crown: a historical sketch of the army medical staff*, 1879.

1076 DREW (*Sir* ROBERT) *and others*. Commissioned officers in the medical services of the British army, 1660–1960. V. 2: 1727–1898. 1968.

> John Laffin, *Surgeons in the field*, 1970.

3. Intelligence

1077 DEACON (RICHARD), *pseud.* of George D. K. McCormick. A history of the British secret service. 1969.

> Jock Haswell (*pseud.* of C. J. D. Haswell), *The first respectable spy; the life and times of Colquhoun Grant, Wellington's head of intelligence*, 1969, is full and well documented.

4. Military Music

1078 FARMER (HENRY GEORGE). History of the Royal artillery band, 1763–1953. 1954.

> Lewis S. Winstock, *Songs and music of the redcoats; a history of the war music of the British army, 1642–1902*, 1970, bibliog., 284–9.

5. DRESS

1079 SMITH (CHARLES HAMILTON). Costume of the army of the British empire. 1815.

1080 LAWSON (CECIL CONSTANT PHILIP). A history of the uniforms of the British army. 1962, in progress.

V. 3 onwards is comprehensive on the period after 1789.

1081 GORDON (LAWRENCE LEE). British battles and medals. 2nd edn. Aldershot. 1850.

See too J. H. Mayo, *Medals and decorations of the British army and navy*, 2 v., 1897; Algernon A. Payne, *A handbook of British and foreign orders, war medals and decorations awarded to the army and navy*, Sheffield, 1911.

G. REGIMENTAL HISTORIES

1082 WHITE (ARTHUR SHARPIN), *comp.* A bibliography of regimental histories of the British army. (Society for Army Historical Research, special publications: Army Museums Ogilby Trust Publications). 1965.

An indispensable guide to an extensive literature. See also British Library, *Catalogue*, 'England', Army, subdivision 'Regiments', under the various branches—cavalry, infantry, etc.

1083 CHICHESTER (HENRY MANNERS) *and* BURGES-SHORT (GEORGE). The records and badges of every regiment and corps in the British army . . . with twenty-four coloured plates and 240 illustrations. 3rd edn. 1902.

VII

NAVAL HISTORY

A. MANUSCRIPT SOURCES

At the beginning of the nineteenth century the management of the Navy involved a far larger and more complex organization than any other branch of government. The general control of policy and operations rested with the Board of Admiralty. The Navy Board, acting in accordance with the general instructions of the Admiralty, was concerned with material, non-combatant personnel, and civil administration, until, in 1832, it was abolished and its responsibilities assumed by the Admiralty operating through new special departments. Also in 1832 the subordinate board of the Commissioners of the Victualling was replaced by a Controller of Victualling. The financial duties of the Treasurer of the Navy, a member of the Navy Board, were transferred to the Paymaster General on the abolition of the office in 1835. A Transport Board was operative during the French wars (1794–1817).

1. Public Record Office

For detailed lists of many of the classes of naval records see the printed P.R.O. *Lists and Indexes*, 18, 1904. The following are some of the more important. classes.

(a) *Admiralty Board*

In-Letters. Secretary's Department. Adm. 1.

Dispatches, letters from commanders-in-chief, captains of ships, and from various departments connected with the navy.

Out-Letters. Adm. 2.

Letters to public offices, to admirals, and to commanders-in-chief of squadrons and stations at home and abroad, to 1815. Continued thereafter in Out-Letters Supplementary (Adm. 13). Owing to severe weeding letters may often be found only in the papers of other departments. Home Office H.O. 28, Admiralty Correspondence, 1782–1840, includes original in-letters and drafts of out-letters; H.O. 29, Admiralty, entry books, 1779–1836, includes entries of out-letters, warrants, instructions.

Minutes of the Board. Adm. 3.

During the nineteenth century minutes were increasingly noted on the in-letters (Adm. 1).

Navy Board Records. Adm. 106.

Minutes; incomplete series of in-letters, from the Admiralty, from public
boards and from naval officers; entry-books of out-letters to the Admiralty,
to public boards (1806–31); standing orders to the dockyards; miscellanea
relating to armaments, stores, visitations of dockyards, and various dockyard
letter-books. This series is complemented by holdings at the National Maritime Museum (*see below*).

(b) *Treasurer of the Navy and Accountant General's Department*

Treasurer's ledgers, to 1836. Adm. 20.
Accountant General's ledgers, from 1826. Adm. 21.
Registers of salaries and pensions. Adm. 22.
Registers of officers on full pay, from 1795. Adm. 24.
Half pay registers. Adm. 25.
Ships' pay books, to 1830. Adm. 31–5.
Ships' musters. Adm. 36–9.

(c) *Transport Department*

Transport records. Adm. 108.

For the most part documents accumulated by the Transport Board (1794–
1817) and thereafter of the transport organization conducted by the Navy
Board and Victualling Office: in-letters, out-letters, minutes, ships and freight
ledgers, letter books of the Transport Office at Deal.

(d) *Victualling Department*

In-Letters. Adm. 109.

Letters from the Admiralty, Navy Board, Treasury and other departments,
victualling yards and stations, 1793–1849; much weeded after 1822.

Register of letters received. Adm. 134.

Brief particulars of each letter with the proceedings taken thereon, 1822–1849:
the sole record for many transactions after 1822, the original letters having
been destroyed.

(e) *Admiralty Medical Department*

Documentation of medical appointments, hospitals, and of prisoners of war,
1796–1833. Adm. 97–105, 132–3.

2. NATIONAL MARITIME MUSEUM

The Museum was established in 1934 for the illustration and study of the maritime history of Great Britain. Its Manuscript Department contains records from
official, semi-official, and private sources. The official section includes Admiralty
orders to the Navy Board and the Victualling Board, the Lieutenants' logs, and

the dockyard records of Portsmouth, Chatham, and Woolwich. In the semi-official class is Lloyd's Register of Shipping from 1834. The private records include the private papers of Sir Francis Austen, Codrington, Collingwood, Cornwallis, Duncan, Exmouth, Foley, Keith, Keppel, Napier, Sir William Parker, and Earl St. Vincent: see Katharine Frances Lindsay-MacDougall, *A guide to the manuscripts at the National Maritime Museum*, 1960. The Department also holds unpublished transcripts deposited by the Navy Records Society, and a microfilm of the Minutes of the Board of Longitude, 1714–1828, preserved at the Royal Observatory, Herstmonceaux.

B. BIBLIOGRAPHY AND CATALOGUES

See Higham (926); Marcus (1104).

1084 MANWARING (GEORGE ERNEST). A bibliography of British naval history. 1930.

> Primarily a guide to MS. materials and to periodical articles; omits individual books but includes composite works. Arranged under author and subject headings. The *Catalogue of naval manuscripts in the library of the Royal United Service Institution*, comp. by H. Garbett, [1914], lists 500 MSS. covering 1636–1864.

1085 MINISTRY OF DEFENCE. Author [and subject] catalogue of the naval library, Ministry of Defence, London. 5 v. Boston. 1967.

> A guide to one of the largest collections of books on naval and maritime affairs. Earlier catalogues of the then Admiralty library, by R. Thorburn, 1875, and W. G. Perrin, 1912, can be helpful. See too the *Official catalogue of the Royal United Services Museum*, 8th edn., ed. by E. L. Hughes, 1932.

1086 NATIONAL MARITIME MUSEUM. Catalogue of the library. 1968, in progress.

> A guide, under subject arrangement, to over 50,000 volumes covering every aspect of maritime affairs; v. 1: voyages and travel; v. 2: pts. 1 and 2: biography; v. 3, pts. 1 and 2: atlases and cartography; v. 4: piracy and privateering.

1087 ALBION (ROBERT GREENHALGH). Naval and maritime history: an annotated bibliography. 4th edn. Mystic, Conn. 1972.

> Louis H. Bolander comp. in three parts an extensive mimeographed *Bibliography of naval literature in the United States Naval Academy library*, [Annapolis, 1929]; it is useful for British naval history.

C. GENERAL WORKS

The Navy Records Society (hereafter NRS) was founded in 1893 for the purpose of printing rare or unpublished works of naval interest; and, up to 1970, has published 115 volumes. All the volumes containing material on the period 1789–1851 have been listed below. Nos. 1–63, 1895–1928, are indexed in Manwaring (1084).

1. SOURCES

1088 PARLIAMENT. Report(s) of the Commissioners appointed by an Act 43

Geo. 3, for inquiring into irregularities, frauds and abuses practised in the naval departments, and in the business of prize agency. [14 reports.] 1802–6.

These, together with the thirteen *Reports of the Commissioners for revising and digesting the civil affairs of H.M. navy*, 1806–9, provide a vast extent of information about naval organization and administration at the start of the nineteenth century.

1089 THE NAVAL CHRONICLE. V. 1–40. 1799–1818. Publ. in half-yearly vols; indexed in Manwaring (1084).

1090 JAMES (WILLIAM). The naval history of Great Britain . . . 1793–1820. 5 v. 1822–4.

Numerous later edns. in 6 v. An invaluable index to the 1886 edn. was prepared by C. G. Toogood and ed. by T. A. Brassey, NRS 4, 1895. The best known of contemporary histories but less accurate is E. P. Brenton, *Naval history of Great Britain, 1793–1820*, new edn., 2 v., 1837. See also John Campbell, *The naval history of Great Britain, including the history and lives of the British admirals*, 2nd edn., 8 v., 1818.

1091 SCHOMBERG (ISAAC). Naval chronology; or, An historical summary of naval and maritime events from the time of the Romans to the treaty of peace, 1802. 5 v. 1802. New edn. rev. and corr. 1815.

Vs. 4 and 5 contain lists of fleets and squadrons, and of admirals and captains; in spite of the title, Schomberg was chiefly concerned with 1750–1800. James Ralfe, *The naval chronology of Great Britain . . . 1803–16*, 3 v., 1820, was intended as a continuation of Schomberg, but on a more extensive scale. Charles Derrick, *Memoirs of the rise and progress of the Royal navy*, 1806, is valuable on non-operational subjects and contains valuable statistics. See too F. P. C. Dupin, *Force navale de la Grande-Bretagne*, 2 v. in 1, Paris, 1825; César Moreau, *Chronological records of the British Royal and commercial navy*, 1827, with tables of shipping, fleet dispositions and other data, culled from official records.

1092 NAUTICAL MAGAZINE. 1832+. Index, 1832–51. 1851.

Deals with the naval and mercantile service, and later on chiefly the latter.

1093 NAPIER (*Sir* CHARLES). The navy; its past and present state. Ed. by Sir William Napier. 1851.

See also Francis Steinitz, *The ship: its origin and progress*, 1849, a rather discursive narrative of naval warfare, with considerable detail for events from 1793.

1094 LAUGHTON (*Sir* JOHN KNOX) *and others, eds.* The naval miscellany. 4 v. NRS 20, 40, 63, 92. 1902–52.

Many letters and documents relating to the period 1793–1815. Nos. 20, 40, and 63 are indexed in Manwaring (1084). William Bowles, *Pamphlets on naval subjects*, 1854, includes pieces written 1830–49.

2. LATER WORKS

1095 BUSK (HANS). The navies of the world; their present state and future capabilities. 1859.

Useful for comparisons.

1096 RAYMOND (XAVIER). Les marines de la France et de l'Angleterre, 1815–63. Paris. 1863.

See also Pierre J. Charliat, *Trois siècles d'économie maritime française*, Paris, 1931. Standard histories on other navies include Cesáreo Fernández Duro, *Armada española*, 9 v., Madrid, 1895–1903 (vs. 8–9 cover 1789–1833); Johannes Cornelis de Jonge, *Geschiedenis van het Nederlandsche zeewezen*, 5 v., Haarlem, 1858–62 (v. 5 covers 1795–1810); E. S. Maclay. *A history of the United States navy*, 1775–1901, new edn., 3 v., N.Y., 1901; R. W. Neeser, *Statistical and chronological history of the United States navy, 1775–1907*, 2 v., N.Y., 1909.

1097 CLOWES (*Sir* WILLIAM LAIRD). The Royal Navy: a history from the earliest times to the present. 7 v. 1897–1903.

Standard, but becoming out-dated. Charles N. Robinson, *The British fleet: the growth, achievements and duties of the navy of the empire*, 1894, is an admirable many-sided study. See also David Hannay, *A short history of the Royal navy, 1217–1815*, 2 v., 1898–[1909], v. 2, *1689–1815*.

1098 COLOMB (PHILIP HOWARD). Naval warfare, its ruling principles and practice, historically treated. 3rd edn. 1899.

1099 BRIDGE (*Sir* CYPRIAN ARTHUR GEORGE). Sea-power, and other studies. 1910.

Collected essays by one of the most illuminating writers on naval subjects. See too Sir Julian S. Corbett, *Some principles of maritime strategy*, 1911, and A. T. Mahan, *Naval strategy*, 1911.

1100 THE MARINER'S MIRROR: the journal of the Society for Nautical Research. 1911+.

Index to 1–35 (1911–48), Camb., 1955. See also *J. of the Roy. United Serv. Instn.* (933).

1101 FIELD (CYRIL). Britain's sea-soldiers: a history of the Royal Marines. 2 v. Liverpool. 1924.

1102 CALLENDER (*Sir* GEOFFREY ARTHUR ROMAINE) *and* HINSLEY (FRANCIS HENRY). The naval side of British history, 1485–1945. 1952.

See also Frank C. Bowen, *The sea: its history and romance*, 4 v., 1924–6, and Sir Herbert W. Richmond, *Statesmen and sea power*, Oxf., 1946, and *National policy and naval strength and other essays*, 1928; Bernard Brodie, *Sea power in the machine age: major naval inventions and their consequences on international politics, 1814–1940*, Princeton, 1944.

1103 LLOYD (CHRISTOPHER). The nation and the navy: a history of naval life and policy. 1954.

See too M. A. Lewis, *The navy of Britain; a historical portrait*, 1948, and *The history of the British navy*, 1959.

1104 MARCUS (GEOFFREY JULES). A naval history of England. 1961, in progress.

V. 2: *The age of Nelson*, deals with 1789–1815; bibliog. 505–20. For sea power in various regions see Oliver Warner, *The sea and the sword; the Baltic: 1630–1945*, 1965;

W. E. F. Ward (2646); G. S. Graham, *Great Britain in the Indian Ocean . . . 1810–1850*, Oxf., 1967; S. W. C. Pack, *Sea power in the Mediterranean*, 1971.

1105 BARTLETT (CHRISTOPHER JOHN). Great Britain and sea power, 1815–53. Oxf. 1963.

G. S. Graham, *The politics of naval supremacy*, Camb., 1965, discusses the consequences and limitations of British naval supremacy.

D. NAVAL OPERATIONS

1106 WARNER (OLIVER). Battle honours of the Royal navy. 1956.

Tabulated list of naval actions, 1588–1953, and details of single ship actions, listed alphabetically. See also Hugh Burdett Money-Coutts, baron Latymer, *Famous duels of the fleet*, 1908, which deals with frigate actions.

1107 ANDERSON (ROGER CHARLES). Naval wars in the Baltic during the sailing ship epoch, 1522–1850. 1950.

See also his *Naval wars in the Levant, 1559–1853*, Liverpool, 1952.

1. 1793–1815

1108 NORIE (JOHN WILLIAM). The naval gazetteer, biographer, and chronologist; containing a history of the late wars, 1793–1801, and 1803–15. New edn. 1827.

See also Sir Charles Ekins, *Naval battles from 1744 to the peace in 1814*, 1824, 2nd edn., 1828.

1109 MAHAN (ALFRED THAYER). The influence of sea power upon the French Revolution and Empire, 1793–1815. 2 v. 1892.

Still of value, though brief on years after 1805. See too Paul Frischauer, *England's years of danger: a new history of the world war, 1792–1815, dramatized in documents*, 1938. Sir Thomas S. Jackson ed., *Logs of the great sea fights, 1794–1805*, 2 v., NRS 16, 18, 1899–1900.

1110 CHEVALIER (ÉDOUARD). Histoire de la marine française sous la première république. Paris. 1886.

Deals with 1789–93, the account being continued to 1815 in his *Histoire de la marine française sous le consulat et l'empire*, Paris, 1886. O. Troude, *Batailles navales de la France*, 4 v., Paris, 1867–8, is a year-by-year description of all engagements. Édouard Desbrière, *1793–1805: projets et tentatives de débarquement aux Îles Britanniques*, 4 v., Paris, 1900–2, contains much detail. For a more general French view see L. Nicolas, *La puissance navale dans l'histoire*, v. 1, Paris, 1958.

1111 PARKINSON (CYRIL NORTHCOTE). War in the Eastern seas, 1793–1815. 1954.

Bibliog. 450–9. Parkinson also ed. *Trade Winds*, 1948, touching on convoy and privateering, and see his *Trade in the Eastern seas, 1793–1813*, Camb., 1937.

1112 KENYON (EDWARD RANULF). Gibraltar under Moor, Spaniard, and Briton. 1911. Repr. 1938.

Lists MS. diaries.

1113 ROSE (JOHN HOLLAND). Lord Hood and the defence of Toulon. Camb. 1922.

1114 WARNER (OLIVER). The glorious first of June. 1961.

1115 DRINKWATER (*Col.* JOHN). A narrative of the proceedings of the British fleet, commanded by Admiral Sir John Jervis. . . . 1797.

A clear account of the battle of St. Vincent, by an eye-witness; 2nd edn., *A narrative of the battle of St. Vincent*, 1840. Christopher Lloyd, *St. Vincent and Camperdown*, 1963, is excellent.

1116 LANUZA CANO (FRANCISCO). Ataque y derrota de Nelson en Santa Cruz de Tenerife; relato historico con arreglo a documentos oficiales de la epoca. [Madrid. 1955].

See also Dionisio de las Cagigas, *El ataque de Nelson a Tenerife, relatado por un marino montañés*, [ed. by Fernando Barreda], Santander, 1936; and Mario Roselli Cecconi, 'Lord Nelson in Corsica et a Teneriffa', *Archivio Storico Corsica*, 16 (1940), 165–77.

1117 JONES (EDWIN HENRY STUART). The last invasion of England. Cardiff. 1950.

On the French landing in Pembrokeshire, 1797. See also his *An invasion that failed: the French expedition to Ireland, 1797*, Oxf., 1950.

1118 BERRY (*Sir* EDWARD). An authentic narrative of the proceedings of H.M.S. squadron, under the command of . . . Nelson, from . . . Gibraltar to the conclusion of the glorious Battle of the Nile. 3rd edn. 1798.

Also by a participant is Cooper Willyams, *A voyage up the Mediterranean in . . . the Swiftsure . . . under the command of Nelson*, 1802. Oliver Warner, *The Battle of the Nile*, 1960, is excellent.

1119 DOUIN (GEORGES). La campagne de Bruix en Méditerranée, mars-août 1799. Paris. 1923.

1120 PARKINSON (CYRIL NORTHCOTE). 'British operations in the Red Sea, 1799–1801', *Roy. Central Asian Soc. J.* 25 (1938), 248–59.

1121 GUTTERIDGE (HAROLD COOKE) *ed.* Nelson and the Neapolitan Jacobins; documents relating to the suppression of the Jacobin revolution at Naples, June 1799. NRS 25. 1903.

See also Constance H. D. Giglioli, *Naples in 1799*, 1903; Francesco Lemmi, *Nelson e Caracciolo, e la Repubblica Napoletana (1799)*, Florence, 1898; J. C. Jeaffreson, *The Queen of Naples and Lord Nelson*, 2 v., 1899; F. P. Badham, *Nelson at Naples; a journal for June 10–30, 1799, refuting recent misstatements of Captain Mahan and Professor J. K. Laughton*, 1900; and Arsenio Amabile, *M. Carolina, Lady Hamilton e O. Nelson nei moti del 1799 a Napoli*, Caserta, 1902.

1122 VIGO (PIETRO). Nelson a Livorno; episodio della guerra tra Francia ed Inghilterra sul finire del secolo XVIII. Siena. 1903.

1123 MACKESY (PIERS). The war in the Mediterranean, 1803–1810. 1957.

Bibliog. 410–17; excellent. See also Charles Auriol (280); Georges Douin, *La Méditerranée, 1803–5*, Paris, 1917; Baron Alberto E. Lumbroso, *Napoleone e il Mediterraneo*, Genoa, 1934; J. H. Rose, 'Napoleon and sea power', *Camb. Hist. J.* 1 (1923–5), 138–57; Walter Frewen Lord, *England and France in the Mediterranean, 1660–1830*, 1901.

1124 LEYLAND (JOHN) ed. Dispatches and letters relating to the blockade of Brest, 1803–5. 2 v. NRS 14, 21. 1899–1902.

1125 ROSE (JOHN HOLLAND) and BROADLEY (ALEXANDER MEYRICK). Dumouriez and the defence of England against Napoleon. 1909.

1126 EINAAR (J. F. E.). Bijdrage tot de kennis van het Engelsch tusschenbestuur van Suriname, 1804–16. Leiden. 1934.

1127 ADMIRALTY. Report of a committee appointed by the Admiralty to examine and consider the evidence relating to the tactics employed by Nelson at ... Trafalgar (Cd. 7120). 1913.

A definitive survey. See also A. H. Taylor, 'Some new aspects of the battle of Trafalgar', *Roy. United Serv. Instn. J.* 82 (1937), 692–709, and 'The battle of Trafalgar', *Mariner's Mirror*, 36 (1950), 281–321. Manuel de Marliani, *Combate de Trafalgar*, 2 pts., Madrid, 1850, gives many interesting side-lights from the Spanish point of view. Of value is Edward Fraser, *The enemy at Trafalgar*, 1906, compiled from French and Spanish dispatches and eye-witness accounts. See too Henri Letuaire, *La bataille de Trafalgar racontée par le commandant Lucas ... 2nd edn. par A. Jacques Parès*, Toulon, 1914.

1128 CORBETT (*Sir* JULIAN STAFFORD). The campaign of Trafalgar. 1910.

Excellent. Also helpful are Édouard Desbrière, *La campagne maritime de 1805: Trafalgar*, 2 pts., Paris, 1907, Eng. trans. by Constance Eastwick, 2 v., Oxf., 1933; R. H. Mackenzie, *The Trafalgar roll*, 1913; Hilary P. Mead, *Trafalgar signals*, 1936; René Maine, *Trafalgar*, Paris, 1955, Engl. trans., 1957; Oliver Warner, *Trafalgar*, 1959.

1129 RYAN (ANTHONY NICHOLAS). 'The navy at Copenhagen in 1807.' *Mariner's Mirror*, 39 (1953), 201–10.

1130 GRAHAM (GERALD SANDFORD) and HUMPHREYS (ROBERT ARTHUR) eds. The navy and South America, 1807–23; correspondence of the commanders-in-chief on the South American station. NRS 104. 1962. See also Beverina, Roberts and Street (356).

1131 PARLIAMENT. A collection of papers relating to the expedition to the Scheldt; presented to Parliament in 1810. 1811.

1132 MAITLAND (*Sir* FREDERICK LEWIS). Narrative of the surrender of Buonaparte and of his residence on board H.M.S. *Bellerophon*; with a detail of the principal events ... between 24th May and 8th August 1815. 2nd edn. 1826. New edn. entitled *The surrender of Napoleon*, ed. by W. K. Dickson, 1904.

See also Félix Barthe, *Réfutation de la relation du Capitaine Maitland touchant l'embarquement de Napoléon, à son bord*, Paris, 1827; *Napoleon's last voyages; being the diaries of*

Admiral Sir Thomas Ussher . . . and John R. Glover . . ., 2nd edn., with introd. and notes by J. H. Rose, 1906.

2. War of 1812

1133 JAMES (WILLIAM). A full and correct account of the chief naval occurrences of the late war between Great Britain and the United States of America. 1817.

See also Abel Bowen, ed., *The naval monument, containing official and other accounts of all the battles fought between the navies of the United States and Great Britain during the late war*, Boston, 1816.

1134 MAHAN (ALFRED THAYER). Sea power in its relations to the War of 1812. 2 v. Boston. 1905.

1135 ROOSEVELT (THEODORE). The naval operations of the war between Great Britain and the United States, 1812–1815. 1910.

See also James Barnes, *Naval actions of the war of 1812*, 1897; C. S. Forester, *The naval war of 1812*, 1957; G. S. Graham, *The empire of the North Atlantic*, 1958; P. Padfield, *Broke and the* Shannon, 1968.

3. 1815–1851

1136 LONGSTAFF (F. V.) *and* LAMB (W. KAYE). 'The Royal navy on the north-west coast, 1813–50.' *Brit. Columbia Hist. Q.* 9 (1945), 1–24, 113–28.

1137 SALAMÉ (ABRAHAM). Narrative of the expedition to Algiers, 1816. 1819.

See Sir Robert L. Playfair, *The scourge of Christendom: annals of British relations with Algiers prior to the French conquest*, 1884.

1138 MARSHALL (JOHN). Narrative of the naval operations in Ava during the Burmese war, in . . . 1824–6. 1830.

See also H. L. Maw, *The early operations of the Burmese war*, 1832.

1139 BOGDANOVITCH (EUGENE). La bataille de Navarin, 1827; d'après les documents inédits des archives imperiales russes. Paris. [1887].

See also *Documents relating to the recall of . . . Sir Edward Codrington from the Mediterranean command in June 1828* [ed. by Sir E. Codrington], priv. pr., 1830, and *Compressed narrative of the proceedings . . . on the Mediterranean station . . . 1827–8*, 1832.

1140 HUNTER (W. PATISON). Narrative of the late expedition to Syria under the command of Admiral Sir Robert Stopford. 2 v. 1842.

See also Sir Charles Napier, *The war in Syria*, 2 v., 1842, and Abraham Crawford, *Reminiscences* (1199).

1141 BINGHAM (JOHN ELLIOT). Narrative of the expedition to China, from the commencement of the war to the present period; with sketches of the manners and customs of that . . . country. 2 v. 1842.

See too W. D. Bernard, *Narrative of the voyages and services of the* Nemesis, *1840–3, and of the combined military and naval operations in China*, 2 v., 1844, and Granville G. Loch, *Closing events of the campaign in China*, 1843.

1142 MACKINNON (LAUCHLAN BELLINGHAM). Steam warfare in the Paraná: a narrative of operations by the combined squadrons of England and France in forcing a passage up that river. 2 v. 1848.

4. PRIVATEERING

See Parkinson (1111), Graham (1104), (1135).

1143 HUTCHINSON (WILLIAM). A treatise on practical seamanship. [Liverpool]. 1777. 4th repr. 1794.

Largely a manual for privateersmen, from experience gained in the Seven Years War.

1144 MARTENS (GEORG FRIEDRICH VON). Essai concernant les armateurs, les prises, et surtout les réprises. Gottingen. 1795.

On privateering law. Eng. trans. by T. H. Horne, 1801. See also (648).

1145 MACLAY (EDGAR STANTON). History of American privateers. 1900.

An earlier account is George Coggeshall, *History of the American privateers*, priv. pr. N.Y., 1856.

1146 MALO (HENRI). Les derniers corsaires, Dunkerque (1715–1815). Paris. 1925.

Malo also ed. *Les corsaires: mémoires et documents inédits*, Paris, 1908.

1147 SNIDER (CHARLES HENRY JEREMIAH). Under the Red Jack; privateers of the maritime provinces of Canada in the War of 1812. 1928.

1148 POWELL (JOHN WILLIAMS DAMER). Bristol privateers and ships of war. Bristol. 1930.

A thorough sound study; bibliog. note, 375–6. See also Williams (2637).

1149 KENDALL (CHARLES WYE). Private man-of-war. 1931.

A general, popular history of privateering. See also E. P. Statham, *Privateers and privateering*, 1910; W. B. Johnson, *Wolves of the Channel*, 1931; H. C. M. Austen, *Sea fights and corsairs of the Indian Ocean; being the naval history of Mauritius, 1715–1810*, Port Louis, Mauritius, 1934.

1150 RUTTER (OWEN). Red ensign, a history of convoy. 1947.

5. SMUGGLING AND PIRACY

1151 CHATTERTON (EDWARD KEBLE). King's cutters and smugglers, 1700–1855. 1912.

See also F. D. Arnold-Forster, *At war with the smugglers: the career of Dr. Arnold's father*, 1936.

1152 JONES (CHARLES GRAY PITCAIRN) *ed.* Piracy in the Levant, 1827–8; selected from the papers of . . . Sir Edward Codrington. NRS 72. 1934.

1153   FOX (GRACE). British admirals and Chinese pirates, 1832–69. 1940.

Bibliog. 209–15. See too Sir John C. D. Hay, *The suppression of piracy in the China sea, 1849*, 1889.

1154   KEPPEL (*Sir* HENRY). The expedition to Borneo of H.M.S. *Dido* for the suppression of piracy; with extracts from the journal of James Brooke of Sarawak. 3rd edn. 2 v. 1847.

1155   GOSSE (PHILIP). The history of piracy. 1932.

On different regions see A. G. Course, *Pirates of the eastern seas*, 1966; Harry Miller, *Pirates of the Far East*, 1970; H. Moyse-Bartlett, *The pirates of Trucial Oman*, 1966.

E. NAVAL VOYAGES

See *N.C.B.E.L.* (2650), v. 2, cols. 1389–486, v. 3, cols. 1669–84.

1156   BLIGH (WILLIAM). A voyage to the South Sea, undertaken by command of His Majesty, for the purpose of conveying the bread-fruit tree to the West Indies, in His Majesty's ship the *Bounty*. 1792. Ed. by Ida Lee. 1920.

Ida Lee also ed. *Captain Bligh's second voyage to the South Sea, 1791–1793*, 1920. For the punitive expedition in search of the mutineers of the *Bounty* see George Hamilton, *A voyage round the world in H.M. frigate* Pandora . . . [*1790–92*], 1793.

1157   VANCOUVER (GEORGE). A voyage of discovery to the north Pacific ocean, and round the world . . . [1790–95] in the *Discovery*, sloop-of-war, and armed tender *Chatham*. [Ed. by J. Vancouver.] 3 v. 1798.

C. F. Newcombe ed., *Menzies' journal of Vancouver's voyage, April to October 1792*, Archives of British Columbia, Memoir 5, Victoria, 1923. See also (1229).

1158   COLNETT (JAMES). A voyage to the South Atlantic and round Cape Horn into the Pacific Ocean, for the purpose of extending the spermaceti whale fisheries. . . . 1798.

1159   BROUGHTON (WILLIAM ROBERT). A voyage of discovery to the north Pacific Ocean . . . in H.M.'s sloop *Providence* . . . [1795–8]. 1804.

Broughton surveyed large parts of the coasts of China, Japan, and Korea.

1160   TURNBULL (JOHN). A voyage round the world . . . [1800–04], in which the author visited the principal islands in the Pacific ocean and the English settlements of Port Jackson and Norfolk Island. 3 v. 1805.

1161   PRIOR (*Sir* JAMES). Narrative of a voyage in the Indian seas; in the *Nisus* frigate, to the Cape of Good Hope, isles of Bourbon, France, and Seychelles; to Madras; and the Isles of Java, St. Paul and Amsterdam . . . [1810–11]. [1812].

Prior also publ., *Voyage along the eastern coast of Africa to Mosambique, Joanna and Quiloa; to St. Helena; to Rio de Janeiro, Bahia and Pernambuco . . .*, 1819.

1162   LAING (JOHN). An account of a voyage to Spitzbergen; containing a full description of that country, of the zoology of the north, and of the Shetland islands; with an account of the whale fishery. 1815.

1163 HALL (BASIL). Account of a voyage of discovery to the west coast of Corea and the Great Loo-Choo island. . . . 1818.

Hall commanded the *Lyra* on the expedition which took the Amherst embassy to China in 1816. See too John McLeod, *Narrative of a voyage in H.M. late ship* Alceste *to the Yellow Sea* . . ., 1817. Hall described his next expedition in *Extracts from a journal written on the coasts of Chile, Peru, and Mexico* . . . [1820–22], 4th edn., 2 v., Edinburgh, 1825.

1164 ROSS (*Sir* JOHN). A voyage of discovery . . . in H.M. ships *Isabella* and *Alexander* for the purpose of exploring Baffin's Bay, and enquiring into the probability of a North-west passage. 1819.

Ross also publ., *Narrative of a second voyage* . . . [*1829–33*], [1834], describing a prolonged stay in the arctic region and the discovery of the northern magnetic pole.

1165 PARRY (WILLIAM EDWARD). Journal of a voyage of discovery to the arctic regions . . . [Apr.–Nov. 1818], in H.M.S. *Alexander* . . . By Alexander Fisher. New voyages and travels, v. 1. 1820.

Parry's next arctic voyage, 1819–20, is described in his *Journal of a voyage for the discovery of a North-West Passage*, 1821, with a supplement by Sir Edward Sabine, 1824, and in Alexander Fisher, *A journal of a voyage of discovery* . . . *in H.M.SS.* Hecla *and* Griper, 1821. See too Parry's *Journal of a second voyage for the discovery of a North-West Passage* . . . [*1821–23*], 2 v., 1824–5, and George F. Lyon, *The private journal of Captain G. F. Lyon, of H.M.S.* Hecla, 1824; Parry, *Journal of a third voyage* . . . [*1824–5*], 1826; Parry, *Narrative of an attempt to reach the North Pole in boats* . . . *attached to H.M. ship* Hecla, *in* . . . *1827*, 1828, and Robert McCormick, *Voyage of discovery in the arctic and antarctic seas and round the world*, 2 v., 1884, section 2. See also (1227).

1166 FRANKLIN (*Sir* JOHN). Narrative of a journey to the shores of the Polar sea. . . [1819–22]. 1823.

Franklin also publ., *Narrative of a second expedition to the shores of the Polar sea* . . . [*1825–7*], 1828. See also (1206).

1167 BEECHEY (FREDERICK WILLIAM). A voyage of discovery towards the North Pole, performed in H.M. ships *Dorothea* and *Trent*, under the command of Captain David Buchan, R.N., 1818; to which is added, a summary of all the early attempts to reach the Pacific by way of the Pole. 1843.

F. W. and H. W. Beechey, *Proceedings of the expedition to explore the northern coast of Africa from Tripoli eastward in 1821–2*, 1828; F. W. Beechey, *Narrative of a voyage to the Pacific and Beerings Strait, to co-operate with the Polar expedition* . . . [*1825–28*], 2 v., 1831.

1168 OWEN (WILLIAM FITZWILLIAM). Narrative of voyages to explore the shores of Africa, Arabia and Madagascar; performed in H.M. ships *Leven* and *Barracouta*, from 1821 to 1826. 2 v. 1833.

1169 BYRON (GEORGE ANSON), *7th baron.* Voyage of H.M.S. *Blonde* to the Sandwich islands . . . [1824–5]. 1826.

1170 WEDDELL (JAMES). A voyage towards the South Pole performed in 1822–24; containing an examination of the Antarctic Sea to the seventy-fourth degree of latitude. . . . 1825.

Weddell, an ex-naval officer, surveyed the South Shetlands and coastal navigation around Tierra del Fuego and Cape Horn.

1171 FITZROY (ROBERT). Narrative of the surveying voyages of H.M. ships *Adventure* and *Beagle* . . . [1826–36], describing their examination of the southern shores of South America; and the *Beagle*'s circumnavigation of the globe. 2 v. 1839.

See also (1204), and Charles Robert Darwin, *Journal of Charles Darwin, naturalist to the* Beagle *(1832–1836)*, 1839, forming v. 3 of this travel account.

1172 WEBSTER (WILLIAM HENRY BAYLEY). Narrative of a voyage to the southern Atlantic Ocean . . . [1828–30] performed in H.M. sloop *Chanticleer.* . . . 2 v. 1834.

1173 BELCHER (*Sir* EDWARD). Narrative of a voyage round the world, performed in H.M. ship *Sulphur*, during the years 1836–1842, including details of the naval operations in China from Dec. 1840 to Nov. 1841. 2 v. 1843.

Belcher also publ., *Narrative of the voyage of H.M.S.* Samarang *during the years 1843–46; employed surveying the islands of the eastern archipelago*, 2 v., 1848.

1174 TROTTER. A narrative of the expedition . . . to the river Niger in 1841 under the command of Captain H. D. Trotter. By William Allen and T. R. H. Thomson. 2 v. 1848.

1175 ROSS (*Sir* JAMES CLARK). A voyage of discovery in the Southern and Antarctic regions . . . [1839–43]. 2 v. 1847.

Another account of this journey is in Robert McCormick, *Voyage of discovery in the arctic and antarctic seas, and round the world*, 2 v., 1884, section 1.

1176 JUKES (JOSEPH BEETE). Narrative of the surveying voyage of H.M.S. *Fly* . . . in Torres Strait, New Guinea and other islands of the eastern archipelago . . . [1842–6]: together with an excursion into the interior of the eastern part of Java. 2 v. 1847.

1177 FORBES (FREDERICK E.). Five years in China; from 1842 to 1847. With an account of the occupation of Labuan and Borneo by her Majesty's forces. 1848.

1178 WALPOLE (FREDERICK). Four years in the Pacific in H.M.S. *Collingwood*, 1844–8. 2 v. 1849.

1179 SEEMANN (BERTHOLD CARL). Narrative of the voyage of H.M.S. *Herald* . . . [1845–51], under the command of Captain H. Kellett . . . being a circumnavigation of the globe, and three cruises to the Arctic regions in search of Sir J. Franklin. 2 v. 1853.

1180 COLLINSON. Journal of H.M.S. *Enterprise*, on the expedition in search of Sir John Franklin's ships by Behring Strait, 1850–55. By Captain B. Collinson. Ed. by T. B. Collinson. 1889.

1181 McCLURE. The discovery of the North-West Passage by H.M.S. *Investigator* [1850–54]. Ed. by Sherard Osborn . . . from the logs and journals of Captain R. J. Le Mesurier McClure. 1856.

1182 RICHARDSON (*Sir* JOHN). Arctic searching expedition; a journal of a boat voyage through Rupert's Land and the Arctic Sea, in search of the Discovery ships under the command of Sir John Franklin. . . . 2 v. 1851.

F. NAVAL BIOGRAPHY

1. BIBLIOGRAPHY AND COLLECTED BIOGRAPHY

1183 JAMES (G. F.). 'Bibliographical aids to research. VI: Collected naval biography.' *Bull. I.H.R.* 15 (1937–8), 162–75.

1184 MARSHALL (JOHN). Royal naval biography. 4 v. and 4 suppl. 1823–35.

Records of the services of surviving naval officers, from the rank of commander upward. See too James Ralfe, *The naval biography of Great Britain . . . during the reign of . . . George III*, 4 v., 1828; Robert Southey, *Lives of the British admirals*, 5 v., 1833–40. W. R. O'Byrne, *A naval biographical dictionary*, 1849, gives the life and service of every living officer; 2nd edn. A–G only, 1861, uncompleted.

1185 FITCHETT (WILLIAM HENRY). Nelson and his captains. 1902.

See also A. M. Broadley and R. G. Bartelot, *The three Dorset captains at Trafalgar: Thomas Masterman Hardy, Charles Bullen, Henry Digby*, 1906; Edward Fraser, *The sailors whom Nelson led*, 1913; Ludovic Kennedy, *Nelson's band of brothers*, 1951; H. G. Thursfield, ed., *Five naval journals, 1789–1817*, NRS 91, 1951.

2. BIOGRAPHY

1186 AUSTEN. Jane Austen's sailor brothers; being the adventures of Sir Francis Austen . . . and Rear-Admiral Charles Austen. By John Henry and Edith C. Hubback. 1906.

1187 BARHAM. Letters and papers of Charles [Middleton], Lord Barham . . . 1758–1813. Ed. by Sir John Knox Laughton. 3 v. NRS 32, 38, 39. 1907–11.

1188 BARRINGTON. The Barrington papers, selected from the letters and papers of Admiral the Hon. Samuel Barrington. Ed. by David Bonner-Smith. 2 v. NRS 77, 81. 1937–41.

1189 BEAVER. The life and services of Captain Philip Beaver. By William Henry Smyth. 1829.

1190 BLIGH. The life of Vice-Admiral William Bligh. By George Mackaness. 2 v. Sydney. 1931. Rev. edn. 1951.

Other lives by Geoffrey Rawson, 1930; Owen Rutter, 1936; Hastings S. Montgomerie, 1937. See also (1156).

1191 BOTELER. Recollections of my sea life, 1808–30, by Captain John Harvey Boteler. Ed. by David Bonner-Smith. NRS 82. 1942.

1192 BRENTON. Memoir of Captain Edward Pelham Brenton . . . with sketches of his professional life . . . observations upon his 'Naval history' and 'Life of the Earl of St. Vincent'. By Sir Jahleel Brenton. 1842.

See also *Memoir of the life and services of Vice-Admiral Sir Jahleel Brenton*, ed. by Henry Raikes, 1846.

1193 BROKE. Admiral Sir P. B. V. Broke . . . a memoir. Comp. by John George Brighton. 1866.

1194 CARDEN. A curtail'd memoir of incidents and occurrences in the life of John Surman Carden, Vice-Admiral in the British navy, written by himself, 1850. Ed. by Christopher T. Atkinson. Oxf. 1912.

1195 COCHRANE. Lord Cochrane, seaman–radical–liberator; a life of Thomas, Lord Cochrane, 10th Earl of Dundonald. By Christopher Lloyd. 1947.

Bibliog. 212–16. See too Cochrane's *Autobiography of a seaman*, 2 v., 1860; Warren S. Tute, *Cochrane; a life of Admiral the Earl of Dundonald*, 1965.

1196 CODRINGTON. Memoir of the life of Admiral Sir Edward Codrington, with selections from his public and private correspondence. Ed. by his daughter, Lady Bourchier. 2 v. 1873.

1197 COLLINGWOOD. A selection from the public and private correspondence of Vice-Admiral Lord Collingwood; interspersed with memoirs of his life. By G. L. Newnham Collingwood. 1828.

There are lives by William C. Russell, 1891, Geoffrey Murray, 1936, D. F. Stephenson, 1948, Oliver Warner, 1968. Edward A. Hughes ed., *The private correspondence . . .*, NRS 98, 1957, covering 1776–1810.

1198 CORNWALLIS. The life and letters of Admiral Cornwallis. By George Frederick Myddelton Cornwallis-West. 1927.

See also Leyland (1124).

1199 CRAWFORD. Reminiscences of a naval officer. By Abraham Crawford. 2 v. 1851.

His recollections of the French wars.

1200 DILLON. A narrative of my professional adventures (1790–1839), by Sir William Henry Dillon. Ed. by Michael Arthur Lewis. 2 v. NRS 93, 97. 1953–6.

1201 DUNCAN. Admiral Duncan. By Lord Camperdown. 1898.

See too Herbert Wrigley Wilson, *Adam Duncan*, [1900].

1202 DURHAM. Memoir of the naval life and services of Admiral Sir Philip C. H. C. Durham. By Alexander Murray. 1846.

1203 ELLIS. Memoirs and services of . . . Sir Samuel Burdon Ellis from his own memoranda. Ed. by Lady Ellis. 1866.

As a young officer of marines Ellis was present at Trafalgar and other important engagements.

1204 FITZROY. Fitzroy of the *Beagle*. By Harold Edward Leslie Mellersh. 1968.

Bibliog. 299–301. See also (1171).

1205 FOLEY. Life and services of Admiral Sir Thomas Foley. By John Beresford Herbert. Cardiff. 1884.

1206 FRANKLIN. Franklin, happy voyages, being the life and death of Sir John Franklin. By Geoffrey Frederick Lamb. 1956.

See also (1166).

1207 FREMANTLE. The Admirals Fremantle. Ed. by Ann Parry. 1971.

Thomas Francis Fremantle served through most of the French wars and was one of Nelson's favourite captains.

1208 GAMBIER. Memorials, personal and historical of Admiral Lord Gambier. By Georgiana, Lady Chatterton. 2 v. 1861.

1209 GARDNER. Recollections of James Anthony Gardner, commander R.N. (1775–1814). Ed. by Sir Richard Vesey Hamilton and John Knox Laughton. NRS 31. 1906.

A primary authority for social life afloat. See too *Above and under hatches*, ed. by Christopher Lloyd, 1957.

1210 HARDY. Nelson's Hardy and his wife. By John Francis Gore. 1935.

Uses unpublished journals and correspondence. A. M. Broadley and R. G. Bartelot, *Nelson's Hardy. His life, letters, and friends*, 1909.

1211 HARGOOD. Memoir of the life and services of Admiral Sir William Hargood; comp. from authentic documents. By Joseph Allen. Priv. pr. Greenwich. 1841.

1212 HOFFMAN. A sailor of King George; the journals of Captain Frederick Hoffman, R.N., 1793–1814. Ed. by A. B. Bevan and H. B. Wolryche-Whitmore. 1901.

1213 HOSTE. Memoirs and letters of Capt. Sir William Hoste. Ed. by Lady Harriet Hoste. 2 v. 1833.

[George Henry Hoste], *Service afloat; or, The naval career of Sir William Hoste*, 1887, is an abridgement with some supplementary material.

1214 HOTHAM. Pages and portraits from the past, being the private papers of Admiral Sir William Hotham. Ed. by A. M. W. Stirling. 2 v. 1919.

1215 HOWE. The life of Richard Earl Howe. By Sir John Barrow. 1838.

1216 KEITH. The Keith papers, selected from the letters and papers of Admiral Viscount Keith. Ed. by William Gordon Perrin and Christopher Lloyd. 3 v. NRS 62, 90, 96. 1927–55.

Alexander Allardyce, *Memoir of . . . Viscount Keith*, Edin. 1882, is unreliable.

1217 KEPPEL. A sailor's life under four sovereigns. By Sir Henry Keppel. 3 v. 1899.

See also Sir Algernon E. West, *Memoir of Sir Henry Keppel*, 1905; Vivian Stuart (*afterw.* Violet Vivian Mann), *The beloved little admiral*, 1967. Keppel entered the navy, 1824.

1218 LEE. Memoirs of the life and services of Sir John Theophilus Lee of the Elms, Hampshire [written by himself]. Priv. pr. 1836.

His life as a midshipman in the 1790s; experiences at the battle of the Nile and further personal adventures, mainly 1797–1815.

1219 LOVELL. Personal narrative of events, 1799–1815. By Vice-Admiral William Stanhope Lovell. 1879.

First publ. anonymously, by 'a captain of the navy', 1837.

1220 MARKHAM. Selections from the correspondence of Admiral John Markham . . . 1801–4 and 1806–7. Ed. by Sir Clements Markham. NRS 28. 1904.

His papers during service at the Admiralty board.

1221 MARTIN. Letters and papers of . . . Sir Thomas Byam Martin. Ed. by Sir Richard Vesey Hamilton. 3 v. NRS 12, 19, 24. 1898–1903.

1222 MOORE. Memoir of Admiral Sir Graham Moore. By Sir Robert W. Gardiner. 1844.

1223 MORESBY. Two admirals . . . Sir Fairfax Moresby . . . (1786–1877), and his son John Moresby; a record of life and service in the British navy for a hundred years. By John Moresby. 1909.

1224 NAPIER. Life and correspondence of Admiral Sir Charles Napier. By Edward H. D. Elers Napier. 2 v. 1862.

See too life by Hugh Noel Williams, 1917.

1225 PARKER. A biographical memoir of Sir Peter Parker. By Sir George Dallas. 1815.

See also Lilian Hare Tucker, 'Sir Peter Parker, commander of H.M.S. *Menelaus* in the year 1814', *Bermuda Hist. Q.* 1 (1944), 189–95.

1226 PARKER. The life of . . . Sir William Parker . . . 1781–1866. By Sir Augustus Phillimore. 3 v. 1876–80.

Abridged as *The last of Nelson's captains*, 1891.

1227 PARRY. Memoirs of . . . Sir W. Edward Parry. By Edward Parry. 1857.

Ann Parry, *Parry of the Arctic*, 1963; bibliog. 232–4. See (1165).

1228 PELLEW. Edward Pellew, Viscount Exmouth, Admiral of the red. By Cyril Northcote Parkinson. 1934.

1229 PENROSE. Lives of Vice Admiral Sir Charles Vinicombe Penrose . . . and Captain James Trevenen. By John Penrose. 1850.

1230 ROBINSON. Sea drift. By Hercules Robinson. Portsea. 1858.

Personal reminiscences; rather slight.

1231 ST. VINCENT. Letters of Admiral of the Fleet the Earl of St. Vincent whilst first lord of the Admiralty, 1801–4. Ed. by David Bonner-Smith. 2 v. NRS 55, 61. 1922–7.

Jedediah S. Tucker, *Memoirs of . . . St. Vincent*, 2 v., 1844, is still of value; other lives by W. V. Anson, 1913, Sir W. M. James, 1950, Evelyn Berckman, 1962.

1232 SAUMAREZ. Memoirs and correspondence of Admiral Lord de Saumarez, from original papers. By Sir John Ross. 2 v. 1838.

A. N. Ryan, ed., *The Saumarez papers; selections from the Baltic correspondence of . . . Saumarez, 1808–1812*, NRS 110, 1968, dealing with operations in the Baltic.

1233 SCONCE. Life and letters of Robert Clement Sconce. Comp. by Sarah S. Bunbury. Priv. pr. 1861.

Letters of the secretary to Admiral Sir John T. Duckworth who commanded in the West Indies through much of the French wars.

1234 SMITH. Life and correspondence of Sir William Sidney Smith. By Sir John Barrow. 2 v. 1848.

See too E. F. L. Russell [Baron Russell of Liverpool], *Knight of the sword; the life and letters of Admiral Sir William Sidney Smith*, 1964.

1235 SPENCER. Private papers of George, 2nd Earl Spencer, first lord of the Admiralty, 1794–1801. Ed. by Julian S. Corbett and H. W. Richmond. 4 v. NRS 46, 48, 58, 59. 1913–24.

1236 SYMONDS. Memoirs of the life and services of Rear-Admiral Sir William Symonds. Ed. by James A. Sharp. 1858.

1237 TOMLINSON. The Tomlinson papers, selected from the correspondence and pamphlets of Captain Robert Tomlinson, R.N., and Vice-Admiral Nicholas Tomlinson. Ed. by John Greville Bullocke. NRS. 74. 1935.

1238 TYLER. Sir Charles Tyler. Admiral of the white. By William Henry Wyndham-Quin. 1912.

1239 VANCOUVER. Surveyor of the sea; the life and voyages of Captain George Vancouver. By Bern Anderson. [1960].

Bibliog. 259–66. See too G. S. Godwin, *Vancouver, a life*, 1930; Richmond, Surrey, Free Public Library, *A list of books, photographs, prints, maps, etc., relating to Captain George Vancouver* [1936]. See also (1157).

1240 WALLIS. Admiral of the fleet Sir Provo W. P. Wallis; a memoir. By John George Brighton. 1892.

1241 WALTERS. Samuel Walters, lieutenant R.N.; his memoirs. Ed. by Cyril Northcote Parkinson. Liverpool. 1949.

1242 WILLOUGHBY. Willoughby the immortal; an account of the life and actions of Rear-Admiral Sir Nesbit Willoughby. by Michael Henry Mason. Oxf. 1969.

1243 WOLSELEY. Memoir of William Wolseley, Admiral of the red. By Mary C. Innes. 1895.

3. NELSON (HORATIO), *Viscount*

(a) *Bibliography and Manuscripts*

The British Library has 91 vols. of Nelson papers, Add. MSS. 34902–92. A few letters parted from this collection are in the Nelson Ward collection at the National Maritime Museum; see also 'Nelson MSS at the National Maritime Museum' by K. F. Lindsay-MacDougall, *Mariner's Mirror*, 41 (1955), 227–32. At the Nelson Museum, Monmouth, are 5 bound vols. of family letters, letter-books, and logs. The Wellcome Historical Medical Library has 15 vols. of papers dealing with ships under the command of Nelson. Harvard University also has some Nelson MSS.

1244 BRITISH MUSEUM. A guide to the manuscripts, printed books . . . . . . exhibited on the occasion of the Nelson centenary. 1905.

See also *The [Fred] Barker collection: manuscripts of and relating to . . . Nelson, chiefly noted by Sir John Knox Laughton*, 1913; Norwich Public Library, *A catalogue of the books, pamphlets, articles, and engravings relating to Nelson in the . . . library*, comp. by G. A. Stephen, Norwich, 1915; Philadelphia Free Library, *An exhibition of autograph letters, books, and relics of Horatio, Lord Nelson, from the collection of Morris Wolf* [Phil.], 1934.

1245 LLOYD'S. The Nelson collection at Lloyd's. Ed. by Warren R. Dawson. 1932.

A catalogue of plate, papers, portraits.

1246 WARNER (OLIVER). Lord Nelson; a guide to reading, with a note on contemporary portraits. 1955.

Lists 68 books, etc., but does not include periodical articles.

(b) *Printed Correspondence*

1247 NELSON. The dispatches and letters of . . . Lord Nelson, [1777–July 1805]. Ed. by Sir Nicholas Harris Nicolas. 7 v. 1844–6.

Standard. *Letters and dispatches of . . . Lord Nelson*, sel. and arr. by Sir John Knox Laughton, 1886, is a selection from Nicolas with a few additions. *Letters of Lord Nelson to Lady Hamilton*, 2 v., 1814, were printed anonymously.

1248 [MORRISON, ALFRED]. The collection of autograph letters and historical documents formed by Alfred Morrison . . . The Hamilton and Nelson papers, 1756–[1815]. 2 v. Priv. pr. 1893–4.

The publication of a collection since dispersed.

1249   NELSON. Nelson's last diary, Sept. 13–Oct. 21, 1805. Ed. by Gilbert Hudson. 1917.

The first accurate transcription from the MSS. in the Probate Registry at Somerset House, London. Oliver Warner, ed., *Nelson's last diary; a facsimile*, 1971.

1250   NELSON. Letters from Lord Nelson. Comp. by Geoffrey Rawson. 1949.

See also *Nelson's letters from the Leeward Islands, and other original documents in the Public Record Office and the British Museum*, ed. by Geoffrey Rawson, with notes by M. A. Lewis, 1953; G. P. B. Naish, ed., *Nelson's letters to his wife and other documents, 1785–1831*, NRS 100, 1958.

(c) *Biographies*

Only a few of the more important biographies of Nelson can be included here. For others consult Callender and Warner (1255).

1251   CLARKE (JAMES STANIER) *and* MACARTHUR (JOHN). Life of . . . Nelson, from his lordship's manuscripts. 2 v. 1809. New edn. 3 v. 1840.

'Official' contemporary biography, still of value.

1252   SOUTHEY (ROBERT). The life of Nelson; ed. with an introd., notes and an appendix, by E. R. H. Harvey. 1953.

Text of the 13th edn. of a classic first publ. in 2 v., 1813.

1253   FORGUES (PAUL ÉMILE DAURAND). Histoire de Nelson d'après les dépêches officielles et ses correspondances privées. Paris. 1860.

The standard French biography.

1254   MAHAN (ALFRED THAYER). Life of Nelson: the embodiment of the sea-power of Great Britain. 2 v. 1897. 2nd edn. 1899.

Valuable for its professional appraisal, as is also Sir W. M. James, *The durable monument: Horatio Nelson*, 1948. See too Russell Grenfell, *Nelson the sailor*, 1949.

1255   OMAN (CAROLA MARY ANIMA). Nelson. 1947.

A brilliant portrayal of the man and his circle, and in many respects the fullest biographical study to date; references in notes, 682–713. Valuable recent studies are Oliver Warner, *A portrait of Lord Nelson*, 1958, and *Nelson's battles*, 1965. See also Sir G. A. R. Callender, *The life of Nelson*, 1912; Renalt Capes, *Poseidon: a personal study of Admiral Lord Nelson*, 1947.

1256   KEATE (EDITH MURRAY). Nelson's wife: the first biography of Frances Herbert, Viscountess Nelson. 1939.

Mary Eyre Matcham, *The Nelsons of Burnham Thorpe; a record of a Norfolk family*, 1911, includes a valuable portrayal of Nelson's father. Margaret and Alfred Gatty, *Recollections of the life of the Rev. A. J. Scott, Lord Nelson's chaplain*, 1842, is also informative.

1257   SICHEL (WALTER SYDNEY). Emma, Lady Hamilton. 1905.

Well documented. J. C. Jeaffreson used the Morrison collection (1248) to write *Lady Hamilton and Lord Nelson*, 2 v., 1888. Joseph Turquan and Jules D'Auriac, *Une aven-*

turière de haut vol: Lady Hamilton . . . et la révolution de Naples, Paris, 1913, trans. as *A great adventuress*, 1914, is full for the Naples period. See too Oliver Warner, *Emma Hamilton and Sir William*, 1960; Hugh Tours, *The life and letters of Emma Hamilton*, 1963. See also (2070).

4. BIOGRAPHY: LOWER DECK

See also (1327).

1258   NICOL. The life and adventures of John Nicol, mariner. [Ed. by John Howell]. Edin. 1822. London. 1937.

Covers 1776–1801, including the battle of the Nile.

1259   WATSON (GEORGE). A narrative of the adventures of a Greenwich pensioner, written by himself. Newcastle. 1827.

1260   [ROBINSON (WILLIAM)]. Nautical economy; or, Forecastle recollections of events during the last war, by a sailor . . . called Jack Nasty-Face. 1836.

1261   BECHERVAISE (JOHN). Thirty-six years of a seafaring life. Portsea. 1839.

He also wrote *A farewell to my old shipmates and messmates . . . by the Old Quarter Master*, Portsea, 1847.

1262   LEECH (SAMUEL). Thirty years from home; or, A voice from the main deck. Boston, Mass. 1843. London. 1851.

1263   RICHARDSON. A mariner of England; an account of the career of William Richardson from cabin boy in the merchant service to warrant officer in the Royal navy, 1780–1819, as told by himself. Ed. by Spencer Childers. 1908.

1264   PEMBERTON (CHARLES REECE). The autobiography of Pel. Verjuice [with an introd. by Eric H. Partridge]. 1929.

1265   HAY. Landsman Hay; the memoirs of Robert Hay, 1789–1847. Ed. by M. D. Hay. 1953.

5. PRISONERS OF WAR

1266   ABELL (FRANCIS). Prisoners of war in Britain, 1756–1815; a record of their lives, their romance and their suffering. 1914.

Ambroise Louis Garneray, *Voyages, aventures et combats: souvenirs de ma vie maritime*, Paris, 1851, deals with his captivity in England, 1806–14.

1267   LEWIS (MICHAEL ARTHUR). Napoleon and his British captives. 1962.

Bibliog. 275–6. Deals with military, naval, and civilian prisoners of war in France.

G. SPECIAL SUBJECTS

1. TACTICS AND WEAPONS

See Bowles (1094).

1268 CORBETT (*Sir* JULIAN STAFFORD). English works on naval tactics, 1750–1850. NRS 35 (1908), 376–9.

Ibid. 380–95, is Corbett's bibliography of *Instructions and signal books, 1650–1830.*

1269 CLERK (JOHN). An essay on naval tactics, systematical and historical. Pt. 1. 1790. Pts. 2, 3, 4. 1797. 2nd edn. Edin. 1804. 3rd edn. with notes by Lord Rodney and an introd. by a naval officer. Edin. 1827.

The first original British work on the subject. Much later it was trenchantly criticized by Capt. Thomas White in *Naval researches: or, A candid inquiry into the conduct of Admirals Byron, Graves, Hood, and Rodney,* 1830, and by Sir Howard Douglas in *Naval evolutions,* 1832.

1270 STEEL (DAVID). A system of naval tactics. 1797.

Pts. 1 and 2 condense S. F. Bigot de Morogues, *Tactique navale,* Paris, 1763, and Jacques Bourdé de Villehuet, *Le manœuvrier,* Paris, 1765, 1769 (transl. by J. H. Jouin de Sauseuil as, *The manœuvrier, or skilful seaman,* 1788). Pt. 3 is on 'the present practice of the British navy'.

1271 SIMMONS (ROBERT). The sea-gunner's vade-mecum; being a new introduction to practical gunnery. 1812.

Sir Howard Douglas, *Treatise on naval gunnery,* 1820, went into a 3rd, greatly enlarged edn., 1851. See too H. J. Paixhans, *On the new wants arising from the introduction of the Paixhans gun in the Royal navy,* 1838; and T. S. Beauchant, *The naval gunner,* 1828.

1272 SIMMONS (THOMAS FREDERICK). Ideas as to the effect of heavy ordnance directed against and applied by ships of war. 1837.

Supplemented by his *A discussion on the present armament of the navy,* 1839.

1273 BIDDLECOMBE (*Sir* GEORGE). Naval tactics, and Trials of sailing . . . [also] the established plan of lights for steam-vessels, and regulations to avoid collision. 1850.

A summary of doctrine at the close of the sailing era. Biddlecombe was also author of *Steam fleet tactics,* 1857. For the first British treatise on steam tactics see Ross (1289).

1274 CORBETT (*Sir* JULIAN STAFFORD) *ed.* Fighting instructions, 1530–1816. NRS 29. 1905.

Corbett also ed. *Signals and instructions, 1776–94, with addenda to vol. 29,* NRS 35, 1908. The introd. is valuable, but needs revision.

1275 ROBERTSON (FREDERICK LESLIE). The evolution of naval armament. 1921.

1276 ANNIS (PHILIP GEOFFREY WALTER). Naval swords; British and American naval edged weapons, 1600–1815. 1970.

See also W. E. May and A. N. Kennard, *Naval swords and firearms,* 1962, and W. E. May and P. G. W. Annis, *Swords for sea service,* 1970.

2. NAVAL ARCHITECTURE

(a) *Bibliography*

1277 INSTITUTION OF NAVAL ARCHITECTS LIBRARY. Catalogue of the Scott collection of books, MSS., prints, and drawings. Comp. by Betty M. Cooper. 1954.

Covers 1532–1896 on shipbuilding and shipping. See also U.S. Library of Congress, *List of references on shipping and shipbuilding,* Wash., 1919.

(b) *Contemporary Publications on Ship Construction*

1278 VIAL DU CLAIRBOIS (HONORÉ SÉBASTIEN). Traité élémentaire de la construction des vaisseaux, à l'usage des élèves de la marine. 2 v. Paris. 1787–1805.

The 3rd pt. was trans. by J. N. Strange, *Elements of naval architecture,* 1846.

1279 SUTHERLAND (WILLIAM). The shipbuilder's assistant; or, Marine architecture. Rev. edn. 1794.

A classic of its time, first publ. 1711. See also Marmaduke Stalkartt, *Naval architecture,* 1781, 1787, 1803; William Hutchinson, *A treatise on naval architecture, founded upon philosophical and rational principles,* 4th edn., 1794.

1280 SOCIETY FOR THE IMPROVEMENT OF NAVAL ARCHITECTURE. Some account of the institution, plan and present state of the Society ... to which is annexed some papers on subjects of naval architecture. 1792.

The society issued an *Address,* 14 Apr. 1791. It prepared a *Catalogue of books on naval architecture,* n.d.; and its committee issued *Reports* in 1794 and 1800. See too *A collection of papers on naval architecture originally communicated through the channel of the ... European Magazine,* 2nd edn., 2 v., 1791–1800. A. W. Johns, 'An account of the society for the improvement of naval architecture', *Trans. Instn. Naval Arch.* 52 (1910), 28–37.

1281 STEEL (DAVID). The elements and practice of rigging and seamanship. 2 v. 1794. New edn. from the 1794 edn. by Claude S. Gill. 1932.

Darcy Lever, *The young sea-officer's sheet-anchor; or, A key to the leading of rigging and to practical seamanship,* Leeds, 1808, [1819], 1835, became a standard manual for nearly fifty years. Sir George Biddlecombe, *The art of rigging ... [based on ... Steel],* 1848; another edn., Salem, Mass., 1925.

1282 ATWOOD (GEORGE). 'The construction and analysis of geometrical propositions ... determining the stability of ships and of other floating bodies.' *Phil. Trans.* 86 (1796), 46–130.

Atwood also wrote, 'A disquisition on the stability of ships', *ibid.* 88 (1798), 201–310. See too A. W. Johns, 'The stability of the sailing warship', *Engineer,* July–Aug. 1922.

1283 SNODGRASS (GABRIEL). Letter to ... Henry Dundas ... on the mode of improving the navy of Great Britain. 1797.

A series of recommendations about ship construction.

1284 CHARNOCK (JOHN). An history of marine architecture . . . of all nations. 3 v. 1800–2.

A highly valuable work, with source materials. See also John Fincham, *A history of naval architecture*, 1851.

1285 GREATHEAD (HENRY). The report of the evidence, and other proceedings in Parliament respecting the invention of the life-boat. 1804.

See also Sir William Hillary, *A plan for the construction of a steam life-boat and also for the extinguishment of fire at sea*, 1824, 2nd edn., 1825.

1286 STEEL (DAVID). The elements and practice of naval architecture . . . 3rd edn. with an appendix, containing the principles and practice of constructing the Royal and mercantile navies, as . . . introduced by Sir Robert Seppings. By John Knowles. 1822.

Excellent detailed study of contemporary ship-building. Seppings wrote, *On a new principle of constructing H.M. ships of war*, 1814; and *A letter . . . to . . . Viscount Melville . . . on the circular sterns of ships of war*, 1822.

1287 MORGAN (WILLIAM) *and* CREUZE (AUGUSTIN) *eds.* Papers on naval architecture and other subjects, connected with naval science. Vs. 1–4 in 3. 1826–32.

Other pubns. about this time included Isaac Blackburn, *A treatise on the science of ship-building*, 1817; Wm. Annesley, *A new system of naval architecture*, 1822; George Harvey, *A treatise on ship-building*, Edin., 1828; Peter Hedderwick, *Treatise on marine architecture*, 2 v., 1830; Oliver Lang, *Improvements in naval architecture*, [Woolwich], 1848.

1288 WHITE (THOMAS). The theory and practice of ship-building. 1848.

See also Steinitz (1093).

(c) *Steam Propulsion*

1289 ROSS (*Sir* JOHN). A treatise on navigation by steam; comprising a history of the steam engine, and an essay towards a system of naval tactics peculiar to steam navigation. 1828. 2nd edn. 1837.

The first naval writer on steamships. See also Sir Robert Spencer Robinson, *The nautical steam engine explained, and its powers and capabilities described for use of the officers of the navy*, 1839, and his *Observations on the steam ships of the Royal navy . . . in a letter to the Earl of Auckland*, 1847; W. J. Williams, *A steam manual for the British navy*, Portsea, 1843; T. J. Main and T. Brown, *The marine steam engine designed chiefly for the use of the officers of H.M. Navy*, 1849, 1852, 1865; E. P. Halsted, *The screw fleet of the navy*, 1850.

1290 RUPERT-JONES (JOHN A.). 'Chronological order of the introduction of steam-propelled vessels in the Royal navy'. *Notes and Queries*, 152 (1927), 327–30, 347–50, 365–7.

(d) *Histories*

1291 JANE (FREDERICK THOMAS). The British battle fleet: its inception and growth throughout the centuries. 1912. 2 v. 1915.

See also Sir Nathaniel Barnaby, *Naval development in the [19th] century*, 1902.

1292 CHATTERTON (EDWARD KEBLE). Sailing ships; the story of their development from the earliest times to the present day. 1909. New edn. 1923.

Sir Alan H. Moore, *Sailing ships of war, 1800–60, including the transition to steam,* 1926, has 90 plates. See also, Sir George C. V. Holmes, *Ancient and modern ships,* 2 v., 1900–6, pt. 1: *Wooden sailing ships;* pt. 2: *The era of steam, iron, and steel;* Romola and R. C. Anderson, *The sailing-ship: six thousand years of history,* 1926; on the controversial designer, Sir William Symonds, see (1236).

1293 CLOWES (GEOFFREY SWINFORD LAIRD). Sailing ships; their history and development. 2nd edn. 2 v. 1931–2.

Various reprints; standard.

1294 CHATTERTON (EDWARD KEBLE). Ship-models. Ed. by Geoffrey Holme. 1923.

Beautifully illus. folio, as is R. M. Nance, *Sailing-ship models,* 2nd edn., 1949; and L. G. C. Laughton, *Old ship figure-heads and sterns,* 1925. August Köster, *Modelle alter Segelschiffe,* Berlin, 1926, was trans., *Ship models of the seventeenth to the nineteenth centuries,* N.Y., 1926. See also C. J. N. Longridge, *The anatomy of Nelson's ships* [1955].

1295 ALBION (ROBERT GREENHALGH). Forests and sea-power: the timber problem of the Royal navy, 1652–1862. Camb., Mass. 1926.

Standard work, linking the economic, diplomatic, colonial and naval aspects; bibliog. 425–69.

1296 BAXTER (JAMES PHINNEY). The introduction of the ironclad warship. Camb., Mass. 1933.

Pp. 1–68 are on the period up to 1851; bibliog. 363–81.

1297 LESLIE (ROBERT CHARLES). Old sea wings, ways, and words, in the days of oak and hemp. 1890. Facs. edn. with introd. by C. R. L. Fletcher and L. G. C. Laughton. 1930.

An excellent introduction to the study of nautical archaeology.

1298 ABELL (*Sir* WESTCOTT). The shipwright's trade. Camb. 1948.

1299 HENDERSON (JAMES). The frigates; an account of the lesser warships of the wars from 1793 to 1815. 1970.

See also Henderson, *Sloops and brigs; an account of the smallest vessels of the Royal navy during the great wars 1793 to 1815,* 1972; Douglas Gordon Browne, *The floating bulwark,* 1963, deals especially with the evolution of ships of the line. See too H. C. B. Rogers, *Troopships and their history,* [1963].

3. Lists of Officers and Ships

1300 NAVY. Steel's original and correct list of the Royal navy, 1782–1816.

Published monthly at first and then quarterly, till 1817, giving lists of all officers, and of all ships showing the captain, 1st lieut., purser, and the stations of those in commission.

1301 THE NAVY LIST. 1814+.

Pub. usually quarterly. Lists of officers on the active list and of all ships; includes the full officer-complement of ships in commission.

1302 NAVY. The commissioned sea officers of the Royal navy, 1660–1815. Comp. by David Bonner-Smith and Michael Arthur Lewis. 3 v. 1954.

1303 WATTS (*Sir* PHILIP). 'The ships of the Royal navy as they existed at the time of Trafalgar'. *Trans. of the Instn. of Naval Architects*, 47 (1905), 285–300.

1304 COLLEDGE (JAMES JOSEPH), *comp.* Ships of the Royal navy; an historical index. 2 v. Newton Abbot. 1969–70.

V. 1, major ships; v. 2, navy-built trawlers, drifters, tugs, and requisitioned ships. Halton S. Lecky, *The King's ships*, 3 v., 1913–14, an alphabetical listing with histories of vessels, suspended publication having reached *Jupiter*. E. E. Sigwart, *Royal fleet auxiliary . . . 1600–1968*, 1969, is a useful handlist of storeships and transports. There are books on H.M.S. *Victory* by Callender, 1914, 2nd edn., 1929; Bertie W. Smith, 1939, and Kenneth Fenwick, 1959; on *Bellerophon* by Edward Fraser, 1909, and C. A. Pengelly, 1966; on *Foudroyant*, by Thomas T. Birbeck, Chepstow, 1966.

1305 HOCKING (CHARLES). Dictionary of disasters at sea during the age of steam, including sailing ships and ships of war lost in action, 1824–1962. 2 v. 1969.

4. OFFICERS AND MEN

(a) Officers

1306 GOSTLING (GEORGE) *ed.* Extracts from the treaties between Great Britain and other . . . states . . . such . . . as relate to . . . the commanders of H.M.'s ships of war. 1792.

1307 A FAIR STATEMENT of the real grievances experienced by the officers and sailors in the navy of Great Britain; with a plan of reform . . . in a letter to Henry Dundas, treasurer of the Navy . . . by a naval officer. 1797.

1308 [DAVIS (JOHN)]. The post-captain; or, The wooden walls well manned, comprehending a view of naval society and manners. 1805. Limited edn. with introd. . . . from the 3rd edn. (1808), by R. H. Case. 1928.

A fictional account.

1309 NAVY. Observations and instructions for the use of the . . . officers of the Royal navy: by a Captain in the Royal navy. 1804. 1807.

1310 AN APPEAL TO HIS MAJESTY, both houses of parliament, and the people . . . against a late rejection of the petition of the captains of the Royal navy, for an augmentation of pay, by Lord Mulgrave . . . by a friend of the navy. 1810.

1311 GLASCOCK (WILLIAM NUGENT). The naval service or officers' manual, for every grade in H.M.'s ships. 2 v. 1836.

The 2nd edn., 1848, includes a note on steam and steam ships.

1312   LIARDET (FRANCIS). Professional recollections on points of seamanship, discipline, etc. Portsea. 1849.

1313   HARRIS (ROBERT). An historical sketch of the several means adopted
for the education of naval officers from 1729 to the present period. 1863.

See also Robert Wall, *Suggestions for the establishment of a naval university*, 1831.

1314   HANNAY (DAVID). Naval courts martial. Camb. 1914.

John Delafons, *A treatise on naval courts martial*, 1805; John McArthur, *Principles and
practice of naval and military courts martial*, 4th edn., 2 v., 1813, and William Hickman,
A treatise on the law and practice of naval courts martial, are contemporary accounts. See
too Peter Burke, *Celebrated naval and military trials*, 1866.

1315   MAHAN (ALFRED THAYER). Types of naval officers, drawn from the
history of the British navy. 1902.

1316   LEWIS (MICHAEL ARTHUR). England's sea-officers; the story of the
naval profession. 1939.

An excellent study.

(b) *Men*

(i) *Regulations*

1317   NAVY. Regulations and instructions relating to H.M. service at sea.
13th edn. 1790. later edns. 1808. 1826. [1833].

1318   PATTON (PHILIP). Strictures on naval discipline, and the conduct of
a ship of war. Edin. 1799.

(ii) *Manning and Discipline*

1319   MARINE SOCIETY. The bye-laws and regulations of the Marine
Society, instituted in 1756, incorporated in 1772 . . . to which is prefixed an
historical account of this institution. 1772. 4th edn. 1792. 6th edn. 1849.

1320   [BUTLER (CHARLES)]. An essay on the legality of impressing seamen.
1777. 2nd edn. 1778. 3rd edn. 1824.

See also Sir T. Byam Martin, *Impressment of seamen, and a few remarks on corporal
punishment, taken from the private memoranda of a naval officer*, 1834.

1321   CLARKE (RICHARD). Plans for increasing the naval force of Great
Britain by rendering the service a more desirable object to officers and seamen.
1795.

See also Thomas Trotter, *A practicable plan for manning the Royal navy and preserving
our maritime ascendancy without impressment, addressed to Admiral Lord Exmouth*,
Newcastle, 1819; and Adderley W. Sleigh, *Nautical reorganisation and increase of the
trading marine; also a practical plan for manning the navy without impressment*, 1840.

1322   HAMILTON (WILLIAM). The navigation laws as they affect the manning of the navy; with suggestions for improving its discipline and the condition of its seamen. [1848].

See also A. P. Eardley-Wilmot, *Manning the navy*, 1849.

1323 HUTCHINSON (J. ROBERT). The press-gang afloat and ashore. 1913.

(iii) *Service Conditions*

1324 STATEMENT OF CERTAIN IMMORAL PRACTICES prevailing in His Majesty's navy. 2nd edn. 1822.

About women on board.

1325 HILLARY (*Sir* WILLIAM). An appeal to the British nation, on the humanity and policy of forming a national institution for the preservation of lives and property from shipwreck. 1823. 5th edn. 1825.

See too Royal National Institution for the Preservation of Life from Shipwreck, *1st Annual report* [1825]; W. O. S. Gilly, *Narratives of shipwrecks of the Royal navy, 1793–1849; comp. from official documents . . .*, 1850; Patrick Howarth, *The Lifeboat story*, 1957.

1326 GRIFFITHS (ANSELM JOHN). Observations on some points of seamanship, with practical hints on naval œconomy, etc. Cheltenham. 1824. 2nd edn. Portsmouth. 1828.

1327 BARKER (MATTHEW HENRY). Greenwich hospital, a series of naval sketches, descriptive of the life of a man-of-war's man. 1826.

See also [Charles McPherson], *Life on board a man-of-war, by 'A British Seaman'*, Glasgow, 1829.

1328 HARRIS (JOHN). Britannia; or, The moral claims of seamen stated and enforced; an essay in three parts. 1837.

1329 MILES (EDMUND). An epitome, historical and statistical, descriptive of the Royal naval service of England . . . with the assistance of L. Miles. 1841. 1844.

With coloured plates.

1330 MATTHEWS (ALFRED). Fire considered as the seaman's scourge; with a glance at the causes of a few of our most serious losses . . . 1795–1864. 1866.

(iv) *Casualties*

1331 HODGES (WILLIAM BARWICK). 'On the mortality arising from naval operations'. *J. Roy. Stats. Soc.* 18 (1855), 201–21.

(v) *Mutinies*

1332 BULLOCKE (JOHN GREVILLE). Sailor's rebellion: a century of naval mutinies. 1938.

Events 1702–1797; bibliog. 305–7.

1333 ANTHONY (IRVIN WHITTINGTON) *ed*. The saga of the *Bounty*: its strange history as related by the participants themselves. N.Y. 1935.

See also Edward Edwards, *Voyage of H.M.S. 'Pandora'* . . . *1790–1*, 1915; Owen Rutter, ed., *The court-martial of the 'Bounty' mutineers*, 1931; *Journal of James Morrison*, with introd. by O. Rutter, 1935. See also Bligh (1156), (1190).

1334 POPE (DUDLEY). The black ship. 1963.

The story of the mutiny on the *Hermione* in the W. Indies, 1797.

1335 GILL (CONRAD). The naval mutinies of 1797. Manchester. 1913.

Classic account of the mutinies at Spithead and the Nore. Contemporary is Philip Patton, *Account of the mutinies at Spithead and St. Helen's* . . . 1797, Edin., n.d.; Sir Charles Cunningham, *A narrative of the occurrences that took place during the mutiny at the Nore*, Chatham, 1829, is a reliable account by a fair-minded eye-witness. See too [W. J. Neale], *History of the mutiny at Spithead and the Nore*, 1842. G. E. Manwaring and B. Dobrée, *The floating republic*, 1935, is admirable.

1336 DUGAN (JAMES). The great mutiny. 1966.

A thorough, well-documented study of the mutiny at Spithead; bibliog. 500–3. See also A. T. Patterson, *The naval mutiny at Spithead, 1797*, Portsmouth, 1968.

(vi) Social Life

1337 FIRTH (*Sir* CHARLES HARDING) *ed*. Naval songs and ballads. NRS 33. 1908.

See also Charles Dibdin, *Sea songs and ballads*, 2 pts., 1877; John Ashton, ed., *Real sailor-songs*, 1891; J. E. Masefield, ed., *A sailor's garland*, 1906; Christopher R. Stone, comp., *Sea songs and ballads*, Oxf., 1906; W. B. Whall, comp., *Sea songs and shanties*, 5th edn., Glasgow, 1926.

1338 LONG (WILLIAM HENRY) *ed*. Naval yarns: letters and anecdotes, comprising accounts of sea fights and wrecks . . . 1616–1831. 1899.

[Matthew Henry Barker], *Tough yarns: a series of naval tales and sketches. By the Old Sailor*. 1835.

1339 PARKINSON (CYRIL NORTHCOTE). Portsmouth point: the British navy in fiction, 1793–1815. 1948.

See too Charles N. Robinson, *The British tar in fact and fiction*, 1909; Harold F. Watson, *The sailor in English fiction and drama, 1550–1800*, N.Y., 1931.

1340 CALLENDER (*Sir* GEOFFREY ARTHUR ROMAINE) *ed*. Spindrift: salt from the ocean of English prose. Camb. 1915.

Selections on the sea and navy from famous English authors. See also Eric W. Bush, ed., *The flowers of the sea: an anthology of quotations, poems and prose*, 1962; Henry Baynham, *From the lower deck; the old navy, 1780–1840*, 1969, an anthology from autobiographical writings.

(vii) Dress

1341 MOLLO (JOHN). Uniforms of the Royal navy during the Napoleonic wars. 1965.

See also Dudley Jarrett, *British naval dress*, 1960; W. E. May, *The dress of naval officers*, 1966.

(viii) *General: Later Works*

1342 KEMP (PETER KEMP). The British sailor; a social history of the lower deck. 1970.

Christopher Lloyd, *The British seaman, 1200–1860; a social survey*, 1968; John Laffin, *Jack Tar*, 1969.

1343 LEWIS (MICHAEL ARTHUR). A social history of the navy, 1793–1815. 1960.

Authoritative; followed by his *The navy in transition, 1814–1864; a social history*, [1965]. S. H. Bonnett, *The price of Admiralty; an indictment of the Royal navy, 1805–1966*, 1968, is largely concerned with conditions of service. See too David Hannay, *Ships and men*, 1910; J. E. Masefield, *Sea life in Nelson's time*, 1905.

5. HEALTH AND NAVAL MEDICINE

1344 LLOYD (CHRISTOPHER) *and* COULTER (JACK L. S.). Medicine in the navy. V. 3: 1714–1815. Edin. 1961. V. 4: 1815–1900. Edin. 1963.

Standard, with full bibliog. C. Lloyd, ed., *The health of seamen; selections from the works of Dr. James Lind, Sir Gilbert Blane and Dr. Thomas Trotter*, NRS 107, 1965.

1345 JOURNAL of the Royal Naval Medical Service. 1915+.

Quarterly. Includes some historical articles, such as Sir H. D. Rolleston, 'Sir William Burnett: the first medical director-general of the Royal navy', 8 (1922), 1–10; H. B. Padwick, 'Some notes on early attempts at prophylaxis against "coast fevers" on the West Africa station', *ibid.* 89–98.

6. NAVIGATION

1346 MOORE (JOHN HAMILTON). The practical navigator and seaman's new daily assistant. 1772. 9th edn. 1791. 20th edn. by J. Dessiou. 1828.

See also John Robertson, *The elements of navigation*, 2 v., 1772, 6th edn., 1796, 7th edn. rev. and corr. by [Renee] Laurence Gwynne, 1806; William Nichelson, *A treatise on practical navigation and seamanship*, 1796; Andrew Mackay, *The theory and practice of finding the longitude at sea or land*, 2 v., 1793, 3rd edn., 1810. Mackay also wrote, *The complete navigator; or, An easy and familiar guide to the theory and practice of navigation*, 1804, 2nd edn., 1810.

1347 RAPER (HENRY). The practice of navigation and nautical astronomy. 3 pts. 1840–[2]. 3rd edn. 1849.

See also Thomas H. Sumner, *A new and accurate method of finding a ship's position at sea by projection on Mercator's chart*, Boston, Mass., 1843.

1348 HEWSON (JOSEPH BUSHBY). A history of the practice of navigation. Glasgow. 1951.

7. NAVAL DICTIONARIES

There is a bibliog. of nautical dictionaries, English and French, by L. G. C. Laughton, in *Mariner's Mirror*, 1 (1911), 84–89, 212–15; of the sea-language, *ibid.* 12 (1926), 335–8.

1349 FALCONER (WILLIAM). A universal dictionary of the marine . . .
To which is annexed, a translation of French sea-terms. 1769.

Many edns. Modernized and enl. by William Burney, 1815, 2nd edn., 1830. Abridged
as *The old wooden walls*, ed. by Claude S. Gill, 1930.

1350 LESCALLIER (DANIEL), *Baron*. Vocabulaire des termes de marine,
anglois et françois. 2 pts. Paris. 1777. New edn. 2 pts. 1783. Another edn.
3 pts. Paris. [1798].

Charles Romme, *Dictionnaire de la marine anglaise, et traduction des termes de la marine
française en anglais*, 2 pts., Paris, 1804.

1351 MOORE (J. J.). The British mariner's vocabulary of technical terms and
sea phrases. 1801. 1805.

1352 YOUNG (ARTHUR). Nautical dictionary. 1846. 2nd edn. 1863.

1353 SMYTH (WILLIAM HENRY). The sailor's word book; an alphabetical
digest of nautical terms. Rev. for the press by Sir E. Belcher. 1867.

'The most useful all-round dictionary of its kind for the sailing navy' (Callender).

8. Administration

See Spencer (1235), St. Vincent (1231), Barham (1187), Graham (220), Croker
(194).

1354 BENTHAM (*Sir* SAMUEL). Naval essays; or, Essays on the management of public concerns as exemplified in the naval department, considered as
a branch of the business of warfare. Essay 1: efficiency of the matériel. Pt. 1.
1828.

See too his *Naval papers and documents referred to in 'Naval essays'*, 8 nos., 1828. Maria
S. Bentham, *The life of Brigadier General Sir Samuel Bentham*, 1862, defended his
work for the navy on the basis of his letters and journals.

1355 HAMILTON (*Sir* RICHARD VESEY). Naval administration. 1896.

Deals with the constitution, character, and functions of the Board of Admiralty and of
the civil departments which it directed; bibliog. 201–7. Sir O. A. R. Murray, 'The
Admiralty', *Mariner's Mirror*, 23 (1937), 13–15, 129–47, 316–31; 24 (1938), 101–4,
204–25, 329–52, 458–78; 25 (1939), 89–111, 216–28, 328–38, provides excellent material.
See also David Bonner-Smith, 'The abolition of the navy board', *ibid.* 31 (1945), 154–9;
Mary E. Condon, 'The establishment of the transport board', *ibid.*, 58 (1972), 69–84;
G. H. Main Thompson, *Admiralty registrars. Some historical notes*, ed. K. C. McGuffie,
1958.

1356 GARDINER (LESLIE). The Board of Admiralty. 1968.

Bibliog. 400–1; a narrative centred on the style of activity of leading personalities.
Christopher Lloyd, *Mr. Barrow of the Admiralty; a life of Sir John Barrow*, 1970, is
important. Barrow wrote his own *Autobiographical memoir*, 1847, and there is a contemporary life by Sir George T. Staunton [1852]. See also Sir John Henry Briggs,
Naval administrations, 1827–92; the experience of 65 years, ed. by Lady Briggs, 1897.

1357 POOL (BERNARD). Navy Board contracts, 1660–1832; contract administration under the Navy Board. 1966.

1358 WISWALL (FRANK LAWRENCE). The development of Admiralty jurisdiction and practice since 1800; an English study with American comparisons. Camb. 1970.

9. FLAGS

1359 POPHAM (*Sir* HOME RIGGS). Telegraphic signals, or marine vocabulary. 1803. With appendix, 1809. 1812. 1816.

1360 PERRIN (WILLIAM GORDON). British flags, their early history, and their development at sea. Camb. 1922.

An indispensable book of reference. See also R. Siegel *Die Flagge*, Berlin, [1912], and William J. Gordon, *Flags of the world*, new edn. ed. by H. Gresham Carr, 1956.

10 MEDALS

1361 LONG (WILLIAM HENRY). Medals of the British navy and how they were won. 1895.

1362 MILFORD HAVEN (LOUIS ALEXANDER MOUNTBATTEN), *1st Marquess of*. British naval medals. Limited edn. 1919.

1363 NATIONAL MARITIME MUSEUM. British and foreign medals relating to naval and maritime affairs. Arranged and indexed by the Earl of Sandwich. 1937. Suppl. 1939. 2nd edn. 1950.

See too W. B. Rowbotham, 'The flag officer's and captain's gold medal, 1794–1815', *Mariner's Mirror* 37 (1951), 260–81.

VIII

ECONOMIC HISTORY

A. BIBLIOGRAPHIES, CATALOGUES, GUIDES, AND JOURNALS

Much material on economic history may also be found in local histories and local record offices (see Chapter XI) and in local newspapers (3493–4). For Public Record Office see (64). For parliamentary papers see Ford and Ford (p. 391), an invaluable guide for the period after 1833; only papers of outstanding importance, or those which appear to be insufficiently known, are listed below. Specialist journals are listed in the appropriate sub-sections. For directories see (3510).

1364 WILLIAMS (JUDITH BLOW). A guide to the printed materials for English social and economic history, 1750–1850. 2 v. N.Y. 1926.

With notes on contents of works listed. Valuable particularly for contemporary pamphlets, for trade journals, and for annual reports and publications of contemporary societies. See also *London Bibliography of the Social Sciences* (7).

1365 ECONOMIC HISTORY REVIEW. Economic History Society. 1927+.

Gives annually extensive lists of economic and social history writings, including many in local journals. *Economica* (London School of Economics), 1921+, is primarily concerned with economics, but contains articles on economic history, and a fair number on the history of economic thought. The *Journal of Economic History*, N.Y., 1941+ devotes much attention to British economic history.

1366 BUSINESS HISTORY. Liverpool. 1958+.

For a general guide see Theodore Cardwell Barker and others, *Business history* (Historical Assoc. Helps for students of history, 59), 1960. For lists of firms' histories see Business Archives Council, *The first five hundred: chronicles and histories of companies ... in the library of the Business Archives Council*, 1959, and Guildhall Library, *London business house histories: a handlist*, [1964]. For a guide to unpublished sources see National Register of Archives, *Sources of business history in reports of the National Register of Archives*, 1, 1964, and annual supplements, 1965+. See also Joyce Margaret Bellamy, *Yorkshire business histories: a bibliography*, 1970, and Horrocks (3610).

1367 COBB (H. S.) 'Sources for economic history amongst the parliamentary records in the House of Lords record office.' *Econ. H.R.*, 2nd ser. 19 (1966–7), 154–74.

1368 LONDON UNIVERSITY LIBRARY. Catalogue of the Goldsmiths' Library of economic literature. *Comp.* Margaret Canney and David Knott. V. 1. Printed books to 1800. V. 2. Printed books 1801–1850. Camb. 1970. 1975.

See also Robert Denis Collison Black, *Catalogue of pamphlets on economic subjects*, *published between 1750 and 1800 and now housed in Irish libraries*, Belfast, 1969, and Rodney P. Sturges, *Economists' papers 1750-1950. A guide to archive and other manuscript sources for the history of British and Irish economic thought*, 1975.

B. GENERAL

I. MODERN GENERAL WORKS

1369 CUNNINGHAM (WILLIAM). The growth of English industry and commerce in modern times. Pt. 1. The mercantile system. Pt. 2. Laissez-faire. Camb. 1882. Another edn. 2 v. 3 pts. 1922–9.

1370 HOBSON (JOHN ATKINSON). The evolution of modern capitalism. A study of machine production. 1894. Rev. edns. 1906, 1917, 1926.

1371 WEBER (ADNA FERRIN). The growth of cities in the nineteenth century: A study in statistics. (Columbia University studies in history, economics, and public law, 11). 1899. Reprinted Ithaca, N.Y. 1963.

See also R. Price Williams, 'The population of London, 1801–1881', *J. Roy. Statistical Soc.* 48 (1885), 349–432 and H. J. Dyos, ed., *The Study of urban history*, etc., 1968.

1372 SOMBART (WERNER). Der moderne Kapitalismus. 2 v. Leipzig. 1902. 2nd edn. 3 v. Munich and Leipzig. 1916–28.

1373 SMART (WILLIAM). Economic annals of the nineteenth century. V. 1, 1801–20, 1910. V. 2, 1821–30, 1917.

Based on *Hansard* reports of debates on economic policy. Similar in character is William Page, ed., *Commerce and industry: a historical review of the economic conditions of the British Empire*, etc., 2 v., 1919.

1374 CLAPHAM (JOHN HAROLD). An economic history of modern Britain. V. 1. The early railway age, 1820–1850. Camb. 1926. 2nd edn. Camb. 1930, reprinted with cor. 1950. V. 2. Free trade and steel, 1850–1886, Camb. 1932. Reprinted with cor. Camb. 1952.

1375 DOBB (MAURICE HERBERT). Studies in the development of capitalism. 1946.

1376 BREBNER (JOHN BARTLET). 'Laissez faire and state intervention in nineteenth century Britain'. *J. Econ. Hist.* 8 (1948) suppl. 59–73.

1377 HAYEK (FRIEDRICH AUGUST VON) *ed.* Capitalism and the historians. 1954.

1378 PRESSNELL (LESLIE SEDDEN) *ed.* Studies in the industrial revolution presented to T. S. Ashton. 1960.

1379 CHECKLAND (SYDNEY GEORGE). The rise of industrial society in England, 1815–1885. 1964.

Bibliog. 431–54. Other short surveys are Charles Ryle Fay, *Great Britain from Adam*

Smith to the present day. An economic and social history, 1928, 5th edn., 1950; William Henry Bassano Court, *A concise economic history of Britain from 1750 to recent times*, Camb. 1954; Thomas Southcliffe Ashton, *An economic history of England; the eighteenth century*, 1955; Arthur Redford, *The economic history of England, 1760–1860*, 2nd edn. rev., 1960; Jonathan David Chambers, *The workshop of the world, British economic history from 1820 to 1880*, 1961; Phyllis Deane, *The first industrial revolution*, 1965; Peter Mathias, *The first industrial nation, an economic history of Britain, 1700–1914*, 1969.

2. STATISTICAL COMPILATIONS

1380 CHALMERS (GEORGE). An estimate of the comparative strength of Britain during the present and four preceding reigns, and the losses of her trade from every war since the revolution. 1782. New edn. cor. 1794. Other edns. 1802, 1804, 1812.

1381 MACPHERSON (DAVID). Annals of commerce, manufactures, fisheries and navigation. 4 v. 1805.

1382 COLQUHOUN (PATRICK). A treatise on the wealth, power and resources of the British empire in every quarter of the world. 1814. 2nd edn. with add. 1815.

Includes an attempt to measure national income.

1383 LOWE (JOSEPH). The present state of England in regard to agriculture, trade and finance. With a comparison of the prospects of England and France. 1822. 2nd edn. 1823.

See also Baron François Pierre Charles Dupin, *The commercial power of Great Britain*, etc., 2 v. 1825 (translated from the French); John Powell, *Statistical illustrations . . . of the British empire*, 1825; Thomas Hopkins, *Great Britain for the last forty years*, etc., 1834.

1384 McCULLOCH (JOHN RAMSAY). A dictionary, practical, theoretical and historical, of commerce and commercial navigation: illustrated with maps and plans. 2 v. 1832. Many later edns.

Compiled with the aid of British consuls abroad. By the same writer, *A descriptive and statistical account of the British empire*, 3rd edn., 2 v., 1847.

1385 PORTER (GEORGE RICHARDSON). The progress of the nation in its various social and economical relations, from the beginning of the nineteenth century to the present time. 3 v. 1836–43. 2nd edn. 1847. 3rd edn. 1851.

By the head of the Statistical Department, Board of Trade, and authoritative. See also *Tables of revenue, population, commerce*, etc., known as Porter's Tables, pub. annually from 1833 to 1852 (in 22 pts.), in Parliamentary papers. John McGregor, *Commercial statistics, a digest of the productive resources, commercial legislation . . . of all nations*, 5 v. 1844–50, is by the Joint Secretary to the Board of Trade.

1386 SPACKMAN (WILLIAM FREDERICK). An analysis of the occupations of the people, showing the relative importance of the agricultural, manufacturing, shipping, colonial, commercial, and mining interests. 1847.

1387 LEVI (LEONE). History of British commerce, and of the economic progress of the British nation, 1763–1870. 1872. 2nd edn. 1880.

1388 MITCHELL (BRIAN REDMAN) with the collaboration of Phyllis Deane. Abstract of British historical statistics. Camb. 1962.

1389 POLLARD (SIDNEY) *and* CROSSLEY (DAVID W.) The wealth of Britain 1085–1966. 1968.

3. Prices, Wages, and the Standard of Living

1390 TOOKE (THOMAS) *and* NEWMARCH (WILLIAM). A history of prices and of the state of the circulation, from 1793 to the present time. 6 v. 1838–57. New edn. with intro. by T. E. Gregory. 1928.

Also Thomas Tooke, *Thoughts and details on the high and low prices of the last thirty years*, 1823.

1391 JEVONS (WILLIAM STANLEY). Investigations in currency and finance. 1884. New edn. abridged. 1909.

Discusses history of prices since 1782.

1392 BOWLEY (ARTHUR LYON). Wages in the United Kingdom in the nineteenth century. Notes for the use of students of social and economic questions. Camb. 1900.

Also A. Hopkinson and A. L. Bowley, 'Bibliography of wage statistics in the United Kingdom in the nineteenth century', *Econ. Rev.* 8 (1898), 504–20.

1393 WOOD (GEORGE HENRY). 'The course of average wages between 1790 and 1860'. *Reports of the British Association for the Advancement of Science*, section F. 1899, 829–30.

Also the same writer's *The history of wages in the cotton trade during the past hundred years*, 1910, and David Chadwick, 'On the rate of wages in Manchester and Salford, and the manufacturing districts of Lancashire, 1839–59', *Statistical Soc. J.* 23 (1860), 1–36.

1394 SAUERBECK (AUGUSTUS). The course of average prices of general commodities in England. [1894.] New edn. 1908.

Index numbers, 1818–1907.

1395 LAYTON (WALTER THOMAS). An introduction to the study of prices, with special reference to the history of the nineteenth century. 1912. 3rd edn. written jointly with Geoffrey Crowther. 1938.

1396 SILBERLING (N. J.). 'British prices and business cycles, 1779–1850'. *Rev. Econ. Statistics*, preliminary vol. 5 suppl. 2 (1923), 219–62.

Based on prices current.

1397 TUCKER (RUFUS S.) 'Real wages of artisans in London, 1729–1935.' *Jour. American Statistical Assoc.* 31 (1936), 73–84.

1398 SCHUMPETER (ELIZABETH BOODY). 'English prices and public finance, 1660–1882.' *Rev. Econ. Statistics*, 20 (1938), 21–37.

On the relationship between price movements and government borrowing.

1399 BEVERIDGE (*Sir* WILLIAM HENRY) *and others*. Prices and wages in England from the twelfth to the nineteenth century. V. 1. 1939.

1400 PHELPS-BROWN (E. H.) *and* HOPKINS (SHEILA V.) 'Seven centuries of the price of consumables compared with builders' wage rates.' *Economica*, new ser. 23 (1956), 296–314.

1401 HOBSBAWM (E. J. E.) *and* HARTWELL (R. M.). 'The standard of living during the industrial revolution: a discussion.' *Econ. H.R.* 2nd ser. 16 (1963–4), 119–46.

The most recent statement of the arguments. See Sir Robert Giffen, *The progress of the working classes in the last half century*, 1884; T. S. Ashton, 'The standard of life of the workers in England, 1790–1830' in Hayek (1377); E. J. E. Hobsbawm, 'The British standard of living 1790–1850', *Econ. H.R.*, 2nd ser. 10 (1957–8), 46–68; A. J. Taylor, 'Progress and poverty in Britain, 1780–1850: a reappraisal', *History*, 45 (1960), 16–31; R. M. Hartwell, 'The rising standard of living in England, 1800–1850', *Econ. H.R.*, 2nd ser. 13 (1960–1), 397–416.

4. ECONOMIC GROWTH AND FLUCTUATIONS

1402 HOBSON (CHARLES KENNETH). The export of capital. 1914. New edn. 1920.

Also Leland Hamilton Jenks, *The migration of British capital to 1875*, 1927, reprinted 1963, and the same writer's 'British experience with foreign investments', *J. Econ. Hist.* 4 (1944), supp., 68–79.

1403 SHANNON (H. A.) 'Bricks—a trade index, 1785–1849.' *Economica*, n.s. 1 (1934), 300–18.

1404 KONDRATIEFF (N. D.) 'The long waves in economic life.' *Rev. Econ. Statistics*, 17 (1935), 105–15.

1405 SMITH (WALTER BUCKINGHAM) *and* COLE (ARTHUR HARRISON). Fluctuations in American business, 1790–1860. (Harvard Econ. Studies, 50.) Camb., Mass. 1935.

1406 ROUSSEAUX (PAUL). Les mouvements de fond de l'économie anglaise, 1800–1913. Louvain, 1938.

1407 SCHUMPETER (JOSEPH ALOIS). Business cycles. A theoretical, historical and statistical analysis of the capitalist process. 2 v. 1939.

1408 HOFFMANN (WALTHER GUSTAV). Wachstum und Wachstumsformen der englischen Industriewirtschaft von 1700 bis zur Gegenwart. (Probleme der Weltwirtschaft, 63.) Jena. 1940.

Trans. with title *British industry, 1700–1950* by W. O. Henderson and W. H. Chaloner,

Oxf. 1955. For comment see J. F. Wright, 'An index of the output of British industry since 1700', *J. Econ. Hist.* 16 (1956), 356–64, and W. A. Cole 'The measurement of industrial growth', *Econ. H.R.*, 2nd ser. 11 (1958–9), 309–15.

1409 WARD-PERKINS (CHARLES NEVILLE). 'The commercial crisis of 1847.' *Oxf. Econ. Papers.* 2 (1950), 75–84.

Also Alexander Baring, Baron Ashburton, *The financial and commercial crises considered*, 1847, and David Morier Evans, *The commercial crisis, 1847–1848*, 1848, 2nd edn. rev. and enl. 1849.

1410 ROSTOW (WALT WHITMAN). The process of economic growth. Oxf. 1953. 2nd edn. Oxf. 1960.

Followed by Rostow, *The stages of economic growth*, etc., Oxf., 1960. For comment see M. M. Postan, 'Economic growth', *Econ. H.R.*, 2nd ser. 6 (1953–4), 78–83. and A. K. Cairncross, 'The stages of economic growth', *ibid.* 13 (1960–1), 450–8. Also W. W. Rostow, ed., *The economics of take-off into sustained growth. Proceedings of a conference held by the International Economic Association*, 1963.

1411 GAYER (ARTHUR DAVID), ROSTOW (WALT WHITMAN), *and* SCHWARTZ (ANNA JACOBSON). The growth and fluctuation of the British economy, 1790–1850. An historical, statistical and theoretical study of Britain's economic development, 2 v. Oxf. 1953.

For comment see R. C. O. Matthews, 'The trade cycle in Britain, 1790–1850', *Oxf. Econ. Papers*, 6 (1954), 1–32. Also, a preliminary work, W. W. Rostow, *British economy of the nineteenth century*, Oxf., 1948.

1412 MATTHEWS (ROBERT CHARLES OLIVER). A study in trade cycle history. Economic fluctuations in Great Britain, 1833–42. Camb. 1954.

1413 CAIRNCROSS (ALEXANDER K.) *and* WEBER (BERNARD). 'Fluctuations in building in Great Britain, 1785–1849.' *Econ. H.R.*, 2nd ser. 9 (1956–7), 283–97.

See also H. J. Habakkuk, 'Fluctuations in house building in Britain and the United States in the nineteenth century', *J. Econ. Hist.* 22 (1962), 198–230; Jeffrey G. Williamson, 'The long swing: comparisons and interactions between the British and American balance of payments, 1820–1913'; *ibid.* 22 (1962), 21–46; John Parry Lewis, *Building cycles and Britain's growth, incorporating material of the late Bernard Weber*, 1965; and Brinley Thomas (1748).

1414 ASHTON (THOMAS SOUTHCLIFFE). Economic fluctuations in England, 1700–1800. Oxf. 1959.

1415 YOUNGSON (ALEXANDER JOHN), *originally* A. J. Y. BROWN. Possibilities of economic progress. Camb. 1959.

1416 DEANE (PHYLLIS) *and* COLE (WILLIAM ALAN). British economic growth, 1688–1959. (Univ. of Cambridge department of applied economics. Monographs 8.) Camb. 1962. 2nd edn. Camb. 1967.

For comment see J. F. Wright, 'British economic growth, 1688–1959', *Econ. H.R.*, 2nd ser. 18 (1965–6), 397–412.

1417 SUPPLE (BARRY EMMANUEL). The experience of economic growth. Case studies in economic history. N.Y. 1963. Repr. 1966.

1418 HIGGINS (J. P. P.) *and* POLLARD (SIDNEY). Aspects of capital investment in Great Britain, 1750–1850; a preliminary survey. Report of a conference held at the University of Sheffield, 5–7 January, 1969. 1971.

See also Sidney Pollard, 'Investment, consumption and the industrial revolution', *Econ. H.R.*, 2nd ser. 11 (1958–9), 215–26.

1419 HARTWELL (RONALD MAX) *ed.* The industrial revolution. Oxf. 1970.

Essays on a variety of topics.

C. FINANCIAL AND COMMERCIAL ORGANIZATION

1. TAXATION

1420 McCULLOCH (JOHN RAMSAY). A treatise on the principles and practical influence of taxation and the funding system. 1845. 3rd edn. Edin. 1863.

1421 DOWELL (STEPHEN). A history of taxation and taxes in England from the earliest times to the present day. 4 v. 1884. 2nd edn. 4 v. 1888.

A catalogue of tax changes. See also Sir John Sinclair, *The history of the public revenue of the British empire*, 3rd edn., 3 v., 1803–4, v. 2 being mostly on Pitt; César Moreau, *Chronological records of British finance* [1828]; Sir Stafford Northcote, *Twenty years of financial policy*, etc., 1862, on the years 1842–61; Sydney Charles Buxton, *Finance and politics: an historical study, 1783–1885*, 2 v., 1888. William Kennedy, *English taxation, 1640–1799, an essay on policy and opinion* (L.S.E. studies in economic and political science, 33), 1913, reprinted 1964, discusses theories of taxation accepted in the 18th century. Angus Whiteford Acworth, *Financial reconstruction in England, 1815–1822*, 1925, deals with taxation and the national debt. James Frederick Rees, *A short fiscal and financial history of England, 1815–1918*, 1921, summarizes the main events. Figures of public income and expenditure 1688–1869 are summarized in H.C. 1868–9 (450), XXXV.

1422 CANNAN (EDWIN). The history of local rates in England in relation to the proper distribution of the burden of taxation. (L.S.E. Studies in Political and Economic Science 1.) 1896, 2nd edn. enl. 1912.

See also Interdepartmental committee on social and economic research, *Guides to official sources*, 3, *Local government statistics*, 1953; E. P. Hennock, 'Finance and politics in urban local government in England, 1835–1900', *Hist. J.* 6 (1963), 212–25.

1423 HARGREAVES (ERIC LYDE). The national debt. 1930. Reprinted 1966.

Bibliog. 297–9. See also Robert Hamilton, *An inquiry concerning the rise and progress . . . of the national debt of Great Britain*, Edin. 1813, 3rd edn. Edin. 1818.

1424 HOPE-JONES (ARTHUR). Income tax in the Napoleonic wars. Camb. 1939.

Also Albert Farnsworth, *Addington, author of the modern income tax*, 1951. On Napoleonic expenditure see Walter M. Stern, 'United Kingdom expenditure by votes of supply, 1793–1817', *Economica*, new ser. 17 (1950), 196–210. See also Henry Beeke, *Observations on the produce of the income tax and on its proportion to the whole income of Great Britain*, etc., 1799, new edn. enl., 1800, and P. K. O'Brien, 'British incomes and property in the early nineteenth century', *Econ. H.R.*, 2nd ser. 12 (1959–60), 255–67, a study of information which can be extracted from income tax returns.

1425 PARNELL (*Sir* HENRY) *4th bart*. On financial reform. 1830. 3rd edn. 1831. 4th edn. 1832.

Proposed reductions in indirect taxation and the reintroduction of income tax: also Sir Samuel Bentham, *Financial reform scrutinized, in a letter to Sir Henry Parnell, Bart.*, *M.P.*, 1830, which recommends cost accounting, competition for contracts, prompt payment etc., and [Benjamin Sayer], *An attempt to shew the justice and expediency of substituting an income or property tax for the present taxes*, etc., 1831, rev. edn., 1833. For the 1840s see Torrens (1790).

1426 SELIGMAN (EDWIN ROBERT ANDERSON). The income tax: A study of the history, theory and practice of income taxation at home and abroad. N.Y. 1911. 2nd edn. rev. and enl. N.Y. 1914.

Also his *The shifting and incidence of taxation*, 5th edn., N.Y., 1927, with bibliog. See also Fakhri Shehab (Shihàb), *Progressive taxation: a study in the development of the progressive principle in the British income tax*, Oxf., 1953.

1427 RICHARDS (RICHARD DAVID). 'The lottery in the history of English government finance.' *Econ. Hist.* 3 (1934–7), 57–76.

By the same author, 'The Exchequer bill in the history of English government finance', *ibid.* 3 (1934–7), 193–211. For the Treasury and tax administration generally see (455).

1428 HELLEINER (KARL FERDINAND). The imperial loans. A study in financial and diplomatic history. Oxf. 1965.

Also William Newmarch, *On the loans raised by Mr. Pitt during the first French war, 1793–1801; with some statements in defence of the method of funding employed*, 1855, which includes a detailed account of each loan.

1429 SABINE (BASIL ERNEST VYVYAN). A history of income tax. 1966.

The best account of the British tax.

2. CURRENCY AND BANKING

(a) *General*

1430 GREGORY (THEODORE EMANUEL GUGENHEIM) *ed*. Select statutes, documents and reports relating to British banking, 1832–1928. 2 v. 1929.

The most important parliamentary papers on banking are *Report of the Lords' committee of secrecy, ordered to be printed 28 April, 1797*, reprinted H.C. 1810 (17) III; *Report of the Commons . . . on . . . the restriction of payments in cash, 1797*, reprinted H.C. 1826 (926) III, both on the suspension of cash payments, 1797; *Report from the select committee on the high price of gold bullion*, H.C. 1810 (349) III, and reprinted by Edwin Cannan, *The paper pound of 1797–1821*, etc., 1919; *Report from the secret committee . . . with reference to the expediency of resuming cash payments*, H.C. 1819 (202, 282) III,

House of Lords' committee on the same subject, 1–2 reps. H.C. 1819 (291) III, all recommending the resumption of cash payments. On the growth of joint-stock banking see *Select committee on promissory notes in Scotland and Ireland* (3914), and *Report of the committee on joint-stock banks*, H.C. 1836 (591) IX. On central banking see *Report from the committee of secrecy on the renewal of the Bank of England charter*, H.C. 1831–2 (722) VI, and *Report of the select committee on banks of issue*, H.C. 1840 (602) IV, and H.C. 1841 (366, 410) V. The *Report of the select committee on the usury laws*, H.C. 1818 (376) VI, reprinted 1845 (611) XII, and H.C. 1821 (410) IV attacked the legal restrictions on rates of interest.

(b) Development of Monetary Theory

1431 THORNTON (HENRY). An enquiry into the nature and effects of the paper credit of Great Britain. 1802.

Reprinted, with his other writings and speeches, 1939, ed. F. A. von Hayek (Library of economics, section 1, no. 2).

1432 KING (PETER) *7th baron*. Thoughts on the restriction of payments in specie at the Banks of England and Ireland. [1803.]

1433 RICARDO (DAVID). The high price of bullion a proof of the depreciation of banknotes. 1810. 4th edn. with appendix answering criticisms, 1811.

Reprinted *Works* (1787), v. 3. Also on the bullionist controversy, William Huskisson, *The question concerning the depreciation of our currency stated and examined*, 1810, 7th edn. 1811, new edn., 1819 (Huskisson was a member of the Bullion Committee); William Blake, *Observations on the principles which regulate the course of exchange; and on the present depreciated state of the currency*, 1810; Charles Bosanquet, *Practical observations on the report of the Bullion Committee*, 1810, an attack on the committee; David Ricardo, *Reply to Mr. Bosanquet's practical observations*, etc., 1811, reprinted in *Works*, v. 3.

1434 ATTWOOD (THOMAS). A letter to the Right Honourable Nicholas Vansittart on the creation of money, and on its action upon national prosperity. Birmingham. 1817.

Also *Prosperity restored*, etc., 1817, *The Scotch banker . . . on banking, currency*, etc., *republished from the Globe newspaper*, etc., both pub. anonymously, 1828. Attwood's monetary theory is discussed by S. G. Checkland, 'The Birmingham economists, 1815–1850', *Econ. H.R.*, 2nd ser. 11 (1948–9), 1–19, and Asa Briggs, 'Thomas Attwood and the economic background of the Birmingham political union', *Camb. Hist. J.* 9 (1948), 190–216. For Attwood's life see C. M. Wakefield, *Life of Thomas Attwood*, 1885. For a similar attack on the return to cash payments by a spokesman of the landed interest see Charles Callis Western, *A letter to the earl of Liverpool on the cause of our present embarrassments and distress*, etc., 1826.

1435 JOPLIN (THOMAS). An essay on the general principles and present practice of banking, in England and Scotland. Newcastle-upon-Tyne. 1822. 5th edn. 1826. 6th edn. 1827.

In favour of joint stock banking. See also his *An analysis and history of the currency question; together with an account of the origin and growth of joint stock banking in England*, 1832. For Joplin and the National Provincial bank see (1445).

1436 GILBART (JAMES WILLIAM). The history and principles of banking. 1834. 2nd edn. 1835. 3rd edn. 1837.

Also *A practical treatise on banking, containing an account of the London and country banks*, etc., 1827, 3rd edn. 1834. For Gilbart and the Westminster Bank see (1445).

1437 PALMER (JOHN HORSLEY). The causes and consequences of the pressure on the money-market; with a statement of the action of the Bank of England from 1st October 1833 to 27th December, 1836. 1837.

Defence of the bank: Horsley Palmer was Governor, 1830–2.

1438 GILBART (JAMES WILLIAM). An inquiry into the causes of the pressure on the money market during the year 1839. 1840.

1439 NORMAN (GEORGE WARDE). Remarks upon some prevalent errors, with respect to currency and banking, and suggestions to the legislature and the public as to the improvement in the monetary system. 1838.

Statement of the tenets of the currency school; so also is Samuel Jones Loyd, *Thoughts on the separation of the departments of the Bank of England*, 1844. For the opposing banking school see Thomas Tooke, *An inquiry into the currency principle*, etc., 1844, and John Fullarton, *On the regulation of currencies*, etc., 1844, and in reply, Robert Torrens, *The principles and practical operation of Sir Robert Peel's Bill of 1844 explained and defended against the objections of Tooke, Fullarton and Wilson*, 1848. See also Loyd (1777).

1440 MACLEOD (HENRY DUNNING). The theory and practice of banking with the elementary principles of currency, prices, credit, and exchanges. 2 v. 1855–6.

1441 [McCULLOCH (JOHN RAMSAY) *ed.*] A select collection of scarce and valuable tracts and other publications, on paper currency and banking. 1857.

1442 FETTER (FRANK WHITSON). Development of British monetary orthodoxy, 1797–1875. Camb., Mass. 1965.

Other general studies are Robert Harry Inglis Palgrave, *Bank rate and the money market . . . in England, France, Germany, Holland and Belgium, 1844–1900*, 1903; Ralph George Hawtrey, *A century of bank rate*, 1938, reprinted 1962 (mostly on the later 19th century); Charles Rist, *Histoire des doctrines relatives au crédit et à la monnaie*, etc., Paris and Liège, 1938, trans. by Jane Degras as *History of monetary and credit theory*, 1940; Elmer Wood, *English theories of central banking control, 1819–1858. With some account of contemporary procedure* (Harvard Economic Studies, 64), Camb., Mass., 1939; Edward Victor Morgan, *The theory and practice of central banking, 1797–1913*, Camb., 1943; Karl Heinrich Niebyl, *Studies in the classical theories of money*, N.Y., 1946; Thomas Southcliffe Ashton and Richard Sidney Sayers, eds., *Papers in English monetary history*, Oxf., 1953, including nine papers on the period 1789–1851; Emmanuel Coppieters, *English banknote circulation 1694–1954*, The Hague, 1955; Alfred Bernard Cramp, *Opinion on bank rate, 1822–60*, [1962].

(c) Banking Histories

1443 PRICE (FREDERICK GEORGE HILTON). A handbook of London bankers. 1876.

Includes historical information.

1444 BASTER (ALBERT STEPHEN JAMES). The Imperial banks. 1929.

By the same author, *The international banks*, 1935.

1445 WITHERS (HARTLEY). National Provincial bank, 1833–1933. 1933.

For the other joint-stock banks, see Wilfred Frank Crick and John Edwin Wadsworth, *A hundred years of joint stock banking*, 1936, on the Midland; Theodore Emanuel Gugenheim Gregory assisted by Annette Henderson, *The Westminster bank through a century*, 2 v., 1936; Richard Sidney Sayers, *Lloyds bank in the history of English banking*, Oxf., 1957; George Chandler, *Four centuries of banking* . . . [a history of] *Martin's Bank Ltd*, v. 1, 1964. Joseph Sykes, *The amalgamation movement in English banking, 1825–1924*, 1926, is a general study.

1446 KING (WILFRID THOMAS COUSINS). History of the London discount market: with an introduction by T. E. Gregory. 1936.

1447 CLAPHAM (*Sir* JOHN HAROLD). The Bank of England: a history, 1694–1914. 2 v. Camb. 1944.

See also Andreas Michael Andréadès, *Essai sur le fondation et l'histoire de la Banque d'Angleterre*, etc., 2 v., Paris, 1904, trans. with title *History of the Bank of England 1640 to 1903* by Christabel Meredith, 1909, 2nd edn. 1924, also Wilfrid Marston Acres, *The Bank of England from within, 1694–1900*, 2 v., 1931.

1448 PRESSNELL (LESLIE SEDDEN). Country banking in the industrial revolution. Oxf. 1956.

See also *T. Twigg's corrected list of the country-bankers of England and Wales*, etc., 1830; George Rae, *The country banker: his clients, cares and work. From an experience of forty years*, 1885, 7th edn., 1930; Maberly Phillips, *A history of banks, bankers, and banking in Northumberland, Durham, and North Yorkshire, illustrating commercial developments of the north of England from 1775 to 1894*, 1894; John Hughes, *Liverpool banks and bankers, 1760–1837*, etc., Liverpool, 1906; Robert Eadon Leader, *The Sheffield banking company limited. An historical sketch. 1831–1916*, Sheffield, 1916; Thomas Southcliffe Ashton, 'The bill of exchange and private banks in Lancashire, 1790–1830', *Econ. H.R.*, 1st ser. 15 (1944–5), 25–35; John Alfred Stuart Leighton Leighton-Boyce, *Smiths the bankers, 1658–1958*, 1958. For two Quaker banking firms see David E. Swift, *Joseph John Gurney: banker, reformer and Quaker*, Middletown, Conn., 1962, and Audrey Mary Taylor, *Gilletts, bankers at Banbury and Oxford: A study in local economic history*, Oxf., 1964.

(d) *Currency*

1449 FEAVEARYEAR (ALBERT EDGAR). The pound sterling. A history of English money. Oxf. 1931. 2nd edn. rev. by E. V. Morgan. Oxf. 1963.

Also Robert Mushet, *An enquiry into the effects produced on the national currency . . . by the Bank Restriction Bill*, etc., 1810, and Frank Whitson Fetter, 'Legal tender during the English and Irish bank restrictions', *J. Political Economy*, 58 (1950), 241–53.

1450 CRAIG (*Sir* JOHN). The Mint. A history of the London Mint from A.D. 287 to 1948. 1953.

Also William Arthur Shaw, *The history of currency, 1252 to 1894. Being an account of the gold and silver monies and monetary standards of Europe and America*, [1895], 2nd edn., 1896.

1451 MATHIAS (PETER). English trade tokens: the industrial revolution illustrated. 1962.

3. BUSINESS ORGANIZATION

1452 SELECT COMMITTEE ON LAWS RELATING TO MERCHANTS, AGENTS AND FACTORS. H.C. 1823 (452) IV.

For treatises on commercial law see 615–22.

1453 EVANS (DAVID MORIER). The city; or, The physiology of London business; with sketches on 'change and at the coffee houses. 1845.

An amusing account of the London business community.

1454 FINDLAY (J. A.) The Baltic Exchange, being a short history of the Baltic mercantile and shipping exchange from the days of the old coffee house. [1927.]

By a former secretary of the exchange; concentrates on notable personalities.

1455 HUNT (BISHOP CARLETON). The development of the business corporation in England, 1800–1867. (Harvard economic studies, 52.) Camb., Mass. 1936.

Also Ronald Ralph Formoy, *The historical foundations of modern company law*, 1923; George Herberton Evans, *British corporation finance, 1775–1850. A study of preference shares* (Johns Hopkins Univ. studies in historical and political science, extra volumes, n.s. 23), Baltimore, 1936; Armand Budington Dubois, *The English business company after the Bubble Act*, N.Y., 1938; Colin Arthur Cooke, *Corporation, trust and company. An essay in legal history*, Manchester, 1950, primarily a legal study. See also J. B. Jefferys, 'The denomination and character of shares 1855–1885' in *Essays in economic history*, I, ed. E. M. Carus-Wilson, 1954, 344–57, and H. A. Shannon, 'The coming of general limited liability', *ibid.* 358–79.

1456 SMITH (RAYMOND). Sea-coal for London. History of the coal factors in the London market. 1961.

1457 MORGAN (EDWARD VICTOR) and THOMAS (WILLIAM ARTHUR). The Stock Exchange: its history and functions. [1962.]

For contemporary guides to the investor see William Fairman, *The stocks examined and compared: or, A guide to purchasers in the public funds*, 1795, 3rd edn., 1798, 7th edn., 1824; [Thomas Mortimer] *Every man his own broker: or, A guide to the Stock Exchange*, 13th edn. 1801, a more general description of how business is conducted; John Taylor, *Statements respecting the profits of mining in England, considered in relation to the prospects of mining in Mexico*, etc., 1825, in effect an advertisement for investors in Mexico; Henry English, *A compendium of useful information relating to the companies formed for working British mines*, etc., 1826, and the same writer's *Complete view of joint-stock companies formed during the years 1824 and 1825, being six hundred and twenty four in number*, 1827, information, by a broker, of capital, dividends, high and low prices, bankers, and solvency; Charles Fenn, *A compendium of the English and foreign funds and the principal joint stock companies*, etc., 1837, 4th edn. rev. 1854, 16th edn. rev. 1898, a substantial work. See also J. R. Killick and W. A. Thomas, 'The provincial stock exchanges, 1830–1870', *Econ. H.R.*, 2nd ser. 23 (1970), 96–111.

4. INSURANCE

1458 RAYNES (HAROLD ERNEST). A history of British insurance. 1948.

For bibliogs. see William Witt Blackstock, *The historical literature of sea and fire insurance in Great Britain, 1547–1810*, Manchester, 1910, and Institute of Actuaries, *Catalogue of the library*, 1935.

1459 BAILY (FRANCIS). An account of the several life assurance companies established in London, 2nd edn. 1811.

For fire insurance, Francis Boyer Relton, *An account of the fire insurance companies . . . including the Sun Fire Office: also of Charles Povey*, etc., 1893.

1460 WRIGHT (CHARLES) *and* FAYLE (CHARLES ERNEST). A history of Lloyd's, from the founding of Lloyd's coffee house to the present day. 1928.

Standard. See also Frederick Martin, *The history of Lloyd's and of marine insurance in Great Britain*, 1876, and Ralph Straus, *Lloyd's, a historical sketch*, 1937, a short popular account. Information on underwriting is contained in *The Report of the Select Committee on Act 6 Geo. I and on the means of effecting marine insurance in Great Britain*, H.C. 1810 (226) IV, reprinted H.C. 1824 (298) VII.

1461 DICKSON (PETER GEORGE MUIR). The Sun insurance office, 1710–1960. The history of two and a half centuries of British insurance. 1960.

See also, for other companies, Sir Charles Robert Bignold, *Five generations of the Bignold family, 1761–1947, and their connection with the Norwich Union*, 1948, more substantial than Robert Norman William Blake, *Esto perpetua: Norwich Union Life Insurance Society*, etc., 1958; Bernard Drew, *The London Assurance; a second chronicle*, 1949; Maurice Edward Ogborn, *Equitable assurances: the story of life assurance in the experience of the Equitable Life Assurance Society, 1762–1962*, 1962; Barry Supple, *The Royal Exchange Assurance. A history of British insurance, 1720–1970*, Camb. 1970.

1462 COX (PETER RICHMOND) *and* STORR-BEST (ROBERT HUGH). Surplus in British life assurance. Actuarial control over its emergence and distribution during 200 years. Camb. 1962.

A clear account of the development of actuarial control. For contemporary works see Joshua Milne (actuary to Sun Life Assurance), *A treatise on the valuation of annuities . . . on the construction of tables of mortality*, etc., 2 v., 1815; Charles Babbage, *A comparative view of the various institutions for the assurance of lives*, 1826; Augustus De Morgan, *Essay on probabilities*, (3097); Edward Sang, *Essays on life assurance*, Edin., 1852; David Jones, *On the value of annuities and reversionary payments* (Library of useful knowledge), 2 v., 1843, enl. edn. 2 v., 1844. For actuarial criticism of friendly societies see (1472).

5. OTHER TOPICS

(a) *Building Societies*

1462A GOSDEN (PETER HENRY JOHN HEATHER). Self-help. Voluntary associations in the nineteenth century. 1973.

Ranges widely over the field of building societies, co-operation, friendly societies, etc.

1463 CLEARY (ESMOND JOHN). The building society movement. 1965.

Bibliog. 313–15. See also Ashworth (2573.)

1464 SCRATCHLEY (ARTHUR). A treatise on benefit building societies, containing remarks upon the erroneous tendency of many of the societies at present in existence. 1849. Another edn. 1867.

Also R. Kerr, *Building societies, their advantages; a refutation of attacks made upon them,* etc., 1844, and W. G. Rimmer, 'Alfred Place Terminating Building Society, 1825–43', *Thoresby Soc. pubs.* 46 (1959–63), 303–30.

(b) *Co-operation*

1465 HOLYOAKE (GEORGE JACOB). The history of co-operation in England: its literature and its advocates. 2 v. (V. 1. The pioneer period, 1812 to 1844; v. 2, The constructive period, 1845 to 1878.) Manchester. 1875–7. Rev. edn. 1906.

The standard authority. For William Lovett see (2322), for Dr. King of Brighton see (2514).

1466 POTTER (BEATRICE) *afterwards* WEBB. The co-operative movement in Great Britain. 1891. Reprinted 1930.

Other general histories are Benjamin Jones, *Co-operative production* . . . etc., 2 v., Oxf., 1894; George Douglas Howard Cole, *A century of co-operation,* Manchester, 1947; Arnold Bonner, *British co-operation* . . . *the history, principles and organisation of the British co-operative movement.* Manchester, 1961. Sidney Pollard, 'Nineteenth century co-operation: from community building to shopkeeping', in *Essays in Labour history,* ed. Asa Briggs and John Saville, 1960, pp. 74–112.

1467 GRAY (JOHN). A lecture on human happiness; being the first of a series of lectures on that subject, in which will be comprehended a general review of the causes of the existing evils of society . . . To which are added the articles of agreement drawn up and recommended by the London Co-operative Society for the formation of a community on principles of mutual co-operation. 1825. Reprinted (Reprints of scarce tracts in economic and political science, 2), 1931.

1468 THOMPSON (WILLIAM). An inquiry into the principles of the distribution of wealth most conducive to human happiness; applied to the newly proposed system of voluntary equality of wealth. 1824. New edn. 1850.

Also by Thompson, pub. anonymously, *Labor rewarded. The claims of labor and capital conciliated; or, How to secure to labor the whole product of its exertions. By one of the idle classes,* 1827, and *Practical directions for the speedy and economical establishment of communities on the principles of mutual co-operation,* etc., [1830]. For Thompson's life see Richard Keir Pethick Pankhurst, *William Thompson, 1775–1833, Britain's pioneer socialist, feminist, and co-operator,* 1954. For Owen and Bray see (524), (1770).

(c) *Friendly Societies*

1469 GOSDEN (PETER HENRY JOHN HEATHER). The friendly societies in England, 1815–1875. Manchester [1961].

Standard. Bibliog. 245–58.

1470 [ROSE (*Rt. Hon.* GEORGE).] Observations on the Act for the relief and encouragement of friendly societies. 1794.

Sir Frederick Morton Eden, *Observations on friendly societies for the maintenance of the industrious classes, during sickness, infirmity, old age and other exigencies,* 1801, describes the working of societies in the 1790s.

1471 SELECT COMMITTEE ON LAWS RESPECTING FRIENDLY SOCIETIES. Report and evidence. H.C. 1825 (522) IV, and H.C. 1826–7 (558) III.

John Tidd Pratt, *The law relating to friendly societies comprising the statute 10 Geo. IV Cap. 56*, 1829, later edns. 1834, 1838, 1846, 1873. Pratt became registrar of friendly societies, 1846. For later changes see *Select committee on friendly societies bill*, report and evidence, H.C. 1849 (458) XIV, and *Select committee on friendly societies*, H.C. 1852 (531) V.

1472 NEISON (FRANCIS G. P.) Observations on Odd-Fellow and friendly societies. 1847. 13th edn. rev. and enl. 1851.

Demonstrates that contributions should vary according to members' ages and health. For Neison on vital statistics see (1694). See also Charles Ansell, *A treatise on friendly societies, in which the doctrine of interest of money, and the doctrine of probability, are practically applied to the affairs of such societies*, etc., Library of Useful Knowledge, 1835; Henry Ratcliffe, *Observations on the rate of mortality . . . for various trades, occupations and localities . . . from the experience of . . . the Independent Order of Odd-Fellows, Manchester Unity*, etc. Manchester, 1850.

1473 MOFFREY (ROBERT WILLIAM). A century of Oddfellowship. Being a brief record of the rise and progress of the Manchester Unity of Independent Order of Odd-Fellows, from its foundation to the present time. Manchester. 1910.

1474 FULLER (MARGARET DOROTHY). West country friendly societies. An account of village benefit clubs and their brass pole heads. Lingfield. 1964.

Bibliog. 159–167. With many good illustrations.

(d) *Savings Banks*

1475 HORNE (H. OLIVER). A history of savings banks. 1947.

Bibliog. 394–8. See also Rt. Hon. George Rose, *Observations on banks for savings*, 1816, 4th edn. enl. 1817, and report and evidence of *Select committees, on savings of the middle and working classes* and *on savings banks*, H.C. 1850 (508, 649) XIX. Albert Fishlow, 'The trustee savings banks, 1817–1861', *J. Econ. Hist.* 21 (1961), 26–40, discusses depositors, scale of deposits, etc. See also (3913).

(e) *Accounting*

1476 BROWN (RICHARD) *ed*. A history of accounting and accountants. Edin. 1905.

See also David Murray, *Chapters in the history of book-keeping, accountancy and commercial arithmetic*, Glasgow, 1930; Ananias Charles Littleton and Basil Selig Yamey, eds., *Studies in the history of accounting*, 1956; S. Pollard, 'Capital accounting in the industrial revolution', *Yorkshire Bull. of Econ. and Social Res.* 15 (1963), 75–91.

1477 HAMILTON (ROBERT). An introduction to merchandize: containing a complete system of arithmetic, a system of algebra, book-keeping in various forms, an account of the trade of Great Britain. 2 v. Edin. 1777–9. 3rd edn. cor. and rev. Edin. 1797. New edn. Edin. 1820.

Also Patrick Kelly, *Elements of book-keeping . . . adapted to the use of schools*, 1801, and his *The universal cambist, and commercial instructor*, etc., 2 v., 1811, 2nd edn., 2 v., 1821, 2nd edn. rev., 1835. William Tate, *The modern cambist; forming a manual of foreign exchanges, in the . . . operations of bills of exchange and bullion, with numerous formulae*, etc., 3rd edn. 1836, 23rd edn. 1893, became a standard work.

(f) Retail Trade

1478 ALEXANDER (DAVID). Retailing in England during the Industrial Revolution. 1970.

D. OVERSEAS COMMERCE AND SHIPPING

1. GENERAL DESCRIPTION AND STATISTICS

1479 POPE (CHARLES). A practical abridgement of the customs and excise laws, relative to the import, export and coasting trade of Great Britain and her dependencies. 2nd edn. 1814.

A compilation which ran through many editions. See also (456), and Rupert C. Jarvis, *Customs letter books of the port of Liverpool, 1711–1813*, Manchester, Chetham Soc. 3rd ser. 6, 1956.

1480 McCULLOCH (JOHN RAMSAY). A treatise on the principles, practice and history of commerce. 1831.

1481 BOURNE (HENRY RICHARD FOX). English merchants: memoirs in illustration of the progress of British commerce. 2 v. 1866.

Biogs. of individuals and groups of merchants, London and provincial. On particular firms see Sydney George Checkland, 'Corn for S. Lancashire and beyond, 1780–1800; the firm of Corrie, Gladstone and Bradshaw', *Business Hist.* 2 (1959–60), 4–20, and the same writer's *The Gladstones* (2240). See also David M. Williams, 'Merchanting in the first half of the nineteenth century: the Liverpool timber trade', *Business Hist.* 8 (1966), 103–21. On Leeds merchants, see Richard George Wilson, *Gentlemen merchants. The merchant community in Leeds, 1700–1830*, Manchester, 1971, and the same writer's 'The fortunes of a Leeds merchant house, 1780–1820', *Business Hist.* 9 (1967), 70–86, on a firm exporting to South America.

1482 SCHLOTE (WERNER). Entwicklung und Strukturwandlungen des englischen Aussenhandels von 1700 bis zur Gegenwart. Jena. 1938.

Trans. with title *British overseas trade from 1700 to the 1930s*, by W. O. Henderson and W. H. Chaloner, Oxf., 1952; primarily concerned with statistical measurement of trade.

1483 PARKINSON (CYRIL NORTHCOTE) *ed.* The trade winds: a study of British overseas trade during the French wars, 1793–1815. 1948.

Essays on different trades, insurance, ports, seamen, etc.

1484 ROSTOW (WALT WHITMAN). 'The terms of trade in theory and practice.' *Econ. H.R.*, 2nd ser. 3 (1950–1), 1–20.

Continued by 'The historical analysis of the terms of trade', *ibid.* 4 (1951–2), 53–76.

1485 IMLAH (ALBERT H.) Economic elements in the 'Pax Britannica'. Studies in British and foreign trade in the nineteenth century. Camb., Mass. 1958.

Also 'Real values in British foreign trade, 1798–1853', *Jour. Econ. Hist.* 8 (1948), 133–52, and 'The terms of trade of the United Kingdom, 1798–1913', *ibid.* 10 (1950), 170–94, and 'British balance of payments and export of capital, 1816–1913', *Econ. H.R.*, 2nd ser. 5 (1952–3), 208–39.

1486   JARVIS (RUPERT C.) 'Official trade and revenue statistics.' *Econ. H.R.*, 2nd ser. 17 (1964–5), 43–62.

Explains how statistics were compiled *c.* 1660–1850 and how they may be interpreted.

2. TRADE TO PARTICULAR REGIONS

1487   ODDY (J. JEPSON). European commerce . . . detailing the produce, manufactures, and commerce of Russia, Prussia, Sweden, Denmark, and Germany . . . with a general view of the trade . . . and navigation of the United Kingdom of Great Britain and Ireland. 1805.

1488   BUCK (NORMAN SYDNEY). The development of the organization of Anglo-American trade, 1800–1850. (Theodore L. Glasgow memorial publication fund, 8.) New Haven., Conn. 1925.

Also Ralph Willard Hidy, *The house of Baring in American trade and finance; English merchant bankers at work, 1763–1861* (Harvard studies in business history, 14), Cambridge, Mass., 1949.

1489   CAMPBELL (MARJORIE WILKINS). The North West Company. Toronto. 1957.

For Hudson's Bay Company see Rich (4437).

1490   ARMYTAGE (FRANCES). The free port system in the British West Indies: a study in commercial policy, 1766–1822. 1953.

Valuable. See also F. L. Benns, *The American struggle for the British West India carrying trade, 1815–1830*, Bloomington, Ind., 1923; J. Holland Rose, 'British West India commerce as a factor in the Napoleonic War', *Camb. Hist. J.* 3 (1929–31), 34–46.

1491   CURTIN (PHILIP DE ARMOND). The Atlantic slave trade: a census. Madison, Wis. 1969.

Bibliog. 299–311. By the same author, 'The British sugar duties and West Indian prosperity', *J. Econ. Hist.* 14 (1954), 157–64; S. G. Checkland, 'John Gladstone as trader and planter', *Econ. H.R.*, 2nd ser. 7 (1954–5), 216–29, also 'Finance for the West Indies, 1780–1815', *ibid.*, 2nd ser. 10 (1957–8), 461–9; R. B. Sheridan, 'The commercial and financial organization of the British slave trade, 1750–1807', *Econ. H.R.*, 2nd ser. 11 (1958–9), 249–63, deals with London's part in financing the trade: see also his 'The West India sugar crisis and British slave emancipation, 1830–1833', *J. Econ. Hist.* 21 (1961), 539–51; D. Eltis, 'The traffic in slaves between the British West Indian colonies, 1807–1833', *Econ. H.R.*, 2nd ser. 25 (1972–3), 55–64. The commercial state of the colonies and of British trade were extensively investigated by Commons' select committees, H.C. 1807 (65) III, 1808 (178, 278, 300, 318) IV, and by the committees investigating the slave trade and slavery: see Anti-Slavery (pp. 329–30) and Pares (4453).

1492   RIPPY (JAMES FREDERICK). British investments in Latin America, 1822–1949. A case study in the operations of private enterprise in retarded regions. Minneapolis. 1959.

See also Edgar Turlington, *Mexico and her foreign creditors*, N.Y., 1930; Judith Blow

Williams, 'The establishment of British commerce with Argentina', *Hispanic American Hist. Rev.* 15 (1935), 43–64; Dorothy Burne Goebel, 'British trade to the Spanish colonies, 1796–1823', *A.H.R.* 43 (1938), 288–320; Robert Arthur Humphreys, *British consular reports on the trade and politics of Latin America, 1824–1826*, Camden 3rd ser. 63, 1940; Dorothy Burne Goebel, 'British American rivalry in the Chilean trade, 1817–1820', *J. Econ. Hist.* 2 (1942), 190–203; Herbert Heaton, 'A merchant adventurer in Brazil, 1808–1818', *ibid.* 6 (1946), 1–23, on John Luccock, exporter of woollens from Leeds; H. S. Ferns, 'Investment and trade between Britain and Argentina in the nineteenth century', *Econ. H.R.*, 2nd ser. 3 (1950–1), 203–18, and the same writer's 'The beginnings of British investment in Argentina', *ibid.*, 2nd ser. 4 (1951–2), 341–52; Robert G. Albion, 'Capital movement and transportation. British shipping and Latin America, 1806–1914', *J. Econ. Hist.* 11 (1951), 361–74.

1493 WOOD (ALFRED CECIL). A history of the Levant Company. 1935.

On trade to the Near East in the 19th century see Puryear (336).

1494 MACPHERSON (DAVID). The history of the European commerce with India. 1812.

The history of the East India company is given in Cyril Henry Philips (4616), and Scott (*ibid.*). For the economic development of India see (4555), (4622–4).

1495 PARKINSON (CYRIL NORTHCOTE). Trade in the eastern seas, 1793–1813. Cambridge. 1937.

Bibliog. 393–414. See also the same writer's (1111).

1496 GREENBERG (MICHAEL). British trade and the opening of China, 1800–42. Camb. 1951.

Based on the papers of Jardine, Matheson & Co. For the later period see John King Fairbank, *Trade and diplomacy on the China coast, 1842–1854*, Cambridge, Mass., 1964. See also Sir James Matheson, *The present position and prospects of the British trade with China*, etc., 1836, and Hoh-Cheung Mui and Lorna H. Mui, 'The commutation act and the tea trade in Britain, 1784–1793', *Econ. H.R.*, 2nd ser. 16 (1963–4) 234–53.

3. The Shipping Industry, and Ports

1497 FAYLE (CHARLES ERNEST). A short history of the world's shipping industry. 1933.

See also César Moreau, *Chronological records of the British Royal and commercial navy*, 1827. William Schaw Lindsay, *History of merchant shipping and ancient commerce*, 4 v., 1874–6, is of value for the 19th century. See also R. J. Cornewall-Jones, *The British merchant service*, etc., 1898; Adam Willis Kirkaldy, *British shipping; its history, organization and importance*, 1914; Hubert Moyse-Bartlett, *A history of the merchant navy*, 1937; Charles Robert Vernon Gibbs, *British passenger liners of the five oceans*, etc., 1963. For a general bibliog. see Albion (1087). For shipbuilding see (1585–7), for steam propulsion (1289–90).

1498 ANNALS OF LLOYD'S REGISTER. Centenary edition. 1934.

Fuller than the more recent George Blake, *Lloyd's Register of Shipping, 1760–1960* [1960]. Frederic C. Lane, 'Tonnages, medieval and modern', *Econ. H.R.*, 2nd ser. 17 (1964–5), 213–33, is a useful guide to the technicalities of shipping statistics. Leonard Harris, *London General Shipowners' society, 1811–1961*, [1962], is very short, but based on the minutes of the society. For an account of the Mercantile Marine Department of the Board of Trade see Prouty (460).

1499 NORTH (DOUGLASS). 'Ocean freight rates and economic development, 1750–1913.' *J. Econ. Hist.* 18 (1958), 537–55.

1500 JONES (*Sir* CLEMENT WAKEFIELD). Pioneer shipowners. 2 v. [1935–8.]

See also Ernest Andrew Ewart (*pseud.* Boyd Cable), *A hundred years' history of the P. & O. Peninsular and Oriental Steam Navigation Company, 1837–1937*, 1937, and Thomas Alexander Bushell, *Royal mail: a centenary history of the Royal Mail Line, 1839–1939* [1939], and, on the East India Company, Cotton (4615).

1501 FARR (GRAHAME EDGAR) *ed.* Records of Bristol ships, 1800–1838. Vessels over 150 tons. (Bristol Record Soc. Pubs. 15.) Bristol. 1950.

Extracted from Bristol custom house register of shipping and other sources. For Liverpool see George Chandler, *Liverpool shipping; a short history*, 1960, and Rupert C. Jarvis (1479), and, with Robert Craig, *Liverpool registry of merchant ships* (Chetham Soc. remains, 3rd ser. 15), Manchester, 1954, 1967. Also David Alan Stevenson, *The world's lighthouses before 1820*, 1959. For lifeboats see (1285), for parliamentary papers on safety at sea, see Ford and Ford (p. 391), 57–8.

1502 OWEN (*Sir* DAVID JOHN). The origin and development of the ports of the United Kingdom. [1939.] 2nd edn. rev. 1948.

See also Sir Joseph Guinness Broodbank, *History of the Port of London*, 2 v., 1921, Aytoun Ellis, *Three hundred years on London river. The Hay's Wharf story, 1651–1951*, 1952. For Glasgow see (4005–7), for minor ports see chap. on local history.

4. COMMERCIAL POLICY

(Arranged roughly in chronological order of subject-matter: for collections of commercial treaties see (253).)

1503 SCHUYLER (ROBERT LIVINGSTON). The fall of the old colonial system. A study in British free trade, 1770–1870. N.Y. 1945.

1504 EHRMAN (JOHN PATRICK WILLIAM). The British government and commercial negotiations with Europe, 1783–1793. Camb. 1962.

1505 BOLTON (G. C.) 'Some British reactions to the Irish Act of Union.' *Econ. H.R.*, 2nd ser. 18 (1965–6), 367–75.

1506 CROUZET (FRANÇOIS). L'économie britannique et le blocus continental, 1806–1813, 2 v. Paris. 1958.

See also Alexander Baring, *An inquiry into the causes and consequences of the Orders in Council; and an examination of the conduct of Great Britain towards the neutral commerce of America*, 1808; Henry Peter Brougham, *The speech of Henry Brougham, Esq., before the House of Commons, Friday April 1 in support of the petitions from London, Liverpool and Manchester against the Orders in Council*, etc., 1808. *Minutes of evidence relating to Orders in Council*, H.C. 1808 (117) X, H.C. 1812 (210) III, also contain a good deal of general economic information. See also Eli Filip Heckscher, *The Continental system. An economic interpretation*, Oxf., 1922, and A. N. Ryan, 'Trade with the enemy in the Scandinavian and Baltic ports during the Napoleonic War: for and against', *Trans. Roy. Hist. Soc.* 5th ser. 12 (1962), 123–40.

1507 SELECT COMMITTEE ON FOREIGN TRADE. H.C. 1820 (300) II,
and Lords' Committee. H.C. 1820 (269) III, H.C. 1821 (186, 535, 746) VI.
Report of Lords' committee H.C. 1821 (476) VII.

Largely concerned with the timber duties: for the committee on timber of 1835 see
H.C. 1835 (519) XIX.

1508 CLAPHAM (JOHN HAROLD). 'The last years of the Navigation Acts.'
E.H.R. 25 (1910), 480–501, 687–707.

See also John Lewis Ricardo, *The anatomy of the navigation laws*, 1847, and William
Schaw Lindsay, *Letters on the Navigation Laws: (reprinted from the Morning Herald)*:
etc., 1849. See also Arthur Reginald Marsden Lower, 'From Huskisson to Peel: a study
in mercantilism', in *Essays in modern English history in honor of Wilbur Cortez Abbott*,
Cambridge, Mass., 1941. For Huskisson see (209).

1509 THE CORN LAWS. An authentic report of the late discussions in the
Manchester Chamber of Commerce on the destructive effects of the Corn
Laws. 1839.

Discussion of the effects of the corn laws on trade. James Wilson, *Influences of the corn
laws, as affecting all classes of the community and particularly the landed interests*, 1839,
2nd and 3rd edns., 1840, is an influential pamphlet by the founder of *The Economist*.
John Ramsay McCulloch, *Statements illustrative of the policy and probable consequences
of the proposed repeal of the existing corn laws, and the imposition . . . of a moderate fixed
duty*, etc., 1841, is an important pamphlet, arguing that repeal would reduce 'the
frequency and intensity of revulsions'. See also William Rathbone Greg, *Not over-
production, but deficient consumption the source of our sufferings*, 1842. For Anti-corn-
law league see (111), (143), for agriculture and the corn laws (1659–63).

1510 McGREGOR (JOHN). The commercial and financial legislation of
Europe and America; with a pro-forma revision of the taxation and the
customs tariff of the United Kingdom. 1841.

For a general discussion of the development of commercial policy, 1830–42, see Brown
(460).

1511 CALKINS (W. N.) 'A Victorian free trade lobby.' *Econ. H.R.*, 2nd ser.
13 (1960–1), 90–104.

On the Liverpool Financial Reform Association, 1848 and after.

1512 HABAKKUK (HROTHGAR JOHN). 'Free trade and commercial
expansion.' *Camb. Hist. British Empire*. V. 2. Camb. 1940.

Also John Gallagher and Ronald Robinson, 'The imperialism of free trade', *Econ. H.R.*,
2nd ser., 6 (1953–4), 1–15.

1513 PLATT (DESMOND CHRISTOPHER ST. MARTIN). Finance,
trade and politics in British foreign policy, 1815–1914. Oxf. 1968.

1514 SEMMEL (BERNARD). The rise of free trade imperialism: classical
political economy and the empire of free trade and imperialism, 1750–1850.
Camb. 1970.

Criticized by D. C. M. Platt, 'Further objections to an "Imperialism of free trade",
1830–60', *Econ. H.R.*, 2nd ser., 26 (1973), 77–91. See also W. M. Mathew, 'The
imperialism of free trade: Peru, 1820–70', *ibid.*, 2nd ser., 21 (1968), 562–79, a case study.

1515 WILLIAMS (JUDITH BLOW). British commercial policy and trade expansion 1750–1850. Oxf. 1973.

5. COMMERCIAL BODIES AND OPINIONS

1516 WRIGHT (GEORGE HENRY). Chronicles of the Birmingham Chamber of Commerce A.D. 1813–1913 and of the Birmingham Commercial Society A.D. 1783–1812. Birmingham. [1913.]

1517 MINCHINTON (WALTER EDWARD). Politics and the port of Bristol in the eighteenth century. The petitions of the Society of Merchant Venturers 1698–1803. (Bristol Record Soc. pubs. 23). 1963.

Also *Trade of Bristol in the eighteenth century*, ed. by the same writer (Bristol Record Soc. pubs. 20), 1957. See also Charles Malcolm MacInnes, *A gateway of empire*, Bristol, 1939, bibliog. 437–43, reprinted 1968. For Merchant Venturers see John Latimer, *The History of the Society of Merchant Venturers of the City of Bristol*, Bristol, 1903.

1518 REDFORD (ARTHUR). Manchester merchants and foreign trade, 1794–1858. (Manchester University pubs, Economic History Ser. 11). 1934.

See also Elijah Helm, *Chapters in the history of the Manchester Chamber of Commerce*, etc., [1902], and Gerald Berkeley Hertz (afterwards Hurst), *The Manchester politician*, *1750–1912*, 1912.

1519 CHECKLAND (S. G.) 'Economic attitudes in Liverpool, 1793–1807.' *Econ. H.R.*, 2nd. ser. 5 (1952–3), 58–75.

Also his 'American versus West Indian traders in Liverpool, 1793–1815', *J. Econ. Hist.* 18 (1958), 141–60.

E. INDUSTRIAL REVOLUTION, INDUSTRY, TECHNOLOGY

1. GENERAL WORKS

1520 ASHTON (THOMAS SOUTHCLIFFE). The industrial revolution, 1760–1830. 1948.

Bibliog. 162–4. See also the same writer's 'The industrial revolution', Studies in bibliography, 3, *Econ. H.R.*, 1st ser. 5 (1934–5), 104–19, reprinted as *The industrial revolution. A study in bibliography*, Economic History Soc.'s bibliogs., pamphlets 3, 1937, reprinted 1964. Notable interpretations of the industrial revolution are Arnold Toynbee, *Lectures on the industrial revolution in England*, 1884, 2nd edn. 1887, new edn. 1908; Paul Joseph Mantoux, *La révolution industrielle au XVIIIᵉ siècle*, Paris, 1906, trans. and rev. as *The industrial revolution in the eighteenth century*, 1928, rev. edn. with preface by T. S. Ashton, 1961; Lilian Charlotte Ann Knowles, *The industrial and commercial revolutions in Great Britain during the nineteenth century*, 1921; John Lawrence le Breton Hammond and Lucy Barbara Hammond, *The rise of modern industry*, 1925. For more recent discussion see R. M. Hartwell, 'Interpretations of the industrial revolution in England', *J. Econ. Hist.* 19 (1959), 229–49 and his 'The causes of the industrial revolution; an essay in methodology', *Econ. H.R.*, 2nd ser. 18 (1965–6), 164–82, also Michael Walter Flinn, *Origins of the industrial revolution*, 1966.

1521 BABBAGE (CHARLES). On the economy of machinery and manufactures. 1832. 4th edn. 1835.

Descriptive as well as theoretical. For descriptions of processes see also Andrew Ure, *A dictionary of arts, manufactures, and mines, containing a clear exposition of their principles and practice*, 1839, later edns. 1843, 1853, 1860, 1867, 1875–8, George Phillips Bevan, ed., *British manufacturing industries*, 13 v., 1875. For a modern account see Abbott Payson Usher, *The history of mechanical inventions*, N.Y., 1929, rev. edn., Camb., Mass., 1954. For Babbage's life see (1622).

1522 SELECT COMMITTEE ON MANUFACTURES, COMMERCE AND SHIPPING. H.C. 1833 (690) VI.

Contains material on a wide variety of industries.

1523 URE (ANDREW). The philosophy of manufactures. 1835. Later edn. 1847.

The most notable contemporary champion of industrialism.

1524 PRITCHARD (ANDREW). A list of all the patents for inventions, in the arts, manufactures etc. etc. etc. granted in England during the present century, including those now in force. 1841.

Also lists patentees and dates. For patent law see (621). See also *Select committee on extending the copyright of designs*, H.C. 1840 (442) VI.

1525 ARMSTRONG (*Sir* WILLIAM GEORGE), *and others*. The industrial resources of the Tyne, Wear, and Tees. 1864.

1526 SMILES (SAMUEL). Men of invention and industry. 1884.

Including the lives of Murdock, Koenig, the Walters, William Clowes, and Bianconi.

1527 TUPLING (GEORGE HENRY). The economic history of Rossendale. Manchester. 1927. (Univ. of Manchester Economic History Ser. 4.) 1927.

1528 COURT (WILLIAM HENRY BASSANO). The rise of the midland industries, 1660–1838. 1938. Reprinted, 1953.

See also Samuel Timmins, ed., *The resources, products, and industrial history of Birmingham and the midland hardware district: . . . by the local industries committee of the British Association . . . in 1865*, 1866, Richard Bissell Prosser, *Birmingham inventors and inventions*, etc., Birmingham, 1881, an account of every Birmingham patent down to 1830 and of important trades to 1852. On Birmingham small arms see Barbara M. D. Smith, 'The Galtons of Birmingham: Quaker gun merchants and bankers, 1702–1831', *Business history*, 9 (1967), 132–50.

1529 HENDERSON (WILLIAM OTTO). Britain and industrial Europe 1750–1870. Studies in British influence on the industrial revolution in western Europe. Liverpool. 1954. 2nd edn. 1965.

By the same author, *J. C. Fischer and his diary of industrial England, 1814–1851*, 1966, and *Industrial Britain under the Regency*, 1968, diaries of four western European visitors to Britain.

1530 TRINDER (BARRIE S.). The industrial revolution in Shropshire. Chichester. 1973.

1531 RAYBOULD (T. J.) The economic emergence of the Black Country. A study of the Dudley estate. Newton Abbot. 1973.

1532 HUDSON (KENNETH). Industrial archaeology. 1963.

Bibliog. 164–72. See also David Marshall Smith, *The industrial archaeology of the East Midlands, Nottinghamshire, Leicestershire and the adjoining parts of Derbyshire*, 1965; Kenneth Hudson, *The industrial archaeology of southern England, Hampshire, Wiltshire, Dorset, Somerset and Gloucestershire east of the Severn*, 1965; John Percival Masterman Pannell, *The techniques of industrial archaeology*, Newton Abbot, 1966. The *Journal of industrial archaeology*, 1964+ should also be consulted. See also Brian Bracegirdle, ed., *The archaeology of the industrial revolution*, 1973 and (2948).

1533 POLLARD (SIDNEY). The genesis of modern management. A study of the industrial revolution in Great Britain. 1965.

By the same author, 'Fixed capital in the industrial revolution in Britain', *J. Econ. Hist.* 24 (1964), 299–314.

1534 MUSSON (ALBERT EDWARD) *and* ROBINSON (ERIC). Science and technology in the industrial revolution. Manchester. 1969.

2. Textiles and Clothing

(a) *Cotton*

1535 BAINES (EDWARD). History of the cotton manufacture in Great Britain. [1835.]

See also Richard Guest, *A compendious history of the cotton-manufacture: with a disproval of the claim of Sir Richard Arkwright to the invention of its ingenious machinery*, Manchester, 1823; Andrew Ure, *The cotton manufacture of Great Britain systematically investigated*, 2 v., 1836, 2nd edn., 1861; Richard Burn, *Statistics of the cotton trade, arranged in a tabular form; also a chronological history of the various inventions, improvements*, etc. [1847], tables of prices, exports, employees, etc.; Thomas Ellison, *The cotton trade of Great Britain: including a history of the Liverpool cotton market and of the Liverpool Cotton Brokers' Association*, 1886.

1536 CHAPMAN (*Sir* SYDNEY JOHN). The Lancashire cotton industry. A study in economic development. (University of Manchester econ. ser. 1.) Manchester. 1904.

Bibliog. 277–304, including summaries of parliamentary papers, to 1837. See also George William Daniels, *The early English cotton industry*, etc. (University of Manchester hist. ser. 36), 1920; Arthur J. Taylor, 'Concentration and specialisation in the Lancashire cotton industry, 1825–1850', *Econ. H.R.*, 2nd ser. 1 (1948–9), 114–22; Mark Blaug, 'The productivity of capital in the Lancashire cotton industry during the nineteenth century', *Econ. H.R.*, 2nd ser. 13 (1960–1), 358–81. Questions of location are discussed in H. B. Rodgers, 'The Lancashire cotton industry in 1840', *Trans. Inst. Brit. Geographers*, 28 (1960), 135–53. N. B. Harte and K. G. Ponting, eds., *Textile history and economic history. Essays in honour of Miss Julia de Lacy Mann*, Manchester, 1973, includes essays on cotton and woollen textiles. See also Smelser and Collier (1809).

1537 CHAPMAN (STANLEY DAVID). The early factory masters: the transition to the factory system in the Midlands textile industry. Newton Abbot. 1967.

See also William Radcliffe, *Origin of the new system of manufacture commonly called 'Power Loom Weaving'*, etc., Stockport, 1828, 2nd edn. with additions, 1840; Gilbert J. French, *The life and times of Samuel Crompton, inventor of the spinning machine called the mule*, Manchester, 1859, 2nd edn. Manchester, 1860; George Unwin, Arthur Hulme, and George Taylor, *Samuel Oldknow and the Arkwrights, The industrial revolutions at Stockport and Marple*, (Univ. of Manchester, Econ. Hist. ser. 1), Manchester, 1924, repr. 1968; Robert Sucksmith Fitton and Alfred Powell Wadsworth, *The Strutts and the Arkwrights, 1758–1830. A study of the early factory system*, Manchester, 1959, bibliog. 349–53; Jean Lindsay, 'An early industrial community: the Evans cotton mill at Darley Abbey, Derbyshire, 1783–1810', *Business Hist. Rev.* 34 (1960), 277–301; Rhodes Boyson, *The Ashworth cotton enterprise*, Oxf. 1970; C. M. Lee, *A cotton enterprise 1795–1840: a history of McConnel and Kennedy, fine cotton spinners*, Manchester, 1972.

1538 TURNBULL (GEOFFREY). A history of the calico printing industry of Great Britain. Ed. by John G. Turnbull. Altrincham. 1951.

For dye-stuffs see (1601).

1539 EDWARDS (MICHAEL M.). The growth of the British cotton trade, 1780–1815. Manchester. 1967.

(b) *Linen*

1540 RIMMER (WILLIAM GORDON). Marshalls of Leeds, flax spinners, 1788–1886. Camb. 1960.

See also John Horner, *The linen trade of Europe during the spinning-wheel period*, Belfast, 1920. For linen in Scotland see (3920), and in Ireland (4162).

(c) *Woollen and Worsted*

1541 BISCHOFF (JAMES). A comprehensive history of the woollen and worsted manufactures, and the natural and commercial history of sheep. 2 v. 1842.

See also James Burnley, *The history of wool and woolcombing*, 1889; Sir John Harold Clapham, *The woollen and worsted industries*, 1907; Ephraim Lipson, *The history of the woollen and worsted industries*, 1921. The report and evidence of the *Select Committee on the state of the woollen manufacture of England* contain much material on the later 18th century, H.C. 1806 (268, 268 a) III. See Harte and Ponting (1536).

1542 JAMES (JOHN). History of the worsted manufacture in England from the earliest times. 1857.

See also William Cudworth, *Worstedopolis: a sketch history of the town and trade of Bradford*, Bradford, 1888; J. H. Clapham, 'The transference of the worsted industry from Norfolk to the West Riding', *Econ. J.* 20 (1910), 195–210; Walter Onslow Garnett, *Wainstall Mills: the history of I & I Calvert Ltd., 1821–1951*, Halifax, 1951; Eric Milton Sigsworth, *Black Dyke Mills: A history with introductory chapters on the development of the worsted industry in the nineteenth century*, Liverpool, 1958, bibliog. 371–5; S. D. Chapman, 'The pioneers of worsted spinning by power', *Business hist.*, 7 (1964–5), 97–116.

1543 JUBB (SAMUEL). The history of the shoddy trade: its rise, progress, and present condition. 1860.

Largely concerned with Batley.

1544 CRUMP (WILLIAM BUNTING) ed. The Leeds woollen industry, 1780–1820. (Thoresby Soc. pubs. 32.) Leeds. 1931.

Also on the West Riding, Herbert Heaton, 'Benjamin Gott and the industrial revolution in Yorkshire', *Econ. H.R.* 3 (1931–2), 45–66; William Bunting Crump and Sarah Gertrude Ghorbal, *History of the Huddersfield woollen industry* (Tolson memorial museum pubs. handbook 9), Huddersfield, 1935; William Bunting Crump, *The little hill farm, Calder valley*, Halifax, 1938, on the domestic system round Halifax; Herbert Heaton, 'Yorkshire cloth traders in the United States, 1770–1840', *Thoresby Miscellany*, 2, 225–87 (Thoresby Soc. pubs. 37), Leeds, 1945; Frederick J. Glover 'The rise of the heavy woollen trade of the West Riding of Yorkshire in the nineteenth century', *Business hist.* 4 (1961–2), 1–21, and the same writer's 'Government contracting, competition and growth in the heavy woollen industry', *Econ. H.R.*, 2nd ser. 16 (1963–4), 478–98, both mainly concerned with Wormald's of Dewsbury. The report and evidence of the *Select committee on the stamping of woollen cloths*, H.C. 1821 (437), VI are mainly concerned with the organization of the industry in the Leeds area.

1545 PONTING (KENNETH GEORGE). A history of the West of England cloth industry. 1957.

Bibliog. 157–62. Also Alfred Plummer, ed., *The Witney blanket industry. The records of the Witney blanket weavers*, 1934, Robert Percy Beckinsale, ed., *The Trowbridge woollen industry as illustrated by the stock books of John and Thomas Clark, 1800–1824* (Wiltshire Archaeol. and Natural Hist. Soc. Rec. branch, 6), Devizes, 1951, and Hubert Fox, *Quaker homespun. The life of Thomas Fox of Wellington, serge maker and banker, 1747–1821*, 1958. Julia de Lacy Mann, *The cloth industry in the west of England from 1640 to 1880*, Oxf., 1971, bibliog. 341–58.

(d) Silk and Hosiery

1546 WARNER (*Sir* FRANK). The silk industry of the United Kingdom: its origin and development. [1921.]

A vast amount of information was collected by the *Select committee on the silk trade*, H.C. 1831–2 (678) XIX. See also Gerald Berkeley Hertz (afterwards Hurst), 'The English silk industry in the eighteenth century', *E.H.R.* 24 (1909), 710–27; J. H. Clapham, 'The Spitalfields acts, 1773–1824', *Econ. J.* 26 (1916), 459–71; D. M. Smith, 'The silk industry of the East Midlands', *East Midland Geographer*, 3 (1962), 20–38, on the area round Derby. For Coventry industry see (3704). See also Donald Cuthbert Coleman, *Courtaulds: an economic and social history, v. 1, The nineteenth century, silk and crepe*, 1969.

1547 FELKIN (WILLIAM). A history of machine-wrought hosiery and lace manufacture. 1867.

Information was collected by two *Select committees on framework knitters' petitions*, H.C. 1812 (247, 349) II, and H.C. 1819 (193) V. See also Gravenor Henson, *The civil, political, and mechanical history of the framework-knitters in Europe and America*, Nottingham, 1831, Frederick Arthur Wells, *The British hosiery trade. Its history and organization*, 1935, Arthur James Pickering, *The cradle and home of the hosiery trade*, etc., ed. H. W. Chandler, Hinckley, 1940 (on Hinckley). See also Blackner (3664), and for the Luddites (99).

(e) Hats and Shoes

1548 DONY (JOHN GEORGE). A history of the straw hat industry. Luton. 1942.

On felt hats Phyllis M. Giles, 'The felt-hatting industry c. 1500–1850 with special reference to Lancashire and Cheshire', *Trans. Lancashire and Cheshire Antiq. Soc.* 69 (1959), 104–32.

1549 RIMMER (WILLIAM GORDON). 'The Leeds leather industry in the nineteenth century.' *Thoresby Miscellany,* 13, pt. II, 119–64. (Thoresby Soc. pubs. 46.) Leeds. 1960.

For information on tanning and shoemaking see *Select committees on leather duties,* H.C. 1812–13 (128) IV, *Select Committee on laws relating to manufacture of leather,* H.C. 1816 (386) VI, *Select Committee on hides and skins,* H.C. 1824 (323) VII. See also G. B. Sutton, 'The marketing of ready made footwear in the nineteenth century', *Business hist.* 6 (1963–4), 93–112, on the firm of C. & J. Clark, from 1825, and Roy Church, 'Messrs Gotch and sons and the rise of the Kettering footwear industry', *ibid.* 8 (1966), 140–9.

3. Mining

(a) *Coal*

1550 WIGAN PUBLIC LIBRARY. Index catalogue of books and papers relating to mining, metallurgy and manufactures. By Henry Tennyson Folkard. Southport. 1880.

A substantial catalogue. For works on miners see (1739), for Wales see (3811–2) for safety lamp (1620).

1551 MURCHISON (*Sir* RODERICK IMPEY). The Silurian system, with descriptions of the coal-fields and overlying formations. 2 v. 1839.

Geological description of area from Midlands to Pembrokeshire. Also John Holland, *The history and description of fossil fuel, the collieries, and coal trade of Great Britain,* 1835, another edn., 1841, Edward Hull, *The coal-fields of Great Britain: their history, structure and duration. With notices of the coal-fields of other parts of the world,* 1861, later edns., 1873, 1881, 1905.

1552 BAINBRIDGE (WILLIAM). A practical treatise on the law of mines and minerals. 1841. Later edns., 1856, 1867, 1878, 1900, all enl.

1553 DUNN (MATTHIAS). An historical, geological, and descriptive view of the coal trade of the north of England. Newcastle upon Tyne. 1844.

Substantial information on contemporary workings.

1554 GALLOWAY (ROBERT LINDSAY). A history of coal mining in Great Britain. 1882.

Also the same writer's *Annals of coal mining and the coal trade,* 1898, enl. edn. which continues annals 1835–50, 1904. See also Charles Beaumont, *A treatise on the coal trade,* 2 pts., 1789. There is much information in House of Commons Reports from committees, 1800, 1st ser. 10, 537–650, in the *Select committee on state of the coal trade in the port of London,* H.C. 1830 (663) VIII, and in the report of the *Lords' committee on the coal trade of the United Kingdom,* H.C. 1830 (9) VIII.

1555 ASHTON (THOMAS SOUTHCLIFFE) *and* **SYKES (JOSEPH).** The coal industry of the eighteenth century. (University of Manchester pubs. econ. hist. ser. 5.) Manchester. 1929.

1556 SWEEZY (PAUL MARLOR). Monopoly and competition in the English coal trade, 1550–1850. (Harvard econ. ser. 63.) Camb., Mass. 1938.

Also Arthur J. Taylor, 'Combination in the mid-nineteenth century coal industry', *Trans. Roy. Hist. Soc.*, 5th ser. 3 (1953), 23–40, and 'The sub-contract system in the British coal industry' in *Studies in the industrial revolution presented to T. S. Ashton*, ed. Leslie Sedden Pressnell, 1960, 215–35. On individual owners and collieries see David Spring, 'The earls of Durham and the Great Northern coal field, 1830–1880', *Canadian Hist. Rev.* 33 (1952), 237–53; W. G. Rimmer, 'Middleton colliery near Leeds, 1770–1830', *Yorkshire Bull. Econ. and Social Research*, 7 (1955), 41–58; J. T. Ward, 'West Riding landowners and mining in the nineteenth century', *ibid.* 15 (1963), 61–74.

(b) *Other Mines*

1557 HUNT (ROBERT). British mining. A treatise on the history, discovery, practical development and future prospects of metalliferous mines in the United Kingdom. 1884. 2nd edn. 1887.

1558 BARTON (DENYS BRADFORD). A history of copper mining in Cornwall and Devon. Truro. 1961.

Also, by the same author, *A historical survey of the mines and mineral railways of East Cornwall and West Devon*, Truro, 1964. Geological information is given in Richard Thomas, *Report of a survey of the mining district of Cornwall, from Chasewater to Camborne*, 1819, and Joseph Henry Collins, *Observations on the west of England mining region*, etc. (Trans. Roy. Geological Soc. Cornwall, 14), Plymouth, 1912. See also Alfred Kenneth Hamilton Jenkin, *The Cornish miner, an account of his life above and underground from early times*, 1927, repr. 1948, 1962, on tin mining, and his *Mines and miners of Cornwall*, Truro, 1961–6, 12 pts., describing mines in different areas.

1559 GOUGH (JOHN WIEDHOFF). The mines of Mendip. Oxf. 1930.

On lead mining.

1560 HARRIS (JOHN RAYMOND). The copper king: **a** biography of Thomas Williams of Llanidan. Liverpool. 1964.

Mining in Cornwall and Wales. See also the *Report from the Committee appointed to enquire into the state of the copper mines and copper trade*, etc., 1799, reports from committees, H.C. 10.

1561 RAISTRICK (ARTHUR) *and* JENNINGS (BERNARD). A history of lead-mining in the Pennines. 1965.

Also Thomas Sopwith, *An account of the mining districts of Alston Moor, Weardale and Teesdale*, etc., Alnwick, 1833, mostly concerned with lead-mining, G. G. Hopkinson, 'Five generations of Derbyshire lead-mining and smelting, 1729–1858', *J. Derbyshire Archaeol. and Natural Hist. Soc.* 78 (1958), 9–24, on the Barker family, Richard Antony Hugh O'Neal, comp. *Derbyshire lead and lead mining: a bibliography*, Derby, 1956, 2nd edn. enl. Matlock, 1960. See also Christopher John Hunt, *The lead miners of the northern Pennines, in the 18th and 19th centuries*, Manchester, 1970. For Welsh lead mining see (3813–4).

4. METAL INDUSTRIES

1562 AITCHISON (LESLIE). A history of metals. 2 v. 1960.

See also Pierre Armand Dufrenoy and Jean Baptiste A. L. L. Élie de Beaumont, *Voyage métallurgique en Angleterre, ou . . . mémoires sur le gisement, l'exploitation et le traitement des minerais*, etc., 2 v. and atlas, Paris, 1827, 2nd edn. Paris, 1837, and John Holland, *A treatise on the progressive improvement and present state of manufactures in metal*, 3 v., 1831–4, 2nd edn. rev. Robert Hunt, 1853. V. 1 and 2 are concerned with iron and steel, v. 3 with other metals: they describe a wide variety of manufactured goods, grates, locks, machines, etc. See also John Percy, *Metallurgy. The art of extracting metals from their ores, and adapting them to various purposes of manufacture*, v. 1–3, 5 (v. 4 never printed), 1861–80.

1563 ASHTON (THOMAS SOUTHCLIFFE). Iron and steel in the industrial revolution. (University of Manchester, Econ. Hist. Ser. 2.) Manchester. 1924. 2nd edn. 1951.

On the industry to c. 1815. See also David Mushet, *Papers on iron and steel, practical and experimental*, etc., 1840; Harry Scrivenor, *A comprehensive history of the iron trade*, etc., 1841, new edn. 1854, repr. 1967, the standard contemporary account; Ludwig Beck, *Geschichte des Eisens*, etc., 5 v., 1884–1903 (v. 3 on 18th century and v. 4 on industry to 1860). See also Alan Birch, *The economic history of the British iron and steel industry, 1789–1879*, etc., 1967.

1564 RAISTRICK (ARTHUR). Dynasty of iron-founders; the Darbys and Coalbrookdale. 1953.

1565 SMILES (SAMUEL). Industrial biography: iron-workers and toolmakers. 1863. New edn. 1879. New edn. ed. Lionel Thomas Caswall Rolt. 1967.

Includes lives of Mushet, Neilson, Bramah, Henry Maudslay, Joseph Clement, R. W. Fox, Matthew Murray, Richard Roberts, Whitworth, Nasmyth, Fairbairn. For the Walker family see Arthur Henry John, *Minutes relating to Messrs Samuel Walker and co.*, etc., Council for the Preservation of Business Archives, pubs. 2, 1951.

1566 LLOYD (GODFREY ISAAC HOWARD). The cutlery trades. An historical essay in the economics of small-scale production. 1913.

See also Robert Eadon Leader, *History of the company of cutlers in Hallamshire, in the county of York*, 2 v., Sheffield, 1905–6.

1567 HAMILTON (HENRY). The English brass and copper industries to 1800 . . . with an introduction by Sir William Ashley. 1926. 2nd edn. with additional introduction by John Raymond Harris. 1967.

1568 ASHTON (THOMAS SOUTHCLIFFE). An eighteenth-century industrialist; Peter Stubs of Warrington, 1756–1806. Manchester. 1939. Repr. 1961.

Stubs was a file-maker.

1569 FORESTIER-WALKER (EVELYN RODNEY). A history of the wire rope industry of Great Britain. Sheffield Federation of Wire Rope Manufacturers. 1952.

1570 MINCHINTON (WALTER EDWARD). The British tinplate industry. A history. Oxf. 1957.

1571 WILSON (RONALD ELIOT). Two hundred precious metal years. A history of the Sheffield Smelting Company Limited, 1760–1960. 1960.

Bibliog. 297–303.

1572 HOGG (OLIVER FREDERICK GILLILAN). The Royal Arsenal. Its background, origins and subsequent history. 2 v. 1963.

V. 1, to 1850, contains much on war production.

1573 CHURCH (ROY A.). Kenrick's in hardware: a family business, 1791–1966. Newton Abbot. 1971.

1574 JONES (S. R. H.). 'Price associations and competition in the British pin industry, 1814–40'. *Econ. H.R.*, 2nd ser. 26 (1973), 237–53.

5. MECHANICAL ENGINEERING AND SHIPBUILDING

(a) *General*

1575 ARMYTAGE (WALTER HARRY GREEN). A social history of engineering. 1961.

See also Aubrey Frederic Burstall, *A history of mechanical engineering*, 1963.

1576 THE NEWCOMEN SOCIETY FOR THE STUDY OF THE HISTORY OF ENGINEERING AND TECHNOLOGY. *Trans.* 1922+.

Contains annually 'Analytical bibliography of the history of engineering and applied science', until v. 25, 1945–7.

1577 ROE (JOSEPH WICKHAM). English and American toolbuilders. 1918.

Includes Samuel Bentham, Mark Isambard Brunel, Henry Maudslay, Fairbairn, and Nasmyth. See also Samuel Smiles, *Lives of the engineers, with an account of their principal works*, etc., 3 v., 1861–2, containing lives of Rennie, Telford, Stephenson. On Bentham see Keith Reginald Gilbert, *The Portsmouth block-making machinery. A pioneering enterprise in mass production* (Science Museum), 1965.

(b) *Steam Engines*

1578 LORD (JOHN). Capital and steam-power, 1750–1800. 1923.

Bibliog. 238–42. See also A. E. Musson and E. Robinson, 'The early growth of steam power', *Econ. H.R.*, 2nd ser. 11 (1958–9), 418–39, and the same authors' 'The origins of engineering in Lancashire', *J. Econ. Hist.* 20 (1960), 209–33.

1579 DICKINSON (HENRY WINRAM). A short history of the steam engine. Camb. 1939.

Among contemporary works see Charles Frederick Partington, *An historical and descriptive account of the steam engine*, etc., 2 pt., 1822; John Farey, *A treatise on the steam engine, historical practical and descriptive*, 1827, a careful and substantial account; Dionysius Lardner, *The steam engine familiarly explained . . . with plain maxims for railway speculators*, 1827, 8th edn., rev., 1851; Robert Stuart, *pseud.* of Robert Stuart Meikleham, *Historical and descriptive anecdotes of steam engines, and of their inventors and improvers*, 2 v., 1829; Elijah Galloway, *History and progress of the steam engine . . . to which is added . . . minute descriptions of all the various improved boilers . . . by Luke Herbert*, 1831; William Pole, *A treatise on the Cornish pumping engine*, etc., 3 pt., 1844; Charles Frederick T. Young, *Fires, fire-engines, and fire brigades, with a history of manual and steam fire engines*, etc., 1866.

1580 NAPIER. Men and machines. A history of D. Napier and son, engineers, Ltd., 1808–1958. By Charles Henry Wilson and William Reader. 1958.

1581 NASMYTH. James Nasmyth, engineer, an autobiography. Ed. by Samuel Smiles. 1883.

Also A. E. Musson, 'James Nasmyth and the early growth of mechanical engineering', *Econ. H.R.*, 2nd ser. 10 (1957–8), 121–7.

1582 STEPHENSON. The life of George Stephenson, railway engineer. By Samuel Smiles, 1857.

See also James G. H. Warren, *A century of locomotive building, by Robert Stephenson and co., 1823–1923*, Newcastle upon Tyne, 1923, and Lionel Thomas Caswall Rolt, *George and Robert Stephenson. The railway revolution*, 1960, bibliog. 338–42, 2nd edn. with title, *The railway revolution: George and Robert Stephenson*, 1962.

1583 TREVITHICK. Life of Richard Trevithick, with an account of his inventions. By Francis Trevithick. 1872.

1584 WATT. James Watt and the steam engine. By Henry Winram Dickinson and Rhys Jenkins. Oxf. 1927.

See also James Patrick Muirhead, ed., *The origin and progress of the mechanical inventions of James Watt*, 3 v., 1854; Samuel Smiles, *Lives of Boulton and Watt, principally from the original Soho mss.*, etc., 1865; Thomas Humphrey Marshall, *James Watt (1736–1819)*, 1925; Erich Roll, *An early experiment in industrial organization: being a history of the firm of Boulton and Watt, 1775–1805*, 1930; Henry Winram Dickinson, *James Watt, craftsman and engineer*, Camb., 1936; the same author's *Matthew Boulton*, Camb., 1937; Lionel Thomas Caswall Rolt, *James Watt*, 1962. See also Eric Robinson and Douglas McKie, *Partners in science. Letters of James Watt and Joseph Black*, Camb., Mass., 1970.

(c) *Shipbuilding, including Wooden Ships*

1585 SELECT COMMITTEE ON EAST INDIA-BUILT SHIPPING. H.C. 1813–14 (115) VIII.

Contains much information on shipbuilding. See also Henry Green and Robert Wigram, *Chronicles of Blackwall yard*, pt. 1, 1881; J. W. Smith and T. S. Holden, *Where ships are born: Sunderland, 1346–1946, a history of shipbuilding on the River Wear*, Sunderland, 1946; John Raymond Harris, 'Copper and shipping in the eighteenth century', *Econ. H.R.*, 2nd ser. 19 (1966–7), 550–68. Relevant material is published in the *Mariners' Mirror* (1100). For general bibliog. see (1087).

1586 SMITH (EDGAR CHARLES) A short history of naval and marine engineering. 1938.

See also Hereward Philip Spratt, *Handbook of the collection illustrating marine engineering, pt. 2. Descriptive catalogue*, Science museum, 1953. For steam propulsion see (1289–90).

1587 FAIRBAIRN. Life of Sir William Fairbairn Bart, F.R.S. LL.D. D.C.L., partly written by himself, Ed. Sir William Pole. 1877. [1876].

6. CIVIL ENGINEERING AND BUILDING

For railway contractors see (1643).

1588 KIRBY (RICHARD SHELTON) *and* LAURSON (PHILIP GUS-
TAVE). The early years of modern civil engineering. New Haven. 1932.

1589 FAIRBAIRN (*Sir* WILLIAM). An account of the construction of the
Britannia and Conway tubular bridges, with a complete history of their progress. 1849.

1590 MATTHEWS (WILLIAM). Hydraulia; an historical and descriptive
account of the water works of London, and the contrivances for supplying
other great cities, in different ages and countries. 1835.

1591 SANDSTRÖM (GÖSTA HERBERT EDWARD). The history of
tunnelling: underground workings through the ages. 1963.

> See also David Lampe, *The tunnel. The story of the world's first tunnel under a navigable
> river dug beneath the Thames, 1824–42*, 1963, a short popular account.

1592 BRUNELS. Memoir of the life of Sir Mark Isambard Brunel. By
Richard Beamish. 1862.

> For I. K. Brunel see Isambard Brunel, *The life of Isambard Kingdom Brunel, civil
> engineer*, 1870, and Lionel Thomas Caswall Rolt, *Isambard Kingdom Brunel*, 1957.

1593 LOCKE. The life of Joseph Locke, civil engineer, M.P., F.R.S. By
Joseph Devey. 1862.

> Worked with George Stephenson on the Liverpool and Manchester railway.

1594 RENNIE. Autobiography of Sir John Rennie, F.R.S., past president of
the Institution of Civil Engineers; comprising the history of his professional
life. Ed. by C. G. C. Rennie, 1875.

> See also Cyril Thomas Goodman Boucher, *John Rennie, 1761–1821. The life and work
> of a great engineer*, Manchester [1963].

1595 TELFORD. The life of Thomas Telford, civil engineer, written by
himself. Ed. by John Rickman. 1838.

> See also Sir Alexander Gibb, *The story of Telford. The rise of civil engineering*, 1935,
> Lionel Thomas Caswall Rolt, *Thomas Telford*, 1958. See also M. C. Hill, 'Iron and
> steel bridges in Shropshire, 1788–1901', *Trans. Shropshire Archaeol. Soc.* 56 (1957–60),
> 104–24, relating to bridges built while Telford was county surveyor.

1596 COONEY (E. W.). 'The origins of the Victorian master builders.' *Econ.
H.R.*, 2nd ser. 8 (1955–6), 167–76.

> On business organization. See also Robert Keith Middlemas, *The master builders*, 1963,
> mainly concerned with the later 19th century. Two technical treatises on building are
> Thomas Tredgold, *Elementary principles of carpentry . . . to which is added, An essay on
> the nature and properties of timber*, etc., 1820, 7th edn. 1886, and the same author's
> *Principles of warming and ventilating public buildings, dwelling houses, manufactories,
> hospitals, hot-houses*, 1824, 2nd edn. improved 1824. See (2941), (2945), (3764).

7. OTHER INDUSTRIES (in alphabetical order)

(a) *Brewing*

1597 MATHIAS (PETER). The brewing industry in England, 1700–1830. Camb. 1959.

See also Richard Shannon, *A practical treatise on brewing, distilling and rectification,* etc., 4 pt., 1805, and James Baverstock, *Treatise on brewing . . . and on malting,* 1824. The report and evidence of the *Select committee on public breweries,* H.C. 1818 (399) III, and 1819 (220) V, are substantial. Alfred Barnard, *The noted breweries of Great Britain and Ireland,* 4 v. [1889–91], contains information on the history of individual firms. See also (4166) on Guinness, and (2566–70) and (3983) on temperance.

(b) *Chairmaking*

1598 MAYES (LEONARD JOHN). The history of chair making in High Wycombe. 1960.

(c) *Chemicals*

1599 CLOW (ARCHIBALD) *and* CLOW (NAN LOUISE). The chemical revolution: A contribution to social technology. 1952.

Bibliog. 633–61. Covers a very wide range. Frank Sherwood Taylor, *A history of industrial chemistry,* 1957, is concerned with scientific rather than industrial history. See also Ludwig Fritz Haber, *The chemical industry during the nineteenth century, a study of the economic aspect of applied chemistry in Europe and North America,* Oxf., 1958, bibliog., 261–80. On particular industries see Albert Frederick Calvert, *Salt in Cheshire,* 1915, Sydney Herbert Higgins, *A history of bleaching,* 1924, Albert Edward Musson, *Enterprise in soap and chemicals; Joseph Crosfield and Sons Ltd., 1815–1965,* Manchester, 1965. 'Autobiographical memoir of Joseph Jewell, 1763–1846', ed. Arthur Walter Slater, *Camden Miscellany,* 22, Camden 4th ser. 1, (1964), 113–78, is concerned with fine chemical manufacture by the firm of Howard, Jewell, and Gibson.

(d) *Clocks and Watches*

1600 BAILLIE (GRANVILLE HUGH). Watchmakers and clockmakers of the world. 1929. 2nd edn. 1947.

Lists clockmakers, as does Frederick James Britten, *Old clocks and watches and their makers,* etc., 1899, 7th edn. by G. H. Baillie, C. Clutton, and C. Ilbert, 1956, repr. with cor. 1969. Also by Baillie is *Clocks and watches, an historical bibliography,* 1951. Much information on the industry is contained in the report and evidence of the *Select committee on watchmakers' petitions,* H.C. 1817 (504) VI, and 1818 (135) IX.

(e) *Dyestuffs*

1601 FAIRLIE (SUSAN). 'Dyestuffs in the eighteenth century'. *Econ. H.R.,* 2nd ser. 17 (1964–5), 488–510.

Factual account of dyestuffs in use. Also on this subject is Donovan Arthur Dawe, *Skilbecks: Drysalters, 1650–1950,* 1950.

(f) *Gas and Lighting*

1602 CHANDLER (DEAN) *and* LACEY (A. DOUGLAS). The rise of the gas industry in Britain. 1949.

See also Friedrich Christian Accum, *A practical treatise on gas-light*, etc., 1815, 4th edn. 1818, and his *Description of the process of manufacturing coal gas for the lighting of streets, houses, and public buildings; with . . . plans of the . . . apparatus now employed at the gas works in London*, 1819, 2nd edn. 1820; Thomas S. Peckston, *The theory and practice of gas-lighting*, etc., 1819; William Matthews, *An historical sketch of the origin, progress, and present state, of gas-lighting*, 1827; Samuel Clegg jun., *A practical treatise on the manufacture and distribution of coal-gas, 1841*, 4th edn. much enl. 1866. General accounts are given by Charles Hunt, *A history of the introduction of gas lighting*, 1907, and E. F. Armstrong, 'Murdock centenary lecture', *Trans. Inst. Gas Engineers*, 88 (1939), 933–1000. Malcolm Falkus discusses the extent of urban gas undertakings in 'The British gas industry before 1850', *Econ. H.R.*, 2nd ser. 19 (1966–7), 494–508. On other forms of lighting see Sir David Brewster, *Account of a new system of illumination for lighthouses*, Edin., 1827, recommending lenses in place of reflectors, [John Scoffern] *The chemistry of artificial light: including the history of wax, tallow, and sperm candles, and the manufacture of gas*, etc., 1860, Stirling Everard, *History of the Gas, Light and Coke Company, 1812–1949*, 1949, and William Thomas O'Dea, *The social history of lighting*, 1958.

(g) *Glass*

1603 BARKER (THEODORE CARDWELL). Pilkington Brothers and the glass industry. 1960.

See also David Reginald Guttery, *From broad glass to cut crystal. A history of the Stourbridge glass industry*, 1956.

(h) *Pottery*

1604 WEDGWOOD (JOSIAH CLEMENT) *Baron Wedgwood.* **Staffordshire pottery and its history. 1913.**

See also Simeon Shaw, *History of the Staffordshire potteries*, etc., Hanley, 1829, containing a number of errors but valuable for early history of the industry; Harold Owen, *The Staffordshire potter*, 1901; Percy Walter Lewis Adams, *A history of the Adams family of North Staffordshire, and of their connection with the development of the potteries*, 1914, supplemented by *Notes on some North Staffordshire families*, etc., Tunstall [1931]; N. J. G. Pounds, 'The discovery of china clay', *Econ. H.R.*, 2nd ser. 1 (1948–9), 20–33; Neil McKendrick, 'Josiah Wedgwood: an eighteenth-century entrepreneur in salesmanship and marketing techniques', *ibid.*, 2nd ser. 12 (1959–60), 408–33; Desmond Eyles, *Royal Doulton, 1815–1965. The rise and expansion of the Royal Doulton potteries*, 1965, which shows the firm's expansion into drain pipes and sanitary fittings in the 1840s. See also Leonard Whiter, *Spode: a history of the family, factory and wares from 1733 to 1833*, 1970. John Thomas, *The rise of the Staffordshire potteries*, Bath, 1971, is based on research carried out in the 1930s. For the Wedgwood family see Meteyard (2204), for other works which are mainly for the collector, (3005–12).

(i) *Printing and Paper*

1605 PLANT (MARJORIE). The English book trade. An economic history of the making and sale of books. 1939. 2nd edn. 1965.

Also James John Barnes, *Free trade in books: a study of the London book trade since 1800*, Oxf. 1964.

1606 MUSSON (ALBERT EDWARD). 'Newspaper printing in the industrial revolution.' *Econ. H.R.*, 2nd ser. 10 (1957–8), 411–26.

See also Thomas Curson Hansard, *Typographia: . . . the origin and progress of the art of printing*, etc., 1825; Charles Frederick Partington, *The printer's complete guide: containing a sketch of the history and progress of printing*, 1825; B. W. E. Alford, 'Government expenditure and the growth of the printing industry in the nineteenth century', *Econ. H.R.*, 2nd ser. 17 (1964–5), 96–112.

1607 COLEMAN (DONALD CUTHBERT). The British paper industry, 1495–1860. A study in industrial growth. Oxf. 1958.

See also Thomas Balston, *William Balston, paper manufacturer, 1759–1849*, 1954 [1955].

(j) *Others*

1608 DEERR (NOËL). The history of sugar. 2 v. 1949. 1950.

1609 ALFORD (BERNARD WILLIAM ERNEST). W. D. and H. O. Wills, and the development of the U.K. tobacco industry, 1786–1965. 1973.

8. TECHNOLOGY (other than industries included above)

(a) *General*

1610 HUDSON (DEREK) *and* LUCKHURST (KENNETH WILLIAM). The Royal Society of Arts, 1754–1954. 1954.

Includes appendix with a list of pubs. of the society. See also the detailed and comprehensive *A history of the Royal Society of Arts*, by Sir Henry Trueman Wood, 1913. See also the *Transactions of the society for the encouragement of arts, manufactures and commerce*, v. 1–57, 1784–1851. Blow Williams (1364), v. 2, section XIV, 1–35 gives a substantial list of contemporary works on inventions.

1611 SINGER (CHARLES), HOLMYARD (ERIC JOHN) *and others*. A history of technology. V. 4. The industrial revolution, c. 1750–c. 1850. Oxf. 1958.

There is also an abridged one-vol. version, ed. Thomas Kingston Derry and Trevor Illtyd Williams, *A short history of technology: from earliest times to A.D. 1900*, Oxf., 1960.

1612 CROWTHER (JAMES GERALD). Scientists of the industrial revolution—Joseph Black, James Watt, Joseph Priestley, Henry Cavendish. 1962.

See also, by the same author (3206), John Desmond Bernal, *Science and industry in the nineteenth century*, 1953, and (3090).

1613 HABAKKUK (HROTHGAR JOHN). American and British technology in the nineteenth century. The search for labour-saving inventions. Camb. 1962.

1614 SCHOFIELD (ROBERT EDWIN). The Lunar Society of Birmingham: a social history of provincial science and industry in eighteenth-century England. Oxf. 1963.

See also A. E. Musson and E. Robinson, 'Science and industry in the late eighteenth century', *Econ. H.R.*, 2nd ser. 13 (1960–1), 222–44, on the Lunar society and the Manchester Literary and Philosophical society.

1615 FERGUSON (EUGENE SHALLCROSS). Bibliography of the history of technology. Society for the history of technology, monographs 5. Camb. (Mass.) 1968.

1616 RAISTRICK (ARTHUR). Quakers in science and industry, being an account of the Quaker contributions to science and industry during the 17th and 18th centuries. 1950. Reprinted 1968.

See also (862).

(b) *Electricity, Telegraphy*

1617 DUNSHEATH (PERCY). A history of electrical engineering. 1962.

See also Alfred Smee, *Elements of electro-metallurgy*, etc., 1841, 2nd edn. 1843, 3rd edn. enl. 1851, which includes discussion of galvanism, batteries, electrotype, and daguerrotypes.

1618 FAHIE (JOHN JOSEPH). A history of electric telegraphy, to the year 1837. Chiefly compiled from original sources, and hitherto unpublished documents. 1884.

By the same author, *A history of wireless telegraphy, 1838–1899*, etc., 1899. Both are standard histories. For bibliog. see Sir Francis Ronalds, (3188).

1619 SABINE (ROBERT). The electric telegraph. 1867.

Describes practical applications of telegraphy. William T. Jeans, *Lives of the electricians, professors Tyndall, Wheatstone and Morse*, 1887, is mainly concerned with railway telegraphy. Paul Fleury Mottelay (3188) is concerned only with the period before Faraday, for whom see (3198). See also Geoffrey Hubbard, *Cooke and Wheatstone and the invention of the electric telegraph*, 1965.

(c) *Other Topics*

1620 DAVY (*Sir* HUMPHRY). On the safety lamp for coal miners; with some researches on flame. 1818.

For Davy generally see (3214).

1621 KATER (HENRY) *and* LARDNER (DIONYSIUS). A treatise on mechanics. 1830. New edn. 1849.

Includes discussion of practical application to pulleys, capstans, etc.

1622 BABBAGE (CHARLES). Passages from the life of a philosopher. 1864.

A recent life is Maboth Moseley, *Irascible genius. A life of Charles Babbage, inventor*, 1964. The Babbage papers are in the British Library, correspondence, 20 v., Add. MSS. 37182–201, misc. papers 37202–5.

1623 GERNSHEIM (HELMUT) *and* GERNSHEIM (ALISON). The history of photography. From the earliest use of the camera obscura in the eleventh century up to 1914. 1955.

See also Arthur Harold Booth, *William Henry Fox Talbot. Father of photography* [1965].

1624 GIBBS-SMITH (CHARLES HARVARD). Sir George Cayley's aeronautics, 1796–1855. 1962.

Also John Laurence Pritchard, *Sir George Cayley: the inventor of the aeroplane* [1961].

9. Exhibition of 1851

1625 OFFICIAL ILLUSTRATED CATALOGUE OF THE GREAT EXHIBITION. 4 v. 1851.

See also Robert Hunt, *Hunt's handbook to the official catalogues . . . of the great exhibition*, 2 v., 1851, an officially approved commentary. John Tallis, *Tallis' history and description of the Crystal Palace, etc. Illustrated*, 3 v. [1852], has illustrations drawn from contemporary daguerrotypes. John Timbs, *The year book of facts in science and art.* etc., annually from 1838 to 1873, contains for 1851 an extra volume, *The year book of facts on the Great Exhibition of 1851*, a useful account of the exhibition and its history. *Dickinson's comprehensive pictures of the Great Exhibition of 1851*, etc., 1854, contains 55 lithographs of the exhibition. See also (2991), and Grant (3762).

1626 ROYAL SOCIETY OF ARTS. Lectures on the results of the Great Exhibition of 1851, delivered before the society of arts, manufactures and commerce at the suggestion of H.R.H. Prince Albert. 1st ser. 1852, 2nd ser. 1853.

1627 HALTERN (UTZ). Die Londoner Weltausstellung von 1851. Münster. 1971.

The most thorough account: see also Kenneth William Luckhurst, *The story of exhibitions*, 1951. For Sir Henry Cole see (2353).

F. INTERNAL TRANSPORT

1. General Works and Bibliography

1628 JOURNAL OF TRANSPORT HISTORY. Leicester. 1953+.

Lists pubs. on transport history. See also L. C. Johnson, 'Historical records of the British transport commission', *Jour. Transport Hist.* 1 (1953–4), 82–96, also Maurice Bond, 'Materials for transport history amongst the records of parliament', *ibid.* 4 (1959–60), 37–52, and H. J. Dyos, 'Transport history in university theses', *ibid.* 4 (1959–60), 161–73. See also *Transport History*, v. 1+. Newton Abbot, 1968+.

1629 PRIESTLEY (JOSEPH). Historical account of the navigable rivers, canals, and railways throughout Great Britain. 1831.

Includes a large map of canals, natural resources, etc.

1630 JACKMAN (WILLIAM T.). The development of transportation in modern England. 2 v. Camb. 1916.

Bibliog. 750–811: standard. Also see Edwin A. Pratt, *A history of inland transport and communication in England*, 1912; Charles Ely Rose Sherrington, *A hundred years of transport, 1830–1933*, 1934, 9th edn. repr. 1969; Christopher Ivor Savage, *An economic history of transport*, 1959. Also Philip Sidney Bagwell, *The transport revolution from 1770*, 1974.

1631 BARKER (THEODORE CARDWELL) *and* ROBBINS (RICHARD MICHAEL). A history of London transport. V. 1: the nineteenth century. 1963.

Contemporary information is given in report and evidence of *Select Committee on the Hackney Coach office*, H.C. 1830 (515) X.

2. ROADS

1632 ORDISH (THOMAS FAIRMAN). 'History of metropolitan roads.'
London Topographical Society Record, 8 (1913), 1–92.

Gives a general account of road improvement in late 18th and early 19th centuries. See
also Benjamin Winstone, *Extracts from the minutes of Epping and Ongar highway trust . . .
1769–1870*, 1891, Percy Russell, *A Leicestershire road—Harborough to Loughborough*,
1934, and Francis Herbert Maud, *The Hockerill highway; . . . a stretch of the Norwich
road*, Colchester, 1957.

1633 McADAM (JOHN LOUDON). Remarks on the present system of
roadmaking. Bristol. 1816. Eighth edition revised with an appendix and report
from the Select Committee of the House of Commons, June, 1823, with
extracts from the evidence. 1824.

Also Roy Pember-Devereux (*pseud.* of Margaret Rose Roy Pember-Devereux), *John
Loudon McAdam. Chapters in the history of highways*, 1936.

1634 ALBERT (WILLIAM). The turnpike road system in England, 1663–
1840. Camb. 1972.

3. CANALS

1635 HADFIELD (ELLIS CHARLES RAYMOND). British canals. An
illustrated history. 1950. 2nd edn. rev. 1959. 4th edn. Newton Abbot. 1969.

Forms an intro. to the series, *The canals . . .*, Newton Abbot, 1966+, a series of regional
studies, which includes his *The canals of southern England*, 1955, *The canals of South
Wales and the border*, 1960, *The canals of the East Midlands* and *The canals of the West
Midlands*, both pub. Newton Abbot, 1966.

1636 STERN (WALTER M.). 'The Isle of Dogs canal. A study in early
public investment.' *Econ. H.R.*, 2nd ser. (1951–2), 359–71.

1637 CARY (JOHN). Inland navigation; or, Select plans of the several
navigable canals throughout Great Britain, accompanied with abstracts of the
different Acts of Parliament relative to them. 1795.

Also John Phillips, *A general history of inland navigation, foreign and domestic; containing
a complete account of the canals already executed in England, with considerations on those
projected*, etc., 1792, new edn. 1795, 4th edn. 1803.

4. RAILWAYS

1638 OTTLEY (GEORGE). A bibliography of British railway history. 1965.

Also Jack Simmons, 'Railway history in English local records', *J. Transport Hist.* 1
(1953–4), 155–169, and D. B. Wardle, 'Sources for the history of railways at the Public
Record office', *ibid.* 2 (1955–6), 214–34. For locomotive building see (1578–84), for
civil engineering (1588–95), for railway stations (2948).

1639 HERAPATH'S RAILWAY MAGAZINE. 1835–1904.

The most famous early railway journal, monthly to August 1839, thereafter weekly:
title changes, May 1835–March 1836, *The Railway Magazine*, March 1836–August

1839, *The Railway Magazine and Annals of Science*, August 1839, *The Railway magazine and commercial journal*. For other journals see Ottley and Williams (1364), v. 1, 469. For timetables see *Bradshaw's British railways guide and hotel directory*, 1841–1961.

1640 ACWORTH (*Sir* WILLIAM MITCHELL). The railways of England. 1889.

Standard, and still probably the best general account. Nicholas Wood, *A practical treatise on rail-roads and interior communications in general*, etc., 1825, 2nd edn. 1832, 3rd edn. 1838 discusses engineering and technical aspects, Dionysius Lardner, *Railway economy, a treatise on the new art of transport*, etc., 1850 reprinted 1968, includes general management down to railway buffets; John Francis, *A history of the English railway, its social relations and revelations, 1820–1845*, 2 v., 1851, is also a general study. Henry Grote Lewin, *Early British railways, a short history of their origin and development, 1801–1844* [1925], and *The railway mania and its aftermath, 1845–1852*, etc., 1936, repr. 1968, are both standard. See also Cuthbert Hamilton Ellis, *British railway history. An outline from the accession of William IV to the nationalization of railways*, v. 1, 1830–1876, 1954, and for a short general survey Jack Simmons, *The railways of Britain: an historical introduction*, 1961, 2nd edn., 1968.

1641 WILLIAMS (FREDERICK SMEETON). The Midland railway, its rise and progress. A narrative of modern enterprise. [1876.] 5th edn. 1888. Repr. 1968 with intro. by C. R. Clinker.

Also Clement Edwin Stretton, *The history of the Midland railway*, 1901, and Eric George Barnes, *The rise of the Midland railway . . . 1844–1874*, 1966. Standard histories of other important companies include, Charles Herbert Grinling, *History of the Great Northern railway, 1845–1902*, 2nd edn. 1903, Oswald Stevens Nock, *The Great Northern railway*, 1958, Wilfred L. Steel, *The history of the London & North Western railway*, 1914, William Weaver Tomlinson, *The North Eastern railway, its rise and development* [1915], Edward Terence MacDermot, *History of the Great Western railway*, v. 1, 1833–1863, 1927, 2nd edn. rev. C. R. Clinker, 1964, George Stead Veitch, *The struggle for the Liverpool and Manchester railway*, Liverpool, 1930, Chapman Frederick Dendy Marshall, *History of the Southern railway*, 1936, criticized as unreliable, 2nd edn. rev. and enl., R. W. Kidner, 2 v., 1963, Cecil John Allen, *The Great Eastern railway*, 1955, 2nd edn. 1956, 3rd edn. 1961, George Dow, *Great Central*, v. 1, The progenitors 1813–1863, 1959.

1642 CLEVELAND-STEVENS (EDWARD). English railways: their development and their relation to the state. 1915.

Also James John Scott, *Railway practice in parliament, The law and practice of railway and other private bills*, etc., 1846; Sir William Hodges, *The law relating to railways*, etc., 1847, 2nd edn., 1855; Gustav Cohn, *Untersuchungen über die englische Eisenbahnpolitik*, 3 pt., Leipzig, 1874–83; Henry Parris, *Government and the railways in nineteenth century Britain*, 1965; Geoffrey Alderman, *The railway interest*, Leicester, 1973.

1643 HELPS (*Sir* ARTHUR). Life and labours of Mr. Brassey, 1805–1870. 1872.

The railway contractor. See also Frederick McDermott, *The life and work of Joseph Firbank J.P. D.L., railway contractor*, 1887; Olinthus John Vignoles, *Life of C[harles] B[lacker] Vignoles . . . soldier and civil engineer . . . a reminiscence of early railway history*, 1889; Sir Alfred Edward Pease, ed., *The diaries of Edward Pease, the father of English railways*, 1907; Richard Stanton Lambert, *The Railway King, 1800–1871: A study of George Hudson and the business morals of his time*, etc., 1934; Terence Richard Gourvish, *Mark Huish and the London and North Western Railway*, Leicester, 1972. See also Terry Coleman, *The railway navvies*, etc., 1965. For the Brunels see (1577), (1592).

1644 HAWKE (GUY RICHARD). Railways and economic growth in England
and Wales, 1840–1870. Oxf. 1970.

See also B. R. Mitchell, 'The coming of the railway and United Kingdom economic
growth', *J. Econ. Hist.* 24 (1964), 315–36; Harold Pollins, 'The finances of the Liverpool and Manchester railway', *Econ. H.R.*, 2nd ser. 5 (1952–3), 90–7; 'The marketing
of railway shares in the first half of the nineteenth century', *ibid.*, 2nd ser. 7 (1954–5),
230–9; 'Railway contractors and the finance of railway development in Britain', *J.
Transport Hist.* 3 (1957–8), 41–51. See also G. R. Hawke and M. C. Reed, 'Railway
capital in the United Kingdom in the nineteenth century', *Econ. H.R.*, 2nd ser. 22
(1969), 269–86. Also M. C. Reed, *Investment in railways in Britain, 1820–44*, 1974.

G. AGRICULTURE AND ITS PRODUCTS, FISHING

1. BIBLIOGRAPHIES, ENCYCLOPAEDIAS, JOURNALS

1645 PERKINS (WALTER FRANK). British and Irish writers on agriculture. Lymington. 1929. 2nd edn. Lymington. 1932. 3rd edn. Lymington.
1939.

See also Ministry of Agriculture and Fisheries library, *Chronological list of early agricultural works in the library*, ed. by George Edwin Fussell, 1930; Mary S. Aslin, *Library
catalogue of printed books and pamphlets on agriculture published between 1471 and 1840*
(catalogue of the library at Rothamsted), 2nd rev. edn. [Harpenden] 1940; Frederick
Arthur Buttress, ed., *Agricultural periodicals of the British Isles, 1681–1900, and their
location*, Camb., 1950. Royal Agricultural Society, *Survey of agricultural libraries in
England and Scotland*, 1957, describes holdings in 46 libraries. See also two bibliographical articles by G. E. Fussell, 'English agriculture from Arthur Young to William
Cobbett', *Econ. H.R.*, 1st ser. 6 (1935–6), 214–22, and 'English agriculture from Cobbett
to Caird (1830–80), *ibid.* 15 (1944–5), 79–85.

1646 LOUDON (JOHN CLAUDIUS). An encyclopaedia of agriculture:
comprising the theory and practice of the valuation, transfer, laying out,
improvement, and management of landed property; the latest improvements;
a general history of agriculture in all countries; and a statistical view of its
present state. 1825. 3rd edn. 1835.

See also Arthur Young, *The farmer's calendar, containing the business necessary to be performed on various kinds of farms during every month of the year*, 1771, new edn. 1804;
Sir John Sinclair, *The code of agriculture; including observations on gardens, orchards,
woods and plantations*, 1817, 3rd edn., 1821; William Cobbett, *Cottage economy, containing information relative to the brewing of beer, making of bread, keeping of cows, pigs,
bees*, etc., 1822, 17th edn., 1850 (for bibliog. of Cobbett see Pearl (188)); Cuthbert
William Johnson, *The farmer's encyclopaedia . . . embracing all the most recent discoveries in agricultural chemistry, adapted to the comprehension of unscientific readers*,
1842; Henry Stephens, *The book of the farm; detailing the labours of the farmer, farm-
steward, plough-man, shepherd, hedger, cattle-man, field-worker, and dairy-maid*, 3 v.,
1844, 2nd edn., 2 v., 1851, containing much on Scottish practice.

1647 AGRICULTURAL HISTORY. Pub. Agricultural History Society.
Chicago. 1927+.

1648 AGRICULTURAL HISTORY REVIEW. Pub. British Agricultural
History Society. 1953+.

2. General Works

See also Salaman (4178).

1649 CHAMBERS (JONATHAN DAVID) *and* MINGAY (GORDON EDMUND). The agricultural revolution, 1750–1880. 1966.

Also standard is Rowland Edmund Prothero, Baron Ernle, *English farming past and present*, 1912; 6th edn., with intro. by G. E. Fussell and O. R. McGregor, 1961, contains bibliog. to 1961 by O. R. McGregor, XCI–CXV. For review see E. L. Jones, 'English farming before and during the nineteenth century', *Econ. H.R.*, 2nd ser. 15 (1962–3), 145–52.

1650 YOUNG (ARTHUR). Annals of agriculture and other useful arts. 46 v. 1784–1815.

For bibliog. see George Douglas Amery, 'The writings of Arthur Young', *Jour. Royal Agricultural Soc. England* 85 (1924), 175–205. See also Arthur Young, *Tours in England and Wales, selected from the Annals of Agriculture*, Reprints of scarce tracts in economic and political science, 14, 1932. For biog. see (2087).

1651 MARSHALL (WILLIAM). The rural economy of Norfolk. 2 v. 1787.

Followed by *The rural economy of Yorkshire*, 2 v., 1788, . . . *Gloucestershire*, 1789, . . . *Midland counties*, 1790, . . . *West of England*, 1796, . . . *Southern counties*, 1798. For bibliog. of Marshall, who has a high reputation as commentator, see Perkins (1645), 96–7.

1652 DAVIS (RICHARD). A general view of the agriculture of the county of Oxford. 1794.

One of the first of a large no. of county reports to the Board of Agriculture, listed in Perkins (1645), 176–7 and in B.L. Cat. under 'London III, Board of Agriculture'. The Board and its reports suffered much contemporary criticism; see John Somerville, 15th Baron Somerville, *The system followed during the last two years by the Board of Agriculture further illustrated*, etc., 1800. Thomas Stone, *A letter to . . . Lord Somerville, late President of the Board of Agriculture, with a view to shew the inutility of . . . that institution*, 1800, William Marshall, *A review of the reports to the Board of Agriculture; from the northern departments of England*, York, 1808, followed by similar criticisms of the reports on the western counties, 1810, eastern counties, 1811, midlands, 1815, southern counties, 1817. For full bibliog. see Perkins (1645), 97. In defence of the Board see Arthur Young, *On the advantages which have resulted from . . . the Board of Agriculture*, etc., 1809. For Sir John Sinclair and the Board see (2140).

1653 CAIRD (JAMES). English agriculture in 1850–51. 1851. 2nd edn. 1852.

Originally pub. as series of letters to *The Times*. See also his *High farming under liberal covenants, the best substitute for protection*, 1848, 5th edn., 1849.

1654 WATSON (JAMES ANDERSON SCOTT). The history of the Royal Agricultural Society of England, 1839–1939. [1939.]

Samuel Parkes, *A letter to the farmers and graziers of Great Britain*, etc., 1819, 4th edn. enl., 1819 lists 103 agricultural socs. in England and Wales.

1655 COPPOCK (J. T.) 'The statistical assessment of British agriculture.' *Agricultural Hist. Rev.* 4 (1956), 4–21.

On government collection of agricultural statistics. On the crop returns collected by the

Home Office in 1801 see David Thomas, 'The acreage returns of 1801: a test of accuracy', *B.B.C.S.* 18 (1959–60), 379–83; W. E. Minchinton, 'Agriculture in Gloucestershire during the Napoleonic wars', *Trans. Bristol and Gloucestershire Archaeol. Soc.* 68 (1949), 165–183; David Williams, 'The acreage returns of 1801 for Wales', *B.B.C.S.* 14 (1950–2), 54–68; K. G. Davies and G. E. Fussell, 'Worcestershire in the acreage returns for 1801', *Trans. Worcestershire Archaeol. Soc.* 27 (1950), 15–23, and Grigg (1686).

1656 **SLICHER VAN BATH (BERNARD HENDRIK).** De agrarische geschiedenis van West-Europa 500–1850. Utrecht and Antwerp. [1960.]

Trans., with title *The agrarian history of western Europe, 500–1850*, by Olive Ordish, 1963. Discusses British agriculture in its European setting. See also G. E. Fussell, 'Low Countries' influence on British farming', *E.H.R.* 74 (1959), 611–22.

1657 **ORWIN (CHRISTABEL SUSAN) and WHETHAM (EDITH HOLT).** History of British agriculture, 1846–1914. 1964.

1658 **JONES (ERIC LIONEL).** Seasons and prices. The role of the weather in English agricultural history. 1964.

Chronological summary of the seasons 1728–1911. See also M. J. R. Healy and E. L. Jones, 'Wheat yields in England, 1815–59', *Jour. Roy. Statistical Soc.* ser. A, 125 (1962), 574–9, estimating yields in bushels to the acre from samples collected by Sandars (corn merchant): the same information used by Tooke (1390). E. L. Jones, 'The agricultural labour market in England, 1793–1872', *Econ. H.R.*, 2nd ser. 17 (1964–5), 322–38, discusses the market in relation to seasonal variations. See also Susan Fairlie, 'The corn laws and British wheat production, 1829–76', in *Econ. H.R.*, 2nd ser. 22 (1969), 88–116.

3. Government Policy and the Corn Trade

For politics and the corn laws see (111), (143), for corn laws and international trade (1509).

1659 **BARNES (DONALD GROVE).** A history of the English corn laws, from 1660–1846. 1930.

With chronological list of contemporary pamphlets and periodicals 303–28, and secondary works 328–31. See also Cornelius Walford, 'The literature of famines and the corn laws', *J. Statistical Soc.* 42 (1879), 247–65.

1660 **FAY (CHARLES RYLE).** The corn laws and social England. Camb. 1932.

1661 **LAWSON-TANCRED (MARY).** 'The Anti-league and the corn law crisis of 1846.' *Hist. J.* 3 (1960), 162–83.

Also on the landed interest see Edward Stillingfleet Cayley, *Reasons for the formation of the Agricultural Protection society*, etc., 1844, D. C. Moore, 'The corn laws and high farming', *Econ. H.R.*, 2nd ser. 18 (1965–6), 544–61, J. T. Ward, 'West Riding landowners and the corn laws', *E.H.R.* 81 (1966), 256–72. For protection societies immediately after 1815 see David Spring and Travis L. Crosby, 'George Webb Hall and the Agricultural Association', *J. of British Studies*, 2 no. 1 (1962), 115–31.

1662 **FAIRLIE (SUSAN).** 'The nineteenth-century corn law reconsidered.' *Econ. H.R.*, 2nd. ser. 18 (1965–6), 562–75.

Assesses the economic effects of protection 1815–46. Among notable contemporary pamphlets see Sir James Robert George Graham, 2nd bart., *Corn and currency; in an address to the land owners*, 1826, 3rd edn., 1827, blaming the return to cash payments for distress.

1663 SELECT COMMITTEE ON THE CORN LAWS. H.C. 1813–14 (339) III.

Also H. L. committee, 1st and 2nd reps. H.C. 1814–15 (26) V. See also *Select committee on agricultural distress*, H.C. 1820 (255) II, 1821 (668) IX, and 1822 (165, 346) V, *Select committee on present state of agriculture*, H.C. 1833 (612) V, and *Select committee on state of agriculture* of 1836, 1st–3rd reps. H.C. 1836 (79, 189, 465) VIII, H.L. committee of 1837, H.C. 1837 (464) V. All these contain much general agricultural information. Not parliamentary papers, but prepared by the Board of Trade's Comptroller of corn returns, are William Jacob, *Report on the trade in foreign corn and on the agriculture of northern Europe*, 1826, and *Tracts relating to the corn trade and corn laws*, etc., 1828, which were the main source of information on foreign sources of supply. On bread supply in towns and on internal corn trade see *Select committee on the high price of provisions* 1st–6th reps. H.C. 1801 (174) II, and H.L. committee, 1st–7th reps. H.C. 1801 (11, 23, 37, 82, 84, 137) II, *Select committee on manufacture, sale, and assize of bread*, H.C. 1814–15 (186) V, *Select committee on regulation of the sale of corn in the United Kingdom* H.C. 1834 (517) VII. The shortages of 1795 are discussed by Walter M. Stern, 'The bread crisis in Britain, 1795–96', *Economica*, new ser. 31 (1964), 168–87.

4. LAND TENURE

(a) *Enclosures*

1664 CHALONER (WILLIAM HENRY). 'Bibliography of recent work on enclosure, the open fields, and related topics.' *Agricultural Hist. Rev.* 2 (1954), 48–52.

Includes a list of handlists of county enclosure awards prepared by William Edward Tate, also listed in West (3514). See also W. E. Tate, 'Some unexplored records of the enclosure movement', *E.H.R.*, 57 (1942), 250–63, and B. A. English, ed., *Handlist of West Riding enclosure awards*, Leeds, 1965. On enclosure commissioners see Maurice W. Beresford, 'Commissioners of enclosure', *Econ. H.R.*, 1st ser. 16 (1945–6), 130–40, and his 'Minutes of enclosure commissions', *Bull. Inst. Hist. Res.* 21 (1946–8), 59–69. W. S. Rogers, 'West Riding commissioners of enclosure, 1729–1850', *Yorkshire Archaeol. Jour.* 40 (1961), 401–19, discusses their social and political background. See also William Edward Tate, *The English village community and the enclosure movements*, 1967.

1665 GENERAL REPORT ON ENCLOSURES, drawn up by order of the Board of Agriculture. 1808.

1666 GONNER (EDWARD CARTER KERSEY). Common land and in-closure. 1912.

See also Arthur Henry Johnson, *The disappearance of the small landowner*, Oxf., 1909. His disappearance has been contested by later writers: see E. Davies, 'The small land-owner, 1780–1832, in the light of the land tax assessments', *Econ. H.R.*, 1st ser. 1 (1927), 87–113, reprinted Carus-Wilson, 270–94; H. G. Hunt, 'Landownership and enclosure, 1750–1830', *Econ. H.R.*, 2nd ser. 11 (1958–9), 497–505, who argues that large land-owners increased their acreage in villages enclosed at this time; G. E. Mingay, 'The size of farms in the eighteenth century', *ibid.* 14 (1961–2), 469–488, arguing for a decrease in numbers of farms of less than 100 acres, and the same writer's 'The land tax assessments and the small landowner', *ibid.* 17 (1964–5), 381–388, criticizing the weight of interpretation placed on the assessments.

1667 TATE (WILLIAM EDWARD) *ed.* Parliamentary land enclosures in the county of Nottingham during the 18th and 19th centuries, 1743–1868. Thoroton Soc. rec. ser. 5. Nottingham. 1935.

Other local studies are V. M. Lavrovsky, 'Parliamentary enclosures in the county of Suffolk, (1797–1814)', *Econ. H.R.*, 1st ser. 7 (1936–7), 186–208, and H. G. Hunt, 'The chronology of parliamentary enclosure in Leicestershire', *ibid.*, 2nd ser. 10 (1957–8), 265–72.

1668 CHAMBERS (JONATHAN DAVID). 'Enclosure and labour supply in the industrial revolution.' *Econ. H.R.*, 2nd ser. 5 (1952–3), 319–43.

(b) *Landownership*

1669 MARSHALL (WILLIAM). On the landed property of England, an elementary and practical treatise; containing the purchase, the improvement and the management of landed estates. 1804.

See also J. S. Bayldon, *The art of valuing rents and tillages, wherein is explained the manner of valuing the tenant's rights on entering and quitting farms, in Yorkshire and the adjoining counties*, etc., 1823; Lewis Kennedy and T. B. Grainger, *The present state of the tenancy of land in Great Britain, shewing the principal customs and practices between incoming and outgoing tenants*, etc., 1828; Humphry William Woolrych, *A treatise on the law of waters, and of sewers*, etc., 1830, dealing with canals, fishing rights, mills, etc. For game laws, and land law generally see (631–5). See also *Select committee on the game laws*, H.C. 1845 (602) XII, and 1846 (463 I–II) IX, pt. i and ii.

1670 RETURN OF OWNERS OF LAND. H.C. 1874 LXXII. Pt. III.

The value of this survey for the preceding century is fully discussed by Thompson (1805). It provided the basis of John Bateman, *The great landowners of Great Britain and Ireland*, 4th edn., 1883, repr. with intro. by David Spring, Leicester, 1971.

1671 BRODRICK (*Hon.* GEORGE CHARLES). English land and English landlords. An enquiry into the origin and character of the English land system. 1881. Repr. 1968.

On estate management see David Spring, *The English landed estate in the nineteenth century: its administration*, Baltimore [1963], bibliog. 195–204, and Eileen Spring, 'The settlement of land in nineteenth-century England', *American Journal of Legal History*, 8 (1964), 209–23. Also John Oxley Parker, ed., *The Oxley Parker papers. From the letters and diaries of an Essex family of land agents in the nineteenth century*, Colchester [1964]. See also B. A. Holderness, 'Landlord's capital formation in East Anglia, 1750–1870', *Econ. H.R.*, 2nd ser. 25 (1972), 434–47, and John Towers Ward and Richard George Wilson, eds., *Land and industry*, Newton Abbot [1971], and Thompson (1805).

1672 MATHER (FREDERICK CLARE). After the Canal Duke. A study of the estates . . . of the third Duke of Bridgewater . . . 1825–1872. Oxf. 1970.

Similar in general scope is Eric Richards, *Leviathan of wealth: the Sutherland fortune in the industrial revolution*, 1973. The decline of the Grenvilles, dukes of Buckingham, is discussed in F. M. L. Thompson, 'The end of a great estate', *Econ. H.R.*, 2nd ser. 8 (1955–6), 36–52, and David and Eileen Spring, 'The fall of the Grenvilles, 1844–1848', *Huntington Library Quarterly*, 19 (1955–6), 165–90.

(c) *Tithe*

1673 PRINCE (HUGH COUNSELL). 'The tithe surveys of the mid-nineteenth century.' *Agricultural Hist. Rev.* 7 (1959), 14–26.

See also E. A. Cox and B. R. Dittmer, 'The tithe files of the mid-nineteenth century', *ibid.* 13 (1965), 1–16. On the law of tithes see Easterby (757).

5. TECHNIQUES

1674 JOHNSTONE (JOHN). An account of the mode of draining land, according to the system practised by the late Mr. Joseph Elkington. Edin. 1797. 4th edn. 1814. New edn. 1841.

4th edn. is much enl. and entitled *A systematic treatise on the theory and practice of draining land*, etc. See also George Edwin Fussell, 'The evolution of field drainage', *Bath and West Soc. J.*, 6th ser. 4 (1929–30), 59–72.

1675 WRIGHT (THOMAS). The art of floating land as is practised in the county of Gloucester. 1799.

Also Eric Kerridge, 'The sheepfold in Wiltshire and the floating of the water-meadows', *Econ. H.R.*, 2nd ser. 6 (1953–4), 282–9.

1676 DAVY (*Sir* HUMPHRY). Elements of agricultural chemistry, in a course of lectures for the Board of Agriculture. 1813. 2nd edn. 1814. 5th edn. 1836.

1677 MARTYN (THOMAS). The gardener's and botanist's dictionary, corrected and newly arranged by Thomas Martyn. 2 v. 4 pt. 1807.

Is a new edn. of Philip Miller, *The gardener's dictionary*, 2 v. 1731–9, 8th edn, 1768. See also John Claudius Loudon, *An encyclopaedia of gardening*, etc., 1822, 4th edn. 1826, John Lindley, *The theory of horticulture; or, An attempt to explain the principal operations of gardening upon physiological principles*, 1840, 2nd edn. rev. and enl., 1855, George William Johnson, *A dictionary of modern gardening*, 1846, and later edns. down to 1917, which became standard, Hon. Alicia Margaret Tyssen Amherst, afterwards Cecil, *A history of gardening in England*, 1895, 3rd edn. enl., 1910, includes history of Roy. Horticultural Soc.

1678 BENNETT (RICHARD) *and* ELTON (JOHN). History of corn milling. 4 v. 1898–1904.

See also Harold Witty Brace, *History of seed-crushing in Great Britain*, 1960.

1679 TROW-SMITH (ROBERT). English husbandry. From the earliest times to the present day. 1951.

1680 FUSSELL (GEORGE EDWIN). The farmer's tools, 1500–1900. The history of British farm implements, tools and machinery before the tractor came. 1952.

See also Robert Ritchie, *The farm engineer, a treatise on barn machinery, particularly on the application of steam and other motive powers to the thrashing machine*, Glasgow, 1849; W. Harwood Long, 'The development of mechanization in English farming', *Agricultural Hist. Rev.* 11 (1963), 15–26; Robert Arthur Whitehead, *Garretts of Leiston* [1965], an early firm of agricultural machinery manufacturers. George Bourne (*pseud.* of George

Sturt), *The wheelwright's shop*, Camb. 1923, though it refers to the later 19th century, gives a first-hand account of wheelwrights' and blacksmiths' work.

1681 TROW-SMITH (ROBERT). A history of British livestock husbandry 1700–1900. 1959.

Bibliog. 327–339. See also G. E. Fussell, 'The size of English cattle in the eighteenth century', *Agric. Hist.* 3 (1929), 160–81, Harold Burnell Carter, *His Majesty's Spanish flock. Sir Joseph Banks and the merinos of George III of England*, Sydney, Norwich, 1964, and Kenneth John Bonser, *The drovers; who they were and how they went*, etc., 1970.

6. LOCAL STUDIES

1682 GARNETT (FRANK WALLS). Westmorland agriculture 1800–1900. Kendal. 1912.

1683 RICHES (NAOMI). The agricultural revolution in Norfolk. Chapel Hill. [N.C.] 1937. Reprinted 1967.

See also Richard Noverre Bacon, *The report on the agriculture of Norfolk*, etc., 1844, and R. A. C. Parker, 'Coke of Norfolk and the agricultural revolution', *Econ. H.R.*, 2nd ser. 8 (1955–6), 156–66.

1684 DARBY (HENRY CLIFFORD). The draining of the fens. Camb. 1940.

1685 HOSKINS (WILLIAM GEORGE) *ed*. Studies in Leicestershire agrarian history. *Trans. Leicestershire Archaeol. Soc.* 24 (1948).

Essays by different authors, including Hoskins, 'The Leicestershire crop returns of 1801', 127–53. See also Hoskins, *The Midland peasant. The economic and social history of a Leicestershire village*, 1957, on Wigston Magna.

1686 THIRSK (JOAN). English peasant farming. The agrarian history of Lincolnshire from Tudor to recent times. 1957.

See also William Henry Wheeler (3638), and David Brian Grigg, *The agricultural revolution in south Lincolnshire*, Camb. 1966.

1687 THIRSK (JOAN) *and* IMRAY (JEAN) *eds*. Suffolk farming in the nineteenth century. (Suffolk Rec. Soc. 1) Ipswich. 1958.

1688 DAVIES (CLARICE STELLA). The agricultural history of Cheshire 1750–1850. (Chetham Soc. 3rd. ser. 10.) Manchester. 1960.

1689 HARRIS (ALAN HENRY). The rural landscape of the East Riding of Yorkshire, 1700–1800. A study in historical geography. 1961.

See also June A. Sheppard, 'East Yorkshire's agricultural labour force in the mid nineteenth century', *Agricultural Hist. Rev.* 9 (1961), 43–54.

7. FISHING

1690 HOLDSWORTH (EDMUND WILLIAM HUNT). Deep sea fishing and fishing boats. 1884.

See also James Travis Jenkins, *The herring and the herring fisheries*, 1927, mostly concerned with Scotland, Harold Adams Innis, *The cod fisheries: the history of an international economy*, New Haven and Toronto, 1940, and Charles Latham Cutting, *Fish saving. A history of fish processing from ancient to modern times*, 1955.

H. POPULATION

1691 [MALTHUS (THOMAS ROBERT)]. An essay on the principle of population as it affects the future improvement of society with remarks on the speculations of Mr. Godwin, M. Condorcet and other writers. 1798. 2nd edn. much enl. and modified, with title *An essay on the principle of population, or, A view of its past and present effects on human happiness*, 1803. Later edns. 1803, 1806, 1817, 1826.

For discussion see James Bonar, *Malthus and his work*, 1885, 2nd edn., 1924; Joseph J. Spengler, 'Malthus' total population theory: a restatement and reappraisal', *Canadian J. Econ.* 11 (1945), 83–110 and 234–64; Kenneth Smith, *The Malthusian controversy*, 1951; David V. Glass, ed., *An Introduction to Malthus*, 1953, essays by various authors; George F. McCleary, *The Malthusian population theory*, 1953; Joseph Stassart, *Malthus et la population*, Liège, 1957; David Edward Charles Eversley, *Social theories of fertility and the Malthusian debate*, Oxf., 1959. See also for full bibliog. (1753).

1692 CENSUS OF GREAT BRITAIN. H.C. 1801 (140) VI and H.C. 1801–2 (9, 112) VI–VIII.

For subsequent censuses see, for 1811, H.C. 1812 (316–17) XI–XII; for 1821, H.C. 1822 (502) XV; for 1831, H.C. 1833 (149) XXXVI–VIII; for 1841, H.C. 1841 (sess. 2) (52) II; H.C. 1843 [496] XXII–III; H.C. 1844 (587–8) XXVII (occupational tables); and for 1851, H.C. 1852–3 (1631–3) LXXXV–VII; H.C. 1852–3 (1691) LXXXVIII (2 v.), 1852–3 [1690] LXXXIX (religious worship), and H.C. 1852–3 [1692] XC (education). The 1851 census for Ireland is contained in H.C. 1852–3 XCI–II. See, for a general guide, Interdepartmental committee on social and economic research, guides to official sources 2, *Census of Great Britain, 1801–1931*, 1951. For discussion of their accuracy see Lucy Barbara Hammond, 'Urban death rates in the early nineteenth century', *Econ. Hist.* 1 (1928), 419–28, and David V. Glass, 'A note on the under-registration in Britain in the nineteenth century', *Population Studies*, 5 (1951), 70–88. For extent of emigration see (1747). On John Rickman see (2188).

1693 GENERAL REGISTER OFFICE. Annual reports of the Registrar-General of births, deaths and marriages in England (England and Wales). 1839+.

Full list of references given in Ford and Ford (391), p. 148. Deficiencies in parish registers were discussed by the *Select committee to consider the general registration of births, marriages and deaths*, H.C. 1833 (669) XIV. See also M. J. Cullen, 'The making of the civil registration act of 1836', *J. of Eccles. Hist.* 25 (1974), 39–59; W. G. Lumley, 'Observations upon the statistics of illegitimacy', *Jour. Royal Statistical Soc.* 25 (1862), 219–74.

1694 FARR (WILLIAM). Vital statistics; a memorial volume of selections from the reports and writings of William Farr. Ed. Noel A. Humphreys. 1885.

See also Francis G. P. Neison, *Contributions to vital statistics, being a development of the rate of mortality and the laws of sickness . . . with an inquiry into the influence of locality on health*, 1845, 2nd edn. 1846, 3rd edn. 1846, 3rd edn. 1857.

1695 GRIFFITH (GROSVENOR TALBOT). Population problems of the age of Malthus. Camb. 1926.

See also G. Udny Yule, 'The growth of population and the factors which control it', *Jour. Roy. Statistical Soc.* 88 (1925), 1–58; and T. H. Marshall, 'The population problem during the industrial revolution; a note on the present state of the controversy', *Econ. Hist.* 2 (1929), and 'The population of England and Wales from the industrial revolution to the Great War', *Econ. H.R.* 5 (1935), 65–77, both reprinted in *Essays in economic history*, ed. E. M. Carus-Wilson, 1954, 306–30 and 331–43.

1696 POPULATION STUDIES. Pub. by Population Investigation Committee. 1947+.

See E. A. Wrigley, ed., *Nineteenth century society. Essays in the use of quantitative methods for the study of social data*, Camb., 1972. Many of the essays are based on data from the census returns.

1697 GLASS (DAVID VICTOR). 'The population controversy in eighteenth century England. Pt. 1. The background.' *Population Studies*, 6 (1952–3), 69–91.

For recent discussion see John T. Krause, 'Changes in English fertility and mortality, 1781–1850', *Econ. H.R.*, 2nd ser. 11 (1950), 52–70, arguing for an increase in fertility down to 1821; K. H. Connell (4187); H. J. Habakkuk, 'The English population in the eighteenth century', *Econ. H.R.*, 2nd ser. 6 (1953–4), 117–33, also considering the possibility of an increase in fertility; John T. Krause, 'Some neglected factors in the English industrial revolution', *J. Econ. Hist.* 19 (1959), 528–40; H. J. Habakkuk, *Population growth and economic development since 1750*, Leicester, 1971.

1698 McKEOWN (THOMAS) *and* BROWN (R. G.). 'Medical evidence related to English population changes in the eighteenth century.' *Population studies*, 9 (1955–6), 119–41.

Doubts the effects of medical improvements in reducing mortality, but considers reduction in death rate more likely than increase in birth rate. P. E. Razzell, 'Population changes in the eighteenth century. A reinterpretation', *Econ. H.R.*, 2nd ser. 18 (1965–6), 312–32, emphasizes the extent of inoculation against smallpox in the 18th century.

1699 BONER (HAROLD ANDERSON). Hungry generations: the nineteenth century case against Malthusianism. Columbia. N.Y. 1955.

On the popular response to Malthus see Francis Place, *Illustrations and proofs of the principle of population including an examination of the proposed remedies of Mr. Malthus, and a reply to the objections of Mr. Godwin and others*, 1822, Michael Sadler, *The law of population; a treatise in six books in disproof of the superfecundity of human beings*, etc., 2 v., 1830. See also (1965).

1700 EVERSLEY (DAVID EDWARD CHARLES). 'A survey of population in an area of Worcestershire from 1660–1850 on the basis of parish records.' *Population Studies*, 10 (1956–7), 253–79.

1701 HOLLINGSWORTH (THOMAS HENRY). The demography of the British peerage. Supp. to *Population Studies*, 18 (1964–5).

By the same author, 'A demographic study of British ducal families', *Population studies*, 11 (1957–8), 4–26.

1702 GLASS (DAVID VICTOR). Numbering the people. The eighteenth century population controversy and the development of census and vital statistics in Britain. Farnborough, Hants. 1973.

I. LABOUR

1. GENERAL

See also (1966).

1703 REDFORD (ARTHUR). Labour migration in England, 1800–50. (University of Manchester pubs., Econ. Hist. ser. 3.) Manchester. 1926. 2nd edn. rev. W. H. Chaloner, 1964.

See also E .J. E. Hobsbawm, 'The tramping artisan', *Econ. H.R.*, 2nd ser. 3 (1950–1), 299–320.

1704 BULLETIN FOR THE STUDY OF LABOUR HISTORY. Sheffield. 1960+.

1705 STERN (WALTER MARCEL). The porters of London. 1960.

1706 HILTON (GEORGE WOODMAN). The truck system, including a history of the British truck acts, 1465–1960. Camb. 1960.

1707 BYTHELL (DUNCAN). The hand-loom weavers: a study in the English cotton industry during the industrial revolution. Cambridge. 1969.

2. OLD POOR LAW

1708 WEBB (SIDNEY JAMES) *and* WEBB (BEATRICE). English poor law history. 3 v. 1927–9. Reprinted 1963. Being v. 7–9 of *English local government* (466).

See also Michael Nolan, *A treatise of the laws for the relief and settlement of the poor,* 1805, 2 v., 4th edn. 1825, and Sir George Nicholls, *A history of the English poor law,* etc., 2 v. 1854, 3 v. 1898–9. Nicholls was a poor law commissioner, 1834, and secretary to the Poor Law Board, 1847. See also (1691) and *Philanthrophy* (pp. 311–13).

1709 EDEN (*Sir* FREDERICK MORTON). The state of the poor. 3 v. 1797. Abridged edn. with intro. by A. G. L. Rogers. 1928. Facsimile of edn. of 1797, 1966.

See also David Davies, *The case of labourers in husbandry stated and considered,* Bath, 1795; Patrick Colquhoun, *A treatise on indigence,* etc., 1806; William Hale, *Letter to Samuel Whitbread, Esq. . . . on the distresses peculiar to the poor of Spitalfields,* 1806, a description of a parish in which ratepayers themselves are starving; Samuel Whitbread, *Substance of a speech on the poor laws . . . with an appendix,* 1807, 2nd edn. 1807; Thomas Robert Malthus, *A letter to Samuel Whitbread Esq. M.P. on his proposed . . . amendment of the poor laws,* 1807.

1710 SELECT COMMITTEE ON POOR LAWS. H.C. 1817 (462) VI, 1818 (107, 237, 358) V, 1819 (529) II.

M. W. Flinn, 'The poor employment act of 1817', *Econ. H.R.*, 2nd ser. 14 (1961–2), 82–92.

1711   HAMPSON (ETHEL MARY). The treatment of poverty in Cambridge-shire, 1597–1834. Camb. 1934.

Other local studies include Edward Rigby, *Further facts relating to the care of the poor, and the management of the workhouse in the city of Norwich*, etc., Norwich, 1812; Arthur Wilfred Ashby, *One hundred years of poor law administration in a Warwickshire village* [Tysoe], (Oxford studies in social and legal hist. 3), 1912; Frederick George Emmison, *The relief of the poor at Eaton Socon, 1706–1834* (Bedfordshire Hist. Rec. Soc. pubs. 15), Aspley Guise, 1933; *Sussex poor law records*, a catalogue, ed. Jane M. Coleman, Chichester, 1960.

1712   POYNTER (JOHN RIDDOCH). Society and pauperism; English ideas on poor relief, 1795–1834. 1969.

A short discussion is also given by John Duncan Marshall, *The old poor law, 1795–1834*, prepared for Economic History Society, 1968.

3. NEW POOR LAW

1713   ROYAL COMMISSION ON ADMINISTRATION AND PRACTI-CAL OPERATION OF THE POOR LAWS. Rep. and appendices. H.C. 1834 (44) XXVII–XXXVIII. Report only, repr. H.C. 1884–5 (347) XXXII.

Much information on development of policy is contained in *Annual reports* of Poor Law Commissioners, 1835–48, subsequently of Poor Law Board, 1849–71: full references given in Ford and Ford (391), pp. 145–6.

1714   KAY (JAMES PHILLIPS), *afterwards* KAY-SHUTTLEWORTH. The training of pauper children. A report published by the Poor Law Commissioners in their fourth annual report. 1839.

1715   BAXTER (GEORGE R. WYTHEN). The book of the Bastiles; or, the history of the working of the new poor-law. 1841.

A violent attack, with many extracts from newspapers and pamphlets: valuable general guide to anti-poor-law writings.

1716   LUMLEY (WILLIAM GOLDEN). A collection of statutes of general use relating to the relief of the poor, with notes. 2 v. 1843–52.

1717   KNIGHT (FREDERIC WINN). The parochial system versus centralization: statistics of close and open parishes: effects of settlement and removal, 1854. 2nd edn. 1854.

1718   BLAUG (MARK). 'The myth of the old poor law and the making of the new.' *Jour. Econ. Hist.* 23 (1963), 151–84.

For illustration see also his 'The poor law report re-examined', *J. Econ. Hist.* 24 (1964), 229–45. Defends the old poor law from criticisms of commissioners. For illustration of myth see Harriet Martineau, *Poor laws and paupers illustrated*, 4 pt., 2 v., 1833–4, stories showing the damage done by the allowance system. See also H. L. Beales, 'The new poor law', in *Essays in economic history*, v. 3, ed. E. M. Carus-Wilson, 1962; J. D. Marshall, 'The Nottinghamshire reformers and their contribution to the new poor law', *Econ. H.R.*,

2nd ser. 13 (1960–1), 382–96; David Roberts, 'How cruel was the Victorian poor law?' *Hist. Jour.* 6 (1963), 97–107; R. A. Lewis, 'William Day and the poor law commissioners', *University of Birmingham Hist. J.* 9 (1963–4), 163–96; Michael E. Rose, 'The allowance system under the new poor law', *Econ. H.R.*, 2nd ser. 19 (1966–7), 607–20; Nicholas C. Edsall, *The anti-poor law movement, 1834–44*, Manchester, 1971.

4. FACTORY LEGISLATION

1719　WARD (JOHN TREVOR). The factory movement, 1830–1855. 1962.

Now standard. See also Alfred (*pseud.* of Samuel Kydd), *The history of the factory movement, from the year 1802 to the enactment of the ten hours' bill in 1847*, 2 v., 1857, Richard Whately Cooke Taylor, *The modern factory system*, 1891, by a factory inspector, and Beatrice Leigh Hutchins and Amy Harrison, *A history of factory legislation*, 1903.

1720　SELECT COMMITTEE ON CHILDREN IN MANUFACTORIES. H.C. 1816 (397) III.

Sir Robert Peel's committee. Also *Select committee on children in manufactures*, H.C. 1831–2 (706) XV (Sadler's committee), which was followed by *Royal Commission on employment of children in factories*, 1st and 2nd reports and evidence, H.C. 1833 (450) XX, and (519) XXI, supplementary reports, H.C. 1834 (167) XIX–XX. Among comments see Michael Thomas Sadler, *Factory statistics. The official tables appended to the report of the Select Committee on the ten-hours factory bill vindicated etc.*, 1836, Samuel Taylor Coleridge, *Two addresses on Sir Robert Peel's Bill (April, 1818)*, ed. and intro. Edmund Gosse, 1913. For Chadwick see (2551).

1721　BLINCOE. A memoir of Robert Blincoe, an orphan boy; sent from the workhouse of St. Pancras, London, to endure the horrors of a cotton mill, through his infancy and youth, with a minute detail of his sufferings, being the first memoirs of the kind published. By John Brown. Manchester. 1832.

A notable piece of propaganda. See also Frances Trollope, *The life and adventures of Michael Armstrong, the factory boy*, 3 v., 1840, a novel, reprinted 1968, and *A narrative of the experience and sufferings of W[illiam] D[odd], a factory cripple, written by himself*, 2nd edn. 1841. Also by Dodd, *The factory system illustrated*, 1842 and *The labouring classes of England*, 2nd edn., Boston, Mass., 1848.

1722　FIELDEN (JOHN). The curse of the factory system. [1836.]

Also Robert Hyde Greg, *The factory question considered in relation to its effects on the health and morals of those employed in factories*, etc., 1837, a defence of the factory owners; also see Holland (143) and (1523).

1723　EDUCATIONAL PROVISIONS OF THE FACTORIES ACT. Factory inspectors' reports. H.C. 1839 (42) XLII.

1724　SELECT COMMITTEE ON THE ACT FOR THE REGULATION OF MILLS AND FACTORIES. 1–6 reports H.C. 1840 (203, 227, 314, 334, 419, 504) X, and H.C. 1841 (56) IX.

Ashley's committee. Leonard Horner (factory inspector), *On the employment of children in factories . . . in the United Kingdom, and in some foreign countries*, 1840, is an amplification of his evidence to it. Followed by *Royal commission on employment of children in mines and manufactories*, H.C. 1842 [380–2] XV–XVII, and 1843 [430–2] XIII–XV, index, 1845 [608] XLII. Other working conditions under discussion at this time include *Select committee on shipwrecks of timber ships*, H.C. 1839 (333) IX, *Select committee on shipwrecks of British vessels*, H.C. 1843 (549, 581) IX, and William Augustus Guy, *Case of the journeymen bakers*, etc., 1848 and *On the health of night-men*, etc., [1848]. For Ashley (later Shaftesbury) see (2518).

1725 OASTLER (RICHARD). The Fleet Papers; being letters to Thomas Thornhill from Richard Oastler his prisoner in the Fleet. With occasional communications from friends. 3 v. 1841–3.

See also standard biography Cecil Herbert Driver, *Tory radical: The life of Richard Oastler*, Oxf. 1946. Also on Ten Hours' agitation see George Jacob Holyoake, *The life of Joseph Rayner Stephens, preacher and political orator* [1881], and John Clifford Gill, *The Ten Hours parson. Christian social action in the eighteen-thirties*, 1959, the life of the Rev. G. S. Bull of Byerley.

1726 THOMAS (MAURICE WALTON). The early factory legislation, a study in legislative and administrative action. Leigh on Sea. 1948.

On the work of the inspectorate. See on mines R. K. Webb, 'A Whig inspector: H. S. Tremenheere', *J. Modern Hist.* 27 (1955), 352–64. Bernice Martin, 'Leonard Horner: a portrait of an inspector of factories', *International Review of Social History* 14 (1969), 412–43. Reports of factory inspectors, 1834+, are listed in Ford and Ford, (391), pp. 145–6.

1727 BLAUG (MARK). 'The classical economists and the factory acts— a re-examination.' *Quart. J. Economics*, 72 (1958), 211–26.

1728 POLLARD (SIDNEY). 'Factory discipline in the industrial revolution.' *Econ. H.R.*, 2nd ser. 16 (1963–4), 254–71.

See also Neil McKendrick, 'Josiah Wedgwood and factory discipline', *Hist. Jour.* 4 (1961), 30–55, and Chapman (1537).

5. TRADE UNIONS

1729 WEBB (SIDNEY JAMES) *and* WEBB (BEATRICE). The history of trade unionism. 1894. Rev. edn. 1920.

Standard. See also George Howell, *Labour legislation, labour movements and labour leaders*, 1902, 2nd edn., 2 v., 1905; Robert Yorke Hedges and Allan Winterbottom, *The legal history of trade unionism*, 1930; Arthur Aspinall, *The early English trade unions: documents from the Home Office papers in the Public Record Office*, 1949. Henry Mathison Pelling, *A history of British trade unionism*, 1963, though short on the early 19th century, has an up-to-date bibliog. 271–8. For Luddites see (99) and Thompson (1810), for Dorchester labourers Loveless (2619).

1730 SELECT COMMITTEE ON ARTIZANS AND MACHINERY. H.C. 1824 (51) V.

Investigated effects of combination laws (chairman Joseph Hume). Followed by *Select committee on combination laws*, H.C. 1825 (417) IV. See also M. Dorothy George, 'The combination laws', *Econ. H.R.*, 1st ser. 6 (1935–6), 172–8.

1731 POSTGATE (RAYMOND WILLIAM). The builders' history. [1923.]

1732 GEORGE (M. DOROTHY). 'The London coal-heavers: attempts to regulate waterside labour in the eighteenth and nineteenth centuries.' *Econ. Hist.* 1 (1926–9), 229–48.

Also D. J. Rowe, 'The strikes of the Tyneside keelmen in 1809 and 1819', *Internat. Rev. of Social Hist.* 13 (1968), 58–75.

1733 WARBURTON (WILLIAM HENRY). The history of trade union organisation in the north Staffordshire potteries. 1931.

Also Roger von Boch, *Geschichte der Töpferarbeiter von Staffordshire im 19 Jahrhundert*, Stuttgart, 1899.

1734 JEFFERYS (JAMES BAVINGTON). The story of the engineers, 1800–1945. [1946.]

1735 HOWE (ELLIC). The London compositor. Documents relating to wages, working conditions and customs of the London printing trade, 1785–1900. 1947.

Also Ellic Howe, *The London bookbinders, 1780–1806*, 1950, and Albert Edward Musson, *The Typographical Association, origins and history up to 1949*, 1954.

1736 COLE (GEORGE DOUGLAS HOWARD). Attempts at general union. A study in British trade union history, 1818–1834. 1953.

Also W. H. Oliver, 'The consolidated trades' union of 1834', *Econ. H.R.*, 2nd ser. 17 (1964–5), 77–95, and two articles by I. J. Prothero, 'London Chartism and the trades', *ibid.*, 2nd ser. 24 (1971), 202–17, and 'William Benbow and the concept of the "general strike" ', *Past and Present* 63 (1974), 132–71.

1737 POLLARD (SIDNEY). A history of labour in Sheffield. Liverpool. 1959.

Opens with a chapter on situation in 1851. Bibliog. 344–65.

1738 TURNER (HERBERT ARTHUR). Trade union growth, structure and policy. A comparative study of the cotton unions. 1962.

Also W. E. Minchinton, 'The beginnings of trade unionism in the Gloucestershire woollen industry', *Trans. Bristol and Gloucester Archaeol. Soc.* 70 (1951), 126–41, and Norman H. Cuthbert, *The Lace Makers Society, A study of trade unionism in the British lace industry, 1760–1960*, Nottingham, 1960; R. G. Kirby and A. E. Musson, *The voice of the people: John Doherty, trade unionist, radical and factory reformer*, Manchester, 1975.

1739 WILLIAMS (JAMES ECCLES). The Derbyshire miners. A study in industrial and social history. 1962.

Bibliog. 890–8. See also Richard Fynes, *The miners of Northumberland and Durham; A history of their social and political progress*, Blyth, 1873, Sidney James Webb, *The story of the Durham miners, 1662–1921*, 1921, and Cyril E. Hart, *The free miners of the royal forest of Dean and hundred of St. Briavels*, etc., Gloucester, 1953, and Raymond Challinor and Brian Ripley, *The Miners' Association. A trade union in the age of the Chartists*, 1968.

6. EMIGRATION

For Scotland see Macmillan (3910) and for Wales (3838), and for Ireland (4190).

1740 LIBRARY OF CONGRESS. A list of books with references to periodicals on immigration. *Comp.* Appleton Prentiss Clark Griffin. 3rd. edn. Washington. 1907.

1741 HOLDITCH (ROBERT). The emigrant's guide to the United States of America; containing the best advice and directions respecting the voyage, preservation of health, choice of settlement, etc. 1818.

Similar guides are John Knight, *The emigrant's best instructor*, etc., Manchester, 1818, William Kingdom, *America and the British colonies . . . the comparative advantages and disadvantages each country offers for emigration*, 1820, Joseph Pickering, *Inquiries of an emigrant . . . an English farmer . . . [who] . . . traversed the United States and Canada*, etc., 4th edn., 1832.

1742 SELECT COMMITTEE ON EMIGRATION. H.C. 1826 (404) IV. 3 further reports H.C. 1826–7 (88, 237, 550) V.

1743 JOHNSON (STANLEY CURRIE). A history of emigration from the United Kingdom to North America, 1763–1912. 1913.

Bibliog. 356–76. See also E. C. Guillet, *The great migration: the Atlantic crossing by sailing ship since 1770*, Toronto, 1937.

1744 COWAN (HELEN I.). British emigration to British North America, 1783–1837. (University of Toronto studies. History and economics. 4. No. 2.) [Toronto] 1928. Rev. edn. [Toronto.] 1961.

1745 CARROTHERS (WILLIAM ALEXANDER). Emigration from the British Isles, with special reference to the development of the overseas dominions. 1929.

See also George Frederic Plant, *Oversea settlement. Migration from the United Kingdom to the dominions*, 1951.

1746 HANSEN (MARCUS LEE). The Atlantic migration, 1607–1860. A history of the continuing settlement of the United States. Camb. Mass. 1941.

Bibliog. 309–71. Also Edith Abbott, *Historical aspects of the immigration problem: select documents*, Chicago, 1926; Robert Ernst, *Immigrant life in New York city, 1825–1863*, N.Y. 1949; Rowland Tappan Berthoff, *British immigrants in industrial America, 1790–1950*, Camb. Mass., 1953, bibliog. 215–75; F. Thistlethwaite, ' The Atlantic migration of the pottery industry', *Econ. H.R.*, 2nd ser. 11 (1958–9), 264–78.

1747 CARRIER (NORMAN HENRY) *and* JEFFERY (JAMES R.). External migration. A study of the available statistics, 1815–1950. 1953.

1748 THOMAS (BRINLEY). Migration and economic growth. A study of Great Britain and the Atlantic economy. (National Inst. of Econ. and Social Res., Econ. and Social studies, 12.) Camb. 1954.

1749 SHEPPERSON (WILBUR STANLEY). British emigration to North America. Projects and opinions in the early Victorian period. Oxf. 1957.

Bibliog. 267–93.

1750 MACDONAGH (OLIVER ORMOND GERARD MICHAEL). A pattern of government growth, 1800–60. The passenger acts and their enforcement. 1961.

1751 JOHNSTON (H. J. M.) British emigration policy, 1815–30. Oxf. 1972.

1752 ERICKSON (CHARLOTTE JOANNE). Invisible immigrants: the adaptation of English and Scottish immigrants to 19th century America. [1972.]

Discusses and reprints letters sent home by British emigrants.

J. ECONOMIC THOUGHT

For currency and banking see (1430–42).

1. GENERAL SURVEYS AND BIBLIOGRAPHIES

1753 McCULLOCH (JOHN RAMSAY). The literature of political economy, a classified catalogue of select publications. 1845. Repr. (Reprints of Scarce Works on Political Economy, 5.) 1938.

See also Keitaro Amano, *Bibliography of the classical economics*, pt. 1, Science Council of Japan, division of economics, commerce, and business administration, economic ser. 27, Tokyo, 1961, covering Adam Smith and Ricardo. Also for contemporary periodical writing, F. W. Fetter, 'The authorship of economic articles in the *Edinburgh Review*, 1802–1846', *J. Polit. Econ.* 61 (1953), 232–59; 'The economic articles in the *Quarterly Review* and their authors, 1809–1852', *ibid.* 66 (1958), 47–64 and 154–70; 'The economic articles in *Blackwood's Edinburgh Magazine* and their authors, 1817–53', *Scottish J. Polit. Econ.* 8 (1960), 85–107, 213–31; 'Economic articles in the *Westminster Review* and their authors, 1824–51', *J. Polit. Econ.* 70 (1962), 570–96.

1754 CANNAN (EDWIN). A history of the theories of production and distribution in English political economy from 1776 to 1848. 1893. 2nd edn. 1903. Repr. 1953.

Also his *A review of economic theory*, 1929.

1755 TAUSSIG (FRANK WILLIAM). Wages and capital. An examination of the wages fund doctrine. N.Y. 1896. Repr. 1932. 1968.

1756 GIDE (CHARLES) *and* RIST (CHARLES). Histoire des doctrines économiques depuis les physiocrates jusqu'à nos jours. Paris. 1909. 2nd edn. Paris 1913. 3rd edn. Paris 1926.

Trans. with title *A history of economic doctrines*, etc., by R. Richards, 1915, 2nd edn. with additional matter from the latest French edns. trans. Ernest F. Row, 1948.

1757 BEER (MAX). Pioneers of land reform. 1920.

See also Walter H. G. Armytage, *Heavens below. Utopian experiments in England 1560–1960*, 1961.

1758 WALKER (HELEN MARY). Studies in the history of statistical methods, with special reference to certain educational problems. Balt. 1929.

See also works on insurance (1458–62). Philip Abrams, *The origins of British sociology, 1834–1914*, 1968, has a chapter on the statistical inquiries of the 1830s. See also M. J. Cullen, *The statistical movement in early Victorian Britain. The foundations of empirical social research*, Hassocks, 1975.

1759 VINER (JACOB). Studies in the theory of international trade. [1937.]

1760 MacGREGOR (DAVID HUTCHISON). Economic thought and policy. 1949.

1761 ROBBINS (LIONEL CHARLES) *Baron*. The theory of economic policy in English classical political economy. 1952.

1762 SCHUMPETER (JOSEPH ALOIS). History of economic analysis. Ed. from MS. by Elizabeth Boody Schumpeter. 1955.

1763 LINK (ROBERT GRANT). English theories of economic fluctuations, 1815–1848. Columbia studies 598. 1959.
Chapters on Attwood, Malthus, Joplin, Wilson, Tooke, and J. S. Mill.

1764 TUCKER (GRAHAM SHARDALOW LEE). Progress and profits in British economic thought, 1650–1850. Camb. 1960.

1765 CORRY (BERNARD ALEXANDER). Money, saving and investment in English economics, 1800–1850. 1962.
Bibliog. 174–185.

1766 WINCH (DONALD NORMAN). Classical political economy and colonies. 1965.

1767 GRAMPP (WILLIAM DYER). Economic liberalism. 2 v. 1965.
V. 2 is relevant to the period 1789–1851.

1768 COATS (ALFRED WILLIAM) *ed*. The classical economists and economic policy. 1971.
Essays by different writers Ricardo, Senior, etc., and on the relationship between economic thought and legislation.

2. PARTICULAR ECONOMIC INSTITUTIONS AND WRITERS (in alphabetical order)

For Royal Statistical Society see (36).

1769 BENTHAM. Jeremy Bentham's economic writings. Critical edn. by Werner Stark. 3 v. 1952–4.
Based on printed works and unpublished manuscripts.

1770 BRAY (JOHN FRANCIS). Labour's wrongs and labour's remedy; or, The age of might and the age of right. Leeds. 1839. Repr. 1931.
Also *A voyage from Utopia*, ed. and introd. M. F. Lloyd-Prichard, 1957. This reply to criticisms of *Labour's wrongs and labour's remedy* was written 1840 and discovered in manuscript in 1937.

1771 CHALMERS (THOMAS). On political economy in connexion with the moral state and moral prospects of society. Glasgow. 1822. 2nd edn. Glasgow. 1832.

1772 ECONOMIST. Economist centenary book, 1843–1943. Oxford. 1943.

Essays by various writers. On its first editor, James Wilson, see Emilie Isabel Barring-ton, *The servant of all. Pages from the life of James Wilson*, 2 v., 1927.

1773 GRAY (JOHN). The economic doctrines of John Gray, 1799–1883. By Janet Kimball. (Catholic University of America Studies in economics. 21.) Washington. 1948.

1774 HODGSKIN (THOMAS). Labour defended against the claims of capital, or, The unproductiveness of capital proved with reference to the present combinations of journeymen. 1825. 3rd edn. rev. reprinted with intro. by G. D. H. Cole. 1922.

See also Hodgskin's *Popular political economy*, etc., 1827, *The natural and artificial right of property contrasted*, etc., pub. anonymously, 1832, and Élie Halévy, *Thomas Hodgskin, 1787–1869*, 1903, trans. and ed. Arthur John Taylor, 1956.

1775 HORNER (FRANCIS). The economic writings of Francis Horner in the *Edinburgh Review*, 1802–6. Ed. and intro. by Frank Whitson Fetter. (Reprints of scarce works on political economy. 13.) 1957.

1776 LONGFIELD (MOUNTIFORT). Lectures on political economy, delivered in Trinity and Michaelmas terms, 1833. Dublin 1834. Repr. (Reprints of scarce tracts in econ. and polit. science. 8.) 1931.

Also *Three lectures on commerce and one on absenteeism, delivered in . . . 1834*, etc., 1835, repr. (Reprints of scarce works on political economy, 4), 1938.

1777 LOYD (SAMUEL JONES). *1st baron Overstone*. The correspondence of Lord Overstone. Edited by Denis Patrick O'Brien. 3 v. Camb. 1971.

1778 McCULLOCH (JOHN RAMSAY). The principles of political economy; with a sketch of the rise and progress of the science. Edin. 1825. 2nd edn. enl. 1830.

See also Denis P. O'Brien, *J. R. McCulloch; a study in classical economics*, 1970, and (1384), (1420), (1480).

1779 MAITLAND (JAMES) *8th Earl of Lauderdale*. An inquiry into the nature and origin of public wealth, and into the means and causes of its increase. 1804. 2nd edn. gtly. enl. 1819.

See also (1780) for a modern discussion of his work.

1780 MALTHUS (THOMAS ROBERT). Principles of political economy considered with a view to their practical application. 1820. 2nd edn. 1836. Re-issue, Oxf. 1951.

See also *An inquiry into the nature and progress of rent*, etc., 1815, *The measure of value stated and illustrated, with an application of it to the alterations in the value of the English currency since 1790*, 1823, *Definitions in political economy*, 1827, Morton Paglin, *Malthus and Lauderdale. The anti-Ricardian tradition*, N.Y., 1961. For Malthus on population see (1691), for a bibliog. see (1753).

1781 MANCHESTER STATISTICAL SOCIETY. Economic and social
investigations in Manchester, 1833–1933. A centenary history of the Manchester
Statistical Society. By Thomas Southcliffe Ashton. 1934.

See also William Dyer Grampp, *The Manchester school of economics*, 1960.

1782 [MARCET (JANE)]. Conversations on political economy; in which the
elements of that science are familiarly explained. 1816. 2nd edn. 1817. 5th edn.
1824.

Explained to children.

1783 MARTINEAU (HARRIET). Illustrations of political economy. 9 v.
1832–4.

Illustrated in fiction.

1784 MILL (JAMES). Elements of political economy. 1821. 2nd edn. 1824.
3rd edn. rev. 1826.

Also *Commerce defended. An answer to the arguments by which Mr. Spence, Mr. Cobbett
and others have attempted to prove that commerce is not a source of national wealth*, 1808.
See also Donald N. Winch, *James Mill: selected economic writings*, Edin., 1966.

1785 MILL (JOHN STUART). Principles of political economy, with some
of their applications to social philosophy. 2 v. 1848. Rev. edns. 1849. 1852.
1857. 1862. 1865. 1871. Critical edn. by Sir William James Ashley. 1909.

Also *Essays on some unsettled questions of political economy*, 1844. The *Principles* are
repr. as v. II and III of the *Collected works*, ed. J. M. Robson, and the *Essays* in v. IV
and V. For full bibliog. and *Collected works* see (2815).

1786 POLITICAL ECONOMY CLUB, founded in London 1821. Minutes
of proceedings, 1899–1920, roll of members, and questions discussed, 1821–
1920, with documents bearing on the history of the club. (Political Economy
Club. Proceedings 6.) 1921.

Includes extracts from diaries of J. L. Mallet between 1823 and 1837 and J. L Prévost,
1838–52, reporting discussions.

1787 RICARDO. The works and correspondence of David Ricardo. Ed. by
Piero Sraffa and Maurice Herbert Dobb. 10 v. Cambridge. 1951–5.

Also earlier edns. by Edward Carter Kersey Gonner, of *Principles of political economy
and taxation*, 1891, repr. 1895, and of *Economic Essays*, 1923. See also Oswald St. Clair,
A key to Ricardo, 1957, and Mark Blaug, *Ricardian economics: A historical study* (Yale
studies in economics, 8), New Haven, 1958, bibliog. 243–61.

1788 SENIOR (NASSAU WILLIAM). An outline of the science of political
economy. 1836. 2nd edn. 1850. 6th edn. 1872. Reprinted (Library of economics. Classics of economic thought. 1) 1938.

For discussion see Marian Bowley, *Nassau Senior and classical economics*, 1937, for
biog. Samuel Leon Levy, *Nassau W. Senior, the prophet of modern capitalism*, 1943.

1789 SPENCE. The address of the Spencean philanthropists. [1816.]

Advocates of the communal ownership of land. See also (520).

1790 TORRENS (ROBERT). The Budget. On commercial and colonial policy. 2 pt. 1844.

Coll. edn. of tracts pub. 1841–3. Also important, *An essay on the production of wealth*, etc., 1821, and *Colonization of South Australia*, 1835, 2nd edn., 1836. For discussion see Lionel Charles Robbins, Baron Robbins, *Robert Torrens and the evolution of classical economics*, 1958, bibliog. 259–347, and T. W. Hutchison, 'Robert Torrens and classical economics', *Econ. H.R.*, 2nd ser. 11 (1958–9), 316–21 (Essays in bibliography and criticism, XXXVIII).

1791 WHATELY (RICHARD). Introductory lectures on political economy, being part of a course delivered in Easter term MDCCCXXXI. 1831–2. 3rd edn. rev. 1847. 4th edn. rev. and enl. 1855.

IX

SOCIAL HISTORY

A. SOCIAL CONDITIONS

1. General Works

See Wrigley (1696).

1792 CARR-SAUNDERS (ALEXANDER MORRIS) *and* WILSON (PAUL ALEXANDER). The professions. Oxf. 1933.

W. J. Reader, *Professional men. The rise of the professional classes in nineteenth century England*, 1966. For lawyers see (583), (587), for civil servants (451), for doctors (2528), for army (932), (934), for navy (1316), for clergy (723), (725) and Pugh (3150) on the foundation of the Royal College of Veterinary Surgeons, and Francis Michael Longstreth Thompson, *Chartered surveyors: the growth of a profession*, 1968.

1793 FAY (CHARLES RYLE). Life and labour in the nineteenth century. Camb. 1920. 4th edn. Camb. 1947.

A general survey.

1794 INTERNATIONAL REVIEW OF SOCIAL HISTORY. V. I+. Assen. Netherlands. 1956+.

Previously *International Review of Social History*, v. 1–4, Leiden, 1936–9, which absorbed *Bulletin of the International Institute of Social History*, v. 1–10, Amsterdam, 1932–5.

1795 READER (WILLIAM JOSEPH). Life in Victorian England. 1964.

A popular general account: in the same series, Sir Arthur Wynne Bryant, *The age of elegance, 1812–22*, 1950, and Reginald James White, *Life in Regency England*, 1963. See also John Ashton (1875).

1796 HARRISON (BRIAN). 'Underneath the Victorians.' *Victorian Studies*, 10 (1966–7), 239–62.

Surveys the Victorian literature of sex. See Vicinus (1964).

1797 PERKIN (HAROLD). The origins of modern English society, 1780–1880. 1969.

1798 HARRISON (JOHN FLETCHER CLEWS). The early Victorians, 1832–51. 1971.

1799 BURNETT (JOHN). Useful toil: autobiographies of working people from the 1820s to the 1920s. 1974.

2. RURAL SOCIETY

1800 HOWITT (WILLIAM). The rural life of England. 2 v. 1838. 2nd edn. rev. 1840.

By the same author, *The boy's country book; being the real life of a country boy*, 1839, descriptive of the Peak district. See also Alexander Somerville, *The whistler at the plough, containing travels, statistics, and descriptions of scenery and agricultural customs in most parts of England*, etc., 1852–3.

1801 HASBACH (WILHELM). Die englischen Landarbeiter in den letzten hundert Jahren und die Einhegungen. (Schriften des Vereins für Sozialpolitik, 59.) Leipzig. 1894.

English trans. by Ruth Kenyon, *A history of the agricultural labourer* (L.S.E. Studies in Econ. and Polit. Science, 15), 1908, reprinted 1920, 1966.

1802 HAMMOND (JOHN LAWRENCE LE BRETON) *and* HAMMOND (LUCY BARBARA). The village labourer, 1760–1832. A study in the government of England before the Reform Bill. 1911. 4th edn. 1927. Another edn. 2 v. 1948.

See also Richard Heath, *The English peasant. Studies historical, local, and biographic*, 1893, a description, based on observation, mainly on the 1870s but with some earlier history, and George Edwin Fussell, *The English rural labourer . . . from Tudor to Victorian times*, 1949, bibliog. 152–60.

1803 FUSSELL (GEORGE EDWIN) *and* FUSSELL (KATHLEEN ROSEMARY). The English countrywoman: a farmhouse social history, A.D. 1500–1900. 1953.

By the same authors, *The English countryman, his life and work, A.D. 1500–1900*, 1955. See also Harold John Massingham, *The English countryman; a study of the English tradition*, 1942, and, for a contemporary picture, Anne Hughes, *The diary of a farmer's wife, 1796–7*, comp. Suzanne Beedell [1965].

1804 BOVILL (EDWARD WILLIAM). English country life, 1780–1830. 1962.

See also Mary Russell Mitford, *Our Village*, sketches of country life first pub. *Lady's Magazine*, 1819, first coll. edn. 5 v., 1824–32, many later edns., and Sabine Baring-Gould, *Old country life*, 1890.

1805 THOMPSON (FRANCIS MICHAEL LONGSTRETH). English landed society in the nineteenth century. 1963.

Based on a detailed analysis of estate accounts. See also Gordon Edmund Mingay, *English landed society in the eighteenth century*, 1963. For landowners see also (1669–72). John Kersley Fowler, *Echoes of old county life, being recollections of sport, politics, and farming in the good old times*, 1892, county society in Buckinghamshire.

1806 HOBSBAWM (ERIC JOHN ERNEST) *and* RUDÉ (GEORGE E.) Captain Swing. 1969.

Also Alfred James Peacock, *Bread or blood; a study of the agrarian riots in East Anglia in 1816*, 1965, and J. P. D. Dunbabin, *Rural discontent in nineteenth century Britain*, 1974. See also Darvall. (99).

3. Urban Society

1807 HAMMOND (JOHN LAWRENCE LE BRETON) *and* HAMMOND (LUCY BARBARA). The town labourer, 1760–1832. The new civilisation. 1917. 2nd edn. 1920.

By the same authors, *The skilled labourer, 1760–1832*, 1919, 2nd edn., 1920, and *The age of the Chartists, 1832–1854. A Study of discontent*, 1930, all notable examples of the 'pessimistic' interpretation of the effects of industrialism.

1808 JOHNSON (LEONARD GEORGE). Social evolution of industrial Britain. Liverpool. 1959.

1809 SMELSER (NEIL JOSEPH). Social change in the industrial revolution. An application of theory to the Lancashire cotton industry, 1770–1840. 1959.

Discusses the effects of technological development on family structure and on social tension in the industry. See also Frances Collier, *The family economy of the working classes in the cotton industry, 1784–1833*, ed. Robert Sucksmith Fitton (from a thesis originally written 1920–1), Manchester [1964], and Michael Anderson, *Family structure in nineteenth century Lancashire*, Camb. 1972.

1810 THOMPSON (EDWARD PALMER). The making of the English working class. 1963.

A massive survey, from the corresponding societies of the 1790s to the reform bill agitation. See also Robert Featherstone Wearmouth, *Some working class movements of the nineteenth century*, 1948 [1949], emphasizing Methodist influence, and sympathetic to it, Asa Briggs, 'The language of "class" in early nineteenth century England' in *Essays in labour history*, etc., ed. Asa Briggs and John Saville, 1960, 43–73, and Eric John Ernest Hobsbawm, *Labouring men; studies in the history of labour*, 1964. For bibliog. see E. Dolléans and M. Crozier, *Mouvement ouvrier et socialiste; chronique et bibliographie*, 5 v., Paris, 1950–9. For early socialist political thought see (524), (537), (1757), for Luddites (99).

1811 URBAN HISTORY NEWSLETTER. 1+. Leicester. 1963+.

Continued by *Urban history yearbook*, Leicester, 1973+. See also Harold James Dyos, ed., *The study of urban history*, 1968, and, with Michael Wolff, eds., *The Victorian City: images and realities*, 2 v., 1973, a massive survey with many illustrations, but mainly on the second half of the century.

1812 THOMPSON (EDWARD PALMER). 'Time, work-discipline and industrial capitalism.' *Past and Present*, 38 (1967), 56–97.

1813 HOLLIS (PATRICIA) *ed*. Class and conflict in nineteenth century England, 1815–1850. 1973.

Also John Foster, *Class struggle and the Industrial Revolution. Early industrial capitalism in three English towns* [1974].

4. Condition of England Question

See also Mayhew (3765).

1814 ALVAREZ ESPRIELLA (DON MANUEL). [*Pseud.* of Robert Southey.] Letters from England, by Don Manuel Alvarez Espriella. Translated

from the Spanish. 3 v. 1807. Another edn. with intro. by Jack Simmons.
1951.

See also Robert Southey, *Sir Thomas More, or, Colloquies on the progress and prospects
of society*, 2 v., 1829, 2nd edn. 1831.

1815 KAY (JAMES PHILLIPS), *afterwards* KAY-SHUTTLEWORTH. The
moral and physical condition of the working classes employed in the cotton
manufacture in Manchester. 1832. 2nd edn. enl. 1832. Repr. Manchester.
1969.

1816 BULWER *afterwards* BULWER LYTTON (EDWARD GEORGE
EARLE LYTTON) *Baron Lytton*. England and the English. 2 v. 1833.

1817 GASKELL (P.). The manufacturing population of England, its moral,
social and physical condition, and the changes which have arisen from steam
machinery. 1833.

See also his *Artisans and machinery: the moral and physical condition of the manufacturing
population considered with reference to mechanical substitutes for human labour*, 1836, a
study of the effects of the mills on the structure of family life.

1818 [WAKEFIELD (EDWARD GIBBON).] England and America. A comparison of the social and political state of both nations. 1833.

1819 WADE (JOHN). History of the middle and working classes, with a
popular exposition of the economical and political principles which have
influenced the condition of the industrious orders. Also an appendix of prices.
1833.

1820 SYMONS (JELINGER COOKSON). Arts and artisans at home and
abroad; with sketches of the progress of foreign manufactures. Edin. 1839.

1821 BURET (ANTOINE EUGENE). De la misère des classes laborieuses
en Angleterre et en France: de la nature de la misère, de son existence, de ses
effets. 2 v. Paris. 1840.

1822 LESTER (CHARLES EDWARDS). The glory and shame of England.
2 v. 1841.

An attack on English conditions, gambling, poverty, etc.

1823 ADSHEAD (JOSEPH). Distress in Manchester. Evidence of the state of
the labouring classes in 1840–42. 1842.

Detailed local statistical inquiry.

1824 BAMFORD (SAMUEL). Walks in south Lancashire, and on its borders.
Blackley. 1844.

1825 CLARKSON (THOMAS). The grievances of our mercantile seamen,
a national and crying evil. 1845

1826 ENGELS (FRIEDRICH). Die Lage der arbeitenden Klasse in England. Nach eigner Anschauung und authentischen Quellen. Leipzig. 1845.

English trans. *The condition of the working class in England in 1844*, N.Y. 1887, London, 1892, new trans. and edn. by W. O. Henderson and W. H. Chaloner, Oxf. 1958.

1827 KAY (JOSEPH). The social condition and education of the people in England and Europe; shewing the results of the primary schools and the division of landed property in foreign countries. 2 v. 1850.

1828 BEAMES (THOMAS). The rookeries of London, past, present, and prospective. 1850.

1829 GREEN (SAMUEL GOSNELL). The working classes of Great Britain: their present condition and the means of their improvement and elevation. [1850.]

1830 LUDLOW (JOHN MALCOLM) *and* JONES (LLOYD). The progress of the working classes, 1832–1867. 1867.

A general survey of social legislation, improvement, newspapers, temperance, etc.

5. British Travellers in Britain

See also bibliogs. in Williams (1364) and Anderson (3515).

1831 MAVOR (WILLIAM FORDYCE). The British tourists, comprehending the most celebrated tours in the British Islands. 6 v. 1798–1800. 3rd edn. 1809.

Summaries of the more popular tours: v. 5 and 6 are concerned with years after 1790. See also Esther Moir, *The discovery of Britain: the English tourists, 1540 to 1840*, 1964, with extensive bibliog. of tours, 157–178.

1832 SKRINE (HENRY). Two successive tours throughout the whole of Wales with several of the adjacent English counties. 1798.

1833 WARNER (RICHARD). A walk through some of the western counties of England. Bath. 1800.

Also the same writer's *A tour through the northern counties of England, and the borders of Scotland*, 2 v., Bath, 1802, and *A tour through Cornwall, in the autumn of 1808*, Bath, 1809.

1834 PHILLIPS (*Sir* RICHARD). Personal tour through the United Kingdom; describing living objects and contemporaneous interests. Nos. 1, 2 [1828.]

Mainly on the midlands.

1835 COBBETT (WILLIAM). Rural rides, in the counties of Surrey, Kent, Sussex, Hants, Berks, Oxford, Bucks, Wilts, Somerset, Gloucester, Hereford, Salop, Worcester, Stafford, Leicester, Hertford, Essex, Suffolk, Norfolk, Cambridge, Huntingdon, Nottingham, Lincoln, York, Lancaster, Durham, and Northumberland in the years 1821, 1822, 1823, 1825, 1826, 1829, 1830: with economical and political observations relative to matters applicable to, and illustrated by, the state of those counties respectively. 2 v. 1830. Later edns. 1853. 2 v. 1885. Modern edn. ed. by G. D. H. and Margaret Cole, 3 v., 1930.

1836 HEAD (*Sir* GEORGE). A home tour through the manufacturing districts and other parts of England, in the summer of 1835. 1836. New edn. 2 v. 1840. Reprinted 1968.

Also in continuation, *A home tour through various parts of the United Kingdom*, etc., 1837, 2nd edn. 2 v., 1840.

1837 MACRITCHIE (WILLIAM). Diary of a tour through Great Britain in 1795. Ed. David MacRitchie, 1897.

1838 BYNG (JOHN), *later 5th Viscount Torrington*. The Torrington diaries, containing the tours through England and Wales of the Hon. John Byng . . . between the years 1781 and 1794. Ed. by Cyril Bruyn Andrews, with an introduction by John Beresford. 4 v. 1934–8.

6. Overseas Travellers in Britain

1839 LETTS (MALCOLM HENRY IKIN). As the foreigner saw us. 1935.

Also Edward Smith, *Foreign visitors in England, and what they have thought of us*, etc., 1889. On American visitors see Robert Ernest Spiller, *The American in England during the first half century of independence*, N.Y. [1926], and Robert Balmain Mowat, *Americans in England*, Cambridge, Mass., 1935. On French travellers see Margery E. Elkington, *Les relations de société entre l'Angleterre et la France, 1814–30*, Paris, 1929, Ethel Jones *Les voyageurs français en Angleterre de 1815 à 1830*, Paris, 1930, and Margaret Isobel Bain, *Les voyageurs français en Ecosse, 1770–1830, et leurs curiosités intellectuelles*, Paris, 1931. See also Margery Weiner, *The French exiles, 1789–1815*, 1960. For German travellers see Robert Elsasser *Über die politischen Bildungsreisen der Deutschen nach England (vom achtzehnten Jahrhundert bis 1815)*, Heidelberg, 1917 (Heidelberger Abhandlungen zur mittleren und neueren Geschichte, 51), and William Douglas Robson-Scott, *German travellers in England, 1400–1800*, Oxf., 1953. The value of these travellers' evidence is discussed in Radzinowicz (2581). See also bibliogs. in Anderson (3515), and for Italian exiles Wicks (314).

1840 LA TOCNAYE (—— DE). Promenade autour de la Grande Bretagne par un officier français emigré. Edin. 1795. 2nd edn. 1801.

1841 MEISTER (JACQUES HENRI). Letters written during a residence in England. Translated from the French of Henry Meister. (Together with a letter from the Margravine of Anspach to the author.) 1799.

French title, *Souvenirs de mes voyages en Angleterre en 1789 et 1792*, Zurich, 1795. General praise of British political institutions.

1842 NEMNICH (PHILIPP ANDREAS). Beschreibung einer im Sommer 1799 von Hamburg nach und durch England geschenen Reise. Tübingen. 1800.

Also *Neueste Reise durch England, Schottland, und Irland, hauptsächlich in Bezug auf Produkte, Fabriken, und Handlung*, Tübingen, 1807. Both works are strongly economic in content.

1843 FIÉVÉE (JOSEPH). Lettres sur l'Angleterre, et réflexions sur la philosophie du XVIIIe siècle. Paris. 1802.

1844 GOEDE (CHRISTIAN AUGUST GOTTLIEB). England, Wales,
Irland und Schottland. 2 edn. 5 pt. Dresden. 1806.
Eng. trans., *The stranger in England, or, Travels in Great Britain*, 3 v., 1807.

1845 SVEDENSTIERNA (ERICH THOMAS). Reise durch einen Theil von
England und Schottland in den Jahren 1802 und 1803, besonders in berg- und
hüttenmännischer, technologischer und mineralogischer Hinsicht. Aus dem
Schwedischen, mit einigen Anmerkungen und Erlauferungen von J. G.
Blumhof. Marburg and Cassel. 1811. Translated by Ernest L. Dellow, with
a new intro. by M. W. Flinn. Newton Abbot. 1973.

1846 LÉVIS (PIERRE MARC GASTON *duc de*). L'Angleterre au commencement du dix-neuvième siècle. Paris. 1814.
Comments on crime, religion, social conditions.

1847 PILLET (RENÉ MARTIN). L'Angleterre vue à Londres et dans ses
provinces pendant un séjour de dix années, dont six comme prisonnier de
guerre. Paris. 1815. English edn. Boston. Mass. 1818.
Strongly anti-British.

1848 [SIMOND (LOUIS).] Journal of a tour and residence in Great Britain
during the years 1810 and 1811, by a French traveller. 2 v. Edin. 1815.

1849 SAY (JEAN-BAPTISTE). De l'Angleterre et les Anglais. London and
Paris. 1815.
Eng. trans. by John Richter, *England and the English people*, rev. and enl. 1816.

1850 SILLIMAN (BENJAMIN). A journal of travels in England, Holland,
and Scotland . . . in the years 1805 and 1806. 1st edn. 2 v. N.Y. 1810. 2nd
edn. Boston. 1812. 3rd edn. New Haven. 1820.

1851 GRISCOM (JOHN). A year in Europe, comprising a journal of observations in England, Scotland, Ireland, France, Switzerland, the north of Italy
and Holland. In 1818 and 1819. 2 v. N.Y. 1823. 2nd edn. 1824.

1852 BLANQUI (JERÔME ADOLPHE). Voyage d'un jeune Français en
Angleterre et en Écosse, pendant l'automne de 1823. Paris. 1824.

1853 MONTULÉ (ÉDOUARD DE). Voyage en Angleterre et en Russie
pendant les années 1821, 1822, et 1823. 2 v. Paris. 1825.

1854 MEIDINGER (HEINRICH). Reisen durch Grossbritannien und Irland
vorzüglich in topographischer, kommerzieller, und statistischer Hinsicht. 2 v.
Frankfurt-am-Main. 1828.
Very substantial economic descriptions.

1855 STAËL-HOLSTEIN (AUGUSTE LOUIS DE). Lettres sur l'Angleterre. Paris. 1825. New edn. Paris. 1829.

Eng. trans. *Letters on England*, 1825, 2nd edn. 1830: mostly a commentary on upper-
class life.

1856 CUSTINE (ASTOLPHE *Marquis de*). Mémoires et voyages, ou,
Lettres écrites à diverses époques, pendant des courses en Suisse, en Calabre,
en Angleterre et en Écosse. 2 v. Paris. 1830.

1857 PÜCKLER-MUSKAU (*Prince* HERMANN LUDWIG HEINRICH
VON). Briefe eines Verstorbenen. Ein fragmentarisches Tagebuch aus England, Wales, Irland und Frankreich, geschrieben in den Jahren 1828 und 1829.
4 v. Stuttgart. 1831.

Trans., together with earlier material, by Sarah Austin as *Tour in England, Ireland and
France in the years 1825, 1826, 1827, 1828, and 1829*, 4 v., 1832, new edn. from this
trans. ed. E. M. Butler, *A Regency visitor, the English tour of Prince Pückler-Muskau ...
1826–28*, 1957.

1858 LEMERCHER DE LONGPRÉ (CHARLES), *Baron d'Haussez*. La
Grande Bretagne en mil huit cent trente trois. 2 v. Brussels. 1833.

Eng. trans. *Great Britain in 1833*, 2 v., 1833.

1859 MELFORT (ÉDOUARD, *comte de*). Impressions of England. 2 v. 1836.

1860 RAUMER (FRIEDRICH LUDWIG GEORG VON). England im
Jahre 1835. 2 v. Leipzig. 1836.

Followed by *England im Jahre 1841*, Leipzig, 1842. Eng. trans., *England in 1835*, by
Sarah Austin and [H. E. Lloyd], 3 v., 1836, and *England in 1841* trans. H. E. Lloyd, 2
v., 1842.

1861 COLTON (CALVIN). Four years in Great Britain. 2 v. N.Y. 1835.

Foreign correspondent of the *New York Observer*.

1862 COOPER (JAMES FENIMORE). England; with sketches of society in
the metropolis. 3 v. 1837.

1863 FISK (WILLBUR). Travels on the continent of Europe, in England,
Ireland, Scotland, France. N.Y. 1838.

1864 HUMPHREY (HEMAN). Great Britain, France and Belgium: a short
tour in 1835. 2 v. N.Y. 1838.

Interested in religion, charities, and teetotalism.

1865 KOHL (JOHANN GEORG). Reisen in England und Wales. 3 v.
Dresden and Leipzig. 1844.

Trans. Thomas Roscoe as *Travels in England and Wales*, Bristol, 1845. repr. 1968.

1866 FAUCHER (LÉON LEONARD JOSEPH). Études sur l'Angleterre.
2 v. Paris. 1845.

1867 CARUS (CARL GUSTAV). England und Schottland im Jahre 1844.
2 v. Berlin. 1845.

> Trans. S. C. Davison as *The king of Saxony's journey through England and Scotland in the year 1844,* 1846.

1868 GREELEY (HORACE). Glances at Europe; in a series of letters during
the summer of 1851, including notices of the Great Exhibition or World's
Fair. N.Y. 1851.

1869 BREMER (FREDRIKA). England in 1851; or, Sketches of a tour in
England. Trans. from the German by L. A. H. Boulogne. 1853.

1870 EMERSON (RALPH WALDO). English traits. 1856.

1871 FOSCOLO. Ugo Foscolo. An Italian in Regency England. By Eric
Reginald Pearce Vincent. Camb. 1953.

1872 TOCQUEVILLE (ALEXIS CHARLES HENRI MAURICE CLÉREL
Comte de). Voyages en Angleterre, Irlande, Suisse et Algérie. Ed. J. P. Mayer.
Œuvres completes v. 5. Paris. 1958.

> Trans. George Lawrence and J. P. Mayer as *Journeys to England and Ireland,* 1958.

B. SOCIAL AND DOMESTIC

1. GENERAL MANNERS AND CUSTOMS

See also Pargellis and Medley (2), 1778.

1873 GROSE (FRANCIS). A provincial glossary, with a collection of local
proverbs, and popular superstitions. 1787. 2nd edn. cor. and enl. 1790. New
edn. cor. 1811.

> Also, by the same author, *A classical dictionary of the vulgar tongue,* 1785, rev. and cor.
> by Pierce Egan, 1823. See also James Hardy Vaux, *A new and concise vocabulary of the
> flash language,* 1819, and Jon Bee (*pseud.* of John Badcock), *Slang. A dictionary of the
> turf, the ring, the chase, the pit, of bon ton and the varieties of life,* 1823. See also Wilfred
> Bonser, ed., *Proverb literature; a bibliography of works relating to proverbs,* Folk Lore
> Society, 1930, and, for early investigation of the subject, Richard Mercer Dorson, *The
> British folklorists; a history,* 1968, bibliog. 442–60.

1874 DOYLE (RICHARD). Manners and customs of ye Englyshe. To which
be added some extracts from Mr. Pips hys Diary, contrybuted by P. Leigh.
[1849.]

> Illustrations of railway buffet, cricket, dining on whitebait, and other contemporary
> scenes.

1875 ASHTON (JOHN). Old times: a picture of social life at the end of the
eighteenth century. 1885.

> Political and anecdotal. Ashton wrote many similar works, among them *The dawn of the
> nineteenth century in England,* etc., 2 v., 1886 [1885], and *Gossip in the first decade of
> Victoria's reign,* 1903. Similar in style is Edwin Beresford Chancellor, *Life in Regency
> and early Victorian times, . . . 1800–1850,* 1926 [1927].

1876 TRAILL (HENRY DUFF) *ed.* Social England, a record of the progress of the people in religion, laws, learning, arts, industry, commerce, science, literature, and manners, from the earliest times to the present day. 6 v. 1893–7. Illus. edn. ed. by H. D. Traill and James S. Mann. 6 v. 1901–4.

1877 QUENNELL (MARJORIE *and* CHARLES HENRY BOURNE). A history of everyday things in England. V. 3. 1733–1851. 1933.

1878 STEEL (ANTHONY). Jorrocks's England. 1932.

Other general studies include Esmé Wingfield-Stratford *The squire and his relations,* 1956, Owen Chadwick, *Victorian miniature,* 1960. See also (1804) and (1906).

1879 JOHNSON (REGINALD BRIMLEY). Manners makyth man; an anthology from the great writers illustrating English manners and customs throughout the centuries. 1927.

See also Jane Webb (afterwards Mrs. Loudon), *The lady's country companion; or, how to enjoy country life rationally,* 1845, 4th edn., 1852, *The habits of good society; a handbook of etiquette for ladies and gentlemen,* etc. [1859].

1880 PARREAUX (ANDRÉ). Daily life in England in the reign of George III; translated [from the French] by Carola Congreve. 1969. (Fr. edn. Paris. 1966.)

2. FOOD, DRINK, TOBACCO, SERVANTS

1881 BRAGGE (WILLIAM). Bibliotheca nicotiana: a catalogue of books about tobacco. [Birmingham.] 1874. 2nd edn. enl. 1880.

See also Egon Caesar, Count Corti, *A history of smoking,* trans. Paul England, 1931, Hugh McCausland, *Snuff and snuff boxes,* 1951, Mark Hamilton Freer Chaytor, *The Wilsons of Sharrow: the snuff makers of Sheffield,* Sheffield, 1962.

1882 OXFORD (ARNOLD WHITAKER). English cookery books to the year 1850. Oxf. 1913.

Other bibliogs. are Katherine Golden Bitting, *Gastronomic bibliography,* San Francisco, 1939, André Louis Simon, *Bibliotheca gastronomica,* etc., 1953, usefully arranged with subject indexes.

1883 SIMON (ANDRÉ LOUIS). Bibliotheca vinaria. 1913.

See also Cyrus Redding, *A history and description of modern wines,* 1833, 2nd edn. 1836, 3rd edn. 1871, an exhaustive and standard work.

1884 [RUNDELL (MARIA ELIZABETH).] A new system of domestic cookery. By a lady. 1809. 64th edn. Remodelled and improved by E. Roberts. 1840.

Other notable or informative cookery books include William Kitchiner, *Apicius redivivus; or, The cook's oracle,* etc., 1817, 6th edn., 1823, also his *The art of invigorating and prolonging life by food, clothes . . . methods to prevent and relieve indigestion . . . to which is added, The pleasure of making a will. Finis coronat opus,* 1821. See also *A new system of practical domestic economy,* 3rd edn. rev. 2 pt., 1823, Eliza Acton, *Modern cookery in all its branches,* 1845, 6th edn., 1846. *The magazine of domestic economy,* 1836–42, continued as *The magazine of domestic economy and family review,* 1843–4, is a general magazine of household management.

1885 CARÊME (MARIE ANTONIN). French cookery; comprising l'art de
la cuisine française; le pâtissier royal; le cuisinier parisien. Trans. by William
Hall. 1836.

Elaborate recipes by the chef to Talleyrand. Also see, for high-class cookery, Thomas
Masters, *The ice book, being a compendious and concise history of everything connected with
ice*, 1844.

1886 SOYER (ALEXIS). The gastronomic regenerator. 1–4th edns. 1846.

A contemporary best-seller. By the same writer, *The modern housewife or ménagère*, etc.,
1849. For his life see *Memoirs of Alexis Soyer*, etc., ed. F. Volant and J. R. Warren,
1859, and Helen Morris, *Portrait of a chef; the life of Alexis Soyer sometime chef to the
Reform Club*, Cambridge, 1938.

1887 DRUMMOND (JACK CECIL) *and* WILBRAHAM (ANNE). The
Englishman's food; a history of five centuries of English diet. 1939.

On the same subject, John Burnett, *Plenty and want; a social history of diet in England
from 1815 to the present day*, 1966. On vegetarianism see Joseph Ritson, *An essay on
abstinence from food as a moral duty*, 1802, and John Frank Newton, *The return to nature,
or, A defence of the vegetable regimen*, 1811. See also Daniel Carr, *The necessity of brown
bread for digestion, nourishment, and sound health, and the injurious effects of white bread*,
1847. Benjamin Thompson, Count Rumford, *An essay on food and particularly on feeding
the poor, exhibiting the science of nutrition*, etc., new edn. by Sir R. Musgrave, Dublin,
1847. On food adulteration see Frederick Accum, *Treatise on the adulteration of food and
culinary poisons . . . and methods of detecting them*, 1820, a mass of detailed information
on current practices, Peter Lund Simmonds, *Coffee as it is and as it ought to be*, 1850, and
Frederick Arthur Filby, *A history of food adulteration and analysis*, 1934.

1888 JEKYLL (GERTRUDE). Old English household life. 1925. New edn.
with add. by Sydney Robert Jones. 1939.

See also Esther Hewlett (afterwards Copley), *Cottage comforts*, etc., Oxf. 1825, 17th edn.
1841, general housekeeping advice to young labourers.

1889 HECHT (JOSEPH JEAN). The domestic servant class in eighteenth-
century England. 1956.

See also John Coakley Lettsom, *Hints to masters and mistresses respecting female servants*,
1800, urging humane treatment, [Thomas Cosnett], *The footman's directory and butler's
remembrancer*, etc., 1823, Samuel and Sarah Adams, *The complete servant*, 1825, Mrs.
William Parkes, *Domestic duties*, etc., 2nd edn. 1825, and *The servant's guide and family
manual*, 1830. *The guide to service*, 17 pt. in 4 v., 1838–44, consists of individual tracts
concerning governesses, farm servants, clerks, bank clerks, in addition to domestic
servants. See also James Williams, *The footman's guide*, etc., 4th edn., 1847.

3. DRESS

1890 COLAS (RENÉ). Bibliographie générale du costume et de la mode. 2 v.
Paris. 1933.

1891 PYNE (WILLIAM HENRY). The costume of Great Britain. 1808.

Coloured plates, unusual in giving illustrations of working class dress.

1892 BOEHN (ULRICH VON). Menschen und Moden im neunzehnten
Jahrhundert. 4 v. 1908–19.

Trans. by M. Edwardes with title *Modes and manners of the nineteenth century*, and two additional chapters by Grace Thompson, 4 v., 1927. See also Max von Boehn, *Modes and manners; ornaments; lace, fans, gloves, walking-sticks, parasols, jewelry, and trinkets* [1929].

1893 HOLLAND (VYVYAN BERESFORD). Handcoloured fashion plates, 1770–1899. 1955.

Contains lists of fashion periodicals and bibliog. information. See also Isabel Stevenson Monro and Dorothy E. Cook, *Costume index: a subject index to plates and to illustrated text*, N.Y., 1937, suppt. by Isabel Stevenson Monro and Kate M. Monro, N.Y., 1937. Doris Langley Moore, *Woman in fashion*, 1950, photographs period costumes from the author's collection worn by living models. Charles Harvard Gibbs-Smith, *The fashionable lady in the nineteenth century*, 1960, is based on the collections in the Victoria and Albert Museum.

1894 COSTUME: the journal of the Costume Society. V. 1+. 1967+.

See also the Society's *Annual Conference proceedings*, no. 1+, 1968+.

1894A CUNNINGTON (CECIL WILLETT) *and* CUNNINGTON (PHILLIS). A handbook of English costume in the eighteenth century. 1957.

By the same authors, *Handbook of English costume in the nineteenth century*, 1959, 3rd edn., 1970; both are indispensable. By the same authors and Charles Beard, *A dictionary of English costume (900–1900)*, 1960, a dictionary of terms used. Works on special aspects include George Walker, *The tailor's masterpiece*, [1838?], *The workwoman's guide, containing instructions . . . in cutting out and completing those articles of wearing apparel . . . which are usually made at home, etc., By a Lady*, 1838, Mary J. Howell, *Handbook of millinery*, etc., 1847. Equally detailed technical studies by modern writers include Iris Brooke, *English children's costume since 1775*, etc., 1930, Cecil Willett Cunnington and Phillis Cunnington, *The history of underclothes*, 1951, and three books by Norah Waugh, *Corsets and crinolines*, 1954, *The cut of men's clothes 1600–1900*, 1964, and *The cut of women's clothes, 1600–1930*, 1968, and Phillis Cunnington and Alan Mansfield, *English costume for sports and outdoor recreation from the sixteenth to the nineteenth centuries*, 1969.

4. Sports and Pastimes

(a) *General*

1895 HIGGINSON (ALEXANDER HENRY). British and American sporting authors; their writings and biographies. 1951. Bibliog. by Sydney R. Smith, 399–437.

An admirable introduction. See also Ralph Henry Nevill, *Old English sporting prints*, 1923, and his *Old English sporting books*, 1924, and Charles Francis George Richard Schwerdt, *Hunting, hawking, shooting, illustrated in a catalogue of books, manuscripts, prints and drawings*, 3 v., privately printed, 1928.

1896 ADAMS (JOHN). An analysis of horsemanship, teaching the whole art of riding. 3 v. 1805.

1897 DANIEL (WILLIAM BARKER). Rural sports. 4 v. New edn. with suppt. 1812–13.

See also Henry Alken, *The national sports of Great Britain*, 1821, magnificent coloured plates of all sports, including bear and bull-baiting, written with a humanitarian tendency, John Mayer, gamekeeper, *The sportsman's directory . . . containing abstracts of the last game laws*, 4th edn., 1823, *Pierce Egan's book of sports and mirror of life*, etc., 2 v., 1832, Delabre P. Blaine, *An encyclopaedia of rural sports*, new edn. rev. and cor. by 'Harry Hieover' (*pseud.* of Charles Bindley), 1852.

1898 NEW SPORTING MAGAZINE. 19 v. 1831–40. New ser. 60 v. 1841–70.

Both Nimrod and Surtees contributed to this: see (1906). Other magazines include *Sporting magazine, or, Monthly calendar of the turf, the chace*, etc., v. 1–50, 1793–1817, v. 51–100, 1817–42, third ser. 1843–70, *The Annals of sporting and fancy gazette*, 13 v. 1822–8, *Bell's life in London and Sporting Chronicle*, 1822–88.

1899 ASH (EDWARD CECIL). Dogs: their history and development. 2 v. 1927.

Classic history of various breeds. See also *The sportsman's cabinet, or, A correct delineation of the various dogs used in the sports of the field*, by 'A veteran sportsman' [i.e. William Taplin], 2 v., 1803–4.

1900 MALCOLMSON (ROBERT W.). Popular recreations in English society, 1700–1850. Camb. 1973.

(b) *Field Sports*

1901 HAWKER (PETER). Instructions to young sportsmen in all that relates to guns and shooting. 1814. 6th edn. cor. and enl. 1830. 9th edn. further improved. 1844.

By the same author, *The diary of Colonel Peter Hawker, 1802–1853*, with intro. by Sir Ralph Payne-Gallwey, 2 v., 1893. On the game laws see Chester Kirby, 'The English game law system', *A.H.R.* 38 (1932–3), 240–62, and his 'The attack on the English game laws', *Jour. Mod. Hist.* 4 (1932), 18–37, and (634). On sporting guns see (1048).

1902 SCROPE (WILLIAM). The art of deer stalking, illustrated by a narrative of a few days' sport in the forest of Atholl. 1838.

Illustrated by Edwin and Charles Landseer and the author.

1903 HARTING (JAMES EDMUND). Bibliotheca accipitraria; a catalogue of books, ancient and modern, relating to falconry. 1891.

See also Francis Henry Salvin and William Brodrick, *Falconry in the British Isles*, 1855, 2nd edn. 1873.

1904 WESTWOOD (THOMAS) *and* SATCHELL (THOMAS). Bibliotheca piscatoria, a catalogue of books on angling, the fisheries and fish culture. 1883. Supp. by Robert Bright Marston. 1901.

See also bibliog. in Daniel (1897).

1905 SCOTT (GEORGE RYLEY). The history of cockfighting [1957?]

See also William Sketchley, *The cocker, containing every information to the breeders and amateurs of . . . the game cock*, etc., 1814.

1906 BOVILL (EDWARD WILLIAM). The England of Nimrod and Surtees, 1815–1854. 1959. Bibliog. 174–6.

For 'Nimrod' (Charles James Apperley), see *My life and times*, ed. with additions by

Edward William Dirom Cuming, Edin., 1927, with bibliog. of his works. For Surtees see *Robert Smith Surtees (creator of Jorrocks), 1803–1864, by himself and E. D. Cuming*, Edin., 1924, based on a MS. autobiography written *c.* 1864 and first pub. 1924, also Frederick Watson, *Robert Smith Surtees; a critical study*, 1933, bibliog. 274–9, with list of Surtees' works. Other hunting biogs. are *Reminiscences of Thomas Assheton Smith, Esq.*, by John Eardley Wilmot, 6th edn. with intro. by Sir Herbert Maxwell, 1902, and *Squire Osbaldeston, his autobiography*, ed. E. W. D. Cuming, 1926, based on a MS. written 1856. Technical treatises include John Cook, *Observations on fox-hunting and the management in the kennels and in the field*, 1826, new edn. 1922, Robert Thomas Vyner, *Notitia venatica; a treatise on foxhunting. To which is added a compendious kennel stud book*, 1841. For histories of hunts see Thomas Francis Dale, *The history of the Belvoir hunt*, Westminster, 1899, Thomas Guy Frederick Paget, *The Melton Mowbray of John Ferneley, 1782–1860*, Leicester, 1931, and Colin Dare Bernard Ellis, *Leicestershire and the Quorn hunt*, Leicester, 1951.

(c) Racing and Steeplechasing

1907 COOK (*Sir* THEODORE ANDREA). History of the English turf. 3 v. [1901–4.]

See also James Christie Whyte, *History of the British turf, from the earliest period to the present day*, 2 v., 1840, James Rice, *History of the British turf from the earliest time to the present day*, 2 v., 1879, William Day, *Reminiscences of the turf with anecdotes and recollections of its principal celebrities*, 2nd edn., 1886, Thormanby (*pseud.* of Willmott Dixon), *Kings of the turf; memoirs and anecdotes of distinguished owners*, etc., 1898. Racing biographies include John Kent, junior, *Racing life of Lord George Cavendish Bentinck, M.P.* ed. Francis Lawley, 1892, and Thomas Henry Bird, *Admiral Rous and the English turf, 1795–1877*, 1939.

1908 CAWTHORN (GEORGE JAMES) *and* HEROD (RICHARD S.). Royal Ascot, its history and associations. Rev. and enl. edn. 1900.

1909 ORCHARD (VINCENT). Tattersalls: two hundred years of sporting history. 1953.

1910 MORTIMER (ROGER). The Jockey Club. 1958.

See also Robert Black, *The Jockey Club and its founders in three periods*, 1891.

(d) Outdoor Games

1911 NOEL (EVAN BAILLIE) *and* CLARK (JAMES OSCAR MAX). A history of tennis. 2 v. 1924.

1912 ALTHAM (HARRY SURTEES) *and* SWANTON (ERNEST WILLIAM). A history of cricket. New edn. 1938. 3rd edn. 1947. 4th edn. 1948.

1st edn., by Altham alone, 1926. See also Frederick Lillywhite, *Lillywhite's illustrated handbook of cricket*, 1844, and his *Frederick Lillywhite's cricket scores and biographies of celebrated cricketers from 1764*, etc., 1862; Sir Jeremiah Colman, *The noble game of cricket, illustrated from drawings, prints*, etc., in the collection of Sir Jeremiah Colman, privately printed, 1941, a book of plates; John Arlott, ed., *From Hambledon to Lords; the classics of cricket, John Nyren, Charles Cowden Clarke, the Rev. James Pycroft, the Rev. John Mitford*, 1948, and the same editor's '*The middle ages of cricket; being sketches of the players' by William Denison*, 'Cricket recollections' *from Oxford memories by James Pycroft. The whole assembled, ed. and discussed by John Arlott* [1949]; Sir Pelham Francis Warner, *Gentlemen v. Players, 1806–1849*, 1950; Rowland Bowen, *Cricket, a history of its growth and development*, 1970.

1913   DARWIN (BERNARD). A history of golf in Britain. 1952.

See also James Bell Salmond, *The story of the R. & A. being the history of the first 200 years of the Royal and Ancient Golf Club of St. Andrews,* 1956.

1914   MARPLES (MORRIS). A history of football. 1954.

See also (1916).

(e) *Other Sports*

1915   EGAN (PIERCE). Boxiana: or, Sketches of ancient and modern pugilism. Nos. 1–21. 1812–[13]. 2 v. 1818. 5 v. 1812–[29].

Henry Downes Miles, *Pugilistica: being one hundred and forty-four years of the history of British boxing,* 3 v. [1880–1], v. 1 to 1820, v. 2, 1814–35, v. 3, 1835–63, and Pierce Egan, *Every gentleman's manual; a lecture on the art of self-defence,* etc., 1845. Also John Ford, *Prizefighting: the age of Regency boximania,* Newton Abbot, 1971.

1916   SHEARMAN (*Sir* MONTAGUE). Athletics and football. Badminton Library. 3rd edn. 1889.

1917   THIMM (CARL ALBERT). A complete bibliography of the art of fence as practised by all European nations from the earliest period to the present day. 1891.

See also Rowland Ingram, *Reflections on duelling,* 1804.

1918   CLARK (RONALD W.). The Victorian mountaineers. 1953.

See also Sir Charles Fellows, *A narrative of an ascent to the summit of Mont Blanc, of the 25th July, 1827,* 1827.

1919   HEATON (PETER). Yachting: a history. 1955. Bibliog. 271–3.

See also Montague John Guest and William Biggs Boulton, *The Royal Yacht Squadron; memorials of its members,* etc. 1903.

1920   CLEAVER (HYLTON REGINALD). A history of rowing. 1957. Bibliog. 245–8.

See also Walter Bradford Woodgate, *Boating,* 1888 (Badminton library), and George Carr Drinkwater and Terence Robert Beaumont Sanders, *The University Boat Race official centenary history, 1829–1929,* 1929.

(f) *Indoor Games*

1921   KENTFIELD (EDWIN). The game of billiards, scientifically explained and practically set forth, etc., 1839.

1922   ASHTON (JOHN). The history of gambling in England. 1898.

Andrew Steinmetz, *The gaming table; its votaries and victims,* etc., 2 v. 1870, and (1952), (2572).

1923   JESSEL (FREDERIC). A bibliography of works in English on playing cards and gaming. 1905.

1733 entries and analytical index. See also *Faro, and rouge et noir; the mode of playing*

. . . *extracted from De Moivre*, etc., 1793, Charles Pigott, *Pigott's new Hoyle* . . . *containing rules and instructions for playing twenty games*, etc., 1800, Thomas Matthews, *Advice to the young whist player*, 7th edn. 1813, 18th edn. 1828, James Burney, *An essay by way of lecture on the game of whist*, 1821, and many subsequent edns. For the many edns. of Hoyle see a series of articles by Julian Marshall in *N. & Q.*, 9th s., v. 2–6, 1888–90.

1924 SERGEANT (PHILIP WALSINGHAM). A century of British chess. 1934.

1925 WHITEHOUSE (FRANCIS REGINALD BEAMAN). Table games of Georgian and Victorian days. 1951. 2nd edn. rev. Royston. 1971.

See also Robert Charles Bell, *Board and table games from many civilizations*, 2nd edn., 2 v., Oxf., 1969.

1926 WINDER (ROLAND). Check list of the older books on conjuring in the library of Roland Winder as at December, 1966. Leeds. [1967.]

(g) Dancing

1927 BEAUMONT (CYRIL WILLIAM). A bibliography of dancing. 1929.

Confined to B.L. books; alphabetically arranged. See also Paul David Magriel, *A bibliography of dancing; a list of books and articles on the dance and related subjects*, N.Y., 1936.

1928 GUEST (IVOR FORBES). The romantic ballet in England, its development, fulfilment and decline. 1954.

See also Felicitée Sheila Forrester, *Ballet in England; a bibliography and survey c. 1700–June 1966*, etc., Library Assoc. Bibliogs. 9, 1968.

1929 RICHARDSON (PHILIP JOHN SAMPEY). The social dances of the nineteenth century in England. 1960.

See also Thomas Wilson, *An analysis of country dancing*, etc., 1808, and his *A companion to the ball room*, etc., 1816, Henri Cellarius, *The drawing room dances*, 1847.

(h) Theatre

(For opera see (3050). General bibliogs. and histories, together with the lives of actors who were also playwrights are listed under Drama.)

(i) Bibliographies and Journals

1930 THEATRE NOTEBOOK, a quarterly journal of the history and technique of the British theatre. Pub. by Society for theatre research. 1945+.

The society also republishes theatrical classics in its annual volumes.

1931 LOEWENBERG (ALFRED) *ed*. The theatre of the British Isles, excluding London. 1950.

Lists towns alphabetically, followed by their theatres. See also (3837).

1932 STOTT (RAYMOND TOOLE). Circus and allied arts: a world bibliography, 1500–1962, based mainly on circus literature in the British Museum, the Library of Congress, the Bibliothèque Nationale and on his own collection. 3 v. Derby. 1958–62.

1933 NICHOLSON (WATSON). The struggle for a free stage. 1906.

On the patent theatres. See also Frederick Howard, 5th earl of Carlisle, *Thoughts upon the present condition of the stage and upon the construction of a new theatre*, 1808.

1934 WYNDHAM (HENRY SAXE). The annals of Covent Garden theatre from 1732 to 1897. 2 v. 1906.

Standard. Other theatre histories are Cyril Maude, *Haymarket theatre, some records and reminiscences*, ed. R. Maude, 1903, Austin Brereton, *The Lyceum and Henry Irving*, 1903, which includes a chronological account of the theatre from 1772, John Booth, *A century of theatre history, 1816–1916. The 'Old Vic.'*, 1917.

1935 SOUTHERN (RICHARD). The Georgian playhouse. 1948.

With many illustrations. Also his *The Victorian theatre*, Newton Abbot, 1970, Edward Wedlake Brayley, *Historical and descriptive accounts of the theatres of London. Illustrated with a view of each theatre*, etc., 1826, and Charles Dibdin, the younger, *The history and illustrations of the London theatres*, etc., 1826, with measured drawings, sections, etc., of the theatres.

1936 RICE (CHARLES). The London theatre in the eighteen-thirties. Ed. Arthur Colby Sprague and Bertram Shuttleworth. (Soc. Theatre Research, annual pubn. 2.) 1950.

Excerpts from Rice's MS. Dramatic register of the patent theatres, now part of the Harvard theatre coll. Rice was a British Museum attendant and spare-time theatre enthusiast. See also Erroll Sherson, *London's lost theatres of the nineteenth century, with notes on plays and players seen there*, 1925. See also Grant (3762).

1937 SAXON (ARTHUR HARTLEY). Enter foot and horse. A history of hippodrama in England and France. 1968.

1938 MAYER (DAVID). Harlequin in his element; the English pantomime, 1806–1836. Camb. (Mass.) 1969.

1939 BETTY. The story of the strange life of Master Betty. By Giles William Playfair. 1967.

1940 COOKE. Memoirs of George Frederick Cooke, late of the Theatre Royal, Covent Garden. By William Dunlap. 2 v. 1913.

1941 GRIMALDI. Memoirs of Joseph Grimaldi. Ed. by 'Boz' [*pseud.* of Charles Dickens]. 2 v. 1838. Another edn. 1853.

1942 KEAN. The life of Edmund Kean. By Barry Cornwall [*pseud.* of Bryan Walter Procter]. 2 v. 1835.

Also standard, Frederick W. Hawkins, *The life of Edmund Kean*, etc., 2 v., 1869. See also Harold Newcomb Hillebrand, *Edmund Kean*, 1933, acute and comprehensive, and Giles William Playfair, *Kean: the life and paradox of the great actor*, 1950. For his son, Charles Kean, see *The life and theatrical times of Charles Kean*, etc., by John William Cole, 2 v., 1859.

1943 KELLY. Reminiscences of Michael Kelly of the King's Theatre and the Theatre Royal, Drury Lane, including a period of nearly half a century. By Theodore Hook, from materials furnished by Kelly. 2 v. 1826.

On his niece Fanny Kelly, Basil Francis, *Fanny Kelly of Drury Lane*, 1950.

1944 KEMBLE. Memoirs of the life of John Philip Kemble, esq., including a history of the stage from the time of Garrick. By James Boaden. 2 v. 1825.

Also Herschel Clay Baker, *John Philip Kemble; the actor in his theatre*, Camb. Mass., 1942. On his niece, the daughter of Charles Kemble, Leota S. Driver, *Fanny Kemble*, Chapel Hill, N.C., 1933, with full bibliog. of her writings and the family's history, 243–55.

1945 MACREADY. Macready's reminiscences and selections from his diaries and letters. Ed. Sir William Frederick Pollock Bt. 2 v. 1875.

Standard but heavily censored extracts from Macready's MS. diaries. William C. Toynbee, *Diaries of William Charles Macready, 1833–1851*, 2 v., 1912, is fuller but omits early reminiscences. See also William Archer, *William Charles Macready*, 1890, and John Courtenay Trewin, *Mr. Macready . . . Illustrated from the Raymond Mander and Joe Mitchenson theatre collection*, 1955, which prints further previously unpub. extracts; bibliog. 253–6.

1946 SIDDONS. Memoirs of Mrs. Siddons, interspersed with anecdotes of authors and actors. By James Boaden. 2 v. 1827.

Also Thomas Campbell, *Life of Mrs. Siddons*, 2 v., N.Y., 1834.

1947 VESTRIS. [Mrs. Charles James Mathews.] Mme. Vestris and her times. By Charles E. Pearce. [1923.]

Standard.

5. CLUBS

1948 TIMBS (JOHN). Club life of London; with anecdotes of the clubs, coffee houses, and taverns of the metropolis during the seventeenth, eighteenth, and nineteenth centuries. 2 v. 1866. New edns. 1872, 1908.

See also [Charles Marsh], *The clubs of London; with anecdotes of their members, sketches of character, and conversations*, 2 v., 1828, *The London clubs; their anecdotes and history, private rules and regulations*, 1853; Thomas Hay Sweet Escott, *Club makers and club members* [1914]; Edwin Beresford Chancellor, *Memorials of St. James's Street*, etc., 1922; Grant (3762).

1949 ATHENAEUM. History of the Athenaeum, 1824–1925. (Based on materials collected by the late H. R. Tedder.) By Thomas Humphry Ward. 1926.

1950 BROOKS'S. Memorials of Brooks's from the foundation of the club, 1764, to the close of the nineteenth century. Compiled from the records of the club. 1907.

Also Henry Swanston Eeles and Albert Edward Spencer, 7th earl Spencer, *Brooks's, 1764–1964*, 1964.

1951 CARLTON. The Carlton Club. By Sir Charles Petrie. 1955.

1952 CROCKFORD'S. Crockford's; or, The goddess of chance in St. James's Street, 1824–1844. By Arthur Lee Humphreys. 1953.

1953 REFORM. The Reform Club: its founders and architect, 1836–1886. By Louis Alexander Fagan. 1887.

1954 WHITE'S. The history of White's. By [William Biggs Boulton]. 2 v. 1892.

Also Percy Colson, *White's 1693–1950*, etc., 1951.

6. INNS AND COFFEE HOUSES

1955 RICHARDSON (ALBERT EDWARD) *and* EBERLEIN (HAROLD DONALDSON). The English inn, past and present; a review of its history and social life. 1925.

See also Peter Boyle, *The publican's daily companion*, etc., 1795, and (1597).

1956 LILLYWHITE (BRYANT). London coffee houses: a reference book of coffee houses of the seventeenth, eighteenth, and nineteenth centuries. 1963.

7. FREEMASONRY

1957 GOULD (ROBERT FREKE). The history of freemasonry. 6 v. 1884–7. 4 v. N.Y., Cincinnati and Chicago. [1884?–9.] 3rd edn. rev. and ed. by the Rev. Herbert Poole. 4 v. 1951.

For bibliogs. see William James Hughan, *Histories of lodges (England)*, 1892, and his *Histories of lodges (Scotland)*, Glasgow, 1892; Henry Josiah Whymper, *A catalogue of . . . works on freemasonry*, 1891; John Lane, *Masonic records, 1717–1894*, 2nd edn., 1895; Sir Algernon Tudor-Craig, comp., *Catalogue of manuscripts and library at Freemasons' Hall in the possession of the United Grand Lodge of England*, 1938.

8. COACHES AND CARRIAGES, SPAS AND WATERING-PLACES

See also Inland Transport (1630), and particular resorts under *Local History*.

1958 MOORE (HENRY CHARLES). Omnibuses and cabs; their origin and history. 1902. [1901.]

1959 McCAUSLAND (HUGH). The English carriage. 1948.

See also William Felton, *A treatise on carriages*, 2 v., 1794–5, and *Supplement*, 1796, and William Bridges Adams, *English pleasure carriages . . . with an analysis of the construction of the common roads and railroads, and the public vehicles used on them*, 1837.

1960 ELLIS (CUTHBERT HAMILTON). Nineteenth century railway carriages in the British Isles, from the eighteen-thirties to the nineteen hundreds. 1949.

For railway bibliog. see Ottley (1638).

1961 VALE (HENRY EDMUND THEODORIC). The mail coach men of the late eighteenth century. 1960.

See also Charles Thomas Samuel Birch Reynardson, '*Down the road*', or, *Reminiscences of a gentleman coachman*, 1875, 2nd edn., 1875. Tom Bradley, *The old coaching days in Yorkshire*, Leeds, 1889, and William Charles Arlington Blew, *Brighton and its coaches*, etc., 1894 [1893], are solidly informative local studies. See too Charles George Harper, *Stage coach and mail in days of yore: a picturesque history of the coaching age*, 2 v., 1903, and Stella Margetson, *Journey by stages; some account of the people who travelled by stage-coach and mail in the years between 1660 and 1840*, 1967.

1962 GRANVILLE (AUGUSTUS BOZZI). The spas of England and principal sea-bathing places. 3 v. 1841.

Richard Metcalfe, *The rise and progress of hydropathy in England and Scotland*, 1912.

9. WOMEN AND CHILDREN

(a) *General*

1963 MILNE (JOHN DUGUID). Industrial and social position of women in the middle and lower ranks. 1857.

Also Georgiana Hill, *Women in English life from medieval to modern times*, 2 v., 1896.

1964 CUNNINGTON (CECIL WILLETT). Feminine attitudes in the nineteenth century. 1935.

Also Janet Dunbar, *The early Victorian woman; some aspects of her life (1837–1857)*, 1953. Martha Vicinus, ed., *Suffer and be still. Women in the Victorian age*, Indiana U.P., 1972, includes valuable bibliog. article, 173–206.

1965 BANKS (JOSEPH AMBROSE). Prosperity and parenthood; a study of family planning among the Victorian middle classes. 1954.

Followed by J. A. and Olive Banks, *Feminism and family planning in Victorian England*, Liverpool, 1964.

1966 HEWITT (MARGARET). Wives and mothers in Victorian industry. 1958.

Standard. Also Wanda Fraiken Neff, *Victorian working women; an historical and literary study of women in British industries and professions, 1832–1850*, 1929, and Ivy Pinchbeck, *Women workers and the industrial revolution, 1750–1850*, 1930.

1967 PINCHBECK (IVY) *and* HEWITT (MARGARET). Children in English society. 2 v. 1969, 1973.

V. II goes from the 18th century to the Children Act, 1948.

(b) *Women's Rights*

1968 BLEASE (WALTER LYON). The emancipation of English women. 1910. New and rev. edn. 1913.

See also Ida Beatrice O'Malley, *Women in subjection: a study of the lives of English women before 1832*, [1933].

1969 WOLLSTONECRAFT (MARY). Vindication of the rights of women. 1792.

See Emma Rauschenbusch Clough, *A study of Mary Wollstonecraft and the rights of women*, 1898, and (2163).

1970 WAKEFIELD (PRISCILLA). Reflections on the present condition of
the female sex with suggestions for its improvement. 1798.

Other works include William Thompson, *Appeal of one half of the human race, women,
against the pretensions of the other half, men*, etc., 1825; Elizabeth Sandford, *Female
improvement*, 2 v., 1836, 3rd edn., 1848, and her *Woman in her social and domestic character*, 1831, 6th edn., 1839; Sarah Ellis, *The women of England*, 1838, 9th edn. [1850?],
and her *The wives of England*, etc. [1839?]; [Sarah Lewis], *Woman's mission*, 2nd edn.,
1839, and many subsequent edns. A Woman, *Woman's rights and duties*, etc., 2 v., 1840,
is more aggressively feminist than most works. See also Artemas Bowers Muzzey, *The
English maiden; her moral and domestic duties*, 1841; 'P. M. Y.', 'Woman and her social
position', *Westminster Review*, 35 (1841), 24–52; Benjamin Parsons, *The mental and
moral dignity of woman*, 1842; Marion Reid, *A plea for women*, etc., Edin. 1842, on the
need for education and equality of civil rights; Ann Richelieu Lamb, afterwards
Dryden, *Can woman regenerate society?* 1844.

1971 GREY (MARIA GEORGINA) *and* SHIRREFF (EMILY A. E.).
Thoughts on self culture. 2 v. 1850.

On the need for education.

1972 [SHAW (WILLIAM).] Affectionate pleading for English oppressed
female workers. 1850.

Also Anon., *Slop shops and slop workers*, 1850; both on sweated industries of the East
End.

1973 NORTON (*the hon.* CAROLINE ELIZABETH SARAH). English laws
for women in the nineteenth century. 1854.

On Mrs. Norton see Jane Gray Perkins, *The life of Mrs. Norton*, 1909, and Alice Acland
Caroline Norton, 1948.

(c) *Female Accomplishments*

1974 THE LADIES' DIARY: or, The woman's almanack, containing many
delightful and entertaining particulars, peculiarly adapted for the use and
diversion of the fair-sex. 1704–1840.

Other women's magazines include *The Lady's Magazine*, etc., 1770–1832, continued
1832–7 as *The Lady's Magazine and Museum of Belles Lettres*, and continued 1838–47 as
*The Court Magazine and Monthly Critic, and Ladies' Magazine and Museum of Belles
Lettres*; also *The Lady's Monthly Museum; or, Polite repository of amusement and instruction ... By a Society of Ladies*, 1798–1811, continued as *The Ladies' Monthly Museum*,
1812–28, the *Ladies' Museum*, 1829–32, and then incorporated with *The Lady's Magazine*, etc., as above.

1975 THE YOUNG LADY'S BOOK; a manual of elegant recreations, exer-
cises and pursuits. 1829.

See also Mrs. Alexander Walker, *Female beauty, as preserved and improved by regimen,
cleanliness, and dress*, etc., 1837, and A. F., *The ladies' pocket book of etiquette*, 7th edn.,
1840.

C. THE COURT

1. SOURCES

Major collections of royal family correspondence are printed in Aspinall, *George III* (146) and *George, Prince of Wales* (197). For court officials see (445). For the sovereigns see entries in *Political Biography*.

1976 HARCOURT. The Harcourt papers. Ed. by Edward William Harcourt. 14 v. (50 copies printed for private circulation.) Oxf. [1876–1903.]

V. 4: Lady Harcourt's memoirs of the years 1788–9; v. 5: Mrs. Harcourt, autobiographical anecdotes, 1792–5; v. 6: Memoirs of George Simon, second Earl Harcourt (1736–1809), with many letters from members of the royal family; vv. 8 and 11–14: Harcourt family correspondence, including a few more royal letters, 1789–1851. See also 'Mrs. Harcourt's diary of the court of George III' [1788–90], *Philobiblon Soc. Misc.* 13 (1871–2).

1977 GREVILLE. The diaries of Colonel the Hon Robert Fulke Greville, equerry to . . . King George III. Ed. by Frank McKno Bladon. 1930.

The diaries cover the years 1781, 1788–9, 1794. For court life in these years see also Burney (D'Arblay) (2102).

1978 CLARKE. Authentic memoirs of Mrs. Clarke. By Elizabeth Taylor. 1809.

Well embroidered. Mrs. Clarke's relations with the Duke of York are also described in *A circumstantial report of the evidence and proceedings upon the charges preferred against . . . the Duke of York*, 1809; and *The rival princes; or, A faithful narrative of facts relating to Mrs. M. A. Clarke's political acquaintance with Colonel Wardle, Major Dodd, etc.*, who were concerned in the charges against the Duke of York, 2 v., 1810.

1979 MURRAY. Recollections from 1803 to 1837. With a conclusion in 1868. By the Hon. Amelia Murray. 1868.

Includes letters of Queen Charlotte to Lady George Murray, the writer's mother, a lady-in-waiting, 1808–13, and court anecdotes; light.

1980 CHARLOTTE. Letters of the Princess Charlotte, 1811–1817. Ed. by Arthur Aspinall. 1949.

The brief life of the Regent's daughter is sketched in Robert Huish, *Memoirs of her Royal Highness, Charlotte Augusta*, 1818. *The autobiography of Miss Knight, Lady companion to Princess Charlotte*, ed. by Roger Fulford, 1960, includes some correspondence and is valuable. See also 'The tragedy at Claremont: letters from Prince Leopold (uncle to Queen Victoria) to his sister the Gräfin Mensdorff-Pouilly now in the possession of her grandson Count Oversdorf', ed. and tr. by Osbert Lancaster, *Cornhill Magazine*, May 1937.

1981 BURY [*formerly* CAMPBELL]. The diary of a lady-in-waiting. By Lady Charlotte Bury. Being the diary illustrative of the times of George the fourth interspersed with original letters from the late Queen Caroline and from other distinguished persons. Ed. with an introd. by A. Francis Steuart. 2 v. 1908.

Valuable. The anonymous 4-v. edn. of 1838–9 includes a few passages omitted by Steuart.

1982 SOPHIA-CHARLOTTE. Memoirs of . . . Sophia-Charlotte, Queen of Great Britain. From authentic documents. By John Watkins. 1819.

Popular but informative, as is also Walley C. Oulton, *Authentic and impartial memoirs of her late Majesty, Charlotte, Queen of Great Britain and Ireland,* 1819.

1983 CAROLINE. Memoirs of her late Majesty, Queen Caroline, consort of King George IV. By Joseph Nightingale. 3 v. 1820–2.

See too Robert Huish, *Memoirs of . . . Caroline, Queen of Great Britain,* 2 v., 1821, and the report of the commissioners of inquiry, *The Book; or, The proceedings and correspondence upon the subject of the inquiry into the conduct of the Princess of Wales,* 1813.

1984 YORK. A biographical memoir of . . . Frederick, Duke of York and Albany. . . . With numerous anecdotes of the royal family. By John Watkins. 1827.

1985 CLARENCE. Mrs. Jordan and her family; being the unpublished correspondence of Mrs. Jordan and the Duke of Clarence, later William IV. Ed. by Arthur Aspinall. 1951.

1986 BROWNLOW. The eve of Victorianism: reminiscences of the years 1802 to 1834. By Emma Sophia [Cust], countess Brownlow. 1940.

Incorporates *Slight reminiscences of a septuagenarian from 1802 to 1815,* 2nd edn., 1867. Anecdotal and mainly on the years after 1815. The writer was a lady of the bedchamber to Queen Adelaide.

1987 KNIGHTON. Memoirs of Sir William Knighton . . . keeper of the privy purse during the reign of . . . George the fourth. Including his correspondence with many distinguished personages. By [Dorothea] Lady Knighton. 2 v. 1838.

Memoirs and letters concerning family, court, and society, *c.* 1800–1836.

1988 RUSH. A residence at the court of London. By Richard Rush, envoy extraordinary and minister plenipotentiary from the United States of America, from 1817 to 1825. 3rd edn. 1873.

Not diplomatic memoirs but an account of the life of the court during his residence.

1989 WILLIAM IV. Glimpses of King William IV and Queen Adelaide. In letters of the late Miss Clitheroe of Boston House, Middlesex. With a brief account of Boston House and the Clitheroe family. By G. Cecil White. 1902.

Intimate anecdotes of the king and queen by private friends who visited them, 1830–37.

1990 CUMBERLAND. Letters of the King of Hanover to Viscountess Strangford. With an historical note by E. M. Coxe and an introd. by Charles Whibley. 1925.

1991 BLOOMFIELD. Reminiscences of court and diplomatic life. By Georgiana, baroness Bloomfield. 2 v. 1883.

Describes her life as maid-in-waiting to Queen Victoria, 1842–4, and then as wife of the British ambassador at St. Petersburg, 1845–51.

1992 PYNE (WILLIAM HENRY). The history of the royal residences of
Windsor Castle, St. James's Palace, Carlton House, Kensington Palace, Hampton Court, Buckingham House and Frogmore. 3 v. 1819.

Thomas Faulkner, *History and antiquities of Kensington, interspersed with biographical anecdotes of royal and distinguished personages, and a descriptive catalogue of the collection of pictures in the palace, from a survey made by the late B. West*, 1820.

2. LATER WORKS

For collective biography of the later Hanoverian queens, see Pargellis and
Medley (2), 2003.

1993 FITZGERALD (PERCY). The good queen Charlotte. 1899.

Constance Hill, *Fanny Burney at the court of queen Charlotte*, 1912, is full and valuable on the years 1788–91. Olwen Hedley, *Queen Charlotte*, 1975, is judicious.

1994 FITZHERBERT. Life and letters of Mrs. Fitzherbert. By Shane Leslie.
2 v. 1939–40.

V. 1, biography, v. 2, the letters. Charles Langdale, *Memoirs of Mrs. Fitzherbert*, 1856, was a vindication by her cousin, but written without access to her papers. These were first made available for W. H. Wilkins, *Mrs. Fitzherbert and George IV*, 2 v., 1905. See too Anita Leslie, *Mrs. Fitzherbert*, 1960.

1995 RICHARDSON (JOANNA). The disastrous marriage: a study of George
IV and Caroline of Brunswick. 1960.

A queen of indiscretions. The tragedy of Caroline of Brunswick, queen of England, trans. by Frederick Chapman from the Italian of Graziano P. Clerici, 1907, includes material from Italian archives. Lewis Melville, *An injured queen. Caroline of Brunswick*, 2 v., 1912, and Sir Edward Parry, *Queen Caroline*, 1930, attempt vindication; other lives are by Howard Cox, 1939, and E. E. P. Tisdall, 1939. See too Roger Fulford, *The trial of queen Caroline*, 1967.

1996 STUART (DOROTHY MARGARET). Daughter of England: a new
study of Princess Charlotte of Wales and her family. 1951.

Lady Rose Weigall, *A brief memoir of Princess Charlotte of Wales*, 1874, includes some letters. Dormer Creston, *The Regent and his daughter*, 1932, 5th edn., 1947, is useful. G. J. Renier, *The ill-fated princess. The life of Charlotte, daughter of the Prince Regent, 1796–1817*, 1932, uses Dutch sources and links the subject to the diplomatic background. Barbara Luttrell, *The prim romantic: a biography of Ellis Cornelia Knight, 1758–1837*, 1965, is a helpful study of the princess's companion.

1997 FOTHERGILL ([ARTHUR] BRIAN). Mrs. Jordan: portrait of an
actress. 1965.

Based on fuller sources than Clare Jerrold, *The story of Dorothy Jordan*, 1914.

1998 HOPKIRK (FRANCES MARY ELIZABETH). Queen Adelaide. 1946.

Popular. Mary F. Sandars, *The life and times of queen Adelaide*, 1915, is factual and pedestrian.

1999 FULFORD (ROGER THOMAS BALDWIN). Royal dukes: the father
and uncles of Queen Victoria. 1933.

Bibliog. 312–17; based on material in the royal archives. Individual lives of George III's sons include: A. H. Burne, *The noble duke of York*, 1949, focused almost exclusively on his military career; H. Van Thal, *Ernest Augustus, Duke of Cumberland and King of Hanover*, 1936; G. M. Willis, *Ernest Augustus, Duke of Cumberland and King of Hanover*, 1954; Anthony Bird, *The damnable Duke of Cumberland*, 1966; W. J. Anderson, *The life of . . . the Duke of Kent and his correspondence with the De Salaberry family, extending from 1791 to 1814*, Toronto, 1870; David Duff, *Edward of Kent*, 1938; Mollie Gillen, *The Prince and his Lady*, 1970, a study of the duke of Kent and Mme St. Laurent; Sir J. H. Reynett, *A short memoir of . . . Adolphus Frederick, Duke of Cambridge*, 1858. On Cambridge's son (b. 1819) see *George Duke of Cambridge: a memoir of his private life, based on the journals and correspondence*, ed. by Edgar Sheppard, 2 v., 1906; the most recent biog., Giles St. Aubyn, *The Royal George*, 1963, adds a little more on his early life from family papers. On the duke of Sussex's eldest son, see A. C. Douglas Firth, *The case of Augustus d'Este*, Camb., 1948. See also George IV (197), William IV (216).

2000 STUART (DOROTHY MARGARET). The daughters of George III. 1939.

Based on the royal archives. See too Morris Marples, *Six royal sisters: the daughters of George III*, 1969. P. C. Yorke, ed., *Letters of Princess Elizabeth*, 1898. On Princess Sophia see Lucille Iremonger, *Love and the Princess*, 1958; and on the youngest sister, W. S. Childe-Pemberton, *The romance of Princess Amelia . . . including extracts from private and unpublished papers*, 1910.

2001 WILLIAMS (NEVILLE JAMES). The royal residences of Great Britain; a social history. 1960.

Ernest Law, *The history of Hampton Court Palace*, 3 v., 1885–91; *Kensington Palace, the birthplace of the queen, illustrated. Being an historical guide to the staterooms, pictures and gardens*, 1899; Sir O. F. Morshead, *Windsor Castle*, 1951, and *George IV and Royal Lodge*, 1965. See also Hope (2967).

D. BIOGRAPHY

D.N.B. (2010) is the principal collection, very fully weighted on the nineteenth century. Entries in sections 1–5 below provide guidance and sources for biographical information. See also listings in *Local History*, and in *Wales, Scotland*, and *Ireland*.

1. BIBLIOGRAPHY AND GUIDES

2002 KAMINKOW (MARION J.). A new bibliography of British genealogy with notes. Baltimore. 1965.

A much fuller analysis of the literature, and more up to date, than H. G. Harrison, *A select bibliography of English genealogy, with brief lists for Wales, Scotland and Ireland*, 1937 (a manual for students). G. Gatfield, *Guide to printed books and manuscripts relating to English and foreign heraldry and genealogy*, 1892, has useful references to MSS. collections, as has also R. Sims, *Manual for the genealogist, topographer, antiquary, and legal professor*, 2nd edn., 1861.

2003 MARSHALL (GEORGE WILLIAM). The genealogist's guide to printed pedigrees. 1879. 4th edn. Guildford. 1903.

Supplemented by J. B. Whitmore, *A genealogical guide . . . in continuation of Marshall's . . .*, 1953. For pedigrees in the old county and local histories see C. Bridger, *Index to pedigrees . . .*, 1867.

2004 PHILLIMORE (WILLIAM PHILLIMORE WATTS), *comp.* An index to changes of name . . . 1760 to 1901. 1905.

2005 THOMSON (THEODORE RADFORD). A catalogue of British family histories. [1928.] 2nd edn. [1935.]

2006 MATTHEWS (WILLIAM). British diaries; an annotated bibliography of British diaries written between 1442 and 1942. Berkeley and Los Angeles. 1950.

Followed by his *British autobiographies: an annotated bibliography of British autobiographies published or written before 1951*, Berkeley and Los Angeles, 1955. Both include references to MSS. as well as imprints.

2007 HYAMSON (A. M.). A dictionary of universal biography of all ages and of all peoples. 2nd edn. 1951.

A guide to location of biographical information in 24 standard biographical dictionaries, and ready reference to dates of birth and death of many thousands of individuals. *Biography Index: a cumulative index to biographical material in books and magazines*, N.Y., 1946+, with four-yearly cumulations, deals primarily with the United States but includes British personalities.

2008 SLOCUM (ROBERT BIGNEY). Biographical dictionaries and related works; an international bibliography of collective biographies, bibliographies, collections of epitaphs, selected genealogical works. Detroit. 1967.

Comprehensive. Phyllis M. Riches, *An analytical bibliography of universal collected biography, comprising books published in the English tongue in Great Britain and Ireland, America and the British dominions*, 1934, covers limited but useful ground.

2009 WAGNER (ANTHONY RICHARD). English genealogy. Oxf. 1960.

Standard guide on the social and technical contexts of genealogical inquiry. See too W. P. W. Phillimore, *How to write the history of a family: a guide for the genealogist*, 2nd edn., 1888, and *A Supplement . . .*, 2nd edn., 1900.

2. General

2010 STEPHEN (LESLIE) *and* LEE (SIDNEY) *eds.* Dictionary of national biography. 63 v. 1885–1901.

Standard. Supplements, 1901, 1912; *Dictionary . . . 1912–1921*, 1927; reprint, 22 v., 1908–9. To be used with *Corrections and additions . . . cumulated from the Bulletin of the Institute of Historical Research*, 1966. F. Boase, *Modern English Biography*, 3 v., and 3 suppl., Cass reprint, 6 v., 1965, includes about 30,000 short sketches of persons dying between 1851 and 1900, supplementing *D.N.B.*, especially for less well-known persons. See too *A new biographical dictionary of 3000 contemporary public characters, British and foreign, of all ranks and professions*, 2nd edn., 3 v., 1825; *The Georgian era: memoirs of the most eminent persons who have flourished in Great Britain from the accession of George the first to the demise of George the fourth*, 4 v., 1832–4. The *Gentleman's Magazine* (31) is a principal source for obituary notices, which are relatively full, 1789–1815, but then become brief, and also for notices of births, marriages, and preferments. For other obituary notices see the *European Magazine* (28), *The Scots Magazine*, 79 v., 1739–1817; *The Monthly Repository*, 36 v., 1806–37 (with varying titles) for Protestant dissenters. Lists of obituaries in the *Annual Register* (22) are indexed to 1819 in *General Index to Dodsley's Annual Register . . . to 1819*, 1826. T. Cooper and E. Walford, comp., *The*

Register and magazine of biography . . . *1869*, 2 v., 1869; See too Index Society, *Index of obituary notices for the year* . . ., annual, 1878–1882.

2011   HAYDN (JOSEPH TIMOTHY). The book of dignities. 1851. 3rd edn., with index. 1894.

Cumulated lists of the holders of the more important public offices. For contemporary lists of office-holders see (445).

2012   WHO'S WHO? 1849+.

Covering slightly different ground is A. B. Thom, *The upper ten thousand*, 1875+.

2013   BURKE (JOHN). A genealogical and heraldic history of the commoners of Great Britain and Ireland. 4 v. 1833–8.

Continued as *A genealogical and heraldic dictionary of the landed gentry of Great Britain and Ireland*; published irregularly. The 1846 edn. has an index of individuals. That part relating to Irish families in the 9th edn. was separately printed as Sir John Bernard Burke, *A genealogical and heraldic history of the landed gentry of Ireland*, 1893, and thenceforward published as a separate work under that title. John R. Magrath ed., *Index to the pedigrees in Burke's Commoners originally prepared by Mr. George Ormerod in 1840*, Oxf., 1907. See too J. L. Sanford and M. W. Townsend, *The great governing families of England*, 2 v., 1865, and E. Walford, *County families of the United Kingdom, or Royal Manual of the titled and untitled aristocracy of England and Wales, Scotland, and Ireland*, 1860 and irregularly to 1870, thereafter annual.

2014   BURKE (JOHN) *and* BURKE (*Sir* JOHN BERNARD). The Knightage of Great Britain and Ireland. 1841.

W. A. Shaw, comp., *The knights of England*, 2 v. in 3 and index vol., 1906.

2015   HUNTER (JOSEPH). Familiae minorum gentium. Ed. by John William Clay. 4 v. 1894–6. Harleian Soc. v. 37–40.

Mainly north-country families.

2016   MISCELLANEA GENEALOGICA ET HERALDICA and the British archivist, 1866–1938. 31 v. 1868–1938.

See also *The Genealogist*, 45 v., 1877–1922, *The Genealogists' Magazine*, 1925+.

3. COLLECTIVE BIOGRAPHY

(a) *Memoirs*

2017   BOYD (MARK). Reminiscences of fifty years. 1871.

Recollections of politicians, literary figures, and others from William Pitt onwards.

2018   [GRANT (JAMES)]. Random recollections of the House of Lords from the year 1830 to 1836, including personal sketches of the leading members. 1836.

Grant also wrote *Random recollections of the House of Commons*, 1836, and *The British senate in 1838*, 1838.

2019 HALL (SAMUEL CARTER). A book of memories of great men and women of the age from personal acquaintance. 1871.

Notes on over 100 literary and political figures of his time. His *Retrospect of a long life*, 2 v., 1883, includes further vignettes and anecdotes.

2020 JERDAN (WILLIAM). Men I have known. 1866.

Sketches of some 50 figures, mainly literary.

2021 PATMORE (PETER GEORGE). My friends and acquaintances. Being memorials, mind-portraits and personal recollections of deceased celebrities of the nineteenth century with selections from their unpublished letters. 1855.

On Lamb, Thomas Campbell, Lady Blessington, R. Plumer Ward, Horace and James Smith, William Hazlitt, Laman Blanchard, R. B. and Thomas Sheridan.

2022 REDDING (CYRUS). Past celebrities whom I have known. 2 v. 1866.

Redding also wrote *Personal reminiscences of eminent men*, 3 v., 1867.

2023 SHEE (WILLIAM ARCHER). My contemporaries, 1830–1870. 1893.

Social gossip culled from his diaries.

(b) *Essays and Compilations*

2024 [CHALMERS (GEORGE)]. Parliamentary portraits; or, Characters of the British senate. 2 v. 1795.

See also *Public Characters... 1798/99... 1809/10*, 10 v., 1799–1809; Thomas Barnes, *Parliamentary portraits*, 1815; William Miller, *Biographical sketches of British characters recently deceased; commencing with the accession of George IV*, 2 v., 1826. T. H. Ward, ed., *Men of the reign*, 1885, containing brief biogs. of noted men deceased since 1837.

2025 THE ANNUAL BIOGRAPHY AND OBITUARY. 21 v. 1817–37.

C. R. Dodd's *The annual biography... 1842*, 1843, ceased publication after one issue. J. P. Edwards, ed., *Lives of the illustrious (The biographical magazine)*, 7 v., 1852–5, contains notices of about 200 persons, mostly British.

2026 BAGEHOT (WALTER). Biographical studies ... ed. by Richard Holt Hutton. 1881. New edn. with index. 1907.

Brilliant sketches of leading politicians. Lord Brougham, *Historical sketches of statesmen who flourished in the time of George III*, 3 v., 1839–43, is often illuminating. W. C. Taylor, *The modern British Plutarch*, N.Y., 1846, has sketches of 38 notable men of the time.

2027 COCHRANE (ROBERT), *comp.* The treasury of modern biography; a gallery of literary sketches of eminent men and women of the nineteenth century. Edin. 1881.

Partly reprinted extracts from contemporary essays, partly original contributions, on about 100 persons; treatment often more extended than *D.N.B.*

2028 COLERIDGE (HARTLEY). Lives of northern worthies. 3 v. 1833. New edn. ed. by Derwent Coleridge. 1852.

2029 COURTENAY (WILLIAM PRIDEAUX). Eight friends of the great. 1910.

Includes notices of John Taylor, Scrope Davies, Lord Webb Seymour, Lydia White, Lord John Townshend.

2030 ELWOOD (ANNE KATHARINE). Memoirs of the literary ladies of England from the commencement of the last century. 2 v. 1843.

2031 HAZLITT (WILLIAM). The spirit of the age; or, contemporary portraits. 1825.

18 essays on literary personalities. See also R. H. Horne, ed., *A new spirit of the age*, 2 v., 1844.

2032 KIRBY (CHESTER). The English country gentleman; a study of nineteenth century types. [1937.]

Includes Lord George Bentinck, Grantley Berkeley, the fifth Duke of Richmond, Sir John Bennet Lawes.

2033 LEY (JAMES WILLIAM THOMAS). The Dickens circle. A narrative of the novelist's friendships. 1918.

2034 MELVILLE (LEWIS). The Beaux of the Regency. 2 v. 1908.

Melville's *Regency Ladies*, 1926, contains 20 sketches.

2035 WELFORD (RICHARD). Men of mark twixt Tyne and Tweed. 3 v. 1895.

Notices on some 500 individuals, originally printed in the *Newcastle Weekly Chronicle*.

2036 WALPOLE (SPENCER). Studies in biography. 1907.

Includes sketches of Peel, Cobden, Disraeli.

4. Peers and Baronets

See the bibliographies of reference books on the peerage in Kaminkow (2002) and Hollingsworth (1701).

2037 C[OKAYNE] (G[EORGE] E[DWARD]). The complete peerage. New edn. rev. and much enlarged by Vicary Gibbs. 13 v. 1910–59.

Concise biogs. of title-holders and their wives only. *Collins's peerage of England . . . continued to the present time*, by Sir Egerton Brydges, 9 v., 1812, provides biogs. of more noteworthy later Georgian collaterals and cadets.

2038 BURKE (*Sir* JOHN BERNARD) *and others*. A genealogical and heraldic dictionary of the peerage and baronetage of the British Empire. 1826+.

At irregular intervals till 1847, thereafter annual. See also their *Genealogical history of the dormant, abeyant, forfeited, and extinct peerages of the British Empire*, 1831, 3rd edn., 1846, new edn., 1883.

2039 DEBRETT (JOHN). The peerage of England, Scotland, and Ireland. 1802+.

2040 DOYLE (JAMES WILLIAM EDMUND). The official baronage of England. 3 v. 1886.

2041 C[OKAYNE] (G[EORGE] E[DWARD]). The complete baronetage [1611–1800]. 5 v. Exeter. 1900–6.

Index, Exeter, 1909. Has inaccuracies and omissions. See also John Debrett, *The Baronetage of England*, 2 v., 1808, and later issues published irregularly; and Sir J. B. Burke and others, *Genealogical and heraldic history of the extinct and dormant baronetcies of England, Ireland, and Scotland*, 1841, new edn., 1866, offset reprint, 1964.

5. SCHOOL AND UNIVERSITY LISTS

See Jacobs (3316). The works listed below give further biographical data beyond the institution's records. Some school lists with very few entries for the period have been omitted.

(a) *Universities*

2042 CAMBRIDGE. Alumni cantabrigienses. Comp. by John and John Archibald Venn. Pt. 2 (1752–1900). 6 v. Camb. 1940–54.

2043 OXFORD. Alumni oxonienses . . . 1715–1886. Ed. by Joseph Foster. 4 v. 1888.

(b) *Schools*

Listed in alphabetical order.

2044 BLUNDELL'S. The register of Blundell's school. By Arthur Fisher. 2 pt. Exeter. 1904. 1932.

Pt. 1: The register, 1770–1882. Mainly west country people.

2045 BROMSGROVE. The Old Bromsgrovian register, together with a brief history . . . of Bromsgrove school. Bromsgrove. 1910.

2046 BURY ST. EDMUNDS. Biographical list of boys educated at King Edward VI free grammar school, Bury St. Edmunds, from 1550 to 1900. Suffolk Green Books no. 13. Bury St. Edmunds. 1908.

2047 CHARTERHOUSE. The Charterhouse register, 1769–1872. Comp. by R. L. Arrowsmith. 1974.

2048 DURHAM. Durham school register. Ed. by Thomas Harold Burbidge. 3rd edn. Camb. 1940.

2049 ETON. The Eton College Register, 1753–1790. Ed. by Richard Arthur Austen-Leigh. Eton. 1921.

For post-1790 see H. E. C. Stapylton, *The Eton school lists from 1791 to 1850 . . . with notes*, 2nd edn. with index of names, 1864.

2050 FELSTED. Alumni Felstedienses . . . 1564 . . . 1931. Ed. by Francis Steele Moller. 1931.

2051 HAILEYBURY. Memorials of old Haileybury college. By Frederick Charles Danvers and others. Westminster. 1894.

Includes a register of students, 1806–57, with notes on their services in India.

2052 HARROW. The Harrow school register, 1571–1800. Ed. by William Townsend Jackson Gun. 1934.

Continued in R. C. Welch, ed., *The Harrow school register, 1800–1911,* 3rd edn., 1911.

2053 MANCHESTER. The admission register of the Manchester school. Ed. by Jeremiah Finch Smith. Chetham Soc. 3 v. 1866–74.

V. 1: 1730–75; v. 2: 1776–1807; v. 3: 1807–37; with excellent biographical detail.

2054 MERCHANT TAYLORS'. Merchant Taylors' school register, 1561–1934. Ed. by Mrs. Ernest Parsons Hart. 2 v. 1936.

2055 MILL HILL. The register of Mill Hill school, 1807–1926. By Ernest Hampden-Cook. 1926.

2056 NEWCASTLE. Register of the royal grammar school of Newcastle-upon-Tyne, 1545–1954. Ed. by Brian Dodd Stevens. Gateshead. 1955.

2057 REPTON. Repton school register. By Minna Messiter. Repton. 1910.

2058 RUGBY. Rugby school register. V. 1: 1675–1857. By Godfrey A. Solly. Rugby. 1933.

2059 ST. PAUL'S. The admission registers of St. Paul's school . . . 1748 . . . 1876. Ed. by Robert Barlow Gardiner. 1884.

2060 SEDBERGH. The Sedbergh school register, 1546 to 1909. Ed. by Bernard Wilson. Leeds. 1909.

2061 SHERBORNE. The Sherborne register. Camb. 1937.

2062 SHREWSBURY. Shrewsbury school register. V. 1: 1798–1908. Ed. by John Ernest Auden. Shrewsbury. 1928.

2063 SIDCOT. Sidcot school. Register of old scholars, 1808–1958. By Mary Douglas Blaschko. Winscombe. 1958.

2064 STONYHURST. Stonyhurst biographical dictionary. Pt. 1: 1774–1825. Pt. 2: 1826–50 (A–K). n.d.

Made-up sets with typescript title-pages, made up from extracts from the Stonyhurst Magazine, various issues from Dec. 1929 to Dec. 1938. At I. H. R., London.

2065 TONBRIDGE. The register of Tonbridge school . . . 1553 to 1820. Ed. by Walter Gray Hart. 1935.

Continued and supplemented by W. O. Hughes-Hughes, ed., *The register of Tonbridge school from 1820 to 1893,* 1893, which includes some lists of before 1820.

2066 UPPINGHAM. Uppingham school roll, 1824–1931. 6th issue. 1932.

Roll by years of entry, with brief biog. notes.

2067 WESTMINSTER. The record of old Westminsters. Ed. by George Fisher Russell Barker and Alan Herbert Stenning. 2 v. 1928.

2068 WINCHESTER. Winchester college 1836–1906. A Register. By John Bannerman Wainewright. Winchester. 1907.

T. F. Kirby, comp., *Winchester scholars*, 1888, listing pupils from 1393, for the period 1789–1851 lists entrants year by year with brief biog. notes.

2069 WOLVERHAMPTON. Wolverhampton grammar school register, 1515–1920. Ed. by Hubert Robert Thomas and John Ryan. Wolverhampton. [1927.]

6. Correspondence, Journals, Memoirs, and Biographies

(Arranged roughly in chronological order of content.) For collections of letters, etc., in which the main interest is political, see *Political history* (146–242), and for other particular interests see under respective sections. See too Matthews (2006), Simpson (4281).

2070 HAMILTON. Sir William Hamilton. Envoy extraordinary. By [Arthur] Brian Fothergill. 1969.

Court, society, and diplomacy in the middle years of George III's reign. See also (1248) and (1257).

2071 CAMPBELL (JOHN DOUGLAS SUTHERLAND), *9th duke of Argyll, ed.* Intimate society letters of the eighteenth century. 2 v. 1910.

V. 2 includes letters on military, political, social, and estate affairs, 1789–1843, from the Argyll MSS.

2072 WHITEFOORD. The Whitefoord papers . . . of Colonel Charles Whitefoord and Caleb Whitefoord from 1739 to 1810. Ed. by William Albert Samuel Hewins. Oxf. 1898.

Correspondence 1789–1810, including letters of Thomas Coutts, the banker.

2073 HAWTREY. The history of the Hawtrey family. By Frances Molesworth Hawtrey. 2 v. 1903.

Family correspondence, late 18th and 19th centuries, of a family with wide clerical and educational connections.

2074 TAYLOR. Memoirs of the principal events in the life of Henry Taylor of North Shields. 1811.

His contacts with Trinity House and concern with navigation on the Tyne in the 1790s.

2075 ADAMS. William Adams, an old English potter: with some account of his family and their productions. Ed. by William Turner. 1904.

Work and life in Staffs. in the later Georgian period. See also Lewis Adams (1604).

2076   PALMERSTON. Portrait of a whig peer; compiled from the papers of the 2nd viscount Palmerston, 1739–1802. By Brian Connell. 1957.

2077   JONES. Diary of the Revd. William Jones, 1777–1821. Ed. with an introd. by Octavius Francis Christie. 1929.

2078   HUTTON. Reminiscences of a gentlewoman of the last century; letters of Catherine Hutton. By Catherine Hutton Beale. Birmingham. 1891.

Memoirs and letters, 1769–1846, of a dau. of William Hutton, the historian of Birmingham.

2079   SHARP. Memoirs of Granville Sharp, esq., composed from his own manuscripts. By Prince Hoare. 1820. 2nd edn. 2 v. 1828.

2080   SMITH. A book for a rainy day; or, Recollections of the events of the years 1766–1833. By John Thomas Smith. Ed. with introd. and notes by W. Whitten. 1905.

Recollections of persons and incidents in the realms of art, literature and the theatre by a keeper of prints at the British Museum.

2081   TAYLOR. The Taylors of Ongar; a portrait of an English family of the eighteenth and nineteenth centuries. By Doris May Armitage. Camb. 1939.

Family life in a middle-class household with literary interests; the writers for children, Ann Gilbert (*née* Taylor, 1782–1866) and Jane Taylor (1783–1824). Josiah Gilbert, ed., *Autobiography and other memorials of Mrs. Gilbert,* 1874, including the account of her childhood and early life at Lavenham and Colchester, 1782–1813.

2082   HARDY. Memoir of Thomas Hardy, founder of and secretary to the London Corresponding Society . . . written by himself. 1832.

Mainly on his activities in the 1790s.

2083   WARD. Benenden letters: London, country, and abroad, 1753–1821. Ed. by Charles Frederic Hardy. 1901.

Family correspondence of William Ward of Benenden, including his letters from France while a hostage after 1803.

2084   BENTINCK. A history of Welbeck Abbey and its owners. By Arthur Stanley Turberville. 2 v. 1939.

V. 2: 1755–1879, on the 3rd duke of Portland and members of his family.

2085   CHURCHILL. The later Churchills. By Alfred Leslie Rowse. 1958.

The dukes of Marlborough and their family circle.

2086   TAYLOR. Records of my life; by the late John Taylor, esq. 2 v. 1832.

A journalist's gossipy impressions of later Georgian personalities.

2087   YOUNG. The autobiography of Arthur Young with selections from his correspondence. Ed. by Matilda [Barbara] Betham-Edwards. 1898.

Journals and letters, 1755–1820. J. G. Gazley, *The life of Arthur Young, 1741–1820,* Phil., 1973, is excellent.

2088 TWINING. Recreations and studies of a country clergyman of the eighteenth century, being selections from the correspondence of the Rev. Thomas Twining [1761–1803]. Ed. by Richard Twining, the younger. 1882.

Includes letters about music to Dr. Burney. *Selections from the papers of the Twining family*, 1887, prints letters of 1778–1844.

2089 WOODFORDE. The diary of a country parson: the Rev. James Wood-forde (1758–1802). Ed. by John Baldwin Beresford. 5 v. 1924–31.

V. 3–5, 1788–1802, a detailed picture of a country parson's daily life.

2090 BOWDLER. Memoir of the life of John Bowdler. [By Thomas Bowdler]. 1824.

Letters and discourses, 1764–1815; discussion of social questions.

2091 STRUTT. The Strutt family of Terling, 1650–1873. By Charles Richard Strutt. Priv. printed. 1939.

Includes correspondence of Joseph Holden Strutt, M.P. (1758–1845), and other members of his family.

2092 HEBER. Dear Miss Heber, an eighteenth century correspondence. Ed. by Francis Bamford. 1936.

Letters to Mary Heber of Weston Hall, Northants, 1765–1806, containing personal, social and political gossip. For family correspondence of her kindred, the Hebers of Hodnit, Salop, and Marton, Yorks., see (3384).

2093 COKE. Coke of Norfolk and his friends. By Anna Maria Diana Wilhel-mina (Pickering) Stirling. New edn. 1912.

Correspondence 1777–1837; illustrative of social life on a great estate; the editing is unreliable.

2094 ROE. The private memorandums of William Roe of Withdean . . . Sussex. Ed. by Charles Thomas-Stanford. Priv. printed. Brighton. 1928.

From his notebooks and diary, 1775–1809; his career, estate management, country life and work, and local affairs.

2095 CRAVEN. The beautiful Lady Craven. The original memoirs of Elizabeth, baroness Craven, afterwards Margravine of Anspach . . . 1750–1828. Ed. by Alexander Meyrick Broadley and Lewis Melville. 2 v. 1914.

The memoirs themselves are of the 1780s but the introduction is a substantial biography, with much material on her later career.

2096 BURGES. Selections from the letters and correspondence of Sir James Bland Burges . . . sometime under-secretary of state for foreign affairs. With notices of his life. Ed. by James Hutton. 1885.

His period at the foreign office, 1789–1795, and his life subsequently till 1824.

2097 CRABBE. Life of the Rev. George Crabbe . . . with his letters and journals. By the Revd. George Crabbe, his son. V. 1 of The poetical works. 1834.

New edns., 1932 with introd. by E. M. Forster, and 1947 with introd. by Edmund Blunden. His life and social circle, 1754–1832.

2098 WALKER. The life of John Walker, M.D. By John Epps. 2nd edn. 1832.

Life of a medical man of humble origins, with much information about social conditions at the end of the 18th century.

2099 LENNOX. The life and letters of Lady Sarah Lennox, 1745–1826, daughter of Charles, 2nd duke of Richmond, and successively the wife of Sir Thomas Charles Bunbury, bt., and of the Hon. George Napier. Ed. by the countess of Ilchester and Lord Stavordale. 2 v. 1901–2. New edn. in one v. 1902.

Includes letters 1789–1817 and extracts from Mrs. Fox's journal concerning the death of C. J. Fox.

2100 DRUMMOND. The Drummonds of Charing Cross. By Hector Bolitho and Derek Peel. 1967.

Personal and business correspondence of a leading banking family, late 18th and 19th centuries.

2101 HAM Elizabeth Ham, by herself, 1783–1820. Ed. with an introd. by Eric Gillett. 1945.

Her life as a child and young woman among the yeomen and lesser gentry of Dorset.

2102 BURNEY. Diary and letters of Madame d'Arblay. Ed. by [Charlotte Frances Barrett]. 7 v. 1842–6. New edn. 7 v. 1854. 4 v. 1893. Ed. by Henry Austin Dobson with preface and notes. 6 v. 1904–5.

V. 5–6 of Dobson's edn. cover 1792–1840; journals and letters, mainly personal but some on literary matters. Joyce Hemlow and others ed., *A catalogue of the Burney family correspondence, 1749–1878*, 1971, and see Joyce Hemlow and others, *The journals and letters of Fanny Burney (Madame d'Arblay)*, 1972, in progress, which will supersede previous editions. Reginald B. Johnson, *Fanny Burney and the Burneys*, 1926, includes letters of Susan Burney, 1787–99, and some additions to the diaries. Christopher Lloyd, *Fanny Burney*, 1936, uses unpublished correspondence in the Ferrers collection. Lives by Averyl Edwards, 1948, and Joyce Hemlow, with bibliog., 496–502, Oxf., 1958. See also Hill (1993).

2103 BRUDENELL. The Brudenells of Deene. By Joan Wake. 1953.

Letters and other material about the court and about county society in Wilts., 1789–1851.

2104 GURNEY. The Gurneys of Earlham. By Augustus John Cuthbert Hare. 2 v. 1895.

Correspondence, 1783–1880, of a Quaker family, personal and social. See also (855).

2105 POWYS. Passages from the diary of Mrs. Philip Lybbe Powys of Hardwicke house, Oxon . . . 1756 to 1808. Ed. by Emily J. Climenson. 1899.

Memoirs of her travels around England, 1789–1808.

2106 NOEL. The Noels and the Milbankes. Their letters for twenty-five years. By Malcolm Elwin. 1967.

Gentry society, life in London and Yorkshire, 1767–92, substantial on 1788–92.

2107 TRENCH. The remains of the late Mrs. Trench. Selections from her journals, letters, and other papers. Ed. by her son, the dean of Westminster. [Richard Chenevix Trench.] 1862.

Life and literary career of Melesina Trench (1768–1827).

2108 FRY. Katharine Fry's book. Ed. by Jane Vansittart. 1966.

Autobiographical and family history, by a daughter of Elizabeth Fry (2604).

2109 BERNARD. The Bernards of Abington and Nether Winchendon. By Sophia Elizabeth Higgins. 4 v. 1903–4.

V. 3–4 deal with the careers of the children of governor Sir Francis Bernard, especially Sir John Bernard, Scrope Bernard, M.P., and Thomas Bernard, the philanthropist. Correspondence 1780–1828 includes letters of Hannah More and William, Lord Grenville.

2110 JOLLIFFE. The Jolliffes of Staffordshire and their descendants. By Lord Hylton. 1892.

Correspondence and journals, touching on private and public affairs, late 18th and early 19th centuries.

2111 FRANCIS. The Francis letters, by Sir Philip Francis and other members of the family [1754–1818]. Ed. by Beata Francis and Eliza Keary. 2 v. 1901.

V. 2, letters on personal and family matters, 1789–1814, many of them addressed to Lord and Lady Thanet. See also (164).

2112 BEAUFOY. Leaves from a beech tree. By Gwendolyn Beaufoy. Oxf. 1930.

Family history of the Beaufoys, including correspondence on personal and public matters, 1756–1828.

2113 BENTHAM. The correspondence of Jeremy Bentham [1752–1832]. Ed. by Timothy L. S. Sprigge, Ian R. Christie, and others. V. 1+. 1968, in progress.

A full collection, illustrating his personal and public concerns, his family affairs and friendships. The life and letters in Bowring (652) v. 10–11, is inadequate. There are biographies by C. M. Atkinson, 1905, and J. L. Stocks, 1933. C. W. Everett, *The education of Jeremy Bentham*, 1931, stops at 1792. A. T. Milne, comp., *Catalogue of the MSS of Jeremy Bentham in the library of University College London*, 2nd rev. edn., 1962. On Bentham's brother, Russian brigadier-general, and inspector-general of naval works, 1795–1807, see Maria S. Bentham (1354).

2114 PEPYS. A later Pepys, the correspondence of Sir William Weller Pepys, bt., master in chancery, 1758–1825, with Mrs. Chapone, Mrs. Hartley, Mrs. Montagu, Hannah More . . . and others. Ed. by introd. and notes by Alice C. C. Gaussen. 2 v. 1904.

2115 MALMESBURY. A series of letters of the first earl of Malmesbury, his family and friends, from 1745 to 1820. Ed. by the earl of Malmesbury. 2 v. 1870.

Miscellaneous political gossip. See too *Malmesbury diaries* (275); v. 3–4 include court, social and political information, 1782–1820.

2116 LYSONS. Memoir and select letters of Samuel Lysons, V.P.R.S., V.P.S.A., 1763–1819. By Lindsay Fleming. Oxf. 1934.

Correspondence 1785–1819, mainly about his archaeological pursuits.

2117 NARES. A versatile professor. Reminiscences of the Rev. E[dward] Nares. Ed. by George C. White. 1903.

His career, social life, historical and antiquarian studies, and notes on politics, 1762–1841.

2118 BECKFORD. The life and letters of William Beckford of Fonthill. By Lewis Melville. 1910.

Letters 1761–1841, from the duke of Hamilton's papers. Other letters in J. W. Oliver, *The life of William Beckford*, 1932. Guy Chapman, *Beckford*, 1937, is admirable. See too H. A. N. Brockman, *The caliph of Fonthill*, 1956; Boyd Alexander, *Life at Fonthill. From the correspondence of William Beckford*, 1957, and *William Beckford: England's wealthiest son*, 1962.

2119 WHALLEY. Journals and correspondence of Thomas Sedgewick Whalley. Ed. by Hill Wickham. 2 v. 1863.

V. 2, letters 1786–1828; correspondents include Anna Seward, Mrs. Piozzi, Martha and Hannah More; literary, social and personal.

2120 TOWNSEND. Memoirs of the Rev. John Townsend. Founder of the asylum for the deaf and dumb. 1828.

His life and his educational and charitable work in London slums, 1757–1826.

2121 GRAY. Papers and diaries of a York family, 1764–1839. Ed. by Mrs. Edwin Gray. 1927.

Life of a York solicitor and his family, with politically progressive and philanthropic interests.

2122 MORE. Memoirs of the life and correspondence of Mrs. Hannah More. By William Roberts. 4 v. 1834.

Letters, 1773–1828. Arthur Roberts, ed., *Letters of Hannah More to Zachary Macaulay*, 1860, and *Mendip annals: or, A narrative of the charitable labours of Hannah and Martha More*, 2nd edn., 1859. Mary Gwladys Jones, *Hannah More*, 1952, a critical scholarly study, supersedes other lives. On her interest in education see Weeks (3355).

2123 BELSHAM. Memoirs of the late . . . Thomas Belsham. By John Williams. 1833.

Life of a unitarian minister, teacher and writer, including extracts from his diaries, 1779–1826.

2124 MORDAUNT. The Mordaunts: an eighteenth century family. By Elizabeth Hamilton. 1965.

Correspondence of the 8th baronet and his family, 1789–c. 1830.

2125 CHEVEREL. The Cheverels of Cheverel Manor. Ed. by Lady Newdigate-Newdigate. 1898.

Letters, 1776–1800, illustrative of county society, of Lady Newdigate, second wife of Sir Roger Newdigate of Arbury, War.

2126 THRALE-PIOZZI. Thraliana, the diary of Mrs. Hester Lynch Thrale (later Mrs. Piozzi), 1776–1809. Ed. by Katharine C. Balderston. 2 v. Oxf. 1942.

From the MSS. in the Huntington Library; v. 2, 1784–1809. Letters of Mrs. Piozzi are printed in Edward Mangin, *Piozziana, or, Recollections of the late Mrs. Piozzi by a friend*, 1833, and A. Hayward, *Autobiography, letters and literary remains of Mrs. Piozzi (Thrale)*, 2 v., Boston, 1861. O. G. Knapp, ed., *The intimate letters of Hester Piozzi and Penelope Pennington, 1788–1821*, 1914. James L. Clifford, *Hester Lynch Piozzi (Mrs. Thrale)*, Oxf., 1941, select bibliog., 470–3, is scholarly.

2127 RITSON. The letters of Joseph Ritson. By Sir Harry Nicolas. 2 v. 1833.

Correspondence on literary matters, 1776–1803. See Bertrand H. Bronson, *Joseph Ritson, scholar-at-arms*, 2 v., Berkeley, 1938.

2128 BERRY. The Berry papers; being the correspondence hitherto unpublished of Mary and Agnes Berry (1763–1852). Ed. by Lewis Melville. 1914.

Letters 1790–1850, but little after 1817. Principal correspondents are Mrs. Damer, Edward Jerningham, John Playfair, Mrs. Howe, the 6th duke of Devonshire; also letters from Mary to Agnes written from Paris in 1816; personal, social, and political gossip. Theresa Lewis, *Extracts from the journals and correspondence of Miss Berry . . . 1783–1852*, 3 v., 1866, is a full and valuable social record.

2129 BUTLER. The Hamwood papers of the ladies of Llangollen and of Caroline Hamilton. Ed. by Eva Mary Bell. 1930.

Diaries and correspondence of Lady Eleanor Butler, Sarah Ponsonby, and Caroline Hamilton, 1774–1831.

2130 PINKERTON. The literary correspondence of John Pinkerton, esq., now first printed from the originals in the possession of Dawson Turner. 2 v. 1830.

Letters, 1775–1815, mainly on literary and scholarly matters.

2131 LONG. Records and letters of the family of the Longs of Longville, Jamaica, and Hampton Lodge, Surrey. By Robert Mowbray Howard. 2 v. 1925.

Much correspondence on personal, public, and military affairs, 1789–1851, among members of the family living in England or in the armed forces.

2132 MELBOURNE. In whig society, 1775–1818; compiled from the hitherto unpublished correspondence of Elizabeth, viscountess Melbourne, and Emily Lamb, countess Cowper, afterwards viscountess Palmerston. By Mabell, countess of Airlie. 1921.

Correspondence of the mother of prime minister, Lord Melbourne, and her daughter. Elizabeth Jenkins, *Lady Caroline Lamb*, 1932, prints family letters of Melbourne's wife, 1805–28.

2133 HOLLAND. The journal of Elizabeth, Lady Holland, 1791–1811. Ed. by the earl of Ilchester. 2 v. 1908.

Ilchester also ed., *The Spanish journal of Elizabeth, Lady Holland*, 1910, including an appendix of letters sent to Lord Holland, 1808, from various British agents in the Peninsula; *Elizabeth, Lady Holland to her son*, 1946, letters, 1821–1845; and *The journal of the Hon. Henry Edward Fox (afterwards fourth and last Lord Holland), 1818–1830*,

1923. Lady Seymour, ed., *The 'pope' of Holland House. Selections from the correspondence of John Whishaw and his friends, 1813–1840*, 1906. Marie [Fox], Princess Liechtenstein, *Holland House*, 2 v., 1874, prints many letters, 1741–1825; more informative are the earl of Ilchester, *The home of the Hollands, 1605–1820*, 1937 (mainly on the reign of George III) and *Chronicles of Holland House, 1820–1900*, 1937 (mainly on 1820–50). Lloyd [Charles] Sanders, *The Holland House circle*, 1908, is useful but based only on printed material. Sonia Keppel, *The sovereign lady*, 1974, is an up-to-date biographical study of Lady Holland and her family.

2134 DEVONSHIRE. The two duchesses: Georgiana, duchess of Devonshire; Elizabeth, duchess of Devonshire. Family correspondence . . . 1777–1859. Ed. by Vere Foster. 2nd edn. 1898.

Family affairs and political gossip. For further letters see *Georgiana: extracts from the correspondence of Georgiana, duchess of Devonshire*, ed. by the earl of Bessborough, 1955; *Hary-O: the letters of Lady Harriet Cavendish, 1796–1809*, ed. by Sir George Leveson Gower and Iris Palmer, 1940. Dorothy M. Stuart, *Dearest Bess*, 1955, is a valuable portrait of the second duchess, using her unpublished journals. See too Hugh Stokes, *The Devonshire House circle*, 1917, and Marjorie Villiers, *The grand Whiggery*, 1939. For the family correspondence of Georgiana's sister see the earl of Bessborough and A. Aspinall, eds., *Lady Bessborough and her family circle*, 1940, and E. C. Mayne, *A regency chapter: Lady Bessborough and her friendships*, 1939. On the 6th duke's circle see Markham (2977).

2135 STUART. Gleanings from an old portfolio, containing some correspondence between Lady Louisa Stuart and her sister Caroline, countess of Portarlington, and other friends and relations. Ed. by Mrs. Godfrey Clark [Alice Georgina Caroline (Strong) Clark]. 3 v. Edin. 1895.

Letters on family and social affairs in the Bute circle, 1778–1813. James A. Home, ed., *Lady Louisa Stuart: selections from her manuscripts*, N.Y., 1899, includes her correspondence with Sir Walter Scott, 1826–30, and her letters to Mrs. Lockhart; Home also ed. *Letters of Lady Louisa Stuart to Miss Louisa Clinton*, 2 v., Edin., 1901–3 (letters, 1817–1834). See too Susan Charlotte Buchan [Lady Tweedsmuir], *Lady Louisa Stuart: her memories and portraits*, 1932. On the family of her brother, general Charles Stuart, see Violet Stuart-Wortley, *Highcliffe and the Stuarts*, 1927, letters, 1794–1843.

2136 FRAMPTON. The journal of Mary Frampton from the year 1779 until the year 1846 including various interesting and curious letters, anecdotes, etc., relating to events which occurred during that period. Ed. with notes by Harriet Georgiana Mundy. 1885.

Includes correspondence of the connections of the earl of Ilchester, and other personalities of the court circle and of county society.

2137 BARBAULD. Georgian chronicle; Mrs. Barbauld and her family. By Betsy Rodgers. 1958.

With an appendix of letters, 1779–1850. Mrs. Herbert Martin ed., *Memories of seventy years*, 1883, being the memoirs of Mrs. Barbauld's great-niece, Anna Letitia (Aikin) Le Breton, including some family letters.

2138 PERCY. The Percy Letters. [Vol. 1.] The correspondence of Thomas Percy and Edmund Malone. Ed. by Arthur Tillotson. Louisiana State Univ. 1944.

Letters, 1789–1811; social, literary and political gossip. Alice C. C. Gaussen, *Percy: prelate and poet*, 1908, includes extracts from family letters of the 1790s.

2139 JERNINGHAM. The Jerningham letters (1780–1843). Being excerpts from the correspondence and diaries of . . . Lady Jerningham and of her daughter, Lady Bedingfield. Ed. with notes by Egerton Castle. 2 v. 1896.

Family and social affairs. Ernest Betham ed., *A house of letters, being excerpts from the correspondence of Miss Charlotte Jerningham . . . Lady Jerningham, Coleridge, Lamb, Southey, Bernard, and Lucy Barton and others, with Matilda Betham*, 1905.

2140 SINCLAIR. The correspondence of the right honourable Sir John Sinclair, bt. . . . ed by himself. 2 v. 1831.

A haphazard collection of letters from 1781 to illustrate the range of his contacts, from a much more extensive archive in family hands. Rosalind Mitchison, *Agricultural Sir John. The life of Sir John Sinclair of Ulbster, 1754–1835*, 1962, is excellent.

2141 SIBBALD. The memoirs of Susan Sibbald (1783–1812). Ed. by Francis Paget Hett. 1926.

Family, social, and personal; Cornwall, Bath, Scotland, London.

2142 CHALMERS. The public life of George Chalmers. By Grace Amelia Cockroft. 1939.

Bibliog. 216–30. A loyalist refugee from America, he was colonial agent for the Bahamas, 1792–1804, and chief clerk to the board of trade, 1786–1825, and engaged in literary pursuits.

2143 SEWARD. Letters of Anna Seward. 6 v. Edin. 1811.

1784–1807, to George Hardinge, William Hayley, Lady Eleanor Butler, Edward Jerningham, Thomas Park, Revd. T. S. Whalley, Sir Walter Scott; personal and literary. See Margaret Ashmun, *The singing swan*, New Haven, 1931.

2144 JESUP. Extracts from the memoranda and letters of Mary Jesup. 1842.

Life in a Quaker family, 1787–1835.

2145 SPENCER-STANHOPE. Annals of a Yorkshire House from the papers of a macaroni (Walter Spencer-Stanhope) and his kindred. By Anna Maria Wilhelmina Stirling. 2 v. 1911. See also (2223).

2146 SHELLEY. The diary of Frances Lady Shelley, 1787–1873. Ed. by Richard Edgcumbe. 2 v. 1912–13.

2147 WYNDHAM. A family history 1688–1837. The Wyndhams of Somerset, Sussex and Wiltshire. By Hugh Archibald Wyndham. 1950.

Includes narrative and correspondence touching on the family and public affairs, estate management and country life of the 3rd earl of Egremont and his circle, 1789–1837.

2148 MALONE. Life of Edmund Malone, editor of Shakespeare. With selections from his manuscript anecdotes. By Sir James Prior. 1860.

Includes correspondence and memoirs, *c.* 1790–1810. See also (2138).

2149 CREWE. The Crewe papers. Section 1: Letters from Mr. Windham to Mrs. Crewe. *Miscellanies of the Philobiblon Society*. 1865–6.

1790–1809, on social and political matters.

2150 WHITE. The life of Joseph Blanco White. Ed. by John Hamilton Thom. 1845.

1775–1841; autobiography interspersed with correspondence with divines and men of letters.

2151 BETTS. The Betts of Wortham in Suffolk, 1480–1905. By Katharine Frances Doughty. 1912.

Local gentry; their involvement in public affairs, 1789–1851.

2152 HICKS-BEACH. A Cotswold family: Hicks and Hicks-Beach. By Susan Emily Hicks-Beach. 1909.

Family correspondence and history, 1789–1851, with letters of Sydney Smith.

2153 ATKINSON. The life and adventures of an eccentric traveller. By Charles Atkinson. York. 1818.

Autobiographical account of a military surgeon's travels in England.

2154 TAYLOR. A memoir of the life and writings of the late William Taylor of Norwich. . . . Ed. by John Warden Robberds. 2 v. 1843.

His life and correspondence, 1765–1836, including letters of Robert Southey and Sir Walter Scott; mainly literary.

2155 AUSTIN. Three generations of Englishwomen. Memoirs and correspondence of Mrs. John Taylor, Mrs. Sarah Austin, and Lady Duff Gordon. By Janet Ross. 2 v. 1888.

Mrs. Austin was the wife of John Austin, the jurist.

2156 FLETCHER. Autobiography of Mrs. Fletcher, with . . . letters and other family memorials. [Ed. by her daughter, Lady Richardson]. Carlisle. 1874.

Wife of the Scottish reformer, Archibald Fletcher (1746–1828); social life and literary interests in Scotland and Yorkshire; contacts with Wordsworth, Mrs. Barbauld and the Aikin family; a substantial record, 1780–1850.

2157 OPIE. Memorials of the life of Amelia Opie, selected and arranged from her letters, diaries and other manuscripts. By Cecilia Brightwell. 2nd edn. Norwich. 1854.

The personal and literary friendships of a Norfolk novelist (1769–1833).

2158 BIGLAND. Memoir of the life of J[ohn] Bigland . . . Written by himself. 1830.

Amusing record of a self-taught Yorkshire educationist and antiquarian.

2159 BRYDGES. The autobiography . . . of Sir Samuel Egerton Brydges. 2 v. 1834.

Life of the bibliographer and genealogist, 1762–1837.

2160 BOWER. The diaries and correspondence of Anna Catherina Bower. Priv. printed. 1903.

Mainly letters to her, 1780–1799, from her friends among the lesser gentry society of Dorset; personal and social gossip.

2161 GORDON. Personal memoirs; or, Reminiscences of men and manners at home and abroad during the last half-century . . . By Pryse Lockhart Gordon. 2 v. 1830.

Anecdotal, but interesting on London literary society.

2162 LINLEY. The Linleys of Bath. By Clementina Black. 1911.

Family history, 1789–1835, including a few letters of R. B. Sheridan.

2163 WOLLSTONECRAFT. Memoirs of Mary Wollstonecraft Godwin. By William Godwin. 1798.

Mainly 1787–97. See R. M. Wardle, *Mary Wollstonecraft. A critical biography*, Lawrence, Kansas, 1952, and *Godwin and Mary; letters of William Godwin and Mary Wollstonecraft*, Lawrence, Kansas, 1967. On Godwin see (521). Claire Tomalin, *The life and death of Mary Wollstonecraft*, 1974. See also (1969).

2164 FOSTER. The life and correspondence of John Foster. Ed. by Jonathan Edwards Ryland. 2 v. 1846.

Baptist minister and essayist, 1770–1843; letters illustrative of his life and social environment, 1790–1843.

2165 GILBERT. Beyond the blaze. A biography of Davies Gilbert. By Arthur C. Todd. 1967.

Life, 1767–1839, of an M.P. and president of the Royal Society, with literary, antiquarian and geological interests.

2166 GLENBERVIE. The diaries of Sylvester Douglas, Lord Glenbervie. Ed. by Francis Bickley. 2 v. 1928.

Political and social memorials of a minor politician recorded day by day, Dec. 1793–Feb. 1819. For some additional material, see Walter S. Sichel, *The Glenbervie journals*, 1910.

2167 CARY. Memoir of the Rev. Henry Francis Cary, M.A., translator of Dante. With his literary journal and letters. By the Rev. Henry Cary. 2 v. 1847.

Life, 1772–1844, travel, family, literary affairs.

2168 POOLE. Thomas Poole and his friends. By Margaret E. Sandford. 2 v. 1888.

Life, 1765–1837, of a self-educated tanner of whiggish leanings, a friend of the Lake poets. See (2282).

2169 FARINGTON. The Farington diary, 1793–1821. Ed. by James Greig. 8 v. 1922–8.

A mine of miscellaneous information noted by the painter, Joseph Farington.

2170 STANLEY. The girlhood of Maria Josepha Holroyd [Lady Stanley of Alderley]. Recorded in letters of a hundred years ago: from 1776 to 1796. Ed. by Jane Henrietta Adeane. 1896. 2nd edn. 1897.

Family letters, mostly of 1791–6. Jane H. Adeane also ed. *The early married life of Maria Josepha, Lady Stanley, with extracts from Sir John Stanley's 'Praeterita'*, 1899, including memoirs and letters, 1766–1823. Nancy Mitford, ed., *The ladies of Alderley; being the letters of Maria Josepha and her daughter-in-law Henrietta-Maria during the years 1841–1850*, 1967.

2171   WYNNE. The Wynne diaries. Ed. by Anne Fremantle. 3 v. 1935–40.

Diaries and letters, 1780–1820, of Elizabeth, Eugenia, and Harriet Wynne; family, naval, social affairs, foreign travel.

2172   ROSCOE. The life of William Roscoe. By Henry Roscoe. 2 v. 1833.

Career of the Liverpool author and radical reformer, 1752–1831. See too G. Chandler *William Roscoe of Liverpool*, 1953.

2173   RUMNEY. From the Old South Sea House; being Thomas Rumney's letter book, 1796–1798. Ed. by Abraham Wren Rumney. 1914.

Material on the life of a Westmorland yeoman (1764–1835). A. W. Rumney, *Tom Rumney of Mellfell . . . by himself, as set out in his letters and diary*, Kendal, 1936, reprints the letters and includes extracts from his accounts, 1814–1833, and full reproduction of his diaries, 1805–6.

2174   SHARPE. Letters from and to Charles Kirkpatrick Sharpe. Ed. by A. Allardyce. With a memoir by W. K. R. Bedford. 2 v. 1888.

Correspondence, 1798–1850, regarding his literary and antiquarian pursuits; a friend of Sir Walter Scott.

2175   BURN. James Burn; the 'Beggar Boy': an autobiography . . . With glimpses of English social, commercial, and political history during . . . 1802–1882. 1882.

Life of a poverty-stricken vagrant who became a tradesman and tavern keeper.

2176   SEWELL. The life and letters of Mrs. [Mary] Sewell. By Mary Bayly. 3rd edn. 1889.

Interesting on Quakerism and country life in the early 19th century.

2177   BRUMMELL. The life of George Brummell, Esq. By William Jesse. 1844. Revised edn. 1886. New edn. 1927.

The main source; includes some letters. Lewis Melville, *Beau Brummell, his life and letters*, 1924, and Kathleen Campbell, *Beau Brummell*, 1948, include some further material.

2178   FRERE. John Hookham Frere and his friends. By Gabrielle Festing. 1899.

Social circle of a minor diplomat and author, a friend of Canning.

2179   WALDEGRAVE. The three ladies Waldegrave and their mother. By Violet Biddulph. 1938.

Family correspondence of the sisters in the 1790s; letters of Hugh Seymour, R.N.; sidelights on the later careers of the duke of Gloucester and of Mrs. Fitzherbert, and on the Seymour adoption.

2180 ROBERTS. Autobiography and select remains. By Samuel Roberts. 1849.

His life, verses, and reformist pamphlets, 1763–1848.

2181 WARE. The life and correspondence of Samuel Hibbert Ware. By Mary Clementine Hibbert Ware. Manchester. 1882.

Family, social, and local affairs, Edinburgh and Manchester, 1782–1848.

2182 BRONTË. A man of sorrow; the life, letters and times of the Rev. Patrick Brontë, 1777–1861. By John Lock and William Thomas Dixon. 1965.

See also (2718).

2183 THELWALL. The life of John Thelwall. By his widow. 1837.

Includes sections of an autobiographical memoir written after the treason trials of 1794. See too C. Cestre, *John Thelwall, a pioneer of democracy and social reform in England during the French Revolution*, 1906.

2184 WAY. The Ways of yesterday. Being the chronicles of the Way family from 1307 to 1885. By Anna Maria Wilhelmina Stirling. 1930.

Mainly a study, with the correspondence, of the career and family affairs of the Revd. Lewis Way, 1772–1840.

2185 PAGET. The Paget brothers, 1790–1840. Ed. by Lord Hylton. 1918.

Family letters.

2186 MACAULAY. The life and letters of Zachary Macaulay. By Viscountess Knutsford. 1900.

Letters, 1791–1838. See Charles Booth, *Zachary Macaulay*, 1934.

2187 BRIDGEWATER. The Bridgewater millions. A candid family history. By Bernard Falk. 1942.

The social circle of the inheritors of the duke of Bridgewater's estate.

2188 RICKMAN. The life and letters of John Rickman. By Orlo Williams. 1912.

Career of the statistician who managed the early censuses.

2189 SHERWOOD. The life of Mrs. Sherwood. Ed. by Sophia Kelly. 1854.

Career of a dau. of George Butt, chaplain to George III; social worker and authoress; associations with Henry Martyn, Elizabeth Fry, Wilberforce. See too F. J. Harvey Darton, *The life and times of Mrs. Sherwood (1775–1851), from the diaries of Captain and Mrs. Sherwood*, 1910, and Naomi Royde Smith, *The state of mind of Mrs. Sherwood*, 1946. On the career of her sister as a clergyman's wife and writer of children's tales, see *The life of Mrs. Cameron: partly an autobiography and from her private journals*, ed. by Charles Cameron, 1862.

2190 TINDALL. Family memorials. Ed. by M. A. Harris. Priv. printed. Leighton Buzzard. 1869.

Life in Yorkshire Quaker society.

2191 MARSDEN. A brief memoir of the life and writings of . . . William Marsden, written by himself, with notes from his correspondence. 1838.

Literary and social, and some notes on his career as secretary to the admiralty, 1794–1807.

2192 CARTER. Memoirs of a working man. With an introduction by Charles Knight. 1845.

Life of a tailor, John (or Thomas) Carter, 1792 to *c.* 1840.

2193 LUCAS. A Quaker journal. Being the diary and reminiscences of William Lucas of Hitchin, 1804–1861. Ed. by Gilbert Ernest Bryant and George Philip Baker. 2 v. 1934.

Personal and family life of a Hertfordshire brewer.

2194 CARRINGTON. The Carrington diary (1797–1810). Ed. by William Branch-Johnson. 1956.

Notes by a farmer of Bramfield, who held various parish offices.

2195 CANNING. The story of two noble lives: being memorials of Charlotte, countess Canning, and Louisa, marchioness of Waterford. By Augustus J. C. Hare. 3 v. 1893.

Letters, 1801–90, on personal, social, and political topics.

2196 GREY. A family chronicle, derived from notes and letters selected by Barbarina, the Hon. Lady Grey. Ed. by Gertrude Lyster. 1908.

Family correspondence, mainly of Barbarina, Lady Dacre; social and political gossip, 1793–1888.

2197 SUFFIELD. A memoir of the life of Edward, third Baron Suffield. By Richard Mackenzie Bacon. Norwich. 1838.

Letters, 1794–1835, on family and local affairs, parliament and prison reform.

2198 SCORESBY. The life of William Scoresby. By Robert Edmund Scoresby Jackson. 1861.

The varied life of an arctic navigator who became an explorer and scientist, and a clergyman.

2199 WILLIAMS WYNN. Correspondence of Charlotte Grenville, Lady Williams Wynn, and her three sons. Ed. by Rachel Leighton. 1920.

Letters, 1795–1832, concerning the Wynn and Grenville circle, with much political gossip; she was a sister of William, Lord Grenville. *Diaries of a lady of quality from 1797 to 1844,* ed. by A. Hayward, 1864, is an edition of the memoranda of anecdotes made by her daughter, Frances Williams Wynn.

2200 WILLIAMS WYNN. Memorials of Charlotte Williams Wynn. 1877.

2201 TURNER. Sir Hilgrove Turner, 1764–1843. Soldier and courtier under the Georges. By Arthur F. Loveday. Dover. 1964.

Diaries and letters, 1800–31.

2202 PATTLE. Julia Margaret Cameron: A Victorian family portrait. By Brian Hill. 1973.

Affairs of the Anglo-Indian family of Pattle in the early nineteenth century.

2203 ALBEMARLE. Fifty years of my life. By George Thomas, 6th earl of Albemarle. 2 v. 1876.

V. 1 includes royal correspondence, 1805–10; v. 2, his journals during the Waterloo campaign, his travels and social life.

2204 WEDGWOOD. A group of Englishmen (1795–1815), being records of the younger Wedgwoods and their friends, embracing the discovery of photography. . . . By Eliza Meteyard. 1871.

Includes material on the Coleridges and Darwins. See too Henrietta E. Litchfield, ed., *Emma Darwin: a century of family letters, 1792–1896*, 1904.

2205 BAMFORD. Passages in the life of a radical [Samuel Bamford]. Ed. by Henry Dunckley. 2 v. 1893.

Includes Samuel Bamford's *Early days*, first publ. 1849. The career of a radical weaver and writer, 1788–1872. New edn. entitled *The autobiography of Samuel Bamford*, ed with intro. by W. H. Chaloner, 2 v., 1967.

2206 THOMASON. Sir Edward Thomason's memoirs during half a century. 2 v. 1845.

Life of a Birmingham metalware manufacturer; letters, 1796–1843.

2207 TERRY. The diaries of Dummer. Ed. by Anna Maria Wilhelmina Stirling. 1934.

Diaries and reminiscences, 1795–1861, of Stephen Terry (1774–1867); education, and country life in Hampshire.

2208 THORNTON. Marianne Thornton, 1797–1887; a domestic biography. By Edward Morgan Forster. 1956.

Includes her recollections of the Clapham circle.

2209 WHARNCLIFFE. The first Lady Wharncliffe and her family, 1799–1856. Ed. by Caroline Grosvenor and Lord Stuart of Wortley. 2 v. 1927.

Social and political gossip.

2210 ROBINSON. Diary, reminiscences and correspondence of Henry Crabb Robinson. Ed. by Thomas Sadler. 3 v. 1869. 3rd rev. edn. 2 v. 1872.

From the papers in Dr. Williams's library. Edith J. Morley, ed., *Henry Crabb Robinson on books and their writers*, 3 v., 1938, and *The correspondence of Henry Crabb Robinson with the Wordsworth circle* [1801–60], 2 v., 1927. See too Edith J. Morley, *The life and times of . . . Robinson*, 1935; John Milton Baker, *Henry Crabb Robinson, of Bury, Jena*, The Times, *and Russell Square*, 1937, bibliog. 245–50.

2211 TAYLOR. Autobiography of [Sir] Henry Taylor. 2 v. 1885.

A friend of the lake poets and of the Benthamites, author, and colonial office official. E. Dowden ed., *The correspondence of Sir Henry Taylor*, 1888; letters, 1823–53.

2212   WAKE. The reminiscences of Charlotte, Lady Wake. Ed. by Lucy Wake. 1909.

Society life in Derbyshire, Worcestershire, and Northants, 1800–1887.

2213   DUDLEY. Letters to Ivy [Helen D'Arcy Stewart] from the first earl of Dudley. Ed. by Samuel Henry Romilly. 1905.

Political and social gossip, 1801–32. [Edward Copleston] ed., *Letters of the earl of Dudley to the bishop of Llandaff*, 1840; letters, 1814–23, literary and political matters.

2214   THOMSON. George Thomson. The friend of Burns. His life and correspondence. By Cuthbert Hadden. 1898.

Letters, 1803–47; Burns, Sir Walter Scott, Beethoven, and others.

2215   LYTTELTON. Correspondence of Sarah [Spencer], Lady Lyttelton, 1787–1870. Ed. by Mrs. Hugh Wyndham. 1912.

Letters, 1804–68, rich in social and political gossip; she held court appointments, 1837–50. On her family see Betty Askwith, *The Lytteltons*, 1975.

2216   RICHARDSON. Recollections, political, literary, dramatic, and miscellaneous, of the last half century. By John Richardson, Ll.B. 2 v. 1856.

2217   ROGERS. Recollections of the table-talk of Samuel Rogers. [Ed. by Alexander Dyce.] 1856. 1887.

Records conversations of Burke, Fox, and Horne Tooke. This book together with [William Sharpe], *Recollections, by Samuel Rogers*, 1859, was the basis of *Reminiscences and table-talk of . . . Rogers*, ed. by George Herbert Powell, 1903. P. W. Clayden, *The early life of Samuel Rogers*, 1887, includes letters, 1780–1802, and was cont. in *Rogers and his contemporaries*, 2 v., 1889, with letters, 1803–55; other letters in Carl P. Barbier, *Samuel Rogers and William Gilpin: their friendship and correspondence*, 1959. See too R. E. Roberts, *Samuel Rogers and his circle*, 1910, and (2385).

2218   SADLER. Memoirs of the life and writings of Michael Thomas Sadler. By Robert Benton Seeley and W. Burnside. 1842.

Business life in Yorkshire and social and political reform, *c.* 1800–35.

2219   SALISBURY. The Gascoyne heiress. The life and diaries of Frances Mary Gascoyne-Cecil, 1802–39. By Carola Oman. 1968.

Extensive material from diaries, 1822–38.

2220   YOUNG. A memoir of Charles Mayne Young, tragedian, with extracts from his son's journal. By Julian Charles Young. 2 v. 1871.

A rather brief memoir of C. M. Y., with a few letters, 1777–1856; mainly autobiographical notes and journals of his son, 1806–70.

2221   WARD. Peeps into the past, being passages from the diary of Thomas Asline Ward. Ed. by Alexander B. Bell and Robert Eadon Leader. 1909.

Diaries and letters, 1804–71, principally before 1852; personal, social and political affairs, mainly in Yorkshire.

2222 HERON. Notes, by Sir Robert Heron, baronet. 1851.

His life, social circle, reflections; mainly of interest after 1810.

2223 SPENCER-STANHOPE. The letter-bag of Lady Elizabeth Spencer-Stanhope, compiled from the Cannon Hall papers, 1806–1873. By Anna Maria Wilhelmina Stirling. 2 v. 1913.

On the family circle of the Spencer-Stanhopes and Cokes see also Spencer Pickering, ed., *Memoirs of Anna Maria Wilhelmina Pickering*, priv. printed, 1903.

2224 SEDGWICK. Life and letters of the Reverend Adam Sedgwick. By John Willis Clark and Thomas McKenny Hughes. 2 v. Camb. 1890.

Letters, 1807–68; Cambridge life and the study of geology.

2225 SOMERSET. Correspondence of two brothers: Edward Adolphus, eleventh duke of Somerset and his brother Lord Webb Seymour; 1800–1819 and after. By Helen Guendolen Ramsden. 1906.

Letters and diaries, mainly social. See too W. H. Mallock and Gwendolen Ramsden, eds., *Letters, remains and memoirs* [1804–85] *of Edward Adolphus Seymour, twelfth duke of Somerset*, 1893.

2226 STAUNTON. Memoirs of . . . the public life of Sir George Thomas Staunton, bt. 1856.

Life of a politician and diplomat.

2227 MORGAN. Memoirs, autobiography, diaries and correspondence of Lady Morgan. Ed. by William Hepworth Dixon. 2 v. 1862.

Literary and social life in England and Ireland. See too Sydney, Lady Morgan, *Passages from my autobiography*, 1859, including some letters mainly of 1818–19.

2228 REDDING. Fifty years recollections. By Cyrus Redding. 3 v. 1858.

Informative memoirs of a journalist; London literary and theatrical society. Supplemented by his *Yesterday and today*, 3 v., 1863. See also (2022).

2229 ADOLPHUS. Recollections of the public career and the private life of the late John Adolphus, the eminent barrister and historian, with extracts from his diaries. By Emily Henderson. 1871.

Includes his account of his contacts with the duke of Sussex.

2230 TEIGNMOUTH. Reminiscences of many years. By Charles John [Shore] Lord Teignmouth. 2 v. 1878.

Full of detail about persons and events, especially in Bristol and Yorkshire.

2231 MONTEFIORE. Diaries of Sir Moses and Lady Montefiore. Ed. by Louis Loewe. 2 v. 1890.

Public diaries, 1812–83; financial business, his work for humanitarian societies and for Jewish emancipation abroad, notes on contemporary politics and court life.

2232 WORMELEY. Recollections of Ralph Randolph Wormeley. By Mary Elizabeth Wormeley, *afterwards* Latimer. N.Y. 1879.

London and Essex; naval, social, and political up to the Reform Act of 1832; member of an American loyalist family.

2233 WILSON. The memoirs of Harriet Wilson. Written by herself. 2 v. 1909. New edn. ed. by J. Laver. 1929.

Highly coloured recollections of a celebrated courtesan, *c.* 1800-25.

2234 WEETON. Miss Weeton: journal of a governess. Ed. by Edward Hall. 2 v. 1936-9.

V. 1: 1807-11; v. 2: 1811-25.

2235 WESTMORLAND. The correspondence of Priscilla, countess of Westmorland. Ed. by Rose Weigall. 1909.

Social, political, and diplomatic affairs, 1812-70. For her correspondence with Wellington see (201), and on her diplomat husband (283).

2236 WATSON. James Watson. By William James Linton. New Haven. 1879.

Life of a radical printer and author, 1799-1874.

2237 TUKE. Samuel Tuke, his life, work and thoughts. By Charles Tylor. 1900.

Includes correspondence and diaries of a York Quaker philanthropist, 1784-1857. W. K. and E. M. Sessions, *The Tukes of York*, 1971, is a brief family history.

2238 TRANT. The journal of Clarissa Trant, 1800-1832. Ed. by Clara Georgina Luard. 1925.

Diaries, at home and abroad, 1811-32, of the very observant daughter of one of Wellington's brilliant peninsular commanders.

2239 OWEN. Threading my way; 27 years of autobiography. By Robert Dale Owen. 1874.

The early life, 1801-27, of the son of Robert Owen (524).

2240 GLADSTONE. The Gladstones: a family biography, 1764-1851. By Sydney George Checkland. 1971.

Liverpool commercial life and the family background of W. E. Gladstone (230).

2241 JERDAN. The autobiography of William Jerdan. 4 v. 1852-3.

The life and milieu of a London journalist; excellent. See also (2020).

2242 LENNOX. Drafts on my memory: being men I have known, things I have seen, places I have visited. By William Pitt Lennox. 2 v. 1866.

Voluble; possibly untrustworthy; followed by his *My recollections from 1806 to 1873*, 2 v., 1874; *Celebrities I have known*, 1st ser., 2 v., 1876, 2nd ser., 2 v., 1877; social, sporting, and theatrical life.

2243 MILNES. The life, letters and friendships of R. Monckton Milnes, first Lord Houghton. By Thomas Wemyss Reid. 2nd edn. 2 v. 1890.

Family letters from 1809, and correspondence with many notable political and literary figures, including Peel, Gladstone, Wordsworth, C. J. MacCarthy, Sydney Smith, Thomas Carlyle. See too James Pope-Hennessy, *Monckton Milnes: the years of promise, 1809-51*, 1950.

2244 TILKE. An autobiographical memoir . . . and a full description of his mode of treating diseases. By Samuel Westcott Tilke. 1840.

Country life, bakery business, and herbalism, 1794–1840.

2245 THOMSON. The autobiography of an artisan. By Christopher Thomson. 1847.

Includes much about working-class life in Yorkshire.

2246 STEPHEN. Sir James Stephen . . . letters with biographical notes. By Caroline Emelia Stephen. Priv. printed. 1906.

Private and family life of an under-secretary of state for the colonies; letters, 1810–59. See also (4305).

2247 TAYLOR. Autobiography of a Lancashire lawyer, being the life and recollections of John Taylor, attorney at law. Bolton. 1883.

Letters and diaries, 1811–1883; personal, professional, and local interest.

2248 STEGGALL. A real history of a Suffolk man. By John Henry Steggall. Ed. by Richard Cobbold. 1857.

Life of a runaway schoolboy who became a curate in Suffolk.

2249 SMART. Leaves from the journals of Sir George [Thomas] Smart. Ed. by Hugh Bertram Cox and C. L. E. Cox. 1907.

Life of a musician, 1776–1867, from autobiographical writings and journals.

2250 SCOTT. An Englishman at home and abroad, 1792–1828. Ed. by Ethel Mann. 1930.

Diaries of a philanthropist and traveller, John Barber Scott (1792–1862).

2251 RICHARDSON. Records of a Quaker family: the Richardsons of Cleveland. By Anne Ogden Boyce. 1889.

2252 RAFFLES. Memoirs of the life and ministry of the Rev. Thomas Raffles. By Thomas Stamford Raffles. 1864.

Social, scholarly, and parish activities at Liverpool over a period of fifty years.

2253 LUKE. Early years of my life. By Jemima Thompson, *afterwards* Luke. 1900.

Life in the Brixton area, mission work and infant education, early 19th century.

2254 LONDONDERRY. Frances Anne: the life of Frances Anne, marchioness of Londonderry, and her husband, Charles, third marquess of Londonderry. By Edith Vane-Tempest-Stewart, marchioness of Londonderry. 1958.

Family, social, political, and diplomatic gossip in the circle of Castlereagh's half-brother.

2255 HUNT. Memoirs of Henry Hunt, esq., written by himself in H.M. jail at Ilchester. 3 v. 1820–22.

Records of the life of the Wiltshire radical agitator (1773–1835). See also Robert Huish, *The history of the private and political life of Henry Hunt*, 2 v., 1835–6.

2256 HOWARD. Reminiscences for my children. By Catharine Mary Howard. 4 v. Carlisle. 1836–8.

Upper class country life in Cumberland; v. 1 includes accounts of country houses in the north, v. 2 is largely concerned with travels in France, 1814–15.

2257 ROMILLY. Romilly-Edgeworth letters, 1813–1818. With an introd. and notes by Samuel Henry Romilly. 1936.

Mainly the letters of Anne, wife of Sir Samuel Romilly (576).

2258 HOOKER. The Hookers of Kew, 1785–1911. By Mea Allan. 1967.

Family life and careers of the botanists Sir William and Sir Joseph Dalton Hooker.

2259 STURGE. Memoirs of Joseph Sturge. By Henry Richard. 1864.

Letters and other papers, 1804–59; social and political. See too Stephen Hobhouse, *Joseph Sturge, his life and work*, 1919.

2260 HOBHOUSE. Recollections of a long life. By John Cam Hobhouse. Ed. by Lady Dorchester. 6 v. 1909–11.

Notes on personal, social, and political matters, 1809–51.

2261 JAMES. Life of commander Henry James. By Edmund Grindall Festing. 1899.

Naval and social interest; includes use of his sea diaries, 1814–38.

2262 SEWELL. Autobiography of Elizabeth M[issing] Sewell. Ed. by Eleanor L. Sewell. 1907.

Life *c.* 1815–98; childhood in the household of a land agent.

2263 PALMERSTON. The letters of Lady Palmerston; selected and edited from the originals at Broadlands and elsewhere. By Tresham Lever. [1957.]

Letters, 1816–69, mainly on social affairs. Other material in the countess of Airlie, *Lady Palmerston and her times*, 2 v., 1922. See also (217).

2264 HILL. Frederic Hill: an autobiography of fifty years in times of reform. Ed. by Constance Hill. 1894.

Includes family letters and diaries, 1783–1899; social life in Birmingham and Edinburgh, of a brother of Rowland Hill (2265) and Matthew Davenport Hill (572).

2265 HILL. The life of Sir Rowland Hill . . . and the history of penny postage. By Sir Rowland Hill and George Birkbeck Hill. 2 v. 1880.

Eleanor C. Smyth, *Sir Rowland Hill. The story of a great reform*, 1907, adds material on his private life. On the post office see (462).

2266 GRANVILLE. Letters of Harriet countess Granville, 1810–1845. Ed. by [Edward] Frederick Leveson Gower. 2 v. 1894.

See also (171).

2267 RATTENBURY. Memoirs of a smuggler, compiled from his diary and journal; containing the principal events in the life of John Rattenbury. Sidmouth. 1837.

2268 NEWTON. The diary of Benjamin Newton. Ed. by Charles Pears Fendall and Ernest Addenbrooke Crutchley. Camb. 1933.

Personal and parish life of a country parson, 1816–18.

2269 GALT. The autobiography of John Galt. 2 v. 1833.

Followed by *The literary life and miscellanies of John Galt*, 3 v., 1834; memoirs of a man with an extensive acquaintance and a varied life, but deficient in dates and definiteness of detail. Jennie W. Aberdein, *John Galt*, 1936.

2270 DYOTT. Dyott's diary, 1781–1845; a selection from the journal of William Dyott, sometime general in the British army and aide-de-camp to his Majesty King George III. Ed. by Reginald Welbury Jeffery. 1907.

Much detail on court and county society as well as military affairs.

2271 JONES. Reminiscences of the public life of Richard Lambert Jones. Priv. printed. 1863.

Notes on the career of a member of the common council of London, 1819–44, and on London development.

2272 HODGSON. Memoir of the Rev. Francis Hodgson. Ed. by James Hodgson. 2 v. 1878.

Life, 1781–1852, of a scholar and divine, provost of Eton, a correspondent of Byron, Moore, Merivale, and other literary men.

2273 HONE. William Hone. His life and times. By Frederick William Hackwood. 1912.

The career of a lively pamphleteer and bookseller, 1780–1842.

2274 WATKIN. Absalom Watkin: extracts from his journal, 1814–56. Ed. by A. E. Watkin. 1920.

Business, literary and political matters, mainly Lancashire.

2275 COX. Recollections of Oxford. By George Valentine Cox. 1868.

On Oxford life and personalities, 1789–1860.

2276 WOOD. A memoir of the right hon. William Page Wood, Baron Hatherley, with selections from his correspondence. By William Richard Wood Stephens. 2 v. 1883.

V. 1, letters from 1818, and material on his early practice and political and social connections.

2277 NEUMANN. The diary of Philipp Von Neumann, 1819–1850. Trans. and ed. by Edwin Beresford Chancellor. 2 v. 1928.

Neumann noted much social and political information during his residences in England.

2278 WILSON. Memoirs of George Wilson. By Jessie Aitken Wilson. Edinburgh. 1860.

From letters and journals, 1818–59, of the regius professor of technology at Edinburgh.

2279 JOHNSTON. Extracts from Priscilla Johnston's journal. Carlisle. 1862.

She belonged to the Quaker circle at Earlham; references to the Frys and Gurneys.

2280 GROSVENOR. Lady Elizabeth and the Grosvenors. Life in a whig family, 1822–1839. By Gervase Huxley. 1965.

2281 COOPER. The life of Sir Astley Cooper, Bart. By Bransby Blake Cooper. 2 v. 1843.

Social and court gossip and sketches from his notebooks of distinguished contemporaries.

2282 COLERIDGE. The story of a Devonshire house. By Lord Coleridge. 1905.

Biographical studies, with letters, of various members of the Coleridge family. See also: on the poet's wife, Stephen Potter, ed., *Minnow among tritons. Mrs. S. T. Coleridge's letters to Thomas Poole, 1799–1834*, 1934; on her daughter [Edith Coleridge], ed., *Memoirs and letters of Sarah Coleridge*, 2 v., 1873, including letters, 1833–51. A. D. Coleridge, *Eton in the forties, by an old colleger*, 1896, is a pleasant and substantial account of his education.

2283 CLIVE. From the diary and family papers of Mrs. Archie Clive (1801–1873). Ed. by Mary Clive. 1949.

Social life among the west midland gentry.

2284 AUSTEN. Austen papers, 1704–1856. Ed. by Richard Arthur Austen-Leigh. Priv. printed. Colchester. 1942.

On various members of Jane Austen's family. More concerned with her milieu than her literary career are Mary Constance Hill, *Jane Austen, her home and her friends*, 1902, and Geraldine E. Mitton, *Jane Austen and her times*, 1905. See also (1186), (2714).

2285 BALLANTINE. Some experiences of a barrister's life [1812–67]. By William Ballantine. 1883.

2286 BARBER. A memoir, mainly autobiographical. By James Henry Barber. Ed. by H. M. D[oncaster]. 1903.

Quaker society in Yorkshire; career in banking, 1820–47.

2287 GRATTAN. Beaten paths: and those who trod them. By Thomas Colley Grattan. 2 v. 1862.

Anecdotes about members of his circle of acquaintances, including Thomas Moore, Thomas Campbell, Coleridge, Wordsworth.

2288 JEKYLL. Correspondence of . . . Joseph Jekyll with his sister-in-law, Lady Gertrude Sloane Stanley, 1818–1838. Ed. with a brief memoir by Algernon Bourke. 1894.

Well-informed social gossip and sidelights on politics.

2289 NEWMAN. Newman family letters. Ed. by Dorothea Mozley. 1962.

Letters of the family circle of John Henry Newman, largely those of his sister Harriet, mainly of the years 1821–52.

2290 SOPWITH. Thomas Sopwith . . . with excerpts from his diary. By Benjamin Ward Richardson. 1891.

Life of a Newcastle engineer (1803–79), based on diaries from 1822.

2291 SKINNER. A journal of a Somerset rector, John Skinner, A.M., antiquary, 1772–1839. Ed. by Howard Coombs and Arthur Nesham Bax. 1930.

Camerton parish affairs, 1822–32.

2292 MARTINEAU. Harriet Martineau's autobiography: with memorials by Maria Weston Chapman. 3 v. 1877.

R. K. Webb, *Harriet Martineau: a radical Victorian*, 1960, is scholarly, with letters and other additional material. Theodora Bosanquet, *Harriet Martineau*, 1927, is less thorough, but written with insight. On Harriet's brother see James Drummond and C. B. Upton, *The life and letters of James Martineau*, 2 v., 1902; v. 1, on 1805–69.

2293 BOWRING. Autobiographical recollections of Sir John Bowring. With a brief memoir by Lewin B. Bowring. 1877.

On his involvement in the Benthamite circle, and other activities.

2294 SMITH. The working man's way in the world; being the autobiography of a journeyman printer. [By Charles Manby Smith.] 1853.

A good picture of working-class life; includes a first-hand account of the Bristol riots of 1831.

2295 BUCKINGHAM. Autobiography of James Silk Buckingham. 1855.

Records of an adventurous life; he was later concerned with journalism, politics, social reform, and philanthropy. See too R. E. Turner, *James Silk Buckingham, 1786–1855. A social biography*, 1934.

2296 BUNBURY. Life, letters, and journals of Sir Charles James Fox Bunbury. Ed. by Frances Joanna Bunbury. Priv. printed 1894.

Mrs. Henry Lyell, ed., *The life of Sir Charles James Fox Bunbury, Bart.*, 2 v., 1906.

2297 TODD. Matthew Todd's journal; a gentleman's gentleman in Europe 1814–1820. Ed. with an introd. by Geoffrey Trease. 1968.

2298 BYRON. The life and letters of Anne Isabella, Lady Noel Byron, from unpublished papers in the possession of the late Ralph, earl of Lovelace. . . . With an introd. and epilogue by Mary countess of Lovelace. By Ethel Colburn Mayne. 1909.

Letters and other family papers, *c.* 1812–59.

2299 CALVERT. An Irish beauty of the regency. Compiled from . . . the unpublished journal of the Hon. Mrs. Calvert, 1789–1822. By Alice Elizabeth Blake. 1911.

2300   CARLYLE. Reminiscences by Thomas Carlyle. Ed. by James Anthony Froude. 1881. 2nd edn. ed. by Charles Eliot Norton. 1887.

His family, and literary friendships; Southey, Wordsworth, Jeffrey. Froude also wrote the old standard Life: *Thomas Carlyle: a history of the first forty years of his life, 1795–1834*, 2 v., 1882, and *Thomas Carlyle: a history of his life in London, 1834–1881*, 2 v., 1884. The fullest Life is by David Alec Wilson and David Wilson MacArthur, 6 v., 1923–34, under titles, *Carlyle till marriage, 1795–1826; Carlyle to 'The French Revolution', 1826–1837; Carlyle on Cromwell and others, 1837–1848; Carlyle at his zenith, 1848–1853; Carlyle to three score and ten, 1853–1865;* and *Carlyle in old age, 1865–1881.* C. E. Norton, ed., *Early letters of Thomas Carlyle, 1814–1826*, 2 v., 1886, and *Letters of Thomas Carlyle, 1826–1836*, 2 v., 1888. Alexander Carlyle, ed., *New Letters of Thomas Carlyle*, 2 v., 1904, and *Letters of Thomas Carlyle to John Stuart Mill, John Sterling and Robert Browning*, 1923, and *The love letters of Thomas Carlyle and Jane Welsh Carlyle*, 2 v., 1909. See too Trudy Bliss, ed., *Thomas Carlyle: Letters to his wife,* 1953. J. Slater, ed., *The correspondence of Emerson and Carlyle*, 1964; E. W. Marrs jun., ed., *The Letters of Thomas Carlyle to his brother Alexander, with related family letters,* Camb., Mass., 1968. Thea Holme, *The Carlyles at home*, 1965. For Carlyle's political thought see (529) and for his historical writing (3429).

2301   CHARLTON. The recollections of a Northumbrian lady, 1815–66: The memoirs of Barbara Charlton (*née* Tasburgh), wife of William Henry Charlton of Hesleyside, Northumberland. Ed. by Lionel Evelyn Oswald Charlton. 1949.

Memoirs and letters; life in Roman Catholic landed society, 1805–66.

2302   GRAHAM. Parties and pleasures; the diaries of Helen Graham, 1823–6. Ed. by James E. M. Irvine. 1957.

Life in upper-class society, mainly at Stirling and Edinburgh.

2303   COWTAN. Passages from the autobiography of a 'Man of Kent'. [By Robert Cowtan]. 1866.

Life, 1817–65, in Canterbury and London.

2304   HOWARD. Three Howard sisters: selections from the writings of Lady Caroline Lascelles, Lady Dover, and Countess Gower, 1825–1833. Ed. by Maud, Lady Leconfield, and revised and completed by John Gore. 1955.

2305   DISBROWE. Old days in diplomacy. By Charlotte Anne Albinia Disbrowe. 1903.

Recollections of life in a diplomat's family by a dau. of Sir Edward C. Disbrowe; family letters, 1809–51.

2306   EDEN. Miss Eden's letters. Ed. by Violet Dickinson. 1919.

Correspondence, 1814–63, of Emily Eden, a close friend of the 4th earl of Clarendon.

2307   WILSON. An autobiography; letters and remains of the author of 'The Listener' [Caroline Wilson, *née* Fry]. 1848.

Life in Kent and London, 1787–1846.

2308   GOLDSWORTHY. Recollections of Taunton. By Edward Francis Goldsworthy. 1883.

2309 HOWITT. Victorian samplers: William and Mary Howitt. By Carl Ray Woodring. 1952.

See too Margaret Howitt, *An autobiography*, ed. by Margaret Howitt, 2 v., 1889.

2310 HUME. Life of James Deacon Hume. By Charles Badham. 1859.

Career, 1774–1842; customs service from 1791, joint secretary, board of trade, 1828–40.

2311 KITTO. Memoirs of John Kitto . . . from his letters and journals. By Jonathan Edwards Ryland. 1856.

A career from humble beginnings to post of printer to the Church Missionary Society; informative on the condition of the poor.

2312 LEWIS. Letters of Sir George Cornewall Lewis, bart, to various friends. Ed. by Sir Gilbert Frankland Lewis. 1870.

Mainly social gossip, early Victorian period.

2313 SOLLY. 'These eighty years'; or, the story of an unfinished life. By Henry Solly. 2 v. 1893.

1813 onwards; contacts with chartists and philosophical radicals.

2314 SOMERVILLE. Personal recollections, from early life to old age, of Mary Somerville. With selections from her correspondence. Ed. by Martha Somerville. 1873.

Her life, 1780–1872, family, and pursuit of scientific knowledge.

2315 WALMSLEY. The life of Sir Joshua Walmsley. By Hugh Mulleneux Walmsley. 1879.

Life, 1794–1871; business and philanthropy in Liverpool; association with radical politicians.

2316 WHEWELL. The life and selections from the correspondence of William Whewell, D.D., late master of Trinity College, Cambridge. By Mrs. Stair Douglas. 1881.

Isaac Todhunter, *William Whewell . . . an account of his writings with selections from his literary and scientific correspondence*, 2 v., 1867.

2317 YONGE. Charlotte Mary Yonge: her life and letters. By Christabel Rose Coleridge. 1903.

Interesting on her early personal and family life in Hampshire and elsewhere.

2318 WHITE. The record of my life: an autobiography. By Henry White. Cheltenham. 1889.

Farm life as a boy; his career as a servant, grocer, itinerant waiter.

2319 VIZETELLY. Glances back through seventy years; autobiographical and other reminiscences. By Henry Vizetelly. 2 v. 1893.

V. 1, 1820–57; lively, graphic memoirs of boyhood and early life in London; apprenticeship as wood-engraver; early Victorian press.

2320 WELD. Lulworth and the Welds. By Joan Berkeley. Gillingham. 1971.

Material on a leading Catholic family in the early nineteenth century.

2321 RUSSELL. Lady John Russell: a memoir, with selections from her diary
and correspondence. Ed. by Desmond MacCarthy and [Mary] Agatha Russell.
1910.

Early Victorian society, court and politics.

2322 LOVETT. Life and struggles of William Lovett in his pursuit of bread,
knowledge, and freedom. 1876. Ed. with a preface by R. H. Tawney. 2 v.
1920. Repr. 1967.

2323 SHORE. The journal of [Margaret] Emily Shore. 1898.

Family life and cultural pursuits, 1831–9, of a youthful member of a literary family.

2324 ROMILLY. Cambridge diary, 1832–42. Selected passages from the
diary of the Rev. Joseph Romilly. Ed. by John Patrick Tuer Bury. 1967.

2325 WALTON. Random recollections of the midland circuit. By Robert
Walton. 1869.

Memoirs relating to his career as barrister and judge.

2326 LINTON. Memories. By William James Linton. 1895.

Life, 1812–97, of a wood-engraver and chartist. See also F. B. Smith, *Radical artisan.*
William James Linton, 1973.

2327 KINGSLEY. Charles Kingsley, his letters and memories of his life. By
Frances Eliza Kingsley. 2 v. 1877.

V. 1, his education and life as a curate up to 1851.

2328 VINCENT. Henry Vincent, a biographical sketch. By William Dorling.
With a preface by Mrs. Vincent. 1879.

His involvement in chartism, and his lecturing.

2329 COOPER. Thomas Cooper, the chartist (1805–1892). By Robert Joseph
Conklin. Manila. 1935.

See too *The life of Thomas Cooper, written by himself,* 1872, repr. with intro. by John
Saville, Leicester, 1971, for his involvement in chartism in Leicester.

2330 HOLLAND. Recollections of past life. By Sir Henry Holland, bt. 1870.

He associated with the Holland House circle and later became a court physician.

2331 RICHMOND. Memoir of Charles Gordon Lennox, fifth duke of Richmond. [By Lord William Pitt Lennox.] 1862.

Family, social, and political, 1791–1860. On the duke see also John Kent, jun., *Records
and reminiscences of Goodwood and the dukes of Richmond,* 1896.

2332 GUTTERIDGE. Lights and shadows in the life of an artisan. By Joseph
Gutteridge. Coventry. 1893.

Life of a ribbon-weaver, 1816+.

2333 GASKELL. Mrs. Gaskell, homes, haunts and stories. By Esther Alice Chadwick. 1913.

See also (2731).

2334 COLLIER. An old man's diary, forty years ago. By John Payne Collier. Priv. printed. 4 pts. 1871-2.

Personal and literary memoirs of a journalist, focused on one year, 1832-3.

2335 ALFORD. Life, journals and letters of Henry Alford. Ed. by Frances Alford. 1873.

Life, 1810-71, personal, social, literary and clerical; notes on politics and on the tractarian movement.

2336 MACKAY. Forty years recollections. By Charles Mackay. 1877.

Supplemented by his *Through the long day*, 1887. A journalist's memories, literary and political, from *c.* 1830.

2337 ASHFORD. Life of a licensed victualler's daughter written by herself. [By Mary Ann Ashford]. 1844.

Life of a domestic servant, early 19th century.

2338 BAGOT. Links with the past. By Sophia Louisa Bagot. 1901.

Snippets in family letters on society and change in Staffordshire.

2339 BERKELEY. My life and recollections. By Grantley Fitzhardinge Berkeley. 4 v. 1865-6.

County society and sport.

2340 BUCKLEY. A village politician. By John Buckley. With an introd. by A. J. Mundella. 1897.

A good general impression of rural working-class life around the 1840s but names and places have been disguised.

2341 CHATTERTON. Memoirs of Georgiana, Lady Chatterton. With some passages from her diary. By Edward Heneage Dering. 1878.

A minor literary figure; contacts with Wilberforce, Hannah More, Samuel Rogers, R. Monckton Milnes, and others.

2342 LAMINGTON. In the days of the dandies. By Alexander Cochrane, 1st baron Lamington. Ed. with introd. by Sir Herbert Maxwell. 2nd edn. 1906.

Memoirs of high society in the 1840s.

2343 LANGDON. The life of Roger Langdon. Told by himself. With additions by his daughter Ellen. [1909.]

2344 CROWE. Reminiscences of thirty-five years of my life. By Sir Joseph Archer Crowe. 1895.

By a correspondent of the *Morning Chronicle* and *Daily News* in the 1840s.

2345 EASTLAKE. Journals and correspondence of Lady Eastlake. Ed. by Charles Eastlake Smith. 2 v. 1895.

V. 1 includes memoirs of literary society in Edinburgh and London in the 1840s.

2346 FARRER. Some Farrer memorials. By Thomas Henry, Lord Farrer. 1923.

Family and social life, with letters of the 1830s and 1840s.

2347 FORSTER. Life of the right honourable William Edward Forster. By Thomas Wemyss Reid. 2 v. 1888.

V. 1: the young Bradford businessman and social reformer of the 1840s.

2348 FOX. Memoirs of old friends: being extracts from the journals and letters of Caroline Fox, of Penjerrick, Cornwall, from 1835 to 1871. Ed. by Horace N. Pym. 1882.

Local electioneering, politics and literary life. The 2nd edn., 1882, includes fourteen letters of J. S. Mill. See Henry W. Harris, *Caroline Fox*, 1944.

2349 SPENCER. An autobiography. By Herbert Spencer. 2 v. 1904.

V. 1, includes much on his life as an engineer and radical publicist in the 1840s.

2350 FROST. Forty years' recollections, literary and political. By Thomas Frost. 2 v. 1880.

His accounts of chartism and other radical political activity. See too his *Reminiscences*, 1886.

2351 GREGORY. Autobiography of Sir William [Henry] Gregory. Ed. by Lady Gregory. 1894.

Includes anecdotes of Daniel O'Connell, Sir Robert Peel, Disraeli, Lord George Bentinck.

2352 GUEST. Lady Charlotte Guest: extracts from her journal, 1833–1852. Ed. by the earl of Bessborough. 1950.

Social affairs, and notices of local chartist activities and other events, from the diaries of the wife of a South Wales iron master.

2353 COLE. Fifty years of public works of Sir Henry Cole [1808–1882] . . . accounted for in his deeds, speeches and writings. [Ed. and completed by A. S. and H. L. Cole.] 2 v. 1884.

Life of an official in the record commission of 1831 and then in the Public Record Office; an associate of J. S. Mill, Charles Buller, and George Grote.

2354 HOLYOAKE. Sixty years of an agitator's life. By George Jacob Holyoake. 2 v. 1892.

Includes his memories of the Birmingham political union and of chartism. See too Joseph MacCabe, *Life and letters of George Jacob Holyoake*, 2 v., 1908.

2355 RUSKIN. The order of release. The story of John Ruskin, Effie Gray and John Everett Millais, told for the first time in their unpublished letters. Ed. by Sir William James. 1947.

Letters, c. 1847–54. See also (2747).

2356 COUSINS. Extracts from the diary of a workhouse chaplain. By Denis Lewis Cousins. 1847.

The experiences of a workhouse chaplain in the 1840s.

2357 MALMESBURY. Memoirs of an ex-minister. By James Howard Harris, 3rd earl of Malmesbury. 2 v. 1884. edn. in 1 v. 1885.

Includes social and political gossip for the 1840s.

2358 TROLLOPE. What I remember. By Thomas Adolphus Trollope. 3 v. 1887–89.

Chatty reminiscences of his contacts in literary and political circles. For the early life of his more famous younger brother, see Anthony Trollope, *An autobiography*, ed. H. M. Trollope, 2 v., 1883, also ed. by Michael Sadleir, rev. edn., 1947.

2358A RUSSELL. Lord William Russell and his wife, 1815–1846. By Georgiana Blakiston. 1972.

7. British Travellers, Explorers, and Residents Abroad

For arctic and antarctic exploration see *Naval Voyages* (1156–82). For naval and land exploration in the region of Australasia see Ferguson (4686) and Hocken (4749), for Canada (4327, 4328), for India Dodwell (4570), and for Southern Africa (4519–4520). For other references to MSS. and works cited in section 6 see Matthews (2006).

(a) *General*

2359 COX (EDWARD GODFREY). A reference guide to the literature of travel. 3 v. Seattle. 1948–50.

Lists accounts of travels to 1800. V. 1: The Old World; v. 2: The New World; v. 3: Great Britain. V. 2 and 3 include valuable lists of general reference works. *N.C.B.E.L.* (2650), v. 2, *1660–1800*, cols. 1389–1486, and v. 3, *1800–1900*, cols. 1669–84, list travels, arranged by regions.

2360 MURRAY (JOHN). 'The origin and history of Murray's handbooks for travellers.' *Murray's Magazine* 6 (1889), 623–9.

The first of these handbooks, *A handbook for travellers on the continent*, etc., by John Murray III, was issued in 1836.

2361 BAKER (JOHN NORMAN LEONARD). History of geographical discovery and exploration. 1931. Rev. edn. 1937.

Standard.

2362 MAXWELL (CONSTANTIA ELIZABETH). The English traveller in France, 1698–1815. 1932.

2363 BROWN (WALLACE CABLE). 'The popularity of English travel books about the Near East, 1775–1825.' *Philological Q.* 15 (1936), 70–80.

See also his 'English travel books and minor poetry about the Near East, 1775–1825', *ibid.* 16 (1937), 249–71, and Henry R. Fedden, *English travellers in the Near East*

(Writers and their work, 97), 1958. Probably the best-known work on the Near East of this period is Alexander William Kinglake, *Eothen*, 1844.

2364   PUDNEY (JOHN SLEIGH). The Thomas Cook story. 1953.

Also William Fraser Rae, *The business of travel: a fifty years' record of progress*, 1891. Cook's tours began in 1841.

(b) *Europe*

2365   ELLIOTT. Journal of my life during the French revolution. By Grace Dalrymple Elliott. 1858.

Based on her diaries, 1789–1801; her adventures in Paris.

2366   MOORE. A journal during a residence in France. By Dr. John Moore. 2 v. 1793.

Reports on military and political affairs and disturbances, Aug.–Dec. 1792, by a travelling companion of Lord Lauderdale.

2367   RUSSELL. The Russells of Birmingham in the French revolution and in America, 1791–1814. By Samuel Henry Jeyes. 1911.

2368   GUTHRIE. A tour performed in the years 1795–6, through the Taurida or Crimea . . . in a series of letters. By Maria Guthrie. 1802.

2369   PAUL. Journal of a party of pleasure. By Sir John Dean Paul. 1802.

Account of a visit to Paris.

2370   SKENE. Italian journey. By James Skene. With an introd. by Sir H. J. C. Grierson. 1937.

His travels in Italy, Sept. 1802–Mar. 1803.

2371   WILMOT. The Russian journals of Martha and Catherine Wilmot, 1803–8. Ed. with an introd. and notes by the marchioness of Londonderry and H. M. Hyde. 1934.

2372   MACGILL. Travels in Turkey, Italy and Russia, during the years 1803–1806. With an account of some of the Greek islands. By Thomas MacGill. 2 v. 1808.

2373   CARR. A northern summer; or, Travels round the Baltic, through Denmark, Sweden, Russia, Prussia, and part of Germany in . . . 1804. By Sir John Carr. 1805.

Carr also pub. *Descriptive travels in the southern and eastern parts of Spain and the Balearic Isles in . . . 1809*, 1811.

2374   REEVE. Journal of a residence at Vienna and Berlin. By Dr. Henry Reeve. 1877.

Court life, eminent acquaintances, and events, during 1805–6.

2375 JOHNSTON. Travels through part of the Russian empire and the country of Poland along the southern shores of the Baltic. By Robert Johnston. 1815.

2376 COCKERELL. Travels in southern Europe and the Levant. By Charles Robert Cockerell. Ed. by Samuel Pepys Cockerell. 1903.

His travels, including meeting with Byron, 1810–17.

2377 CLARKE. Travels in various countries of Europe, Asia and Africa. By Edward Daniel Clarke. 6 v. 1810–23. New edn., 11 v. 1816–24.

Observations of a travelling tutor.

2378 BRIDGEMAN (G. A. F. H.) (*Earl of Bradford*). Letters from Portugal, Spain, Sicily and Malta in 1812, 13, and 14. Priv. printed. 1875.

Lord John Russell accompanied Bridgeman on this tour.

2379 KNOX. Memoirs of a vanished generation, 1813–1855. By Alice Elizabeth Blake. 1909.

Correspondence and affairs of members of the family of Knox, resident mainly in France; social, embassy circles.

2380 JAMES. Journal of a tour in Germany, Sweden, Russia and Poland, during . . . 1813 and 1814. By John Thomas James. 2 v. 1816. 3rd edn. 2 v. 1918.

2381 BIRKBECK. Notes of a journey through France. By Morris Birkbeck. 1815.

Summer 1814; an interest in people and in economic activities.

2382 MAYNE. The journal of John Mayne during a tour on the continent upon its reopening after the fall of Napoleon. Ed. by John Mayne Colles. 1909.

His tour Aug. 1814–Mar. 1815.

2383 MAXWELL. My adventures. By Col. Montgomery Maxwell. 2 v. 1845.

Much social gossip relating to his experiences in Italy, 1814–15.

2384 SOUTHEY. Journal of a tour in the Netherlands. [By Robert Southey]. Ed. by William Robertson Nicoll. Boston. 1902. London. 1903.

A very full account of his travels, Sept.–Oct. 1815.

2385 ROGERS. The Italian journal of Samuel Rogers. Ed. with an account of Rogers' life and of travel in Italy, 1814–1821, by John Rigby Hale. 1956.

2386 FRYE. After Waterloo: reminiscences of European travel, 1815–1819. Ed. by Salomon Reinach. 1908.

From the travel diaries of Major William Edward Frye.

2387	MATTHEWS. The diary of an invalid. By Henry Matthews. 1819.

Travels in southern Europe, Sept. 1817–June 1819.

2388	YEARDLEY. Memoir and diary of John Yeardley, minister of the gospel. Ed. by Charles Tylor. 1859.

Yeardley, a Quaker, settled in Germany in 1821, and travelled extensively there and in Norway and Russia.

2389	FOSTER. The journal of Emily Foster. By Mary A. Foster. Ed. by Stanley Thomas Williams and Leonard B. Beach. Oxf. 1928.

Her travels in Germany, Mar. 1821–Aug. 1823.

2390	BENSON. Sketches of Corsica. By Robert Benson. 1825.

His diary during a business mission, Oct.–Dec. 1823.

2391	BEATTIE. Journal of a residence in Germany. By William Beattie. 2 v. 1831.

He stayed on various occasions as medical attendant to the duke and duchess of Clarence, June 1822–Oct. 1826.

2392	HOGG. Two hundred and nine days. By Thomas Jefferson Hogg. 2 v. N.Y. 1827.

Continental travels, Aug. 1825–Feb. 1826.

2393	BRYDGES. Recollections of foreign travel, on life, literature and self-knowledge. By Sir Samuel Egerton Brydges. 2 v. 1825.

2394	SWAN. Journal of a voyage up the Mediterranean. By Charles Swan. 2 v. 1826.

His travels and sightseeing while chaplain on H.M.S. *Cambrian*, Oct. 1824–Sept. 1825.

2395	BEST. Four years in France; or, Narrative of an English family's residence. By Henry Digby Best (*afterwards* Beste). 1826.

Best also pub. *Italy as it is; or, Narrative of an English family's residence*, 1828, *and Personal and literary memorials*, 1829, including further anecdotes of his travels.

2396	JONES. Travels in Norway, Sweden, Finland, Russia and Turkey; also the coasts of the Sea of Azov and of the Black Sea. By George Matthew Jones. 2 v. 1827.

2397	MALTHUS. The travel diaries of Thomas Robert Malthus. Ed. by Patricia James. Camb. 1966.

His journeys in Scandinavia, 1799, on the Continent, 1825, and in Scotland, 1826.

2398	WESTMINSTER. Diary of a tour in Sweden, Norway and Russia. With letters. By Elizabeth Mary, marchioness of Westminster. 1879.

Her travels and meetings with royalty and high society, May–Nov. 1827.

2399 BUCKINGHAM AND CHANDOS. The private diary of Richard, Duke of Buckingham and Chandos. 3 v. 1862.

His travels, mainly in Italy, and contacts with English people there, Sept. 1827–Aug. 1829.

2400 COBBETT. A ride of eight hundred miles in France. By James Paul Cobbett. 1824.

Cobbett also pub. *Journal of a tour in Italy, and also in part of France and Switzerland*, 1830.

2401 BADCOCK. Rough leaves from a journal kept in Spain and Portugal during the years 1832, 1833 and 1834. By Lt. Col. Lovell Badcock. 1835.

Travels and experiences of a military observer during the civil wars in the Peninsula.

2402 LAING. Journal of a residence in Norway. By Samuel Laing. 1837.

A business man's account, July 1834–Apr. 1836.

2403 DE ROS. Journal of a tour in the principalities, Crimea, and countries adjacent to the Black Sea . . . 1835–36. By William Lennox, 23rd baron De Ros. 1855.

The explorations of a minor diplomat, July 1835–Jan. 1836.

2404 BELL. Journal of a residence in Circassia. By James Stanislaus Bell. 2 v. 1840.

A business man's travels and residence, Apr. 1837–Feb. 1840.

2405 FRY. Elizabeth Fry's journeys on the continent, 1840–1841. Ed. by Reginald Brimley Johnson. 1931.

Her tour visiting Quaker circles in the Low Countries, Denmark and Germany, Feb. 1840–Sept. 1841.

2406 TRENCH. Diary of travels in France and Spain, chiefly in the year 1844. By Francis Trench. 2 v. 1845.

Sept. 1843–Sept. 1844. Trench also pub. *A walk round Mont Blanc*, 1847.

2407 FRANCIS. Notes from a journal kept in Italy and Sicily . . . 1844–46. By John George Francis. 1847.

Largely about his antiquarian and literary interests.

2408 QUILLINAN (*formerly* WORDSWORTH). Journal of a few months' residence in Portugal. By Dorothy Quillinan. 2 v. 1847.

Her travels and residence, May 1845–May 1846.

(c) *The Levant, Arabia, and Asia*

See also (2372), (2376), (2377), (2396), (2404), (2428), (2432).

2409 FORSTER. A journey from Bengal to England through the northern parts of India, Kashmire, Afganistan and Persia, and into Russia by the Caspian Sea. By George Forster. 2 v. 1798.

2410   LEAKE. Journal of a tour in Asia Minor [in 1800]; with comparative remarks on the ancient and modern geography of that country. By William Martin Leake. 1824.

2411   MORIER. A journey through Persia, Armenia and Asia Minor to Constantinople in . . . 1808 and 1809. By James Justinian Morier. 1812.

This minor diplomat serving in the Middle East also pub. *A second journey . . . to Constantinople between . . . 1810 and 1816*, 1818; both works include accounts of British diplomatic activity in Persia.

2412   BURCKHARDT. Travels in Syria and the Holy Land. By John Lewis Burckhardt. Ed. by W. M. Leake. 1822.

W. M. Leake also ed. Burckhardt's *Travels in Nubia*, 1819, and Sir W. Ouseley ed. his *Travels in Arabia*, 1829. See too Katharine Sim, *Desert traveller; the life of Jean Louis Burckhardt*, 1969, bibliog. 419–23; *Scheik Ibrahim (Johann Ludwig Burckhardt); Briefe an Eltern und Geschwister*, ed. by Carl Burckhardt-Sarasin and Hansrudolf Schwabe-Burckhardt, Basel, 1956.

2413   STANHOPE. Memoirs of lady Hester Lucy Stanhope; as related by herself in conversations with her physician. Ed. by Charles Lewis Meryon. 3 v. 1845.

The duchess of Cleveland, *The life and letters of lady Hester Stanhope*, priv. printed, 1897, new edn. 1914, is from the family papers. Frank Hamel, *Lady Hester Stanhope; new light on her life and love affairs*, 1913, adds new information. Ian Bruce, *The Nun of Lebanon. The love affair of lady Hester Stanhope and Michael Bruce*, 1951, deals mainly with *c.* 1810–16, using Bruce MSS.

2414   RICH. Narrative of a journey to the site of Babylon in 1811. . . ., memoir on the ruins . . . second memoir on the ruins with a narrative of a journey to Persepolis. By Claudius James Rich. Ed. by his widow. 1839.

On Rich's archaeological activities see (3400).

2415   KINNEIR. Journey through Asia Minor, Armenia, and Koordistan in . . . 1813 and 1814. With remarks on the marches of Alexander, and the retreat of the Ten Thousand. By John Macdonald Kinneir. 1818.

2416   TURNER. Journal of a tour in the Levant. By William Turner. 3 v. 1820.

Account by a foreign office official in Egypt and Syria, 1813–16.

2417   FRASER. Narrative of a journey into Khorasan in . . . 1821 and 1822, including some account of the countries to the north east of Persia. By James Baillie Fraser. 1825.

Fraser also pub. *Travels and adventures in the Persian provinces on the southern banks of the Caspian Sea; with an appendix containing short notices on the geology and commerce of Persia*, 1826; *A winter's journey . . . from Constantinople to Tehran, with travels through various parts of Persia*, 2 v., 1838; *Travels in Koordistan, Mesopotamia, etc., including an account of parts of those countries hitherto unvisited by Europeans*, 2 v., 1840.

2418 SADLIER. Diary of a journey across Arabia from El Khatif . . . to Yambo . . . during the year 1819. By G. Forster Sadlier. Comp. from the records of the Bombay government by P. Ryan. Bombay. 1866.

2419 CONOLLY. Journey to the north of India, overland from England, through Russia, Persia, and Affghaunistaun. By Arthur Conolly. 2 v. 1834.

2420 BURNES. Travels into Bokhara; being the account of a journey from India to Cabool, Tartary and Persia; also narrative of a voyage on the Indus . . . in the years 1831, 1832, and 1833. By Sir Alexander Burnes. 3 v. 1834.

Twice reprinted. Burnes also pub. *Cabool; being a personal narrative of a journey to, and residence in that city, in . . . 1836, 7 and 8,* 1842. For a modern study see J. D. Lunt, *Bokhara Burnes,* 1969.

2421 HAMILTON. Researches in Asia Minor, Pontus and Armenia; with some account of their antiquities and geology. By William John Hamilton. 2 v. 1842.

2422 CHESNEY. The expedition for the survey of the rivers Euphrates and Tigris . . . 1835, 1836 and 1837 . . . vols. 1, 2. By Francis Rawdon Chesney. 1850.

No more publ. Chesney later wrote, *Narrative of the Euphrates expedition,* 1868. See too W. F. Ainsworth, *Researches in Assyria, Babylonia, and Chaldaea; forming part of the labours of the Euphrates expedition,* 1838, and *A personal narrative of the Euphrates expedition,* 2 v., 1888. There is a *Life* of Chesney by Louisa Chesney and Jane O'Donnell, 1885.

2423 AINSWORTH. Travels and researches in Asia Minor, Mesopotamia, Chaldea, and Armenia. By William Francis Ainsworth. 2 v. 1842.

See too Ainsworth's *Travels in the track of ten thousand Greeks,* 1844.

2424 BRANT. 'Journey through a part of Armenia and Asia Minor in . . . 1835.' By James Brant. *J. of the Royal Geographical Soc.,* 6, 1836, 187–223.

Brant also pub. 'Notes of a journey through a part of Kurdistan . . . 1838', *ibid.* 10, 1841, 341–434.

2425 MONTEFIORE. Notes from a private journal of a visit to Egypt and Palestine. By Lady Judith Montefiore. 1836.

2426 RAWLINSON. 'Notes on a march from Zohab . . . to Khujistan (Susiana), and . . . through the province of Luristan to Kirmanshah in . . . 1836.' By Sir Henry Creswicke Rawlinson. *J. of the Royal Geographical Soc.* 9, 1839, 26–116.

Rawlinson also wrote 'Notes on a journey from Tabriz through Persian Kurdistan . . .', *ibid.* 10, 1841, 1–64, 65–158. On his archaeological interests see (3399).

2427 FELLOWS. A journal written during an excursion in Asia Minor. By Sir Charles Fellows. 1839.

Fellows also pub. *An account of discoveries in Lycia, being a journal kept during a second excursion in Asia Minor,* 1841.

(d) *Africa north of the Zambesi*

2428 BROWNE. Travels in Africa, Egypt and Syria . . . 1792 to 1798. By William George Browne. 1799.

Largely about his expedition to Darfur, 1793–6.

2429 PARK. Travels in the interior districts of Africa: performed under the direction and patronage of the African Association, in . . . 1795, 1796 and 1797. By Mungo Park. With an appendix. . . . By Major Rennell. 1799.

John Whishaw ed. *The journal of a mission to the interior of Africa, in* . . . *1805*, 1815, including a biographical sketch. See L. G. Gibbon [James Leslie Mitchell], *Niger; The life of Mungo Park*, Edinburgh, 1934, and S. L. Gwynn, *Mungo Park and the quest of the Niger*, 1934.

2430 BROUGHTON. Six years residence in Algiers. By Elizabeth Broughton. 1839.

Life and observations of a consul's wife, 1806–12.

2431 SALT. A voyage to Abyssinia, and travels into the interior of that country . . . 1809 and 1810. . . . By Henry Salt. Bulmer. 1814.

See J. J. Halls, *The life and correspondence of Henry Salt*, 2 v., 1834.

2432 IRBY (CHARLES LEONARD) *and* MANGLES (JAMES). Travels in Egypt and Nubia, Syria and Asia Minor . . . [1817 and 1818]. 1823.

2433 TUCKEY. Narrative of an expedition to explore the river Zaire, usually called the Congo, in South Africa, in 1816 . . . to which is added the journal of Professor Smith. By James Kingston Tuckey. 1818.

2434 LYON. A narrative of travels in northern Africa . . . [1818–20]; accompanied by geographical notices of Soudan, and of the course of the Niger. By George Francis Lyon. 1821.

2435 GRAY. Travels in western Africa in the years 1818 [to] 21, from the river Gambia . . . to the river Niger. . . . By William Gray and ——— Dochard. 1825.

2436 LAING. Travels in Timannee, Kooranko, and Soolima countries in western Africa. By Alexander Gordon Laing. 1825.

For Laing's letters 1824–6 see the Hakluyt Society, 2nd ser., v. 123, *Missions to the Niger*, v. 1, 1964, 123–394. A. Bonnel de Mézières, *Le Major A. Gordon Laing, Tombouctou 1826*, Paris, 1912, cites sources in Arabic texts. See too Robert Gaffiot, *Le Major A. Gordon Laing à Tombouctou, 1826*, Dakar, 1931.

2437 DENHAM. Missions to the Niger, v. 2–4: The Bornu mission, 1822–25, pt. 1–3. The Hakluyt Society, 2nd series, v. 128–30. Camb. 1966.

Prints the travel accounts of Dixon Denham and his associates, Hugh Clapperton and Walter Oudney.

2438 CLAPPERTON. Journal of a second expedition into the interior of Africa, from the Bight of Benin to Soccatoo. By Hugh Clapperton. 1829.

2439 LANDER. Records of captain Clapperton's last expedition to Africa . . . with the subsequent adventures of the author. By Richard Lemon Lander. 2 v. 1830.

For Lander's second expedition, 1830–1, with his brother John, see *Journal of an expedition to explore the . . . Niger*, ed. by A. B. B[echer], 3 v., 1832, and R. Huish, *The travels of Richard and John Lander . . . from unpublished documents*, 1836. His last journey is recorded in Macgregor Laird and R. A. K. Oldfield, *Narrative of an expedition into the interior of Africa, by the river Niger . . . [1832–4]*, 2 v., 1837.

2440 RICHARDSON (JAMES). Travels in the great desert of Sahara, in 1845 and 1846; including a description of the oases and cities of Ghat, Ghadames and Mourzuk. 2 v. 1848.

Richardson also pub. *Narrative of a mission to central Africa performed in the years 1850–51*, 1853.

(e) *Far East*

See also Morrell (4782).

2441 STAUNTON (*Sir* GEORGE LEONARD). An authentic account of an embassy from the king of Great Britain to the Emperor of China. . . . 2 v. 1797.

An account of the embassy of Lord Macartney. J. L. Cranmer-Byng ed. *An embassy to China. Being the journal kept by Lord Macartney during his embassy to the emperor Ch'ien-Lung, 1793–1794*, [1962]. Sir John Barrow, Macartney's comptroller, pub. *Travels in China*, 1804, and *A voyage to Cochin China*, 1806, and a life of Macartney (4527).

2442 ELLIS (*Sir* HENRY). Journal of the proceedings of the late embassy to China. 2 v. 1818.

An account of Earl Amherst's mission, 1816–17.

2443 CRAWFURD (JOHN). Journal of an embassy . . . to the courts of Siam and Cochin China. 2 v. 1828.

Crawfurd also pub. *Journal of an embassy to the court of Ava*, 2nd edn., 2. v., 1834.

2444 DAVIDSON (G. F.). Trade and travel in the Far East; or, Recollections of twenty-one years passed in Java, Singapore, Australia, and China. 1846.

2445 EARL (GEORGE WINDSOR). The Eastern Seas, or voyages and adventures in the Indian archipelago . . . [1832–34], comprising a tour of Java, visits to Borneo, the Malay Peninsula, Siam, etc; also an account of the present state of Singapore, with observations on the commercial resources of the archipelago. 1837.

2446 FORTUNE (ROBERT). Three years wanderings in the northern provinces of China. 1847.

2447 SMITH (GEORGE). A narrative of an exploratory visit to each of the consular cities of China, and to the islands of Hong Kong and Chusan in behalf of the Church Missionary Society . . . [1844–6]. 1847.

Smith was consecrated bishop of Victoria, Hong Kong, 1847; he had been concerned to observe the moral, social and political condition of the peoples he visited.

(f) *The United States*

See Allan Nevins, *America through British eyes*, N.Y., 1948, bibliog., 503–19.

2448 WANSEY (HENRY). The journal of an excursion to the United States of North America in the summer of 1794. Salisbury. 1796.

2449 BAILY (FRANCIS). Journal of a tour in unsettled parts of North America . . . [1796–97]. Ed. by Augustus de Morgan. 1856.

2450 DAVIS (JOHN). Travels of four years and a half in the United States . . . [1798–1802]. 1803.

2451 DOUGLAS (THOMAS) *5th earl of Selkirk*. Lord Selkirk's diary 1803–1804. A journal of his travels in British North America and the north-eastern United States. Ed. by P. C. T. White. Champlain Soc. v. 35. 1958.

2451A FOSTER (*Sir* AUGUSTUS JOHN) *Bart*. Jeffersonian America: notes on the United States of America collected in the years 1805-6-7 and 11–12 by Sir Augustus John Foster, Bart. Ed. with an intro. by Richard Beale Davis. San Marino, Calif. 1954.

2452 ASHE (THOMAS). Travels in America, performed in 1806, for the purpose of exploring the rivers Alleghany, Monongahela, Ohio, and Mississippi. 3 v. 1808.

2453 LAMBERT (JOHN). Travels through Lower Canada and the United States of North America . . . [1806–8]. 3 v. 1810.

2454 MELISH (JOHN). Travels in the United States . . . [1806–11]. 2 v. Phil. 1812.

2455 KENDALL (EDWARD AUGUSTUS). Travels through the northern parts of the United States . . . [1807–8]. 3 v. N.Y. 1809.

2456 BRADBURY (JOHN). Travels in the interior of America . . . [1809–11]; including a description of Upper Louisiana together with the states of Ohio, Kentucky, Indiana and Tennessee, with the Illinois and Western Territories. . . . Liverpool. 1817.

2457 HALL (FRANCIS). Travels in Canada and the United States in 1816 and 1817. 1818.

2458 COBBETT (WILLIAM). A year's residence in the United States of America. 3 v. 1819.

2459 FEARON (HENRY BRADSHAW). Sketches of America. A narrative of a journey of five thousand miles through the eastern and western states of America contained in eight reports. . . . 1818.

This investigation on behalf of prospective migrants fell into competition with that conducted by Birkbeck; see Morris Birkbeck, *Notes on a journey in America from the coast of Virginia to the territory of Illinois*, 1818, and *Letters from Illinois*, 1818.

2460 DUNCAN (JOHN M.). Travels through part of the United States and Canada in 1818 and 1819. 2 v. Glasgow. 1823.

2461 WOODS (JOHN). Two years residence in the settlement on the English Prairie, in the Illinois country. 1822.

2462 BLANE (WILLIAM NEWNHAM). An excursion through the United States and Canada . . . 1822–23. 1824.

2463 HALL (BASIL). Travels in North America in the years 1827 and 1828. 3 v. Edinburgh. 1829.

For his wife's impressions see *The aristocratic journey. Being the outspoken letters of Mrs. Basil Hall . . .*, ed. by Una Pope-Hennessy, 1931.

2464 HAMILTON (THOMAS). Men and manners in America. Edinburgh. 1833.

At the time one of the most widely discussed accounts of the United States. Also an influential best-seller, although exaggerated and misleading, was Frances Trollope *Domestic manners of the Americans*, 2 v., 1832.

2465 ABDY (EDWARD STRUTT). Journal of a residence and tour in the United States of North America . . . April 1833 to October 1834. 3 v. 1835.

2466 MURRAY (CHARLES AUGUSTUS). Travels in North America . . . 1834–36, including a summer residence with the Pawnee tribe of Indians . . . and a visit to Cuba and the Azores Islands. 2 v. N.Y. 1839.

2467 MARTINEAU (HARRIET). A retrospect of western travel. 3 v. 1838.

An account of her sojourn in 1834–6.

2468 MARRYAT (FREDERICK). A diary in America, with remarks on its institutions. 3 v. 1839.

2469 DAUBENY (CHARLES GILES BRIDLE). Journal of a tour through the United States and in Canada . . . [1837–38]. Priv. printed. Oxford. 1843.

2470 STURGE (JOSEPH). A visit to the United States in 1841. 1842.

2471 BUCKINGHAM (JAMES SILK). America, historical, statistic and descriptive. 3 v. 1841.

Further accounts of Buckingham's travels, 1837–40, followed in *The eastern and western states of America*, 3 v., 1842, and *The slave states of America*, 2 v., 1842.

2472 DICKENS (CHARLES). American notes for general circulation. 2 v. 1842.

2473 FARNHAM (THOMAS JEFFERSON). Travels in the great western prairies, the Anahuac and Rocky Mountains, and in the Oregon territory. 2 v. 1843.

2474 FEATHERSTONHAUGH (GEORGE WILLIAM). Excursion through the slave states from Washington on the Potomac to the frontier of Mexico. 2 v. 1844.

2475 LYELL (*Sir* CHARLES). Travels in North America; with geological observations on the United States, Canada and Nova Scotia. 2 v. 1845.

See also Sir C. Lyell, *A second visit to the United States of North America*, 2 v., 1849.

2476 RUXTON (GEORGE AUGUSTUS FREDERICK). Adventures in Mexico and the Rocky mountains. 1847.

A minor classic of frontier life, as was also his *Life in the Far West*, Edinburgh, 1849.

2477 PLAYFAIR (ROBERT). Recollections of a visit to the United States and British provinces of North America . . . [1847–9]. Edinburgh. 1856.

2478 LEWIS (JOHN DELAWARE), *pseud.* of J. Smith of Smith Hall. Across the Atlantic. 1850.

(g) *Latin America*

See Bernard Naylor, *Accounts of nineteenth century South America. An annotated checklist of works by British and United States observers*, 1969; C. H. Gardiner, 'Foreign travellers' accounts of Mexico, 1810–1910', *The Americas*, 8 (1951–2), 321–51. See also Hall, *Journal* (1163), Ruxton (2476).

2479 WATERTON (CHARLES). Wanderings in South America, the North West of the United States, and the Antilles, in 1812, 1816, 1820 and 1824. 1825.

Mainly on the region of Venezuela.

2480 STEVENSON (WILLIAM BENNET). Narrative of twenty years residence in South America . . . containing travels in Arauco, Chili, Peru, and Columbia. 3 v. 1825.

2481 CALDCLEUGH (ALEXANDER). Travels in South America . . . [1819–21], containing an account of . . . Brazil, Buenos Ayres and Chile. 2 v. 1825.

2482 GRAHAM (MARIA) [*Lady* Callcott]. Journal of a voyage to Brazil and residence there during parts of the years 1821, 1822, 1823.

By the tutor to Dona Maria, dau. of the Emperor Pedro I; she also pub. *Journal of a residence in Chili . . . 1822. And a voyage from Chili to Brazil in 1823*, 1824.

2483 BULLOCK (WILLIAM). Six months residence and travels in Mexico; containing remarks on the present state of New Spain. . . . 1824.
Account of a naturalist's trip during 1822.

2484 WARD (HENRY GEORGE). Mexico in 1827. 2 v. 1828.
A leading account, by the British minister resident, 1823–4, 1825–7.

2485 PROCTOR (ROBERT). Narrative of a journey across the cordillera of the Andes, and of a residence in Lima and other parts of Peru . . . [1823–4]. 1825.

2486 HAMILTON (JOHN POTTER). Travels through the interior provinces of Colombia. 2 v. 1827.

2487 HEAD (*Sir* FRANCIS BOND). Rough notes taken during some rapid journeys across the pampas and among the Andes. 1826.

2488 ANDREWS (JOSEPH). Journey from Buenos Ayres, through the provinces of Cordova, Tucuman, and Salta, to Potosi . . . Arica . . . Santiago de Chili and Coquimbo . . . [1825–6]. 2 v. 1827.

2489 BEAUFOY (MARK). Mexican illustrations, founded on facts; indicative of the present condition of society, manners, religion, and morals, among the Spanish and native inhabitants of Mexico: with observations upon the government and resources of the republic of Mexico, as they appeared during part of the years 1825, 1826 and 1827. . . . 1828.

2490 LYON (GEORGE FRANCIS). Journal of a residence and tour in the republic of Mexico in . . . 1826, with some account of the mines in that country. 2 v. 1828.

2491 MIERS (JOHN). Travels in Chile and La Plata. 2 v. 1826.

2492 DUNN (HENRY). Guatemala; or the republic of central America in 1827–8. 1829.

2493 THOMPSON (GEORGE ALEXANDER). Narrative of an official visit to Guatemala from Mexico. 1829.

2494 MAW (HENRY LISTER). Journal of a passage from the Pacific to the Atlantic, crossing the Andes in the northern provinces of Peru, and descending the river Marañon or Amazon. 1829.

2495 SMYTH (WILLIAM) *and* LOWE (FREDERICK). Narrative of a journey from Lima to Para, across the Andes and down the Amazon. 1836.

2496 HAWKSHAW (JOHN). Reminiscences of South America: from two and a half years' residence in Venezuela. 1838.

2497 SCARLETT (PETER CAMPBELL). South America and the Pacific: comprising a journey across the pampas and the Andes, from Buenos Ayres to Valparaiso, Lima, and Panama. 2 v. 1838.

2498 YOUNG (THOMAS). Narrative of a residence on the Mosquito Shore ... [1839–41], with an account of Truxillo, and the adjacent islands of Bonacca and Roatan. 1842.

2499 DUNLOP (ROBERT GLASGOW). Travels in central America, being a journal of nearly three years in the country. 1847.

2500 COULTER (JOHN). Adventures on the western coast of South America and the interior of California. 2 v. 1847.

2501 BYAM (GEORGE). Wanderings in some of the western republics of America, with remarks on the cutting of the great ship canal through central America. 1850.

E. SOCIAL POLICY

1. General Works

2502 ROBERTS (FREDERICK DAVID). Victorian origins of the British welfare state. New Haven. 1960.

An indispensable detailed study of administrative developments in the second quarter of the nineteenth century. The early chapters of D. Fraser, *The evolution of the British welfare state*, 1973, provide a thoughtful summary. See too M. Bruce, *The coming of the welfare state*, 2nd edn., 1965, Geoffrey B. A. M. Finlayson, *England in the 1830s: decade of reform*, 1969, and John Trevor Ward, ed., *Popular movements c. 1830–1850*, 1970. For the constitutional background see Parris (452) and Lubenow (453).

2. Philanthropy

(a) General

2503 OWEN (DAVID EDWARD). English philanthropy, 1660–1960. Cambridge. Mass. 1964.

A full and standard history. See also George Jacob Holyoake, *Self-help a hundred years ago*, 1888, containing material on a variety of philanthropic and co-operative enterprises of the Napoleonic period; Benjamin Kirkman Gray, *A history of English philanthropy. From the dissolution of the monasteries to the taking of the first census*, 1905, a standard general history; Betsy Rodgers, *Cloak of charity. Studies in eighteenth century philanthropy* 1949; Margaret Bayne Simey, (Lady Simey), *Charitable effort in Liverpool in the nineteenth century*, Liverpool, 1951; Agnes Freda Young and Elwyn Thomas Ashton, *British social work in the nineteenth century*, 1956; Brian Harrison, 'Philanthropy and the Victorians', *Victorian Studies* 9 (1965–6), 353–74.

2504 COMMISSIONERS OF INQUIRY CONCERNING CHARITIES in England and Wales. Reports, 1818 to 1837. 32 reports scattered through *Parl. papers*, 1819 (83) X–A to 1840 (219) XIX, Part I, 1.

Indexed in *Parl. papers*, 1840 (279) XIX. For charities in London see Anthony Highmore, *Pietas Londinensis*, etc., 2 v., 1810, 1814, an extensive list of privately supported institutions, continued in his *Philanthropia metropolitana*, etc., 1822, and Sampson Low, *The charities of London . . . their origin and design, progress, and present position*, 1850. For the provinces see [John Wade], *An account of the public charities in England and Wales, abridged from the reports of his Majesty's Commissioners*, etc., 1828. There is much material in the *V.C.H.*, and the older town histories.

2505 FEARON (JOHN PETER). The endowed charities; with some suggestions for further legislation regarding them. 1855.

Includes a general history of 19th-century policy and legislation. Henry Peter Brougham, Baron Brougham and Vaux, *A letter to Sir Samuel Romilly . . . upon the abuse of charities*, 1st–11th edns., 1818, is a criticism of the effect of indiscriminate charity. See also George Williams Keeton, *The modern law of charities*, 1962, and Gareth Hywel Jones, *History of the law of charity, 1532–1827*, Camb., 1969.

2506 BROWN (FORD KEELER). Fathers of the Victorians. The age of Wilberforce. Camb. 1961.

A discussion of the evangelical movement in philanthropy. See also Howse (745).

2507 HEASMAN (KATHLEEN JOAN). Evangelicals in action. An appraisal of their social work in the Victorian era. 1962.

For general works on Evangelicals see (745); for Christian Socialism see (722).

2508 SOCIETY FOR BETTERING THE CONDITION AND INCREASING THE COMFORTS OF THE POOR. Reports of the Society. 1798–1840.

Founded by Wilberforce, Sir Thomas Bernard, and others. Associated with it was the Association for the Relief of the Manufacturing and Labouring Poor, *Reports*, 1813–17.

2509 SOCIETY FOR THE SUPPRESSION OF MENDICITY. (*Later* London mendicity society.) Reports. 1819–[1959].

2510 ALLEN. Life of William Allen, with selections from his correspondence. 3 v. 1846.

Quaker philanthropist; partner of Robert Owen in New Lanark, and in the firm of Allen and Hanbury. Helena Hall, *William Allen, 1770–1843: member of the Society of Friends*, Haywards Heath, 1953. For Quaker philanthropy in general see (864).

2511 BERNARD. The life of Sir Thomas Bernard, Baronet. By James Baker. 1819.

2512 GISBORNE (THOMAS). The principles of moral philosophy investigated, and applied to the constitution of civil society. 4th edn. corr. and enl. 1798.

See also his *An enquiry into the duties of men in the higher and middle classes of society in Great Britain*, 1794, 6th edn., 2 v., 1811. Gisborne was a friend of Hannah More (2122) and Wilberforce (121).

2513 HEY. The life of William Hey, Esq., F.R.S. [With extracts from his writings.] By John Pearson. 2 v. 1822. 2nd edn. 1823.

Evangelical surgeon and philanthropist in Leeds.

2514 KING. Co-operation's prophet. The life and letters of Dr. William King of Brighton with a reprint of 'The Co-operator', 1828–1830. By Thomas William Mercer. Manchester. 1947.

An associate of William Allen and Mrs. Fry.

2515 LETTSOM. Lettsom: his life, times, friends and descendants. By James Johnston Abraham. 1933.

See also John Coakley Lettsom, *Hints designed to promote beneficence, temperance, and medical science*, 3 v., 1801, another edn., enl. 3 v., 1816, a series of essays on social problems and notable philanthropists.

2516 MÜLLER. A narrative of the Lord's dealings with G. M. written by himself. By Georg Friedrich Müller. 2 pt. 1837. 1841.

Also Arthur Tappan Pierson, *George Müller of Bristol*, 1899. Müller founded the Bristol Orphanage, 1835–6.

2517 REED. Memoirs of the life and philanthropic labours of Andrew Reed, with selections from his journals. Ed. Andrew Reed Jr. and Sir Charles Reed. 1863.

Founder of London Orphan Asylum, Infant Asylum, Reedham Orphan Asylum, between 1815 and 1847, and Hospital for Incurables, 1855.

2518 SHAFTESBURY. The life and work of the seventh earl of Shaftesbury, K.G. By Edwin Hodder. 3 v. 1886.

Also John Lawrence le Breton Hammond and Lucy Barbara Hammond, *Lord Shaftesbury*, 1923, Geoffrey Francis Andrew Best, *Shaftesbury*, 1964, and Georgina Battiscombe, *Shaftesbury, a biography of the seventh Earl, 1801–1885*, 1974. For his speeches see Anthony Ashley Cooper, 7th earl of Shaftesbury, *Speeches . . . upon subjects having relation chiefly to the claims and interests of the labouring classes. With a preface*, 1868.

2519 WILLIAMS. The life of Sir George Williams. By Sir John Ernest Hodder Williams. 1906. Rev. edn. with title, *The father of the Red Triangle*, 1918.

Founder of the Young Men's Christian Association, 1844. See also Laurence Locke Doggett, *A history of the Young Men's Christian Association*, 2 v., N.Y., 1919–22; Clyde Binfield, *George Williams and the Y.M.C.A.*, 1973.

(b) *Special Topics*

2520 [COLQUHOUN (PATRICK).] Suggestions offered to the public for the purpose of reducing the consumption of bread corn. 1799. 2nd edn. 1800.

Detailed instructions for the running of a soup-kitchen.

2521 Thoughts on means of alleviating the miseries attendant upon common prostitution. [1799.]

2522 HOYLAND (JOHN). A historical survey of the customs, habits, and present state of the gypsies; designed to promote the amelioration of their condition. York. 1816.

A factual account, based on the author's investigations. Also Walter Simson, *A history of the gypsies: with specimens of the gypsy language*, ed. J. Simson, 1865. For general bibliog. see George F. Black, *A gypsy bibliography*, etc., privately printed, Edin., 1909, and the *Journal of the Gypsy Lore Society*, Edin. 1888+, in progress.

2523 MONTGOMERY (JAMES). The chimney-sweeper's friend, and climbing-boy's album. 1824.

A collection of evidence of ill treatment, etc. See also Society for Superseding the Necessity of Climbing Boys, *Reports*, 2nd edn., 1804, 22nd, 1838, and their *A short account of the proceedings of the society*, 1816. The question was investigated by a select committee in 1817, H.C. 1817 (400) VI. A modern survey is George Lewis Phillips, *England's climbing-boys. A history of the long struggle to abolish child labor in chimney-sweeping* (pub. 5 of the Kress Library of Business and Economics) Boston, Mass. [1949], with bibliog. 57–61.

2524 RITCHIE (JOHN M.). Concerning the blind: being a historical sketch of organized effort on behalf of the blind in Great Britain, and some thoughts concerning the mental life of a person born blind. 1930.

With an appendix giving histories of institutions for the blind, 1800–50. See also Henry John Wagg, *A chronological survey of work for the blind*, etc., 1932, bibliog., 199–207.

2525 NICHOLS (REGINALD HUGH) *and* WRAY (FRANCIS ASLETT). The history of the Foundling Hospital. 1935.

2526 MOSS (ARTHUR W.) Valiant crusade; The history of the R.S.P.C.A. 1961.

Based on the society's records. See also Brian Harrison, 'Animals and the state in nineteenth-century England', *E.H.R.* 88 (1973), 786–820.

3. HEALTH

(a) *Medical Services*

2527 HODGKINSON (RUTH GLADYS). The origins of the National Health Service; the medical services of the new Poor Law, 1834–1871. Wellcome Historical Medical Lib., n.s., 11. 1967.

(i) *Doctors*

For general reference and histories of medical societies see *Medicine* (pp. 382–6).

2528 POYNTER (FREDERICK NOËL LAWRENCE) *ed.* The evolution of medical practice in Great Britain. 1961.

2529 WHITE (*Sir* WILLIAM HALE). Great doctors of the nineteenth century. 1935.

Also Major Greenwood, *Some British pioneers of social medicine* (Univ. of London Heath Clark Lectures), 1946. For Jenner see (3117).

2530 BUDD. William Budd, the Bristol physician and epidemiologist. By Edward Wilberforce Goodall. 1936.

2531 CROSSE. A surgeon in the early nineteenth century: the life and times of John Green Crosse, M.D., F.R.C.S., F.R.S., 1790–1850. By Victoria Mary Crosse. 1968.

The life of a provincial surgeon in Norfolk, based on his diaries.

2532 CURRIE. Memoir of the life, writings and correspondence of James Currie, M.D., F.R.S. of Liverpool. By William Wallace Currie. 2 v. 1831.

Also gives a valuable picture of provincial cultural life. See also R. D. Thornton, *James Currie, the entire stranger, and Robert Burns*, 1963, bibliog. 409–23.

2533 DUNCAN. Duncan of Liverpool. Being an account of the work of Dr. W. H. Duncan, medical officer of health of Liverpool, 1847–1863. By William Mowll Frazer. 1947.

2534 HASTINGS. The life and times of Sir Charles Hastings, founder of the British Medical Association. By William Henry McMenemey. 1959.

2535 SIMON. Sir John Simon, 1816–1904, and English social administration. By Royston Lambert. 1963.

Also Sir John Simon, *Personal recollections*, 1894.

2536 SOUTHWOOD SMITH. Dr. Southwood Smith: a retrospect. By Gertrude Lewes. 1898.

2537 THACKRAH. The life work and times of Charles Turner Thackrah, surgeon and apothecary of Leeds, 1795–1833. By Andrew Meiklejohn. 1957.

2538 WAKLEY. The life and times of Thomas Wakley, founder and first editor of the 'Lancet', member of Parliament for Finsbury, and coroner for West Middlesex. By Sir Samuel Squire Sprigge. 1897.

Also useful for radical politics.

(ii) *Nurses and Hospitals*

2539 ABEL-SMITH (BRIAN). A history of the nursing profession. 1960.

Brief on early 19th century. Also Herbert Ritchie Spencer, *The history of British midwifery from 1650 to 1800*, 1927, and Agnes Elizabeth Pavey, *The story of the growth of nursing as an art, a vocation, and a profession*, 1938, 5th edn. 1959.

2540 POYNTER (FREDERICK NOËL LAWRENCE) *ed*. The evolution of hospitals in Britain. 1964.

With a valuable bibliography of hospital history, comp. E. Gaskell, 255–279. See also John Howard, *An account of the principal lazarettos in Europe*, etc., Warrington, 1789, 2nd edn., enl. London, 1791; Sir Henry Charles Burdett, *Hospitals and asylums of the world*, etc., 4 v., 1891–3; Brian Abel-Smith, *The hospitals, 1800–1948: A study in social administration in England and Wales*, 1964, brief for early 19th century. See also (3982), (Edinburgh and Glasgow), and (4239), (Dublin).

2541 MOORE (*Sir* NORMAN). The history of St. Bartholomew's hospital. 2 v. 1918.

For other London hospitals see *An account of the British Lying-in Hospital . . . in*

Brownlow Street, etc., 1808; Edward Geoffrey O'Donoghue, *Bridewell Hospital, palace, prison, schools* 2 v., 1923, 1929; George Benjamin Golding, *The origin, plan, and operations of the Charing Cross Hospital . . . erected 1831 by the late Benjamin Golding, M.D.*, 1867; Hector Charles Cameron, *Mr. Guy's hospital, 1726–1948*, 1954; Archibald Edmund Clark-Kennedy, *The London, A study in the voluntary system*, 2 v., 1962, 1964; Sir William James Erasmus Wilson, *The history of the Middlesex Hospital*, etc., 1845; Edward Treacher Collins, *The history and traditions of the Moorfields Eye Hospital*, etc., 1929; Frederick George Parsons, *The history of St. Thomas's hospital*, etc., 3 v., 1932–6.

2542 [BUNCE (JOHN THACKRAY).] The Birmingham General Hospital and Triennial Musical Festivals. Birmingham. [1858.]

Histories of other notable provincial hospitals (in alphabetical order of places) are George Munro Smith, *A history of the Bristol Royal Infirmary*, Bristol, 1917; Stephen Towers Anning, *The General Infirmary at Leeds, I, the first hundred years, 1767–1869*, 1963; Thomas Herbert Bickerton, *A medical history of Liverpool from the earliest days to the year 1920*, ed. H. R. Bickerton and R. M. B. MacKenna, 1936, which deals with public health and all medical services; William Brockbank, *Portrait of a hospital, 1752–1948 . . . the Royal Infirmary, Manchester*, 1952; Edward Mansfield Brockbank, *Sketches of the lives and work of the Honorary Medical Staff of the Manchester Infirmary . . . to 1830*, etc., Manchester, 1904, continued by William Brockbank, *The honorary medical staff of the Manchester Royal Infirmary, 1830–1948*, Manchester [1965]; Frederick Stancliffe Stancliffe, *The Manchester Royal Eye Hospital, 1814–1964; a short history*, Manchester [1964]; John Harley Young, *St. Mary's Hospitals, Manchester, 1790–1963*, 1964; Alexander George Gibson, *The Radcliffe Infirmary*, 1926; John Daniel Leader, *1797–1897. Sheffield General Infirmary, now . . . the Sheffield Royal Infirmary*, etc., Sheffield, 1897; William Henry McMenemey, *A history of the Worcester Royal Infirmary*, 1947.

(iii) *Lunacy*

2543 JONES (KATHLEEN). Lunacy, law and conscience, 1744–1845. The social history of the care of the insane. 1955.

Bibliog. 227–34. See also her *A history of the mental health services*, 1972, and William Parry Jones, *The trade in lunacy; a study of private madhouses in England in the eighteenth and nineteenth centuries*, 1972. In 1848 these cared for 50 per cent of the insane. See also Daniel Hack Tuke, *Chapters in the history of the insane in the British Isles*, etc., 1882. Parliamentary inquiries include *Report on the state of criminal and pauper lunatics*, H.C. 1807 (39) II, *Select Committee on madhouses in England*, H.C. 1814–5 (299) IV, and H.C. (227, 398, 451) VI, *Select Committee on pauper lunatics in the county of Middlesex* H.C. 1826–7 (557) VI.

2544 TUKE (SAMUEL). Description of the Retreat, an institution near York, for insane persons of the Society of Friends. Containing an account of its origin and progress, the modes of treatment, and a statement of cases. York. 1813.

Reprinted 1964, with an intro. by Richard Alfred Hunter and Ida Macalpine (Psychiatric monographs 7), also John Thurnam, *Observations and essays on the statistics of insanity . . . to which are added the statistics of the Retreat, near York*, 1845. On other asylums see Caleb Crowther, *Observations on the management of madhouses illustrated by occurrences in the West Riding and Middlesex Asylums*, pt. 1, 1838, pt. 2, 1841, pt. 3, 1849; Edward Geoffrey O'Donoghue, *The story of Bethlehem Hospital from its foundation in 1247*, 1914; Charles Newenham French, *The story of St. Luke's Hospital*, etc., 1951; Nesta Roberts, *Cheadle Royal Hospital, A bicentenary history*, Altrincham, 1967.

2545 HUNTER (RICHARD ALFRED) *and* MACALPINE (IDA). Three
hundred years of psychiatry, 1535–1860. A history presented in selected
English texts. 1963.

James Cowles Prichard, *A treatise on insanity, and other disorders affecting the mind*,
1835, was long the standard work. See also Flugel (3152).

2546 CONOLLY. A memoir of John Conolly, M.D., D.C.L., comprising
a sketch of the treatment of the insane in Europe and America. By Sir James
Clark. 1869.

Physician at Hanwell, 1839–52. See also John Conolly, *An inquiry concerning the indica-
tions of insanity*, etc., 1830, reprinted 1964 with intro. by Richard Hunter and Ida
Macalpine (Psychiatric monographs, 4), *The construction and government of lunatic
asylums and hospitals for the insane*, etc., 1847, and *The treatment of the insane without
mechanical restraints*, 1856.

(iv) *Pharmacy*

2547 POYNTER (FREDERICK NOËL LAWRENCE) *ed*. The evolution of
pharmacy in Britain. 1965.

Also George Edward Trease, *Pharmacy, a history*, 1964.

(b) *Public Health*

(i) *Administration*

2548 BUER (MABEL CRAVEN). Health, wealth, and population in the
early days of the industrial revolution. 1926.

A comprehensive and standard work.

2549 FRAZER (WILLIAM MOWLL). A history of English public health,
1834–1939. 1950.

See also Beatrice Leigh Hutchins, *The public health agitation, 1833–48*, 1909; Sir Arthur
Newsholme, *Evolution of preventive medicine*, 1927; George Rosen, *A history of public
health*, (M.D. Monographs on Medical History, 1), [1958]; Colin Fraser Brockington,
Public health in the nineteenth century, 1965. See also (3108–50) for general medical
history, (1344–5) for medicine in the navy, and (1075) for medicine in the army.

2550 HENNOCK (E. P.) 'Urban sanitary reform a generation before Chadwick?' *Econ.H.R.*, 2nd ser. X (1957–8), 113–19.

A reply to B. Keith-Lucas, 'Some influences affecting the development of sanitary
legislation in England', *Econ. H.R.*, 2nd ser. VI (1953–4), 290–6. See also Henry Harris,
'Manchester's board of health in 1796', *Isis*, 28 (1938), 26–37.

2551 CHADWICK. The life and times of Sir Edwin Chadwick. By Samuel
Edward Finer. 1952.

Also Richard Albert Lewis, *Edwin Chadwick and the public health movement, 1832–1854*,
1952. Both works are admirable. See also *The health of nations, a review of the works of
Sir Edwin Chadwick. With a biographical dissertation*, by Benjamin Ward Richardson,
2 v., 1887. For attacks on Chadwick and the General Board of Health see Joshua
Toulmin Smith, *The laws of England relating to public health*, etc., 1848, and, by the
same author (374); also Henry Wyldbore Rumsey, *Essays on state medicine*, 1856,
criticizing the Board's indifference to medical opinion.

2552 SIMON (*Sir* JOHN). English sanitary institutions, reviewed in the course of their development, and in some of their political and social relations. 1890. 2nd edn. 1897.

By the same author, *Public health reports, edited for the Sanitary Institute of Great Britain, by Edward Seaton, M.D.*, 2 v., 1887. V. 1 contains City of London reports, v. 2 reports to Privy Council. For Simon's life see (2535).

2553 HEALTH OF TOWNS. Select Committee report and evidence. H.C. 1840 (384) XI.

This was followed by the *Report on the sanitary condition of the labouring population of Great Britain*, by Edwin Chadwick and others on behalf of Poor Law Commissioners, H.L. 1842 XXVI–XXVIII, reprinted Edin. [1965] with intro. by M. W. Flinn, and *Royal Commission on large towns and populous districts*, H.C. 1844 [572] XVII, and H.C. 1845 [602, 610] XVIII. This last includes reports on particular towns by inspectors, in appendices. Many similar reports by private individuals are reported in early numbers of *Journal of Royal Statistical Soc.*, 1839+ (36).

2554 HEALTH OF TOWNS ASSOCIATION. Report of the sub-committee on the answers returned to questions addressed to the principal towns of England and Wales, and on the objections from corporate bodies to the Public Health Bill. 1848.

One of the assoc.'s many publications.

2555 HEALTH OF TOWNS. Select Committee report and evidence on the effect of interment of bodies in towns. H.C. 1842 (327) X.

Also Edwin Chadwick, *Supplementary report on interment in towns*, H.C. 1843 [509] XII, see also George Alfred Walker, *Gatherings from grave-yards*, etc., 1839, one of the earliest attacks on the problem.

2556 JEPHSON (HENRY). The sanitary evolution of London. 1907.

See also Health of London Association, *Report . . . on the sanitary condition of the metropolis*, etc., 1847 (the result of a questionnaire circulated to 3000 persons); Hector Gavin, *Sanitary ramblings; being sketches . . . of Bethnal Green*, etc., 1848; General Board of Health, *Report on a general scheme for extra-mural sepulture, with particular reference to the Metropolis*, H.C. 1850 [1158] XXI; Sir John Simon, *Reports relating to the sanitary condition of the City of London*, 1854; Metropolitan Commission of Sewers [*Reports and other documents issued . . . February 1848 to March 1856*], 2 v., 1848–56. For full bibliog. and general discussion of London see Lambert (2535).

2557 DICKINSON (HENRY WINRAM). Water supply of Greater London. 1954.

Also John Wright, *The Dolphin; or, Grand Junction Nuisance*, etc., 1827, an attack on the water companies; Sir William Clay, *Remarks on the water supply of London*, 1849, in defence of the companies; General Board of Health, *Report on the supply of water to the metropolis*, H.C. 1850 [1218, 1281–4] XXII; Henry Charles Richards and William Henry Christopher Payne, *The metropolitan water supply*, 1891, 2nd edn. ed. J. H. Soper, 1899; T. F. Reddaway, 'London in the nineteenth century. III. The fight for a water supply', *Nineteenth Century and After*, 148 (1950), 118–30.

2558 NEWLANDS (JAMES). Liverpool past and present in relation to sanitary operations. Liverpool. 1859.

Also W. T. McGowen, *Sanitary legislation, with illustrations from experiences in Liverpool*, Liverpool, 1859; also (2532), (2533), and Bickerton (2542).

2559 SEWERAGE AND CLEANSING OF THE SITES OF TOWNS. General Board of Health minutes of information. H.C. 1852 [1535] XIX.

Technical information on the design of sewers, water-closets etc. Also George Drysdale Dempsey, *Rudimentary treatise on the drainage of towns and buildings*, etc., 1849, 3rd edn., 1865.

2560 GIBSON (EDWARD H.). 'Baths and washhouses in the English public health agitation, 1839–48.' *Jour. of the Hist. of Medicine*, 9 (1954), 391–406.

(ii) *Epidemics and Occupational Diseases*

2561 CREIGHTON (CHARLES). A history of epidemics in Britain. 2 v. Camb. 1891. 1894.

Reprinted 2 v., 1965, with additional material by David Edward Charles Eversley, E. Ashworth Underwood, Lynda Overall; the classic work on the subject. Also William Heberden, *Observations on the increase and decrease of certain diseases and particularly of the plague*, 1801. Robert Willan, *Reports on the diseases in London, particularly during the years 1796, 97, 98, 99, and 1800*, 1801, and Thomas Bateman, *Reports on the diseases of London, and the state of the weather, from 1804 to 1816*, etc., 1819, are both based on reported cases. J. R. Brownlee, 'The health of London in the eighteenth century', *Proc. Roy. Soc. Medicine*, 18 (1925), Epidemiology section, 73–85, discusses deaths from particular diseases. See also Thomas Shapter, *Remarks on the mortality of Exeter*, 1844, and for works on population, (1691–1702).

2562 EPIDEMIC CHOLERA OF 1848 AND 1849. General Board of Health report. H.C. 1850 [1273–5] XXI.

General survey and reports of particular towns. See also William Budd, *Malignant cholera; its mode of propagation and its prevention*, and John Snow, *On the mode of communication of cholera*, 1849, 2nd edn. much enl., 1855, and reprinted under the title, *Snow on cholera . . . Together with a biographical memoir by B. W. Richardson . . . and an introduction by Wade Hampton Frost*, N.Y. 1936. Budd and Snow argued independently that the disease was water-borne: for Budd's life see (2530).

2563 SHAPTER (THOMAS). The history of the cholera in Exeter in 1832. 1849.

A notable description of an historical epidemic; see also Edward Headlam Greenhow, *Cholera in Tynemouth in 1831–2; 1848–9; and 1853* [1855], and M. Darcy, *The first spasmodic cholera epidemic in York, 1832* (Borthwick papers no. 46), York, 1974. Charles Kingsley's *Two years ago*, Camb. 1857, is a novel on the subject. For modern discussion see Asa Briggs, 'Cholera and society in the nineteenth century', *Past and Present*, no. 19 (1961), 76–96, Finer and Lewis (2551) and Lambert (2535). Norman Longmate, *King cholera*, 1966, is a popular account.

2564 OLIVER (*Sir* THOMAS) ed. Dangerous trades. The historical, social and legal aspects of industrial occupations as affecting health, by a number of experts. 1902.

A wide-ranging work of reference. See also Charles Turner Thackrah, *The effects of the principal arts, trades, and professions . . . on health and longevity: with a particular reference to the trades and manufactures of Leeds*, 1831, 2nd edn., greatly enl., 1832. For Thackrah's life see (2537). George Calvert Holland, *The vital statistics of Sheffield*, 1843, contains much material on industrial diseases. For bakers see Guy (1724), for chimney sweeps (2523).

2565 McDONALD (J. C.). 'The history of quarantine in Britain during the
nineteenth century.' *Bull. Hist. Medicine*, 25 (1951), 22–44.

See also General Board of Health report on quarantine H.C. 1849, (1070) XXIV, and
on yellow fever H.C. 1852 (1473) XX. These deprecate the value of quarantine, holding
that the essential condition of an epidemic is an 'epidemic atmosphere'.

4. Social Problems

(a) *Temperance*

2566 HARRISON (BRIAN). Drink and the Victorians: the temperance
question in England, 1815–1872. 1971.

And, with Barrie Trinder, *Drink and sobriety in an early Victorian town: Banbury,
1830–1860, E.H.R.* Suppt. 4, Harlow, 1969. Norman Richard Longmate, *The water-
drinkers; a history of temperance*, 1968, is a short popular account. For a very extensive
modern bibliog. see Brian Harrison, 'Drink and sobriety in England, 1815–72: a critical
bibliography', *Internat. Review of Social History*, 12 (1967) 204–76. See also (1864).

2567 WILSON (GEORGE BAILEY). Alcohol and the nation. (A contribution to the study of the liquor problem in the United Kingdom from 1800 to
1935.) 1940.

See also Samuel Couling, *History of the temperance movement in Great Britain and
Ireland*, 1862, James Dawson Burns, *Temperance history. A consecutive narrative of the
rise, development and extension of the temperance reform*, 2 v. [1889–91], is a standard
account, as is Peter Turner Winskill, *The temperance movement and its workers*, 4 v.,
Edin., 1892. Henry Carter, *The English temperance movement: a study in objectives . . .,
v. 1, The formative period, 1830–1899*, 1933, is a short survey.

2568 WEBB (SIDNEY JAMES) *and* WEBB (BEATRICE). The history of
liquor licensing in England, principally from 1700 to 1830. 1903.

Reprinted 1963 as v. XI of *English local government* (466). [Patrick Colquhoun], *Observations and facts relative to licensed alehouses in the city of London and its environs*, 1794,
2nd edn., 1796, was an attack on the large numbers of ill-conducted houses; *Select
committee on sale of beer by retail*, H.C. 1830 (253) X, recommended 'free trade in beer';
Select committee on sale of beer, H.C. 1833 (416, 585, 664) XV, contains a mass of information on licensing; *Select committee on sale of beer* (a Lords' committee), H.C. 1850
(398) XVIII, contains much criticism of effects of 'free trade'.

2569 LIVESEY (JOSEPH). The life and teachings of Joseph Livesey, comprising his autobiography, with an introductory review of his labours by John
Pearce. 2 pts. [1886.]

See also Livesey's *Reminiscences of early teetotalism*, Preston, 1868. Connected with
Livesey is the first teetotal publication in England, *The Preston Temperance Advocate*,
Preston, 1837.

2570 LONDON TEMPERANCE SOCIETY *afterwards* BRITISH AND
FOREIGN TEMPERANCE SOCIETY. Reports. 1831+.

(b) *Sunday observance; Betting*

2571 SELECT COMMITTEE ON OBSERVANCE OF SABBATH DAY.
Report and evidence, H.C. 1831–2 (697) VII.

Gives a vivid picture of London life. See also *Select committee on the carriage of goods and merchandise on canals, navigable rivers on Sundays*, H.L. 1841 (92) XXI, *Select committee on Sunday trading in the Metropolis*, H.C. 1847 (666) IX, and the House of Lords' committee on the same subject, H.C. 1850 (441) XIX.

2572 SELECT COMMITTEE ON GAMING. Report and evidence. H.C. 1844 (297) VI.

Also House of Lords' committee, 1–3 reps. H.C. 1844 (468, 544, 604) VI. Investigation of legal regulation of gaming houses, betting at races, etc., with evidence from the Metropolitan Police. See also Cecil Henry L'Estrange Ewen, *Lotteries and sweepstakes ... their introduction, suppression, and re-establishment in the British Isles*, 1932, and on a more gossipy level, John Ashton, *A history of English lotteries*, 1893.

5. Housing and Town Planning

2573 ASHWORTH (WILLIAM). The genesis of modern British town planing. A study in the economic and social history of the nineteenth and twentieth centuries. 1954.

Also his 'British industrial villages of the nineteenth century', *Econ.H.R.*, 2nd ser. 3 (1950–1), 378–87. See also Colin John Bell and Rose Bell, *City fathers; the early history of town planning in Britain*, 1969; Stanley David Chapman, ed., *The history of working class housing; a symposium*, Newton Abbot, 1971; John Nelson Tarn, *Working class housing in 19th century Britain* (Architectural Assn. Papers, 7), 1971, and his *Five per cent. philanthropy. An account of housing in urban areas, 1840–1914*, Camb., 1974; Enid Gauldie, *Cruel habitations. A history of working class housing, 1780–1918*, 1974. See also (1811).

2574 BUILDING REGULATION AND IMPROVEMENT OF BOROUGHS. Report of select committee. H.C. 1842 (372) X.

Also William Hosking, *A guide to the proper regulation of building in towns*, etc., 1848, a technical study. *The Select committee on public walks*, H.C. 1833 (448) XV, is an early discussion of that subject.

2575 BUCKINGHAM (JAMES SILK). National evils and practical remedies, with the plan of a model town. [1849].

2576 ROBERTS (HENRY). The dwellings of the labouring classes, their arrangement and construction. 1850. 3rd edn. 1854. 6th edn. 1867.

Pub. in connection with the Society for Improving the Condition of the Labouring Classes: it contains plans, elevations, discussions of densities. See also the same writer's *Model houses for families built in connection with the Great Exhibition of 1851, by command of Prince Albert* [1851].

2577 SMITH (THOMAS SOUTHWOOD). Results of sanitary improvement illustrated by the operation of the Metropolitan Societies for Improving the Dwellings of the Industrial Classes; the working of the Common Lodging Houses Act. 1854.

A report on provincial towns as well as London.

2578 HOLE (JAMES). The homes of the working classes with suggestions for their improvement. [Leeds.] 1866.

On Hole see John Fletcher Clews Harrison, *Social reform in Victorian Leeds; the work of James Hole, 1820–1895*, Thoresby Soc. Monographs 3, 1954, publication 100. See also William Gordon Rimmer, 'Working men's cottages in Leeds, 1770–1840', *Thoresby Soc. Miscellany*, 13, pt. 2 (1960), 165–99.

2579 SMITH (EDWARD). The peasant's home, 1760–1875. 1876.

2580 WINSTANLEY (DAVID). A schoolmaster's notebook, being an account of a nineteenth century experiment in social welfare. Ed. by Edith and Thomas Kelly. (Chetham Society Remains, 3rd ser. 8.) 1957.

An interesting account of housing management in Miles Platting, Manchester.

6. LAW AND ORDER

(a) *General*

For a guide to the Home Office papers see (64).

2581 RADZINOWICZ (LEON). A history of English criminal law and its administration from 1750. 4 v. 1948–68.

A full and authoritative account, dealing with the theory of penology, development of penal law, police reform, and enforcement. Each vol. has a full bibliog., including a list of parliamentary debates, 1785–1832 (v. 1, 753–60). Other bibliogs. are New York Public Library, *List of works relating to criminology*, N.Y., 1911, and Sir John Ghest Cumming, *A contribution towards a bibliography dealing with crime and cognate subjects*, Calcutta, 3rd edn., 1935. For treatises on criminal law see (624–30), for law reports (555–6).

2582 TOBIAS (JOHN JACOB). Crime and industrial society in the nineteenth century. 1967.

(b) *Penal Reform*

2583 GRUENHUT (MAX). Penal reform. A comparative study. Oxf. 1948.

A general study of Europe and America. See also Richard Standish Elphinstone Hinde, *The British penal system, 1773–1950*, 1951, and James Heath, *Eighteenth century penal theory*, 1963, a collection of extracts from the writings of penal reformers, Beccaria, Bentham, Romilly, Howard, and others. For Bentham see (652), Mackintosh (575), Romilly (576), Howard (Pargellis and Medley, 2217), Peel and criminal law (200).

(i) *Capital Punishment*

For parliamentary papers on criminal law see Ford and Ford (391). See also *Philanthropy*.

2584 MONTAGU (BASIL). The opinions of different authors upon the punishment of death, selected by Basil Montagu. 3 v. 1809–12.

Montagu founded, in association with William Allen (2510) and others, the Society for the Diffusion of Knowledge upon the Punishment of Death, and the Improvement of Prison Discipline: see the Society's *Reports of the Committee*, 1818–32.

2585 ROMILLY (*Sir* SAMUEL). Observations on the criminal law of England, as it relates to capital punishments, and on the mode in which it is administered. 1810. 2nd edn. 1811. 3rd edn. 1813.

2586 MILLER (JOHN). An inquiry into the present state of the statute and criminal law of England. 1822.

2587 SOCIETY FOR THE DIFFUSION OF INFORMATION ON THE SUBJECT OF CAPITAL PUNISHMENTS. Punishment of death: a series of short articles to appear occasionally in numbers designed for general circulation. Nos. 1–15. [1831.]

Society founded 1829.

2588 WAKEFIELD (EDWARD GIBBON). Facts relating to the punishment of death in the metropolis. 1831. 2nd edn. With appendix. 1832.

Wakefield had spent 3 years in Newgate, and gives a grim account of the effect of executions on prisoners, which made a strong public impact.

2589 WOOLRYCH (HUMPHRY WILLIAM). The history and results of the present capital punishments in England; to which are added full tables of convictions, executions, etc. 1832.

2590 LAURENCE (JOHN). A history of capital punishment, with special reference to capital punishment in Great Britain. [1932].

(ii) *Debt*

2591 NEILD (JAMES). An account of the rise, progress, and present state, of the Society for the discharge and relief of persons imprisoned for small debts throughout England and Wales. 1802.

See also Matthew Robinson, *The insolvent debtors' guide, containing full directions to persons under imprisonment for debt*, etc., 1817, and [Frederick William Naylor Bayley] *Scenes and stories by a clergyman in debt*, etc., 3 v., 1835, a novel. See also *Select Committee to consider bankrupt laws*, H.C. 1817 [486] I and H.C. 1818 (127, 276, 277) VI. For later Parliamentary papers see Ford and Ford (391), 45, for legal treatises (616).

(iii) *Corporal punishment*

2592 Observations on the offensive and injurious effect of corporal punishment. 1827.

For military flogging see (1062), (1066).

(iv) *Juveniles*

2593 PHILANTHROPIC SOCIETY instituted in London, September 1788, for the prevention of crimes. Reports 1789+.

The society was still in existence in 1848, and concerned itself with juveniles. See also *Report of the committee for investigating the causes of the alarming increase of juvenile delinquency*, 1816; on Glasgow, Brebner (3978), and *Report by the directors of the Glasgow society for repressing juvenile delinquency*, Glasgow, 1839, Thomas Beggs, *An inquiry into the extent and causes of juvenile depravity*, etc., 1849. Beggs had been secretary to the Health of Towns Association.

2594 JUVENILE OFFENDERS AND TRANSPORTATION. Report of House of Lords' Select Committee on Criminal Law. H.C. 1847 (447, 534) VII.

2595 CARPENTER (MARY). Reformatory schools for the children of the perishing and dangerous classes, and for juvenile offenders. 1851.

See also her *Juvenile delinquents, their condition and treatment*, 1853, and Joseph Estlin Carpenter, *The life and work of Mary Carpenter*, 1879.

(v) *Prisons*

2596 WEBB (SIDNEY) *and* WEBB (BEATRICE). English prisons under local government. 1922. Reprinted 1963 as v. 6 of English Local Government.

Other general works on prisons include Walter Lowe Clay, *The prison chaplain: a memoir of the Rev. John Clay, B.D. . . . with selections from his reports and correspondence, and a sketch of prison discipline in England*, Cambridge, 1891; Henry Mayhew and John Binny, *The criminal prisons of London and scenes of prison life*, 1862, with many striking illustrations; Derek Lionel Howard, *The English prisons. Their past and their future*, 1960.

2597 BENTHAM (JEREMY). Panopticon; or The inspection-house; containing the idea of a new principle of construction. 3 v. 1791.

The panopticon was discussed by the *Select Committee on the laws relating to penitentiary houses*, H.C. 1810–11 (199, 207), III.

2598 PAUL (*Sir* GEORGE ONESIPHORUS). Proceedings of the grand juries, magistrates, and other noblemen and gentlemen of the county of Glocester on designing and executing a general reform in the construction and regulation of prisons for the said county. Gloucester. 1808.

See also *General regulations for inspection and controul of all the prisons . . . for the county of Glocester*, etc. 2 pt. Gloucester, 1791.

2599 NEILD (JAMES). State of the prisons in England, Scotland, and Wales, with documents, observations, and remarks. 1812.

Important. Neild continued John Howard's work (see Pargellis and Medley, 2217).

2600 STATE OF THE GAOLS OF THE CITY OF LONDON. Select committee reports. H.C. 1813–14 (157) IV, 1814–15 (152) IV, 1818 (275, 392) VIII, 1819 (109) XI.

2601 BUXTON (*Sir* THOMAS FOWELL). An inquiry whether crime and misery are produced or prevented, by our present system of prison discipline. 2 pt. 1818. 5th edn. 1818.

An important work, leading to the formation of the Society for the Improvement of Prison Discipline and for the Reformation of Juvenile Offenders. See Society's *Reports*, 1818–32, which reported on prisons in the manner of Howard and Neild. See also Charles Buxton, *Memoirs of Sir Thomas Fowell Buxton*, etc., 1848, and R. H. Mottram, *Buxton the liberator*, 1945. Also associated with the society was *Peter Bedford, the Spitalfields philanthropist*, by William Tallack, 1865.

2602 GURNEY (JOSEPH JOHN). Notes on a visit made to some of the prisons in Scotland and the north of England in company with Elizabeth Fry. With some general observations on the subject of prison discipline. 1819.

Brother of Elizabeth Fry; for his life see (855).

2603 PRISONS. Copies of all reports, and the schedule (B) transmitted to the Secretary of State from the several counties, cities, towns, in England and Wales, under the provisions of the 'Gaol Act' of 4 Geo. IV, c. 64. H.C. 1824 (104) XIX.

Detailed reports continued annually until superseded by annual reports of inspectors of prisons, 1836. The first report of the inspectors was attacked in Peter Laurie, *Prison discipline and secondary punishments. Remarks on the first report of the inspector of prisons*, 1837.

2604 FRY (ELIZABETH). Observations on the visiting, superintendence, and government of female prisoners. 1827.

See also Katharine Fry and Rachel E. Cresswell, *Memoir of the life of Elizabeth Fry, with extracts from her journal and letters.* 2 v., 1847; Thomas Timpson, *Memoirs of Mrs. Elizabeth Fry . . . With a biographical sketch of her brother, J. J. Gurney, Esq.*, 2nd edn. with additions, 1847; Susanna Corder, *Life of Elizabeth Fry. Compiled from her journal . . . and from various other sources*, 1853. Two modern accounts are Janet Payne Whitney, *Elizabeth Fry, Quaker heroine*, Boston, 1936, London, 1937, and John Henry Somerset Kent, *Elizabeth Fry*, 1962.

2605 SECONDARY PUNISHMENTS. Report of select committee. H.C. 1831 (276) VII, 1831–2 (547) VII.

Followed by HL *committee on gaols and houses of correction in England and Wales*, 1st and 2nd reps. H.C. 1835 (438–9) XI, 3rd–5th reps. H.C. 1835 (440–1) XII. This committee received evidence from Mrs. Fry and others.

2606 JEBB (*Sir* JOSHUA). Modern prisons: their construction and ventilation. 1844.

Related to Pentonville, and influential on subsequent prison construction. Jebb was surveyor-general of convict prisons at this time: for surveyor-general's reports see Ford and Ford (391), 108–9.

2607 MARTIN (SARAH). A brief sketch of the life of the late Miss S. Martin, of Great Yarmouth; with extracts from the parliamentary reports on prisons; her own prison journals, etc., etc. Yarmouth. 1844.

Also [George Mogridge], *Sarah Martin, the prison visitor of Great Yarmouth: the story of a useful life* [1872].

2608 MACONOCHIE (ALEXANDER). Crime and punishment. The mark system, framed to mix persuasion with punishment. 1846.

Also his *Prison discipline*, 1856. Marks were to be given as rewards for work performed. See also (4696).

2609 SELECT COMMITTEE ON PRISON DISCIPLINE. Report and evidence. H.C. 1850 (632) XVII.

2610 CHESTERTON (GEORGE LAVAL). Revelations of prison life; with an enquiry into prison discipline and secondary punishments. 2 v. 1856. 3rd edn. 1857.

See also Joseph Kingsmill, *A commonsense view of the treatment of criminals, especially those sentenced to transportation*, etc., 1850.

2611 BRANCH-JOHNSON (WILLIAM). The English prison hulks. 1957.

See also George Peter Holford, *Statements and observations concerning the hulks*, etc., 1826. Much information was collected by the *Select Committee on the laws relating to penitentiary houses*, 3rd rep., H.C. 1812 (306) II, and by the *Select committee on the treatment and condition of convicts in the hulks at Woolwich*, H.C. 1847 [831 I–II] XVIII.

2612 SMITH (ANN DOROTHEA). Women in prison. A study in penal methods. 1962. Bibliog. 345–56.

2613 RHODES (ALBERT JOHN). Dartmoor prison. A record of 126 years of prisoner of war and convict life, 1806–1932. 1933.

Also Sir Basil Thomson, *Dartmoor prison*, 1907. Other prison histories are George Peter Holford, *An account of the general penitentiary at Millbank*, 1828; Arthur George Frederick Griffiths, *Memorials of Millbank and chapters in prison history*, 2 v., 1875, another edn., 1884, also his *The chronicles of Newgate*, 2 v., 1884; Charles Gordon [*pseud.* of John Ashton], *The Old Bailey and Newgate* [1902]. Joseph Adshead, *Prisons and prisoners*, 1845, is on Pentonville, as are Joseph Kingsmill, *Chapters on prisons and prisoners*, 1850, 2nd edn. 1852, 3rd edn. 1854, and John Thomas Burt, *Results of the system of separate confinement, as administered at the Pentonville prison*, 1852. See also John Field, *Prison discipline; the advantages of the separate system . . . in the new county gaol of Reading*, 1846, another edn. 2 v., 1848, Joseph Horsfall Turner, *The annals of Wakefield house of correction*, etc., Bingley, 1904, a documented history of a county gaol, and T. J. Walker, *The depot for prisoners of war, Norman Cross*, 1913.

(vi) *Transportation*

2614 SHAW (ALAN GEORGE LEWERS). Convicts and the colonies: a study of penal transportation from Great Britain and Ireland to Australia and other parts of the British Empire. 1966.

See also Bénigne Ernest Poret, Marquis de Blosseville, *Histoire des colonies pénales de l'Angleterre dans l'Australie*, Paris, 1831; Eris Michael O'Brien, *The foundation of Australia (1786–1800); a study in English criminal practice and penal colonization in the eighteenth century*, 1936, 2nd edn. 1950; Leslie Lloyd Robson, *The convict settlers of Australia; An enquiry into the origin and character of the convicts transported to New South Wales and Van Diemen's Land, 1787–1852*, 1965, a study of the English background of a 5 per cent sample of convicts.

2615 BATESON (CHARLES). The convict ships, 1789–1868. Glasgow. 1959.

Also Thomas Reid, *Two voyages to New South Wales and Van Diemen's Land*, etc., 1822, Colin Arrott Browning, *England's exiles; or . . . instruction and discipline, as carried into effect during the voyage to the penal colonies*, etc., 1842.

2616 WHATELY (RICHARD). Remarks on transportation, and on a recent defence of the system, in a second letter to Earl Grey. 1834.

See, in reply, Sir George Arthur, *Defence of transportation, in a reply to the remarks of the Archbishop of Dublin*, 1835. Whately led the attack on transportation which was investigated by select committees in 1832 (2605), and (the Molesworth Committee), 1837, H.C. 1837 (518) XIX, and H.C. 1838 (669) XXII. See also John Dunmore Lang, *Transportation and colonisation*, 1837, and, a strong attack on the convicts' case, James Mudie, *The felonry of New South Wales*, 1837.

2617 MACONOCHIE (ALEXANDER). Thoughts on convict management, and other subjects connected with the Australian penal colonies. Hobart Town. 1838.

Reprinted Hobart Town, 1839, as *Australiana; thoughts on convict management,* etc. See Sir John Vincent William Barry, *Alexander Maconochie of Norfolk Island. A study of a pioneer in penal reform,* etc., 1958, and the same writer's *The life and death of John Price. A study of the exercise of naked power,* 1964, the life of Maconochie's brutal successor.

2618 MELVILLE (HENRY). Australasia and prison discipline. 1851.

2619 BARRINGTON (GEORGE). A voyage to Botany bay, with a description of the country, manners, customs, religion, etc., of the natives: to which is added his life and trial. 2 pt. [1795?]

Republished N.Y. [1803] as *A voyage to New South Wales* (by a reformed thief). Among many memoirs see *Memoirs of James Hardy Vaux,* 2 v., 1819, 2nd edn. 1827, another edn., 1830; George Loveless, *Victims of Whiggery; being a statement of the persecutions experienced by the Dorsetshire labourers,* etc., 1837, 8th edn., 1838; Marcus Andrew Hislop Clarke, *His natural life* (a novel), Melbourne, 1874; George Louis Becke, ed., *Old convict days,* 1899, a novel; James Scott, *Remarks on a passage to Botany Bay, 1787–1792,* etc., William Dixson foundation pubns. 1, 1963; John Frederick Mortlock, *Experiences of a convict transported for twenty-one years,* ed., G. A. Wilkes and A. G. Mitchell, 1965; John Easty, *Memorandum of the transactions of a voyage from England to Botany Bay, 1787–1793; A First Fleet journal,* William Dixson foundation pubns. 4, 1965, also Mitchel (4129).

(c) *Police and Public Order*

For Ireland see (4134).

2620 CRITCHLEY (THOMAS ALAN). A history of police in England and Wales, 900–1966. 1967.

Also William Lauriston Melville Lee, *A history of police in England,* 1901; Charles Reith, *The police idea. Its history and evolution in England in the eighteenth century and after,* 1938, on police history to 1829; the same writer's *British police and the democratic ideal,* 1943, on 1829–40, and *A new study of police history,* 1956.

2621 RITSON (JOSEPH). The office of constable: being an entirely new compendium of law concerning that ancient minister for the conservation of the peace. 1791. 2nd edn. enl. 1815.

Similar manuals are Society for the Suppression of Vice, *The constable's assistant: being a compendium of the duties and powers of constables and other police officers,* 1808, 3rd edn. 1818, 4th 1831, both with additions; John William Willcock, *The office of constable . . with an account of their institution and appointment,* 1827; Joseph Chitty, *A summary of the office and duties of constables,* 1836, 2nd edn. 1837, 3rd enl. 1844, which includes the duties of the borough police. See also (477), (484).

2622 [COLQUHOUN (PATRICK).] A treatise on the police of the metropolis explaining the various crimes and misdemeanors which at present are felt as a pressure upon the community; and suggesting remedies for their prevention. 1796. 6th edn. corr. and enl. 1800. 7th edn. 1806.

Classic study. See also his *A treatise on the commerce and police of the river Thames,* etc., 1800. For biographies see Iatros (*pseud.* of Grant David Yeats), *A biographical sketch of the life and writings of P. Colquhoun, Esq.*, 1818, and Ralph Pieris, *The contributions of Patrick Colquhoun to social theory*, 1954.

2623 POLICE OF THE METROPOLIS. Report of select committee. 1799.

Followed by *Select committee on the nightly watch and police of the metropolis, Report*, H.C. 1812 (127) II, and by a further series of select committee reports, H.C. 1816 (510) V, 1817 (233, 484) VII, 1818 (423) VIII, 1822 (440) IV, 1828 (533) VI.

2624 ARMITAGE (GILBERT). The history of the Bow Street runners, 1729–1829. 1912. New edn. [1932.]

See also Percy Hetherington Fitzgerald, *Chronicles of Bow Street Police-office. With an account of the magistrates, 'runners', and police; and a selection of the most interesting cases*, 2 v., 1888, Henry Goddard, *Memoirs of a Bow Street Runner, . . . with an introduction by Patrick Pringle*, 1956.

2625 MOYLAN (*Sir* JOHN FITZGERALD). Scotland yard and the Metropolitan police. 1929. Rev. and enl. edn. 1934.

Also Douglas Gordon Browne, *The rise of Scotland yard. A history of the Metropolitan police*, 1956, and Geoffrey Belton Cobb, *The first detectives, and the early career of Richard Mayne, commissioner of police*, 1957, [1958].

2626 HART (JENIFER M.) 'The reform of the borough police, 1835–1856.' *E.H.R.* 70 (1955) 411–427.

See also *Royal Commission on the establishment of a constabulary force in the counties of England and Wales, 1st Report*, H.C. 1839 [169], XIX.

2627 MATHER (FREDERICK CLARE). Public order in the age of the Chartists. Manchester. [1959.]

Edward Wise, *The law relating to riots and unlawful assemblies*, etc., 1848, 3rd edn. 1889, 4th edn. 1907. On public order and the Luddites see Darvall and Peel (99).

(d) *Crime*

2628 RAYNER (JOHN L.) *and* CROOK (G. T.) *eds*. The complete Newgate calendar. 5 v. 1926.

Also A. F., *The criminal recorder, or, Biographical sketches of notorious public characters . . . by a student of the Inner Temple*, 4 v., 1804–9. 2nd edn. 1815. For Newgate see Gordon (2613). See also Tobias (2582).

2629 REDE (LEMAN THOMAS). York castle in the nineteenth century, being an account of all the principal offences committed in Yorkshire from the year 1800 to the present period, with the lives of the capital offenders. Leeds. 1831.

Also *Criminal chronology of York castle . . . commencing March 1st 1379, to the present time*, etc., York, 1867.

2630 PLINT (THOMAS). Crime in England, its relation, character and extent, as developed from 1801 to 1848. 1851.

A statistical analysis of the incidence and causes of crime. Also Frederic Hill, *Crime: its amount, causes and remedies*, 1853.

2631 RIBTON-TURNER (CHARLES JAMES). A history of vagrants and vagrancy, and beggars and begging. 1887.

Also Frank Wadleigh Chandler, *The literature of roguery*, 2 v., 1907, and on Dickens and crime, Collins (2728). George Ives, *A history of penal methods, criminals, witches, lunatics*, 1914. For smugglers and pirates see (1151–5).

7. ANTI-SLAVERY

Works primarily concerned with conditions in the slave colonies are listed at pp. 553–60; those on the economic workings of the system at (1491).

(a) *General*

2632 DUMOND (DWIGHT LOWELL). A bibliography of anti-slavery in America. Ann Arbor, Mich. [1961.]

See also the bibliog. in (1364). Elizabeth Donnan, ed., *Documents illustrative of the history of the slave trade to America*, 4 v., Wash., 1930–5, reprinted 1965, contains, in v. 2, *The eighteenth century*, a small amount on the period.

2633 KLINGBERG (FRANK JOSEPH). The anti-slavery movement in England; a study in English humanitarianism. Yale Historical Pubns Misc. 17. New Haven, Conn. 1926.

A standard general account, as are three volumes by William Law Mathieson, *British slavery and its abolition, 1823–38*, 1926, *Great Britain and the slave trade, 1839–1865*, 1929, and *British slave emancipation, 1838–49*, 1932. Two other older works, written in the liberal tradition, are Sir Reginald Coupland, *The British anti-slavery movement*, 1933, and Charles Malcolm MacInnes, *England and slavery*, Bristol, 1934. Daniel Pratt Mannix and Malcolm Cowley, *Black cargoes: a history of the Atlantic slave trade, 1518–1865*, 1963. Edith F. Hurwitz, *Politics and the public conscience*, 1973.

2634 WILLIAMS (ERIC EUSTACE). Capitalism and slavery. Chapel Hill, N.C. 1944.

The classic statement of the thesis that slavery was abolished when it was no longer economically worth' while; extensively discussed in *The transatlantic trade from West Africa*, Centre of African studies, Univ. of Edin. [1965]. For more recent criticism see Roger T. Anstey, 'Capitalism and slavery, a critique', *Econ.H.R.*, 2nd ser., 21 (1968), 307–20, and his excellent study, *The Atlantic slave trade and British abolition 1760–1810*, 1975.

(b) *Anti-Slavery Leaders*

For Brougham see (207), for T. F. Buxton (2601), for J. J. Gurney (855), for Zachary Macaulay (2186), for Romilly (576), for Roscoe (2172), for Granville Sharp (2079), for Sir James Stephen (2246), for Sturge (2259), for Wilberforce (151).

2635 CLARKSON. Thomas Clarkson; the friend of slaves. By Earl Leslie Griggs. 1936.

Bibliog. including list of Clarkson's works, 199–204. See also Thomas Taylor, *A biographical sketch of Thomas Clarkson, with a concise historical outline of the abolition of slavery . . . with occasional brief strictures on the misrepresentation of him contained in* The life of William Wilberforce, 1839, 2nd edn. 1847, and James Elmes, *Thomas Clarkson: a monograph, being a contribution towards the history of the abolition of the slave trade and slavery*, 1854.

(c) *The Slave Trade and its Abolition*

2636 CLARKSON (THOMAS). The history of the rise, progress, and accomplishment of the abolition of the African slave-trade by the British parliament. 2 v. 1808.

The development of the campaign may be traced in the same writer's *An essay on the comparative efficiency of regulation or abolition, as applied to the slave trade*, 1789, in the *Minutes of the evidence taken before a committee of the House of Commons . . . respecting the African slave trade*, Accounts and papers, 1791, v. 34, papers 745–8. See Eric Eustace Williams, 'The British West Indian slave trade after its abolition in 1807', *Jour. of Negro Hist.* 27 (1942), 175–91, and Alan M. Rees, 'Pitt and the achievement of abolition', *ibid.* 39 (1954), 167–84. See especially Anstey (2634).

2637 WILLIAMS (GOMER). History of the Liverpool privateers and letters of marque with an account of the Liverpool slave trade. 1897.

Standard and very substantial. See also Averil Mackenzie-Grieve, *The last years of the English slave trade, Liverpool, 1750–1807*, [1941], and *Liverpool and slavery: an historical account of the Liverpool–African slave trade . . . by a genuine 'Dicky Sam'*, Liverpool, 1884. Also on Liverpool, Jean Trepp, 'The Liverpool movement for the abolition of the slave trade', *Jour. of Negro Hist.* 13 (1928), 265–85, and Smithers and Touzeau (3625).

(d) *The Campaign for Emancipation*

2638 AFRICAN INSTITUTION. Reports of the Committee. 1807+.

The B.L. has those of 1807–18 and 1824. The institution was founded in 1807 and was superseded in 1823 by the newly founded and more powerful Society for the Abolition of Slavery throughout the British Dominions, which pub. annual *Reports* and the *Anti-Slavery Monthly Reporter*, 1827–36, and (a representative tract) *The slave colonies of Great Britain or, A picture of negro slavery drawn by the Colonists themselves; being an abstract of the various papers recently laid before Parliament . . . by the Society*, 1825, reprinted by Sutra branch of the California State Library, Occasional papers, reprint ser. 22, 2 pt., 1940.

2639 STEPHEN (JAMES). The slavery of the British West Indies delineated. 2 v. 1824–30.

A classic statement of the case for emancipation, answered by Alex. Barclay, *A practical view of the present state of slavery in the West Indies*, 2 v., 1828. See also Thomas Clarkson's important pamphlet, *Thoughts on the necessity of improving the condition of the slaves in the British colonies, with a view to their ultimate emancipation*, 1823, and John Henry Howard, *The laws of the British colonies in the W. Indies and other parts of America, concerning real and personal property and manumission of slaves*, 2 v., 1827.

2640 SELECT COMMITTEE TO CONSIDER MEASURES FOR . . . THE EXTINCTION OF SLAVERY. H.C. 1831–2 (721) XX.

The *Select committee on the expediency of supplying the West Indian colonies with free labourers from the East, Report and evidence*, H.C. 1810–11 (225) II, is also relevant. See also the *Select commitee on the working of the apprenticeship system, Reports and evidence*, H.C. 1836 (560) XV, and 1837 (510) VII.

2641 THOME (JAMES A.) *and* KIMBALL (J. H.). Emancipation in the West Indies. 2nd edn. N.Y. 1838.

Also Richard R. Madden. *A twelve months' residence in the West Indies*, 2 v., 1835, an account by one of the magistrates sent to supervise emancipation, and Joseph Sturge and T. Harvey, *The West Indies in 1837*, 1838.

2642 STEPHEN (*Sir* GEORGE). Anti-slavery recollections; in a series of letters addressed to Mrs. Beecher Stowe, written . . . at her request. 1854.

An account of the development of the agitation: see also N. B. Lewis, *The abolitionist movement in Sheffield, 1823–1833*, Manchester, 1934.

(e) *The Suppression of the Slave Trade*

2643 THE BRITISH AND FOREIGN ANTI-SLAVERY SOCIETY. The Anti-Slavery Reporter. 1839+.

Also the Aborigines' Protection Society, founded 1837, pub. *Annual Reports*, 1838–46: printed in the society's *Colonial Intelligencer or Aborigines' Friend*, 1847–51. The two societies amalgamated in 1909.

2644 SELECT COMMITTEE ON THE SLAVE TRADE. 1–4 reports. H.C. 1847–8 (272, 366, 536, 623) XXII, and H.C. 1849 (308, 410) XIX.

Also the House of Lords' Committee, H.L. 1850 (53, 590), IX.

2645 BETHELL (LESLIE). The abolition of the Brazilian slave trade: Britain, Brazil and the slave trade question, 1807–1869. Camb. 1970.

On the problem of Brazilian slavery see Sir Thomas Fowell Buxton, *The African slave trade and its remedy*, 1839, 2nd edn., 1840, and J. Gallagher, 'Fowell Buxton and the New African policy, 1838–42', *Camb. Hist. J.* 10 (1950), 36–58 (Buxton proposed the making of anti-slave trade treaties with inland African tribes). Also on Brazil, George William Alexander, *Letters on the slave trade, slavery, and emancipation*, 1842.

2646 TEMPERLEY (HOWARD). British anti-slavery, 1833–1870. 1972.

New and authoritative. See also William Edward Burghardt du Bois, *The suppression of the African slave trade to the United States of America, 1638–1870*, Camb., Mass., 1896; Christopher Lloyd, *The navy and the slave trade: the suppression of the African slave trade in the 19th century*, 1949; William Ernest Frank Ward, *The Royal Navy and the Slavers; the suppression of the Atlantic slave trade*, 1969.

(f) *Other Topics*

See also Coupland (4549).

2647 ADAM (WILLIAM). The law and custom of slavery in British India, in a series of letters to Thomas Fowell Buxton, Esq. 1840.

See also British and Foreign Anti-Slavery Soc., *A brief view of slavery and the slave trade in British India*, 1841.

2648 SCHUYLER (ROBERT LIVINGSTON). 'The constitutional claims of the British West Indies; the controversy over the Slave Registry Bill of 1815.' *Political Science Q.* 40 (1925), 1–36.

2649 TINKER (HUGH RUSSELL). A new system of slavery: the export of Indian labour overseas, 1830–1920. Oxf. 1974.

X

CULTURAL HISTORY

A. LITERATURE

The purpose of this section is to give a short guide to standard works, together with books published too recently for inclusion in *N.C.B.E.L.*

1. BIBLIOGRAPHY AND JOURNALS

2650 NEW CAMBRIDGE BIBLIOGRAPHY OF ENGLISH LITERA-
TURE. Ed. George Grimes Watson. V. II: 1660–1800. Camb. 1971. V. III:
1800–1900. Camb. 1969.

> Lists works up to *c.* 1967. It extends to newspapers, history, philosophy, and travel, and
> locates MS. sources for major writers. Current work is listed in the English Association's
> *The year's work in English studies*, 1919–20+, annual, and the *Annual bibliography of
> English language and literature*, v. 4, Camb. 1923+, pub. by the Modern humanities
> research association. (V. 1–3, 1920–2, were pub. with title *Bibliography of English lan-
> guage and literature*.) See also William S. Ward, comp. *A bibliography of literary reviews
> in British periodicals, 1798–1820*, 2 v., N.Y., 1972.

2650A REVIEW OF ENGLISH STUDIES. V. 1+. 1925+.

2651 ALTICK (RICHARD DANIEL) *and* MATTHEWS (WILLIAM R.).
Guide to doctoral dissertations in Victorian literature, 1886–1958. Urbana.
Ill. 1960.

2652 GHOSH (JYOTISH CHANDRA) *and* WITHYCOMBE (ELIZA-
BETH GIDLEY). Annals of English literature, 1475–1925. 2nd edn. Oxf. 1961.

> Lists the main books published in each year. Bent's *Monthly literary advertiser*, 1826+,
> attempted to produce a list of new books every year. On a minor subject Frederick
> Winthrop Faxon, *Literary annuals and gift books; a bibliography with a descriptive intro-
> duction*, Bost. 1912.

2653 BATESON (FREDERICK NOEL WILSE). A guide to English literature. 1965.

> Arthur Garfield Kennedy and Donald B. Sands, *A concise bibliography for students of
> English*, 4th edn. Stanford, Calif., 1960, is a guide to general works, as is Donald Frederick
> Bond, *A reference guide to English studies*, Chicago, 1962.

2654 BAILEY (RICHARD W.) *and* BURTON (DOLORES M.). English
stylistics; a bibliography. Camb. Mass. 1968.

2. HISTORIES OF LITERATURE AND CRITICISM

For Scotland see (3950–63), for Ireland (4197–208).

2655 ELTON (OLIVER). A survey of English literature, 1780–1830. 2 v. 1912.

> Continued by *A survey of English literature, 1830–1880*, 2 v., 1920.

2656 HARVEY (*Sir* HENRY PAUL) *ed.* The Oxford companion to English literature. Oxf. 1932. 4th edn. rev. by Dorothy Eagle, Oxf. 1967.

2657 BAUGH (ALBERT CROLL). History of the English language. N.Y. 1935. 2nd edn. 1959.

2658 WELLEK (RENÉ). A history of modern criticism: 1750–1950. New Haven, Conn. V. 1. The later eighteenth century. 1955. V. 2. The romantic age. 1955. V. 3. The age of transition, 1966.

The first 3 v. of a 5-v. history. See also George Edward Bateman Saintsbury, *A history of English criticism*, Edin., 1911, and William Kurtz Wimsatt and Cleanth Brooks, *Literary criticism; a short history*, N.Y. and London, 1957. For a short guide see George Grimes Watson, *The literary critics*, Harmondsworth, 1962.

2659 DAICHES (DAVID). A critical history of English literature. 2 v. N.Y. 1960. Repr. 4 v. London. 1968.

Also S. C. Chew, 'The nineteenth century and after', forming pt. 4 of Albert Croll Baugh, ed., *A literary history of England*, N.Y., 1948, London, 1950, and Joseph Ellis Baker, ed., *The reinterpretation of Victorian literature*, Princeton, 1950, a wide-ranging volume of essays by different writers.

2660 RENWICK (WILLIAM LINDSAY). English literature, 1789–1815. Oxf. 1963.

Continued by Ian Robert James Jack, *English literature, 1815–1832*, Oxf. 1963, forming v. 9 and 10 of the Oxford History of English literature, eds. F. P. Wilson and Bonamy Dobrée. V. 11 has not yet appeared. Both contain full critical bibliogs.; Jack's, pp. 458–631, especially so.

2661 HAYDEN (JOHN O.) The romantic reviewers, 1802–1824. 1969.

With appendices of reviewing periodicals, works reviewed, and authors where known. See also R. G. Cox, 'The great reviews', *Scrutiny*, 6 (1937), 2–20 (on criticism of the poets) and 155–75 (on the novelists), and Thomas Crawford, *The Edinburgh Review and romantic poetry, 1802–29*, University College bulletin 47, English ser. 8, Auckland, N.Z., 1955, and (3955).

3. ROMANTICISM

See also (2962).

2662 LOGAN (JAMES VENABLES) *et al. eds.* Some British romantics; a collection of essays. Edited by J. V. Logan, John E. Jordan, and Northrop Frye. Columbus, Ohio. 1966.

The most recent of a series pub. by the Modern Language Association of America outlining bibliographies and recent research on particular writers. Ernest Bernbaum, *Guide through the romantic movement*, N.Y., 1930, new edn. N.Y., 1949, covers similar ground. 'The romantic movement, a selective and critical bibliography' appeared annually in *English literary history*, Johns Hopkins Univ., Baltimore, 1937–49, then in *Philological Quarterly*, Iowa State Univ., Iowa, 1950–64, and since 1965 as suppl. to *English Language Notes*, Univ. of Colorado, Boulder, Colorado.

2663 BABBITT (IRVING). Rousseau and romanticism. Boston. 1919.

On romanticism in general. See also Jacques Barzun, *Romanticism and the modern age*, Boston, 1943, rev. edn. with title *Classic, romantic, and modern*, N.Y., 1962.

2664 BIRKHEAD (EDITH). The tale of terror; a study of the Gothic romance. 1921.

See also Friedrich Brie, *Exotismus der Sinne; eine Studie zur Psychologie der Romantik* (Heidelberger Akademie der Wissenschaften, Abhandlung 3), Heidelberg, 1920; Alice M. Killen, *Le roman terrifiant, ou, roman noir de Walpole à Anne Radcliffe et son influence sur la littérature française jusqu'en 1840* (Bibliothèque de littérature comparée, 4), Paris, 1923; Eino Railo, *The haunted castle: a study of the elements of English romanticism*, 1927; Paul Yvon, *Le gothique et la renaissance gothique en Angleterre* (1750–1880), Caen, Paris, 1931; Devendra Prasad Varma, *Gothic flame, being a history of the Gothic novel in England*, etc., 1957. Further material may be found in Montague Summers, *A Gothic bibliography*, 1941.

2665 PRAZ (MARIO). The romantic agony. Translated from the Italian by Angus Davidson. 1933. Repr. 1950.

2666 BALDENSPERGER (FERNAND). '"Romantique", ses analogues et ses équivalents: tableau synoptique de 1650 à 1810.' *Harvard studies and notes in philology and literature*, 19 (1937), 13–105.

Elaborate discussion of the meanings of the word. Arthur Oncken Lovejoy, 'On the discrimination of romanticisms', *P.M.L.A.* 39 (1924), 229–53, and 'The meaning of romanticism for the historian of ideas', *Journal of the History of Ideas*, 2 (1941), 257–78, René Wellek, 'The concept of "Romanticism" in literary history', *Comparative literature*, 1 (1949), 1–23 and 147–72, and 'Romanticism re-examined' in his *Concepts of Criticism*, New Haven, 1963, 199–221, discuss whether there was a 'romantic movement' forming a coherent body of ideas, and whether it extended to England.

2667 BUSH (JOHN NASH DOUGLAS). Mythology and the romantic tradition in English poetry. (Harvard studies in English, 18.) Camb. Mass. 1937. Repr. N.Y. 1957.

2668 DYKES (EVA BEATRICE). The negro in English romantic thought, or, A study of sympathy for the oppressed. Wash. 1942.

2669 BATE (WALTER JACKSON). From classic to romantic. Premises of taste in eighteenth century England. Camb. Mass. 1946. Repr. London. 1961.

2670 BOWRA (*Sir* MAURICE). The romantic imagination. 1950.

2671 ABRAMS (MEYER HOWARD). The mirror and the lamp; romantic theory and the critical tradition. N.Y. 1953. London. 1960.

2672 GÉRARD (ALBERT). L'idée romantique de la poésie en Angleterre; études sur la théorie de la poésie chez Coleridge, Wordsworth, Keats et Shelley. (Bibliothèque de la Faculté de philosophie et lettres de l'Université de Liège, 136.) Paris. 1955.

2673 PIPER (HERBERT WALTER). The active universe; pantheism and the concept of Imagination in the English romantic poets. 1962.

2674 HAYTER (ALETHEA). Opium and the romantic imagination. 1968.

Also Meyer Howard Abrams, *The milk of paradise; the effect of opium visions on the works of De Quincey, Crabbe, Francis Thompson and Coleridge* (Harvard Honours theses in English, 7), Camb., Mass., 1934.

2675 REIMAN (DONALD H.) *ed.* The Romantics reviewed. 3 pts. N.Y.
1972.

Reprints contemporary reviews: pt. A, Lake poets, pt. B, Byron and Regency society,
pt. C, Shelley, Keats, and London radical writers.

2676 WATSON (JOHN RICHMOND). Picturesque landscape and English
romantic poetry. 1970.

See (2837), (2900), Tooley (3464), and (3516).

4. FOREIGN LITERARY RELATIONS

See also Chapter IX, sections A.6 and D.7.

2677 MORAUD (MARCEL IAN). Le romantisme français en Angleterre de
1814 à 1848. Contribution à l'étude des rélations littéraires entre la France et
l'Angleterre dans la première moitié du XIXe siècle. (Bibliothèque de la
revue de littérature comparée, v. 90.) Paris. 1933.

Also Albert Elmer Hancock, *The French revolution and the English poets*, etc., N.Y., 1899;
Charles Cestre, *La révolution française et les poètes anglais (1789–1909)*, Dijon, Paris,
1906; Allene Gregory, *The French revolution and the English novel*, N.Y., 1915, on
novelists of the war period; Marian Gladys Devonshire, *The English novel in France,
1830–1870*, 1929, repr. 1967.

2678 FARLEY (FRANK EDGAR). Scandinavian influences in the English
romantic movement. (Studies and notes in philology and literature, 9.)
Boston. 1903.

2679 PRICE (LAWRENCE MARSDEN). English>German literary influences; bibliography and survey. (University of California Pubns. in modern
philology, 9.) Berkeley. 1919.

Also Jean-Marie Carré, *Goethe en Angleterre*, 2 v., Paris, 1920, (v. 2 is a bibliog.); Frank
Woodyer Stokoe, *German influence in the English romantic period, 1788–1818, with
special reference to Scott, Coleridge, Shelley, and Byron*, Camb., 1926; Walter Franz
Schirmer, *Der Einfluss der deutschen Literatur auf die englische im 19 Jahrhundert*, Halle,
1947; Bayard Quincy Morgan and Alexander Rudolf Hohlfeld, eds., *German literature
in British magazines, 1750–1860*, Madison, 1949. For bibliogs. see Robert Pick,
Schiller in England, 1787–1960. A bibliography, etc. (Pubs. of the English Goethe Soc.
n.s. 30), 1961, and Bayard Quincy Morgan, *A critical bibliography of German literature
in English translation, 1481–1927*, 2nd edn. rev. 1938. For English influence in Germany,
Lawrence Marsden Price, *The reception of English literature in Germany*, Berkeley,
1932, principally on Scott, Byron, and Dickens in this period.

2680 WALTER (FÉLIX). La littérature portugaise en Angleterre à l'époque
romantique. (Bibliothèque de la revue de littérature comparée, v. 36.) Paris.
1927.

2681 SIMMONS (ERNEST JOSEPH). English literature and culture in
Russia (1553–1840). (Harvard studies in comparative literature, 12.) Camb.
Mass. 1935.

2682 SPENCER (TERENCE). Fair Greece, sad relic; literary philhellenism from Shakespeare to Byron. 1954.

Bibliog. 299–301.

2683 GLENDINNING (NIGEL). 'Spanish books in England, 1800–1850.' *Trans. Cambridge Bibliog. Soc.* 3 (1960), 70–92.

2684 BRAND (CHARLES PETER). Italy and the English romantics; the Italianate fashion in early nineteenth century England. Camb. 1957.

Bibliog. 235–59. Also Roderick Marshall, *Italy in English literature, 1755–1815: origins of the romantic interest in Italy*, N.Y., 1934; Harry W. Rudman, *Italian nationalism and English letters; figures of the risorgimento and Victorian men of letters*, 1940; Herbert Gladstone Wright, *Boccaccio in England from Chaucer to Tennyson*, 1957. See also (1871), (2958).

5. POETRY

2685 RAYSOR (THOMAS MIDDLETON) ed. The English Romantic poets; a review of research. (Modern Language Assoc. of America, Revolving Fund, ser. 18.) N.Y. 1950. Rev. edn. N.Y. 1956.

Bibliogs. and reviews of research on particular writers: also Frederick Everett Faverty, ed., *The Victorian poets; a guide to research*, Camb., Mass., 1956, 2nd edn., Camb., Mass., 1968 (M.L.A.A. Victorian group), Carolyn Washburn Houtchens and Lawrence Huston Houtchens, eds., *The English Romantic poets and essayists; a review of research and criticism* (M.L.A.A. Revolving Fund, ser. 20), N.Y., 1957 and Logan (2662). See also Meyer Howard Abrams, ed., *English Romantic poets; modern essays in criticism*, N.Y., 1960.

2686 COURTHOPE (WILLIAM JOHN). History of English poetry. 6 v. 1895–1910.

Other older standard works are George Edward Bateman Saintsbury, *A history of English prosody*, etc., 3 v., 1906–10; Andrew Cecil Bradley, *Oxford lectures on poetry*, 1909, including 'The long poem in the age of Wordsworth', 177–208; Arthur Symons, *The romantic movement in English poetry*, 1909.

2687 BATESON (FREDERICK NOEL WILSE). English poetry and the English language; an experiment in literary history. Oxf. 1934.

2688 LEAVIS (FRANK RAYMOND). Revaluation: tradition and development in English poetry. 1936.

2689 FAIRCHILD (HOXIE NEALE). Religious trends in English poetry. 6 v. N.Y. 1939–68.

V. 3, *1780–1830; Romantic faith*, N.Y., 1949, and v. 4, *1830–1880; Christianity and Romanticism in the Victorian era*, N.Y., 1957, are relevant.

2690 BRADNER (LEICESTER). Musae anglicanae: a history of Anglo-Latin poetry, 1500–1925. (M.L.A.A. General ser. 10.) N.Y. 1940.

2691 SHUSTER (GEORGE NAUMAN). The English ode from Milton to Keats. (Columbia University studies in English and comparative literature, 150.) N.Y. 1940.

2692 KNIGHT (GEORGE WILSON). The starlit dome; studies in the poetry of vision. 1941. Repr. 1959.

2693 WARREN (ALBA H.) English poetic theory, 1825–1865. (Princeton studies in English, ser. 29.) Princeton. 1950.

2694 PERKINS (DAVID). The quest for permanence; the symbolism of Wordsworth, Shelley and Keats. Camb. Mass. 1959.

6. The Novel

2695 SADLEIR (MICHAEL THOMAS HARVEY). XIX century fiction; a bibliographical record, based on his own collection. 2 v. 1951.

The most accurate guide to the subject. Andrew Block, *The English novel, 1740–1850, A catalogue including prose romances, short stories and translations of foreign fiction*, 1939, has been much criticized for inaccuracy; see also Lucien Leclaire, *General analytical bibliography of the regional novelists of the British Isles, 1800–1950*, Paris, 1954. Other reference works are Inglis Freeman Bell and Donald Baird, *The English novel, 1578–1956; a checklist of twentieth century criticisms*, Denver [1958], and Arthur Lionel Stevenson, *Victorian fiction; a guide to research*, Camb. Mass., 1964 (pub. by Modern Languages Assoc. of America). See also *Nineteenth century fiction*, v. 4+, Los Angeles, 1949+ (v. 1–3 were pub. at Berkeley with title *The Trollopian*, 1945–8). For Irish novels see (4198).

2696 BAKER (ERNEST ALBERT). The history of the English novel. 10 v. 1924–39. Repr. N.Y. 1952.

Descriptive accounts of a great many novels.

2697 TOMPKINS (JOYCE MARJORIE SANXTER). The popular novel in England, 1770–1800. 1932.

See also Dorothy Blakey, *The Minerva press, 1790–1820*, 1939, which produced novels for the circulating libraries, Margaret Dalziel, *Popular fiction 100 years ago; an unexplored tract of literary history*, 1957, and Robert Donald Mayo, *The English novel in the magazines, 1740–1815, with a catalogue of 1375 magazine novels and novelettes*, Evanston, Ill., 1962, and (3302).

2698 ROSA (MATTHEW WHITING). The silver-fork school; novels of fashion preceding *Vanity Fair*. (Columbia University studies in English and comparative literature, 123.) N.Y. 1936.

Bibliog. 211–18. Also Robert Palfrey Utter and Gwendolyn Bridges Needham, *Pamela's daughters*, N.Y., 1936.

2699 SHEPPERSON (ARCHIBALD BOLLING). The novel in motley; a history of the burlesque novel in English. Camb. Mass. 1936.

2700 TILLOTSON (KATHLEEN). Novels of the eighteen-forties. 1954.

See also Louis Cazamian, *Le roman social en Angleterre, 1830–1850; Dickens—Disraeli —Mrs Gaskell—Kingsley*, Paris, 1904, repr. 2 v., Paris, 1935, a substantial work including other novelists, English trans. by Martin Fido with title *The social novel in England*, 1973, and Joseph Ellis Baker, *The novel and the Oxford movement* (Princeton studies in English, 8), Princeton, 1932.

2701 PRAZ (MARIO). The hero in eclipse in Victorian fiction; translated from the Italian by Angus Davidson. 1956.

2702 LUKÀCS (GYÖRGY). The historical novel. Trans. Hannah and Stanley Mitchell. 1962.

2703 HOLLINGSWORTH (KEITH). The Newgate novel, 1830–1847; Bulwer, Ainsworth, Dickens, and Thackeray. Detroit. 1963.

2704 COLBY (ROBERT ALAN). Fiction with a purpose; major and minor nineteenth century novels. Bloomington, Ind. [1967].

7. OTHER SUBJECTS

2705 BROADUS (EDMUND KEMPER). The laureateship: a study of the office of poet laureate in England, with some account of the poets. Oxf. 1921.

2706 WALKER (HUGH). English satire and satirists. 1925.

2707 BABCOCK (ROBERT WITBECK). The genesis of Shakespeare idolatry, 1766–1799; a study in English criticism of the late eighteenth century. Chapel Hill, N.C. 1931.

Also Franz Walther Ebisch and Levin Ludwig Schücking, *A Shakespeare bibliography*, Oxf., 1931, suppl., Oxf., 1937.

2708 KITCHIN (GEORGE). A survey of burlesque and parody in English. 1931.

2709 KÖKERITZ (HELGE). 'English pronunciation as described in short-hand systems of the 17th and 18th centuries.' *Studia Neophilologica*, 7 (1934–5), 73–146.

Also Astrid Sturzen-Becker, 'Some notes on English pronunciation about 1800', *ibid.* 14 (1941–2), 301–30.

2710 SAUNDERS (JOHN WHITESIDE). The profession of English letters. 1964.

Bibliog. 249–56.

2711 REED (JOSEPH WAYNE). English biography in the early nineteenth century, 1801–1838. (Yale studies in English, 160.) New Haven, Conn. 1966.

Bibliog. 167–70. Also Waldo Hilary Dunn, *English biography*, 1916, and Edgar Johnson, *One mighty torrent; the drama of biography*, N.Y. 1937, repr. N.Y. 1955, both more general in scope.

2712 SUSSMAN (HERBERT LEWIS). Victorians and the machine; the literary response to technology. Camb. Mass. 1968.

Bibliog. 237–43. On Carlyle, Dickens, Ruskin, and others.

8. Authors

Some authors who are treated in Pargellis and Medley are not included here. See also chapters on Scotland, Wales, and Ireland in this work for writers of predominantly local interest. For Kingsley see (530), for Carlyle see (529), for Newman (779–80), for Maria Edgeworth (4200), for Fanny Burney see (2102), and Pargellis and Medley (2) 2183, 2454.

2713 AINSWORTH. William Harrison Ainsworth and his friends. By Stewart Marsh Ellis. 1911.

2714 AUSTEN. Jane Austen; facts and problems. The Clark lectures, Trinity College, Cambridge. By Robert William Chapman. Oxf. 1948.

Chapman also edited Jane Austen's *Works*, 6 v. Oxf., 1923–54, *Jane Austen's letters to her sister Cassandra and others*, 2 v. Oxf., 1932, 2nd edn. Oxf., 1952, and *Jane Austen; a critical bibliography*, 2nd edn., Oxf., 1955. For criticism see Mary Madge Lascelles, *Jane Austen and her art*, Oxf., 1939. See also Barry Roth and Joel Weinsheimer, *An annotated bibliography of Jane Austen studies, 1952–1972*, Charlottesville, Va, 1973, and Marilyn Speers Butler, *Jane Austen and the war of ideas*, Oxf., 1975.

2715 BEDDOES. Thomas Lovell Beddoes, the making of a poet. By Henry Wolfgang Donner. Oxf. 1935.

Donner also ed. Beddoes' *Works*, including his letters, 1935.

2716 BLAKE. The life of William Blake. By Mona Wilson. 1927. New edn. 1948.

The main source for Blake's life is Alexander Gilchrist, *Life of W. Blake*, 'Pictor Ignotus', etc., 2 v., 1863, new edn. by Ruthven Todd, 1945. Geoffrey Keynes has ed. *The writings of William Blake*, 3 v., 1925, and *The letters of William Blake*, 1956. For the most recent criticism see Kathleen Raine, *Blake and tradition*, 2 v., Princeton, 1969, bibliog. 324–42. See also Gerald E. Bentley and Martin K. Nurmi, *A Blake bibliography*, Minneapolis, 1964, and Gerald E. Bentley, *Blake records*, Oxf., 1969, a collection of contemporary references to Blake. For his work as an artist see (2909).

2717 BLESSINGTON. Blessington-D'Orsay, a masquerade. By Michael Sadleir. Rev. edn. 1947.

Also Richard Robert Madden, *The literary life and correspondence of the Countess of Blessington*, 2nd edn. 3 v., 1855, and Alfred Morrison, *The Blessington papers* (Catalogue of the collection of autograph letters formed by Alfred Morrison, 2nd ser. v. 2), 1895.

2718 BRONTËS. The four Brontës; the lives and works of Charlotte, Branwell, Emily, and Anne Brontë. By Lawrence Hanson and Elizabeth Mary Hanson. 1949.

Also Fannie Elizabeth Ratchford, *The Brontës' web of childhood*, N.Y., 1941. On Charlotte see Elizabeth Cleghorn Gaskell, *The life of Charlotte Brontë*, 2 v., 1857, and Winifred Gérin, *Charlotte Brontë: the evolution of genius*, Oxf., 1967, repr. 1969. On Emily, Charles Simpson, *Emily Brontë*, 1929, and Jacques Blondel, *Emily Brontë; expérience spirituelle et création poétique*, Paris, 1956. See also Winifred Gérin, *Anne Brontë*, 1959, *Branwell Brontë*, 1961, and *Emily Brontë*, Oxf., 1971. Also *The Transactions of the Brontë Society*, Bradford, 1895+.

2719 BROWNING. The life of Robert Browning. With notices of his writings, his family, and his friends. By William Hall Griffin, completed and ed. by Harry Christopher Minchin. 1910. 3rd edn. rev. and enl. 1938.

The standard edn. of the *Works* was ed. Frederick George Kenyon, 10 v. 1910 (the 'Centenary edition'). *The Letters of Robert Browning collected by Thomas J. Wise,* ed. Thurman L. Hood, New Haven, 1933 and *The letters of Robert Browning and Elizabeth Barrett Barrett, 1845–1846,* ed. Elvan Kintner, Cambridge, Mass., 1970: for other letters scattered in a number of works consult *N.C.B.E.L.* and Leslie Nathan Broughton, Clark Sutherland Northup and Robert Pearsall, *Robert Browning; a bibliography, 1830–1950* (Cornell studies in English, 39), Ithaca, 1953. See also William Clyde De Vane, *A Browning handbook,* rev. edn. 1937. For criticism see Robert Langbaum, *The poetry of experience,* 1957.

2720 BULWER (*later* BULWER-LYTTON). Bulwer: a panorama, Edward and Rosina, 1803–1836. By Michael Sadleir. 1931.

Also *The life, letters, and literary remains of Edward Bulwer, Lord Lytton, by his son* (Edward Robert Bulwer, 1st Earl of Lytton), 2 v., 1883, and *The life of Edward Bulwer, first Lord Lytton, by his grandson* (Victor Alexander George Robert Bulwer-Lytton, 2nd Earl of Lytton), 2 v., 1913.

2721 BURNS. Robert Burns. By David Daiches. 1952. Rev. edn. 1966.

James Kinsley, *The poems and songs of Robert Burns,* 3 v., Oxf., 1968, is the standard critical edn. See also Thomas Crawford, *Burns; a study of the poems and songs,* 1960, and J. W. Egerer, *A bibliography of Robert Burns,* 1964. See also Thornton (2532).

2722 BYRON. Byron; a biography. By Leslie Alexis Marchand. 3 v. [1958.]

The standard edn. of the *Poetical Works* is by Ernest Hartley Coleridge, 7 v., 1905. *Letters and journals* were ed. Rowland E. Prothero, 6 v., 1898–1901. Other letters are in *Lord Byron's correspondence chiefly with Lady Melbourne, Mr. Hobhouse, the Hon. Douglas Kinnaird and P. B. Shelley,* ed. John Murray, 2 v., 1922, and Peter Quennell, *Byron, A self portrait . . . with hitherto unpublished letters,* 2 v., 1950; a new, definitive edn. of the letters and journals, also by Marchand, is in progress, 1973+. See also Robert Charles Etienne Georges Escarpit, *Lord Byron, un tempérament littéraire* (Les grandes études, 7), 2 v., Paris, 1956–7, and Edward John Mawby Buxton, *Byron and Shelley, the history of a friendship,* 1968.

2723 CAMPBELL. The life and letters of Thomas Campbell. By William Beattie. 1849.

Also Cyrus Redding, *Literary reminiscences and memoirs of Thomas Campbell,* 1860. The *Complete poetical works* were ed. J. Logie Robertson, Oxf., 1907.

2724 CLARE. John Clare, his life and poetry. By John William Tibble and Anne Tibble. 1956.

New edn. rev., with title, *John Clare, a life,* 1972. J. W. Tibble also ed. the *Poems,* 2 v., 1935, and, with Anne Tibble, *The letters,* 1951, and *The prose,* 1951. See also Geoffrey Grigson, *Poems of John Clare's madness,* 1949.

2725 COLERIDGE. The collected works of Samuel Taylor Coleridge. General ed. Kathleen Coburn, and sponsored by the Bollingen Foundation. Princeton. 1969+.

In progress. At present standard edn. of Coleridge's *Biographia literaria* is by J. Shawcross, 2 v., Oxf., 1907, and of the *Poetical works* is by Ernest Hartley Coleridge,

1912. The *Collected letters* are ed. by Earl Leslie Griggs, 6 v., Oxf., 1956–71, and the *Notebooks* by Kathleen Coburn, 1957, in progress. John Livingston Lowes, *The road to Xanadu; a study in the ways of the imagination*, 1927, 2nd rev. edn., 1951, and J. R. de. J. Jackson, *Method and imagination in Coleridge's criticism*, 1969 are notable studies. See also Sir Edmund Kerchever Chambers, *Samuel Taylor Coleridge; a biographical study*, Oxf., 1938 and John Bernard Beer, *Coleridge the visionary*, 1959, a general study. See also (526) and (716).

2726 CRABBE. Un poète réaliste anglais, George Crabbe, 1754–1832. By René Huchon. Paris. 1906. Trans. Frederick Clarke. 1907.

The standard edn. of the poems is by Adolphus William Ward, 3 v., Camb. 1905–7; also *New poems*, ed. Arthur Pollard, Liverpool, 1960. See also Lilian Haddakin, *The poetry of Crabbe*, 1955, and Robert Lyall Chamberlain, *George Crabbe*, N.Y., 1965.

2727 DE QUINCEY. Thomas De Quincey, a biography. By Horace Ainsworth Eaton. N.Y. 1936.

The *Collected writings* were ed. David Masson, 14 v., Edin., 1889–90; see also *The posthumous works*, etc., with intro. and notes by Alexander H. Japp, 2 v., 1891, and *New essays ... His contributions to the* Edinburgh Saturday Post, *and the* Edinburgh Evening Post, *1827–1828*, ed. Stuart M. Tave, Princeton, 1966. The most recent study is Françoise Moreux, *Thomas de Quincey; la vie, l'homme, l'œuvre* (Publications de la faculté des lettres et sciences humaines de Paris, série 'Recherches', v. 12), Paris, 1964, bibliog. 583–610.

2728 DICKENS. The life of Charles Dickens. By John Forster. 3 v. 1872–4. New edn. by A. J. Hoppé. 2 v. 1966.

Standard: see also Edgar Johnson, *Charles Dickens, his tragedy and triumph*, 2 v., N.Y., 1952, 2 v., London, 1953. The standard edn. of the novels is *The Oxford illustrated Dickens*, 1947+. *The letters of Charles Dickens*, ed. Madeline House and Graham Storey, Oxf., 1965+, in progress, will supersede *The letters . . . edited by his sister-in-law* [*Georgina Hogarth*] *and his eldest daughter* [*Mamie Dickens*], 3 v., 1880–2; see also Kenneth Joshua Fielding, *The speeches of Charles Dickens*, Oxf., 1960. Aspects of his work are dealt with in Humphry House, *The Dickens world*, 1941, the novels in relation to their social setting; George Harry Ford, *Dickens and his readers; aspects of novel-criticism since 1836*, Princeton, 1955, London, 1965; John Butt and Kathleen Tillotson, *Dickens at work*, 1957; Philip Collins, *Dickens and crime* (Cambridge studies in criminology, 17), and his *Dickens and education*, 1963; and Robert Garis, *The Dickens theatre; a reassessment of the novels*, Oxf., 1965. See also the *Dickensian*, v. 1+, 1905+.

2729 D'ISRAELI. Curiosities of literature, edited with a memoir and notes by his son, the Right Hon. B. Disraeli. 3 v. 1858.

Also James Ogden, *Isaac D'Israeli*, Oxf., 1969. Benjamin Disraeli's novels are discussed by Blake (234): all, except *Lothair* and *Endymion*, date from before 1851.

2730 ELLIOTT. Ebenezer Elliott (the corn-law rhymer), 1781–1849. A commemorative brochure. By A. A. Eaglestone, E. R. Seary and G. L. Phillips. Sheffield. [1949.]

With bibliog. of his writings. *Corn law rhymes* were first pub. 1831.

2731 GASKELL. Elizabeth Gaskell: her life and work. By Annette Brown Hopkins. 1952.

See the Knutsford edn. of her works, ed. Adolphus William Ward, 8 v., 1906; *Mary Barton*, dealing with industrial Manchester, was pub. anonymously, 1848. *The letters of Mrs Gaskell* have been ed. by J. A. V. Chapple and Arthur Pollard, Manchester, 1966. Arthur Pollard, *Mrs. Gaskell, novelist and biographer*, Manchester, 1965.

2732 HAZLITT. The life of William Hazlitt. By Percival Presland Howe. 1922. 3rd rev. edn. 1947.

Howe also ed. the *Complete works*, 21 v. and index, 1930–4. See also Herschel Clay Baker, *William Hazlitt*, 1962, bibliog. 477–80. See also (2763).

2733 HEMANS. Memorials of Mrs. Hemans, with illustrations of her literary character from her private correspondence. By Henry Fothergill Chorley. 2 v. 1836.

Also *The works of Mrs Hemans with a memoir of her life by her sister*, 7 v., 1839.

2734 HOGG. James Hogg: a critical study. By Louis Simpson. 1962.

Other studies are Edith C. Batho, *The Ettrick shepherd*, 1927, and *The life and letters of James Hogg*, by Alan Lang Strout, Lubbock, Texas, 1946. The most complete edn. of the works is by Thomas Thomson, 2 v., 1865.

2735 HOOD. Thomas Hood. By John Cowie Reid. 1963. Bibliog. 268–75.

The *Complete poetical works*, ed. Walter Copeland Jerrold, 1906, and *The letters of Thomas Hood. From the Dilke papers in the British Museum*, ed. Leslie Alexis Marchand, New Brunswick, 1945. See also John Louis Edwin Clubbe, *Victorian forerunner, the later career of Thomas Hood*, Durham, N.C., 1968.

2736 HOOK. Theodore Hook and his novels. By Myron Franklin Brightfield. Camb. Mass. 1928.

2737 HUNT. Leigh Hunt; a biography. By Edmund Charles Blunden. 1930.

Also Louis Landré, *Leigh Hunt (1784–1859); contribution à l'histoire du Romantisme anglais*, 2 v., Paris, 1935–6, and *The autobiography of Leigh Hunt*, ed. Jack Eric Morpurgo, 1950. The *Correspondence* was ed. Thornton Hunt, 2 v., 1862, and the *Poetical works* by Humphrey Sumner Milford, Oxf., 1923. Lawrence Huston Houtchens and Carolyn Washburn Houtchens, eds., *Leigh Hunt's literary criticism*, N.Y., 1956 and *Political and occasional essays*, 1962. See also (2762).

2738 KEATS. John Keats. By Walter Jackson Bate. Camb. Mass. 1963. Repr. with corr. 1967.

Also Robert William Victor Gittings, *John Keats, the living year*, etc., 1954, and *John Keats*, 1968. Hyder Edward Rollins, ed., *The letters of John Keats, 1814–1821*, 2 v., Camb., Mass., 1958, and, related to Keats, *The Keats circle; letters and papers 1816–1878*, 2 v., Camb., Mass., 1948, repr. 1965, and *More letters and poems of the Keats circle*, Camb., Mass., 1955. The standard edn. of the *Poetical works* is by Heathcote William Garrod, 2nd edn., Oxf., 1958. See also Ian Robert James Jack, *Keats and the mirror of art*, Oxf., 1967.

2739 LAMB. The life of Charles Lamb. By Edward Verrall Lucas. 2 v. 1905. 5th edn. 1 v. rev. 1921.

The *Works of Charles and Mary Lamb* were also ed. by Lucas, 7 v., 1903–5. V. 6 and 7 are letters. New edn. in 3 v., 1935. See also (2766).

2740 LANDOR. Landor: a replevin. By Malcolm Elwin. N.Y. 1941. London. 1958. Bibliog. 471–7.

Also standard is Robert Henry Super, *Walter Savage Landor: a biography*, 1957. The standard edn. of the *Complete works* is by T. Earle Welby and Stephen Wheeler, 16 v., 1927–36.

2741   LEWIS ('MONK'). Life and correspondence of M. G. Lewis, author of 'The Monk', 'Castle Spectre', etc., with many pieces in prose and verse never before published. [By H. Baron-Wilson.] 2 v. 1839.

See also (2664). Louis Francis Peck, *A life of Matthew G. Lewis*, Camb., Mass., 1961.

2742   MITFORD. MITFORD (MARY RUSSELL). Recollections of a literary life, or, Books, places, and people. 3 v. 1852.

See also A. G. L. L'Estrange, ed., *The life of Mary Russell Mitford in a selection of her letters*, 3 v., 1870. Vera Watson, *Mary Russell Mitford* [1949], the most substantial and recent biog., lists earlier lives and letters, xiii–xv, and her writings, 312–13.

2743   MONTGOMERY. Memoirs of James Montgomery. By John Holland and James Everett. 1855.

Sheffield poet and journalist: his *Poetical works* were pub. in 4 v., 1841.

2744   MOORE. The harp that once. By Howard Mumford Jones. N.Y. 1937.

The *Poetical works . . . collected by himself* were pub. 10 v. 1840–1. See also *Memoirs, journal, and correspondence*, etc., ed. Lord John Russell, 8 v., 1853–6, and *The letters of Thomas Moore*, ed. Wilfred S. Dowden, 2 v., Oxf., 1964.

2745   PEACOCK. Un épicurien anglais: Thomas Love Peacock. By Jean Jacques Mayoux. Paris. 1933.

The standard edn. of the works is the Halliford edn., 10 v., 1924–34, ed. Herbert Francis Brett Brett-Smith and C. E. Jones, of which v. 1 is a biography. See also Howard Mills, *Peacock; his circle and his age*, Camb., 1969.

2746   RADCLIFFE. Ann Radcliffe: a biography. By Aline Grant. Denver. [1951.]

See also (2664).

2747   RUSKIN. Ruskin, the great Victorian. By Derrick Leon. 1949.

Bibliog. 583–6. Sir Edward Tyas Cook and Alexander Wedderburn ed. a massive edn. of the *Works*, 39 v., 1900–11. Sources for Ruskin's life are his unfinished autobiography, *Praeterita*, etc., 3 v., Orpington, 1885–9, repr. 1 v., 1949, and William Gershom Collingwood, *The life and work of John Ruskin*, 2 v., 1893. Other modern lives are by Reginald Howard Wilenski (1933) and Joan Evans (1954). Joan Evans and John Howard Whitehouse ed. *The diaries of John Ruskin*, 3 v., Oxf., 1956–9. Van Akin Burd has ed. *The Ruskin family papers. The correspondence of John James Ruskin, his wife and their son John, 1801–1843*, v. 1, 1801–37, v. 2, 1837–43, Cornell, 1973. The greater part of Ruskin's life falls outside the period of this bibliog. For his drawings see (2894); for *Modern Painters* (2851).

2748   SCOTT. Sir Walter Scott; the great unknown. By Edgar Johnson. 2 v. 1970.

The earlier standard lives are John Gibson Lockhart, *Memoirs of the life of Sir Walter Scott, Bart.*, 7 v., Edin., 1837–8, 10 v. (rev. slightly), 1839, and repr. in 5 v., 1900, and

Sir Herbert John Clifford Grierson, *Sir Walter Scott Bart.; a new life*, etc., 1938. The standard edn. of the novels is the Dryburgh *Waverley Novels*, 25 v., 1892–4, and of the *Poetical Works* that ed. Andrew Lang, 2 v., 1895. The *Journal of Sir Walter Scott* was ed. by John Guthrie Tait and William Mathie Parker, 3 v., Edin., 1936–46, repr. in 1 v., 1950; a more recent edn. is by W. E. K. Anderson, Oxf., 1972. See also Wilfred Partington, *The private letter books of Sir Walter Scott*, 1930, and *Sir Walter's post bag; more sidelights from his unpublished letter-books*, 1932, and H. J. C. Grierson, *The letters of Sir Walter Scott*, 12 v., 1932–7. See also James C. Corson, *A bibliography of Sir Walter Scott . . . 1797–1940*, 1943. See also (2791) and (3958).

2749 SHELLEY. Shelley. By Newman Ivey White. 2 v. N.Y. 1940. London. 1947.

The standard edn. of the *Complete works* is by Roger Ingpen and Walter E. Peck, 10 v., 1926–9 (the Julian edition). The *Notebooks* were ed. Harry Buxton Forman, 3 v., Boston, 1911, and the *Letters* by Frederick L. Jones, 2 v., Oxf., 1964 (v. 1, Shelley in England, v. 2, Shelley in Italy). See also Arthur Montague D'Urban Hughes, *The nascent mind of Shelley*, Oxf., 1947, and Kenneth Neill Cameron, *The young Shelley; genesis of a radical*, 1951, and the same writer's *Shelley and his circle . . . a complete edition of the manuscripts . . . of the Carl H. Pforzheimer library*, New York, 8 v., Camb., Mass., 1961+. For recent criticism see Neville Rogers, *Shelley at work; a critical inquiry*, Oxf., 1956, 2nd edn., Oxf., 1967.

2750 SOUTHEY. Life and correspondence of Robert Southey. By Cuthbert C. Southey. 6 v. 1849–50.

See *The poetical works . . . collected by himself*, 10 v., 1838. Other lives are *The early life of Robert Southey, 1774–1803*, by William Haller, N.Y., 1917, and Jack Simmons, *Southey*, 1945. For correspondence see John Wood Warter, *Selections from the letters of Robert Southey*, 4 v., 1856, Edward Dowden, *Correspondence with Caroline Bowles, to which are added, Correspondence with Shelley and Southey's Dreams*, 1881. Kenneth Curry, *New letters of Robert Southey*, 2 v., N.Y., 1964. Geoffrey Carnall, *Robert Southey and his age; the development of a conservative mind*, Oxf., 1960, concentrates on political thought.

2751 STERLING. The life of John Sterling. By Thomas Carlyle. 1851.

2752 TENNYSON. Alfred Tennyson. By Sir Charles Bruce Locker Tennyson. 1949.

Also Hallam Tennyson, 2nd Baron Tennyson, *Alfred Lord Tennyson, a memoir*, 2 v., 1897, who also ed. the standard Eversley edn. of the *Poems*, 9 v., 1907–8. For criticism see Paull Franklin Baum, *Tennyson sixty years after*, Chapel Hill, N.C., 1948, and John Killham, *Tennyson and the Princess; reflections of an age*, 1958, discussing the *Princess* (1847) in relation to contemporary attitudes towards women. Ralph Wilson Rader, *Tennyson's Maud: the biographical genesis* (Perspectives in criticism, 15), Berkeley and Los Angeles, 1963, is of biographical importance. For the poet's family background see Sir Charles Tennyson and Hope Dyson, *The Tennysons. Background to genius*, 1974.

2753 THACKERAY. Thackeray: the uses of adversity (1811–1846). By Gordon Norton Ray. 1955.

Continued by *Thackeray: the age of wisdom (1847–1863)*, 1958. Ray has also ed. *The letters and private papers of William Makepeace Thackeray*, 4 v., 1945–6, and *Thackeray's contributions to the* Morning Chronicle, *now first reprinted*, Urbana, Ill., 1955. For criticism see Geoffrey Tillotson, *Thackeray the novelist*, Camb., 1954.

2754   WORDSWORTH. William Wordsworth, a biography. By Mary Moorman. 2 v. Oxf. 1957, 1965.

The poetical works were ed. Ernest de Selincourt and Helen Darbishire, 5 v., Oxf., 1940–9. Ernest de Selincourt also ed. *The Journals of Dorothy Wordsworth*, 2 v., 1941, and the *Letters of William and Dorothy Wordsworth*, 4 v., Oxf., 1935–9. A new edn. is in progress, *The early years, 1787–1805*, rev. Chester L. Shaver, Oxf., 1967, *The middle years*, pt. I, 1806–11, rev. Mary Moorman, Oxf., 1969, pt. II, 1812–20, rev. Mary Moorman and Alan G. Hill, Oxf., 1970. A recent work on Wordsworth's philosophical ideas is Melvin Rader, *Wordsworth; a philosophical approach*, Oxf., 1967.

B. DRAMA

See also *Theatre* (chapter IX, section B. 4 (h)).

1. BIBLIOGRAPHIES, CATALOGUES, REFERENCE WORKS

2755   OXBERRY (WILLIAM). Oxberry's dramatic biography and histrionic anecdotes. Ed. Catherine E. Oxberry. 5 v. 1825–6.

Also *Oxberry's dramatic biography and histrionic anecdotes; or, The green room spy*, new ser., 2 v., 1927.

2756   BRITISH DRAMA LEAGUE. The player's library; the catalogue of the library of the British Drama League. 2nd edn. 1950. 1st suppl. 1951. 2nd suppl. 1954.

The fullest bibliog. of English plays and books. See also Robert William Lowe, *A bibliographical account of English theatrical literature from the earliest times to the present day*, N.Y., 1888. See also Blanch Merritt Baker, *Theatre and allied arts; a guide to books dealing with . . . the drama and theatre*, etc., N.Y., 1952, and James Fullarton Arnott and John William Robinson, *English theatrical literature, 1559–1900; a bibliography*, 1970.

2757   NICOLL (JOHN RAMSAY ALLARDYCE). A history of English drama, 1660–1900. 2nd edn. 6 v. Camb. 1952–9. V. 3. Late eighteenth century drama, 1750–1800. 2nd edn. Camb. 1952. V. 4. Early nineteenth century drama, 1800–1850. 2nd edn. Camb. 1955.

An indispensable guide to the subject. A large part of each vol. consists of a handlist of plays with authors and places and dates of performance, wherever known. Bibliog. of collections of printed plays, v. 4, 248. Lists of London and provincial theatres, with short hist. details, v. 3, 229–30, v. 4, 222–44.

2758   STRATMAN (CARL JOSEPH). A bibliography of British dramatic periodicals. N.Y. 1962.

Two long-lasting periodicals, among many begun in this period, were *The Theatrical Observer*, 1821–76, and *The Theatrical Journal*, 1837–73.

2759   BRITISH MUSEUM. Catalogue of additions to the manuscripts. Plays submitted to the Lord Chamberlain. 1964.

Plays submitted before 1824 are now in the Huntington Library, California; see Dougald William Macmillan, *Catalogue of the Larpent plays in the Huntington Library*, Huntington Lib. lists, 4. San Marino, Calif., 1939.

2760 KINDERMANN (HEINZ). Theatergeschichte Europas. V. 6. Romantik. Salzburg. 1964. V. 7. Realismus. Salzburg. 1965.

Each contains a chap. on England.

2761 STRATMAN (CARL JOSEPH). Bibliography of English printed tragedy, 1565–1900. Carbondale, Ill. 1966.

2. General History and Criticism

2762 HUNT (JAMES HENRY LEIGH). Critical essays on the performers of the London theatres, including general observations on the practise [*sic*] and genius of the stage. 1807.

Continued by *Leigh Hunt's dramatic criticism, 1808–1831*, ed. Lawrence Huston Houtchens and Carolyn Washburn Houtchens, N.Y., 1949.

2763 HAZLITT (WILLIAM). A view of the English stage. 1818. Another edn. by W. Spencer Jackson. 1906.

Reprints his dramatic criticisms from *The Times*, the *Examiner*, the *Champion*, and the *Morning Chronicle*. Also issued, 2nd edn., 1851, with title *Criticisms and dramatic essays*.

2764 TOMLINS (FREDERICK GUEST). A brief view of the English drama from the earliest times to the present day, with suggestions for elevating the present condition of the art and of its professors. 1840.

2765 DIBDIN (JAMES C.). The annals of the Edinburgh stage, with an account of the rise and progress of dramatic writing in Scotland. Edin. 1888.

2766 LAMB (CHARLES). The dramatic essays of Charles Lamb. Ed. Brander Matthews. 1891.

2767 FILON (AUGUSTIN). The English stage; an account of Victorian drama. Trans. Frederic Whyte. 1897.

2768 CHILD (HAROLD HANNYNGTON). 'Nineteenth century drama.' *Camb. Hist. Eng. Lit.* 13, Camb. 1916, 255–74.

2769 ARCHER (WILLIAM). The old drama and the new; an essay in re-valuation. 1923.

Strongly attacks the standards of early 19th century drama.

2770 WATSON (ERNEST BRADLEE). Sheridan to Robertson; a study of the nineteenth century London stage. Camb. Mass. 1926.

2771 DUBOIS (ARTHUR EDWIN). The beginnings of tragic comedy in the drama of the nineteenth century. Baltimore. 1934.

2772 NICOLL (JOHN RAMSAY ALLARDYCE). The English theatre; a short history. 1936. Rev. edn. 1948.

By the same author, *The development of the theatre*, etc., 1927, rev. edn. 1948. Both standard.

2773 REYNOLDS (ERNEST RANDOLPH). Early Victorian drama (1830–1870). Camb. 1936.

A useful general survey, as is George Rignal Rowell, *The Victorian theatre; a survey*, 1956, bibliog. 159–89.

2774 KLEMM (WERNER). Die englische Farce im 19 Jahrhundert. Bern. 1946.

2775 EVANS (BERTRAND). Gothic drama from Walpole to Shelley. (Univ. of California pubns. in English, 18.) Berkeley and Los Angeles. 1947.

2776 CLINTON-BADDELEY (VICTOR CLINTON). The burlesque tradition in the English theatre after 1660. 1952.

2777 SOUTHERN (RICHARD). Changeable scenery. Its origin and development in the British theatre. 1952.

See also Lily Bess Campbell, *A history of costuming between 1660 and 1823* (Univ. of Wisconsin studies in lang. and lit. 2), Madison, 1918.

2778 MERCHANT (WILLIAM MOELWYN). Shakespeare and the artist. 1959.

On the presentation of Shakespeare at different epochs. See also George Clinton Densmore Odell, *Shakespeare from Betterton to Irving*, 2 v., N.Y., 1920. Repr. 1966.

2779 KNIGHT (GEORGE WILSON). The golden labyrinth; a study of British drama. 1962.

2780 BOOTH (MICHAEL RICHARD). English melodrama. 1965.

Also Frank Rahill, *The world of melodrama*, 1967, bibliog. 315–25.

3. DRAMATISTS

For Cumberland, Inchbald, O'Keeffe, see Pargellis and Medley, 2421, 2427, 1930. For Sheridan see Pargellis and Medley, 2433 also (162). See also (1939–47).

2781 BAILLIE. The life and works of Joanna Baillie. By Margaret S. Carhart. (Yale studies in English literature, 64.) New Haven. 1923.

2782 BYRON. The dramas of Lord Byron: a critical study. By Samuel Claggett Chew. Baltimore. 1915.

2783 COLMAN. George Colman the younger, 1762–1836. By Jeremy Felix Bagster-Collins. N.Y. 1946.

Also Richard Brinsley Peake, *Memoirs of the Colman family, including their correspondence with the most distinguished personages of their time*, 2 v., 1841.

2784 DIBDIN. Professional and literary memoirs of Charles Dibdin the Younger. Ed. from the original manuscripts by George Speaight. (Society for theatre research annual volume, 1955–6.) 1956.

Also Thomas John Dibdin (brother of Charles Dibdin the younger), *The reminiscences of Thomas Dibdin, of the Theatre Royal, Covent-garden, Haymarket*, 1827.

2785 FITZBALL. Thirty-five years of a dramatic author's life. By Edward Fitzball. 2 v. 1859.

2786 HOLCROFT. The life of Thomas Holcroft written by himself, continued from his diary, notes and other papers by William Hazlitt, and now newly edited with introduction and notes by Elbridge Colby. 1925.

First pub. 3 v. 1816. See also Holcroft's *Narrative of facts, relating to a prosecution for high treason*, 1795. E. Colby, comp., *A bibliography of Holcroft*, [N.Y.], 1922.

2787 KNOWLES. Sheridan Knowles and the theatre of his time. By Leslie Howard Meeks. Bloomington. Ind. 1933.

2788 MATURIN. Charles Robert Maturin, his life and works. By Niilo Idman. 1923.

2789 PLANCHÉ. The recollections and reflections of J. R. Planché, a professional autobiography. 2 v. 1872.

2790 REYNOLDS. The life and times of Frederick Reynolds, written by himself. 2 v. 1826.

2791 SCOTT. Sir Walter Scott's novels on the stage. By Henry Adelbert White. (Yale studies in English 76.) New Haven. 1927.

2792 TAYLOR. Tom Taylor and the Victorian drama. By Winton Tolles. (Columbia University studies in English and comparative literature, 148.) N.Y. 1940.

C. PHILOSOPHY

For writers on political thought see (517–42).

1. BIBLIOGRAPHY AND PERIODICALS

2793 BRIE (G. A. DE) *ed.* Bibliographica philosophica, 1934–1945. 2 v. Utrecht and Brussels. 1950–4.

V. 1, history of philosophy, v. 2, philosophy. Current writing is listed in *Bibliographie de la philosophie*, Paris, 1937–9, 1954+, pub. by Institut international de collaboration philosophique, and *Répertoire bibliographique de la philosophie*, Louvain, 1949+, quarterly. For 19th century works see Benjamin Rand, *Bibliography of philosophy, psychology, and cognate subjects*, 2 v., N.Y., 1905, repr. 1949, and Gilbert Varet, *Manuel de bibliographie philosophique*, 2 v., Paris, 1956. The standard writers are listed, for the period 1660–1800, in *N.C.B.E.L.* 2, cols. 1833–94 and for 1800–1900 in *N.C.B.E.L.* 3, cols. 1509–99.

2794 BAUMGARDT (DAVID). Philosophical periodicals; an annotated world list. Wash. 1952.

The major British journal is *Mind*, v. 1+, 1876+. See also the *Journal of Philosophy*, N.Y., v. 1+, 1904+, the *Philosophical Review*, v. 1+, Boston, N.Y., 1892+, the *Journal of Philosophy*, N.Y. v. 1+, 1904+, *Philosophy, the journal of the British institute of philosophy*, v. 1+, 1926+ (from 1926 to 1930 *Journal of Philosophical studies*) and the *Journal of the history of ideas*, v. 1+, Lancaster, Pa., 1940+. All are now indexed in the *International index to periodicals* (17).

2. General Histories

2795 UEBERWEG (FRIEDRICH) *ed.* Grundriss der Geschichte der Philosophie von Thales bis auf die Gegenwart. 12th edn. 5 v. Berlin. 1923–8.

V. 5, *Die Philosophie des Auslandes vom Beginn des 19 Jahrhunderts bis auf die Gegenwart*, by T. K. Oesterreich, 12th edn., Berlin, 1928. Other general histories are Harald Höffding, *A history of modern philosophy*, etc., trans. from the German by B. E. Meyer, 2 v., 1900; William Ritchie Sorley, *A history of English philosophy*, Camb., 1920, repr. 1937; Emile Bréhier, *Histoire de la philosophie*, 2 v., Paris, 1926–34, supp. vols. 1948, 1949; Rudolf Metz, *A hundred years of British philosophy*, ed. John Henry Muirhead, 1938; Frederick Charles John Paul Copleston, *A history of philosophy*, 1947–66. V. 8, *Bentham to Russell*, refers to the period of this bibliography.

2796 EDWARDS (PAUL) *ed.* The encyclopaedia of philosophy. 8 v. 1967.

3. Special Subjects

2797 STEPHEN (*Sir* LESLIE). History of English thought in the eighteenth century. 2 v. 1876. 3rd edn. 2 v. 1902, repr. 1927, 1962.

2798 BURY (JOHN BAGNELL). The idea of progress; an inquiry into its origin and growth. 1920.

2799 GILBERT (KATHARINE EVERETT) *and* KUHN (HELMUT). A history of esthetics. N.Y. 1939. Bloomington. Ind. 1954.

Also Walter John Hipple, *The beautiful, the sublime and the picturesque in eighteenth-century British aesthetic theory*, Carbondale, Ill., 1957, bibliog. 377–84.

2800 WILLEY (BASIL). Nineteenth-century studies; Coleridge to Matthew Arnold. 1949.

On religious and moral ideas. Other more general works on the history of ideas are Christopher John Holloway, *The Victorian sage*, etc., 1953 (on Carlyle, George Eliot, Disraeli, Newman); Walter Edwards Houghton, *The Victorian frame of mind*, New Haven, 1957; Shirley Robin Letwin, *The pursuit of certainty: David Hume, Jeremy Bentham, John Stuart Mill, Beatrice Webb*, 1965; John Burrow, *Evolution and society; a study in Victorian social theory*, 1966.

2801 PUCELLE (JEAN). L'idéalisme en Angleterre de Coleridge à Bradley. Neuchatel. 1955.

On Carlyle, Sterling, and J. Grote. Also John Henry Muirhead, *The Platonic tradition in Anglo-Saxon philosophy. Studies in the history of idealism in England and America*, 1931.

2802 GRAVE (SELWYN ALFRED). The Scottish philosophy of common sense. Oxf. 1960.

Also Gladys Bryson, *Man and society: the Scottish inquiry of the eighteenth century*, Princeton, 1945, and Thomas Edmund Jessop, *A bibliography of David Hume and of Scottish philosophy from Francis Hutcheson to Lord Balfour*, 1938.

2803 KNEALE (WILLIAM) *and* KNEALE (MARTHA). The development of logic. Oxf. 1962.

Bibliog. 743–51.

2804 MACINTYRE (ALASDAIR CHALMERS). A short history of ethics. N.Y. 1966. L. 1967.

Also Henry Sidgwick, *Outlines of the history of ethics for English readers*. 1886. 6th edn., 1931.

4. PHILOSOPHERS

For Reid see Pargellis & Medley (2), 2539; for de Morgan (3097).

2805 BENTHAM. Deontology; or, The science of morality in which the harmony and coincidence of duty and self interest, virtue and felicity, prudence and benevolence, are explained and exemplified. From the MSS. of Jeremy Bentham, arranged and edited by John Bowring. 2 v. 1834.

Other philosophical writings, printed in John Bowring's edn. of the *Works* (652), are *A fragment on ontology*, written 1813, 1814, 1821, printed v. VIII, 192–211, *A table of the springs of action*, etc., written 1815, printed v. I, 195–219, and *Essay on logic*, written 1816 (?), printed v. VIII, 213–93. See also *Chrestomathia* (3267) and the *Introduction to the principles of morals and legislation* (523). For discussion see David Baumgardt, *Bentham and the ethics of today with Bentham manuscripts hitherto unpublished*, Princeton, 1952, also Letwin (2800). For Bentham's life see (2113).

2806 BOOLE (GEORGE). The mathematical analysis of logic, being an essay towards a calculus of deductive reasoning. Camb. 1847. Facsimile reprint. Oxf. 1948.

2807 BROWN (THOMAS). Observations on the Zoonomia of Erasmus Darwin, M.D. Edin. 1798.

Also *Observations on the nature and tendency of the doctrine of Mr. Hume, concerning the relation of cause and effect* [1805], 3rd edn. rev. and enl. with title *Inquiry into the relation of cause and effect*, Edin., 1818; *Lectures on the philosophy of the human mind*, 4 v. Edin., 1820, 8th edn., *with a memoir . . . by David Welsh*, Edin., 1834.

2808 CARLYLE. Carlyle and German thought, 1819–34. By Charles Frederick Harrold. New Haven. 1934. (Yale studies in English, 82.)

2809 COLERIDGE. The philosophical lectures of S. T. Coleridge, hitherto unpublished. Edited by Kathleen Coburn. 1949.

See also Alice Dorothea Snyder, *Coleridge on logic and learning, with selections from the unpublished manuscripts*, New Haven, 1929, and, edited by the same writer, *S. T. Coleridge's Treatise on method, as published in the Encyclopaedia Metropolitana*, etc., 1934. For commentary see John Henry Muirhead, *Coleridge as philosopher*, 1930 and Elisabeth Winkelmann, *Coleridge und die Kantische Philosophie*, etc., Palaestra, 184, Leipzig, 1933. For general Coleridge bibliog. see (2725), for constitutional and religious thought see (526), (716).

2810 GODWIN. Godwin's moral philosophy; an interpretation of William Godwin. By David Hector Monro. 1953.

2811 HAMILTON (*Sir* WILLIAM). Lectures on metaphysics and logic. Eds.
H. L. Mansel and John Veitch. 4 v. Edin. 1859–60. 2nd edn. rev. 4 v. 1861–6.

Also *Discussions on philosophy and literature, education, and university reform, chiefly from the Edinburgh Review*, etc., 1852, 3rd edn., 1866. For J. S. Mill's criticism see (2815).

2812 HERSCHEL (*Sir* JOHN FREDERICK WILLIAM). A preliminary discourse on the study of natural philosophy. 1830.

On the philosophy of science.

2813 KANT. Immanuel Kant in England, 1793–1838. By René Wellek. Princeton. 1931.

2814 MILL (JAMES). Analysis of the phenomena of the human mind. 2 v. 1829. New edn. with notes illustrative and critical by A. Bain, A. Findlater and G. Grote. Ed. with add. notes by John Stuart Mill. 2 v. 1869.

On associationist psychology; also *Fragment on Mackintosh*, 1835. See Alexander Bain, *James Mill, a biography*, 1882; for political economy (1784), for political life, Hamburger (534).

2815 MILL (JOHN STUART). Collected works. Ed. Francis Ethelbert Louis Priestley and others. Toronto. 1963+. In progress.

Many of his more important occasional writings were collected in *Dissertations and discussions*, 4 v., 1859–75; see also *An examination of Sir William Hamilton's philosophy*, etc., 1865, 6th edn., 1889. More recent reprints include *The spirit of the age* ed. and intro. Friedrich August von Hayek, Chicago, 1942 (articles originally appearing in the *Examiner*, 1831), and *Mill on Bentham and Coleridge*, ed. Frank Raymond Leavis, 1950. For political economy and general bibliog. of his writings see N. MacMinn, J. R. Hainds, and J. M. McCrimmon, *Bibliography of the published writings of J. S. Mill*, Evanston, Ill., 1945. Mill's best-known political writing was pub. after 1851.

2816 MILL (JOHN STUART). A system of logic, ratiocinative and inductive, being a connected view of the principles of evidence and the methods of scientific investigation. 2 v. 1843. 9th edn. 2 v. 1875.

For discussion see Oskar Alfred Kubitz, *The development of John Stuart Mill's system of logic*, Urbana, Ill., 1932 (Illinois studies in social sciences, 18), and Reginald Jackson, *An examination of the deductive logic of John Stuart Mill*, 1941.

2817 MILL (JOHN STUART). Autobiography. Ed. Helen Taylor. 1873. New edn. by Jack Stillinger, 1971.

See also *Autobiography, published from the original manuscript in the Columbia University Library*, with a preface by John Jacob Coss, 1924, repr. 1960, and *The early draft of John Stuart Mill's autobiography*, ed. Jack Stillinger, Urbana, Ill., 1961. The standard modern Life is by Michael St. John Packe, 1954, bibliog. 532–42. See also Friedrich August von Hayek, *John Stuart Mill and Harriet Taylor: their correspondence and subsequent marriage*, 1951; Ruth Borchard, *John Stuart Mill: the man*, 1957; Anna Jean Mill, ed., *John Mill's boyhood visit to France* . . ., 1820–1 [1960]. Francis Edward Mineka has ed. the *Earlier letters of J. S. Mill, 1812–1848*, 2 v., Toronto, 1963 (v. 12, 13 of the *Collected works*), and with Dwight N. Lindley, the *Later letters* . . . *1849–73*, 4 v., 1972, being v. 14–17 of the *Collected works*. See also Bruce Mazlish, *James and John Stuart Mill*, 1975.

2818 ANSCHUTZ (R. P.). The philosophy of J. S. Mill. Oxf. 1953.

Discusses all aspects of his thought. For contemporary criticism see John Grote, *An examination of the utilitarian philosophy* [of J. S. Mill], ed. J. B. Major, 1870, and Alexander Bain, *John Stuart Mill, a criticism; with personal recollections*, 1882. See also Emery Edward Neff, *Carlyle and Mill: an introduction to Victorian thought*, N.Y., 1924; Karl Britton, *J. S. Mill*, 1953; Iris Wessel Mueller, *John Stuart Mill and French thought*, Urbana, Ill., 1956, particularly on his relations with Comte and Tocqueville; Alan Ryan, *The philosophy of John Stuart Mill*, 1970; Henry J. McCloskey, *J. S. Mill: a critical study*, 1971.

2819 PAINE (THOMAS). The age of reason. 1793.

2820 STEWART (DUGALD). Elements of the philosophy of the human mind. 1792. 3rd edn. cor. 1808.

His most influential work. Stewart's *Collected works* were ed. by Sir William Hamilton, 11 v., 1854–60.

2821 WHATELY (RICHARD). Elements of logic, comprising the substance of the article in the Encyclopaedia Metropolitana; with additions. 1826. 9th edn. rev. 1848.

For Whately's life see (701).

2822 WHEWELL (WILLIAM). The elements of morality, including polity. 2 v. 1845. 4th edn. with supp. Camb. 1864.

See also (3085).

D. FINE AND APPLIED ART

1. BIBLIOGRAPHIES, ENCYCLOPAEDIAS, BIOGRAPHICAL DICTIONARIES, JOURNALS

2823 GRAVES (ALGERNON). A dictionary of artists who have exhibited works in the principal London exhibitions from 1760 to 1893. 1895. Repr. 1970.

Lists names of artists, where they exhibited and dates, providing a key to his other works, *The Royal Academy of Arts, a complete dictionary of contributors and their work . . . 1769 to 1904*, 8 v., 1905–6, and *The British Institution 1806–1867, a complete dictionary of contributors and their work*, etc., 1908, reprinted 1970, which list individual works. His *A century of loan exhibitions, 1813–1912*, 5 v., 1913–15, lists paintings (old masters and contemporary works) and their owners at the time of exhibition. Samuel Redgrave, *A dictionary of artists of the English school; painters, sculptors, architects, engravers, and ornamentalists*, 1874, new edn. rev., 1878, repr. 1970, is also a useful work of reference; see also Allan Cunningham, *The lives of the most eminent British painters, sculptors, and architects*, 6 v., 1829–33, rev. edn. 3 v., 1879–80.

2824 REES (THOMAS MARDY). Welsh painters, engravers and sculptors, 1527–1911. 1912.

2825 STRICKLAND (WALTER GEORGE). A dictionary of Irish artists. 2 v. Dublin. 1913.

2826 THE BURLINGTON MAGAZINE FOR CONNOISSEURS. 1903+.

The most scholarly of similar publications. *The Connoisseur: an illustrated magazine for collectors*, 1901+, deals with furniture, paintings, and objets d'art.

2827 THIEME (ULRICH) *and* BECKER (FELIX). Allgemeines Lexikon der bildenden Künstler von der Antike bis zur Gegenwart. V. 1–37. Leipzig. 1907–50.

Comprehensive and standard. Michael Bryan, *Dictionary of painters and engravers*, 2 v., 1816, new edn. rev. and enl. by G. C. Williamson, 5 v., 1903–4 is also standard and useful for this period. Emmanuel Bénézit, *Dictionnaire critique et documentaire des peintres, sculpteurs, dessinateurs et graveurs*, new edn., 8 v., Paris, 1948–55, is less full, though more up to date than Thieme–Becker.

2828 THE WALPOLE SOCIETY. Oxf. 1912+.

Concentrates on British art history.

2829 THE ART INDEX . . . 1929+. N.Y. 1933+.

Indexes about 130 art periodicals by author and subject and includes all fine arts.

2830 BIBLIOGRAPHY OF THE HISTORY OF ART. 1934+. Camb. 1936+.

Originally pub. with title *Annual bibliography of the history of British art*, and prepared by the Courtauld Institute, University of London. V. 6, 1956, the most recent, covers publications 1946–8: comprehensive.

2831 JOURNAL OF THE WARBURG AND COURTAULD INSTITUTES. 1939+.

2832 NATIONAL GALLERY. National gallery catalogues. The British school. By Martin Davies. 1946. 2nd edn. rev. 1959.

2833 TATE GALLERY. Catalogue; British school. 25th edn. with supplement 1937–46. 1947.

2834 ENCYCLOPAEDIA OF WORLD ART. 15 v. 1959+. In progress.

The English version of *Enciclopedia universale dell'arte*, Venice and Rome, 1958+. Shorter and simpler works include Leonard Gerald Gwynne Ramsey, ed., *The concise encyclopaedia of antiques*, 5 v., 1955–61, and Herbert Cecil Ralph Edwards and L. G. G. Ramsey, eds., *The Connoisseur period guides to the houses, decoration, furnishing, and chattels of the classic periods, The late Georgian period, 1760–1810*, 1956, *The Regency period, 1810–1830*, 1958, *The early Victorian period, 1830–60*, 1958.

2835 NEW YORK METROPOLITAN MUSEUM OF ART. Library. Library catalogue. 25 v. Boston. Mass. 1960.

2. GENERAL WORKS

(a) *Histories and Critical Studies*

2836 BOASE (THOMAS SHERRER ROSS). English art, 1800–70. Oxford history of art. V. 10. Oxf. 1959.

2837 HUSSEY (CHRISTOPHER EDWARD CLIVE). The picturesque: studies in a point of view. 1927. Repr. with new preface by the author. 1967.

Influential contemporary writers include Archibald Alison (Pargellis & Medley 2554), Richard Payne Knight, *The landscape; a didactic poem*, etc., 1794, 2nd edn., 1795, and *An analytical inquiry into the principles of taste*, 1805, 4th edn., 1808: see Jean Jacques Mayoux, *Richard Payne Knight et le pittoresque; essai sur une phase esthetique*, Paris, 1933. Also Sir Uvedale Price, 1st bart., *An essay on the picturesque as compared with the sublime and the beautiful; and on the use of studying pictures for the purpose of improving real landscape*, 2 v., 1794-8, another edn. 3 v., 1810, and William Gilpin, author of *Three essays on picturesque beauty*, etc., 1792, *Remarks on forest scenery*, etc., 2 v., 1794, on whom see William Darby Templeman, *The life of William Gilpin*, etc., Urbana, 1939 (Illinois studies in language and literature, v. 24, no. 34), bibliog. 307-25. See also (2662-76), (2799), (2900), (2949), (2979), Tooley (3464), and (3516).

2838 WHITLEY (WILLIAM THOMAS). Artists and their friends in England, 1700-1799. 2 v. 1928.

Continued by the writer's *Art in England, 1800-1820*, Camb. 1928, and *Art in England, 1821-37*, Camb., 1930, a general account of artists' lives, exhibitions, etc.

2839 FOSTER (*Sir* WILLIAM). 'British artists in India, 1760-1820.' *Walpole Soc.* 19 (1930-31), 1-88.

See also Mildred Archer, *British drawings in the India Office library*, 2 v., 1970, which catalogues nearly 11,000 drawings, including work of Chinnery, the Daniells, and Edward Lear.

2840 STEEGMAN (JOHN). The rule of taste from George I to George IV. 1936.

Continued by *Consort of taste, 1830-1870*, 1950. See also Beverly Sprague Allen, *Tides in English taste (1619-1800)*, etc., Camb., Mass., 1937.

2841 KLINGENDER (FRANCIS DONALD). Art and the Industrial Revolution. 1947. New edn. rev. Arthur Elton. 1968.

2842 HALE (JOHN RIGBY). England and the Italian Renaissance; the growth of interest in its history and art. 1954.

2843 SMITH (BERNARD). European vision and the South Pacific, 1768-1850; a study in the history of art and ideas. Oxf. 1960. Bibliog. 258-74.

2844 IRWIN (DAVID). English neoclassical art; studies in inspiration and taste. 1966. Bibliog. 171-212.

(b) *Patronage, Collectors, Institutions*

2845 WAAGEN (GUSTAV FRIEDRICH). Works of art and artists in England. 3 v. 1838.

Trans. from the German by H. E. Lloyd. Also by Waagen, *Treasures of art in Great Britain*, etc., 4 v., 1854-7, trans. Lady Eastlake, accounts of the growth and contents of the major collections. For the previous generation see Charles Molloy Westmacott, *British galleries of painting and sculpture, comprising a general historical and critical catalogue*, etc., 1824.

2846 PYE (JOHN). Patronage of British art, an historical sketch; comprising an account of the rise and progress of art and artists in London, from the beginning of the reign of George the Second: together with a history of the Society for the management and distribution of the Artists Fund . . . 1810 to . . . 1827. 1845.

On Sir George Beaumont, the notable patron and collector, see William Angus Knight, *Memorials of Coleorton*, etc., 2 v., 1887, and Margaret Greaves, *Regency patron: Sir George Beaumont*, 1966, a short life. On patronage outside London, see Trevor Fawcett, *The rise of English provincial art . . . 1800-30*, Oxf., 1974.

2847 SMITH (THOMAS). Recollections of the British Institution for promoting the fine arts in the United Kingdom; with . . . biographical notices of the artists who have received premiums . . . 1805-1859. 1860.

2848 HOLMES (*Sir* CHARLES) *and* BAKER (CHARLES HENRY COLLINS). The making of the National Gallery, 1824-1924. 1924.

2849 REITLINGER (GERALD ROBERTS). The economics of taste. V. I. The rise and fall of picture prices, 1760-1960. 1961. Bibliog. 503-6. V. II. The rise and fall of objets d'art prices since 1750. 1963.

Based on sale room records. On Christie's see William Roberts, *Memorials of Christie's, a record of art sales from 1766 to 1896*, 2 v., 1897, and Henry Currie Marillier, '*Christie's*', *1766 to 1925*, 1926.

2850 HUTCHISON (SIDNEY CHARLES). The history of the Royal Academy, 1768-1968. 1968. Bibliog. 245-7.

Of older histories, the basic account is William Sandby, *History of the Royal Academy of Arts . . . with biographical notices of all the members*, 1862.

3. PAINTING

(a) *General Studies*

2851 [RUSKIN (JOHN).] Modern painters: their superiority in the art of landscape painting to all the ancient masters proved by examples of the true, the beautiful and the intellectual from the works of modern artists, especially from those of J. M. W. Turner R.A. By a graduate of Oxford. V. 1. 1843. 2nd edn. 1844. 3rd edn. 5 v. 1846-60. (Ruskin's name appears on the title-page of v. 3-5.)

2852 REDGRAVE (RICHARD) *and* REDGRAVE (SAMUEL). A century of painters of the English school, with critical notices of their works and an account of the progress of art in England. 2 v. 1866. 2nd edn. abridged and brought up to date. 1890. New edn. based on that of 1890 with title *A century of British painters*, 1947.

See also Charles Henry Collins Baker, *British painting*, Boston, 1933, and Maurice Harold Grant, *A chronological history of the old English landscape painters (in oil) from the XVIth century to the XIXth century*, new rev. and enl. edn. 8 v., Leigh-on-Sea, 1957-61.

2853 GILBEY (*Sir* WALTER). Animal painters of England from the year 1650. A brief survey of their lives and works. 3 v. 1910–11.

The basic study: short lives in dictionary form. See also Walter Shaw Sparrow, *British sporting artists from Barlow to Herring*, 1922, repr. 1965, *Angling in British art*, etc., 1923, and *A book of sporting painters*, 1931, the last with biog. information on a large number of painters. For a general survey see Basil Taylor, *Animal painting in England from Barlow to Landseer*, 1955.

2854 MARILLIER (HENRY CURRIE). The Liverpool school of painting, an account of the Liverpool academy from 1810 to 1867 with memoirs of the principal artists. 1904.

2855 DICKES (WILLIAM FREDERICK). The Norwich school of painting, being a full account of the Norwich exhibitions, the lives of the painters, the lists of their respective exhibits and descriptions of the pictures. [1906.]

2856 CURSITER (STANLEY). Scottish art to the close of the nineteenth century. 1949. Bibliog. 129–30.

See also Sir James Lewis Caw, *Scottish painting past and present, 1620–1908*, Edin., 1908.

2857 REYNOLDS (ARTHUR GRAHAM). Painters of the Victorian scene. 1953.

See also Odette Aubrat, *La peinture de genre en Angleterre de la mort de Hogarth (1764) au Préraphaélisme (1850)*, Paris [1934], bibliog. 159–72, and Sacheverell Sitwell, *Narrative pictures, a survey of English genre and its painters*, 1937.

2858 FOSKETT (DAPHNE). British portrait miniatures: a history. 1963. Bibliog. 185–8.

Also Basil Somerset Long, *British miniaturists*, 1929, which lists a large number of miniaturists, and Arthur Graham Reynolds, *English portrait miniatures*, 1952. Daphne Foskett, *A dictionary of British miniature painters*, 2 v., 1972, supersedes and amplifies Long.

2859 REYNOLDS (ARTHUR GRAHAM). Victorian painting. 1966.

(b) *Painters*

For Cosway, Hoppner, Morland, Raeburn, Reynolds, Romney, and Zoffany, all of whom were alive in this period, see Pargellis and Medley (2).

2860 BEECHEY. Sir William Beechey, R.A. By William Roberts. 1907.

2861 CHINNERY. George Chinnery, 1774–1852, artist of the China coast; with a foreword by Alice Winchester. By Henry and Sidney Berry-Hill. Leigh-on-Sea. 1963.

2862 BONINGTON. Bonington. By the Hon. Andrew Shirley. 1940.

See also A. Dubuisson, *Richard Parkes Bonington: his life and work*, trans. C. E. Hughes, 1924.

2863 COLLINS. Memoirs of the life of William Collins R.A. With selections from his journal and correspondence. By William Wilkie Collins. 2 v. 1848.

2864 CONSTABLE. Correspondence. Ed. with intro. and notes by Ronald Brymer Beckett. 6 v. (Suffolk Rec. Soc. Pubns. 4, 6, 8, 10–12.) [Ipswich.] 1962–8.

Also by Beckett, *John Constable and the Fishers: the record of a friendship*, 1952. The standard contemporary life is Charles Robert Leslie, *Memoirs of the life of John Constable R.A.*, etc., ed. Hon. Andrew Shirley, 1937, and by Jonathan Mayne, 1951. See also Victoria and Albert Museum, *Catalogue of the Constable collection*, by Arthur Graham Reynolds, 1960, and also by Reynolds, *Constable: the natural painter*, 1965. See also (2889), (2912).

2865 CROME. John Crome. By Derek and Timothy Clifford. 1968. Bibliog. 285–9.

Also Charles Henry Collins Baker, *Crome . . . With an introduction by C. J. Holmes*, 1921.

2866 EASTLAKE (*Sir* CHARLES LOCK). Contributions to the literature of the fine arts. 1848. 2nd ser. with a memoir by Lady Eastlake. 1870.

Director of the National Gallery from 1855, and the dominant figure in the artistic life of the time.

2867 ETTY. Life of William Etty. By Alexander Gilchrist. 2 v. 1855.

Also Dennis Larry Ashwell Farr, *William Etty*, 1958, with catalogue of Etty's works.

2868 FRITH. My autobiography and reminiscences. By William Powell Frith. 3 v. 1887–8.

A short abridgement has been ed. by Nevile Wallis with title, *A Victorian canvas; the memoirs of W. P. Frith*, etc., 1957.

2869 FUSELI. The life and writings of Henry Fuseli Esq. M.A., R.A., the former written, and the latter edited, by John Knowles. 3 v. 1831.

See also Frederick Antal, *Fuseli studies*, 1956. On his drawings see Paul Leonhard Ganz, *The drawings of Henry Fuseli*, 1949, and Caryll Nicolas Peter Powell, *The drawings of Henry Fuseli*, 1951.

2870 HAYDON (BENJAMIN ROBERT). The diary of Benjamin Robert Haydon. Ed. William Bissell Pope. 5 v. Camb. Mass. 1960–3.

Standard. Also, by Haydon, *Lectures on painting and design*, etc., 2 v., 1844–6, *Life of Benjamin Robert Haydon, historical painter from his autobiography and journals*, ed. and comp. Tom Taylor, 2 v., 1853, new edn. by Edmund Blunden, 2 v., 1927, *Correspondence and table talk, with a memoir by his son, Frederic Wordsworth Haydon*, 2 v., 1876. For a short modern life see Eric Beardsworth George, *The life and death of Benjamin Robert Haydon, historical painter, 1786–1846*, 1948, 2nd edn. with add. by Mary Dorothy George, Oxf., 1967.

2871 LANDSEER. Sir Edwin Landseer. [Being the third edn. of 'The early works of Sir Edwin Landseer, extended'.] By Frederic George Stephens. 1880.

Also William Cosmo Monkhouse, *The works of Sir Edwin Landseer . . . With a history of his art-life* [1879–80], and for a catalogue, Algernon Graves, *Catalogue of the works of the late Sir Edwin Landseer, R.A.*, 1875.

2872   LAWRENCE. Lawrence. By Sir Walter Armstrong. 1913.

The contemporary official life is D. E. Williams, *The life and correspondence of Sir Thomas Lawrence*, etc., 2 v., 1831. See also *Sir Thomas Lawrence's letter-bag. With recollections of the artist by Miss Elizabeth Croft*, ed. George Somes Layard, 1906, and O. G. Knapp, ed., *An artist's love story told in the letters of Sir Thomas Lawrence, Mrs Siddons, and her daughters*, 1904, letters 1797–1803. For a modern study see Kenneth John Garlick, *Sir Thomas Lawrence*, 1954, and the same writer's *A catalogue of the paintings, drawings, and pastels of Sir Thomas Lawrence* (Walpole Soc. pubns. 39), 1964.

2873   LEAR. Edward Lear as a landscape draughtsman. By Philip Hofer. 1967.

Also Angus Davidson, *Edward Lear, landscape painter and nonsense poet, 1812–1888*, 1968.

2874   LESLIE. Autobiographical recollections. By the late Charles Robert Leslie. Edited with a prefatory essay on Leslie as an artist and selections from his correspondence by Tom Taylor. 2 v. 1860.

2875   MARTIN. John Martin, 1789–1854: his life and works. By Thomas Balston. 1947.

See also William Feaver, *The art of John Martin*, Oxf., 1975.

2876   PALMER. The letters of Samuel Palmer. By Raymond George Lister. 2 v. Oxf. 1975.

By the same author, *Samuel Palmer*, 1975. These together supersede Alfred Herbert Palmer, *The life and letters of Samuel Palmer, painter and etcher*, 1892. See also Geoffrey Edward Harvey Grigson, *Samuel Palmer. The visionary years*, 1947, with catalogue, 155–94.

2877   SCOTT. Memoir of David Scott R.S.A., containing his journal in Italy, notes on art, and other papers. By William Bell Scott. Edin. 1850.

Also John Miller Gray, *David Scott, R.S.A., and his works. With a catalogue*, etc., Edin., 1884.

2878   SHEE. Life of Sir Martin Archer Shee, president of the Royal Academy, F.R.S., D.C.L. By his son Martin Archer Shee. 2 v. 1860.

2879   STOTHARD. Thomas Stothard, R.A. An illustrated monograph. By A. C. Coxhead. 1906.

Also Anna Eliza Bray, *The life of Thomas Stothard R.A.*, etc., 1851. Stothard was also notable as a book illustrator.

2880   STUBBS. Stubbs. By Basil Taylor, 1971.

See also Pargellis & Medley (2), 2604.

2881   TURNER. The life of J. M. W. Turner, R.A. By Alexander Joseph Finberg. Oxf. 1939. 2nd edn. rev. Oxf. 1961.

Standard: lists paintings and water-colours exhibited during Turner's lifetime, 456–520. The same writer also compiled the National Gallery's *Complete inventory of the drawings of the Turner Bequest*, etc., 1909. The official contemporary life by Walter Thornbury,

The life of J. M. W. Turner, etc., 2 v., 1862, repr. 1969, has been severely criticized. Recent works include Jack Lindsay, *J. M. W. Turner, his life and work; a critical biography*, and Arthur Graham Reynolds, *Turner*, 1969. See also Tate Gallery, *Turner, 1775–1851*, 1974.

2882 WARD. James Ward R.A. His life and works, with a catalogue of his engravings and pictures. By Cecil Reginald Grundy. (Connoisseur extra no.) 1909.

2883 WEST. The life, studies, and works of Benjamin West. By John Galt. 2 v. 1820.

2884 WILKIE. The life of Sir David Wilkie, his journals, tours and critical remarks on works of art and a selection from his correspondence. By Allan Cunningham. 3 v. 1843.

See also Lord Ronald Charles Sutherland Leveson Gower, *Sir David Wilkie*, 1902.

4. DRAWINGS AND WATER-COLOURS

(a) *General Studies*

2885 ROGET (JOHN LEWIS). History of the Old Water-Colour society, now the Royal Society of Painters in Water-Colours. 1891.

Authoritative for the first half of the 19th century.

2886 BRITISH MUSEUM. Catalogue of drawings by British artists, and artists of foreign origin working in Great Britain, preserved in the department of prints and drawings in the British museum. By Robert Laurence Binyon. 4 v. 1898–1907.

New edn. in progress, but 19th century vol. not yet published. See also Arthur Ewart Popham, *A handbook to the drawings and water-colours in the Department of Prints and Drawings, British Museum*, 1939.

2887 MEYER-SÉE (ROBERT RENÉ). English pastels, 1750–1830. Paris. 1911.

2888 FINBERG (ALEXANDER JOSEPH). The English water colour painters. [1906.]

One of the pioneer studies. Also standard are Cecil Eldred Hughes, *Early English water-colour*, 1913, 3rd edn. rev. and ed. Jonathan Mayne, 1950, and Robert Laurence Binyon, *English water-colours*, 1933, 2nd edn., 1944.

2889 VICTORIA AND ALBERT MUSEUM. Catalogue of water colour paintings by British artists and foreigners working in Great Britain. Rev. edn. 1927. Suppl. with acquisitions to the end of 1950. 1951.

Includes the massive Constable bequest.

2890 WILLIAMS (IOLO ANEURIN). Early English watercolours and some cognate drawings by artists born not later than 1785. 1952.

Includes a number of minor figures. See also Henri Lemaître, *Le paysage anglais à l'aquarelle, 1760–1851*, Paris [1955], bibliog. 445–54, and Derek Clifford, *Watercolours of the Norwich school*, 1965.

2891 HARDIE (MARTIN). Water-colour painting in Britain. Ed. Dudley Snelgrove with Jonathan Mayne and Basil Taylor. V. 1. The eighteenth century. 1966. V. 2. The Romantic period. 1967. V. 3. The Victorian period. 1968. Standard.

(b) *Artists*

2892 COTMAN. Life of John Sell Cotman. By Sydney Decimus Kitson. 1937.

Also Victor Rienaecker, *John Sell Cotman, 1782–1842*, Leigh-on-Sea, 1953, bibliog. 155.

2893 GIRTIN. The art of Thomas Girtin. By Thomas Girtin and David Loshak. 1954. Bibliog. 125–6.

Also Jonathan Mayne, *Thomas Girtin*, 1949.

2894 RUSKIN. The drawings of John Ruskin. By Paul H. Walton. Oxf. 1972.

2895 VARLEY. John Varley of the 'Old Society'. By Adrian Bury. Leigh-on-Sea. 1946.

5. Engraving

(a) *Bibliographies, Catalogues, Journals*

2896 BRITISH MUSEUM. Catalogue of engraved British portraits preserved in the Department of prints and drawings in the British Museum. By Freeman Marius O'Donoghue and Henry Mendelssohn Hake. 6 v. 1908–25.

2897 THE PRINT-COLLECTOR'S QUARTERLY. V. 1–7, N.Y., Bost. 1911–17; v. 8+, London 1921+.

Complete index, volumes 1–23, 1911–1936, 1936.

2898 LEVIS (HOWARD COPPUCK). A descriptive bibliography of the most important books in the English language, relating to the art and history of engraving and the collecting of prints. 1912.

See also Frank Weitenkampf, *Prints and their production; a list of works in the New York public library*, N.Y., 1916, arranged according to subject. For books with coloured plates see Martin Hardie, *English coloured books*, 1906, and Tooley (3464).

2899 BUSHNELL (GEORGE HERBERT). Scottish engravers; a biographical dictionary of Scottish engravers and of engravers who worked in Scotland to the beginning of the nineteenth century. Oxf. 1949.

2900 ABBEY (JOHN ROLAND). Scenery of Great Britain and Ireland in aquatint and lithography, 1770–1860, from the library of J. R. Abbey; a bibliographical catalogue. [Storrington, Sussex.] 1952.

See also his *Life in England in aquatint and lithography, 1770–1860*, etc., 1953, and *Travel . . . 1770–1860*, v. 1, *World, Europe, Africa*, v. 2, *Asia, Oceania, Antarctica, America*, 1957, all descriptive of the author's notable collections. For a large collection of early illustrated books see Henry E. Curran and Charles Robertson, *Ex bibliotheca Hugh Frederick Hornby, catalogue of the art library bequeathed . . . to the Free Public Library of the city of Liverpool*, Liverpool, 1906. See also Tooley (3464.)

(b) *General Works*

2901 GRAY (BASIL). The English print. 1937.

The most useful introduction to the subject. Arthur Mayger Hind, *A short history of engraving and etching*, 1908, 3rd edn. rev. 1923, bibliog. 393–419, is the standard British authority. Jean Laran, and others, *L'estampe*, 2 v., Paris, 1959, bibliog. v. 1, 263–72, is the standard general history. (V. 2 consists of plates.)

2902 SMITH (JOHN CHALONER). British mezzotinto portraits. 4 v. 1878–83.

See also Alfred Charles Whitman, *Nineteenth century mezzotinters*, 3 v., 1903–7, Cyril James Humphries Davenport, *Mezzotints*, 1904, and Charles E. Russell, *English mezzotint portraits and their states*, etc., 2 v., 1926.

2903 PRIDEAUX (SARAH TREVERBIAN). Aquatint engravings; a chapter in the history of book illustration. 1909.

2904 BLISS (DOUGLAS PERCY). A history of wood engraving. 1928. Repr. 1964.

2905 SILTZER (FRANK). The story of British sporting prints. 1925. Enl. 1929.

2906 TWYMAN (MICHAEL). Lithography 1800–1850. The techniques of drawing on stone in England and France and their application to works of topography. 1970.

See also Joseph Pennell and Elizabeth Robins Pennell, *Lithography and lithographers*, 1898.

(c) *Engravers and Publishers*

2907 ACKERMANN. Rudolph Ackermann . . . with a selected list of his publications in the New York Public Library. By William J. Burke. N.Y. 1935.

2908 BEWICK. Thomas Bewick. By Montague Weekley. 1953.

See also *A memoir of Thomas Bewick, written by himself*, Newcastle upon Tyne, 1862, ed. with intro. by Montague Weekley, 1961 and by Iain Bain, Oxf. 1975. See also Sydney Roscoe, *Thomas Bewick; a bibliography raisonné of editions of the 'General history of quadrupeds', the 'History of British birds' and the 'Fables of Aesop' issued in his lifetime*, 1953. For reproductions see Robert Hutchinson, *1800 woodcuts by Thomas Bewick*, etc., 1962.

2909 BLAKE. The art of William Blake. By Sir Anthony Frederick Blunt. 1959. Bibliog. 115–18.

See also Sir Geoffrey Langdon Keynes, *Engravings by William Blake; the separate plates, a catalogue raisonné,* etc., Dublin, 1956, and, containing many reproductions, his *William Blake's engravings,* 1950. For particular books see *Illustrations of the book of Job,* ed. G. L. Keynes and Robert Laurence Binyon, N.Y., Pierpont Morgan library, 1935, G. L. Keynes, *William Blake's illustrations to the Bible,* Clairvaux, 1957, Albert Sutherland Roe, *Blake's illustrations to the Divine Comedy,* Princeton, 1953. G. L. Keynes's *A study of the illuminated books of William Blake; poet, printer, prophet,* 1965, contains excellent colour reproductions and a general intro. For his drawings see G. L. Keynes, *Pencil drawings by William Blake,* 1927, and *Blake's pencil drawings,* 2nd ser., 1956. For Blake generally see Pargellis and Medley (2), 2342–6 and (2716).

2910 CALVERT. Edward Calvert. By Raymond George Lister. Camb. 1966.

Primarily a wood-engraver.

2911 DANIELL. The Daniells; artists and travellers. By Thomas Sutton. 1954.

Their best-known work is perhaps their illustrations to Richard Ayton's *A voyage round Great Britain,* etc., 8 v., 1814–25. They also worked in India: see (2839).

2912 LUCAS. The published mezzotints of David Lucas after John Constable, R.A. A catalogue and historical account. By the Hon. Andrew Shirley. Oxf. 1930.

With the correspondence of Constable and Lucas.

2913 TURNER. The history of Turner's Liber Studiorum. With a new catalogue raisonné. By Alexander Joseph Finberg. 1924.

Also William George Rawlinson, *The engraved work of J. M. W. Turner, R.A.,* 2 v., 1908, 1913.

6. CARICATURE

(a) *General Works*

2914 BRITISH MUSEUM. Catalogue of prints and drawings in the British museum. Division 1. Political and personal satires. Ed. by Frederic George Stephens, Edward Hawkins, and Mary Dorothy George. 11 v. 1870–1954.

Vols. 6–11 cover the period 1789–1832.

2915 GEORGE (MARY DOROTHY). English political caricature; a study of opinion and propaganda. V. 1. To 1792. V. 2. 1793–1832. 2 v. 1959.

By the same author, *Hogarth to Cruikshank; social change in graphic satire,* 1967. See also Graham Everitt, *English caricaturists and graphic humourists of the nineteenth century,* etc., 1886, 2nd edn., 1893.

(b) *Caricaturists*

2916 BROWNE (HABLOT KNIGHT) ['PHIZ']. Phiz illustrations from the novels of Charles Dickens. By Albert Johannsen. Chicago. [1956.]

Technical discussion of the plates. See also David Croal Thomson, *Life and labours of Hablot Knight Browne,* 'Phiz', 1884.

2917   CRUIKSHANK (ISAAC, ISAAC ROBERT, *and* GEORGE). The three
Cruikshanks; a bibliographical catalogue. By Frederick Marchmont (*pseud.* of
Hugh Arthur Torriano.) 1897.

For Isaac see Edward Bell Krumbhaar, *Isaac Cruikshank; a catalogue raisonné, with a
sketch of his life and work*, Phil. [1966], bibliog. 174–5; for his son George, George
William Reid, *A descriptive catalogue of the works of George Cruikshank*, etc., 3 v., 1871,
with many illustrations; William Blanchard Jerrold, *The life of George Cruikshank*, etc.,
2 v., 1882; Albert Mayer Cohn, *George Cruikshank; a catalogue raisonné of the work
executed during the years 1806–77*, etc., 1924, standard.

2918   DOYLE (JOHN ['HB'] *and* RICHARD). The seven years of William IV.
A reign cartooned by John Doyle. By George Macaulay Trevelyan. 1952.

Selected from Doyle's *Political sketches of H.B.*, 8 v., 1829+. For his son Richard see
[Richard Doyle], *A journal kept . . . in the year 1840*, etc., 1885, facsimile edn. with
many illustrations, and Daria Hambourg, *Richard Doyle*, 1948.

2919   GILLRAY. Mr. Gillray, the caricaturist; a biography. By Draper Hill.
1965.

See also James Gillray, *The genuine works of James Gillray, engraved by himself*, 2 v.,
1830, Thomas Wright and Robert Harding Evans, *Historical and descriptive account of
the caricatures of James Gillray*, 1851, and Thomas Wright and Joseph Grego, eds., *The
works of James Gillray*, etc. [1873].

2920   KAY. A series of original portraits and caricature etchings by the late
J. Kay. By Hugh Paton. 2 v. Edin. 1838. New edn. 2 v. Edin. 1877.

2921   LEECH. John Leech, his life and work. By William Powell Frith. 2 v.
1891.

See also Frederic George Kitton, *John Leech, artist and humourist, a biographical
sketch*, 1883. For a catalogue see Grolier Club, *Catalogue of an exhibition of . . . John
Leech . . . with an introduction by Stanley Kidder Wilson*, N.Y., 1914.

2922   ROWLANDSON. Thomas Rowlandson; his life and art. A documentary
record. By Bernard Falk. [1949.]

Also Joseph Grego, *Rowlandson the caricaturist*, etc., 2 v., 1880, Ronald Paulson, *Rowlandson; a new interpretation*, 1972, and John Hayes, *Rowlandson; watercolours and
drawings*, 1972.

7. SCULPTURE

(a) *General Works*

2923   WHINNEY (MARGARET DICKENS). Sculpture in Britain, 1530–
1830. Harmondsworth. 1964. Bibliog. 281–4.

2924   ESDAILE (KATHARINE ADA). English monumental sculpture since
the Renaissance. 1927.

By the same author, *English church monuments, 1510–1840*, 1946.

2925 GUNNIS (RUPERT). Dictionary of British sculptors, 1660–1851. 1953.

(b) *Sculptors*

2926 CHANTREY. Sir Francis Chantrey, R.A., recollections of his life, practice, and opinions. By George Jones. 1849.

Also John Holland, *Memorials of Sir Francis Chantrey*, Sheffield, 1851, critical of Jones.

2927 FLAXMAN. John Flaxman, 1755–1826. By William George Constable. 1927.

See also John Flaxman, *Lectures on sculpture . . . with a brief memoir of the author*, 1829, 2nd edn. enl. [1838], and *The drawings of Flaxman in the Gallery of University College, London. . . . With . . . an introductory essay . . . by Sidney Colvin*, 1876, and Margaret Dickens Whinney and Rupert Gunnis, *The collection of models by John Flaxman, R.A. at University College, London; a catalogue and introduction*, 1967.

2928 GIBSON. The biography of John Gibson, R.A., sculptor, Rome. By Thomas Matthews. 1911.

Also [Lady] Elizabeth Eastlake, ed., *Life of John Gibson*, 1870.

2929 NOLLEKENS. Nollekens and his times, comprehending a life of that sculptor and memoirs of several contemporary artists, from the time of Roubiliac, Hogarth and Reynolds to that of Fuseli, Flaxman and Blake. By John Thomas Smith. 2 v. 1828. New edn. by G. W. Stonier. 1945. Another edn. 1949.

8. ARCHITECTURE

For architectural descriptions of particular areas see in the appropriate sections of Local history, Scotland, Wales, or Ireland. See also Pevsner (3523).

(a) *Bibliographies, Catalogues, Dictionaries, Journals*

2930 GWILT (JOSEPH). An encyclopaedia of architecture, historical, theoretical and practical. 1842. Many later edns.

2931 THE BUILDER, AN ILLUSTRATED WEEKLY MAGAZINE. 1842+.

2932 ROYAL INSTITUTE OF BRITISH ARCHITECTS. Catalogue of the Royal Institute of British Architects' Library. [By H. V. Molesworth Roberts.] 2 v. 1937–8.

Classified by authors and subjects. See also the *Catalogue of the drawings collection of the Royal Institute of British Architects*, 1966+, in progress.

2933 COLVIN (HOWARD MONTAGU). A biographical dictionary of English architects, 1660–1840. 1954.

2934 ARCHITECTURAL HISTORY; the journal of the Society of Architectural Historians. V. 1+. York. 1958+.

Also the *Journal* of the American Society of Architectural Historians, Crawfordsville,

Indiana, v. 1+, 1942+. The *Architectural Review for the artist and craftsman*, v. 1+ (2 v. annually), 1897+, contains much material on architectural history. *Country life illustrated*, 1897+, has contained in recent years valuable illustrated articles on English country houses.

2935 COLUMBIA UNIVERSITY. Architectural library. Catalog of the Avery Memorial Architectural Library of Columbia University. 6 v. Boston. 1958.

2936 COLVIN (HOWARD MONTAGU). A guide to the sources of English architectural history. Rev. edn. Newport, Isle of Wight. 1967.

(b) *General Works*

2937 RUSKIN (JOHN). The seven lamps of architecture. With illustrations drawn and etched by the author. 1849. 2nd edn. 1855.

2938 GOODHART-RENDEL (HARRY STUART). English architecture since the Regency; an interpretation. 1953.

Also Christopher Reginald Turnor, *Nineteenth century architecture in Britain*, 1950, Peter Ferriday, ed., *Victorian architecture*, 1963, essays by different writers, and Robert Furneaux Jordan, *Victorian architecture*, Harmondsworth, 1966.

2939 SUMMERSON (*Sir* JOHN NEWENHAM). Architecture in Britain, 1530–1830. 1953. 4th edn. rev. and enl. Harmondsworth. 1963. Bibliog. 363–70.

Standard. See also his *Georgian London* (3767).

2940 HITCHCOCK (HENRY-RUSSELL). Early Victorian architecture in Britain. 2 v. (V. I text; v. II illustrations.) (Yale Historical Pubns. History of Art, 9.) New Haven, Conn. 1954.

Standard. By the same author, *Architecture, nineteenth and twentieth centuries*, Harmondsworth, 1958, bibliog. 463–72.

(c) *Special Subjects*

2941 RICHARDSON (CHARLES JAMES). A popular treatise on the warming and ventilation of buildings. 1837.

2942 RICHARDSON (ALBERT EDWARD). Monumental classic architecture in Great Britain and Ireland during the eighteenth and nineteenth centuries. [1914.]

On banks, public buildings, etc.

2943 GOTCH (JOHN ALFRED) *ed.* The growth and work of the Royal Institute of British architects, 1834–1934. 1934. Rev. edn. [1935].

Also on the profession, Barrington Lawrence Burnett Kaye, *The development of the architectural professions in Britain; a sociological study*, 1960, and Frank Jenkins, *Architect and patron, a survey of professional relations and practice in England from the sixteenth century to the present day*, 1961.

2944 ADDLESHAW (GEORGE WILLIAM OUTRAM) *and* ETCHELLS (FREDERICK). The architectural setting of Anglican worship; an inquiry into the arrangements for public worship in the Church of England from the Reformation to the present day. 1948.

See also Marcus Whiffen, *Stuart and Georgian churches; the architecture of the Church of England outside London, 1603–1837,* 1948, and (727).

2945 GLOAG (JOHN) *and* BRIDGWATER (DEREK). A history of cast iron in architecture. 1948.

For designs see Lewis Nockalls Cottingham, *The smith and founder's director,* etc., 1823, and John Frederick Harris, *English decorative ironwork from contemporary source books, 1610–1836; a collection of drawings and pattern books,* 1960, with examples from Cottingham, John Young, Henry Shaw and A. W. N. Pugin.

2946 GIEDION (SIEGFRIED). Space, time, and architecture, the growth of a new tradition. Camb. Mass. 1949. 5th edn. Camb. Mass. 1967.

Standard, on the general background to the development of modern architecture, and with some discussion of early town planning.

2947 HUSSEY (CHRISTOPHER EDWARD CLIVE). English country houses. V. II. Mid-Georgian, 1760–1800. 1956. V. III. Late-Georgian, 1800–1840. 1958.

Replaces Henry Avray Tipping, *English homes, period VI. Vol. 1. Late Georgian, 1760–1820,* 1926. Also see Albert Edward Richardson and Charles Lovett Gill, *Regional architecture of the west of England,* 1924, and (3767).

2948 RICHARDS (JAMES MAUDE). The functional tradition in early industrial buildings. [1958.]

See also Christian Barman, *An introduction to railway architecture,* 1950, and Carroll L. V. Meeks, *The railway station; an architectural history,* New Haven, Conn. 1956 (Yale Historical Pubns. History of Art, 11), on Europe and the U.S.

2949 CLIFFORD (DEREK). A history of garden design. 1962. Bibliog. 220–4.

See also Repton (2979). Other contemporary works on landscape gardening include John Claudius Loudon, *Hints on the formation of gardens and pleasure grounds,* etc., 1812, and his *Suburban gardener and villa companion,* 1838, also Richard Morris, *Essays on landscape gardening,* 1825, George William Johnson, *A history of English gardens,* 1829. For a modern history see also Ralph Dutton, *The English garden,* 1937.

2950 GIROUARD (MARK). The Victorian country house. Oxf. 1971.

2951 CROOK (JOSEPH MORDAUNT) *and* PORT (MICHAEL HARRY). The history of the King's works. V. VI. 1783–1851. Ed. by Howard Montagu Colvin. 1973.

Contains accounts of works at Windsor, the British Museum, Buckingham Palace, the Houses of Parliament, and other places.

(d) *Styles*

2952 RICHARDSON (GEORGE). The new Vitruvius Britannicus, consisting of plans and elevations of modern buildings . . . in Great Britain. 2 v. 1802–8.

2953 GANDY (JOSEPH). The rural architect, consisting of various designs
for country buildings, accompanied with ground plans, estimates and descriptions. 1805.

2954 LUGAR (ROBERT). The country gentleman's architect; containing a
variety of designs for farm houses and farm yards of different magnitudes,
arranged on the most approved principles. 1807.

Influential in advocating Gothic.

2955 BRITTON (JOHN). The architectural antiquities of Great Britain,
represented and illustrated in a series of views, elevations, plans, sections, and
details of various ancient English edifices; with historical and descriptive
accounts of each. 5 v. 1807–26.

Important in adapting public taste to Gothic. See also (3516) for illustrated topographical works.

2956 RICKMAN (THOMAS). An attempt to discriminate the styles of English architecture from the Conquest to the Reformation . . . With notices of
eight hundred English buildings; preceded by a sketch of the Grecian and
Roman orders. 1817. 7th edn. Oxf. 1881.

An influential investigation of architectural history, dividing Gothic into 'early English',
'decorated', and 'perpendicular' periods.

2957 ROBINSON (PETER FREDERICK). Rural architecture, or, A series
of designs for ornamental cottages. 1823. 4th edn. 1836.

Influential in recommending Gothic.

2958 HUNT (THOMAS FREDERICK). Archittetura campestre, displayed
in lodges, gardeners' houses . . . in the modern or Italian style. 1827.

Hunt's designs in the Italian manner. Charles Parker, *Villa rustica . . . selected
from buildings and scenes in the vicinity of Rome and Florence, and arranged for rural
and domestic dwellings*, 1848, illustrates actual Italian buildings and suggests their
adaptation.

2959 COCKERELL (CHARLES ROBERT) *and others*. Antiquities of Athens
and other places in Greece, Sicily etc., supplementary to the Antiquities of
Athens by J. Stuart and N. Revett. 1830.

2960 GOODWIN (FRANCIS). Domestic architecture . . . A series of designs
in the Grecian, Italian and Old English styles. 1833–4. Re-issued as Rural
Architecture, 1835.

Recommends Gothic for small houses (cottages, parsonages) and Greek for public
buildings. John Claudius Loudon, *An encyclopaedia of cottage, farm and villa architecture and furniture*, 1833, new edn. 1836, provides an anthology of the picturesque.

2961 HAKEWILL (JAMES). An attempt to determine the exact character of
Elizabethan architecture. 1835.

See also Charles James Richardson, *The architectural remains of Elizabeth and James I*,
1838, and Thomas Frederick Hunt, *Exemplars of Tudor architecture adapted to modern
habitations*, etc., 1830, for practical applications.

2962 CLARK (*Sir* KENNETH). The Gothic revival; an essay in the history of taste. 1928. 3rd edn. 1962.

An important near-contemporary account, giving details of many buildings, is Sir Charles Lock Eastlake, *A history of the Gothic revival; an attempt to show how the taste for medieval architecture which lingered in England during the last two centuries has since been encouraged and developed*, 1872., repr. 1971, ed. J. M. Crook. For Pugin see (2978).

2963 CLARKE (BASIL FULFORD LOWTHER). Church builders of the nineteenth century; a study of the Gothic Revival in England. 1938.

Also White, *The Cambridge movement* (729). The manual of the church restorers was *The Ecclesiologist*, v. 1–30, Camb. 1841–5, Lond. 1846–68. For stained glass see [Charles Winston], *An inquiry into the differences of style observable in ancient glass paintings, especially in England*, Oxf. 1847, 2nd edn. 1867.

2964 PILCHER (DONALD ELE). The Regency style. 1947.

2965 CROOK (JOSEPH MORDAUNT). The Greek revival: neo-classical attitudes in British architecture, 1760–1870. 1972.

(e) *Buildings*

2966 RUTTER (JOHN). A description of Fonthill Abbey and demesne. 6th edn. 1822.

By the same author, *Delineations of Fonthill and its Abbey*, 1823.

2967 HOPE (*Sir* WILLIAM HENRY ST. JOHN). Windsor Castle, an architectural history. 2 v. and portfolio of plans. 1913.

Also William Henry Pyne, *The history of the royal residences* (1992) I, *Windsor and Frogmore*, 1819, and Jeffry Wyatt (afterwards Sir Jeffry Wyatville), *Illustrations of Windsor Castle . . . ed. by* H. Ashton, 2 v., 1841.

2968 HASTINGS (MAURICE). Parliament House. The chambers of the House of Commons. 1950.

2969 MUSGRAVE (CLIFFORD). Royal Pavilion: an episode in the romantic. Brighton. 1951. Rev. and enl. edn. 1959.

2970 WHITBREAD (SAMUEL) *intro*. Southill, a regency house. 1951.

Essays by different writers on the home of the Whitbread family.

2971 HARRIS (JOHN FREDERICK), DE BELLAIGUE (GEOFFREY) *and* MILLAR (OLIVER). Buckingham Palace. 1968.

(f) *Architects*

2972 BARRY. Life and works of Sir Charles Barry. R.A. F.R.S. By Alfred Barry. 1867.

2973 DANCE. George Dance, architect, 1741–1825. By Dorothy Nancy Stroud. 1971.

2974 HOLLAND. Henry Holland; his life and architecture. By Dorothy Nancy Stroud. 1966.

2975 MYLNE. Robert Mylne, architect and engineer, 1733 to 1811. By Sir Albert Edward Richardson. 1955.

2976 NASH. John Nash, architect to King George IV. By Sir John Newenham Summerson. 1935. 2nd edn. 1950.

> Also Terence Davis, *The architecture of John Nash*, etc., 1960, and the same writer's *John Nash; the Prince Regent's architect*, 1966.

2977 PAXTON. The works of Sir Joseph Paxton, 1803–65. By George Fletcher Chadwick. 1962.

> See also Violet Rosa Markham, *Paxton and the bachelor Duke*, 1935.

2978 PUGIN. Pugin; a mediaeval Victorian. By Michael Trappes-Lomax. 1932.

> With lists of his buildings pp. 331–45, and writings 346–50. Of greatest general interest are Augustus Welby Northmore Pugin, *Contrasts*, etc., 1836, 2nd edn. 1841, repr. 1969, and *An apology for the revival of Christian architecture in England*, 1843. See also Benjamin Ferrey, *Recollections of A. N. Welby Pugin and his father, Augustus Pugin. With notices of their works*, 1861, and Denis Rolleston Gwynn, *Lord Shrewsbury, Pugin, and the Catholic revival*, 1946.

2979 REPTON. Humphry Repton. By Dorothy Nancy Stroud. 1962.

> Of Repton's works see *Sketches and hints on landscape gardening*, 1794, new edn. by John Nolen, 1907, and *The landscape gardening and landscape architecture of the late Humphry Repton*, etc., ed. John Claudius Loudon, 1840.

2980 SOANE. The architecture of Sir John Soane; with an introduction by Professor Henry-Russell Hitchcock. By Dorothy Nancy Stroud. 1961.

> See also Arthur Thomas Bolton, ed., *The works of Sir John Soane*, etc. (Soane museum pubns. 8) [1924], *The portrait of Sir John Soane, . . . set forth in letters from his friends (1775–1837)*, 1927, and *Lectures on architecture . . . from 1809 to 1836* (Soane museum pubns. 14), 1929.

2981 WILKINS. Haileybury and the Greek revival; the architecture of William Wilkins, R.A. By Joseph Mordaunt Crook. [Leicester. 1964.]

2982 WYATT. James Wyatt, architect, 1746–1813. By Antony Dale. Oxf. 1936. New edn. 1956.

2983 WYATVILLE. Sir Jeffry Wyatville, architect to the King. By Derek Linstrum. Oxf. 1973.

9. FURNITURE AND INTERIOR DECORATION

(a) *Bibliographies, Catalogues, Dictionaries, Journals*

2984 MACQUOID (PERCY) *and* EDWARDS (HERBERT CECIL RALPH). The dictionary of English furniture from the middle ages to the late Georgian period. 3 v. 1924–7. New edn. rev. and enl. by H. C. R. Edwards [Ralph Edwards]. 3 v. 1954.

The most important work of reference. Ralph Edwards and Margaret Jourdain, *Georgian cabinet-makers*, 1944, 3rd edn. rev., 1955, illustrates a collection of documented furniture of both well-known and lesser-known cabinet makers.

2985 VICTORIA AND ALBERT MUSEUM. Catalogue of English furniture and woodwork. V. 4. Georgian. By Herbert Cecil Ralph Edwards. 1931.

2986 HEAL (*Sir* AMBROSE). The London furniture makers, from the Restoration to the Victorian era, 1660–1840: a record of 2,500 cabinet makers, upholsterers, carvers and gilders. 1953.

2987 FURNITURE HISTORY SOCIETY. Furniture history. V. 1+. Leeds. 1965+. Annual.

(b) *General Works*

2988 FASTNEDGE (RALPH). English furniture styles from 1500 to 1830. Harmondsworth. 1955.

The best introduction. Percy Macquoid, *A history of English furniture*, 4 v., 1904–8, though once standard, is now dated. Other general histories are John Charles Rogers, *English furniture*, 1923, 3rd edn. rev. and enl. by Margaret Jourdain, 1959, and Robert Wemyss Symonds, *Furniture making in seventeenth and eighteenth century England; an outline for collectors*, 1955, standard. Peter Ward-Jackson, *English furniture designs of the eighteenth century* (Victoria and Albert Museum pubns.), 1958, is important and includes a bibliog. of the principal 18th century pattern books. See also Elizabeth Aslin, *Nineteenth century English furniture*, 1962. For particular buildings see (2969–71).

2989 JOURDAIN (MARGARET). English decoration and furniture of the later XVIIIth century (1760–1820) . . . its development and characteristic forms. 1922.

By the same author, *English interiors in smaller houses from the Restoration to the Regency, 1660–1830* [1923], *English interior decoration, 1500 to 1830; a study in the development of design*, 1950, and Margaret Jourdain and Fred Rose, *English furniture: the Georgian period (1750–1830)*, 1953.

2990 SUGDEN (ALAN VICTOR) *and* EDMONDSON (JOHN LUDLAM). A history of English wallpaper, 1509–1914. 1925.

Also Eric Arthur Entwisle, *The book of wallpaper; a history and an appreciation*, 1954, and his *A literary history of wallpaper*, 1960, a collection, in chronological order, of literary and trade directory references.

2991 PEVSNER (NIKOLAUS BERNHARD LEON). High Victorian design; a study of the exhibits of 1851. 1951.

For detailed coloured lithographs see Matthew Digby Wyatt, *The industrial arts of the nineteenth century. A series of illustrations of the choicest specimens produced by every nation*, etc., 2 v., 1851. See also (1625–7).

2992 SYMONDS (ROBERT WEMYSS) *and* WHINERAY (BRUCE BLUNDELL). Victorian furniture. 1962.

Also Frederic Gordon Roe, *Victorian furniture* [1952].

2993 JOURDAIN (MARGARET). Regency furniture, 1795–1830. 1934. New edn. rev. and enl. by Ralph Fastnedge. 1965.

Indispensable. See also Brian Reade, *Regency antiques*, 1953, John Frederick Harris, ed., *Regency furniture designs from contemporary source books, 1803–1826*, etc., 1961 (including the work of Sheraton, Hope, Ackermann, P & M. A. Nicholson and George Smith), and Clifford Musgrave, *Regency furniture, 1800–1830*, 1961.

2994 WILLS (GEOFFREY). English looking-glasses; a study of glass frames and makers (1670–1820). Foreword by John Hayward. 1965.

2995 CROFT-MURRAY (EDWARD). Decorative painting in England, 1537–1837. V. 2. The eighteenth and early nineteenth centuries. 1971.

(c) *Cabinet Makers and Designers*

2996 ADAM. The furniture of Robert Adam. By Eileen Harris. 1963.

The first scholarly account. For the brothers Adam see Pargellis and Medley 2675–7.

2997 HEPPLEWHITE. The cabinet-maker and upholsterer's guide; or, Repository of designs for every article of household furniture. By A. Hepplewhite and Co. 1788. Abridged edn. with title, Hepplewhite furniture designs, with introduction by Herbert Cecil Ralph Edwards, 1947.

2998 HOPE. Thomas Hope, 1769–1831, and the neo-classical idea. By David Watkin. 1969.

See also *Household furniture and interior decoration executed from designs by Thomas Hope*, 1807.

2999 SHERATON. Sheraton furniture. By Ralph Fastnedge. 1962.

See also Thomas Sheraton, *The cabinet maker and upholsterer's drawing book*, 1791–4, 2nd edn. 1794, 3rd, 1802, also abridged edn. with title *Sheraton furniture designs*, with intro. by Herbert Cecil Ralph Edwards, 1945.

3000 SMITH (GEORGE). A collection of designs for household furniture and interior decoration in the most approved and elegant taste. 1808.

See also his *The cabinet maker and upholsterer's guide, drawing book, and repository*, 1826.

10. Textiles and Carpets

3001 HUNTON (W. GORDON). English decorative textiles: tapestry and chintz, their design and development from the earliest times to the nineteenth century. 1930.

See also Cyril George Edward Bunt and Ernest Arthur Rose, *Two centuries of English chintz, 1750–1950, as exemplified by the productions of Stead, McAlpine and Co.*, Leigh-on-Sea, 1957. For a short but authoritative guide see [Peter Floud] *English printed textiles 1720–1836*, 1960, and Victoria and Albert Museum, *Catalogue of a loan exhibition of English chintz*, etc., 1960, which contains a list of pattern books.

3002 KENDRICK (ALBERT FRANK). English needlework. 1933. 2nd edn. rev. and much re-written, by Patricia Wardle, 1967. Bibliog. 200–2.

See also Barbara Morris, *Victorian embroidery*, 1962, bibliog. 219–20, 225.

3003 TATTERSALL (CREASSEY EDWARD CECIL). A history of British carpets from the introduction of the craft until the present day. Benfleet [Essex]. 1934.

3004 WARDLE (PATRICIA). Victorian lace. 1968. Bibliog. 267–70.

II. CERAMICS

See also (1604) for economic history.

(a) *Bibliographies, Catalogues, Journals*

3005 SOLON (LOUIS MARC EMMANUEL). Ceramic literature: an analytical index to the works published in all languages on the history and technology of the ceramic art. 1910.

3006 ENGLISH CERAMIC CIRCLE. Transactions. 1931+.

From 1928–31 known as the English Porcelain circle.

3007 HONEY (WILLIAM BOWYER). European ceramic art from the end of the Middle Ages to about 1815; a dictionary of factories, artists, technical terms, et cetera. 2 v. 1949–52.

For marks, the most recent and comprehensive work is Geoffrey Arthur Godden, *Encyclopaedia of British pottery and porcelain marks*, 1964. See also John Patrick Cushion and William Bowyer Honey, *Handbook of pottery and porcelain marks*, 1956, 2nd edn. 1958, 3rd edn. rev. 1965.

(b) *General Works*

3008 JEWITT (LLEWELLYNN F. W.). The ceramic art of Great Britain. 2 v. 1878. 2nd edn. 1883.

Contains a great deal of information on individual firms, which is near-contemporary for Victorian productions. For Wedgwood see (2204); for Doulton (1604).

3009 HONEY (WILLIAM BOWYER). English pottery and porcelain. 1933. 5th edn. rev. R. J. Charleston. 1962.

Standard. See also Geoffrey Bemrose, *Nineteenth century English pottery and porcelain*, 1952, and Geoffrey Arthur Godden, *British pottery and porcelain, 1780–1850*, 1963, bibliog. 186–9.

3010 WAKEFIELD (HUGH GEORGE). Victorian pottery. 1962.

Also George Bernard Hughes, *Victorian pottery and porcelain*, 1959, new edn. 1967.

3011 HUGHES (GEORGE BERNARD). English pottery and porcelain figures. 1964.

Also Thomas Balston, *Staffordshire portrait figures of the Victorian age*, 1958, suppl. 1963, and Arthur Lane, *English porcelain figures of the eighteenth century*, 1961. See also Patterson David Gordon Pugh, *Staffordshire portrait figures and allied subjects of the Victorian era*, 1970.

3012　CHARLESTON (ROBERT JESSE) *ed.* English porcelain, 1745–1850. 1965.

Chapters on different factories, with full bibliogs. by specialist writers. Also William Bowyer Honey, *Old English porcelain: a handbook for collectors*, 1928, new edn. 1948; Geoffrey Arthur Godden, *Victorian porcelain*, 1961, bibliog. 215–16; Dennis George Rice, *Rockingham ornamental porcelain*, 1965; Geoffrey Arthur Godden, *Minton pottery and porcelain of the first period, 1793–1850*, 1968, and his *Illustrated guide to Lowestoft porcelain*, 1969.

12. GLASS

See also (1603) for economic history.

3013　DUNCAN (GEORGE SANG). Bibliography of glass (from the earliest records to 1940). Ed. by Violet Dimbleby. 1960.

See also *Journal of the society of glass technology*, v. 1+, Sheffield, 1917+.

3014　WESTROPP (MICHAEL SEYMOUR DUDLEY). Irish glass; an account of glass-making in Ireland from the XVIth century to the present day. 1920.

3015　THORPE (WILLIAM ARNOLD). A history of English and Irish glass. 2 v. 1929.

Standard. Also Henry James Powell, *Glass-making in England*, Camb., 1923, E. M. Elville, *English table glass*, 1951, bibliog. 267–9, and the same writer's *English and Irish cut glass, 1750–1950*, 1953, also Hugh George Wakefield, *Nineteenth century British glass*, 1961.

3016　BEARD (GEOFFREY WILLIAM). Nineteenth century cameo glass; with a foreword by E. Barrington Haynes, Newport, Mon., 1956.

13. DECORATIVE METALWORK AND JEWELLERY

3017　CHAFFERS (WILLIAM). Hall marks on gold and silver plate. 1863. 10th edn. rev. and enl. by C. A. Markham. 1922.

Standard; bibliog. 374–83. Also standard are Sir Charles James Jackson, *English goldsmiths and their marks*, 1905, 2nd edn. rev. and enl., 1921, repr., N.Y., 1964, and Wilfred Joseph Cripps, *Old English plate, ecclesiastical, decorative and domestic: its marks and makers*, 1878, 12th edn., 1967.

3018　JACKSON (*Sir* CHARLES JAMES). An illustrated history of English plate, ecclesiastical and secular . . . from the earliest known examples to the latest of the Georgian period. 2 v. 1911.

Standard.

3019　BRADBURY (FREDERICK). History of old Sheffield plate, being an account of the origin, growth, and decay of the industry. 1912.

Standard. It also deals with Britannia metal manufacture. Sheffield plate was ousted by electro-plating *c.* 1840.

3020 YOUNG (W. A.). Old English pattern books of the metal trades. A descriptive catalogue of the collection in the [Victoria and Albert] museum. 1913.

Includes door furniture.

3021 COTTERELL (HOWARD HERSCHEL). Old pewter, its makers and marks in England, Scotland and Ireland; an account of the old pewterer and his craft etc. 1929. Repr. 1963.

Standard. Pewter tended to be supplanted, as a cheap substitute for silver, towards the end of the 18th century by Britannia metal.

3022 OMAN (CHARLES CHICHELE). English domestic silver. 1934. 6th edn. 1965.

See also Charles Heathcote Tatham, *Designs for ornamental plate*, etc., 1806; Gerald Taylor, *Silver*, Harmondsworth, 1956, 2nd edn., Harmondsworth, 1963, bibliog. 285–97; Patricia Wardle, *Victorian silver and silver-plate*, etc., 1963.

3023 JOHN (WILLIAM DAVID). Pontypool and Usk japanned wares. With the early history of the iron and tinplate industries at Pontypool. Newport, Mon. 1953.

3024 STORR. Paul Storr, the last of the goldsmiths; with a foreword by Charles Oman. By Norman Mosley Penzer. 1954.

3025 FINLAY (WILLIAM IAN ROBERTSON). Scottish gold and silver work. 1956.

3026 OMAN (CHARLES CHICHELE). English church plate, 597–1830. 1957.

Standard.

3027 BRADFORD (ERNLE DUSGATE SELBY). English Victorian jewellery. 1959. New edn. 1967.

Margaret Flower, *Victorian jewellery*, etc., 1951, is less technical and more concerned with changes in fashion.

E. MUSIC

1. BIBLIOGRAPHIES, CATALOGUES, DICTIONARIES, AND JOURNALS

3028 GROVE (*Sir* GEORGE). Dictionary of music and musicians. 4 v. 1879–89. 5th edn. rev. Eric Walter Blom. 9 v. 1954. Suppl. vol. to 5th edn. containing bibliogs. to 1959. 1961.

Standard.

3029 BRITISH MUSEUM. Catalogue of printed music published between 1487 and 1800 now in the British Museum. 2 v. (V. 1 and suppl.) 1912. 2nd suppl. by William C. Smith. 1940.

Accessions lists of music published both before and after 1800 have been issued annually since 1956. In addition the *British Catalogue of Music* (published under the auspices of the B.N.B.) has been published annually since 1957. See also *Handlist of music published in some British and foreign periodicals between 1787 and 1848, now in the British Museum* [by Unity Sherrington], 1962, Augustus Hughes-Hughes, *Catalogue of manuscript music in the British Museum*, 3 v., 1908–9, repr. 3 v., 1966, and William Barclay Squire, *Catalogue of the King's music library. British Museum*, 3 v., 1927–9, mostly of 18th-century works.

3030 THE MUSICAL QUARTERLY. N.Y. 1915+.

Index, 1915 thru 1959 by Herbert K. Goodkind, N.Y., 1960, has both author and subject indexes.

3031 BLUME (FRIEDRICH) *ed*. Die Musik in Geschichte und Gegenwart. Allgemeine Enzyklopädie der Musik. Cassel. 1949+. In progress.

12 v. have been published to date (1970): comprehensive and authoritative. For single-volume encyclopaedias see Percy Alfred Scholes, *The Oxford companion to music*, etc. 1938, 19th edn. 1970, rev. John Owen Ward, and Oscar Lee Thompson, *The international cyclopaedia of music and musicians*, 9th edn. rev. Robert Sabin, 1964.

3032 HUMPHRIES (CHARLES) *and* SMITH (WILLIAM C.). Music publishing in the British Isles from the earliest times to the middle of the nineteenth century; a dictionary of engravers, printers, publishers and music sellers, with an historical introduction. 1954.

For one of the best-known publishers see Novello and Co., *A century and a half in Soho*, etc. [1961].

3033 SCHNAPPER (EDITH B.) *ed*. The British union-catalogue of early music before the year 1801; a record of the holdings of over one hundred libraries throughout the British Isles. 2 v. 1957.

3034 BAKER (THEODORE). Baker's biographical dictionary of musicians. 5th edn. completely rev. by Nicolas Sloninsky. N.Y. 1958.

For minor British composers see James Duff Brown and Stephen Samuel Stratton, *British musical biography*, etc., Birmingham, 1897.

3035 KING (ALEXANDER HYATT). Some British collectors of music, c. 1601–1960. Camb. 1963.

2. CONTEMPORARY TREATISES

3036 KING (MATTHEW PETER). General treatise on music, particularly on harmony or thorough bass and its application in composition. 1800.

3037 SHIELD (WILLIAM). An introduction to harmony. 1800. 2nd edn. [1814?]

See also his *Rudiments of thorough bass for young harmonists . . . being an appendix to the Introduction to harmony* [1815?]

3038 CALLCOTT (JOHN WALL). A musical grammar. 1806. 3rd edn. 1817, another edn. 1883.

For long the standard elementary introduction. See also (3349).

3039 CROTCH (WILLIAM). Elements of musical composition, comprehending the rules of thorough bass, and the theory of tuning. 1812.

3040 DAY (ALFRED). A treatise on harmony. 1845. 2nd edn. with appendix by G. A. McFarren. 1885.

3. HISTORIES OF MUSIC

(a) *General*

3041 MAITLAND (JOHN ALEXANDER FULLER). English music in the nineteenth century. 1902.

3042 WALKER (ERNEST). A history of music in England. Oxf. 1907. 3rd edn. rev. and enl. by Sir Jack Allan Westrup. Oxf. 1952.

Bibliog. 403–14. Henry Davey, *History of English music*, 1895, 2nd edn. rewritten [1921], was long a standard work. More recent histories are Eric Walter Blom, *Music in England*, 1942, and Percy Marshall Young, *A history of British music*, 1967.

3043 OXFORD HISTORY OF MUSIC. V. 5. The Viennese period. By William Henry Hadow. 1931. V. 6. The Romantic period. By Edward Dannreuther. 1931.

(b) *Special Subjects*

3044 CAZALET (WILLIAM WAHAB). History of the Royal Academy of Music, compiled from authentic sources. 1854.

3045 CHAPPELL (WILLIAM). Popular music of the olden time. 2 v. 1855–9.

A pioneer study of English folk music. See also Margaret Dean-Smith, *A guide to English folk-song collections, 1822–1952, with an index to their contents, historical annotations and an introduction*, Liverpool, 1954. For Scottish folk music see Francis Collinson, *The traditional and national music of Scotland*, 1966.

3046 BARRETT (WILLIAM ALEXANDER). English glees and part songs; an inquiry into their historical development. 1886.

Also David Baptie, *Sketches of the English glee composers*, etc. [1896], short biographies *c.* 1735–1866.

3047 FOSTER (MYLES BIRKET). History of the Philharmonic Society of London. 1813–1912. 1912.

A substantial account, describing its connection with Beethoven.

3048 FELLOWES (EDMUND HORACE). English cathedral music from Edward VI to Edward VII. 1941. New edn. rev. Sir Jack Allan Westrup, 1969.

For a fierce attack on contemporary standards see Samuel Sebastian Wesley, *A few words on cathedral music and the musical system of the church, with a plan of reform*, 1849, repr. 1961. For biographical material see John Ebenezer West, *Cathedral organists past and present . . . of the cathedrals, chapels royal, and principal collegiate churches of the United Kingdom, from about the period of the Reformation until the present day*, 1899, and Myles Birket Foster, *Anthems and anthem composers*, 1901. For general histories see

John Skelton Bumpus, *A history of English cathedral music*, 2 v., 1908; Erik Reginald Routley, *The music of Christian hymnody*, 1957; Arthur James Brummell Hutchings, *Church music in the nineteenth century*, 1967. See also Kenneth H. MacDermott, *The old church gallery minstrels . . . 1660–1860*, 1948. For hymns see (922–5).

3049 RUSSELL (JOHN F.) *and* ELLIOT (J. H.). The brass band movement. 1936.

3050 LOEWENBERG (ALFRED). Annals of opera, 1597–1940. Camb. 1943. 2nd edn. rev. and corr. by Frank Walker. 2 v. Geneva. 1955.

Details and dates of productions.

3051 FARMER (HENRY GEORGE). A history of music in Scotland. 1947.

Standard, and concerned with music other than folk music.

3052 SHAW (HAROLD WATKINS). The Three Choirs Festival; the official history of the meetings of the Three Choirs of Gloucester, Hereford, and Worcester, c. 1713–1953. 1954.

Bibliog. note pp. x–xi lists earlier works on festival.

3053 MACKERNESS (ERIC DAVID). A social history of English music. 1964.

Relates music to social and industrial background.

4. BIOGRAPHIES AND MEMOIRS

For Smart see (2249).

3054 BALFE. Balfe, his life and work. By William Alexander Barrett. 1862.

3055 BERLIOZ. Berlioz in London. By A. W. Ganz. 1950.

3056 CHORLEY (HENRY FOTHERGILL). Thirty years' musical recollections. Ed. with intro. by Ernest Newman. 1926.

First pub. in 2 v., 1862. See also Chorley's *Autobiography, memoir and letters*, ed. Henry G. Hewlett, 2 v., 1873. Chorley was a music critic and both works contain much general gossip.

3057 HAYDN. The collected correspondence and London note books of Joseph Haydn. By Howard Chandler Robbins Landon. 1959.

3058 JULLIEN. The life of Jullien. By Adam von Ahn Carse. 1951.

Jullien was a conductor and concert promoter.

3059 LUMLEY (BENJAMIN). Reminiscences of the opera. 1864.

Lumley was for 20 years director of Her Majesty's Theatre.

3060 MENDELSSOHN. Felix Mendelssohn and his times. By Heinrich Eduard Jacob. Trans. Richard and Clara Winston. 1963.

See also Rosamund Brunel Gotch, *Mendelssohn and his friends in Kensington*, 1934.

3061 PHILLIPS (HENRY). Musical and personal recollections during half a century. 2 v. 1864.

Phillips was a celebrated singer.

3062 WESLEY. Samuel Wesley, musician; the story of his life. By James Thomas Lightwood. 1937.

See also Eliza Wesley, *Letters of Samuel Wesley to Mr. Jacobs . . . relating to the introduction into this country of the works of John Sebastian Bach*, 1875, covering the years 1808–16. For both Wesley and his son, Samuel Sebastian, see Erik Reginald Routley, *The musical Wesleys*, 1968, and S. S. Wesley (3048).

5. THE ORCHESTRA AND INSTRUMENTS

3063 MARCUSE (SIBYL). Musical instruments; a comprehensive dictionary. N.Y. 1964. L. 1966.

Bibliog. 603–8. See also Curt Sachs, *The history of musical instruments*, 1942, and Victoria and Albert Museum, *Catalogue of musical instruments*, 2 v., 1968 (v. 1, *Keyboard instruments* by Raymond Russell, and v. 2, *Non-keyboard instruments*, by Anthony Baines). Bibliogs.

3064 MORRIS (WILLIAM MEREDITH). British violin makers. A biographical dictionary of British makers of stringed instruments and bows and a critical description of their work. 2nd edn. 1920.

3065 JAMES (PHILIP BRUTTON). Early keyboard instruments from their beginnings to the year 1820. 1930.

3066 CARSE (ADAM VON AHN). The orchestra from Beethoven to Berlioz; a history of the orchestra in the first half of the 19th century, and of the development of orchestral baton conducting. Camb. 1948.

3067 BAINES (ANTHONY). Woodwind instruments and their history. 1957.

3068 CLUTTON (CECIL) *and* NILAND (WALTER AUSTIN JOHN). The British organ. 1963.

Bibliog. 305. See also Michael I. Wilson, *The English chamber organ: history and development 1650–1850*, Oxf., 1968.

3069 SUMNER (WILLIAM LESLIE). The pianoforte. 1966. 3rd edn. with corr. 1971.

Bibliog. 205–16. See also Rosamond Evelyn Mary Harding, *The pianoforte, its history traced to the Great Exhibition of 1851*, Camb., 1933, and Ernest Closson, *History of the piano*, trans. Delano Ames, 1947, bibliog. 137–48, by the director of the Musée du Conservatoire royal de Bruxelles, which houses a notable collection of keyboard instruments.

F. SCIENCE

Works on technological developments are listed under *Economic History*.

1. GENERAL

(a) *Bibliography and Periodicals*

3070 CATALOGUE of scientific papers, compiled by the Royal Society of London. Camb. 1867+.

1st ser., v. 1–6: *1800–1863*, 1867–72; 2nd ser., v. 7–8: *1864–1873*, 1877–9; 3rd ser., v. 9–11: *1874–1883*, 1891–6; v. 12: *suppl. 1800–1883*, 1902; 4th ser., vol. 13–19: *1884–1900*, 1914–25. *Subject index, 1800–1900* [ed. by T. Herbert McLeod], 4 v., Camb., 1908–14, covers mathematics, mechanics, and physics.

3071 ROYAL SOCIETY OF LONDON. Philosophical transactions. 1665+.

The Society has a valuable archive and library. For a list of the officers and members see *The record of the Royal Society of London*, rev. edn., 1940. Charles Richard Weld, *A history of the Royal Society*, 2 v., 1848, is comprehensive; see too Sir Henry George Lyons, *The Royal Society, 1660–1940*, Camb., 1944, and Dorothy Stimson, *Scientists and amateurs: a history of the Royal Society*, N.Y., 1948; and, for the leading personality of the time, Hector Charles Cameron, *Sir Joseph Banks, K.B., P.R.S., the autocrat of the philosophers*, 1952. On Banks's correspondence see (3082).

3072 YOUNG (THOMAS). A course of lectures on natural philosophy and the mechanical arts. 2 v. 1807. New edn. by P. Kelland. 1845.

Most of v. 2 is a critical catalogue of works on 'natural philosophy and the mechanical arts'; a useful summary of contemporary ideas on many questions of science.

3073 POGGENDORFF (JOHANN CHRISTIAN). Biographisch-literarisches Handwörterbuch zur Geschichte der exacten Wissenschaften. Bd. 1–6 in 10. Leipzig. 1863–1940. Fac. rep. Ann Arbor Mich. 10 v. 1945.

Bd. 1–2 include 60,000 titles up to 1857.

3074 SCIENCE MUSEUM, LONDON. Catalogue of the science library in the South Kensington museum. 1891. Supp. 1895.

See too *Classified list of bibliographies in the science library bibliographical series*, 1946; *A list of current periodicals on the history of science* [bibliog. ser. no. 721], 1953. Henry Carrington Bolton, comp., *A catalogue of scientific and technical periodicals* (1665 to 1895), 2nd edn., Wash., 1897, fuller than Samuel Hubbard Scudder, *Catalogue of scientific serials of all countries . . . 1633–1876*, Camb., Mass., 1879. See too D. McKie, 'The scientific periodicals from 1665 to 1798', *Philosophical Mag. Commemoration number* (1948), 122–132.

3075 SUBJECT LIST OF WORKS on general science, physics, sound, music, light, microscopy, and philosophical instruments, in the library of the Patent Office. 1903.

The Commrs. of patents for inventions pub., *Abridgements of specifications relating to optical, mathematical, and other philosophical instruments; including nautical, astronomical, and meteorological instruments, A.D. 1636–1866*, 1875.

3076 ISIS: international review devoted to the history of science and civilization. Bruges, Bern. 1913+.

See *Isis cumulative bibliography. A bibliography of the history of science formed from Isis
critical bibliographies 1–90, 1913–1965*, edited by Magda Whitrow, 1971, in progress.

3077 QUELLEN UND STUDIEN zur Geschichte der Mathematik, Astronomie und Physik. Berlin. 1930+.

Abt. A: *Quellen*, 1–4, 1930–6; Abt. B: *Studien*, 1–4, 1929–38.

3078 OSIRIS: Studies on the history and philosophy of science, and on the
history of learning and culture. Bruges. 15 v. 1936–68.

3079 ANNALS OF SCIENCE: A quarterly review of the history of science
since the renaissance. 1936+.

3080 BRITISH SOCIETY FOR THE HISTORY OF SCIENCE. Bulletin.
2 v. 1949–60.

Continued as *British journal for the history of science*, Keston, Kent, 1962+.

3081 SARTON (GEORGE). Horus: a guide to the history of science: a first
guide to the history of science with introductory essays on science and tradition.
Waltham, Mass. 1952.

François Russo, *Histoire des sciences et des techniques; bibliographie*, Paris, 1954; John
Leonard Thornton and R. I. J. Tully, *Scientific books, libraries, and collectors; a study
of bibliography and the book trade in relation to science*, 1954.

(b) *Sources*

3082 BANKS. The Banks letters. A calendar of the manuscript correspon-
dence of Sir Joseph Banks preserved in the British Museum, The British
Museum Natural History, and other collections in Great Britain. Edited by
Warren Royal Dawson. 1958.

Also supplements in the *Bulletin of the British Museum (Natural History)*, historical
series 3, no. 2 (1962), 41–70, no. 3 (1965), 71–93.

3083 BABBAGE (CHARLES). Reflections on the decline of science in England, and on some of its causes. 1830.

3084 HERSCHEL (*Sir* JOHN FREDERICK WILLIAM). A preliminary
discourse on the study of natural philosophy. 1830.

3085 WHEWELL (WILLIAM). History of the inductive sciences from the
earliest to the present time. 3 v. 1837. Rev. edn. 4 v. 1847–57.

Whewell also wrote, *The philosophy of the inductive sciences founded upon their history*,
2 v., 1840, rev. edn., 1847. There are lives of him with selected corr. by Isaac Todhunter,
1876, and Janet M. Douglas, 1882 (2316).

(c) *Later Works*

3086 MERZ (JOHN THEODORE). A history of European thought in the
nineteenth century. 4 v. 1896–1914.

V. 1–2 deal with science. A guide to discoveries is Ludwig Darmstaedter, *Handbuch zur*

Geschichte der Naturwissenschaften und der Technik, in chronologischen Darstellung, Berlin, 1908.

3087 SCHUSTER (ARTHUR) *and* SHIPLEY (ARTHUR E.). Britain's heritage of science. 1917.

Charles Singer, *A short history of science to the nineteenth century*, Oxf., 1949, places the period well in its context. For the end of the eighteenth century, see Abraham Wolf, *A history of science, technology, and philosophy in the eighteenth century*, 2nd edn. rev. by D. McKie, 1952.

3088 DAMPIER (*Sir* WILLIAM CECIL), *formerly* WHETHAM. A history of science and its relations with philosophy and religion. Camb. 4th edn. 1948.

3089 HOWARTH (OSBERT JOHN RADCLIFFE). The British Association for the advancement of science: a retrospect, 1831–1931. 1931.

Thomas Martin, *The Royal Institution*, 3rd edn., 1961. See also, on the Royal Dublin Society, (4149).

3090 CARDWELL (DONALD STEPHEN LOWELL). The organisation of science in England: a retrospect. Rev. edn. 1972.

3091 DEACON (MARGARET). Scientists and the sea, 1650–1900. A study of marine science. 1971.

2. MATHEMATICS

(a) *Bibliography*

3092 NEW YORK PUBLIC LIBRARY. List of works on the history of mathematics. *N.Y.P.L. Bull.* 7 (1903), 464–95.

Royal society, *Catalogue of scientific papers, 1800–1900*, subject index, v. 1: Pure mathematics, ed. by Herbert McLeod, Camb., 1908, includes 40,000 titles.

3093 BIBLIOTECA MATHEMATICA. Zeitschrift für Geschichte der mathematischen Wissenschaften. 30 v. in 28. Stockholm, 1884–9; Leipzig, 1900–15.

3094 MAY (KENNETH O.). Bibliography and research manual of the history of mathematics. Toronto. 1973.

See too N. G. Parke, *Guide to the literature of mathematics and physics*, 2nd rev. edn., 1959.

(b) *Sources*

3095 IVORY (*Sir* JAMES). 'On the attractions of homogeneous ellipsoids', *Phil. Trans.* 1809, 345–72.

Ivory was skilled in applying the infinitesimal calculus to physical investigations. See also his 'On the attractions of an extensive class of spheroids', *ibid.* 1812, 46–82, followed by a number of other papers during the ensuing thirty years.

3096 GREEN (GEORGE). Mathematical papers; with a brief memoir. Ed. by Norman MacLeod Ferrers. 1871.

3097   DE MORGAN (AUGUSTUS). Elements of arithmetic. 1830.

One of a number of important mathematical works which include, *Essays on probabilities*, 1838; *The differential and integral calculus*, 1842; *Formal logic*, 1847; *Trigonometry and double algebra*, 1849. Sophia Elizabeth de Morgan, *Memoir of Augustus de Morgan*, 1882, includes a list of his writings. [*De Morgan*] *On the syllogism and other logical writings*, ed. by Peter Heath, 1965, reprints his works with the exception of *Formal Logic*.

3098   PEACOCK (GEORGE). A treatise on algebra. Camb. 1830.

3099   SYLVESTER (JAMES JOSEPH). 'An analytical development of Fresnel's optical theory of crystals.' *Phil. Mag.* 3rd ser. 11 (2), 1837, 461–9, 537–41.

3100   BOOLE (GEORGE). 'Exposition of a general theory of linear transformations.' *Camb. Math. J.* 3 (1841–3), pt. 13, 1–20, pt. 15, 106–19.

Boole published numerous other papers in this journal before 1851 and also *The mathematical analysis of logic*, Camb., 1847.

3101   HAMILTON (*Sir* WILLIAM ROWAN). Lectures on quaternions. 1853.

Deals with studies begun in the 1840s. Hamilton's *Mathematical papers* were ed. by A. W. Conway and J. L. Synge, 2 v., Camb., 1931–40. See also R. F. Graves, *Life of Sir William Rowan Hamilton*, 3 v., 1882–9.

3102   SALMON (GEORGE). A treatise on conic sections. 1847.

The leading textbook of the subject for half a century.

3103   STOKES (*Sir* GEORGE GABRIEL). Mathematical and physical papers. 5 v. Camb. 1880–1905.

Sir J. Larmor, ed., *Memoir and Scientific correspondence of . . . Sir G. G. Stokes*, 2 v., Camb., 1907.

(c) *Histories*

3104   MACFARLANE (ALEXANDER). Lectures on ten British mathematicians of the nineteenth century. N.Y. 1916.

3105   MILLER (GEORGE ABRAM). Historical introduction to mathematical literature. N.Y. 1916.

3106   BELL (ERIC TEMPLE). The development of mathematics. N.Y. 1940.

See also David E. Smith, *History of mathematics*, 2 v., 1923.

3107   KLINE (MORRIS). Mathematical thought from ancient to modern times. N.Y. 1972.

3. MEDICINE

See also (2527–65)

(a) *Bibliography*

3108   INDEX-CATALOGUE of the library of the Surgeon-General's office. 16 v. Wash. 1880–95. 2nd ser. 21 v. 1896–1916. 3rd ser. 10 v. 1918–32. 4th ser. v. 1+, 1936 in progress.

3109 OSLER (*Sir* WILLIAM). Bibliotheca Osleriana. A catalogue of books illustrating the history of medicine and science, collected, arranged and annotated . . . and bequeathed to McGill university. Oxf. 1929.

3110 LE FANU (WILLIAM RICHARD). British periodicals of medicine: a chronological list. Baltimore. 1938.

3111 WELLCOME RESEARCH INSTITUTION, LONDON. A catalogue of printed books in the Wellcome Historical Medical Library. V. 1. 1962, in progress.

V. 2: *Books printed from 1641 to 1850, A–E*, 1966. The Library also pub., *Current work in the history of medicine*, 1954, in progress, quarterly. See also, *Catalogue of western manuscripts on medicine and science in the Wellcome historical library*, v. 2: *MSS. written after 1650*, 2 pts., 1973.

3112 MORTON (LESLIE THOMAS DENNIS). A medical bibliography: an annotated check-list of texts illustrating the history of medicine. 3rd edn. 1970.

Estelle Brodman, *The development of medical bibliography*, Washington, 1954, provides a comprehensive survey of medical bibliography since 1500.

3113 THORNTON (JOHN LEONARD) *and others, comps.* A select bibliography of medical biography. Library Assoc. bibliographies no. 3. 1961.

(b) *Sources*

3114 YOUNG (THOMAS). 'Observations on vision.' *Phil. Trans.* 1793, 169–81.

His paper 'On the mechanism of the eye', *ibid.* 1801, 23–88, included the first scientific description of astigmatism. See also (3190).

3115 BAILLIE (MATTHEW). The morbid anatomy of some of the most important parts of the human body. 1793.

Ten *fasciculi* of engravings in illustration of this work were pub. 1799–1803. The first systematic textbook of the subject. See too William Heberden, *Commentaries on the history and cure of diseases*, 2nd edn., 1803.

3116 WILLAN (ROBERT). On cutaneous diseases. V. 1. 1796–1808.

By a founder of modern dermatology; no more publ. His work was continued by Thomas Bateman in his *Delineations of cutaneous diseases*, 1817.

3117 JENNER (EDWARD). An enquiry into the causes and effects of the variolae vaccinae. 1798.

Announced the discovery of vaccination. See W. R. Le Fanu, *A bio-bibliography of Edward Jenner, 1749–1823*, 1951.

3118 DAVY (*Sir* HUMPHRY). Researches, chemical and philosophical, chiefly concerning nitrous oxide . . . and its respiration. 1800.

Further discussions of anaesthesia were by Henry Hill Hickman, *A letter on suspended animation*, Ironbridge, 1824; and by the leading gynaecologist, Sir James Young Simpson, 'Discovery of a new anaesthetic agent, more efficient than sulphuric ether' *Lond.*

Med. Gaz., n.s. v (1847), 934–7. Simpson was a pioneer in the use of chloroform. See Frederick F. Cartwright, *The English pioneers of anaesthesia: Beddoes, Davy, and Hickman*, Bristol, 1952.

3119 COLLES. Selections from the works of Abraham Colles, consisting chiefly of his practical observations on the venereal disease, and on the use of mercury. Ed. with annotations by Robert McDonnell. 1881.

3120 COOPER (*Sir* ASTLEY PASTON). The anatomy and surgical treatment of abdominal hernia. 2nd edn. 2 pts. 1827.

An outstanding contribution on this subject. He was also a pioneer in surgery of the ear and of the vascular system; Russell Claude Brock, *The life and work of Astley Cooper*, 1952.

3121 BELL (*Sir* CHARLES). A system of dissections, explaining the anatomy of the human body, the manner of displaying the parts, and their varieties in disease. With plates. 2 v. Edin. 1798–1803.

The most important British work in the field in the early nineteenth century. His other leading works include *A system of operative surgery*, 2 v. 1807–9; *Idea of a new anatomy of the brain* [1811]; *The nervous system of the human body*, 1830. His brother, John Bell, also eminent in the development of surgical anatomy, was part author with him of *Anatomy [of the human body]*, 4 v., 1793–1803, and *Principles of surgery*, 2 v., 1801, 4 v., 1826.

3122 BADHAM (CHARLES). Observations on the inflammatory affections of the mucous membrane of the bronchiae. 1808.

3123 BURNS (ALLAN). Observations on some of the most frequent and important diseases of the heart. Edin. 1809.

There is a biog. by J. B. Henrick, 1935. Also on the vascular system are Joseph Hodgson, *A treatise on the diseases of arteries and veins*, 1815; Thomas Hodgkin, 'On the retroversion of the valves of the aorta', *Lond. Med. Gaz.* 3 (1828–9), 433–43; Sir Dominic John Corrigan, 'On permanent patency of the mouth of the aorta, or inadequacy of the aortic valves', *Edin. Med. and Surg. J.* 37 (1832), 225–45; Andrew Buchanan, 'On the coagulation of blood and other fibriniferous liquids', *Lond. Med. Gaz.* n.s. 1 (1845), 617–21.

3124 PARKINSON (JAMES). An essay on the shaking palsy. 1817.

Convenient reprint in MacDonald Critchley, *James Parkinson, 1755–1824, A bicentenary volume of papers dealing with Parkinson's disease*, 1955.

3125 BRODIE (*Sir* BENJAMIN COLLINS). Pathological and surgical observations on diseases of the joints. 1818.

The most important work of a head of the profession in London who was a prolific contributor to medical journals. There is a biog. by Timothy Holmes, 1897.

3126 PARRY (CALEB HILLIER). Collections from the unpublished medical writings of . . . [C. H. Parry]. Ed. by Charles Henry Parry. 2 v. 1825.

3127 BRIGHT (RICHARD). Reports of medical cases selected with a view of illustrating the symptoms and cure of diseases by a reference to morbid anatomy. 2 v. in 3. 1827–31.

'Observations on jaundice', 'Observations on abdominal tumours', *Guy's Hosp. Rep.* 1 (1836), 604–37, 3 (1838), 401–60.

3128   HALL (MARSHALL). 'On the reflex functions of the medulla oblongata and medulla spinalis.' *Phil. Trans.* 1833, 635–65.

Charlotte Hall, *Memoirs of Marshall Hall*, 1861.

3129   STOKES (WILLIAM). A treatise on the diagnosis and treatment of diseases of the chest. Pt. i. Dublin. 1837.

No more publ. Sir William Stokes, *William Stokes, his life and work*, 1898.

3130   ADDISON (THOMAS) *and* MORGAN (JOHN). An essay on the operation of poisonous agents upon the living body. 1829.

The first book in English on this subject. See *A collection of the published writings of . . . T[homas] Addison* [New Sydenham soc.], 1868.

3131   COPLAND (JAMES). A dictionary of practical medicine. 3 v. 1834–59.

3132   TAYLOR (ALFRED SWAINE). Elements of medical jurisprudence. V. 1. 1836. 3rd edn. 1849.

No more publ.

3133   HODGKIN (THOMAS). Lectures on the morbid anatomy of the serous and mucous membranes. 2 v. 1836–40.

3134   WATSON (*Sir* THOMAS). Lectures on the principles and practices of physic. 2 v. 1843.

Robert James Graves, *A system of clinical medicine*, Dublin, 1843, was by one of the then leaders of the medical profession in Ireland.

3135   BOWMAN (*Sir* WILLIAM). Lectures on the parts concerned in the operations on the eye, and on the structure of the retina. 1849.

Bowman's *Collected Papers* were ed. by J. Burdon Sanderson and J. W. Hulke, 2 v., 1892.

(c) Later Works

3136   GARRISON (FIELDING HUDSON). An introduction to the history of medicine. Phil. & Lond. 1913. 4th edn. 1929.

The best reference work in English for biog. data and important discoveries. Johann Hermann Baas, *Grundriss der Geschichte der Medicin*, Stuttgart, 1876, English trans. by H. E. Handerson, N.Y., 1889, remains valuable for its continental treatment, though not always reliable. Sir William Osler, *The evolution of modern medicine*, New Haven, 1921, stresses the great discoveries. Douglas J. Guthrie, *A history of medicine*, 1945, rev. edn. with supp. 1958, includes a classified bibliog. See too C. Singer and E. A. Underwood, *A short history of medicine*, 2nd edn., Oxf., 1962.

3137   CHAPLIN (THOMAS HANCOCK ARNOLD). Medicine in England during the reign of George III. 1919.

3138   LAIGNEL-LAVASTINE (MAXIME). *ed.* Histoire générale de la médicine, de la pharmacie, de l'art dentaire et de l'art vétérinaire. 3 v. Paris. 1934–49.

Of particular value for its illustrations.

3139 BARRETT (CHARLES RAYMOND BOOTH). The history of the Society of Apothecaries of London. 1905.

3140 COMRIE (JOHN DIXON). History of Scottish medicine to 1860. 2nd edn. 2 v. 1932.

3141 LITTLE (ERNEST MUIRHEAD). History of the British Medical Association, 1832–1932. 1932.

For provincial societies see Sir D'Arcy Power, ed., *British medical societies*, 1939.

3142 FLEETWOOD (JOHN). History of medicine in Ireland. Dublin. 1951.

3143 GRAY (JAMES). History of the Royal Medical Society, 1737–1937. Ed. by Douglas J. Guthrie. Edin. 1952.

3144 NEWMAN (CHARLES). The evolution of medical education in the nineteenth century. 1957.

A study confined to the subject in England. Stephen Paget, *Memoirs and letters of Sir James Paget*, 8th imp. of 3rd edn., 1903, gives a good account of the life and training of a doctor in the early nineteenth century.

3145 BULLETIN OF THE HISTORY OF MEDICINE. Baltimore. 1933+.

The organ of the American Assoc. of the Hist. of Medicine and the Johns Hopkins Inst. of the Hist. of Medicine; includes articles on British social medicine, as does the *Journal of the history of medicine*, N.Y., 1946+.

3146 COPE ([VINCENT] ZACHARY). The Royal college of surgeons of England. A history. 1959.

See [V. G. Plarr], *Plarr's lives of the fellows of the Royal college of surgeons of England*, rev. by Sir D'Arcy Power, W. G. Spencer, and G. E. Cask, 2 v., Bristol, 1930.

3147 CLARK (*Sir* GEORGE). A history of the Royal college of physicians of London. 3 v. Oxf. 1964–72.

V. 2 covers the early nineteenth century. See William Munk, *The roll of the Royal college of physicians of London*, 2nd edn., rev. and enl., 4 v., 1878, continued in G. H. Brown, *Lives of the Fellows of the Royal college of physicians of London, 1826–1925*, 1955. Munk also wrote the biog. of the president of the college, 1820–44: *The life of Sir Henry Halford, Bt.*, 1895.

3148 CLARKE (EDWIN). *Ed.* Modern methods in the history of medicine. 1971.

A valuable examination of techniques of inquiry.

(d) *Dentistry*

3149 TOMES. Sir John Tomes: a pioneer of British dentistry. By V. Zachary Cope. 1961.

(e) *Veterinary Medicine*

3150 PUGH (LESLIE PENRHYS). From farriery to veterinary medicine, 1785–1795. Camb. 1962.

4. PSYCHOLOGY

See also *Lunacy* (2543–6).

(a) *Bibliography and General Works*

3151 HARVARD UNIVERSITY. Department of psychology and social relations. The Harvard list of books in psychology. Compiled and annotated by the psychologists in Harvard University. 3rd edn. Camb. Mass. 1964.

3152 BORING (EDWIN GARRIGUES). A history of experimental psychology. 1929. 2nd edn. N.Y. [1950.]

Other general histories are George Sidney Brett, *A history of psychology*, 3 v., 1912–21; Gardner Murphy, *An historical introduction to modern psychology*, 1929, rev. edn., N.Y., 1951; John Carl Flugel, *A hundred years of psychology, 1833–1933*, 1933, 3rd edn. rev. by D. J. West, 1964, bibliog. 359–74.

(b) *Special Subjects*

3153 COMBE (GEORGE). Essays on phrenology, or, An inquiry into the principles and utility of the system of Drs. Gall and Spurzheim and into the objections made against it. 1819.

See also *The Phrenological Journal*, 1823–47, and Charles Gibbon, *Life of George Combe, author of 'The constitution of man'*, 2 v., 1878.

3154 BRAMWELL (JOHN MILNE). Hypnotism, its history, practice, and theory. 1903. New edn. 1960.

Early studies of hypnotism, rejected by orthodox medical journals, were pub. in *The Zoist; a journal of cerebral physiology and mesmerism*, 1843–56. See also the pioneer study of James Braid, *Neurypnology, or, The rationale of nervous sleep, etc.*, new edn., with biog. notice of Braid, by Arthur Edward Waite, 1899; James Esdaile, *Mesmerism in India, and its practical application in surgery and medicine*, 1846.

3155 WARREN (HOWARD CROSBY). A history of the association psychology. 1921.

3156 ZILBOORG (GREGORY), *in collaboration with* George W. Henry. A history of medical psychology. N.Y. 1941.

5. ASTRONOMY

(a) *Bibliography*

3157 HOUZEAU (JEAN CHARLES) *and* LANCASTER (ALBERT BENOIT MARIE). Bibliographie générale de l'astronomie . . . jusqu'en 1880. 2 v. in 3. Bruxelles. 1882–9.

Over 42,000 titles, elaborately arranged chronologically by subject. V. 2 is a guide to periodicals. Royal Astronomical Society, *Catalogue of the library*, 1850, lists 2,500 titles; see also edn. by W. H. Wesley, 1886, and *Supplementary catalogue . . .*, 1900, 1926.

(b) *Sources*

See also Ivory (3095), Hamilton (3101).

3158 HERSCHEL (*Sir* WILLIAM). The scientific papers of Sir William Herschel . . . including early papers hitherto unpublished; collected and edited under the direction of a joint committee of the Royal Society and the Royal Astronomical Society. 2 v. 1912.

On his work and that of his sister, see Mrs. John Herschel, *Memoir and correspondence of Caroline Herschel*, 1876; Agnes M. Clerke, *The Herschels and modern astronomy*, 1895; Constance Anne (Herschel) Lubbock, ed., *The Herschel chronicle; the life-story of William Herschel and his sister Caroline Herschel*, Camb., 1933; J. B. Sidgwick, *William Herschel, explorer of the heavens*, 1953; Angus Armitage, *William Herschel*, 1962.

3159 CAVENDISH (HENRY). 'Experiments to determine the density of the earth.' *Phil. Trans.*, 1798, 469–526.

3160 WOLLASTON (WILLIAM HYDE). 'A method of examining refractive and dispersive powers by prismatic reflection.' *Phil. Trans.*, 1802, 365–80.

In all he published over fifty papers on pathology, physiology, chemistry, optics, mineralogy, crystallography, astronomy, electricity, mechanics, and botany.

3161 BRINKLEY (JOHN). Elements of astronomy. 1808. 6th edn. Dublin. 1845.

3162 GROOMBRIDGE (STEPHEN). A catalogue of circumpolar stars, reduced to Jan. 1, 1810. Ed. by G. B. Airy. 1838.

3163 PEARSON (WILLIAM). An introduction to practical astronomy . . . 2 v. 1824–9.

3164 BAILY (FRANCIS). Astronomical tables and formulae . . . 1827.

There is a *Memoir* of Baily, with notices of his writings, by Sir John Herschel, 1845.

3165 AIRY (*Sir* GEORGE BIDDELL). Gravitation: an elementary explanation of the principal perturbations in the solar system. 1834.

Airy's *Autobiography* with a list of his papers was ed. by W. Airy, Camb. 1896.

3166 BRITISH ASSOCIATION for the advancement of science. Catalogue of stars . . . reduced to Jan. 1, 1850. . . . [Superintended by F. Baily.] 1845.

3167 HERSCHEL (*Sir* JOHN FREDERICK WILLIAM). Results of astronomical observations made during the years 1834–8 at the Cape of Good Hope. 1847.

Herschel also pub. *Outlines of astronomy*, 1849.

3168 PARSONS (WILLIAM), *3rd earl of Rosse*. Scientific papers . . . collected and republished by C. A. Parsons, 1926.

3169 ADAMS (JOHN COUCH). Scientific papers. Ed. by W. G. Adams. 2 v.
Camb. 1896–1900.

See G. B. Airy, 'Account of some circumstances historically concerned with the discovery of the planet exterior to Uranus', *Monthly notices of the Royal Astronomical Soc.* 7
(1847), 121–52, 268–70.

(c) *Later Works*

3170 CLERKE (AGNES MARY). A popular history of astronomy during the
nineteenth century. 1885. 4th edn. 1902.

See too H. C. MacPherson, *A century's progress in astronomy*, Edinburgh, London,
1906; W. W. Bryant, *A history of astronomy*, 1907; E. W. Maunder, *The royal observatory, Greenwich*, 1900; J. L. E. Dreyer, and H. H. Turner, *History of the Royal Astronomical Society, 1820–1920*, 1923.

3171 KING (HENRY CHARLES). The history of the telescope. 1955.

6. GEOLOGY

(a) *Bibliography*

See also H. B. Woodward (3186).

3172 MARGERIE (EMMANUEL DE). Catalogue des bibliographies géo-
logiques. Paris. 1896.

Edward Bennett Mathews comp. a supplement, *Catalogue of published bibliographies in
geology*, 1896–1920, Wash., 1923. See too Louis Jean Rodolphe Agassiz, *Bibliographia
zoologiae et geologiae* . . . cor., enl. and ed. by H. E. Strickland, 4 v., 1848–54; Henry
White and Thomas W. Newton, *A catalogue of the library of the Museum of practical
geology and geological survey*, 1878; British Museum, *Catalogue of the books in the
department of mineralogy*, 1881. Catalogues of the library of the Geological Society of
London were pub. in 1846 with supplements 1856, 1860, 1863 (subject arrangement),
and 1881 (alph. list of authors). See too John Challinor, *The history of British geology.
A bibliographical study*, Newton Abbot, 1971.

(b) *Sources*

3173 HUTTON (JAMES). The theory of the earth, or, an investigation of the
laws observable in the composition, dissolution and restoration of land upon
the globe. Rev. edn. 2 v. 1795.

Part of a third volume, edited by Sir A. Geikie, was first publ. in 1899: the foundation
work of modern geology. On Hutton see V. A. Eyles in *Proc. Roy. Soc. Edin.*, 63 B
(1950), 377–86. His ideas were developed and popularized by John Playfair; see Playfair's *Works, with a memoir of the author*, ed. by James G. Playfair, 4 v., Edin., 1822.
Among Hutton's chief early critics were John Williams (*Natural history of the mineral
kingdom*, 2 v., Edin., 1789) and Richard Kirwan (*Geological essays*, 1799). See Sir Edward
Battersby Bailey, *James Hutton—the founder of modern geology*, 1967; *James Hutton's
System of the earth* . . ., with an introd. by V. A. Eyles (Contributions to the history of
geology, ed. by George W. White, v. 5), Darien, Conn., 1970.

3174 JAMESON (ROBERT). System of mineralogy. . . . 3 v. Edin. 1804–8.
3rd enl. edn. 3 v. 1820.

His later works included *Manual of mineralogy*, 1821. See L. Jameson, 'Biographical memoir of the late Prof. Robert Jameson', *Edin. New. Phil. J.* 57 (1854), 1–49. He supported the views of Werner. These were attacked by, among others, the experimentalist, Sir James Hall; see his papers in *Trans. Roy. Soc. Edin.* for 1805, 1812, 1826.

3175 SMITH (WILLIAM). A geological map of England and Wales. . . . 1815.

The founder of modern stratigraphical geology; also wrote *Strata identified by organized fossils*, 1816, and *Stratigraphical system of organized fossils*, 1817. See T. Sheppard, 'William Smith, his maps and memoirs', *Proc. Yorks Geol. Soc.* 19 (1917), 75–253; also separate imprint, 1920.

3176 MACCULLOCH (JOHN). A description of the Western Isles of Scotland. . . . 3 v. 1819.

Followed by his *The Highlands and Western Islands of Scotland*, 4 v., 1824, which was strongly attacked in James Browne, *A critical examination of Dr. Macculloch's work on the Highlands*, etc., Edin., 1825, 2nd edn., Edin., 1826. See V. A. Eyles, 'John Macculloch, F.R.S., and his geological map: an account of the first geological survey of Scotland', *Annals of Science* 2 (1937), 114–29.

3177 SEDGWICK (ADAM). 'On the physical structure of those formations which are immediately associated with the primitive ridge of Devonshire and Cornwall.' *Trans. Camb. Phil. Soc.* 1 (1819), 89–146.

John Willis Clark and Thomas McKenny Hughes, *Life and letters of Adam Sedgwick*, 2 v., Camb., 1890, gives, pp. 591–604, a list of his writings.

3178 BUCKLAND (WILLIAM). Reliquiae diluvianae, or, Observations on the organic remains contained in caves, fissures, and diluvial gravel, attesting the action of a universal deluge. 1823.

Buckland later maintained his thesis in *Geology and mineralogy considered with reference to natural theology*, 2 v., 1836. There is a *Life and correspondence*, by his da., Elizabeth O. Gordon, 1894. See his papers in Geological Society *Transactions, passim*.

3179 GEOLOGICAL SOCIETY OF LONDON. Transactions. 1811–45.

The *Transactions* were succeeded by the *Quarterly Journal*, 1845+. George Wareing Ormerod comp., *A classified index to the transactions, proceedings, and quarterly journal of the . . . society*, 2nd edn. 1870, supplement, 1876.

3180 LONSDALE (WILLIAM). 'On the oolitic district of Bath.' *Trans. Geol. Soc.* 2nd ser., 3, pt. ii (1832), 241–76.

Also, 'On the age of limestones of South Devonshire', *Trans. Geol. Soc.*, 2nd ser., 5, pt. iii (1840), 721–38.

3181 LYELL (*Sir* CHARLES). Principles of geology. 1 v. 1830–33.

This work demolished Mosaic theories of cosmology. It was supplemented by *Elements of geology*, 1838. Katharine M. Lyell, *Life and letters and journals of Sir Charles Lyell*, 2 v., 1881. Sir Edward B. Bailey, *Charles Lyell*, 1962. Leonard G. Wilson, ed., *Sir Charles Lyell's scientific journals on the species question*, 1970, and see his *Charles Lyell. The years to 1841: the revolution in geology*, 1973.

3182 MURCHISON. The life of Sir Roderick Impey Murchison. By Sir Archibald Geikie. 2 v. 1875.

Includes a list of his writings (vol. 2, 353–67). He was secretary and then president of the Geological Society, to the *Transactions* of which he was a prolific contributor.

3183   DARWIN (CHARLES [ROBERT]). Geology of the voyage of the Beagle.
. . . 3 pts. 1842–6.

Pt. 1: *The structure and distribution of coral reefs* (an outstanding contribution to the
subject); pt. 2: *Geological observations on the volcanic islands*; pt. 3: *Geological observation
on South America.*

3184   OWEN (*Sir* RICHARD). A history of British fossil mammals and birds.
1846.

He also wrote *A history of British fossil reptiles,* 4 v., 1849–84.

3185   FORBES. Life and letters of J[ames] D[avid] Forbes. By John Campbell
Shairp, P. J. Tait, and A. A. Reilly. 1873.

On the career of a leading investigator into glaciation; see too J. Tyndall, *Professor
Forbes and his biographers,* 1873. Forbes collected his articles in *Occasional papers on the
theory of glaciers,* Edin., 1859.

(c) *Later Works*

3186   ZITTEL (KARL ALFRED VON). History of geology and palaeontology
to the end of the nineteenth century; trans. by M. M. Ogilvie-Gordon. 1901.

Horace B. Woodward, *History of geology,* 1911, is a brief survey. Sir Archibald Geikie,
The founders of geology, 2nd edn., 1905, is valuable; see also H. B. Woodward, *The
history of the Geological Society of London,* 1908; Sir John Flett, *The first hundred years
of the Geological Survey of Great Britain,* 1937. Influence on contemporary thought is
discussed in Charles Coulston Gillispie, *Genesis and geology: a study in the relation of
scientific thought, natural theology, and scientific opinion in Great Britain (1790–1850),*
Camb. Mass., 1951, bibliog. 231–58.

3187   CHORLEY (RICHARD J.), DUNN (ANTHONY J.), *and* BECKIN-
SALE (ROBERT P.). The history of the study of landforms, or the development of geomorphology. V. 1: Geomorphology before Davis. 1964.

Full treatment on the nineteenth century up to the 1880s; full section bibliographies.

7. PHYSICS

(a) *Bibliography*

3188   SUBJECT LIST of works on general physics (including measuring, cal-
culating and mathematical instruments, and meteorology) in the library of the
Patent Office. 1914.

Herbert MacLeod ed. for the Royal Soc., a *Catalogue of scientific papers, 1880–1900;
subject index, vol. 3, physics,* 2 v., Camb., 1912–14. Sir Francis Ronalds, comp., *Catalogue
of books relating to electricity, magnetism, and the electric telegraph . . .,* ed. by Alfred
James Frost, 1881. See too Paul Fleury Mottelay, *Bibliographical history of electricity
and magnetism, chronologically arranged,* 1922, covering work in this field up to 1822.
See Parke (3094).

(b) *Sources*

3189   CAVENDISH (HENRY). The scientific papers of . . . Cavendish. Ed.
by J. C. Maxwell and Sir Edward Thorpe with contributions by Sir Joseph
Larmor and Charles Chree. 2 v. Camb. 1921.

Arthur J. Berry, *Henry Cavendish. His life and scientific work,* 1960.

3190 YOUNG (THOMAS). 'On the theory of light and colours.' *Phil. Trans.* (1802), 12–48.

One of several papers on light and optics. See also (3114). See Herbert Spencer Robinson, 'Thomas Young: a chronology and a bibliography, with estimates of his work and character', *Med. life* 36 (1929), 527–40; Frank Oldham, *Thomas Young*, 1933.

3191 DALTON (JOHN). 'Extraordinary facts relating to the vision of colours.' *Mem. Lit. and Phil Soc. Manchester*, 5 (1798), pt. 1, 28–45.

3192 THOMPSON (BENJAMIN), *Count Rumford.* 'An enquiry concerning the nature of heat, and the mode of its communication.' *Phil. Trans.* (1804), 77–182.

See his *Complete Works*, 5 v., 1870–5.

3193 DALTON (JOHN). The theory of chemical proportions and chemical action of electricity. 1814.

On Dalton see also (3210).

3194 LESLIE (*Sir* JOHN). An experimental inquiry into the nature and propagation of heat. 1804.

3195 DANIELL (JOHN FREDERIC). 'On a new register-pyrometer, for measuring the expansion of solids, and determining the higher degrees of temperature upon the common thermometric scale.' *Phil. Trans.* (1830), 257–86.

3196 BREWSTER (*Sir* DAVID). A treatise on optics. 1831.

See too his *A Treatise on magnetism* forming the articles under that head in the 7th edition of the *Encyclopaedia Britannica*, Edin. 1837.

3197 FORBES (JAMES DAVID). 'Researches on the conducting power of the metals for heat and electricity.' Roy. Soc. of Edinburgh, *Transactions*, v. 1. 1845.

See the index for other short articles in this volume, *passim*, reporting his studies on heat. For his life see (3185).

3198 FARADAY (MICHAEL). Experimental researches in electricity. Reprinted from the Philosophical Transactions of 1831–52, with other electrical papers from the proceedings of the Royal Institution, the Quarterly Journal of Science, and the Philosophical Magazine. 3 v. 1839–55.

Thomas Martin, ed., *Faraday's diary*, 8 v., 1932–6. Georg W. A. Kahbaum and Francis V. Darbishire, eds., *The letters of Faraday and Schoenbein, 1836–1864*, 1899. L. Pearce Williams, ed., *The selected correspondence of Michael Faraday*, 2 v., Camb., 1971. J. Tyndall, *Faraday as a discoverer*, 1868, includes personal recollections. Henry Bence-Jones, *Life and letters of Faraday*, 2 v., 1870. Silvanus Phillips Thompson, *Faraday, his life and work*, 1898. Recent studies include Thomas Martin, *Faraday's discovery of electromagnetic induction*, 1949; James Kendall, *Michael Faraday, man of simplicity*, 1955; Leslie P. Williams, *Michael Faraday, a biography*, 1965. A. E. Jeffreys comp., *Michael Faraday. A list of his lectures and published writings*, 1960.

3199   GROVE (*Sir* WILLIAM ROBERT). 'On the gas voltaic battery. Voltaic action of phosphorous, sulphur and hydrocarbons.' *Phil. trans.* (1845), 351–61.

A number of his minor works are collected in the 6th edn. of his *The correlation of physical forces*, 1874.

3200   THOMSON (WILLIAM), *1st baron Kelvin*. 'On an absolute thermometric scale founded on Carnot's theory of the motive power of heat, and calculated from Regnault's observations.' *Proc. Camb. Phil. Soc.* 1, no. 5 (1848), 66–71.

He also publ. papers on the dynamical theory of heat in *Proc. Roy. Soc. Edin.* v. 3 (1851), *passim*, and *Phil. Mag.* 4th ser. 4 (1852), 8–21, 105–17, 168–76. Sir Joseph Larmor arranged his collected *Mathematical and physical papers*, 6 v., Camb., 1882–1911. Life by Arthur P. Young, 1948; D. K. C. MacDonald, *Faraday, Maxwell, and Kelvin*, 1965.

3201   STOKES (*Sir* GEORGE GABRIEL). The dynamical theory of diffraction. 1849.

See his *Mathematical and physical papers*, 5 v., Camb., 1880–1905. Sir Joseph Larmor, ed., *Memoir and scientific correspondence of* [*Sir G. G.*] *Stokes*, 2 v., Camb., 1907.

3202   JOULE (JAMES PRESCOTT). Scientific papers. 2 v. 1884–7.

Alex. Wood, *Joule and the study of energy*, 1925.

(c) *Later Works*

3203   CAJORI (FLORIAN). A history of physics in its elementary branches, including the evolution of physical laboratories. N.Y. 1899. Rev. edn. 1929.

3204   WHITTAKER (*Sir* EDMUND TAYLOR). History of the theories of aether and electricity. 1910. New edn. v. 1. 1951.

3205   CREW (HENRY). The rise of modern physics. 2nd edn. Balt. 1935.

3206   CROWTHER (JAMES GERALD). British scientists of the nineteenth century. 1935.

Studies of Davy, Faraday, Joule, Thomson. See also Alex. MacFarlane, *Lectures on ten British physicists of the nineteenth century*, N.Y., 1919; D. M. Turner, *Makers of science. Electricity and magnetism*, 1927. W. Wilson, *A hundred years of physics*, 1950, deals with developments since the beginning of Victoria's reign.

8. CHEMISTRY

(a) *Bibliography*

3207   BOLTON (HENRY CARRINGTON). A select bibliography of chemistry, 1492–1892. Wash. 1893.

1st supp. 1899, 2nd supp. 1904, list of dissertations, 1901 [Smithsonian Miscellaneous Collections, v. 36, 39, 41, 44]. See too *Subject list of the works on chemistry (including alchemy, electro-chemistry and radioactivity) in the library of the Patent Office*, 1911; John Ferguson, ed. *Bibliotheca chemica*, 2 v., Glasgow, 1906; *Catalogue of the library of the Chemical Society of London*, 1903.

(b) *Sources*

See also Maxwell, *Cavendish* (3189), Faraday (3198).

3208 PRIESTLEY (JOSEPH). Scientific correspondence; ed. with notes by Henry Carrington Bolton. N.Y. 1892.

John F. Fulton and Charlotte H. Peters, *Works of Joseph Priestley, 1733–1804; preliminary short title list*, New Haven, 1937; J. A. Passmore, ed., *Priestley's writings on philosophy, science, and politics*, 1965; R. E. Schofield, ed., *A scientific autobiography of Joseph Priestley, 1733–1804. Selected scientific correspondence* [1966].

3209 NICHOLSON (WILLIAM). A dictionary of chemistry.... 2 v. 1795.

Also, *Dictionary of practical and theoretical chemistry*, 1808. He edited (and contributed to) the *Journal of Natural philosophy, Chemistry and the Arts*, 5 v., 1797–1802, n.s. 36 vols., 1802–[1813].

3210 DALTON (JOHN), WOLLASTON (WILLIAM HYDE), and THOMSON (THOMAS). Foundations of the atomic theory: comprising papers and extracts by John Dalton, William Hyde Wollaston, ... and Thomson (1802–1808). Alembic club reprints no. 2. Edin. 1899.

Dalton's works include over 100 papers in the *Memoirs of the Literary and Philosophical Soc. of Manchester*. A. L. Smyth comp., *John Dalton, 1766–1844. A bibliography of works by and about him*, Manch., 1966. The main work in which his theories were systematically expounded was *A new system of chemical philosophy*, 2 v., 1808–27. On him see Robert Angus Smith, *Memoir of John Dalton; a history of the atomic theory up to his time*, 1856, with a list of his pubs., pp. 253–63; J. P. Millington, *John Dalton*, N.Y., 1906; E. M. Brockbank, *John Dalton: some unpublished letters....* Manch., 1944; Frank Greenaway, *John Dalton and the atom*, 1966; D. S. L. Cardwell, *John Dalton and the progress of science*, Manch. 1968; Elizabeth C. Patterson, *John Dalton and the atomic theory*, N.Y., 1970. Wollaston's outstanding contribution was his paper, 'A synoptic scale of chemical equivalents', *Phil. Trans.* (1814), 1–22. Thomas Thomson, *A system of chemistry*, 4 v., Edin., 1802, incorporated Dalton's theory in the 3rd edn. (5 v., 1807); on Thomson see Herbert S. Klickstein, 'Thomas Thomson: pioneer historian of chemistry', *Chymia*, 1 (1948), 37–53, with a bibliog. of his chief pubs. on the history of chemistry, mainly in *Annals of Philosophy*, and J. R. Partington, 'Thomas Thomson, 1773–1852', *Annals of Science*, 6 (1948–50), 115–26. For background, and controversy, about atomic theory see William Higgins, *A comparative view of the phlogistic and antiphlogistic theories*, 2nd edn., 1791, and his *Experiments and observations on the atomic theory and electrical phenomena*, Dublin, 1814, reprinted in T. S. Wheeler, and J. R. Partington, *The life and work of William Higgins, Chemist (1763–1825)*, 1960.

3211 [PROUT (WILLIAM)]. 'On the relation between the specific gravities of bodies in their gaseous state and the weights of their atoms'. *Annals of Phil.* 6 (1815), 321–30.

3212 TURNER (EDWARD). Elements of chemistry.... 1827.

3213 DANIELL (JOHN FREDERIC). An introduction to the study of chemical philosophy. 1839.

3214 DAVY (*Sir* HUMPHRY). Collected works; ed. by John Davy, with a life. 9 v. 1839–40.

Joshua C. Gregory, *The scientific achievements of Sir Humphry Davy*, 1930; Anne

Treneer, *The mercurial chemist. A life of Sir Humphry Davy*, 1963; Sir Harold B. Hartley, *Humphry Davy*, [1966]. June Z. Fullmer, *Sir Humphrey Davy's published works*, 1970, is a full annotated bibliography.

3215   FOWNES (GEORGE). Manual of elementary chemistry, theoretical and practical. 1844.

He also wrote *Chemical tables*, 1846, and *Introduction to qualitative analysis*, 1846.

3216   WILLIAMSON (ALEXANDER WILLIAM). 'Theory of aetherification'. *Lond. Edin. and Dublin Phil. mag. and journ. of sciences*, 37, (1850), 350–6.

G. C. Foster, 'Alexander William Williamson', *J. Chem. Soc.* 87 (1905), 605–18.

3217   GRAHAM (THOMAS). Chemical and physical researches . . . with preface and analytical contents by Robert Angus Smith. Edin. 1876.

See too R. A. Smith, *The life and work of Thomas Graham*, Glasgow, 1884.

3218   FRANKLAND (*Sir* EDWARD). Experimental researches in pure, applied and physical chemistry. 1877.

(c) *Later Works*

3219   PARTINGTON (JAMES RIDDICK). A history of chemistry, 4 v. 1961–4. v. 4: 1800 to the present.

See also D. P. Mellor, *The evolution of the atomic theory*, 1971.

3220   CHYMIA. Annual studies in the history of chemistry. v. 1+. Phil. 1948+.

3221   CROSLAND (MAURICE PIERRE). Historical studies in the language of chemistry. 1962.

Useful guidance on symbols and terminology.

3222   WEEKS (MARY ELVIRA). Discovery of the elements. 7th edn. completely revised and new material added, by Henry M. Leicester. Easton, Pa. 1968.

Useful chronological list of discoveries; attention given to minor researchers; valuable chapter bibliographies.

9. BIOLOGY

(a) *Bibliography*

See also Agassiz (3172).

3223   BRITISH MUSEUM (Natural History). Catalogue of the books, manuscripts, maps and drawings. Comp. by Bernard Barham Woodward. 5 v. 1903–15.

90,000 titles. A series of suppl. have been published since 1922. The only completed volume of Wilhelm Engelmann, *Bibliotheca historico-naturalis*, Leipzig, 1846, deals with works on anatomy and physiology produced between 1700 and 1846 in most European countries and in Britain. Casey Albert Wood, *An introduction to the literature of verte-brate zoology*, Montreal, 1931, is based mainly on the various libraries of McGill University. There are various specialist bibliographies in the *Journal* of the Society for the bibliography of natural history, 1936+.

3224 LINNEAN SOCIETY of London. Catalogue of the printed books and pamphlets in the library. . . . New edn. 1925.

See too *Catalogue of the manuscripts in the library of the Linnean Society*, v. 1, 1934, in progress.

3225 DEAN (BASHFORD). Bibliography of fishes. Enl. and ed. by C. R. Eastman. N.Y. 3 v. 1916–23.

3226 MULLENS (WILLIAM HERBERT) and SWANN (HARRY KIRKE). A bibliography of British ornithology from the earliest times to the end of 1912, including biographical accounts of the principal writers and bibliographies of their published works. 1917.

Mullens and Swann, with F. C. R. Jourdain, also comp., *A geographical bibliography of British ornithology*, 6 pts., 1919–20. See too Reuben Myron Strong, *A bibliography of birds*, 3 v., Chicago, 1939–46.

(b) *Sources*

3227 LINNEAN SOCIETY OF LONDON. Transactions. V. 1+. 1791+.

Also *Proceedings*, v. 1+, 1849+. *The Journal of the proceedings of the Linnean Society: zoology, botany*, v. 1–8, 1857–65, was continued in two series for *zoology* and for *botany*, v. 9+, 1867+; now respectively *The Zoological J.* and *The Botanical J. of the Linnean Society*, 1969+. See too *Memoirs* of the Wernerian Natural History Soc., 8 v., Edin., 1811–39; *Proceedings*, of the Zoological Soc. of London, 1831+; Roy. Entomological Soc. of London, *Transactions*, 1834+, *Journal of proceedings*, 10 v., 1841–6.

3228 DARWIN (ERASMUS). Zoonomia; or the laws of organic life. 2 v. 1794–6.

Ernst Krause, *Erasmus Darwin*, tr. by W. S. Dallas, 1879, is a good discussion of Darwin's theory of evolution. Hesketh Pearson, *Doctor Darwin*, Toronto, 1930; D. G. King-Hele, *Erasmus Darwin*, 1963, and *The essential writings of Erasmus Darwin*, 1968.

3229 BROWN (ROBERT). Prodromus florae novae Hollandiae et Insulae Van Diemen. 1810.

His discovery of the cell nucleus was reported in his 'Observations on the organs and mode of fecundation in Orchidaceae and Asclepiadaceae', *Trans. Linn. Soc. 1829–32*, 16 (1832), 685–746.

3230 MAGAZINE OF NATURAL HISTORY and journal of zoology, botany, mineralogy, geology, and meteorology. V. 1–9, n.s. 1–4, 1828–40.

Then merged with the *Companion to the Botanical Magazine* as the *Annals and Magazine of Natural History*, 1841+.

3231 OWEN (*Sir* RICHARD). Memoir on the pearly nautilus. 1832.

His pubs. incl. *Descriptive and illustrated catalogue of the physiological series of comparative anatomy contained in the museum of the Royal College of Surgeons*, 5 v. in 6, 1833–40;

Odontography, 2 v. and atlas, 1840–45; *On the archetype and homologies of the vertebrate skeleton*, 1848; *On the nature of limbs*, 1849. Richard Startin Owen, *Life of Sir Richard Owen*, 2 v., 1894, rev. edn., 1970.

3232 GOULD (JOHN). The birds of Europe. 5 v. 1832–37.

Richard Bowdler Sharpe, comp., *An analytical index to the works of the late John Gould, F.R.S.*, 1893, including a biographical memoir.

3233 DARWIN (CHARLES [ROBERT]). ed. Zoology of the voyage of H.M.S. Beagle. 5 pts. 1839–43.

Other accounts of scientific expeditions include, Philip Parker King, *Narrative of a survey of the intertropical and western coasts of Australia . . . between . . . 1818 and 1822*, 2 v. in 8, 1827; John Richardson, John E. Gray, and others, *Zoology of Captain Beechey's voyage . . . in H.M.S. Blossom, in the years 1825 . . . 1828*, 1830–39; *Zoology of the voyage of H.M.SS. Erebus and Terror . . . during . . . 1839–43*, 2 v., 1844–75; *The zoology of the voyage of H.M.S. Samarang*, 1848–9; *Zoology and botany of the voyage of H.M.S. Sulphur*, 1844. See *List of the books, memoirs, and miscellaneous papers, by J. E. G[ray]*, with a prefatory note by J. Saunders, priv. printed, 1872.

3234 DARWIN (CHARLES [ROBERT]). The foundations of the origin of species : two essays written in 1842 and 1844 by Charles Darwin; ed. by his son, Francis Darwin. Camb. 1909.

Nora Barlow, ed., *Charles Darwin's diary of the voyage of H.M.S. Beagle*, Camb., 1933; Francis Darwin, ed., *The life and letters of Charles Darwin, including an autobiographical chapter*, 3 v., 1887, and, with A. C. Seward, *More letters of Charles Darwin*, 2 v., 1903; Nora Barlow, ed., *Darwin and Henslow. The growth of an idea. Letters 1831–1860*, 1967. See Peter R. Bell, *Darwin and biological work: some aspects reconsidered*, Camb., 1959; Sir Gavin R. De Beer, *Charles Darwin and A. R. Wallace. Evolution by natural selection*, 1963; R. B. Freeman, *The works of Charles Darwin. An annotated bibliographical handlist*, 1965.

3235 FORBES (EDWARD). A history of British star-fishes, sea urchins and other animals of the class echinodermata. 1841.

George Wilson and Arch. Geikie, *Memoir of Edward Forbes, F.R.S.*, 1861, incl. a list of his writings, pp. 575–83.

3236 CHAMBERS (ROBERT). Vestiges of the natural history of creation. 2 v. 1844. Repr. with introd. by Gavin de Beer. Leicester. 1969

An outspoken and eccentric statement of a belief in evolution, which anticipated Darwin's *Origin of Species* by 16 years.

3237 HUXLEY (THOMAS HENRY). 'On the anatomy and affinities of the family of medusae'. *Phil. Trans.* (1849), 413–34.

Leonard Huxley, *The life and letters of T. H. Huxley*, 2 v., 1900, incl. a full list of his published works. Cyril Bibby, *Scientist extraordinary*, Oxf., 1972.

(c) *Later Works*

3238 SINGER (CHARLES JOSEPH). A history of biology. A general introduction to the study of living things. 2nd edn. 1950.

Henry Alleyne Nicholson, *Natural history, its rise and progress in Britain as developed in the life and labours of leading naturalists*, 1886.

3239 MITCHELL (PETER CHALMERS). Centenary history of the zoological society of London, 1929.

3240 GAGE (ANDREW THOMAS). History of the Linnean Society of London, 1938.

3241 ROOK (ARTHUR) ed. The origins and growth of biology. 1958.

See also Jane M. Oppenheimer, *Essays in the history of embryology and biology*, 1967.

(d) *Microscopy*

3242 LISTER (JOSEPH JACKSON). 'On some properties in achromatic object-glasses applicable to the improvement of the microscope'. *Phil. Trans.* (1830), 187–200.

See Alfred N. Disney, Cyril F. Hill and Wilfred E. W. Baker, *Origin and development of the microscope*, 1928; Reginald S. Clay and Thomas H. Court, *History of the microscope . . . up to the introduction of the achromatic microscope*, 1932. Quekett Microscopical Club library *Catalogue*, 1929, incl. 3,550 titles.

10. BOTANY

(a) *Bibliography*

3243 SCIENCE MUSEUM OF LONDON, Library. Bibliographies on pure and applied botany and related subjects (bibliog. ser. no. 144). 1932.

Catalogue of the library of the Royal Botanic Gardens, Kew [comp. Benj. Daydon Jackson], 1899, supp. 1919; Alfred Rehder, *The Bradley bibliography: a guide to the literature of the woody plants of the world published before the beginning of the twentieth century*, 5 v., Camb., Mass., 1911–18; H. R. Hutchinson, ed. for the Royal Horticultural Soc., *The Lindley library: catalogue of books, pamphlets, manuscripts and drawings*, 1927; there are suppl. in the society's *Journal*.

3244 NISSEN (CLAUS). Die botanische Buchillustration. Ihre Geschichte und Bibliographie. 2 v. Stuttgart. 1951–[1952].

(b) *Sources*

See Royal Society (3071), Linnean Society (3224), Brown (3229), Darwin (3234).

3245 THE BOTANICAL MAGAZINE or flower garden displayed. V. 1+. 1787+.

Title *Curtis's Botanical Magazine*, 1801+. On its first editor see W. Hugh Curtis, *William Curtis, 1746–1799*, Winchester, 1941.

3246 WOODVILLE (WILLIAM). Medical botany, containing . . . descriptions, with plates, of all the medicinal plants . . . comprehended in the catalogues of the materia medica. . . . 3 v. and supp. 1790–4.

3247 SOWERBY (JAMES) *and* SMITH (*Sir* JAMES EDWARD). English botany. 37 v. 1790–1814.

Smith was the founder of the Linnean Soc.; other valuable works by him are: *Flora Britannica*, 3 v., 1800–4; *Introduction to physiological and systematic botany*, 1807 (numerous later edns.); *English flora*, 4 v., 1824–8. Pleasance Smith, *Memoir and corre-spondence of . . . Smith*, 2 v., 1832.

3248 INGENHOUSZ (JAN). An essay on the food of plants and the renovation of soils. 1796.

The discoverer of photo-synthesis. See Howard S. Reed, 'Jan Ingenhousz, plant physiologist . . .', *Chronica Botanica*, 2 (1949), 285–393.

3249 KNIGHT (THOMAS ANDREW). 'Experiments and observations on the motion of the sap in trees'. *Phil. Trans.*, 1804, 183–90.

George Bentham and John Lindley ed., *A selection from the physiological and horticultural papers . . . by . . . Thomas Andrew Knight*, 1841.

3250 HOOKER (*Sir* WILLIAM JACKSON). Journal of a tour in Iceland in the summer of 1809. 1811.

One of the earliest of a series of important pubs. His son, Joseph Dalton Hooker, also eminent as a botanist, wrote, *A sketch of . . . Sir William Jackson Hooker*, 1903. See too Leonard Huxley, *Life and letters of Sir Joseph Dalton Hooker*, 2 v., 1918, incl. a list of works. W. B. Turrill, *Joseph Dalton Hooker, botanist, explorer and administrator* [1963].

3251 LINDLEY (JOHN). An introduction to the natural system of botany. 1830.

A statement of the challenge to the Linnean system. His *Fossil flora of Great Britain* (with William Hutton) 3 v., 1831–7, was for long a standard work. His chief work was *The vegetable kingdom*, 1846.

3252 BERKELEY (MILES JOSEPH). Gleanings of British *algae*; being an appendix to the *Supplement to English botany* [by Sir W. J. Hooker], 1833.

He contributed v. 6, *Fungi*, 1836, to Hooker's edn. of *British flora*.

3253 HENSLOW (JOHN STEVENS). The principles of descriptive and physiological botany. 1835.

A teacher of Charles Darwin and collaborator of Sir W. J. Hooker at Kew; on him see Leonard Jenyns, *Memoir of John Stevens Henslow*, 1862.

3254 BENTHAM (GEORGE). Labiatarum genera et species; or, a description of the genera and species of plants of the order Labiatae. Issued in parts. 1832–6.

Benjamin Daydon Jackson, *George Bentham*, 1906.

3255 HENFREY (ARTHUR). Outlines of structural and physiological botany. 1847.

(c) *Later Works*

3256 GREEN (JOSEPH REYNOLDS). A history of botany in the United kingdom from the earliest times to the end of the nineteenth century. 1914. Rev. edn. 1931.

3257 OLIVER (FRANCIS WALL) *ed.* Makers of British botany. A collection of biographies by living botanists. Camb. 1913.

Includes sketches of Robert Brown, Sir William Hooker, J. S. Henslow, John Lindley, William Griffith, Arthur Henfrey, W. H. Harvey, M. J. Berkeley, J. D. Hooker. James Britten and George Simonds Boulger, *A biographical index of British and Irish botanists*, 1893; 1st supp. 1899, 2nd supp. 1905. 2nd edn. rev. and completed by A. B. Rendle, 1931.

11. ANTHROPOLOGY AND ETHNOLOGY

See Buckland (3178), Chambers (3236).

3258 KEESING (FELIX MAXWELL). Cultural change: an analysis and bibliography of anthropological sources to 1952. Stanford, Cal. London. 1953.

Chronological bibliog. from 1800, pp. 97–242.

3259 PENNIMAN (THOMAS KENNETH). A hundred years of anthropology, 1935.

2nd rev. edn., 1952, with bibliog. 457–500. Charles White, *An account of the regular gradation in man, and in different animals and vegetables; and from the former to the latter*, 1799, marked an important stage in the growth of anthropometry. James Cowles Prichard, *Researches into the physical history of man*, 2nd edn., 2 v., 1826, broached evolutionary ideas which he suppressed in later editions; his *The natural history of man*, 1843, was monumental. See too Sir William Lawrence, *An introduction to comparative anatomy and physiology, being the two introductory lectures . . .*, 1816, and *Lectures on physiology, zoology, and the natural history of man*, 1819, in 2 v., 1822. The Ethnological Soc. of London began its *Journal*, 1848.

G. EDUCATION

1. BIBLIOGRAPHY

3260 HIGSON (CONSTANCE WINIFRED JANE) *ed.* Sources for the history of education; a list of material (including school books) contained in the libraries of the institutes and schools of education, together with works from the libraries of the universities of Nottingham and Reading. 1967.

Sections on history are to be found in: Annie Margaret Blackwell, *A list of researches in education and educational psychology presented for higher degrees . . . from 1918 to 1948*, 1950; George Baron, *A bibliographical guide to the English educational system*, 3rd rev. edn., 1965; Thomas Kelly, ed., *A select bibliography of adult education in Great Britain*, 2nd edn., 1962; Ann Christophers, *An index to nineteenth-century British educational biography*, 1965. See also *N.C.B.E.L.* (2650) and Curtis (3300). For school registers see (2044–69) and Jacobs (3316).

3261 THE BRITISH JOURNAL OF EDUCATIONAL STUDIES. 1953+.

Includes a number of bibliographical articles on the history of various branches of education.

3262 THE BRITISH EDUCATION INDEX. 1954+.

Comprehensive annual union list of articles in periodicals. There is material on Great Britain in the American *Education Index*, 1929+.

3263　WALLIS (PETER JOHN). Histories of old schools; a revised list for England and Wales. Newcastle on Tyne. 1966.

Covers schools already in existence by 1700. For a select list of histories of other schools see Curtis (3300).

2. GENERAL

(a) *Sources*

(i) *Educational Treatises*

3264　DARWIN (ERASMUS). A plan for the conduct of female education in boarding schools. 1797.

A subject further discussed in: Hannah More, *Strictures on the modern system of female education*, 1799; Mary Wollstonecraft, *A vindication of the rights of women . . .*, 1792.

3265　EDGEWORTH (MARIA *and* RICHARD LOVELL). Essays on practical education. 2 v. 1798.

Other discussions of teaching methods include Richard Lovell Edgeworth, *Essays on professional education*, 1809; Henry Dunn, *Popular education; or, The normal school manual . . .*, 1837; David Stow, *The training system of education*, 1840.

3266　LANCASTER (JOSEPH). Improvements in education, as it respects the industrious classes of the community. . . . 1803.

This, and his second pamphlet, *An account of the progress of Joseph Lancaster's plan for the education of poor children and the training of masters for country schools*, [1809], form the chief exposition of his monitorial system. See too Andrew Bell, *An experiment in education, made at the male asylum at Madras*, 1797.

3267　BENTHAM (JEREMY). Chrestomathia. . . . 1816.

Repr. in *Works*, ed. Bowring (523), v. 8, 5–191. Proposals for the application of Lancaster's system to higher branches of education.

3268　MILL (JAMES). Essays on . . . education . . . reprinted . . . from the supplement to the Encyclopaedia Britannica. 1818.

The only systematic exposition of the ideas of the Utilitarians. See W. H. Burston, 'James Mill on the aims of education', *Cambridge Journal*, 6, 1952, 79–101, and *James Mill on philosophy and education*, 1973.

3269　[HILL (MATTHEW DAVENPORT)]. Plans for the goverment and liberal instruction of boys, in large numbers; drawn from experience. 1822.

An account of the school at Hazelwood for upper and middle class children run by Rowland Hill according to the theories of Pestalozzi.

3270　OWEN (ROBERT DALE). An outline of the system of education at New Lanark. Glasgow. 1824.

3271　BROUGHAM (HENRY). Practical observations upon the education of the people, addressed to the working classes and their employers. 1825.

This powerful plea for mechanics' institutes ran through nineteen editions in three months. See too Timothy Claxton, *Hints to mechanics, on self-education and mutual instruction*, 1839, and James Hole, *An essay on the history and management of literary scientific and mechanics' institutes* . . ., 1853.

3272 MAYO (CHARLES). Observations on the establishment and direction of infant schools. 1827.

By the advocate of the application of Pestalozzi's principles to infant teaching.

3273 WILDERSPIN (SAMUEL). Early discipline illustrated; or, The infant system progressing and successful. 1832.

3274 LOVETT (WILLIAM) *and* COLLINS (JOHN). Chartism; a new organization of the people. 1840. Repr. with intro. by A. Briggs. Leicester. 1969.

About half the pamphlet is concerned with schemes of popular education.

(ii) *Contemporary Reports*

See also, on missionary societies, (898–905).

3275 OF THE EDUCATION OF THE POOR, being the first part of a digest of the reports of the Society for Bettering the Condition of the Poor. [Ed. with a preface by Sir Thomas Bernard.] 1809.

Descriptions of schools.

3276 NATIONAL SOCIETY FOR PROMOTING THE EDUCATION OF THE POOR. . . . Annual reports. 1812+.

3277 POLE (THOMAS). A history of the origin and progress of adult schools. . . . Bristol. 1814.

3278 CARLISLE (NICHOLAS). A concise description of the endowed grammar schools in England and Wales; ornamented with engravings. 2 v. 1818.

Descriptions, of varying quality, of 475 schools.

3279 MANCHESTER STATISTICAL SOCIETY. Report of the committee . . . on the state of education in the borough of Bury, Lancashire, in July 1835. 1835.

One of a number of surveys carried out by the society, covering Manchester, Salford, Liverpool, York, Hull, and other districts during the 1830s.

3280 THE CENTRAL SOCIETY OF EDUCATION. Papers. 3 v. 1837–1839.

Much material on schools and other educational agencies.

3281 COMMITTEE OF THE PRIVY COUNCIL ON EDUCATION. Minutes of the committee with appendices and plans of school houses. 1839/40–1857/8. 1840+.

See also Sir James Phillips Kay Shuttleworth, *Public education, as affected by the minutes of the committee of privy council from 1846 to 1852* . . ., 1853; and *Four periods of public education as reviewed in 1832–1839–1846–1862* . . . 1862.

3282 KAY (JOSEPH). The education of the poor in England and Europe. 1846.

Results of an inquiry undertaken for the university of Cambridge with a view to promoting reforms.

3283 CENSUS. 1851. Education: England and Wales. 1854.

Command paper [1692]; report and tables.

3284 MACLURE (JOHN STUART), *comp.* Educational documents: England and Wales, 1816–1963. 1965.

(iii) *Government and Education*

3285 HILL (FREDERIC). National education; its present state and prospects. 2 v. 1836.

A factual account, illustrating the problem rather than advocating policies.

3286 DUNN (HENRY). National education, the question of questions, being an apology for the Bible in schools for the nation. 1838.

An early ranging shot against ideas of state control, as was also James Shergold Boone, *The educational economy of England, part I. On the external economy of education; or the means of providing instruction for the people,* 1838.

3287 POWELL (BADEN). State education considered with reference to prevalent misconceptions on religious grounds. 1840.

A condemnation of sectarian rivalries in education by the Savilian professor of geometry at Oxford.

3288 BURGESS (RICHARD). National education considered. 1842.

A discussion of the need to expand provision of schools for working-class children.

3289 HOOK (WALTER FARQUHAR). On the means of rendering more efficient the education of the people. A letter to the Lord Bishop of St. David's. 1846.

This strong plea for more state management of education went through ten edns. in five years and stirred up much controversy.

3290 COMBE (GEORGE). Remarks on national education. 1847.

One of several pamphlets by him supporting a system of state secular education.

3291 BAINES (EDWARD). Letters to . . . Lord John Russell . . . on state education: with an appendix. . . . 1846.

An eloquent statement of opposition to plans for government control of education. See also his widely circulated *Alarm to the nation, on the unjust, unconstitutional and dangerous measure of state education proposed by the government,* 1847.

3292 CROSBY HALL lectures on education. [1848].

Lectures attacking plans for state control given under the auspices of the Congregational board of education.

(b) *Later Works*

3293 SEXTON (ALEXANDER HUMBOLDT). The first technical college. A sketch of the history of the Andersonian. Glasgow. 1894.

3294 BINNS (HENRY BRYAN). A century of education. The centenary history of the British and Foreign School Society, 1808–1908. 1908.

3295 PATERSON (ALICE). The Edgeworths; a study of later eighteenth century education. 1914.

3296 ARCHER (RICHARD LAWRENCE). Secondary education in the nineteenth century. Camb. 1921.

3297 ROBSON (ADAM HENRY). The education of children engaged in industry, 1833–76. 1931.

3298 RICH (ROWLAND WILLIAM). The training of teachers in England and Wales in the nineteenth century. 1933.

More recent, but much briefer on the period, is Asher Tropp, *The school teachers; the growth of the teaching profession in England and Wales from 1800 to the present day*, 1957.

3299 MACK (EDWARD CLARENCE). Public schools and British opinion, 1780 to 1860: an examination of the relationship between contemporary ideas and the evolution of an English institution. 1938.

Thomas William Bamford, *The rise of the public schools . . .*, 1967, provides a brief straightforward outline of developments after 1837.

3300 CURTIS (STANLEY JAMES). History of education in Great Britain. 1948. 7th edn. 1967.

Standard, with valuable bibliog. Chaps. V–VII deal with the period, 1789–1851.

3301 POLLARD (HUGH M.). Pioneers of popular education, 1760–1850. 1956.

Bibliog. 281–93. Samuel Edwin Maltby, *Manchester and the movement for national elementary education, 1800–1870*, Manchester, 1918, is excellent. See also Amy M. Gilbert, *The work of Lord Brougham for education in England*, Chambersburg, Pa., 1922.

3302 ALTICK (RICHARD DANIEL). The English common reader: a social history of the mass reading public, 1800–1900. 1957.

Also valuable are: Amy Cruse, *The Englishman and his books in the early nineteenth century*, [1930], and *The Victorians and their books*, 1935; Robert Kiefer Webb, *The British working class reader, 1790–1840. Literary and social tension*, 1955; William Louis James, *Fiction for the working man, 1830–1850 . . .*, 1963.

3303 MURPHY (JAMES). The religious problem in English education: the crucial experiment. 1959.

Examines the experience of Liverpool, *c.* 1827–1870. For general surveys of the approach to education of particular churches, see Henry James Burgess, *Enterprize in education; the story of the work of the established church in the education of the people prior to 1870,*

1958; C. K. F. Brown, *The church's part in education, 1833–1941*, 1942; Horace Frederick Mathews, *Methodism and the education of the people, 1791–1851*, 1949; Frank Cyril Pritchard, *Methodist secondary education: a history . . .*, 1950; William Alexander Campbell Stewart, *Quakers and education, as seen in their schools in England*, 1953. See also McLachlan (796) and Barnes (889).

3304 CURTIS (STANLEY JAMES) *and* BOULTWOOD (MYRTLE EMMA AMELIA). An introductory history of English education since 1800. 1960.

Standard. Older surveys still of value are Clive Howard Barnard, *A history of English education from 1760*, 2nd rev. edn. 1961; John William Adamson, *English education, 1789–1902*, Camb. 1930.

3305 SIMON (BRIAN). Studies in the history of education, 1780–1870. 1960.

Substantial scholarly survey of growth in elementary and 'middle class' education. For other treatment see John Hurt, *Education in evolution. Church, state, society, and popular education, 1800–1870*, 1971, and Peter Gordon, *The Victorian school manager: a study in the management of education, 1800–1902*, 1974.

3306 HARRISON (JOHN FLETCHER CLEWS). Learning and living, 1790–1960: a study in the history of the English adult education movement. 1961.

Mabel Tylecote, *The mechanics' institutes of Lancashire and Yorkshire before 1851*, Manchester, 1957, is outstanding for scholarly detail. Thomas Kelly, *A history of adult education in Great Britain*, Liverpool, 1962, is standard.

3307 CURTIS (STANLEY JAMES) *and* BOULTWOOD (MYRTLE EMMA AMELIA). A short history of educational ideas. 4th edn. 1965.

3308 BISHOP (GEORGE DANIEL). Physics teaching in England from early times up to 1850. [1962.]

3309 BELL (QUENTIN). The schools of design. 1963.

Deals with the argument over art training for industrial workers.

3310 PRITCHARD (DAVID G.). Education and the handicapped, 1760–1960. 1963.

Fully documented study. Bibliog. 222–38.

3311 BALL (NANCY). Her Majesty's inspectorate, 1839–49. (Birmingham Univ. Institute of Education. Educational monographs 6.) 1963.

Detailed and scholarly. Bibliog. 257–63. Edward Leslie Edmonds, *The school inspector*, 1962, is a standard outline.

3312 SILVER (HAROLD). The concept of popular education: a study in ideas and social movements in the early nineteenth century. 1965.

Detailed, with use of the Robert Owen papers. See too Archibald Edward Dobbs, *Education and social movements, 1700–1850*, 1919, and William A. C. Stewart and W. P. McCann, *The educational innovators, 1750–1880*, 1967.

3313 TOWNSEND (JOHN ROWE). Written for children: an outline of children's literature. 1965.

Bibliog. 152–4. See also Mary Florence Thwaite, *From primer to pleasure: an introduction to the history of children's books in England* . . ., 1963, bibliog. 263–79; Sheila A. Egoff, *Children's periodicals of the nineteenth century: a survey and bibliography*, 1951.

3314 KAMM (JOSEPHINE). Hope deferred: girls' education in English history. 1965.

Chaps. 9–12 relate to the early 19th century.

3315 STURT (MARY). The education of the people: a history of primary education in England and Wales in the nineteenth century. 1967.

Older standard treatments are Charles Birchenough, *History of elementary education in England and Wales from 1800 to the present day*, 1914; Frank Smith, *A history of English elementary education, 1760–1902*, 1931.

3. UNIVERSITIES

(a) *Bibliographies and Catalogues*

3316 JACOBS (PHYLLIS MAY), *comp*. Registers of the universities, colleges, and schools of Great Britain and Ireland: a list. 1964.

3317 BARTHOLOMEW (AUGUSTUS THEODORE). Catalogue of the books and papers for the most part relating to the university, town and county of Cambridge, bequeathed to the university by J. W. Clark. Camb. 1912.

See too Robert Bowes, *A catalogue* (3539).

3318 BRIGGS (GRACE MARGARET) *ed*. The William W. Clary Oxford collection: a descriptive catalogue. Oxford. 1956.

A supplementary catalogue was edited in 1965 by Catherine King Firman.

(b) *Sources*

(i) *Manuscript*

3319 MADAN (FALCONER). Rough list of manuscript materials relating to the history of Oxford contained in the printed catalogues of the Bodleian and college libraries. Oxf. 1887.

By the same author, *Notes on Bodleian manuscripts relating to Cambridge*, pt. I, *Town and university*, Camb. 1931. *The Oxford deeds of Balliol college*, ed. H. E. Salter, Oxf. 1913, includes much about sites and properties.

3320 PEEK (HEATHER ELINOR) *and* HALL (CATHERINE PRISCILLA). The archives of the university of Cambridge: an historical introduction. Camb. 1962.

(ii) *Printed*

3321 GUNNING (HENRY). Reminiscences of the university, town and county of Cambridge, from the year 1780. 2 v. 1854.

Ends at 1830. See also Cox (2275).

3322 [COPLESTON (EDWARD)]. A reply to the calumnies of the Edinburgh Review against Oxford, containing an account of studies pursued in that university. Oxf. 1810.

3323 WHEWELL (WILLIAM). On the principles of English university education. 1837.

By the same author, *Of a liberal education in general: and with particular reference to the leading studies of the university of Cambridge,* 2nd edn., 1850.

3324 Report of Her Majesty's Commissioners appointed to inquire into the state, discipline, studies and revenues of the university and colleges of Oxford. 1852. [P.P. 1852 [1482] xxii.]

Followed shortly by the *Report . . . [on] the university and colleges of Cambridge* [P.P. 1852–3 [1559] xliv].

3325 HAMILTON (*Sir* WILLIAM). Discussions on philosophy and literature, education and university reform. 1852.

3326 PATTISON (MARK). 'Oxford studies'. In *Oxford essays, contributed by members of the university,* 1885, pp. 251–310.

3327 QUILLER-COUCH (LILIAN M.) *ed.* Reminiscences of Oxford by Oxford men, 1559–1850. *Oxf. Hist. Soc.* Oxf. 1892.

3328 SHADWELL (LIONEL LANCELOT). Enactments in parliament specially concerning the universities of Oxford and Cambridge . . . and the colleges of Winchester, Eton, and Westminster. *Oxf. Hist. Soc.* 4 v. Oxf. 1912.

(c) *Later Works*

For Scottish and Irish universities, see *Scotland* (4044–8) and *Ireland* (4273). For Oxford and Cambridge colleges, consult *The college history series,* published by Robinson, 1899, and Pargellis and Medley, p. 359. For Oxford colleges see also Vivian Hubert Howard Green, *Oxford common room: a study of Lincoln college and Mark Pattison,* 1957; William Conrad Costin, *The history of St. John's college, Oxford, 1598–1860,* Oxf. Hist. Soc., [1958]. For Cambridge colleges see also Anthony Bedford Steel, *The custom of the room: or, early wine books of Christ's college, Cambridge,* Camb. [1951]; Patrick Bury, *The college of Corpus Christi and of the Blessed Virgin Mary: a history from 1822 to 1952,* Camb., 1952; Edward Miller, *Portrait of a college: a history of the college of Saint John the Evangelist,* Camb., 1961.

3329 TILLYARD (ALFRED ISAAC). A history of university reform, from 1800 A.D. to the present time. With suggestions towards a complete scheme for the university of Cambridge. Camb. 1913.

Michael Sanderson, ed., *The universities in the nineteenth century,* 1975, is a useful collection of documents.

3330 MALLET (*Sir* CHARLES EDWARD). A history of the university of Oxford. 3 v. [1924-7.]

V. 3, *Modern Oxford*, is full on the 19th century. For university politics see William Reginald Ward, *Victorian Oxford*, 1965.

3331 BURNS (CECIL DELISLE). A short history of Birkbeck college, university of London. 1924.

3332 BELLOT (HUGH HALE). University college, London, 1826-1926. 1929.

3333 HEARNSHAW (FOSSEY JOHN COBB). The centenary history of King's college, London. 1929.

3334 WHITING (CHARLES EDWIN). The university of Durham. 1932.

3335 WINSTANLEY (DENYS ARTHUR). Early Victorian Cambridge. Camb. 1940.

Percy Cradock, *Recollections of the Cambridge union, 1815-1939*, 1953.

3336 HILKEN (THOMAS JOHN NORMAN). Engineering at Cambridge university: 1783-1965. Camb. 1967.

4. LIBRARIES AND MUSEUMS

3337 BURTON (MARGARET) *and* VOSBURGH (MARION E.). A bibliography of librarianship: classified and annotated guide to the library literature of the world (excluding Slavonic and Oriental languages). 1934.

Includes sections on history. See too David Murray, *Museums, their history and their use, with a bibliography and list of museums in the United Kingdom*, 3 v., Glasgow, 1904.

3338 [CLARKE (WILLIAM).] ed. Repertorium bibliographicum; or, Some account of the most celebrated British libraries. 2 v. 1819.

3339 EDWARDS (EDWARD). Lives of the founders of the British museum; with notices of its chief augmentors and other benefactors, 1570-1870. 2 v. 1870.

Other material on the history of libraries in his *Memoirs of Libraries*, 2 v., 1859, and *Libraries and founders of libraries*, 1865. See also biog. (3356).

3340 MACRAY (WILLIAM DUNN). Annals of the Bodleian library, Oxford ... 1598 ... 1867. 2nd edn. enl. Oxf. 1890.

3341 ESDAILE (ARUNDELL JAMES KENNEDY). The British Museum library: a short history and survey; with an introduction by Sir Frederick Kenyon. 1946.

Standard. There is useful information in Robert Cowtan, *Memories of the British Museum*, 1872, and George F. Barwick, *The British Museum Reading Room*, 1929. See also Panizzi (3356).

3342 KELLY (THOMAS). Early public libraries: a history of public libraries in Great Britain before 1850. 1966.

Chap. bibliogs. with histories of individual libraries. John Minto, *A history of the public library movement in Great Britain and Ireland*, 1932, bibliog. 343–4, is a standard outline. See also C. B. Oldman, W. A. Munford and S. Nowell-Smith, *English libraries, 1800–1850*, 1958—lectures on the British Museum, on libraries of mechanics' institutes, and on the London Library.

3343 MUNBY (ALAN NOEL LATIMER). Macaulay's library: being the twenty-eighth lecture on the David Murray Foundation in the university of Glasgow. . . . Glasgow. 1966.

See too McLachlan, *Nonconformist Library* (796).

5. BIOGRAPHY

See also works on Brougham (207), Ewart (222), Newman (780), Pattison (771), Raikes (737).

3344 JUDGES (ARTHUR VALENTINE) *ed.* Pioneers of English education: a course of lectures given at King's College, London. 1952.

See also Frederick Douglas How, *Six great schoolmasters*, 1904.

3345 ARNOLD. The life and correspondence of Thomas Arnold. By Arthur Penrhyn Stanley. 2 v. 1844.

A. P. Stanley also ed. Arnold's *Misc. works*, 1845. Thomas William Bamford, *Thomas Arnold*, 1960, has notes and refs., 213–25.

3346 BELL. The life of the Rev. Andrew Bell. . . . By Robert and Charles Cuthbert Southey. 3 v. 1844.

3347 BIRKBECK. George Birkbeck, pioneer of adult education. By Thomas Kelly. Liverpool. 1957.

Bibliog. 340–63.

3348 BUTLER. The life and letters of Dr Samuel Butler. By Samuel Butler. 2 v. 1896.

3349 CURWEN. Memorials of John Curwen. Compiled by his son John Spencer Curwen. With a chapter on his home life by his daughter, Mrs Banks. 1882.

Life of the pioneer of the sol-fa method of musical instruction.

3350 EDWARDS. Edward Edwards, 1812–1886: portrait of a librarian. By William Arthur Munford. 1963.

Bibliog. 229–32. Edwards's quarrel with Panizzi led to his dismissal from the British Museum in 1850.

3351 JOWETT. The life and letters of Benjamin Jowett, M.A., master of Balliol College, Oxford. By Evelyn Abbott and Lewis Campbell. 2 v. 1897.

Jowett was a tutor at Balliol from 1838. His papers there were consulted for Geoffrey Faber, *Jowett. A portrait with background*, 1958.

3352 KAY-SHUTTLEWORTH. The life and work of Sir James Kay-Shuttleworth. . . . By Frank Smith. 1923.

Disappointing but indispensable. Barry Cambray Bloomfield, comp., *A handlist of the papers in the deed box of Sir J. P. Kay-Shuttleworth, 1804–77*, 1961.

3353 KNIGHT. 'Charles Knight: an educational pioneer.' By T. L. Jarman. *Journal of Adult Education*, 6 ii (1932–4), 176–85.

3354 LANCASTER. The practical parts of Lancaster's 'Improvements' and Bell's 'Experiment'. Ed. by David Salmon. Camb. 1932.

3355 MORE. Hannah More's interest in education and government. By Luther Courtney Weeks. [Waco, Texas.] 1929.

For biog. see (2122).

3356 PANIZZI. Prince of librarians: the life and times of Antonio Panizzi of the British Museum. By Edward Miller. 1967.

Bibliog. 335–45; includes much material for the history of the museum library.

3357 PHILLIPPS. Portrait of an obsession: the life of Sir Thomas Phillipps, the world's greatest book collector. Adapted by Nicolas Barker from the five volumes of 'Phillipps Studies' [by Alan Noel Latimer Munby]. 1967.

3358 STOW. Memoir of the life of David Stow, founder of the training system of education. By William Fraser. 1868.

3359 WILDERSPIN. 'Samuel Wilderspin and the early infant schools.' By W. P. McCann. *British J. of Educational Studies*, 14 (1965–6), 188–204.

H. SCHOLARSHIP

For the Study of British folklore see (1873).

1. GENERAL WORKS

3360 DANIEL (GLYN EDMUND). A hundred years of archaeology. 1950.

For British archaeology in this period see *Archaeologia; or, Miscellaneous tracts relating to antiquity*, 1770+, indexes v. 1–15, 1809, v. 16–30, 1844, and 1–50, 1889, and, on his pioneer excavations, Sir Richard Colt Hoare, *The ancient history of South [and North] Wiltshire*, 2 v., 1812–21, and *Tumuli Wiltunenses; a guide to the barrows on the plains of Stonehenge*, Shaftesbury, 1829. See also Joan Evans, *A history of the Society of Antiquaries*, Oxf., 1956, which gives an account of papers read, and contemporary interests.

3361 AARSLEFF (HANS). The study of language in England, 1780–1860. Princeton. 1967.

Studies the development from the 'philosophically orientated preoccupations of the 1780s to the philological concerns of the 1860s'. A general survey of the study of European and Asian languages is given by Holger Pedersen, *Linguistic science in the nineteenth century*, trans. John Webster Spargo, Camb., Mass., 1931.

3362 SANDYS (*Sir* JOHN EDWIN). 'Scholars, antiquaries and biblio-
graphers' *Camb. Hist. Eng. Lit.* v. 12. Camb. 1915. Chapter 15. Bibliog.
479–523.

A short introduction. *N.C.B.E.L.* v. 2 lists the writings of major authors, literary
studies cols. 1741–1819, and classical and oriental studies cols. 1819–32. *N.C.B.E.L.*
v. 3, for the period after 1800, lists English studies only, cols. 1635–68: for 19th cent.
classical and oriental scholarship see *C.B.E.L.* 3, 993–1021.

2. BIBLICAL CRITICISM

3363 METZGER (BRUCE MANNING). The text of the New Testament.
Its transmission, corruption, and restoration. Oxf. 1964.

3364 STRAUSS (DAVID FRIEDRICH). The life of Jesus critically examined.
Trans. by Marian Evans, afterwards Cross. 1846.

This translation of David Friedrich Strauss, *Das Leben Jesu*, 4th edn. Tübingen, 1840,
introduced the higher criticism to the British public.

3365 ALFORD (HENRY). The Greek testament, with a critically revised
text, prolegomena, and a critical and exegetical commentary. 1849–61.

3366 TREGELLES (SAMUEL PRIDEAUX). An account of the printed
text of the Greek New Testament, with remarks on its revision upon critical
principles. Together with a collation of the critical texts of Griesbach, Scholz,
Lachmann, and Tischendorf, with that in common use. 1854.

Tregelles travelled extensively in search of the earliest texts. His edn. and translation
of the book of Revelation was pub. 1844. His edn. of *The Greek New Testament . . .
edited from the ancient authorities*, etc., which occupied the rest of his life, was pub.
1857–79.

3. CLASSICAL SCHOLARSHIP

(a) *Textual and Historical Studies*

3367 SANDYS (*Sir* JOHN EDWIN). A history of classical scholarship. 3 v.
Camb. 1908.

See also Robert Maxwell Ogilvie, *Latin and Greek; a history of the influence of the classics
on English life, from 1600 to 1918*, 1964. For Blomfield and Burgess see (700), (739).

3368 CLARKE (MARTIN LOWTHER). Greek studies in England, 1700 to
1830. Camb. 1945.

Includes list of trans. from Greek authors, 1700–1830, and biog. notes on scholars in
the same period. See also Finley Melville Kendall Foster, *English translations from the
Greek; a bibliographical study* (Columbia Univ. Studies in English and Comparative
Literature), N.Y. 1918.

3369 MUSEUM CRITICUM, or, Cambridge classical researches. Camb.
1813–26.

The journal of the Porsonian school, considered of a higher standard than its rival, the
Classical Journal, 1810–29.

3370 MOSS (JOSEPH WILLIAM). A manual of classical bibliography. 2 v. 1825. 2nd edn. 2 v. 1837.

Lists edns. for collectors, with comments. For translations see Frank Seymour Smith, *The classics in translation. An annotated guide to the best translations of the Greek and Latin classics into English,* 1930, also *N.C.B.E.L.,* v. 2. Cols. 1485–1502.

3371 GROTE. George Grote; a biography. By Martin Lowther Clarke. 1962.

Primarily on his classical scholarship. Harriet Grote, *The personal life of George Grote,* 1873, lays more emphasis on his political life. Grote's *History of Greece,* 8 v., was pub. 1846–56.

3372 PARR. Dr. Parr; a portrait of the Whig Dr. Johnson. By Warren Derry. Oxf. 1966.

Bibliog. 352–9. See also (688).

3373 PORSON. Richard Porson; a biographical essay. By Martin Lowther Clarke. 1937.

See also John Selby Watson, *Life of Richard Porson,* etc., 1861.

(b) *Classical Archaeology*

See also (2959), (2965).

3374 GELL (*Sir* WILLIAM). The topography of Troy and its vicinity, illustrated and explained by drawings and descriptions. 1804.

Gell also wrote *The geography and antiquities of Ithaca,* 1807, *The itinerary of Greece,* 1810, *The itinerary of the Morea,* 1817, and *Pompeiana, the topography, edifices and ornaments of Pompeii,* 1817–19, 2nd edn., including *the result of excavations since 1819,* 2 v., 1832.

3375 LEAKE (WILLIAM MARTIN). The topography of Athens, with some remarks on its antiquities. 1821.

Also *Journal of a tour in Asia Minor,* etc., 1824, *Travels in the Morea,* 3 v. 1830, and *Travels in Northern Greece,* 4 v., 1835. Leake was a colonel of artillery, making a geographical survey in Greece, 1804–7. See John Howard Marsden, *A brief memoir of . . . William Martin Leake,* 1864.

3376 MILLINGEN (JAMES V.). Ancient unedited monuments. Painted Greek vases, . . . statues, busts, bas-reliefs and other domains of Grecian art from collections in various countries illustrated and explained. 3 pt. 1822–6.

Also his *Ancient coins of Greek cities and kings from various collections principally in Great Britain illustrated and explained,* 1831.

3377 MICHAELIS (ADOLF THEODOR FRIEDRICH). Ancient marbles in Great Britain. Camb. 1882.

Standard. See also William Linn St. Clair, *Lord Elgin and the marbles,* 1967.

4. OLD AND MIDDLE ENGLISH STUDIES

3378 KENNEDY (ARTHUR GARFIELD). A bibliography of writings on the English language from the beginning of printing to the end of 1922. Camb. Mass. and New Haven. 1927.

Supplemented by Robin Carfrae Alston, *A bibliography of the English language from the invention of printing to the year 1800*, Leeds, 1965+, in progress.

3379 STEEVES (HARRISON ROSS). Learned societies and English literary scholarship in Great Britain and the United States. N.Y. 1913.

Societies important for the publication of early English texts include the Roxburghe Club (1812), on which see the Hon. Clive Bigham, *The Roxburghe Club: its history and its members, 1812–1927*, Oxf. 1928, the Bannatyne Club (1823+) in Edinburgh, the Royal Society of Literature (1825), the Surtees Society (1834), whose pubs. related to the north of England and southern Scotland, the Camden Society (1838), the Percy Society (1840), primarily concerned with early English ballads and popular literature. The Philological Society (1842), *Proceedings*, 5 v., 1844–54, and *Transactions*, 1854+, later sponsored the preparation of the *New English Dictionary*. The *Retrospective review and historical and antiquarian magazine*, ed. Henry Southern and Nicholas Harris Nicolas, 14 v., 1820–6, 2nd ser. 1827, 1828, popularized medieval literature.

3380 ADAMS (ELEANOR NATHALIE). Old English scholarship in England from 1566–1800. Yale studies in English 55. New Haven. 1917.

3381 BOSWORTH (JOSEPH). A dictionary of the Anglo-Saxon language. 1838.

3382 COLLIER (JOHN PAYNE). Notes on the life of John Payne Collier with a complete list of his works and an account of such Shakespeare documents as are believed to be spurious. By Henry Benjamin Wheatley. 1884.

3383 HALLIWELL (*afterwards* Halliwell-Phillipps). Halliwelliana: a bibliography of the publications of James Orchard Halliwell-Phillipps. By Justin Winsor. Camb. Mass. 1881.

Son-in-law of Sir Thomas Phillipps, and chiefly active in Shakespearian studies and the development of Stratford-on-Avon.

3384 HEBER. The Heber letters, 1783–1832. By Richard Hugh Cholmondeley. 1950.

Book collector.

3385 KEMBLE. J. M. Kemble and Old English scholarship (with a bibliography of his writings). By Bruce Dickins. (Sir Israel Gollancz memorial lecture, 1938.)

3386 NARES. A glossary, or collection of words, phrases, names and allusions to customs, proverbs, etc. which have been thought to require illustrations in the work of English authors, particularly Shakespeare and his contemporaries. By Robert Nares. 1822.

Rev. edn. by J. O. Halliwell and T. Wright, 2 v., 1859, later edns., 2 v., 1882, 2 v., 1905.

3387 PHILLIPPS. Phillipps studies. By Alan Noel Latimer Munby. 5 v. Camb. 1951–60.

See also the abridged version by Nicolas Barker, *Portrait of an obsession* (3357).

3388 THORPE (BENJAMIN). R. C. Rask. A grammar of the Anglo-Saxon tongue translated from the Danish by Benjamin Thorpe. 1830.

Thorpe later edited and translated many Anglo-Saxon historical and literary works.

3389 TURNER (SHARON). The history of the Anglo-Saxons, from their first appearance above the Elbe, to the death of Egbert. 1799.

V. 2, 1802, with altered title 'to the Norman conquest. In four volumes'. V. 3, 1802, v. 4. 1805. 2nd edn. enl. and corr., 2 v., 1807. The first important history of the period.

5. ORIENTAL STUDIES

(a) *General*

3390 ROYAL ASIATIC SOCIETY. Transactions. 1827–34. Journal. 1834+.

For the early history of the society and a catalogue of articles see Frederick Eden Pargiter, *Royal Asiatic Society centenary volume, 1823–1923*, 1923. See also the Society for the Publication of Oriental Texts' pubns., 1842–8.

3391 ARBERRY (ARTHUR JOHN). British orientalists. 1943.

A short introduction. See also Bernard Lewis and P. M. Holt, eds. *Historians of the Middle East*, 1962, a series of essays. For a general bibliog. see James Douglas Pearson, *Oriental and Asian bibliography, an introduction with some reference to Africa*, 1966. See also the *Bulletin of the School of Oriental and African Studies*, 1917+.

(b) *Egyptology*

3392 SALT (HENRY). Essay on Dr. Young's and M. Champollion's phonetic system of hieroglyphics; with some additional discoveries, by which it may be applied to decipher the names of the ancient kings of Egypt and Ethiopia. 1825.

Salt was consul-general in Egypt, 1815–27, and discovered the Abu Simbel inscriptions, 1817.

3393 HAY (ROBERT) *of Linplum*. Catalogue of the Egyptian antiquities belonging to the late Robert Hay. 1869.

Also *Illustrations of Cairo*, 1840. Hay's archaeological drawings and part of his diary are in the British Library, Add. MSS. 29812–60, 31054.

3394 WILKINSON (*Sir* JOHN GARDNER). Manners and customs of the ancient Egyptians. Illustrated by drawings. 2 series. 6 v. 1837–41.

Popularized Egyptology. Wilkinson also wrote *Materia hieroglyphica . . . the Egyptian pantheon, and the succession of the Pharaohs . . . to the conquest of Alexander*, 2 pt., Malta, 1828.

(c) *Assyriology*

3395 PALLIS (SVEND AAGE). The antiquity of Iraq. A handbook of Assyriology. Copenhagen. 1956.

Chaps. 2–6 contain a detailed account of the 19th-century growth of the subject.

3396 HINCKS (EDWARD). 'On the first and second kinds of Persepolitan writing.' *Trans. Royal Irish Academy*, 21 (1841), 114–31.

Also 'On the three kinds of Persepolitan writing', *ibid.* 233–48, and 'On the Khorsabad inscriptions', *ibid.* 22 (1850), 3–72. Hincks identified the Assyrian as a Semitic language, and discovered the Persian cuneiform vowel system, working independently of Rawlinson.

3397 LAYARD (*Sir* AUSTEN HENRY). Nineveh and its remains: with an account of a visit to the Chaldean Christians of Kurdistan, and the Yezidis or devil worshippers, and an enquiry into the manners and arts of the ancient Assyrians. 2 v. 1849.

Repr., abridged, with intro. by H. W. F. Saggs, 1970. See also Layard's *Autobiography and letters . . . until his appointment as H.M. Ambassador at Madrid*, ed. Hon. William N. Bruce, 2 v., 1903 and Nora Benjamin Kubie, *Road to Nineveh*, etc., N.Y. 1964, London, 1965.

3398 PORTER (*Sir* ROBERT KER). Travels in Georgia, Persia, Armenia, ancient Babylonia, . . . during the years 1817, 1818, 1819 and 1820. With numerous engravings. 2 v. 1821–2.

3399 RAWLINSON (HENRY CRESWICKE). The Persian cuneiform inscription at Behistun, deciphered and translated with a memoir on Persian inscriptions in general and that of Behistun in particular. Repr. from *Jour. of Royal Asiatic Soc.* 1846–51.

Also 'On the inscriptions of Assyria and Babylonia', *Jour. Royal Asiatic Soc.* 12 (1850), 401–83, on the 'Babylonian' version of the Behistun inscription. See also George Rawlinson, *A memoir of Major General Sir H. C. Rawlinson*, 1898.

3400 RICH (CLAUDIUS JAMES). Memoir on the ruins of Babylon. 1815.

Also *Second memoir on Babylon*, etc., 1818, and *Narrative of a residence in Koordistan and on the site of ancient Nineveh*, 1836. Rich's surveys of these sites were the first and provided the basis for Layard's expedition in 1842.

(d) *Persian Studies*

3401 OUSELEY (*Sir* WILLIAM). Travels in various countries of the East, more particularly Persia. 3 v. 1819–23.

Relating to travels 1810–13. He had previously pub. *Persian miscellanies: an essay to facilitate the reading of Persian manuscripts*, etc., 1795, *The oriental collections . . . illustrating the history and antiquities, the arts, sciences and literature of Asia*, 3 v., [1797–9], and a number of translations (see *C.B.E.L.*). By his brother, Sir Gore Ouseley, *Biographical notices of Persian poets with critical and explanatory remarks. With memoir by James Reynolds*, 1846.

3402 MALCOLM (*Sir* JOHN). The history of Persia from the most early period to the present time, containing an account of the religion, government, usages and character of the inhabitants of that kingdom. 2 v. 1815.

(e) *Arabic*

3403 LEWIS (BERNARD). British contributions to Arabic studies. 1941.

3404 LANE (EDWARD WILLIAM). An Arabic–English lexicon. 5 pt. 1863–74.

Lane had worked on this in Cairo 1842–9. He had previously pub. *The thousand and one nights*, 3 v. 1839–41, the first accurate translation, and *Selections from the Kur-àn*, 1843. See also Stanley Lane-Poole, *Life of Edward William Lane*, 1877.

(f) *Indian Studies*

3405 WINTERNITZ (MORIZ). A history of Indian literature. 2nd edn. 3 v. Calcutta. 1959.

3406 MARSHALL (PETER JAMES) *ed*. The British discovery of Hinduism in the eighteenth century. 1970.

Reprints eight late 18th-century writings with an intro.

3407 ASIATIC SOCIETY OF BENGAL. Asiatick researches. Calcutta, 1788–1839. Journal. Calcutta. 1832+.

The society pub. texts in *Bibliotheca Indica*, Calcutta, 1848+. See Sibadas Chaudhuri, *Index to the publications . . . 1788–1953*, Calcutta, 1956, and *Centenary review . . . from 1784 to 1883*, 4 pt. Calcutta, 1885.

3408 CAREY (WILLIAM). The Bible, translated from the original tongues by W. Carey and — Fountain. Bengali. 1801.

Carey, a Baptist missionary at Serampore, and his associates also translated the Bible into Sanskrit (1811), Hindi (1812), and Telugu (1821). They also published grammars and dictionaries of Bengali, Mahratta, Punjabi and other vernacular languages. See S. Pearce Carey, *William Carey, D.D., Fellow of Linnean Society*, 1923.

3409 COLEBROOK (HENRY THOMAS). A digest of Hindu law on contracts and successions. Translated from the Sanscrit. 4 v. Calcutta. 1798.

His essay, 'On the Vedas', *Asiatick Researches*, 1805, was the first to give reliable information about them. He also published a Sanskrit grammar (1805) and dictionary (1808), and translations for which see *N.C.B.E.L.*

3410 JONES (*Sir* WILLIAM). Institutes of Hindu law or, The ordinances of Manu. Calcutta. 1794.

For his translations from Sanskrit see *The works of Sir William Jones*, ed. by John Shore, Lord Teignmouth, and Lady Jones, 6 v., 1799, 2 suppl. v. 1801. Jones' *Letters* have been ed. by Garland Cannon, 2 v., Oxf., 1970; there are lives by Cannon, 1964, and S. N. Mukherjee, 1968.

3411 MILL (JAMES). The history of British India. 3 v. 1817. 3rd edn. 6 v. 1826.

3412 WILKINS (*Sir* CHARLES). A grammar of the Sanskṛita language. 1808.

For his Sanskrit translations see *C.B.E.L.*

(g) *China and the Far East*

3413 CHINESE REPOSITORY. 20 v. Canton. 1832–51.

Local news; articles on Chinese history and culture, etc.

3414 DAVIS (*Sir* JOHN FRANCIS). The Chinese: a general description of the empire of China and its inhabitants. 1836.

Also *Chinese novels translated from the originals, to which are added proverbs and moral maxims*, 1822.

3415 MARSDEN (WILLIAM). Dictionary of the Malayan language. 1812.

Also *A grammar of the Malayan language*, 1812, and *Numismata orientalia*, 1823–5.

3416 MARSHMAN (JOSHUA). Dissertation on the characters and sounds of the Chinese language. [Serampore? 1810?]

Also *Elements of Chinese grammar*, Serampore, 1814. He also trans. *The works of Confucius, containing the original text, with a translation*, 1809.

3417 MEDHURST (WALTER HENRY). Chinese and English dictionary; containing all the words in the Chinese Imperial Dictionary, arranged according to the Radicals. 2 v. Batavia. 1842–3.

3418 MORRISON (ROBERT). A dictionary of the Chinese language in three parts. Part the first, containing Chinese and English, arranged according to the Radicals; part the second, Chinese and English arranged alphabetically, and part the third, English and Chinese. 3 pt. Macao. 1815–23.

Also [Chinese title] [The Bible] *translated into Chinese by Robert Morrison and William Milne*, 21 v., [Malacca] 1823. See also Eliza Morrison, *Memoirs of the life and labours of Robert Morrison D.D. with critical notices of his works by S. Kidd*, 2 v., 1839.

I. HISTORIOGRAPHY

1. SOURCES

3419 PRIESTLEY (JOSEPH). Lectures on history, and general policy; to which is prefixed, An essay on a course of liberal education for civil and active life. Birm. 1788. 2 v. 1793. New edn. 1826.

3420 DALES (SAMUEL). An essay on the study of the history of England. 1809.

Representative of a lay view; an army officer's bibliography for English history from the beginning to modern times.

3421 BOONE (JAMES SHERGOLD). An essay on the study of modern history. . . . 1821. New edn. 1822.

Urges the addition of history to the Oxford curriculum.

3422 TAYLOR (ISAAC). The process of historical proof: exemplified and explained with observations on the peculiar points of the Christian evidence. 1828.

Exposition of common principles of historical investigation, applied first to study of Herodotus and then to the New Testament. Lighter in touch is Richard Whately, *Historic doubts relative to Napoleon Buonaparte* (659).

3423 NICOLAS (*Sir* NICHOLAS HARRIS). Observations on the state of historical literature. . . . 1830.

Discusses the need to make documents available to historians; critical of the Record Commission of 1800–30. See also, *Report from the Select Committee appointed to inquire into the affairs of the Record Commission and the present state of the records of the United Kingdom*, H.C. 1836 (565) xvi.

3424 VAUGHAN (HENRY HALFORD). Two general lectures on modern history, delivered on inauguration. . . . 1849.

An Oxford regius professor on the nature and purpose of history. William Torrens McCullagh, *On the use and study of history*, Dublin, 1842, was pitched to the level of mechanics' institutes.

3425 STODDART (*Sir* JOHN). An introduction to the study of universal history. Two dissertations . . . 2nd rev. edn. 1850.

2. LATER WORKS

3426 GOOCH (GEORGE PEABODY). History and historians in the nineteenth century. 1913. Rev. edn. 1952.

Chaps. XV–XVII deal with British historians in the period. Some brief additional material is in James Westfall Thompson and Bernard J. Holm, *A history of historical writing*, 2 v., N.Y., 1942, v. 2, *The eighteenth and nineteenth centuries*. On Hallam, see *Some modern historians of Britain; essays in honor of R. L. Schuyler*, ed. Herman Ausubel, N.Y., 1951; and on Stanhope, Aubrey Norris Newman, *The Stanhopes of Chevening*, 1969.

3427 HAILE (MARTIN) [*pseud. of* HALLÉ (MARIE)] *and* BONNEY (EDWIN). The life and letters of John Lingard, 1771–1851. [1911.]

3428 PEARDON (THOMAS PRESTON). The transition in English historical writing, 1760–1830. N.Y. 1933.

Excellent. Bibliog. 311–31.

3429 YOUNG (LOUISE MERWIN). Thomas Carlyle and the art of history. Phil. Oxf. 1939.

Methodical discussion, with valuable notes and bibliog.

3430 FIRTH (*Sir* CHARLES HARDING). A commentary on Macaulay's History of England. 1938. 2nd imp. 1964.

The standard biog. is Trevelyan (228). Richmond Croom Beatty, 'Macaulay and Carlyle', *Philolog. Quart.* 18 (1939), 25–34, fills some gaps. Giles St. Aubyn, *Macaulay*, 1952, is a brief, urbane introductory sketch.

3431 DOCKHORN (KLAUS). Der deutsche Historismus in England; ein Beitrag zur englischen Geistesgeschichte des 19 Jahrhunderts. Göttingen. 1950.

Exhaustive on English study of classical antiquity. For a criticism see Duncan Forbes, 'Historismus in England', *Cambridge Journal*, 4 (1951), 387–400.

3432 FORBES (DUNCAN). The liberal Anglican idea of history. Camb. 1952.

3433 BUTTERFIELD (*Sir* HERBERT). George III and the historians. 1957.

Analyses approaches of British historians to events after the accession of George III. Similar in treatment is Hedva Ben Israel, *English historians on the French Revolution*, Camb., 1968. See too Pieter Geyl, *Debates with historians*, Groningen, London, 1955.

3434 PREYER (ROBERT). Bentham, Coleridge and the science of history. Bochum-Langendreer. 1958.

J. MAPS

For county maps and roadbooks see (3518–21). Guides to maps of particular areas are classified under those areas, e.g. (3984–5), Scotland, and (3754), London.

I. BIBLIOGRAPHIES, CATALOGUES, JOURNALS

3435 ROYAL GEOGRAPHICAL SOCIETY. Catalogue of the map room of the Royal Geographical Society. 1882.

Includes both MS. and printed maps, including a complete set of the 1st edn. of the 6″ Ordnance Survey.

3436 PHILLIPS (PHILIP LEE). A list of geographical atlases in the Library of Congress, with bibliographical notes. 6 v. Wash. 1909. In progress.

V. 5 and 6 are by Clara Egli Le Gear. Two more vols. are projected.

3437 MAP COLLECTORS' SERIES. Published by Map Collectors' Circle. 1963+.

Issued in pamphlet form it contains many articles on the cartography of particular areas. Note also Ronald Vere Tooley, *A dictionary of mapmakers, including cartographers, geographers, publishers, engravers, etc. from earliest times to 1900*, pub. in parts in the Series, II (1964–5), 16; III (1965–6), 28; IV (1967–8), 40; and V (1968–9), 50, covering the letters A–G.

3438 BRITISH MUSEUM. Catalogue of printed maps, charts, and plans. Photolithographic edn. complete to 1964. 15 v. 1967.

See also *Catalogue of maps, prints, drawings etc., forming the geographical and topographical collections . . . of . . . King George the Third, and presented . . . to the British Museum*, 1829, and *Catalogue of the manuscript maps, charts, and plans, and of the topographical drawings in the British museum*, 3 v., 1844–61, repr. 1962.

3439 PUBLIC RECORD OFFICE. Maps and plans in the Public Record office. V. 1. British Isles, c. 1410–1860. 1967.

Includes early maps relating to Ordnance Survey and maps of 18th and 19th century London.

3440 NATIONAL MARITIME MUSEUM. Catalogue of the library. 4 v. 1968–72.

V. 3 is a catalogue of atlases.

2. Atlases

3441 KITCHIN (THOMAS) *and others*. New universal atlas. 1773.

Many later edns.

3442 RENNELL (JAMES) New universal atlas. 1799.

3443 CARY (JOHN). Cary's new universal atlas, containing distinct maps of all the principal states and kingdoms throughout the world. 1808.

For a full bibliog. account of this atlas see Fordham's *Life* (3518), pp. 77–82.

3444 ARROWSMITH (JOHN). The London atlas of universal geography. 1835[–36]. Other edns. 1842[–52], 1858.

Aaron Arrowsmith (1750–1823) and his nephew John, who took over the business in 1823, published a large number of regional maps culminating in this atlas.

3. General Works

3445 BROWN (BASIL J. W.). Astronomical-atlases, maps and charts; an historical and general guide. 1932.

3446 BROWN (LLOYD ARNOLD). The story of maps. Boston, Mass. 1949. 1951.

Bibliog. 341–73. See also Gerald Roe Crone, *Maps and their makers; an introduction to the history of cartography*, 1953, 2nd edn. 1962, 3rd, 1966.

4. Special Subjects

3447 RENNELL (JAMES). Sketch of the northern part of Africa, exhibiting the geographical information collected by the African Association. 1790[–92].

3448 CLOSE (*Sir* CHARLES FREDERICK) *afterwards* ARDEN-CLOSE. The early years of the Ordnance Survey. Chatham. 1926. Repr. Newton Abbot. 1969.

See also R. A. Skelton, 'Origins of the Ordnance Survey of Great Britain', *Geographical Journal*, 128 (1962), 406–30, and for a general account John Brian Harley, *The historian's guide to ordnance survey maps, reprinted from 'The Amateur Historian' with additional material* [1965]. For the work of the survey see William Mudge and Isaac Dalby, *An account of the operations carried on for accomplishing a trigonometrical survey of England and Wales*, 3 v. 1799–1811, followed by *Ordnance Trigonometrical Survey of Great Britain and Ireland. Account of observations and calculations . . . Drawn up by Capt. A. R. Clarke . . . under the direction of Lt. Col. H. James*, 1858. Published maps begin with the 1″ map of Kent in 1801. The British Museum map room possesses preliminary drawings for the 1st edn. as a whole which may antedate published versions by ten or more years.

3449 PHILLIMORE (REGINALD HENRY), *comp.* Historical records of the survey of India. 1945+. In progress.

V. I–IV, covering the years to 1843, have been pub. 1945–58. Previous maps of India were based on the work of James Rennell, who surveyed Bengal, 1764–77, and whose *Memoir of a map of Hindoustan*, 1783, 2nd edn. 1785, enl. edn. 1794, was the basis of maps until the 19th-century surveys. See also Sir Clements R. Markham, *A memoir on the Indian surveys*, 2nd edn. 1878, and India Office, *Catalogue of manuscript and printed reports, field books, memoirs, maps . . . of the Indian surveys*, 1878.

3450 STEVENS (HENRY) *and* TREE (ROLAND). 'Comparative cartography exemplified in an analytical and bibliographical description of nearly one hundred maps and charts of the American continent published in Great Britain during the years 1600 to 1850', in *Essays honoring Lawrence C. Wroth*, 1951, 305–63. Repr. Map Collectors' Series IV (1967), 39.

See also H. R. Holmden, *Catalogue of maps, plans and charts in the Map room of the Dominion archives*, Ottawa, 1912 (Pub. of the Canadian archives, 8), also Henry Raup Wagner, *The cartography of the northwest coast of America to the year 1800*, Berkeley, 1937, and Don. W. Thomson, *Men and meridians; the history of surveying and mapping in Canada, v. 1, Prior to 1867*, Ottawa, 1966, bibliog. 304–12.

3451 BAILEY (*Sir* EDWARD BATTERSBY). Geological survey of Great Britain. 1952. Bibliog. vi–vii.

Geological survey of Great Britain, *Memoirs*, 1846+, are valuable on superficial geology, water supplies, and economic geology. For William Smith and John Macculloch see (3175), (3176).

3452 ROBINSON (ADRIAN HENRY WARDLE). Marine cartography in Britain; a history of the sea chart to 1855. With a foreword by Vice-Admiral Sir John Edgell, F.R.S. Leicester. 1962.

Also G. S. Ritchie, *The Admiralty chart. British naval hydrography in the nineteenth century*, 1967. For the work of the Admiralty see Llewellyn Styles Dawson, *Memoirs of hydrography, including brief biographies of the principal officers . . . between 1750 and 1885*, 2 pt., Eastbourne, [1883,] 1885, supplemented by Sir Archibald Day, *The Admiralty hydrographic service, 1795–1919*, pub. Ministry of Defence, 1967, bibliog. 350–9. For published charts see Admiralty Hydrographic department, *A catalogue of charts, plans, and views*, etc., 1825, and frequent editions thereafter. The Hydrographic department, Ministry of Defence, Taunton, has a large collection MS. and engraved, arranged topographically. The Naval library, Ministry of Defence, London, has a large collection of printed charts and atlases.

K. PRINTING

I. BIBLIOGRAPHY

See Jack (2660).

3453 BIGMORE (EDWARD CLEMENTS) *and* WYMAN (CHARLES WILLIAM HENRY). A bibliography of printing, with notes and illustrations. 3 v. 1880–86.

Comprehensive for its time. Later guides include: St. Bride Foundation Institute,

Catalogue of the technical reference library of works on printing and the allied arts, 1919; National Book League, *Books about books: catalogue of the library* . . ., 1955, suppl. Jan. 1954–June 1956, and monthly accession lists; London School of Economics, *Classified catalogue of a collection of works on publishing and bookselling in the British library of political and economic science*, 1961; John M. Wing Foundation, *Dictionary catalogue of the history of printing from the foundation*, 6 v., Boston, Mass., 1962.

2. GENERAL WORKS

3454 TIMPERLEY (CHARLES HENRY). Encyclopaedia of literary and typographical anecdote; being a chronological digest of the most interesting facts illustrative of the history of literature and printing . . . second edition, to which are added, a continuation to the present time, comprising recent biographies, chiefly of booksellers. 1842.

3455 THE LIBRARY; a quarterly review of bibliography. 1889+.

Indexed, with [London] Library association and Bibliographical society publications in George Watson Cole, *An index to bibliographical papers* . . . *London, 1877–1932*, Chicago, 1933.

3456 HOWE (ELLIC) *ed.* The trade: passages from the literature of the printing craft, 1550–1935, selected by E. Howe. 1943.

3457 GLAISTER (GEOFFREY ASHALL). Glossary of the book; terms used in paper-making, printing, bookbinding and publishing with notes on illuminated manuscripts, bibliophiles, private presses and printing societies . . . 1960.

Bibliog. 477–84. Printed in U.S.A. as *An encyclopaedia of the book*, Cleveland, 1960.

3458 JOURNAL of the Printing Historical Society. V. 1+. 1965+.

3459 CLAIR (COLIN). A history of printing in Britain. 1965.

Fuller on the early 19th century than Henry Robert Plomer, *A short history of English printing, 1476–1898*, rev. edn., 1920. Phyllis Margaret Handover, *Printing in London from 1476 to modern times* . . ., 1960, is informative. See also Howe (1735).

3460 TWYMAN (MICHAEL). Printing, 1770–1970; an illustrated history of its development and uses in England. 1970.

3. THE ART OF THE BOOK

(a) *General*

On music publishing see (3032).

3461 STOWER (CALEB). The printer's grammar, or introduction to the art of printing; containing a concise history of the art. 1808. Repr., English bibliographical sources, ed. D. F. Foxon, series 3, no. 4, 1965.

For other professional handbooks see T. C. Hansard, *Typographia* (1606) and Charles Henry Timperley, *The printer's manual* . . ., 1838, repr. English bibliog. sources, ed. Foxon, series 3, no. 7, 1965.

3462 REED (TALBOT BAINES). A history of the old English letter foun-
dries, with notes historical and bibliographical on the rise and progress of
English typography. New edn. rev. and enl. by A. F. Johnson. 1952.

See too John Findlay McRae, *Two centuries of typefounding: annals of the letter foundry
established by William Caslon . . .*, 1920.

3463 UPDIKE (DANIEL BERKELEY). Printing types; their history, forms,
and use; a study in survivals. 3rd edn. 2 v. Camb. Mass. 1962.

The most comprehensive work on the history of type design. Nicolette Mary Gray,
Nineteenth century ornamental types and title pages, 1938, deals with 'expressive' types.
The most complete catalogue of type-founders' specimens is William Turner Berry
and Alfred Forbes Johnson, *Catalogue of specimens of printing types by English and
Scottish printers and founders, 1665–1830*, new edn., 1962.

3464 JAMES (PHILIP BRUTTON). English book illustration, 1800–1900.
1947.

3465 TOOLEY (RONALD VERE). English books with coloured plates,
1790–1860; a bibliographical account of the most important books illustrated
by English artists in colour aquatint and colour lithography. 1954.

(b) *Printers and Presses*

3466 LIEBERMAN (ELIZABETH KOLLER), *comp.* The first check-log of
private press names. White Plains. N.Y. 1960. 3rd edn. 1962.

Lists 1,200 names of presses, 1475–1960.

3467 MARTIN (JOHN). A bibliographical catalogue of books privately
printed. . . . 2nd edn. 1854.

British presses only, largely on the period 1780–1853.

3468 ANDERSON (JOHN). Catalogue of early Belfast printed books, 1694
to 1830. Belfast. [1886.] Enl. edn. Belfast. 1890. Supplements, 1894, 1902.

3469 HILSON (J. LINDSAY). Berwick-upon-Tweed typography, 1753–
1900. Priv. printed. [1902.]

3470 JONES (IFANO). A history of printing and printers in Wales to 1810
and of successive and related printers to 1923; also, A history of printing and
printers in Monmouthshire to 1923. Cardiff. 1925.

3471 WARREN (ARTHUR). The Charles Whittinghams, printers. N.Y.
1896.

3472 ROBERTS (SYDNEY CASTLE). A history of the Cambridge university
press, 1521–1921. Camb. 1921.

See also Robert Bowes, *Biographical notes on the University printers from the commencement of printing in Cambridge to the present time.* [Camb. 1886].

3473 MACLEHOSE (JAMES). The Glasgow university press, 1638–1931, with some notes on Scottish printing in the last three hundred years. Glasgow. 1931.

3474 HART (HORACE). Charles Earl Stanhope and the Oxford University Press. Reprint, Printing Historical Society, pubs. 2. 1966.

3475 TWYMAN (MICHAEL) *and* ROLLINSON (WILLIAM). John Soulby, printer, Ulverston; a study of the work printed by John Soulby, father and son, between 1796 and 1827 . . . (Reading University. Museum of English rural life, pubs.) Reading. 1966.

3476 DOUGHTY (DENNIS WILLIAM). The Tullis press, Cupar, 1803–1849. (Abertay Historical Society, pubs. 12.) Dundee. 1967.

(c) *Publishers*

For Scottish publishers see (3953–3958).

3477 SMILES (SAMUEL). A publisher and his friends. Memoir and correspondence of . . . John Murray, with an account of the origin and progress of the house, 1768–1843. 2 v. 1891.

3478 KEYNES (*Sir* GEOFFREY LANGDON). William Pickering, publisher; a memoir and a hand-list of his editions. 1924.

3479 MORISON (STANLEY). John Bell, 1745–1831; bookseller, printer, publisher, typefounder, journalist, &c. Camb. 1930.

3480 BLUNDEN (EDMUND CHARLES). Keats's publisher: a memoir of John Taylor, 1781–1864. 1936.

Tim Chilcot, *A publisher and his circle: the life and work of John Taylor*, 1972.

3481 BESTERMAN (THEODORE) *ed.* The publishing firm of Cadell and Davies; select correspondence and accounts, 1793–1836. 1938.

3482 MERRIAM (HAROLD GUY). Edward Moxon, publisher of poets. (Columbia Univ. Studies in English and comparative literature.) N.Y. 1939.

3483 PIKE (G. HOLDEN). John Cassell. 1894.

3484 GETTMANN (ROYAL ALFRED). A Victorian publisher; a study of the Bentley papers. Camb. 1960.

4. BOOKSELLERS AND THEIR TRADE

3485 MUMBY (FRANK ARTHUR). Publishing and bookselling; a history from the earliest times to the present day. 4th edn. 1956. 5th edn. Part I: to 1870, by F. A. Mumby, part II: 1870-1970, by Ian Norrie. 1974.

Standard. Thin on period, but with useful bibliog. Henry Curwen, *A history of book-*

sellers, the old and the new, 1873, is old-fashioned but informative. See also Barnes and Plant (1605).

3486 RIVINGTON (SEPTIMUS) *ed*. The publishing family of Rivington. 1919.

3487 COLLINS (ARTHUR SIMONS). The profession of letters; a study of the relation of author to patron, publisher and public, 1780–1832. 1928. N.Y. 1929.

3488 SMITH (GEORGE) *and* BENGER (FRANK). The oldest London bookshop: a history of two hundred years. 1928.

5. ALLIED SUBJECTS

See, on paper (1607); on copyright, (622).

3489 HOBSON (ANTHONY ROBERT ALWYN). The literature of book-binding. (The Book, no. 2.) 1954.

A select bibliography.

3490 RAMSDEN (CHARLES). Bookbinders of the United Kingdom (outside London), 1780–1840. [1954.]

A comprehensive directory, as is also his *London bookbinders, 1780–1840*, 1956. On organization of the trade see Howe and Child (1735).

3491 MIDDLETON (BERNARD CHESTER). A history of English craft bookbinding technique. 1963.

See too Michael Sadleir, *The evolution of publishers' binding styles, 1770–1900*, 1930; and Lionel Seabrook Darley, *Bookbinding then and now; a survey of the first hundred and seventy-eight years of James Burn and company*, 1959.

3492 WESTBY-GIBSON (JOHN). The bibliography of shorthand. 1887.

An unannotated alphabetical list. The leading practitioner's survey of the development of early 19th-century systems is Sir Isaac Pitman, *History of shorthand*, 1847, 4th edn. [1918].

L. NEWSPAPERS

1. BIBLIOGRAPHIES AND LISTS

See *N.C.B.E.L.* (2650), v. 2, cols. 1353–70, v. 3, cols. 1755–1884.

3493 [MUDDIMAN (JOSEPH GEORGE).] Tercentenary handlist of English and Welsh newspapers, magazines and reviews. The Times. 1920. New edn. 1933.

A chronological list, with an index.

3494 PRICE (WARREN C.). The literature of journalism: an annotated bibliography. Minneapolis and London. [1959.]

Notes on individual newspapers and journalists. William S. Ward, *British periodicals and newspapers, 1789–1832. A bibliography of secondary sources*, Kentucky univ. press, [?1973].

2. GENERAL

3495 BOURNE (HENRY RICHARD FOX). English newspapers; chapters in the history of journalism. 2 v. 1887.

Inadequate, but still the most useful general history. Alexander Andrews, *The history of British journalism from the foundation of the newspaper press in England, to the repeal of the Stamp Act in 1855*, 2 v., 1859, has inaccuracies. Personal information was used in Frederick Knight Hunt, *The fourth estate . . .*, 2 v., 1850, and in James Grant, *The newspaper press*, 3 v., 1871. Harold Herd, *The march of journalism: the story of the British press from 1622 to the present day*, 1952, adds a little but is brief on the period 1789–1851. See also Ian R. Christie, 'British newspapers in the later Georgian age', *Myth and Reality in late-eighteenth-century British politics and other papers*, 1970, pp. 311–33.

3496 MORISON (STANLEY). The English newspaper. Some account of the physical development of journals printed in London between 1622 and the present day. Camb. 1932.

Excellent outline on questions of journalistic presentation.

3. SPECIAL ASPECTS

3497 ASPINALL (ARTHUR). Politics and the press, c. 1780–1850. 1949.

Bibliog. 385–92. On left-wing newspapers see also Simon Maccoby, 'Newspaper politics: a footnote to nineteenth century history', *Politics*, I (1934–5), 200–14.

3498 BURTON (KENNETH GEORGE). The early newspaper press in Berkshire, 1723–1855. Privately printed. Reading. 1954.

3499 READ (DONALD). Press and people, 1790–1850: opinion in three English cities. 1961.

Deals principally with the press in Leeds, Manchester, and Sheffield.

3500 HOLLIS (PATRICIA). The pauper press. A study of working class radicalism of the 1830s. 1970.

Excellent. J. H. Wiener, *The war of the unstamped . . . 1830–1836*, Ithaca, N.Y., 1969, is also valuable.

4. INDIVIDUAL JOURNALS

3501 [MORISON (STANLEY).] The history of the Times. V. I, 'The Thunderer' in the making, 1785–1841. 1935. V. II, The tradition established, 1841–1884. 1939.

Thorough and well documented. On the two early great editors see Derek Hudson, *Thomas Barnes of* The Times, *with selections from his critical essays never before reprinted*, ed. Harold Child, Camb. 1943, and Arthur Irwin Dasent, *John Thadeus Delane, editor of 'The Times': his life and correspondence . . .*, 2 v., 1908.

3502 MILLS (WILLIAM HASLAM). The Manchester Guardian: a century of history. 1921.

A journalistic account, of limited value. See also David Ayerst, *'Guardian': biography of a newspaper*, 1971.

3503 HINDLE (WILFRID). The Morning Post, 1772–1937. Portrait of a newspaper. [1937.]

3504 STOUT (GEORGE D.). The political history of Leigh Hunt's *Examiner*. 1949.

3505 HANDOVER (PHYLLIS MARGARET). A history of the 'London Gazette', 1665–1965. 1965.

3506 CHRISTIE (IAN RALPH). 'James Perry of the *Morning Chronicle*, 1756–1821.' *Myth and Reality in late-eighteenth-century British politics and other essays*, 1970, pp. 334–58, and Ivon Asquith, 'Advertising and the press . . . James Perry and the *Morning Chronicle* 1790–1821', *Hist. J.* 18 (1975), 703–24.

XI

LOCAL HISTORY

Many of the older local histories, and the earlier volumes of the *Victoria County Histories*, give scant attention to the nineteenth century. (Some histories of the early industrial districts are an exception.) More useful sources are sometimes to be found in local newspapers (3493), in parliamentary papers (see Ford and Ford (391) above and Powell (3508)), in the Public Record Office (64), as well as more specialized or local repositories (3509). For agriculture, industries, and communications see *Economic History*, chapter VIII, section G. For local government see chapter III, section D.

A. BIBLIOGRAPHY, CATALOGUES, AND GUIDES

3507 HUMPHREYS (ARTHUR LEE). A handbook to county bibliography: being a bibliography of bibliographies relating to the counties and towns of Great Britain and Ireland. 1917.

The *Economic History Review* (1365) has published annual lists of works on economic history, containing much local history, since 1927; the *Subject index to periodicals*, subseq. *British humanities index* (19) classifies articles under county headings, 1954+.

3508 GROSS (CHARLES). A bibliography of British municipal history, including gilds and parliamentary representation. Harvard hist. studies 5. N.Y. 1897. 2nd edn. with a preface by Geoffrey Haward Martin. Leicester. 1966.

Supplemented by Geoffrey Haward Martin and Sylvia McIntyre, *A bibliography of British and Irish municipal history*, v. 1: *General works*, Leicester, 1972, in progress. Other general guides are William Raymond Powell, *Local history from blue books; a select list of the sessional papers of the House of Commons*, Hist. Assoc. Helps for Students of History, 64, 1962; Maurice Bond, *The records of Parliament; a guide for genealogists and local historians* [Canterbury], 1964; Alan Rogers, *This was their world: approaches to local history*, B.B.C., 1972, and William Brewer Stephens, *Sources for English local history*, Manchester, 1973.

3509 REDSTONE (LILIAN JANE) *and* STEER (FRANCIS WILLIAM) *eds*. Local records: their nature and care. 1953.

See also Frederick George Emmison and Irvine Gray, *County records (Quarter sessions, Petty sessions, Clerk of the Peace and Lieutenancy)*, rev. edn., Hist. Assoc. Helps for Students of History, 62, 1961. For local societies see Sir Robert Somerville, *Handlist of record publications* (British Records Assoc. Pubs. pamphlets 3), 1951; Historical MSS. Commission, *List of record repositories in Great Britain*, 5th edn., rev. by Felicity Ranger, 1973; Sara E. Harcup, *Historical, archaeological and kindred societies in the British Isles: a list*, 1965.

3510 NORTON (JANE ELIZABETH) *ed*. Guide to the national and provincial directories of England and Wales, excluding London, published before 1856. (Roy. Hist. Soc. Guides and Handbooks 5). 1950.

Designed to complement Goss (3753) on London. See also David Frederick Radmore and Sandra Payne, *Guide to the directories of the West Midlands to 1850*, 1971, and Society of Genealogists, *A catalogue of directories and poll books in the possession of the Society of Genealogists*, ed. J. M. Sims, 1964.

3511   GOMME (GEORGE LAURENCE) *ed*. The Gentleman's magazine library: being a classified collection of the chief contents of the Gentleman's magazine from 1731–1868. 29 v. in 30. 1883–1905.

3512   SOCIETY OF GENEALOGISTS. A catalogue of parish register copies in the possession of the Society of Genealogists. Rev. enl. edn. 1963.

To be used in conjunction with the society's *National index of parish register copies*, 1939, new edn., by Donald John and A. E. F. Sheel, in progress, 1968+. See also Anthony John Camp, *Wills and their whereabouts being a thorough revision and extension of the previous work of the same name by B. G. Bouwens*, Canterbury, 1953. For genealogies see William Berry, *County genealogies*, 8 v. 1830–42.

3513   NUNN (GEORGE WALTER ARTHUR) *ed*. British sources of photographs and pictures. 1952.

3514   HOSKINS (WILLIAM GEORGE). Local history in England. 1959.

Also Ralph Bernard Pugh, *How to write a parish history*, 1954; Joscelyne Finberg, *Exploring villages*, 1958; John West, *Village records*, 1962. Frederick William Kuhlicke and Frederick George Emmison, *Local history handbook* (Hist. Assoc. Helps for Students of History, 69), 4th edn., 1969, is also useful. For local government see (466), (476), (507–8), and Gomme (p. 74).

B. TOPOGRAPHY, GAZETTEERS, ROAD BOOKS, MAPS

3515   ANDERSON (JOHN PARKER). The book of British topography: a classified catalogue of the topographical works in the library of the British Museum relating to Great Britain and Ireland. 1881.

Other guides are George Edwin Fussell, *The exploration of England. A select bibliography of travel and topography: 1570–1815*, 1935; Edward Godfrey Cox, *A reference guide to the literature of travel*, v. 3, *Great Britain* (Univ. of Washington pubs. 12), Seattle, 1949, lists works published before 1800 only; *A catalogue of ten thousand tracts and pamphlets . . . collected . . . by . . . William Upcott and John Russell Smith*, 1878, and Walter Vernon Daniell and Frederick J. Nield, *Manual of British topography, etc.*, 1909, two sale catalogues, somewhat disorganized in arrangement. See also (2900).

3516   BRAYLEY (EDWARD WEDLAKE), BRITTON (JOHN), NIGHTINGALE (JOSEPH), *and others*. The beauties of England and Wales: or Delineations, topographical, historical, and descriptive, of each county. 18 v. 1801–15.

There are many such collections, among them George Alexander Cooke, *The modern British traveller; or, tourist's pocket directory . . . of all the counties in England, Scotland and Wales, as also the adjacent islands*, 47 v. [1802?–1810?]; Thomas Kitson Cromwell, *Excursions through England and Wales, Scotland and Ireland*, 12 v., 1818 [–1822]. Among the fine illustrated books of the period see Samuel Middiman, *Select views in*

Great Britain, 1784–1813 [1814?]; Samuel Ireland, *Picturesque views on the river Thames etc.*, 2 v., 1792; Joseph Wilkinson, *Select views in Cumberland, Westmorland, and Lancashire*, 1810, with an anonymous introduction which is the first version of Wordsworth's *Description . . . of the Lakes*, 1822; Philippe Jacques de Loutherbourg, *The romantic and picturesque scenery of England and Wales etc.*, 1805; John Preston Neale, *Views of the seats of noblemen and gentlemen in England, Wales, Scotland, and Ireland, from drawings*, 6 v., 1818–23, 2nd Series, 5 v., 1824–9.

3517 LEWIS (SAMUEL). A topographical dictionary of England . . . and the islands of Guernsey, Jersey, and Man. 4 v. 1831. 3rd edn. 5 v. 1835. 5th edn. 4 v. and atlas. 1842. 7th edn. 4 v. 1848–9.

The most valuable of the early gazetteers. Also Daniel and Samuel Lysons, *Magna Britannia etc.*, 6 v., [1806]–22, James Bell, *A new and comprehensive gazetteer of England and Wales etc.* 8 pts., Glasgow and Edinburgh, 1836, which gives populations according to census of 1831, and parliamentary franchises according to reform act of 1832. James A. Sharp, *A new gazetteer; or topographical dictionary of the British Islands . . . with a reference under every name to the sheet of the Ordnance Survey*, etc., 2 v., 1852, gives information for the end of the period on railways, manufactures, poor law unions.

3518 FORDHAM (*Sir* HERBERT GEORGE). The roadbooks and itineraries of Great Britain, 1570 to 1850. A catalogue with an introduction and a bibliography. Camb. 1924.

Also Dorothy Ballen, *Bibliography of roadmaking and roads in the United Kingdom* (Studies in Econ. and Polit. Science, bibliogs., 3), 1914. Among popular roadbooks see John Ogilby and William Morgan, *The traveller's pocket book; or, Ogilby and Morgan's book of the roads, improved and amended*, 24th edn., 1794, of a work first published in 1676; Daniel Paterson, *A new and accurate description of all the direct and principal cross roads in Great Britain*, 1771, 18th edn. ed. Edward Mogg, with title *Paterson's roads, being an entirely original and accurate description etc.*, 1826; John Cary, *Cary's traveller's companion*, 1790. For the history of these works see Sir H. G. Fordham, 'John Ogilby, his "Britannia" and the British itineraries of the eighteenth century', *The Library*, Bibliog. Soc. Trans. 4th ser. 6 (1925–6), 157–78; ' "Paterson's Roads", Daniel Paterson, his maps and itineraries, 1738–1825', *loc. cit.* 5 (1924–5), 333–56; *John Cary, engraver, map, chart, and print-seller and globe-maker, 1754 to 1835. A bibliography*, Camb., 1925. For guide books see Walley Chamberlain Oulton, *The traveller's guide . . . comprising a complete topography of England and Wales*, 2 v., 1805; Adam and Charles Black, *Black's picturesque tourist and road book of England and Wales*, Edin., 1843; John Murray, *A handbook for travellers in Devon and Cornwall. With maps*, 1851, the first of a long series.

3519 TOOLEY (RONALD VERE). Maps and map-makers. 2nd rev. edn. 1952.

Contains a full list of county bibliogs., 72–85. See also Thomas Chubb (62), Sir H. G. Fordham, *Hand-list of catalogues and works of reference relating to carto-bibliography and kindred subjects for Great Britain and Ireland, 1720 to 1927*, Camb., 1928, Elizabeth M. Rodger, *The large scale county maps of the British Isles, 1596–1850: a union list compiled in the map section of the Bodleian library*, Oxf., 1960. Harold Whitaker, *The Harold Whitaker collection of county atlases, road-books and maps, presented to the University of Leeds: a catalogue*, Leeds, 1947, is a good general guide to early maps, as is Audrey M. Lambert, 'Early maps and local studies', *Geography*, 41 (1956), 167–77. For Ordnance survey see (3448), and for maps in the P.R.O. (3439).

3520 GREENWOOD (CHARLES) *and* GREENWOOD (JOHN). Atlas of the counties of England from actual surveys made from the years 1817 to 1833. 1834.

A beautifully prepared atlas. Another useful atlas is *Pigot and Co's British atlas*, [1839].

3521 LOBEL (MARY DOREEN) *ed.* Historic towns: maps and plans of towns and cities in the British Isles, with historical commentaries, from earliest times to 1800. [Oxf.] 1969+.

Also Angela Fordham, *Town plans of the British Isles, series appearing in atlases from 1580–1850,* Map Collectors' Circle, Map Collectors' series (1965/6), 22.

C. COUNTY AND TOWN HISTORIES

1. General Works

Counties are listed alphabetically, and towns alphabetically within the counties. The local government areas are those which existed down to 1 April, 1974.

3522 PAGE (WILLIAM), DOUBLEDAY (H. ARTHUR), *and others, eds.* The Victoria history of the counties of England. 1900+.

In progress. Complete county histories, and those more recent volumes which deal fully with the 19th century, are listed separately below.

3523 PEVSNER (*Sir* NIKOLAUS BERNHARD LEON) *and others.* The buildings of England. Harmondsworth. 1951–74.

The *Reports* of the Royal Commission on Historical Monuments now include buildings down to 1851.

3524 BRIGGS (ASA). Victorian cities. 1963.

Also on 19th-century towns see Charles Ryle Fay, *Round about industrial Britain, 1830–1860* (The Toronto lectures), Toronto, 1952.

2. Counties

3525 BEDFORDSHIRE. CONISBEE (LEWIS RALPH). A Bedfordshire bibliography, with some comments and biographical notes. (Bedfordshire Hist. Soc. pubns.) Aspley Guise. 1962. Suppt. 1967.

See also Joyce Godber, *History of Bedfordshire,* pub. Bedfordshire County Council, 1969, also Bedfordshire County Council, *Guide to the Bedfordshire Record Office,* Bedford, 1957, and *Guide supplement, 1957–62* [1963]. Extracts from Quarter Sessions records are printed in W. J. Hardy and William Page, *Notes and extracts from the county records,* v. 1, Bedford, 1907. *V.C.H.* Bedfordshire is complete. See also Joyce Godber and P. A. Kennedy, *Guide to the Russell estate collections for Bedfordshire and Devon to 1910,* Bedford, 1966.

3526 —— BEDFORD. BLYTH (THOMAS ALLEN). The history of Bedford and visitor's guide. [1873.]

3527 —— LUTON. AUSTIN (WILLIAM). The history of Luton and its hamlets. 2 v. Newport. Isle of Wight. 1928.

3528 BERKSHIRE. READING CENTRAL PUBLIC LIBRARY. Local collection. Catalogue of books and maps relating to Berkshire. Reading. 1958.

See also Felix Hull, comp., *Guide to the Berkshire Record Office,* Reading, 1952. Early

19th-century Berkshire politics are discussed in Gash (437). For newspapers see (3498). *V.C.H.* Berkshire is complete.

3529 —— ABINGDON. TOWNSEND (JAMES). News of a country town. Being extracts from *Jackson's Oxford Journal* relating to Abingdon, 1753–1835. 1914.

3530 —— MAIDENHEAD. WALKER (JOHN WESLEY) *ed.* A calendar of the ancient charters and documents of the corporation of Maidenhead. Maidenhead. 1908.

3531 —— NEWBURY. MONEY (WALTER). History of the ancient town and borough of Newbury in the county of Berks. Oxf. 1887.

3532 —— READING. CHILDS (WILLIAM MacBRIDE). The town of Reading during the early part of the nineteenth century. (University College of Reading studies in local history.) Reading. 1910.

See also J. Man, *History of Reading*, 1816, and two volumes of reminiscences, Peter Hampson Ditchfield, *Reading seventy years ago; a record of events 1813–1819*, Reading, 1887, and [William Silver Darter], *Reminiscences of Reading. By an octogenarian*, Reading, 1889. Mary Russell Mitford's *Belford Regis, or, Sketches of a country town*, 3 v., 1835, is about Reading.

3533 —— WANTAGE. PHILIP (KATHLEEN). Victorian Wantage. Wantage 1968.

3534 —— WINDSOR. BOND (MAURICE FRANCIS). A guide to books about Windsor castle and borough. [Windsor. 1946.]

Also Shelagh Mary Bond, comp., *Handlist of the records of the royal borough of New Windsor*, Windsor, 1959; Robert Richard Tighe and James Edward Davis, *Annals of Windsor: being a history of the castle and town, with some account of Eton and places adjacent*, 2 v., 1858; George Martin Hughes, *A history of Windsor forest, Sunninghill, and the Great Park*, 1890.

3535 BUCKINGHAMSHIRE. GOUGH (HENRY). Bibliotheca Buckinghamiensis: a list of books relating to the county of Buckingham. Aylesbury. 1890.

The most recent bibliog. available. For records see Buckinghamshire Record Society, Lists and indexes no. 1, *A handlist of the Stowe collection in the Huntington library*, California, comp. John Gilbert Jenkins, Jordans 1956; no. 2, *A handlist of Buckinghamshire estate maps*, comp. Elizabeth Mary Elvey, Jordans, 1963. See also Buckinghamshire Record Office, Occasional pubns. 1, *Education records*, Aylesbury, 1961, and 3, *Catalogue of maps, 1440–1850*, Aylesbury, 1961. A valuable compilation, from contemporary newspapers, is Robert Gibbs, *Buckinghamshire; a record of local occurrences and general events, chronologically arranged*, 4 v., Aylesbury, 1878–82. *V.C.H.* Buckinghamshire is complete. Richard W. Davis, *Political change and continuity, 1760–1885: A Buckinghamshire study*, Newton Abbot, 1972, is excellent. See also, for enclosures (1664).

3536 —— AYLESBURY. GIBBS (ROBERT). Buckinghamshire; a history of Aylesbury with its borough and hundreds, the hamlet of Walton, and the electoral division. Aylesbury, 1885.

3537 —— HIGH WYCOMBE. ASHFORD (LEONARD JOHN). The history of the borough of High Wycombe from its origins to 1880. 1960.

3538 —— STONY STRATFORD. HYDE (FRANCIS EDWIN) *and* MARKHAM (SIDNEY FRANK). A history of Stony Stratford and the immediate vicinity. 1948.

3539 CAMBRIDGESHIRE. CAMBRIDGESHIRE COUNTY LIBRARY. Cambridgeshire: an annotated list of books, maps, prints, pamphlets and other material in the Cambridgeshire county library local history collection. Comp. P. R. Gifford. Cambridge. 1961.

Also see Isle of Ely County Library, *Hereward's Isle, books on the Fenland*, comp. Walter Ernest Dring, 4th edn., 1962, and Robert Bowes, *A catalogue of books printed at, or relating to, the University, town and county of Cambridge from 1521 to 1893*, Cambridge, 1894. See also (1664) (enclosures). On county history see (1684), and Henry Clifford Darby, *The Cambridge Region*, Cambridge, 1938, and on the fens, Samuel Henry Miller and Sydney Barber Josiah Skertchly, *The Fenland past and present*, 1878, and Bayne (3648).

3540 —— CAMBRIDGE. V.C.H. CAMBRIDGESHIRE. V. III. The City and University of Cambridge. Ed. by John Peter Charles Roach. 1959.

Includes Helen Maud Cam, 'The City of Cambridge', 1–149. See also Charles Henry Cooper, *Annals of Cambridge*, 5 v., Cambridge, 1842–1908.

3541 —— WISBECH. WATSON (WILLIAM). An historical account of the ancient town and port of Wisbech, in the Isle of Ely, in the county of Cambridge. Wisbech. 1827.

Neil Walker and Thomas Cradock, *The history of Wisbech and the Fens*, Wisbech, 1849.

3542 CHANNEL ISLANDS. DURAND (RALPH) Guernsey: present and past. Guernsey. 1933.

See also Jonathan Duncan, *The history of Guernsey, with occasional notices of Jersey, Alderney, and Sark, and biographical sketches*, 1841; F. C. Lukis, 'The growth of St. Peter Port in the early nineteenth century', *Société Guernésiaise Reports and Transactions*, 12, part 2 (1935), 153–70; J. P. Warren, 'Guernsey in the eighteen-thirties', *ibid.* 13, pt. 3 (1939), 268–83.

3543 —— JERSEY. BALLEINE (GEORGE REGINALD). A history of the island of Jersey from the cave men to the German occupation and after. 1950.

Bibliog. 333–6. See also Eugene Duprey, 'Essai de bibliographie jersiaise' in *Société Jersiaise Bulletin*, 4 (1899), 151–92, and 5 (1902), 57–72. Other accounts of 19th-century Jersey are *Caesarea; the island of Jersey* 1840; Charles le Quesne, *A constitutional history of Jersey*, 1856; Arthur Charles Saunders, *Jersey in the 18th and 19th centuries*, Jersey, 1930; Ralph Mollet, *Chronology of Jersey*, Jersey, 1949; Charles Ryle Fay, *The Channel Islands and Newfoundland*, Cambridge, 1961, predominantly on Jersey's trade with Newfoundland.

3544 CHESHIRE. ORMEROD (GEORGE). The history of the county palatine and city of Chester. 3 v. 1819. 2nd edn. rev. and enl. by Thomas Helsby. 3 v. 1882.

See also John Henry Cooke, *Bibliotheca Cestriensis*, etc., Warrington, 1904; William

Williams Mortimer, *The history of the hundred of Wirral, with a sketch of the city and county of Chester*, etc., 1847, which also contains information on 19th cent. Birkenhead; Dorothy Sylvester and Geoffrey Nulty, eds., *The historical atlas of Cheshire*, etc., Chester 1958, rev. edn. 1966; see also (1688), Baines and Fairbairn (3611), and Emery and Beard (3676).

3545 —— CHESTER. FENWICK (GEORGE LEE). A history of the ancient city of Chester from the earliest times. Chester. 1896.

Bibliog. 445–60. Joseph Hemingway, *History of the city of Chester, from its foundation to the present time*, 2 v., Chester, 1831, contains much 19th-century material.

3546 —— CONGLETON. STEPHENS (WILLIAM BREWER) *ed*. History of Congleton published to celebrate the 700th anniversary of the granting of the charter to the town. Manchester. 1970.

3547 —— CREWE. CHALONER (WILLIAM HENRY). The social and economic development of Crewe, 1780–1923. (University of Manchester Econ. Hist. Ser. 14.) Manchester. 1950.

Bibliog. ix–xiv.

3548 —— MACCLESFIELD. DAVIES (CLARICE STELLA) *ed*. A history of Macclesfield. Manchester. [1961.]

Bibliog. 380–90.

3549 —— STOCKPORT. HEGINBOTHAM (HENRY). Stockport, ancient and modern. 2 v. 1882–1892.

See also Unwin *et al.* (1537).

3550 CORNWALL. ROWE (WILLIAM JOHN). Cornwall in the age of the industrial revolution. Liverpool. 1953.

Bibliog. 337–45. Also Richard Pearse, *The ports and harbours of Cornwall: an introduction to the study of eight hundred years of maritime affairs*, St. Austell [1963], bibliog. 153–6. The standard bibliography, George Clement Boase and William Prideaux Courtney, *Bibliotheca Cornubiensis*, 3 v., 1874–82, is now very old. For Cornish archives see Margaret J. Groombridge, 'Cornish archives', *Royal Cornwall Polytechnic Society Annual Report*, 118 (1951), 27–9, 119 (1952), 26–8, 120 (1953), 32–4, 124 (1957), 18–20. The society has published many papers on local industrial history in recent years; see *Index to the annual reports of the society* [1896–1957], [1960]. The most substantial survey of the county for the 19th century is [Joseph Polsue], *A complete parochial history of the county of Cornwall, compiled from the best authorities, and corrected and improved from actual survey*, 4 v., 1867–72; see also Charles Sandoe Gilbert, *An historical (and topographical) survey of the county of Cornwall*, 2 v., Plymouth Dock, 1817–20; William Penaluna, *Historical survey of the County of Cornwall*, 2 v., Helston, 1838; Walter Hawken Tregellas, *Cornish worthies: sketches of some eminent Cornish men and families*, 2 v., 1884; George Clement Boase, *Collectanea Cornubiensia: a collection of biographical and topographical notes relating to the county of Cornwall*, Truro, 1890. Alfred Kenneth Hamilton Jenkin, *News from Cornwall, with a memoir of William Jenkin*, 1951, is based on letters written 1790–1820. For Cornish parliamentary history see (426), (434), for mining see (1558), for agriculture see Marshall (3563).

3551 —— FALMOUTH. THOMAS (RICHARD). History and description of the town and harbour of Falmouth. Falmouth. 1827.

3552 —— HELSTON. TOY (HENRY SPENCER). The history of Helston. 1936.

3553 —— LAUNCESTON. ROBBINS (*Sir* ALFRED FARTHING). Launceston, past and present: a historical and descriptive sketch. Launceston. 1888.

3554 —— PENZANCE. COURTNEY (LOUISE). Half a century of Penzance, 1825–1875. From notes by John Sampson Courtney. Penzance. 1878.

See also George Bown Millett, *Penzance past and present*, Penzance, 1880.

3555 —— ISLES OF SCILLY. MATTHEWS (GORDON FORRESTER). The Isles of Scilly: a constitutional, economic and social survey of the development of an island people from early times to 1900. 1960.

Bibliog. 247–50.

3556 CUMBERLAND. BOUCH (CHARLES MURRAY LOWTHER) *and* JONES (GWILYM PEREDUR). A short economic and social history of the Lake counties, 1500–1830, with contributions by R. W. Brunskill. Manchester. 1962.

Based on a wide range of sources. See also Henry Wigston Hodgson, ed., *A bibliography of the history and topography of Cumberland and Westmorland*, Joint archives committee for Cumberland, Westmorland and Carlisle Record Office, 1968, also (3706). See also Fred. Barnes and James Leslie Hobbs, *Handlist of newspapers published in Cumberland, Westmorland and North Lancashire* (Cumberland and Westmorland Antiquarian and Archaeol. Soc., Tract ser., 14), Kendal, 1951. William Whellan, *The history and topography of the counties of Cumberland and Westmorland*, Pontefract, 1860, and Henry Lonsdale, *The worthies of Cumberland*, 6 v., 1867–75, contain substantial 19th-century information. For social life see William Dickinson, *Cumbriana, or fragments of Cumbrian life*, 1875; *Tom Rumney of Mellfell* (2173); C. M. L. Bouch, *Prelates and people of the lake counties, a history of the diocese of Carlisle, 1133–1933*, Kendal, 1948; Edward Hughes, *North country life in the eighteenth century*, ii, *Cumberland and Westmorland, 1700–1830*, 1965. See also John Duncan Marshall, *Old Lakeland: some Cumberland social history*, Newton Abbot [1971]. For parliamentary history see (434).

3557 —— CARLISLE. CREIGHTON (MANDELL). Carlisle. 1889.

3558 —— WIGTON. CARRICK (THOMAS WILLIAM). History of Wigton, Cumberland, from its origin to the close of the nineteenth century. Carlisle. 1949.

3559 DERBYSHIRE. ORMEROD (JAMES). Derbyshire; a select catalogue of books about the county. Derby. 1930.

Also Derby County Library, *A list of books about the county* [Derby 1953]. John Charles Cox, ed., *Calendar of the records of the county of Derby*, 1899, lists much 19th-century material; see also the *Annual Reports* of the Derbyshire Record Office, Derby, 1962+. The *Journal* of the Derbyshire Archaeol. and Natural History Soc. publishes articles on 19th-century subjects. General histories are Stephen Glover, *The history of the county of Derby*, 2 v., Derby, 1829, and John Charles Cox, *Three centuries of Derbyshire annals*, 2 v., 1890. For industries see Fitton and Wadsworth (1537), for mining Hopkinson and O'Neal (1561), for miners (1739), for county government (472).

3560 —— BUXTON. HEAPE (ROBERT GRUNDY). Buxton under the Dukes of Devonshire. 1948.

3561 —— CHESTERFIELD. [HALL (GEORGE)]. The history of Chester-field, with particulars of the hamlets contiguous to the town, and accounts of Chatsworth, Hardwick, and Bolsover castle. Enl. and ed. by Thomas Ford. 1839.

3562 —— DERBY. DAVISON (A. W.). Derby: its rise and progress. 1906.

Also Stephen Glover, *The history of the borough of Derby*, Derby, 1843.

3563 DEVONSHIRE. HOSKINS (WILLIAM GEORGE). Devon. (A new survey of England. V. 2). 1954.

With full and critical bibliog. of the county, 554–71. See also James Davidson, *Bibliotheca Devoniensis; a catalogue of the printed books relating to the county of Devon*, Exeter, 1852, supplement, Exeter, 1862. For archives see Devon Record Office and Exeter Diocesan Record Office, *Annual reports*, 1962+. Thomas Moore, *The history of Devonshire, from the earliest period to the present*, 2 v., 1829–31, and William Marshall, *The rural economy of the west of England including Devonshire and parts of Somersetshire, Dorsetshire and Cornwall*, 2 v., 1796, are general surveys. For Exeter diocese see Robert James Edmund Boggis, *A history of the diocese of Exeter*, Exeter, 1922. See also Eric Raymond Delderfield, *The Raleigh country, a brief history of Exmouth, Budleigh Salterton, East Budleigh, Otterton, Bicton, Lympstone and Topsham*, repr., Exmouth, 1949; Edwin A. G. Clark, *The ports of the Exe estuary, 1660–1860: a study in historical geography*, Exeter, 1960; Bryan Desmond Greenway Little, *Exeter, Crediton, Cullompton, Exmouth, Ottery St. Mary, Tiverton and Topsham*, 1953, mainly concerned with architecture. For Exmoor see Edward Terence MacDermot, *The history of the forest of Exmoor*, Taunton, 1911, and Charles Stewart Orwin, *The reclamation of Exmoor forest*, 1929. For Devon parliamentary history see (434), for Russell estates, Godber and Kennedy (3525).

3564 —— BARNSTAPLE. GARDINER (WILLIAM FRANCIS). Barnstaple: 1837–97. Barnstaple. 1897.

For the earlier period see Joseph Besley Gribble, *Memorials of Barnstaple*, Barnstaple, 1830.

3565 —— DARTMOUTH. RUSSELL (PERCY). Dartmouth; a history of the port and town. 1950.

3566 —— DEVONPORT. WORTH (RICHARD NICHOLLS). History of the town and borough of Devonport, sometime Plymouth Dock. Plymouth. 1870.

3567 —— EXETER. HOSKINS (WILLIAM GEORGE). Industry, trade, and people in Exeter, 1688–1800. (University of Exeter history of Exeter research group. Monograph 6.) Manchester. 1935.

In the same series, Monograph 10, Allan Brockett, *Nonconformity in Exeter, 1650–1875*, Manchester, 1962. James Cossins, *Reminiscences of Exeter fifty years since*, 2nd edn., with additions, Exeter, 1878. For the end of the period see Robert Newton, *Victorian Exeter*, Leicester, 1968. For social conditions see Shapter (2561), (2563).

3568 —— EXMOUTH. DELDERFIELD (ERIC RAYMOND). Exmouth milestones; a history. Exmouth. 1948.

3569 —— PLYMOUTH. WALLING (ROBERT ALFRED JOHN). The story of Plymouth. 1950.

See also Plymouth Public Libraries, *A guide to the archives department of Plymouth City Libraries*, pt. I, Plymouth [1962]. Earlier histories are Llewellynn Frederick William Jewitt, *A history of Plymouth*, 1873; Richard Nicholls Worth, *History of Plymouth from the earliest period to the present time*, new and enl. edn., Plymouth, 1871, 1890; Henry Francis Whitfield, *Plymouth and Devonport in times of war and peace*, Plymouth, 1900.

3570 —— TEIGNMOUTH. GRIFFITHS (GORDON DOUGLAS) and GRIFFITHS (EDITH GRACE CHALMERS). History of Teignmouth. 1965.

3571 —— TIVERTON. HARDING ([WILLIAM]). The history of Tiverton in the county of Devon. 2 v. Tiverton. 1845-7.

3572 —— TORQUAY. RUSSELL (PERCY). A history of Torquay and the famous anchorage of Torbay. Torquay. 1960.

For a contemporary account see Octavian Blewitt, *The panorama of Torquay; a descriptive and historical sketch of the district comprised between the Dart and the Teign*, 2nd edn., 1833.

3573 DORSET. DOUCH (ROBERT). A handbook of local history: Dorset. Bristol. 1952. 1st edn. repr. with suppl. of add. and corrections to 1960. 2 v. Bristol. 1962.

A valuable bibliog. and guide to research materials: see also Charles Herbert Mayo, *Bibliotheca Dorsetiensis*, 1885. John Pouncy, *Dorsetshire photographically illustrated* [1857], is noteworthy. For county government see (469), (489); for agriculture see Marshall (3563). On Portland see Joseph Harold Bettey, *The island and royal manor of Portland . . . 1750–1851*, Portland and Bristol, 1970.

3574 —— POOLE. SYDENHAM (JOHN). The history of the town and county of Poole, from the earliest period to the present time. Poole. 1839.

Bernard C. Short, *Poole; the romance of its later history.* [1932].

3575 DURHAM (County). THOMPSON (HENRY). A reference catalogue of books relating to the counties of Durham and Northumberland. Pt. 1, historical and topographical. Newcastle. 1888.

General histories, containing much 19th-century material, are John Sykes, *Local records, or, Historical register of remarkable events which have occurred exclusively in the counties of Durham and Northumberland, Newcastle-upon-Tyne, and Berwick-upon-Tweed*, Newcastle, 1824, 2nd edn. continued to 1832 by John Latimer, 2 v., Newcastle, 1833; Eneas Mackenzie and M. Ross, *The historical, topographical, and descriptive view of the county palatine of Durham*, 2 v., Newcastle, 1834; William Fordyce, *The history and antiquities of the county palatine of Durham*, etc., 2 v., Newcastle, 1855-7; Richardson (3656). See also Anthony Ian Doyle, *Maps of Durham, 1607–1872, in the University Library*, Durham, 1954. For parliamentary history see (434), for miners, Webb (1739).

3576 —— DARLINGTON. LONGSTAFFE (WILLIAM HYLTON DYER). The history and antiquities of the parish of Darlington in the bishopric. Darlington. 1854.

3577 —— GATESHEAD. LUMLEY (DAVID). The story of Gateshead town, from the earliest age to the mid-Victorian. Newcastle. 1932.

Also Francis William David Manders, *A history of Gateshead*, Gateshead, 1973, and Mackenzie (3660).

3578 —— HARTLEPOOL. SHARP (*Sir* CUTHBERT). History of Hartlepool by the late Sir Cuthbert Sharp, Kt., F.S.A.; being a reprint of the original work, published in 1816, with a supplemental history, to 1851 inclusive. Hartlepool. 1851.

Also Robert Wood, *West Hartlepool, the rise and development of a Victorian new town*, Hartlepool, 1967.

3579 —— SOUTH SHIELDS. HODGSON (GEORGE B.) The borough of South Shields from the earliest period to the close of the nineteenth century. Newcastle. 1903.

3580 —— STOCKTON. RICHMOND (THOMAS). The local records of Stockton and the neighbourhood; or, A register of memorable events, chronologically arranged, which have occurred in and near Stockton ward and the north-eastern parts of Cleveland. 1868.

See also John Brewster, *The parochial history and antiquities of Stockton-upon-Tees*, 1796, 2nd edn. 2 pts, 1829, continued by Henry Heavisides, *The annals of Stockton-upon-Tees, with biographical notices*, Stockton, 1865.

3581 —— SUNDERLAND. POTTS (TAYLOR). Sunderland, a history of the town, port, trade and commerce. Sunderland. 1892.

See also George Garbutt, *A historical and descriptive view of the parishes of Monkwearmouth and Bishopwearmouth, and the port and borough of Sunderland*, Sunderland, 1819; Arnold Levy, *History of the Sunderland Jewish community*, 1956; Helen Gertrude Bowling, *Some chapters on the history of Sunderland*, Sunderland, 1969. For shipbuilding see Smith and Holden (1585).

3582 ESSEX. V.C.H. ESSEX. Bibliography. 1959.

Supplement by Dagenham public libraries, Dagenham, 1962. See also Dagenham public libraries, *Essex and Dagenham*, etc., 2nd edn. Dagenham, 1961; Frederick George Emmison, *Guide to the Essex record office*, Chelmsford, 2nd edn., 1969 (Essex record office pubs., 51), and in the same ser., no. 7; E. J. Erith, *Catalogue of Essex parish records, 1240–1894, with a supplement of Nonconformist charities, societies, and school records, 1341–1903*, Chelmsford, 1950, 2nd edn. rev. F. G. Emmison, Chelmsford, 1966. Valuable for the 19th century are Duffield William Coller, *The people's history of Essex*, etc. [Chelmsford, 1861], and Edward Walford, *Greater London; a narrative of its history, its people, and its places*, rev. edn. [1898], an account of suburbs then outside the Metropolitan area. See also Philip Benton, *The history of the Rochford hundred*, nos. 1–58, Rochford, 1867–8, and Bayne (3648). For local government see (513), for highways Winstone and Maud (1632).

3583 —— COLCHESTER. CROMWELL (THOMAS KITSON). History and description of the ancient town and borough of Colchester, in Essex. 2 v. 1825.

3584 —— DAGENHAM. SHAWCROSS (JOHN PETER). A history of Dagenham in the county of Essex. 1904.

3585 —— EAST AND WEST HAM. STOKES (ALFRED). East Ham. From village to county borough. 3rd edn. East Ham. 1933.

Also Archer Philip Crouch, *Silvertown and neighbourhood (including East and West Ham): a retrospect*, 1900.

3586 GLOUCESTERSHIRE. AUSTIN (ROLAND). Catalogue of the Gloucestershire collection: books, pamphlets and documents in the Gloucester public library relating to the county, cities, towns and villages of Gloucestershire. Gloucester. 1928.

Also Sir Francis Adams Hyett and William Bazeley, *The bibliographer's manual of Gloucestershire literature*, 3 v., Gloucester, 1895–7, supplement, by Sir Francis Hyett and Roland Austin, Gloucester, 1915–16, and [Roland Austin] comp., *Catalogue of Gloucestershire books collected by Sir Francis Hyett . . . in the Shire Hall*, [Gloucester, 1949]. Other guides are Irvine Egerton Gray and Alexander Thomas Gaydon, *Gloucestershire quarter sessions archives, 1660–1889, and other official records*, etc., Gloucester, 1958; I. E. Gray and Elizabeth Ralph, *Guide to the parish records of . . . Bristol and the county of Gloucester*, Bristol and Gloucestershire Archaeol. Soc., records section, 5, Bristol, 1962. The society's *Transactions*, Gloucester, 1876+, publish 18th- and 19th-century articles. See also Henry George Nicholls, *The Forest of Dean, an historical and descriptive account*, 1858, also his *The personalities of the Forest of Dean*, 1863, and Cyril Hart, *The industrial history of Dean*, Newton Abbot, 1971. See also Esther Moir, *Local government in Gloucestershire, 1775–1800. A study of the justices of the peace*, Bristol and Gloucestershire Archaeol. Soc. Records Section, Bristol, 1969. For parliamentary history see W. R. Williams (Pargellis and Medley, 434); for prisons see (2598).

3587 —— BRISTOL. MATHEWS (EDWARD ROBERT NORRIS) *ed.* Bristol bibliography; a catalogue of the books, pamphlets, collectanea, etc., relating to Bristol, contained in the central reference library. Bristol. 1916.

May be supplemented by Elizabeth Ralph, *Guide to the Bristol Archives Office*, Bristol, 1971. The most comprehensive general history is John Latimer, *The annals of Bristol* in the eighteenth century, [Frome?] 1893, continued by *The annals of Bristol in the nineteenth century*, 2 v., Bristol, 1887–1902. See also Walter Ison, *The Georgian buildings of Bristol*, 1952, and Shepherd (3674). For local government see (491); for economic history see (1501), (1507).

3588 —— CHELTENHAM. HART (GWEN). A history of Cheltenham. Leicester. 1965.

Also Contem Ignotus (*pseud.* of Richard Glover), *The golden decade of a favourite town . . . 1843–53*, 1884, Edith M. Humphris and Edwin Charles Willoughby, *At Cheltenham Spa, or, Georgians in a Georgian town*, 1928.

3589 —— GLOUCESTER. BOND (FREDERICK). The history of Gloucester; and descriptive account of the same city and its suburbs. Gloucester. 1848.

3590 ——TETBURY. LEE (ALFRED THEOPHILUS). The history of the town and parish of Tetbury, in the county of Gloucester. 1857.

3591 —— TEWKESBURY. BENNETT (JAMES). The history of Tewkesbury. 1830.

3592 HAMPSHIRE. GILBERT (HENRY MARCH) *and* GODWIN (GEORGE NELSON). Bibliotheca Hantoniensis. Southampton. [1891.]

Continued by Sumner Wilson, *Supplementary Hampshire bibliography*, Southampton, 1897, and Richard George Davis, 'A second supplement to Hampshire bibliography', *Hampshire Field Club, Papers and proceedings*, 5 (1904–6), 127–36, 229–39. These three are repr. with other bibliogs. by Raymond V. Turley as, *Hampshire and Isle of Wight bibliographies*, [Winchester, 1975]. Robert Mudie, *Hampshire; its past and present condition, and future prospects*, 3 v., Winchester, 1838, includes the Isle of Wight. *V.C.H.* Hampshire is complete. On the New Forest see Heywood Sumner, *New Forest bibliography*, 2nd edn. ed. by W. Frank Perkins, Lymington, 1935, and H.M.S.O., *Report of the New Forest Committee*, 1947 (H.M.S.O. reference, .7245). For parliamentary history see (434).

3593 —— PORTSMOUTH. GATES (WILLIAM GEORGE). The history of Portsmouth, a naval chronology. Portsmouth. 1931.

See also Portsmouth Corporation, *The city of Portsmouth; records of the corporation, 1835–1927*, ed. W. G. Gates, Portsmouth, 1928; Lake Allen, *The history of Portsmouth*, 1817; Henry and Julian Slight, *Chronicles of Portsmouth*, 1828, which includes an account of the dockyard.

3594 —— SOUTHAMPTON. PATTERSON (ALFRED TEMPLE). A history of Southampton, 1700–1914. V. 1. An oligarchy in decline, 1700–1835. V. 2. The beginnings of modern Southampton, 1836–1867. Southampton records ser. 11, 14. Southampton. 1966–71.

See also in the same series, v. 10, his *A selection from the Southampton corporation journals, 1815–35, and borough council minutes, 1835–7*, 1965; also *Guide to the records of the corporation and absorbed authorities in the civic record office* (Southampton records ser. 1), Southampton, 1964; and for a short account Fossey John Cobb Hearnshaw, *A short history of Southampton*, Oxf., 1910.

3595 HEREFORDSHIRE. COUNTY LIBRARY: LOCAL HISTORY SECTION. Herefordshire books: a select list of books in the local collection of the Herefordshire county libraries. [Hereford.] 1955.

Frederick Bodenham, *The bibliographer's manual of Herefordshire literature*, Hereford, 1890, may also be consulted. For parliamentary history see W. R. Williams (Pargellis and Medley, 434).

3596 HERTFORDSHIRE. JOHNSON (WILLIAM BRANCH). Local history in Hertfordshire, and a Hertfordshire local history directory. Hitchin. 1964.

Also Hertfordshire Local History Council, county bibliography, pt. 1, *Hertfordshire newspapers, 1722–1955*, compiled by Mary Florence Thwaite, [Hertford], 1955, and pt. 2, by the same writer, *Periodicals and transactions relating to Hertfordshire: a short guide and subject index*, Bengeo, 1959; H. R. Wilton Hall, *Catalogue of the 'Lewis Evans' collection of books and pamphlets relating to Hertfordshire*, 2 pt., St. Albans, 1906–8. For records see William le Hardy, *Guide to the Hertfordshire record office. Part 1. Quarter sessions and other records*, Hertford, 1961. Robert Clutterbuck, *The history and antiquities of the county of Hertford*, 3 v., 1815–27, is a general survey. *V.C.H.* Hertfordshire is complete. See also William Urwick, *Nonconformity in Herts*, 1884. For county government see (474); for social life (2077), (2194).

3597 —— HERTFORD. TURNOR (LEWIS). History of the ancient town and borough of Hertford. Hertford. 1830.

3598 —— HITCHIN. HINE (REGINALD LESLIE). The history of Hitchin. 2 v. 1927–9.

Also his *Hitchin worthies, four centuries of English life*, 1932.

3599 —— ST. ALBANS. TOMS (ELSIE). The story of St. Albans. St. Albans. 1962.

Also Arthur Ernest Gibbs, *The corporation records of St. Albans, with lists of mayors, high stewards, members of parliament*, St. Albans, 1890.

3600 HUNTINGDONSHIRE. COUNTY LIBRARY. Catalogue of the local history collection. Huntingdon. 1950.

Also Herbert E. Norris, *Catalogue of the Huntingdonshire books*, Cirencester, 1895, and Huntingdonshire County Archives Committee, *Guide to the Huntingdonshire record office*, ed. George Hugo Findlay, Huntingdon, 1958. *V.C.H.* Huntingdonshire is complete.

3601 ISLE OF MAN. CUBBON (WILLIAM) *ed.* A bibliographical account of works relating to the Isle of Man with biographical memoranda and copious literary references. 2 v. 1933–9.

See also Joseph Train, *An historical and statistical account of the Isle of Man, from the earliest times to the present date*, 2 v., Douglas, 1845, and Robert Henry Kinvig, *A history of the Isle of Man*, 2nd edn., Liverpool, 1950. For constitution see (516).

3602 KENT. COUNTY LIBRARY. Local history catalogue, 1939. Maidstone. 1939.

Also Archibald John Gritten, *Catalogue of books . . . in the local collection . . . of Margate public library*, Margate, 1934; Gillingham public libraries, *Local history catalogue*, Gillingham, 1951, *supplement*, 1955; Brian Burch, *A bibliography of printed material relating to Bromley, Hayes and Keston, in the county of Kent*, Bromley, 1964. A more extensive, but early, bibliog. is John Russell Smith, *Bibliotheca Cantiana*, 1837. See also Felix Hull, *Guide to the Kent county archives office*, Kent County Council County Archives Committee, Maidstone, 1958, and *First supplement . . . 1957–1968*, Maidstone, 1971. Later accessions are listed annually in *Archaeologia Cantiana*. Samuel William Henry Ireland, *England's topographer; or, A new and complete history of the county of Kent; from the earliest records to the present time*, 4 v., 1828–30, contains contemporary material. For parliamentary history see (423).

3603 —— CHATHAM. PRESNAIL (JAMES). Chatham: the story of a dockyard town and the birthplace of the British navy. Chatham. 1952.

3604 —— DEAL. LAKER (JOHN). History of Deal. Deal. 1917.

3605 —— DOVER. LYON (JOHN). The history of the town and port of Dover, and of Dover castle; with a short account of the Cinque ports. 2 v. Dover. 1813–14.

Also *Horn's description of Dover, containing a concise account of the castle, heights, harbour, and town*, Dover, 1817.

3606 —— GRAVESEND. CRUDEN (ROBERT PEIRCE). The history of the town of Gravesend in the county of Kent and of the port of London. 1843.

3607 ——MARGATE. OULTON (WALLEY CHAMBERLAIN). Picture of Margate and its vicinity. 1820.

3608 —— TONBRIDGE. NEVE (ARTHUR HENRY). The Tonbridge of yesterday. Rev. edn. Tonbridge. 1934.

3609 —— TUNBRIDGE WELLS. MELVILLE (LEWIS), *pseud.* of Lewis Saul Benjamin. Society at Royal Tunbridge Wells in the eighteenth century and after. 1912.

See also Paul Amsinck, *Tunbridge Wells and its neighbourhood*, 1810, with fine illustrations, and Margaret Barton, *Tunbridge Wells* [1937].

3610 LANCASHIRE. MANCHESTER JOINT COMMITTEE ON THE LANCASHIRE BIBLIOGRAPHY. The Lancashire bibliography. Manchester. 1968+.

To date seven volumes have appeared, including George Henry Tupling, *Lancashire directories, 1684–1957*, rev. and enl. Sidney Horrocks, Manchester, 1968, and Sidney Horrocks, ed., *Lancashire acts of Parliament, 1266–1957*, Manchester, 1969, *Lancashire business histories*, Manchester, 1971, *Lancashire family histories*, Manchester, 1972, and *Registers*, Manchester, 1973. See also Henry Fishwick, *The Lancashire library . . . topography, biography, history*, etc., 1875. For archives see Reginald Sharpe France, *Guide to the Lancashire record office*, Lancashire rec. pub. 2, 2nd edn., Preston, 1962, and the record office's *Annual reports*, 1951+, which list accessions. The Chetham Society's *Publications*, and the annual *Transactions* of the Lancashire and Cheshire Antiquarian Society and of the Historic Society of Lancashire and Cheshire, publish material on the 19th century. For social history of Lancashire see (1826), (1866), for enclosures (1664), for engineering (1578).

3611 —— BAINES (THOMAS) *and* FAIRBAIRN (*Sir* WILLIAM). Lancashire and Cheshire, past and present; a history and description of the palatine counties of Lancaster and Chester, with an account of the rise and progress of manufactures and commerce, and civil and mechanical engineering in these districts by William Fairbairn. 2 v. [1868–9.]

Concentrates on 19th century. See also Edward Baines, *History of the county palatine and duchy of Lancaster*, etc., 4 v., 1836, new rev. and enl. edn. ed. by James Croston, 5 v., 1888–93, and among many descriptions, John Aikin, *A description of the country from thirty to forty miles round Manchester*, 1795, reprinted 1968; John Corry, *The history of Lancashire*, 2 v., 1825; William Henry Pyne, *Lancashire illustrated in a series of views*, 1831; Edwin Butterworth, *A statistical sketch of the county palatine of Lancaster*, 1841; William Cooke Taylor, *Notes of a tour in the manufacturing districts of Lancashire*, 1842, partly anti-corn-law propaganda; [Cyrus Redding and others], *An illustrated itinerary of the county of Lancaster*, 1842, reissued as *A pictorial history of the county of Lancaster*, 1844; Roy Millward, *Lancashire; an illustrated essay on the history of the landscape*, Making of the English landscape, 3, 1955. See also Francis Espinasse, *Lancashire worthies*, 1st and 2nd ser., 1874–7; Thomas Ellison Gibson, *Lydiate Hall and its associations*, 1876, on Roman Catholics; Benjamin Nightingale (795), on non-conformity. *V.C.H.* Lancashire is complete. For local government see (483), for parliamentary history see Bean (434).

3612 —— ALLERTON. BROWN (RONALD STEWART). A history of the manor and township of Allerton in the county of Lancaster. Liverpool. 1911.

Refers to the Roscoe family.

3613 —— ASHTON-UNDER-LYNE. BOWMAN (WINIFRED MARY). England in Ashton-under-Lyne. Ashton-under-Lyne. 1960.

See also Edwin Butterworth, *An historical account of the towns of Ashton-under-Lyne, Stalybridge, and Dukinfield*, Ashton, 1842, and George F. Foster, ed., *Ashton-under-Lyne: its story through the ages.* [1947].

3614 —— BARROW-IN-FURNESS. MARSHALL (JOHN DUNCAN). Furness and the industrial revolution; an economic history of Furness (1711–1900) and the town of Barrow (1757–1897) with an epilogue. Barrow-in-Furness. 1958.

3615 —— BLACKBURN. MILLER (GEORGE CALVERT). Blackburn: the evolution of a cotton town. Blackburn. [1952.]

Bibliog. 438–9. Also William Alexander Abram, *Parish of Blackburn, county of Lancashire; a history of Blackburn, town and parish*, Blackburn, 1877.

3616 —— BLACKPOOL. THORNBER (WILLIAM). An historical and descriptive account of Blackpool and its neighbourhood. 2nd edn. Blackpool. 1844.

3617 —— BOLTON. SPARKE (ARCHIBALD). Bibliographia Boltoniensis: being a bibliography, with biographical details of Bolton authors, and the books written by them, from 1550 to 1912; books about Bolton; and those printed in the town from 1785 to date. Manchester. 1913.

Also Peter Armstrong Whittle, *Bolton-le-Moors, and the townships in the parish*, Bolton, 1855; Benjamin Thomas Barton, *Historical gleanings of Bolton and district*, 3 v., Bolton, 1881–3 (based on the Bolton *Daily Chronicle*). William Brimelow, *Political and parliamentary history of Bolton*, Bolton, 1882, reprinted from the *Bolton Journal*, and James Clegg, *Annals of Bolton; history, chronology, politics, parliamentary and municipal polls*, Bolton, 1888, together give an exceptionally full picture of early 19th-century municipal politics. A modern work is Charles Harold Saxelby, ed., *Bolton survey*, 1953.

3618 —— BURNLEY. BENNETT (WALTER). The history of Burnley. Pt. 3. 1650–1850. Burnley. 1948.

3619 —— BURY. BARTON (BENJAMIN THOMAS). History of the borough of Bury and neighbourhood, in the county of Lancaster. Bury. [1874.]

3620 —— CARTMEL. STOCKDALE (JAMES). Annales Caermoelenses; or annals of Cartmel. Ulverston. 1872.

3621 —— COLNE. CARR (JAMES). Annals and stories of Colne and neighbourhood. Rev. edn. Manchester. 1878.

3622 —— FYLDE. PORTER (JOHN). History of the Fylde of Lancashire. Fleetwood and Blackpool. 1876.

3623 ——HASLINGDEN. ASPIN (CHRISTOPHER). Haslingden, 1800–1900; a history. 2nd edn. Haslingden. [1963.]

3624 —— LANCASTER. SCHOFIELD (MAURICE MARPLES). Outlines of an economic history of Lancaster from 1680 to 1860. (Transactions of Lancashire branch Hist. Assoc., 1 and 2.) Pt. 1. 1946. Pt. 2. [1952.]

Also William Oliver Roper, *Materials for the history of Lancaster*, 2 v., Chetham Soc. n.s. v. 61, 62. Manchester. 1907.

3625 —— LIVERPOOL. CHANDLER (GEORGE). Liverpool. 1957.

Full bibliog. 473–96. See also Liverpool public libraries, *Liverpool prints and documents; catalogue of maps, plans, views, portraits, memoirs, literature*, ed., Peter Cowell, Liverpool, 1908. Standard histories are Thomas Baines, *History of the commerce and town of Liverpool, and of the rise of manufacturing industry in the adjoining counties*, 1852, Sir James Allanson Picton, *Memorials of Liverpool*, 2 v., 2nd edn., 1875. See also [James Wallace], *A general and descriptive history . . . of the town of Liverpool . . . its government, police, antiquities, and modern improvements*, 1795; William Moss, *The Liverpool guide, including a sketch of the environs, with a map of the town*, 2nd edn., 1797; Henry Smithers, *Liverpool, its commerce, statistics, and institutions; with a history of the cotton trade*, Liverpool, 1825; Richard Brooke, *Liverpool as it was during the last quarter of the eighteenth century, 1775 to 1800*, Liverpool, 1853, mostly on local politics; James Touzeau, *The rise and progress of Liverpool from 1551 to 1835*, 2 v., Liverpool, 1910, also on politics and government; John Ramsay Bryce Muir, *A history of Liverpool*, Liverpool, 1907, bibliog. 341–9; François Vigier, *Change and apathy; Liverpool and Manchester during the industrial revolution*, 1970; Francis Edwin Hyde, *Liverpool and the Mersey; an economic history of a port, 1700–1970*, Newton Abbot, 1971. See also two volumes of reminiscences, [James Aspinall] *Liverpool a few years since, By an old stager*, Liverpool, 1852, and James Stonehouse, *The streets of Liverpool*, Liverpool, [1870]; and on growth of the city see Quentin Hughes, *Seaport; architecture and townscape in Liverpool*, 1964. For local government see (504), (510); for social conditions (2532), (2533), Simey (2503), Bickerton (2542); for William Roscoe (2172); for slave trade (2637); for shipping Chandler (1501); for banks Hughes (1448); for merchants (1519); on dissent (795).

3626 —— MANCHESTER. FRANGOPULO (NICHOLAS JOSEPH) *ed.* Rich inheritance: a guide to the history of Manchester. Manchester. 1962.

Contains an up-to-date bibliog., 295–305. Manchester lacks a modern general history. *The Manchester Review*, Manchester, 1936+, publishes articles touching on 19th-century Manchester and the John Rylands library and the city public library contain 19th-century MSS. Earlier histories still worth consultation include Archibald Prentice, *Historical sketches and personal recollections of Manchester*, 1851, written from a radical point of view and beginning in 1792; John Reilly, *The history of Manchester*, 2 v., Manchester, 1861, in the same tradition; William Edward Armitage Axon, *The annals of Manchester; a chronological record from the earliest times to the end of 1885*, Manchester, 1886, and his *Cobden as a citizen; a chapter in Manchester history*, 1907; James Butterworth, *The antiquities of the town, and a complete history of the trade of Manchester*, etc., Manchester, 1822, with much technical information on cotton; James Wheeler, *Manchester, its political, social and commercial history, ancient and modern*, 1836; Benjamin Love, *The handbook of Manchester*, etc., Manchester, 1842; Léon Faucher, *Manchester in 1844; translated from the French with copious notes by a member of the Manchester Athenaeum*, etc., 1844; George Edwin Bateman Saintsbury, *Manchester*, etc., 1887; Léon Soutierre Marshall, *The development of public opinion in Manchester, 1780–1820*, Syracuse N.Y., 1946. Mrs. Elizabeth Cleghorn Gaskell, *Mary Barton, a tale of Manchester life*, 2 v., 1848, is about Manchester. Useful information may be found in Richard Wright Procter, *Memorials of Manchester streets*, Manchester, 1874, and *Memorials of bygone Manchester, with glimpses of the environs*, Manchester, 1880; Josiah Thomas Slugg, *Reminiscences of Manchester fifty years ago*, Manchester, 1881; Thomas Swindells, *Manchester streets and Manchester men*, 5 v., Manchester, 1906–8. On architecture see Cecil Stewart, *Stones of Manchester*, 1956, together with his *The architecture of Manchester; an index of the principal buildings and their architects, 1800–1900*, Manchester, 1956. For local government see (487), (503), (509), for parliamentary history (431), for social history (1815), (1817), (1823), (2542), for Peterloo (105), for Anti-corn-law league (111), for Chamber of Commerce (1518), for Manchester School and for Manchester Statistical Society (1781), for education Maltby (3301), for newspapers (3499), (3502).

3627 —— OLDHAM. BUTTERWORTH (EDWIN). Historical sketches of Oldham, with an appendix containing the history of the town to the present time. Oldham. 1856.

Giles Shaw, ed., *Local notes and gleanings; Oldham and neighbourhood in byegone times*, Oldham, 1887–9. See also Foster (1813).

3628 —— PRESTON. HARDWICK (CHARLES). History of the borough of Preston and its environs, in the county of Lancaster. Preston. 1857.

Peter Whittle, *A topographical, statistical and historical account of the borough of Preston*, 2 v., Preston, 1821–37. Anthony Hewitson, *History of Preston*, Preston, 1883, repr. Wakefield, 1969. For local government see (448), for parliamentary history see Dobson (Pargellis and Medley, 434), for temperance (2569). H. W. Clemesha, *A bibliography of . . . Preston*, Preston, 1923, is brief but helpful.

3629 —— ROCHDALE. ROBERTSON (WILLIAM). Rochdale past and present; a history and guide. Rochdale. 1875.

Rebe Prestwick Taylor, *Rochdale retrospect*, etc., ed. Ernest Taylor, 1956.

3630 —— ROSSENDALE. NEWBIGGING (THOMAS). History of the forest of Rossendale. 1868.

See also (1527).

3631 —— ST. HELENS. BARKER (THEODORE CARDWELL) *and* HARRIS (JOHN RAYMOND). A Merseyside town in the industrial revolution: St. Helens, 1750–1900. Liverpool. 1954.

See also (1603).

3632 —— SOUTHPORT. BAILEY (FRANCIS ARTHUR). A history of Southport. Southport. 1955.

Bibliog. 220–3.

3633 —— ULVERSTON. PARK (JAMES). Some Ulverston records. Ulverston. 1932.

3634 —— WARRINGTON. BEAMONT (WILLIAM). Walks about Warrington towards the beginning of the present century. Warrington. 1887.

Also Warrington Municipal Museum, *Catalogue of the reference library*, by Charles Madeley, Warrington 1898, supplement, 1908.

3635 —— WIGAN. FOLKARD (HENRY TENNYSON). Wigan and district; a local record. Wigan. 1916.

A classified local bibliog.

3636 LEICESTERSHIRE. LEE (JOHN MICHAEL). Leicestershire history: a handlist to printed sources in the libraries of Leicester. (Leicester University, Vaughan College paper 4), Leicester 1958. Corrections and additions 1959.

See also C. V. Kirkby, *Catalogue of the books, pamphlets, maps, views, mss. etc. relating to Leicestershire . . . in the Central Reference Library*, Leicester, [1893], and the *Annual Reports* of the Leicestershire record office, 1955+, which list accessions. *V.C.H.* Leicestershire, ii, 1954, contains articles by John Henry Plumb on 'Political history, 1530–1885', 102–35, and by Joan Thirsk on 'Agrarian history, 1540–1950', 199–254; *V.C.H.* Leicestershire, iii, 1955, is devoted to Leicestershire industries. See also William George Hoskins, *Leicestershire. An illustrated essay on the history of the landscape*, 1957. For hunting see Dale, Paget (1906), for transport Russell (1632), for hosiery industry (1547) for agriculture (1685), for enclosures Hunt (1667).

3637 ——— LEICESTER. PATTERSON (ALFRED TEMPLE). Radical Leicester, 1780–1850. Leicester. 1954.

For bibliog. and list of corporation archives see Leicester Museums and Art Gallery, *The records of the corporation of Leicester*, Leicester, 1956. See also Robert Read, *Modern Leicester; . . . with an original history of corporation undertakings*, 1881; Robert William Greaves, *The corporation of Leicester, 1689–1836*, 1939; bibliog. 145–52. *V.C.H.* Leicestershire, iv, *The city of Leicester*, 1958. For local government see (492), for parliamentary history (429).

3638 LINCOLNSHIRE. CORNS (ALBERT REGINALD). Bibliotheca Lincolniensis; a catalogue of the books, pamphlets, etc., relating to the city and county of Lincoln, preserved in the reference department of the city of Lincoln public library. Lincoln, 1904.

Lincolnshire archives committee, *Archivist's reports*, 1948+, list accessions; Lincolnshire local history society, *Local history: its interest and value*, Lincoln, 1949 is a useful introduction to the county. On local politics see R. J. Olney, *Lincolnshire politics, 1832–1885*, Oxf., 1973. See also Bartholomew Howlett, *A selection of views in the county of Lincoln*, 1801; Mary Saunders, *Lincolnshire in 1835*, displayed in a series of nearly a hundred engravings, etc., Lincoln, 1835; and A. R. Maddison, ed., *Lincolnshire pedigrees* (Harleian soc. v. 50–2, 55) 4 v., 1902–6. For the Holland division see William Marrat, *The history of Lincolnshire, topographical, historical, and descriptive*, 3 v., Boston, 1814–16; for the Isle of Axholme, William Brocklehurst Stonehouse, *The history and topography of the Isle of Axholme; being that part of Lincolnshire which is west of Trent*, 1839; for north Lincolnshire, Samuel Sidney, *Railways and agriculture in North Lincolnshire; rough notes of a ride over the track of the Manchester, Sheffield, Lincolnshire and other railways*, 1848; for the Lincolnshire fens, William Henry Wheeler, *A history of the fens of South Lincolnshire*, 1868, and James Sandby Padley, *The fens and floods of mid-Lincolnshire*, Lincoln, 1882. For agriculture see (1686), for enclosures (1664).

3639 ——— BOSTON. THOMPSON (PISHEY). The history and antiquities of Boston, and the villages of Skirbeck, Fishtoft, Freiston, Butterwick, Benington, Leverton, Leake and Wrangle. 1856.

3640 ——— GRIMSBY. GILLETT (EDWARD). A history of Grimsby. 1970.

Also Gordon Jackson, *Grimsby and the Haven Company, 1796–1846*, Grimsby, 1971.

3641 ——— LINCOLN. HILL (*Sir* JAMES WILLIAM FRANCIS). Georgian Lincoln. Cambridge. 1966.

Continued in his *Victorian Lincoln*, Camb., 1974.

3642 —— STAMFORD. DRAKARD (JOHN). The history of Stamford, in the county of Lincoln, comprising its ancient, progressive, and modern state. Stamford. 1822.

Also Alan Rogers, *The making of Stamford*, Leicester, 1965.

3643 MIDDLESEX. ROBBINS (RICHARD MICHAEL). Middlesex. (New survey of England, 1.) 1953.

Bibliog. 397-417. See also Greater London Council Record Office, *Guide to the Middlesex sessions records, prepared for the Standing Joint Committee of the County of Middlesex,* 1965; Middlesex County Record Office, *Annual reports of the county archivist,* 1961+. Of earlier surveys see James Thorne, *Handbook to the environs of London,* 2 pts., 1876 Walford (3582) and (3770).

3644 —— BRENTFORD. FAULKNER (THOMAS). The history and antiquities of Brentford, Ealing, and Chiswick. 1845.

Also Fred. Alfred Turner, *History and antiquities of Brentford*, Brentford, 1922.

3645 ——ENFIELD. ROBINSON (WILLIAM). The history and antiquities of Enfield, in the county of Middlesex. 2 v. 1823.

3646 —— TOTTENHAM. ROBINSON (WILLIAM). The history and antiquities of the parish of Tottenham in the county of Middlesex. 2 v. 2nd edn. Tottenham. 1840.

3647 —— UXBRIDGE. REDFORD (GEORGE) *and* RICHES (THOMAS HURRY). The history of the ancient town of Uxbridge, containing copies of interesting public documents. Uxbridge. 1818.

3648 NORFOLK. DARROCH (ELIZABETH) *and* TAYLOR (BARRY). A bibliography of Norfolk history. University of East Anglia. 1975.

Now largely supersedes Jeremiah James Colman, *Bibliotheca Norfolciensis*, comp. John Quinton, Norwich, 1896, a catalogue of Colman's library, now in the possession of Norwich corporation. See also Walter Rye, *An index to Norfolk topography*, Index society pubns. 10, 1881, continued by *Appendix . . . forming an index to parishes mentioned in books published or written since that date*, Rye's Norfolk handlists, 2nd series, 1, Norwich, 1916; Walter Rye, *Norfolk families*, 2 pt., Norwich, 1913, 1915. For general histories see [John Chambers], *A general history of the county of Norfolk,* etc., 2 v, Norwich, 1829; A. D. Bayne, *Royal illustrated history of Eastern England, civil, military, political, and ecclesiastical,* Yarmouth, [1873]; Charles Mackie, *Norfolk annals; a chronological record . . . Compiled from the files of the 'Norfolk Chronicle',* 2 v., Norwich [1901]. See also (471) for local government and (2089) (2197) for social history, and for agriculture (1683).

3649 —— KING'S LYNN. HILLEN (HENRY J.) History of the borough of King's Lynn, 2 v. Norwich. [1907.]

3650 —— LETHERINGSETT. COZENS-HARDY (BASIL). The history of Letheringsett in the county of Norfolk: with extracts from the diary of Mary Hardy, 1773-1809. Norwich [1957.]

3651 —— NORWICH. BAYNE (A. D.) Norwich. A comprehensive history of Norwich. Norwich. 1869.

See also William Hudson and John Cottingham Tingey, *Revised catalogue of the records of the city of Norwich*, Norwich, [1898], George Arthur Stephen, *Guide to the study of Norwich: a select bibliography of the principal books . . . in the Norwich Public Library*, Norwich, 1914, 2nd edn. 1919. [John Stacy] *A topographical and historical account of the city and county of Norwich, its antiquities and modern improvements*, Norwich and Lynn, 1819. See also (502).

3652 —— YARMOUTH. PALMER (CHARLES JOHN). The history of Great Yarmouth, designed as a continuation of Manship's history of that town. 1856.

Also his *The perlustration of Great Yarmouth, with Gorleston and Southtown*, 3 v., Yarmouth, 1872–5, and John Preston, *The picture of Yarmouth*, Yarmouth, 1819.

3653 NORTHAMPTONSHIRE. TAYLOR (JOHN). A catalogue of a special collection of printed books relating to particular towns, parishes, seats, quaint customs, historical events, family history *etc.* and referring to the history of the county of Northampton in general, 1800–1884. Northampton. 1884.

Derived from his monumental *Bibliotheca Northantonensis*, Northampton, *c.* 1870, which is very rare. Taylor's own collections are in Northampton public library. See also P. I. King, *Summary guide to the Northamptonshire record office*, Northampton, 1954 and *Annual reports* of the county archivist, 1952+. *Northamptonshire past and present*, Northampton, 1948+, is useful. See also George Baker, *The history and antiquities of the country of Northampton*, 2 v., 1822-41, and Longden (723). For parliamentary history see Forrester (Pargellis and Medley, 434).

3654 —— KETTERING.

For local government see (511) for footwear industry (1549).

3655 —— NORTHAMPTON. MARKHAM (CHRISTOPHER ALEXANDER) *and* COX (JOHN CHARLES). The records of the borough of Northampton. 2 v., Northampton. 1898.

3656 NORTHUMBERLAND. NEWCASTLE UPON TYNE PUBLIC LIBRARIES. Local catalogue of material concerning Newcastle and Northumberland as represented in the central public library, Newcastle upon Tyne. Ed. Basil Anderton. Newcastle. 1932.

Supplemented by H. A. Taylor, *Northumberland history: a brief guide to records and aids in Newcastle upon Tyne*, Newcastle, 1963. A monumental county history is *A history of Northumberland issued under the direction of the Northumberland county history committee*, 15 v., Newcastle, 1893–1940. See also Eneas Mackenzie, *An historical, topographical, and descriptive view of the county of Northumberland, and of those parts of the county of Durham . . . north of the river Tyne*, 2nd edn., 2 v., Newcastle, 1825; Moses Aaron Richardson, *The local historian's table book of remarkable occurrences . . . connected with the counties of Newcastle upon Tyne, Northumberland, and Durham*, 8 v., 1841–6; John William House, *North eastern England: population movements and the landscape since the early nineteenth century* (King's college, Department of Geography, Research series, 1), Newcastle, 1954. See also for parliamentary history (430), (434), for coal mines, Fynes (1739) for shipping (1525).

3657 —— BERWICK ON TWEED. FULLER (JOHN). The history of

Berwick upon Tweed, including a short account of the villages of Tweed-
mouth and Spittal. Edinburgh. 1799.

3658 —— BLYTH. WALLACE (JOHN). The history of Blyth from the
Norman conquest to the present day. Blyth. 1862.

Also Christopher Edmund Baldwin, *The history and development of the port of Blyth,*
Newcastle, 1929.

3659 —— CULLERCOATS. TOMLINSON (WILLIAM WEAVER).
Historical notes on Cullercoats, Whitley, and Monkseaton. With a descriptive
memoir of the coast from Tynemouth to St. Mary's Island. 1893.

3660 —— NEWCASTLE. MIDDLEBROOK (SYDNEY). Newcastle upon
Tyne: its growth and achievement. Newcastle. 1950.

Contemporary descriptions, with much information on industrial growth include [John
Hodgson?], *The picture of Newcastle upon Tyne, containing a guide to the town and . . .
a description of the coal mines,* Newcastle, 1807, repr. 1969; Eneas Mackenzie, *A
descriptive and historical account of . . . Newcastle upon Tyne, including the borough of
Gateshead,* 2 v., Newcastle, 1827; Moses Aaron Richardson, *Descriptive companion
through Newcastle upon Tyne and Gateshead,* Newcastle, 1838; Thomas Oliver, *The
topographical conductor . . . to Newcastle and Gateshead,* etc., Newcastle, 1851; Thomas
Crawford, *Nineteenth century notes on Walker,* Newcastle, 1904. See also Lyall Wilkes
and Gordon Dodds, *Tyneside classical. The Newcastle of Grainger, Dobson, and Clayton*
[1964]. For local government see (493).

3661 NOTTINGHAMSHIRE. BOROUGH OF NOTTINGHAM. Free
public libraries. List of books in the reference library. Ed. by John Potter
Briscoe. Nottingham. 1909.

Supplemented by Nottinghamshire county library, *Nottinghamshire: county library
local history collection,* Nottingham, 1953, and James Ward, *A descriptive catalogue of
books . . . in the library of J. Ward,* Nottingham, 1892, supplement, 1898. For archives,
P. A. Kennedy, *Guide to the Nottinghamshire county records office,* Nottingham, 1960,
supplemented by *Annual reports* of county archivist, 1957+, and *Annual reports* of
Archives department, City of Nottingham public libraries: see also John Thomas
Godfrey, *Manuscripts . . . in the possession of Mr. James Ward,* 1900. For 19th-century
histories see Thomas Bailey, *Annals of Nottinghamshire,* etc., 4 v., [1852–5]; Cornelius
Brown, *Lives of Nottinghamshire worthies,* etc., 1882; Robert Mellors, *Men of Notting-
ham and Nottinghamshire,* etc., Nottingham, 1924. Among modern works Alfred Cecil
Wood, *A history of Nottinghamshire,* Nottingham, 1947; Kenneth George Tweedale
Meaby, *Nottinghamshire: extracts from the county records of the eighteenth century,*
Nottingham [1947]; Jonathan David Chambers, *The vale of Trent, 1670–1800: a
regional study of economic change,* Economic history review suppl. 3 [1957], and his
Nottinghamshire in the eighteenth century: a study of life and labour under the squirearchy,
1932, 2nd edn. 1966. See also (1547), (1667), and Meredith (3719).

3662 —— MANSFIELD. GROVES (WILLIAM HORNER). The history of
Mansfield. Nottingham. 1894.

3663 —— NEWARK. BROWN (CORNELIUS). A history of Newark-on-
Trent. 2 v. Newark. 1904–7.

Also his *The annals of Newark-on-Trent,* etc., 1879.

3664 —— NOTTINGHAM. WOOD (ALFRED CECIL). 'Nottingham, 1835–1865.' *Trans. Thoroton Soc.* 59 (1955), 1–83.

The printed *Records* (485), are also valuable for the town's general history; also John Blackner, *The history of Nottingham, embracing its antiquities, trade, and manufactures,* etc., Nottingham, 1815; John F. Sutton, *The date book of remarkable and memorable events connected with Nottingham and its neighbourhood, 1750–1850,* 1852; William Howie Wylie, *Old and new Nottingham,* 1853; Duncan Gray, *Nottingham through 500 years: a short history of town government,* 1949, 2nd edn., 1960; Roy Anthony Church, *Economic and social change in a midland town: Victorian Nottingham, 1815–1900,* 1966; Malcolm Ian Thomis, *Politics and society in Nottingham, 1785–1835,* Oxf. 1969.

3665 OXFORDSHIRE. CORDEAUX (EDWARD HAROLD) *and* MERRY (DENIS HARRY). A bibliography of printed works relating to Oxfordshire, excluding the city and university of Oxford. Oxf. 1955.

Additions and corrigenda are published in *Bodleian Library Record.* See also Oxfordshire County Record Office Record Pubs., No. 4, *Summary catalogue of the privately deposited records in the Oxfordshire County Record Office,* Oxford, 1966, and Peter Spencer Spokes, *Summary catalogue of manuscripts in the Bodleian Library relating to the city, county, and university of Oxford: accessions from 1916 to 1962,* Oxford Hist. Soc. Pub. n.s. 17, Oxf., 1964. See also for local government (470).

3666 —— BANBURY. BEESLEY (ALFRED). The history of Banbury, including copious and antiquarian notes of the neighbourhood. [1841.]

See also Taylor (1448), and Harrison and Trinder (2566).

3667 —— DEDDINGTON. COLVIN (HOWARD MONTAGU). A history of Deddington. 1963.

3668 —— OXFORD. FASNACHT (RUTH). A history of the City of Oxford. Oxf. 1954.

See also Mary Grizel Hobson, *Oxford Council Acts, 1752–1801* (Oxford Hist. Soc. pubs. n.s. 15), Oxf. 1962, and references to the university, pp. 406–8 above.

3669 RUTLAND. V.C.H. RUTLAND.

Complete.

3670 SHROPSHIRE. BEDDOWS (HARRY THOMAS) *ed.* Catalogue of local books and pamphlets in the Shrewsbury Free Public Library together with a calendar of the MSS, other than charters and deeds, preserved in the same library by W. G. Dimock Fletcher. Shrewsbury. 1903.

Also Salop County Council, *A guide to the Shropshire records,* comp. Mary C. Hill, 1952, Geoffrey Charles Cowling, *A descriptive list of the printed maps of Shropshire, A.D. 1577–1900,* Shrewsbury, 1959, For general history see Charles Hulbert, *The history and description of the county of Salop,* Providence Grove, 1837. For local government see (473), for industrialization (1530), and Hill (1595).

3671 —— MADELEY. RANDALL (JOHN). History of Madeley, including Ironbridge, Coalbrookdale, and Coalport. Madeley. 1880.

See also (1564).

3672 —— SHREWSBURY. OWEN (HUGH) *and* BLAKEWAY (JOHN BRICKDALE). A history of Shrewsbury. 2 v. 1825.

Also *Calendar of the muniments and records of the borough of Shrewsbury*, Shrewsbury, 1896, and (434).

3673 SOMERSET. GREEN (EMANUEL). Bibliotheca Somersetiensis; a catalogue of books, pamphlets, single sheets, and broadsheets, in some way connected with the county of Somerset. 3 v. Taunton. 1902.

See also Arthur Lee Humphreys, *Somersetshire parishes; a handbook of historical reference to all places in that county*, 2 v., 1906; Somerset County Council Records Committee, *Inventory of parochial documents in the diocese of Bath and Wells and the county of Somerset*, ed. John Edward King, Taunton, 1938, and *Somerset in manuscript: notes on the main archive groups preserved in the Somerset Record Office*, etc., Taunton, 1959; Leslie Ernest John Brooke, *Somerset newspapers, 1725–1960* [Yeovil], 1960. William Phelps, *The history and antiquities of Somersetshire*, etc., 2 v., 1836–9, contains 19th-century material. See also Marshall, C. S. Orwin (3563).

3674 —— BATH. SHUM (FREDERICK). A catalogue of Bath books on the hot mineral springs of Bath from the sixteenth century to the twentieth century. Bath. 1913.

May be supplemented by Bath Public Libraries, *Bath guides, directories and newspapers*, Bath, 1962. See also Thomas Hosmer Shepherd, *Bath and Bristol, with the counties of Somerset and Gloucester, displayed in a series of views*, etc., 1829; Rowland Mainwaring, *Annals of Bath from the year 1800 to the passing of the new Municipal Act*, Bath, 1838, a detailed political history; John Earle, *A guide to the knowledge of Bath, ancient and modern*, 1864; Walter Ison, *The Georgian buildings of Bath from 1700 to 1830*, 1948.

3675 —— BRIDGWATER. POWELL (ARTHUR HERBERT). Bridgwater in the later days. Bridgwater. 1908.

Also Sydney Gardnor Jarman, *A history of Bridgwater*, 1889.

3676 STAFFORDSHIRE. SIMMS (RUPERT). Bibliotheca Staffordiensis, or, A bibliographical account of books and other printed material relating to— printed or published in—or written by a native, resident, or person deriving a title from any portion of the county of Stafford Lichfield. 1894.

Supplemented by Stafford Public Library, *Staffordshire: a list of books in Stafford Public Library*, Stafford, 1953. Norman Emery and D. R. Beard, *Current bibliography of published material relating to north Staffordshire and south Cheshire*, v. 1, no. 1, Stoke on Trent, 1964, and the same authors' *Staffordshire directories; a union list of directories relating to the geographical county of Stafford*, Stoke on Trent, 1966. See also William Pitt, *A topographical history of Staffordshire; including its agriculture, mines, and manufactures . . . with a succinct account of the rise and progress of the Staffordshire potteries*, 2 v., Newcastle under Lyme, 1817; Henry Carlos Wedgwood, *Romance of Staffordshire, a series of sketches*, 3 v., 1877–9; John Alfred Langford, C. S. Mackintosh and James Carpenter Tildesley, *Staffordshire and Warwickshire past and present*, 4 v. [1884], a very full account of the 19th century; Phil Drabble, *Black Country*, 1952. *V.C.H.* Staffordshire, viii, 1963, ed. J. G. Jenkins, gives a detailed account of the 19th century Potteries: *V.C.H.* Staffordshire, ii, 1967, ed. J. G. Jenkins and M. W. Greenslade, deals with the coal, iron and metal industries. For Potteries also see (1604), for parliamentary history see J. C. Wedgwood, *Staffordshire Parliamentary history*, v. 3, 1934, for Black Country see (1528), (1531), for local government (512).

3677 —— BILSTON. LAWLEY (GEORGE T.). A history of Bilston, in the county of Stafford; a record of its archaeology, ecclesiology, etc. Bilston. 1893.

3678 —— BURTON ON TRENT. MOLYNEUX (WILLIAM). Burton on Trent, its history, its waters and its breweries. [1869.]

3679 —— CANNOCK CHASE. HACKWOOD (FREDERICK WILLIAM). The chronicles of Cannock Chase. 1903.

3680 —— SEDGLEY. HACKWOOD (FREDERICK WILLIAM). Sedgley researches. 1898.

Also E. A. Underhill, *The story of the ancient manor of Sedgley* [Sedgley, 1942].

3681 —— STAFFORD. ROXBURGH (ALAN L. P.) Stafford. Being a reprint, with revisions, of articles published in the 'Staffordshire Chronicle'. Stafford. 1948.

3682 —— STOKE ON TRENT. WARRILLOW (ERNEST JAMES DALZELL). A sociological history of the city of Stoke on Trent. Stoke on Trent. 1960.

See also his *History of Etruria* ... *1760–1951*, Hanley, 1952; and John Ward, *The borough of Stoke-upon-Trent* ... *also the manorial history of Newcastle under Lyme*, 1843.

3683 —— WALSALL. HOMESHAW (ERNEST JAMES). The corporation of the borough and foreign of Walsall. Walsall. 1960.

Bibliog. 172–7. Also his *The industrial history of Walsall*, Walsall, 1953.

3684 —— WEDNESBURY. EDE (JOHN FREDERICK). History of Wednesbury. [Wednesbury. 1962].

3685 —— WEST BROMWICH. HACKWOOD (FREDERICK WILLIAM). A history of West Bromwich, reprinted from the 'Midland Sun'. Birmingham. 1895.

3686 —— WILLENHALL. TILDESLEY (NORMAN WILLIAM). A history of Willenhall. Willenhall. [1952.]

Also Frederick William Hackwood, *The annals of Willenhall*, Wolverhampton, 1908.

3687 —— WOLVERHAMPTON. MANDER (GERALD POYNTON). A history of Wolverhampton to the early nineteenth century. Ed. and completed by Norman William Tildesley. [Wolverhampton.] 1960.

See also George T. Lawley, *The bibliography of Wolverhampton etc.*, Bilston, 1890, Alfred Hinde, *A handy history of Wolverhampton and guide to the district*, 1884, William Highfield Jones, *Story of the municipal life of Wolverhampton*, 1903. Industrial Development Committee, *The story of a midland town*, 1908.

3688 SUFFOLK. IPSWICH FREE LIBRARY. Catalogue of books in the reference department. Ed. by Henry Ogle. Ipswich. 1906.

See also Ipswich and East Suffolk Record Office, *Parish records survey: report of the survey in . . . East Suffolk and in the archdeaconries of Ipswich and Suffolk* [Ipswich] 1963; Augustine Page, *A supplement to the Suffolk traveller*, etc., Ipswich, 1843; Alfred Inigo Suckling, *The history and antiquities of the county of Suffolk*, 2 v., 1846–8; *Index*, Ipswich, 1952; John Glyde, *Suffolk in the nineteenth century: physical, social, moral, religious and industrial*, 1856, a very full and useful account, as is A. D. Bayne (3648). Walter Arthur Copinger, *The manors of Suffolk*, etc., 7 v., v. 1, London, 1905, v. 2–7, Manchester, 1908–11. For enclosures see Lavrovsky (1667), for agriculture (1687).

3689 —— IPSWICH. GLYDE (JOHN). The moral, social, and religious condition of Ipswich in the middle of the nineteenth century . . . with a sketch of its history, rise and progress. Ipswich. 1850.

Also George Rix Clarke, *The history and description of . . . Ipswich*, etc., Ipswich, 1830; John Wodderspoon, *A new guide to Ipswich*, etc., Ipswich, 1842.

3690 SURREY. GUILDFORD PUBLIC LIBRARY. Reference dept. Catalogue of works in the library relating to the county of Surrey. [Guildford.] 1957.

Also William Myson, *Surrey newspapers; a handlist and tentative bibliography*, Wimbledon [1961]; M. Y. Williams, *Short guide to the Surrey collection*, 1965, descriptive of the Minet library, Camberwell; Surrey County Council, Records and ancient monuments committee, *Guide to archives and other collections of documents relating to Surrey*, 6 v., Surrey Record Soc. Pub., nos. 23–4, 26, 28–9, 31–2. Thomas Allen, *History of the counties of Surrey and Sussex . . . illustrated by a series of views engraved . . . by Nathaniel Whittock*, 2 v., 1829, is a general survey; *V.C.H.* Surrey is complete. For local government see (475).

3691 —— GUILDFORD. CARTER (HECTOR). Guildford freemen's books, 1655–1933. Guildford. 1963.

3692 —— MORTLAKE. ROSE (CHARLES MARSHALL). Nineteenth century Mortlake and East Sheen: a factual history. 1961.

3693 SUSSEX. BUTLER (GEORGE SLADE). Topographica Sussexiana: an attempt towards forming a list of the various publications relating to the county of Sussex. [1866.]

May be supplemented by Eastbourne public libraries, *Catalogue of the local collection, comprising books on Eastbourne and Sussex*, Eastbourne, 1956. See also West and East Sussex County Councils, *Descriptive report on the Quarter Sessions, and the official and ecclesiastical records in the custody of the County Councils of West and East Sussex*, etc., compiled by B. Campbell Cooke (Record pub. 2), 1954. Both county councils have published full catalogues of archives and estate accounts in recent years, among them West Sussex County Council, *The Cowdray archives*, ed. Alan Arthur Dibben, 2 pt., Chichester, 1960; *The Mitford archives*, ed. Francis William Steer, Chichester, 1961; *The Hawkins papers*, ed. Francis William Steer, Chichester, 1963; *The Lavington estate archives*, ed. Francis W. Steer, Chichester, 1964; *Goodwood estate archives*, ed. Francis W. Steer and J. E. Amanda Venables, 2 v., Chichester, 1970, 1972; and the East Sussex County Council, *The Glynde Place archives a catalogue*, ed. Richard F. Dell, Lewes, 1965, and *The Danny archives*, ed. Judith A. Wooldridge, Lewes, 1966. See also John Comber, comp. *Sussex genealogies*, 3 v., Cambridge, 1931–3; John Docwra Parry, *An historical and descriptive account of the coasts of Sussex . . . forming also a guide to all the watering places*, Brighton, 1833, and on Romney marsh, William Holloway, *The history of Romney marsh from its earliest formation to 1837*, etc., 1849. For general survey see Allen (3690), for enclosures (1664).

3694 —— BRIGHTON. GILBERT (EDMUND WILLIAM). Brighton: old ocean's bauble. 1954.

Also John Ackerson Erredge, *History of Brighthelmston . . . with a chronological table of local events*, Brighton, 1862; John George Bishop, *A peep into the past—Brighton in the olden time, with glances at the present*, 1880; Sir Osbert Sitwell and Margaret Barton, *Brighton*, 1935; Antony Dale, *Fashionable Brighton, 1820–60*, 1947, and *The history and architecture of Brighton*, Brighton, 1950; See also Musgrave (2969).

3695 —— CHICHESTER. The Chichester papers. Chichester. 1955+.

Pamphlets on aspects of Chichester's history. No. 38 is an index, *Articles and notes about Chichester in Sussex archaeological collections*, (*v. 1–100*) and *Sussex Notes and Queries*, (*v. 1–15*), ed. Francis William Steer, 1963. For local government see (495).

3696 —— EASTBOURNE. WRIGHT (JOHN CHARLES). Bygone Eastbourne. 1902.

3697 —— HASTINGS. COUSINS (HENRY). Hastings of bygone days— and the present. Hastings. 1911.

3698 —— LEWES. See (434).

3699 —— RYE. EAST SUSSEX COUNTY RECORD OFFICE. The records of Rye corporation; a catalogue edited by Richard F. Dell. Lewes. 1962.

See also William Holloway, *History and antiquities of the ancient town and port of Rye in Sussex*, 1847.

3700 —— SEAFORD. EAST SUSSEX COUNTY RECORD OFFICE. Records of the corporation of Seaford. Ed. by Francis William Steer. Lewes. 1959.

3701 ——WINCHELSEA. EAST SUSSEX COUNTY RECORD OFFICE. Winchelsea corporation records: a catalogue. Ed. by Richard F. Dell. Lewes. 1963.

3702 WARWICKSHIRE. WILSON (ROGER BURDETT). A handlist of books relating to the county of Warwick. Birmingham. 1955.

A short guide. See also Paul D. Harvey and H. Thorpe, *The printed maps of Warwickshire, 1576–1900*, Warwickshire County Council Records Committee, Warwick, 1959; Thomas Sharp, *An epitome of the county of Warwick*, etc., 1835; Elihu Burritt, *Walks in the Black country and its green borderland*, 1868. For parliamentary history see Langford (3676), for local government (482), for enclosures (1664).

3703 —— BIRMINGHAM. BIRMINGHAM PUBLIC LIBRARIES. Reference department. Catalogue of the Birmingham collection, including printed books and pamphlets, manuscripts, maps, views, portraits. Birmingham. 1918. Supplement, 1918–31, comp. by Herbert Maurice Cashmore. Birmingham. 1931.

A full and massive bibliog. See also Benjamin Walker, 'Birmingham directories', *Birmingham Archaeol. Soc. Trans. and Proc.*, 58 (1937), 1–36; Sir Ernest Varvill Hiley and Francis Cecil Minshull, *Index to local legislation of the corporation of Birmingham*,

Birmingham, 1920. The standard modern histories are Conrad Gill and Asa Briggs, *History of Birmingham*, 2 v., Oxford, 1952, (v. 1, Manor and borough to 1865 is by Conrad Gill), and *V.C.H.* Warwickshire, vii, *The City of Birmingham*, ed., William Brewer Stephens, Oxford, 1964. Nineteenth-century histories include Charles Pye, *A description of modern Birmingham . . . including Warwick and Leamington*, Birmingham [1820]; *The history of Birmingham by William Hutton, F.A.S., with considerable additions*, 6th edn., 1835, by James Guest; John Alfred Langford, *A century of Birmingham life; or A chronicle of local events, from 1741 to 1841*, 2 v., 2nd edn., 1871, continued in his *Modern Birmingham and its institutions; a chronicle of local events, from 1841 to 1871*, 2 v., 1873-7, E. Edwards, *Personal recollections of Birmingham and Birmingham men. Reprinted from the Birmingham Daily Mail, with . . . additions*, Birmingham, 1877; Robert Kirkup Dent, *Old and new Birmingham; a history of the town and its people*, 3 v., Birmingham, 1879-80; also his *The making of Birmingham; being a history of the rise and growth of the midland metropolis*, 1894. Two journals containing articles on the area are Birmingham Archaeological Society *Transactions and Proceedings*, 1870+, *Index* to v. 1-69 comp. Dorothy May Norris, Birmingham, 1954, and *Birmingham University Historical Journal* (40). For local government see (499), for Joseph Parkes (223), for Lunar Society (1614), Thomas Attwood and Birmingham economists (1434), for Chamber of Commerce (1516), for industrial history (1528).

3704 —— COVENTRY. PREST (JOHN MICHAEL). The industrial revolution in Coventry. 1960.

See also Alice Lynes, *Coventry's story; a select booklist*, etc., Coventry City Libraries local history pamphlets 4, Coventry, 1960. Benjamin Poole, *Coventry: its history and antiquities . . . illustrated by W. Fred. Taunton*, 1870, is a substantial 19th-century history.

3705 ——LEAMINGTON. DUDLEY (THOMAS BRISCOE). From chaos to charter: a complete history of Royal Leamington Spa, from the earliest times to the Charter of Incorporation. 1896.

3706 WESTMORLAND. HINDS (JAMES PITCAIRN). Bibliotheca Jacksoniana; catalogue. Kendal. 1909.

See also Thomas Rose, *Westmorland, Cumberland, Durham and Northumberland illustrated. From original drawings by T. Allom, G. Pickering* etc., 1832-5. For agriculture see (1682), for parliamentary history (434). See also the relevant works at (3556).

3707 —— KENDAL. NICHOLSON (CORNELIUS). The annals of Kendal; being a historical and descriptive account of Kendal and its environs, with biographical sketches of many eminent personages connected with the town. Kendal. 1832.

3708 WILTSHIRE. GODDARD (EDWARD HUNGERFORD) *ed.* Wiltshire bibliography; a catalogue of printed books, pamphlets and articles bearing on the history, topography and natural history of the county. [1929.]

See also Wiltshire Archaeological and Natural History Society Records Branch, v. 5, *List of Wiltshire borough records earlier in date than 1836*, ed. Maurice Gilbert Rathbone, Devizes, 1951; Wiltshire County Record Committee, *Guide to the records in the custody of the clerk of the peace for Wiltshire*, ed. Maurice Gilbert Rathbone, Trowbridge, 1959; *Guide to the county council, parish, poor law and other official records in the Wiltshire County Record Office*, ed. Pamela Stewart, Trowbridge, 1961. *V.C.H.* Wiltshire, v (1957), ed. Elizabeth M. Crittall, contains articles on county government and parliamentary history. For enclosures see (1664).

3709 —— CORSLEY. DAVIES (MAUD FRANCES). Life in an English village; an economic and historical survey of the parish of Corsley in Wiltshire. 1909.

An unusually detailed village history produced under the supervision of Beatrice Webb.

3710 —— DEVIZES. CUNNINGTON (EDWARD BENJAMIN HOWARD). Some annals of the borough of Devizes, 1791–1835. Devizes. 1925.

See also [Henry Bull or James Waylen] *A history, military and municipal, of the ancient borough of the Devizes,* etc., 1859 and *V.C.H.* Wiltshire, v. 10.

3711 —— MARLBOROUGH. STEDMAN (ALFRED REDVERS). Marlborough and the upper Kennet country. Marlborough. 1960.

3712 —— SALISBURY. V.C.H. A history of Wiltshire. Ed. by Elizabeth M. Crittall. v. 6. 1962.

Pages 69–180 give the history of Salisbury.

3713 —— SWINDON. GRINSELL (LESLIE VALENTINE) *and others.* Studies in the history of Swindon. Swindon. 1950.

See also William Morris, *Swindon fifty years ago,—more or less.* Swindon, [1885].

3714 WORCESTERSHIRE. BURTON (JOHN RICHARD) *and* PEARSON (FRANK SHAKESPEARE). Bibliography of Worcestershire. (Worcestershire Hist. Soc. Pubs.) 3 pt. Oxford. 1898. 1903.

See also Ettwell Augustine Bracher Barnard, *List of printed papers and miscellanea (with index)* . . . *in the Prattinton collections of Worcestershire history in the possession of the Society of Antiquaries,* 1932; Worcestershire Record Office, *Annual Reports* of county archivist, Worcester, 1947+, list accessions. T. C. Turberville, *Worcestershire in the nineteenth century; a complete digest of facts occurring in the county since the commencement of the year 1800,* 1852, is a full history. *V.C.H.* Worcestershire is complete. For enclosures see (1664).

3715 —— DUDLEY. CHANDLER (GEORGE) *and* HANNAH (IAN CAMPBELL). Dudley: as it was and as it is today. 1949.

See also Charles Francis George Clark, *Curiosities of Dudley and the Black country,* 1881.

3716 —— KIDDERMINSTER. BURTON (JOHN RICHARD). A history of Kidderminster, with short accounts of some neighbouring parishes. 1890.

3717 —— MALVERN. SMITH (BRIAN S.). A history of Malvern. [Leicester.] 1964.

3718 —— WORCESTER. WOOF (RICHARD). Catalogue of manuscript records and printed books in the library of the corporation of Worcester, with an appendix of local records not in the custody of the corporation. Worcester. 1874.

See also McMenemy (2542).

3719 YORKSHIRE. YORKSHIRE ARCHAEOLOGICAL SOCIETY. Catalogue of the printed books and pamphlets in the library of the Yorkshire archaeological society. Comp. by George Edward Kirk. 2 v. in 1. Wakefield. 1935–6. Supplement, 1 Dec. 1932—30 Nov. 1939.

Accessions lists have been pub. annually since 1948. See also Edward Hailstone, *Catalogue of a collection of historical and topographical works . . . relating to the county of York*, Bradford, 1858; William Boyne, *The Yorkshire library*, 1869; [Butler Wood], *Catalogue of the books and pamphlets relating to Yorkshire in the central reference library, Bradford*, Bradford, 1892, which concentrates on the West Riding; York public library, *List of books in the local collection relating to the city and county of York*, York, 1912, arranged analytically; Leeds public libraries, *Leeds and Yorkshire; a guide to the collections*, Leeds, 1947. For the East Riding see Arthur Geoffrey Dickens and Kenneth Austin Macmahon, *A guide to regional studies on the East Riding of Yorkshire and the City of Hull*, Hull, 1956. See also George Ebenezer Laughton and Lorna Rutherford Stephen, eds., *Yorkshire newspapers: a bibliography, with locations*, Harrogate, 1960, and Sheffield city council libraries committee, *Catalogue of the Arundel Castle manuscripts . . . relating to the Yorkshire, Nottingham and Derbyshire estates of the Dukes of Norfolk*, etc., ed. Rosamond Meredith, Sheffield, 1965.

3720 YORKSHIRE. MAYHALL (JOHN). The annals of Yorkshire from the earliest period to the present time. 2 v. Leeds. [1866].

Other general histories are Edward Baines, *History, directory and gazetteer of the county of York*, 2 v., Leeds, 1822–3; Thomas Langdale, *A topographical dictionary of Yorkshire*, etc., 2nd edn., Northallerton, 1822; Thomas Allen, *A new and complete history of the county of York*, 3 v., 1828–31; Henry Schroeder, *The annals of Yorkshire from the earliest period to the present time*, 2 v., Leeds, 1851, 1852; Thomas Baines, ed., *Yorkshire past and present; a history and description of the three Ridings*, etc., 2 v., 1871–7. On the East Riding see T. Bulmer, *History, topography and directory of East Yorkshire (with Hull)*, etc., Preston, 1892; George Poulson, *The history and antiquities of the seigniory of Holderness*, etc., 2 v., Hull, 1840–1; Alan Harris (1689). For the North Riding see Thomas Dunham Whitaker, *An history of Richmondshire*, etc., 2 v., 1823: *V.C.H.*, North Riding is complete. For the West Riding see T. D. Whitaker, *The history and antiquities of the deanery of Craven*, 1805, and his *Loidis and Elmete . . . the lower portions of Aredale and Wharfdale, together with the entire vale of Calder* etc., Leeds, 1816; Joseph Hunter, *South Yorkshire, the history and topography of the deanery of Doncaster*, etc., 2 v., 1828–31; William Odom, *Hallamshire worthies. Characteristics and work of notable Sheffield men and women*, Sheffield, 1926. See also A. D. Orange, *Philosophers and provincials: the Yorkshire philosophical society from 1822 to 1844*, York, 1973. For enclosures see (1664), for agriculture (1689), for industries (1540–4), (1561), for parliamentary history (425), (428), (434).

3721 —— BEVERLEY. DENNETT (J.). Beverley borough records, 1575–1821. Yorkshire archaeological society. Record series 84. Huddersfield. 1933.

See also Ivan Hall and Elisabeth Hall, *Historic Beverley*, York, 1973, an excellent collection of photographs, and for local government (494).

3722 —— BINGLEY. TURNER (JOSEPH HORSFALL). Ancient Bingley; or Bingley, its history and scenery. Bingley. 1897.

See also Harry Speight, *Chronicles and stories of Bingley and district*, 1904.

3723 —— BIRSTALL. CRADOCK (HENRY COWPER). A history of the ancient parish of Birstall. 1933.

3724 —— BRADFORD. JAMES (JOHN). The history and topography of Bradford (in the county of York), with topographical notices of its parish. 1841.

Also his *Continuation and additions to the history of Bradford and its parish*, 1866. See also Edward Collinson, *The history of the worsted trade and historic sketch of Bradford*, 1854; James Burnley, *Phases of Bradford life; a series of pen and ink sketches* [1871]; William Scruton, *Pen and pencil pictures of old Bradford*, Bradford, 1889; four works by William Cudworth, *Round about Bradford; a series of sketches descriptive and semi-historical*, Bradford, 1876, *Historical notes on the Bradford corporation*, Bradford, 1881, *Histories of Bolton and Bowling (townships of Bradford)*, Bradford, 1891, *Manningham, Heaton and Allerton (townships of Bradford)*, Bradford, 1896. Bradford lacks a comprehensive history: further material is given by Keith George Elliott Harris, ed., *Catalogue of the library of the Bradford Historical and Antiquarian Society*, 1957. See also (1542).

3725 —— BRIGHOUSE. MITCHELL (REGINALD). Brighouse: portrait of a town. Brighouse. 1953.

3726 —— DONCASTER. TOMLINSON (JOHN). Doncaster from the Roman occupation to the present time. 1887.

3727 —— GIGGLESWICK. BRAYSHAW (THOMAS) *and* ROBINSON (RALPH MOSLEY). A history of the ancient parish of Giggleswick. 1932.

3728 —— GOOLE. PORTEOUS (JOHN DOUGLAS). The company town of Goole; an essay in urban genesis. Univ. of Hull. Occasional Papers in geography, 12. Hull. 1969.

3729 —— HALIFAX. CRABTREE (JOHN). A concise history of the parish and vicarage of Halifax in the county of York. Halifax. 1836.

See also Joseph Horsfall Turner, *Halifax books and authors*, Brighouse, 1906.

3730 —— HARROGATE. GRAINGE (WILLIAM). The history and topography of Harrogate and the forest of Knaresborough. 1871.

3731 —— HONLEY. JAGGER (MARY A.). The history of Honley and its hamlets from the earliest time to the present. Huddersfield. [1914].

3732 —— HOOTON PAGNELL. RUSTON (ARTHUR GOUGH) *and* WITNEY (DENIS). Hooton Pagnell: the agricultural evolution of a Yorkshire village. 1934.

Also Charles Edwin Whiting, *The accounts of the churchwardens, constables, overseers of the poor and overseers of the highways of the parish of Hooton Pagnell, 1767–1820* (Yorkshire Archaeol. Soc. Rec. Ser. 97) [Leeds], 1938.

3733 —— HUDDERSFIELD. SYKES (DANIEL FREDERICK EDWARD). The history of Huddersfield and vicinity. Huddersfield. 1898.

Also his *The history of the Colne valley*, Slaithwaite, 1906, and Roy Brook, *The story of Huddersfield*, 1968. For woollen industry see Ghorbal (1544).

3734 —— HULL. SHEAHAN (JAMES JOSEPH). History of the town and port of Kingston-upon-Hull. 2nd edn. Beverley. 1866.

Fuller than 1st edn., 1864. See also *V.C.H.*, Yorkshire, East Riding I, *The city of Kingston upon Hull*, ed. Keith Allison, 1969.

3735 —— LEEDS. WARDELL (JAMES). The municipal history of the borough of Leeds, in the county of York. Leeds. 1846.

Leeds lacks an adequate general history. See Edward Parsons, *The civil, ecclesiastical, literary, commercial . . . history of Leeds, Bradford, Wakefield, Dewsbury, Otley . . .*, 2 v., Leeds, 1834, *An historical guide to Leeds and its environs*, Leeds, 1858; Richard Vickerman Taylor, *The biographia Leodiensis . . . the worthies of Leeds and neighbourhood*, 1865–7. Edward Baines, *The life of Edward Baines by his son*, 1851 (proprietor of the *Leeds Mercury* from 1801), Sir Thomas Wemyss Reid, *A memoir of John Deakin Heaton, M.D. of Leeds*, 1883, deal with public life. For Dr. Hook see (706), for newspapers (3499), for Thackrah (2537), (2564), for woollen industry (1544), for flax (1540), for leather (1549), for housing (2578), for merchant community, Wilson (1481). In recent years the Thoresby Society has published material on 19th-century Leeds. See especially Kenneth J. Bonser and Harold Nichols, *Printed maps and plans of Leeds*, Thoresby Soc. pubs. 47, Leeds, 1960, and William Gordon Rimmer, 'The industrial profile of Leeds, 1740–1840', Thoresby Soc. pubs. 113, *Miscellany* 14, pt. 2, Leeds, 1967, 130–57, and by the same author, 'Occupations in Leeds, 1841–1941', *ibid.* 158–78.

3736 —— MALTON. HUDLESTON (NIGEL ANDREW). History of Malton and Norton. Scarborough. 1962.

See also (434).

3737 —— MIDDLESBROUGH. LILLIE (WILLIAM). The history of Middlesbrough. An illustration of the evolution of English industry. Middlesbrough. 1968.

3738 —— MORLEY. SMITH (WILLIAM) *junior*. Rambles about Morley, with descriptive and historic sketches; also an account of the rise and progress of the woollen manufacture in this place. 1866.

See also his *Morley, ancient and modern*, Leeds, 1886.

3739 —— NORTHALLERTON. SAYWELL (JOSEPH LEMUEL). The history and annals of Northallerton, Yorkshire, with notes and voluminous appendix. Northallerton. 1885.

3740 —— PUDSEY. RAYNER (SIMEON). The history and antiquities of Pudsey. Ed. by W. Smith. 1887.

3741 —— ROTHERHAM. GUEST (JOHN). Historic notices of Rotherham: ecclesiastical, collegiate, and civil. Worksop. 1879.

3742 —— SCARBOROUGH. BAKER (JOSEPH BROGDEN). The history of Scarborough from the earliest date. 1882.

See also Arthur Rowntree, ed., *The history of Scarborough*, 1931.

3743 —— SEDBERGH. THOMPSON (WILLIAM). Sedbergh, Garsdale, and Dent. Leeds. 1892.

3744 —— SHEFFIELD. ODOM (WILLIAM). A bibliography of Sheffield history. Sheffield. 1930.

Supplemented by Sheffield city libraries, department of local history and archives, *Basic books on Sheffield history*, 4th edn., Sheffield, 1966, and *Guide to the manuscript collections* (72). Mary Walton, *Sheffield: its story and its achievements*, Sheffield, 3rd edn., 1952 is a good general history. Older works include Joseph Hunter, *Hallamshire: the history and topography of the parish of Sheffield* . . ., new edn. by Alfred Gatty, Sheffield, 1869; Alfred Gatty, *Sheffield past and present*, Sheffield, 1873; Robert Eadon Leader, ed., *Reminiscences of old Sheffield, its streets and its people*, Sheffield, 1875, also his *Sheffield in the eighteenth century*, Sheffield, 1901; John Parker and Sir Henry George Ward, *Chapters in the political history of Sheffield, 1832–1849; consisting of letters from Mr. J. Parker M.P. and Mr. H. G. Ward M.P.*, Sheffield, 1884; Matthew Henry Habershon, *Chapeltown researches; archaeological and historical*, etc., 1893, which has material on iron industry; John Daniel Leader, ed., *The records of the Burgery of Sheffield, commonly called the Town Trust*, 1897, with *Supplement, 1848–1955*, ed. Edward Bramley, 1957. For social conditions see Holland (2564), for industries (1566), (1571), for newspapers (3499).

3745 —— SPEN VALLEY. PEEL (FRANK). Spen valley past and present. Heckmondwike. 1893.

Contains material on Luddites: see also (99).

3746 —— WAKEFIELD. TAYLOR (THOMAS). The history of Wakefield in the county of York, the rectory manor, with biographical and other notices of some of the persons connected therewith. Wakefield. 1886.

Also Henry Clarkson, *Memories of merry Wakefield; an octogenarian's recollections*, etc., Wakefield, 1887.

3747 —— WHITBY. YOUNG (GEORGE). A history of Whitby and Streoneshalh abbey; with a statistical survey of the vicinity to the distance of twenty-five miles. 2 v. Whitby. 1817.

Also Francis Kildale Robinson, *Whitby; its abbey and the principal parts of the neighbourhood*, etc., Whitby, 1860.

3748 —— YORK. V.C.H. Yorkshire, v. The City of York. Ed. by Peter M. Tillott. 1961.

See also Charles Brunton Knight, *A history of the city of York*, 1944; Alan Armstrong, *Stability and change in an English county town: a social study of York, 1801–51*, Camb., 1974. For the Retreat see (2544).

D. LONDON

This section deals with the areas included in the scope of the Metropolis Local Management Act, 1855 (roughly the same as the area of the London County Council down to 1965), and particular districts are listed alphabetically, as far as possible by the names of the vestries concerned. Works on the Port of London, on communications, and on the City as a financial centre are listed in Economic History; works on police, on public health administration, and on clubs and inns in Social History. The London theatre is to be found in Cultural History.

1. BIBLIOGRAPHY, CATALOGUES, AND GUIDES

3749 SMITH (RAYMOND). The city of London; a select book list. 1951.

Should be supplemented, for areas outside the city boundaries, by Library Assoc. Reference and Special Libraries section, S.E. Group, *The county of London: a select booklist compiled by the senior staff of the Guildhall Library* (Aids to reference service, 1), 1959. Raymond Smith, 'London local collections', *Journal of Documentation*, 5 (1949), 19–30, is an invaluable survey of a complicated subject. See also John Merriman Sims, *London and Middlesex published records; a handlist* (London Rec. Soc. Occasional Pubns, 1), 1970.

3750 LONDON COUNTY COUNCIL LIBRARY. Members' library catalogue. V. 1. London history and topography. 1939.

The best full-scale printed bibliography. See also L.C.C. Record Office, *Guide to the records in the London County Record Office, pt. 1, Records of the predecessors of the L.C.C., except the Boards of Guardians*, by Ida Darlington, 1962. (Records of the London vestries were inherited by the metropolitan boroughs.) See also Greater London Record Office, *A survey of the parish registers of the diocese of London, Inner London area*. [By Joan Coburn.] [1969]. (G.L.C. pubn. 199.) The L.C.C. and later the G.L.C. have published annual accessions lists of books and documents, 1958+.

3751 CORPORATION OF LONDON. Guildhall library. A guide to the records in the Corporation of London Records Office and the Guildhall Library Muniment Room. Comp. by Philip Edmund Jones and Raymond Smith. 1951.

See also Guildhall Library handlists, *Vestry minutes of parishes within the city of London*, 1958, 2nd edn., 1964; *Churchwardens' accounts of parishes within the city of London*, 1960, new edn., 1969; *London rate assessments and inhabitants' lists*, etc., 1961; *Parish registers; a handlist, part 1, Registers of Church of England parishes within the city of London*, 1963, 2nd edn. rev. and enl. 1966, 3rd edn., 1972; *Part II, Registers of Church of England parishes outside the city of London: non-parish registers and registers of foreign denominations, burial ground records*, 1964; *London business house histories*, 1964; *A handlist of poll-books and registers of electors in Guildhall library*, 1970. The Guildhall library maintains a full, up-to-date, classified card catalogue of London history.

3752 LONDON COUNTY COUNCIL. London statutes. V. 1. 1750–1888. Comp. by Sir George Laurence Gomme and Seager Berry. [1907.]

For parliamentary papers on London see Ford and Ford (391) 16–24. For works on London government see Gross (3508).

3753 GOSS (CHARLES WILLIAM FREDERICK). The London directories, 1677–1855: a bibliography with notes on their origin and development. 1932.

3754 DARLINGTON (IDA) *and* HOWGEGO (JAMES). Printed maps of London, circa 1553–1850. 1964.

See also *A catalogue of maps, plans, and views of London, Westminster, and Southwark, collected and arranged by Frederick Crace*, ed. John Gregory Crace, 1878.

3755 HENNESSY (GEORGE). Novum repertorium ecclesiasticum parochiale Londinense or, London diocesan clergy succession from the earliest times to the year 1898. 1898.

On the London Baptists see Whitley (812).

2. General History and Topography

3756 RUDÉ (GEORGE E.) Hanoverian London, 1714–1808. 1971.

Bibliog. 256–61. In the same series (*The history of London*), and by the general editor, Francis Henry Wollaston Sheppard, *London, 1808–1870: the infernal wen*, 1971, bibliog. 391–404.

3757 BESANT (*Sir* WALTER). Survey of London. 10 v. 1902–12.

A large-scale popular work. For a recent general study see John Terence Coppock and Hugh Counsell Prince, eds., *Greater London*, 1964. For population see Williams (1371).

3758 CORPORATION OF THE CITY OF LONDON. The corporation of London. 1950.

For the City corporation see Henry Hunter, *The history of London and its environs*, 2 v., 1811, which contains much political information on 1790–1811; William John Loftie, *A history of London*, 2 v., 1883–4, 2nd edn., 2 v., 1884; Reginald Robinson Sharpe, *London and the kingdom; a history derived mainly from the archives at Guildhall*, 3 v., 1894–5, a standard political history of the city in its relations with the crown and parliament; Charles Welch, *Modern history of the city of London . . . from 1760 to the present day*, 1896, also primarily concerned with the City corporation; Sir George Laurence Gomme, *London in the reign of Victoria, 1837–97* (Victorian era series), 1898, an intelligent study by an officer of the L.C.C.; William Alexander Robson, *The government and misgovernment of London*, 1939, 2nd edn. [1948]. For the livery companies see William Herbert, *History of the twelve great livery companies* of London, etc., 1837. See also (500) and (2625).

3759 HARBEN (HENRY A.). A dictionary of London; being notes topographical and historical relating to the streets and principal buildings in the city of London. 1918. [1917.]

An authoritative work. Other similar dictionaries are John Lockie, *Lockie's topography of London*, etc., 1810; Charles Knight, *London*, 6 v., 1841–4; George Walter Thornbury and Edward Walford, *Old and new London: a narrative of its history, its people, and its places*, 6 v., 1873–8; Henry Benjamin Wheatley and [Peter Cunningham], *London past and present*, 3 v., 1891, new edn. 1930; George Hamilton Cunningham, *London, being a comprehensive survey of the history . . . of buildings and monuments, arranged under streets in alphabetical order*, 1927; William Kent, *An encyclopaedia of London*, 1937, 2nd edn., ed. Richard Gladstone, 1951; *London topographical record*, published irregularly 1899+. Bermondsey public library has a good topographical and historical collection.

3. Social History

3760 ACKERMANN (RUDOLPH). The microcosm of London, or London in miniature. 3 v. 1808–11. Re-ed. 3 v. 1904.

Other works chiefly notable for their illustrations are [Richard Phillips], *Modern London; being the history and present state of the British metropolis*, etc., 1804; Robert Wilkinson, *Londina illustrata*, 2 v., 1819–25; John Britton and Augustus Charles Pugin, *Illustrations of the public buildings of London*, etc., 2 v., 1823–8; [James Elmes], *Metropolitan improvements; . . . being a series of views . . . from . . . drawings by T. H. Shepherd*, etc., 1827, another edn. 1847; [James Elmes] *London and its environs . . . illustrated by . . . drawings by T. H. Shepherd*, 1829; John Tallis, *Tallis's London street views*, 1839, a series of street elevations drawn to scale; Thomas Shotter Boys, *Original views of London as it is . . . with historical and descriptive notices . . . by Charles Ollier*, 2 v. 1842, reprinted with additional notes by James Laver, 2 v., Guildford [1954–5]; Burlington

Fine Arts Club, *Catalogue of a collection of early drawings and pictures of London,* etc., 1920, which includes reproductions of works by Constable, Girtin, Samuel Scott, etc.

3761 TWEEDIE (ETHEL BRILLIANA). Hyde Park. 1908.

Also on parks and pleasure gardens, James Granville Southworth, *Vauxhall gardens, a chapter in the social history of England,* N.Y. 1941; Walter Sidney Scott, *Bygone pleasures of London,* 1948.

3762 [CLARKE (WILLIAM)] Everynight book; or, Life after dark. By the author of 'The Cigar'. 1827.

Also James Grant, *The Great Metropolis,* 1836, 2nd edn. 1837, and his *Sketches in London,* 1838. *London as it is today. Where to go and what to see during the Great Exhibition,* 1851, also describes where to stay and what to pay. John Timbs, *Curiosities of London,* etc., 1855, includes nearly fifty years' personal recollections.

3763 SMITH (JOHN THOMAS). Etchings of remarkable beggars, itinerant traders, and other persons of notoriety in London and its environs. 1815.

Illustrations. See also his *Vagabondiana; or, Anecdotes of mendicant wanderers through the streets of London,* 1817, new edn. 1874; and his *The cries of London: exhibiting several of the itinerant traders of ancient and modern times . . . With a memoir and portrait of the author* [the memoir by J. B. Nichols], 1839. On street cries generally see Charles Hindley, *A history of the cries of London, ancient and modern,* 2nd edn., enl. and rev. [1884], and Andrew White Tuer, *Old London street cries, and the cries of today,* 1885.

3764 SMITH (ALBERT RICHARD) *ed.* Gavarni in London: sketches of life and character. 1849.

Gavarni, a French illustrator, was in London in 1849.

3765 MAYHEW (HENRY). London labour and the London poor; a cyclopaedia of the condition and earnings of those that *will* work, those that *cannot* work and those that *will not* work. 1851. Later edns. 1861, 1862, 1864, 1865.

Originally published in the *Morning Chronicle.* A different series of selections, mostly appearing for the first time, have been pub. by Edward Palmer Thompson and Eileen Yeo as *The unknown Mayhew; selections from the* Morning Chronicle, *1849–1850,* 1971. There are also three volumes of selections from the collected edn. of 1861, by Peter Quennell, *Mayhew's London,* 1949, *London's Underworld,* 1950, and *Mayhew's characters,* 1951. On the slums see also Thomas Beames (1828); and John Garwood, *The million peopled city; or, One half of the people of London made known to the other half,* 1853: for a modern survey see H. J. Dyos, 'The slums of Victorian London', *Victorian Studies,* 11 (1967), 1–40.

3766 GEORGE (MARY DOROTHY). London life in the XVIIIth century. 1925. 2nd edn. 1930.

3767 SUMMERSON (*Sir* JOHN NEWENHAM). Georgian London. 1945. Rev. edn. 1962.

Standard. See also Albert Edward Richardson and Charles Lovett Gill, *London houses from 1660 to 1820; a consideration of their architecture and detail,* 1911; the Hon. Elizabeth Hilton Young and the Hon. Wayland Hilton Young, *Old London churches,* 1956; Donald James Olsen, *Town planning in London: the eighteenth and nineteenth centuries* (Yale Hist. Pubns, Misc. Series, 80), 1964, primarily a study of the Bedford and Foundling Hospital estates; Hermione Hobhouse, *Thomas Cubitt; master builder,*

1971. London County (now Greater London Council) and London Survey Committee, *Survey of London*, 1900+, in progress, is a massive and definitive study of the areas covered.

4. London Districts

3768 ROSE (MILLICENT). The East End of London. 1951.

3769 ALLEN (THOMAS). The history and antiquities of London, Westminster, Southwark, and parts adjacent. V. 5 by Thomas Wright. 5 v. 1827–37.

3770 HOWITT (WILLIAM). The northern heights of London; or, Historical associations of Hampstead, Highgate, Muswell Hill, Hornsey and Islington. 1869.

3771 CAMBERWELL. ALLPORT (DOUGLAS). Collections illustrative of the geology, history, antiquities, and associations of Camberwell, and the neighbourhood. Camberwell. 1841.

See also Harold James Dyos, *Victorian suburb, a study of the growth of Camberwell*, Leicester, 1961. The main growth of Camberwell took place after 1851.

3772 CHELSEA. BEAVER (ALFRED). Memorials of old Chelsea; a new history of the village of palaces. 1892.

A comprehensive history. Also standard is Thomas Faulkner, *An historical and topographical description of Chelsea and its environs*, Chelsea, 1829.

3773 CLERKENWELL. PINKS (WILLIAM JOHN). The history of Clerkenwell. 1865. 2nd edn. 1881.

3774 FULHAM. FAULKNER (THOMAS). An historical and topographical account of Fulham, including the hamlet of Hammersmith. 1813.

See also his *The history and antiquities of the parish of Hammersmith*, 1839. Charles James Fèret, *Fulham old and new, being an exhaustive history of the ancient parish of Fulham*, 3 v., 1900, contains great quantities of somewhat disorganized material.

3775 GREENWICH. HASTED (EDWARD). Hasted's history of Kent, corrected, enlarged and continued to the present time from the manuscript collections of T. Streatfeild, and other sources. Ed. by H. H. Drake. Pt. 1, The Hundred of Blackheath. 1886.

Roughly covers Deptford, Greenwich, Lewisham, and Woolwich. See also John Kimbell, *An account of the legacies, gifts, rents, fees, etc.,* . . . *of the parish of St. Alphege, Greenwich* [1816], more general in treatment than its title suggests.

3776 HACKNEY. ROBINSON (WILLIAM). The history and antiquities of the parish of Hackney. 2 v. 1842–3.

Also his *The history and antiquities of the parish of Stoke Newington*, etc., 1842, and Benjamin Clarke, *Glimpses of ancient Hackney and Stoke Newington*, etc. [1894].

3777 HAMPSTEAD. THOMPSON (FRANCIS MICHAEL LONG-
STRETH). Hampstead. Building a borough, 1650–1964. 1974.

See also Thomas James Barratt, *The annals of Hampstead*, 3 v., 1912, and Ernest
Frederick Oppé, *Hampstead, a London town*, 1951.

3778 ISLINGTON. LEWIS (SAMUEL). The history and topography of
the parish of St. Mary, Islington. 1842.

Based on John Nelson, *The history and antiquities of the parish of Islington*, 3rd edn.,
1829.

3779 KENSINGTON. FAULKNER (THOMAS). The history and antiquities of Kensington. 1820.

Also standard is William John Loftie, *Kensington, picturesque and historical*, 1888.
Florence Margaret Gladstone, *Notting Hill in bygone days* [1924], deals with north
Kensington.

3780 LAMBETH. ALLEN (THOMAS). The history and antiquities of the
parish of Lambeth and the archiepiscopal palace, including biographical
sketches. 1827.

An interesting political history is given in George Hill, *The electoral history of the
borough of Lambeth since its enfranchisement in 1832*, 1879.

3781 PADDINGTON. ROBINS (WILLIAM). Paddington, past and present.
[1853.]

3782 POPLAR. COWPER (BENJAMIN HARRIS). A descriptive, historical
and statistical account of Millwall, commonly called the Isle of Dogs. 1853.

3783 ROTHERHITHE. BECK (EDWARD JOSSELYN). Memorials to
serve for a history of the parish of St. Mary, Rotherhithe. Camb. 1907.

3784 ST. GEORGE, HANOVER SQUARE. WHEATLEY (HENRY
BENJAMIN). Round about Piccadilly and Pall Mall; or A ramble from the
Haymarket to Hyde Park, consisting of a retrospect of the various changes that
have occurred in the Court End of London. 1870.

See also George Clinch, *Mayfair and Belgravia, being an . . . account of the parish of St.
George, Hanover Square*, 1892.

3785 ST. GILES IN THE FIELDS. PARTON (JOHN). Some account of
the hospital and parish of St. Giles in the Fields, Middlesex. 1822.

An important compilation and account of parish administration, by a former vestry
clerk, written in answer to Rowland Dobie, *The history of the united parishes of St. Giles-
in-the-Fields and St. George, Bloomsbury, combining strictures on their parochial government*, 1829, 2nd edn., 1834. See also George Clinch, *Bloomsbury and St. Giles: past and
present*, etc., 1890, and Olsen (3767).

3786 ST. MARYLEBONE. COX-JOHNSON (ANN) *comp.* Handlist to the
Ashbridge collection on the history and topography of St. Marylebone. 1959.

The standard history is Thomas Smith, *A topographical and historical account of the
parish of St. Marylebone*, 1833. See also George Clinch, *Marylebone and St. Pancras*
etc., 1890, and for local government (514).

3787 ST. PANCRAS. MILLER (FREDERICK). Saint Pancras past and present; being historical, traditional, and general notes of the parish. 1874.

3788 SOHO. CARDWELL (JOHN HENRY) *et al*. Two centuries of Soho, its institutions, firms, and amusements. By the clergy of St. Anne's, Soho. 1898.

3789 SOUTHWARK. BOWERS (ROBERT WOODGER). Sketches of Southwark old and new. 1905.

For Southwark elections see (423), David J. Johnson, *Southwark and the City*, 1969, includes discussion of the 19th century.

3790 WANDSWORTH. PARSONS (THOMAS). The chronicles of Clapham (Clapham common). [1929.]

3791 WESTMINSTER. WALCOTT (MACKENZIE EDWARD CHARLES). The memorials of Westminster; the city, royal palaces, houses of Parliament, Whitehall. A new edition, with an appendix and notes. 1851.

For Westminster elections see (424), (427), for local government (501).

3792 WOOLWICH. VINCENT (WILLIAM THOMAS). The records of the Woolwich district. 2 v., Woolwich. [1888–90.]

See also (1052), (3775).

XII

WALES

A. BIBLIOGRAPHY, CATALOGUES, AND GUIDES

Including general periodicals. For local journals and record socs. consult Somerville (3871), and (3793).

3793 UNIVERSITY OF WALES, Board of Celtic Studies, History and Law Committee. A bibliography of the history of Wales. 2nd edn. Cardiff. 1962.

Supplements are pub. periodically in *B.B.C.S.* (3797). An admirable and indispensable bibliog.

3794 TRANSACTIONS OF THE HONOURABLE SOCIETY OF CYMMRODORION. 1893+.

Also *Y Cymmrodor. Embodying the transactions of the Cymmrodorion society of London*, pub. irregularly, 1877+. For the history of the society see (3833).

3795 BOWEN (IVOR) *ed*. The statutes of Wales. 1908.

Collections of all acts of Parliament and parts thereof which refer to Wales. See also Thomas Ieuan Jeffreys Jones, *Acts of Parliament concerning Wales, 1714–1901* (Wales University Board of Celtic Studies, Hist. and Law Ser. 17), Cardiff, 1959.

3796 BIBLIOTHECA CELTICA. A register of publications relating to Wales and the Celtic peoples and languages. Series 1 and 2. 11 v. 1909–38. Series 3. 1954+.

Also *Subject index to Welsh periodicals*, Cardiff, 1934+, ed. Arthur Ap Gwynn and Idwal Lewis. V. 1 relates to 1931.

3797 BULLETIN OF THE BOARD OF CELTIC STUDIES. University of Wales. History and law section. Cardiff. 1921+.

3798 NATIONAL LIBRARY OF WALES. JOURNAL. Aberystwyth. 1939+.

Has pub. handlists of MSS. since 1940: for indexes see pt. XII, sections I and II, and pt. XXI. See also John Humphreys Davies, *Catalogue of Manuscripts, v. I. Additional manuscripts in the collections of Sir John Williams*, Aberystwyth, 1921, and William Llewelyn Davies, *The National Library of Wales; a survey of its history*, Aberystwyth, 1937.

3799 WELSH HISTORY REVIEW. Cardiff. V. I+. 1960+.

3800 NATIONAL MUSEUM OF WALES. A survey of portraits in Welsh houses. V. I. North Wales. V. II. South Wales. By John Steegman. Cardiff. 1957. 1962.

B. GENERAL HISTORY

3801 WILLIAMS (DAVID). A history of modern Wales. 1950.

Standard. See also Sir John Rhys and David Brynmor-Jones, *The Welsh people. Chapters on their origin, history, laws, language, literature and characteristics*, 1st and 2nd edns. 1900, 3rd edn. 1902, 4th edn. 1906. Also standard are Robert Thomas Jenkins, *Hanes Cymru yn y ddeunawfed ganrif*, Cardiff, 1928, and the same writer's *Hanes Cymru yn y bedwaredd ganrif ar bymtheg*, etc., Cardiff, 1933 (histories of Wales in the 18th and 19th centuries respectively). For the French landing of 1797 see (1117), also Hugh John Owen, *Merioneth volunteers and local militia during the Napoleonic wars, 1795–1816*, Dolgelley, 1934.

C. POLITICAL AND CONSTITUTIONAL HISTORY

For Chartism in Wales see Williams and Gunn (113).

3802 WILLIAMS (WILLIAM RETLAW). The parliamentary history of the principality of Wales from the earliest times to the present day, 1541–1895. Brecknock. 1895.

Biographical details of M.P.s. By the same writer, *The history of the great sessions in Wales, 1542–1830*, Brecknock, 1899. See also John Vyrnwy Morgan, *Welsh political and educational leaders of the Victorian era*, 1908.

3803 EVANS (THOMAS). The background of modern Welsh politics, 1789–1846. Cardiff. 1936.

On Samuel Roberts see Glanmor Williams, *Samuel Roberts, Llanbrynmair*, Cardiff, 1950. Henry Richard, *Letters on social and political conditions of the principality of Wales* [1866] contains historical material. For newspapers see R. D. Rees, 'South Wales and Monmouthshire newspapers under the Stamp Acts', *Welsh Hist. Rev.* 1 (1960–3), 301–24.

3804 JONES (DAVID J. V.) Before Rebecca. Popular protests in Wales, 1793–1835. 1973.

D. ECONOMIC HISTORY

1. GENERAL

3805 DODD (ARTHUR HERBERT). The industrial revolution in North Wales. Cardiff. 1933. 2nd edn. Cardiff. 1951.

3806 JOHN (ARTHUR HENRY). The industrial development of South Wales, 1750–1850: an essay. Cardiff. 1951.

With bibliog. of MS. sources, 193–4. Also on South Wales see Thomas William Booker, *Prize treatise on the mineral basin of Glamorgan*, 1834; Henry Austin Bruce, 1st Baron Aberdare, *The present condition and future prospects of the working classes in South Wales*, 1851, reprinted 1896 in his *Lectures and addresses*; David Rhys Phillips, *The history of the vale of Neath*, Swansea, 1925; T. M. Hodges, 'Early banking in Cardiff', *Econ. H.R.*, 1st ser. 18 (1947–8), 84–114; Evan David Lewis, *The Rhondda valleys: a study in industrial development, 1800 to the present day*, 1959, with substantial bibliog. 287–303.

3807 DODD (ARTHUR HERBERT). The character of early Welsh emigration to the United States. Cardiff. 1953.

2. MINING AND METAL INDUSTRIES

3808 GRANT-FRANCIS (GEORGE). The smelting of copper in the Swansea district from the time of Elizabeth to the present day. Swansea. 1867. 2nd edn. London. 1881.

Also Martin Phillips, *The copper industry in the Port Talbot district*, Neath, 1935. See also John Rowlands, *Copper mountain*, Llangefni, 1966, and (1560).

3809 WILKINS (CHARLES). The history of the iron, steel, tin-plate, and other trades of Wales. Merthyr Tydfil. 1903.

Also Edwin F. Roberts, *A visit to the iron works and environs of Merthyr Tydfil in 1852*, 1853; John Lloyd, *The early history of the old South Wales iron works, 1760–1840*, 1906; John Philip Addis, *The Crawshay dynasty: a study in industrial organization and development, 1765–1867*, Cardiff, 1957; Madeleine Elsas, ed., *Iron in the making: Dowlais Iron Company letters, 1782–1860*, Cardiff, 1960. For the Guest family of Dowlais see (2352).

3810 NORTH (FREDERICK JOHN). The slates of Wales. National Museum of Wales. Cardiff. 1925. 3rd edn. Cardiff. 1946.

See also William Williams, of Llandegai, *Observations on the Snowdon mountains*, etc., 1802; William John Parry, *Chwareli a chwarelwyr Cymru* (Welsh quarries and quarrymen), Carnarvon, 1897; Sir William Llewelyn Davies, *The memoirs of Samuel Holland, one of the pioneers of the North Wales slate industry* (Merioneth Hist. and Record Soc. Extra Pubns, ser. 1, no. 1 [1952]).

3811 MORRIS (JOHN HENRY) *and* WILLIAMS (LAWRENCE JOHN). The South Wales coal industry, 1841–1875. Cardiff. 1958.

See also Charles Wilkins, *The South Wales coal trade and its allied industries from the earliest days to the present time*, Cardiff, 1888, with detailed histories of firms; James Edmund Vincent, *John Nixon, pioneer of the steam coal trade in South Wales. A memoir*, 1900; Elizabeth Phillips, *A history of the pioneers of the Welsh coalfield*, Cardiff, 1925; Frederick John North, *Coal and the coalfields in Wales* (National Museum of Wales), Cardiff, 1926, mainly a geological account. For North Wales see George Geoffrey Lerry, *The collieries of Denbighshire, past and present*, Wrexham and Oswestry, 1946.

3812 EVANS (ERIC WYN). The miners of South Wales. Cardiff. 1961.

On trade union history. See also Ignotus (*pseud.*), *The last thirty years in a mining district, or, Scotching and the candle versus lamp and trades unions*, 1867.

3813 NORTH (FREDERICK JOHN). Mining for metals in Wales. Cardiff. 1962.

3814 LEWIS (WILLIAM JOHN). Lead mining in Wales. Cardiff. 1967.

3. TRANSPORT

3815 DODD (ARTHUR HERBERT). 'The roads of North Wales, 1750–1850.' *Archaeologia Cambrensis*, 80 (1925), 121–48.

3816 BARRIE (DEREK STIVEN MAXWELTON). The Taff Vale railway. 2nd edn. South Godstone, Surrey. 1950.

Also George Geoffrey Lerry, *Henry Robertson, pioneer of railways into Wales*, Oswestry, 1949, concerned with transport of coal in the Wrexham area.

3817 HADFIELD (CHARLES). The canals of South Wales and the border. 1960.

4. AGRICULTURE

3818 BOARD OF AGRICULTURE. General view of the agriculture of North Wales and of each of the counties of South Wales. 8 reports. 1794–6.

By John Clark, John Fox, Charles Hassall, George Kay, Thomas Lloyd, and the Revd. D. Turner. Followed by Walter Davies, *A general view of the agriculture and domestic economy of North Wales*, 1810, and his *A general view of the agriculture and domestic economy of South Wales*, 2 v., 1814. For the Board of Agriculture see (1652).

3819 JOHNES (THOMAS). A Cardiganshire landlord's advice to his tenants. Bristol. 1800.

Advice on agricultural improvement, cheese-making, etc. For the life of Johnes see Elisabeth Inglis-Jones, *Peacocks in Paradise*, 1950.

3820 BOWEN (IVOR). The great enclosures of common lands in Wales. 1914.

Contains a list of private acts of parliament for enclosure, 1733–1885.

3821 THOMAS (*Sir* DANIEL LLEUFER). Bibliographical (and other) memoranda, being an appendix to the Report of the Royal Commission on land in Wales. 1896.

Also his *The Welsh Land Commission, a digest of its report*, 1896.

3822 HUGHES (PHILIP GWYN). Wales and the drovers. The historic background of an epoch. 1943.

See also J. Llefelys Davies, 'The livestock trade in West Wales in the nineteenth century', *Aberystwyth Studies*, 13 (1934), 85–105.

3823 WILLIAMS (DAVID). The Rebecca riots; a study in agrarian discontent. Cardiff. 1955.

3824 THOMAS (DAVID). Agriculture in Wales during the Napoleonic Wars: a study in the geographical interpretation of historical sources. Cardiff. 1963.

See also Francis Jones, 'Some farmers of bygone Pembrokeshire', *Trans. Cymmrodorion Soc.* (1943–4), 133–51, on agricultural improvement; D. J. V. Jones, 'The corn riots in Wales, 1793–1801', *Welsh Hist. Rev.* 2 (1964–5), 323–50; David Williams, 'The acreage returns of 1801 for Wales', *B.B.C.S.* 14 (1950), 54–68 and 139–54, and *ibid.* 17 (1956), 50–2; W. E. Minchinton, 'The agricultural returns of 1800 for Wales', *ibid.* 21 (1965–6), 74–93.

E. SOCIAL HISTORY

1. BIOGRAPHIES

For family histories see *Bibliography of History of Wales* (3793), 2–6.

3825 HONOURABLE SOCIETY OF CYMMRODORION. Y bywgraffiadur Cymreig hyd 1940. Ed. by Sir John Edward Lloyd and Robert Thomas Jenkins 1953.

Welsh national dictionary of biography, in Welsh. The English version with title *Dictionary of Welsh biography down to 1940*, etc., Oxf. 1959, incorporates revisions and improvements. Both supersede any earlier collections, but for the 19th century see also Robert Williams, Canon of St. Asaph, *A biographical dictionary of eminent Welshmen*, etc., Llandovery, 1852; Thomas Nicholas, *Annals and antiquities of the counties and county families of Wales*, 2 v., 1872; Thomas Mardy Rees, *Notable Welshmen, 1700–1900*, etc., Carnarvon, 1908; Thomas Rowland Roberts, *Eminent Welshmen*, Cardiff and Merthyr Tydfil, 1908.

2. WELSH LITERATURE

For printing in Wales see (3470).

3826 ASHTON (CHARLES). Hanes llenyddiaeth Gymreig, 1650–1850. Liverpool. [1893.]

History of Welsh literature, 1650–1850.

3827 BALLINGER (*Sir* JOHN). The Bible in Wales, a study in the history of the Welsh people. 1906.

3828 DAVIES (JOHN HUMPHREYS). A bibliography of Welsh ballads printed in the eighteenth century. 1911.

See also Thomas Parry, *Baledi'r ddeunawfed ganrif*, Cardiff, 1935 (Ballads of the eighteenth century), Arthur Stanley Davies, *The ballads of Montgomeryshire; life in the eighteenth century*, Welshpool, 1938.

3829 ROBERTS (ROBERT). Life and opinions of Robert Roberts, a wandering scholar, as told by himself. Ed. John Humphreys Davies. Cardiff. 1923.

3830 DAVIES (DAVID). The influence of the French revolution on Welsh life and literature. Carmarthen. 1926.

Includes bibliog. of books relating to the influence of the revolution on Welsh life and literature by Bob Owen, ix–xxvi. See also John James Evans, *Dylanwad y chwyldro Ffrengig ar lenyddiaeth Cymru*, Liverpool, 1928 (influence of the French revolution on Welsh literature).

3831 BELL (HAROLD IDRIS). The development of Welsh poetry. Oxf. 1936.

3832 PARRY (THOMAS). Hanes llenyddiaeth Gymraeg hyd 1900. Cardiff. 1944. 3rd edn. 1953.

Eng. trans. by Harold Idris Bell, with title *A history of Welsh literature*, Oxf. 1955.

3833 JENKINS (ROBERT THOMAS) *and* RAMAGE (HELEN MY-FANWY). A history of the Honourable Society of Cymmrodorion, and of the Gwyneddigion and Cymreigyddion Societies, 1751–1951. (Y Cymmrodor. 50.) 1951.

Also William Davies Leathart, *The origin and progress of the Gwyneddigion Society of London*, 1831.

3. WELSH LIFE

3834 ROBERTS (PETER). The Cambrian popular antiquities; or, An account of some traditions, customs, and superstitions of Wales, with observations. 1815.

3835 HUGHES (WILLIAM JOHN). Wales and the Welsh in English literature from Shakespeare to Scott. 1924.

3836 PEATE (IORWERTH CYFEILIOG). The Welsh house: a study in folk culture. 1940. 2nd edn. rev. 1944.

3837 PRICE (CECIL). English theatre in Wales in the eighteenth and early nineteenth centuries. Cardiff. 1948.

3838 CONWAY (ALAN) *ed.* The Welsh in America: letters from the immigrants. Cardiff. 1961.

See also (3807).

F. LOCAL HISTORY

For full bibliog. see *Bibliography of History of Wales* (3793), Section B. Also Topography (3515–21).

1. TOPOGRAPHY AND TRAVEL

3839 FORDHAM (*Sir* GEORGE). 'The road-books of Wales, with a catalogue, 1775–1850.' *Archaeologia Cambrensis* 82 (1927), 276–91.

For a short guide see Samuel Leigh, *Leigh's guide to Wales and Monmouthshire*, etc., 1831, 2nd edn. 1833, 3rd edn. 1835, 4th edn. 1839.

3840 CARDIFF PUBLIC LIBRARY. Handlist of manuscript tours in Wales, original drawings and sketch books, and illustrated works on the scenery of Wales, in the Cardiff public library. Cardiff. 1933.

3841 WARNER (RICHARD). A walk through Wales in August 1797. Bath. 1798. 3rd edn. Bath. 1799.

See also his *A second walk through Wales . . . in August and September, 1798*, Bath, 1799, 2nd edn. Bath, 1800, containing a fair amount of social and economic description; John Thomas Barber, *A tour through South Wales and Monmouthshire*, etc., 1803; John Evans, *Letters written during a tour through South Wales . . . in 1803*, etc., 1804; Benjamin Heath Malkin, *The scenery, antiquities, and biography of South Wales, from materials collected . . . in the year 1803*, 1804; Edward Donovan, *Descriptive excursions*

through South Wales and Monmouthshire, in the year 1804 and the four preceding summers,
2 v., 1805; George Nicholson, *The Cambrian traveller's guide*, Stourport, 1808, 2nd
edn. 1813, 3rd 1840; Charles Frederick Cliffe, *The book of South Wales*, 1847, 2nd edn.
1848; Richard Fenton, *Tours in Wales, 1804–13*, ed. from his MS. journals in Cardiff
Public Library, by John Fisher, 1917.

2. COUNTY AND TOWN HISTORIES

3842 BRECKNOCK. JONES (THEOPHILUS). A history of the county of
Brecknock. 2 v. Brecknock. 1805–9. Enl. edn. 4 v. Brecknock. 1909–30.

Also Edwin Poole, *The illustrated history and biography of Brecknockshire from the
earliest times to the present day*, Brecknock, 1886, with full 19th-century coverage.

3843 CARDIGAN. JONES (GLYN LEWIS). Llyfryddiaeth Ceredigion,
1600–1964; a bibliography of Cardiganshire. 3 v. Aberystwyth. 1967. Suppt.
1964–8. 1970.

V. 1 localities; v. 2 and 3 local authors.

3844 CARMARTHEN. LLOYD (JOHN EDWARD) *ed*. A history of
Carmarthenshire edited by the London Carmarthenshire society. 2 v. Cardiff.
1935–9.

3845 DENBIGH. DENBIGHSHIRE COUNTY LIBRARY. Bibliography
of the county. Pt. 2. Historical and topographical sources. 2nd edn. rev. and
enl. Ruthin. 1951. Suppt. for 1951–7. 1959.

3846 —— WREXHAM. PALMER (ALFRED NEOBARD). A history of the
older nonconformity of Wrexham and its neighbourhood. Wrexham. [1888.]

Also his *History of the town of Wrexham, its houses, streets, fields and old families*, Wrexham, 1893, together forming the 3rd and 4th parts of his exhaustive *History of the town
and parish of Wrexham*.

3847 FLINTSHIRE. FLINT. TAYLOR (HENRY). Historic notices, with
topographical and other gleanings descriptive of the borough and county
town of Flint. 1883.

3848 GLAMORGAN. BRIDGEND. RANDALL (HENRY JOHN). Bridgend; the story of a market town. Newport. 1955.

A scholarly study, with full coverage of the 19th century.

3849 —— CARDIFF. CHAPPELL (EDGAR LEYSHON). History of the
port of Cardiff. Cardiff. 1939.

See also John Hobson Matthews and others, eds., *Cardiff records*, 6 v., Cardiff, 1898–
1911. V. 4–5 relate to the years 1789–1851.

3850 —— MERTHYR TYDFIL. WILKINS (CHARLES). The history of
Merthyr Tydfil. Merthyr Tydfil. 1867.

See also Gwyn A. Williams, 'The making of radical Merthyr, 1800–36', *Welsh Hist.
Rev.* 1 (1960–3), 161–87; D. J. V. Jones, 'The Merthyr riots of 1831', *ibid.* 3 (1966–7),
173–205; Glanmor Williams, ed., *Merthyr politics*, Cardiff, 1966.

3851 —— PORT TALBOT. BISCOE (CLIVE). Port Talbot, a bibliographical guide. Port Talbot. 1968.

3852 —— SWANSEA. JONES (WILLIAM HENRY). History of the port of Swansea. Carmarthen. 1922.

See also Glyn Roberts, *The municipal development of the borough of Swansea to 1900*, Cardiff, 1940.

3853 MONMOUTHSHIRE. MONMOUTHSHIRE ARCHIVES COMMITTEE. Guide to the Monmouthshire record office. By W. H. Baker. Newport. 1959.

See also Cyril James Oswald Evans, *Monmouthshire: its history and topography*, Cardiff. [1954].

3854 —— NEWPORT. JONES (BRYNMOR PIERCE). From Elizabeth I to Victoria. The government of Newport (Mon.), 1550–1850. Newport, Mon. 1957. Bibliog. 213–19.

3855 MONTGOMERY. WILLIAMS (RICHARD). Montgomeryshire worthies. Newtown. 1884. 2nd edn. 1894.

3856 PEMBROKE. MILFORD HAVEN. REES (*Sir* JAMES FREDERICK). The story of Milford. Cardiff. 1954.

G. RELIGIOUS HISTORY

1. GENERAL

3857 REES (THOMAS). History of Protestant non-conformity in Wales, from its rise in 1633 to the present time. 1861. 2nd edn. rev. 1888.

A substantial account. See also [Arthur James Johnes], *An essay on the causes which have produced dissent from the Established Church in the principality of Wales*, 1835, on abuses in the church, repr. with add. preface, 1870.

3858 GRIFFITH (DOROTHI MARY). Nationality in the Sunday school movement. Bangor. 1925.

3859 WILLIAMS (DAVID). 'The census of religious worship of 1851 in Cardiganshire.' *Ceredigion*, 4, (1961), 113–28.

With general comments on the census in Wales.

2. DENOMINATIONS IN WALES

3860 HUGHES (JOHN). Methodistiaeth Cymru sef hanes blaenorol a gwedd bresenol y methodistiaid calfinaidd. 3 v. Wrexham. 1851–6.

Also William Williams, of Swansea, *Welsh Calvinistic Methodism*, etc., 1856, 2nd edn. enl. 1884, a short digest of John Hughes: see also for a general account, David Erwyd Jenkins, *Calvinistic Methodist holy orders*, Caernarvon, 1911. For individual ministers see Joseph Evans, *Biographical dictionary of ministers and preachers of the Welsh*

Calvinistic Methodist body or Presbyterians of Wales . . . to . . . 1850, Caernarvon, 1907.
See also Thomas Charles Edwards, *Bywyd a llythyrau Lewis Edwards*, 1901 (life and
letters of Lewis Edwards, editor of *Y Traethodydd*, 1845–55), and David Erwyd
Jenkins, *Life of the Rev. Thomas Charles B.A. of Bala*, 3 v., Denbigh, 1908. Useful
material may also be found in *Cylchgrawn Cymdeithas Hanes y Methodistiaid
Calfinaidd*, (journal of the Welsh Calvinistic Methodist society), 1916+.

3861 TRAFODION CYMDEITHAS HANES Y BEDYDDWYR CYM-
REIG. 1907+.

Transactions of the Welsh Baptist Historical society; also Edwin Paxton Hood, *Christ-
mas Evans, the preacher of Wild Wales*, 1881, and John James Evans, *Morgan John Rhys
a'i amserau*, Cardiff, 1935 (Morgan John Rhys and his times).

3862 JONES (HUGH). Hanes Wesleyaeth yng Nghymru. 4 v. Bangor. 1911–13.

History of Welsh Wesleyan Methodism. See also David Young, *The origin and history
of Methodism in Wales and the borders*, 1893, concerned with Wesleyans.

3863 Y COFIADUR. Cylchgrawn Cymdeithas Hanes Annibynwyr Cymru.
Wrexham. 1923+.

Magazine of the historical society of the Welsh Independents. Also Thomas Rees and
John Thomas, *Hanes Eglwysi Annibynol Cymru*, 5 v., Liverpool and Dolgelley, 1871–91
(history of the Welsh Independent Church).

3864 JONES (DAVID AMBROSE). A history of the church in Wales.
Carmarthen. 1926.

Also Alfred Edwards, *Landmarks in the history of the Welsh church*, 1912. J. Conway
Davies, 'The records of the church in Wales', *Nat. Lib. Wales Jour.* 4 (1945–6), 1–34,
describes categories of archives (about two million documents) transferred to National
Library of Wales in 1944. For parish registers see *Bibliog. Hist. Wales*, 66–9. For biogs.
of Burgess see (739), for Coplestone (696), for Thirlwall (704), and John Connop
Thirlwall, *Connop Thirlwall, historian and theologian*, 1936.

3865 ATTWATER (DONALD). The Catholic church in modern Wales.
A record of the past century. 1935.

H. EDUCATION

3866 PHILLIPS (*Sir* THOMAS). Wales: the language, social condition,
moral character, and religious opinions of the people, considered in their
relation to education. 1849.

Still standard: a reply to the *Report of the Royal Commission of inquiry into Welsh
education*, 1846. In defence of the Commission see William Williams, M.P., *Letter to
Lord John Russell on the report of the Commissioners*, etc., 1848, and *A second letter to
Lord John Russell on the present defective state of education in Wales*, 1848. See also
Cadwalader Tawelfryn Thomas, *Cofiant Ieuan Gwynedd*, Dolgelley, n.d. (life of Ieuan
Gwynedd, i.e. Evan Jones) and Thomas Gwynn Jones, *Cofiant Thomas Gee*, Denbigh,
1913 (life of Thomas Gee).

3867 ROBERTS (H. P.). 'Non-conformist academies in Wales.' *Soc. of
Cymmrodorion Trans.* (1928–9), 1–98.

Substantial. See also Ebenezer Thomas Davies, *Monmouthshire schools and education to
1870*, Newport, 1957.

XIII

SCOTLAND

A. BIBLIOGRAPHIES, CATALOGUES, GUIDES, AND JOURNALS

3868 HANCOCK (PHILIP DAVID). A bibliography of works relating to Scotland, 1916–1950. 2 v. Edin. [1959–60.]

For earlier works see Mitchell and Cash (3984). See also George Fraser Black, *A list of works relating to Scotland* [New York Public Library], N.Y. 1916. A list of articles on Scotland has been published annually in the October number of the *Scottish Historical Review* since 1959.

3869 SCOTTISH HISTORICAL REVIEW. Glasgow, 1904+.

3870 LIVINGSTONE (MATTHEW). A guide to the public records of Scotland deposited in H.M. General Register House, Edinburgh. Edin. 1905.

Continued by William Angus, 'Accessions of public records to the Register House since 1905', *S.H.R.* 26 (1947), 26–46, and by annual reports in *S.H.R.* since 1952. As a general guide see Henry M. Paton, *The Scottish records, their history and value* (Hist. Assoc. of Scotland, pamphlets n.s. 7), Edin., 1933.

3871 TERRY (CHARLES SANFORD). A catalogue of the publications of Scottish historical and kindred clubs and societies, and of the volumes relative to Scottish history, issued by His Majesty's Stationery office, 1780–1908. Glasgow. 1909.

This, with his *An index to the papers relating to Scotland, described or calendared in the Historical MSS. Commission's reports*, Glasgow, 1908, was continued, 1908–27, by Cyril Matheson, Aberdeen, 1928. For a short and convenient guide see British Records Association, *Handlist of Scottish and Welsh record publications*, ed. Sir Robert Somerville (Pamphlets, 4), 1954.

3872 NATIONAL LIBRARY OF SCOTLAND. Catalogue of manuscripts acquired since 1925. 3 v. Edin. 1938–68.

Including Melville papers. Apart from these, the largest 19th-century collections are literary, namely the Abbotsford, Constable and Cadell, and Carlyle collections.

3873 FERGUSON (JOAN PRIMROSE SCOTT). Scottish newspapers held in Scottish libraries. Edin. 1956.

3874 FERGUSON (JOAN PRIMROSE SCOTT). Scottish family histories held in Scottish libraries. Edin. 1960.

See also Margaret Stuart and James Balfour Paul, *Scottish family history: a guide to works of reference on the history and genealogy of Scottish families*, etc., Edin., 1930, and (4065).

B. GENERAL HISTORY

3875 PRYDE (GEORGE SMITH). Scotland from 1603 to the present day. 1962.

> Bibliog. 333–42. Standard, devoting a good proportion of space to the 19th century. Earlier, predominantly political, outlines are Sir Henry Craik, *A century of Scottish history from the days before the '45 to those within living memory*, 2 v. 1901, 1911; Peter Hume Brown, *History of Scotland. V. 3 From . . . 1689 to . . . 1843*, Camb. 1909; Sir Robert Sangster Rait and George Smith Pryde, *Scotland* (Nations of the Modern World), 1934, new edn. revised by G. S. Pryde, 1954, bibliog. 323–9. William Law Mathieson, *The awakening of Scotland, . . . 1747 to 1797*, Glasgow, 1910, and his *Church and reform in Scotland . . . 1797 to 1843* give good coverage to religious movements.

3876 MEIKLE (HENRY WILLIAM). Scotland and the French Revolution. Glasgow. 1912.

> Bibliog. 282–307. A detailed political account. See also J. R. Western, 'The formation of the Scottish militia in 1797', *S.H.R.* 34 (1955), 1–18.

3877 SAUNDERS (LAURANCE JAMES). Scottish democracy, 1815–1840: the social and intellectual background. 1950.

3878 SMOUT (THOMAS CHRISTOPHER). A history of the Scottish people, 1560–1830. 1969.

> Bibliog. and notes 521–51.

C. POLITICAL AND CONSTITUTIONAL HISTORY

1. PARLIAMENT AND POLITICS

3879 FERGUSON (ROBERT). The proposed reform of the counties of Scotland impartially examined; with observations on the conduct of the delegates. Edin. 1792.

> A plea for reform.

3880 FLETCHER (ARCHIBALD). A memoir concerning the origin and progress of the reform proposed in the internal government of the Royal Burghs of Scotland. Edin. 1819.

> Fletcher defended Gerrald and the other 'friends of the people' in 1793. See Mrs. Eliza Fletcher (his wife), *Autobiography*, etc., ed. Lady Richardson, Edin., 1875.

3881 WILKIE (T.). The representation of Scotland. Parliamentary elections since 1832; representation before 1832; distribution of seats since the union. Paisley. 1895.

> On modes of election see Arthur Connell, *A treatise on the election laws in Scotland, to which is added an historical inquiry concerning the municipal constitution of towns and boroughs*, Edin. 1827. The case for reform is argued in 'Parliamentary representation of Scotland', *Edinburgh Review*, 52 (1830–1), 208–27. On elections after 1832 see *Fictitious votes in Scotland*, Select Committee 1st report, H.C. 1837 (215) XII, 2nd report H.C. 1837–8 (590) XIV, *Roxburghshire petition*, Select Committee, H.C. 1837–8 (152 I-II)

XII, and W. Ferguson, 'The Reform Act (Scotland) of 1832; intention and effect', *S.H.R.* 45 (1966), 105–14, and J. I. Brash, ed., *Papers on Scottish election politics, 1832–1854* (Scottish Hist. Soc. 4th s., v. 11), Edin., 1974. For the Scottish representative peers see (400).

3882 COWAN (ROBERT McNAIR WILSON). The newspaper in Scotland, 1815–60. Glasgow. 1946.

See also David Croal, *Early recollections of a journalist, 1832–1859*, Edin. and Haddington, 1898.

3883 ALISON. Some account of my life and writings; an autobiography. Ed. by his daughter-in-law Lady Alison. 2 v. 1883.

On Sir Archibald Alison, 1st bart., brother of William Pulteney Alison, the Scottish poor law reformer.

3884 BLACK. Memoirs of Adam Black. Ed. by Alexander Nicolson. Edin. 1885.

Of the publishing firm of A. & C. Black. Black was also a central figure in Edinburgh Whig politics in the mid 19th century.

3885 COCKBURN. Memorials of his time. By Henry Thomas, Lord Cockburn. Edin. 1856. New edn. with intro. by his grandson Harry A. Cockburn. 1909.

Supplemented by *Journal of Henry Cockburn, being a continuation of the memorials of his time 1831–54*, 2 v. Edin. 1874, and *Some letters . . . with pages omitted from the Memorials*, ed. Harry A. Cockburn, Edin. 1932. Also by Lord Cockburn, *Letters . . . [on] the affairs of Scotland, from Henry Cockburn . . . to Thomas Francis Kennedy M.P.* 2 v. 1874, and *An examination of the trials for sedition which have hitherto occurred in Scotland*, 2 v., Edin. 1888 (on the state trials of 1793–4, 1819–20, and 1848–9). Taken together these works give a most valuable picture of Edinburgh Whig politics, particularly in the years 1830–2. See also Karl Miller, *Cockburn's Millenium*, 1975.

3886 DUNDAS. The Arniston memoirs; three centuries of a Scottish house, 1591–1838, edited from the family papers. Ed. by George William Thomson Omond. Edin. 1887.

3887 ERSKINE. The Honourable Henry Erskine, lord advocate for Scotland . . . compiled from family papers. By Alexander Fergusson. 1882.

3888 JEFFREY. Life of Lord Jeffrey, with a selection from his correspondence. By Henry Thomas, Lord Cockburn. Edin. 1852. New edn. 1874.

Jeffrey was one of the founders of the *Edinburgh Review*, and editor 1803–29.

3889 McLAREN. The life and work of Duncan McLaren. By John Beveridge Mackie. 2 v. 1888.

Prominent in Edinburgh Whig politics after 1832.

3890 MUIR. The life of Thomas Muir Esq., of Huntershill, who was tried for sedition . . . with a full report of his trial. By Peter Mackenzie. Glasgow. 1831.

See also Frank Clune, *The Scottish martyrs, their trials and transportation to Botany bay*, 1969.

3891 NAPIER. Macvey Napier MSS. 21 v. B.L. Add. MSS. 34611–31.

Macvey Napier succeeded Jeffrey as editor of the *Edinburgh Review*.

2. LAW

3892 MAXWELL (LESLIE) *and* MAXWELL (WILLIAM HAROLD). Scottish law to 1956. Together with a list of Roman law books in the English language. (Legal bibliography of the British Commonwealth of Nations. V. 5.) 2nd edn. 1957.

See also *An introductory survey of the sources and literature of Scots law*, by various authors ed. Hector McKechnie (Stair Society 1), Edin., 1936, and *The public general statutes affecting Scotland . . . 1707 to 1847*, 3 v., Edin., 1876–1947, an authoritative work.

3893 PATON (GEORGE CAMPBELL HENDERSON) *ed.* An introduction to Scottish legal history. By various authors. (Stair Society, 20.) Edin. 1958.

Outlines the development of legal institutions and of particular branches of Scots law. See also Malcolm Ronald McLarty and G. C. H. Paton, eds., *A source book and history of administrative law in Scotland, by various authors*, 1956, and William Murray Gloag and Robert Candlish Henderson, *Introduction to the law of Scotland*, Edin., 1927, 6th edn. rev. by Andrew Dewar Gibb and Norman M. L. Walker, Edin., 1956, a text book of Scottish law.

3894 HUME (DAVID). Commentaries on the law of Scotland, respecting the description and punishment of crimes. 2 v. Edin. 1797. Later edn. with supp. by Benjamin Robert Bell, 2 v. Edin. 1844.

Hume's lectures have been edited by G. C. H. Paton, *Baron David Hume's lectures, 1786–1822*, 6 v. (Stair Society, v. 5, 13, 15, 17–19.) Edin. 1939–58.

3895 MORISON (WILLIAM MAXWELL). The decisions of the Court of Session ... digested under proper heads in the form of a dictionary. 42 v. Edin., 1811.

See also Patrick Shaw, *Digest of cases decided in the supreme courts of Scotland from 1800 to 1868; and on appeal by the House of Lords from 1726–1868, being a new edition of the digest from 1800 to 1852 by Messrs. Macpherson, Bell and Lamond, advocates*, rev. consol. and cont. to 1868 by Andrew Beatson Bell and William Lamond, Edin., 1869.

3896 CLERK (*Sir* JOHN) *and* SCROPE (JOHN). Historical view of the forms and powers of the court of exchequer in Scotland, to which is added . . . rules of procedure and certain minutes of court relating thereto. Edin. 1820.

3897 BELL (GEORGE JOSEPH). Principles of the law of Scotland, for the use of students in the University of Edinburgh. Edin. 1829. 10th edn. Edin. 1899.

By the same writer, *Commentaries on the laws of Scotland, and on the principles of mercantile jurisprudence*, 2nd edn., Edin., 1810, 7th edn., Edin., 1870.

3898 BRUNTON (GEORGE) *and* HAIG (DAVID). An historical account of the senators of the College of justice from its institution in 1532. 1832.

3899 LAW COMMISSION (SCOTLAND). 1st report of Royal Commission. H.C. 1834 (295) XXVI, 2nd report H.C. 1835 [63] XXXV, 3rd report H.C. 1837–8 [114] XXIX, 4th report H.C. 1840 [241] XX.

A massive general investigation. Other government inquiries include *Select Committee on Scotch entails*, H.C. 1828 (198, 404) VII, H.C. 1829 (102) III, and H.C. 1833 (109) XVI, *Select Committee on Supreme Court of Judicature*, H.C. 1840 (332) XIV. The *Edinburgh Review* published a series of informed articles critical of Scottish administration of justice. See 'Proposed reform of the Court of Session', 9 (1806–7), 462–92; 'Nomination of Scottish juries', 38 (1823), 226–34; 'Criminal law of Scotland', 41 (1825), 450–64; 'Scotch entails', 43 (1825–6), 442–61; 'Scottish judicial reforms—law of Scotland and England', 51 (1830), 114–44; 'Scottish law of evidence', 57 (1833), 96–106; 'Scottish criminal jurisprudence and procedure', 83 (1846), 196–223.

3900 OMOND (GEORGE WILLIAM THOMSON). The lord advocates of Scotland from the close of the fifteenth century to the passing of the reform bill. 2 v. Edin. 1883.

A series of biographies; followed by his *The lord advocates of Scotland. Second series, 1834–1880*, 1914. A contemporary attack on the lord advocate, who often acted as election manager on behalf of the London government, is 'Office of lord advocate of Scotland', *Edinburgh Review*, 39 (1824), 363–92.

3901 GRANT (*Sir* FRANCIS JAMES) *ed.* The Faculty of Advocates in Scotland, 1532–1943, with genealogical notes. (Indices and calendars of records issued by the Scottish Record Soc. Part CXLV.) Edin. 1944.

3. ADMINISTRATION

3902 HUTCHESON (GILBERT). Treatise on the offices of justice of peace; constable; commissioner of supply and commissioner under comprehending acts, in Scotland; with occasional observations upon other municipal jurisdictions. 2 v. Edin. 1806. 2nd edn. 4 v. Edin. 1809.

See also George Tait, *A summary of the powers and duties of a Justice of the Peace in Scotland*, Edin. 1813, later edns. 1815, 1817, 1821, 1828, William Blair, *The Scottish justices' manual*, Edin. 1834, and on local maladministration, *Report on the administration of the law in the Justice-of-Peace court, Glasgow*, H.C. 1841 (Session 2) (9) II.

3903 PRISONS IN SCOTLAND. Select Committee, report and evidence. H.C. 1826 (381) V.

Also *Select Committee on regulation of assessment for Scottish prisons*, H.C. 1845 (460) XIII, contains much administrative information.

3904 ROYAL COMMISSION ON MUNICIPAL CORPORATIONS IN SCOTLAND H.C. 1835 (30–31) XXIX, and H.C. 1836 (32, 34) XXIII.

Mabel Atkinson, *Local government in Scotland*, 1904, has a little information on this period.

3905 IRONS (JAMES CAMPBELL). Manual of the law and practice of the Dean of Guild court, with synopsis of the law relating to building restrictions, servitudes. Edin. 1895.

Dean of Guild courts, in the royal burghs only, were concerned in this period with building regulations, removal of obstructions, etc.

3906 TURNER (STANLEY HORSFALL). The history of local taxation in Scotland. 1908.

Discusses parochial poor relief and burghal rating.

D. ECONOMIC HISTORY

1. BIBLIOGRAPHY

3907 MARWICK (WILLIAM HUTTON). 'A bibliography of Scottish economic history.' *Econ. H.R.* 3 (1931), 117–37.

Continued and brought up to date by the same author in *Econ. H.R.*, 2nd ser., 4 (1951–2), 376–82 and *Econ. H.R.* 2nd ser., 16 (1963–4), 147–54. William Robert Scott, *Scottish economic literature to 1800*, Glasgow, 1911, is primarily concerned with the writings of the economists. The *Scottish Journal of Political Economy*, Edin., 1954+, also contains articles on economic history.

2. GENERAL WORKS

3908 CAMPBELL (ROY HUTCHESON). Scotland since 1707. The rise of an industrial society. Oxf. 1965.

Bibliog. 327–46. Another essential general study is Henry Hamilton, *An economic history of Scotland in the eighteenth century*, Oxf. 1963, bibliog. 421–30. See also William Hutton Marwick, *Economic developments in Victorian Scotland*, 1936, bibliog. 279–91, and a short outline by the same author, *Scotland in modern times. An outline of economic and social development since the Union of 1707*, 1964.

3909 MACKINTOSH (JOHN). The history of civilisation in Scotland. 4 v. 1888. New edn. partly rewritten. Paisley. 1896.

V. 4 contains information about particular manufactures. Similar statistical information, in this case largely compiled from government records, is in François Pierre Charles, Baron Dupin, *The commercial power of Great Britain*, etc., 2 v. 1825.

3910 MACDONALD (DONALD FERGUSON). Scotland's shifting population, 1770–1850. Glasgow. 1937.

See also George Seton, *Sketch of the history and imperfect condition of the parochial records of births, deaths and marriages in Scotland, in illustration of the important advantages which would be derived from the introduction of a system of compulsory registration*, Edin., 1854. On Irish immigration see James Edmund Handley, *The Irish in Scotland, 1798–1845*, Cork, 1943, bibliog. 303–13, and his *The Irish in modern Scotland*, Cork, 1947, bibliog. 328–37. David Stirling Macmillan, *Scotland and Australia, 1788–1850*, Oxf., 1967, is a study of Scottish immigration and economic enterprise in Australia.

3911 PAYNE (PETER L.) *ed.* Studies in Scottish business history. 1967.

3. BANKING AND COMMERCE

3912 KERR (ANDREW WILLIAM). History of banking in Scotland. Glasgow. 1884. 2nd edn. 1902. 4th edn. rev. 1926.

Standard. See also Robert Somers, *The Scotch banks and system of issue including translation of 'Les banques d'Ecosse by L. Wolowski'*, Edin., 1873, and William Graham, *The one pound note in the rise and progress of banking in Scotland*, Edin., 1886.

3913 DUNCAN (HENRY). An essay on the nature and advantages of parish banks. Edin. 1815.

A detailed account of the working of the first savings bank, established by Duncan, minister of Ruthwell, 1810.

3914 PROMISSORY NOTES IN SCOTLAND AND IRELAND. Report of select committee. H.C. 1826 (402) III, H.C. 1826–7 (245) VI.

A comment on the Act of 1826 is given by Malachi Malagrowther (*pseud.* of Sir Walter Scott), *Thoughts on the proposed change of currency, and other late alterations, as they affect, or are intended to affect, the kingdom of Scotland*, Edin., 1826.

3915 REID (JOHN). Manual of the Scottish stocks and British funds, with a list of the joint stock companies in Scotland. 3rd edn. Edin. 1841. 4th edn. Edin. 1842.

3916 MALCOLM (CHARLES ALEXANDER). The bank of Scotland, 1695–1945. Edin. [1948.]

Other histories of particular banks are Charles William Boase, *A century of banking in Dundee, being the annual balance sheets of the Dundee banking company from 1764 to 1864*, 2nd edn., Edin., 1867; James Lawson Anderson, *The story of the Commercial Bank of Scotland . . . 1810 to 1910*, Edin., 1910; Neil Munro, *The history of the Royal Bank of Scotland, 1727–1927*, Edin., 1928 (privately printed); Sir Robert Sangster Rait, *The history of the Union Bank of Scotland*, Glasgow, 1930.

4. INDUSTRY

3917 HAMILTON (HENRY). The industrial revolution in Scotland. Oxf. 1932.

See also Roy Hutcheson Campbell, 'The industrial revolution. A revision article', *S.H.R.* 46 (1967), 37–55. David Bremner, *The industries of Scotland, their rise, progress, and present condition*, Edin., 1869, has a series of chapters on particular industries. Information on Scottish industries may also be found in the *Select Committee on manufactures, commerce and shipping* (1522), and in government inquiries on factories and mines (1724).

3918 BALD (ROBERT). A general view of the coal trade of Scotland. Edin. 1812.

A solid and informative account by a mining expert. A later account by a geologist is David Milne, *Memoir of the Mid-Lothian and East-Lothian coalfields*, Edin., 1839. See also Baron F. Duckham, *A history of the Scottish coal industry, v. 1, 1700–1815*, Newton Abbot 1970.

3919 CLELAND (JAMES). Historical account of the steam engine and its application in propelling vessels. Glasgow. 1825.

With appendices listing engines at work in factories, collieries, and steam-boats round Glasgow in 1825. See also John Strang, *Progress, extent, and value of steamboat building and marine engine making on the Clyde*, etc., Glasgow, 1852. See also Smiles (1565), (1577) and Fairbairn (1587), (1589).

3920 WARDEN (ALEXANDER JOHNSTON). The linen trade, ancient and modern. 1864. 2nd edn. 1867.

A solid account by a merchant. See also Enid Gauldie, ed., *The Dundee textile industry, 1790–1885*, Scottish Hist. Soc., 4th ser. 6, Edin., 1969.

3921 BLAIR (MATTHEW). The Paisley thread industry and the men who created and developed it, with notes concerning Paisley, old and new. Paisley. 1907.

By the same author, *The Paisley shawl and the men who produced it*, Paisley, 1904.

3922 SMITH (JOHN). Old Scottish clockmakers from 1453 to 1850. 2nd edn. rev. and enl. Edin. 1921.

Lists known firms.

3923 CAMPBELL (ROY HUTCHESON). Carron Company. [1961.]

Very much slighter are John Lees Carvel, *The Coltness Iron Company*, etc., Edin., 1948, and Augustus Muir, *The story of Shotts*, etc., Edin. [1954].

5. COMMUNICATIONS

3924 TELFORD (THOMAS). A survey and report of the coasts and central Highlands of Scotland. [1803.]

Telford worked on roads and harbours in the north of Scotland and constructed the Caledonian Canal. See Robert Southey, *Journal of a tour in Scotland in 1819*, etc., ed. Charles Harold Herford, 1929. Southey accompanied Telford and was an observant and factual reporter. For Telford generally see (1595).

3925 WILLIAMSON (JAMES). The Clyde passenger steamer. Its rise and progress during the nineteenth century. Glasgow. 1904.

Also Robert Gillespie, *Glasgow and the Clyde*, Glasgow, 1876, and John Rankin, *A history of our firm. Being some account of the firm of Pollok, Gilmour and co. and its off-shoots and connections, 1804–1820*, 2nd edn., rev., Liverpool, 1921.

3926 PRATT (EDWIN A.). Scottish canals and waterways. 1922.

Bibliog. 284–92. A substantial account, including information on docks. See also Sir William Fairbairn, Bt., *Remarks on canal navigation illustrative of the advantages of the use of steam*, 1831. See also Jean Lindsay, *The canals of Scotland*, 1968.

3927 NOCK (OSWALD STEVENS). Scottish railways. 1950.

See also Sir William Mitchell Acworth, *The railways of Scotland . . . with a glance at their past*, etc., 1890, and J. R. Kellett, 'Glasgow's railways, 1830–80; a study in "natural growth"', *Econ. H.R.* 2nd ser. 17 (1964), 354–68.

3928 SIMMONS (JACK). 'The Scottish records of the British Transport Commission.' *Jour. Transport Hist.* 3 (1957–8), 158–67.

3929 HALDANE (ARCHIBALD RICHARD BURDON). New ways through the glens. [1962.]

Bibliog. 235–7; an account of road building in the Highlands. By the same writer, *The drove roads of Scotland*, 1952, bibliog. 245–53. See also *Annual reports* of the commissioners for making and repairing roads and bridges in Scotland, 1st rep. H.C. 1803–4 (108) VI, and *Select Committee on statute labour in Scotland*, H.C. 1836 (430) XVIII, a consideration of the finance of upkeep. William Pagan, *Road reform. A plan for abolishing turnpike tolls and statute labour assessments, and for providing the funds necessary . . . by an annual rate on horses*, Edin., 1845, 3rd edn. Edin., 1857, is on the same subject.

6. Agriculture and Fisheries

3930 SYMON (JAMES ALEXANDER). Scottish farming, past and present. 1958.

A general survey, with valuable chronological bibliography, 435–52, including a full list of Board of Agriculture surveys. James Edmund Handley, *Scottish farming in the eighteenth century*, 1953, also with substantial bibliography, 288–306, is authoritative. See also his *The agricultural revolution in Scotland*, Glasgow, 1963, bibliog. 294–311.

3931 ROBERTSON (GEORGE). Rural recollections; or, The progress of improvement in agriculture and rural affairs. Irvine. 1829.

An important source. See also William M'Combie, *Cattle and cattle breeders*, 1867, later edns. 1869, 1875, 1886, reminiscences by a breeder in East Lothian.

3932 THOMSON (JAMES). The value and importance of the Scottish fisheries, comprehending fully every circumstance connected with their present position. 1849.

See also Robert Charles Fraser, *A letter . . . on the most effectual means of improvement of the coasts and Western Islands of Scotland, and the extension of the fisheries*, 1803, and the *Report* of the House of Lords' select committee on salmon fisheries in Scotland, H.C. 1842 (522) XIV. The Royal Commission on Sea Fisheries of 1866 also collected information on the period before 1851; see H.C. 1866 [3596–3596/1] XVII–XVIII.

3933 MORGAN (VALERIE). 'Agricultural wage rates in late eighteenth-century Scotland.' *Econ. H.R.* 2nd ser. 24 (1971), 181–201.

7. The Highland Economy

3934 GRAY (MALCOLM). The Highland economy, 1750–1850. 1957.

Bibliog. 263–71. See also his bibliographical article, 'Settlement in the Highlands, 1750–1850' in *Scottish Studies*, 6 (1962), 145–54. For a full contemporary description see John Walker, *An economical history of the Hebrides and Highlands of Scotland*, 2 v., Edin., 1808. For attempts at agricultural improvement see *Prize essays and transactions of the Highland and Agricultural Society of Scotland*, 6 v., Edin., 1799–1824, and Alexander Ramsay, *History of the Highland and Agricultural Society of Scotland*, etc., 1879.

3935 IRVINE (ALEXANDER). An inquiry into the causes and effects of emigration from the Highlands and western islands of Scotland, with observations on the means to be employed for preventing it. Edin. 1802.

Thomas Douglas, 5th earl of Selkirk, settled Highland emigrants in Prince Edward Island, 1803; see his *Observations on the present state of the Highlands of Scotland; with a view of the causes and probable consequences of emigration*, 1805, and Robert Brown, *Strictures and remarks on the Earl of Selkirk's Observations*, etc., Edin., 1806, also Margaret I. Adam, 'The cause of the Highland emigrations of 1783–1803', *S.H.R.* 17 (1920), 73–89.

3936 LOCH (JAMES). An account of the improvements on the estate of Sutherland belonging to the Marquess and Marchioness of Stafford. 1815.

Followed by his longer *An account of the improvements on the estates of the Marquess of Stafford ... with remarks*, 1820. Loch was economic adviser to the Marquess of Stafford (later 1st Duke of Sutherland). His drastic policy of resettling the tenants provoked most bitter feeling. See Donald Macleod, *History of the destitution in Sutherlandshire*, Edin., 1841, a reprint of letters which had appeared in the *Edinburgh Weekly Chronicle* in 1841 attacking the clearances. Alexander Mackenzie, *The history of the Highland clearances*, Inverness, 1883, strongly supports the crofters and reprints Macleod, with title *Gloomy memories of the Highlands*. Thomas Sellar, *The Sutherland evictions of 1814*, etc., 1883, is a defence of Patrick Sellar, the author's father, who had been factor on the estates. Donald Sage, *Memorabilia domestica; or, Parish life in the north of Scotland*, ed. by his son Donald Fraser Sage, Wick, 1889, 2nd edn., 1899, is a balanced account by a minister on the Sutherland estates, written in 1840 and published posthumously. For a recent evaluation see Eric S. Richards, 'The prospect of economic growth in Sutherland at the time of the clearances, 1809 to 1813', *S.H.R.* 49 (1970), 154–71, and 'Structural change in a regional economy: Sutherland and the industrial revolution, 1780–1830', *Econ. H.R.*, 2nd ser. 26 (1973), 63–76. R. J. Adam, ed., *Papers on Sutherland estate management, 1802–1816* (Scottish Hist. Soc., 4th s., 8 and 9), 2 v., Edin., 1972. See also (1672).

3937 ALISON (WILLIAM PULTENEY). Observations on the famine of 1846–7, in the Highlands of Scotland and in Ireland. 1847.

Also James Bruce, *Destitution in the Highlands. Letters ... Reprinted from the Scotsman newspaper*, Edin., 1847, Robert Somers, *Letters from the Highlands; or, The famine of 1847*, 1848. 'An eye witness' [i.e. Thomas M'Lauchlan], *The depopulation system in the Highlands*, etc., Edin., 1849, discusses extent of clearances outside Sutherland.

3938 CREGEEN (ERIC R.). Argyll estate instructions. Mull, Morvern, Tiree, 1771–1805 (Scottish Hist. Soc. 4th ser. 1.) Edin. 1964.

Estate papers of the 'improving' 5th Duke of Argyll. John Philip Wellesley Gaskell, *Morvern transformed. A highland parish in the nineteenth century*, Camb., 1968, is a substantial study of the estate after it had been partly sold by the 6th Duke, a friend of the Prince Regent. See, finally, George Douglas Campbell, 8th Duke of Argyll, *Crofts and farms in the Hebrides. Being an account of the management of an island estate for 130 years*, Edin., 1883. More general works on the Highlands are listed at (3990).

8. POOR LAW

3939 CORMACK (ALEXANDER ALLAN). Poor relief in Scotland. An outline of the growth and administration of the poor laws in Scotland, from the middle ages to the present day. Aberdeen. 1923.

See also Charles Stewart Loch, 'Poor relief in Scotland: its statistics and development, 1791 to 1891', *Jour. Royal Statistical Soc.* 61 (1898), 271–370. By the secretary to the Charity Organization Society, it places strong emphasis on self-help. See also Thomas Hamilton, *Poor relief in South Ayrshire, 1700–1845*, 1942.

3940 BURNS (ROBERT). Historical dissertations on the law and practice of Great Britain, and particularly of Scotland with regard to the poor. 2nd edn. enl. Glasgow. 1819.

Substantial and factual. See also David Monypenny, *Remarks on the poor laws, and on the method of providing for the poor in Scotland*, Edin., 1834, 2nd edn. with add., Edin., 1836. Until 1845 the management of the poor was the responsibility of the heritors and kirk sessions in every parish, who provided for them through church collections. For the working of the system see Committee of the General Assembly, *Report on the management of the poor in Scotland*, H.C. 1839 [177] XX, Poor Law Commissioners' *Report on the sanitary condition of the labouring population, Scotland*, 1842 (H.L.) XXVIII, *Select committee on the treatment of the unemployed and destitute inhabitants of Paisley*, H.C. 1843 (115) VII, *Royal commission report on the administration and practical operation of the poor laws*, Scotland, H.C. 1844 [557] XX.

3941 ALISON (WILLIAM PULTENEY). Observations on the management of the poor in Scotland, and its effects on the health of the great towns. 1840. 2nd edn. 1840.

Alison opened the campaign for the adoption of the English poor law in Scotland, in opposition to Thomas Chalmers (see 4030). See also, among many pamphlets, Robert Burns, *A plea for the poor of Scotland*, etc., Paisley, 1841, *Pictures of pauperism. The condition of the poor described by themselves in 50 genuine letters, addressed by paupers to the agent of the Glasgow association in aid of the poor*, Glasgow, 1847; James Begg, *Pauperism and the poor laws*, etc., 1849.

3942 NICHOLLS (*Sir* GEORGE). A history of the Scotch poor law, in connexion with the condition of the people. 1856.

For administrative details see John Guthrie Smith, *Digest of the law of Scotland relating to the poor*, Edin., 1859, and Robert Peel Lamond, *The Scottish poor laws; their history, policy, and operation*, Edin., 1870, new edn. enl., Glasgow, 1892.

9. Labour History

3943 SOCIETY FOR THE STUDY OF LABOUR HISTORY. Scottish committee. An interim bibliography of the Scottish working class movement, and of other labour records held in Scotland. Ed. by Ian McDougall. Edin. 1965.

See also, particularly on early trade union history, Thomas Johnston, *The history of the working classes in Scotland*, Glasgow, 1922, 3rd edn., Glasgow, 1935, a frankly partisan study, and William Hutton Marwick, 'Early trade unionism in Scotland', *Econ. H.R.* 5 (1935), 87–95, and his 'The beginnings of the Scottish working class movement in the nineteenth century', *International Rev. for Social Hist.* 3 (1938), 1–24. For Scottish Chartism see Wright (113).

3944 OWEN (ROBERT). Report to the county of Lanark of a plan for relieving public distress. Glasgow. 1821. Another edn. 1832.

See also his *An address . . . to the inhabitants of New Lanark on the first of January, 1816*, 1816. For Owen's life and other works, see (524).

3945 RICHMOND (ALEXANDER BAILEY). Narrative of the condition of the manufacturing population and the proceedings of government which led to the state trials in Scotland. Glasgow. 1825.

Richmond was believed to be a government spy and was strongly attacked by Ten Pounder (*pseud.* of Peter Mackenzie), *An exposure of the spy system pursued in Glasgow during the years 1816–17–18–19 and 20*, etc., Glasgow, 1833. See also John Stevenson, *A true narrative of the radical rising in Strathaven*, Glasgow [1835], which refers to a rising in 1820. See also P. Berresford Ellis and Seumas Mac a' Ghobhainn, *The Scottish insurrection of 1820*, 1970, criticized by W. M. Roach, *S.H.R.* 50 (1971), 86–9, and in his 'Alexander Richmond and the radical reform movements in Glasgow in 1816–17', *S.H.R.* 51 (1972), 1–19.

3946 MARSHALL (JAMES). The trial of Thomas Hunter, Peter Hacket, Richard M'Niel, James Gibb, and William M'Lean, the Glasgow cotton-spinners, before the High Court of Justiciary at Edinburgh. Edin. 1838.

A verbatim report. A great deal of material was presented to the Select Committee on combination of workmen, H.C. 1837-8 (488 and 646) VIII.

3947 WARD (JOHN TREVOR). 'The factory reform movement in Scotland.' *S.H.R.* 41 (1962), 100–23.

See also (1720), and the Scottish evidence on handloom weavers in H.C. 1839 (159) XLII.

E. SOCIAL HISTORY

1. BIOGRAPHICAL COLLECTIONS

3948 ANDERSON (WILLIAM). The Scottish nation, or, The surnames, families, literature, honours, and biographical history of the people of Scotland. 3 v. Edin. 1863.

See also Robert Chambers, *A biographical dictionary of eminent Scotsmen,* 4 v., Glasgow, 1834, new edn. by Revd. Thomas Thomson, 5 v., Glasgow, 1855.

3949 PAUL (JAMES BALFOUR) *ed.* The Scots peerage; founded on Wood's edition of Sir Robert Douglas's peerage of Scotland; containing an historical and genealogical account of the nobility of that kingdom. 6 v. Edin. 1904–14.

2. LITERARY AND INTELLECTUAL HISTORY

For Adam Black see (3884). For Burns, Campbell, Hogg, and Scott see *Literature,* for music see Collinson (3045).

3950 CRAIG (DAVID). Scottish literature and the Scottish people, 1680–1830. 1961.

William Lindsay Renwick, (2660) has a chapter (VII) on Scottish literature. See also Kurt Wittig, *The Scottish tradition in literature,* 1958.

3951 GRANT (*Mrs.* Anne *of Laggan*). Letters from the mountains. 3 v. 1806.

Reflections on the influence of romantic landscape; it ran through many edns. in the early 19th century.

3952 LOCKHART (JOHN GIBSON). Peter's letters to his kinsfolk. 3 v. Edin. 1819.

Critical and amusing descriptions of Edinburgh society, written with the assistance of 'Christopher North' (John Wilson).

3953 KEIR (DAVID EDWIN). The House of Collins, the story of a Scottish family of publishers from 1789 to the present day. 1952.

The firm was a pioneer of cheap publishing.

3954 TREDREY (FRANK D.). The House of Blackwood, 1804–1954: the history of a publishing firm. 1954.

An earlier history, containing much correspondence, is *Annals of a publishing house, v. 1 & 2, William Blackwood and his sons,* etc., by Margaret Oliphant Oliphant Edin., 1897, *v. 3, John Blackwood,* by Mrs. Gerald (Mary) Porter, Edin., 1898. Comments on the Blackwood circle are to be found in Nathaniel Parker Willis, *Pencillings by the way,* 3 v., 1835, and Sir George Brisbane Scott Douglas, *The Blackwood group* (Famous Scots series) [1897], which prints lives of John Galt, John Wilson, D. M. Moir, Miss Ferrier, Michael Scott, Thomas Hamilton.

3955 CLIVE (JOHN LEONARD). Scotch reviewers. The Edinburgh Review, 1802–1815. 1957.

3956 BLACKIE (AGNES ANNA COVENTRY). Blackie and sons, 1809–1959; a short history of the firm. 1959.

3957 CHAMBERS (ROBERT). Memoir of Robert Chambers. With autobiographic reminiscences of William Chambers. By William Chambers. 1872. 13th edn. 1884.

New edn. with title *Memories of the Chambers brothers,* etc., ed. Derek Maggs, 1967. The firm published *Chambers' Edinburgh Journal,* Edin., 1832 +.

3958 CONSTABLE. Archibald Constable and his literary correspondents; a memorial by his son. By Thomas Constable. 3 v. Edin. 1873.

Scott's publishers.

3959 GILLIES (ROBERT PEARSE). Memoirs of a literary veteran from 1794 to 1849. 3 v. 1851.

3960 LOCKHART. The life and letters of John Gibson Lockhart. By Andrew Lang. 2 v. 1897.

For full bibliog. see Jack (2660), 578–9.

3961 MACKENZIE. A Scottish man of feeling; some account of Henry Mackenzie . . . of the golden age of Burns and Scott. By Harold William Thompson. 1931.

Bibliog. 424–39.

3962 MILLAR. John Millar of Glasgow, 1735–1801, his life and thought and his contributions to sociological analysis. By William Christian Lehmann. (Glasgow Univ. Social and Econ. Studies. 4.) Camb. 1960.

3963 WILSON (JOHN), Christopher North; a memoir of John Wilson. By Martha H. Gordon. 2 v. Edin. 1862. New edn. Edin. 1879.

Wilson contributed to *Blackwood's Magazine* under the pseudonym of Christopher North. See also Elsie Swann, *Christopher North,* 1934, which uses additional material to that in Mrs. Gordon's biography.

3. SOCIAL CONDITIONS

3964 HAMILTON (ELIZABETH). The cottagers of Glenburnie; a tale for the farmer's ingle-nook. Edin. 1808. New edn. Edin. 1885.

A realistic novel of the manners of the small farmer class.

3965 [GALT (JOHN)]. Annals of the parish; or, The chronicle of Dalmailing. Edin. 1821. Many later edns.

The notable description of country life, which continues to 1810. Galt's *The Provost*, Edin., 1822, new edn. ed. Ian A. Gordon, Oxf., 1973, gives an equally vivid picture of local government. For full bibliog. see Jack (2660) and (2269).

3966 THOM (WILLIAM). Rhymes and recollections of a hand-loom weaver. 1844. 2nd edn. with add. 1845.

3967 SOMERVILLE (ALEXANDER). The autobiography of a working man. By one who has whistled at the plough. 1848. Many later edns.

3968 MILLER (HUGH). My schools and schoolmasters, or The story of my education. Edin. 1854. 18th edn. 1871.

Self-educated geologist and man of letters, who had begun life as a stonemason.

3969 RAMSAY (EDWARD BANNERMAN). Reminiscences of Scottish life and character. 1st ser. 2nd edn. 1858. 2nd ser. 1861.

A collection of anecdotes, discussions of dialect usages, cookery, etc.; a very popular contemporary work, the 1st ser. reaching its 22nd edn. by 1874.

3970 SOMERVILLE (THOMAS). My own life and times, 1741–1814. Edin. 1861.

3971 VICTORIA (*Queen*). Leaves from the journal of our life in the Highlands, from 1848 to 1861. To which are prefixed and added extracts from the same journal giving an account of earlier visits to Scotland and tours in England and Ireland, and yachting excursions. Ed. by Sir Arthur Helps. 1868.

3972 COCKBURN (HENRY THOMAS, *Lord*). Circuit journeys. Edin. 1888. 2nd edn. Edin. 1889.

Covers the years 1837–54.

3973 STRACHEY (JANE MARIA, *Lady*) ed. Memoirs of a Highland lady. The autobiography of Elizabeth Grant of Rothiemurchus, afterwards Mrs. Smith of Baltiboys, 1797–1830. 1898. 2nd edn. 1911. New and rev. edn. by Angus Davidson. 1950.

A first-hand account of life on a Speyside estate.

3974 HALDANE (ELIZABETH SANDERSON). The Scotland of our fathers. A study of Scottish life in the nineteenth century. 1933.

3975 HORN (BARBARA L. H.) *ed.* Letters of John Ramsay of Ochtertyre, 1799–1812. (Scottish Hist. Soc. Pubs. 4th ser. 3.) Edin. 1966.

Illustrates the urban and rural life of the Scottish gentry.

4. SOCIAL POLICY

(a) *General*

3976 FERGUSON (THOMAS). The dawn of Scottish social welfare. A survey from medieval times to 1863. 1948.

Also Stewart Mechie, *The Church and Scottish social development, 1780–1870*, 1960, which discusses housing, education, poor laws, and temperance.

3977 MACGILL (STEVENSON). Discourses and essays on subjects of public interest. Edin. 1819.

Reprints his *Remarks on prisons*, Glasgow, 1810, and *On lunatic asylums*, Glasgow, 1810. On MacGill's life as a social reformer and theologian see Robert Burns, *Memoir of the Rev. Stevenson MacGill, D.D.*, Edin., 1842.

3978 BREBNER (WILLIAM). Letter to the Lord Provost on the expediency of a house of refuge for juvenile offenders. Glasgow. 1829.

3979 SMITH (JOHN). The grievances of the working classes, and the pauperism and crime of Glasgow with their causes, extent, and remedies. Glasgow. 1846.

See also Henry Miller, *Papers relative to the state of crime in the city of Glasgow*, etc., Glasgow, 1840. Social conditions in Edinburgh are described in George Bell, *Day and night in the wynds of Edinburgh*, 1st–3rd edns., Edin., 1849, and his *Blackfriars' Wynd analyzed*, Edin., 1850. On Dundee see George Lewis, *The state of St. David's parish, with remarks on the moral and physical statistics of Dundee*, Dundee, 1841.

(b) *Public Health and Medical Services*

3980 BROTHERTON (JOHN HOWIE FLINT). Observations on the early public health movement in Scotland. (London School of Hygiene and Tropical Medicine, Memoir 8.) 1952.

Contemporary studies include Robert Cowan (physician to the Glasgow Royal Infirmary), *Vital statistics of Glasgow*, Glasgow and Edin., 1838, Alexander Watt, *Vital statistics of Glasgow for 1843, 1844*, Glasgow, 1846, and James Stark, *Report on the mortality of Edinburgh and Leith for the six months June-November, 1846*, Edin., 1846.

3981 RUSSELL (JAMES BURN). Public health administration in Glasgow; a memorial volume. Ed. by Archibald Kerr Chalmers. 1905.

3982 TURNER (ARTHUR LOGAN). Story of a great hospital. The Royal Infirmary of Edinburgh, 1729–1929. 1937.

See also Glasgow Royal Asylum for Lunatics, *Annual reports of the directors*, Glasgow, 1818+, and Moses Steven Buchanan, *History of the Glasgow Royal Infirmary from its commencement in 1787 to the present time*, Glasgow, 1832.

(c) *Temperance*

3983 DUNLOP (JOHN). Autobiography of John Dunlop. (Dunlop papers. 1.)
1932.

> Founder of the temperance movement in Scotland. See also his *Artificial drinking usages
> of North Britain*, listing social drinking conventions, 4th edn. with large add., Greenock,
> 1836. Thomas Welsh Hamilton, *The temperance reformation in Scotland with special
> reference to John Dunlop and Greenock*, Greenock, 1929, is a simple account. See also
> *Public houses in Scotland. Petition of ministers for the better observance of the Lord's day*,
> H.C. 1846 (457) XV, and a formidable tract, William Logan, *The moral statistics of
> Glasgow*, Glasgow, 1849. For William Collins, also active in the movement, see (3953).

F. LOCAL HISTORY

I. TOPOGRAPHICAL AND GENERAL

(a) *Bibliographies and Catalogues*

3984 MITCHELL (*Sir* ARTHUR) *and* CASH (CALEB GEORGE). A contribution to the bibliography of Scottish topography. 2 v. Edin. 1917.

> V. 1 is a guide to local history, v. 2 is primarily topographical. See also Sir Arthur
> Mitchell, *A list of travels and tours in Scotland, 1296 to 1900*, Edin., 1902, repr. from v.
> XXXV of the *Proceedings of the Society of Antiquaries of Scotland*, 1901.

(b) *General Works*

3985 ORDNANCE SURVEY OF THE UNITED KINGDOM. Catalogue
of the 6 inch and 25 inch county maps and town plans of Scotland, and of the
one-inch and smaller scale maps and other publications of the Ordnance
Survey of the United Kingdom to 1st April 1913. 1913.

> Lists, pp. 40–1, the large-scale (5 and 10 feet to the mile) maps prepared for Scottish
> towns, usually in connection with water and drainage schemes in the 1850s. The first
> one-inch survey of Scotland was published 1857. For earlier maps see Rodger (3519)
> and John Elliot Shearer, *Old maps and map makers of Scotland*, Stirling, 1905, and
> Harry R. G. Inglis, John Mathieson, and C. B. B. Watson, *The early maps of Scotland*,
> *with an account of the Ordnance survey*, Edin., 1934, 2nd edn., Edin., 1936.

3986 SINCLAIR (*Sir* JOHN) *ed*. The statistical account of Scotland, drawn
up from the communications of the ministers of the different parishes. 21 v.
Edin. 1791–9.

> Sinclair analysed this material to some extent in his *General report of the agricultural
> state and political circumstances of Scotland*, 5 v., with app., Edin., 1814, and in his
> *Analysis of the statistical account of Scotland*, 2 v., 1825. Rosalind Mitchison (2140) is an
> admirable modern biography. A similar survey was made in *The new statistical account
> of Scotland, by the ministers of the respective parishes*, 15 v., 1845, summarized by James
> Hooper Dawson, *An abridged and statistical history of Scotland*, 1853.

3987 LEWIS (SAMUEL). A topographical dictionary of Scotland. 2 v. 1846.

> George Chalmers, *Caledonia . . .*, 1807–24, new and better edn., 7 v. and index, Paisley,
> 1887–94, 1902, is a similar work, but contains less information on the 19th century.
> Illustrated works include *Scotia depicta . . . illustrated in a series of finished etchings by
> James Fittler, A.R.A. . . . from accurate drawings . . . by John Claude Nattes*, 1804;

William Beattie, *Scotland illustrated in a series of views . . . by . . . T. Allom, W. H. Bartlett and H. McCulloch,* 1838.

3988 COBBETT (WILLIAM). Cobbett's tour in Scotland and in the four northern counties of England in the autumn of the year 1832. 1833.

3989 WORDSWORTH (DOROTHY). Recollections of a tour made in Scotland A.D. 1803. Ed. by John Campbell Shairp. Edin. 1894.

3990 MACKENZIE (WILLIAM COOK). A short history of the Scottish Highlands and Isles. Paisley. 1906. 3rd edn. Paisley. 1908.

A general history: new edn. with title *Highlands and Isles of Scotland. An historical survey,* 1937. David Stewart, *Sketches of the character, manners and present state of the Highlanders of Scotland,* 2 v., Edin., 1822, new edn. Inverness, 1886, contains information on the Highland regiments. For physical description see Macculloch (3176). Sir John Scott Keltie, ed., *A history of the Scottish Highlands, Highland clans and Highland regiments, with an account of the Gaelic language, literature and music* 2 v., 1875, is standard.

3991 CADELL (HENRY MOUBRAY). The story of the Forth. Glasgow. 1913.

3992 DUNBAR (JOHN G.) The historic architecture of Scotland. [1966.]

Also George Hay, *The architecture of Scottish post-Reformation churches, 1560–1843,* Oxf., 1957.

2. INDIVIDUAL COUNTIES AND TOWNS

(Counties are arranged alphabetically, and towns under the appropriate county.) The *Third statistical account of Scotland* includes in each case a bibliography and history of the town or county concerned. To date (1975) there have been published Ayrshire, Fife, East Lothian, Aberdeen (city), Glasgow, Dunbartonshire, Aberdeenshire, Lanarkshire, Argyllshire, Banffshire, Renfrewshire and Bute, Dumfriesshire, Peeblesshire and Selkirkshire, Moray and Nairn, Clackmannan, Edinburgh, and Kirkcudbright and Wigton.

3993 ANGUS. WARDEN (ALEXANDER JOHNSTON). Angus or Forfarshire, the land and people, descriptive and historical. 5 v. Dundee. 1880–5.

3994 —— DUNDEE. [BEATTS (JOHN MACLEAN).] The municipal history of the royal burgh of Dundee. Dundee. 1873. 2nd edn. Dundee, 1878.

James Thomson, *The history of Dundee,* etc., Dundee, 1847, new edn. by J. Maclaren, *continued to the present time,* Dundee, 1874, is also a substantial history. For social conditions see Lewis (3979).

3995 ABERDEENSHIRE. JOHNSTONE (JAMES FOWLER KELLAS). A concise bibliography of the history, topography, and institutions of the shires of Aberdeen, Banff, and Kincardine. (Aberdeen Univ. Studies. 66.) Aberdeen. 1914.

See also Aberdeen Public Library, *Catalogue of the local collection,* comp. George Milne

Fraser, Aberdeen, 1914, an extensive collection. Also Alexander Smith, *A new history of Aberdeenshire*, Aberdeen and Edin., 1875.

3996 —— ABERDEEN. KENNEDY (WILLIAM). Annals of Aberdeen, from the reign of King William the Lion to the end of 1818. 2 v. 1818.

Includes local statistics and information on whaling. William Robbie, *Aberdeen, its traditions and history, with notices of some eminent Aberdonians*, Aberdeen, 1893, and Victoria Elizabeth Clark, *The port of Aberdeen*, etc., Aberdeen, 1921, are both good.

3997 AYRSHIRE. SHAW (JAMES EDWARD). Ayrshire, 1745–1950. A social and industrial history of the county, compiled for the Ayrshire Archaeological and Natural History Society. 1953.

Also published by the society, (Collections, 5), [Ayr], 1959, and ed. John Strawhorn, *Ayrshire at the time of Burns*, a useful collection of contemporary extracts with lists of local officials.

3998 CAITHNESS. MOWAT (JOHN). A new bibliography of the county of Caithness. Wick. 1940.

3999 CLACKMANNANSHIRE. GIBSON (WILLIAM). Reminiscences of Dollar, Tillicoultry, and other districts adjoining the Ochils. 2nd edn. Edin. 1883.

4000 DUNBARTONSHIRE. IRVING (JOSEPH). The history of Dunbartonshire ... to the present time. Dumbarton. 1857. Rev. edn. by John Irving, 3 pt. Dumbarton. 1917.

See also Thomas Johnston, *Old Kirkintilloch*, Kirkintilloch, 1937.

4001 EAST LOTHIAN. JAMIESON (JAMES H.) *and* HAWKINS (ELEANOR). Bibliography of East Lothian. Edin. 1936.

4002 FIFE AND KINROSS. MACKAY (AENEAS JAMES GEORGE). 'List of books relating to Fife and Kinross.' *Edin. Bibliographical Soc. Pubns.*, v. 3, pt. 1 (1895–8), 1–30. Edin. 1899.

See also Erskine Beveridge, *A bibliography of works relating to Dunfermline and the west of Fife*, Edin. Bibliographical Soc. Pubns., v. 5, Dunfermline, 1901.

4003 —— ST. ANDREWS. BAXTER (JAMES HOUSTON). Collections towards a bibliography of St. Andrews. (Univ. of St. Andrews Library Pubns. 1.) St. Andrews. 1926.

4004 INVERNESS-SHIRE. ANDERSON (PETER JOHN). A concise bibliography of the printed and MS. material on the history, topography and institutions of the burgh, parish and shire of Inverness. (Aberdeen Univ. Studies. 73.) Aberdeen. 1917.

Sir James Cameron Lees, *A history of the county of Inverness, mainland*, Edin., 1897, is a good county history. James Barron, *The Northern Highlands in the nineteenth century, Newspaper index and annals*, 3 v., Inverness, 1903–7, consists of extracts from the *Inverness Courier*, 1800–56, and is a mine of local information. See also Alexander Nicolson, *History of Skye*, Glasgow, 1930.

4005 LANARKSHIRE. GLASGOW. TODD (GEORGE EYRE). History of
Glasgow. V. 3. From the Revolution to the Reform Act. Glasgow. 1934.

Forms v. 3 of Robert Renwick and Sir John Lindsay's *History of Glasgow*, Glasgow,
1921–43, the standard history. Other general histories are George MacGregor, *The
history of Glasgow, from the earliest period to the present time*, Glasgow, 1881, valuable for
political history, and Charles Allen Oakley, *The Second City*, 1946, a short introduction.
Important contemporary sources are James Cleland, *Annals of Glasgow*, 2 v., Glasgow,
1816, and the same writer's *Enumeration of the inhabitants of . . . Glasgow and the county
of Lanark*, 1917. See also John Strang, *Glasgow and its clubs*, Glasgow, 1856, 3rd enl.
edn., Glasgow, 1864, and *Memories and portraits of one hundred Glasgow men*, Glasgow,
1886. For social conditions see (3977–9), for pauperism (3941), for labour history
(3944–5).

4006 ——— ——— STEWART (GEORGE). Progress of Glasgow. A sketch of the
commercial and industrial increase of the city during the last century, as
shown in the records of the Glasgow Chamber of Commerce and other
authentic documents. Glasgow. 1883.

Glasgow lacks an adequate economic history. For commercial organization see George
Crawfurd, *A sketch of the rise and progress of the Trades' House of Glasgow*, Glasgow,
1858; [W. H. Hill and Andrew Scott], *View of the Merchants' House of Glasgow*,
Glasgow, 1866. (The Merchants' and Trades' houses together had also composed the
town council before municipal reform.) See also James R. Anderson, *The burgesses and
guild brethren of Glasgow* (Scottish Rec. Soc. Pubn. 66), Edin., 1935; James Deas, *The
river Clyde. An historical description of the rise and progress of the Harbour of Glasgow, and
of the improvement of the river from Glasgow to Port-Glasgow*, Glasgow, 1876.

4007 ——— ——— MARWICK (*Sir* JAMES DAVID) *and* RENWICK
(ROBERT) *eds*. Extracts from the records of the burgh of Glasgow. 11 v.
Glasgow 1908–16.

V. 8–11 covering the years 1781–1891 were edited by Renwick alone. See also his
Abstracts of charters and documents relating to the City of Glasgow, A.D. 1833–1872,
Glasgow, 1917. Also on local administration see Sir James Bell, Bt., and James Paton,
Glasgow: its municipal organization and administration, Glasgow, 1896, and Sir James
David Marwick, *The River Clyde and the Clyde burghs*, Glasgow, 1909, both substantial
works.

4008 MIDLOTHIAN. EDINBURGH. ANDERSON (JOHN). A history of
Edinburgh from the earliest period to the completion of the half century, 1850.
1856.

Annals, with biographical notices. See also *Edinburgh, 1329–1929*, Edin., 1929, an
official history, comp. by David Robertson, Marguerite Wood, and Frank C. Mears.
Particular aspects of the city's history are dealt with in James Colston, *The Edinburgh
and district water supply*, Edin., 1890; William Norrie, *Edinburgh newspapers past and
present*, Earlston, 1891; James Campbell Irons, *Leith and its antiquities*, 2 v., Edin.
[1898]; Alexander Heron, *The rise and progress of the company of Merchants of the city of
Edinburgh, 1681–1902*, Edin., 1903. *The book of the Old Edinburgh Club*, 1908+, in
progress, gen. index to v. 1–20, 1936, is a miscellany of local history. See also Charles
Brodie Boog Watson, ed., *Roll of the Edinburgh burgesses and guild-brethren, 1761–1841*
(Scottish Rec. Soc. Pubns. 68), Edin., 1933, and David Robertson, *The Princes Street
proprietors*, Edin., 1935, primarily concerned with local administration. Alexander John
Youngson (formerly A. J. Y. Brown), *The making of classical Edinburgh, 1750–1840*,
Edin., 1966, is an important study relating architectural and economic history. For
social history see (3952–60), for public health, see Bell (3979). For maps see William
Cowan and C. B. B. Watson, *The maps of Edinburgh, 1544–1929*, Edin., 1932.

4009 ORKNEY. CURSITER (JAMES WALLS) *ed.* List of books and pamphlets relating to Orkney and Shetland. Kirkwall. 1894.

George Barry, *The history of the Orkney Islands*, Edin., 1805, includes chapters descriptive of Orkney at the time of writing.

4010 PEEBLES-SHIRE. BUCHAN (JAMES WALTER) *ed.* A history of Peebles-shire. 3 v. Glasgow. 1925–7.

4011 PERTHSHIRE. PERTH. MARSHALL (THOMAS HAY). The history of Perth, from the earliest period to the present time. Perth. 1849.

4012 RENFREWSHIRE. GREENOCK. SMITH (ROBERT MURRAY). The history of Greenock. Greenock. 1921.

4013 —— PAISLEY. BROWN (ROBERT). The history of Paisley to 1884. 2 v. Paisley. 1886.

Also William Musham Metcalfe, *A history of Paisley, 600–1908*, Paisley, 1909. See also (3921).

4014 ROSS AND CROMARTY. BAIN (ROBERT). History of the ancient province of Ross from the earliest to the present time. Dingwall. 1899.

4015 SELKIRKSHIRE. GALASHIELS. HALL (ROBERT). The history of Galashiels. Galashiels. 1898.

4016 STIRLINGSHIRE. NIMMO (WILLIAM). A general history of Stirlingshire. 2nd edn. 2 v. 1817. 3rd edn. enl. and brought up to the present time by R. Gillespie, 1880.

Also William B. Cook and David B. Morris, eds., *The Stirling guildry book . . . 1592–1846*, Stirling, 1916, deals with municipal administration.

G. RELIGIOUS HISTORY

1. BIBLIOGRAPHY

4017 MACGREGOR (MALCOLM BLAIR). The sources and literature of Scottish church history. Glasgow. 1934.

A bibliog. of printed sources. For manuscripts see Thomas Burns, *Church property*, Edin., 1905, which lists records of the General Assembly, synods, presbyteries, and kirk-sessions.

2. CHURCH OF SCOTLAND

4018 THE PRINCIPALL ACTS of the solemne generall assembly of the Kirk of Scotland (1638–1841+). Edin. 1639–1841+.

4019 DUNLOP (ALEXANDER MURRAY). Parochial law. Edin. 1830.

The law relating to the manse, the poor law, ecclesiastical patronage, parochial schools, etc. Alexander Taylor Innes, *The law of creeds in Scotland*, 2nd edn., Edin., 1867, deals with both the established and other churches. On teinds see (758).

4020 ROYAL COMMISSION ON RELIGIOUS INSTRUCTION (SCOT-
LAND). 1st report H.C. 1837 (31) XXI; 2nd–4th reports 1837–8 [109]
XXXII, [113, 122] XXXIII; 5th–9th reports 1839 [152] XXIII, [153] XXIV,
[154] XXV [162, 164] XXVI.

A massive parish-by-parish survey of church buildings and attendance. For the 1851
religious census in Scotland see P.P. (1854) LIX, 301–46.

4021 SCOTT (HEW). Fasti ecclesiae Scoticanae: the succession of ministers
in the parish churches of Scotland from . . . 1560. 3 v. Edin. 1866–71. New
edn. rev. and continued to the present time. 8 v. Edin. 1915–50.

4022 FLEMING (JOHN ROBERT). A history of the Church in Scotland,
1843–1929. V. 1. 1843–1874. Edin. 1927–33.

The standard history. A useful short history is John Henderson Seaforth Burleigh, *A
church history of Scotland*, 1960. The older standard history is John Cunningham, *The
church history of Scotland from the commencement of the Christian era to the present
century*, 2 v., Edin., 1859, 2nd edn., 2 v., Edin., 1882. See also Andrew James Campbell,
Two centuries of the Church of Scotland, 1707–1920 (Hastie Lectures, Univ. of Glasgow),
Paisley, 1930, and Andrew L. Drummond and James Bulloch, *The Scottish Church; the
age of the moderates, 1688–1843*, Edin., 1973, and Mathieson (3875).

4023 MACINNES (JOHN). The evangelical movements in the Highlands of
Scotland, 1688 to 1800. Aberdeen. 1951.

Also John Mackay, *The Church in the Highlands . . . 563–1843*, 1914, and Colin Mac-
naughton, *Church life in Ross and Sutherland from . . . 1688 to the present time*, etc.,
Inverness, 1915, on the parish of Tain. For the Lowlands see James Tait, *Two centuries
of Border church life*, etc., Kelso, 1889.

4024 HEWAT (ELIZABETH GLENDINNING KIRKWOOD). Vision and
achievement, 1796–1956. A history of the foreign missions of the churches
united in the Church of Scotland. 1960.

See also Jessy J. Matheson, *A memoir of Greville Ewing*, 1843, who was first secretary of
the Edinburgh Missionary Society, 1796, and Andrew Landale Drummond, *The Kirk
and the Continent*, Edin., 1956, a study of relations with reformed churches in Europe,
and of Church of Scotland congregations on the Continent.

3. THE DISRUPTION

4025 HENDERSON (GEORGE DAVID). Heritage. A study of the Disruption. 1943.

A short modern summary. Standard accounts by moderate supporters of the Established
Church are James Bryce, *Ten years of the Church of Scotland from 1833 to 1843*, 2 v.,
1850, and Alexander Turner, *The Scottish secession of 1843*, etc., Edin., 1859. The best
account from the side of the Free Church is Robert Buchanan, *The ten years' conflict*,
etc., 2 v., Glasgow, 1849. Detailed narratives of events are to be found in William Maxwell
Hetherington, *Narrative of proceedings in the General Assembly of the Church of Scotland,
1842*, Edin., 1842, and *Proceedings of the General Assembly of the Free Church of Scotland, 1843*, Edin., 1843. See also G. I. T. Machin, 'The Disruption and British politics,
1834–43', *S.H.R.* 51 (1972), 20–51.

4026 BROWN (THOMAS). Annals of the Disruption. Edin. 1877.

An account of the later careers of the Free Church ministers and their congregations, written from contemporary narratives. On the same subject is Norman Lockhart Walker, *Chapters from the history of the Free Church of Scotland*, 1895.

4027 BEGG. Memoirs of James Begg. D.D., minister of Newington Free Church, Edinburgh, including autobiographical chapters by Dr. Begg. By Thomas Smith. 2 v. Edin. 1885–8.

4028 BUCHANAN. Robert Buchanan D.D. An ecclesiastical biography. By Norman Lockhart Walker. 1877.

4029 CAMPBELL (JOHN M'LEOD). Memorials of John M'Leod Campbell, D.D. Being selections from his correspondence. Edited by his son, the Rev. Donald Campbell. 2 v. 1877.

Minister of Row, Dunbartonshire, 1825–30, ejected for heresy, 1830. The Row case was one of the subjects of dispute within the Church.

4030 CHALMERS (THOMAS). Memoirs of the life and writings of Thomas Chalmers, D.D. By William Hanna. 4 v. 1849–52.

Also Hugh Watt, ed., *The published writings of Dr. Thomas Chalmers, 1780–1847. A descriptive list*, Edin., 1943. Chalmers was the leading figure in the Free Church.

4031 ERSKINE *of Linlathen.* Erskine of Linlathen. Selections and biography. By Henry Frank Hornby Henderson. 1899.

Also William Hanna, ed., *Letters of Thomas Erskine of Linlathen*, etc., 2 v., Edin., 1877. Erskine was an influential follower of Campbell.

4032 GUTHRIE. Autobiography of Thomas Guthrie and memoir by his sons. By David K. Guthrie and Charles John Guthrie. 2 v. 1874. Another edn. 1877.

Guthrie joined the Free Church, 1843, and was a promoter of Ragged Schools.

4033 MACLEOD. Memoir of Norman MacLeod D.D. 2 v. 1876. 2nd edn. 1877.

A founder of the Evangelical Alliance, 1847.

4. OTHER DENOMINATIONS

4034 McKERROW (JOHN). History of the Secession Church. Rev. and enl. edn. Glasgow. 1841. Edin. 1848.

See also David Scott, *Annals and statistics of the original Secession Church till its disruption and union with the Free Church of Scotland in 1852*, Edin. [1886].

4035 STRUTHERS (GAVIN). The history of the rise, progress and principles of the Relief Church. Glasgow. 1843.

The Relief Church, founded in 1761, united in 1847 with the main body of the United Secession Church to form the United Presbyterian Church. See Robert Small, *History of the congregations of the United Presbyterian Church from 1733 to 1900*, 2 v., Edin., 1904.

4036 GRUB (GEORGE). An ecclesiastical history of Scotland. 4 v. Edin. 1861.

The standard history of the episcopalians. See also John Skinner, *Annals of the Scottish*

Episcopacy from ... *1788 to* ... *1816 (with a memoir of Bishop Skinner)*, Edin., 1818; William Perry, *The Oxford Movement in Scotland*, Cambridge, 1933; Frederick Goldie, *A short history of the Episcopal Church in Scotland from the Restoration to the present time* etc., 1951. Among biographies see William Walker, *Life of the Rt. Rev. George Gleig* ... *Bishop of Brechin*, etc., Edin., 1878, the same writer's *The life of* ... *Alexander Jolly* ... *Bishop of Moray*, 2nd edn. enl., 1878, and his *The life and times of John Skinner Bishop of Aberdeen*, Aberdeen, 1887.

4037 BELLESHEIM (ALPHONS). History of the Catholic Church of Scotland. Trans. by D. Oswald Hunter Blair. 4 v. Edin. 1887–90.

See also Frederick Odo Blundell, *The Catholic Highlands of Scotland*, 2 v., 1909–17, and Peter Frederick Anson, *The Catholic Church in modern Scotland*, *1560–1937*, 1937. Both works discuss the evolution of individual congregations. Also by Anson, *Underground Catholicism in Scotland 1622–1878*, Montrose, 1970.

4038 YUILLE (GEORGE) *ed*. History of the Baptists in Scotland. Glasgow. [1926.]

4039 ESCOTT (HARRY). A history of Scottish Congregationalism. Glasgow. 1960.

Bibliog. 378–88. See also Alexander Haldane, *Memoirs of the lives of Robert Haldane of Airthrey, and of his brother James Alexander Haldane*, 1852. Both were founders of Congregationalism in Scotland.

H. EDUCATION

1. Schools and Generally

4040 KERR (JOHN). Scottish education, school and university, from early times to 1908. Camb. 1910.

Also John Strong, *A history of secondary education in Scotland*, etc., Oxf., 1909, and Henry Macdonald Knox, *Two hundred and fifty years of Scottish education, 1696–1946*, 1953, bibliog. 242–6, a useful survey of schools only.

4041 CHRISTISON (ALEXANDER). The general diffusion of knowledge one cause of the prosperity of North Britain. Edin. 1802.

A plea that more should be spent on education. Other reforming writings include George Lewis, *Scotland a half-educated nation, both in the quantity and quality of her educational institutions* (Glasgow Educational Assoc. 1), Glasgow, 1834; James Simpson, *The philosophy of education, with its practical application to a system and plan of popular education as a national object*, 2nd edn., Edin., 1836; Robert Buchanan, *The schoolmaster in the Wynds, or, How to educate the masses*, 3rd edn., Glasgow, 1850. For Andrew Bell see John Miller Dow Meiklejohn, *An old educational reformer, Dr. Andrew Bell*, 1881.

4042 RUSK (ROBERT ROBERTSON). The training of teachers in Scotland —an historical review. Edin. 1928.

For David Stow see Fraser (3358).

4043 MASON (JOHN). A history of Scottish experiments in rural education, from the eighteenth century to the present day. (Publications of the Scottish Council for Research in Education. 7.) 1935.

Makes substantial use of the records of the Scottish S.P.C.K. Bibliog. of MSS. and printed sources, 191–5. Two earlier important histories are Alexander Wright, *The history of education and of the old parish schools of Scotland*, Edin., 1898, and James Grant, *History of the burgh and parish schools of Scotland*, 1876, mostly on the period before 1800. The Scottish Council for Research in Education has published a series of local historical studies, J. C. Jessop, *Education in Angus, an historical survey*, etc. (Pubn. 2), 1931; Ian James Simpson, *Education in Aberdeenshire before 1872* (Pubn. 25), 1947; William Boyd, *Education in Ayrshire through seven centuries* (Pubn. 45), 1961; Andrew Bain, *Education in Stirlingshire* (Pubn. 51), 1965. See also James Anderson Russell, *History of education in the Stewartry of Kirkcudbright*, etc., Newton-Stewart, 1951, and R. K. Webb, 'Literacy among the working classes in nineteenth century Scotland', *S.H.R.* 33 (1954), 100–14.

2. UNIVERSITIES

4044 MORGAN (ALEXANDER). Scottish university studies. 1933.

On the growth of the Scottish university system as a whole. See also George Elder Davie, *The democratic intellect; Scotland and her universities in the nineteenth century* (Edin. Univ. Pubns. Hist. Phil. and Econ. 12), Edin. [1961]. See also the *Royal Commission on the state of universities of Scotland*, H.C. 1831 (310) XII. For evidence on Edinburgh see H.C. 1837 [92] XXXV, on Glasgow H.C. 1837 [93] XXXVI and H.C. 1839 [175] XXIX, on St. Andrews, H.C. 1837 [94] XXXVII and H.C. 1846 [717] XXIII, and on Aberdeen H.C. 1837 [95] XXXVIII, H.C. 1837–8 [123] XXXIII and 1839 [176] XXIX.

4045 ABERDEEN. Collections towards a bibliography of the universities of Aberdeen. By Peter John Anderson. (Edin. Bibliog. Soc. Pubns. 8.) Edin. 1907.

See also Sir Robert Sangster Rait, *The universities of Aberdeen, a history*, Aberdeen, 1895, and Peter John Anderson, ed., *Studies in the history and development of the University of Aberdeen* (Aberdeen Univ. Studies, 19), Aberdeen, 1900.

4046 EDINBURGH. A short history of the University of Edinburgh, 1556–1889. By David Bayne Horn. Edin. 1967.

Also David Laing, ed., *A catalogue of the graduates in the faculties of arts, divinity, and law, of the University of Edinburgh, since its foundation*, Edin., 1858; Sir Alexander Grant, *The story of the University of Edinburgh during its first three hundred years*, 2 v., 1884; Alexander Morgan, ed., *University of Edinburgh; charters, statutes and acts of the town council and the senatus, 1583–1858*, with historical intro. by Robert Kerr Hannay, Edin., 1937.

4047 GLASGOW. The University of Glasgow, 1451–1951. A short history. By John Duncan Mackie. Glasgow. 1954.

See also William Innes Addison, ed., *A roll of the graduates of the University of Glasgow from . . . 1727 to . . . 1897; with short biographical notes*, Glasgow, 1898, and the same writer's *The matriculation albums of the University of Glasgow from 1728 to 1858*, Glasgow, 1913, also David Murray, *Memories of the old college of Glasgow* (Glasgow Univ. Pubns. 3), Glasgow, 1927.

4048 ST. ANDREWS. The University of St. Andrews. A short history. By Ronald Gordon Cant. Edinburgh. 1946.

Also James Maitland Anderson ed., *The matriculation roll of the University of St. Andrews, 1747–1897*, 1905, and *Duncan Dewar, a student of St Andrews 100 years ago: his accounts. With a commentary by . . . Sir Peter Redford Lang*, Glasgow, 1926.

XIV

IRELAND

A. BIBLIOGRAPHY, CATALOGUES, AND GUIDES

Including general periodicals. For parliamentary papers after 1833, see Ford and Ford (391), 116–34, a section devoted to Irish papers.

4049 EAGER (ALAN ROBERT). A guide to Irish bibliographical material: being a bibliography of Irish bibliographies and some sources of information. 1964.

A bibliography of 3,803 items. *List of works in the New York Public Library relating to Ireland, the Irish language and literature*, etc., N.Y., 1905, is partly arranged according to subject; [F. J. P. Burgoyne] *Catalogue of the books in the Irish section of the Linen Hall library, Belfast*, Belfast, 1917, is a valuable classified bibliography. [William Shaw Mason], *Bibliotheca Hibernicana: or, A descriptive catalogue of a select Irish library, collected for the Right Hon. Robert Peel*, Dublin, 1823, is a useful small collection of contemporary works, notably on public affairs and topography. Homer L. Calkin, 'The United States government and the Irish; a bibliographical study of research materials in the U.S. national archives', *Irish Historical Studies*, 9 (1954–5), 28–52, concentrates on immigration and consular reports. *A catalogue of the Bradshaw collection of Irish books in the University library, Cambridge*, is primarily concerned with literature, as is Richard Irvine Best, *Bibliography of Irish philology and of printed Irish literature*, Dublin, 1913, continued by his *Bibliography of Irish philology and manuscript literature. Publications 1913–41*, Dublin, 1942. For a short guide see Edith Mary Johnston, *Irish history: a select bibliography*, Historical Assn., 1969. New pubns. are listed in *Irish Publishing Record*, Dublin 1968+.

4050 ELMES (ROSALIND M.). Catalogue of engraved Irish portraits, many in the Joly collection of original drawings. National Library of Ireland. Dublin. [1937.]

4051 VICARS (*Sir* ARTHUR EDWARD). Index to the prerogative wills of Ireland, 1536–1810. Dublin. 1897.

4052 IRISH MANUSCRIPTS COMMISSION, DUBLIN. Catalogue of publications issued and in preparation, 1928–1962. Dublin. 1962.

James Hogan, *The Irish Manuscripts Commission*, Irish Historical series, 1, Cork, 1954, is a general description. The Commission publishes, irregularly, *Analecta Hibernica*, Dublin, 1930+, which reports on private manuscript collections: v. 14, 15, 20 contain surveys of documents in private keeping, 1944–58.

4053 IRISH STATE PAPER OFFICE, DUBLIN.

Contains the correspondence of the Irish central executive (Dublin Castle).

4054 BELFAST PUBLIC LIBRARIES. Bibliographic dept. Finding list of books added to the stock of the Irish and local history collection before 1956. Belf. 1964.

Part I, authors and titles arranged alphabetically; part II, classified subject index.

4055 NATIONAL LIBRARY OF IRELAND, DUBLIN. Annual reports of the council of trustees. Dublin. 1930+.

List major accessions, including manuscripts.

4056 PUBLIC RECORD OFFICE OF IRELAND, DUBLIN. Reports of the Deputy Keeper. Dublin. 1869+.

List accessions. Margaret Griffith, 'A short guide to the Public Record Office of Ireland', *Irish Historical Studies*, 8 (1952–3), 45–58, is indispensable. See also Robert Henry Murray, *A short guide to the principal classes of documents preserved in the Public Record Office*, S.P.C.K. Helps for students of history, 7, 1919, and Herbert Wood, 'The public records of Ireland before and after 1922', *Trans. Roy. Hist. Soc.* 4th ser. 13 (1930), 17–49.

4057 PUBLIC RECORD OFFICE OF NORTHERN IRELAND, BELFAST. Reports of the Deputy Keeper. 1927+.

The volumes for 1924 and 1925 were published by the Northern Ireland Ministry of Finance. The reports list accessions of MSS.

4058 ROYAL IRISH ACADEMY. Transactions (1785–1906). Dublin. 1787–1907. Proceedings. Dublin. 1836+.

Indexed by Robert Lloyd Praeger, *Index to the serial publications of the Royal Irish Academy . . . 1786 to 1906 inclusive*, Dublin, 1912, and *Index . . . 1907–1932*, Dublin, 1934.

4059 ROYAL SOCIETY OF ANTIQUARIES OF IRELAND. Transactions and Journal. Dublin. 1849+.

Founded 1849 as the Kilkenny Archaeological Society. Indexes, v. 1–19 (1849–89), Dublin, 1902; v. 21–40 (1891–1910), Dublin, 1915.

4060 TRINITY COLLEGE, DUBLIN. Catalogue of the manuscripts in the library of Trinity college, Dublin. By Thomas Kingsmill Abbott. Dublin. 1900.

4061 HISTORICAL STUDIES. 1958+.

Papers read to Irish conferences of historians.

4062 IRISH COMMITTEE OF HISTORICAL SCIENCES. Bulletin. Nos. 1–59. Dublin. 1939–48. New series, nos. 60–99. 10 v. Dublin. 1952–65.

Reports of meetings and conferences of Irish historians.

4063 IRISH HISTORICAL STUDIES. The joint journal of the Irish historical society and the Ulster society for Irish historical studies. Dublin. 1938+.

Contains from 1936 annual lists of writings and annual lists of completed theses, on Irish history.

4064 POWER (JOHN). List of Irish periodical publications (chiefly literary) from 1729 to the present time. [1866.]

See also Ernest Reginald McClintock Dix, *Irish bibliography. Tables relating to some Dublin newspapers of the eighteenth century showing what volumes of each are extant and where access can be had to them in Dublin*, Dublin, 1910. The general history of the subject is sketched in Richard Robert Madden, *The history of Irish periodical literature, from the end of the seventeenth to the middle of the nineteenth century*, 2 v., 1867, repr. 1968, which is mostly on the eighteenth century: the MS. notes for the years 1800–40 are in the Public Library, Pearse Street, Dublin. See also A. Albert Campbell, *Belfast newspapers, past and present*, Belfast, 1921, and *N.C.B.E.L.* (2650).

4065 FALLEY (MARGARET DICKSON). Irish and Scotch-Irish ancestral research. A guide to genealogical records, methods and sources in Ireland. 2 v. Evanston, Ill. 1962.

V. 1: Repositories and records; v. 2: Bibliography and family index. See also Brian de Breffny, *Bibliography of Irish family history and genealogy*, Dublin, 1974.

4066 HAYES (RICHARD JAMES) *ed.* Manuscript sources for the history of Irish civilisation. 11 v. Boston. 1965.

4067 MOODY (THEODORE WILLIAM). Irish historiography, 1936–70. 1971.

Chapters by different writers: the 19th-century chapter, 71–102, is by Helen F. Mulvey. See also Queen's University of Belfast, Institute of Irish Studies, *Theses on subjects relating to Ireland presented for higher degrees, 1950–67*, Belfast, 1968.

B. GENERAL HISTORY

4068 LECKY (WILLIAM EDWARD HARTPOLE). A history of Ireland in the eighteenth century. 5 v. 1892. Repr. 1908–12.

Standard. See also James Anthony Froude, *The English in Ireland in the eighteenth century*, 3 v. 1872–4.

4069 PLOWDEN (FRANCIS PETER). An historical review of the state of Ireland, from the invasion of that country under Henry II to its union with Great Britain on the 1st of January, 1801. 2 v. 1803.

Continued by his *History of Ireland from its union with Great Britain in January 1801 to October 1810*, 3 v., Dublin, 1811, which expresses the disappointment of loyal Irish Catholics with the Union. On the period before 1800 see also Caesar Litton Falkiner, *Studies in Irish history and biography, mainly of the eighteenth century*, 1902.

4070 O'CONNOR (*Sir* JAMES). History of Ireland, 1798–1924. 2 v. 1925.

Other general histories are Stephen Lucius Gwynn, *The history of Ireland*, 1923; Edmund Curtis, *A history of Ireland*, 1936, 6th edn. rev., 1950; Patrick Sarsfield O'Hegarty, *A history of Ireland under the Union, 1801 to 1922*, 1952, strongly nationalist in interpretation; Brian Inglis, *The story of Ireland*, 1956; James Camlin Beckett, *A short history of Ireland*, 1952, rev. edn., 1958.

4071 McDOWELL (ROBERT BRENDAN). Irish public opinion, 1750–1800. 1944.

Bibliog. 261–93. Followed by his *Public opinion and government policy in Ireland 1801–46*, 1952, bibliog. 261–92. Both books are more general studies than their titles suggest, and contain excellent bibliographies. On the period to 1829 see also David Alfred Chart, *Ireland from the union to Catholic emancipation, a study of social, economic and administrative conditions 1800–1829*, 1910.

4072 WAKEFIELD (EDWARD). An account of Ireland, statistical and political. 2 v. 1812.

Standard, and very substantial. See also George Barnes, *Statistical account of Ireland founded on historical facts*, Dublin, 1811; César Moreau, *The past and present statistical state of Ireland*, 1827; Gustave de Beaumont, *L'Irlande; sociale, politique, et religieuse*, 2 v., Paris, 1839, trans. and ed. W. C. Taylor, 2 v., 1839; George Lewis Smyth, *Ireland: historical and statistical*, 3 v., 1844–9.

4073 SENIOR (NASSAU WILLIAM). Journals, conversations and essays relating to Ireland. 2 v. 1868.

These begin with Ireland in 1843.

4074 O'BRIEN (RICHARD BARRY). Fifty years of concessions to Ireland, 1831–1881. 2 v. [1883–5.]

Written from the point of view of a Home Ruler. See also George John Shaw Lefevre, Baron Eversley, *Peel and O'Connell: a review of the Irish policy of Parliament from the Act of Union to the death of Sir Robert Peel*, 1887. Godfrey Locker Lampson, *A consideration of the state of Ireland in the nineteenth century*, 1907, is strongly anti-British and contains a mass of material; Emil Strauss, *Irish nationalism and British democracy*, 1951, is a Marxist interpretation. Philip Nicholas Seton Mansergh, *The Irish question, 1840–1921*, 3rd edn., 1975, is a rewritten and enl. version of his *Ireland in the age of reform and revolution*, 1940, which takes account of recent work.

4075 CRONNE (HENRY ALFRED), MOODY (THEODORE WILLIAM) *and* QUINN (DAVID BEERS) *eds*. Essays in British and Irish history in honour of James Eadie Todd. 1949.

4076 CURTIS (EDMUND) *and* McDOWELL (ROBERT BRENDAN) *eds*. Irish historical documents, 1172–1922. 1943.

4077 SENIOR (HEREWARD). Orangeism in Ireland and Britain, 1795–1836. (Studies in Irish history, 2nd ser. 4.) 1966.

4078 BECKETT (JAMES CAMLIN). The making of modern Ireland, 1603–1923. 1966.

Probably the most useful short introduction.

C. POLITICAL AND CONSTITUTIONAL HISTORY

1. THE IRISH PARLIAMENT, 1789–1800

4079 THE JOURNALS OF THE HOUSE OF COMMONS of the kingdom of Ireland, 18th May, 1613 – 2nd August, 1800. With appendix and index. 20 v. Dublin. 1796–1800.

Debates are recorded in *The parliamentary register: or, History of the proceedings and debates of the House of Commons of Ireland* (1781–1800), 20 v., Dublin, 1784–1800. On the Irish parliament see also William Wenman Seward, *Collectanea politica . . . George the III to the present time*, 3 v., Dublin, 1801–4, and James Mullalla, *A view of Irish affairs since . . . 1688 to the close of . . . 1795*, 2 v., Dublin, 1795.

4080 JOURNALS OF THE HOUSE OF LORDS of the kingdom of Ireland from ... 1634 to ... 1800. 8 v. Dublin. 1779–1800.

4081 BALL (JOHN THOMAS). Historical review of the legislative systems operative in Ireland ... (1172–1800). 1888.

On elections see Somerset Richard Lowry-Corry, Earl of Belmore, *Parliamentary memoirs of Fermanagh, county and borough from 1613 to 1885*, Dublin, 1885; Robert Malcolmson, *The Carlow parliamentary roll ... shire ... and ... borough* [to 1872] Dublin, 1872; the Hon. John Meade, *The county of Down election*, 1805, an illustrated account of the contest between the Downshire and Londonderry interests. For modern discussion see J. H. Whyte, 'The influence of the Catholic clergy on elections in nine-teenth-century Ireland', *E.H.R.* 75 (1960), 239–59, and 'Landlord influence at elections in Ireland, 1760–1885', *ibid.* 80 (1965), 740–60; Edith M. Johnston, 'The state of the Irish House of Commons in 1791', *Proceedings of the Royal Irish Academy*, 59 (1957), section C, 1–56; P. Jupp, 'County Down elections, 1783–1831', *Irish Hist. Studies*, 18 (1972–3), 177–206.

4082 BOLTON (GEOFFREY CURGENVEN). The passing of the Irish Act of Union. A study in parliamentary politics. Oxf. 1966.

Sir Charles Coote, *History of the Union of the kingdoms of Great Britain and Ireland*, etc., 1802, concentrates on the debates in the Irish parliament. Thomas Dunbar Ingram, *History of the legislative union of Great Britain and Ireland*, 1887, minimizes British electoral corruption; John Gordon Swift Macneill, *How the Union was carried*, 1887, is written from the opposite point of view. See also Joseph Robert Fisher, *The end of the Irish parliament*, 1911. McDowell, *Irish public opinion* (4071) has a good bibliog. of pamphlets and debates.

4083 BARRINGTON (*Sir* JONAH). Historic memoirs of Ireland, comprising secret records of the national convention, the rebellion, and the union, with delineation of the principal characters connected with these transactions. 1833.

See also the same writer's *Rise and fall of the Irish nation*, Paris, 1833, 2nd edn., Dublin, 1853, and his *Personal sketches of his own times*, 3 v., 1827–32, 3rd edn., 2 v., 1869.

4084 BERESFORD. The correspondence of the Right Hon. John Beresford, illustrative of the last thirty years of the Irish parliament. Ed. by William Beresford. 2 v. 1854.

4085 BURKE. Edmund Burke and Ireland. By Thomas Henry Donald Mahoney. 1960.

Written with access to the Burke MSS. in Sheffield. See also his *Letters, speeches and tracts on Irish affairs*, collected and arranged by Matthew Arnold, 1881.

4086 CHARLEMONT. Memoirs of the political and private life of James Caulfeild, earl of Charlemont. By Francis Hardy. 1810. 2nd edn. 2 v. 1812.

See also the life by Maurice James Craig, *The volunteer earl*, 1948. For Charlemont's correspondence see (77).

4087 CURRAN. The life of the Right Honourable John Philpot Curran, late master of the rolls in Ireland. By his son, William Henry Curran. 2 v. 1819.

See also Thomas Osborne Davis, *The speeches of ... with memoir and historical notices*, Dublin, 1845; William O'Regan, *Memoirs of the legal, literary and political life of ... J. P. Curran*, etc., 1817; Charles Phillips, *Recollections of Curran and some of his cotem-poraries*, 1822.

4088 DAY. Mr. Justice Day of Kerry, 1745–1841: a discursive memoir. By Ella Blanche Day. Exeter. 1938.

Day was a friend of Grattan: this biography gives a picture of opinions among the landed gentry.

4089 GRATTAN. Memoirs of the life and times of the Rt. Hon. Henry Grattan. By his son, Henry Grattan. 5 v. 1839–46.

See also *The speeches of . . . in the Irish, and in the imperial parliament*, 4 v., 1822, and *Miscellaneous works*, both edited by his son, Henry Grattan, 1822. For a short, modern, life see Stephen Lucius Gwynn, *Henry Grattan and his times*, Dublin, 1939. See also 'Forbes letters' by Thomas Joseph Kiernan in *Analecta Hibernica*, 8 (1938), 315–71. Forbes was a political subordinate of Grattan, and prepared material for his speeches.

2. The United Irishmen and the Politics of the 1790s

See Cornwallis (172), Abercromby (954), Moore (990).

4090 SIMMS (SAMUEL). 'A select bibliography of the United Irishmen, 1791–8.' *Irish Historical Studies*, 1 (1938), 158–80.

For Emmet's rebellion see Francis Stephen Bourke, 'The rebellion of 1803; an essay in bibliography', in *Bibliog. Soc. Ireland*, 5 (1933), 13–16.

4091 JACOB (ROSAMOND). The rise of the United Irishmen, 1791–94. 1937.

See also Robert Brendan McDowell, 'The personnel of the Dublin Society of United Irishmen, 1791–4', *Irish Historical Studies* 2 (1941), 12–53, and his 'United Irish plans of parliamentary reform, 1793', *ibid.* 3 (1942), 39–59.

4092 MADDEN (RICHARD ROBERT). The United Irishmen: their lives and times. 7 v. 1842–6. 2nd edn rev. Dublin. 1858.

A classic. See also his *Ireland in '98: sketches of the principal men of the time*, ed. John Bowles Daly, 1888.

4093 MUSGRAVE (*Sir* RICHARD). Memoirs of the different rebellions in Ireland. Dublin. 1801. 3rd edn. 2 v. Dublin. 1802.

A loyalist account, dedicated to Cornwallis: for the opposite view see William James McNeven, *Pieces of Irish history illustrative of the condition of the Catholics of Ireland, of the . . . United Irishmen* etc., N.Y., 1807. The Revd. James Bentley Gordon, *History of the rebellion in Ireland in the year 1798*, etc., 1803, is more impartial. For modern general accounts see Patrick Brendan Bradley, *Bantry Bay; Ireland in the days of Napoleon and Wolfe Tone*, 1931, and the Hon. Thomas Pakenham, *The year of liberty*, etc., 1968, criticized for its ignoring of Ulster. Local aspects are discussed in Edward Hay, *History of the insurrection in . . . Wexford*, etc., Dublin, 1803, and Charles Dickson, *The Wexford rising in 1798*, etc., Tralee, 1956, and his *Revolt in the North: Antrim and Down in 1798*, 1960; also Richard Francis Hayes, *The last invasion of Ireland: when Connacht rose*, Dublin, 1937. On the French expeditions see Georges Servières, 'Épisode de l'expédition (1798) d'Irlande', *Revue historique* 93 (1907), 46–73; on Napper Tandy, Nuala Costello, *Two diaries of the French expedition, 1798* (Analecta Hibernica, 11), Dublin, 1941 and (1117). For a chronological narrative see Lecky (4068).

4094 FITZPATRICK (WILLIAM JOHN). Secret service under Pitt. 2nd edn. enl. 1892.

Summarizes his earlier works on F. Higgins, proprietor of the *Freeman's Journal*, agent of the government. For another informer see *The life of Thomas Reynolds*, by his son, Thomas Reynolds, 2 v., 1839.

4095　McDOWELL (ROBERT BRENDAN). 'The Fitzwilliam episode.' *Irish Historical Studies* 15 (1966–7), 115–30.

4096　COMMITTEE OF SECRECY of the House of Commons. 1st and 2nd reports, H.C. 1801 (39, 71) III.

4097　RIDGEWAY (WILLIAM) A report of the proceedings in cases of high treason, at a court of oyer and terminer under a special commission in the months of August, September, 1803. 2 v. Dublin. 1803.

The trials of Emmet and his associates. For the trials of the United Irish leaders see (566).

4098　BYRNE. Memoirs of Miles Byrne, commander in Wexford and Wicklow, 1798–1800. Ed. Stephen Lucius Gwynn. 2 v. 1907.

4099　DRENNAN. The Drennan letters: being a selection from the correspondence which passed between William Drennan, and his brother-in-law and sister, Samuel and Martha McTier, during the years 1776–1819. Ed. by David Alfred Chart. Belfast. 1931.

4100　DWYER. The life of Michael Dwyer, with some account of his companions. By Charles Dickson. Dublin. 1944.

4101　EMMET. The life and times of Robert Emmet, Esq. By Richard Robert Madden. Dublin. 1847.

See also Thomas Addis Emmet, *The Emmet family, with some incidents relating to Irish history*, New York, 1898; David James O'Donoghue, *Life of Robert Emmet*, Dublin, 1902; John J. Reynolds, *Footprints of Emmet*, Dublin, 1903 (with interesting photographs of places associated with Emmet); Helen Landreth, *The pursuit of Robert Emmet*, Dublin, 1949, uses fresh sources of information.

4102　FITZGERALD. The life and death of Lord Edward Fitzgerald. By Thomas Moore. 2 v. 1831. Later edns., 1875, 1897. (Published under title, *Memoirs of Lord Edward Fitzgerald*.)

See also Patrick Byrne, *Lord Edward Fitzgerald*, Dublin, 1955, and Gerald Campbell, *Edward and Pamela Fitzgerald*, 1904.

4103　McCRACKEN. The life and times of Mary Ann McCracken; 1770–1866: a Belfast panorama. By Mary McNeill. Dublin. 1960.

Wife of Henry Joy McCracken.

4104　HAMILTON ROWAN. Autobiography of Archibald Hamilton Rowan. With additns. and notes by William Hamilton Drummond. Dublin. 1840.

4105　WOLFE TONE. The life of Theobald Wolfe Tone, founder of the United Irish Society . . . with his political writings and fragments of his Diary.

. . . Narratives of his trial, defence before the court martial, and death. Ed. by his son, William Theobald Wolfe Tone. 2 v. Washington. 1826.

Much fuller than the edition published in England, 1827. A full later edition is Richard Barry O'Brien, *The autobiography of Theobald Wolfe Tone*, 2 v., 1893; Frank MacDermot, *Theobald Wolfe Tone; a biographical study*, 1939; M. J. MacManus, 'Bibliography of Theobald Wolfe Tone', *Dublin Magazine*, n.s. 15 (1940), 52–64.

3. CATHOLIC EMANCIPATION

4106 GWYNN (DENIS ROLLESTON). The struggle for Catholic emancipation (1750–1829). 1928.

4107 EDWARDS (ROBERT DUDLEY) *ed.* 'The minute book of the Catholic Committee, 1773–92', *Archivium Hibernicum*, 9 (1942), 3–172.

On the movement in the eighteenth century see also Patrick Rogers, *The Irish volunteers and Catholic emancipation (1778–1793) a neglected phase of Ireland's history*, 1934; Myles Vincent Ronan, 'Archbishop Troy's correspondence with Dublin Castle', *Archivium Hibernicum*, 11 (1944), 1–30.

4108 REYNOLDS (JAMES ALOYSIUS). The Catholic emancipation crisis in Ireland, 1823–29. Yale Hist. Pubns. Miscellany, 60. 1954.

A standard history, with full bibliography, especially of the extensive pamphlet literature. The *Dublin Review* 184 (1929) is a centenary number on emancipation: see particularly George O'Brien, 'O'Connell and the Ireland in which he lived', 182–93, and Basil Whelan, 'Behind the scenes of Catholic emancipation', 295–328. For some preliminaries see P. Jupp, 'Irish parliamentary elections and the influence of the Catholic vote, 1801–20', *Hist. J.* 10 (1967), 183–96. See also (104), (888), (4081).

4109 WYSE (*Sir* THOMAS). Historical sketch of the late Catholic association of Ireland. 2 v. 1829.

Contains important documents, as do the *Proceedings of the Catholic association in Dublin from May 13, 1823 to Feb. 11, 1825*, 1825. See also Amicus Hibernicus, *An authentic review of the principles, measures, and designs of the Catholic association etc.*, 1825, and Bishop James Doyle, *An essay on the Catholic claims etc.*, Dublin, 1826.

4110 SELECT COMMITTEE ON DISTURBANCES. First report of select committee to enquire into the nature and extent of the disturbances which are now subject to the provisions of the Insurrection Act. H.C. 1824 (372) VIII; minutes of evidence, 1825 (20) VII; minutes of Lords' committee, 1825 (200) VII; 1825 (129) VIII, (181, 521) IX; 1826 (40) V.

This massive inquiry was mainly concerned with disorders arising from the Catholic question, though other problems were also investigated: see also William Phelan and Mortimer O'Sullivan, *Digest of evidence . . . [on] . . . state of Ireland, 1824–5*, 1826.

4111 CLONCURRY. Personal recollections of the life and times of Valentine, Lord Cloncurry. By Valentine Browne Lawless, 2nd Baron Cloncurry. Dublin. 1849.

Also William John Fitzpatrick, *Life, times and contemporaries of Lord Cloncurry*, Dublin, 1855.

4112 O'CONNELL. The Liberator. Daniel O'Connell and the Irish party, 1830–1847. By Angus Macintyre. 1965.

His correspondence is being ed. by Maurice Rickard O'Connell, *The correspondence of Daniel O'Connell*, v. 1, 1792–1814, v. 2, 1815–1823, Shannon, 1972: an earlier edn is by William John Fitzpatrick, 2 v., 1888. His son, John O'Connell, ed. *The life and speeches of Daniel O'Connell, M.P.*, 2 v., Dublin, 1846, and *Select Speeches of . . . O'Connell*, 2 v., Dublin, 1854–5; see also his *Recollections and experiences during a parliamentary career from 1833 to 1848*, 2 v., 1849. Mary Frances Cusack, ed., the *Speeches*, 2 v., 1875; her *Life*, 1872, is uncritical but based on MSS. W. Fagan, *The life and times of . . . O'Connell*, 1847, using much contemp. printed material, ends at 1837. There are personal impressions in William Joseph O'Neill Daunt, *Personal recollections of . . . O'Connell*, 1848, and William Forbes Taylor, *A Munster Farmer's reminiscences of O'Connell*, n.d. For O'Connell's beginnings, Arthur Houston, *Daniel O'Connell: his early life and journal, 1795–1802*, 1906, is of value. Other lives are by J. A. Hamilton, 1888, Michael Mac-Donagh, 1903, and Denis Gwynn, 1930. See too M. MacDonagh, *Daniel O'Connell and the story of Catholic Emancipation*, 1929, and *Daniel O'Connell. Nine centenary essays*, ed. by Michael Tierney, Dublin, 1949. See also Lawrence John McCaffrey, *Daniel O'Connell and the repeal year*, Lexington, Univ. of Kentucky Press, 1966.

4113 PLUNKET. Life, letters and speeches of Lord Plunket. By his grandson, the Hon. David Plunket, 2 v. 1867.

Also John Cashel Hoey, ed. (with a memoir) *Speeches of . . . at the Bar and in the Senate*, Dublin, 1856.

4114 SHEIL. Memoirs of the Right Hon. Richard Lalor Sheil. Ed. by William Torrens McCullagh. 2 v. 1855.

See also Sheil's *Sketches legal and political*, ed. with notes by Marmion W. Savage, 2 v. 1855, which are concerned with politics of the eighteen twenties.

4115 WYSE. Sir Thomas Wyse, 1791–1862. The life and career of an educator and diplomat. By James Johnston Auchmuty. 1939.

See also (4276).

4. POLITICS, 1829–51, AND THE REPEAL MOVEMENT

4116 SELECT COMMITTEE ON STATE OF IRELAND. Rep., minutes of evidence, H.C. 1831–2 (677) XVI.

On the tithe agitation. See also (4252).

4117 LARGE (DAVID). 'The House of Lords and Ireland in the age of Peel, 1832–50'. *Irish Historical Studies*, 9 (1955), 367–99.

4118 O'CONNELL (DANIEL). Letters to the reformers of England on the Reform Bill for Ireland. 1832.

4119 NOWLAN (KEVIN BARRY). The politics of repeal, a study in the relations between Great Britain and Ireland, 1841–50. (Studies in Irish history, 2nd ser. 3.) 1964.

Bibliography, with a full discussion of manuscript sources for this period, 232–41. See also (4081).

4120   BRODERICK (JOHN F.). The Holy See and the Irish movement for the repeal of the Union with England, 1829–1847. Analecta Gregoriana, v. 55, series facultatis historiae ecclesiasticae, sectio B, no. 9. Rome. 1951.

4121   LOYAL NATIONAL REPEAL ASSOCIATION OF IRELAND. Reports of the parliamentary committee of the association, 1844–6. Dublin. 1844–6.

See also the Association's *Repeal Prize Essays*, 4 pt., Dublin, 1845. Of an earlier date see William Joseph Battersby, *The fall and rise of Ireland, or The repealer's manual*, 2nd edn., Dublin, 1834. General accounts of the repeal agitation are given by William Joseph O'Neill Daunt, *Ireland and her agitators*, Dublin, 1845, new edn., 1867, and the same writer's *Eighty-five years of Irish history 1800–1885*, 2 v., 1886.

4122   DUFFY (*Sir* CHARLES GAVAN). Young Ireland. A fragment of Irish history, 1840–45. 2 v. Final revision. 1896.

V. 2 was first issued in 1883 as *Four years of Irish history*. See also the same writer's *My life in two hemispheres*, 2 v., 1898. On the disputes within the repeal movement see James Winder Good, 'O'Connell and repeal', in *Dublin Review*, 184 (1929), 218–28; John Henry Whyte, 'Daniel O'Connell and the repeal party', *Irish Hist. Studies*, 2 (1941), 297–315; Randall Clarke, 'The relations between O'Connell and the Young Irelanders', *ibid.* 3 (1942), 18–33, and B. A. Kennedy, 'Sharman Crawford's federal scheme for Ireland', in (4075). For the literary work of Young Ireland see (4207).

4123   THE NATION. Dublin. 1842–8.

The journal of Young Ireland. See Kevin M. McGrath, 'Writers in *the Nation*, 1842–45', *Irish Historical Studies*, 6 (1948–9), 189–223.

4124   BUTT. The road of excess. By Terence de Vere White. Dublin. [1964.]

4125   DAVIS. Thomas Davis, the memoirs of an Irish patriot, 1840–1846. By Sir Charles Gavan Duffy. 1890.

See also Theodore William Moody, *Thomas Davis, 1840–45*, 1945, which discusses *The Nation* at some length; M. J. MacManus, *Thomas Davis and Young Ireland*, Dublin, 1945, essays by various hands: and review article by Kevin Barry Nowlan, 'Writings in connection with Thomas Davis and the Young Ireland centenary, 1945', *Irish Hist. Studies*, 5 (1945), 265–72.

4126   DOHENY (MICHAEL) The felon's track, or history of the attempted outbreak in Ireland, embracing the leading events in the Irish struggle from the year 1843 to the close of 1848. Original edition with D'Arcy M'Gee's narrative of 1848. Ed. with preface by Arthur Griffith. 1914.

Also Denis Rolleston Gwynn, *Young Ireland and 1848*, Cork, and Oxf., 1949; Revd. Philip Fitzgerald, *Personal recollections of the insurrection at Ballingarry in July, 1848*, Dublin, 1861.

4127   LALOR. James Fintan Lalor, patriot and political essayist. Collected writings. Ed. by L. Fogarty. 2nd edn. Dublin. 1947.

4128   MEAGHER. Meagher. By Robert G. Athearn. University of Colorado Studies. Series in history, no. 1. 1949.

See also Arthur Griffith, *Meagher of the Sword etc.*, 1916, Meagher's speeches, recollections, and a narrative of the 1848 rising; and Denis Rolleston Gwynn, *Thomas Francis Meagher*, Dublin, 1962, a useful summary of the present state of knowledge on events in 1848.

4129 MITCHEL. Life of John Mitchel. By William Dillon. 2 v. 1888.

See also Mitchel's *Jail Journal*, ed. by Arthur Griffith, Dublin, 1913, a diary of transportation to Tasmania, and a powerful piece of anti-British writing. See also Lefroy (4141) and Hogan (4222).

5. Law and Administration

4130 McDOWELL (ROBERT BRENDAN). The Irish administration, 1801–1914. Studies in Irish history, 2nd series, 2. 1964.

On the period before 1800 see Edith Mary Johnston, *Great Britain and Ireland, 1760–1800: a study in political administration*, St. Andrews university pubns., 55, 1963; also Sir John Thomas Gilbert, ed., *Documents relating to Ireland (1795–1804): official account of secret service money*, Dublin, 1893. Lists of officials, M.P.s etc., are given in Rowley Lascelles, *Liber Munerum publicorum Hiberniae (1152–1827); or, The establishments of Ireland*, Record Commission, 2 v., 1824–30; see also James L. J. Hughes, ed., *Patentee officers in Ireland, 1173–1826* (Irish MSS. Commission), Dublin, 1960, which serves as index to parts of Lascelles. Richard Barry O'Brien, *Dublin Castle and the Irish people*, 2nd edn., 1912, is a general account of the executive. See also Robert Shipkey, 'Problems of Irish patronage during the chief secretaryship of Peel, 1812–18', *Hist. J.* 10 (1967), 41–56.

4131 MacDONAGH (MICHAEL) *the Younger*. The Viceroy's post-bag. Correspondence hitherto unpublished of the earl of Hardwicke, first lord lieutenant of Ireland after the Union. 1904.

On the office of chief secretary see J. L. J. Hughes, 'The chief secretaries in Ireland, 1566–1921', *Irish Historical Studies*, 8 (1952–3), 59–72. On Peel, chief secretary, 1812–18, see Gash (200). On the office of under-secretary see (Lady) Isabella Augusta Gregory, ed., *Mr. Gregory's letter-box, 1813–30*, 1898, and John Ferguson MacLennan, *Memoir of Thomas Drummond, under-secretary to the Lord Lieutenant of Ireland, 1835–40*, and Richard Barry O'Brien, *Life and Letters of Thomas Drummond*, 1889.

4132 INGLIS (BRIAN). The freedom of the press in Ireland, 1784–1841. (Studies in Irish history, 6) 1954.

See also (3497).

4133 MacANALLY (*Sir* HENRY WILLIAM WATSON). The Irish militia, 1793–1816: a social and military study. 1949.

4134 BROEKER (GALEN). Rural disorder and police reform in Ireland, 1812–36. (Studies in Irish history. 2nd ser. 8.) 1970.

Also Robert Curtis, *The history of the Royal Irish Constabulary*, 1869, 2nd edn., 1871.

4135 KIERNAN (THOMAS JOSEPH). History of the financial administration of Ireland to 1817. 1930.

See also Windham Thomas Wyndham Quin, 4th earl of Dunraven, *An historical study of the finances of Ireland before the Union and after, etc.*, 1912. Sir Henry Cavendish, Bart., *A statement of the public accounts of Ireland*, 1791, gives figures of the yield of taxes, pensions, etc., The *Select committee on the public income and expenditure of Ireland*, 1st rep. H.C. 1810–11 (262) V; 2nd H.C. 1812 (376) V; 3rd 1812–13 (309) VI; and 4th 1814–15 (214) VI, is an investigation of Irish finance at the Union. The *Royal Commission on fees, gratuities, perquisites and emoluments etc. in public offices in Ireland*, 14 reports 1806–14, is a vast administrative inquiry which concentrated on the machinery of revenue collection, and was followed by the *Royal Commission ... into the collection and management of the revenue arising in Ireland*, 22 reports, 1822–30, listed in McDowell (4130), 305–7. See also Hibernicus, (pseud.) *A letter to the Rt. Hon. Sir John Newport ... on ... the appointment of a parliamentary commission ... into the abuses ... of the revenue in Ireland*, Dublin, 1821, and John Finlay, *Letters addressed to the Irish government on local taxes, the Irish collieries etc.*, Dublin, 1822, which argues that Ireland is over-taxed.

4136   IRISH GRAND JURY PRESENTMENTS. Reports from select committee. H.C. 1814–15 (283) VI; 1816 (374, 435) IX; 1819 (353) VII; 1822 (359, 413) VII; 1826–27 (555) III.

The grand juries voted local taxes (the county cess). The *Select committee on the survey and valuation of Ireland*, H.C. 1824 (445, 360) VIII proposed a revaluation, carried out after 1826. The papers relating to this are now in the Irish Public Record Office. For later parliamentary papers see Ford and Ford (391).

4137   NUN (RICHARD) *and* WALSH (JOHN EDWARD). The powers and duties of justices of the peace in Ireland, and of constables as connected therewith. 2 v. 2nd edn. Dublin. 1844.

4138   WEBB (JOHN JOSEPH) Municipal government in Ireland, medieval and modern. Dublin. 1918.

Very slight in treatment of this period. See also Peter Gale, *An inquiry into the ancient corporate system of Ireland*, etc. 1834. The reports of the *Royal Commission on municipal corporations in Ireland* are listed by Ford and Ford (391), 117–18.

4139   MAXWELL (LESLIE F.) *and* MAXWELL (WILLIAM HAROLD). Irish law to 1956. Sweet and Maxwell's legal bibliography of the British Commonwealth of Nations, v. 4. 2nd edn. 1957.

4140   THE STATUTES AT LARGE, passed in the parliaments held in Ireland: from the third year of Edward the second, A.D. 1310, to the fortieth year of George the third, A.D. 1800. 20 v. Dublin. 1786–1801.

The revised edn. ed. William Fitzpatrick Cullinan, 1885, does not include statutes repealed after 1800. For the years after 1800 see Andrew Newton Oulton, *Index to the statutes at present in force in, or affecting, Ireland, from the year 1310–1836*, continued by annual supplements, 1837–49. See also a short summary, Isaac Saunders Leadam, *Coercive measures in Ireland, 1830–80* [1881]. For reports of state trials see (556).

4141   SMYTH (CONSTANTINE JOSEPH). Chronicle of the law officers of Ireland containing lists of the lord chancellors and keepers of the great seal, masters of the rolls ... from the earliest period. Dublin. 1839.

See also James Roderick O'Flanagan, *The lives of the lord chancellors and keepers of the great seal of Ireland, from the earliest times to the reign of Queen Victoria*, 2 v., 1870; Francis Elrington Ball, *The judges in Ireland, 1221–1921*, 2 v., 1926; Thomas Lefroy, *Memoir of chief justice Lefroy, by his son*, etc., Dublin, 1871; Edward Blackburne, *Life of the Rt. Hon. Francis Blackburne, late lord chancellor of Ireland*, 1874.

4142 McDOWELL (ROBERT BRENDAN) 'The Irish courts of law, 1801–1914.' *Irish Historical Studies* 10 (1956–7), 363–91.

See also the reports of the *Royal Commission respecting Irish courts of justice*, 21 reports, 1817–31 (listed in McDowell (4130), p. 306), which investigated temporal and ecclesiastical courts.

D. ECONOMIC HISTORY

1. BIBLIOGRAPHY

4143 PRENDEVILLE (P. L.). 'A select bibliography of Irish economic history: Pt. 2, The seventeenth and eighteenth centuries.' *Econ. H. R.* 3 (1931–2), 402–416. Pt. 3. 'The nineteenth century'. *Ibid.* 4 (1932), 81–90.

See also Robert Denis Collison Black, 'A selective bibliography of economic writings by members of Trinity College, Dublin', *Hermathena*, 66 (1945), 55–68. Extensive bibliographies, particularly of the very large pamphlet literature on Irish economic problems, can be found in Black (4147), Connell (4187), and O'Brien (4144).

2. GENERAL

4144 CULLEN (LOUIS MICHAEL). Anglo-Irish trade, 1660–1800. Manchester. 1968.

See also the essays by different writers which he ed. in *The formation of the Irish economy*, Cork, 1969. These revise the nationalist interpretation found in George Augustine Thomas O'Brien, *The economic history of Ireland in the eighteenth century*, Dublin, 1918, and *The economic history of Ireland from the Union to the Famine*, 1921.

4145 GREEN (EDWARD RODNEY RICHEY) The Lagan valley, 1800–1850; a local history of the industrial revolution. 1949.

Bibliog. 164–76.

4146 FREEMAN (THOMAS WALTER). Pre-famine Ireland: a study in historical geography. Manchester. 1957.

Lists Ordnance Survey maps, with dates of publication.

4147 BLACK (ROBERT DENIS COLLISON). Economic thought and the Irish question, 1817–1870. Cambridge. 1960.

Bibliog. 249–92. On the period before 1800 see his 'Theory and policy in Anglo-Irish trade relations, 1775–1800', *Journal of the Statistical Society of Ireland*, 18 (1949–50), 312–26, which discusses economic arguments for and against the Union.

4148 CONNELL (KENNETH HUGH). Irish peasant society. Four historical essays. Oxf. 1968.

On illicit distilling, illegitimacy before the famine, Catholic marriage, and ether drinking in Ulster.

4149 BERRY (HENRY FITZPATRICK). A history of the Royal Dublin society. 1915.

Founded 1731, to promote husbandry and other 'useful arts'. A more recent account, which does not claim to supersede Berry, is Terence de Vere White, *The story of the Royal Dublin Society*, Tralee [1955]. See also *A bibliography of the publications of the Royal Dublin Society from its foundation . . . together with a list of bibliographic material*, 2nd edn., Dublin, 1955.

4150 STATISTICAL AND SOCIAL INQUIRY SOCIETY OF IRELAND. Centenary volume, 1847–1947; with a history of the Society by R. D. Collison Black, and indexes to the Transactions of the Society. Dublin. 1947.

Supersedes Samuel Shannon Millin, *Historical memoirs of the . . . Society*, Dublin, 1920.

4151 BELFAST NATURAL HISTORY AND PHILOSOPHICAL SOCIETY. Centenary volume, 1821–1921. Ed. by Arthur Deane. Belfast. 1924.

4152 CRUMPE (SAMUEL). An essay on the best means of providing employment for the people. To which was adjudged the prize proposed by the Royal Irish Academy. Dublin. 1793.

Among the many contemporary surveys of the Irish economy see the Revd. Dr. Clarke, *The political, commercial and civil state of Ireland. Being an appendix to 'Union or separation'* (by the Revd. Josiah Tucker), etc., 1799, both arguing in favour of free trade; Thomas Newenham, *A view of the natural, political, and commercial circumstances of Ireland*, 1809; John Christian Curwen, *Observations on the state of Ireland*, etc., 2 v., 1818, a very substantial work; 'Hibernicus' (*pseud.* of E. G. MacDonnell), *Practical views and suggestions on the present condition and permanent improvement of Ireland*, Dublin, 1823; William Graydon, *Reflections on the state of Ireland in the nineteenth century*, etc., 2nd edn., 1825; James Ebenezer Bicheno, *Ireland and its economy; being the result of observations made in a tour . . . in the autumn of 1829*, 1830.

4153 SELECT COMMITTEE ON THE LABOURING POOR: H.C. 1823 (561) VI.

A general investigation of the economic situation, as is the *Report of the Select Committee on the state of Ireland*, H.C. 1830 (589, 654, 655, 667) VII. See also (4116), (4191).

4154 LEWIS (GEORGE CORNEWALL). On local disturbances in Ireland; and on the Irish church question. 1836.

4155 BUTT (ISAAC). A voice for Ireland: the famine in the land. What has been done and what is to be done. 1847.

See also the same writer's *Protection to home industry; some cases of its advantages considered*, Dublin, 1846. Butt, at that time a moderately conservative opponent of O'Connell, argues in both these pamphlets for industrial protection.

4156 FOSTER (THOMAS CAMPBELL). Letters on the condition of the people of Ireland. 1846. 2nd edn. 1847.

Discusses the need for capital for agricultural improvement. See also Emmet Larkin, 'Economic growth, capital investment and the Roman Catholic church in nineteenth-century Ireland', *A.H.R.* 72 (1967), 852–84.

3. Currency and Banking

4157 DILLON (MALCOLM). The history and development of banking in Ireland from the earliest times to the present day. 1889.

See also James William Gilbart, *The history of banking in Ireland*, 1836; John Salmon,

'Early Irish bankers and banking', pt. 2, *New Ireland Review*, November, 1899; Frederick George Hall, *The Bank of Ireland, 1783–1946*, Dublin and Oxford, 1949, bibliog. 409–22; Eoin O'Kelly, *The old private banks and bankers of Munster, part I, Bankers of Cork and Limerick cities, Cork*, 1959.

4158 FETTER (FRANK WHITSON). The Irish pound, 1797–1826. A reprint of the report of the committee of 1804 of the House of Commons on the condition of the Irish currency, and an introduction. 1955.

Bibliog. of contemporary works on currency and banking, 125–8. The original report is in H.C. 1803–4 (86) IV; reprinted in H.C. 1810 (28) III and 1826 (407) V. See also Henry Brooke Parnell, *Observations upon the state of the currency in Ireland*, 3rd edn., 1804; and George O'Brien, 'The last years of the Irish currency', *Economic History*, 1927, 249–58. See also the evidence of Daniel Wakefield to the Bullion Committee of 1810 (1430).

4159 MURRAY (ALICE EFFIE). A history of the commercial and financial relations between England and Ireland from the period of the Restoration. 1903.

4. INDUSTRY AND MANUFACTURES

4160 WALLACE (THOMAS). An essay on the manufactures of Ireland, in which is considered to what manufactures her natural advantages are best suited, and what are the best means of improving such manufactures. Dublin. 1798.

4161 KANE (ROBERT). The industrial resources of Ireland. Dublin. 1844.

Chapters on different industries, mineral resources, water power.

4162 GILL (CONRAD). The rise of the Irish linen industry. Oxf. 1925.

See also the Irish chapters of John Horner (1540). S. M. Stephenson, 'On the linen and hempen manufactures in the province of Ulster', *Select papers of the Belfast Literary Society*, Belfast, 1808, describes the locations and technology of the industry; William Charley, *Flax and its products in Ireland*, Belfast, 1862, is a systematic general history. See also the *Proceedings* of the Trustees of the linen and hempen manufactures of Ireland, Dublin, 1784–1828, mostly on the industry in the south, and the Select Committees on the linen trade of Ireland, Reports, H.C. 1822 (560) VII, 1825 (411, 463) V. On both linen and cotton see Hugh McCall, *Our staple manufactures*, Belfast, 1855, 2nd edn. under the title, *Ireland and her staple manufactures*, Belfast, 1870.

4163 ROYAL COMMISSION ON HAND LOOM WEAVERS. Report. Pt. III. West Riding, Ireland, H.C. 1840 (43–II) XXIII.

4164 MONAGHAN (JOHN J.). 'The rise and fall of the Belfast cotton industry.' *Irish Historical Studies*, 3 (1942), 1–17.

4165 WEBB (JOHN JOSEPH). Industrial Dublin since 1698, and the silk industry in Ireland. Dublin. 1913.

4166 LYNCH (PATRICK) *and* VAIZEY (JOHN). Guinness' brewery in the Irish economy, 1759–1876. Cambridge. 1960.

See also Kenneth Hugh Connell, 'Illicit distillation; an Irish peasant industry', *Historical Studies*, III (1961), 58–92.

4167 GRIFFITH (*Sir* RICHARD JOHN, *Bart.*) Geological and mining report on the Leinster coal district. Dublin. 1814.

The author was Inspector-General of H.M. royal mines in Ireland. He also wrote *Geological and mining survey of the Connaught coal district of Ireland*, Dublin, 1818, and *Geological and mining surveys of the coal districts of Tyrone and Antrim*, etc., Dublin, 1829.

4168 WILKINSON (GEORGE). Practical geology and ancient architecture of Ireland. 1845.

A practical description of building materials in use in different parts of Ireland.

5. COMMUNICATIONS

4169 GRIFFITH (RICHARD). Thoughts and facts relating to the increase of agriculture, manufactures, and commerce, by the extension of inland navigation in Ireland. Dublin. 1795.

4170 HERRING (IVOR JACK). 'Ulster roads on the eve of the railway age, *c.* 1800–1840.' *Irish Historical Studies*, ii (1941), 160–88.

See also Mrs. M. A. O'Connell, *Charles Bianconi, a biography, 1786–1875*, 1878, and Molly O'Connell Bianconi and S. J. Watson, *Bianconi, king of the Irish roads*, Dublin, 1962. Bianconi was a very large-scale mail-coach proprietor.

4171 CONROY (JOHN CHARLES). A history of railways in Ireland. 1928.

See also reports of *Commissioners . . . [on] . . . a general system of railways for Ireland*, 1st report, H.C. 1837 (75) XXXIII, 2nd report, 1837–8 (145) XXXV. See also Joseph Lee, 'The provision of capital for early Irish railways', *Irish Historical Studies*, 16 (1968), 33–63.

4172 ANDERSON (ERNEST B.). Sailing ships of Ireland; being a record of Irish sailing ships of the nineteenth century. Dublin. 1951.

See also Sholto Cooke, *The Maiden City and the western ocean: a history of the shipping trade between Londonderry and North America in the nineteenth century*, Dublin. [1960.]

4173 MARMION (ANTHONY). The ancient and modern history of the maritime ports of Ireland. 1855.

4174 McCUTCHEON (WILLIAM ALAN). The canals of the north of Ireland. 1965.

Also Vincent Thomas Hyginn Delany and Dorothy Ruth Delany, *The canals of the south of Ireland*, Newton Abbot, 1966.

6. AGRICULTURE AND FISHING

4175 COMMISSION ON THE NATURE AND EXTENT OF THE BOGS OF IRELAND. Reports 1–4, H.C. 1810 (365) X, 1810–11 (96) VI, 1813–14 (130–131) VI.

Reports of select committees on this subject in H.C. 1810 (148) IV, and H.C. 1835 (329, 573) XX. See also Robert Monteath, *A new and easy system of draining and reclaiming the bogs and marshes of Ireland*, 1829, and Kenneth Hugh Connell, 'The colonization of waste land in Ireland, 1780–1845', *Economic History Review*, 2nd series, 3 (1950–1951), 44–71.

4176 SELECT COMMITTEE ON CORN TRADE BETWEEN GREAT BRITAIN AND IRELAND. H.C. 1801–2 (36) II.

4177 TRIMMER (JOSHUA KIRBY). A brief inquiry into the present state of agriculture in the southern parts of Ireland. 1809.

Continued by his *Further observations on the present state of agriculture and condition of the lower classes*, 1812.

4178 SALAMAN (REDCLIFFE NATHAN). The influence of the potato on the course of Irish history. Dublin. [1944.]

The author discusses Irish potatoes at greater length in his general study, *The history and social influence of the potato*, Camb., 1949. See also Thomas Patrick O'Neill, 'The scientific investigation of the failure of the potato crop in Ireland, 1845–6', in *Irish Historical Studies*, 5 (1946–7), 123–38, and P. M. Austin Bourke, 'The scientific investigation of the potato blight in 1845–6', *ibid.* 13 (1962–63), 26–32. Jasper W. Rogers, *The potato truck system of Ireland*, 2nd edn., 1847, is an attack on the payment of farming debts by potatoes.

4179 O'DONOVAN (JOHN) Economic history of live stock in Ireland. Dublin and Cork, 1940.

4180 PETTY-FITZMAURICE (HENRY WILLIAM EDMUND) *6th marquis of Lansdowne.* Glanerought and the Petty-Fitzmaurices. Oxford. 1937.

An account of the running of a large estate: critical of William Steuart Trench, *Realities of Irish life*, 1868. Trench was agent for the Lansdowne and Bath estates among others. Other documented accounts of landed estates, a subject which has been little studied, are Ada Kathleen Longfield, ed., *The Shapland Carew papers*, Dublin, 1946, and John Barry, ed., 'The Duke of Devonshire's Irish estates, 1794–7, reports by Henry Bowman, agent', *Analecta Hibernica*, 22 (1960), 269–327. See also O. Robinson, 'The London companies as progressive landlords in nineteenth century Ireland', *Econ. H.R.*, 2nd ser. 15 (1962–3), 13–18; David Large, 'The wealth of the greater Irish landowners, 1750–1815', *Irish Historical Studies*, 15 (1966–7), 407–37; William Alexander Maguire, *The Downshire Estates in Ireland. The management of Irish landed estates in the early nineteenth century*, Oxf., 1972, a substantial study, and W. A. Maguire, ed., *Letters of a great Irish landlord: a selection from the estate correspondence of the third Marquess of Downshire, 1809–45*, H.M.S.O., Belfast, 1974. See also John H. Gebbie, ed., *An introduction to the Abercorn letters (as relating to Ireland, 1736–1816)*, Omagh, 1972.

4181 BLACKER (WILLIAM). An essay on the improvement to be made in the cultivation of small farms. Dublin. 1834.

Practical advice by a land agent to tenants on the estates of the Earl of Gosford and Colonel Close. William Blacker's *Prize essay . . . on the management of landed property in Ireland*, Dublin, 1837, is a classic general treatise in favour of small farms. P. Knight, *Erris, in the 'Irish highlands', and the 'Atlantic railway'*, Dublin, 1836, is a detailed account of improvements on two estates in Co. Mayo.

4182 FERGUSON (WILLIAM DWYER) *and* VANCE (ANDREW). The tenure and improvement of land in Ireland considered with reference to the relation of landlord and tenant and tenant-right. Dublin. 1851.

A law text-book. See also George Sigerson, *History of land tenures and land classes of Ireland*, 1871; Richard Barry O'Brien, *The parliamentary history of the Irish land question from 1829–1869*, 1880; Moritz Julius Bonn, *Die englische Kolonization in Irland*, 2 v., Berlin, 1916; John Edwin Pomfret, *The struggle for land in Ireland 1800–1923*. Princeton, 1930.

4183 CONNER (WILLIAM). The true political economy of Ireland: or Rack-rent the one great cause of all her evils: with its remedy. Dublin. 1835.

See also his *Two letters to the editor of the Times on the rack-rent oppression of Ireland*, Dublin, 1846, and John Wiggins, *The 'monster' misery of Ireland*, 1844, who also argues in favour of the extension of tenant right.

4184 DEVON COMMISSION on law and practice in respect to the occupation of land in Ireland. H.C. 1845 [605, 606] XIX, [616] XX, [657] XXI, [672, 673] XXII.

Contains a mass of information on pre-famine agriculture. See also *Digest of evidence* by John Pitt Kennedy, secretary to the commission, 2 v., Dublin, 1847. The commission proposed a tenant right limited to compensation for improvements. On the Ulster Tenant Right association of 1846 see Brian A. Kennedy 'Sharman Crawford on Ulster tenant right, 1846', *Irish Historical Studies*, 13 (1962–63), 246–53, and Nowlan (4119). On agriculture see P. M. Austin Bourke, 'The agricultural statistics of the 1841 census of Ireland. A critical review', *Econ. H.R.* 2nd ser. 18 (1965–6), 376–91.

4185 HANCOCK (WILLIAM NEILSON). Impediments to the prosperity of Ireland. 1850.

On the need for tenant right after the famine, by the professor of economics at Trinity College, Dublin; see also George Poulett Scrope, 'The Irish difficulty and how it must be met', *Westminster and Foreign Quarterly Review* (Jan. 1849) and [Henry Grant], *Ireland's Hour*, 1850, both criticizing the Encumbered Estates Act. See also the notable discussion in Mill's *Principles* (1785). William Bullock Webster, *Ireland, considered as a field for investment or residence*, Dublin, 1852, describes a rise in land values since the passing of the act.

4186 BRABAZON (WALLOP). The deep sea and coast fisheries of Ireland, with suggestions for the working of a fishing company. 1848.

Describes different techniques and gives a history of the fishing bounties.

7. POPULATION

4187 CONNELL (KENNETH HUGH). The population of Ireland, 1750–1845. Oxf. 1950.

Bibliog. 276–86. Also his 'Some unsettled problems in English and Irish population history', *Irish Historical Studies*, 7 (1950–1), 225–34. But see also the criticism of Michael Drake, 'Marriage and population growth in Ireland, 1750–1845', *Econ. H.R.*, 2nd ser. 16 (1963–4), 307–13. An important contemporary authority is Thomas Newenham, *A statistical and historical enquiry into the progress and magnitude of the population of Ireland*, 1805, reviewed by Malthus in *Edinburgh Review*, 12 (1808), 336–55. See also S. H. Cousens, 'Regional death rates in Ireland during the great famine from 1846 to 1851', *Population studies*, 14 (1960–1), 55–74, and Peter Froggatt, 'The census in Ireland of 1813–15', *Irish Historical Studies*, 14 (1964–5), 227–35.

8. FAMINE

4188 EDWARDS (ROBERT DUDLEY) *and* **WILLIAMS (THOMAS DESMOND)** *eds.* The great famine: studies in Irish history, 1845–52. Dublin. 1956.

Bibliog. 499–509. A series of fairly general essays. Standard accounts are John O'Rourke, *The history of the great Irish famine of 1847, with notices of earlier Irish famines*, Dublin

1875, and William Patrick O'Brien, *The great famine in Ireland*, etc., 1896. Cecil Woodham-Smith, *The great hunger*, 1962, is a recent popular account.

4189 TREVELYAN (*Sir* CHARLES EDWARD, *Bart.*) The Irish crisis; being a narrative of the measures for the relief of the distress caused by the great Irish famine of 1846–7. 1848. 2nd edn. 1880.

The standard account of official relief measures, much criticized then and since: see George Poulett Scrope, *The Irish relief measures, past and future*, 1848. Voluntary relief schemes are described in the *Transactions of the Central Relief Committee of the Society of Friends . . . in 1846 and 1847*, Dublin, 1852; Jonathan Pim, *The condition and prospects of Ireland*, Dublin, 1848, by a member of the Friends' Relief Society; William Bennett, *Narrative of a recent journey of six weeks in Ireland*, etc., 1847, a journey on behalf of the Ladies' Relief Committee of the Friends; James Hack Tuke, *A visit to Connaught in the autumn of 1847*, 1847; Robert Alexander Shafto Adair, Baron Waveney, *The winter of 1846–7 in Antrim, with remarks on outdoor relief and colonization*, 1847; Robert Bennet Forbes, *The voyage of the Jamestown on her errand of mercy*, Boston, 1847.

9. EMIGRATION

4190 ADAMS (WILLIAM FORBES). Ireland and Irish emigration to the New World from 1815 to the Famine. New Haven. 1932.

On English emigration policy see reports of the Select Committee on emigration (1742), criticized by Michael Thomas Sadler, *Ireland; its evils, and their remedies; being a refutation of the errors of the Emigration Committee*, etc., 1828. On other aspects of Irish emigration see Barbara M. Kerr, 'Irish seasonal migration to Great Britain, 1800–38', *Irish Historical Studies*, 3 (1942), 365–80; Oliver MacDonagh, 'The Irish Catholic clergy and emigration during the great famine', *Irish Historical Studies*, 5 (1946–7), 287–302; Eilish Ellis, 'State-aided emigration schemes from crown estates in Ireland, c. 1850', *Analecta Hibernica*, 22 (1960), 331–94.

10. POOR LAW AND PUBLIC HEALTH

4191 SELECT COMMITTEE ON CONTAGIOUS FEVER. 1st and 2nd reports, H.C. 1818 (285, 359) VII.

Followed by the *Select Committee . . . as to disease and condition of the labouring poor in Ireland*, H.C. 1819 (314, 409), VIII. See also Francis Rogan, *Observations on the condition of the middle and lower classes in the north of Ireland, as it tends to promote the diffusion of contagious fever, with the history and treatment of the late epidemic disorder*, 1819, a very careful analysis of the spread of disease, as is William Harty, *An historic sketch . . . of the contagious fever epidemic in Ireland during the years 1817, 1818, and 1819*, Dublin, 1820. Francis Barker and John Cheyne, *An account of the . . . fever lately epidemical in Ireland* etc., 2 v., 1821.

4192 NICHOLLS (*Sir* GEORGE). A history of the Irish poor law, in connexion with the condition of the people. 1856.

An early writer who emphasized the need for a new poor law in Ireland was William Parker, *A plan for the general improvement of the state of the poor of Ireland*, Cork, 1816, and *A plea for the poor and industrious*, Cork, 1819. Two major investigations were launched in the 1830s, *Commissioners for inquiring into the conditions of the poorer classes in Ireland*, H.C. 1835 (369) XXXII, 1836 [35–43] XXX–XXXIV, 1837 (68) XXXI, LI. These recommended a programme of public works. Sir George Nicholls submitted three reports, H.C. 1837 (69) LI, 1837–8 (104, 126) XXXVIII, recommending the introduction of the English poor law to Ireland. John Revans, *Evils of the state of Ireland*, 2nd edn. [1837], summarizes the work of the first commission, by its secretary; See also John Pitt Kennedy, *Analysis of projects proposed for the relief of the poor of Ireland*, etc. 1837, and for bibliography and theoretical discussions see Black (4147). George Poulett Scrope, *Letters to Lord John Russell on the expedience of enlarging the Irish poor law to the full extent of the poor law of England*, 1846, argues for fixity of tenure and the English poor law.

II. LABOUR HISTORY

4193 RYAN (WILLIAM PATRICK) Irish labour movement from the 'twenties to our own day. 1919.

Jesse Dunsmore Clarkson, *Labour and nationalism in Ireland*, N.Y., 1925, has a chapter on Dublin and the combination acts.

E. SOCIAL HISTORY

I. BIOGRAPHICAL COLLECTIONS

4194 CRONE (JOHN SMYTH). A concise dictionary of Irish biography. Dublin. 1928. Rev. and enl. edn. Dublin. 1937.

Contains about 3,000 five-line sketches. More specialized is Alfred John Webb, *A compendium of Irish biography: comprising sketches of distinguished Irishmen, and of eminent persons connected with Ireland by office or by their writings*, Dublin, 1878.

4195 HAYES (RICHARD FRANCIS). Biographical dictionary of Irishmen in France. Dublin. 1949.

Bibliog. 319–26.

4196 LECKY (WILLIAM EDWARD HARTPOLE). The leaders of public opinion in Ireland. 1861, New edns. rev. and enl. 2 v. 1871. 1903. 1912.

2. LITERARY AND INTELLECTUAL HISTORY

For Moore see (2744).

4197 BROWN (STEPHEN JAMES MEREDITH). Guide to books on Ireland: pt. 1 prose literature, poetry, music, plays. Dublin. 1912.

No more parts published, but see the same writer's *Ireland in fiction, a guide to historical novels, tales, romances and folklore*, 1916.

4198 FLANAGAN (THOMAS JAMES BONNER). Irish novelists, 1800–1850. Columbia. 1959.

Bibliog. 343–51. Horatio Sheafe Krans, *Irish life in Irish fiction*, Columbia Univ. Studies, 1903, has a wider range than Flanagan.

4199 CARLETON. The life of William Carleton, being his autobiography and letters and an account of his life and writings, from the point at which the autobiography breaks off. By David J. O'Donoghue. 2 v. 1896.

With a bibliography of Carleton's writings.

4200 MARIA EDGEWORTH. Memoirs, begun by himself and concluded by his daughter, Maria Edgeworth. By Richard Lovell Edgeworth. 2 v. 1820. 3rd edn. 1844.

The main source; may be supplemented by Harriet Jessie Butler and Harold Edgeworth, eds., *The black book of Edgeworthstown and other Edgeworth memoirs*, 1585–1817, 1927. The first important life was by Augustus John Cuthbert Hare, *The life and letters of Maria Edgeworth*, 2 v., 1894, and the most recent, Marilyn Speers Butler, *Maria Edgeworth, a literary biography*, Oxf., 1972. See also Michael C. Hurst, *Maria Edgeworth and the public scene: Intellect, fine feeling and landlordism in the age of reform*, 1969, and Christina Colvin, *Maria Edgeworth: letters from England*, Oxf., 1971.

4201 LEVER. The life of Charles Lever. By William John Fitzpatrick. 2 v. 1879.

Also Edmund Downey, *Charles Lever: his life in his letters*, 2 v., 1906. Lever, the novelist, was editor of the *Dublin University Magazine*, 1842–5.

4202 BELFAST LITERARY SOCIETY, 1801–1901; historical sketch with memoirs of some distinguished members. Belfast. 1902.

4203 DUBLIN UNIVERSITY MAGAZINE. Dublin. 1833–77.

See Michael Thomas Harvey Sadler, 'Dublin University Magazine, its history, contents, and bibliography', *Bibliog. Soc. Ireland*, 5 (1938), 59–81.

4204 FOX (CHARLOTTE MILLIGAN). Annals of the Irish harpers. 1911.

Describes the beginning of the revival of Irish music in Belfast, *c.* 1791. See Charlotte Brooke (leader of the movement), *Reliques of Irish poetry . . . by Miss Brooke*, Dublin, 1789, 2nd edn., with a memoir by Aaron Crossley Seymour, 2 v., Dublin, 1816.

4205 McCARTNEY (DONALD). 'The writing of history in Ireland, 1800–30.' *Irish Hist. Studies*, 10 (1957), 347–62.

4206 MADDEN (RICHARD ROBERT). Literary remains of the United Irishmen of 1798, and selections from other popular lyrics of their times. Dublin. 1887.

See also Thomas Crofton Croker, *Songs illustrating the French invasions of Ireland*, Percy Society, v. 21, 1847.

4207 DUFFY (*Sir* CHARLES GAVAN). The ballad poetry of Ireland. 3rd edn. Dublin. 1845.

See also Michael Joseph Barry, ed., *The songs of Ireland*, Dublin, 1845, and Denis Florence McCarthy, *A book of Irish ballads*, Dublin, 1846. Both are pub. in Duffy's Library of Ireland, an organ of the Young Ireland movement.

4208 HAYES (EDWARD) *ed.* Ballads of Ireland. 2 v. 1855.

See also Thomas Crofton Croker, *The popular songs of Ireland etc.*, 1839. Croker's collection of current songs was attacked by Duffy as misrepresenting the 'national minstrelsy of Ireland'. A modern collection is Colm O'Lochlainn, *Irish street ballads*, new edn., 1960.

4209 PETRIE (GEORGE). The ecclesiastical architecture of Ireland. 1845.

A landmark in Irish archaeology.

3. Social Life and Conditions

4210 O'SUILLEABHAIN (SÉAN) A handbook of Irish folklore. Dublin.
1942.

By the archivist to the Irish folklore commission.

4211 CLARK (WILLIAM SMITH). The Irish stage in the county towns,
1720–1800. Oxford. 1965.

4212 BOWDEN (CHARLES TOPHAM). A tour through Ireland. Dublin.
1791.

A description of educated Dublin life; see also Anne Plumptre, *Narrative of a residence
in Ireland during the summer of 1814 and that of 1815,* 1817. On the life of the nobility
and gentry see *Lady Morgan's memoirs* (2227); Mrs. Alice Clark (2135), the memoirs of
an absentee family; Anthony Dymoke Powell, *Barnard letters, 1778–1824,* 1928;
Richard Warwick Bond, ed., *The Marlay letters, 1778–1820,* 1937. See also Lansdowne
(4180), and Day (4088).

4213 LEADBEATER (MARY). The Leadbeater papers. V. 1. The annals of
Ballitore with a memoir of the author. V. 2. Letters and correspondence. 1862.

Country life down to 1818. See also Mary Leadbeater, *Cottage dialogues among the Irish
peasantry,* with notes and preface by Maria Edgeworth, 1811. According to Miss Edgeworth 'It contains an exact representation of the *manner of being* of the lower Irish and
a literal transcript of their language'. For peasant life see also the novels of William
Carleton (4199), himself the product of a hedge school.

4214 [MAXWELL (WILLIAM HAMILTON)]. Wild sports of the west, with
legendary tales and local sketches. 2 v. Illustrated. 1832.

4215 SULLIVAN (ALEXANDER MARTIN). New Ireland. 6th edn. 1878.

Reminiscences of Irish country life *c.* 1800–40.

4216 EVANS (EMYR ESTYN). Irish folk ways. 1957.

A detailed investigation of building and furnishing of cabins, farming implements and
methods, etc., of the Irish peasant.

4217 RYAN (DESMOND). The sword of light: from the four masters to
Douglas Hyde, 1636–1938. 1939.

A study of the decay and revival of the Irish language.

4218 O'SULLIVAN (HUMPHREY). The diary of Humphrey O'Sullivan.
Ed. and trans. by Rev. Michael McGrath. Irish Texts Society. 1936–7.

The diary of a country schoolmaster, written in Gaelic.

4. The Irish Emigrant

Works on emigration policy are listed under economic history (1740–52), and
(4190): those below are concerned with the Irish overseas. For the Irish in
Scotland see Handley (3910).

4219 HIGGINS (PATRICK). The Irish brigades on the continent. Irish library, v. 7. 1908.

Also Mrs. Morgan John (Mary Anne) O'Connell, *The last colonel of the Irish Brigade, Count O'Connell . . . 1745–1833*, 2 v., 1892; and Richard Francis Hayes, *Ireland and Irishmen in the French revolution*, 1932, and (4195).

4220 LEWIS (*Sir* GEORGE CORNEWALL). Report on the state of the Irish poor in Great Britain. Being appendix G to 1st report of Irish poor law enquiry. H.C. 1836 (39) XXXIV.

A general but informative account is given in John Denvir, *The Irish in Britain from the earliest times to the fall and death of Parnell*, 1892.

4221 WITTKE (CARL FREDERICK). The Irish in America. Baton Rouge, Louisiana. 1956.

Bibliog. 295–306. See also Edward Everett Hale, the elder, *Letters on Irish emigration*, Boston, Mass., 1852; John Francis Maguire, *The Irish in America*, 1868; Oscar Handlin, *Boston's immigrants, 1790–1865: a study in acculturation*, Harvard Historical Studies, 50, Cambridge, Mass., 1941.

4222 HOGAN (JAMES FRANCIS). The Irish in Australia. London. 1887.

Patrick Francis Moran, *History of the Catholic church in Australasia*, etc., Sydney [1897], is largely concerned with Irish emigrants. Thomas Joseph Kiernan, *The Irish exiles in Australia*, 1954, and Revd. John H. Cullen, *Young Ireland in exile, the story of the men of '48 in Tasmania*, Dublin and Cork, 1928.

F. LOCAL HISTORY

I. TOPOGRAPHICAL AND GENERAL

4223 O'NEILL (THOMAS PATRICK). Sources of Irish local history. 1st series. Dublin. 1958.

A general survey of a wide variety of material. Other useful guides are John P. Anderson, *The Book of British topography* (3515), and Rosalind M. Elmes, *Catalogue of Irish topographical prints and original drawings*, Dublin, 1943.

4224 FORDHAM (HERBERT GEORGE). 'The road-books and itineraries of Ireland, 1647–1850.' *Bibliog. Soc. of Ireland.* V. 2, no. 4. Dublin. 1923.

Two informative contemporary guide-books are James Fraser, *Guide through Ireland*, etc., Dublin, 1838, and Samuel Leigh, *New pocket road-book of Ireland*, ed. C. C. Hamilton, 1827, which lists mail-coaches.

4225 ORDNANCE SURVEY. Catalogue of the maps and plans and other publications of the Ordnance Survey of Ireland. 1862.

For dates of particular maps see Freeman (4146). See also Daniel Augustus Beaufort, the elder, *Memoir of a map of Ireland, illustrating the topography of that kingdom*, 1792. See J. H. Andrews, *History in the Ordnance map: an introduction for Irish readers*, Dublin, 1974, and *A paper landscape. The Ordnance Survey in nineteenth-century Ireland*, Oxf., 1975.

4226 LEWIS (SAMUEL). A topographical dictionary of Ireland, comprising the several counties, boroughs, corporate, market, and post towns, parishes, and villages, with historical and statistical descriptions. 2 v. 1837.

Also *The Parliamentary gazetteer of Ireland*, 3 v., 1846.

4227 FRASER (ROBERT). Statistical survey of the county of Wexford. 1807.

See also Hely Dutton, *A statistical and agricultural survey of the county of Galway*, 1824. The remaining volumes in the series, are listed by Connell (4187). See also Desmond Clarke, 'The Dublin Society's statistical surveys' in *An Leabharlann*, 15 (1957), 47–54.

4228 MASON (WILLIAM SHAW). A statistical account or parochial survey of Ireland drawn up from the communications of the clergy. 3 v. Dublin. 1814–19.

Mason was secretary to the Board of public records, and produced a survey on the Scottish model. His *Survey, valuation and census of the Barony of Portnehinch, compiled in the year 1819*, Dublin, 1821, was 'a model of a royal statistical survey of Ireland', never carried out. See also Edward Ledwich, *A statistical account of the parish of Aghaboe*, Dublin, 1796.

4229 HALL (SAMUEL CARTER) *and* HALL (ANNA MARIA). Ireland, its scenery, character. 3 v. 1841–3.

A valuable description immediately before the famine, illustrated. Other tours include George Cooper, *Letters on the Irish nation written on a visit to that kingdom in the autumn of 1799*, 1800; John O'Driscol, *Views of Ireland, moral, political, and religious*, 2 v., 1823; Henry David Inglis, *Ireland in 1834; a journey throughout Ireland*, 3rd edn., 2 v., 1835; Hon. Baptist Wriothesley Noel, *Notes of a short tour through the midland counties of Ireland in the summer of 1836*, etc., 1837; Johann Georg Kohl, *Reisen in Irland*, 2 v., Dresden and Leipzig, 1843, translated as *Ireland, Scotland, England*, etc., 1844; Knut Jong Bohn Clement, *Reisen in Irland*, etc., Kiel, 1845; and Tocqueville (1872). Other titles, in this very large class, are to be found in Anderson (3515), Maxwell (Pargellis and Medley, 3569), O'Brien (4144), and Black (4147).

4230 ULSTER JOURNAL OF ARCHAEOLOGY. V. 1–9, 1853–62; 2nd ser., v. 1–17, 1894–1910; Belfast. 1853–1911. 3rd ser., v. 1+, 1938+.

Ramsay Colles, *The history of Ulster from the earliest times to the present day*, 2 v., 1919–20, tends to describe national events as they affected Ulster.

4231 MOODY (THEODORE WILLIAM) *and* BECKETT (JAMES CAMLIN) *eds.* Ulster since 1800: a political and economic survey. 1954.

4232 GUINNESS (DESMOND) *and* RYAN (WILLIAM). Irish houses and castles. [1971].

The Ulster Architectural Heritage Society lists historic buildings, groups of buildings, and areas of architectural importance.

2. INDIVIDUAL COUNTIES AND TOWNS

Counties are arranged alphabetically and towns under the appropriate county. A full local history bibliography is given in Eager (4049), and by William MacArthur, 'Bibliography of histories of Irish counties and towns', *Notes and*

Queries, ser. 11, v. 11–12, ser. 12, v. 1–2, 1915–16. The entries below include only a selection.

4233 ANTRIM. BELFAST. STEVENSON (NORAGH). Belfast before 1820. A bibliography of printed material. Belfast. 1967.

Contains 618 entries. The standard contemporary history is by George Benn, *A history of the town of Belfast . . . to the close of the eighteenth century*, 2 v., Belfast, 1877, 1880, and his *History of the town of Belfast with an accurate account of its former and present state*, Belfast, 1823. For political history, William Bruce and Henry Joy, *Belfast politics*, etc., Belfast, 1794, and Henry Joy, *Historical collections relative to the town of Belfast . . . to the Union*, 1817, are of interest. James Adair Pilson, *History of . . . Belfast and annals of the county Antrim*, Belfast, 1846, contains much contemporary economic information. See also Andrew George Malcolm, *The sanitary state of Belfast*, etc., Belfast, 1852; Sir David John Owen, *A short history of the port of Belfast*, Belfast, 1917 and his *A history of Belfast*, 1921. The earliest directory of Belfast and Lisburn is by Thomas Bradshaw, Belfast, 1819: see also *Martin's Belfast directory*, 1839+, and the *Post Office directory*, 1843+. Charles Edward Bainbridge Brett, *Buildings of Belfast, 1700–1914* [1967], and (4151), (4274–5). Ian Budge and Cornelius O'Leary, *Belfast: approach to crisis. A study of Belfast politics, 1613–1970*, 1973.

4234 —— LISBURN. BAYLY (HENRY). A topographical and historical account of Lisburn. Belfast. 1834.

4235 CORK. CORK HISTORICAL AND ARCHAEOLOGICAL SOCIETY JOURNAL. 1892+.

Contains much local and regional 19th-century material: indexed by Denis J. O'Donoghue, 1892–1940, Cork, 1943, and 1941–60, Cork, 1964; local bibliog. in v. 48, 1943. For Cork city see John Windele, *Historical and descriptive notices of the city of Cork and its vicinity*, Cork, 1840, new edn. rev. James Coleman, Cork, 1910, and William O'Sullivan, *The economic history of Cork city . . . to the act of union*, 1937. James S. Donnelly, Jr., *The land and the people of nineteenth-century Cork: the local economy and the land question* (Studies in Irish History, 2nd ser. 9), 1975, relates mainly to the county.

4236 DONEGAL. DONEGAL ANNUAL. V. 2+. 1948+.

V. 1 has title *County Donegal Historical Society Journal*, and contains a county bibliog. by J. C. T. MacDonagh and Edward MacIntyre, 152–64.

4237 DOWN. KNOX (ALEXANDER). A history of the county of Down from the most remote period to the present day. Dublin. 1875.

Also John Stevenson, *Two centuries of life in Down, 1600–1800*, Belfast, 1920.

4238 DUBLIN (county). BALL (FRANCIS ELRINGTON). A history of the county Dublin: the people, parishes and antiquities from the earliest times to the close of the eighteenth century. 6 v. Dublin. 1902–20.

See also John D'Alton, *The history of the county of Dublin*, Dublin, 1838.

4239 —— (city). CRAIG (MAURICE JAMES). Dublin, 1660–1860. 1962.

An admirable general survey, with much on architecture; bibliog. 342–52. John Hooper Harvey, though shorter, is similar in scope, *Dublin; a study in environment*, 1949. James Malton, *Picturesque and descriptive view of the city of Dublin . . . in 1791*, 1792–9, is notable for its plates. See also *The Dublin Historical Record*, v. 1+, 1938+, pub. by the Old Dublin Society. A standard general history is John Thomas Gilbert, *A history of the city of Dublin*, 3 v., Dublin, 1854–9, and his *Calendar of the ancient records of Dublin, in the possession of the municipal corporation*, etc., 17 v., Dublin, 1889–1916 (v. 15–17, covering 1797–1822, are ed. by Lady Gilbert). Also on administration see the *Reports of the Select Committee on Dublin local taxation*, H.C. 1822 (394) VII, 1823 (356, 549) VI, 1824 (475) VIII, and 1825 (329) V. See also James Whitelaw, *Essay on the population of Dublin, being the result of an actual survey taken in 1798 . . . to which is added the general return . . . in 1804*, Dublin, 1805, important since the MS. survey was destroyed in the Dublin Public Record Office; and Thomas Percy Claude Kirkpatrick and Henry Jellett, *The book of the Rotunda hospital*, etc., 1913. The earliest directory is *Wilson's Dublin directory*, 1751–1837. The *Post Office directory* dates from 1832. Later, *Thom's Irish almanac and official directory*, Dublin, 1844–80, with its statistical introductions, became the most important. See Joseph Dennan, 'The first hundred years of the Dublin directory', *Proc. Irish Bibliog. Soc.*, v. I, no. 7 (1920), 89–108. See also Maxwell (P & M 3569).

4240 GALWAY. A bibliography of county Galway. Galway county library. By Mary Kavanagh. 1965.

The *Galway archaeological and historical society journal*, Galway, 1900+, contains 19th-century material.

4241 KILKENNY. COLEMAN (JAMES). 'Bibliography of the counties of Kilkenny, Carlow and Wicklow.' *Waterford and S.E. Ireland Archaeol. Soc. Journal*, 11 (1907–8), 126–33.

4242 LIMERICK. LENIHAN (MAURICE). Limerick; its history and antiquities, ecclesiastical, civil and military. Dublin. 1866.

See also Patrick Fitzgerald and John James M'Gregor, *The history, topography and antiquities of the county and city of Limerick*, 2 v., Dublin, 1826–7 (v. 2 is topographical).

4243 LOUTH. LOUTH ARCHAEOLOGICAL SOCIETY JOURNAL. Dundalk. 1904+.

Has articles on the 19th century. V. 2 (1908) has a bibliog. of Louth, Meath, Westmeath, and Longford by James Coleman, 24–6.

4244 SLIGO. WOOD–MARTIN (WILLIAM GREGORY). History of Sligo, county and town, from 1688 to the present time. Dublin. 1892.

V. 3 of his *History of Sligo*.

4245 TIPPERARY. GLEESON (*Rev.* JOHN). History of the Ely O'Carroll territory, or ancient Ormond situated in North Tipperary, and north-western King's County, Ireland. Dublin. 1915.

Includes the Famine period.

4246 WATERFORD. WATERFORD AND SOUTH-EAST OF IRELAND ARCHAEOLOGICAL SOCIETY JOURNAL. V. 1–19. Waterford. 1894–1920.

Bibliog. of Waterford, Tipperary, and Wexford in v. 10 (1907), 323–8, by James Coleman.

4247 WEXFORD. KENNEDY (PATRICK). The banks of the Boro: a chronicle of the county of Wexford. 1867.

Description of country life at the beginning of the 19th century.

G. RELIGIOUS HISTORY

1. General

4248 KILLEN (WILLIAM DOOL). The ecclesiastical history of Ireland. From the earliest period to the present times. 2 v. 1875.

See also M. J. Brenan, *An ecclesiastical history of Ireland, from the introduction of Christianity into that country, to the year 1829*, 2 v., Dublin, 1829; new and rev. edn., Dublin, 1864; and James Godkin, *Ireland and her churches*, 1867, a survey written at the time of disestablishment.

2. United Church of England and Ireland

4249 PHILLIPS (WALTER ALISON) *ed.* History of the church of Ireland from the earliest times to the present day. 3 v. 1933–4.

Other general histories are Richard Mant, *History of the Church of Ireland, from the reformation to . . . 1801*, 2 v., 1840, 2nd edn., 1841, and John Thomas Ball, *The reformed church of Ireland (1537–1886)*, 1886, 2nd edn. rev., 1890.

4250 COTTON (HENRY). Fasti ecclesiae Hibernicae; the succession of the prelates and members of the cathedral bodies in Ireland. 5 v. (and Suppl). Dublin. 1845–78.

See also Hugh Jackson Lawlor, *The fasti of St. Patrick's, Dublin*, Dundalk, 1930; and James Blennerhassett Leslie, *Armagh clergy and parishes*, Dundalk, 1911, and similar works on the diocese of Clogher, 1929, Ossory, 1933, Ferns, 1936, Derry, Enniskillen, 1937, Raphoe, Enniskillen, 1940, and, with Henry Biddall Swanzy, *Biographical succession lists of the clergy of the diocese of Down*, Enniskillen, 1936.

4251 PAPERS RELATING TO THE ESTABLISHED CHURCH IN IRELAND. H.C. 1807 (78) V, 1820 (93) I, 1823 (135, 241) XVI.

4252 SELECT COMMITTEE CONCERNING TITHES IN IRELAND. 1st and 2nd reports. H.C. 1831–2 (177, 508) XXI, H.C. 1831–2 (271, 663) XXII.

The MS. tithe applotment books are now in the Dublin P.R.O. and are described, in *Analecta Hibernica* 10 (1941), 295–8, by Robert C. Simington.

4253 COMMISSIONERS OF ECCLESIASTICAL ENQUIRY. H.C. 1831 (93) IX, H.C. 1833 (762) XXI, H.C. 1834 (406, 589) XXIII, H.C. 1836 (246) XXV, H.C. 1837 (500) XXI.

4254 SELECT COMMITTEE ON PREROGATIVE AND ECCLESIASTICAL COURTS. H.C. 1837 (412) VI.

See also McDowell (4130).

4255 MANT (WALTER). Memoirs of the Rt. Rev. Richard Mant, bishop of Down and Connor and of Dromore with an introductory sketch of the history of those dioceses from the beginning of the seventeenth century. Dublin. 1857.

See also Revd. Edward Berens, *A memoir of the life of Bishop Mant*, 1849. Other biographies of Anglican bishops are Arthur Henry William Kenney, *The works of the most reverend William Magee . . . with a memoir of his life*, 1842 (Magee was archbishop of Dublin, 1822–31), and William John Fitzpatrick, *Memoirs of Richard Whately, archbishop of Dublin*, etc., 2 v., 1864, and Elizabeth Whately (707). Whately was archbishop of Dublin 1831–63.

4256 McWALTER (J. G.). The Irish reformation movement in its religious, social, and political aspects. Dublin, 1852.

On Anglican missions to Roman Catholics see also Mrs. A. M. Thompson, *A brief account of . . . the change in religious opinion now taking place in Dingle, and the west of the county of Kerry, Ireland*, 1846; Robert Jocelyn, 3rd earl of Roden, *Progress of the Reformation in Ireland*, 1851; Alexander Dallas, *Story of the Irish church missions*, pt. 1 (no more published) [1867]; Joseph D'Arcy Sirr, *Memoir of . . . Power le Poer Trench, last Archbishop of Tuam*, Dublin, 1845; William Urwick, *Biographic sketches of the late James Digges la Touche*, ed. William Urwick jr., Dublin, 1868; Mrs. Anne Briscoe Dallas, *Incidents in the life and ministry of the Rev. A. R. C. Dallas*, 1871; Mrs. Hamilton Madden, *Memoir of the Rt. Rev. Robert Daly, D.D., lord bishop of Cashel*, Edinburgh, 1875; and *Edward Nangle: the apostle of Achill; a memoir and a history*, by Henry Seddall, 1884. See also (4278).

4257 BROOKE (RICHARD SINCLAIR). Recollections of the Irish church. 1877.

Reminiscences of church life. For the life of the parochial clergy see Revd. Samuel Madden, *Memoir of the life of the Rev. Peter Roe*, etc., Dublin, 1842.

3. ROMAN CATHOLICS

Works on Catholic emancipation are listed at (4106–15).

4258 IRISH CATHOLIC HISTORICAL COMMITTEE. Proceedings. Dublin. 1955+.

Discusses extensively the sources for Irish ecclesiastical history: see 'A handlist of Irish diocesan histories' (1957), 31–37, and Thomas Patrick O'Neill 'Sources for a history of Catholic life in Ireland, 1780–1850' (1959), 19–23.

4259 IRISH ECCLESIASTICAL RECORD. v. 1+. Dublin. 1864+.

Contains historical as well as contemporary material; indexed 1865–1922 by Thomas J. Shaw, 1925.

4260 ARCHIVIUM HIBERNICUM; or, Irish historical records. (Catholic Record Society of Ireland.) Maynooth. 1912+.

4261 COLLECTANEA HIBERNICA. Sources for Irish history. 1958+.

4262 [BATTERSBY (WILLIAM JOSEPH)]. A complete Catholic directory, almanack, and registry. Dublin. 1836+.

A useful, but incomplete, list of Catholic parish registers in existence in 1914 is to be found in *Archivium Hibernicum*, v. 3 (1914), 366–406.

4263 BELLESHEIM (ALPHONS). Geschichte der katholischen Kirche in Irland von der Einführung des Christenthums bis auf die Gegenwart. 3 v. Mainz. 1890–1.

See also James MacCaffrey, *History of the Catholic church in the nineteenth century, 1789–1908*, 2 v., Dublin, 1909, which has much on Ireland.

4264　MacKENNA (THEOBALD). Thoughts on the civil condition and relations of the Roman Catholic clergy, religion, and people in Ireland. Dublin. 1805.

On Catholic disabilities and the payment of the clergy see Revd. John Milner, Bishop of Castabala, *An inquiry into certain vulgar opinions concerning the Catholic inhabitants of Ireland*, etc., 1808; Henry Brooke Parnell, *A history of the penal laws against the Irish Catholics; from the year 1689 to the union*, 1808, 4th edn., 1825; David O. Croly, *An essay . . . on ecclesiastical finance, as regards the Roman Catholic church in Ireland*, Cork, 1834.

4265　MORAN (PATRICK FRANCIS). Spicilegium ossoriense; being a collection of original letters and papers illustrative of the history of the Irish church from the reformation to the year 1800. 3 v. Dublin. 1874–84.

4266　COGAN (ANTHONY). The diocese of Meath, ancient and modern. 3 v. Dublin 1867–70.

A valuable source for the parochial life of the church, printing accounts of episcopal visitations and many letters.

4267　HEALY (JOHN). Maynooth college; its centenary history. Dublin. 1895.

See also Patrick J. Hamill, 'Maynooth students and ordinations, 1795–1895: index', in *Irish Eccl. Record*, ser. 5, 108 (1967), 353–70.

4267 A　MacHALE (JOHN, *Archbishop of Tuam*). The letters of the Most Rev. John MacHale D.D. Dublin. 1847. Another edn. Dublin. 1888.

The most important figure in the Catholic hierarchy: for his life see Bernard O'Reilly, *John MacHale, archbishop of Tuam, his life, times and correspondence*, 2 v., N.Y., 1890. For other leading figures see Revd. George Crolly, *Life of the Most Rev. Dr. Crolly, Archbishop of Armagh and Primate of Ireland*, Dublin, 1851; William John Fitzpatrick, *The life, times, and correspondence of the Rt. Rev. Dr. Doyle, Bishop of Kildare and Leighlin*, 2 v., Dublin, 1861, another edn. 1880; Thomas D'Arcy McGee, *Life of the Right Reverend Edward Maginn*, N.Y., 1863; Peadar Macsuibhne, *Paul Cullen and his contemporaries, with their letters from 1820 to 1902*, 3 v., Naas, Co. Kildare, 1961–5.

4268　MAGUIRE (JOHN FRANCIS). Father Mathew; a biography. 1863. 2nd edn. 1864. Other edns. 1865, 1882.

The classic life of the temperance reformer. See also Revd. Patrick Rogers, *Father Theobald Mathew, apostle of temperance*, Dublin [1943], N.Y. and Toronto, 1945. Other notable figures in Irish Catholic social and educational work include Myles Vincent Ronan, *An apostle of Catholic Dublin, Father Henry Young*, Dublin, 1944 (there is also a life by Lady Georgiana Fullerton, 1874); J. D. Fitzpatrick, *Edmund Rice, founder and first superior general of the brothers of the Christian schools of Ireland*, (Christian Brothers), Dublin, 1945; Roland Burke Savage, *Catherine McAuley, the first Sister of Mercy*, Dublin, 1949. The Christian Brothers were founded 1808 and the Sisters of Mercy, in Dublin, 1827.

4. OTHER DENOMINATIONS

4269　REID (JAMES SEATON). History of the Presbyterian church in Ireland, comprising the civil history of the province of Ulster . . . continued to the present time by William Dool Killen. 3 v. Edin. 1834–53.

See also his *History of the congregations of the Presbyterian church in Ireland*, with intro.

and notes by W. D. Killen, Belfast, 1886, giving names and dates of ministers; Josias Leslie Porter, *The life and times of Henry Cooke*, etc., 1871, on the leading opponent of Arianism in Ulster; A. Albert Campbell, *Irish Presybyterian magazines, past and present, a bibliography*, Belfast, 1919.

4270 CROOKSHANK (CHARLES HENRY). History of Methodism in Ireland. 3 v. Belfast. 1885–8.

See also William Reilly, *A memorial of the ministerial life of Gideon Ouseley, Irish missionary*, etc., 1847.

4271 GRUBB (ISABEL). The Quakers in Ireland, 1654–1900. 1927.

Bibliog. 149–52.

H. EDUCATION

4272 AUCHMUTY (JAMES JOHNSTON). Irish education: a historical survey. 1937.

A short outline account. James Godkin, *Education in Ireland, its history, institutions, systems, statistics, and progress from the earliest times to the present*, Dublin, 1862, is a valuable survey of the national education system and the various voluntary societies.

4273 MAXWELL (CONSTANTIA). A history of Trinity College, Dublin, 1591–1892. Dublin. 1946.

Bibliog. 281–9. Also George Dames Burtchaell and Thomas Ulick Sadleir, eds., *Alumni Dublinensis; a register of students, graduates, professors, and provosts of Trinity college, in the University of Dublin* [1593–1846], 1924, new edn. to 1860, Dublin, 1935; also Robert Brendan McDowell and David Allardyce Webb, 'Trinity College in the age of revolution and reform (1794–1831)', *Hermathena*, 72 (1948), 3–19, and Robert Brendan McDowell, 'Trinity College, Dublin in 1830', pt. 1–4, *Hermathena*, 75 (1950), 1–23; 76 (1950), 1–24; 78 (1951), 22–31; 81 (1953), 63–77.

4274 JAMIESON (JOHN). The history of the Royal Belfast Academical Institution, 1810–1960. Belfast. 1959.

4275 ANDERSON (JOHN). History of the Belfast library and society for promoting knowledge, commonly known as the Linen Hall library. Belfast. 1888.

4276 WYSE (THOMAS). Education reform; or the necessity of a national system of education. V. 1 (no more published). 1836.

Wyse introduced the bill for national education in Ireland in the Commons in 1836; see also Winifrede M. Wyse, *Notes on education reform in Ireland . . . compiled from speeches, letters, etc. . . . of the Rt. Hon. Sir Thomas Wyse, K.C.B.*, Waterford, 1901; Richard P. J. Batterberry, 'Sir Thomas Wyse and mixed education', *Irish Eccl. Record*, 53 (1939), 561–76; 54 (1939), 21–34.

4277 O'RAIFEARTAIGH (T). 'Mixed education and the synod of Ulster, 1831–40'. *Irish Historical Studies*, 9 (1954–5), 281–99.

Also Richard P. J. Batterberry, 'The synod of Ulster and the national board', *Irish Eccl. Record*, 5th ser. 56 (1940), 548–61; 58 (1941), 16–28; 59 (1942), 61–73.

4278 MOORE (HENRY KINGSMILL). An unwritten chapter in the history of education: being the history of the Society for the Education of the Poor of Ireland, generally known as the Kildare Place Society, 1811–31. 1904.

The most famous voluntary Protestant society. See also Herbert McLachlan, 'The Irish academies', *Transactions of Unitarian Hist. Society*, 6 (1936), 91–102. Robert Steven, *An enquiry into the abuses of the chartered schools in Ireland, with remarks upon the education of the lower classes*, etc., 1817, discusses the lack of Protestant education in Gaelic, which is also discussed in Henry Joseph Monck Mason, *History of the origin and progress of the Irish Society, established for . . . the education of the native Irish, through the medium of their own language*, Dublin, 1844. The *Annual reports of Commissioners of Education in Ireland, 1814–31*, report on private endowed schools, controlled by commissioners under an Act of 1813.

4279 BRENAN (MARTIN). Schools of Kildare and Leighlin, A.D. 1775–1835. Dublin, 1935.

Patrick John Dowling, *The hedge schools of Ireland*, Dublin and Cork, [1935].

4280 COMMISSIONERS OF IRISH EDUCATION ENQUIRY, 1826. 1st rep., mins. of evidence, H.C. 1825 (400) XII, 2nd, H.C. 1826–7 (12) XII, 3rd–9th, H.C. 1826–7 XIII.

A major source of information on Irish school education: appendix to 2nd report lists all the schools in Ireland. For the public inquiries of the eighteen-thirties see Ford and Ford (391), 130; also William Tighe Hamilton, *Abstract of the first report of the commissioners on religious and other instruction in Ireland*, 1835.

XV

THE BRITISH EMPIRE

A. BIBLIOGRAPHY

4281 ROYAL COMMONWEALTH (*formerly* Royal Empire) SOCIETY LIBRARY. Subject catalogue . . . by Percy Evans Lewin. 4 v. 1930–7.

V. 1: The British empire generally, and Africa. 1930.

V. 2: The commonwealth of Australia, the dominion of New Zealand, the South Pacific, general voyages and travels, and Arctic and Antarctic regions, 1931.

V. 3: The dominion of Canada and its provinces, the dominion of Newfoundland, the West Indies, and colonial America. 1932.

V. 4: The mediterranean colonies, the Middle East, Indian Empire, Burma, Ceylon, British Malaya, East Indian islands, and the Far East. 1937.

Biographical catalogue of the Library . . . comp. by Donald H. Simpson, 1961, lists all biographical material acquired up to autumn 1960 and periodical articles to the end of 1959. *Subject catalogue* . . ., 7 v., Boston, 1971, is a printing from the catalogue cards, including accessions to March 1971. There is no up-to-date listing in print of the important collection held by the Colonial Office Library, but see *Catalogue of the printed books . . . index of authors*, 1896, and *Supplement*, 1907.

4282 HEWITT (ARTHUR REGINALD). Guide to resources for Commonwealth studies in London, Oxford and Cambridge, with bibliographical and other information. 1957.

A most valuable general account of available printed and MS. material. For documents in the P.R.O. see *The Records of the Colonial and Dominion Offices*, Public Record Office handbooks no. 3, comp. Ralph Bernard Pugh, 1964.

4283 ADAM (MARGARET ISABELLA), *and others, comps.* Guide to the principal parliamentary papers relating to the dominions, 1812–1911 . . . Edin. 1913.

Does not include references to dependencies. See also under Parliamentary Papers (391).

4284 WINKS (ROBIN W.) *ed.* The historiography of the British Empire–Commonwealth. Trends, interpretations, and resources. Durham, N.C. 1966.

A bibliographical survey, under some twenty regional headings.

4285 FLINT (JOHN EDGAR). Books on the British empire and commonwealth; a guide for students. 1968.

B. BRITISH COLONIAL POLICY AND ADMINISTRATION

1. PRINTED SOURCES

4286 MOLESWORTH (*Sir* WILLIAM). Selected speeches . . . on questions relating to colonial policy. Ed. with an introd. by H. N. Egerton. 1903.

There is a *Life* of Molesworth by Millicent Garrett Fawcett, 1901. See also Edith Dobie,

'Molesworth's indictment of the Colonial Office, March 6, 1838', *Pacific Hist. Rev.* 13 (1944), 376–89.

4287 HARLOW (VINCENT TODD) *and* MADDEN (ALBERT FREDERICK McCULLOCH) *eds.* British colonial documents, 1774–1834; select documents. Oxf. 1953.

Fairly comprehensive, as is also Kenneth Norman Bell and William Parker Morrell, eds., *Select documents on British colonial policy, 1830–1860*, Oxf. 1928. Arthur Berriedale Keith, ed., *Selected speeches and documents on British colonial policy, 1763–1917*, 2 vols., 1917, rep. in one v., 1948, deals exclusively with the evolution of representative and responsible government in overseas settlements. George Bennett, ed., *The concept of Empire: Burke to Attlee, 1774–1947*, 2nd edn., 1962, illustrates changing attitudes from speeches and contemporary writings.

2. CONTEMPORARY TREATISES

4288 BROUGHAM (HENRY PETER), *Lord Brougham and Vaux*. An inquiry into the colonial policy of the European powers. 2 v. Edin. 1803.

A controversial exposition of the economic value of colonies.

4289 BAKER-HOLROYD (JOHN), *Lord Sheffield*. Strictures on the necessity of inviolably maintaining the navigation and colonial system of Great Britain. 1804. New edn. much enl. 1806.

Sheffield was a consistent exponent of the old colonial trading system, which was not effectively challenged till after the Napoleonic wars.

4290 HORTON (*Sir* ROBERT JOHN WILMOT). Letters [signed Philalethes] containing observations on colonial policy originally printed in Ceylon in 1832. 1839.

The views of an under-secretary for war and colonies (1821–8). See Douglas Pike, 'Wilmot Horton and the National Colonization Society', *Hist. Studies Australia and New Zealand* 7 (1955–7), 205–10.

4291 BULLER (CHARLES). Responsible government for colonies. 1840.

Repr. in *Charles Buller and responsible government*, with an introd. essay by E. M. Wrong, Oxf., 1926. See also Durham report (4352).

4292 MERIVALE (HERMAN). Lectures on colonization and colonies. 2 v. 1841–2. New edn. 1861. Repr. 1928.

Largely a criticism of the ideas of E. G. Wakefield. Merivale revised the 1861 reprint in the light of his experience as under-secretary in 1848–59. There is a brief memoir of him by Charles Merivale in *Trans. of the Devonshire Assoc.* 16 (1884), 570–80.

4293 WAKEFIELD (EDWARD GIBBON). A view of the art of colonization, in letters between a statesman and a colonist. 1849. New edn. with introd. by James Collier, Oxf. 1914.

The most recent study is Paul Bloomfield, *Edward Gibbon Wakefield: builder of the British Commonwealth*, 1961, bibliog. 354–60. Also see (4698).

4294 LEWIS (*Sir* GEORGE CORNEWALL). An essay on the government of dependencies. 1841. New edn. by C. P. Lucas, Oxf. 1891.

A theoretical treatise, by an active politician.

4295   ROEBUCK (JOHN ARTHUR). The colonies of England: a plan for the government of some portion of our colonial possessions. 1849.

4296   GREY (HENRY GEORGE), *3rd Earl Grey*. The colonial policy of Lord John Russell's administration. 2 v. 1852. 2nd edn. 1853.

A defence of his own administration at the colonial office.

3. LATER WORKS

See also under Colonial Office (461).

4297   EGERTON (HUGH EDWARD). A short history of British colonial policy, 1606–1909. Rev. by A. P. Newton. 12th edn. 1950.

A brief general survey, first pub. 1897, which is still of value. Much material illustrative of theory and propaganda is assembled in Klaus Eugene Knorr, *British colonial theories, 1570–1850*, Toronto, 1963. See too the excellent study of George Radcliffe Mellor, *British imperial trusteeship, 1783–1850*, 1951, bibliog. 457–79.

4298   MACMILLAN (WILLIAM MILLER). The road to self-rule: a study in colonial evolution. 1959.

Suggestive discussion of various aspects of colonial policy, with the main weight on problems of government.

4299   MANNING (HELEN TAFT). British colonial government after the American revolution, 1782–1820. New Haven, London. 1933.

Analyses the survival of the 'old colonial system' into the nineteenth century. See also Gerald Sandford Graham, *Sea Power and British North America, 1783–1820: a study in British colonial policy*, Camb., Mass., 1941. Though largely concerned with an earlier period, V. T. Harlow, *The founding of the second British Empire, 1763–93*, 2 v., 1952–64, is indispensable as a presentation of themes which remained dominant for many years after 1793.

4300   SCHUYLER (ROBERT LIVINGSTON). The fall of the old colonial system: a study in British free trade, 1770–1870. 1945.

Analyses the effect of changing commercial circumstances on British policy.

4301   MANNING (HELEN TAFT). 'Colonial crises before the cabinet, 1829–35.' *Bull. I.H.R.* 30 (1957), 41–61.

See also her papers, 'The colonial policy of the Whig ministers, 1830–7', *Canadian Hist. Rev.* 33 (1952), 203–36, 341–68, and, 'Who ran the British Empire, 1830–1850?' *J. of British Studies* 5 (1965–6), 88–121.

4302   HITCHINS (FRED HARVEY). The colonial land and emigration commission. 1931.

Deals with the work of the commission set up in 1840. See too R. G. Riddell, 'A study in the land policy of the colonial office, 1763–1855', *Canadian Hist. Rev.* 8 (1937), 385–405.

4303   FEATHERSTONE (DONALD F.). Colonial small wars, 1837–1901. 1974.

4304 MORRELL (WILLIAM PARKER). British colonial policy in the age of Peel and Russell. Oxf. new imp. 1966.

Bibliog. 533–40; standard on years 1841–52. A partial sequel is provided in his *British Colonial Policy in the mid-Victorian age. South Africa. New Zealand. The West Indies*, Oxf., 1969. Paul Knaplund, *Gladstone and Britain's imperial policy*, new imp., 1966, touches on Gladstone's passing interest in colonies in this period. See too John M. Ward, 'The colonial policy of Lord John Russell's administration', *Hist. Studies Australia and New Zealand* 9 (1959–61), 244–62.

4305 KNAPLUND (PAUL). James Stephen and the British colonial system, 1813–1847. Madison, Wis. 1953.

Bibliog. 301–7; a well-documented account of the influence of a leading civil servant on colonial policy. See also J. M. Ward, 'The retirement of a Titan. James Stephen, 1847–1850', *J. of Modern Hist.* 31 (1959), 189–205.

4306 KOEBNER (RICHARD). Empire. Camb. 1961.

An analysis of the concept up to the early 19th century; the sequel is R. Koebner and Helmut von Reinhard Schmidt, *Imperialism. The story and significance of a political word, 1840–1960*, Camb., 1964.

4307 CURTIN (PHILIP DE ARMOND). The image of Africa. British ideas and action, 1780–1850. Madison, Wis. 1964.

A valuable examination of the views expressed in contemporary literature, mainly on West Africa.

C. COLONIAL HISTORY (GENERAL)

1. CONTEMPORARY DESCRIPTIONS AND HISTORIES

4308 ADOLPHUS (JOHN). The political state of the British empire, containing a general view of the domestic and foreign possessions of the crown. 4 v. 1818.

4309 MARTIN (ROBERT MONTGOMERY). History of the British colonies. 5 v. 1834–5.

Mainly a descriptive survey.

2. LATER WORKS

4310 LUCAS (*Sir* CHARLES PRESTWOOD) *ed.* A historical geography of the British colonies. 7 v. in 11. 1888–1916.

From 1905 onwards, various vols. were expanded to bring them up to date, and in some cases reached a third edition. Full narrative, with chapter bibliogs.

4311 THE CAMBRIDGE HISTORY OF THE BRITISH EMPIRE. General eds. John Holland Rose, Arthur Percival Newton, Ernest Alfred Benians, and Henry Herbert Dodwell. 8 v. in 9. Camb. 1929–63.

Lengthy detailed treatment by specialist contributors. The valuable bibliogs. include guides to MSS. V. 2: *The growth of the new empire, 1783–1870*, 1940; v. 4; *British India, 1497–1858*, 1929; v. 6: *Canada and Newfoundland*, 1930; v. 7, pt. 1: *Australia*,

1933; pt. 2: *New Zealand*, 1933; v. 8: *South Africa, Rhodesia and the Protectorates*, 2nd edn., 1963.

4312   CARRINGTON (CHARLES EDMUND). The British overseas: exploits of a nation of shopkeepers. 2nd edn. 1968.

An able work of compression. Other surveys are J. A. Williamson, *A short history of British expansion*, v. 2: *The modern empire and commonwealth*, rev. 6th edn., 1967; John Ramsay B. Muir, *A short history of the British commonwealth*, v. 2: *The modern commonwealth*, 8th edn. 1954. See too A. G. L. Shaw, ed., *Great Britain and the colonies*, 1970.

4313   BURT (ALFRED LEROY). The evolution of the British empire and commonwealth from the American revolution. Boston. [Mass.] 1956.

Also of value is Paul Knaplund, *The British empire, 1815–1939*, 1942.

3. Special Subjects

For Christian missions in the colonies see (898–910)

(a) *Economic History*

4314   KNOWLES (LILIAN CHARLOTTE ANN) *and* KNOWLES (CHARLES MATTHEW). The economic development of the British overseas empire. 3 v. 1924–36.

V. 1 on the empire as a whole, and on the tropical colonies and India (2nd edn. 1928); v. 2 (1930) includes Canada; v. 3 (1936), South Africa. Charles Malcolm MacInnes, *An introduction to the economic history of the British empire*, 1935, is a briefer general survey. Special topics are treated in Geoffrey B. Masefield, *A short history of agriculture in the British colonies*, Oxf., 1950; Robert Chalmers, *A history of currency in the British colonies*, 1893.

(b) *Law and Institutions*

See Sweet and Maxwell, v. 7 (547)

4315   CLARK (CHARLES). A summary of colonial law, the practice of the Court of appeals from the plantations and of the laws and their administration in all the colonies. 1834.

Invaluable. Arthur Mills, *Colonial constitutions*, 1856, is useful but incomplete. Martin Wight, *The development of the legislative council, 1606–1945*, 1946, is brief but excellent.

(c) *Migration and Native Peoples*

4316   CUMPSTON (INA MARY). Indians overseas in British territories, 1834–1854. 1953.

Includes a detailed discussion of British legislation in relation to these movements of peoples. For movements of British peoples see (1744), (1745), (1747), (1749), (4370).

(d) *Colonial Servants (general)*

4317   ARTHUR (*Sir* GEORGE). The Arthur papers; being the Canadian papers, mainly confidential, private and demi-official . . . in the MS. collection of the Toronto Public Libraries. Ed. by Charles R. Sanderson. 3 v. Toronto. 1957–9.

Corr. 1822–1850, but mainly 1838–41. Arthur was lieut. governor Van Diemen's Land, 1823–37, Upper Canada, 1838–41; governor of Bombay, 1842. See also Michael C. I. Levy, *Governor George Arthur, a colonial benevolent despot*, Melbourne, 1953.

4318 COLBORNE, *afterwards* **SEATON.** The life of John Colborne, field marshal Lord Seaton. By George Charles Smith. 1903.

Colborne was governor of Upper Canada from 1830 to 1838, and of the Ionian Islands, 1843–9; *cr.* Baron Seaton, 1838, after putting down the Canadian revolt.

4319 COLE. Memoirs of Sir [Galbraith] Lowry Cole . . . Edited by Maud Lowry Cole and Stephen Gwynn. 1934.

Prints extracts from his correspondence. Cole was governor of Mauritius 1823–8 and of Cape Colony 1828–33.

4320 ELGIN. Letters and journals of James, eighth earl of Elgin. Ed. by Theodore Walrond. 1872.

Elgin served as governor of Jamaica, 1842, and governor-general of Canada, 1847–54. Other corr. for the Canadian period is in *The Elgin-Grey papers, 1846–52*, ed. with notes and appendices by Sir A. G. Doughty, Ottawa, 1937. Lives by Sir John G. Bourinot, Toronto, 1903, G. M. Wrong, 1905, and William P. M. Kennedy, 1926, deal mainly with his period in Canada. There is more on his earlier career in John L. Morison, *The eighth earl of Elgin: a chapter in nineteenth-century imperial history*, 1928.

4321 MAITLAND. The colonial administration of Sir Thomas Maitland. By Cyril Willis Dixon. 1939.

Bibliog. 261–74. Deals with Maitland's governorships in Ceylon (1806–11), Malta (1813–15), Ionian Isles (1815–24). Maitland was also c. in c. Mediterranean from 1815; see too Walter F. Lord, *Sir Thomas Maitland: The mastery of the Mediterranean*, 1897.

4322 METCALFE. The life and correspondence of Charles, Lord Metcalfe . . . from unpublished letters and journals. By Sir John William Kaye. Rev. edn. 2 v. 1858.

Metcalfe held a series of posts in India, 1808–38; was governor of Jamaica, 1839–42; governor-general of Canada, 1843–5. Edward J. Thompson, *The life of Charles, Lord Metcalfe*, 1937, bibliog. 419–28, is a scholarly survey.

D. THE BRITISH NORTH AMERICAN COLONIES

1. BIBLIOGRAPHY

(a) *Manuscripts*

4323 LAMB (WILLIAM KAYE) *and* **GORDON (ROBERT S.).** Union list of manuscripts in Canadian repositories. Ottawa. 1968.

A general guide to whereabouts of collections, not full detail on their contents. Publications of the Archives of Canada include (no. 2) *Inventory of military documents in the Canadian Archives; prepared by Lieut. Col. Cruikshank*, Ottawa, 1910, and (no. 10) *A guide to the documents in the manuscript room at the public archives of Canada*, comp.

David W. Parker, v. 1, Ottawa, 1914 (no more published). Public Archives of Canada, Manuscript Division, General inventory: manuscripts, Ottawa, 1971, in progress, includes holdings of microfilms and other copies. David W. Parker, *Guide to the materials for United States history in Canadian archives*, Wash., 1913, includes material for Canadian–U.S. relations. Toronto Public Libraries, *Guide to the manuscript collections in the ... libraries* [comp. by Donalda Putnam and Edith Firth], Toronto, 1954, lists mainly material for Upper Canada.

4324 MATTESON (DAVID MAYDOLE). List of manuscripts concerning American history preserved in European libraries. Wash. 1925.

Although chiefly concerned with the United States includes material relating to Canada, as do also: Carl Russell Fish, *Guide to the materials for American history in Roman and other Italian archives*, Wash., 1911; Waldo Gifford Leland, *Guide to materials for American history in the libraries and archives of Paris*, 2 v., Wash., 1932–43. See also particularly, Crick and Alman (74).

(b) *Printed Sources*

4325 CANADA. PUBLIC ARCHIVES. Reports. 1883+. Ottawa. 1884+.

Continues series published 1872–80 in the reports of the department of agriculture. The principal series for source materials. An index vol. for 1872–1908 was published in 1909.

4326 CHAMPLAIN SOCIETY. Publications. 1+. Toronto. 1907+.

Valuable record material from manuscripts and contemporary imprints. Hudson's Bay Record Society, Publications, 1+, Toronto and London, 1938+, contain material from the Hudson's Bay Co. records. See too A. P. C. Griffin, *Bibliography of American historical societies (the United States and the Dominion of Canada)*, vol. 2, A. H. A. annual report for 1905, 2nd edn., Wash., 1907, for publications of historical societies down to 1905 with table of contents of each vol.; *Historical societies in the United States and Canada; a handbook*, comp. C. Crittenden and Doris Godard, Wash., 1944.

(c) *Printed Works*

4327 TANGHE (RAYMOND) *comp*. Bibliography of Canadian bibliographies. Toronto. 1960.

Supplements, 1960, 1961, 1962. Includes ref. to many lists available only in typescript in various university schools of librarianship. Of major importance are the R.C.S. Library, *Subject Catalogue* (4281), v. 3, and the bibliog. to v. 6 of *C.H.B.E.* (4311). Frances Maria Staton and Marie Tremaine, ed., *A bibliography of Canadiana: being items in the public library of Toronto ... relating to the early history and development of Canada*, Toronto, 1934, a selective and annotated list of source books covering 1534–1867 arranged chronologically; Supplement 1, by Gertrude M. Boyle and Marjorie Colbeck, Toronto, 1959. William F. E. Morley, ed., *Canadian local histories to 1950: a bibliography*, Toronto, 1967, in progress; v. 1 deals with the Atlantic provinces.

4328 TREMAINE (MARIE). A bibliography of Canadian imprints, 1751–1800. Toronto. 1952.

Includes official pubs. Frances M. Staton comp. for Toronto Public Libraries, *Books and pamphlets published in Canada up to ... 1837 ... in the ... library*, Toronto, 1916, suppls., 1919, 1926. Magdalen Casey, comp., *Catalogue of pamphlets in the Public Archives of Canada*, v. 1: 1493–1877 (publn. of the Public Archives of Canada no. 13), Ottawa, 1931. Olga Bernice Bishop, comp., *Publications of the governments of Nova*

Scotia, Prince Edward Island, New Brunswick, *1758–1952*, Ottawa, 1957, and *Publications of the government of the Province of Canada, 1841–1867*, Ottawa, 1963. Still of value, despite incompleteness, is George Barthéleme Faribault, *Catalogue d'ouvrages sur l'histoire de l'Amérique et en particulier sur celle du Canada*, Quebec, 1837. William Matthews, comp., *Canadian diaries and autobiographies*, Berkeley, 1950, includes also unpublished items. For printed material relating to cultural history Reginald Eyre Watters, *A check list of Canadian literature and background materials, 1628–1950* Toronto, 1959, is especially valuable.

4329 CANADIAN HISTORICAL REVIEW. V. 1+. Toronto. 1920+.

Quarterly, continued from annual *Review of historical publications relating to Canada*, Toronto, 1897–1919; decennial indexes. Apart from articles and reviews gives quarterly listing of recent publications relating to Canada. In recent years the *Revue d'histoire de l'Amérique française*, v. 1+, Montreal, 1947+, has ceased to be almost exclusively concerned with pre-1763. See too Canadian Historical Association, *Annual reports*, 1922+, Ottawa, 1923+.

2. POLITICAL HISTORY

(a) *General Histories*

See *C.H.B.E.* (4311), v. 6.

4330 [HIND (HENRY YOULE) *and others*]. Eighty years' progress of British North America. 1863.

Methodical and substantial. Of more contemporary accounts, John McGregor, *Historical and descriptive sketches of the maritime colonies of British America*, 1828, reports personal observation; Joseph Bouchette, *The British dominions in North America*, 2 v., 1831, is a topographical and statistical description comp. from docs. in the Surveyor-General's office; Thomas Rolph, *A descriptive and statistical account of Canada*, 2nd edn., 1841, was for the information of immigrants. See too William Henry Smith, *Canada: past, present, and future; being a historical, geographical, geological, and statistical account of Canada West*, 2 v., Toronto, 1851. *Early travellers in Canada, 1791–1867*, sel. and ed. by Gerald M. Craig, Toronto, 1955, includes a valuable intro. essay.

4331 KINGSFORD (WILLIAM). The history of Canada. 10 v. London, Toronto. 1887–98.

Long the standard history; v. 7–10 provide detailed narrative, 1779–1841. Thomas Chapais, *Cours d'histoire du Canada* [1760–1846], 8 v., Quebec, 1919–34, is well balanced.

4332 SHORTT (ADAM) *and* DOUGHTY (ARTHUR GEORGE) *eds.* Canada and its provinces. 23 v. Toronto. 1914–17.

A comprehensive collaborative work; v. 23 is the index and includes list of MSS. and bibliog. The *Canadian Centenary Series*, ed. W. L. Morton and D. G. Creighton, now in progress, will eventually provide a replacement.

4333 GARNEAU (FRANÇOIS-XAVIER). Histoire du Canada. 3 v. 1845–6; 8th edn. rev. and enl. by Hector Garneau. 9 v. Montreal. 1944–6.

A presentation from the French-Canadian viewpoint. The edition most fully representing the author's mind is the 4th, 4 v., Montreal, 1882–3. On a smaller scale are Sir J. G. Bourinot, *Canada under British rule, 1760–1905*, rev. with an add. section by G. M. Wrong, Camb., 1909, and Jean Bruchési, *Histoire du Canada pour tous*, t. 2, *Le régime anglais*, 2nd edn., Montreal, 1940. Lionel Adolphe Groulx, *Histoire du Canada français*, 4 v., Montreal, is an interpretative survey; v. 3 relates to 1760–1848.

4334 AUDET (FRANÇOIS JOSEPH). Canadian historical dates and events, 1492–1915. Ottawa. 1917.

Dates of events and appointments, and lists of office-holders.

4335 MARTIN (CHESTER). Foundations of Canadian nationhood. Toronto. 1955.

Other general surveys giving modern summary treatment of the period 1789 to 1851 include D. G. Creighton, *Dominion of the North*, 1958; A. R. M. Lower, *Canadians in the making: a social history* . . ., Toronto, 1958; Edgar McInnis, *Canada*, 2nd edn., Toronto, 1959; J. B. Brebner, *Canada*, Ann Arbor, 1960.

4336 CLARK (SAMUEL DELBERT). Movements of political protest in Canada, 1640–1940. Toronto. 1959.

A valuable detailed survey of the internal politics of the various north American colonies.

4337 STANLEY (GEORGE FRANCIS GILMAN) *and* JACKSON (HAROLD M.). Canada's soldiers: the military history of an unmilitary people. Rev. edn. Toronto. 1960.

4338 KERR (DONALD GORDON GRADY) *ed.* Historical atlas of Canada. Toronto. 1961.

4339 WALLACE (WILLIAM STEWART) *comp.* The Macmillan dictionary of Canadian biography. 3rd rev. and enl. edn. 2 v. Toronto. 1963.

Can be supplemented from the *Encyclopaedia Canadiana*, 10 v., Ottawa, 1957–8, which includes historical articles and many biographical notes not available elsewhere.

(b) *1789–1815*

4340 RIDDELL (WILLIAM RENWICK). The life of John Graves Simcoe. Toronto. 1926.

Simcoe was lieut.-governor of Upper Canada, 1791–6. E. A. Cruikshank, ed., *The correspondence of . . . Simcoe . . . 1789–1796*, 5 v., Toronto, 1923–31.

4341 CARON (IVANHOË). La colonisation de la province de Quebec. V. 2: Les cantons de l'Est, 1791–1815. Quebec. 1927.

See too Michel Brunet, 'Les Canadiens et la France révolutionnaire', *Revue d'Histoire de l'Amérique française* 13 (1959–60), 467–75; Jean-Pierre Wallot, 'La querelle des prisons (Bas-Canada, 1805–1807)', *ibid.* 14 (1960–1), 61–86; Lawrence A. H. Smith, '*Le Canadien* and the British constitution, 1806–10', *Canadian Hist. Rev.* 38 (1957), 93–108.

4342 CRUIKSHANK (ERNEST ALEXANDER). The political adventures of John Henry; the record of an international imbroglio. Toronto. 1936.

The career of an adventurer and secret agent in the years leading up to the war of 1812.

4343   LUCAS (*Sir* CHARLES PRESTWOOD). The Canadian war of 1812. Oxf. 1906.

With maps. Compiled from war dispatches of both sides. See also L. L. Babcock, *The war of 1812 on the Niagara frontier*, New York, 1927; E. A. Cruikshank, ed., *The documentary history of the campaign on the Niagara frontier in 1814*, 9 v., Welland, 1896–1908, and *Documents relating to the invasion of Canada and the surrender of Detroit*, Ottawa, 1913; William C. H. Wood, ed., *Select British documents of the Canadian war of 1812*, 3 v. in 4, Toronto, 1920–8.

4344   TUPPER (FERDINAND BROCK). The life and correspondence of Major-General Sir Isaac Brock. 2nd edn. 1847.

From the private papers of the British c.-in-c. at the beginning of the war of 1812. E. A. Cruikshank, ed., 'Some unpublished letters from General Brock', *Ontario Hist. Soc. Papers and Records*, 13 (1915), 8–23. See Lady Matilda Edgar, *General Brock*, Toronto, 1905; 2nd edn. rev. by E. A. Cruikshank, 1926.

(c) *1815–1840*

4345   HOUSE OF COMMONS. Report of the select committee appointed to enquire into the state of the civil government of Canada. 1828. VII. 569, pp. 375–730.

Sir Robert J. W. Horton, *Exposition and defence of Earl Bathurst's administration of the affairs of Canada when Colonial Secretary during . . . 1822–1827*, 1838, is a comment on the report by the under-sec. under Bathurst. See William Ormsby, 'The problem of Canadian union, 1822–8', *Canadian Hist. Rev.* 39 (1958), 277–95.

4346   CANADA. PUBLIC ARCHIVES. Calendar of the Dalhousie papers. Toronto. 1939.

Mainly on the period 1816–1828, for most of which Dalhousie was captain-general and governor-in-chief in British N.A.

4347   KILBOURN (WILLIAM). The firebrand: William Lyon Mackenzie and the rebellion in Upper Canada. 1958.

Charles Lindsey, *Life and times of William Lyon Mackenzie*, 2 v., Toronto, 1862, used family papers; there is a condensed edn. by G. G. S. Lindsey, Toronto, 1908. Margaret Fairley, ed., *The selected writings of . . . Mackenzie*, 1824–1837, Toronto, 1960. See too R. A. Mackay, 'The political ideas of William Lyon Mackenzie', *Canadian J. of Economics and Political Science*, 3 (1937), 1–22; Lillian F. Gates, 'The decided policy of William Lyon Mackenzie', *Canadian Hist. Rev.* 40 (1959), 185–208. On the background of Mackenzie's agitation, see Manning (4299). F. H. Armstrong, 'William Lyon Mackenzie, first mayor of Toronto: a study of a critic in power', *Canadian Hist. Rev.* 48 (1967), 309–31, is an interesting assessment.

4348   GOURLAY (ROBERT FLEMING). Banished Briton and Neptunian; being a record of the life, writings, principles and projects of Robert Gourlay. 39 pts. Boston. 1843.

Rare. See William Renwick Riddell, 'Robert (Fleming) Gourlay', *Ontario Hist. Soc. Papers and Records* 14 (1916), 5–133, and E. A. Cruikshank, 'The government of Upper Canada and Robert Gourlay', *ibid.* 23 (1926), 65–179.

4349   TORONTO PUBLIC LIBRARY. The rebellion of 1837–38: a bibliography of the sources of information in the . . . library. Comp. Frances M. Staton. Toronto. 1924.

Lists 1,500 items. Also important is *Bibliography of materials at the . . . archives . . . relating to the rebellion of 1837–8*, Report of the Canada Public Archives for 1939, pp. 63–138, Ottawa, 1940.

4350 FILTEAU (GÉRARD). Histoire des patriotes. 3 v. Montreal. 1938–42.

A full study, opinionated but well documented. W. S. Wallace, *The family compact: a chronicle of the rebellion in Upper Canada*, Toronto, 1915, provides a general introduction, though now somewhat outdated. Émile Dubois, *Le feu de la Rivière-du-Chêne: étude historique sur le mouvement insurrectionel de 1837 au nord de Montréal*, St. Jérôme, 1937, is fully documented, but one-sided. See too Edwin C. Guillet, *The lives and times of the patriots: an account of the rebellion in Upper Canada, 1837–8, and the patriot agitation in the United States, 1837–42*, Toronto, 1938, with chapter bibliogs. and an appendix of docs. Still worth consulting is John C. Dent, *The story of the Upper Canadian rebellion; largely derived from original sources and documents*, 2 v., Toronto, 1885.

4351 RUMILLY (ROBERT). Papineau. Paris. 1934.

The most considerable biography; accurate, though little concerned with ideas, for which see Eve Circé-Côté, *Papineau. Son influence sur la pensée canadienne*, Montreal, 1924. A recent assessment is Fernand Ouellet, 'Papineau dans la révolution de 1837–8', *Canadian Hist. Assoc. Report* for 1958, pp. 13–34; see also his *Louis-Joseph Papineau: a divided soul* (Canadian Hist. Ass. booklet 11), Ottawa, 1960.

4352 LUCAS (*Sir* CHARLES PRESTWOOD). Lord Durham's report on the affairs of British North America. 3 v. Oxf. 1912.

The standard edn. Sir Reginald Coupland, *The Durham report*, Oxf., 1945, is an abridged version with intro. and notes. There is a French-Canadian edn. by Marcel-Pierre Hamel, Quebec, 1948. *Report of the Public Archives of Canada . . . for 1923*, Ottawa, 1924, appendix B, 11–410, lists Durham's papers in Canada relating to the insurrection of 1837–8. R. C. Watt, 'The political prisoners in Upper Canada, 1837–38', *E.H.R.* 14 (1926), 526–55, deals with the end of the rising and of Durham's mission. See also Buller (4291). For various aspects of the British approach to Canadian problems see three books by Peter C. Burroughs, *The colonial reformers and Canada, 1830–1849*, Toronto, 1969, *British attitudes towards Canada, 1822–1849*, Toronto, 1971, and *The Canadian crisis and British colonial policy, 1828–1841*, 1972.

4353 HEAD (*Sir* FRANCIS BOND). A narrative . . . 3rd edn. 1839.

An attempt at self-exculpation by the Lieut.-Governor of Upper Canada after the publication of the Durham report. On him see Sydney Jackman, *Galloping Head: the life of . . . Sir Francis Bond Head*, 1958.

(d) *1840–1851*

4354 KINCHEN (OSCAR ARVLE). Lord Russell's Canadian policy: a study in British heritage and colonial freedom. Lubbock [Texas]. 1945.

Penetrating on Russell's admin. at the colonial office, 1839–41. For a Canadian attack on the Canada Act see Sir John Beverley Robinson, *Canada, and the Canada bill*, 1840; Robinson was a member of the family compact—on him see the Life by Charles Walker Robinson, 1904. Governor-general's letters to Russell, 1839–41, are printed in *Letters from Lord Sydenham . . . to . . . Lord John Russell*, ed. by Paul Knaplund, 1931. Adam Shortt, *Lord Sydenham*, 1926, deals mainly with his Canadian career from the Canadian archives; but see also Poulett Thomson (219). I. M. Abella, 'The "Sydenham Election" of 1841', *Canadian Hist. Rev.* 47 (1966), 326–43, examines the consolidation of the governor-general's power in face of whig opposition.

4355 MORISON (JOHN LYLE). British supremacy and Canadian self-government, 1839–1854. Glasgow. 1919.

An excellent description of Canadian constitutional development. Rosa W. Langstone, *Responsible government in Canada*, 1931, is of value. Other aspects of the development of institutions are treated in John E. Hodgetts, *Pioneer public service: an administrative history of the United Canadas, 1841–1867*, Toronto, 1955, and C. P. Stacey, *Canada and the British army, 1846–1871: a study in the practice of responsible government*, rev. edn., 1963. See also William G. Ormsby, *The emergence of the federal concept in Canada, 1839–45*, Toronto, 1969.

4356 CARELESS (JAMES MAURICE STOCKFORD). The union of the Canadas: the growth of Canadian institutions, 1841–1857. Toronto. 1967.

Masterly treatment with attention to economic and social change, and especially good on the politics of the upper province. The old comprehensive survey, with a heavy Whig bias, is J. C. Dent, *The last forty years*, 1881, and for near-contemporary French Canadian interpretations see L. P. Turcotte, *Le Canada sous l'union, 1841–67*, 2 v., Quebec, 1871–2, and A. Gérin-Lajoie, *Dix ans au Canada, 1840–1850*, Quebec, 1888.

4357 GLAZEBROOK (GEORGE PARKIN de TWENEBROKES). Sir Charles Bagot in Canada: a study in British colonial government. 1929.

Bagot was governor-general 1841.

4358 WILSON (GEORGE EARL). The life of Robert Baldwin: a study in the struggle for responsible government. Toronto. 1933.

Other biographical studies illustrating the Whig approach to politics in this period are R. S. Longley, *Sir Francis Hincks: a study of Canadian politics, railways, and finance in the nineteenth century*, Toronto, 1943, and J. M. S. Careless, *Brown of the Globe*; v. 1: *The voice of Upper Canada, 1818–59*, Toronto, 1959. Jacques Monet, 'La Crise Metcalfe and the Montreal election, 1843–1844', *Canadian Hist. Rev.* 44 (1963), 1–19, shows how politicians of both main parties conceived of responsible government, and George Metcalfe, 'Draper conservatism and responsible government in the Canadas, 1836–1847', *ibid.* 42 (1961), 300–24, illuminates the neglected conservative aspect of Canadian politics after union. See also Metcalfe (4322) and Elgin (4320).

4359 MONET (JACQUES). 'French Canada and the Annexation Crisis, 1848–1850'. *Canadian Hist. Rev.* 47 (1966), 249–64.

C. D. Allin and G. M. Jones, *Annexation, preferential trade and reciprocity . . .*, Toronto, 1912, treats this crisis more from the economic viewpoint.

3. SPECIAL TOPICS

(a) *Constitutional History*

4360 KENNEDY (WILLIAM PAUL McCLURE) *ed.* Statutes, treaties and documents of the Canadian constitution, 1759–1915. Toronto. 1918.

Standard; includes more docs. for the period up to 1849 than the 2nd edn. of 1930. Much fuller collections are: *Documents relating to the constitutional history of Canada: 1759–91*, sel. and ed. by Adam Shortt and Arthur G. Doughty, 2 pt., 2nd edn., Ottawa, 1918; *Documents . . . 1791–1818*, sel. and ed. by A. G. Doughty and D. A. McArthur,

Ottawa, 1914; *Documents . . . 1819–1828*, sel. and ed. by A. G. Doughty and Norah Story, 4 v., Ottawa, 1914–35. See too H. E. Egerton and W. L. Grant, *Canadian constitutional development, shown by selected speeches and despatches, with introductions and explanatory notes*, 1907.

4361 A collection of the Acts passed in the Parliament of Great Britain and other public acts relating to Canada 1759–1834.

A made-up set in the Brit. Library, London. [Canada] *Index to Dominion and provincial statutes from the earliest period . . . 1916*, Montreal, 1918; Aemilius Irving, *An index to the statutes of Canada . . . 1840–50, comprising all the acts passed, in force and repealed in Upper-Lower Canada, with a chronological index*, Toronto, 1850. See also Sweet and Maxwell (547), v. 3.

4362 CANADA. PARLIAMENT. Journals of the legislative assembly of the province of Canada. v. 1–26, 1841–66. Kingston. 1842–67.

General index to the journals . . . 1841–1851, comp. by Alfred Todd, Montreal, 1855. *Journals of the legislative council . . .*, v. 1–26, Quebec, 1841–66.

4363 KENNEDY (WILLIAM PAUL McCLURE). The constitution of Canada, 1534–1937. 2nd edn. 1938.

The standard constitutional history. Chester Martin, *Empire and commonwealth: studies in governance and self-government in Canada*, Oxford, 1929, is mainly a survey of developments in various provinces.

(b) *Economic History*

4364 INNIS (HAROLD ADAMS) *and* LOWER (ARTHUR REGINALD MARSDEN) *eds*. Select documents in Canadian economic history, 1783–1885. Toronto. 1933.

A substantial collection. General histories with chapters on 1789–1851 are Mary Quayle Innis, *An economic history of Canada*, new edn., Toronto, 1954, and W. T. Easterbrook and H. G. Aitken, *Canadian economic history*, Toronto, 1956. Donald Grant Creighton, *The empire of the St. Lawrence: a study in commerce and politics*, Toronto, 1956, is a reissue, with a new preface, of his *The commercial empire of the St. Lawrence, 1760–1850*, Toronto, 1937. G. N. Tucker, *The Canadian commercial revolution, 1845–1851*, New Haven, 1936, is thorough and well judged. Of value is C. D. W. Goodwin, *Canadian economic thought: the political economy of a developing nation, 1814–1914*, 1961.

4365 BRECKENRIDGE (ROELIFF MORTON). A history of banking in Canada. Wash. 1910.

See too his earlier study, *The Canadian banking system, 1817–1890*, Toronto, 1894.

4366 SMITH (WILLIAM). The history of the post office in British North America, 1639–1870. Camb. 1920.

4367 INNIS (HAROLD ADAMS). The fur trade in Canada; an introduction to Canadian economic history. Rev. edn. Toronto. 1956.

Innis also wrote *The cod fisheries*, rev. edn. Toronto, 1954; both books relate to U.S.-Canadian relations.

4368 GLAZEBROOK (GEORGE PARKIN de TWENEBROKES). History of transportation in Canada. Toronto. 1938.

G. R. Stevens, *Canadian national railways*, 2 v., Toronto, 1960–2, v. 1: Sixty years of trial and error [1836–96]. While much railway promotion went on in the late 1840s, little line had been laid before 1851.

4369 CREIGHTON (DONALD GRANT). 'The commercial class in Canadian politics, 1792–1840'. *Canadian Political Science Assoc. papers . . .*, 5 (1933), 43–61.

4370 MACDONALD (NORMAN). Canada, 1763–1841, immigration and settlement: the administration of the imperial land regulations. 1939.

Thorough treatment in relation to both economic development and politics; bibliog. 531–59. M. L. Hansen, *The mingling of the Canadian and American peoples*, New Haven, 1940, has interesting material on the peopling of Ontario and the west. See also Cowan (1744), Guillet (1743), Hansen (1746).

(c) *Relations with the United States*

See also (339–349).

4371 CANADA. DEPARTMENT OF EXTERNAL AFFAIRS. Treaties and agreements affecting Canada in force between H.M. and the United States of America . . . 1814–1925. Ottawa. 1927.

Includes also subsidiary docs. William R. Manning, ed., *Diplomatic correspondence of the United States: Canadian relations, 1784–1860*, 4 v., Wash., 1940–5.

4372 KEENLEYSIDE (HUGH LLEWELLYN) *and* BROWN (GERALD S.). Canada and the United States: some aspects of their historical relations. 2nd edn. New York. 1952.

Other general studies are James M. Callahan, *American foreign policy in Canadian relations*, N.Y., 1937, and E. W. McInnis, *The unguarded frontier: a history of American-Canadian relations*, N.Y., 1942. Some specific questions are covered in Fred Landon, *Western Ontario and the American frontier*, Toronto, 1941; Albert B. Corey, *The crisis of 1830–42 in Canadian-American relations*, New Haven, 1941; J. R. Baldwin, 'The Ashburton-Webster boundary settlement', *Canadian Hist. Assoc. Report* of 1938, pp. 121–33.

(d) *Religious and Cultural History*

4373 WALSH (HENRY HORACE). The Christian church in Canada. Toronto. 1956.

See too Samuel D. Clark, *Church and sect in Canada* [1760–1900], Toronto, 1948; J. E. Sanderson, *The first century of Methodism in Canada, 1775–1883*, 2 v., Toronto, 1908–10; C. B. Sissons, *Egerton Ryerson; his life and letters*, 2 v., Toronto, 1937–47. P. Carrington, *The Anglican church in Canada*, Toronto, 1963.

4374 BAKER (RAY PALMER). A history of English-Canadian literature to the confederation: its relation to the literature of Great Britain and the United States. Camb. Mass. 1920.

Jean Lunn, 'Canadian newspapers before 1821, a preliminary list', *Canadian Hist. Rev.* 25 (1944), 417–20, reprinted Toronto, 1944.

4375 TORY (HENRY MARSHALL) *ed*. A history of science in Canada. Toronto. 1939.

John Joseph Heagerty, *Four centuries of medical history in Canada; and a sketch of the medical history of Newfoundland*, 2 v., Bristol, 1928.

4376 HUBBARD (ROBERT HAMILTON). An anthology of Canadian art. Toronto. 1960.

Coloured prints, and a bibliog. note, 167–9.

4. Regions

(a) *Newfoundland and Labrador*

4377 PRIVY COUNCIL. Judicial Committee. In the matter of the boundary between the dominion of Canada and the colony of Newfoundland in the Labrador peninsula, between the dominion of Canada of the one part and the colony of Newfoundland of the other part. 12 v. 1926–7.

Of particular interest is pt. 9, v. 4, of the joint appendix, *Documents relating to the history of Newfoundland*.

4378 ANSPACH (LEWIS AMADEUS). A history of the island of Newfoundland; containing a description of the island, the Banks, the fisheries and trade . . . and the coast of Labrador. Priv. printed. 1819.

Valuable for its descriptions from first-hand knowledge but untrustworthy as history.

4379 PROWSE (DANIEL WOODLEY). A history of Newfoundland, from the English, colonial, and foreign records. 1895. 2nd edn. rev. and cor. 1896.

The most comprehensive and best documented of the older histories, but the historical judgements are unreliable. Charles Pedley, *The history of Newfoundland . . . to . . . 1860*, 1863, is a useful survey. See too William G. Gosling, *Labrador: its discovery, exploration, and development*, 1910.

4380 McLINTOCK (ALEXANDER HARE). The establishment of constitutional government in Newfoundland, 1783–1832: a study of retarded colonization. 1941.

Excellent, as is its recent sequel, Gertrude E. Gunn, *The political history of Newfoundland, 1832–1864*, Toronto, 1966.

4381 MACFARLAND (RAYMOND). A history of the New England fisheries. New York. 1911.

See also Innis, *Fisheries* (1690).

4382 HOWLEY (MICHAEL FRANCIS). Ecclesiastical history of Newfoundland. Boston. 1888.

Principally a history of the Catholic church, but notice taken of other churches.

(b) *Prince Edward Island*

4383 MORGAN (JEAN E.). A bibliography of descriptive and historical material relating to Prince Edward Island (typescript, McGill Univ. Lib. School). Montreal. 1940.

4384 THE ACTS of the general assembly of Prince Edward Island from 1773 [to 1862]. 2 v. Charlotte Town. 1862.

For government publications see Bishop (4328).

4385 STEWART (JOHN). An account of Prince Edward Island . . . 1806.

Substantial, and informative on geography and land-distribution.

4386 WARBURTON (ALEXANDER BANNERMAN). A history of Prince Edward Island from . . . 1534 until . . . 1831. St. John [New Brunswick]. 1923.

The first quarter of Frank MacKinnon, *The government of Prince Edward Island*, Toronto, 1951, traces constitutional dev. up to 1851. Andrew H. Clark, *Three centuries and the Island* . . ., Toronto, 1959, is an historical geography, particularly valuable for its extensive footnotes and bibliog. 226–57.

(c) *Cape Breton Island*

4387 BROWN (RICHARD). A history of the island of Cape Breton. 1869.

(d) *Nova Scotia*

For government publications see Bishop (4328).

4388 NOVA SCOTIA. Commission of Public Records. Catalogue of manuscript documents arranged, bound and catalogued . . . together with a list of books of entry . . . 1710–1867. Halifax. 1877. Another edn. 1886.

Nova Scotia Public Archives, *A calendar of official correspondence and legislative papers* . . . *1802–15*, comp. by Margaret Ells, Halifax, 1936. Canada Public Archives, *Report*, *1894*, pp. 1–573; *Calendar of papers relating to Nova Scotia* [1603–1801], Ottawa, 1895; *Report*, *1946*, appendix: *Nova Scotia State Papers. Calendar of Nova Scotia Official Correspondence*, *1. Nova Scotia A, 1802–1820*; Ottawa, 1947; *Report*, *1947*, idem, *1820–1836*, Ottawa, 1948; *Report 1948*, appendix, idem, *1. Nova Scotia A, 1837–40*, *2. Colonial Office Series C.O. 218*, 1768–1842, Ottawa, 1949; *Report*, *1949*, appendix, *Nova Scotia Despatches (1834–1867)*, Ottawa, 1950.

4389 NOVA SCOTIA HISTORICAL SOCIETY. (Reports and) Collections. Halifax. 1897+.

Prints journals and records in full; index to v. 1–32 in v. 33 (1961).

4390 NOVA SCOTIA. PUBLIC ARCHIVES. A directory of the members of the legislative assembly . . . 1758–1958. With an intro. by C. Bruce Fergusson. Halifax. 1958.

4391 HALIBURTON (THOMAS CHANDLER). An historical and statistical account of Nova Scotia, 2 v. Halifax, 1829.

Useful descriptive material. See also W. S. Moorsom, *Letters from Nova Scotia; comprising sketches of a young country*, 1830.

4392 CAMPBELL (GEORGE GRAHAM). The history of Nova Scotia. Toronto. 1948.

A summary account. More full is David Allison, *History of Nova Scotia*, 3 v., Halifax, 1916; v. 3, by C. E. Tuck, is sub-titled *Biographical sketches of representative citizens*.

Beamish Murdoch, *A history of Nova Scotia or Acadie,* 3 v., Halifax, 1865–7, prints documents, but ends at 1827. See too Duncan Campbell, *Nova Scotia, in its historical, mercantile and industrial relations,* Montreal, 1873, and Sir J. G. Bourinot, *Builders of Nova Scotia: a historical review,* Toronto, 1900.

4393 BURROUGHS (PETER). 'The search for economy: imperial administration of Nova Scotia in the 1830s'. *Canadian Hist. Rev.* 49 (1968), 24–43.

4394 ROY (JAMES ALEXANDER). Joseph Howe: a study in achievement and frustration. Toronto. 1935.

A scholarly study of the champion of responsible government in Nova Scotia; bibliog. 333–40.

4395 LIVINGSTONE (W. ROSS). Responsible government in Nova Scotia. A study of the constitutional beginnings of the British Commonwealth. Iowa. 1930.

Scholarly, based on MSS. sources; bibliog. 265–72. J. M. Beck, *The government of Nova Scotia,* Toronto, 1957, has a substantial historical section.

4396 MARTELL (JAMES STUART). Immigration to and emigration from Nova Scotia, 1815–1838. Halifax. 1942.

An anthology from newspapers and documents, with an intro. essay.

(e) *New Brunswick*

For government publications see Bishop (4328).

4397 MacFARLANE (WILLIAM GOODSOE). New Brunswick bibliography: the books and writers of the province. St. John. 1895.

4398 NEW BRUNSWICK HISTORICAL SOCIETY. Collections. 1894+.

Irregular; none pub. 1930–55; includes letters, papers, and journals. W. O. Raymond, ed., *Winslow papers, 1776–1826,* St. John, 1901, principally the corr. of Edward Winslow (1765–1815), judge of the supreme court of N. Brunswick.

4399 ATKINSON (WILLIAM CHRISTOPHER). A historical and statistical account of New Brunswick, with advice to emigrants. 3rd edn. Edinburgh. 1844.

One of the more informative contemporary accounts. See also Abraham Gesner, *New Brunswick, with notes for emigrants . . .,* 1847.

4400 MacNUTT (WILLIAM STEWART). New Brunswick. A history: 1784–1867. Toronto. 1963.

A thorough, scholarly survey. See also his articles, 'New Brunswick's age of harmony; the administration of Sir John Harvey', *Canadian Hist. Rev.* 32 (1951), 105–25, and 'The coming of responsible government to New Brunswick', *ibid.* 33 (1952), 111–28. An older detailed account is James Hannay, *History of New Brunswick,* 2 v., St. John, 1909. Esther C. Wright, *The Loyalists of New Brunswick,* Fredericktown, 1955, is a valuable social survey of the colony at the end of the 18th century.

4401 KERR (DONALD GORDON GRADY). Sir Edmund Head: a scholarly governor. Toronto. 1954.

Head was governor of New Brunswick, 1847–54.

(f) *Quebec and the French Canadians*

4402 ARCHIVES DE LA PROVINCE DE QUÉBEC. Inventaires. Beauceville. 1917+.

Vols. so far pub. deal mainly with the period of French rule, but there is some early 19th-century material. See also the excellent series of the *Rapports de l'archiviste de la province de Québec*, 1920/21+, Quebec, 1921+.

4403 DIONNE (NARCISSE EUTROPE). Québec et Nouvelle France. Bibliographie. 4 v. and suppl. Quebec. 1905–12.

[V. 1]: *Inventaire chron. des livres . . . publiés en langue française dans la province de Québec . . . 1764–1905; v. 2: . . . ouvrages publiés a l'étranger en diverse langues sur Québec et la Nouvelle France . . . 1534–1906; v. 3: . . . publiés en langue anglaise dans la province de Québec . . . 1764–1906; v. 4: Cartes, plans, atlas . . . 1508–1908.* Suppl. covers the years 1904–12. Philip Garigue, *A bibliographical introduction to the study of French Canada*, Montreal, 1956, gives a classified listing of nearly 3,000 books and articles. Gustave Lanctôt, *L'œuvre de la France en Amérique du Nord; bibliographie sélective et critique*, Montreal, Paris, 1951, has extremely valuable critical notes.

4404 THE LITERARY AND HISTORICAL SOCIETY OF QUEBEC. Index to the archival publications, 1824–1924. Quebec. 1923.

4405 WADE (HUGH MASON). The French Canadians, 1760–1967. 2nd rev. edn. 2 v. Toronto. 1968.

A massive and valuable study. See too L. A. Groulx, *La pénétration du continent américain par les canadiens français, 1763–1846*, Montreal, 1939.

4406 CHRISTIE (ROBERT). A history of the late province of Lower Canada [1791–1841]. 6 v. Quebec. 1848–55.

Chiefly political and parliamentary history, based partly on personal knowledge and also on documents some of which were later destroyed; invaluable. E. J. Hutchins, 'The maintenance of imperial influence in French Canada (1791–1840)', *Revue d'Histoire des Colonies*, 26 (1933), 17–49, is a scholarly commentary but without references.

4407 MANNING (HELEN TAFT). The revolt of French Canada, 1800–1835: a chapter in the history of the British commonwealth. 1962.

An important work of interpretation. See also Elizabeth Nish, ed., *Racism or responsible government: the French Canadian dilemma of the 1840s*, Toronto, 1967.

4408 DESJARDINS (JOSEPH). Guide parlementaire historique de la province de Québec, 1792 à 1902. Quebec. 1902.

A valuable handbook, lists and introd. essays. F. J. Audet and F. Surveyer, *Les députés au premier parlement du Bas-Canada, 1792–6*, Montreal, 1946, provides useful biographical essays.

4409 QUEBEC. Legislative Council. Journals. V. 1–15. Quebec. 1792–1837.

The provincial statutes of Lower Canada, 14 v., Quebec, 1792–1836. A complete index to the Ordinances and Statutes of Lower Canada to [1817], Quebec, 1817; *A continuation of the index . . . to* [1832], Quebec, 1832. For governors' proclamations see (4419).

4410 ATHERTON (WILLIAM HENRY). Montreal, 1535–1914. 3 v. Montreal. 1914.

V. 2 deals with British rule, 1760–1914, with full analysis of the city's economic, cultural, and social development.

4411 OUELLET (FERNAND). Histoire économique et sociale du Québec, 1760–1850: structures et conjoncture. Montreal. Paris. 1966.

Breaks new ground in the establishment of quantitative bases for analysis of society in the province. On the seigniorial system see: W. B. Munro, ed., *Documents relating to the seignorial tenure in Canada, 1598–1854*, Toronto, 1908; and, *The seigniorial system in Canada: a study in French colonial policy*, N.Y., 1907; G. M. Wrong, *A Canadian manor and its seigneurs* [1761–1861], Toronto, 1908; Jean-Pierre Wallot, 'Le régime seigneurial et son abolition au Canada', *Canadian Hist. Rev.* 50 (1969), 367–93.

4412 AUDET (LOUIS-PHILIPPE). La système scolaire de la province de Québec. 6 v. Quebec. 1951–6.

V. 5: Les écoles élémentaires dans le Bas Canada, 1800–63; v. 6: La situation scolaire à la veille de l'union, 1836–40.

(g) *Ontario*

4413 ONTARIO. BUREAU OF ARCHIVES. Report, 1+. Toronto. 1903+.

4414 KINGSFORD (WILLIAM). The early bibliography of the province of Ontario . . . Toronto. 1892.

Fully annotated; covers 1783–1840. Ontario Historical Society, Papers and Records, v. 1+, Toronto, 1899+, prints docs.; index to v. 1–32 in v. 33 (1939); title changed to *Ontario History*, with v. 39 (1947).

4415 GOURLAY (ROBERT). Statistical account of Upper Canada, compiled with a view to a grand system of emigration. 3 v. 1822.

Includes docs. A biographical account of interest is Samuel Strickland, *Twenty-seven years in Canada West . . .*, ed. by Agnes Strickland, 1853.

4416 MIDDLETON (JESSE EDGAR) and LANDON (FRED). The province of Ontario: a history, 1615–1927. 5 v. Toronto. 1927–8.

Standard. V. 3–5 contain biographical material.

4417 CRAIG (GERALD M.). Upper Canada: The formative years. 1784–1841. Toronto. 1963.

Bibliog. 299–310. First vol. to appear of the Canadian Centenary Series (4332). Aileen Dunham, *Political unrest in Upper Canada, 1815–36*, 1927, is excellent.

4418 SMITH (WILLIAM). Political leaders of Upper Canada. Toronto. 1931.

Based on original material, though not documented. Conway E. Cartwright, ed., *Life and Letters of . . . Richard Cartwright*, Toronto, 1876, prints corr. of a leading merchant and politician.

4419   ONTARIO. BUREAU OF ARCHIVES. Proclamations of the Governors and Lieutenant Governors of Quebec, 1760–1791, and of the Lieutenant Governors of Upper Canada, 1792–1840. With portraits. (Report no. 4.) Toronto. 1907.

The journals of the legislative assembly of Upper Canada . . . 1792[–1824] (Bureau of Archives reports 6, 8–11) Toronto, 1911–15; *The journal of the house of assembly of Upper Canada . . .* [1829–1838], 17 pt. York [Toronto], 1829–38; *General index to the journals, 1825–1839/40*, Montreal, 1848; *Table of the provincial statutes in force, or which have been in force in Upper Canada, in their chronological order. . . . With a continuation of the index to the statutes in force, etc. to . . . 1856*, Toronto, 1856.

4420   PATERSON (GILBERT CLARENCE). Land settlement in Upper Canada, 1783–1840. Toronto. 1921.

William Canniff, *History of the settlement of Upper Canada*, Toronto, 1869, preserves much oral tradition. On Talbot's colonizing work, see Fred Coyne Hamil, *Lake Erie baron: the story of Colonel Thomas Talbot*, Toronto, 1955. There is also an older study, *The Talbot regime*, by C. O. Ermatinger, St. Thomas, 1904. James Henry Coyne, ed., *The Talbot papers*, in *Roy. Soc. Canada Trans.* 3rd series, section 2 (1907), 15–210. See also F. C. Hamil, *The valley of the lower Thames, 1640–1850*, Toronto, 1951.

4421   GUILLET (EDWIN CLARENCE). Early life in Upper Canada. Toronto. 1933. Repr. 1963.

A very full study of social conditions to 1870, with much on economic history; over 300 illus. and bibliog. 735–55. Richard B. Splane, *Social Welfare in Ontario, 1791–1893: a study of public welfare administration*, Toronto, 1965, has a good deal on early developments before 1851.

4422   FIRTH (EDITH G.) ed. The town of York, 1793–1815 [Documents]. Toronto. 1962. The town of York, 1815–1834: a further collection of documents . . . Toronto. 1966.

Edith G. Firth also ed. *Early Toronto newspapers, 1793–1867* (with intro. by Henry C. Campbell), a catalogue with historical notes and plates. See also T. W. Acheson, 'The nature and structure of York commerce in the 1820s', *Canadian Hist. Rev.* 50 (1969), 406–28.

4423   MOIR (JOHN S.). Church and state in Canada West: three studies in the relation of denominationalism and nationalism, 1841–1867. Toronto. 1959.

Deals with the clergy reserves and the education question. A. N. Bethune, *Memoir of the Rt. Rev. John Strachan . . .*, Toronto, 1870, is a life of the first bishop of Toronto. For Strachan's corr., mainly of *c.* 1812–20, see *The John Strachan letter-book: 1812–34*, ed. George W. Spragge, Toronto, 1946.

4424   HODGINS (JOHN GEORGE). The establishment of schools and colleges in Ontario, 1792–1910. 3 v. Toronto. 1910.

Hodgins also ed. *Documentary history of education in Upper Canada . . . 1791 to . . . 1876*, 28 v., Toronto, 1894–1910, of which v. 1–10 cover 1791–1852 in great detail using both official and private papers; and *Historical and other papers, documents illustrative of the educational system of Ontario, 1792–1872*, 4 v., Toronto, 1911–12. V. 1 covers 1792–1852, but there is also relevant material out of date order in v. 2–4.

4425 CANNIFF (WILLIAM). The medical profession in Upper Canada, 1783–1850: an historical narrative, with original documents relating to the profession. Toronto. 1894.

Contains much biographical as well as general historical info.

(h) *The Canadian West*

(i) *General*

4426 CANADA. PUBLIC ARCHIVES. The Canadian North-West; its early development and legislative records. Minutes of the councils of the Red River colony and the Northern Department of Rupert's land. Ed. by Edmund Henry Oliver. Ottawa. 1914–15.

4427 TORONTO. PUBLIC LIBRARIES. The Canadian North West: a bibliography of the sources of information in the reference library . . . in regard to the Hudson's Bay Company, the fur trade and the early history of the Canadian North West. Comp. by Frances M. Staton. Toronto. 1931.

4428 MORTON (ARTHUR SILVER). A history of the Canadian West to 1870: being a history of Rupert's Land, the Hudson's Bay Company's Territory, and of the North West Territory. 1938.

A monumental work of detail based on original sources. Still worth consulting are George Dugas, *L'Ouest Canadien . . . à 1822*, Montreal, 1896, English version entitled *The Canadian West . . . to the year 1822*, Montreal, 1905, and his sequel, *Histoire de l'Ouest Canadien de 1822 à 1869*, Montreal, 1906; Norman Fergus Black, *History of Saskatchewan and the old North West*, 2nd edn., Regina [1913].

4429 RICH (EDWIN ERNEST). The fur trade and the Northwest to 1857. Toronto. 1967.

See also (1489).

4430 WADE (MARK SWEETEN). Mackenzie of Canada: The life and adventures of Alexander Mackenzie, discoverer. Edin. London. 1927.

Wade made use of family papers. Less full is Hume Wrong, *Sir Alexander Mackenzie: explorer and fur trader*, Toronto, 1927.

4431 MORICE (ADRIEN GABRIEL). Histoire de l'église catholique dans l'ouest Canadien, du Lac Supérieur au Pacifique, 1659–1915. 4 v. Winnipeg. 1928.

Material on the years 1789–1851 is in v. 1 and 2.

(ii) *The Prairie Region*

4432 PEEL (BRUCE BRADEN). A bibliography of the prairie provinces to 1953. Toronto. 1956. Suppl. Toronto. 1963.

680 pp. Marjorie Morley comp. *A bibliography of Manitoba, from holdings in the legislative assembly of Manitoba*, mimeo., Winnipeg, 1953.

4433 WALLACE (WILLIAM S.). Documents relating to the North West Company [1772–1827]. Toronto. 1934.

Bibliog. 506–13. See too, Elliott Coues, ed., *New light on the early history of the greater Northwest: the manuscript journals of Alexander Henry . . . and of David Thompson . . . 1799–1814*, 3 v., 1897; Louis R. Masson, ed., *Les bourgeois de la compagnie du Nord-Ouest; récits de voyages, lettres et rapports inédits relatifs au Nord-Ouest Canadien*, 2 v., Quebec, 1889–90, facs. rep., N.Y., 1960. See also Campbell (1489).

4434 GUNN (DONALD) *and* TUTTLE (CHARLES R.). History of Manitoba from the earliest settlement to . . . [1870]. Ottawa. 1880.

Old-fashioned, but full of detail. W. L. Morton, *Manitoba: a history*, Toronto, 1957, bibliog. 501–5, is excellent but brief on the years up to 1851.

4435 PRITCHETT (JOHN PERRY). The Red River Valley, 1811–1849: a regional study. 1942.

Thorough, detailed examination of the history of the Selkirk settlement; bibliog. 272–9. Chester Martin, *Lord Selkirk's work in Canada*, Oxf., 1916, is valuable; see too his guide, *Red River settlement: papers in the Canadian archives relating to the pioneers* [Ottawa], 1910. John Morgan Gray, *Lord Selkirk of Red River*, 1963, is based on docs. but without references. See also (3935).

4436 HISTORICAL AND SCIENTIFIC SOCIETY OF MANITOBA. Publications (Transactions). v. 1–72. Winnipeg. 1882–1904. New series, v. 1+. Winnipeg. 1926+. Papers. v. 1+. Winnipeg. 1945. +.

(iii) *The Hudson's Bay Company's Territory*

See also (4429).

4437 RICH (EDWIN ERNEST). The history of the Hudson's Bay Company, 1670–1870. 2 v. 1958–9.

Standard; with chapter bibliogs. On company leaders see Richard Gill Montgomery, *The white headed eagle: John McLoughlin, builder of an empire*, N.Y., 1935, and A. S. Morton, *Sir George Simpson, overseas governor of the . . . Company . . .*, Toronto, 1944. *The Letters of John McLoughlin from Fort Vancouver . . .*, were ed. by E. E. Rich, 3 v., Toronto, 1941–4. See also John S. Galbraith, *The Hudson's Bay Company as an imperial factor, 1821–1869*, Berkeley, 1957, bibliog. 479–87.

(iv) *The Pacific Coast*

4438 MACKENZIE. First Man West; Alexander Mackenzie's journal of his voyage to the Pacific Coast of Canada in 1793. Ed. by Walter Sheppe. Montreal. 1963.

For another leading pioneer of exploration and settlement, see *The letters and journals of Simon Fraser, 1806–1808*, ed. by W. Kaye Lamb, Toronto, 1960.

4439 SCHOLEFIELD (ETHELBERT OLOF STUART) *and* HOWAY (FREDERICK WILLIAM). British Columbia, from the earliest times to the present. 4 v. Vancouver. 1914.

V. 1 is a detailed and discursive narrative for the period up to 1851. Older works worth consulting include: H. H. Bancroft, *History of British Columbia, 1792–1887*, San Francisco, 1887; Alexander Begg, *History of British Columbia . . .*, Toronto, 1894;

Adrien Gabriel Morice, *The history of the northern interior of British Columbia . . .
1660–1880*, Toronto, 1904. F. W. Howay's briefer work, *British Columbia: the making
of a province*, Toronto, 1928, has select bibliog.

4440 ORMSBY (MARGARET ANCHORETTA). British Columbia: a
history. Toronto. 1958.

Brief treatment of period to 1851; bibliog. 527–34. See too *British Columbia and the
United States: the North Pacific slope from fur trade to aviation*, by F. W. Howay, W. N.
Sage, and H. F. Angus, Toronto, New Haven, 1942.

4441 BRITISH COLUMBIA HISTORICAL QUARTERLY. V. 1+.
Victoria. 1937+.

E. THE WEST INDIES

1. GENERAL

(a) *Bibliography*

See Royal Commonwealth Society Library, *Subject Catalogue . . .*, (4281), v. 3,
pp. 503–634. For the anti-slavery movement see (2638–2642).

4442 BELL (HERBERT CLIFFORD) *and* PARKER (DAVID W.), *and
others*. Guide to British West Indian archive materials, in London and in the
islands, for the history of the United States. Wash. 1926.

Lists to 1815. There are some corrections and additions in R. Pares, 'Public records in
British West India islands', *Bull. I.H.R.* 7 (1929–30), 149–57; see also Baker (4484),
(4487), Chandler (4468). L. J. Ragatz comp., *A guide to the official correspondence of the
governors of the British West India colonies with the Secretary of State, 1763–1833*, 1923;
A check list of House of Commons sessional papers relating to the British West Indies . . .,
1763–1834, 2nd edn., 1930; and *A check list of House of Lords sessional papers . . .*, 2nd
edn., 1932. Eric [Eustace] Williams comp., *Documents on British West Indian history,
1807–1833*, Port-of-Spain, 1952, a selection from the P.R.O. relating to Barbados,
British Guiana, Jamaica, and Trinidad; and The *British West Indies at Westminster*,
pt. I, *1789–1823*, 1954, comprising extracts from parliamentary debates.

4443 RAGATZ (LOWELL JOSEPH). A guide for the study of British
Caribbean history, 1763–1834, including the abolition and emancipation
movements. Wash. 1932.

V. 3, A.H.A. annual report for 1930; a comprehensive guide to material, MSS. and
printed. F. Cundall, *Bibliography of the West Indies, excluding Jamaica*, Kingston, 1909,
is valuable, covering not only the British islands. See too *List of works in the New York
Public Library relating to the West Indies*, N.Y., 1912, repr. from *N.Y.P.L. Bull.*, v. 16,
nos. 1, 3, 8, Jan.–Aug. 1912; Waldo Lincoln, *List of newspapers of the West Indies and
Bermuda in the library of the American Antiquarian Society*, Worcester [Mass.], 1926;
West India Committee Library, *Catalogue*, 1941, rich in pamphlet material on slavery
and emancipation; Elsa V. Goveia, *A study on the historiography of the British West
Indies to the end of the nineteenth century*, México, 1956; A. E. Gropp, *Guide to libraries
and archives in Central America and the West Indies, Panama, Bermuda, and British
Guiana*, New Orleans, 1941. For recent publications see *Current Caribbean Bibliography*,
published annually by the Caribbean Commission, Port-of-Spain, 1951+.

(b) *Histories*

4444 SOUTHEY (THOMAS). Chronological history of the West Indies. 3 v. 1827.

V. 3, 1784–1816; haphazard, but includes useful collection of documents. G. Pinckard, *Notes on the West Indies*, 2 v., 1816, is vivid and well informed, mainly on Barbados and Guiana. John Williamson, *Medical and miscellaneous observations relative to the West India islands*, 2 v., Edin., 1817, was based on fourteen years' residence in Jamaica. Sir William Young, *The West India Commonplace Book*, 1807, is a politician's working collection of memoranda from debates and official documents.

4445 THE WEST INDIAN REPORTER. nos. 1–41. 1827–32.

Organ of the West India Committee; pub. intermittently. The Committee published *British colonial slavery compared with that of pagan antiquity*, 1833.

4446 CARMICHAEL (*Mrs.* A. C.). Domestic manners and social condition of the white, coloured, and negro population of the West Indies. 2 v. 1833.

By a planter's wife; strong local bias. Other good accounts from personal observation are Sir James E. Alexander, *Transatlantic sketches . . .*, 2 v., 1833, and Trelawny Wentworth, *The West India sketch book*, 2 v., 1834.

4447 AUGIER (FITZROY RICHARD) *and* **GORDON (SHIRLEY C.).** Sources of West Indian history. 1962.

A useful anthology, from documents and contemporary accounts.

4448 BURNS (*Sir* ALAN CUTHBERT M.). History of the British West Indies. Rev. 2nd edn. 1965.

Standard; bibliog. 797–808. J. H. Parry and P. M. Sherlock, *A short history of the West Indies*, 1956, is an excellent introduction. Vere Langford Oliver, *Caribbeana*, 6 v., 1909–19, is packed with genealogical information. On the West India Regiment see books by James E. Caulfeild, 1899, and Alfred B. Ellis, 1885.

4449 CARIBBEAN STUDIES. Rio Piedras, Puerto Rico. V. 1+. 1962+.

Pub. annually by the Institute of Caribbean Studies; contains articles and bibliog. lists. The *Caribbean Quarterly*, v. 1+, Port-of-Spain, 1949+, pub. irregularly, includes articles mainly on the British islands.

4450 MURRAY (DAVID JOHN). The West Indies and the development of colonial government, 1801–1834. Oxf. 1965.

An important study from primary material; bibliog. 233–56. The *Reports of the Commission of enquiry into the administration of civil and criminal justice in the West Indies*, 6 v., 1825–9, contain much information. See too accounts of the laws and constitutions of the islands by John Henry Howard, 2 v., 1827, and Henry I. Woodcock, 2nd edn. with corr., 1838.

4451 DAVY (JOHN). The West Indies before and since slave emancipation . . . founded on notes and observations collected during a three years' residence [1845–8]. 1854.

Reliable, excellent on economic matters. For the controversy over protection of sugar, see Zachary Macaulay, *East and West India sugar*, 1823, answered in Joseph Marryat, *A reply to the arguments contained in various publications recommending an equalization of the duties on East and West Indian sugar*, 1823; also Alex. Macdonnell, *Colonial commerce*, 1828.

4452 RAGATZ (LOWELL JOSEPH). Statistics for the study of British Caribbean economic history, 1763–1833. 1928.

An important collection. John Lowndes, *The coffee-planter*, 1807, is an instruction manual. See too Edgar L. Erickson, 'The introduction of East Indian coolies into the British West Indies', *J. of Modern Hist.* 6 (1934), 127–46. On trade see (1490).

4453 RAGATZ (LOWELL JOSEPH). The fall of the planter class in the British Caribbean, 1763–1833; a study in social and economic history. N.Y. and London. 1928.

Standard; bibliog. 461–90. His *Absentee landlordism in the British Caribbean, 1750–1833* Baltimore, 1931, is authoritative. R. Pares, *A West India fortune*, 1950, is a valuable account of the plantation-owning Pinney family. See too M. G. Smith, 'Some aspects of social structure in the British Caribbean about 1820', *Social and Economic Studies* [Kingston], v. 1, no. 4 (1953), 55–79.

4454 CALDECOTT (ALFRED). The church in the West Indies. 1898.

Deals with the Anglican church. See too F. P. L. Josa, *English church history of the West India province*, Georgetown, 1910. On Methodist missions in the West Indies see the life of Thomas Coke by Warren A. Candler, Nashville [Tenn.] 1923. F. J. Klingberg, 'The Lady Mico charity schools in the British West Indies, 1835–1842', *J. of Negro Hist.* 24 (1939), 291–344, deals with negro education.

2. SEPARATE AREAS

(a) *Jamaica*

4455 CUNDALL (FRANK). Bibliographia Jamaicensis: a list of Jamaica books and pamphlets, magazine articles, newspapers, and maps, most of which are in the library of the Institute of Jamaica. Kingston. 1902. Suppl. 1908.

C. V. de Bross Black, 'The archives of Jamaica', *Caribbean Quarterly*, 3 (1953), 130–5, is a general description. See too Agnes M. Butterfield, 'Notes on the records of the Supreme Court, the Chancery, and the Vice-admiralty courts of Jamaica', *Bull. I.H.R.* 16 (1938–9), 88–99. Philip Wright comp. *Monumental Inscriptions of Jamaica*, 1966.

4456 JAMAICA. Assembly. Journals . . . 1663–[1826]. 15 v. Jamaica. 1811–29.

V. 15 is an index volume. See too *The votes of the . . . assembly, 1784–1866*, 82 v., St. Iago de la Vega, 1785–1867.

4457 JAMAICA. Statutes. The laws of Jamaica; comprising all the acts in force, 1681–1837. 9 v. St. Iago de la Vega. 1802–37.

J. E. R. Stephens ed., *Supreme Court decisions of Jamaica and privy council decisions, 1774–1923*, 1924.

4458 JAMAICA ALMANACK. Pub. annually during period 1789–1851.

4459 STEWART (JOHN). A view of the past and present state of the island of Jamaica. Edin. 1823.

Based on twenty-one years' experience, critical in treatment, as is also Gilbert Mathison,

Notices respecting Jamaica in 1808–1810, 1811. On the Maroons, see R. C. Dallas, *History of the Maroons*, 2 v., 1803, and *The proceedings of the governor and assembly in regard to the Maroon negroes*, 1796. There is a modern study, Carey Robinson, *The Fighting Maroons of Jamaica*, Glasgow, 1969. Matthew G. Lewis, *Journal of a West India proprietor kept during a residence in . . . Jamaica* [1815–17], 1834, repr. ed. by Mona Wilson, 1929, is one of the best records of its kind; see too F. Cundall ed., *Lady Nugent's journal* [1801–15], 3rd edn., 1939.

4460 BRIDGES (GEORGE WILSON). The annals of Jamaica. 2 v. 1828.

A defence of the planter interests against emancipationists. For descriptions during the period of change after emancipation see B. M'Mahon, *Jamaica plantership*, 1839; *West Indies: extracts from the journal of J. Candler whilst travelling in Jamaica*, 2 pt., 1840–1; J. M. Phillippo, *Jamaica. Its past and present state*, 1843, ed. with a new intro. by Philip Wright, 1969; Sir John Bigelow, *Jamaica in 1850: or, The effects of sixteen years of freedom on a slave colony*, 1851. Graham Knox, 'British colonial policy and the problems of establishing a free society in Jamaica, 1838–65', *Caribbean Studies*, v. 2, no. 4 (1962–3), 3–13, is a well-documented survey.

4461 GARDNER (WILLIAM JAMES). A history of Jamaica from its discovery . . . to 1872. New edn. by A. W. Gardner. 1909.

A first-rate history based on local archive materials. F. Cundall, *Historic Jamaica*, Kingston, 1915, describes historic sites and monuments. A modern survey is C. V. de Bross Black, *The story of Jamaica*, 1965, with bibliog. 239–43. P. De Armond Curtin, *Two Jamaicas: the role of ideas in a tropical colony, 1830–1865*, Camb. [Mass.] 1955, bibliog. 218–32, is a valuable discussion of social structure and social concepts. Some material on a connected island group is in G. S. S. Hirst, *Notes on the history of the Cayman Islands*, 3 pt., Kingston, 1910–[12].

4462 JAMAICAN HISTORICAL REVIEW. Kingston. 1945+.

Journal of the Jamaica Historical Society; about one no. a year.

4463 MILNER (THOMAS HUGHES). The present and future state of Jamaica considered. 1839.

One of the best contemporary discussions about the functioning of government in Jamaica. For description see *The political constitution of Jamaica, including the judicial and ecclesiastical establishments of that colony, and its annual laws in force for 1844*, 1844.

4464 EISNER (GISELA). Jamaica, 1830–1930; a study in economic growth. Manchester. 1961.

Bibliog. 381–90. On the years before 1830, U. B. Phillips, 'A Jamaica slave plantation [1791–6]', *A.H.R.* 19 (1914), 543–58, is one of the best accounts of the management of a Caribbean estate. Anton V. Long, *Jamaica and the new order, 1827–1847*, Kingston, 1956, and D. G. H. Hall, *Free Jamaica, 1838–1865; an economic history*, New Haven, 1959, deal with the period of transition. For particular aspects see D. G. H. Hall, 'The apprenticeship period in Jamaica, 1834–1838', *Caribbean Quarterly*, v. 3, no. 3 (1953), 142–66; R. V. Sires, 'Negro labour in Jamaica in the years following emancipation', *J. of Negro Hist.* 25 (1940), 484–97, and 'The Jamaica slave insurrection loan, 1832–1863', *ibid.* 27 (1942), 295–319. F. Cundall, 'The press and printers of Jamaica prior to 1820', *American Antiquarian Soc. Proc.* 26 (1916), 290–412, includes a bibliog. guide; and see his *A history of printing in Jamaica from 1717 to 1834*, Kingston, 1935. See also Michael Craton and James Walvin, *A Jamaican plantation. The history of Worthy Park, 1670–1970*, 1970.

4465 ELLIS (JOHN BOURNE). The diocese of Jamaica: a short account of its history, growth and organization. 1913.

On the Church of England; the diocese was created in 1824. For other denominations see Rudolph A. L. Knight, *Liberty and progress: a short history of the Baptists of Jamaica*, Kingston, 1938; E. B. Underhill, *Life of James Mursell Phillippo*, 1881; Henry B. Foster, *Rise and progress of Wesleyan-Methodism in Jamaica*, 1881; J. H. Buchner, *The Moravians in Jamaica . . . 1754–1854*, 1854; J. A. P. M. Andrade, *A record of the Jews in Jamaica, from the English conquest to the present time*, Kingston, 1941.

4466 WRIGHT (RICHARDSON LITTLE). Revels in Jamaica, 1682–1838. N.Y. 1937.

Informative account of public entertainment in the colony.

(b) Bahamas

4467 CRATON (MICHAEL). A history of the Bahamas. 1962. 2nd edn. 1968.

Standard, with good bibliog.

(c) Barbados

4468 CRUICKSHANK (J. GRAHAM). 'A bibliography of Barbados.' *J. of the Barbados Museum and Hist. Soc.* 2 (1934–5), 155–65, 220–5; 3 (1935–6), 20–5.

M. J. Chandler, *A guide to records in Barbados*, Oxf., 1965; lists government and private records and collections. See too *Laws of Barbados*, v. 1; *1646–1854*, 1855.

4469 SCHOMBURGK (*Sir* ROBERT HERMANN). The history of Barbados; comprising a geographical and statistical description of the island. 1848.

Encyclopaedic and scholarly. For recent valuable articles see *J. of the Barbados Museum and Hist. Soc.*, v. 1 +, 1933 +.

4470 STARKEY (OTIS PAUL). The economic geography of Barbados; a study of the relationships between environmental variations and economic development. N.Y. 1939.

A comprehensive survey; bibliog. 213–19. Claude Levy describes 'Barbados: the last years of slavery, 1823–1833', in *J. of Negro Hist.* 44 (1959), 308–45. J. H. Bennett, *Bondsmen and bishops*, Berkeley, 1958, examines slavery and apprenticeship on the Codrington plantations, and F. J. Klingberg, *Codrington chronicle*, Berkeley, 1949, is a scholarly study of Codrington college. James E. Reece and C. G. Clark Hunt, eds., *Barbados diocesan history . . . [1825–1925]*, 1928, is antiquarian but informative.

(d) Bermuda

4471 WILLIAM (WILLIAM FRITH). An historical and statistical account of the Bermudas, from their discovery to the present time. 1848.

The author used local records. Sir Reginald Gray comp., *Acts of the legislature of the islands of Bermuda, 1690–1883*, 2 v., 1884, and an *Index to the acts . . . 1690–1896*, 1896. See also the *Bermuda Historical Quarterly*, v. 1 +, 1944 +. A. T. Tucker ed. *Correspondence and letters of a Bermuda merchant, 1779–1799*, Hamilton, 1930.

(e) *British Guiana*

4472 HISS (PHILIP HANSON). A selective guide to the English literature on the Netherlands West Indies; with a supplement on British Guiana. N.Y. 1943.

Vincent Roth, 'Bibliography of British Guiana' [Georgetown (?)], 1948—typescript, on microfilm at various major libraries. C. V. de Bross Black, *Report on the archives of British Guiana*, Georgetown, 1955.

4473 BRITISH GUIANA. LAWS. The laws of British Guiana chronologically arranged from the year 1580 to 1880. New rev. edn. Georgetown. 6 v. in 7. 1870–82.

4474 SCHOMBURGK (*Sir* ROBERT HERMANN). A description of British Guiana. 1840.

More reliable than H. G. Dalton, *The history of British Guiana*, 2 v., 1855. Barton Premium (*pseud.*), *Eight years in British Guiana . . . 1840–1848*, 1850, touches especially on trade questions.

4475 RODWAY (JAMES). History of British Guiana from . . . 1668 to the present time. 3 v. Georgetown. 1891–4.

Standard, as is Sir Cecil Clementi, *A constitutional history of British Guiana*, 1937. L. M. Penson, 'The making of a crown colony: British Guiana, 1803–1833', *Trans. Roy. Hist. Soc.* 4th ser., 9 (1926), 107–34, treats of a formative period. Rawle Farley discusses various economic developments in papers in *Caribbean Q.* 3 (1953), 101–9, *Social and Econ. Studies* [Kingston], 2, no. 4 (1954), 87–103, and *Revista de Historia de America*, 39 (1955), 21–59. There are histories of the East India immigrants by Peter Ruhomon, Georgetown, 1947, and Dwarka Nath, 1950. M. Moohr, 'The economic impact of slave emancipation in British Guiana, 1832–1852', *Econ. H.R.*, 2nd ser., 25 (1972), 588–606.

4476 FARRAR (THOMAS). Notes on the history of the church in Guiana. Berbice. 1892.

See too E. A. Wallbridge, *The Demerara martyr: memoirs of the Rev. John Smith*, 1843, re-ed. with add. material by J. Graham, by V. Roth, Georgetown, 1943.

(f) *British Honduras*

4477 BLISS INSTITUTE, *Belize*. A bibliography of published material on the country as found in the national collection in the central library . . . Belize. 1964. Supp. 1966.

Sir J. A. Burdon, ed., *Archives of British Honduras . . . being extracts and précis from records, with maps*, 3 v., 1931–5, is haphazard but useful, including documents since destroyed. The *Revista del archivo y biblioteca nacionales de Honduras*, Tegucigalpa, 1904+, has been since 1927 the organ of the Society of geography and history of the Honduras.

4478 HENDERSON (GEORGE). An account of the British settlement of Honduras. 2nd edn. 1811.

Comprehensive. A. R. Gibbs, *British Honduras: an historical and descriptive account of the colony from its settlement*, 1883, made good use of local newspaper material. S. Caiger, *British Honduras past and present*, 1951, is summary and has inaccuracies. There is brief factual information in Robert Cleghorn. *A short history of Baptist missionary work in British Honduras, 1822–1939*, 1939. See R. A. Humphreys (362).

(g) *Trinidad and Tobago*

4479 TRINIDAD. PUBLIC LIBRARY. Catalogue of books. Port-of-Spain. 1892. Supps. for 1893–4–5.

4480 TRINIDAD. LAWS. Laws of Trinidad, 1831–1848. The orders in council and ordinances of the council of government. 1852.

G. L. Garcia comp., *Laws of Trinidad, 1832–1896*, Port-of-Spain, 1898.

4481 CARMICHAEL (GERTRUDE). The history of the West Indian islands of Trinidad and Tobago, 1498–1900. 1961.

References, 319–62. E. E. Williams, *History of the people of Trinidad and Tobago*, Port-of-Spain, 1962; bibliog. 285–8.

4482 FRASER (LIONEL MORDAUNT). History of Trinidad from 1781 to [1839]. 2 v. Port-of-Spain. [1891]–6.

Includes numerous excerpts from official correspondence. Donald Wood, *Trinidad in transition: the years after slavery*, 1968, bibliog. 305–10, is a fully documented detailed scholarly study of the period 1838–70. C. R. Ottley, *The story of Port-of-Spain, capital of Trinidad*, Trinidad, 1962, is a brief municipal history. Charles Reis, *A history of the constitution or government of Trinidad from the earliest times . . . with notes*, v. 1, Trinidad [1929]. Trinidad Historical Society, *Publications*, no. 1+, n.d.+, form an important though uneven source for printed documents.

4483 WOODCOCK (HENRY ILES). A history of Tobago. Ayr. 1867.

Informative. C. R. Ottley, *The complete history of . . . Tobago*, Port-of-Spain, 1946, is a brief survey. English Protestant Church of Tobago, *Register of baptisms, marriages, deaths, from 1781 to 1817*, Port-of-Spain, 1936.

(h) *Leeward Islands*

4484 BAKER (EDWARD CECIL). A guide to records in the Leeward Islands. Oxf. 1965.

Archives of the islands of Antigua, Montserrat, Nevis, St. Christopher, and the Virgin Is.

4485 OLIVER (VERE LANGFORD). The history of the island of Antigua . . . to the present time. 3 v. 1894–9.

Mainly genealogical. *The laws of the island of Antigua, consisting of the Acts of the Leeward Islands* [1690–1798], *and the Acts of Antigua* [1668–1845], 4 v., 1805–46. Mrs. Flannigan, sometimes Flanagan, *Antigua and the Antiguans*, 2 v., 1844, gives an entertaining picture of contemporary society. Robson Lowe, *The Codrington correspondence, 1743–1851*, priv. print. 1951, includes material on plantation business; and see U. B. Phillips, 'An Antigua plantation, 1769–1818', *North Carolina Hist. Rev.* 3 (1926), 439–45.

4486 ST. CHRISTOPHER. STATUTES. The Statutes of the islands of St. Christopher and Anguilla [1711–1857]. St. Christopher. 1857.

Laws of Nevis from 1681 to 1861 inclusive, comp. by H. C. Huggins, 1862, excludes laws which had become inoperative. S. B. Jones, *Annals of Anguilla, British West Indies*,

1650–1923, Basseterre, 1937, is slight. On Montserrat see T. S. English, *Ireland's only colony*, Montserrat, 1930. *Letters from the Virgin Islands*, 1843, comprises rather anecdotal correspondence of a resident official during the 1820s.

(i) *Windward Islands*

4487 BAKER (EDWARD CECIL). A guide to records in the Windward Islands. Oxf. 1968.

Archives of the islands of Grenada, St. Vincent, St. Lucia, and Dominica.

4488 DOMINICA. Laws of the island of Dominica [1763–1859]. 2 v. Dominica. 1858–60.

4489 GRENADA. The laws of Grenada and the Grenadines [1766–1852]. Grenada. 1852.

There are accounts of the insurrection of 1795 by Gordon Turnbull, Edin., 1795, and John Hay, 1823, and a modern study in the last ch. of R. P. Devas, *The history of the island of Grenada*, Grenada, 1964. W. D. Davis, *A practical summary of the constitution of . . . Grenada*, Grenada [1837], is a valuable survey.

4490 ST. LUCIA. Laws at present in force . . . 1853.

Includes French eighteenth-century law, and British ordinances from 1826. Henry H. Breen, *St. Lucia: historical, statistical, and descriptive*, 1844, is excellent.

4491 ST. VINCENT. Laws of . . . St. Vincent and its dependencies from the first establishment of a legislature to . . . 1821. 2 pt. St. Vincent. 1811–23.

See too *Laws of St. Vincent*, 2 v., 1884, which includes only acts still operative at date of publication. Charles Shephard, *An historical account of the island of Saint Vincent*, 1831, is largely concerned with the Carib war of 1795.

F. THE ATLANTIC ISLANDS

(a) *Falkland Islands*

4492 CAWKELL (M. B. R.) *and others.* The Falkland Islands. 1960.

Slight, but useful bibliog. 232–44. Sets of papers regarding the islands were published by the Colonial Office in 1841 and 1843. V. F. Boyson, *Falkland Islands*, Oxf., 1924, is rather general, but has bibliog. 391–8. R. R. Caillet-Blois, *Una tierra Argentina: las Islas Malvinas; ensayo basado en una nueva y desconocida documentacion*, 2nd edn., Buenos Aires, 1952, bibliog. 427–53, explains the Argentine claim. See also J. C. J. Metford, 'Falklands or Malvinas?—The background to the dispute', *International Affairs*, 44 (1968), 463–81, and Goebel (261).

(b) *Ascension*

4493 HART-DAVIS (DUFF). Ascension. The story of a South Atlantic island. 1972.

Bibliog. 230–4.

(c) *St. Helena*

4494 KITCHING (GEOFFREY CHARLES). A St. Helena bibliography.
St. Helena. 1937.

T. H. Brooke, *History of the island of St. Helena, from its discovery by the Portuguese to ... 1806*, 2nd edn., 1824, by an official of long residence, has a descriptive opening chapter and about fifty pages on the period 1788–1806. Philip Gosse, *St. Helena, 1501–1938*, 1938, bibliog. 433–8.

(d) *Tristan da Cunha*

4495 BRANDER (JAN). Tristan da Cunha, 1506–1902. 1940.

See also Margaret Mackay, *Angry island. The story of Tristan da Cunha (1506–1963)*, 1963.

G. EUROPE

1. HELIGOLAND

4496 LINDEMANN (EMIL). Das deutsche Helgoland. Berlin-Charlotten-
burg. 1913.

A general account, including a short historical survey, a chronology of events, and a brief bibliog. William G. Black, *Heligoland and the islands of the North Sea*, 1888, is descriptive, with slight historical matter. For the British seizure of the island see Navy Records Society, *Naval Miscellany*, v. 1, 1902, 375–86.

2. MEDITERRANEAN

See Lewin (4281), v. 4, and W. F. Lord (1123).

4497 MONK (WINSTON FRANCIS). Britain in the Western Mediterranean. 1953.

An outline. Walter Frewen Lord, *The lost possessions of England: essays in imperial history*, 1896, is informative on Corsica and the Ionian islands.

(a) *Gibraltar*

4498 GARRATT (GEOFFREY THEODORE). Gibraltar and the Mediterranean. 1939.

Standard outline. Wilbur C. Abbott (264) includes *c.* 1,000 bibliog. entries.

(b) *Corsica*

4499 JOLLIVET (MAURICE). Les Anglais dans la Méditerranée: une
royaume anglo-corse. Paris. 1896.

See also Lord (4497), ch. 8.

(c) *Capri*

4500 KNOWLES (*Sir* LEES). The British in Capri, 1806–1808. 1918.

A narrative based on dispatches and private correspondence.

(d) *Malta*

4501 DONALDSON (GORDON). A handlist of manuscripts in the British Isles relating to Malta. Malta. 1950.

For local documents see Giuseppe Gatt, 'Gli archivi di Malta durante il periodo della occupazione francese e i primi anni della dominazione inglese', *Archivio Storico di Malta*, nuova ser. 9 (1938), 411–28. B. W. Beeley comp., *A bibliography of the Maltese islands (provisional draft)*, Durham, 1959, circulated as duplicated typescript. Donald H. Simpson comp., *A checklist of British official publications relating to Malta, 1801–1950*, Malta, 1954, also in *Melita Historica*, v. 1, no. 3 (1954).

4502 ETON (WILLIAM). Authentic materials for a history of the people of Malta. Malta. 1827.

Reprint of three pamphlets of 1802–7 by a British official, informative on the beginning of the British regime. Other leading contemporary accounts are Andrew Bigelow, *Travels in Malta and Sicily*, Boston, 1831; G. P. Badger, *Description of Malta and Gozo*, Malta, 1838; John Davy, *Notes and observations on the Ionian islands and Malta*, 2 v., 1842.

4503 VIVIANI (LEONARDO). Storia di Malta. 2 v. in 3. Turin. 1933.

A detailed, substantial study of Malta in the international situation of the Revolutionary and Napoleonic wars, using Neapolitan archives and Maltese MSS. collections. V. 2 concerns Britain and Malta. Piero Pieri, *La questione di Malta e il governo napoletano, 1798–1803*, Florence, 1927, also reflects Italian viewpoints. William Hardman, *The history of Malta during the period of French and British occupation, 1798–1815*, ed. J. Holland Rose, 1909, is an important collection of documents. For a different viewpoint see Sir Augusto Bartolo, *The sovereignty of Malta and the nature of its title*, Malta, 1909. For the British governor, 1813–15, see Maitland (4321).

4504 SMITH (HARRISON). Britain in Malta. 2 v. Malta. 1953.

V. 1 deals with constitutional developments in the nineteenth century; bibliog. 240–56. Sir Themistocles Zammit, *Malta, the islands and their history*, Valetta, 1929, is a general account. Mario Manlio Rossi, *La dominazione inglese a Malta fino al 1860*, Portici, 1935, is critical of British rule. Albert V. Laferla, *British Malta*, 2 v., Malta, 1938–47 is well documented and readable; standard; v. 1 spans 1800–1872. Charles A. Price, *Malta and the Maltese: a study in nineteenth century migration*, Melbourne, 1954, is an important work, with much information on social and economic conditions.

4505 MELITA HISTORICA. Valetta. 1952+.

Journal of the Maltese historical society; pub. irregularly.

(e) *Ionian Islands*

4506 LEGRAND (ÉMILE L. J.). Bibliographie Ionienne: description raisonnée des ouvrages publiés par les grecs des Sept Îles ou concernant ces îles du quinzième siècle a l'annee 1900. 2 v. Paris. 1910.

Supplement by Nakes Pierres, Athens, 1966.

4507 GUILLAUME DE VAUDONCOURT (FRÉDÉRIC). Memoirs on the Ionian islands considered in a commercial, political-military point of view. Translated by William Walton. 1816.

Substantial. Also important for its first-hand information is Sir Charles James Napier, *The colonies . . . of the Ionian islands in particular*, 1833. See too Davy (4502).

4508 HIDROMENOS (ANDREAS M.). Πολιτικη 'ιστορια της 'Επτανησου, *1815–1864* . . . 2nd edn. Corfu. 1935.

There is much incidental information from Napier's private correspondence in W. F. P. Napier, *The life and opinions of General Sir Charles James Napier*, 4 v., 1857, v. 1, pp. 285–436. See also Dixon and Lord (4321) and Lord (4497), ch. 10.

H. AFRICA

1. General

See Royal Commonwealth Society Library Catalogue (4281).

4509 ROBINSON (A. M. LEWIN). A bibliography of African bibliographies covering territories south of the Sahara. 4th edn. Duplicated. South African Public Library, Grey bibliographies no. 7. Cape Town. 1961.

Anthea Garling, *Bibliography of African bibliographies* [duplicated], Camb. 1968.

4510 HERTSLET (*Sir* EDWARD). The map of Africa by treaty. 2 v. 1894.

2. West Africa

(a) General

4511 FAGE (JOHN DONNELLY). A history of West Africa. An introductory survey. Camb. 1969.

Standard. C. W. Newbury, *British policy towards West Africa. Select Documents, 1786–1874*, Oxf., 1965, is indispensable. E. C. Martin, *The British West Africa settlements, 1750–1821. A study in local administration*, 1927, bibliog. 167–77. T. O. Elias, *Ghana and Sierra Leone; the development of their laws and constitutions*, 1962, has brief historical surveys. On commerce see J. B. Williams, 'The development of British trade with West Africa, 1750 to 1850', *Political Science Q.* 50 (1935), 194–213.

(b) Regions

(i) Gambia

4512 GRAY (*Sir* JOHN MILNER). A history of the Gambia. Camb. 1940.

Full use of documents. H. A. Gailey, *A history of the Gambia*, 1964, bibliog. 218–22, gives a brief survey.

(ii) Sierra Leone

4513 LUKE (HARRY CHARLES). A bibliography of Sierra Leone, preceded by an essay on the origin, character, and peoples of the colony and protectorate. 2nd edn. Oxf. 1925.

Christopher Fyfe, *A history of Sierra Leone*, 1962, bibliog. 621–39, standard, is supplemented by his *Sierra Leone inheritance*, 1964, containing illustrative documents.

(iii) Gold Coast

4514 CARDINALL (ALLAN WOLSEY). A bibliography of the Gold Coast. Accra. [1932.]

4515 METCALFE (GEORGE EDGAR) *ed.* Great Britain and Ghana. Documents of Ghana history, 1807–1957. 1964.

Substantial on the years to 1851. John J. Crooks, *Records relating to the Gold Coast settlements from 1750 to 1874*, Dublin, 1923, includes material from Company records. Brodie Cruikshank, *Eighteen years on the Gold Coast*, 2 v., 1853, is a major contemporary account; the writer became a member of the legislative council.

4516 CLARIDGE (WILLIAM WALTON). A history of the Gold Coast and Ashanti, from the earliest times to the commencement of the twentieth century. With an intro. by Sir Hugh Clifford. 2 v. 1915.

Substantial. A. B. Ellis, *History of the Gold Coast*, 1893, is old-fashioned but full of detail. C. C. Reindorf, *History of the Gold Coast and Asante*, 2nd edn., 1951, makes good use of native tradition. W. E. F. Ward, *A history of Ghana*, 2nd rev. edn., 1958, bibliog. 13–14, provides summary modern treatment. See too G. E. Metcalfe, *Maclean of the Gold Coast. The life and times of George Maclean, 1801–1847*, 1962.

(iv) *Niger Delta*

4517 BURNS (*Sir* ALAN CUTHBERT). History of Nigeria. 7th edn. 1969.

Britain was involved in this area though it was not yet colonized. See too Arthur N. Cook, *British enterprise in Nigeria*, Philadelphia, 1943, bibliog. 291–319, and K. O. Diké, *Trade and politics in the Niger delta, 1830–85*, Oxf., 1956.

3. SOUTHERN AFRICA

(a) *Bibliography*

4518 BOTHA (COLIN GRAHAM). The public archives of Southern Africa, 1652–1910. Cape Town. 1928.

Local archive collections. The provincial archives, which are responsible for the records of the pre-Union colonies, are situated at Cape Town, Pretoria, Pietermaritzburg, and Bloemfontein. The archives at Cape Town include records of the first British occupation of the Cape, 1795–1803, of the Batavian Republic, 1803–6, and of the second British occupation and development of the Crown Colony after 1806. Those at Pietermaritzburg include records before the annexation in 1843 (see under (d) (ii)). The publications of the Van Riebeeck Society (Cape Town, 1918+) are mainly editions of source material, some of it from private collections, and are indispensable. Una Long, *An index to authors of unofficial, privately-owned manuscripts relating to the history of South Africa, 1812–1920; with copies, summaries, and extracts of documents*, 1947, includes biographical notes.

4519 MENDELSSOHN (SIDNEY). South African bibliography; being the catalogue raisonné of the Mendelssohn library of works relating to South Africa. 2 v. 1910.

Typescript additions in 3 v., 1910–14. copious annotations. Other collections are listed in C. A. Fairbridge and John Noble, *Catalogue of books relating to South Africa*, Cape Town, 1886; C. A. Fairbridge, *The Fairbridge library*, priv. printed, Edin., 1904; G. M. Theal, *Catalogue of books and pamphlets relating to Africa south of the Zambesi in the English, Dutch, French, and Portuguese languages*, Cape Town, 1912, new imp. 1963. Afrikaans literature from its beginning in 1861 is listed in P. J. Nienaber, *Bibliografie van Afrikaanse boeke*, 1943+. C. F. J. Muller, F. A. Van Jaarsveld, and T. Van Wijk comp., *A select bibliography of South African history*, Pretoria, 1966 (215 pp.), with subject and period arrangement. A. A. Roberts, *A South African legal bibliography*,

Pretoria, 1942, includes European literature on Roman and Roman Dutch law of relevance to South Africa. See also Lewin (4281). South African imprints since 1959 are listed in the *South African national bibliography*, quarterly with annual cumulations, Pretoria, 1960+.

(b) *Description*

4520 SCHMIDT (KATHE MARGARET) *comp.* Bibliography of personal accounts of the Cape of Good Hope in printed books, 1715–1850. Cape Town. 1955.

Typescript; copies available in some major libraries. An excellent listing, with items arranged chronologically and evaluated. A few of the most important accounts are: Sir John Barrow, *Travels into the interior of southern Africa* [1797–8], 2nd edn., 1806; M. H. C. Lichtenstein, *Travels in southern Africa* [1803–6], reprint of the translation by Anne Plumptre, 2 v., Cape Town, 1928–30; W. J. Burchell, *Travels in the interior of southern Africa*, 2 v., 1822–4; George Thompson, *Travels and adventures in southern Africa*, 2 v., 1827; Harriet Ward, *Five years in Kaffirland*, 1848. Details from the viewpoint of government house are given in Lady Anne Barnard, *South Africa a century ago*, *1797–1801*; pt. 1: *Letters . . .*, pt. 2: *Extracts from a journal . . .*, sel. and ed. by H. J. Anderson, with a memoir by W. H. Wilkins, Oxf. [1925]; see too Dorothea Fairbridge, *Lady Anne Barnard at the Cape of Good Hope, 1797–1802*, Oxf., 1924, and A. M. Lewin Robinson, ed., *The letters of Lady Anne Barnard to Henry Dundas . . . 1793–1803*, *together with her journal* (South African biographical and historical studies 17), Cape Town, 1973.

(c) *History*

(i) *General*

See Cole (4319)

4521 CAPE OF GOOD HOPE. Records of the Cape Colony from February 1793. By George McCall Theal. 36 v. 1897–1905.

Material from the Public Record Office, London. Theal also comp., *Catalogue of documents from 16 September 1795 to 21 February 1803, in the collection of colonial archives at Cape Town*, Cape Town, 1880. V. 5 of *Kaapse argiefstukke. Kaapse plakkaat boek*, Cape Town, 1944+, contains the proclamations of the British governors, 1795–1803. E. M. Jackson ed. the colony's *Statutes, 1652–1905*, 4 v., 1906; v. 1 covers the period. See also Walter Harding, *The Cape of Good Hope government proclamations from 1806 to 1825 as now in force and unrepealed and the ordinances . . . 1825 to 1844*, 4 v., Cape Town, 1845; *Rules and orders of the courts of judicature in the colonies of the Cape of Good Hope and Western Australia*, 1841. Guides and published records of the Boer communities which moved out of the jurisdiction of the colony include *Transvaal archief*. *Beredeneerde inventarissen van de oudste archief-groepen der Zuid-Afrikaanse Republiek*, by P. L. A. Goldman, Pretoria, 1927; *Transvaalse argiefstukke. Staatsekretaries, inkomende stukke, 1850–1853*, by D. W. Krynauw and H. S. Pretorius, Pretoria, 1949; *Notule van die volksraad van die Suid-Afrikaanse Republik*, ed. J. H. Breytenbach and H. S. Pretorius, 6 v., Cape Town, 1949–56.

4522 CORY (*Sir* GEORGE EDWARD). The rise of South Africa: a history of the origin of South African colonization and of its development towards the East from the earliest times to 1857. 5 v. 1910–30.

A final six chapters of v. 6 were pub. in *Archives Year Book* (4524), 1939, pt. 1, Cape Town, 1940. Also on the grand scale, G. M. Theal, *History of South Africa, 1795–1872*, 5 v., 1919–27, covers an area wider than the present republic.

4523 CAMBRIDGE HISTORY OF THE BRITISH EMPIRE. V. 8: South Africa, Rhodesia and the High Commission Territories. [2nd edn.] General ed. Eric A. Walker. Camb. 1963.

Bibliog. 917–1017. Eric A. Walker, *A history of Southern Africa*, 3rd edn., 1957, is a standard general survey; bibliog. 925–45. Other important general histories are *Geskiedenis van Suid-Afrika*, by A. J. H. Van Der Walt and others, Cape Town, 1965, bibliog. 593–607, and *The Oxford History of South Africa*, ed. by Monica Wilson and L. Thompson, v. 1: *South Africa to 1870*, Oxf., 1969, bibliog. 447–72.

4524 ARCHIVES YEAR BOOK FOR SOUTH AFRICAN HISTORY. Cape Town. 1938+.

Usually two volumes a year, including both articles and longer works of book-length; indispensable.

4525 EYBERS (GEORGE VON WELFLING) *ed*. Select constitutional documents illustrating South African history, 1795–1910. 1918.

A comprehensive, well-chosen collection. P. J. Venter, *Landdros en heemrade (1682–1827)*, Archives Year Book, 3, pt. 2 (1940), is a study of local administration, relating its breakdown to the Boer migrations.

4526 MILLAR (ANTHONY KENDAL). Plantagenet in South Africa: Lord Charles Somerset. 1965.

A sympathetic study of the most controversial of the governors [1812–26]. There is indispensable material in *The autobiography of the late Sir Andries Stockenstrom, bart.*, ed. C. W. Hutton, 2 v., Cape Town, 1887, facsim. rep. 1964. Less important is *The autobiography of Lieut. General Sir Harry Smith*, ed. G. C. Moore Smith, 2 v., 1901.

(ii) *Studies of Subjects and Periods*

4527 WAGNER (MARY ST. CLAIR). The first British occupation of the Cape of Good Hope, 1795–1803: a bibliography. (University of Cape Town School of Lib. bibliog. series). Cape Town. 1946.

Duplicated typescript copies available in some major libraries. See also *The Keith Papers* (1216), i. 205–474; Sir John Barrow, *Some account of the public life . . . of the Earl of Macartney*, 2 v., 1807; and on the British return in 1806, *The Naval Miscellany*, v. 3, Nav. Rec. Soc. (1928), 191–285.

4528 VAN DER MERWE (PETRUS JOHANNES). Die Noordwaartse beweging van die Boere voor die Groot Trek, 1770–1842. The Hague. 1937.

Well-documented study with full bibliog.

4529 EDWARDS (ISOBEL EIRLYS). Towards emancipation: a study in South African slavery. Cardiff. 1942.

4530 VAN OORDT (JAN WILLEM GERBRANDT). Slagtersnek: een bladzijde uit de voorgeschiedenis der Zuid Afrikaansche Republiek. Amsterdam. Pretoria. 1897.

A full collection of the papers is in *The rebellion of 1815, generally known as Slachters Nek*, ed., H. C. V. Leibbrandt, Cape Town, 1902.

4531 EDWARDS (ISOBEL EIRLYS). The 1820 settlers in South Africa:
a study in British colonial policy. 1934.

A penetrating, fully documented study; bibliog. 156–70. *Philipps, 1820 settler; his
letters,* ed. A. Keppel-Jones, Pietermaritzburg, 1960, contains valuable material. General
accounts of the settlers' experiences are given in H. E. Hockly, *The story of the British
settlers of 1820 in South Africa,* 2nd edn., Cape Town, 1957, and Dorothy E. Rivett-
Carnac, *Thus came the English in 1820,* 1961. On development at Knysna see Patricia
Storrar, *George Rex: death of a legend,* Johannesburg, 1974.

4532 WALKER (ERIC ANDERSON). The Great Trek. 5th edn. 1965.

Standard. Older works worth consulting are G. M. Theal, *History of the Boers in South
Africa,* 1887; Henry Cloete, *History of the great Boer trek,* 2nd edn., 1899; J. C. Voigt,
Fifty years of the history of the Republic in South Africa, 2 v., 1899. *Voortrekker-argief-
stukke 1829–1849,* by H. S. Pretorius and others, Pretoria, 1937, is a collection of
documents.

4533 GALBRAITH (JOHN SEMPLE). Reluctant empire: British policy on
the South African frontier, 1834–54. Berkeley. 1963.

Bibliog. 277–86. A study from the viewpoint of Whitehall well based on the archives;
also well documented is C. F. J. Muller, *Die Britse owerheid en die Groot Trek,* 2nd edn.,
Johannesburg, 1963, bibliog. 301–26.

4534 HATTERSLEY (ALAN FREDERICK). The convict crisis and the
growth of unity: resistance to transportation in South Africa and Australia,
1848–53. Pietermaritzburg. 1965.

Mainly focused on South Africa and dealing with a significant preliminary to the move
towards representative government in Cape Colony.

4535 DE KIEWIET (CORNELIUS WILLEM). British colonial policy and
the South African Republics, 1848–1872. 1929.

4536 NEUMARK (SOLOMON DANIEL). Economic influences on the
South African frontier, 1652–1836. Stanford. 1957.

A valuable study, linking economic conditions with migration. On other aspects of
economic life see E. H. D. Arndt, *Banking and currency development in South Africa,
1652–1927,* Cape Town, 1928, bibliog. 507–19; C. G. W. Schumann, *Structural
changes and business cycles in South Africa, 1806–1936,* 1938; R. F. M. Immelman,
*Men of Good Hope: the romantic story of the Cape Town Chamber of Commerce, 1804–
1954,* Cape Town, 1955. See Knowles (4314).

4537 SMITHERS (ALAN J.). The Kaffir wars, 1779–1877. 1974.

4538 SCHAPERA (ISAAC) *ed.* Select bibliography of South African native
life and problems. 1941.

The emphasis is ethnological, but some historical material is listed. W. M. Macmillan,
The Cape Colour question: an historical survey, 1927, and *Bantu, Boer, and Briton: the
making of the South African native problem,* 1929 (rev. and enl. edn., Oxf., 1963),
received scholarly critical challenge in J. S. Marais, *The Cape Coloured people, 1652–
1937,* 1939.

4539 HINCHCLIFF (PETER). The Anglican Church in South Africa; an account of the history and development of the Church of the Province of South Africa. 1963.

Bibliog. 251–62; more up-to-date but more summary than C. Lewis and Gertrude E. Edwards, *Historical records of the Church of the Province of South Africa*, 1934. S. P. Engelbrecht, *Geskiedenis van die Nederduits hervormde kerk van Afrika*, Cape Town, 1953, is a comprehensive account. There is a brief account of the Baptists in ch. 1 of H. J. Batts, *The story of a hundred years, 1820–1920; being the history of the Baptist church in South Africa*, Cape Town [1922]. On religious missions, see D. K. Clinton, *The South African melting pot: a vindication of missionary policy, 1799–1836*, 1937, and V. Ellenberger, *A century of mission work in Basutoland, 1833–1933*, Morija, 1938.

4540 MALHERBE (ERNEST GIDEON). Education in South Africa (1652–1922); a critical survey of educational administration in the Cape, Natal, Transvaal and the Orange Free State. Cape Town. 1925.

A substantial survey, with good bibliog. 483–504. See also *Onderwys in Suid-Afrika, 1652–1956*, ed. J. C. Coetzee, Pretoria, 1958.

4541 MANDELBROTE (JOYCE C.). The Cape Press, 1838–1850: a bibliography. Cape Town. 1945.

Duplicated typescript; a chronological listing of imprints, arranged alphabetically for each year. L. H. Meurant, *Sixty years ago; or, Reminiscences of the struggle for the freedom of the press in South Africa*, Cape Town, 1885, facsim. rep. 1963, is a first-hand account.

4542 BURROWS (EDMUND HARTFORD). A history of medicine in South Africa up to the end of the nineteenth century. Cape Town. 1958.

4543 LEWCOCK (RONALD [BENTLEY]). Early nineteenth century architecture in South Africa: a study of the interaction of two cultures, 1795–1837. Cape Town. 1963.

Finely illustrated, and comprehensive references and bibliog.

(iii) *Natal*

4544 WEBB (COLIN DE B.) *comp*. A guide to the official records of the colony of Natal. Pietermaritzburg. 1965.

Duplicated typescript. For published records see *Notule Natalse Volksraad (met bylae), 1838–1845* (South African Archival Records, Natal, no. 1), Cape Town, 1953; *Records of the Natal Executive Council, 1846–1852* (S.A.A.R., Natal, nos. 2–4), 3 v., Cape Town, 1960–63; G. M. Theal, *Basutoland Records*, 3 v., Cape Town, 1883, v. 1: *1833–1852*.

4545 O'BYRNE (SHELAGH PATRICIA MARY), *comp*. The colony of Natal to the Zulu war, 1843–78; a bibliography. Cape Town. 1965.
Duplicated typescript.

4546 BIRD (JOHN). The annals of Natal, 1495–1845. 2 v. Pietermaritzburg. 1888.

A valuable collection of printed documents and verbal depositions. See too J. C. Chase, *Natal, a reprint of all the authentic notices and public documents* [1494–1843], 2 pt., Grahamstown, 1843; W. J. D. Moodie, *Ordinances, proclamations, etc., relating to the colony of Natal, 1836–55*, 2 v., Pietermaritzburg, 1856. For a contemporary description see J. E. Methley, *The new colony of Port Natal*, 2nd edn., 1850.

4547 BROOKES (EDGAR HARRY) *and* **WEBB (COLIN DE B.). A history of Natal. Pietermaritzburg. 1965.**

Notes on sources, 307–54. Standard, but summary on period. Studies in greater detail are, A. F. Hattersley, *The British settlement of Natal; a study in imperial migration,* Camb., 1950, and *More annals of Natal,* 1936, an anthology of personal accounts. See too Hector M. Robertson, 'The 1849 settlers in Natal', *South African J. of Economics* v. 17 (1949), 274–88, 416–42.

4548 RITTER (ERNST AUGUST). Shaka Zulu: the rise of the Zulu empire. 1955.

Other studies of the African side of the border conflicts on the frontier of Natal are D. R. Morris, *The washing of the spears: a history of the rise of the Zulu nation under Shaka and its fall in the Zulu war of 1879,* 1966; P. Becker, *Rule of fear: the life and times of Dingane, king of the Zulu,* 1964, and *Path of blood: the rise and conquests of Mzilikazi, founder of the Matabele tribe of Southern Africa,* 1962.

4. EAST AFRICA

4549 GRAY (*Sir* JOHN). The British in Mombasa, 1824–26; being the history of Captain Owen's protectorate. (Kenya History Society transactions, v. 1.) 1957.

The wider context of outside interest in East Africa is treated in Reginald Coupland, *East Africa and its invaders* [to 1856], Oxf., 1938, and Mabel V. Jackson, *European powers and south-east Africa: a study of international relations on the south-east coast of Africa, 1796–1856,* 1942. For the African background see also R. Oliver and G. Mathew, *History of East Africa,* v. 1, Oxf., 1963, and K. Ingham, *A history of East Africa,* 1962.

5. MAURITIUS AND THE SEYCHELLES

See Cole (4319).

4550 TOUSSAINT (AUGUSTE) *and* **ADOLPHE (H.). Bibliography of Mauritius (1502–1954), covering the printed records, manuscripts, archivalia, cartographic material. Port Louis. 1956.**

About 9,000 entries, including a number of references to the Seychelles.

4551 PITOT (ALBERT). L'Isle Maurice, 1810–1833. 3 v. Port Louis. 1910–14.

See too D. Napal, comp., *Les Constitutions de l'Île Maurice* (Mauritius Archives Pubs.), Port Louis, 1962; Auguste Toussaint, *Une cité tropicale. Port-Louis de l'Île Maurice,* Paris, 1966; G. A. North Coombes, *The evolution of sugar cane culture in Mauritius,* Port Louis, 1937.

I. INDIA

1. BIBLIOGRAPHY

Consult the bibliogs. in Lewin (4281), *The Cambridge History of India,* v. 5 (4570), and the section 'East Indies' in the B.L. Catalogue. On Indian studies see (3405–12).

(a) *Manuscripts*

4552 WAINWRIGHT (MARY DOREEN) *and* MATTHEWS (NOEL) *comp.* A guide to western manuscripts and documents in the British Isles relating to South and South East Asia. 1965.

S. C. Sutton, *A guide to the India Office Library with a note on the India Office records,* 1967, explains classifications and has an appendix listing gifts and deposits. S. C. Hill, *Catalogue of the Home Miscellaneous Series of the India Office records,* 1927, gives detail. Joan C. Lancaster, *Guide to lists and catalogues of the India office records,* 1966. Mary Thatcher, comp., *Cambridge South Asian Archive. Records of the British period in South Asia relating to India, Pakistan, Ceylon, Burma, Nepal and Afghanistan, held in the Centre of South Asian Studies, University of Cambridge,* 1973.

4553 GHOSE (SAILEN). Archives in India. History and Assets. Calcutta. 1963.

Explains the organization of the archives in India; includes a list of printed selections from the records and of guides to various groups. For detail see Donald A. Low, J. C. Iltis, and M. D. Wainwright, *Government archives in South Asia. A guide to national and state archives in Ceylon, India, and Pakistan,* Camb., 1969; *A handbook of the records of the government of India in the Imperial Record Department* [now the National Archives of India], *1748–1859,* Calcutta, 1925; *List of treaties, engagements and sanads in the custody of the Imperial Record Department,* Simla, 1941; *Catalogue of the English records, 1758–1858, preserved in the Historical record room of the government of Bengal,* 3 pt., Calcutta, 1922–5; Edmond Gaudard, *Catalogue des manuscrits des anciennes archives de l'Inde française,* 8 v., Paris, 1926–36.

(b) *Printed Sources*

4554 WILSON (PATRICK). 'Bibliographical article: a survey of bibliographies on Southern Asia'. *J. of Asian Studies.* 18 (1959), 365–76.

4555 GREAT BRITAIN. PARLIAMENT. Annual lists and general index of the parliamentary papers relating to the East Indies published . . . 1801 to 1907. 1909.

See too *A classified list of reports and other publications in the record branch of the India Office,* 1913. Particularly informative on all aspects of British activity in India are the successive Reports of the House of Commons Select Committees on the affairs of the East India Company: 1st R., H.C. 1808 (261) III, 2nd R., H.C. 1810 (363) V, 3rd R. H.C. 1810–11 (250) VII, 4th R., H.C. 1812 (280) VI, 5th R., H.C. 1812 (377) VII; H.C. 1830 (644, 655) V. H.C. 1830 (646) VI, containing a Lords' Committee Report; Minutes of evidence 1831 (320) V and (320 B–E) VI, 1831–2 (734) VIII and (735) I–VI, IX–XIV.

4556 INDIA OFFICE. Catalogue of the library. 22 pt. 1888–1936.

Collections in the Indian National Library, Calcutta, are listed in its *Catalogue of printed books in European languages,* Calcutta, 1941, in progress, and *Catalogue of periodicals, newspapers and gazettes* [comp. by Benoy Sen Gupta], Calcutta, 1956. See too Margaret H. Case, *South Asian history, 1750–1950. A guide to periodicals, dissertations, and newspapers,* Princeton, 1968; and the indexes in the *Centenary volume of the Royal Asiatic Society of Great Britain and Ireland, 1823–1923,* comp. by F. E. Pargiter, 1923. B. S. Kesavan and V. Y. Kulkarni, general eds., *The national bibliography of Indian literature, 1901–1953,* v. 1, New Delhi, 1962, lists pubs. in Assamese, Bengali, English, and Gujarati. For imprints since 1958 see *The Indian national bibliography,* Calcutta, 1959+, annual cumulations.

4557 DATTA (KALIKINKAR). A survey of recent studies on modern Indian history. Patna. 1957.

Includes mention of theses then in progress. C. H. Philips, ed., *Historians of India, Pakistan, and Ceylon,* 1961, discusses missionaries' accounts.

2. GENERAL HISTORY

(a) *Sources*

4558 FIRMINGER (WALTER KELLY) *ed.* The fifth report from the Select committee of the House of Commons on the affairs of the East India company. Dated 28th July, 1812. 3 v. Calcutta, 1917–8.

Standard authority on Indian land tenures, judicial, and police system.

4559 MALCOLM (*Sir* JOHN). The political history of India, 1784–1823. 2 v. 1826. 2nd edn. 1911.

A valuable account by a participant, whose information often has the value of an original source.

4560 CALCUTTA GAZETTE. Selections from the *Calcutta Gazettes* of the years 1784–1823, showing the political and social condition of the English in India. V. 1–3 by W. S. Seton-Karr; v. 4–5 by H. D. Sandeman. Calcutta. 1864–9.

In sequel is *The days of John Company: selections from Calcutta Gazette, 1824–1832;* comp. and ed. by Anil C. Das Gupta, Calcutta, 1959.

4561 ASIATIC JOURNAL AND MONTHLY REGISTER for British India. V. 1–28, n.s. 1–40. 1816–43.

Further series were pub. under various titles, 1843–50, when it merged with *Simmonds colonial magazine.*

4562 HAMILTON (WALTER). The East-India gazetteer; containing particular descriptions of . . . Hindostan and the adjacent countries, India beyond the Ganges, and the Eastern Archipelago. 1815. 2nd edn. 2 v. 1828.

4563 JACQUEMONT (VICTOR VINCESLAS). Voyage dans l'Inde . . . pendant les années 1828–1832 . . . journal. 4 v. Paris. 1835–1844.

See too *Letters from India, 1829–1832; being a selection from the correspondence of Victor Jacquemont;* trans. with introd. by Catherine A. Phillips, 1936.

4564 SUTHERLAND (JOHN). Sketches of the relations subsisting between the British government in India and the different native states. Calcutta. 1837.

Brief, but well informed, notable for its almost synoptic presentation with careful analysis of variant forms of relationship.

4565 MORLEY (WILLIAM HOOK). An analytical digest of all the reported cases decided in the supreme courts of judicature in India, in the courts of the Hon. East India Company, and on appeal from India by H.M. in council. 3 v. 1849–52.

4566 MANUEL (R. A.) *comp*. A comprehensive, alphabetical and analytical index to all the acts repealed and unrepealed of the legislative councils of the Governor General of India, the governors of Bombay and Madras, and the lieut. governor of Bengal, to 1873. Calcutta. 1874.

4567 AITCHISON (*Sir* CHARLES UMPHERSTON) *ed*. A collection of treaties, engagements, and sunnuds relating to India and neighbouring countries. Calcutta. 7 v. 1862–5.

Another edn. rev. and continued up to the present time by Lieutenant A. C. Talbot [with an index by M. Belletty], 8 v., 1876–8. Other edns. and continuations, 11 v., Calcutta, 1892; 13 v., 1909 [to 1 June 1906]. The standard collection for reference on diplomatic engagements.

4568 PHILLIMORE (REGINALD HENRY) *comp*. Historical records of the survey of India. 4 v. Dehra Dun. 1945–59.

A miscellany of information of military, fiscal, and geographical interest. See also (3449).

4569 MUIR (RAMSAY) *ed*. The making of British India, 1756–1858. 2nd edn. Manchester. 1951.

Other valuable collections of documents include Sir George Anderson and M. Subedar, *The last days of the Company: a source book of Indian history 1818–1858*, 2 v., 1918–21; *Select documents of the British period of Indian history, in the collection of the Victoria Memorial, Calcutta*, ed. D. C. Ganguly, Calcutta, 1958. C. H. Dharker, ed., *Lord Macaulay's legislative minutes*, Madras, 1946.

(b) *Later Works*

4570 THE CAMBRIDGE HISTORY OF INDIA. V. 5: British India, 1497–1858. Ed. by Henry H. Dodwell. Camb. 1929.

A standard one-vol. history of British rule, with indispensable bibliogs. Other good general surveys are J. Allan, Sir T. W. Haig, and H. H. Dodwell, *The Cambridge shorter history of India*, Camb., 1934; Edward J. Thompson and G. T. Garratt, *Rise and fulfilment of British rule in India*, 1934; R. C. Majumdar and others, *An advanced history of India*, 2nd edn., 1956; P. E. Roberts, *History of British India under the company and the crown*, 3rd edn. ed. by T. G. P. Spear, 1952; Vincent A. Smith, *The Oxford history of India*, 3rd edn. ed. T. G. P. Spear, Oxf., 1967; Michael Edwardes, *British India, 1772–1947. A survey of the nature and effects of alien rule*, 1967. James Burgess, *The chronology of modern India . . . 1494–1894*, Edin., 1913, is convenient for reference.

4571 MISRA (G. S.). British foreign policy and Indian affairs. 1788–1815. 1964.

For treatment of the French presence in this period see Siba P. Sen, *The French in India, 1763–1816*, Calcutta, 1958. See also M. E. Yapp (338).

4572 BUCKLAND (CHARLES EDWARD). Dictionary of Indian biography. 1906.

See also *The men who ruled India*, by Philip Woodruff, *pseud*. of Philip Mason, 2 v., 1953–4, pt. 1: *The founders* [to 1858].

4573 JOURNAL OF INDIAN HISTORY. Allahabad. V. 1+. 1921+.

Useful for book reviews and some articles with historical content is the *Calcutta Review*,

v. 1+, Calcutta, 1844+; index to v. 1–50, 1873. Other journals include the Royal
Asiatic Society, Bombay Branch, *Journal*, v. 1+, Bombay, 1844+, and n.s. v. 1+,
1925+; Bombay Historical Society, *Journal*, v. 1+, Bombay, 1928+.

**4574 BEARCE (GEORGE DONHAM). British attitudes towards India, 1784–
1858. 1961.**

James Mill, *The history of British India*, 3 v., 1817, 5th edn. with notes and continuation
by Horace H. Wilson, 10 v., 1858, has been the most influential of British historical
writings on India during the nineteenth century. Other accounts well representing the
contemporary view are Edward Thornton, *The history of the British empire in India*,
6 v., 1841–5, 2nd edn., 1858, and Henry Beveridge, *A comprehensive history of India*,
3 v., 1858–62.

(c) *Biography: Governors General*

See also Metcalfe (4322).

**4575 CORNWALLIS (G.G. 1786–93, 1805). Lord Cornwallis. Dispatches of
Lord Cornwallis from India, 1790–2, 1805. Ed. with an intro. by Sir George
William Forrest. 2 v. Oxf. 1926.**

V. 1: introduction; v. 2: documents. See also (172). A. Aspinall, *Cornwallis in Bengal*,
Manchester, 1931, examines administrative and judicial reforms, commercial expansion
and the foundation of Penang.

**4576 SHORE (G.G. 1793–8). The private record of an Indian governor-
generalship: the correspondence of Sir John Shore . . . with Henry Dundas
. . . 1793–1798. Ed. by Holden Furber. Camb., Mass. 1933.**

Charles J. Shore, 2nd baron Teignmouth, *Memoir of the life and correspondence of John
Lord Teignmouth by his son*, 2 v., 1843.

**4577 WELLESLEY (G.G. 1798–1805). The despatches, minutes and corres-
pondence of the Marquess Wellesley during his administration in India. Ed.
by Robert Montgomery Martin. 5 v. 1836–7.**

*A selection from the despatches, treaties, and other papers of . . . Wellesley . . . during his
government of India* was ed. by S. J. Owen, Oxf., 1877. Papers captured by the French
were later published as *History of all the events and transactions . . . in India . . . by . . .
the Marquess of Wellesley*, 1805. See Paul E. Roberts, *India under Wellesley*, 1929. Critical from an Indian viewpoint is B. N. Mehta, 'Lord Wellesley's policy and its reversal',
J. of Indian History, 32 (1954), 171–90. See also (196).

**4578 MINTO (G.G. 1807–13). Lord Minto in India: life and letters . . . from
1807 to 1814 . . . Ed. by the Countess of Minto. 1880.**

See also (166). Shilendra K. Singh, 'Minto, Baillie, and Saadut Ali, 1807–1813', *J. of
Indian History*, 30 (1952), 235–44; 31 (1953), 57–73, 119–33, 259–70.

**4579 HASTINGS (G.G. 1813–23). The private journal of the Marquess of
Hastings . . . Governor General . . . in India; edited by his daughter, the Marchioness of Bute. 2 v. 1858.**

The East India Company pub. *Papers regarding the administration of the Marquis of
Hastings in India*, 1824. H. T. Prinsep, *History of the political and military transactions
in India during the administration of the Marquess of Hastings, 1813–1823*, 2 v., 1825,
is an authoritative contemporary survey. A good modern study is Mohan Sinha Mehta,
Lord Hastings and the Indian states, Bombay, 1930.

4580 AMHERST (G.G. 1823–8). RITCHIE (ANNE ISABELLA) (*Lady* THACKERAY) *and* EVANS (RICHARDSON). Lord Amherst and the British advance eastwards to Burma. Oxf. 1894.

4581 BENTINCK (G.G. 1828–35). BOULGER (DEMETRIUS CHARLES) Lord William Bentinck. Oxf. 1892.

4582 AUCKLAND (G.G. 1836–42). TROTTER (LIONEL JAMES). The Earl of Auckland. Oxf. 1893.

Partisan in its indictment of Auckland's policy.

4583 ELLENBOROUGH (G.G. 1842–4). IMLAH (JAMES ALBERT HENRY). Lord Ellenborough: a biography. . . . Camb. Mass. 1939.

Standard; bibliog. 275–84. Ellenborough's *A political diary, 1828–1830*, ed. by Lord Colchester, 2 v., 1881, covers his years at the Board of Control. Colchester also ed. *History of the Indian administration of Lord Ellenborough in his correspondence with the Duke of Wellington* . . . [and] *Lord Ellenborough's letters to the Queen*, 1874. See too *India under Lord Ellenborough . . . a selection from the hitherto unpublished papers and secret despatches*, ed. by Sir Algernon Law, 1926.

4584 HARDINGE (G.G. 1844–7). HARDINGE (CHARLES STEWART), 2nd Viscount. Viscount Hardinge. Oxf. 1891.

4585 DALHOUSIE (G.G. 1848–56). LEE-WARNER (*Sir* WILLIAM). The life of the Marquis of Dalhousie. 2 v. 1904.

See too *Private letters of the Marquess of Dalhousie*, ed. J. G. A. Baird, 1910.

3. BRITISH EXPANSION AND RELATIONS WITH NATIVE STATES

See also appropriate entries in section 2 (*c*)

4586 SARKAR (*Sir* JADUNATH). Fall of the Mughal empire. 4 v. Calcutta. 1932–50.

V. 4 carries the story with thoroughness from 1789 to the British occupation of Delhi in 1803.

4587 THOMPSON (EDWARD JOHN). The making of the Indian princes. 1943.

Bibliog. 288–94; traces British policy towards the later 'protected' states in the period 1799–1819.

4588 KHAN (MOHIBBUL HASAN). History of Tipu Sultan. Calcutta. 1951.

Deals with British relations with Mysore to 1799. For a later period see Kasi N. Venkatasubba Sastri, *The administration of Mysore under Sir Mark Cubbon, 1834–1861*, 1932.

4589 BILGRAMI (*Saiyid* HUSAIN) *and* WILLMOTT (C.) *comp.* Historical and descriptive sketch of His Highness the Nizam's dominions. 2 v. Bombay. 1883–4.

4590   SARKAR (*Sir* JADUNATH) *and others, eds.* English records of Maratha history. Poona residency correspondence. 15 v. Bombay. 1936–53.

From MSS. at the Alienation office, Poona. See Govind S. Sardesai, *Handbook to the records in the Alienation Office, Poona,* Bombay, 1933. Standard is Govind S. Sardesai, *The new history of the Marathas,* 3 v., Bombay, 1946–8; v. 3 deals with the years 1772–1848. James Duff, *A history of the Mahrattas,* 3 v., 1826, rev. edn. by S. M. Edwardes, is a classic not yet superseded. See also Pratul C. Gupta, *Baji Rao II and the East India Company, 1796–1818,* 1939, and *The last Peshwa and the English commissioners, 1818–1851,* Calcutta, 1944; Rustom D. Choksey, *A history of British diplomacy at the court of the Peshwas, 1786–1818, based on English records of Mahratta history,* Poona, 1951; ed., *The last phase: selections from the Deccan Commissioners' files . . . 1815–1818,* Bombay, 1848; ed., *Period of transition: selections from the Deccan Commissioners' files . . . 1818–1826,* Poona, 1945; and *The aftermath . . . 1818–1826: with select documents . . . on the administrative and judicial organisation of Maharashtra by the British,* Bombay, 1950.

4591   GHOSH (BISWANATH). British policy towards the Pathans and the Pindaris in Central India, 1805–1818. Calcutta. 1966.

4592   BANERJEE (ANIL CHANDRA). The Rajput states and the East India company. Calcutta. 1951.

On period 1790 to 1818; partly original work, partly anthology. H. C. Batra, *The relations of Jaipur state with East India company, 1803–1858,* Delhi, 1958.

4593   BHUYAN (SURYYA KUMAR). Anglo-Assamese relations, 1771–1826. Gauhali. 1949.

Standard work, dealing with relations up to the British conquest.

4594   LANDON (PERCEVAL). Nepal. 2 v. 1928.

Standard. A more recent survey is Sir Francis Tuker, *Gorkha,* 1957. Bhairava D. Sanwal, *Nepal and the East India company,* 1965, deals mainly with the period 1792–1858, using the national archives of India. Sir William W. Hunter, *Life of Brian Houghton Hodgson,* 1896, is an account of the British resident at Katmandu, 1833–44.

4595   BANERJEE (ANIL CHANDRA). The eastern frontier of British India, 1784–1826. 2nd edn. Calcutta. 1946.

A well-documented study of events leading to the first Anglo-Burmese war in 1824. See also *The Crawfurd Papers,* Bangkok, 1915, for John Crawfurd's mission to Siam in 1821.

4596   HUTTENBACK (ROBERT A.). British relations with Sind, 1799–1843: an anatomy of imperialism. 1962.

Well documented. P. N. Khera, *British policy towards Sind up to the annexation, 1843,* rev. enl. edn. Lahore, 1963, is a critical essay using Punjab govt. records. H. T. Lambrick, *Sir Charles Napier and Sind,* Oxf., 1952, is exhaustive and authoritative; see too his *John Jacob of Jacobabad,* 1960.

4597   COLVIN (*Sir* AUCKLAND). John Russell Colvin, the last lieut. governor of the North West under the company. Oxf. 1895.

A defence of his father from charges of responsibility for the Afghan war of 1838–42.

4598   SINGH (KHUSHWANT). A history of the Sikhs. 2 v. 1963–7.

V. 1: 1469–1839; v. 2: 1839–1964. Bikrama Jit Hasrat, *Anglo-Sikh relations 1799–1849.*

A reappraisal of the rise and fall of the Sikhs, Hoshiarpur, 1968, is valuable, as is also Khushwant Singh, *Ranjit Singh. Maharaja of the Punjab*, 1962. Hari Ram Gupta, ed., *Panjab on the eve of the Sikh war*, Hoshiarpur, 1956, using the letters from British informants at Lahore. Ganda Singh ed., *Private correspondence relating to the Anglo-Sikh wars, being private letters of Lords Ellenborough, Hardinge, Dalhousie, and Gough, and of political assistants, addressed to Sir Frederick Currie as British resident at Lahore*, Amritsar, 1955. John L. Morison, *Lawrence of Lucknow, 1806–1857*, 1934, includes his involvement in the annexation of the Punjab. Jagmohan Mahajan, *Circumstances leading to the annexation of the Punjab, 1846–1849*, Allahabad, 1949, is critical of British policy.

4. MILITARY HISTORY

(a) *Sources*

4599 COCKLE (MAURICE JAMES DRAFFEN). A catalogue of books relating to the military history of India. Simla. 1901.

4600 DODWELL (EDWARD) *and* MILES (JAMES SAMUEL) *comps.* Alphabetical list of the officers of the Indian army, 1760–1837. 1838.

They also comp. *Alphabetical list of the medical officers of the Indian army . . . 1764–1838*, 1839. See too V. C. P. Hodson, *Officers of the Bengal army*, 4 v., 1927–47, a biographical dictionary.

4601 MACKENZIE (*Major* RODERICK). A sketch of the war with Tippoo Sultaun . . . 1789 to 1792. 2 v. Calcutta. 1793–4.

Includes interesting material about army supply services. For the last campaign against Tippoo in 1799 see James Salmond, *A review of the origin, progress, and result of the . . . war . . . in Mysore*, 1800; and on this and some later campaigns, Wellington, *Dispatches* (201), and Jac Weller, *Wellington in India*, 1972.

4602 BLACKER (VALENTINE). Memoir of the operations of the British army in India during the Mahratta war of 1817, 1818 and 1819. 1821.

4603 KAYE (*Sir* JOHN WILLIAM). History of the war in Afghanistan. 4th edn. 3 v. 1890.

Comp. from the unpub. letters and journals of political and military officers; remains the principal authority.

4604 THACKWELL (EDWARD JOSEPH). Narrative of the second Seikh war in 1848–1849. 1851.

Chatty, but includes a valuable appendix of dispatches.

(b) *Later Works*

4605 GREY (CHARLES). European adventurers of Northern India 1785–1849. Ed. by H. L. O. Garrett. Lahore. 1929.

See too H. G. Keene, *Hindustan under free lances, 1770–1820; sketches of military adventure*, 1907.

4606 QURESHI (MOHAMMED IBRAHIM). The First Punjabis: history of the First Punjab Regiment, 1759–1956. Aldershot. 1958.

E. G. Phythian-Adams, *The Madras Regiment, 1758–1958*, Wellington, Madras, 1958.

4607 YOUNG (HENRY AYERST). The East India company's arsenals and manufactories. Oxf. 1937.

A study in military supply, with notice of the industry sustaining it.

4608 LOW (CHARLES RATHBONE). History of the Indian navy, 1613–1863. 2 v. 1877.

4609 KAYE (*Sir* JOHN WILLIAM). Lives of Indian officers. New edn. 2 v. 1904.

Deals with twelve leading figures. Biographies and memoirs are numerous—W. H. Wilkin, *The life of Sir David Baird,* 1912; H. W. Pearse, *Memoir of the life and military services of Viscount Lake . . . 1744–1808,* 1908; T. H. McGuffie, 'Report on the military papers of Field Marshal Sir George Nugent', *Bull. I.H.R.* 21 (1946–8), 225–32; William Cook Mackenzie, *Colonel Colin Mackenzie; first surveyor-general of India,* 1952; Sir F. J. Goldsmid *Sir James Outram; a biography,* 2 v., 1880; L. J. Trotter, *The Bayard of India: a life of General Sir James Outram,* 1903; *Memoirs and letters of Col. Armine Simcoe Henry Mountain,* ed. by his wife, 1857; *The military memoirs of Lieut. General Sir Joseph Thackwell,* arranged . . . by H. C. Wylly, 1908; Sir Robert S. Rait, *The life and campaigns of Hugh, 1st Viscount Gough, Field-Marshal,* 2 v., 1903; Dennis Holman, *Sikander Sahib: the life and times of James Skinner, 1778–1841,* 1961.

4610 NORRIS (JAMES ALFRED). The first Afghan war, 1838–1842. Camb. 1967.

5. EAST INDIA COMPANY

(a) *Sources*

4611 EAST INDIA COMPANY. A list of the names of those members of the United Company of Merchants of England trading to the East Indies who stood qualified as voters on the Company's books. 16 pt. 1773–1852.

Charles Hardy comp. *A register of ships employed in the service of the . . . East India Company from . . . 1760,* latest edition, 1820; continued in *A supplement to a register . . . to the conclusion of the commercial charter,* 1835, which lists ships for the years 1819–1833. See too *The East India Register and Directory,* ann. 1803–1844, then *East India Register and army list,* 1845–1860.

4612 AUBER (PETER). An analysis of the constitution of the East India Company. 1826. Suppl. 1828.

Standard. Also valuable is *Selection of papers from the records at the East India House relating to the revenue, police, civil, and criminal justice under the Company's governments in India,* 4 v., 1820–6.

4613 MALCOLM (*Sir* JOHN). The government of India. 1833.

Written with a view to reforms in the system of government. F. J. Shore, *Notes on Indian affairs,* 2 v., 1837, dealt more with changing views on policy.

(b) *Later Works*

4614 KAYE (JOHN WILLIAM). The administration of the East India company. 1853.

A pioneer work still worth consulting, with an emphasis on policy rather than organization.

4615 COTTON (*Sir* HARRY EVANS AUGUSTE). East Indiamen: the East India company's maritime service. Ed. by Sir Charles Fawcett. 1949.

4616 MISRA (BANKEY BIHARI). The central administration of the East India company, 1773–1834. Manchester. 1960.

Standard. Cyril H. Philips, *The East India Company, 1784–1834*, repr. Manchester, 1961, is authoritative on internal politics and relations with the government. Philips also ed. *Correspondence of David Scott . . . 1787–1805*, 2 v., Royal Hist. Soc. Camden 3rd ser., vv. 75, 76 (1951), and, with D. Philips, comp. 'Alphabetical list of directors of the East India company, 1758–1858', *J. Roy. Asiatic Soc. of Great Britain and Ireland* (1941), 325–36. See also Sir J. W. Kaye, *The life and correspondence of Henry St. George Tucker, late accountant general of Bengal and chairman of the East India company*, 1854. Holden Furber, *John Company at work*, 1948, examines intensively the decade 1783–93.

4617 EMBREE (AINSLIE THOMAS). Charles Grant and the British rule in India. 1962.

Bibliog. 295–311; a valuable study of one of the company's policy-makers.

4618 KEITH (ARTHUR BERRIEDALE) *ed.* Speeches and documents on Indian policy, 1750–1921. 2 v. 1922.

See too J. K. Majumdar, ed., *Indian speeches and documents on British rule, 1821–1918*, 1937; A. C. Banerjee, *Indian constitutional documents*, v. 1: *1757–1858*, 2nd edn., Calcutta, 1948.

4619 KEITH (ARTHUR BERRIEDALE). A constitutional history of India, 1600–1935. 2nd edn. 1937.

Standard. An excellent general survey though brief on the period. Mariadas Ruthnaswamy, *Some influences that made the British administrative system in India*, 1939, is a well-documented study. Patrick J. Thomas, *The growth of federal finance in India; being a survey of India's public finances, 1833–1939*, 1939, supplements Misra (4616) on this subject.

4620 O'MALLEY (LEWIS SIDNEY STEWARD). The Indian civil service. 1601–1930. 1931.

A good general account, focused more on persons and less on analysis than the chapter in Misra (4616). Akshoy K. Ghosal, *Civil service in India under the East India company: a study in administrative development*, Calcutta, 1944, pays especial attention to training.

4621 CURZON (GEORGE NATHANIEL) *Marquess*. British government in India. 2 v. 1925.

Tells the story of the viceroys and government houses.

6. SPECIAL SUBJECTS

(a) *Economic and Social History*

4622 DUTT (ROMESH CHUNDER). The economic history of India under early British rule, from the rise of the British power in 1757 to . . . 1837. 2nd edn. 8th imp. 1956.

A classic, first published 1902; continued in his *The economic history of India in the Victorian age*, 2nd edn. 8th imp., 1956.

4623   BANERJEA (PRAMATHANATH). Indian finance in the days of the company. 1928.

Methodical treatment and useful appendices. Baden H. Baden-Powell, *The land-systems of British India*, 3 v., Oxford, 1892, is a copious manual of land-tenure and systems of land-revenue administration. See too P. Banerjea, *A history of Indian taxation*, 1930.

4624   DURGA PARSHAD (IGNATIUS). Some aspects of Indian foreign trade, 1757–1893. 1932.

Well documented, bibliog. 226–32. Holden Furber, 'The beginnings of American trade with India, 1784–1812', *New England Q.* 11 (1938), 235–65, surveys an important development. See also K. N. Chaudhuri, 'India's foreign trade and the cessation of the East India Company's trading activities, 1828–1840', *Econ. H. R.* 2nd series, 19 (1966–7), 345–63; H. B. Morse, *Chronicles of the East India Company trading to China, 1635–1834*, 2 v., Oxf., 1926–9; H. R. C. Wright, *East Indian economic problems in the age of Cornwallis and Raffles*, 1961.

4625   THORNER (DANIEL). Investment in empire. British railway and steam shipping enterprise in India, 1825–1849. Phil. 1950.

4626   KINCAID (DENNIS CHARLES ALEXANDER). British social life in India, 1608–1937. 1938.

A broad but vivid treatment of the subject.

4627   DUBOIS (JEAN ANTOINE). Hindu manners, customs, and ceremonies . . . translated from the French and edited by H. K. Beauchamp. 3rd edn. repr. Oxf. 1947.

Records observations made in the early nineteenth century. John H. Hutton, *Caste in India; its nature, function, and origins*, 3rd edn., 1961, is standard. Also excellent is Govind S. Ghurye, *Caste and class in India*, 2nd edn., Bombay, 1957, which discusses the impact of British rule.

4628   TUKER (*Sir* FRANCIS). The yellow scarf: the story of the life of Thuggee Sleeman, or, Major General Sir William Henry Sleeman, 1788–1856, of the Bengal Army and the Indian political service. 1961.

4629   BALLHATCHET (KENNETH A.). Social policy and social change in Western India, 1817–1830. 1957.

4630   CHAUDHURI (SASHI BHUSAN). Civil disturbances during the British rule in India, 1765–1857. Calcutta. 1955.

(b) *Cultural History*

4631   MAYHEW (ARTHUR INNES.) The education of India: a study of British educational policy in India, 1835–1920. 1926.

A more recent general study is Shridhar N. Mukerji, *History of education in India* (*modern period*), 3rd edn., Baroda, 1957; bibliog. 326–31.

4632   CHATTERTON (EYRE). A history of the Church of England in India since the early days of the East India company. 1924.

Standard. A. I. Mayhew, *Christianity and the government of India*, 1929, examines the relations of missionaries and officials. Iqbal Singh, *Rammohun Roy: a bibliographical inquiry into the making of modern India.* v. 1: *The first phase*, Bombay, 1958, deals with intellectual interpenetration of Christianity and Hinduism.

4633 STOKES (ERIC). The English Utilitarians and India. Oxf. 1959.

Traces the influence of British thinkers on British administrators, but not on the Indian educated class. K. Ingham, *Reformers in India, 1793–1833*, Camb., 1956, examines the connections between Christian missions and social reform.

4634 O'MALLEY (LEWIS SIDNEY STEWARD) *ed.* Modern India and the West: a study of the interaction of their civilizations. 1941.

Deals with cultural aspects.

4635 PAKISTAN. Board of Editors. A history of the freedom movement (being the story of Muslim struggle for the freedom of Hind-Pakistan), 1707–1947. V. 1: 1707–1831. Karachi. 1957.

4636 BARNS (MARGARITA D.). The Indian press: a history of the growth of public opinion in India. 1940.

Bibliog. 476–9. Useful on governmental attitudes and the struggle for the freedom of the press.

4637 NILSSON (STEN). European architecture in India, 1750–1850. Transl. by Agnes George and Eleanore Zettersten. 1968.

7. Regions

(a) *Assam*

4638 ANTROBUS (HINSON ALLAN). A history of the Assam company, 1839–1953. Edin. 1957.

Deals with the main economic development of Assam, from the company's records.

(b) *Bengal, with Bihar and Orissa*

4639 HUNTER (*Sir* WILLIAM WILSON). Bengal MS. records; a selected list of 14,136 letters in the board of revenue, Calcutta, 1782–1807, with an historical dissertation and analytical index. 4 v. 1894.

Brief calendar illustrating land rights and status of cultivators. For other groups of records see: *Catalogue of the English records 1758–1858 preserved in the Historical record room of the Government of Bengal*, Calcutta, 1922: *Select index to general letters to and from the court of directors . . . preserved in the Bengal secretariat record room*, 4 v., 1924–7, with subtitles referring to various departmental groups. See too Bengal Record Room, *Bibliography of Bengal records, 1632–1858; list of English records relating to the company's administration in Bengal which can be consulted in print*, 2nd edn., Calcutta, 1925.

4640 BENGAL PAST AND PRESENT. Journal of the Calcutta historical society. Calcutta. 1907+.

See too *Royal Asiatic Society of Bengal Journal*, Calcutta, 1829+, title varies.

4641 O'MALLEY (LEWIS SIDNEY STEWART). History of Bengal, Bihar and Orissa under British rule. Calcutta. 1925.

Bibliog. 776–9; a useful outline. See also Sir Jadunath Sarkar, ed., *History of Bengal*, v. 2: *The Muzlim period*, Dacca, 1948.

4642 SINHA (NARENDRA KRISHNA). The economic history of Bengal from Plassey to the permanent settlement. 2 v. Calcutta. 1956–62.

For various aspects, see Hari R. Ghosal, *Economic transition in the Bengal presidency* (*1793–1833*), Patna, 1950; Amales Tripathi, *Trade and finance in the Bengal presidency, 1793–1833*, Bombay, 1956, bibliog. 267–78; Kshitish C. Chaudhuri, *The history and economics of the land system in Bengal*, Calcutta, 1927.

(c) *Bombay, with Sind*

4643 BOMBAY RECORD OFFICE. Descriptive catalogue of the secret and political department series, 1755–1820. Comp. by V. G. Dighe. Bombay. 1954.

See also *A handbook of Bombay government records*, by A. F. Kindersley, Bombay, 1921.

4644 COLEBROOKE (*Sir* THOMAS EDWARD). Life of . . . Mountstewart Elphinstone, 2 v. 1884.

Treats of the career of a distinguished governor (1819–27). G. W. Forrest, ed., *Selections from the minutes and other official writings of . . . Elphinstone*, 1884, from the Bombay secretariat records. On his successor see Sir J. W. Kaye, *Life and correspondence of Sir John Malcolm*, 2 v., 1856. Also valuable is F. G. D. Drewitt, *Bombay in the days of George IV: memoirs of Sir Edward West*, 2nd edn., 1935, chief justice of the King's court during its conflict with the company.

4645 CADELL (*Sir* PATRICK ROBERT). History of the Bombay army. 1938.

Mainly a history of campaigns.

4646 KUMAR (RAVINDER). Western India in the nineteenth century. A study in the social history of Maharashtra. 1968.

See also R. Kumar, 'The rise of the rich peasants in Western India', and 'The new Brahmans of Maharashtra', in *Soundings in Modern South Asian history*, ed. Donald A. Low, 1968, pp. 25–58, 95–130.

4647 YOUNG (KEITH). Scinde in the forties: being the journal and letters of Colonel Keith Young, C.B., sometime Judge-Advocate-General in India. Edited by Arthur F. Scott. 1912.

(d) *Central India*

4648 LUARD (CHARLES ECKFORD). A bibliography of the literature dealing with the Central India agency. 1908.

Sir Richard Jenkins, *Report on the territories of the Rajah of Nagpore*, Calcutta, 1827, and Sir John Malcolm, *A memoir of Central India*, 3rd edn., 2 v., 1832, are the two leading contemporary accounts. H. N. Sinha, ed., *Selections from the Nagpur residency records at the Central Provinces secretariat*, 3 v., Nagpur, 1950–3, for the period 1799–1817.

(e) *Madras*

4649 DODWELL (HENRY HERBERT). Report on the Madras records. Madras. [1916].

4650 PRINSEP (CHARLES CAMPBELL). Record of services of the honourable East India company's civil servants in the Madras presidency, 1741–1858. 1885.

Chronological lists of office-holders with brief biogs. Edward Dodwell and J. S. Miles comps. *Alphabetical list of the hon. E.I.C.'s Madras civil servants . . . 1780–1839*, 1839.

4651 GLEIG (GEORGE ROBERT). The life of Sir Thomas Munro . . . with extracts from his correspondence and private papers. 3 v. 1830. Rev. condensed edn. 1849.

Munro was governor, 1820–7. See T. H. Beaglehole, *Thomas Munro and the development of administrative policy in Madras, 1792–1818: the origins of 'the Munro system'*, Camb., 1966; K. N. Venkatasubba Sastri, *The Munro system of British statesmanship in India*, Mysore, 1939, is a selection of documents; bibliog. 332–49.

4652 WILSON (WILLIAM JOHN). History of the Madras army. 5 v. Madras 1882–9.

See also H. M. Vibart, *The military history of the Madras engineers and pioneers from 1743 up to the present time*, 2 v., 1881–3. See also Phythian-Adams (4606).

4653 SARADA-RAJU (A.). Economic conditions in the Madras presidency, 1800–1850. Madras. 1941.

G. H. Hodgson, *Thomas Parry, free merchant, Madras, 1768–1824*, Madras, 1938, includes business and private correspondence. See too P. J. Thomas and B. Natarajan, 'Economic depression in the Madras presidency (1825–1854)', *Econ. H.R. 7* (1936), 67–75.

(f) *Northwest Provinces*

4654 DEWAR (DOUGLAS). A hand-book to the English pre-mutiny records in the government record rooms of the United Provinces of Agra and Oudh. Alahabad. [1919].

Dharma Bhanu, *History and administration of the North-western provinces . . . 1803–1858*, Agra, 1957, deals with the later Agra province. Michael Edwardes, *The orchid house: splendours and miseries of the kingdom of Oudh, 1827–1857*, 1960, bibliog. 209–11, is a vivid account of a state finally taken over by the British in 1856. See too Babu R. Misra, *Land revenue policy in the United Provinces under British rule*, Benares, 1942; T. G. P. Spear, *Twilight of the Mughuls: studies in late Mughul Delhi*, Camb., 1951; Purnandu Basu, *Oudh and the East India Company, 1785–1801*, Lucknow, 1943.

(g) *Punjab*

4655 PUNJAB GOVERNMENT RECORD OFFICE. A catalogue of the . . . Office publications. Comp. by Muhammad Sadullah. Lahore. 1942.

8. Arakan, Tenasserim, and Relations with Ava

4656 TRAGER (FRANK N.) *ed.* Annotated bibliography of Burma. New Haven. Conn. 1956.

Lists over 1,000 items. A. F. M. Abdul Ali, 'Burma records in the imperial record department (1753–1859)', *J. of the Burma Research Soc.* Rangoon, 20, pt. 2 (1930), 53–8, gives a general description.

4657 PEMBERTON (*Captain* ROBERT BOILEAU). Report on the Eastern frontier of British India, with an appendix and maps. With a supplement by Dr. Bayfield. Calcutta. 1835.

Topographical and military. The supplement is *Historical review of the political relations between the British government in India and the empire of Ava* . . . comp. by G. T. Bayfield, rev. by Lieut. Col. Henry Burney. Journals of various residences at the court of Ava were published by Michael Symes, 1800, Hiram Cox, 1821, John Crawfurd, 1828. See too *Michael Symes: Journal of his second embassy to the court of Ava in 1802*, ed. by D. G. E. Hall, 1955, and D. G. E. Hall, 'Burney's comments on the court of Ava, 1832', *Bull. S.O.A.S.* 20 (1957), 305–14.

4658 BURMA. Report on the progress of Arakan under British rule from 1826 to 1875. Rangoon. 1876.

4659 BURMA. Selected correspondence of letters issued from and received in the office of the commissioner, Tenasserim division . . . 1825–26 to 1842–43. Rangoon. 1928.

4660 WOODMAN (DOROTHY). The making of Burma. 1962.

Bibliog. 577–82. G. W. De Rhé-Philipe, *A narrative of the first Burmese war, 1824–6*, Calcutta, 1905, prints reports and dispatches. W. S. Desai, *History of the British residency in Burma, 1826–1840*, Rangoon, 1939, is a detailed scholarly account. J. S. Furnivall, *The fashioning of Leviathan: the beginnings of British rule in Burma*, Rangoon, 1939, is a valuable account of the early British administration in Tenasserim.

4661 BRUCE (GEORGE). The Burma wars, 1824–1886. 1973.

J. CEYLON

For Bibliog. see (4281–5, 4673).

1. Guides to Manuscripts

4662 CEYLON: GOVERNMENT ARCHIVES DEPT. The Government archives department and its contents in brief. Nuwara Eliya, Ceylon. 1962.

Duplicated typescript; lists categories of records, and pub. and unpub. indexes. The Dept. also pub. in same form *Index to the records of the executive council of Ceylon, 1802–1931*, Nuwara Eliya, 1962. See too Historical Manuscripts Commission of Ceylon, *Report*, Colombo, 1933+, and *Bulletin*, Colombo, 1937+.

2. Sources

4663 CORDINER (JAMES). A description of Ceylon . . . with narratives of a tour round the island in 1800, the campaign in Candy in 1803, and a journey to Ramisseram in 1804. 2 v. 1807.

A valuable account by the chaplain to the garrison at Colombo, 1799–1804, though biased in favour of North; Cordiner incorporated material from the journals of various officials. James Steuart, *Notes on Ceylon and its affairs during . . . 38 years, ending in 1855*, 1862, gives miscellaneous information, including notes on the pearl fisheries.

4664 MENDIS (GARRETT CHAMPNESS) *ed.* The Colebrook-Cameron papers: documents on British colonial policy in Ceylon, 1796–1833. 2 v. 1956.

Simon G. Perera, ed., *The Douglas Papers*, Colombo, 1933, a report drawn up in 1800 for Dundas preparatory to the setting up of Crown colony government.

4665 CHITTY (SIMON CASIE). The Ceylon gazetteer. Colombo. 1834.

An encyclopaedia of the island, with much material of historical value.

3. LATER WORKS

4666 MILLS (LENNOX ALGERNON). Ceylon under British rule, 1795–1932; with an account of the East India Company's embassies to Kandy, 1762–97. 1933.

An indispensable, scholarly survey; bibliog. 286–96. Standard histories with briefer treatment of the period are G. C. Mendis, *Ceylon under the British*, 3rd rev. edn., Colombo, 1952, and E. F. C. Ludowyk, *The modern history of Ceylon*, 1966, with select bibliog.

4667 ROYAL ASIATIC SOCIETY, CEYLON BRANCH. Journal. 1845+. Colombo. 1859+.

J. F. W. Gore comp. *Index* to v. 1–11 of the journals and proceedings comprising nos. 1–41 (1845–90), Colombo, 1895. Recent vols. contain scholarly work. See too *University of Ceylon Review*, Colombo, 1943+; *Ceylon Historical J.*, Dehiwela, 1951+; *Ceylon J. of Historical amd Social Studies*, Peradeniya, 1958+.

4668 DE SILVA (COLVIN REGINALD). Ceylon under the British occupation, 1795–1833. V. 1: Its political and administrative development. 3rd edn. Colombo. 1952.

A well-documented account. L. J. B. Turner, *Collected papers on the history of the maritime provinces of Ceylon, 1795–1805*, 1923, is thorough and comprehensive. G. Nypels, *Hoe Nederland Ceilon verloor*, The Hague, 1908, treats the British conquest from the Dutch point of view; see too Violet M. Methley, 'The Ceylon expedition of 1803', *TRHS*, 4th ser., 1 (1918), 92–128. Sir Paulus E. Pieris, *Tri Sinhala, the last phase, 1796–1815*, 2nd edn. 1945, gives a detailed account of British relations with the kingdom of Kandy until its collapse. For Maitland's administration see (4321).

4669 PIERIS (*Sir* PAULUS EDWARD). Sinhale and the patriots, 1815–1818. Colombo. 1950.

Detailed study incorporating much Kandian lore and tradition; bibliog. 702–8. R. L. Brohier, *The golden age of military adventure in Ceylon: an account of the Uva rebellion, 1817–1818*, Colombo, 1933, is popular in style.

4670 HARDY (STANLEY MAURICE). 'Wilmot-Horton's government of Ceylon, 1831–1837'. *Univ. of Birmingham Hist. J.* 7 (1959–60), 180–99.

An important study of a critic of the Colebrooke-Cameron proposals.

4671 JENNINGS (*Sir* W. IVOR) *and* TAMBIAH (HENRY WINBOOH). The dominion of Ceylon; the development of its laws and constitution. 1952.

Includes some historical material; bibliog. 305–7. J. R. Toussaint, *Annals of the Ceylon civil service*, Colombo, 1935, is presented mainly in the form of biographical vignettes. G. K. Pippet, *A history of the Ceylon police*, v. 1: *1795–1870*, Colombo, 1938, is based on documents with substantial citation. P. M. Bingham, *History of the public works department* . . . *1796–1913*, 3 v., Colombo, 1921–3.

4672 DE SILVA (KINGSLEY MUTHUMUNI). Social policy and missionary organizations in Ceylon, 1840–1855. 1965.

A well-documented study covering the clash between missionaries and Buddhists; bibliog. 301–14.

K. EAST INDIES AND HONG KONG

1. BIBLIOGRAPHY

4673 HAY (STEPHEN N.) *and* CASE (MARGARET H.) *eds*. Southeast Asian history: a bibliographic guide. N.Y. 1962.

Covers Burma, Ceylon, and Malaysia. H. R. Cheeseman, *Bibliography of Malaya*, 1959, is supplemented in the *Annual Reports of the British Association of Malaya, supplements*, 1959+. K. G. Tregonning, ed., *Malaysian historical sources: a series of essays on historical material mainly in Malaya or Malaysia*, Singapore, 1962. D. G. E. Hall, ed., *Historians of South East Asia*, 1961. See also L. A. Mills (4676).

2. GENERAL HISTORY

4674 HALL (DANIEL GEORGE EDWARD). A history of South-East Asia. 3rd edn. 1968.

The standard history of the whole region; bibliog. 899–929.

4675 JOURNAL OF SOUTHEAST ASIAN HISTORY. Singapore. 1960+.

4676 MILLS (LENNOX ALGERNON). British Malaya, 1824–67. Rev. edn. with an introd. chapter by D. K. Bassett and a bibliog. by C. M. Turnbull. 1966.

Turnbull's bibliog. is full and critical, covering MSS. records, bibliographies, and a comprehensive annotated list of contemporary accounts published between 1786 and 1867. Victor Purcell, *The Chinese in Malaya*, 1948, touches on aspects of British administration.

4677 MALAYA IN HISTORY. *Formerly* The Malayan Historical J. Kuala Lumpur. 1954+.

4678 TARLING (NICHOLAS). British policy in the Malay Peninsula and Archipelago, 1824–1871. 1969.

Thorough, well-documented study. Also important are Tarling, *Anglo-Dutch rivalry* (368), and *Piracy and politics in the Malay world. A study of British imperialism in nineteenth-century south-east Asia*, Melbourne, 1963, dealing mainly with 1800–1850; K. G. Tregonning, *The British in Malaya. The first forty years, 1786–1826*, Tucson, Arizona, 1965, bibliog., 173–8.

4679 BUCKLEY (CHARLES BURTON). An anecdotal history of old times in Singapore. Kuala Lumpur. 1965.

Reprint of a classic compilation which cites much contemporary material on years 1819–1867. C. D. Cowan, ed., 'Early Penang and the rise of Singapore, 1805–1832', *Royal Asiatic Society Malayan Branch J.* 23, ii (1950), pp. 1–210, documents mainly from the E.I. Co. records. H. J. Marks, *The first contest for Singapore, 1819–1824*, The Hague, 1959, makes full use of Dutch material.

4680 RAFFLES. Raffles of the Eastern Isles. By Charles Edward Wurtzburg. Ed. for publication by Clifford Witting. 1954.

Bibliog. 755–69; the most complete biography. See too J. S. Tay, 'The attempts of Raffles to establish a British base in South-East Asia, 1818–1819', *J. of Southeast Asian Hist.* 1, ii (1960), 30–46. *The journal of Thomas Otho Travers, 1813–1820*, ed. John Bastin, Singapore, 1960, is a record of one of Raffles's *aides*.

4681 BASTIN (JOHN STURGUS). The native policies of Sir Stamford Raffles in Java and Sumatra: an economic interpretation. Oxf. 1957.

Bastin also ed. *The British in West Sumatra (1685–1825)*, Kuala Lumpur, 1965.

4682 WILLI (JOHANNES) of *Gais*. The early relations of England with Borneo, to 1805. Langensalza. 1922.

Mainly on the 18th century but includes some material on the period. S. Baring-Gould and C. A. Bampfylde, *A history of Sarawak under its two white rajahs, 1839–1908*, 1909, is an accurate and valuable account by a member of the rajah's administration. Sir Steven Runciman, *The white rajahs: a history of Sarawak from 1841 to 1946*, Camb., 1960, bibliog. 302–7, is based on the Brooke archives. See also Graham Irwin, *Nineteenth-century Borneo; a study in diplomatic history*, The Hague, 1955, bibliog. 218–42, a well-documented study of British and Dutch policies in Borneo.

4683 ENDACOTT (GEORGE BEER). A history of Hong Kong. 1958.

Standard; select bibliog. 311–12. Also by Endacott are *A biographical sketch book of early Hong Kong*, Singapore, 1962, and *An Eastern Entrepot. A collection of documents illustrating the history of Hong Kong*, 1964. E. J. Eitel, *Europe in China: The history of Hong Kong from the beginning to ... 1882*, 1895, is old-fashioned but informative. Austin Coates, *Prelude to Hong Kong*, 1966, has valuable material on the period leading up to annexation. G. R. Sayer, *Hong Kong: Birth, adolescence and coming of age*, 1937, treats the years 1841–62 in some detail.

L. AUSTRALIA

1. BIBLIOGRAPHY

4684 AUSTRALIA. NATIONAL LIBRARY. Guide to collections of manuscripts relating to Australia. Canberra. 1965, in progress.

A loose-leaf union catalogue, giving brief details of collections, public and private, and location of MSS. or of microfilm copies. Phyllis Mander-Jones, ed., *Manuscripts in the British Isles relating to Australia, New Zealand and the Pacific*, Canberra, 1973, lists a vast body of material in public collections, societies, firms, and private hands. The Scottish Record Office has issued duplicated lists, *Material relating to Australia and New Zealand in the ... office*, 2 pt., Edinburgh, 1965.

4685 AUSTRALIA. NATIONAL LIBRARY. Australian bibliographical centre. Australian bibliography and bibliographical services. Canberra. 1960.

A general guide to indexes and bibliographies, including index vols. of periodicals, accession lists, and an appendix of works then in preparation. Shorter but more up-to-date is D. H. Borchardt, *Australian bibliography: a guide to the principal sources of information*, 2nd edn. rev. and enlarged, Melbourne, 1966.

4686 FERGUSON (JOHN ALEXANDER) *ed*. Bibliography of Australia. 6 v. Sydney. 1941–65, in progress.

Indispensable; lists under year of publication for 1784–1900 not only all books with an Australian imprint, regardless of subject-matter, but also all books wherever published that touch on the subject of Australia. An excellent selective bibliog. is in v. 2 of the Commonwealth Society catalogue (4281). There are bibliographies of French, Dutch, and German literature on Australia by L. L. Politzer, Melbourne, 1952, 1953. The Australian National Library produced, *Annual catalogue of Australian publications*, nos. 1–25, 1936–1960, continued as *Australian national bibliography*, 1961+; and *Union list of newspapers in Australian libraries*, pt. 2: *Newspapers published in Australia*, Canberra, 1960, suppl. and index, 1961–4. Ida Leeson, *The Mitchell Library, Sydney; historical and descriptive notes*, Sydney, 1936, gives a general description of the most important classes of material in this collection. J. Dindinger, *Missionsliteratur von Australien und Ozeanien, 1525–1950*, Freiburg, 1955, gives an exhaustive listing in chronological order of publication.

2. GENERAL HISTORY

(a) *Sources*

4687 THE HISTORICAL RECORDS OF AUSTRALIA. Ed. by Frederick Watson. 35 v. Sydney. 1914–25.

Ser. 1: governors' despatches . . . 1788–1848, 26 v.
Ser. 3: despatches and papers relating to the settlement of the states, 1803–1830, 6 v.
Ser. 4: legal papers; section A, v. 1, 1786–1827.
  Ser. 2 was not published. Charles M. H. Clark and L. J. Pryor, ed., *Select documents in Australian history, 1788–1850*, 1950; Clark also ed. a more general collection, *Sources of Australian history*, 1957. For Wakefield's writings on Australia, see *The collected works of Edward Gibbon Wakefield*, ed. M. F. Lloyd-Prichard, 1968.

(b) *Later Works*

4688 AUSTRALIAN DICTIONARY OF BIOGRAPHY. General ed. Douglas Pike. V. 1: 1788–1850; A–H; v. 2: 1788–1850; I–Z. Melbourne. 1966. 1967.

There is much historical material in *The Australian Encyclopaedia*, ed. Alec H. Chisholm, 10 v., Sydney, 1958.

4689 ROYAL AUSTRALIAN HISTORICAL SOCIETY. Journal and proceedings. Sydney. V. 1+. 1901+.

Index v. 1–42, 1958. *Historical Studies Australia and New Zealand*, v. 1, Melbourne, 1940+, includes annual listings of writings on Australian and New Zealand history.

4690 CAMBRIDGE HISTORY OF THE BRITISH EMPIRE (4311). V. 7, pt. 1: Australia. Camb. 1933.

Standard; bibliog. 645–718. George Wm. Rusden, *History of Australia*, 3 v., Melbourne, 1897, is old-fashioned but full of detail. Sir Ernest Scott, *A short history of Australia*, 8th edn., Melbourne, 1950, is a good introduction. C. M. H. Clark, *A history of Australia*, v. 1: *From the earliest times to the age of Macquarie*; v. 2: *New South Wales and Van Dieman's land, 1822–1838*, Melbourne, 1962, 1968, sums up recent scholarship.

4691 EDDY (JOHN J.). Britain and the Australian Colonies, 1818–1831: the technique of government. Oxf. 1969.

Examines problems arising when transportation ceased to be the primary purpose served by Australia. Michael Roe, *The quest for authority in Eastern Australia, 1835–51*, Melbourne, 1965, deals with political and with moral and intellectual attitudes in the period leading up to responsible government. Peter Burroughs, *Britain and Australia, 1831–1855. A study in imperial relations and crown lands administration*, Oxf., 1967, discusses a major issue regarding imperial authority.

3. Special Subjects

(a) *Exploration and Discovery*

4692 FAVENC (ERNEST). The history of Australian exploration from 1788 to 1888. Sydney. 1888.

Old-fashioned but one of the best general accounts of land expeditions; see also his *The explorers of Australia and their life-work*, Christchurch, 1908. Anthologies include Sir Ernest Scott, ed., *Australian discovery*, 2 v., 1929; Ida Lee, *Early explorers in Australia*, 1925; Kathleen Fitzpatrick, *Australian explorers: a selection from their writings*, 1958. A. C. and F. T. Gregory, *Journals of Australian explorations*, Brisbane, 1884, relates to Western Australia.

4693 MACK (JAMES DECKER). Matthew Flinders, 1774–1814. 1966.

Full scholarly study, bibliog. 254–62. K. A. Austin, *The voyage of the Investigator, 1801–3, Commander Matthew Flinders, R.N.*, 1964, complements Mack. K. M. Bowden, *George Bass, 1771–1803*, Melbourne, 1952, is about one of Flinders's leading associates.

4694 WILLIAMS (GWENNETH). South Australian exploration to 1856. Adelaide. 1919.

With maps and guide to sources. For the north see Dora Howard, 'The English activities on the north coast of Australia in the first half of the nineteenth century', *Proc. Royal Geographical Society of Australia, South Aust. Branch*, v. 33 (1933), 21–194. George Mackaness, ed., *Fourteen journeys over the Blue Mountains of New South Wales, 1813–1841*, 3 pt., priv. printed, Sydney, 1950–1, and *The discovery and exploration of Moreton Bay and the Brisbane River (1799–1823)*, 2 pt., priv. printed, Sydney, 1956. Biographies of leading explorers by land include M. J. L. Uren and R. Stephens, *Waterless horizons . . . life-story of Edward John Eyre . . .*, Melbourne, 1941; A. H. Chisholm, *Strange new world: the adventures of John Gilbert and Ludwig Leichhardt*, 2nd edn., Sydney, 1955; Catherine D. Cotton, *Ludwig Leichhardt and the Great South Land*, Sydney, 1938; J. H. L. Cumpston, *Thomas Mitchell, surveyor general and explorer*, 1954; M. Langley, *Sturt of the Murray. Father of Australian exploration*, 1969; Helen M. E. Heney, *In a dark glass: the story of Paul Edmond Strzelecki*, Sydney, 1962. L. L. Politzer, comp. *Bibliography of literature on Dr. Ludwig Leichhardt*, priv. printed, Melbourne, 1953. See also George A. Wood, *The discovery of Australia*, 1922; T. Dunbabin, *The making of Australia*, 1922.

(b) *Settlement*

On British criminal practice and penal colonization see O'Brien (2614); on convict ships Bateson (2615); on social origins of the convict settlers Robson (2614).

4695 WHITE (CHARLES). Early Australian history: convict life in New South Wales and Van Diemen's Land. Bathurst. 1889.

Highly coloured, but full of detail. Recent studies of individual adventurers are Frank Clune and P. R. Stephensen, *The Viking of Van Diemen's Land: the stormy life of Jorgen Jorgensen*, 1954, bibliog. 477–82; *The secrets of Alexander Harris; a frank autobiography* . . ., with an introd. by . . . Grant Carr-Harris and a preface by Alec H. Chisholm, Sydney, 1961. On Irish exiles and immigrants see (4222).

4696 FORSYTH (WILLIAM DOUGLASS). Governor Arthur's convict system: Van Diemen's Land, 1824–36. A study in colonization. 1935.

4697 MADGWICK (ROBERT BOWDEN). Immigration into Eastern Australia, 1788–1851. 1937.

Bibliog. 252–60; deals only with free settlers. On hardships of the immigrants see Caroline Chisholm, *Emigration and transportation relatively considered in a letter, dedicated, by permission, to Earl Grey*, 1847, 3rd edn., 1847, and Margaret Kiddle, *Caroline Chisholm* (4727). See also Richard C. Mills, *The colonization of Australia (1829–42): The Wakefield experiment in empire building*, 1915, rep. 1968, and studies of Wakefield by Richard Garnett, 1898, A. J. Harrop, 1928, Irma O'Connor, 1929. On Scottish immigrants see Macmillan (3910).

4698 ROBERTS (STEPHEN HENRY). History of Australian land settlement (1788–1920). Melbourne. 1924.

A good general account. Roberts also wrote *The squatting age in Australia, 1835–1847*, Melbourne, 1935, rep. 1964. For more specialist treatment see Wilfrid Oldham, *The land policy of South Australia from 1830 to 1842*, Adelaide, 1917; K. Buckley, 'E. G. Wakefield and the alienation of crown land in New South Wales to 1847', *The Economic Record* [Melbourne], v. 33 (1957), 80–96; T. M. Perry, *Australia's first frontier: the spread of settlement in New South Wales, 1788–1829*, Melbourne, 1963. See also James Collier, *The pastoral age in Australasia*, 1911, and Bloomfield (4293).

4699 WHITE (CHARLES). History of Australian bushranging. 2 v. Sydney. 1900–6.

V. 1, to 1862; standard. See too G. E. Boxall, *The story of the Australian bushrangers*, Sydney, 1959.

(c) *Constitutional and Legal History*

See also Sweet and Maxwell (547).

4700 SWEETMAN (EDWARD). Australian constitutional development. Melbourne. 1925.

Bibliog. 444–8; detailed on the period to 1856. F. L. W. Wood, *The constitutional development of Australia*, 1933, is a briefer, more general survey. J. M. Ward, *Earl Grey and the Australian colonies, 1846–1857: a study of self-government and self-interest*, Melbourne, 1958, bibliog. 471–90, is valuable.

4701 MELBOURNE (ALEXANDER CLIFFORD VERNON). Early constitutional development in Australia: New South Wales, 1788–1856. 1934.

Standard. Other regions are dealt with in B. T. Finniss, *The constitutional history of
South Australia . . .* [1836–57], 1886; W. A. Townsley, *The struggle for self-government
in Tasmania, 1842–1856*, Hobart, 1951.

4702 BEDFORD (RUTH). Think of Stephen – a family chronicle. Sydney.
1954.

Includes biog. of Sir Alfred Stephen, author of authoritative legal works in the 1840s.

(d) *Economic History*

4703 SHANN (EDWARD OWEN GIBLIN). An economic history of Australia. Camb. 1930. Repr. Melbourne. 1948.

An excellent general survey. More detailed are B. Fitzpatrick, *British imperialism and
Australia, 1783–1833*, 1939, bibliog. 382–6, and *The British Empire in Australia: an
economic history, 1834–1939*, 2nd edn. Melbourne, 1949. Sir T. A. Coghlan, *Labour
and industry in Australia*, 4 v., repr. 1969, is standard. On other aspects see S. J. Butlin,
Foundations of the Australian monetary system, 1788–1851, Melbourne, 1953, bibliog.
555–73, and *Australia and New Zealand Bank: the Bank of Australia and the Union
Bank of Australia Ltd., 1828–1951*, 1961. See also D. S. Macmillan, *The debtors' war:
Scottish capitalists and the economic crisis in Australia, 1841–1846*, Melbourne, 1960,
and *Scotland and Australia* (3910).

4704 HARTWELL (RONALD MAX). The economic development of Van
Diemen's Land, 1820–1850. Melbourne. 1954.

Bibliog. 255–66; comprehensive. For both Tasmania and N.S.W., *Clyde Company
papers*, ed. Philip L. Brown, 5 v., 1941–63, is valuable. Brown also ed. *The narrative of
George Russell*, 1935, the journal of a manager of the Clyde Company.

4705 GREGSON (JESSE). The Australian agricultural company, 1824–1875.
Sydney. 1907.

Agricultural development in N.S.W. C. T. Burfitt, *History of the founding of the wool
industry in Australia*, Sydney, 1907, is a brief survey. A. Barnard, *The Australian wool
market, 1840–1900*, Melbourne, 1958, gives some statistics for the 1840s. E. Dunsdorfs,
The Australian wheat-growing industry, 1788–1948, Melbourne, 1956, gives comprehensive treatment.

(e) *Religious History*

4706 BORDER (JOSEPH THOMAS ROSS). Church and state in Australia,
1788–1872: a constitutional study of the Church of England in Australia. 1962.

Valuable, though with some inaccuracies. There is material for N.S.W. in James Bonwick, *Australia's first preacher: the Rev. Richard Johnson* [1898]; *Some letters of Rev.
Richard Johnson*, ed. G. Mackaness, 2 pt., Sydney, 1954; F. T. Whitington, *William
Grant Broughton, bishop of Australia*, Sydney, 1936. G. H. Jose, *The Church of England
in South Australia, 1836–1905*, 3 v., Adelaide, 1937–55, is summary; F. T. Whitington,
Augustus Short, first bishop of Adelaide, Adelaide, 1887, makes extensive use of Short's
journals. Constance L. M. Hawtrey, *The availing struggle*, Perth, 1949, outlines the
development of the church in W. Australia, and see *Wollaston's Picton journal* and
Wollaston's Albany Journals, ed. Canon A. Burton and P. U. Henn, Perth, 1948–54.
John Barrett, *That better country; the religious aspect of life in eastern Australia*, 1966,
touches on more general religious themes.

4707   O'FARRELL (PATRICK). The Catholic Church in Australia. A short
history, 1788–1966. Sydney. 1968.

The first really scholarly work on the subject. O'Farrell and D. O'Farrell, ed., *Documents in Australian Catholic History*, v. 1: *1788–1884*, 1969. See too T. L. Suttor, *Hierarchy and democracy in Australia, 1788–1870: the formation of Australian Catholicism*, Melbourne, 1965.

4708   KING (JOSEPH). Ten decades: the Australian centenary story of the
London Missionary Society. [1895.]

(f) *Cultural History*

4709   AUSTIN (ALBERT GORDON). Australian education, 1788–1900:
church, state and public education in colonial Australia. Melbourne. 1961.

Bibliog. 263–74. His arguments are supported and illustrated in his *Select documents in Australian education, 1788–1900*, Melbourne, 1963; see too his *George William Rusden and national education in Australia, 1849–1862*, Melbourne, 1958. R. Fogarty, *Catholic education in Australia, 1806–1950*, 2 v., Melbourne, 1959, is definitive. On separate colonies see A. Barcan, *A short history of education in New South Wales*, Sydney, 1965; D. C. Griffiths, *Documents on the establishment of education in New South Wales, 1789–1880*, Melbourne, 1957; D. H. Rankin, *The history of the development of education in Western Australia, 1829–1923*, Perth, 1926, and *The history of the development of education in Victoria, 1836–1936*, Melbourne, 1939.

4710   NADEL (GEORGE HANS). Australia's colonial culture: ideas, men
and institutions in mid-nineteenth century Eastern Australia. Melbourne.
1957.

Bibliog. 289–95; deals with the period 1830–60.

4711   GREEN (HENRY MACKENZIE). A history of Australian literature,
pure and applied . . . until 1950. 2 v. Sydney. 1961.

V. 1; 1789–1923.

4712   SMITH (BERNARD WILLIAM). Place, taste and tradition: a study of
Australian art since 1788. Sydney. 1945.

Bibliog. 272–5. Some rather different ground, with other plates, is covered in his *Australian painting, 1788–1960*, 1962.

4713   HERMAN (MORTON). The early Australian architects and their work.
1954.

4714   [SYDNEY MORNING HERALD]. A century of journalism: the *Sydney
Morning Herald* and its record of Australian life, 1831–1931. Sydney. 1931.

George H. Pitt, *The press in South Australia, 1836–1850*, Adelaide, 1946, is a brief survey.

4715   GANDEVIA (BRYAN HALE). An annotated bibliography of the history
of medicine in Australia. Sydney. [1955.]

(g) *Aborigines*

4716 GREENWAY (JOHN). Bibliography of the Australian aborigines and the native peoples of Torres Strait to 1959. Sydney. 1963.

Over 10,000 entries; no evaluation. E. J. Foxcroft, *Australian native policy: its history, especially in Victoria*, Melbourne, 1941, bibliog. 158–62, touches also on N.S.W.; for other regions see P. M. C. Hasluck, *Black Australians: a survey of native policy in Western Australia, 1829–1897*, Melbourne, 1942; C. Turnbull, *Black war: the extermination of the Tasmanian aborigines*, Melbourne, 1948.

4. SEPARATE COLONIES

See also references to separate colonies in preceding sections.

(a) *New South Wales*

4717 NEW SOUTH WALES. ARCHIVES AUTHORITY. Concise guide to the State Archives of New South Wales. Sydney. 1970.

No. 13 in the series of guides to the State Archives. Other guides cover particular classes.

4718 BLADEN (FRANK MURCOTT) *and* **BRITTON (A.)** *eds.* Historical records of New South Wales. [1762–1811.] 7 v. in 11. Sydney. 1892–1901.

Prints valuable collection of documents from the P.R.O., London. For legislation see *Acts and ordinances of the Governor and Council of New South Wales, and Acts of Parliament enacted for, and applied to, the colony*, comp. by Thomas Callaghan, 3 v., Sydney, 1844–52.

4719 WHITE (HAROLD RODERICK) *comp.* A first-fleet index. Southport, Queensland. 1960.

There are recent reprints of various first-fleet journals: *The voyage of Governor Phillip to Botany Bay*, facs. rep. Melbourne, 1950; Watkin Tench, *Sydney's first four years*, with introd. and notes by L. F. Fitzhardinge, Sydney, 1961; John White, *Journal of a voyage to New South Wales*, with a biog. introd. by Rex Rienits, ed. by Alec H. Chisholm, Sydney, 1962. See also Scott, Easty (2619).

4720 CUMPSTON (J. S.). Shipping arrivals and departures, Sydney, 1788–1825. Canberra. Priv. pub. 1964.

An invaluable reference work, impeccable in research and documentation.

4721 BONWICK (JAMES). First twenty years of Australia: a history founded on official documents. 1882.

Old-fashioned and sometimes biased, but full of detail. H. J. Rumsey, comp., *The pioneers of Sydney Cove*, Sydney, 1937, a list with biog. details. G. Mackness, *Admiral Arthur Phillip, founder of New South Wales, 1738–1814*, Sydney, 1937, bibliog. 479–92, is the best life.

4722 EVATT (HERBERT VERE). Rum rebellion: a study of the overthrow of Governor Bligh by John Macarthur and the New South Wales Corps. Reset edn. 1955.

G. Mackaness, ed., *Some correspondence of . . . Bligh*, Sydney, 1949, and *Fresh light on*

Bligh . . . some unpublished correspondence, Sydney, 1953; see also lives (1190). M. H. Ellis, *John Macarthur*, Sydney, 1955, bibliog. 533–40, is excellent.

4723 ELLIS (MALCOLM HENRY). Lachlan Macquarie: his life, adventures and times. 3rd edn. Sydney. 1958.

Bibliog. 531–40. See also Marion Phillips, *A colonial autocracy: New South Wales under Governor Macquarie, 1810–1821*, 1900; Marjorie F. Barnard, *Macquarie's world*, 2nd edn. Melbourne, 1949; *Lachlan Macquarie . . . journals of his tours in New South Wales and Van Diemen's Land, 1810–1822*, Sydney, 1956. A. C. V. Melbourne, *William Charles Wentworth*, Brisbane, 1934, is a brief life of a leading critic of Macquarie.

4724 ONSLOW (ELIZABETH MACARTHUR) *comp*. Some early records of the Macarthurs of Camden. Sydney. [1915].

Includes documents on the early wool industry; valuable for economic and social life. Other varied sketches of life in the colony include M. B. Eldershaw (*pseud.*), *The life and times of Capt. John Piper*, Sydney, 1939; M. H. Ellis, *Francis Greenway*, 1949; R. H. Goddard, *The life and times of James Milson*, Melbourne, 1955; Marnie Bassett, *The Governor's lady: Mrs. Philip Gidley King*, 2nd edn., 1956.

4725 GILCHRIST (ARCHIBALD) *comp*. John Dunmore Lang, chiefly autobiographical, 1799–1878: cleric, writer, traveller, statesman, pioneer of democracy in Australia; an assembling of contemporary documents. 2 v. Melbourne. 1951.

For politics in the 1840s see also the detailed treatment in Ruth Knight, *Illiberal Liberal: Robert Lowe in New South Wales, 1842–50*, Melbourne, 1966.

4726 CURREY (CHARLES HERBERT). Sir Francis Forbes; the first chief justice of the supreme court of New South Wales. 1968.

4727 THERRY (*Sir* ROGER). Reminiscences of thirty years residence in New South Wales and Victoria. 1863.

A lively but biased account of life in the colony in the 1830s and 1840s by a one-time judge of the supreme court. F. J. Meyrick, *Life in the bush, 1840–1847: a memoir of Henry Howard Meyrick*, 1939, is based on letters. Margaret L. Kiddle, *Caroline Chisholm*, 2nd edn. Melbourne, 1957, depicts society and immigration.

4728 CLUNE (FRANK PATRICK). Saga of Sydney: the birth, growth and maturity of the mother city of Australia. Rev. edn. Sydney. 1963.

A topographical arrangement embodying historical material. Alan Birch and David S. Macmillan ed., *The Sydney scene, 1788–1960*, Melbourne, 1962, an anthology of extracts from newspapers and contemporary accounts. George W. D. Allen, ed., *Early Georgian: extracts from the journal of George Allen (1800–1877)*, Sydney, 1958, an engaging record of the trivialities of life in Sydney.

(b) *Victoria*

4729 MELBOURNE UNIVERSITY. Victorian historical documents; pt. 1: An outline list of documents mainly in the Public Library of Victoria and relating to the history of Victoria. Melbourne. 1949.

J. J. Shillinglaw, ed., *Historical records of Port Phillip: the first annals of the colony of Victoria*, Melbourne, 1879, documents dealing with early exploration and settlement,

1802–4. For the period after the establishment of the separate colony see Office of the Registrar General, Victoria, *Statistical notes on the progress of Victoria*, comp. by W. H. Archer, 2 pt., pt. 1, 2nd edn. rev. and corr., Melbourne, 1861.

4730 VICTORIAN HISTORICAL MAGAZINE. V. 1+. Melbourne. 1911+.

Index v. 1–25, 1911–54, consolidated by E. M. Christie, Melbourne, 1956.

4731 LABILLIÈRE (FRANCIS PETER). Early history of . . . Victoria. 2 v. 1878.

A full and careful account. Also detailed is James Bonwick, *Port Phillip settlement*, 1883. R. V. Billis and A. S. Kenyon, *Pastures new: an account of the pastoral occupation of Port Phillip*, Melbourne, 1930, is excellent and their *Pastoral pioneers of Port Phillip*, 1932, is a biographical dictionary of pastoral licensees of the crown followed by an alphabetical list of the Port Phillip runs.

4732 TURNER (HENRY GYLES). A history of the colony of Victoria. 2 v. 1904.

V. 1: 1797–1854; based partly on oral evidence of men active in the colony before 1854. The centenary celebrations council, Victoria, *Victoria—the first century: an historical survey*, Melbourne, 1934, provides a useful outline. Alan Gross, *Charles Joseph La Trobe*, Melbourne, 1956, is a life of the chief administrator, 1839–54. Edward Jenks, *The government of Victoria (Australia)*, 1891, is a constitutional history with much material on the period to 1851.

4733 FINN (EDMUND). The chronicles of early Melbourne. 2 v. Melbourne. 1888.

Anecdotal but interesting. See too W. Westgarth, *Personal recollections of early Melbourne and Victoria*, Melbourne, 1888; *Georgiana's journal: Melbourne a hundred years ago*, ed. by Hugh McCrae, 1967. J. A. Grant and G. Serle, *The Melbourne scene, 1803–1956*, Melbourne, 1957, prints extracts from newspapers and memoirs.

4734 BONWICK (JAMES). John Batman, the founder of Victoria. Melbourne. 1867.

Memoirs and correspondence illustrating the life of the colony include: *Letters from Victorian pioneers*, ed. T. F. Bride, Melbourne, 1898; J. C. Hamilton, *Pioneering days in Western Victoria*, Melbourne, 1923; *A homestead history; being the reminiscences and letters of Alfred Joyce of Plaistow and Norwood*, ed. G. F. James, 2nd edn., Melbourne, 1949; *The correspondence of John Cotton*, ed., G. Mackaness, 3 pt., Sydney, 1953. Studies include N. F. Learmonth, *The Portland Bay settlement . . . 1800–1851*, Portland, Victoria, 1934; Marnie Bassett, *The Hentys: an Australian colonial tapestry*, 1954; Margaret Kiddle, *Men of yesterday: a social history of the western district of Victoria, 1834–90*, Melbourne, 1961, bibliog. 557–61.

(c) *South Australia*

4735 CROWLEY (FRANK KEBLE). South Australian history. A survey for research students. 1966.

Largely supersedes Thomas Gill, *Bibliography of South Australia*, Adelaide, [1886].

4736 SOUTH AUSTRALIANA. A journal for the publication and study of South Australian historical and literary manuscripts. Adelaide. V. 1+. 1962+.

See also *The White collection: an annotated catalogue of the papers of John White* [1787–1860], Adelaide, 1960.

4737   PRICE (ARCHIBALD GRENFELL). The foundation and settlement of
South Australia, 1829–45. Adelaide. 1924.

Bibliog. 249–52. Price also wrote *Founders and pioneers of South Australia*, Adelaide,
1929, bibliog. 255–60, a series of biographical essays. Individual lives include E. Hodder,
George Fife Angas: father and founder of South Australia, 1891; *The founding of South
Australia as recorded in the journals of Robert Gouger*, ed. E. Hodder, 1898; G. C. Mor-
phett, *Sir James Hurtle Fisher*, Adelaide, 1955, a life of the first resident commissioner.
James Rutherford, *Sir George Grey*, 1961, bibliog. 671–89, is comprehensive; Grey was
governor, 1841–5. See also Geoffrey Dutton, *Founder of a city: the life of colonel William
Light . . . founder of Adelaide*, Melbourne, 1960, bibliog. 303–9. Thomas Worsnop,
History of the city of Adelaide, Adelaide, 1878, was written by the then town clerk from
documents. Douglas Pike, *Paradise of dissent: South Australia, 1829–1857*, 1957,
emphasizes the interreaction of political and religious attitudes.

4738   PRICE (ARCHIBALD GRENFELL). The history and problems of the
Northern Territory, Australia. Adelaide. 1930.

A brief survey down to 1871.

(d) *Western Australia*

4739   CROWLEY (FRANK KEBLE). The records of Western Australia [a
bibliography]. Duplicated edn. Perth. 1953.

A guide to documents and publications, and with a list of relevant bibliographies. More
limited is F. G. Steere, *Bibliography of books, articles, and pamphlets dealing with Western
Australia since its discovery in 1616*, Perth, 1923.

4740   WESTERN AUSTRALIA. Registry department. Statistical view of
ninety-nine years' progress in Western Australia, 1829–1927/8; compiled from
official sources. Perth. 1929.

4741   FREMANTLE. Diary and letters of Admiral Sir C. H. Fremantle
relating to the founding of the colony of Western Australia, 1829. Edited by
T. F. Fremantle, 3rd baron Cottesloe. 1928.

For other biographical information see G. F. Moore, *Diary . . . of an early settler in
Western Australia*, 1884; E. O. G. Shann, *Cattle chosen: the story of the first group settlement in Western Australia, 1829–1841*, 1926, based on letters and diaries; *Early days
in Western Australia; being the letters and journal of lieut. H. W. Bunbury*, ed. W. St.
Pierre Bunbury and W. P. Morrell, 1930; M. J. L. Uren, *Land looking west: the story
of governor James Stirling in Western Australia*, 1948; Alexandra Hasluck, *Portrait with
background: a life of Georgiana Molloy*, Melbourne, 1955.

4742   BATTYE (JAMES SYKES). Western Australia: a history from its
discovery to the inauguration of the commonwealth. Oxf. 1924.

Standard. J. K. Hitchcock, *The history of Fremantle . . . 1829–1929*, Fremantle, 1929;
T. P. Field, *Swanland, 1829–1956; the agricultural districts, Western Australia*, Lexington, Ky., 1957.

(e) *Queensland*

4743   COOTE (WILLIAM). History of the colony of Queensland. V. 1: 1770–
1859. Brisbane. 1882.

Old-fashioned, but gives outline narrative. H. S. Russell, *The genesis of Queensland*,

Sydney, 1888, is a detailed account of early exploration and settlement. See too J. F. Hogan, *The Gladstone colony*, 1898; R. L. Jack, *Northmost Australia: three centuries of exploration, discovery, and adventure in and round the Cape York Peninsula, Queensland*, 2 v. [1921]; *Journal of the Historical Society of Queensland*, Brisbane, v. 1+, 1914+.

(f) *Tasmania*

4744 FLINN (ELIZABETH). The history, politics and economy of Tasmania in the literature, 1856–1959. Hobart. 1961.

A bibliog. arranged under subject heads with author and title entry indexes. A. Morton comp. *Register of papers published in the Tasmanian journal and the papers and proceedings of the Royal Society of Tasmania . . . 1841 to 1885*, Hobart, 1887.

4745 TASMANIA, UNIVERSITY. Report on the historical manuscripts of Tasmania. 5 pts. in one v. Hobart. 1964.

Calendars various collections. See Tasmania, State Archives, *Guide to the public records of Tasmania*; section 1: *Colonial secretary's office record group*; section 2: *Governor's office record group, 1816–1953*; section 3: *Convict department record group*, duplicated, Hobart, 1957–65. Anne McKay, ed., *Journals of the Land Commissioners for Van Diemen's Land, 1826–8*, Hobart, 1962. See also *Records of the Queen Victoria Museum, Launceston*, v. 1, no. 1–v. 3, 1942–52, new ser. no. 1, 1952, in progress.

4746 WEST (JOHN). The history of Tasmania. 2 v. Launceston. 1852.

Old-fashioned but indispensable; the author had access to private papers. James Fenton, *A history of Tasmania from its discovery*, Hobart, 1884, gives a general outline. R. W. Giblin, *The early history of Tasmania*, 2 v., 1928–39, is standard for the period up to 1818.

4747 FITZPATRICK (KATHLEEN). Sir John Franklin in Tasmania, 1837–1843. Melbourne. 1949.

Bibliog. 399–402; excellent. Clarence R. Collins, *Saga of settlement: a brief account of the life and times of lieutenant colonel David Collins*, Perth [1957], deals with the founder of Hobart. *Bobby Knopwood and his times*, ed. Mabel Hookey, Hobart, 1929, is from the diaries of Collins's chaplain; see also W. H. Hudspeth, *An introduction to the diaries of the Rev. Robert Knopwood and G. T. W. B. Boyes*, Hobart, 1955. *Friendly mission: the Tasmanian journals and papers of George Augustus Robinson, 1829–34*, ed. N. J. B. Plomley [Hobart], 1966, bibliog. 1051–5, is a mine of information on settlers and aborigines.

M. NEW ZEALAND

1. BIBLIOGRAPHY

4748 NEW ZEALAND. Department of internal affairs. A guide to the Dominion archives. Wellington. 1953.

Gives a preliminary listing of the principal groups of archives, now supplemented by *Preliminary Inventories*, nos. 1–9, Wellington, 1953–61, of which no. 1: *Archives of the Governor General*; no. 2: *Archives of the New Zealand Company*; no. 3: *Archives of the army department*; no. 9: *Archives of the Old Land Commission*; the remainder list archives for districts. In 1966 the department issued *National Archives of New Zealand: a review and summary of work*, the first of an intended series to include listings of accessions. See also Scottish R.O. (4684).

4749 HOCKEN (THOMAS MORLAND). A bibliography of the literature relating to New Zealand. Wellington. 1909.

Chronological arrangement, some 3,000 titles, standard for list of contemporary accounts; supplement by A. H. Johnstone, Auckland, 1927. W. H. Trimble, *Catalogue of the Hocken Library*, Dunedin, 1912, provides an author and classified catalogue of much of the same material. On missions see Dindinger (4686). There are selective bibliographies in various issues of the *New Zealand official year-book*. James O. Wilson comp. *A finding list of British parliamentary papers relating to New Zealand, 1817–1900*, Wellington, 1960. The N.Z. General Assembly library has issued *A union catalogue of New Zealand newspapers*, 2nd edn. comp. by J. S. Gully, Wellington, 1961, including Australian newspapers relating to N.Z. Austin Graham Bagnall ed., *New Zealand national bibliography to the year 1960*, Wellington, 1970, in progress. The *New Zealand national bibliography*, 1968+, provides annual cumulations for pubs. from 1966.

2. GENERAL HISTORY

(a) *Sources*

4750 McNAB (ROBERT) *ed.* Historical records of New Zealand. 2 v. Wellington. 1908–14.

Documents, 1642–1842, including official papers from the P.R.O., London, and from private collections. R. Carrick, ed., *Historical records, New Zealand South prior to 1840*, Dunedin, 1903, compiled from archives in Australia relating to N.Z.; the editing is not always trustworthy.

4751 DIEFFENBACH (ERNST). Travels in New Zealand. 1843.

By the naturalist to the New Zealand Co.; one of the best accounts published at the time; for others see Hocken (4749). R. A. Cruise, *Journal of a ten months' residence in New Zealand, 1820*, ed. A. G. Bagnall, Christchurch, 1957, is also important. Nancy M. Taylor, ed., *The journal of Ensign Best, 1837–1843*, Wellington, 1966, includes memoirs of the British annexation, as does also E. J. Wakefield, *Adventure in New Zealand from 1839 to 1844*, ed. Sir Robert Stout, 1908. J. Rutherford, ed., *The founding of New Zealand: the journals of Felton Mathew, first surveyor-general . . . 1840–1847*, Dunedin, Wellington, 1940, invaluable for the picture it gives of Hobson's early administration. C. A. Sharp, ed., *The Dillon letters . . . 1842–1853*, Wellington, 1954– , letters of the governor's civil secretary.

4752 MANING (FREDERICK EDWARD). Old New Zealand. New edn. Christchurch. [1948.]

A classic account of life in New Zealand in the 1830s, first publ. 1863. For the life of pioneers in the 1840s see John Webster, *Reminiscences*, Christchurch, 1908; *Dean's letters 1840–1854*, ed. J. Deans, Christchurch, 1954; *The Torlesse papers*, ed. P. B. Maling, Christchurch, 1958.

(b) *Later Works*

See *Historical Studies Australia and New Zealand* (4689).

4753 SCHOLEFIELD (GUY HARDY) *ed.* A dictionary of New Zealand biography. 2 v. Wellington. 1940.

4754 CAMBRIDGE HISTORY OF THE BRITISH EMPIRE (4311). V. 7, pt. 2: New Zealand. Camb. 1933.

Standard; bibliog. 259–90. G. W. Rusden, *History of New Zealand*, 3 v., 1895, and

R. A. A. Sherrin and J. H. Wallace, *Early history of New Zealand*, Auckland, 1890, remain worth consultation. W. P. Reeves, *The long white cloud: Ao Tea Roa*, 4th edn. with additional chapters by A. J. Harrop, 1950, is a classic first pub. 1898. K. Sinclair, *A history of New Zealand*, 1961, is a recent summary.

4755   HARROP (ANGUS JOHN). England and New Zealand: from Tasman to the Taranaki war. 1926.

A scholarly study paying special attention to the New Zealand Company and the development of imperial policy. E. J. Tapp, *Early New Zealand, a dependency of New South Wales, 1788–1841*, Melbourne, 1958, is strongest on administration. E. Ramsden, *Busby of Waitangi, H.M.'s resident at New Zealand, 1833–1840*, Wellington, 1942, bibliog. 377–84, is exhaustive. See too Trevor Williams, 'James Stephen and British intervention in New Zealand, 1838–40', *J. of Modern History*, 13 (1941), 19–35.

4756   BUICK (THOMAS LINDSAY). The Treaty of Waitangi: or how New Zealand became a British colony. 3rd edn. 1936.

Long standard but now somewhat outdated; James Rutherford, *The treaty of Waitangi and the acquisition of British sovereignty in New Zealand, 1840*, Auckland, 1949, is a brief essay.

4757   SCHOLEFIELD (GUY HARDY). Captain William Hobson, first governor of New Zealand. 1934.

A sound biographical study. Also of value is J. C. Beaglehole, *Captain Hobson and the New Zealand Company: a study in colonial administration*, Northampton, Mass., 1928.

3. SPECIAL SUBJECTS

(a) *Exploration and Discovery*

4758   TAYLOR (NANCY M.) *ed.* Early travellers in New Zealand. Oxf. 1959.

A massive and scholarly compendium of early narratives. C. W. N. Ingram and P. O. Wheatley, *Shipwrecks: New Zealand disasters, 1795–1950*, 2nd edn. Wellington, 1951, is valuable for reference. James Cowan, *Sir Donald McLean. The story of a New Zealand statesman*, Dunedin, Wellington, 1940, includes material about exploration and negotiation with the Maoris during the 1840s.

(b) *Colonization*

See Wakefield (4293).

4759   MARAIS (JOHANNES STEPHANUS). The colonization of New Zealand. 1927.

A comprehensive, well-documented study, excessively critical of the New Zealand Co. M. Turnbull, *The New Zealand bubble: the Wakefield theory in practice*, Wellington, 1959, is a valuable short essay. W. R. Jourdain, *Land legislation and settlement in New Zealand*, Wellington, 1925, summarizes the principal land legislation. Lazarus Goldman, *The history of the Jews in New Zealand*, Wellington, 1958, has material on Jewish immigration.

(c) *Constitutional and Legal History*

4760   HIGHT (JAMES) *and* BAMFORD (H. DEAN). The constitutional history and law of New Zealand. Christchurch. 1914.

Old-fashioned but full of information. Jessie I. Hetherington, *New Zealand: its political connection with Great Britain*, 2 v., Dunedin, 1926–7, traces constitutional history up to the attainment of responsible government. On the decade after Waitangi see N. A. Foden, *The constitutional development of New Zealand . . . 1839–1849*, Wellington, 1938. A. H. McLintock, *Crown colony government in New Zealand*, Wellington, 1958, bibliog. 434–58, is thorough and well documented.

(d) *Economic History*

4761 NEW ZEALAND. Department of Statistics. Statistical publications, 1840–1960. Wellington. 1961.

Reference to data in official pubns., newspapers, and monographs. Auckland University, department of economics, *Statistics of New Zealand for the crown colony period, 1840–1852*, duplicated, Auckland [1954].

4762 CONDLIFFE (JOHN BELL). New Zealand in the making: a study of economic and social development. 2nd edn. 1959.

Standard: but no separate treatment of the period up to 1851.

4763 McNAB (ROBERT). Murihiku: history of the South Island of New Zealand and the islands adjacent and lying to the south, 1642–1835. Wellington. 1909.

Deals largely with the whaling and sealing expeditions round the south of New Zealand. See too his *The old whaling days: a history of southern New Zealand . . . 1830–1840*, Christchurch, 1913.

(e) *Religious History*

4764 PURCHAS (HENRY THOMAS). A history of the English church in New Zealand. Christchurch. 1914.

A useful outline. Hugh Carleton, *The life of Henry Williams, archdeacon of Waimate*, ed. and rev. by James Elliott, Wellington, 1948, is valuable for its long excerpts from diaries. John Heber Evans, *Churchman militant: George Augustus Selwyn, bishop of New Zealand and Lichfield*, 1964, bibliog. 277–81, is the best life, but H. W. Tucker, *Memoir of . . . Selwyn*, 2 v., 1879, remains indispensable for its full citation from correspondence.

4765 MORLEY (WILLIAM). History of Methodism in New Zealand. Wellington. 1900.

4766 ELDER (JOHN RAWSON). The history of the Presbyterian Church in New Zealand, 1840–1940. Christchurch. 1940.

4767 KEYS (LILLIAN GLADYS). The life and times of Bishop Pompallier. Christchurch. 1957.

Bibliog. 400–7; a scholarly study of the beginnings of the Roman Catholic church in N.Z.

4768 WILLIAMS (WILLIAM). Christianity among the New Zealanders. 1867.

Indispensable; combining material from the C.M.S. records with personal knowledge, mainly on the period to 1840. Material on missions is considerable and often of more than religious interest. Eric Ramsden, *Marsden and the Missions. Prelude to Waitangi*, Sydney, 1936, is a full, scholarly life of a great mission organizer; see also *The letters and journals of Samuel Marsden, 1765–1838*, ed. John Rawson Elder, Dunedin, 1932; *Marsden's lieutenants*, ed. J. R. Elder, Dunedin, 1934; *Some private correspondence of . . . Marsden*, ed. G. Mackaness, Sydney, 1942; *Marsden and the New Zealand mission; sixteen letters*, ed. P. H. Williams, Otago, 1961. For the work of other missionaries, see (arranged roughly by date of their arrival) *Earliest New Zealand: the journals and correspondence of the Rev. John Butler*, ed. R. J. Barton, Masterton, 1927; J. N. Coleman, *A memoir of the Rev. Richard Davis*, 1865; *The early journals of Henry Williams*, ed. Lawrence M. Rogers, Christchurch, 1961, bibliog. 495–503 (on 1826–40); Frederick W. Williams, *Through ninety years, 1826–1916* [notes on the lives of William and William Leonard Williams], Wellington, 1945; *Missionary life and work in New Zealand, 1833–1862; being the private journal of . . . J. A. Wilson*, ed. C. J. Wilson, Auckland, 1899; H. E. R. L. Wily and H. Maunsell, *Robert Maunsell, a New Zealand pioneer*, Dunedin, 1938; James Buller, *Forty years in New Zealand*, 1878; A. D. Mead, *Richard Taylor. Missionary tramper*, Wellington, 1966. See too H. C. Fancourt, *The advance of the missionaries . . . expansion of the Church Missionary Society mission south of the Bay of Islands, 1833–1840*, Dunedin, 1939.

(f) *Aborigines*

There is much material in the titles under (4768).

4769   COWAN (JAMES). The Maoris of New Zealand. Christchurch. 1910.

Mainly anthropological, but has some historical material. H. M. Wright, *New Zealand 1769–1840: early years of western contact*, Camb., Mass., 1959, is concerned primarily with the European impact on Maori life and outlook, mainly in the Bay Islands. A. G. Bagnall and G. C. Petersen, *William Colenso . . . his life and journeys*, Wellington, 1948, bibliog. 448–60, is a study of an outstanding observer and interpreter of Maori culture.

4770   MILLER (JOHN OWEN). Early Victorian New Zealand: a study of racial tension and social attitudes, 1839–1852. 1958.

Bibliog. 200–9; well documented. See too J. Rutherford, *Hone Heke's rebellion, 1844–1846*, Auckland, 1947; K. Sinclair, *The origins of the Maori wars*, Wellington, 1957; H. G. Miller, *Race conflicts in New Zealand, 1814–1865* [Hamilton], 1966; I. M. Wards, *The shadow of the land. A study of British policy and racial conflict in New Zealand, 1832–1852*, Wellington, 1968.

4. LOCAL HISTORY

4771   BUICK (THOMAS LINDSAY). The French at Akaroa: an adventure in colonization. Wellington. 1928.

4772   MULGAN (ALAN EDWARD). The city of the strait: Wellington and its province. Wellington. 1939.

A centennial history, with much detail on the 1840s.

4773   HOWARD (BASIL). Rakiura: a history of Stewart Island. Dunedin. 1940.

4774   RUTHERFORD (JAMES) *and* SKINNER (WILLIAM HENRY) *eds.* The establishment of the New Plymouth settlement in New Zealand, 1841–1843. New Plymouth. 1940.

4775   ROSS (RUTH M.). New Zealand's first capital. Wellington. 1946.

4776 MEIKLEJOHN (GEORGE MACPHERSON). Early conflicts of press
and government: a story of the first *New Zealand Herald* and of the foundation
of Auckland. Auckland. 1953.

Deals especially with the conflict over the government's first land grants in 1841–2.

4777 McLINTOCK (ALEXANDER HARE). The history of Otago: the
origins and growth of a Wakefield class settlement. Dunedin. 1949.

Bibliog. 791–815; excellent. T. M. Hocken, *The early history of New Zealand*, Wellington, 1914, deals mainly with the settlements at Otago and Canterbury.

4778 ALLAN (RUTH). The history of Port Nelson. Wellington. 1954.

4779 HIGHT (*Sir* JAMES) *and* STRAUBEL (CARL RUDOLPH) *eds*. A
history of Canterbury. V. 1: to 1854. Christchurch. 1957.

Bibliog. 251–68. C. E. Carrington, *John Robert Godley of Canterbury*, Christchurch,
1950, is a life of a leading figure; see too *Letters from early New Zealand by Charlotte
Godley, 1850–1853*, ed. with notes by John R. Godley, Christchurch, 1951.

N. THE PACIFIC ISLANDS

During this period the region of the Pacific islands was an area of British commercial and missionary activity but no territorial annexations took place until
much later in the century.

See Brookes and Ward (369). On missions see Dindinger (4686).

4780 LEESON (IDA). A bibliography of bibliographies of the South Pacific.
1954.

Arranged under both area and subject; helpful introduction. Clyde R. H. Taylor, *A
Pacific bibliography; printed matter relating to the native peoples of Polynesia, Melanesia
and Micronesia*, 2nd edn., Oxf., 1965, is exhaustive; the 'general' sections give guidance
on missions and exploration. L. A. Jore, *Essai de bibliografie du Pacifique*, Paris, 1931,
is of value for areas of French penetration.

4781 SHARP (ANDREW). The discovery of the Pacific islands. Oxf. 1960.

A work of reference, fixing details of discovery from a wide selection of sources; bibliog.
225–8.

4782 MORRELL (WILLIAM PARKER). Britain in the Pacific islands. Oxf.
1960.

Standard. A. A. Koskinen, *Missionary influence as a political factor in the Pacific islands*,
Helsinki, 1953, is the best work on its subject but displays a certain naïvety. John
Davies, *The history of the Tahitian mission, 1790–1830, with supplementary papers from
the correspondence of the missionaries*, ed. C. W. Newbury, Camb., 1961, is excellent. On
Marsden see E. O. Ramsden, 'Marsden and the South Seas', *Roy. Aust. Hist. Soc. J.*
24 (1938) 189–213.

INDEX

Black type indicates a main entry or entries: italics a subject entry.

Moohr, Michael: impact of emancipation in British Guiana, 4475.

Moore, Sir Alan Hilary: sailing ships of war, 1292.

Moore, David Cresap: the reform Act of 1832, 107; the corn laws and high farming, 1661.

Moore, Doris Langley: woman in fashion, 1893.

Moore, George Fletcher: diary, 4741.

Moore, Sir Graham, R.N.: 1222.

Moore, Henry Charles: omnibuses and cabs, 1958.

Moore, Henry Kingsmill: hist. of the Kildare Place society, 4278.

Moore, J. J.: British mariner's vocabulary, 1351.

Moore, John, M.D.: residence in France, 2366.

Moore, Sir John: 990.

Moore, John Hamilton: the practical navigator, 1346.

Moore, Sir Norman: hist. of St. Bartholomew's hospital, 2541.

Moore, Stuart Archibald: hist. and law of the foreshore, 650.

Moore, Thomas: life of Sheridan, 162; 2287; works and correspondence, **2744**; life of Lord E. Fitzgerald, 4102.

Moore, Thomas: hist. of Devonshire, 3563.

Moorman, Mary: letters and biog. of Wordsworth, 2754.

Moorsom, Wm. Scarth: letters from Nova Scotia, 4391.

Moran, Patrick Francis: hist. of Catholic church in Australasia, 4222; spicilegium ossoriense, 4265.

Moraud, Marcel Ian: le romantisme français en Angleterre, 2677.

Moravians: **870**, 4465.

Mordaunt family: 2124.

More, Hannah: works, 735; 2114, 2119, **2122**, 2341; strictures on female education, 3264; and education, 3355.

More, Martha: 2119, 2122.

Moreau, César: on British shipping, 1091, 1497; British finance, 1421; state of Ireland, 4072.

Morelli, Emilia: Mazzini in Inghilterra, 314.

Moreno, Mariano: 356.

Moresby, Sir Fairfax, R.N.: life, 1223.

Moresby, John, R.N.: life, 1223.

Moreux, Françoise: Th. De Quincey, 2727.

Morgan, Alexander: Scottish university studies, 4044.

Morgan, Bayard Quincy: bibliog. of German lit. in English translation, 2679.

Morgan, Edward Victor: theory and practice of central banking, 1442; the stock exchange, 1457.

Morgan, Hector Davies: law of marriage, adultery and divorce, 638.

Morgan, Jean E.: bibliog. of Prince Edward Is., 4383.

Morgan, John: essay on poisonous agents, 3130.

Morgan, John Vyrnwy: Welsh political and educational leaders, 3802.

Morgan, Sydney, Lady Morgan: 2227.

Morgan, Valerie: agric. wage rates in Scotland, 3933.

Morgan, Wm.: papers on naval architecture, 1287.

Morgan, Wm.: travellers' pocket-book, 3518.

Morice, Adrien Gabriel: l'église catholique dans l'ouest canadien, 4431; hist. of British Columbia, 4439.

Morier, James Justinian: travels in the Middle East, 2411.

Morison, John: founders of the London Missionary soc., 901.

Morison, John Lyle: Lord Elgin, 4320; British supremacy and Canadian self-govt., 4355; Lawrence of Lucknow, 4598.

Morison, Stanley: John Bell, 3479; the English newspaper, 3496; hist. of the Times, 3501.

Morison, Wm. Maxwell: the decisions of the court of session, 3895.

Morley: **3738**.

Morley, Charles: guide to research in Russian hist., 254.

Morley, Edith Julia: H. C. Robinson, 2210.

Morley, James Wycliffe Headlam-: dipl. hist., 262.

Morley, John, 1st Viscount Morley of Blackburn: Burke, 161; Gladstone, 230; Cobden, 239.

Morley, Marjorie Gertrude: bibliog. of Manitoba, 4432.

Morley, Wm.: hist. of Methodism in N. Zealand, 4765.

Morley, Wm. F. E.: bibliog. of Canadian local histories, 4327.

Morley, Wm. Hook: Indian law cases, 4565.

Morning Post, the: 3503.

Morocco, relations with: see *Great Britain*.

Morphett, George Cummins: Sir Jas. H. Fisher, 4737.

Morpurgo, Jack Eric: ed. autobiog. of Leigh Hunt, 2737.

Romilly, Anne: letters, 2257.

Romilly, Joseph: Cambridge diary, 2324.

Romilly, Sir Samuel: H. of Commons procedure, 407; biog., 576; capital punishments, 2585.

Romilly, Samuel Henry: letters of Lord Dudley, 2213; Romilly–Edgeworth letters, 2257.

Romme, Charles: naval dict., 1350.

Romney Marsh: **3693**.

Ronalds, Sir Francis: bibliog. of electricity, 3188.

Ronan, Myles Vincent: letters of archbp. Troy, 4107; Father H. Young, 4268.

Rook, Arthur: origins of biology, 3241.

Roose, Edward Mahon: ecclesiastica, 676.

Roosevelt, Theodore: war of 1812, 1135.

Roper, Roper Stote Donnison: law of legacies, 639.

Roper, Wm. Oliver: hist. of Lancs., 3624.

Ropes, John Codman: campaign of Waterloo, 1019.

Rosa, Matthew Whiting: novels of fashion, 2698.

Roscoe family: 3612.

Roscoe, Edward Stanley: Lord Stowell, 577.

Roscoe, Henry: Wm. Roscoe, 2172.

Roscoe, Sydney: bibliog. of T. Bewick, 2908.

Roscoe, Thomas: transl. Kohl's travels, 1865.

Roscoe, Wm.: pamphlets, 128, 131; biog., 2172.

Rose, Charles Marshall: Mortlake, 3692.

Rose, Edward Alan: Methodist circuit plans, 843.

Rose, Ernest Arthur: hist. of English chintz, 3001.

Rose, Fred: hist. of furniture, 2989.

Rose, George: diaries, 152; public expenditure, 446; friendly societies, 1470; savings banks, 1475.

Rose, Hugh Henry, 1st Baron Strathnairn: papers, 244.

Rose, John Holland: Wm. Pitt, 147; third coalition, 281; Napoleon, 940; defence of Toulon, 1113; Napoleon and sea power, 1123; Dumouriez, 1125; W. Indian commerce, 1490; ed. Cambridge hist. of the Br. empire, 4311; ed. hist. of Malta, 4503.

Rose, Michael E.: poor law, 1718.

Rose, Millicent: east end of London, 3768.

Rose, Thomas: illustrations of northern counties, 3706.

Rosen, George: hist. of public health, 2549.

Rosenbach, Abraham S. Wolf: Jewish bibliog., 911.

Rosenblatt, Frank Ferdinand: chartist movement, 113.

Roseveare, Henry: the treasury, 455.

Ross, Charles: Cornwallis, 172.

Ross, George: law of vendors, 615.

Ross, Sir James Clark: Antarctic discovery, 1175.

Ross, Janet: three generations, 2155.

Ross, Sir John: naval discovery, 1164; Admiral Saumarez, 1232; steam navigation, 1289.

Ross, M.: hist. of Durham, 3575.

Ross, Ruth M.: N. Zealand's first capital, 4775.

Rosselli, John: Lord Wm. Bentinck, 174, 298.

Rosselli, Nello: Inghilterra e Sardegna, 314.

Rossendale: 1527, **3630**.

Rossi, Mario Manlio: hist. of Malta, 4504.

Ross-shire: **4014**.

Rostow, Walt Whitman: economic growth, 1410; British economy, 1411; terms of trade, 1484.

Roth, Barry: bibliog. of Jane Austen studies, 2714.

Roth, Cecil: Jewish bibliog., 911; hist. of Jews, 921.

Roth, Vincent: bibliog. of Br. Guiana, 4472.

Rotherham: **3741**.

Rotherhithe: **3783**.

Rothstein, Theodore: labour hist., 112.

Rous, Henry John: 1907.

Rousseau, Izac Jozua: journal of Sir B. D'Urban, 974.

Rousseau, Jean Jacques: 2663.

Rousseaux, Paul: econ. hist., 1406.

Roussin, Henri: Wm. Godwin, 521.

Routley, Erik Reginald: hist. of church music, 3048.

Rowan, Archibald Hamilton: autobiog., 4104.

Rowbotham, Wm. Bevill: naval medals, 1363.

Rowden, Alfred Wm.: primates, 714.

Rowe, David John: London radicalism, 187; keelmen's strikes, 1732.

Rowe, George Stringer: Jabez Bunting, 836.

Rowe, Wm. John: industrial rev. in Cornwall, 3550.

Rowell, Geoffrey: Universalist societies, 874.

Rowell, George Rignal: Victorian theatre, 2773.

Russell, Edward Frederick Langley, 2nd Baron Russell of Liverpool: life of Admiral Sir Wm. Sidney Smith, 1234.

Russell, Elbert: hist. of Quakerism, 861.

Russell, Frances Anna Maria (Lady John): 2321.

Russell, Francis: treatise on arbitration, 620.

Russell, George: narrative, 4704.

Russell, George Wm. Erskine: Sydney Smith, 692; E. B. Pusey, 775.

Russell, Henry Stuart: genesis of Queensland, 4743.

Russell, Ina Stafford: local govt. in Manchester, 503.

Russell, James Anderson: education in Kirkcudbright, 4043.

Russell, James Burn: public health in Glasgow, 3981.

Russell, Lord John: 134, 140; C. J. Fox, 155; biog., 205; English govt., 372; foreign travel, 2378; and colonies, 4296, 4304.

Russell, John F.: the brass band movement, 3049.

Russell, Percy: Leicestershire road, 1632; hist. of Dartmouth, 3565; hist. of Torquay, 3572.

Russell, Rollo: corresp. of Lord J. Russell, 205.

Russell, Lord William: 2358A.

Russell, Wm. Clarke: Admiral Collingwood, 1197.

Russell, Sir Wm. Oldnall: crimes and misdemeanours, 624.

Russia: 141, 145; travellers in, 2368, 2371–3, 2375, 2380, 2388, 2396, 2398, 2403, 2409, 2419; English culture in, 2681; *relations with*: see *Great Britain*.

Russo, François: hist. des sciences, 3081.

Ruston, Arthur Gough: Hooton Pagnell, 3732.

Rüter, Paul: on eastern question, 329.

Rutherford, James: Sir George Grey, 4737; ed. journals of Felton Mathew, 4751; treaty of Waitangi, 4756; Hone Heke's rebellion, 4770; New Plymouth settlement, 4774.

Ruthnaswamy, Mariadas: British system in India, 4619.

Rutland, education in: 3279 (Manchester stat. soc.).

Rutter, John: Fonthill abbey, 2966.

Rutter, Owen: hist. of convoy, 1150; Bligh, 1190; *Bounty* mutineers, 1333.

Ruxton, George Augustus Frederick: travels in America, 2476.

Ryan, Alan: J. S. Mill, 2818.

Ryan, Anthony Nicholas: navy at Copenhagen, 1129; Saumarez papers, 1232; trade with the enemy, 1506.

Ryan, Desmond: the Irish language, 4217.

Ryan, John: Wolverhampton school register, 2069.

Ryan, Wm.: Irish houses, 4232.

Ryan, Wm. Patrick: Irish labour movement, 4193.

Rydjord, John: on Latin American independence, 355, 363.

Rye: 3699.

Rye, Reginald Arthur: libraries of London, p. 3; MSS. in Univ. of London lib., 67.

Rye, Walter: Norfolk families, Norfolk topography, 3648.

Ryerson, Egerton: 4373.

Ryland, Jonathan Edwards: John Foster, 2164; John Kitto, 2311.

Rylands library: handlist of MSS., 71.

Sabine, Basil Ernest Vyvyan: hist. of income tax, 1429.

Sabine, Edward: Sir A. S. Frazer, 975.

Sabine, Robert: the electric telegraph, 1619.

Sachs, Curt: hist. of musical instruments, 3063.

Sadleir, Michael, *pseud.*: see Sadler, Michael [Thomas Harvey].

Sadleir, Thomas Ulick: alumni Dublinenses, 4273.

Sadler, Michael Thomas (d. 1835): law of population, 1699; factory statistics, 1720; biog., 2218; Ireland, evils and remedies, 4190.

Sadler, Michael [Thomas Harvey]: Sheridan, 162; (under *pseud.* of Michael Sadleir), A. Trollope, 2358; bibliog. of 19th century fiction, 2695; Blessington D'Orsay, 2717; Bulwer, 2720; binding styles, 3491; Dublin Univ. magazine, 4203.

Sadler, Thomas: ed. H. C. Robinson's diary, 2210.

Sadlier, G. Forster: travels in Arabia, 2418.

Sadullah, Muhammad: catalogue of Punjab R.O. pubns., 4655.

Saenger, Erwin: ed. Br. union catalogue of periodicals, 15.

Sage, Donald: memorabilia domestica, 3936.

Sage, Walter Noble: hist. of British Columbia, 4440.

St. Albans: **3599**.

St. Andrews golf club: 1913.

St. Andrews University: 4044, 4048.

St. Aubyn, Giles: Duke of Cambridge, 1999; Macaulay, 3430.

Usher, Abbott Payson: hist. of inventions, 1521.

Usk japanned wares: 3023.

Ussher, Sir Thomas, R.N.: diary, 1132.

Usury laws: 1430.

Utter, Robert Palfrey: Pamela's daughters, 2698.

Uxbridge: 3647.

Uzunçarşili, Ismail Hakki: Anglo-Turkish relations, 326.

Vagrancy: 2509, 2631. *See* poverty, beggars.

Vaizey, John: hist. of Guinness' brewery, 4166.

Vale, Henry Edmund Theodoric: mail-coach men, 1961.

Valor ecclesiasticus: 672.

Van Alstyne, Richard Wm.: rising American empire, 340; Palmerston and Central America, 362.

Vance, Andrew: land tenure in Ireland, 4182.

Vancouver, George, R.N.: 1157, 1239.

Van der Merwe, Petrus Johannes: hist. of the Boers, 4528.

Van der Walt, Andries Jacobus Hendrik: geskiedenis van Suid-Afrika, 4523.

Van Diemen's land co.: 4745.

Vane, Charles, 3rd Marquess of Londonderry: *see* Stewart, *afterwards* Vane.

Vane, Frances Anne, Marchioness of Londonderry: 2254.

Van Jaarsveld, F. A.: bibliog. of S. Africa, 4519.

Van Mildert, Wm.: 657, 659, 690.

Van Oordt, Jan Willem Gerbrandt: Slagtersnek, 4530.

Van Riebeeck soc.: pubns., 4518.

Vansittart, Jane: Surgeon James's journal, 1013; Katharine Fry's book, 2108.

Van Thal, Herbert: Duke of Cumberland, 1999.

Van Wijk, Theo: bibliog. of S. Africa, 4519.

Vardon, Thomas: index to statutes, 383.

Varet, Gilbert: bibliog. of philosophy, 2793.

Varley, John: 2895.

Varma, Devendra Prasad: the gothic novel, 2664.

Vassall, Elizabeth, Baroness Holland: letters, journal, 2133.

Vassall, Henry Richard, 3rd Baron Holland: 131, 134; memoirs, 189.

Vaudoncourt, Frédéric Guillaume de: Ionian islands, 4507.

Vaughan, Frank: free church of England, 868.

Vaughan, Henry Halford: lectures on hist., 3424.

Vaux, James Hardy: dict. of slang, 1873; memoirs, 2619.

Vauxhall: 3761.

Veitch, George Stead: parl. reform, 95; Huskisson and Liverpool, 209; Liverpool and Manchester railway, 1641.

Veitch, John: ed. of Hamilton, 2811.

Venables, Juliet Elizabeth Amanda: Goodwood estate archives, 3693.

Venkatasubba Sastri, Kasi Nageswara: Mysore under Cubbon, 4588; the Munro system, 4651.

Venn, John: family annals, 746; alumni Cantab., 2042.

Venn, John Archibald: alumni Cantab., 2042.

Venter, Pieter Johannes: landdros en heemrade, 4525.

Verjuice, Pel., mariner: autobiog., 1264.

Verner, Ruth Wingfield: ed. memoirs of Sir Wm. Verner, 1014.

Verner, Sir Wm.: memoirs, 1014.

Verner, Willoughby: journals of G. Simmons, 997.

Verney, Sir Harry: Sir H. Calvert, 946.

Vestris, Lucia Elizabetta (Mrs. Charles James Mathews): 1947.

Veterinary medicine: 3150.

Vetus, *pseud.*: *see* Sterling, Edward.

Vial du Clairbois, Honoré Sébastien: construction des vaisseaux, 1278.

Vibart, Henry Meredith: Madras engineers, 4652.

Vicars, Sir Arthur Edward: index to Irish wills, 4051.

Vicinus, Martha: Victorian women, 1964.

Victoria (colony): 4709; 4729–34.

Victoria, Queen: **236**, 237, 1991, 3971.

Victoria and Albert Museum: catalogues, 2889, 2985, 3001, 3063.

Victoria hist. of the counties: 3522.

Victorian hist. docs.: 4729.

Victorian hist. magazine: 4730.

Victorian studies: 59.

Vidal de la Blache, Henri Joseph Marie Casimir: l'évacuation de l'Espagne, 1009.

Vidler, Alexander Roper: church hist., 730, 732, 753.

Vienna, congress of: 284, 301.

Vigier, François: change and apathy, 3625.

Vignoles, Charles Blacker: 1643.